Family Law

Family Law

Eighth Edition

P M Bromley
M A (Oxon), LL M (Manchester)

of the Middle Temple, Barrister;
Emeritus Professor of English Law in the University of Manchester

N V Lowe
LL B (Sheffield)

of the Inner Temple, Barrister;
Professor of Law at Cardiff Law School, University of Wales

Butterworths
London, Dublin, Edinburgh
1992

United Kingdom	Butterworth & Co (Publishers) Ltd, 88 Kingsway, LONDON WC2B 6AB and 4 Hill Street, EDINBURGH EH2 3JZ
Australia	Butterworths, SYDNEY, MELBOURNE, BRISBANE, ADELAIDE, PERTH, CANBERRA and HOBART
Belgium	Butterworth & Co (Publishers) Ltd, BRUSSELS
Canada	Butterworths Canada Ltd, TORONTO and VANCOUVER
Ireland	Butterworth (Ireland) Ltd, DUBLIN
Malaysia	Malayan Law Journal Sdn Bhd, KUALA LUMPUR
New Zealand	Butterworths of New Zealand Ltd, WELLINGTON and AUCKLAND
Puerto Rico	Equity de Puerto Rico, Inc, HATO REY
Singapore	Butterworths Asia, SINGAPORE
USA	Butterworth Legal Publishers, AUSTIN, Texas; BOSTON, Massachusetts; CLEARWATER, Florida (D & S Publishers); ORFORD, New Hampshire (Equity Publishing); ST PAUL, Minnesota; and SEATTLE, Washington

A CIP Catalogue record for this book is available from the British Library.

ISBN 0 406 60935 7

Typeset, printed and bound in Great Britain by Butler & Tanner Ltd, Frome and London

Preface

Most changes in this edition have again been to Part II dealing with children. The Children Act 1989, which came into force on 14 October 1991, has brought about the biggest change in both the public law and the private law relating to children ever produced by one statute and, except for much of adoption, has affected every part of this branch of the law. This has necessitated the rewriting and re-ordering of the whole of this Part, and we have no doubt that the importance of children in English family law today has justified our increasing the number of chapters from eight to ten. We have referred to the few reported cases decided under the Act, but for some time it will obviously still be necessary to consider many of the principles laid down under the old law.

A number of other changes in the contents and their presentation should be mentioned. Firstly, the close connection between domestic violence and occupation of the home (emphasised in the Law Commission's Report on these subjects) has led us to conclude that we should no longer defer consideration of the latter topic to the chapter on the matrimonial home (where it could be argued that it logically belongs), but we now deal with both together in the chapter on physical protection. Secondly, the rest of the chapter dealing with the matrimonial home (concerned primarily with ownership, the effects of insolvency and the statutory protection of leasehold tenants) has been completely rewritten in the light of the provisions of the Housing Act 1988 and a number of important decided cases. Thirdly, the assimilation of the legal position of all children, whether their parents are married to each other or not, has made obsolete the former chapter on financial support for members of the family outside marriage and we have scrapped it. Fourthly, we have added a section on the Child Support Act 1991 in Chapter 20. Finally, we have omitted the former section on tax from Chapter 17 because the subjects covered in the last edition have been superseded by the separate taxation of spouses and the loss of certain benefits formerly enjoyed by unmarried cohabitants.

It once more gives us great pleasure to express our thanks to a number of friends and colleagues to whom we are indebted. We should like to thank in particular Mr Michael Jones, Lecturer in Law at Cardiff Law School who did most of the work updating Chapter 21 and Miss Gillian Douglas, Senior Lecturer in Law at Cardiff Law School who provided us with the first draft on the Child Support Act 1991 and generally updated the section on income support. We should also mention the invaluable help offered to us by Professor Margaret Brazier and Mr Martin Davey, both of the University of Manchester, and Dr Richard Ingleby of the University of Melbourne (and currently at the University of Manchester). Finally, but certainly not least, we acknowledge the inestimable assistance of Miss Kathryn Bates who cheerfully undertook the typing for Professor Lowe.

It is also a pleasure to record our thanks to the staff of Butterworths who, as ever, have been unfailingly patient and helpful.

Our division of labour has not changed: Professor Lowe has been responsible for Part II and Chapters 20 and 21 and Professor Bromley for the rest. Naturally, we have both amended our drafts in the light of the other's criticisms and we accept joint responsibility for the whole book.

We have sought to state the law as it stood on 1 May 1992. We have, however, managed to refer to a few cases reported since that date and to the Law Commission's Report on Domestic Violence and Occupation of the Family Home.

P.M.B.
N.V.L.

May 1992

Contents

Table of statutes

References in this Table to *Statutes* are to Halsbury's Statutes of England (Fourth Edition) showing the volume and page at which the annotated text of the Act will be found.

xxviii   *Table of statutes*

List of cases

Part I

Husband and wife

Summary of contents

Chapter 1

Introduction

A. The nature and scope of family law

The meaning of 'family'

The word *family* is one which it is difficult, if not impossible to define.[1] In one sense it means all persons related by blood or marriage; in another it means all the members of a household, including parents and children with perhaps other relations, lodgers and even servants. But both these definitions are far too wide for our purpose. The fact that two persons can claim descent from a common ancestor does not per se affect their legal relations at all: it is relevant for only one purpose, that of intestate succession. Similarly, the legal relationship between the head of a household and his lodgers and servants is contractual and therefore lies outside the scope of this book.

Essentially, the family may be regarded as a basic social unit constituted by at least two people, whose relationship may fall into one of three categories. Most families will consist of three or more members falling into at least two different categories.

First, the relationship may be that of husband and wife or two persons living together in a manner similar to spouses. The large number of people now cohabiting outside marriage has forced the law to take cognisance of this social phenomenon. If an extra-marital union comes to an end by separation or death, the parties and their children may need the same protection as spouses and their children, and consequently the legal position of cohabitants has to a certain extent been assimilated to that of married persons. This will be considered further in the next section, but it must be stressed immediately that rights have been accorded only to those living in a heterosexual relationship: homosexual couples are in no different legal position from two persons (of either sex) who share accommodation out of friendship or convenience.[2]

Secondly, a family may be constituted by a parent living with one or more children.

Thirdly, brothers and sisters or other persons related by blood or marriage may be regarded as forming a family. The relationship, however, has only very limited effects on their legal position, and these arise principally on the death of another member of the family.[3]

Our purpose will be to examine the legal consequences that flow from these relationships. Many of them are personal but others affect financial provision and claims to property. Because the vast majority of families are still based

[1] See further Hoggett and Pearl *The Family, Law and Society* (3rd Edn) pp 1–18.
[2] Cf *Harrogate Borough Council v Simpson* [1986] 2 FLR 91, CA, post, p 848, n 18.
[3] Eg claims under the Fatal Accidents Act (post, p 125), succession rights (post, pp 818–819) and claims to a tenancy under the Rent Act 1977 or the Housing Act 1985 (post, pp 844 and 848).

3

on marriage, we shall start with this subject: how a marriage is contracted and annulled, its legal effects and the consequences of its breakdown. At each stage where it is relevant we shall also contrast the position of spouses and extra-marital cohabitants. We shall then consider the legal consequences of the relationship of parent and child, together with the related subjects of guardians, adopted children, wards of court and children in the care of a local authority. Finally, we shall examine the question of financial provision and the effect of these relationships on property rights.

The function of family law

In this context the law has four distinct but related functions.

Definition and alteration of status

Historically this was the law's main role because it was primarily concerned with the rights which one member of the family could claim over another or over the latter's property. In the case of a man and woman living together, these arose only if they were married, and their legal relationship still depends very largely on their status. Similarly, there were virtually no rights and duties with respect to children unless they were legitimate (which in turn depended on whether their parents were married). A child's status is now of less importance but a fundamental question—who prima facie has parental responsibility for a child—still depends on whether his parents were married to each other when he was born. Questions of status are also of importance in public law, for on them may turn such matters as a person's nationality and right to live in the United Kingdom and claims to contributory social security benefits.

Akin to the courts' power to define status is their power to alter it. Among the most important aspects of this is their jurisdiction to grant divorces and make adoption orders, because a marriage can be dissolved and a child can be legally adopted only by judicial process.

Resolution of disputes

The courts' power to resolve disputes between members of the family is usually called into play when the family unit breaks down. Among the commonest subjects of disputes are the residence and upbringing of children and contact with them and the right to occupy the matrimonial home.

Protection

The protection of the weaker members of the family has two aspects: physical and economic. The former usually raises the more urgent problems and the courts can give protection to the victims of domestic violence (whether wives, husbands, cohabitants, or children) by making non-molestation orders and orders excluding a party from the matrimonial home. As a last resort they may order a child to be taken into the care of a local authority. The economic protection of a member of the family usually assumes importance when the family unit ceases to exist, either through separation or death, and the courts have extensive powers to make orders for financial provision on both these events.

Property adjustment and division

Even though the termination of the family unit may leave the members adequately provided for, justice may nonetheless require the redistribution of their capital assets, and the courts have power to make orders for this purpose on the breakdown of a marriage and, to a more limited extent, on the death of a member of the family. Similarly, if a person dies intestate, his property will have to be distributed, and the law of intestate succession is essentially a part of family law because it provides for the division of a deceased person's property amongst members of his family.

During the past century English family law has shown a steady movement away from the first of these functions to the other three, and today its remedial role is of much greater importance than that of conferring rights. The result has been to give individual judges much greater discretion, for while Parliament and appellate courts can lay down general principles for, say, the resolution of disputes relating to children or the award of financial relief, their application will vary enormously according to the circumstances of each family.

B. Marriage and extra-marital cohabitation

The large increase in the number of couples living together outside marriage has already been noted: in 1989 one in ten cohabiting couples were not married.[4] There are various reasons for this. Some cannot marry because one of them is in the process of obtaining a divorce (or is unable to do so). Some wish to avoid the financial responsibilities attached to marriage. Others wish to postpone the assumption of the legal incidents of marriage and regard cohabitation as a form of trial marriage or merely 'a pre-marital experience'. Some regard marriage as irrelevant and many cohabit because they reject 'the traditional marriage contract and the assumption of the roles which necessarily seem to go with it'.[5]

Until about 20 years ago extra-marital cohabitation gave the parties no rights over and above those possessed by, say, a brother and sister living together. Indeed, they might find themselves, legally speaking, in a worse position because their relationship, involving, as it did, fornication, might deprive them of rights which they might otherwise have. If, for example, a woman contributed a sum towards the purchase of a house in which she was to live with her brother in consideration of his undertaking to have it conveyed into their joint names, she could enforce the contract; if, however, she entered into a similar agreement with a man with whom she was going to cohabit, the illicit purpose of the transaction probably made it unenforceable. Extra-marital sexual intercourse was regarded as immoral and consequently any agreement entered into with this object in view was liable to be struck down as contrary to public policy. In *Upfill v Wright*[6] the plaintiff let a flat to the defendant who was to his knowledge the mistress of a man who intended to

---

[4] General Household Survey 1989, 137.
[5] Freeman and Lyon *Cohabitation without Marriage* p 51. For a much fuller discussion of the question see ibid ch 3; Hoggett and Pearl op cit ch 8. See also Oliver *Why do People live together?* [1982] JSWL 209; O'Donovan 47 MLR 111.
[6] [1911] 1 KB 506.

visit her there. Holding that the plaintiff could not recover the rent, Darling J said:[7]

> 'The flat was let to the defendant for the purpose of enabling her to receive the visits of the man whose mistress she was and to commit fornication with him there. I do not think that it makes any difference whether the defendant is a common prostitute or whether she is merely the mistress of one man...'

As late as 1959 the Court of Appeal expressed the view in *Diwell v Farnes*[8] that any attempt by a woman to claim an interest in a house bought by the man with whom she had been living by spelling out an agreement that they should buy it as a joint venture was doomed to failure because such a contract would be unenforceable as founded on an immoral consideration.

A complete change in the courts' attitude came a decade or so later. In 1972 the Court of Appeal held that the property rights of cohabitants who intended to marry as soon as they were free to do so should be determined in the same way as the rights of spouses.[9] Three years later they held that a cohabitant could rely on a contractual licence to give her a right to occupy a house bought by her former partner.[10] In the same year they reached the more controversial decision that a cohabitant could claim the transmission of a statutory tenancy under the Rent Act as a member of the deceased tenant's family.[11] *Upfill v Wright* itself now appears to have been overruled by the Court of Appeal in *Heglibiston Establishment v Heyman*.[12] The plaintiff had let a flat to the defendant. One of the covenants in the lease provided that the premises should not be used for an immoral purpose. The plaintiff brought proceedings for possession alleging that the tenant was in breach of this covenant by permitting his son to live in the flat with a woman to whom he was not married. The Court of Appeal held that this did not produce a forfeiture: what the clause was aimed at was preventing the premises from being used as a brothel or for the purposes of prostitution. This decision seems to have limited the rule that a contract to promote illicit sexual relationships is contrary to public policy to transactions involving sexual intercourse for a money consideration.

At the same time Parliament started to give claims to cohabitants which could scarcely have been imagined even 25 years before. By enabling a de facto dependant to apply for an order under the Inheritance (Provision for Family and Dependants) Act 1975, it has given a cohabitant the right to claim provision after her (or his) partner's death which she did not have during his lifetime. Provisions of two other Acts apply to 'a man and a woman living with each other in the same household as husband and wife': the Domestic Violence and Matrimonial Proceedings Act 1976 (which enables a county court to grant a non-molestation or ouster injunction to such a person) and the Administration of Justice Act 1982 (which has amended the Fatal Accidents Act 1976 so as to enable a cohabitant to maintain an action

---

[7] At 510.
[8] [1959] 2 All ER 379 at 384 (per Ormerod LJ) and 388 (per Willmer LJ) CA. Cf *Gammans v Ekins* [1950] 2 KB 328, [1950] 2 All ER 140, CA.
[9] *Cooke v Head* [1972] 2 All ER 38, CA. See post, p 595.
[10] *Tanner v Tanner* [1975] 3 All ER 776, CA; post, p 619.
[11] *Dyson Holdings Ltd v Fox* [1976] QB 503, [1975] 3 All ER 1030, CA; post p 842, n 19.
[12] (1977) 121 Sol Jo 851, CA. Only Megaw LJ suggested that *Upfill v Wright* should not be regarded as good law; Brown LJ distinguished it on the facts and Roskill LJ did not find it necessary to decide the point.

under that Act for the death of her (or his) partner). Similarly, the Housing Acts include 'a man or woman who lived with the tenant as husband or wife' among those who can claim a tenancy on the tenant's death.

'Living with each other as husband and wife'

Although it is not easy to see precisely what this expression means, its interpretation (like the interpretation of the corresponding phrase 'living together as husband and wife' in the Social Security Contributions and Benefits Act 1992)[13] has apparently given the courts little difficulty.[14] In the leading case of *Davis v Johnson*[15] members of the House of Lords referred to 'an unmarried housewife',[16] an 'unmarried woman commonly but not very appropriately referred to as "a common law wife"',[17] and 'unmarried partners'.[18] It has never been suggested that they should be holding themselves out as married,[19] although, if they do, this would normally be conclusive. The important question is the manner in which they live together and their reason for doing so: did they intend to live together as husband and wife?[20] Usually the parties will use their financial resources in common, share a social life and have sexual relations, although the absence of the last is not decisive.[1] The inference will be stronger if they have children or intend to marry when this is possible. The duration of the relationship must be of prime importance in any case, and the Administration of Justice Act 1982 and the Housing Act 1985 expressly provide that the parties must have lived together for two years and twelve months respectively to satisfy the statutory requirements. The relationship must be stable:[2] a man or woman living together whilst on holiday or students living together during term time prima facie do not appear to be living with each other as husband and wife. The phrase implies that they must be living together on a day to day basis, and a man living with his wife and visiting another woman regularly could hardly be said to be living with the latter as her husband. It is arguable, however, that the same person could be living with two partners in this relationship simultaneously: if a man living with a wife in London spends a considerable amount of his time on business in Manchester and, whilst there, regularly lives with another

---

[13] S 137(1) (definition of 'unmarried couple'), replacing earlier legislation.

[14] Cf Lord Widgery CJ: 'The phrase ... is so well known that nothing I could say about it could possibly assist in its interpretation hereafter' (*R v South West London Appeal Tribunal, ex p Barnett*, cited in *Crake v Supplementary Benefits Commission* (1980) 2 FLR 264, 266).

[15] [1979] AC 264, [1978] 1 All ER 1132, HL.

[16] Per Lord Kilbrandon at 339 and 1148 respectively.

[17] Per Lord Salmon at 340 and 1149 respectively.

[18] Per Lord Scarman at 347 and 1155 respectively.

[19] Cf *Davis v Johnson*, where the plaintiff does not seem to have passed herself off as the defendant's wife.

[20] *Crake v Supplementary Benefits Commission* (supra) at 267 and 269, where it was held that a man who had moved into an ill woman's house to nurse her was not living with her as her husband; *Robson v Secretary of State for Social Services* (1981) 3 FLR 232, 236, where the fact that both parties were severely handicapped and had moved into the same house to share and so reduce expenditure suggested that they were not living together as husband and wife. Cf *Kingsley v Secretary of State for Social Services* (1983) 4 FLR 143 (woman who lived with her former husband to look after his child not living as his wife).

[1] *Crake v Supplementary Benefits Commission* (supra) at 274; *Kingsley v Secretary of State for Social Services* (supra) at 149.

[2] Cf *Campbell v Secretary of State for Social Services* (1983) 4 FLR 138, where one of the facts leading the court to uphold a decision that the parties were living together as husband and wife was their having applied to the local authority for a joint tenancy.

woman, could they not be said to be living as husband and wife?[3]

The present legal position of cohabitants

The judicial and parliamentary attitude towards extra-marital cohabitation merely reflects the attitude of society generally. But it is not without its critics.[4] Convincing arguments can be put forward on both sides.[5] The strongest reason for giving rights to cohabitants is that, as many unmarried couples are virtually indistinguishable from married ones, the parties (or the survivor) and their children may be as much in need of legal protection as spouses if the union breaks down as a result of separation or is brought to an end by death. This argument is particularly strong if the parties were unable to marry each other for some reason. Against this can be raised a number of counter-arguments. The first is a purely moral one and reflects the old common law position: extra-marital cohabitation is wrong and consequently no legal rights should be granted to those who engage in it. Whilst this view is undoubtedly held by only a minority of people today, its force should not on that account be underestimated, particularly in the light of a possible 'moral backlash'. The second reason for not according rights to cohabitants rests on the indisputable premise that it is in the interests of society generally that the relationship that a couple enter into should be as stable as possible, particularly if they have children. As marriage implies an emotional and legal commitment, marital relationships, it is argued, should be more stable than extra-marital ones. Consequently, by giving to the unmarried rights previously possessed only by the married, the law is weakening the institution of marriage and thus undermining the family. The force of this argument depends on whether the assumption about the comparative stability of marriage is correct, and we have no reliable evidence about this. Finally, it is argued that the law should not force the parties to accept the obligations of marriage they have consciously chosen to reject or confer on them the attendant rights, particularly when it is possible for them, in part at least, to regulate their own legal relationship by contract.[6]

In any case, the extension of rights and obligations to persons living together outside marriage raises the difficult question of defining the class to whom they should be extended. The obvious answer is to limit it to those living with each other as husband and wife. As we have seen, the interpretation of this phrase has not caused difficulty in practice, but there seems little justification for imposing a minimum period of cohabitation (as the Fatal Accidents Act 1976 and the Housing Act 1985 do). The period is bound to be arbitrary and the principle can work injustice: a woman who has been living with a man for 18 months may be as much in need of compensation if he is killed as if she had been living with him for two years. An alternative solution would be to include within the class all who can show financial

---

[3] Cf *Watson v Lucas* [1980] 3 All ER 647, at 651 and 658, CA, where it was said that a man may be a member of two families for the purpose of the Rent Act 1977.

[4] See Freeman and Lyon *Cohabitation without Marriage* ch 7 and the judgments and writers cited at pp 187–190, particularly Deech *The Case against Legal Recognition of Cohabitation* in Eekelaar and Katz *Marriage and Cohabitation in Contemporary Societies.*

[5] See Barton *Cohabitation Contracts* 73–75.

[6] But if cohabitants can so regulate their legal position, why should not spouses be able to do so as well (eg by contracting out of their mutual duty of support)?

dependence. This is the solution adopted by the Inheritance (Provision for Family and Dependants) Act. Its implications would be extensive. If a couple parted, one would be able to claim financial provision from the other (including possibly the transfer of capital assets), and a relationship based on financial dependence could include homosexual couples and other family relations (for example, a brother and sister living together). Whatever test is applied, it could also give rise to a multiplicity of claims, for example by the wife to whom a man is still married and the woman with whom he is living.

English law has adopted a typical compromise and has assimilated the legal position of cohabitants to that of spouses only in isolated fields. This inconsistency no doubt reflects the ambivalence of society generally to the question of cohabitation as well as the number of different reasons that couples have for living together outside marriage. As the number of cohabiting couples increases, the problems resulting from the breakdown of their relationship and the attendant loss of home and support will become more common and more acute. Whatever the difficulties, the introduction of a uniform policy is essential.[7]

The legal position of spouses and cohabitants will be compared throughout this book whenever comparison is relevant, but it may be useful at this stage to summarise the principal ways in which they differ.[8]

(1) Children born to unmarried cohabitants will be illegitimate. Since the passing of the Family Law Reform Act 1987 this has been much less important than formerly. But one important distinction remains: if the parents are unmarried, parental responsibility will automatically vest in the mother only and not in both parents, as it will if they are married.[9]

(2) Although cohabitants may obtain maintenance for children, they have no claim against their partners for maintenance for themselves.[10]

(3) Whilst the court may make property adjustment orders on granting a decree of divorce, nullity or judicial separation, there is no similar power to adjust cohabitants' capital assets. An unmarried person's rights must turn on the application of the general law of property.[11]

(4) On the death of an unmarried partner, the survivor's claims for provision under the Inheritance (Provision for Family and Dependants) Act are weaker than a spouse's.

(5) Unlike a spouse, a cohabitant has no statutory right to occupy the quasi-matrimonial home, but is entitled to remain in it only as an owner or a licensee.

(6) A cohabitant has no succession rights on the death intestate of his or her partner.

(7) Certain social security benefits may be claimed by virtue of a spouse's

---

[7] The Law Commission has apparently been reluctant to undertake the task. See the Foreword to Barton op cit (which was written as a consequence of Law Com No 97).

[8] For an exhaustive comparison (now a little out of date) see Barton op cit ch 2. See also Parry *Law relating to Cohabitation* (2nd Edn).

[9] See post, p 322.

[10] But if the couple have a child or children under the age of 16 and one claims income support for herself (or himself) and the children, a magistrates' court may order the other parent to make payments in respect of both the claimant and the children: Social Security Act 1986, s 24A (added by the Social Security Act 1990, s 8). See post, p 667.

[11] But if one parent brings proceedings against the other for financial provision for a child, the court can order property to be transferred to the claimant for the benefit of the child. See post, p 697.

contributions. This principle does not extend to a cohabitant's contributions.

(8) A transfer of property between spouses (but not between cohabitants) is exempt from inheritance tax and does not attract the immediate payment of capital gains tax.[12]

(9) Usually the spouse of a person who is not a British citizen but who is settled in this country will be permitted to enter and remain here.[13] This principle does not apply to cohabitants.

Cohabitation contracts[14]

It has been suggested that those embarking on cohabitation outside marriage may wish to enter into an agreement defining their rights and obligations and, indeed, that it might be desirable for them to do so. The result would be that their relationship would be terminable by consent or at the will of either party (depending on the terms of the agreement) and that they would be completely free to decide what rights each was to have with respect to property, how their household was to be funded, how assets were to be divided on separation, and so forth. This contrasts with the position of a married couple whose union can be dissolved only by the decree of a court which can then intervene to protect their children and control their financial position and the division of their property.

It is far from clear that the courts would entertain an action based on such an agreement. The party seeking to enforce it would face two possible lines of defence: that it was contrary to public policy (or lacked consideration) and that it could not have been the parties' intention that it should be legally binding.

Public policy

It has already been argued that the rule that contracts tending to promote illicit sexual intercourse will now be struck down only if they are made with prostitutes and the like. In all the cases where contracts with cohabitants or involving cohabitation have been endorsed, however, cohabitation has not been the *sole* consideration, and it must not be assumed that a court will take the same view if it is. There are at least two other reasons for regarding the contract as possibly contrary to public policy. First, any provision for terminating it by agreement or at will contemplates a temporary union, which is likely to be unstable. Secondly, either expressly or by implication it contemplates the conception and birth of children and the court will not have the power (as it does on divorce) to intervene to protect them and, if necessary, a dependent parent on the parties' separation. Against this, however, it must be pointed out that a marriage is now terminable by consent (after two years' separation or immediately if one spouse commits adultery and the other is willing to petition for divorce), that the courts encourage spouses to reach an agreed settlement on divorce, and that unmarried parents can take proceedings to obtain an order relating to the residence and maintenance of children and contact with them.

Whilst, therefore, the position is by no means clear, it is submitted that on balance such contracts should not be regarded as contrary to public policy.

[12] Inheritance Tax Act 1984, s 18; Taxation of Chargeable Gains Act 1992, s 58.
[13] See post, p 145.
[14] See generally Barton op cit; Parry op cit ch 9; Freeman and Lyon op cit 215–220.

They are not likely to encourage people to cohabit who would not do so anyway and, if two people do intend to live together, it is better that they should give some thought to their financial and other arrangements if the union should break down.[15]

Intention to enter into legal relations

We shall see later that in *Balfour v Balfour*[16] the Court of Appeal refused to enforce an agreement by which spouses sought to regularise their domestic affairs during cohabitation because it was presumed that they had no intention to be legally bound. By analogy it could be argued that similar agreements between unmarried cohabitants would be unenforceable, particularly if they were entered into when the parties were already living together. On the other hand, it must be borne in mind that this is the only way in which legal effect can be given to their relationship. It will be strongly urged that the effect of *Balfour v Balfour* should be limited as far as possible, and it certainly should not be extended to unmarried partners if it is clear that they intended to be bound by their agreement.

Terms of the agreement

It is relatively easy for the parties to agree on their respective rights in any property acquired and on their financial obligations towards each other. Difficulty arises when they try to determine their rights and duties with respect to any children they may have. As in the case of married parents, any dispute must be resolved primarily by reference to the children's welfare.[17] Any attempt to determine in advance how far each party is to be responsible for the children's maintenance is likely to produce injustice when it is not known how many children they will have and what each party's financial position and earning capacity will be, although this can be remedied by an application to the court to alter the agreement.[18] A provision that the home in which the parties are living shall be sold on separation could also work hardship for it may leave neither party with enough to acquire any other property and the woman with no accommodation for herself and the children of the union. In the latter case she would obviously be better off if the parties were joint tenants of their home because this would give rise to a trust for sale; if she refused to concur in a sale, the court might take the view that this should be postponed at least until the property was no longer needed as a home for the children.[19]

It is obvious that a clear warning must be given to a couple contemplating making a cohabitation contract. Not only do they run the risk of finding that their agreement is legally unenforceable but it is virtually impossible to draft terms which will operate justly in all circumstances, particularly if they have

---

[15] This is the conclusion reached by Barton op cit, ch 3, Dwyer *Immoral Contracts* 93 LQR 386, 388 and Poulter 124 New LJ 999, 1034. Honoré *Sex Law* 45 argues that a contract might be lawful only if the parties had already decided to live together before making it. Sed quaere? It would still tend to promote or continue their relationship. For the position in the United States see Albano and Schiller *Cohabitation without Formal Marriage in the USA* [1986] Fam Law 43.

[16] [1919] 2 KB 571, CA. See post, p 128.

[17] See post, p 336.

[18] Under the Children Act 1989, Sch 1, paras 10 and 11. See post, pp 663–664.

[19] Cf post, p 602.

children. The only sound piece of advice is that the maximum protection can be obtained by having their home conveyed into joint names, but even this may have the effect of keeping the man from claiming what may be his only capital asset if the court refuses to order a sale so long as the woman needs to reside in it to bring up their children.

C. The courts administering family law

Sometimes a question of family law arises in a case of contract or tort or in a criminal prosecution. For example, it may be necessary to determine whether a woman can claim damages in respect of her husband's death or whether the accused's spouse is a compellable witness. Each of these cases will, of course, be tried in the ordinary civil or criminal courts and no special problem arises. What we are concerned with here are the courts which hear and determine causes raising issues solely of family law, for example the annulment or dissolution of marriage, the residence of children, and financial provision. As one would expect, the High Court has jurisdiction in almost all these matters, but a considerable concurrent jurisdiction has now been given to county courts and magistrates' courts.

The High Court

The High Court's jurisdiction in family matters is derived in part from the ecclesiastical courts. Although they had no power to dissolve a valid marriage, they had exclusive jurisdiction to grant decrees of nullity of marriage, divorce *a mensa et thoro* (equivalent to the modern judicial separation), and restitution of conjugal rights. Obviously this could not long survive the nineteenth century attitude to religious toleration. The Matrimonial Causes Act of 1857 transferred the ecclesiastical jurisdiction in matrimonial causes to a new statutory Divorce Court, which was also empowered to grant divorce by judicial process. In 1875 this jurisdiction was in turn transferred to the High Court and assigned to the Probate, Divorce and Admiralty Division.[20]

The second principal source of the jurisdiction of the High Court in family matters derives from the Court of Chancery. This court, exercising the prerogative power of the Crown as parens patriae, had a general supervisory jurisdiction over minors and, in particular, could make orders with respect to their custody and education, could appoint guardians for them and, by making them wards of court, could exercise a continuing control and supervision of them. This jurisdiction was vested in the Chancery Division when the High Court was created in 1875.[1] In view of this jurisdiction it was natural to add to it the power to make adoption orders when this became possible in 1926.

The Family Division

The fact that two divisions of the High Court possessed the power to make orders with respect to children was really an historical anomaly. It became a positive embarrassment when the two jurisdictions came into conflict as

---

[20] Supreme Court of Judicature Act 1873, s 34.
[1] Ibid.

they could, for example, if an order was sought in divorce proceedings with respect to a child who was already a ward of court. The position was made even more complicated by the fact that custody of a minor could also be claimed in the Queen's Bench Division by habeas corpus. A similar confusion arose in appeals from magistrates' courts which could lie to each of the three divisions of the High Court depending on the nature of the proceedings.[2]

It is obviously desirable to concentrate in one Division jurisdiction to deal with all matters likely to arise when a marriage breaks down. With this object in view, and as a first step perhaps to establishing a new court which could deal with all aspects of family law, section 1 of the Administration of Justice Act 1970 renamed the Probate, Divorce and Admiralty Division as the Family Division of the High Court. All the matters mentioned above, both at first instance and appellate, were transferred to the Family Division together with a number of other aspects of family law.[3] The complete list of business now assigned to the Division will be found in Appendix A, post.

County courts

The first jurisdiction to deal with family matters vested in county courts was in relation to children, and they were given power to make orders under the Guardianship of Infants Act in 1886 and to make adoption orders in 1926. Further powers followed, mainly to make orders with respect to property[4] and under the Inheritance (Provision for Family and Dependants) Act 1975. But the most important extension of county courts' jurisdiction was conferred by the Matrimonial Causes Act of 1967. The enormous increase in the number of divorce petitions during and immediately after the Second World War made it impossible for the High Court judges in London and on assize to get through the cases themselves. Consequently Divorce Commissioners (who were mainly, but not exclusively, county court judges) were appointed to try matrimonial causes in London and certain provincial towns. When it is realised that about two-thirds of all cases were heard by commissioners and over 90% of all cases were undefended, it will be appreciated that an enormous number of undefended petitions were being tried by county court judges. But as they were technically sitting as a part of the High Court, the proceedings had none of the advantages of county court proceedings: for example, solicitors could not settle pleadings and had no right of audience. This anomaly was removed by the Matrimonial Causes Act 1967, which empowered the Lord Chancellor to designate any county court as a divorce county court to hear any undefended matrimonial cause. Experience over the next few years indicated that there was no justification for declining to give county courts jurisdiction in most defended cases, and in practice many cases were being released to county court judges or heard by them sitting as deputy High Court judges. Consequently the Matrimonial and Family Proceedings Act

---

[2] In proceedings under the Guardianship of Minors Act or the Adoption Act, they went to the Chancery Division; in affiliation proceedings, to the Queen's Bench Division; and in proceedings under the Matrimonial Proceedings (Magistrates' Courts) Act, to the Probate, Divorce and Admiralty Division.

[3] See now the Supreme Court Act 1981, Sch 1, as amended. Of the other matters formally assigned to the Probate, Divorce and Admiralty Division probate business (other than non-contentious and common form business) is now assigned to the Chancery Division and admiralty and prize cases are assigned to the Queen's Bench Division.

[4] Eg, under s 17 of the Married Women's Property Act 1882 (post, p 567) and the Matrimonial Homes Act 1967.

1984 now gives divorce county courts jurisdiction to hear all matrimonial causes, both defended and undefended, and all other applications under the Matrimonial Causes Act 1973[5].

All matrimonial causes (that is, actions for divorce, nullity of marriage and judicial separation) must now be commenced in a divorce county court or in the Principal Registry in London (which is a divorce county court for this purpose). Matrimonial causes tried in a county court must be tried in a divorce county court specially designated as a court of trial.[6]

County courts' jurisdiction in matters dealing with children is now more complex. Following the implementation of the Children Act 1989, some have been designated as family hearing centres and some as care centres. These are specialist centres having sole jurisdiction to hear contested cases relating to children. The details will be considered later.[7]

Distribution and transfer of cases between the High Court and county courts

Some family proceedings[8] may be heard in the High Court only and others must be dealt with in that court unless the nature of the issues of fact or law raised makes them more suitable for trial in a county court (for example, because these issues are not complex, difficult or grave or the residence of witnesses makes trial there more convenient).[9] Subject to this the High Court may order family proceedings in that court (other than those under the Children Act or Adoption Act) to be transferred to a county court if, applying these criteria, they should be dealt with there.[10]

Conversely, a county court may order any family proceedings pending before it (other than those under the Children Act or Adoption Act) to be transferred to the High Court if the complexity, difficulty or gravity of the issues justifies such action.[11]

The transfer of cases dealing with children is subject to different rules and will be dealt with later.[12]

Magistrates' courts

The oldest jurisdiction possessed by magistrates in the field of family law related to affiliation orders, by which maintenance for illegitimate children could be obtained from the father. Historically the purpose of such orders was to relieve the poor law authority of the burden of maintaining the child themselves, and this was merely one example of the magistrates' powers to enforce this branch of the law.

Extension of their jurisdiction stems from the administration of the criminal law. Section 4 of the Matrimonial Causes Act of 1878 gave a criminal

---

[5] Matrimonial and Family Proceedings Act 1984, ss 33 and 34.

[6] Ibid, s 33.

[7] See post, p 256.

[8] Ie proceedings which in the High Court are assigned exclusively to the Family Division: Matrimonial and Family Proceedings Act 1984, s 32.

[9] Matrimonial and Family Proceedings Act 1984, s 37; *Practice Direction (Family Division: Distribution of Business)* [1992] 3 All ER 151, qv for details.

[10] Matrimonial and Family Proceedings Act 1984, s 38; Children (Allocation of Proceedings) Order 1991, art 5.

[11] Matrimonial and Family Proceedings Act 1984, s 39; Children (Allocation of Proceedings) Order 1991, art 5; *Practice Direction* (supra). In particular the court must have regard to the capital value of assets involved, substantial allegations of fraud, deception or non-disclosure, and substantial contested allegations of conduct.

[12] See post, p 258.

court, before which a married man had been convicted of an aggravated assault upon his wife, power to make an order that she should no longer be bound to cohabit with him if it felt that her future safety was in peril. The court could also order a husband to pay maintenance to a wife in whose favour such a separation order was made and vest in her the legal custody of any children of the marriage under the age of ten years. In 1886 courts of summary jurisdiction were given a further power to make a maintenance order in favour of a woman whose husband had deserted her and was wilfully refusing or neglecting to maintain her.[13]

Magistrates' domestic jurisdiction was extensively increased in 1895 when they were given much wider powers to make orders on the application of married women. During the next half century a series of Acts, which were collectively known as the Summary Jurisdiction (Separation and Maintenance) Acts 1895 to 1949,[14] gradually extended the grounds on which the wife might apply for an order, enabled the courts to order a married man to pay maintenance in respect of his children, and finally gave a husband a limited power to apply for matrimonial relief himself. The law was again completely overhauled by the Matrimonial Proceedings (Magistrates' Courts) Act of 1960, but the principles underlying this Act, with their emphasis on matrimonial offences and the parties' conduct,[15] fitted ill with the new divorce law introduced in 1971. Stringent criticisms were made of the operation of the courts and the law they administered,[16] and the number of applications to magistrates' courts declined dramatically.[17] The changed situation prompted the Law Commission to review the whole question of matrimonial proceedings in magistrates' courts, and their recommendations[18] formed the basis of the provisions of the Domestic Proceedings and Magistrates' Courts Act of 1978. In addition to overhauling the law relating to maintenance, this Act abolished the magistrates' power to make an order that the complainant should no longer be bound to cohabit with the defendant (which the Law Commission had concluded was of no practical value) and replaced it by a power to make an order forbidding one spouse to use violence against the other or against a child and, if necessary, excluding him from the matrimonial home.

Magistrates' jurisdiction in relation to children was further enlarged in 1925 and 1926, when they were given power to make orders under the Guardianship of Infants Acts and adoption orders respectively. Their current jurisdiction relating to children is governed by the Children Act 1989 and the Adoption Act 1976, and cases may be transferred to and from county courts. The details of this matter will be considered later.[19]

---

[13] Married Women (Maintenance in Case of Desertion) Act 1886.
[14] These were: the Summary Jurisdiction (Married Women) Act 1895; the Licensing Act 1902, s 5; the Married Women (Maintenance) Act 1920; the Summary Jurisdiction (Separation and Maintenance) Act 1925; and the Married Women (Maintenance) Act 1949.
[15] For details, see the 5th Edn of this book, ch 7.
[16] See particularly McGregor, Blom-Cooper and Gibson *Separated Spouses*, and the Report of the Committee on One-parent Families (the Finer Report) 1974, Cmnd 5629.
[17] In 1970 27,905 women applied for orders. The number then declined every year: in 1978 there were 6,851 applications. This is despite the removal (by the Maintenance Orders Act 1968) of the financial limit formerly set on magistrates' orders, which enabled them to make appropriate orders for women whose husbands were relatively well off.
[18] Law Com No 77 (Matrimonial Proceedings in Magistrates' Courts).
[19] See post, p 258.

Family proceedings

Since 1937 there have been special statutory provisions relating to the constitution and procedure of magistrates' courts when they are hearing 'family
proceedings'. These include proceedings under the Domestic Proceedings and
Magistrates' Courts Act 1978, the Children Act 1989 and the Adoption Act
1976.[20] A magistrates' court sitting as a 'family proceedings court' must
consist of not more than three magistrates (including, so far as is practicable,
both a man and a woman) drawn from a special 'family panel'.[1] No one may
be present in the court except the officers of the court, the parties, their legal
representatives, witnesses, other persons directly concerned in the case (such
as welfare officers), representatives of the press, and any other person whom
the court may in its discretion permit to be present.[2] The powers of newspapers and sound and television broadcasting services to report family proceedings are also considerably curtailed.[3]

Proposals for reform: the Family Court

It will be seen that proceedings relating to members of the same family may
take place in a number of courts simultaneously. For example, a wife, having
taken proceedings in a magistrates' court, may then petition for divorce in a
county court; at the same time a child of the family may have been made a
ward in the High Court.[4] This fragmented and overlapping jurisdiction causes
confusion, complicates proceedings, and leads to inconvenience, unnecessary
cost and unreasonable delay.[5] The problem is further compounded by the
fact that the law applied in magistrates' courts is significantly different from
that applied in the higher courts.[6]

As a result, pressure has been building up for a number of years for the
establishment of a unified Family Court. Family Courts have existed in the
United States for some time and have been introduced in Australia and New
Zealand.[7] Impetus for their introduction in this country was given by the
Report of the Committee on One-parent Families (the Finer Report) in 1974.[8]
Little was done to implement the Committee's suggestions for nearly a
decade. In 1983 the Lord Chancellor's Department issued a consultation
paper which was in turn overtaken by the establishment of a review committee
which published its own consultation paper in 1986.[9]

---

[20] Introduced by the Summary Procedure (Domestic Proceedings) Act 1937. See now the
Magistrates' Courts Act 1980, ss 65–74, as amended by the Children Act 1989, Sch 11. For
the full definition of 'family proceedings', see ibid, s 65 as amended. Until the commencement
of the Children Act 1989 such proceedings were known as 'domestic proceedings'. Proceedings
for the enforcement of orders and for the variation of periodical payments do not generally
come within the definition of family proceedings unless the court otherwise orders.

[1] Magistrates' Courts Act 1980, ss 66–68, as amended by the Children Act 1989, Sch 11.

[2] Ibid, s 69. Representatives of the press and 'other persons' may not be present during adoption
proceedings: s 69(3). See Lowe 145 JPN 256.

[3] See ibid, s 71, as amended by the Broadcasting Act 1990, Sch 20.

[4] As occurred in *Re C (Wardship and Adoption)* (1979) 2 FLR 177, CA. See also Hoggett *Family
Courts or Family Law Reform?* 6 LS 1, 3–5.

[5] See the Lord Chancellor's Department's Consultation Paper (1986) and Hoggett loc cit p 5.

[6] Eg magistrates' powers to order financial relief or make a personal protection order are
considerably more limited than those of the High Court or a county court.

[7] See Brown *The Legal Background to the Family Court* [1966] BJ Crim 139 (USA); the Family
Law Act 1975, s 21 (Australia); the Family Courts Act 1980, s 4 (New Zealand).

[8] Cmnd 5629 Pt 4, Ss 13 and 14.

[9] A useful summary of the contents of the paper is to be found in [1986] Fam Law 247.

A fundamental question is what the function of a Family Court should be. In the United States it is frequently seen as fulfilling a therapeutic role, whilst the models put forward by authoritative bodies in this country give it solely adjudicative powers. One of the criticisms levelled against all English matrimonial courts is that the adversarial procedure they adopt merely exacerbates the parties' relationship. The Finer Committee emphasised the importance of conciliation in all family disputes, but they also stressed that the normal safeguards of the judicial process must not be weakened by the court's regarding litigants coming before it as 'clients' or 'patients'. They therefore concluded that, if the parties were unable to reach an agreed solution, 'the Family Court must be an impartial judicial institution, regulating the rights of citizens and settling their disputes according to law'.[10] The court, they argued, should not come into the arena and they envisaged that the tribunal would be able, as now, to call on the services of welfare officers to make the necessary investigations and reports. This underlines another advantage of a unified Family Court: the integration of welfare and other ancillary services. This would get rid of the present confusing involvement of two different welfare officers with the same family if proceedings in a magistrates' court are followed by further proceedings in a county court.[11]

To be effective, a Family Court must have sole jurisdiction in all family matters and apply a uniform law: the court's powers must not depend on the tribunal before which proceedings are brought. This raises another major issue: should there be an entirely new court or could a Family Court be created out of the High Court and county courts?[12] Further, does the lay magistracy have a part to play in a Family Court? The Finer Committee believed that they had 'not only as a source of manpower, but as an equally indispensable source of lay experience and outlook which is a traditional feature in the administration of family law in England and Wales'.[13] A further advantage of including magistrates amongst the members of the tribunal is that they, like circuit judges, sit locally, and it is essential that litigants should have ready access to a local court and that most cases should be dealt with expeditiously and cheaply.[14] All judges, whether professional or lay, should clearly be trained specialists in the field of family law.

The provisions of the Children Act 1989 may prove to be the first step towards the establishment of a Family Court. They not only substitute a uniform code for the former confused and fragmented system of law but also integrate the law relating to disputes within families and the public law affecting children and local authorities. Proceedings for an order under that Act or the Adoption Act may be brought in the High Court, a designated county court or a magistrates' court sitting as a family proceedings court. Certain proceedings (mainly relating to the functions of local authorities)

---

[10] Cmnd 5629, paras 4.285 and 4.283. See generally paras 4.278 et seq.
[11] See ibid, paras 4.315–4.336. The Finer Committee recommended much closer co-operation between the court and the Department of Social Security: see ibid, Pt 4, S 12, and para 4.337.
[12] See the three options put forward by the Review Committee. (The third contemplates the retention of the existing courts with a revised jurisdiction to eliminate overlapping.)
[13] Report para 4.348. But their role has undoubtedly diminished since 1974. See also the proposals of the Association of Magisterial Officers, [1986] Fam Law 250.
[14] It would be necessary to have clear rules to determine the allocation of business between lay and professional judges.

must be begun in a family proceedings court (as were corresponding proceedings before 1991); otherwise parties have, as before, freedom to choose
in which court they will apply for an order although cases may be transferred
both laterally and vertically.[15]

If this is to be taken as a model for a Family Court with jurisdiction over
all family proceedings, it will be seen to satisfy the criteria and by implication
answer the questions set out above. The role of the court is primarily to
adjudicate, although it can take some steps on its own initiative, and the
substantive law is comprehensive and administered uniformly. There is not
a separate court, but existing courts of all tiers, including magistrates' courts,
are involved. When dealing with matters relating to children the tribunal is
composed of specialists—judges of the Family Division, specified county
court judges and magistrates drawn from the family panel—for all of whom
there was an intensive programme of training before the Children Act came
into force. The logical step is to extend these principles to other branches of
family law.[16]

D. The European Convention for the Protection of Human Rights

Although the European Convention for the Protection of Human Rights
and Fundamental Freedoms[17] is not a part of English domestic law, it is
nevertheless beginning to have a significant influence on its development.
Two articles are of particular importance in family law: Article 8, which
provides that everyone has the right to respect for his private and family life,
his home and his correspondence, and Article 12, which provides that men
and women of marriageable age have the right to marry and to found a
family according to the national laws governing the exercise of this right.
Although individuals may not bring a case to the Court of Human Rights
themselves, anyone alleging a violation of the Convention may petition the
Commission after exhausting local remedies, and the Commission may bring
the case before the Court of Human Rights at Strasbourg.[18] A range of
applications has been made by persons in this country. Amongst these may
be mentioned attempts to upset the rules that a husband cannot prevent his
wife from having an abortion[19] and that a transsexual cannot have his birth
certificate altered to record a change of sex or marry a person of the opposite
sex to that which he has assumed.[20] Others have challenged the refusal to let

---

[15] See post, pp 257–258.

[16] This could be helped by the fact that the Lord Chancellor's Department (which has responsibility for administering the High Court and county courts) has now taken over responsibility
for the administration of magistrates' courts: see the Transfer of Functions (Magistrates'
Courts and Family Law) Order 1992. In addition to the articles etc mentioned above, see
Graham Hall 1 Fam Law 6; Turner 4 Fam Law 39; 13 Fam Law 63; Cripps [1984] Fam Law
72; [1987] Fam Law 64; Craven-Griffiths and Sood [1987] Fam Law 96; Allen (ed) *Family
Justice—a structure for the Family Court*; Hoggett and Pearl *The Family, Law and Society* (3rd
Edn) 675–681.

[17] Cmnd 8969 (1953). See Douglas *The Family and the State under the European Convention on
Human Rights* 2 International Journal of Law and the Family 76.

[18] Arts 24–26, 30–32 and 48.

[19] *Paton v United Kingdom* (1980) 3 EHRR 408.

[20] *Rees v United Kingdom* (1986) 9 EHRR 56; *Cossey v United Kingdom* [1991] 2 FLR 492.

a member of the family of a person resident here enter or remain in this country[1] and a local authority's refusal to give access to the case records of a child in their care.[2]

Signatories are bound to change their domestic law if this is found to be in breach of the Convention.[3] Its provisions have been taken into account by the House of Lords in determining a mother's contact with a ward of court[4] and by the draftsman of the Children Act 1989, particularly in dealing with contact with a child in the care of a local authority. It is clear that the future shape of English family law is likely to be determined to an increasing extent by the possibility that an unsuccessful litigant may obtain access to the court as a tribunal of last resort.

---

[1] *Abdulaziz v United Kingdom* (1985) 7 EHRR 471; *Uppal v United Kingdom* (1979) 3 EHRR 391.
[2] *Gaskin v United Kingdom* (1990) 12 EHRR 36. See also *O v United Kingdom* (1987) 10 EHRR 82 (denial of access to child in local authority care).
[3] Art 5(3).
[4] *Re KD* [1988] AC 806, [1988] 1 All ER 577, HL.

Chapter 2

Marriage

A. The nature of marriage

Quite apart from its abstract meaning as the social institution of marriage, 'marriage' has two distinct meanings: the ceremony by which a man and woman become husband and wife or the *act of marrying*, and the relationship existing between a husband and his wife or the *state of being married*.[1] This distinction largely corresponds with its dual aspect of contract and status.

Marriage as a contract

In English law at least, marriage is an agreement by which a man and a woman enter into a certain legal relationship with each other and which creates and imposes mutual rights and duties. Looked at from this point of view, marriage is clearly a contract. It presents similar problems to other contracts—for example, of form and capacity; and like other contracts it may be void or voidable. But it is, of course, quite unlike any commercial contract, and consequently it is sui generis in many respects. In particular we may note the following marked dissimilarities.

(1) The law relating to the capacity to marry is different from that of any other contract.

(2) A marriage may only be contracted if special formalities are carried out.

(3) The grounds on which a marriage may be void or voidable are for the most part completely different from those on which other contracts may be void or voidable.

(4) Unlike other voidable contracts, a voidable marriage cannot be declared void ab initio by rescission by one of the parties but may be set aside only by a decree of nullity pronounced by a court of competent jurisdiction.

(5) A contract of marriage cannot be discharged by agreement, frustration or breach. Apart from death, it can be terminated only by a formal legal act, usually a decree of dissolution (or divorce) pronounced by a court of competent jurisdiction.

Marriage as creating status

This second aspect of marriage is much more important than its first. It creates a status, that is, 'the condition of belonging to a particular class of

[1] Graveson *Status in the Common Law* pp 80–81. Compare the use of the word 'marriage' in the following two sentences: 'The marriage took place yesterday between X and Y' and 'Their marriage has been dissolved'.

persons [ie, married persons] to whom the law assigns certain peculiar legal capacities or incapacities'.[2]

In the first place, whereas the parties to a commercial agreement may make such terms as they think fit (provided that they do not offend against rules of public policy or statutory prohibition), the spouses' mutual rights and duties are very largely fixed by law and not by agreement. An increasing number of these may be varied by consent; for example, the spouses may release each other from the duty to cohabit. But many may still not be altered; thus neither may contract out of his or her power to apply to the court for financial relief in the event of divorce.

Secondly, unlike a commercial contract, which cannot affect the legal position of anyone who is not a party to it, marriage may also affect the rights and duties of third persons and the relationship of the individual with government bodies. So, for example, a person whose negligence causes the death of a married man may be liable in damages to his widow, and a married woman may claim a state retirement benefit by virtue of her husband's contributions.

Definition of marriage

The classic definition of marriage in English law is that of Lord Penzance in *Hyde v Hyde*:[3]

'I conceive that marriage, as understood in Christendom, may ... be defined as the voluntary union for life of one man and one woman to the exclusion of all others.'

It will be seen that this definition involves four conditions.

First, the marriage must be *voluntary*. Thus, as we shall see,[4] it can be annulled if there was no true consent on the part of one of the parties.

Secondly, it must be *for life*. If by marriage 'as understood in Christendom' Lord Penzance was referring to the view traditionally taken in Western Europe by the Roman Catholic Church and some other denominations, his statement is of course unexceptionable. But it does not mean that by English law marriage is indissoluble: divorce by judicial process had been possible in England for over eight years when *Hyde v Hyde* was decided. The gloss put on the dictum by the Court of Appeal in *Nachimson v Nachimson*[5]—that it must be the parties' intention when they enter into the marriage that it should last for life—is unsatisfactory. This may well be the intention of the vast majority, but, if, say, two people enter into a marriage for the sole purpose of enabling a child to be born legitimate, intending never to live together but to obtain a divorce by consent at the earliest opportunity, it cannot be doubted that their union is a marriage by English law.[6] The only interpretation that can be put on Lord Penzance's statement is that the marriage must last for life unless it is previously determined by a decree or some other act of dissolution.[7] If one may draw an analogy (perhaps not very happy) from

---

[2] Allen *Status and Capacity* 46 LQR 277, 288. In this article Sir Carleton Allen critically discusses a number of other definitions of status and analyses this elusive legal concept. See also Graveson op cit.

[3] (1866) LR 1 P & D 130, 133. See further post, pp 59–60.

[4] Post, pp 90 et seq.

[5] [1930] P 217, CA.

[6] See post, p 95.

[7] *Nachimson v Nachimson* (supra) at pp 225, 227 (per Lord Hanworth MR), 235 (per Lawrence LJ), 243–244 (per Romer LJ).

the law of real property, marriage must resemble a determinable life interest rather than a term of years absolute.

Thirdly, the union must be *heterosexual.*

Fourthly, it must be *monogamous*. Neither spouse may contract another marriage so long as the original union subsists.

B. Agreements to marry

A marriage is frequently, although by no means invariably, preceded by an agreement to marry or 'engagement'. At common law such agreements amounted to contracts provided that there was an intention to enter into legal relations (as there probably would not be in the case of an 'unofficial engagement'). Because of their highly personal and non-commercial nature they possessed certain peculiar characteristics, but as a general rule they were governed by the general principles of the law of contract. Consequently if either party withdrew from the engagement without lawful justification, the other could sue for breach of contract. Such actions became rare after the Second World War—and were seldom, if ever, brought by men at all—partly no doubt because of the difficulty of proving damage, but probably largely as the result of a change in social views.[8]

The fact that actions for breach of promise of marriage were still occasionally brought raised the question of their utility. If either party to an engagement was convinced that he (or she) ought not to marry the other, it was highly doubtful whether public policy was served by letting the threat of an action push him into a potentially unstable marriage or by penalising him in damages if he resiled. The Law Commission therefore recommended the abolition of these actions[9] and this recommendation was implemented by section 1 of the Law Reform (Miscellaneous Provisions) Act 1970. This provides that no agreement to marry shall take effect as a legally enforceable contract and that no action shall lie in this country for breach of such an agreement, wherever it was made.

Property of engaged couples

The action of breach of promise of marriage might occasionally fulfil a social function by permitting a party to recover expenses which he had incurred in contemplation of the marriage. To take three examples: the woman might have travelled a considerable distance to marry and live in this country; the man might have bought furniture which he no longer needs; both parties might have spent money and labour in securing a mortgage on the proposed matrimonial home, decorating it and carrying out repairs on it. There is now no remedy at all for the first two types of loss. With respect to the third, engaged couples acquiring property for use in their married life together are in a position little different from that of a newly married couple and consequently section 2(1) of the Law Reform (Miscellaneous Provisions) Act 1970 seeks to give them some protection by enacting:

[8] The civil judicial statistics do not disclose how many actions were brought. Nor do we know how far the existence of the action led to settlements out of court.

[9] Law Com No 26 (Breach of Promise of Marriage) 1969.

'Where an agreement to marry is terminated, any rule of law relating to the rights of husbands and wives in relation to property in which either or both has or have a beneficial interest ... shall apply, in relation to any property in which either or both of the parties to the agreement had a beneficial interest while the agreement was in force, as it applies in relation to property in which a husband or wife has a beneficial interest.'

It therefore follows, for example, that if a man purchases a house in his own name partly with money provided by his fiancée and they enhance its value by doing work on it, the use of her money and her contribution to the improvement of the house will give her the same interest in it as she would have acquired had the parties been married at the time.[10]

In order to bring this subsection into play it will be seen that there must have been an agreement to marry and at least one of the parties to it must have had an interest in the property whilst the agreement was in force. It is not clear what agreements are caught by these words. Given the purpose of the legislation, it seems at first sight that the subsection applies only if there was a legally enforceable contract at common law. In *Shaw v Fitzgerald*,[11] however, Scott Baker J held that all agreements to marry were covered by the Act (whether or not they were formerly enforceable) and consequently an action could be brought under section 2(2)[12] even though the contract would have been regarded as contrary to public policy because one of the parties was married to a third person. If this decision is correct, the test must be whether there was an unconditional agreement to marry. The cause of the termination of the agreement to marry is irrelevant: it may be by consent, by repudiation by one of the parties, or by the death of either of them.

It is possible to interpret this subsection in such a way as to give very extensive rights to the parties to an engagement. In one sense of the word, for example, an intestate man's widow could be said to have *rights* in relation to his estate: it could then be argued that the Act gives similar rights to the fiancée of a man who dies intestate. This was clearly not its intention[13] and it is highly doubtful whether any court would construe it so as to give a party rights in anything but specific items of property.[14] Indeed it is doubtful whether the subsection gives the engaged person much advantage that he or she would not otherwise possess. At common law a man who bought property with his own money and had it conveyed into his fiancée's name was presumed to intend to make a gift like a husband who had property conveyed into his wife's name.[15] Similarly, the legal position of a fiancée can scarcely be weaker than that of an unmarried cohabitant, and the courts have now held that the latter, like a wife, may take a beneficial interest in property to the purchase of which she has contributed.[16] What is more important is that, in the case

---

[10] For the interests taken by spouses in each other's property, see post, pp 569 et seq.

[11] [1992] 1 FLR 357.

[12] See infra and post, p 567.

[13] Cf Law Com No 26, paras 35–42.

[14] Cf *Mossop v Mossop* [1989] Fam 77, 82, [1988] 2 All ER 202, 204, CA.

[15] *Moate v Moate* [1948] 2 All ER 486. See further post, p 574.

[16] See post, p 587. One significant difference is that an engaged person who spends money on improving property in which the other party to the engagement has a beneficial interest may claim a share or enlarged share in the interest by virtue of s 37 of the Matrimonial Proceedings and Property Act 1970 (see post, pp 599–600).

of engaged couples, there is nothing comparable to the power to adjust rights in property that the court has on divorce.[17]

To enable parties to an engagement that has been terminated to settle disputes over property more expeditiously, either of them may now bring summary proceedings under section 17 of the Married Women's Property Act 1882 within three years of the termination of the agreement.[18]

Gifts between engaged couples

At common law a gift made by one party to an engagement to the other in contemplation of marriage could not be recovered by the donor if he was in breach of contract. This meant, for example, that if the man broke off the engagement without legal justification, he could not recover the engagement ring, but he could do so if the woman was in breach of contract.[19]

In conformity with this principle that the parties' rights with respect to property should not depend upon their responsibility for the termination of the agreement, section 3(1) of the Law Reform (Miscellaneous Provisions) Act 1970 now provides:

> 'A party to an agreement to marry who makes a gift of property to the other party on the condition (express or implied) that it shall be returned if the agreement is terminated shall not be prevented from recovering the property by reason only of his having terminated the agreement.'[20]

Whether a particular gift was made subject to an implied condition that it should be returned if the marriage did not take place must necessarily be a question of fact to be decided in each case. Normally birthday presents and Christmas presents will vest in the donee absolutely, whilst property intended to become a part of the matrimonial home (for example, furniture) will be conditional. It is suggested that the general test to be applied should be: was the gift made to the donee as an individual or solely as the donor's future spouse? If it is in the latter class, it will be regarded as conditional, whereas if it is in the former, it will be regarded as absolute and recoverable only in the same circumstances as any other gift—for example, on the ground that it was induced by fraud or undue influence.

The engagement ring is specifically dealt with by the statute. The gift is presumed to be absolute but this presumption may be rebutted by proving that the ring was given on the condition (express or implied) that it should be returned if the marriage did not take place for any reason.[1] One would have thought that by current social convention an engagement ring was still regarded as a pledge and that the presumption ought to have been the other way. As it is, the ring is likely to be recoverable only in the most exceptional circumstances, for example if it can be shown that it was an heirloom in the man's family.

---

[17] *Mossop v Mossop* (supra). See also Law Com No 26, paras 35–42; Cretney 33 MLR 534.

[18] Law Reform (Miscellaneous Provisions) Act 1970, s 2(2). See further, post, p 567.

[19] *Cohen v Sellar* [1926] 1 KB 536; *Jacobs v Davis* [1917] 2 KB 532. There is no direct authority for the position if the agreement was terminated otherwise than by breach, eg, by agreement or death. It was generally assumed that the donor (or his personal representatives) could recover conditional gifts: see *Cohen v Sellar*.

[20] This is an unfortunately worded provision. If the man behaved in such a way as to justify the woman in breaking off the engagement, he could not recover conditional gifts at common law. But as it is she who has strictly terminated the agreement, it is arguable that the statute has no application and he still cannot recover the gift: see Cretney 33 MLR 534.

[1] Law Reform (Miscellaneous Provisions) Act 1970, s 3(2). See further Cretney loc cit.

If a gift in contemplation of marriage is made to one or both of the engaged couple by a third person (as in the case of wedding presents), it is, in the absence of any contrary intention, conditional upon the celebration of the marriage and must therefore be returned if the marriage does not take place for any reason at all.[2] A contrary intention will clearly be shown if the gift is for immediate use before the marriage.

Undue influence

It was formerly believed that the fact that an engaged woman would probably place the greatest confidence in her fiancé raised a presumption in equity that he had exercised undue influence over her with respect to any gift that she made to him or any contract or other transaction that she entered into at his request; consequently if she later sought to set the gift or transaction aside on this ground, the burden immediately shifted to the man to prove that there was in fact no such influence. But the change in relationship between engaged couples during the past century led the Court of Appeal to reconsider the question in *Zamet v Hyman*.[3] All the members of the court were of the opinion that the same rules must be applied today whether it is the man or the woman who secures the benefit. Donovan LJ said simply that the transaction could be set aside only if the party seeking to do so proved affirmatively that he or she had imposed confidence and trust in the other and that the disposition resulted from the abuse of such confidence and trust.[4] Lord Evershed MR (with whose observations Danckwerts LJ agreed) stated the rule more fully. Having said that the court should not necessarily assume the existence of undue influence in every case, he continued:[5]

'In any transaction of the kind of a deed or arrangement or settlement ... made between an engaged couple which upon its face appears much more favourable to one party than the other, ... the court may find a fiduciary relationship ... so as to cast an onus on the party benefited of proving that the transaction was completed by the other party only after full, free and informed thought about it.'

Thus the majority of the Court of Appeal were of the opinion that once a fiduciary relationship has been established, the burden shifts on to the party who might be expected to have exercised undue influence to prove that the transaction was the result of a free exercise of the other's will—a burden which can usually be discharged only by showing that the other received genuinely independent advice.[6] In *Zamet v Hyman* a woman aged 71 became engaged to a man aged 79. Both had children by previous marriages and three days before the marriage she executed a deed by which she relinquished all rights she might have on the husband's intestacy and under the Inheritance (Family Provision) Act in consideration of a sum of £600 payable to her out of the husband's estate on his death. Three years later the husband died intestate and left an estate worth about £10,000. In view of the vast discrepancy between the rights that she had relinquished and the sum she had gained and the fact that she had received virtually no legal advice, all the

[2] See *Jeffreys v Luck* (1922) 153 LT Jo 139.
[3] [1961] 3 All ER 933, CA.
[4] At 942.
[5] At 938.
[6] Cf the position where it is alleged that a parent has exercised undue influence over his child: post, p 644.

members of the court were of the view that the deed could not stand and that she was not bound by it.

C. The contract of marriage

In order that a man and woman may become husband and wife, two conditions must be satisfied: first, they must both possess the capacity to contract a marriage, and secondly, they must observe the necessary formalities.

The original view was that the law of marriage in all its aspects was governed by the lex loci celebrationis on the ground that those administering the law could not be expected to be familiar with any other rule. But in *Brook v Brook*[7] the House of Lords drew a distinction between capacity and formalities. In the words of Lord Campbell LC:[8]

> 'While the forms of entering into the contract of marriage are to be regulated by the lex loci celebrationis, the law of the country in which it is celebrated, the essentials of the contract depend upon the lex domicilii, the law of the country in which the parties are domiciled at the time of the marriage, and in which the matrimonial residence is contemplated.'

Capacity[9]

This question is important for two reasons: to determine whether a person who is not domiciled in this country may lawfully marry here and to determine whether we will recognise the marriage of a person married abroad.

Although capacity to marry is undoubtedly governed by the parties' lex domicilii, it is impossible to state with confidence how this principle will be applied in all cases. In the passage from Lord Campbell's speech in *Brook v Brook* cited above it will be seen that he refers to the country in which the parties are domiciled at the time of the marriage *and* in which they propose to reside. If these coincide, there is no difficulty: if both are domiciled in England and they intend to reside in this country, both must have capacity by English law wherever the marriage takes place. But what if they have different domiciles or intend to set up home in a third country? Two tests have been proposed to solve the problem. By the first, the 'dual domicile test', each party must have capacity by his or her domicile at the time of the ceremony and, if either lacks it, the marriage will be void.[10] It has the advantage of being easy to apply, but it can operate arbitrarily. If, to take the facts of *Radwan v Radwan (No 2)*,[11] a woman domiciled in England contracts in France a polygamous marriage with a man, domiciled in Egypt where such marriages are permitted, and then lives with him in Egypt, it is difficult to see why the marriage should be void because it is forbidden by English law. For this reason the alternative 'intended matrimonial home test' may be preferred. It was thus spelled out by its chief English proponent, Dr Cheshire:[12]

---

[7] (1861), 9 HL Cas 193, HL.
[8] At p 207. See also *Sottomayor v De Barros* (1877) 3 PD 1, 5, CA.
[9] See generally Law Com WP No 89 (Choice of Law Rules in Marriage).
[10] Dicey and Morris *Conflict of Laws* (11th Edn) pp 622 et seq.
[11] [1973] Fam 35, [1972] 3 All ER 1026.
[12] Cheshire and North *Private International Law*, (11th Edn) p 575.

'The basic presumption is that capacity to marry is governed by the law of the husband's domicile at the time of the marriage, for normally it is in the country of that domicile that the parties intend to establish their permanent home. This presumption, however, is rebutted if it can be inferred that the parties at the time of the marriage intended to establish their home in a certain country and that they did in fact establish it there within a reasonable time.'

If one applies this to the facts given above, it will be seen that the marriage will be valid, for the law of Egypt alone will be relevant.[13] The weakness of the test is that it is contrary to basic principle to permit the parties to be able to change their legal capacity merely by conceiving an intention; furthermore if the parties propose to establish their matrimonial home in a country different from that in which the husband is domiciled at the time of the ceremony, one must wait and see whether they carry out their intention, and the validity of the marriage may be in doubt until they do so.

Yet another test was proposed by Lord Simon of Glaisedale in *Vervaeke v Smith*.[14] Drawing a somewhat elusive distinction between the essential and quintessential validity of a marriage, he suggested that the latter might be governed by the law of the territory with which the marriage has the most real and substantial connection. At the time of the marriage the wife was a Belgian national, domiciled in Belgium; applying Belgian concepts of public policy the marriage was void, by English law it was valid. Lord Simon was of the opinion that public policy was a matter of quintessential validity, and as the marriage took place in England, the husband was domiciled here, and the wife intended to reside in this country and apply for British nationality, English law should prevail as that of the territory with which the marriage had the most real and substantial connection. There is only one reported case in which this has been followed. In *Lawrence v Lawrence*[15] at first instance Anthony Lincoln J, faced with a conflict between the dual domicile and intended matrimonial home tests, held that the parties' freedom to marry each other was a matter of quintessential validity and resolved the conflict by applying Lord Simon's test.

The real difficulty is that two principles are pulling in opposite directions. The first is the desire to uphold the validity of an existing union, particularly one which has already lasted for a number of years; the second is the need to have a simple rule which can be applied easily and prospectively, so that the parties can know in advance whether or not they have capacity to enter into a proposed marriage. It is the sophistication of Lord Simon's test (which may involve litigation to determine the law with which the marriage has the

---

[13] Unless it is void because the parties lack capacity by the lex loci celebrationis: see post, p 30.

[14] [1983] 1 AC 145, 165–166, [1982] 2 All ER 144, 158–159, HL.

[15] [1985] Fam 106, [1985] 1 All ER 506. The Court of Appeal did not discuss the applicability of this test ([1985] Fam 106, [1985] 2 All ER 733). See also Fentiman *The Validity of Marriage and the Proper Law* [1985] CLJ 256 and *Activity in the Law of Status* 6 OJLS 353; Smart *Interest Analysis, False Conflicts, and the Essential Validity of Marriage* 14 Anglo-American LR 225. Another test is proposed by Jaffey *The Essential Validity of Marriage in the English Conflict of Laws* 41 MLR 38. He points out that English law would recognise a polygamous marriage which was valid by both parties' lex domicilii even though they came to live in England immediately afterwards. He therefore suggests that a marriage should be void on the ground of polygamy or relationship within the prohibited degrees only if it is void by either party's lex domicilii *and* by the law of the country within which they establish a matrimonial home within a reasonable time after the celebration. As the law relating to non-age is designed to protect the immature, he argues that a marriage should be void only if forbidden by the lex domicilii of the party under age.

most real and substantial connection) and the uncertainty of the intended matrimonial home test that may make both unworkable. The dual domicile test has the merit of being relatively easy to apply and it enables the parties' marital status to be ascertained with certainty at the time of the marriage.[16] At present the balance of judicial authority is in its favour,[17] and two statutory provisions rest on the assumption that it is correct.[18] The intended matrimonial home test is supported by the decision of the Court of Appeal in *De Reneville v De Reneville*[19] and was applied by Cumming-Bruce J in *Radwan v Radwan (No 2)*,[20] although he was careful to limit his decision to the question of capacity to enter into a polygamous union.[1] In the latest case in which the problem was debated, that of *Lawrence v Lawrence*[2] in the Court of Appeal, Ackner and Purchas LJJ held that there was no need to resolve it (although the latter doubted whether the intended matrimonial home test could be generally applied because of the uncertainty of its operation) whilst Sir David Cairns was inclined to the view that a marriage might be valid if either test was satisfied. This may prove to be the solution that judges will adopt in the future: prospectively the parties can tell whether their marriage will be valid by applying the dual domicile test, whilst retrospectively it may be saved by the intended matrimonial home test.[3]

Whatever be the correct test, reference to the *lex domicilii* includes a reference to its relevant conflict of laws rules. In *R v Brentwood Superintendent Registrar of Marriages, ex p Arias*[4] an Italian national who was domiciled in Switzerland and who had obtained a divorce in that country wished to marry in England. By Swiss law capacity to marry is governed by the law of the party's nationality and, as Italian law did not recognise the Swiss divorce, he lacked the capacity to marry in Italy and, therefore, in England too.

The actual decision in this case is no longer law. It is anomalous that we should recognise a divorce but deny the parties to the former marriage the capacity to remarry. The decision in *Ex p Arias* was reversed by section 7 of the Recognition of Divorces and Legal Separations Act 1971; this section has in turn been repealed and the principle extended by section 50 of the Family Law Act 1986. This provides:

'Where, in any part of the United Kingdom—

(a) a divorce or annulment has been granted by a court of civil jurisdiction, or

---

[16] See Law Com WP No 89, paras 3.20 and 3.34–3.36.

[17] *Padolecchia v Padolecchia* [1968] P 314, 336, [1967] 3 All ER 863, 873, following *Schwebel v Unger* (1963) 42 DLR (2d) 622; affd (1964) 48 DLR (2d) 644. See also *Re Paine* [1940] Ch 46; *Pugh v Pugh* [1951] P 482; [1951] 2 All ER 680; and cf *Szechter v Szechter* [1971] P 286, 295, [1970] 3 All ER 905, 913.

[18] Marriage (Enabling) Act 1960, s 1(3); Matrimonial Proceedings (Polygamous Marriages) Act 1972, s 4 (now repealed and re-enacted in the Matrimonial Causes Act 1973, s 11(d)), (post, p 62). See also Morris *Conflict of Laws* (3rd Edn) pp 159 et seq.

[19] [1948] P 100, [1948] 1 All ER 56, CA. See also *Kenward v Kenward* [1951] P 124, 144–146, [1950] 2 All ER 297, 310–11, CA (per Denning LJ); *In the Will of Swan* (1871) 2 VR 47.

[20] [1973] Fam 35, [1972] 3 All ER 1026. See Karsten 36 MLR 291, where the writer points out that the decision is scarcely supported by the authorities on which Cumming-Bruce J relied.

[1] At pp 540 and 1040 respectively.

[2] [1985] Fam 106, [1985] 2 All ER 733, CA.

[3] The Law Commission eventually decided that no legislative changes were desirable because the law is still in the process of development and, although legislation would give certainty, flexibility would be lost: Law Com No 165 (Choice of Law Rules in Marriage), Part II.

[4] [1968] 2 QB 956, [1968] 3 All ER 279.

(b) the validity of a divorce or annulment is recognised by virtue of [Part II of the 1986 Act],[5]

the fact that the divorce or annulment would not be recognised elsewhere shall not preclude either party to the marriage from re-marrying in that part of the United Kingdom or cause the re-marriage of either party (wherever the re-marriage takes place) to be treated as invalid in that part.'

Whilst this provision removes one difficulty, it creates another. Had the husband in *Ex p Arias* gone through a second ceremony of marriage abroad, in 1968 we should have regarded him as married to neither his first nor his second wife. Now we should regard him as validly married to the second while his lex domicilii would regard him as still married to the first.

It is not certain what view an English court would take of the converse situation, that is if a divorce is recognised by the parties' lex domicilii but not in England. If either party remarried in England (or perhaps if the other party to the second marriage were domiciled in England, wherever the marriage took place), we should probably hold the marriage void on the ground that we should have to regard him (or her) as already married.[6] If he remarried elsewhere, however, it would be more consonant with common sense to accept the validity of a marriage which is valid by the parties' lex domicilii. But until all countries accept the same rules of recognition of foreign divorces and annulments, the scandal of the limping marriage[7] will remain.

If the parties' capacity is governed by English law, the courts of this country have consistently declared marriages void where that capacity has been lacking, even though the person concerned would have had capacity by the lex loci celebrationis.[8] But they have not applied this principle consistently in the case of a marriage in England of a person domiciled abroad. Where *neither* party is domiciled in England, they will admittedly regard the marriage as void if the parties lacked capacity by their lex domicilii even though they would have had capacity had they been domiciled in England; but where one of the parties is domiciled in England, the courts will not take account of any incapacity imposed by the lex domicilii of the other party which is not recognised by English law. Hence, if both parties are domiciled in a country where marriage between first cousins is prohibited, such a marriage will be void if celebrated in this country;[9] but if one of them is domiciled in England, the marriage will nevertheless be valid.[10] This distinction has been judicially justified on the grounds that English courts are bound to protect their own

---

[5] For recognition of divorces and annulments see Dicey and Morris *Conflict of Laws* (4th Supplement to 11th Edn) pp 91 et seq; Cheshire and North *Private International Law* (11th Edn) pp 648–685. In certain circumstances an overseas divorce or annulment will be recognised even though it was not obtained by means of any formal proceedings (eg a Muslim talaq).

[6] But in *Schwebel v Unger* (1963) 42 DLR (2d) 622, (1964) 48 DLR (2d) 644 the Supreme Court of Canada held that such a marriage was valid. The case was approved by Simon P in *Padolecchia v Padolecchia* [1968] P 314, 339, [1967] 3 All ER 863, 875. See also Nott *Capacity to marry following Foreign Divorce or Nullity Decrees* 15 Fam Law 199.

[7] Ie a marriage which is regarded as valid in one country but not in another.

[8] *Brook v Brook* (1861) 9 HL Cas 193, HL (prohibited degrees of affinity); *Pugh v Pugh* [1951] P 482, [1951] 2 All ER 680 (nonage); *Sussex Peerage Case* (1844) 11 Cl & Fin 85, HL (Royal Marriages Act 1772).

[9] *Sottomayor v De Barros* (1877) 3 PD 1, CA.

[10] *Sottomayor v De Barros (No 2)* (1879) 5 PD 94, approved by the Court of Appeal in *Ogden v Ogden* [1908] P 46.

nationals and that 'no country is bound to recognise the laws of a foreign state when they work injustice to its own subjects';[11] but the fact that such a marriage may be regarded as void in one country and valid in another is liable to produce greater hardship than it avoids.[12]

There may be two further exceptions to the rule that capacity to marry is governed by the lex domicilii. It is possible that a marriage will be void if the parties lack capacity by the lex loci celebrationis. So far as marriages celebrated in England are concerned, we will not permit a polygamous union to be contracted,[13] and it is scarcely credible that we should permit our marriage laws to be used to enable a marriage to be contracted between persons under the age of 16 or related within the prohibited degrees. This seems to be amply justified on the grounds of public policy. It does not follow, however, that English courts would necessarily take the same view if the marriage took place elsewhere, for example if first cousins, both domiciled in England, married in a country where such marriages were forbidden. Although the principle of reciprocity should compel them to regard the marriage as void if the lex loci did so, we have already seen that this principle is not applied uniformly.[14] The second possible exception is that English law will disregard any incapacity imposed by the lex domicilii if it is penal. It is not clear what incapacities are caught by this rule. It has been held to cover prohibitions against marrying outside one's own caste[15] and against the remarriage of a divorced person;[16] it is submitted that it is really a further example of public policy and would also include prohibitions against marrying persons of a different race and, perhaps, against the marriage of those who have taken vows of celibacy. Clearly, if the marriage was celebrated in England to a person domiciled here, we should disregard the prohibition anyway, and the so called exception may be merely a particular application

---

[11] Per Cotton LJ in *Sottomayor v De Barros* (1877) 3 PD at p 7. But the rule applies to persons *domiciled* in England who may not be British subjects. See also Webb *Some Thoughts on the Place of English Law as* Lex Fori *in English Private International Law* 10 ICLQ 818, at pp 825–829.

[12] The Law Commission are of the view that it should be abolished: Law Com No 165 (Choice of Law Rules in Marriage) para 2.15. But see Clarkson *Marriage in England; favouring the lex fori* 10 Legal Studies 80. For statutory attempts to avoid limping marriages, see the Marriage (Enabling) Act 1960, s 1(3), the Marriage (Prohibited Degrees of Relationship) Act 1986, s 1(7) and the Marriage with Foreigners Act 1906. Under the last named a foreigner marrying a British subject in England and Wales can be required to produce a certificate that there is no impediment to the marriage by foreign law. But the attempt has been wholly ineffective as no Orders in Council have yet been made under the Act. The Law Commission's Working Party rejected the proposal that such certificates should be obligatory on the ground that this would place an undue burden on superintendent registrars: Law Com No 53, Annex, para 57.

[13] See post, p 61.

[14] But in *Breen v Breen* [1964] P 144, [1961] 3 All ER 225, Karminski J would apparently have held a marriage celebrated in Dublin void if the Irish courts had not recognised the validity of a previous English divorce, even though both parties were domiciled in England. For Commonwealth decisions to the contrary, see *In the Will of Swan* (1871) 2 VR (IE&M) 47; *Reed v Reed* (1969) 6 DLR (3d) 617. See also Jaffey 41 MLR 38, 46–47; Bradshaw *Capacity to marry and the Relevance of the* Lex Loci Celebrationis *in Commonwealth Law* 15 Anglo-American LR 112.

[15] *Chetti v Chetti* [1909] P 67.

[16] *Warter v Warter* (1890) 15 PD 152, 155, explaining *Scott v A-G* (1886) 11 PD 128. But this does not apply if the prohibition is purely suspensive to ensure that the decree is not appealed: *Warter v Warter*.

of the principle we have already discussed. But in *Warter v Warter*[17] Hannen P referred to an incapacity 'penal in its character and as such ... inoperative out of the jurisdiction under which it was inflicted'. This is wide enough to oblige us to disregard it wherever the marriage was celebrated and whatever was the domicile of the other party. In the absence of any authority it is submitted that on grounds of public policy we should do so unless the marriage was celebrated in the country of the parties' domicile, when it must be void by any test.[18]

Formalities[19]

English law has rarely departed from the rule that the formal validity of the marriage depends upon the lex loci celebrationis. This is so even though persons domiciled in England may deliberately have gone to another country in order to evade the English rules as to formalities. Hence, the courts of this country always recognised the validity of the 'Gretna Green' marriages since, until the law was altered by statute in 1939, a valid marriage could be contracted in Scotland per verba de praesenti in the presence of a witness, who, at least till a residence requirement was imposed by statute in 1856, was by tradition frequently the blacksmith in the first town over the Border. Similarly, a person resident in England may validly contract a marriage by proxy in a country the law of which permits such marriages,[20] and if the marriage is initially formally invalid by the lex loci, English law will recognise the effect of a local statute retrospectively curing the invalidity.[1] It seems that the lex loci celebrationis includes its conflict rules, so that if the parties do not comply with the municipal law of the place where they are married but the lex loci, applying its own conflict rules, will recognise the marriage as validly contracted, we shall apparently do so as well.[2] This avoids a limping marriage, for which there would be no justification.

---

[17] (1890) 15 PD 152, 155.

[18] But see the view expressed by Lord Simon of Glaisdale in *Vervaeke v Smith* [1983] 1 AC 145, 166, [1982] 2 All ER 144, 159, HL, that public policy is a question for the law of the territory with which the marriage has the most real and substantial connection (ante, p 27). Dicey and Morris *Conflict of Laws* (11th Edn) p 642 suggest that English law might regard the marriage as valid or void according to the view taken by the lex loci celebrationis.

[19] See Law Com WP No 89 (Choice of Law Rules in Marriage), Pt II. Comment on this working paper favoured retention of the present rules: Law Com No 165, para 2.5.

[20] *Apt v Apt* [1948] P 83, [1947] 2 All ER 677, CA; *Ponticelli v Ponticelli* [1958] P 204, [1958] 1 All ER 357.

[1] *Starkowski v A-G* [1954] AC 155, [1953] 2 All ER 1272, HL. Quaere whether the retrospective operation would have been recognised if either party had remarried in the meantime. See further Mendes da Costa *The Formalities of Marriage in the Conflict of Laws* 7 ICLQ 217, at pp 251 et seq; Tolstoy *The Validation of Void Marriages* 31 MLR 656.

[2] Cf *Taczanowska v Taczanowski* [1957] P 301, [1957] 2 All ER 563, CA, where the court would apparently have recognised a marriage celebrated in Italy as valid if the parties had complied with the formalities required by Polish law on the ground that it would have been recognised by the Italian conflict of laws. Formerly English law appears to have regarded a marriage celebrated in a foreign embassy in London as valid provided that both parties were subjects of the ambassador's state: see Cheshire and North *Private International Law* (11th Edn) p 562. Now that the fiction of extra-territoriality is exploded, it is possible that we might no longer recognise such a marriage unless, perhaps, at least one of the parties was a member of the mission: cf *Radwan v Radwan* [1973] Fam 24, [1972] 3 All ER 967. Conversely, subject to certain very stringent conditions the Foreign Marriage Acts 1892 and 1947 (as amended by the Foreign Marriage (Amendment) Act 1988) empower a British ambassador or consul or a Governor, High Commissioner or Resident to solemnize a marriage at his official residence provided that he holds a marriage warrant from the Foreign Secretary and at least one of the

Recognition of common law marriages

English law will also recognise a marriage which is valid at common law if no local form exists at all or if it would be impossible or unreasonable to expect the parties to comply with the lex loci celebrationis in the circumstances. They would undoubtedly be justified in not observing local formalities if, for example, the ceremony was offensive by English standards or the only form available was a polygamous one. A particular application of the same principle is to be seen in the rule, accepted by our courts, that members of occupying belligerent forces cannot be expected to submit to the laws of those they have conquered. This exception is not confined to members of the British forces[3] as can be seen from a series of cases involving the marriage of Polish forces in Europe immediately after the Second World War.[4] It is, however, limited to marriages of which one party is a member of a foreign occupying force or is 'in a foreign country as part of the organisation necessarily or at least commonly set up when there is hostile occupation'.[5] Consequently two civilians who have no connection with the occupying force cannot contract a valid common law marriage and must comply with the lex loci.[6]

In *Taczanowska v Taczanowski*[7] the Court of Appeal applied the common law as the lex fori. This approach is open to the criticism that the validity of the marriage may turn on the court in which it is put in issue: it is difficult by any process of reasoning to see how a marriage celebrated in Italy between two persons domiciled in Poland can be governed by the English common law. A more acceptable explanation is that put forward by Russell LJ in *Preston v Preston:*[8]

> 'Once the lex loci is rejected ... it may well leave it open to a court in this country to recognise as a marriage ... that which by the general law of Christendom was recognised as constituting the basic essence of the marriage contract—the contract per verba de praesenti without further formalities.'

This would also explain what seems to be a further anomaly. Originally at common law a marriage was contracted by mutual declarations, but this rule was later modified and a valid marriage could be contracted only in the

---

parties is a United Kingdom national as defined in s 1 of the 1892 Act (as amended). For the detailed provisions, see Dicey and Morris op cit, pp 612–613; Cheshire and North op cit, pp 563–565.
[3] So far as British forces are concerned, the Foreign Marriage Act 1947, s 2, permits naval, military and air force chaplains and other persons authorised by the Commanding Officer to solemnize marriages in a foreign territory provided that at least one of the parties is a member of the British forces serving in that territory or is employed there in a capacity defined by Order in Council. For details see Dicey and Morris op cit p 611, Cheshire and North op cit p 565.
[4] *Taczanowska v Taczanowski* (supra); *Merker v Merker* [1963] P 283, [1962] 3 All ER 928; *Preston v Preston* [1963] P 411, [1963] 2 All ER 405, CA. Contrast *Lazarewicz v Lazarewicz* [1962] P 171, [1962] 2 All ER 5, where the marriage was held to be void on the ground that the parties had intended, but failed, to comply with the lex loci celebrationis. The problem arose particularly with respect to Poles because of the large number of Polish forces and displaced civilians in Central Europe who refused to return to Poland when it became controlled by a communist government after the War. Many subsequently settled in this country and acquired an English domicile.
[5] Per Ormerod LJ in *Preston v Preston* (supra) at 427 and 411 respectively.
[6] The earlier decision to the contrary in *Kochanski v Kochanska* [1958] P 147, [1957] 3 All ER 142 can no longer be regarded as good law.
[7] [1957] P 301, [1957] 2 All ER 563, CA.
[8] [1963] P 411, 436, [1963] 2 All ER 405, 416, CA.

presence of an episcopally ordained clergyman.[9] It is doubtful whether this requirement ever applied outside England and Ireland; in the type of case we are considering it certainly does not apply if compliance would be impossible, difficult or even inconvenient. Thus in *Penhas v Tan Soo Eng*[10] the Privy Council held that 'in a country such as Singapore, where priests are few and there is no true parochial system, where the vast majority are not Christians, it is neither convenient nor necessary' that a marriage between a Jew and a non-Christian Chinese should be contracted in the presence of an episcopally ordained clergyman.

Characterisation[11]

It is sometimes difficult to decide whether a particular rule should be characterised as relating to capacity or to formalities. The problem arose in *Ogden v Ogden*.[12] A domiciled Frenchman, aged 19, married in England a woman domiciled in this country without obtaining his parents' consent. By French law this meant that he lacked capacity to contract a valid marriage, but by English law parental consent is a question of formality and lack of it will not affect the validity; it therefore became vital to decide which law should govern the question. The Court of Appeal classified parental consent as a part of the ceremony (thus holding the marriage to be valid) apparently on the principle that English law would apply the lex fori to characterise a condition in the case of a marriage celebrated in England. It is submitted that the case was correctly decided on the ground that we should ignore the effect of lack of parental consent on the husband's capacity as he married a woman domiciled in England in this country;[13] but in any event to fall back on the lex fori to characterise the matter is quite indefensible. In order to avoid a limping marriage, one should ask first of all what the relevant law relating to capacity is by the parties' lex domicilii; if this regards lack of parental consent as invalidating the marriage, we must accept and apply the rule. One must then ask what the relevant rule relating to formalities is by the lex loci. In the *Ogden v Ogden* type of case, where consent is relevant by both systems, the marriage will be void if lack of consent deprives either party of capacity by his lex domicilii or if it renders the ceremony a nullity by the lex loci celebrationis.

We must now consider in greater detail the relevant English municipal law.

D. Capacity to marry

In order that a person domiciled in England should have capacity to contract a valid marriage, the following conditions must be satisfied:

    (a) one party must be male and the other female;
    (b) neither party must be already married;

[9] Post, p 39.
[10] [1953] AC 304, PC, following *Wolfenden v Wolfenden* [1946] P 61, [1945] 2 All ER 539.
[11] See Law Com WP No 89 (Choice of Law Rules in Marriage) paras 4.1–4.10; Morris *Conflict of Laws* (3rd Edn) pp 151–153.
[12] [1908] P 46, CA, followed in *Lodge v Lodge* (1963) 107 Sol Jo 437.
[13] See ante, p 29.

(c) both parties must be over the age of 16; and

(d) the parties must not be related within the prohibited degrees of con-
    sanguinity or affinity.[14]

Sex

A new problem, arising out of operations to effect a so-called change of sex,
had to be considered by Ormrod J in *Corbett v Corbett*.[15] The petitioner in
this case was a man; before the marriage the respondent had undergone a
surgical operation for the removal of 'her' male genital organs and the
provision of artificial female organs. After dealing at length with the medical
evidence the learned judge (who was also a qualified medical practitioner)
came to the conclusion that a person's biological sex is fixed at birth (at the
latest) and cannot subsequently be changed by artificial means. That being
so, the respondent, who was male at birth, was not a woman and the marriage
was therefore void.

In this case the respondent was to be regarded as male by three independent
biological criteria: chromosomal, gonadal and genital. There are persons,
however, who are male by one test and female by another. Ormrod J deliberately left open the question of capacity to marry in such cases but he was
inclined to give greater weight to the appearance of the genital organs. It is
at least arguable that such persons are neither male nor female and consequently are legally incapable of marrying anyone of either sex.

It has been suggested that from a social and domestic point of view the
psychological gender of a transsexual such as the respondent in *Corbett v
Corbett* (that is the sex to which the individual feels that he or she belongs)
is of greater importance than biological sex.[16] Accordingly, as the parties to
such a union regard themselves as belonging to opposite sexes (a view
presumably shared by others), a marriage between them should be valid, at
least provided that the transsexual party has undergone surgery of the type
described. The view has also been expressed that section 11(c) of the Matrimonial Causes Act 1973, which requires the parties to be respectively male
and female, would now permit a court to take gender, rather than biological
sex, into account.[17] It is very doubtful, however, whether this result could or
should be achieved in this oblique way. The law relating to consummation

---

[14] A further prohibition is to be found in the Royal Marriages Act 1772, which was passed to
prevent the contracting of highly undesirable marriages by the younger brothers of King
George III. It provides that no descendant of King George II (other than the issue of princesses
who have married into foreign families) may marry without the previous consent of the
Sovereign formally granted under the great seal and declared in Council. Any marriage coming
within the Act, consent to which has not been obtained, will be void; but if the descendant in
question is over the age of 25 and gives twelve months' notice of the intended marriage to the
Privy Council, it may be validly contracted unless both Houses of Parliament have in the
meantime expressly declared their disapprobation of it. For a criticism of the Act and a
discussion of how far (if at all) it has any force today, see Farran *The Royal Marriages Act
1772* 14 MLR 53.

[15] [1971] P 83, [1970] 2 All ER 33; applied in *R v Tan* [1983] QB 1053, [1983] 2 All ER 12, CA
(person born male remains a man for the purposes of the Sexual Offences Acts notwithstanding
a similar 'sex change operation').

[16] See Kennedy *Transsexualism and Single Sex Marriage* 2 Anglo-American Law Review 112;
Armstrong and Walton *Transsexuals and the Law* 140 New LJ 1384.

[17] See Poulter *The Definition of Marriage in English Law* 42 MLR 409, 421–425. S 11 of the
Matrimonial Causes Act 1973 re-enacts s 1 of the Nullity of Marriage Act 1971, which received
the royal assent 17 months after judgment was delivered in *Corbett v Corbett*. See further post,
p 81.

emphasises that English law still regards marriage as a normal heterosexual relationship[18] and it is by no means certain that public opinion would support the change advocated. Although transsexuals can obviously be distinguished from other types of homosexuals, the recognition of any form of homosexual union would mark such a profound departure from the traditional approach of English law that it should be brought about only by an unambiguously worded statute.

Monogamy

As a result of the English view of marriage as a monogamous union, neither party may contract a valid marriage whilst he or she is already married to someone else. If a person has already contracted one marriage, he cannot contract another until the first spouse dies or the first marriage is annulled or dissolved.[19] It follows that a mistaken belief that the first marriage has been terminated, for example, by the death of the spouse, is immaterial: what is relevant is whether it has in fact been terminated. Consequently, the second marriage may be void even though no prosecution for bigamy will lie in respect of it.

Age

Both by canon law and at common law a valid marriage could be contracted only if both parties had reached the legal age of puberty, viz 14 in the case of a boy and 12 in the case of a girl. If either party was under this age when the marriage was contracted, it could be avoided by either of them when that party reached the age of puberty; but if the marriage was ratified (as it would impliedly be by continued cohabitation), it became irrevocably binding.[20]

It is somewhat surprising that this remained the law until well into the present century. In the words of Pearce J:[1]

'According to modern thought it is considered socially and morally wrong that persons of an age, at which we now believe them to be immature and provide for their education, should have the stresses, responsibilities and sexual freedom of marriage and the physical strain of childbirth. Child marriages by common consent are believed to be bad for the participants and bad for the institution of marriage.'

This change of thought led to the passing of the Age of Marriage Act in 1929. Section 1 (now re-enacted in section 2 of the Marriage Act 1949) effected two changes in the law. First, it was enacted that a valid marriage could not be contracted unless both parties had reached the age of 16, and secondly any marriage to which either party was under this age was made *void* and not voidable as before.

The provision that *both* parties must be over the age of 16 is important when the party under that age is not domiciled in England and has capacity

---

[18] See post, pp 85–90 and cf the judgment of Ormrod J in *Corbett v Corbett* [1971] P 83, 106, [1970] 2 All ER 33, 48. The principle has been upheld by the European Court of Human Rights: *Rees v United Kingdom* (1986) 9 EHRR 56; *Cossey v United Kingdom* [1991] 2 FLR 492. See Naldi 137 New LJ 129.

[19] But this does not apply if the first marriage was *void*: post, p 75.

[20] Co Litt 79; Blackstone *Commentaries*, i, 436.

[1] *Pugh v Pugh* [1951] P 482, 492, [1951] 2 All ER 680, 687. See further Law Com No 33 (Nullity of Marriage), paras 16–20; Report of the Latey Committee on the Age of Majority, 1967, Cmnd 3342, paras 166–177.

by his or her own lex domicilii. This is illustrated by *Pugh v Pugh*.[2] A man over the age of 16 and domiciled in England went through a form of marriage in Austria with a girl aged 15. She was domiciled in Hungary, by the law of which country the marriage was valid. It was nevertheless held that it was void since the man had no capacity by English law to marry her.

Prohibited degrees

Most, if not all, civilised states prohibit certain marriages as incestuous. The prohibited relationship may arise from consanguinity (ie, blood relationship) or from affinity (ie, relationship by marriage). Before the Reformation English law adopted the canon law of consanguinity and affinity,[3] but one of the results of the break with the Roman Catholic Church was the adoption of a modified table of prohibited degrees. The new law, which was Levitical in origin,[4] was to be found in a series of statutes,[5] but the vague reference in the statute 32 Hen 8, c 38, to marriages 'prohibited by God's law' left the matter in considerable doubt, and the interpretation of this Act was still the subject of litigation as late as 1861.[6] But there was eventually little doubt that the prohibited degrees were those laid down by Archbishop Parker in 1563 and adopted in 1603 in the ninety-ninth Canon and set out in the Book of Common Prayer.[7] Since 1949 the prohibitions have been statutory and are contained in the First Schedule to the Marriage Act, which, as originally enacted, reproduced Archbishop Parker's Table as qualified by three Acts passed between 1907 and 1931.[8] Since 1949 it has been amended by three other Acts:[9] it is set out in its current form in Appendix B (post, p 854). It is drawn up in two columns, of which the left and right state the persons with whom a man and a woman respectively may not intermarry (subject to certain qualifications noted below in the case of relationships coming within Parts II and III).

Until 1835 a marriage within the prohibited degrees was voidable merely, but the Marriage Act of that year made all such marriages void.

Consanguinity

In the case of consanguinity prohibition is based on moral and eugenic grounds. Most people view the idea of sexual intercourse (and therefore marriage) between, say, father and daughter or brother and sister with abhorrence; furthermore, the more closely the parties are related, the greater

[2] [1951] P 482, [1951] 2 All ER 680.
[3] See Pollock and Maitland *History of English Law*, ii, 383–387. The rules that emerged lacked theological or sociological justification and 'are the idle ingenuities of men who are amusing themselves by inventing a game of skill which is to be played with neatly drawn tables of affinity and doggerel hexameters': ibid, 387.
[4] Leviticus 18.
[5] 25 Hen 8, c 22, 28 Hen 8, c 7, and 32 Hen 8, c 38. All three of these statutes were repealed by 1 Ph & M, c 8, but 1 Eliz 1, c 1, revived 32 Hen 8, c 38, and thus by implication so much of the other two as it referred to. See *R v Chadwick* (1847) 11 QB 173, 2 Cox CC 381; *Wing v Taylor* (1861) 2 Sw & Tr 278.
[6] *Wing v Taylor* (supra).
[7] *Hill v Good* (1674) Vaugh 302, 328. But see *R v Chadwick* (1847) 2 Cox CC at 406.
[8] Deceased Wife's Sister's Marriage Act 1907; Deceased Brother's Widow's Marriage Act 1921; Marriage (Prohibited Degrees of Relationship) Act 1931.
[9] Marriage (Enabling) Act 1960; Children Act 1975, Sch 3; Marriage (Prohibited Degrees of Relationship) Act 1986.

will be the risk of their children inheriting undesirable genetic characteristics. The degrees of relationship based on consanguinity are set out in Part I of the Schedule to the Marriage Act; marriage within these degrees is completely prohibited.[10] Because of the eugenic basis of the prohibition it includes not only relationships traced through the whole blood but also those traced through the half blood,[11] and it is immaterial that the parents of either of the parties (or of any person through whom the relationship is traced) have not been married to each other.[12]

It should be observed that the number of persons between whom marriage is forbidden is greater than those between whom sexual intercourse is a criminal offence under the Sexual Offences Act 1956,[13] although of course all the relationships set out in the latter Act come within the prohibited degrees.

Affinity

In the case of affinity, prohibition was originally based on the theological concept that husband and wife were one flesh, so that marriage with one's sister-in-law was as incestuous as marriage with one's own sister.[14] This view probably commands little support today and justification must now be sought on social and moral grounds. (Some will also have religious objections to certain marriages,[15] but in a pluralist society this must be a matter for the individual's conscience.) Marriage with a near relation of a former spouse is always liable to create tensions within the family, particularly if the spouse is still alive, and the possibility of marriage to a stepchild could in some cases lead to sexual exploitation. Even if this were not so, difficulties could well arise if, say, a man were to become the brother-in-law of his other stepchildren and the stepbrother-in-law of his own children. There is a stronger reason for forbidding marriage with a stepchild to whom the other party has been in loco parentis, for this can readily be seen as an abuse of the relationship. In circumstances of this sort prohibition could be justified on the ground that the function of the marriage laws is to support the family and the relationships that uphold it. On the other hand it must be remembered that degrees of affinity can be created only by marriage: there is nothing to prevent a man from cohabiting with his stepdaughter outside marriage or marrying the daughter (by another man) of a woman with whom he has himself been living.

Wide dissatisfaction with the rules relating to affinity has been expressed for a century, though it was only after bitter controversy that the Deceased Wife's Sister's Marriage Act was passed in 1907 permitting a man to marry his deceased wife's sister, and it was not until 1921 that he was allowed to marry his deceased brother's widow.[16] In 1931 the principle of these two Acts was extended to eight other prohibited degrees of affinity,[17] and in 1960 marriage was allowed within these degrees after a decree of divorce or nullity

---

[10] Marriage Act 1949, s 1(1).
[11] See the definitions of 'brother' and 'sister' in the Marriage Act 1949, s 78(1).
[12] *Hains v Jeffell* (1696) 1 Ld Raym 68; *R v Brighton Inhabitants* (1861) 1 B & S 447.
[13] Ss 10 and 11.
[14] For the same reason in the Middle Ages extra-marital sexual intercourse created prohibited degrees.
[15] See *No Just Cause* (infra) pp 30–32.
[16] Deceased Brother's Widow's Marriage Act 1921.
[17] Marriage (Prohibited Degrees of Relationship) Act 1931.

even though the former spouse was still alive.[18] Further extensive changes were made in 1986 by the Marriage (Prohibited Degrees of Relationship) Act, passed after the publication of *No Just Cause*, the report of a group set up by the Archbishop of Canterbury to consider the problem following four private Acts to permit marriage within the prohibited degrees.[19]

The present law represents a compromise between the conflicting principles mentioned above. The remaining prohibited degrees of affinity are divided into two groups, but in neither case is the prohibition absolute. The first group (set out in Part II of the Schedule to the Marriage Act) is retained in order to protect stepchildren against possible exploitation. A person may not marry his or her stepchild or stepgrandchild unless both parties have attained the age of 21 and the latter was not at any time before reaching the age of 18 a child of the family in relation to the other.[20] 'Child of the family' is defined as a child who has lived in the same household as the other and been treated by the latter as a child of his or her family.[1] It will thus be seen that there is nothing to prevent a man from marrying his stepdaughter if, say, she was brought up by her grandparents so that he was never in loco parentis to her. The inclusion of the second group (set out in Part III of the Schedule) is the result of a compromise between those who, like the majority of the Archbishop's group, saw no reason for prohibiting marriage with a son-in-law or daughter-in-law and those who feared that the possibility of such a union might give rise to sexual rivalry between parent and child and thus undermine family relationships. Consequently a man may not marry his son's wife unless both his son and the son's mother are dead; similarly a woman may not marry her daughter's husband unless both the daughter and the daughter's father are dead. In addition, in either case both parties must be over the age of 21.[2]

E. Formalities of marriage

1. HISTORICAL INTRODUCTION

The history of the English law relating to the formalities of marriage—even the state of the law immediately before the passing of Lord Hardwicke's Act in 1753—is still a matter of considerable doubt.[3] Canon law emphasised the

---

[18] Marriage (Enabling) Act 1960 (adopting the majority recommendation of the Morton Commission 1956, Cmd 9678, Pt XV).

[19] See also Chester and Parry *Reform of the Prohibition on Marriage of Related Persons* 14 Fam Law 237.

[20] Marriage (Prohibited Degrees of Relationship) Act 1986, s 1(1); Marriage Act 1949, s 1(2), (3) and Sch 1, Pt II, as amended by Sch 1 to the Act of 1986.

[1] Marriage (Prohibited Degrees of Relationship) Act 1986, s 1(5); Marriage Act 1949, s 78 (as amended). The phrase 'treated as a child of the family' also appears in the definition of 'child of the family' in the Matrimonial Causes Act 1973 and will presumably be interpreted in the same way: see post, pp 368–369.

[2] Marriage (Prohibited Degrees of Relationship) Act 1986, s 1(3), (4); Marriage Act 1949, s 1(4), (5) and Sch 1, Pt III (as amended).

[3] Cf the conflicting opinions expressed in *R v Millis* (1844) 10 Cl & Fin 534, HL. See Swinburne *Spousals*; Jackson *Formation and Annulment of Marriage* (2nd Edn) ch 2; Pollock and Maitland *History of English Law* ii 362 et seq; the judgment of Sir W Scott in *Dalrymple v Dalrymple* (1811) 2 Hag Con 54; and the opinion of the judges in *Beamish v Beamish* (1861) 9 HL Cas 274, HL.

consensual aspect of the contract and before the Council of Trent in 1563 no religious ceremony had to be performed; all that was necessary was a declaration by the parties that they took each other as husband and wife, either per verba de praesenti (eg 'I take you as my wife [or husband]'), in which case the marriage was binding immediately, or per verba de futuro (eg 'I shall take you as my wife [or husband]'), in which case it became binding as soon as it was consummated. But it early became customary for the marriage to be solemnized in facie ecclesiae after the publishing of banns (unless this was dispensed with by papal or episcopal licence) and with the consent of the parents of either party who was under the age of 21. The marriage would then be contracted at the church door per verba de praesenti in the presence of the priest, after which the parties would go into the church itself for the celebration of the nuptial mass.[4]

It is hardly surprising that the common law favoured the publicity of marriage in facie ecclesiae, for upon the existence of the union might depend many property rights and the identity of the heir at law. Consequently, there developed a curious rule that the wife was not dowable unless she was endowed at the church door,[5] and certain other proprietary disabilities may have followed as well.[6] But in the course of time the reason for the common law insistence upon such a marriage was forgotten. Neither the publishing of banns nor the presence of any other witness was any longer considered necessary; the emphasis shifted on to the presence of the priest (or, after the Reformation, a clerk in holy orders), so that eventually the rule was laid down that a valid marriage at common law could be contracted only per verba de praesenti exchanged in his presence.[7]

But the old marriage per verba de praesenti was not wholly ineffective. Until the middle of the eighteenth century a marriage could be contracted in one of three ways:

(a) In facie ecclesiae, after the publishing of banns or upon a licence, before witnesses, and with the consent of the parent or guardian of a party who was a minor. Such a marriage was obviously valid for all purposes.

(b) Clandestinely, per verba de praesenti before a clerk in holy orders, but not in facie ecclesiae. This, as we have seen, was as valid as if it had been solemnized in facie ecclesiae.

(c) Per verba de praesenti or per verba de futuro with subsequent sexual intercourse, but where the words were not spoken in the presence of an ordained priest or deacon. Whilst such a marriage would no longer produce all the legal effects of coverture at common law, it was nevertheless valid for many purposes. Such a union was indissoluble, so that, if either party to it

---

[4] The marriage service of the Church of England still preserves this ancient form. The first part of the service takes place in the body of the church and consists of the espousals (in which each party replies 'I will') followed by the contracting of the marriage per verba de praesenti. This concludes the civil aspect of the marriage: the remainder of the service is purely religious in character.

[5] Bracton f 303b.

[6] Swinburne op cit.

[7] *R v Millis* (1844) 10 Cl & Fin 534, HL. There is little doubt that the decision was based on a misunderstanding of the medieval law: Pollock and Maitland loc cit. See further Hall *Common Law Marriage* [1987] CLJ 106, pp 112 et seq; Lucas *Common Law Marriage* [1990] CLJ 117. During the Commonwealth, marriages could be celebrated before Justices of the Peace: Jackson op cit pp 59–60.

subsequently married another, the later marriage could be annulled.[8] More-over, either party could obtain an order from an ecclesiastical court calling upon the other to solemnize the marriage in facie ecclesiae.[9]

Lord Hardwicke's Act

It needs little imagination to picture the social evils which resulted from such a state of law. A person who had believed himself to be validly married for years would suddenly find that his marriage was a nullity because of a previous clandestine or irregular union, the existence of which he had never before suspected. Children would marry without their parents' consent, and if the minor was a girl with a large fortune, the old common law rule that a wife's property vested in her husband on marriage made her a particularly attractive catch. The 'Fleet' parsons thrived—profligate clergy who traded in clandestine marriages. By the middle of the eighteenth century matters had come to such a pass that there was a danger in certain sections of society that such marriages would become the rule rather than the exception.[10]

It was to stop these abuses that Lord Hardwicke's Act was passed in 1753.[11] The principle underlying this Act was to secure publicity by enacting that no marriage should be valid unless it was solemnized according to the rites of the Church of England in the parish church of the parish in which one of the parties resided in the presence of a clergyman and two other witnesses.[12] Unless a licence had been obtained, banns had to be published in the parish church of the parish in which each party resided for three Sundays. If either party was under the age of 21, parental consent had to be obtained as well, unless this was impossible to obtain or was unreasonably withheld, in which case the consent of the Lord Chancellor had to be obtained. If these stringent provisions were not observed, the marriage would in the vast majority of cases be void. Furthermore, the Act abolished the jurisdiction of the Ecclesiastical Courts to compel persons to celebrate the marriage in facie ecclesiae if they had contracted a marriage per verba de praesenti or per verba de futuro followed by consummation.

Marriage Act 1823

Whilst Lord Hardwicke's Act effectively put a stop to clandestine marriages in England, it caused an almost greater social evil. For the new law was so stringent and the consequence of failing to observe it—the avoidance of the marriage—so harsh, that many couples deliberately evaded it by getting married in Scotland. This was particularly the case when one of the parties was a minor and parental consent was withheld; so that the 70 years following the passing of the Act saw an increasing number of 'Gretna Green' marriages. It was in an attempt to prevent this that Parliament in 1823 repealed Lord Hardwicke's Act and replaced it by a new Marriage Act. So far as the positive directions of the earlier Act were concerned, viz the necessity of the

---

[8] *Bunting v Lepingwell* (1585) 4 Co Rep 29a. This rule was abrogated by 32 Hen 8, c 38, in 1540 but revived in 1548 by 2 & 3 Ed 6, c 23.

[9] *Bunting v Lepingwell* (supra); *Baxtar v Buckley* (1752) 1 Lee 42.

[10] See Stone *The Family, Sex and Marriage* pp 30–35.

[11] There is no doubt that its main purpose was to protect the property interests of the upper classes: Stone op cit pp 35–37.

[12] Marriages according to the usages of the Society of Friends (Quakers) and according to Jewish rites were exempt from the provisions of the Act.

solemnization of the marriage in the church of the parish in which one of the parties resided after the publication of banns or the grant of a licence, they were re-enacted with only a few minor alterations of detail; where the new Act differed largely was in the effect of non-compliance with these directions. A marriage was now to be void only if both parties *knowingly and wilfully* intermarried in any other place than the church wherein the banns might be published, or without the due publication of banns or the obtaining of a licence, or if they *knowingly and wilfully* consented to the solemnization of the marriage by a person not in holy orders. In all other cases the marriage was to be valid notwithstanding any breach in the prescribed formalities. But if the marriage of a minor, whose parent or guardian had not given his consent, had been procured by fraud, the Attorney-General, on the relation of the parent or guardian, might sue for the forfeiture of any property acquired as a result of the marriage by the party who had perpetrated the fraud.

This Act remained the principal Act governing the formalities of marriage in England for over 125 years. Naturally, it was greatly amended during that time. Thus, jurisdiction to make an order dispensing with parental consent was extended to county courts and magistrates' courts;[13] and in 1930 it became possible for the parties to be married in a church which was the regular place of worship of one of them even though it was the parish church of neither.[14] But two Acts introduced principles which were so radically different from those of the Acts of 1753 and 1823 that they must be mentioned separately.

Marriage Act 1836

The principal criticism raised against the two earlier Acts was that they forced Roman Catholics and Protestant dissenters[15] to go through a religious form of marriage which might well be repugnant to them. The growth of religious toleration generally during the early years of the nineteenth century eventually led to the removal of this grievance by the Marriage Act of 1836.

This Act, together with the Births and Deaths Registration Act which was passed immediately after it, brought into existence the superintendent registrars of births, deaths and marriages, who were empowered to issue certificates to marry as an alternative to the publication of banns or the obtaining of a licence. But the real importance of the Act lay in the fact that it permitted marriages to be solemnized on the authority of a superintendent registrar's certificate (with or without a licence) in other ways than according to the rites of the Church of England. For the first time since the Middle Ages, English law recognised the validity of a marriage, which was purely civil in character and completely divorced from any religious element, by permitting the parties to marry per verba de praesenti in the presence of a superintendent registrar and a registrar of marriages and two other witnesses. The Act went even further by permitting places of worship of members of denominations other than the Church of England to be registered for the solemnization of marriages; and it now became lawful for marriages to be celebrated in these 'registered buildings' in accordance with whatever religious

---

[13] Guardianship of Infants Act 1925, s 9.
[14] Marriage Measure 1930.
[15] Except Quakers who (together with Jews) were still permitted to celebrate their own marriages (see p 40, n 12, ante).

ceremony the members wished to adopt, provided that at some stage the parties took each other as husband and wife per verba de praesenti in the presence of a registrar of marriages and at least two other witnesses.

Marriage Act 1898

The Act of 1836 had removed the legitimate grievance of Roman Catholics and Protestant dissenters; the remaining disability under which they suffered—the necessity of having a registrar present at a religious ceremony—was removed by the Marriage Act of 1898. This Act permitted the trustees or governing body of a registered building to authorise a person to be present at the solemnization of marriages in that building, and henceforth a marriage could be lawfully solemnized there in the presence of an 'authorised person' without a registrar being present at all. Normally, of course, this person would be a minister of the particular denomination, so that the combined effect of the Acts of 1836 and 1898 was to give to the ministers of all religious denominations the power of solemnizing marriages already enjoyed by clergymen of the Church of England.

Marriages Acts 1949–1986

By 1949 the extremely complicated law relating to the formalities of marriage could be found only by reference to more than 40 statutes, quite apart from the case law which had grown up as the result of their judicial interpretation. The purpose of the Marriage Act of that year was to consolidate these enactments in one Act. As a result, nearly twenty of these statutes were repealed in toto and most of the rest were repealed in part. Few changes were made in the substantive law: the only notable exception was that the Attorney-General's power to sue for the forfeiture of property was taken away—a power which the married women's property legislation had, in any case, already made virtually obsolete.

The Act of 1949 has since been amended by a series of Acts,[16] two of which deserve special mention. The Acts of 1836 and 1898 had left those marrying according to the rites of the Church of England one privilege not shared by others: the power to marry in a private building on the authority of a special licence. This anomaly has now been removed. The Marriage (Registrar General's Licence) Act 1970 permits the Registrar General to issue a licence authorising the solemnization of a marriage anywhere if one of the parties is suffering from a serious illness from which he is not expected to recover and cannot be moved to a register office or registered building. The Marriage Act 1983 has gone further and enables a house-bound or detained person to be married in the place where he is confined or detained on the authority of a superintendent registrar's certificate. A change in the law of much wider application was the reduction of the age of majority to 18 by the Family Law

---

[16] The Marriage Act 1949 (Amendment) Act 1954; the Marriage Acts Amendment Act 1958; the Marriage (Enabling) Act 1960; the Marriage (Wales and Monmouthshire) Act 1962; the Marriage (Registrar General's Licence) Act 1970; the Marriage Act 1983; the Marriage (Wales) Act 1986; the Marriage (Prohibited Degrees of Relationship) Act 1986. These Acts (except for that of 1962) and the Marriage Act 1949 are collectively known as the Marriage Acts 1949–1986.

Reform Act 1969, as a result of which anyone over this age may now marry without the consent of any other person.[17]

In addition to laying down the legal requirements relating to the preliminaries to marriage and the place and method of solemnization, the Marriage Acts also regulate the registration of marriages. The details of the relevant law are far too complex to be considered here,[18] but it must be emphasised that proper registration is of extreme importance not only to the parties themselves but also to others (including government departments) who may wish to have evidence of the marriage.[19]

The above outline will have made it clear that the principles underlying the modern law cannot be understood without a knowledge of their historical origin. The law is now hopelessly out of date: proposals for reform will be considered later.[20]

It will be convenient to consider the modern law under two heads: (a) where the marriage is solemnized according to the rites of the Church of England, and (b) where it is solemnized in some other way. Before doing this, however, we must consider the question of consent to the marriage of a person under the age of 18. Finally it will be necessary to discuss marriages in naval, military and air force chapels.

2. MARRIAGES OF PERSONS UNDER THE AGE OF 18

If either party to the marriage is over the age of 16 but under the age of 18, certain persons are normally required to give their express consent to the marriage or are given a power to dissent from it. The purpose of this provision is, of course, to prevent minors' contracting unwise marriages. Doubtless in 1753 Parliament was primarily concerned to see that property did not get into the hands of undesirable suitors; today its object is to cut down the number of potentially unstable unions.[1] Should the marriage be solemnized without consent, the damage will have been done; consequently lack of consent will normally not make the marriage void.[2]

The law relating to those whose consent is required was extensively changed by the Children Act 1989. Normally it will be that of each parent with parental responsibility and each guardian (if any). Hence an unmarried father cannot withhold consent unless he has entered into a parental responsibility agreement or obtained a parental responsibility order. But if a residence order is in force with respect to the child, the consent required is that of the person or persons with whom the child is living or is to live under the order

---

[17] S 2(1). This implements the recommendations of the Latey Committee on the Age of Majority, 1967, Cmnd 3342.
[18] They are contained in Pt IV of the Marriage Act 1949 (as amended by the Marriage Act 1983, Sch 1) and in the Marriage (Registrar General's Licence) Act 1970, s 15.
[19] See Law Com No 53 (Report on Solemnization of Marriage), Annex, para 104. See ibid, paras 105–118 for a critical review of the present law and for suggestions for reform.
[20] Post, pp 57–59.
[1] Report of the Latey Committee, Cmnd 3342, paras 135–177; Eekelaar *Family Security and Family Breakdown* pp 63–64; Priest *Buttressing Marriage* 12 Fam Law 40, 43–45.
[2] Law Com No 53, Annex, para 49. See post, pp 82–83. But this is not the case if the parent or other person publicly dissents on the publication of banns which will then be void: post, p 84.

and not that of parents or guardians.[3] If a care order is in force, the local authority designated in the order must consent *in addition to parents and guardians*. It should be noted that no consent is required at all if the minor is a widow or widower.[4]

It will also be seen from what follows that, if it is impossible to obtain the necessary consent or, more particularly, if the consent is withheld, the consent of the court may be obtained instead. The 'court' for this purpose is the High Court, a county court or a magistrates' court sitting as a 'family proceedings court'.[5]

Marriages by a superintendent registrar's certificate

If the parties propose to marry on the authority of a superintendent registrar's certificate (whether by licence or without licence), the necessary consent or consents must be expressly given. If a person's consent cannot be obtained because he is absent or inaccessible or under any disability (eg, mental illness), it is dispensed with entirely if there is any other person whose consent is also required (as will be the case where both parents must consent); where no other person's consent is required, however, either the Registrar General may dispense with the necessity of any consent or the consent of the court must be obtained. Where any person's consent is *refused*, then the consent of the court must be obtained in any case.[6]

Marriages by the Registrar General's licence

In this case the position is exactly the same as above except that the consent of a person who is absent, inaccessible or under a disability is never automatically dispensed with. The Registrar General has a discretion to dispense with it in all cases, whether or not there is any other person whose consent is required.[7]

Marriages by a common licence

If the parties propose to marry on the authority of a common licence, the necessary consent or consents must be expressly given, and precisely the same rules apply as in the case of marriages by a superintendent registrar's certificate except that, where the only person whose consent is required is absent, inaccessible or under a disability, the necessity of obtaining any consent may be dispensed with by the Master of the Faculties and not by the Registrar General.[8]

[3] If a residence order was in force immediately before the child reached the age of 16 but is no longer in force, the consent required is that of the person or persons with whom he lived or was to live.

[4] Marriage Act 1949, s 3(1), (1A) and (1B), as amended and added by the Children Act 1989, Schs 12 and 15. If the minor is a ward of court, the court's consent must be obtained: ibid, s 3(6).

[5] Ibid, s 3(5), as amended by the Family Law Reform Act 1969, s 2(2), the Domestic Proceedings and Magistrates' Courts Act 1978, Sch 2, and the Justices of the Peace Act 1979, Sch 2; Magistrates' Courts Act 1980, s 65(1)(c). For the meaning of 'family proceedings court', see ante, p 16. There is no statutory right of appeal from an order of the court giving or withholding consent, so that there is no appeal at all from the decision of a magistrates' court: *Re Queskey* [1946] Ch 250, [1946] 1 All ER 717.

[6] Marriage Act 1949, s 3(1). Consent once given can be withdrawn at any time before the solemnization: *Hodgkinson v Wilkie* (1795), 1 Hag Con 262, 265. Quaere whether a superintendent registrar could revoke a certificate on this ground: cf post, p 51, n 14.

[7] Marriage (Registrar General's Licence) Act 1970, s 6.

[8] Marriage Act 1949, s 3(2).

Marriages after the publication of banns

In this case express consent need not be given but

'if any person whose consent to the marriage would have been required ... in the case of a marriage intended to be solemnized otherwise than after the publication of the banns, openly and publicly declares or causes to be declared, in the church or chapel in which the banns are published, at the time of the publication, his dissent from the intended marriage, the publication of the banns shall be void.'[9]

The Act does not expressly empower the court to consent to the marriage in this case. If the court's consent is obtained, therefore, it is probably necessary for the parties to marry on the authority of a common licence or a superintendent registrar's certificate.[10]

3. MARRIAGES ACCORDING TO THE RITES OF THE CHURCH OF ENGLAND

There are two matters to be considered. First, certain preliminary formalities must be observed: a marriage may be solemnized according to the rites of the Church of England (which includes the Church in Wales)[11] only after the publication of banns or on the authority of a common licence, a special licence or a superintendent registrar's certificate.[12] Secondly, the law relating to the ceremony itself must be discussed.

It should be noted that no clergyman is obliged to solemnize the marriage of a divorced person whose former spouse is still alive or to solemnize a marriage which would have been void before the passing of the Marriage (Prohibited Degrees of Relationship) Act 1986 because of the relationship of the parties. Nor can he be forced to permit such a marriage to be solemnized in the church or chapel of which he is the minister.[13]

Publication of banns

Since the purpose of publishing banns is to give publicity to the proposed marriage, they must normally be published in the parish church of the parish in which the parties reside, or if they reside in different parishes, in the parish church of each of the two parishes.[14] But where a party resides in a chapelry (ie a district attached to one of certain specified chapels) or in a parish in which the bishop of the diocese has licensed a public chapel or church building for the publication of banns and the solemnization of marriages (as he may do in a remote part of a parish covering a wide area or if the building is

---

[9] Ibid, s 3(3).

[10] Although it is arguable that, if a person's consent is refused and that of the court is obtained instead, he is no longer 'a person whose consent to the marriage would have been required' and therefore any subsequent dissent will be ineffectual.

[11] Marriage Act 1949, ss 78(2), 80(3). A few technical provisions of the Act do not apply in Wales: see ibid, Sch 6, as amended by the Marriage (Wales and Monmouthshire) Act 1962 and the Marriage (Wales) Act 1986.

[12] Marriage Act 1949, s 5.

[13] Matrimonial Causes Act 1965, s 8(2); Marriage Act 1949, s 5A (added by the Marriage (Prohibited Degrees of Relationship) Act 1986, s 3).

[14] Marriage Act 1949, s 6(1). There are special provisions dealing with changes in parish boundaries, the creation of new parishes, the amalgamation of parishes and benefices, and cases where churches are being repaired or rebuilt or have been injured by war damage: ibid, ss 10, 18, 19 and 23; Pastoral Measure 1983, s 27 and Sch 3, para 14.

shared with other denominations), banns may be published either in that authorised chapel or building or in the parish church,[15] and if he resides in a district in which there is no church or chapel in which divine service is usually held every Sunday, banns may be published in any adjoining parish or chapelry.[16] Banns may be published in Scotland, Northern Ireland or the Republic of Ireland if either party is residing there,[17] or, provided that both parties are British subjects, in certain other parts of the British Commonwealth.[18] If one of the parties is an officer, seaman or marine on a Royal Naval ship *at sea*, banns may be published on board by the chaplain or, if there is no chaplain, by the captain or other officer in command.[19]

If the parties wish to be married in another church or authorised chapel which is the normal place of worship of either of them,[20] banns must be published there as well as in their parish churches.[1]

Manner of publication

Banns must be published on three Sundays during morning service by a clergyman of the Church of England.[2] The form of words is prescribed by the rubric in the Book of Common Prayer.[3]

Names in which banns should be published

Since the purpose of the publication of banns would be defeated if the parties could not be identified, they must be referred to by the names by which they are generally known. This will, of course, usually be their original Christian names and surname, or in the case of a woman who has been previously married, her married surname;[4] but if a person has assumed some other name by which he is generally known, the banns should be published in that name. An example of due publication under an assumed name is to be seen in *Dancer v Dancer*.[5] The wife was the legitimate daughter of Mr and Mrs Knight. When she was aged three, her mother went to live with a man called Roberts by whom she had five children. All the children, including the wife, Jessamine, passed as the legitimate children of Roberts and Mrs Knight (who

---

[15] Marriage Act 1949, s 6(1); Sharing of Church Buildings Act 1969, s 6. See the definition of 'authorised chapel' in the Marriage Act 1949, s 78(1), and see also ibid, s 21. For the licensing of chapels, see s 20, as amended by the Patronage (Benefices) Measure 1986, ss 34(3) and 41 and Sch 5.

[16] Marriage Act 1949, s 6(3). See also s 6(2) and the Pastoral Measure 1983, s 29.

[17] Ibid, s 13.

[18] Marriage of British Subjects (Facilities) Acts 1915 and 1916. See 27 Halsbury's Statutes (4th Edn) 463–466.

[19] Marriage Act 1949, s 14.

[20] As defined in the Marriage Act 1949, s 72. The party must be enrolled on the church electoral roll. For marriages in guild churches in the City of London, see the City of London (Guild Churches) Act 1952, s 22.

[1] Marriage Act 1949, s 6(4).

[2] Ibid, ss 7 and 9. If there is no morning service, banns may be published during the evening service (s 7(1)), and a lay reader may publish banns if there is no clergyman officiating (s 9(2)). A clergyman is entitled to a week's notice in writing before he publishes banns: s 8.

[3] Ibid, s 7(2). 'I publish the banns of marriage between *M* of   and *N* of   . If any of you know cause or just impediment why these two persons should not be joined together in holy matrimony, ye are to declare it. This is the first [second, *or* third] time of asking.'

[4] Per Sir R Phillimore in *Fendall v Goldsmid* (1877) 2 PD 263, 264.

[5] [1949] P 147, [1948] 2 All ER 731. See also *R v Billinghurst* (1814) 3 M & S 250. For the converse case of an undue publication under the original surname, see *Tooth v Barrow* (1854) 1 Ecc & Ad 371.

assumed the name of Roberts) and were known by the name of Roberts; and it was not till she was 17, when Roberts died, that Jessamine discovered that she was not his daughter. She continued to use the name of Roberts, and on the advice of the vicar who published the banns, she was named therein as Jessamine Roberts. It was held that the banns were duly published, for the wife was generally known by that name and the purpose of publishing the banns under it was not to conceal her identity but to avoid any concealment.

In all the cases where it has been held that the banns have not been duly published, there has been some fraudulent intention to conceal the party's identity.[6] The reason for the concealment is immaterial: thus it has been held that there was an undue publication where the parties' intention was to conceal the marriage from the man's relations,[7] and where the man was a deserter from the Royal Field Artillery and had assumed a false name to avoid detection and prosecution.[8] A difficult case is *Chipchase v Chipchase.*[9] A woman, whose maiden surname was Matthews, had married in 1915 a man called Leetch. He had deserted her in 1916 and she had not heard of him since. In 1928 she went through a form of marriage with the petitioner after the publication of banns in the name of Matthews, which she had used for some two years before the marriage and by which she was generally known in the district; her reason for having the banns published in this name was not that she was known by it but that it served to conceal, or at least not to emphasise, the fact that she had been married before. Henn Collins J holding that there had been an undue publication of the banns, said:[10]

'The wife did not conceal her identity from the persons in her parish who knew her by that name, but I think that one of the purposes of the Marriage Act would be defeated if it was open to a person to have banns called in a name by which he was known in the parish when the use of his legal name might lead persons to make uncomfortable inquiries. In my view that is one of the very things against which the Act of Parliament was directed.'

In so far as Henn Collins J held that there must be some intentional concealment before the court will hold that there has not been a due publication, his decision follows the earlier cases. The difficulty is to discover in what name the banns should have been published, for it is submitted that, if she was generally known by the name of Matthews, it would have equally defeated the purposes of the Act to publish the banns under any other name. The common sense answer to this problem is that the banns should have been published under both names in the alternative (ie, Matthews or Leetch) even though there is no precedent for this.

Common licences

Licences dispensing with the necessity of the publication of banns have been granted since the fourteenth century. They are now known as common licences (to distinguish them from special licences granted only by the

---

[6] *Chipchase v Chipchase* [1939] P 391, 398, [1939] 3 All ER 895, 899–900; *Gompertz v Kensit* (1872) LR 13 Eq 369. But if banns are published in a name by which the party is not known at all, there cannot be a due publication even though there is no intention to deceive. See further Jackson *Formation and Annulment of Marriage* (2nd Edn) pp 173–181.

[7] *Tooth v Barrow* (supra).

[8] *Small v Small* (1923) 67 Sol Jo 277.

[9] [1942] P 37, [1941] 2 All ER 560.

[10] At 40 and 562, respectively.

Archbishop of Canterbury) and may be granted by the bishop of a diocese acting through his chancellor or one of the latter's surrogates.[11]

A common licence may be granted for the solemnization of a marriage only in the parish church of the parish, or an authorised chapel in the ecclesiastical district, in which one of the parties has had his or her usual place of residence for fifteen days immediately before the grant of the licence, or in the parish church or authorised chapel which is the usual place of worship of either of the parties.[12] The similarity between the granting of a common licence and the publication of banns is very close: the churches in which the marriage may be solemnized are the same, fifteen days is the period required for the publishing of banns on three successive Sundays, and there appears to be no significant difference between the word 'resides' for the purpose of the publication of banns and the phrase 'usual place of residence' for the purpose of the granting of a common licence.[13] On the other hand, the residence of the other party is immaterial.

Before a licence may be granted, one of the parties must swear (i) that he or she believes that there is no impediment to the marriage, (ii) that either the residence requirement is satisfied or the church in which the marriage is to take place is the regular place of worship of one of them, and (iii) if either of them is a minor, that all consents required by the Act have been obtained or dispensed with, or that the court has consented to the marriage, or that there is no person whose consent is required.[14]

Any person seeking to prevent the granting of a licence may enter a caveat stating the ground of his objection. In such a case the licence may not be granted until the caveat is withdrawn or the ecclesiastical judge with jurisdiction has decided that it ought not to obstruct the grant.[15] Although a caveat is rarely entered, the power to do so might be exercised, for example, by a parent who fears that his minor child may obtain a licence by falsely swearing that his consent to the marriage had been given.

Special licences

A special licence may be granted only by the Archbishop of Canterbury acting through the Master of the Faculties.[16] A special licence differs from any other authorisation to marry according to the rites of the Church of England in that it may permit the parties to marry at any time and in any place;[17] it is, therefore, the only way in which they may marry in a church or chapel in which their banns could not be published or for which a common licence or a superintendent registrar's certificate could not be issued.[18] In

---

[11] Cripps *Church and Clergy* (8th Edn) pp 547–548.

[12] Marriage Act 1949, s 15. If either party resides in a district where there is no church or chapel in which divine service is usually held every Sunday, the licence may authorise the solemnization of the marriage in any adjoining parish or chapelry.

[13] But see McClean *The Meaning of Residence* 11 ICLQ 1153.

[14] Marriage Act 1949, s 16(1).

[15] Marriage Act 1949, s 16(2).

[16] By Roman Catholic canon law the dispensation had to be papal; the power was transferred to the Archbishop of Canterbury by the Ecclesiastical Licences Act 1533. The office of the Master of the Faculties is performed by the Dean of the Arches.

[17] Marriage Act 1949, s 79(6).

[18] But the marriage *ceremony* may be celebrated there after a marriage in a register office: see post, p 52.

practice special licences are granted only in exceptional circumstances.[19]

Superintendent registrar's certificates

A marriage may be solemnized on the authority of a superintendent registrar's certificate in any church or chapel in which banns may be published and which is within the registration district in which either party resides or which is the usual place of worship of either of them.[20] It may also be solemnized in the building in which a house-bound or detained person is confined.[1] The issue of certificates will be discussed below; it should, however, be observed that a marriage in the Church of England may not be solemnized on the authority of a certificate *by licence*.[2]

The solemnization of the marriage

All marriages according to the rites of the Church of England must be solemnized by a clerk in holy orders of that Church in the presence of at least two other witnesses.[3] Except where the marriage is solemnized on the authority of a special licence, it must also be solemnized between 8 am and 6 pm.[4] A marriage following the publication of banns may be solemnized only in one of the churches or authorised chapels in which they have been published; a marriage solemnized on the authority of a common licence or a superintendent registrar's certificate must take place in the church or chapel specified in the licence or certificate (or, in the case of the marriage of a house-bound or detained person, the building specified in the certificate).[5] The marriage must also be solemnized within three months of the completion of the publication of the banns, the grant of the licence or the entry of notice in the superintendent registrar's marriage notice book, as the case may be.[6]

4. MARRIAGES SOLEMNIZED OTHERWISE THAN ACCORDING TO THE RITES OF THE CHURCH OF ENGLAND

All marriages other than those celebrated according to the rites of the Church of England may be solemnized only on the authority of a superintendent registrar's certificate, either without a licence or by licence, or on the authority of the Registrar General's licence.[7] The difference between a certificate

[19] On the average about 250 special licences are granted every year. The cost is £50, which may be waived.
[20] Marriage Act 1949, ss 17 (as amended by the Marriage Act 1983, Sch 1), 34, 35(3). But the marriage may not be solemnized on the authority of a superintendent registrar's certificate without the minister's consent: ibid, s 17.
[1] See post, p 54.
[2] Ibid, s 26(2).
[3] Ibid, ss 22, 25. The precise words of the ceremony need not be spoken by the parties and consent may be given by signs, eg, in the case of a dumb person: *Harrod v Harrod* (1854) 1 K & J 4. The marriage is probably contracted as soon as the parties have taken each other as husband and wife: *Quick v Quick* [1953] VLR 224.
[4] Ibid, ss 4, 75(1)(a).
[5] Ibid, ss 12(1), 15 and 25(a), (d) (as amended by the Marriage Act 1983, Sch 1). For the rearrangement of boundaries etc after banns have been published or a licence issued, see the Pastoral Measure 1983, Sch 3, para 4.
[6] Ibid, ss 12(2), 16(3), 33.
[7] The Marriage Act does not expressly so enact but this is its obvious intention and must be its effect. For arguments to the contrary, see Barton 89 LQR 181 and Hall *Common Law Marriage* [1987] CLJ 106. See also Thompson 90 LQR 28.

simpliciter and a certificate with a licence corresponds roughly to that between banns and a common licence, in that in the latter case the superintendent registrar is concerned with the residence qualification of one party only and the authorisation to marry may be obtained much more quickly. The Registrar General's licence corresponds to a special licence in that it enables the parties to marry elsewhere than in a register office or registered building. As with marriages in the Church of England, it will be necessary to consider separately the law relating to the preliminary formalities and that relating to the marriage ceremony itself.

Issue of a superintendent registrar's certificate without a licence

Notice of the proposed marriage must be given in writing to the superintendent registrar of the registration district in which the parties have resided for at least seven days immediately beforehand, or, if they have resided in different districts, then to the superintendent registrar of each district.[8] The party giving the notice must at the same time make a solemn declaration (i) that he or she believes that there is no impediment to the marriage, (ii) that the residence requirement is satisfied, and (iii) if either of them is a minor, that all consents required by the Act have been obtained or dispensed with, or that the court has consented to the marriage, or that there is no person whose consent is required.[9] The superintendent registrar must then enter the details of the notice in his marriage notice book and display the notice or a copy of it in a conspicuous place in his office for 21 successive days.[10]

As in the case of the granting of a common licence, anyone may enter a caveat against the issue of a certificate. The certificate may not then be issued until either the caveat has been withdrawn or the superintendent registrar or the Registrar General has satisfied himself that it ought not to obstruct the issue of the certificate.[11] Where the objection is that a consent to the marriage of a minor has not been obtained, any person whose consent is required may effectively prevent the marriage by the much simpler means of writing 'forbidden' against the entry in the marriage notice book, in which case the certificate may not be issued unless the consent of the court has been obtained.[12] An objection based on the fact that one of the parties is the other's stepdaughter, stepgranddaughter, stepson or stepgrandson and that the conditions permitting them to intermarry are not satisfied may be made by delivering a written statement to this effect to the superintendent registrar; he may not then issue the certificate until the parties have obtained a declaration from the High Court that the conditions are satisfied and that there is no impediment to the marriage on this ground.[13]

---

[8] Marriage Act 1949, s 27(1). For the matters which the notice must contain, see ss 27(3), 27A, 27B and 27C (as amended and added by the Marriage Act 1983, Sch 1, and the Marriage (Prohibited Degrees of Relationship) Act 1986, Sch 1).

[9] Ibid, s 28. Cf the oath required before a common licence may be granted, ante, p 48. The superintendent registrar is entitled to demand written evidence that the consents required have been given if either party is a minor: Family Law Reform Act 1969, s 2(3).

[10] Ibid, ss 27(4), 31(1).

[11] Ibid, s 29. A person entering a caveat frivolously is liable in damages to the person against whose marriage it was entered.

[12] Ibid, s 30.

[13] Ibid, s 27B(4), (5). Either party may apply for a declaration even though no formal objection has been made.

If no impediment has been shown and the issue of the certificate has not been forbidden, the superintendent registrar must issue it at the end of the 21 days.[14]

As in the case of the publication of banns, a certificate may be issued locally if one of the parties resides in Scotland or Northern Ireland,[15] or, provided that both parties are British subjects, in certain other parts of the British Commonwealth.[16] Similarly, notice of marriage may be given by an officer, seaman or marine borne on the books of one of Her Majesty's ships at sea to the officer commanding the ship, who is empowered to grant a certificate.[17]

Issue of a superintendent registrar's certificate with a licence

The law relating to the issue of a certificate with a licence is the same as that relating to the issue of a certificate simpliciter except in two important respects. First, notice is to be given to only *one* superintendent registrar—that of the registration district in which *either* party has resided for a period of *fifteen* days immediately beforehand.[18] The residence of the other party is irrelevant provided that it is in England or Wales,[19] and the provisions relating to parties resident in other parts of the United Kingdom and the issue of certificates on board warships do not apply. Secondly, the superintendent registrar is not required to display the notice or a copy of it in his office, but, unless an impediment to the marriage has been shown or the issue of the certificate has been forbidden, he must issue the certificate and licence at any time after the expiration of one whole day after the giving of the notice.[20]

Solemnization of the marriage

A marriage on the authority of a superintendent registrar's certificate (whether by licence or without a licence) may be solemnized in a super-intendent registrar's office, in a registered building, in the place where a house-bound or detained person is, or according to the usages of the Society of Friends or of the Jews.[1] In any case the marriage must be solemnized within three months of the entry being made in the marriage notice book; and, unless it is a Quaker or Jewish marriage, it must also be solemnized between 8 am and 6 pm, with open doors and in the presence of at least

---

[14] Ibid, s 31(2). Quaere whether he can revoke the certificate before the marriage is solemnized if he discovers some impediment (eg, that one party is a minor and parental consent has not been given).

[15] Ibid, ss 37 (as amended by the Marriage (Scotland) Act 1977, Schs 2 and 3) and 38. (But not when the other party resides in the Republic of Ireland.)

[16] Marriage of British Subjects (Facilities) Acts 1915 and 1916. See 27 Halsbury's Statutes (4th Edn) 463–466.

[17] Marriage Act 1949, s 39.

[18] Ibid, s 27(2).

[19] The Act specifically states 'whether the persons to be married reside in the same or in different districts' and thus implies that one of these two conditions must be satisfied.

[20] Ibid, s 32. Hence, if notice is given on Monday, the certificate and licence may be issued on Wednesday.

[1] Ibid, s 26(1) (as amended by the Marriage Act 1983, Sch 1). The marriage of a house-bound or detained person may not be solemnized on a certificate by licence. For marriages in the Church of England on a certificate without licence, see ante, p 49.

two witnesses in addition to the superintendent registrar and registrar or, alternatively, the registrar of authorised person.[2]

Marriage in a register office

The parties may marry in the office of the superintendent registrar to whom the notice of the intended marriage was given (or, if notice was given to two superintendent registrars, in the office of either of them), in the presence of the superintendent registrar and also of a registrar of marriages.[3] They must declare that they know of no impediment why they should not be joined in matrimony and then contract the marriage per verba de praesenti.[4] No religious service may be used in a superintendent registrar's office, but, if the parties so wish, the marriage there may be followed by a religious ceremony in a church or chapel. In this case the marriage which is *legally* binding for all purposes is that in the register office.[5] This provision is useful if the parties wish to be married in a private chapel in which banns may not be published (eg, the chapel of an Oxford or Cambridge college) without being put to the expense of obtaining a special licence or in a non-conformist place of worship which is not a registered building.

Marriage in a registered building

Any building which is certified as a place of religious worship[6] may be registered by the Registrar General for the solemnization of marriages.[7] A superintendent registrar may normally issue a certificate or certificate and licence for the solemnization of a marriage in a registered building only within his own district, or, where the marriage is without a licence and the parties reside in different districts, within the district in which either of them resides.[8] In two cases, however, he may issue a certificate (with or without licence) for the solemnization of a marriage in another district. First, he may do so if there is not in the district in which one of the parties resides a registered building in which marriages are solemnized according to the practices of the religious body to which one of them belongs.[9] Secondly, he may issue a certificate for the solemnization of the marriage in a registered building which is the usual place of worship of one of the parties.[10]

---

[2] Ibid, ss 4, 22, 33, 44(2), 45(1), 45A(2), (3) and 75(1)(a) (as amended and added by the Marriage Act 1983, Sch 1). The requirement that the marriage must be solemnized with open doors does not apply to the marriage of a house-bound or detained person.
[3] Ibid, ss 36, 45(1).
[4] Marriage Act 1949, ss 45(1), 44(3). The form of words to be used is: 'I call upon these persons here present to witness that I, *AB*, do take thee, *CD*, to be my lawful wedded wife [or husband].' A Welsh form may be used: s 52. As to marriages of dumb persons, see *Harrod v Harrod*, p 49, n 3 ante.
[5] Ibid, ss 45(2), 46.
[6] Under the Places of Worship Registration Act 1855.
[7] See the Marriage Act 1949, ss 41 and 42, as amended by the Marriage Acts Amendment Act 1958, s 1(1), and the Marriage (Registration of Buildings) Act 1990, s 1(1).
[8] Marriage Act 1949, ss 34 and 36. But no marriage may take place in a registered building without the consent of the minister or one of the trustees, owners, deacons or managers: ibid, s 44(1).
[9] Ibid, s 35(1), as amended by the Marriage Act 1949 (Amendment) Act 1954, s 2. The registered building in which the superintendent registrar authorises the solemnization of the marriage must be in the registration district nearest to the residence of that party in which there is a registered building where marriages may be so solemnized.
[10] Ibid, s 35(2), as amended by the Marriage Act 1949 (Amendment) Act 1954, s 1.

A marriage in a registered building may take place only if there is present a registrar of marriages or an 'authorised person'.[11] It will be recalled that since the Marriage Act of 1898 the trustees or governing body of a registered building have been empowered to authorise a person to be present at a marriage there and thus dispense with the necessity of having a registrar in attendance.[12] The authorised person will, of course, normally be a minister of the particular faith or denomination. The functions of the registrar (or authorised person) are to ensure that certificates (and, if necessary, a licence) have been issued, that the provisions of the Marriage Act relating to the solemnization are complied with, and to register the marriage. The marriage may be in any form provided that, at some stage in the ceremony, a declaration is made similar to that required when the marriage is in a register office, and the parties contract the union per verba de praesenti.[13]

Marriages of house-bound and detained persons

The requirement that the marriage must be solemnized in a register office or a registered building meant that a person could not marry on a superintendent registrar's certificate at all if he was incapable of leaving home or any other building (for example, a hospital or prison) where he happened to be. (Indeed it was not uncommon for a prisoner to be released for a short period to enable him to marry.) As we shall see, the position was partly ameliorated by the provisions of the Marriage (Registrar General's Licence) Act 1970, but these apply only to those who are fatally ill. A much wider relaxation has been afforded by the Marriage Act 1983 which enables a house-bound or detained person to be married in the place where he is for the time being.

A house-bound person is defined as one who, owing to illness or disability, ought not to be moved from the place where he is and who is likely to remain in this condition for three months. A detained person is one who is detained in a mental hospital (otherwise than for short periods for assessment) or prison.[14] Notice of the proposed marriage must be accompanied by a statement signed by a medical practitioner that the person in question satisfies the definition of 'house-bound' or signed by the hospital managers or prison governor identifying the establishment where the person is detained and certifying that there is no objection to the establishment being specified as the place where the marriage is to take place.[15] The house-bound or detained person is deemed to be resident in the place where he is for the time being.[16] A major limitation imposed by the Act is that no marriage may take place

---

[11] Ibid, s 44(2).

[12] See now the Marriage Act 1949, s 43, as amended by the Marriage Acts Amendment Act 1958, s 1(2); the Sharing of Church Buildings Act 1969, Sch 1. An authorised person may be present (and thus dispense with the need of having a registrar) at a marriage in any registered building in the same registration district: Marriage Act 1949, s 44(2)(b). See also ibid, s 44(5).

[13] Marriage Act 1949, s 44(1), (3). A slightly different form of words may be used if the marriage is solemnized in the presence of an authorised person without the presence of a registrar.

[14] Marriage Act 1983, s 1 and Sch 1 (amending the Marriage Act 1949, s 78), qv for the full definition.

[15] Marriage Act 1949, ss 27 and 27A (as amended and added, respectively, by the Marriage Act 1983, Sch 1).

[16] Ibid, s 78(5) (added by the Marriage Act 1983, Sch 1).

under its provisions on the authority of a superintendent registrar's certificate by licence.[17]

The marriage may take place only in the building where the house-bound or detained person is. It may take the form of a civil ceremony or a religious ceremony (including a ceremony according to the rites of the Church of England) but Quaker and Jewish marriages are unaffected by the Act. Unless the marriage is solemnized according to the rites of the Church of England (when the service must be taken by a clerk in holy orders), a registrar must be present and, if the ceremony is a purely civil one, the superintendent registrar must be present as well.[18]

Quaker marriages

The Act of 1949 preserves the right of the Society of Friends to solemnize marriages according to their own usages. Provided that the rules of the Society permit it, a marriage may be contracted in this way even though one or both parties are not members of the Society.[19]

Jewish marriages

The privilege of the Jewish community to celebrate marriages according to their own rites is also preserved. In this case, however, both parties must profess the Jewish religion.[20]

Marriages solemnized on the authority of the Registrar General's licence

Until 1970 the only way in which a person could be married elsewhere than in a church or authorised chapel, a registered building or a register office was on the authority of a special licence. Consequently if he was unable to attend such a building and wished to marry (for example on his deathbed), he had to do so according to the rites of the Church of England. To overcome this difficulty the Marriage (Registrar General's Licence) Act was passed in 1970 to enable the Registrar General to issue a licence authorising the solemnization of a marriage elsewhere than in a register office or registered building. But whereas a special licence can serve one of two purposes—to enable a person to marry even though he is too ill or infirm to be moved and to permit a wedding to take place for purely social reasons in a church or private chapel where the parties' banns could not be published—the Registrar General's licence is intended to serve only the first. Consequently its issue is subject to two important limitations. In the first place, the Registrar General must be satisfied that one of the parties is seriously ill and not expected to recover and that he cannot be moved to a place where the marriage could be solemnized under the provisions of the Act of 1949. Secondly, no such

[17] Ibid, s 26(2) (as amended).
[18] Ibid, ss 17 and 45A (as amended and added); Marriage Act 1983, s 1(6). The same form of words must be used as in a register office. A civil marriage may be followed later by a religious ceremony in a church or chapel: Marriage Act 1949, s 46 (as amended).
[19] Ibid, s 47. This privilege was first granted by the Marriage (Society of Friends) Act 1860. See the *Marriage Regulations* of the Society of Friends; Jackson, *Formation and Annulment of Marriage* (2nd Edn) pp 198–200. The rule that the building in which the marriage is to be solemnized must be within the registration district in which one of the parties resides does not apply to marriages according to the usages of the Society of Friends: s 35(4).
[20] Marriage Act 1949, s 26(1)(d). S 35(4) (see n 19, supra) also applies. See Jackson op cit pp 200–202.

marriage may be solemnized according to the rites of the Church of England.[1]

The details of the preliminary formalities to be observed will be found in the Act. Notice must be given to the superintendent registrar of the registration district in which it is intended to solemnize the marriage; the requirements are much the same as when an application is made for the issue of a superintendent registrar's certificate and licence except that there is no residence qualification and the party giving the notice must produce such evidence as the Registrar General may require that the statutory conditions regarding the health of one party are satisfied and that that person understands the purport of the marriage ceremony.[2] After entering the details in his marriage notice book the superintendent registrar informs the Registrar General of the application; if the latter is satisfied that sufficient grounds exist for the granting of a licence, he must then issue it unless a lawful impediment has been shown or the marriage of a minor has been forbidden.[3]

The marriage must be solemnized in the place stated in the notice of marriage and within *one* month of the entry in the marriage notice book.[4] It may take the form of a civil ceremony in the presence of the superintendent registrar and a registrar,[5] or it may be according to any form or ceremony the parties choose to adopt (other than the rites of the Church of England) in the presence of a registrar. At least two witnesses must be present, and at some stage the parties must make the same declaration and contract the marriage in the same form of words as would be required at a marriage in a register office.[6]

These provisions have obviously been made largely redundant by the provisions of the Marriage Act 1983 which enable a house-bound person to be married at home or in hospital. But there are still two, and possibly three, situations where the Registrar General's licence will be required. First, Quaker and Jewish marriages cannot be solemnized under the 1983 Act but they can be on the Registrar General's licence. Secondly, as the marriage of a house-bound person cannot take place on the authority of a superintendent registrar's certificate by licence, the Registrar's General's licence will have to be sought if there is a danger that the party will die within the 21 days before the certificate could be issued. Thirdly, the wording of the statement which the medical practitioner is required to sign under the 1983 Act implies that the house-bound person is likely to survive for three months;[7] if this strict interpretation is correct, a person cannot be 'house-bound' if he is expected

---

[1] Marriage (Registrar General's Licence) Act 1970, s 1. The Registrar General may remit the fee of £15 in whole or in part if he thinks that the payment would cause hardship to the parties: s 17(1).

[2] Ibid, ss 2 and 3. A registered medical practitioner's certificate is sufficient evidence.

[3] Ibid, ss 2(2) and 4–7. A caveat may be entered with either the superintendent registrar or the Registrar General; in either case, however, only the Registrar General may decide that it should not obstruct the issue of the licence.

[4] Ibid, ss 8 and 9. The marriage does not necessarily have to take place between 8 am and 6 pm: see s 16(4).

[5] As in the case of a marriage in a register office, this may be followed by a religious ceremony which will be of no legal effect: ibid, s 11.

[6] Ibid, s 10. The provisions relating to the presence of a registrar and two witnesses, the declaration, and the form of words to be used do not apply if the marriage is solemnized according to the usages of the Society of Friends or, if both parties profess the Jewish faith, according to Jewish rites. No clergyman of the Church of England may solemnize the marriage.

[7] 'It is likely that it will be the case for at least … three months … that … he ought not to move or be moved from [the place where he is].'

to die within that period. It is much to be regretted that the 1983 Act was not drafted in such a way as to cover these cases and thus eliminate the need for the Registrar General's licence.

5. MARRIAGES IN NAVAL, MILITARY, AND AIR FORCE CHAPELS

Part V of the Marriage Act enables certain persons to marry in naval, military and air force chapels certified as such by the Secretary of State for Defence.[8] The purpose of this is to enable members of the Forces and their daughters to marry in garrison churches, etc. Consequently, in order that a marriage may be solemnized in such a chapel, at least one of the parties must be a serving or former member of one of the regular armed forces or a daughter of such a person.[9] The privilege has since been extended to members of certain Commonwealth and NATO forces and their daughters.[10] If the chapel has been licensed for this purpose by the bishop of the diocese, it may be treated as the parish church of the parish in which it is situated, and banns may be published and marriages solemnized in it provided that at least one of the parties resides in that parish.[11] The Registrar General may also register a chapel so as to enable the superintendent registrar of the district in which it stands to issue a certificate to marry in it (either with or without a licence) according to rites other than those of the Church of England.[12] Subject to these limitations and certain other modifications,[13] the same rules apply to marriages in these chapels as to other marriages.

6. RETROSPECTIVE VALIDATION OF MARRIAGES WHICH ARE VOID BECAUSE OF FORMAL DEFECTS

Although, as we shall see later,[14] failure to observe all the formal requirements of English law does not necessarily invalidate the marriage, certain defects in form will have this effect. The complexities of the English law on this subject have in the past led persons who were morally innocent to go through a form of marriage which has subsequently proved to be a legal nullity. Parliament has from time to time intervened to validate these marriages by curing the informality retrospectively.[15] Although the number of cases in which innocent parties contract a marriage that is void because of formal

---

[8] Replacing the Marriage (Naval, Military and Air Force Chapels) Act 1932. See also the Defence (Transfer of Functions) Act 1964, s 1(2).

[9] Marriage Act 1949, s 68, as amended by the Armed Forces Act 1981, Schs 3 and 5.

[10] Visiting Forces and International Headquarters (Application of Law) Order 1965, arts 3 and 12(2) and Sch 3 (SI 1965 No 1536), as amended.

[11] Marriage Act 1949, s 69. But the parties may not marry in a chapel solely on the ground that it is the usual place of worship of either of them: see Sch 4, Pt I.

[12] Ibid, s 70. 'Authorised persons' may be appointed by the Secretary of State: Sch 4, Pt IV. It seems that the parties may marry there on the ground that no other registered building is available or that it is the regular place of worship of one of them: ibid, Pt III.

[13] See the Marriage Act 1949, Sch 4, as amended by the Marriage Acts Amendment Act 1958, s 1(2).

[14] Post, pp 82–84.

[15] A list of the public general Acts passed for this purpose will be found in 22 Halsbury's Laws of England (4th Edn), 617. Many private Acts have also been passed.

invalidity is not likely to be great today, nevertheless the situation might conceivably arise. Consequently, the Marriages Validity (Provisional Orders) Acts 1905 and 1924 have given the Home Secretary power to make orders for the purpose of curing retrospectively any formal defect in the marriage or of removing any doubt about the validity of a marriage due to informality.[16]

7. PROPOSALS FOR REFORM

It will be seen that the present law relating to the formalities of marriage is still in principle based upon the provisions of Lord Hardwicke's Act of 1753 and the Marriage Act of 1836. It thus reflects the desire to prevent the clandestine marriages which were the disgrace of eighteenth century England. In this respect the law is now hopelessly out of date. Clandestine marriages are no longer the social evil that they were 250 years ago; nor does the modern law effectively prevent them. Provided that both parties are over the age of 18, a marriage can usually be solemnized on a common licence or a superintendent registrar's certificate and licence without the knowledge of the parties' friends and relations. The ease with which people can travel round the country and acquire a new residence makes it virtually impossible for the parents of a determined minor to forbid his marriage before it takes place. Another problem is presented by the speed with which the parties can rush into marriage without giving due thought to the implications of their act. A superintendent registrar's licence may be obtained in 48 hours and a common licence in as many minutes: an extreme case illustrating how a person may be married at literally five minutes' notice may be found in *Cooper v Crane*.[17]

The law has been reviewed twice during the past 20 years, once by a Working Party set up by the Law Commission and the Registrar General in 1973[18] and once in a White Paper in 1990.[19] The earlier review (which was the more extensive) began by saying:[20]

'We have assumed that the purpose of a sound marriage law is to ensure that marriages are solemnised only in respect of those who are free to marry and have freely agreed to do so and that the status of those who marry shall be established with certainty so that doubts do not arise, either in the minds of the parties or in the community, about who is married and who is not. To this end it appears to us to be necessary that there should be proper opportunity for the investigation of capacity (and, in the case of minors, parental consent) before the marriage and that the investigation should be carried out, uniformly for parties to all marriages, by persons trained to perform this function. We suggest that the law should guard

---

[16] Orders made under these Acts are subject to special parliamentary procedure under the Statutory Orders (Special Procedure) Acts 1945 and 1965: SI 1949 No 2393. None has been made in recent years: Law Com No 53, p 65, n 30. There is no power under these Acts to legalise a marriage which is void because of the incapacity of either party.

[17] [1891] P 369. The respondent, who had unknown to the petitioner obtained a licence and arranged the wedding, took her out and, having got her to the church door, threatened to blow his brains out unless she went into the church and married him. It was held that the petitioner had not discharged the burden of proving that her will was overborne and that consequently the marriage was valid.

[18] See Law Com No 53 (Solemnisation of Marriage), 1973.

[19] *Registration: proposals for change*, Cm 939, following a green paper *Registration: a modern service*, Cm 531, 1988. See Bradney [1989] Fam Law 408.

[20] Law Com No 53, Annex, paras 4–5.

against clandestine marriages, that there should be proper opportunity for legal impediments to be declared or discovered, that all marriages should be publicly solemnised and that the marriage should be duly recorded in official registers. At the same time we recognise that a marriage ceremony is an important family and social occasion and we feel that unnecessary and irksome restrictions on its celebration should be avoided.

Moreover, since nearly every person who attains maturity marries at least once and attends numerous marriages of friends and relations and since the marriage creates a status which vitally concerns the public, the law of marriage should be as simple and easily understood as possible.'

They concluded that these aims could be achieved only if the superintendent registrar's certificate became the standard legal authorisation to marry.[1] This would ensure that any necessary investigations would be made by an officer trained to conduct them. Furthermore, the abolition of both common licences and superintendent registrar's licences would achieve some measure of publicity of the parties' intention to marry: the number of cases in which a licence is sought because of genuine urgency is apparently very small.

In its White Paper the Government rejected the proposal to introduce a registrar's certificate[2] as a universal preliminary largely because a working party set up by the General Synod of the Church of England had opposed it, but they agreed that the certificate and licence should be abolished. To meet the few cases of real urgency they recommended that the registrar to whom notice is given should be permitted to reduce the period before the certificate is issued.[3] The reports are at one in recommending that *both* parties should be required to give notice. This would mean that each would have to make a declaration about his or her own age, status, etc, and might reduce the chance of marriage by a person who did not understand the nature of the ceremony or who was under some improper pressure. Both the Working Party and the Government proposed that the person celebrating the marriage should be under a duty to ensure that both parties understand that they are entering into a monogamous marriage and, if their native tongue is not English (or Welsh, where a Welsh form is permitted), that they understand the words used. The Government also recommended that the parties should be able to marry in any district in England and Wales, although each would still have to give notice in the district in which he or she normally resides: they pointed out that a couple may wish to be married near the family home of one of them and the present law encourages deceit to achieve this end.[4] They commented on the dreary appearance of some register offices and proposed that local authorities should be able to provide a choice of 'marriage rooms' for civil ceremonies by contracting, for example, with stately homes and hotels.[5] They also recommended that the civil ceremony could be made

---

[1] But the Church of England could still retain the publication of banns (or the issue of a licence) as an additional *ecclesiastical* formality if it wished.

[2] The White Paper proposes the restructuring of the registration service which would involve the abolition of the separate office of superintendent registrar.

[3] The Working Party recommended that only the Registrar General should have power to reduce the period in order to insulate the person exercising the discretion from pressure and to ensure a uniform exercise.

[4] See Cm 531, para 3.13.

[5] The public would have to be allowed access. Registrars are opposed to holding ceremonies in licensed premises because of problems that could arise if those attending have been drinking.

less bleak by permitting additions 'such as poetry readings ... provided that they do not detract from the dignity of the occasion'.[6]

No Bill to give legislative effect to these proposals has yet been presented, but some of them are clearly desirable. In the end, nothing will deter a minor determined at all costs to marry in the face of parental opposition or a bigamist determined to go through a ceremony with a woman who is convinced that she is entering into a lawful marriage. Nor perhaps is it realistic to devise a rule which would forbid marriage until the parties had known each other for a minimum period of time:[7] at least the requirement that both parties should give notice would remove the possibility of the facts of *Cooper v Crane* occurring again.

F. The recognition of foreign marriages[8]

Monogamous marriages

A marriage will be recognised in this country if it satisfies the definition of marriage formulated by Lord Penzance in *Hyde v Hyde*.[9] Although he referred to 'marriage as it is understood in Christendom', it must not be supposed that this is synonymous with 'a Christian marriage'. If the marriage satisfies the four conditions he laid down, it will be recognised by English courts even though neither party professes the Christian faith provided that each had capacity by the relevant lex domicilii and they complied with the formalities laid down by the lex loci celebrationis.[10]

Most of the cases dealing with the recognition of foreign marriages have in fact been concerned with polygamous unions. It is still an open question how far English courts will recognise monogamous unions which fail to satisfy the other requirements laid down by Lord Penzance or which would have been void for some other reason if they had been contracted in England. It is submitted that the proper test to apply is that formulated by Simon P in *Cheni v Cheni*,[11] where he said:

> 'I believe the true rule to be that the courts of this country will exceptionally refuse to give effect to a capacity or incapacity to marry by the law of the domicile on the ground that to give it recognition and effect would be unconscionable. ...
>
> What I believe to be the true test [is] whether the marriage is so offensive to the conscience of the English court that it should refuse to recognise and give effect to the proper foreign law. In deciding that question the court will seek to exercise common sense, good manners and a reasonable tolerance.'

[6] Readings would have to be approved by the registrar and no religious service should be used.
[7] The Latey Committee doubted whether the problem was as grave as is commonly supposed and were unanimously opposed to any kind of formal betrothal on the ground that this might encourage potentially unstable marriages rather than the reverse. See Cmnd 3342, paras 178–183.
[8] See Hartley *The Policy Basis of the English Conflict of Laws of Marriage* 35 MLR 571.
[9] (1866) LR 1 P & D 130. See further ante, pp 21–22.
[10] *Brinkley v A-G* (1890) 15 PD 76 (marriage between a man domiciled in Ireland and a woman domiciled in Japan before the civil authority in Tokyo recognised as a valid marriage). Otherwise all marriages celebrated between Jews would be invalid. For capacity and formal requirements, see ante, pp 26–33.
[11] [1965] P 85, 98–99, [1962] 3 All ER 873, 882–883.

In that case the court gave recognition to a marriage between an uncle and niece which was valid by the law of the parties' domicile (Egypt) even though it would have been void by English law because they were related within the prohibited degrees.[12] Likewise in *Nachimson v Nachimson*[13] it was held that a marriage celebrated in Russia and intended to be entered into for life came within the *Hyde v Hyde* definition notwithstanding that it could be dissolved by mutual consent declared before a registrar or at the will of either spouse by judicial process. On the other hand it seems inconceivable that English courts would recognise a union between two persons of the same sex; and it is very doubtful whether they would recognise a child marriage, at least unless the parties had ratified it when they were old enough to understand the nature and significance of marriage.[14]

Polygamous marriages[15]

It must be appreciated at the outset that English law regards a marriage as polygamous if either spouse has the capacity to contract further marriages during the subsistence of the first, whether he does so or not. If a party has another spouse, the marriage may be said to be de facto polygamous; unless the contrary is stated, throughout the following discussion the term 'polygamous marriage' will be used to include both a de facto and a de jure (or potentially) polygamous union.

For many years after the decision in *Hyde v Hyde* the courts refused to recognise the validity of any marriage which did not satisfy Lord Penzance's definition.[16] In practice this meant the refusal to recognise polygamous unions—despite the fact that a large part of the civilised world permits polygamy and that the Judicial Committee of the Privy Council was upholding the validity of such unions on appeal from various courts in the Commonwealth. To fail to recognise a marriage which was valid by a man's lex domicilii (which is generally accepted as governing his status) seems the height of absurdity. Moreover, it is clear that Lord Penzance himself had intended no such result. At the end of his judgment he said:[17]

> 'In conformity with these views the Court must reject the prayer for the petition, but ... this decision is confined to that object. This Court [the Divorce Court] does not profess to decide upon the rights of succession or legitimacy which it might be proper to accord to the issue of the polygamous unions, nor upon the rights or obligations in relation to third persons which people living under the sanction of such unions may have created for themselves. *All that is intended to be here decided is that as between each other they are not entitled to the remedies, adjudication, or the relief of the matrimonial law of England.*'

[12] But would the court recognise a marriage if we regarded the relationship as criminally incestuous (eg, between brother and sister)?

[13] [1930] P 217, CA But the court implied that they would not have regarded it as a marriage had it been a mere cloak for casual intercourse, to be dissolved the next day, or if it had conferred no status on the parties (at 233, 244).

[14] See Poulter *Ethnic Minority Customs, English Law and Human Rights* 36 ICLQ 589, 610–611.

[15] See Poulter *English Law and Ethnic Minority Customs* ch 3.

[16] See *Re Bethell* (1888) 38 ChD 220, and the remarks of Avory J in *R v Naguib* [1917] 1 KB 359, 360, CCA. *Re Bethell* is an unsatisfactory case because it is not entirely clear what the ratio decidendi was. A domiciled Englishman went through a form of marriage with Teepoo, a Baralong girl, according to the custom of the Baralong tribe in Bechuanaland. The Baralongs had no religion and practised polygamy. Stirling J, professing to follow *Hyde v Hyde*, held that this marriage was void and that the child born of it was illegitimate.

[17] At 138. Italics supplied.

But it was not until 1946 that the decision in *Hyde v Hyde* was put in its proper context by the Court of Appeal in *Baindail v Baindail*,[18] following earlier dicta of Lord Maugham LC in the *Sinha Peerage Case*.[19] In *Baindail v Baindail* a woman domiciled in England went through a ceremony of marriage in England with a Hindu domiciled in India. She later discovered that he already had a wife in India and petitioned for nullity on the ground that the marriage was bigamous and therefore void. Although the respondent's first marriage was polygamous, it was held that, as it was valid by the law of his domicile, it must be recognised as valid here. The petitioner's contention was therefore sound and her marriage void.

During the past fifty years the attitude of Parliament and the judges towards polygamous marriages has become progressively more liberal. Change has doubtless been hastened by the necessity of doing justice to the large number of immigrants in this country whose marriages are de jure polygamous. In 1968 Lord Parker CJ was able to say that a polygamous marriage is now 'recognised in this country unless there is some strong reason to the contrary'.[20]

What marriages are polygamous?[1]

Whether the marriage is to be regarded as monogamous or polygamous must initially be determined by the lex loci celebrationis.[2] If that law prohibits polygamy (as English law does), all marriages celebrated under it must be monogamous.[3] If a party to such a marriage is permitted to practise polygamy by his lex domicilii, he may nonetheless contract a valid monogamous marriage here provided that he is not already married;[4] if he is already married, a marriage contracted in this country will be void as bigamous.[5] Conversely, if the lex loci permits polygamy, any marriage contracted in that country by a person whose lex domicilii permits him to enter into a polygamous union will be polygamous.[6]

It was at one time believed that if a person whose lex domicilii forbids

---

[18] [1946] P 122, [1946] 1 All ER 342, CA. See also *Srini Vasan v Srini Vasan* [1946] P 67, [1945] 2 All ER 21, where on virtually identical facts Barnard J came to the same decision as the Court of Appeal.

[19] (1939), reported [1946] 1 All ER 348n, HL.

[20] *Mohamed v Knott* [1969] 1 QB 1, 13–14, [1968] 2 All ER 563, 567, citing Dicey and Morris, *Conflict of Laws*: see now ibid (11th Edn) Rule 77. See also *Chaudhry v Chaudhry* [1976] Fam 148, [1975] 3 All ER 687 (affirmed on other grounds, [1976] Fam 148, [1976] 1 All ER 805n, CA); *Re Sehota* [1978] 3 All ER 385; Law Com No 146 (Polygamous Marriages), Part III.

[1] The subject of polygamous marriages is dealt with at length in the standard textbooks on Private International Law and in many articles. See particularly Bartholomew, *Recognition of Polygamous Marriages in Canada*, 10 ICLQ 305; Morris, *The Recognition of Polygamous Marriages in English Law*, 66 Harv LR 961; Mendes da Costa, *Polygamous Marriages in the Conflict of Laws*, 44 Can Bar Rev 293; Hartley, *Polygamy and Social Policy*, 32 MLR 155; 34 MLR 305; Poulter, *Hyde v Hyde—a Reappraisal*, 25 ICLQ 475; Weston, 28 MLR 484; Jackson, *Formation and Annulment of Marriage* (2nd Edn) pp 131–144; Law Com No 42 (Report on Polygamous Marriages) and No 146 (Polygamous Marriages).

[2] *Hussain v Hussain* [1983] Fam 26, [1982] 3 All ER 369, CA; Schuz 46 MLR 653; Pearl [1983] CLJ 26.

[3] See *R v Hammersmith Superintendent Registrar of Marriages, ex p Mir-Anwaruddin* [1917] 1 KB 634, CA; *Maher v Maher* [1951] P 342, 346, [1951] 2 All ER 37, 39.

[4] *Ex p Mir-Anwaruddin* (supra).

[5] *Baindail v Baindail* [1946] P 122, [1946] 1 All ER 342, CA; *Srini Vasan v Srini Vasan* [1946] P 67, [1945] 2 All ER 21.

[6] *Risk v Risk* [1950] P 50, [1950] 2 All ER 973.

polygamy went through a polygamous form of marriage abroad, the marriage would be void by English law.[7] At first sight section 11(d) of the Matrimonial Causes Act 1973[8] appears to give statutory effect to this principle by providing that, if a person domiciled in England enters into a polygamous marriage outside this country after 31st July 1971,[9] the marriage will be void. In *Hussain v Hussain*,[10] however, the Court of Appeal reached the opposite decision. The husband, who was unmarried and domiciled in England, married in Pakistan a woman domiciled in that country. By Pakistani law a man may take a second wife but a woman may not take a second husband. The court held that, as neither party had the capacity to enter into a second marriage whilst that contracted in Pakistan subsisted, the latter was monogamous and therefore valid. The court was careful to limit its decision to marriages celebrated since 1st August 1971 but the argument applies with equal force whenever the marriage was contracted.[11] Whilst we must await an authoritative decision of the House of Lords, section 11(d) appears to apply only if a person domiciled in England marries one whose lex domicilii permits him (or her) to take further spouses in a ceremony designed to produce a polygamous union.

The decision in *Hussain v Hussain* is to be welcomed because it removes an anomaly. It is not uncommon for members of immigrant communities to return to their family's homeland to marry, and it would be unjust to recognise the marriage if the husband retained a domicile in, say, Pakistan but not if he had acquired one in England. On the other hand, if a woman domiciled in England marries in Pakistan a man domiciled there, the marriage will still be polygamous (because the husband may take further wives) and therefore void. This is clearly discriminatory, and the Law Commission recommend that every man and woman domiciled in this country should have capacity to enter into any marriage which is de facto monogamous, even though it is celebrated in a form appropriate to polygamous marriages.[12]

If the marriage is polygamous by the test set out above, it is irrelevant that the parties intended to enter into a monogamous union. Their reservations cannot change the legal effects of their act.[13]

Change of character of marriage

There is no doubt that a marriage which is de jure polygamous but de facto monogamous can be turned into one that is de jure monogamous. It is not sufficient that the parties should intend to effect such a change: there must be some other act or event which brings this about by operation of law such as the birth of a child,[14] a change of religious faith affecting the parties' legal

[7] Cf *Re Bethell* (1888) 38 Ch D 220.
[8] Re-enacting s 4 of the Matrimonial Proceedings (Polygamous Marriages) Act 1972.
[9] Ie after the Nullity of Marriage Act 1971 came into force.
[10] [1983] Fam 26, [1982] 3 All ER 369, CA. See Carter [1982] BYIL 298; Poulter 13 Fam Law 72.
[11] See Stone *Capacity for Polygamy* 13 Fam Law 76. The Law Commission is of the opposite view: Law Com No 146, para 2.13.
[12] Law Com No 146, paras 2.17–2.31.
[13] *Sowa v Sowa* [1961] P 70, [1961] 1 All ER 687, CA. (Parties went through a polygamous form of marriage in Ghana after the husband had presented his bride with a ring and a Bible, symbolising his intention to contract a Christian monogamous marriage. It was held that the marriage was polygamous.)
[14] *Cheni v Cheni* [1965] P 85, [1962] 3 All ER 873; Higgins 26 MLR 205.

status,[15] local legislation changing the character of the marriage,[16] a change of domicile from one permitting polygamy to one forbidding it,[17] or possibly a second ceremony of marriage designed to create a monogamous union.[18]

Presumably the acquisition of an English domicile by a man who already has two or more wives could not affect the validity of these marriages. In *Cheni v Cheni*[19] the parties, who were uncle and niece, had contracted a valid marriage in Egypt when they were domiciled in that country. They later acquired a domicile in England and the wife petitioned for a decree of nullity on the ground that they were related within the prohibited degrees of consanguinity. Simon P held that the marriage was still valid. The principle to be deduced is that the acquisition of an English domicile does not affect the validity of a marriage already contracted: it must therefore follow that a man domiciled here can have a plurality of wives. Such a conclusion is startling; but the alternative view, that a change of domicile will automatically render all the marriages void, is wholly unacceptable.

The converse question—whether an initially monogamous marriage may be converted into a polygamous one—is probably less likely to arise but such authority as there is indicates that such a conversion is possible. In *Cheni v Cheni*[20] Simon P said obiter: 'there are no marriages which are not potentially polygamous, in the sense that they may be rendered so by a change of domicile and religion on the part of the spouses', but he added that it was more reasonable to presume that a polygamous union could be converted into a monogamous one than vice versa. This dictum was followed by the Privy Council in *A-G of Ceylon v Reid*.[1] The respondent was domiciled in Ceylon and his capacity to marry depended upon his religious faith. Whilst he was a Christian he contracted a monogamous Christian marriage. He was then converted to Islam and went through a second ceremony of marriage without having the first dissolved. He was later charged with bigamy and the question of law raised by the relevant penal statute was whether the second marriage was valid or void. The Privy Council held that it was valid for, having changed to the Muslim faith, Reid was now permitted to practise polygamy by the law of Ceylon.

If a man can take further wives following a change of domicile, a fortiori he should be able to do so if his lex domicilii at the time of the monogamous

---

[15] *Sinha Peerage Claim* [1946] 1 All ER 348n, HL (change of Hindu sect from one practising polygamy to one practising monogamy).

[16] *Parkasho v Singh* [1968] P 233, [1967] 1 All ER 737 (Indian statute converting polygamous Sikh marriages into monogamous ones); *R v Sagoo* [1975] QB 885, [1975] 2 All ER 926, CA (Kenyan statute to the same effect).

[17] *Ali v Ali* [1968] P 564, [1966] 1 All ER 664, followed in *R v Sagoo* (supra). Cf *Hussain v Hussain* (supra).

[18] *Amadasun v Amadasun* [1992] 1 FLR 585, 590. In *Ohochuku v Ohochuku* [1960] 1 All ER 253, the parties, who had contracted a potentially polygamous marriage in Nigeria, subsequently went through a second ceremony in England. Wrangham J held that he could dissolve the latter. This decision is questionable: as English courts will recognise the first marriage as a marriage, the second ceremony seems to have been of no legal effect at all (see post, p 236, n 4). See *Amadasun v Amadasun; Parkasho v Singh* (supra) at 242 and 741 respectively; Mendes da Costa 44 Can Bar Rev at 310–311; Furmston 10 ICLQ 180.

[19] [1965] P 85, [1962] 3 All ER 873.

[20] [1965] P 85, 90, [1962] 3 All ER 873, 877. See also *Russ v Russ* [1964] P 315, 326; [1962] 3 All ER 193, 198, CA, where Willmer LJ referred to a marriage between a man domiciled in Egypt and a woman domiciled in England as potentially polygamous.

[1] [1965] AC 720, [1965] 1 All ER 812, PC. Strongly criticised by Koh in 29 MLR 88.

marriage permits him to practise polygamy.[2] In either case the wife's domicile will presumably be irrelevant.[3] This raises the question whether an English court would be prepared to give an immediate release to a woman who had entered into a de facto monogamous marriage and found her position as the first of two or more wives intolerable. It is submitted that sexual intercourse with one's own wife cannot amount to adultery,[4] so that divorce would be possible only if the husband's contracting a second marriage could be said to be such behaviour that the first wife could not reasonably be expected to live with him. In the only reported case in which this point has had to be considered, *Quoraishi v Quoraishi*,[5] the parties, who were Muslims domiciled in Bangladesh, married in Karachi in 1964. They were both doctors: the husband came to England in 1970 and the wife joined him a year or so later. In 1979 the husband married a second wife in Bangladesh. Before this marriage the wife had expressed her reluctance about the proposal, at the last minute she tried to stop the marriage, and afterwards asked her husband to divorce the second wife. When he refused to do so, she left him. He later petitioned for divorce based on her desertion. The Court of Appeal upheld Butler-Sloss J's judgment dismissing the petition and held that in the circumstances the wife had good cause for leaving him. From this it follows that the wife would have been successful had she based a petition for divorce on her husband's behaviour or desertion.[6] All the circumstances must be taken into account. In this case, although both parties were Muslims domiciled in a country which permitted polygamy, the marriage had been de facto monogamous for 15 years, nine of which had been spent in England and Wales, and the wife had never willingly accepted the position. The decision might well have been different if the parties had been less accustomed to English social life and the first wife had entered into the marriage knowing that her husband would probably take a second wife.

Problems created by polygamous marriages

Although polygamous marriages are now generally recognised in this country, we must consider one or two cases in which difficulty may still arise.[7]

---

[2] The point was left open in *Nabi v Heaton* [1981] 1 WLR 1052.

[3] Cf *Onabrauche v Onabrauche* (1978) 8 Fam Law 107. The parties, who were then both domiciled in Nigeria, contracted a polygamous marriage. After the wife had acquired an English domicile, the husband (who was still domiciled in Nigeria) contracted a second marriage. It was held that the wife could not allege that he had committed adultery.

[4] Cf *Onabrauche v Onabrauche* (supra). In *Drammeh v Drammeh* (1970) 78 Ceylon Law Weekly 55, PC, it was held that under the law of the Gambia the first wife could petition for divorce on the ground of the husband's adultery with the second wife. It is submitted that this decision should not be followed in this country.

[5] [1985] FLR 780, CA.

[6] See post, p 207.

[7] Another point that has been left open in the past is whether parties to a polygamous marriage can be together guilty of conspiracy: *Mawji v R* [1957] AC 126, 135–136, [1957] 1 All ER 385, 387, PC. There seems to be no reason why they should not be in the same position as parties to a monogamous marriage. For the position in relation to personal relief as a married man under the Income and Corporation Taxes Act when the taxpayer has more than one wife, see *Nabi v Heaton* [1983] 1 WLR 626, CA, where the Crown consented to an appeal from the decision of Vinelott J, [1981] 1 WLR 1052, and conceded that the taxpayer was entitled to relief with respect to his second wife. For the defence of marital coercion, see post, p 137, n 18.

Matrimonial causes

Hyde v Hyde[8] laid down the rule that matrimonial relief was not open to the parties to a polygamous marriage in this country. This was rigidly enforced for over a century, with the result that English courts would not entertain proceedings for divorce,[9] nullity,[10] or matrimonial relief in a magistrates' court.[11] It will be recalled that this bar operated if the marriage was de jure polygamous, even though it was de facto monogamous; consequently in recent years a large number of immigrants resident in this country but domiciled in, say, Pakistan or Nigeria found themselves unable to obtain any form of matrimonial relief here. Thus a wife, deserted by her husband, could obtain maintenance only by applying for supplementary benefit. Such a situation was clearly intolerable and the position was reversed by section 1 of the Matrimonial Proceedings (Polygamous Marriages) Act 1972, which permits a court to grant matrimonial relief or a declaration concerning the validity of the marriage notwithstanding that it is polygamous.[12]

Most of the problems that the working of this Act is likely to produce will probably flow from the difficulty of applying English matrimonial law to parties who have not been fully integrated into English social life. Although no reliable statistics are available, the number of men in this country with two or more wives is believed to be very small; but if one of the parties to a de facto polygamous marriage seeks matrimonial relief, the court may find itself in an impossible position. Would one wife be justified in leaving the matrimonial home on the ground, for example, that she found it impossible to live with another of her husband's wives? The truth is that English law, designed for monogamous relationships cannot easily be adapted to deal with polygamous ones; Parliament might have done well to exclude de facto polygamous marriages from the Act even though this would have left a small number of spouses unable to obtain any form of matrimonial relief in England even though they were domiciled here.[13]

Bigamy

In *R v Sagoo*[14] it was stated by the Court of Appeal that a marriage which is to be the foundation for a prosecution for bigamy must be a monogamous

[8] (1866), LR 1 P & D 130. See ante, p 60.
[9] *Hyde v Hyde* (1866), LR 1 P & D 130.
[10] *Risk v Risk* [1951] P 50, [1950] 2 All ER 973.
[11] *Sowa v Sowa* [1961] P 70, [1961] 1 All ER 687, CA.
[12] Now repealed and re-enacted by the Matrimonial Causes Act 1973, s 47. The Act implemented the recommendations of the Law Commission: Law Com No 42 (Report on Polygamous Marriages), 1971. 'Matrimonial relief' includes decrees of divorce, nullity, judicial separation, and presumption of death and dissolution of marriage, orders on the ground of wilful neglect to maintain and for the alteration of maintenance agreements, ancillary orders in all such proceedings, and orders under the Domestic Proceedings and Magistrates' Courts Act 1978 and Pt III of the Matrimonial and Family Proceedings Act 1984 (maintenance after foreign divorce etc): Matrimonial Causes Act 1973, s 47(2), as amended by the two Acts mentioned. See also the Family Law Act 1986, Sch 1, para 14.
[13] This was the reason for Mr Neil Lawson's dissent from the majority recommendations of the Law Commission: Law Com No 42, pp 46–47.
[14] [1975] QB 885, 889, [1975] 2 All ER 926, 929, CA. The point was left open in *R v Naguib* [1917] 1 KB 359, 361, CCA, and *Baindail v Baindail* [1946] P 122, 130, [1946] 1 All ER 342, 347, CA. See further Bartholomew *Polygamous Marriages and English Criminal Law* 17 MLR 344; Polonsky *Polygamous Marriage—a Bigamist's Charter* [1971] Crim LR 401; Pearl [1976] CLJ 48; Morse 25 ICLQ 229.

one. The critical question, however, is whether the first union is monogamous at the time of the second ceremony. Hence if, as in *R v Sagoo*, a man contracts a polygamous marriage with W, which is then converted into a monogamous union by local legislation or the man's changing his domicile, and he later goes through a ceremony of marriage with X, he may be convicted of bigamy. If, however, the first marriage is still polygamous at the time of the second ceremony, he apparently commits no criminal offence even though the second marriage is void, for example because it is contracted in England. This distinction is unwarranted. Difficulty arises because a citizen of the United Kingdom and Colonies may be prosecuted for bigamy even though the second marriage is celebrated abroad, and there is no saving for marriages which are valid by the accused's lex domicilii.[15] It is inconceivable, however, that a man would be prosecuted in this country for contracting a lawful second marriage abroad if this is valid by the law of his domicile and the place where it was celebrated.[16] There is no justification whatever for permitting a man who enters into a *void* second marriage to escape conviction for bigamy by pleading that his first marriage was polygamous. The dictum was not essential to the decision in *R v Sagoo*, and it is to be hoped that the House of Lords or Parliament will seize an early opportunity of overruling it.[17]

Rights in property

Problems with respect to rights in property are likely to arise only if the marriage is de facto polygamous. It has been held that one of two widows may apply for an order under the Inheritance (Provision for Family and Dependants) Act 1975:[18] obviously both could apply if necessary. The Matrimonial Homes Act 1983 applies if the marriage is polygamous, whether de jure or de facto.[19] Although the Rent Act and the Housing Acts are silent on the point, it is submitted that two widows who have been living together require the same protection against eviction from the former matrimonial home as one does and that the husband's tenancy should vest in them as joint tenants after his death. Intestate succession presents a more complicated problem: do both widows take £75,000 (or £125,000) each or as joint tenants or tenants in common? In fairness to other beneficiaries, they should not take more than the statutory sum in total, and it seems more just to divide this between them equally as tenants in common.[20]

Social welfare legislation

Refusal to allow benefit to a woman who had been married under a system allowing polygamy resulted in legislation to define the position of spouses in such cases. Under existing regulations a polygamous marriage is to be treated

---

[15] Offences against the Person Act 1861, s 57; British Nationality Act 1948, s 3(1).

[16] Dicey and Morris *Conflict of Laws* (11th Edn) p 669.

[17] The dictum fails to comply with the Court of Appeal's own view that the rules relating to the recognition of the status created by marriage should be the same in criminal law and family law: [1975] QB 885, 890, [1975] 2 All ER 926, 930.

[18] *Re Sehota* [1978] 3 All ER 385.

[19] S 10(2).

[20] The personal chattels would have to be divided equally between them too.

as valid for the purpose of the Social Security Contributions and Benefits Act 1992 at any time while it is monogamous in fact.[1]

The reason for this provision is that contributions and benefits are calculated on the assumption that a man has only one wife at a time. On the other hand, a man cannot be permitted to throw the burden of supporting his wife or wives on the taxpayer merely because his marriage is polygamous and consequently he is bound to support them for the purpose of the Social Security Administration Act 1992 even though the unions are de facto polygamous.[2]

G. Presumption of marriage

It has long been established law that, if a man and woman cohabit and hold themselves out as husband and wife, this in itself raises a presumption that they are legally married.[3] Consequently, if the marriage is challenged, the burden lies upon those challenging it to prove that there was in fact no marriage and not upon those alleging it to prove that it has been solemnized. This may be important, for example, if the parties have been married abroad and have no written or other evidence of the solemnization, or if the validity of the marriage is called into question indirectly when the parties can no longer give evidence, as it may be if the legitimacy of their children is put in issue after their deaths.

A closer examination will show that there are really two presumptions: first, that at some time or other the parties went through a valid form of marriage, and, secondly, that, when they did so, they both had the capacity to marry. This distinction is important when the standard of proof necessary to rebut the presumption is considered.

Presumption of formal validity

The presumption that the parties went through a valid form of marriage may always be rebutted, of course, by proving that they never contracted any marriage at all, and although this will usually be difficult to do by direct evidence, it may be possible to do so by inference.[4] Even if it is not disputed that the parties went through a form of marriage, it may still be alleged that owing to some formal defect the ceremony was a legal nullity. But in this case omnia praesumuntur rite esse acta, and the generally accepted view is that the presumption will not be rebutted unless the evidence to the contrary

---

[1] See s 121 and s 147(5). See also Social Security and Family Allowances (Polygamous Marriages) Regulations, SI 1975 No 561; Child Benefit (General) Regulations, SI 1976 No 965, reg 12. See Pearl [1978–79] JSWL 24; Poulter *English Law and Ethnic Minority Customs* 3.17.

[2] *Din v National Assistance Board* [1967] 2 QB 213, [1967] 1 All ER 750. For liability under the Social Security Administration Act 1992, see post, p 666.

[3] But in a prosecution for bigamy the presumption of the accused's innocence outweighs the presumption of marriage to be drawn from cohabitation and the marriage must be strictly proved by the prosecution: see Smith and Hogan *Criminal Law* (6th Edn) pp 705–706.

[4] As in *Re Bradshaw* [1938] 4 All ER 143, where the presumption was rebutted by evidence that the parties had subsequently intermarried.

satisfies one beyond reasonable doubt that there has been no valid marriage.[5] The number of cases in which this has been done is extremely small.

Presumption of capacity

In *Tweney v Tweney*[6] Pilcher J said:

> 'The petitioner's marriage to the present respondent being unexceptionable in form and duly consummated remains a good marriage until *some* evidence is adduced that the marriage was, *in fact*, a nullity.'

This raises the question: what evidence will suffice for this purpose? Although this point still has to be decided, it is tentatively submitted on the present state of the authorities that, if any evidence is adduced showing that either of the parties lacked capacity, the presumption in favour of the validity of the marriage disappears and the question has to be decided on the balance of probability in the light of all the available evidence. It will usually be easy to determine whether either party was at the time of the marriage under the age of 16 or whether they are related within the prohibited degrees of consanguinity or affinity; difficulty may arise when one of the parties has been previously married and it is alleged that this earlier marriage was still subsisting when the later union was contracted. The common problem is therefore this: A marries X and they later separate; A then marries Y without having the former marriage dissolved and not knowing whether X is still alive. Is the marriage between A and Y to be presumed to be valid?[7]

Whether X was still alive at the time of A's marriage to Y is a question of fact.[8] If X was suffering from a fatal disease when A last heard of him, he may be presumed to have died within a relatively short time; the converse is true if X was a young person in good health. The presumption that the second marriage was valid was rebutted in *Re Peete*.[9] W had separated from her first husband some time before 1916. In that year she was told by his sister that he had been killed in an explosion in a factory where he was employed but that she (the sister) had been unable to identify his body. In 1919 W went through a form of marriage with H. In an application under the Inheritance (Family Provision) Act 1938 by W as H's widow, it was held that she could not succeed. Although there was an initial presumption that the marriage between H and W was valid, there was some evidence that she had not at that time the capacity to marry him, viz the existence of the previous marriage. The sister's statement that the first husband had been killed was clearly inadmissible as it amounted to double hearsay; hence W had remarried only four years after last seeing her first husband and there was no admissible evidence to rebut the presumption that he was still alive after that short period.

If X has been absent for seven years or more and has not been heard of

---

[5] See *Mahadervan v Mahadervan* [1964] P 233, 246, [1962] 3 All ER 1108, 1117, and the cases there cited, particularly *Hill v Hill* [1959] 1 All ER 281, 285, PC; *Piers v Piers* (1849) 2 HL Cas 331, HL, at 362, 370. But in *Re Taylor* [1961] 1 All ER 55, 63, CA, Harman LJ was of the opinion that the evidence in rebuttal should be *firm and clear*.

[6] [1946] P 180, 182, [1946] 1 All ER 564, 565. (Italics supplied.)

[7] The question in dispute may be alternatively whether a previous marriage was validly dissolved: *Gatty v A-G* [1951] P 444.

[8] *Chard v Chard* [1956] P 259, [1955] 3 All ER 721.

[9] [1952] 2 All ER 599. Cf *MacDarmaid v A-G* [1950] P 218, [1950] 1 All ER 497 (first wife presumed to be still alive after three years).

during that time, this may of itself raise a presumption of law that he is dead provided that certain conditions are satisfied. The nature of this presumption was thus stated by Sachs J in *Chard v Chard*:[10]

'Where ... there is no acceptable affirmative evidence that he was alive at some time during a continuous period of seven years or more, then if it can be proved first, that there are persons who would be likely to have heard of him over that period, secondly, that those persons have not heard of him, and thirdly, that all due inquiries have been made appropriate to the circumstances, [X] will be presumed to have died at some time within that period.'

If any of these conditions is missing, the presumption cannot be invoked. In *Chard v Chard* the husband went through a form of marriage with the respondent 16 years after last seeing his first wife. He had spent almost the whole of that time in prison, and there was some evidence that his first wife had also contracted a bigamous marriage. That being so, the husband was not likely to have heard of her during the intervening period and so the first of the three conditions was not satisfied. Hence no presumption was raised that the first wife was dead at the end of the 16 years, and as she would be only 44 years old at the time of the second marriage, the court inferred that she was still alive and granted a decree of nullity in respect of the second marriage. Again, in *Bradshaw v Bradshaw*[11] it was inferred that the first husband was still alive after 19 years' absence. In this case the presumption could not be invoked because the third condition was not satisfied, as the wife had failed to make obvious enquiries about her husband (who, when she last saw him, was a regular soldier) from his Corps records.

These cases were distinguished in *Taylor v Taylor*,[12] where the question in issue was whether a *previous* marriage was to be presumed to have been valid. W went through a form of marriage with G. She later left him and, having discovered facts which led her to conclude that this marriage was void because G was already married to another woman, she went through a form of marriage with H whilst G was still alive. H then petitioned for a decree of nullity on the ground that his marriage to W was void as she had been married to G when it was celebrated. These facts gave rise to conflicting presumptions and Cairns J resolved the problem by 'leaning towards the preservation of existing unions' rather than 'towards the avoiding of existing unions in favour of doubtful earlier and, to all intents and purposes, dead ones.'[13] He accordingly held that the presumption that W was validly married to H was not rebutted. It may be doubted, however, whether he was justified in coming to this conclusion. Had the sole question in issue been the validity of W's marriage to G, the court must have pronounced in its favour in the absence of any evidence to rebut the presumption. The facts indicated that the marriage to H was presumptively void and there was no evidence to rebut

---

[10] [1956] P 259, 272, [1955] 3 All ER 721, 728; criticised by Nokes in 19 MLR 208. See also Treitel *Presumption of Death* 17 MLR 530. The first spouse was presumed to be dead in the following cases: *Tweney v Tweney* [1946] P 180, [1946] 1 All ER 564 (12 years' absence during which exhaustive enquiries had been made); *Re Watkins* [1953] 2 All ER 1113 (25 years' absence); *Bullock v Bullock* [1960] 2 All ER 307 (14 years' absence during which police had sought husband).

[11] [1956] P 274, n.

[12] [1967] P 25, [1965] 1 All ER 872.

[13] At 39 and 881, respectively.

this presumption either. However practically convenient this decision may be, it seems to be logically unsupportable.[14]

H. Declarations of status

The increasing number of immigrants (many of whom visit their countries of origin from time to time) and the ease of international travel mean that many people living in this country have been married or divorced abroad. Occasionally the question of the marital status of a person in this position may be raised—for example, to determine whether he or she is free to marry here or can claim a pension or other benefit as the spouse or widow or widower of another—and legal machinery must be provided to resolve it. This is now done by section 55 of the Family Law Act 1986, which confers a power to make a declaratory order regarding marital status on the High Court and county courts.[15]

An application may be made for one or more of the following declarations:

(a) that a marriage was at its inception a valid marriage;
(b) that a marriage subsisted, or did not subsist, on a given date;
(c) that a divorce, annulment or legal separation obtained outside England and Wales is, or is not, entitled to recognition in this country.[16]

It will be observed that there is no power to apply for a declaration that a marriage was void ab initio: in this case the correct procedure is to petition for a decree of nullity, when the court may make ancillary orders relating to children and financial relief.[17]

Although a declaration will normally be sought by one of the parties to the marriage, others may be legitimately interested in its validity. For example, the trustees of a pension fund may wish to establish whether a woman is the widow of a former employee. Applications for a declaration may therefore be brought by anyone, but the court must refuse to hear a case if it considers that the applicant does not have a sufficient interest in the outcome of the proceedings.[18] In any event it may refuse to make a declaration if to do so would be manifestly contrary to public policy.[19] This appears to give statutory effect to the decision in *Puttick v A-G*,[20] when Baker P refused

---

[14] W could easily have petitioned for a decree of nullity with respect to her first marriage, and the hardship worked in *Re Peete* (ante, p 68) was much greater. It is also submitted that Cairns J applied the wrong standard of proof by requiring decisive evidence to rebut the presumption of capacity.

[15] See also s 63 (meaning of 'court'). These provisions implement the Law Commission's recommendations in Law Com No 132 (Report on Declarations in Family Matters). Previously the power had derived partly from statute (going back to the Legitimacy Declaration Act 1858) and partly from the inherent jurisdiction of the High Court (which was abolished in this respect by s 58(4) of the Family Law Act). There was also a decree of jactitation of marriage which restrained the respondent from wrongfully boasting or asserting that he or she was married to the petitioner. Proceedings for jactitation (which were virtually obsolete) were abolished by s 61 of the Family Law Act 1986.

[16] Family Law Act 1986, s 55(1).

[17] Ibid, s 58(5)(a), (b).

[18] Ibid, s 55(3).

[19] Ibid, s 58(1).

[20] [1980] Fam 1, [1979] 3 All ER 463.

to grant a declaration when the petitioner (better known as Astrid Proll) had entered this country on a forged passport to evade prosecution in Germany, had committed perjury to obtain a superintendent registrar's certificate and licence, and had shown a general disregard of the laws of this country. It is not clear, however, what purpose withholding the decree really served. Granted that the petitioner was validly married, the fact that she had achieved her aim by illegal means seems to be irrelevant: it is not really sensible to compel a person to re-litigate this matter whenever the question is raised.

A declaration is a judgment in rem and binds everyone including the Crown (which may be important if, for example, the applicant is seeking British citizenship or claiming the right to live in this country).[1] Consequently, the Attorney-General is to be given notice of an application and may intervene in any proceedings.[2]

Jurisdiction

The court has jurisdiction only if one of the parties to the marriage is domiciled in England and Wales at the time of the application or has been habitually resident in this country for one year before that date or, alternatively, if one of them is dead and he or she satisfied either of these conditions at the time of his or her death.[3]

Staying of proceedings

The court has a discretionary power to stay any proceedings for a declaration relating to the validity or subsistence of the petitioner's marriage if any proceedings in respect of it or capable of affecting its validity or subsistence are continuing in another jurisdiction.[4] The court must take the same matters into account in deciding whether to order a stay and has the same power to remove a stay as it has in proceedings for divorce. These matters are considered in greater detail later.[5] There are no obligatory stays in proceedings for a declaration.

---

[1] Family Law Act 1986, s 58(2). But no declaration is to affect any judgment or decree already made: s 60(3).
[2] Ibid, ss 59 and 60(2)(c); Family Proceedings Rules 1991, r 3.16(4). Other interested persons may also be required to be made parties: s 60(2)(b).
[3] Ibid, s 55(2). This brings jurisdiction into line with that in nullity: see post, p 78.
[4] Domicile and Matrimonial Proceedings Act 1973, Sch 1, paras 2 and 9. This Act has not been amended to take account of the change in terminology introduced by the 1986 Act (under which the person bringing the proceedings is known as the applicant) or the possibility of an application being made by someone who is not a party to the marriage.
[5] See post, pp 231–233.

Chapter 3

Void and voidable marriages

A. Introductory

1. VOID AND VOIDABLE MARRIAGES

The view of the Roman Catholic Church that marriage is a sacrament inevitably meant that the law relating to marriage would become a part of the canon law, over which the ecclesiastical courts successfully claimed exclusive jurisdiction.[1] This had the most profound effect on subsequent legal developments. Not only were these courts the only tribunals competent to declare whether the parties were validly married, but the Roman Catholic doctrine of the indissolubility of marriage became a tenet of English law.

Whilst this doctrine precluded the courts from granting decrees of divorce, it did not stop them from declaring that, although the parties had gone through a ceremony of marriage, some impediment prevented their acquiring the status of husband and wife. Clearly there was no valid marriage if either of the spouses was already married to somebody else, if they were related within the prohibited degrees, or if one of them did not fully consent to the solemnization. Furthermore, a marriage was not regarded as consummated until the parties had become one flesh by sexual intercourse; consequently, if either of them was impotent, he or she was regarded as lacking capacity to contract the union, which could therefore be annulled. The same principles were applied by the English ecclesiastical courts after the breach with Rome in the sixteenth century. Such marriages were said to be void for, although the parties by going through a ceremony had apparently contracted a marriage, the result of the impediment was that there was never a marriage either in fact or in law. Consequently, the marriage could be formally annulled by a decree of an ecclesiastical court and, even without such a decree, either party was free to contract another union (unless he or she was already married to somebody else). As the marriage was a complete nullity, its validity could also be put in issue by any other person with an interest in so doing, even after the death of one or both of the parties to it. So, for example, after the death of a tenant in fee simple his brother might claim his estate on the ground that the tenant's marriage was void, with the result that his children, being illegitimate, could not inherit and his 'widow', never have been married, could not claim dower.

By the beginning of the seventeenth century, however, the royal courts were obviously becoming concerned at the ease with which marriages could be set aside and the issue bastardised. This was more likely to work injustice after the parties' death, when relevant evidence might no longer be available. By the use of the writ of prohibition, therefore, they cut down the jurisdiction

---

[1] Pollock and Maitland *History of English Law*, ii, 364–366.

of the ecclesiastical courts by forbidding them to annul marriages in certain cases after the death of either party.[2] This had the result of dividing impediments into two kinds: civil and canonical. If the impediment was civil—for example, the fact that one of the parties was married to a third person at the time of the ceremony—the marriage was still void ab initio and its validity could be put in issue by anyone at any time, whether or not the parties were still alive. If the impediment was canonical—for example, the fact that one of the parties was impotent or (until the law was changed in 1835)[3] that they were related within the prohibited degrees—the validity of the marriage could not be questioned after either party had died. The rule thus developed that such a marriage must be regarded as valid unless it is annulled during the lifetime of both parties. Until that time it has the capacity to be turned into a void marriage: in other words, it is voidable. Once a decree of nullity had been pronounced, however, it acted retrospectively and the marriage was then regarded as having been void from the beginning. Consequently, the parties reverted to their pre-marital status and their children were automatically bastardised. The distinction between void and voidable marriages was described by Lord Greene MR in the following words:[4]

'A void marriage is one that will be regarded by every court in any case in which the existence of the marriage is in issue as never having taken place and can be so treated by both parties to it without the necessity of any decree annulling it: a voidable marriage is one that will be regarded by every court as a valid subsisting marriage until a decree annulling it has been pronounced by a court of competent jurisdiction.'

After the introduction of divorce by judicial process in 1857, the voidable marriage came to occupy a position midway between the void marriage and the valid marriage. The annulment of a voidable marriage, like divorce, changes the parties' status by a judicial decree, and whatever the theoretical differences between them are, both are means of terminating a marriage that has broken down. Divorce, however, does not act retrospectively; the parties are still regarded as having been husband and wife up to the time when the decree was made absolute. Some of the inconveniences of the retrospective operation of the decree of nullity of a voidable marriage were removed by statute or avoided by the courts: for example, children of the marriage now remain legitimate[5] and it has never been possible to set aside transactions carried out on the assumption (valid at the time) that the parties to a voidable marriage were husband and wife.[6] Nevertheless, many anomalies remained and the retrospective effect of the decree was artificial and confusing and 'in truth perpetuated a canonical fiction'.[7]

The whole of the law of nullity was reviewed by the Law Commission in 1970.[8] In view of the criticisms that had been levelled against the anomalous nature of the voidable marriage, the Commission examined the question

---

[2] See Jackson *Formation and Annulment of Marriage* (2nd Edn) pp 54–55.

[3] Such marriages were made void by the Marriage Act 1835.

[4] *de Reneville v de Reneville* [1948] P 100, 111, [1948] 1 All ER 56, 60, CA. Professor Newark considered that historically this distinction is incorrect: *The Operation of Nullity Decrees* 8 MLR 203.

[5] See post, p 282.

[6] See post, p 102.

[7] Per Lord Goddard CJ in *R v Algar* [1954] 1 QB 279, 288, [1953] 2 All ER 1381, 1384, CCA.

[8] Law Com No 33.

whether the concept should be abolished altogether and the grounds for annulling a voidable marriage included amongst the facts from which irretrievable breakdown of the marriage might be inferred as the ground for divorce. They rejected the proposal for three reasons. First, certain Christian denominations and their members draw a clear distinction between the annulment and the dissolution of marriage and would be offended if the distinction were blurred. Secondly, some people still associate stigma with divorce and therefore prefer to keep matters involving no moral blame, such as impotence and mental disorder, as grounds for nullity.[9] Thirdly, the bar which then applied to divorce within the first three years of marriage was clearly inappropriate to the grounds for nullity.[10] The Law Commission, however, did make extensive recommendations with the object of resolving uncertainties and removing anomalies. Effect was given to these by the Nullity of Marriage Act 1971, which came into operation on 1st August 1971, and which to a large extent codified the whole of the law of nullity.[11] This Act has in turn been repealed and its provisions re-enacted in the Matrimonial Causes Act 1973.

Distinction between void and voidable marriages

We are now in a position to compare the salient features of the two types of marriage.

Grounds for annulment

Essentially, a marriage will be void if either party lacks capacity to contract it or if the ceremony is formally defective. Until the Nullity of Marriage Act it was doubtful whether lack of consent made a marriage void or voidable; in the case of marriages contracted after 31st July 1971, the Act specifically provides that this will make them voidable.

With the doubtful exception of lack of consent, the only ground on which a marriage could be voidable after 1929[12] was that one of the parties was impotent. The Matrimonial Causes Act of 1937 added four new grounds: the respondent's wilful refusal to consummate the marriage, either party's mental disorder, the respondent's venereal disease, and the respondent wife's pregnancy per alium. Impotence, the four statutory grounds (with some modifications) and lack of consent are the grounds on which a marriage will be voidable today.

---

[9] But this overlooks the fact that moral blame attaches to some of the grounds for nullity (eg, pregnancy per alium).

[10] During the ten years 1976–1984 there were on average just over 1,000 petitions a year. In the years 1985–1990 the average was 567. It is significant that the large drop in 1985 occurred in the first full year in which it became possible to petition for divorce after the first year of marriage. About 85% of all petitions are based on impotence or wilful refusal to consummate.

[11] For the Act generally, see Hall [1971] CLJ 208; Cretney 35 MLR 57.

[12] When the Age of Marriage Act rendered a marriage void if either party was under the age of 16: see ante, p 35.

Necessity for decree

The vital distinction between a void and a voidable marriage is still that the former, being void ab initio, needs no decree to annul it, whilst the latter is in all respects a valid marriage until a decree absolute of nullity is pronounced. Hence if either party dies before a decree is granted, a voidable marriage must be treated as valid for all purposes and for all time.[13] On the other hand, for example, either party to a void marriage may lawfully contract a valid marriage with someone else without having the first marriage formally annulled.

Even though, in the case of a void marriage, a decree of nullity can only be declaratory and cannot effect any change in the parties' status, there may be good reason for obtaining such a decree. In the first place, there may be some doubt whether on the facts or the law applicable the marriage is void: whether, for example, one party was already married or there was a due publication of banns. Secondly, a decree of nullity is a judgment in rem, so that no one may subsequently allege that the marriage is in fact valid. But the most important reason for bringing proceedings is that the court has power on granting a decree to make certain ancillary orders, and a party may therefore present a petition in order, for example, to obtain a property adjustment order or financial provision for herself and any children of the family. As the parties are not married, this is in fact the only way in which the 'wife' may obtain any form of maintenance for itself.

Third parties' rights

From what has been said above, it follows that third parties must treat a voidable marriage as valid unless a decree has been pronounced. On the other hand, if it is alleged that a marriage is void, any person with an interest in so doing may prove as a question of fact that there has never been a marriage at all. Thus, suppose that property is settled on trust for A for life with remainder to his widow or, if he leaves no widow, to B absolutely. A goes through a ceremony of marriage with W who survives him. Even though the marriage between W and A was voidable, B cannot dispute its validity to prove that W is not A's widow; but he can show, even after A's death, that the marriage between them was void and that consequently the remainder over to him takes effect, for W, never having been A's wife, cannot now be his widow. But if a decree of nullity had been pronounced before A's death, then, whether the marriage was void or voidable, everyone is bound by it and W may not now assert that she is A's widow. It is easy to imagine other cases in which the validity of a marriage might be impeached: for example, others interested in property might wish to prove that the alleged marriage had not revoked the will of one of the parties to it.[14]

Conversely, it might be in the interest of one of the parties to the marriage to prove that it was void. Suppose that a testator devises property to W so long as she remains his widow and, if she remarry, to X. W subsequently goes through a ceremony of marriage with K. In the event of a dispute between W and X over the beneficial interest in the property after the

[13] *Re Roberts* [1978] 3 All ER 225, CA (revocation of will executed before marriage).
[14] Cf *Harrod v Harrod* (1854) 1 K & J 4; *Re Peete* [1952] 2 All ER 599; *In the Estate of Park* [1954] P 89, [1953] 2 All ER 408, CA.

ceremony, W clearly succeeds if she can show that the marriage between herself and K is void.[15]

Effect of the decree

If the marriage is void ab initio, the decree does not affect the parties' status at all. In the case of a voidable marriage, the Law Commission sought to remove the difficulties caused by the retrospective effect of the decree by recommending that it should operate to annul the marriage only as respects any time after it had been made absolute and that the marriage should continue to be treated as having existed up to that time. This recommendation was implemented by the Nullity of Marriage Act 1971, but as we shall see, it is by no means clear what the effect of the legislation has been.[16]

2. PETITIONS

Jurisdiction to grant decrees of nullity (whether the marriage was alleged to be void or voidable) was transferred from the ecclesiastical courts to the new Divorce Court set up by the Matrimonial Causes Act of 1857, and was vested in the High Court by the Judicature Act of 1873. Divorce county courts now have jurisdiction to hear all petitions.[17]

It was an established practice in the ecclesiastical courts to permit a petition to be presented not only by one of the parties to the marriage but also, in certain circumstances, by third persons as well. If the parties were related within the prohibited degrees (and presumably if the marriage was bigamous) any member of the public could invoke the so-called criminal jurisdiction of the court to abate a scandal, and if the allegation were found to be true, the court would pronounce a decree of nullity.[18] In other cases a third person could bring proceedings if he had an interest in the validity of the marriage. The interest apparently had to be proprietary or financial,[19] but a 'slight interest' was enough even though it depended on some contingency that was only remotely likely to occur. Successful proceedings were brought by the husband's statutory next of kin, who had an interest under their mother's will contingent on his dying without legitimate issue,[20] and by the wife's father, who had a potential liability under the old poor law to maintain any children she might have if they were indigent and their father could not support them.[1] Proceedings based on the criminal jurisdiction were no longer possible once the ecclesiastical courts ceased to have jurisdiction in matrimonial causes, but the rule that a person with an interest could bring nullity

[15] *Allen v Wood* (1834) 1 Bing NC 8.
[16] See post, pp 100–102.
[17] Matrimonial and Family Proceedings Act 1984, s 33. See further, ante, pp 13–14.
[18] *Turner v Meyers* (1808) 1 Hag Con 414; *Blackmore v Brider* (1816) 2 Phillim 359; *Chick v Ramsdale* (1835) 1 Curt 34.
[19] The relationship of parent and child did not per se entitle the parent to petition unless, perhaps, the child was a minor: *Sherwood v Ray* (1837) 1 Moo PC 353, 397, PCC; *Turner v Meyers* (supra).
[20] *Faremouth v Watson* (1811) 1 Phillim 355.
[1] *Sherwood v Ray* (supra).

proceedings apparently survived and there are dicta in comparatively recent cases indicating that it is still good law.[2]

As early as 1868 it was held that impotence is a matter of personal complaint and consequently could be raised only by the parties to the marriage themselves.[3] This principle applies with equal force to some of the new grounds for nullity, for example the respondent's pregnancy or venereal disease. Although many of the cases referred to in the last paragraph concerned voidable marriages, it is submitted that, now that their annulment has been assimilated much more to divorce, a third person can no longer petition if the marriage is voidable.[4] So far as void marriages are concerned, there seems to be a confusion between two principles: first, that anyone can show that a marriage is (or was) void in any proceedings in which this is relevant and, secondly, that it is open to the parties to obtain a decree of nullity which, as a judgment in rem, binds all the world. There is, however, a fundamental difference between, say, permitting a third person to prove that a marriage was void in order to establish a claim to one party's estate after his death and permitting him to bring proceedings to obtain a judgment *in rem* to this effect before or after the death of the two persons involved. Petitions are now rarely, if ever, brought by strangers and it is urged that the power to do so should be abolished.[5]

3. JURISDICTION OF ENGLISH COURTS

Before 1974 an English court had jurisdiction to pronounce a decree if one of the parties was domiciled in this country on the principle that it could always adjudicate on the status of a person domiciled within the jurisdiction.[6] It also had jurisdiction if both parties were resident in this country because this was the basis of the ecclesiastical courts' jurisdiction which divorce courts now exercise.[7] If the marriage was void, a petition could also be brought if

[2] See the Matrimonial Causes Act 1857, s 22, which provided that the Divorce Court should apply the same principles as the ecclesiastical courts had applied. The rule was regarded as good law by Collingwood J in *J v J* [1953] P 186, [1952] 2 All ER 1129, by Ormrod J in *Kassim v Kassim* [1962] P 224, 234, [1962] 3 All ER 426, 432, and by the Law Commission in Law Com No 33, para 87, and Law Com No 48 (Jurisdiction in Matrimonial Causes), para 50. Its existence is confirmed by implication by the Domicile and Matrimonial Proceedings Act 1973, s 5(3)(c), dealing with the court's jurisdiction after the death of one or both parties: see post, p 78.
[3] *A v B* (1868) LR 1 P & D 559.
[4] See *Re Roberts* [1978] 3 All ER 225, 227 (per Walton J). This view is supported by the fact that it is now expressly provided by statute that the respondent may raise the petitioner's own conduct as a bar in all such cases: see post, pp 96–99. This scarcely makes sense if the petitioner is not the other spouse.
[5] The Law Commission does not support this view: Law Com No 132 (Declarations in Family Matters), paras 3.29–3.32.
[6] *de Reneville v de Reneville* [1948] P 100, [1948] 1 All ER 56, CA. There is no English authority to support the proposition that the court had jurisdiction if the respondent alone was domiciled here, but this was generally accepted to be the position.
[7] *Ramsay-Fairfax v Ramsay-Fairfax*, [1956] P 115, [1955] 3 All ER 695, CA. In fact residence of the respondent alone was apparently sufficient, for the petitioner ipso facto submitted to the jurisdiction by invoking it: *Magnier v Magnier* (1968) 112 Sol Jo 233. But residence of the petitioner alone would not suffice, for in the absence of statutory authority a respondent who was neither domiciled nor resident in this country and whose marriage had not been celebrated here could not be compelled to appear in an English court to answer a petition which might affect his status: *de Reneville v de Reneville* (supra).

the marriage had been celebrated in England and Wales.[8] Additional jurisdiction to pronounce a decree on the wife's petition had been conferred by
statute in two cases: (a) if the husband had deserted the wife or had been
deported and had been domiciled in England and Wales immediately before
the desertion or deportation, and (b) if the wife had been ordinarily resident
in England and Wales for three years before the commencement of the
proceedings.[9]

These rules produced some anomalous results. The fact that a void marriage had been celebrated here sufficed to give the court jurisdiction when
the parties had only a slight connection with this country;[10] the statutory
bases applied only if the wife petitioned; and it is obviously desirable to have
a uniform set of rules applying to both nullity and divorce so that, if necessary,
a cross-petition may be brought and all litigation relating to the marriage
may be disposed of at the same time. This last consideration formed the basis
of the recommendations made by the Law Commission in 1972[11] which were
implemented by the Domicile and Matrimonial Proceedings Act 1973. By
section 5(3) of that Act the court now has jurisdiction in nullity proceedings
if (and only if) either of the parties to the marriage:

'(a) is domiciled in England and Wales on the date when the proceedings are begun;
     or
 (b) was habitually resident there throughout the period of one year ending with
     that date: or
 (c) died before that date and either
     (i) was at death domiciled in England and Wales, or
     (ii) had been habitually resident there throughout the period of one year ending
          with the date of death.'[12]

It will be seen that the same rules now apply whether the marriage is alleged
to be void or voidable and that it is immaterial whether the party domiciled
or resident here is petitioner or respondent.

The court also has jurisdiction if proceedings for divorce, nullity or judicial
separation, over which it has jurisdiction, have already begun, even though
it would no longer have jurisdiction when the nullity petition is presented.[13]
The operation of this provision can be illustrated by the following hypothetical facts. A wife petitions for divorce and the sole ground on which the
court could assume jurisdiction is that she is habitually resident in this
country. She then ceases to be resident here. The husband can cross-petition

---

[8] *Simonin v Mallac* (1860) 2 Sw & Tr 67; *Padolecchia v Padolecchia* [1968] P 314, [1968] 3 All
ER 863. This did not apply if the marriage was voidable: *Ross Smith v Ross Smith* [1963] AC
280, [1962] 1 All ER 344, HL.
[9] (a) was originally enacted by the Matrimonial Causes Act 1937. It was particularly important
when the marriage was alleged to be voidable when the wife's domicile would automatically
be the same as the husband's. (b) was originally enacted by the Law Reform (Miscellaneous
Provisions) Act 1949 following a large number of marriages contracted between English
women and foreign servicemen during the Second World War. Both were re-enacted in s 46
of the Matrimonial Causes Act 1973, now repealed by the Domicile and Matrimonial Proceedings Act 1973, Sch 6.
[10] Cf *Padolecchia v Padolecchia* (supra), where the petitioner, who was domiciled in Italy, went
through a ceremony of marriage with the respondent, who was domiciled in Denmark, whilst
on a short visit to England.
[11] Law Com No 48 (Report on Jurisdiction in Matrimonial Causes).
[12] Para (c) presupposes that the court has jurisdiction to pronounce a decree of nullity after the
death of one or both parties and will therefore apply only if the marriage is void: see ante, p 77.
[13] Domicile and Matrimonial Proceedings Act 1973, s 5(5).

for nullity whilst the divorce proceedings are pending even though he could no longer have brought proceedings if the wife had not previously petitioned herself.

Stays

It is obvious that other matrimonial proceedings between the parties could be brought in another country whilst nullity proceedings are pending here: for example, whilst a wife is petitioning for nullity in this country, her husband might bring proceedings for divorce elsewhere. To prevent embarrassment, the court has a discretionary power to stay nullity proceedings here if before the beginning of the trial it appears that any proceedings in respect of the marriage or capable of affecting its validity or subsistence are continuing in any country outside England or Wales. The law relating to the facts to be taken into account in deciding whether to exercise the discretion, the removal of stays and their effect on ancillary orders is the same as in divorce, and in view of the comparative rarity of petitions for nullity, these matters will be considered when we deal with dissolution.[14]

There are no obligatory stays in nullity proceedings as there are in divorce.[15]

Choice of law

The question of the choice of law to be applied in a nullity suit is exceptionally complicated because most cases will involve the lex loci celebrationis or the parties' lex domicilii. Reference must be made to books on the conflict of laws.

4. DECREES

A decree of nullity is made in two stages: the decree nisi followed by the decree absolute. The rules relating to the application for a decree nisi to be made absolute (including the restrictions imposed where children of the family are involved) are exactly the same as they are in divorce.[16] The marriage is finally annulled when the decree is made absolute and a party to a voidable marriage may not remarry until then.

Whether the marriage is void or voidable, the court has power to make a number of ancillary orders. These will be dealt with in various places in this book; a list of them will be found in Appendix C, post.

[14] See post, pp 231–233.
[15] The reason is that a conflict has always been possible between different jurisdictions in the United Kingdom and in practice this did not give rise to any problems. If the other proceedings are for divorce or judicial separation, the nullity suit should always be disposed of first. See Law Com No 48, para 88.
[16] See post, p 236.

B. Void marriages

1. INTRODUCTORY

We have already seen that a void marriage is strictly speaking a contradiction in terms: to speak of a void marriage is merely a compendious way of saying that, although the parties have been through a ceremony of marriage, they have never acquired the status of husband and wife owing to the presence of some impediment. If they have never been through a ceremony at all, however, their union cannot even be termed a void marriage. This raises the exceptionally difficult problem of what kind of ceremony will be sufficient to enable the court to grant a decree of nullity. The matter may be of considerable practical importance because in certain circumstances the issue of a void marriage can be legitimate and only if the court pronounces a decree does it have power to make orders relating to financial provision for the spouses and the adjustment of their rights in property.

There is no reported case in which the problem has arisen in this form. Obviously, a ceremony cannot produce even a void marriage if it is intended to be no more than a charade and is seen to be such by the parties and spectators, for example the representation of a wedding on the stage. On the other hand, even though the ceremony is formally valid, the marriage will be void if both parties realise that it will not confer on them the status of husband and wife because, for example, one of them is already married.[17] Two difficult cases come between these extremes. The first is that of the ceremony recognised by the law as capable of constituting a marriage which fails to do so because of a formal defect known to both parties. As the Marriage Act 1949 expressly provides that a marriage shall be void in such circumstances, the implication is that it can be the subject of nullity proceedings. The other difficult case is that of the ceremony incapable of constituting a marriage in any circumstances which one or both of the parties nevertheless believe to be valid. This may well be of considerable importance because of the risk that members of immigrant communities may go through religious ceremonies in private houses under the misapprehension that they are thereby contracting a legally recognised marriage. There is some indication that this will not be recognised as even a void marriage. Quashing a conviction for knowingly and wilfully solemnizing a marriage in precisely such circumstances, the Court of Criminal Appeal said:[18]

> 'What, in our judgment, was contemplated by [the Marriage Act] ... in dealing with marriage and its solemnisation, and that to which alone it applies, was the performing in England of a ceremony in a form known to and recognised by our law as capable of producing, when there performed, a valid marriage.'

It is, however, highly undesirable to place a construction on the Act which could leave one party to such a ceremony wholly without means of obtaining financial support from the other. Earlier the Court had said: 'It does not seem to the court that the provisions of the Act have any relevance or application to a ceremony which is not *and does not purport to be* a marriage

---

[17] If, unbeknown to the parties, the first spouse was in fact dead, there seems little doubt that the ceremony would create a valid marriage.

[18] *R v Bham* [1966] 1 QB 159, 169, [1965] 3 All ER 124, 129, CCA. See 81 LQR 474.

of the kind allowed by English domestic law.'[19] This statement was sufficiently wide to cover the point in issue in the case, and it is submitted that it should determine whether the ceremony was such as to enable the court to pronounce a decree of nullity and to grant ancillary relief. The test should be: did either or both of the parties honestly believe that they were contracting a legally valid marriage? Only if both knew that the ceremony could not make them husband and wife by English law should they be in the same position as a couple who cohabit without going through any ceremony at all.

2. GROUNDS ON WHICH A MARRIAGE WILL BE VOID

Section 11 of the Matrimonial Causes Act 1973[20] expressly provides that a marriage celebrated after 31st July 1971 (when the Nullity of Marriage Act 1971 came into force) shall be void only on the grounds there set out. These are all grounds on which a marriage celebrated before that date would be void. In addition, it is probable that lack of consent on the part of one of the parties formerly made a marriage void, in which case a marriage celebrated before 1st August 1971, affected by lack of consent, will remain void.[1]

The present grounds can be divided into two: those relating to capacity and those relating to formal requirements.

Lack of capacity

Obviously lack of capacity to marry will ipso facto make the marriage void. This must be determined in accordance with the principles already discussed.[2]

If the relevant law is English, the marriage will be void on the following grounds:

(a) That the parties are related within the prohibited degrees of consanguinity or, if the conditions set out in the Marriage Act 1949 are not observed, within the prohibited degrees of affinity.[3]

(b) That either of them is under the age of 16.

(c) That either of them is already married.

(d) That they are not respectively male and female. This provision is designed to cover the case of a party who has previously undergone an operation to achieve an alleged change of sex or about whose sex there is genuine doubt.[4] The wording of the Act is sufficiently wide to enable a petition for nullity to be brought where each party knows that both are of the same sex but leads all concerned with the solemnization of the marriage to believe that one of them is of the opposite sex. The point is probably academic, but it is at least questionable whether the court should have power in nullity

---

[19] At 168 and 129, respectively. (Italics supplied.)

[20] Re-enacting the Nullity of Marriage Act 1971, s 1, as amended by the Matrimonial Proceedings (Polygamous Marriages) Act 1972, s 4.

[1] See further post, pp 90–95. It is also possible that a marriage celebrated before 1st August 1971 was void if one of the parties was divorced and the time for appealing against the decree absolute had not expired: see *Dryden v Dryden* [1973] Fam 217, 239, [1973] 3 All ER 526, 542.

[2] Matrimonial Causes Act 1973, s 14(1). See ante, pp 26–31. A marriage may also be void under the Royal Marriages Act 1772: ibid, Sch 1, para 6. See ante, p 34, n 14.

[3] See ante, pp 36–38.

[4] See ante, pp 34–35.

proceedings to order financial relief for the benefit of a party to an overtly homosexual relationship.[5]

(e) That either party to a polygamous marriage celebrated abroad was at the time of the ceremony domiciled in England. This is subject to the overriding principle that a foreign rule of law must be applied instead of the English rule when the conflict of laws so requires.[6] Consequently, if the proper law to apply is that of the proposed matrimonial home, the marriage may still be valid notwithstanding that one of the parties is domiciled in this country.[7]

Formal defects

Whether failure to comply with the formal requirements relating to the marriage ceremony will make the marriage void must be determined by reference to the lex loci celebrationis.[8]

If the marriage is solemnized in England, it is not every defect in the formalities laid down in the Marriage Act that will render the ceremony a nullity. Whilst public policy requires that these formalities should be strictly observed, the consequences of avoiding any marriage where there was some technical defect, however slight, would be socially even more undesirable. English law has effected a compromise between these conflicting demands of public policy with the result that some formal defects will not render the marriage void at all, whilst in the case of the rest the marriage will be void only if *both* parties contracted it with knowledge of the defect. In other words, it is impossible for a person in England innocently to contract a marriage which is void because of a formal defect. The real sanction is afforded by the criminal law, for if a party knowingly fails to comply with the Marriage Act, he will frequently have to make a false oath or declaration which is punishable under the Perjury Act of 1911.[9] This should adequately safeguard the marriage law without prejudicing the position of the innocent spouse.

Defects which will never invalidate a marriage

The Marriage Act 1949 specifically enacts that a marriage shall not be rendered void on any of the following grounds:[10]

    (a) That any of the statutory residence requirements was not fulfilled (whether for the purpose of the publication of banns or of obtaining a common licence or superintendent registrar's certificate);

    (b) That the necessary consents had not been given in the case of the

---

[5] Cf Law Com No 33, paras 30–32.
[6] Matrimonial Causes Act 1973, s 14(1).
[7] See *Radwan v Radwan (No 2)* [1973] Fam 35, [1972] 3 All ER 1026, ante, pp 26–28.
[8] See ante, pp 31–33.
[9] S 3. If a material alteration is made to any document (eg, the date on a superintendent registrar's certificate), this will be punishable under the Forgery Act 1913. See also the Marriage Act 1949, s 75, and the Marriage (Registrar General's Licence) Act 1970, s 16 (punishment of offences relating to the solemnization of marriages).
[10] Ss 24 and 48. See also s 47(3) (authorisation of marriage according to the usages of the Society of Friends), s 71 (evidence of marriages in naval, military and air force chapels) and s 72 (usual place of worship), and the Marriage (Registrar General's Licence) Act 1970, s 12 (marriages solemnized on the Registrar General's licence).

marriage of a minor by common licence or a superintendent registrar's certificate;[11]

(c) That the registered building in which the parties were married had not been certified as a place of religious worship or was not the usual place of worship of either of them; or

(d) That an incorrect declaration had been made in order to obtain permission to marry in a registered building in a registration district in which neither party resided on the ground that there was not there a building in which marriages were solemnized according to the rites of the religious belief which one of them professed.

Although these are the only formal defects which the Act says shall not invalidate a marriage, it is a general rule that, if the irregularity is not one of those which the Act expressly states may invalidate it, the defect will never make the ceremony a nullity.[12] Hence, for example, even though the parties are aware that two witnesses are not present at the ceremony, the marriage will still be perfectly valid.[13]

Defects which may invalidate a marriage

In the following cases only will a failure to comply with the provisions of the Marriage Act make the marriage void, and then only if *both* parties were aware of the irregularity at the time of the ceremony.[14]

In the case of a marriage according to the rites of the Church of England (otherwise than by special licence), the following come within the rule:[15]

(a) That (except in the case of the marriage of a house-bound or detained person) the marriage was solemnized in a place other than a church or chapel in which banns may be published.

(b) That banns had not been duly published, a common licence obtained or a superintendent registrar's certificate duly issued. Since failure to comply with the residence qualification will never invalidate a marriage, an undue publication of banns will usually occur when one or both of the parties have been wrongly named or where there has been no publication at all.[16] But the object of giving publicity to the intended union (which is the purpose of the publication of banns) does not apply to a licence or, apparently, to a certificate; so that provided that either of these was issued for the marriage of the parties which in fact took place, the marriage will not be void even though

---

[11] The Act refers to consents only where the parties are married on the authority of a superintendent registrar's certificate, but the same is true where they are married by common licence: *R v Birmingham* (1828) 8 B & C 29.

[12] *Campbell v Corley* (1856) 28 LTOS 109.

[13] *Campbell v Corley* (supra); *Wing v Taylor* (1861) 2 Sw & Tr 278.

[14] The Act speaks of 'knowingly and wilfully' intermarrying, and it is not clear whether it is sufficient that both parties should know as a question of fact that the formality is not complied with or whether in addition they must know as a question of law that the defect will invalidate the marriage. The point was left open by Lord Penzance in *Greaves v Greaves* (1872) LR 2 P & D 423, 424–425. The former construction seems the more natural even though its adoption would have the effect of invalidating more marriages.

[15] Marriage Act 1949, s 25 (as amended by the Marriage Act 1983, Sch 1).

[16] But there would presumably be an undue publication, eg, if the banns were not published at a service specified in the Act or by a clergyman or authorised lay reader.

one of the parties was designated by a wholly false name.[17]

(c) That, in the case of the marriage of a minor by banns, a person entitled to do so had publicly dissented from the marriage at the time of the publication of the banns.[18]

(d) That more than three months had elapsed from the completion of the publication of the banns, the grant of a common licence or the entry of the notice of marriage in the superintendent registrar's marriage notice book, as the case may be.

(e) That, in the case of a marriage by superintendent registrar's certificate, the ceremony was performed in a place other than the church, chapel or other building specified in the notice of marriage and certificate.

(f) That the marriage was solemnized by a person who was not in Holy Orders.

In the case of other marriages, the following come within the rule:[19]

(a) That due notice of marriage had not been given to the superintendent registrar.[20]

(b) That a certificate and, where it is necessary, a licence had not been duly issued.

(c) That more than three months had elapsed since the entry of the notice in the superintendent registrar's marriage notice book.

(d) That the marriage was not solemnized in the building specified in the notice and certificate.

(e) That the marriage was solemnized in the absence of a superintendent registrar or registrar or (if it was solemnized in a registered building) in the absence of a registrar or authorised person or (in the case of the marriage of a house-bound or detained person) in the absence of a superintendent registrar or registrar whose presence was required.

Proposals for reform

The present rule that a marriage will not be void on the ground of a formal defect unless both parties were aware of it has the advantage that it is impossible for a party mistakenly to contract such a marriage. It also produces uncertainty, however. If there has been some irregularity which could invalidate the marriage, dishonest parties may have the option of deciding whether it is to be regarded as valid or void, for it may be extremely difficult to disprove whatever evidence they give about their knowledge or lack of

---

[17] *Bevan v M'Mahon* (1861) 2 Sw & Tr 230; *Plummer v Plummer* [1917] P 163, CA; *R v Lamb* (1934) 50 TLR 310, CCA; *Puttick v A-G* [1980] Fam 1, [1979] 3 All ER 463 (where the petitioner, better known as Astrid Proll, had entered this country on another woman's passport and was married in the name of an identifiable third person). The application of this principle to the issue of a certificate without licence is surprising because it defeats the purpose of giving publicity to the intended marriage by displaying the notice for 21 days.

[18] Contrast the position where the marriage of a minor is by common licence or a superintendent registrar's certificate: see supra.

[19] Marriage Act 1949, s 49 (as amended by the Marriage Act 1983, Sch 1). The same rules apply mutatis mutandis if the marriage is solemnized on the authority of the Registrar General's licence: Marriage (Registrar General's Licence) Act 1970, s 13. In particular, such a marriage will be void if the parties knowingly and wilfully intermarry more than *one* month after the entry of notice.

[20] Ie, in the due form. Notice in a false name does not invalidate the notice or the marriage: see supra.

knowledge of the defect at the time of the ceremony. Similar uncertainty could surround the validity of the marriage of the scrupulous 'for most people have no difficulty in sincerely convincing themselves that what they would like to have occurred is what in fact occurred'.[1] Consequently the Law Commission have come to the conclusion that the test of whether a marriage is void on the ground of formal irregularity should be objective and not depend on the parties' knowledge or complicity. Their detailed recommendations depend on the proposals they make for reform relating to the formalities of marriage: essentially they believe that the number of defects which will invalidate a marriage should be kept to the minimum required to ensure that the social purpose lying behind the need for formalities is satisfied.[2]

C. Voidable marriages

1. GROUNDS ON WHICH A MARRIAGE WILL BE VOIDABLE

The six grounds on which a marriage celebrated after 31st July 1971 will be voidable are now set out in section 12 of the Matrimonial Causes Act 1973.[3] Five of these grounds are, with two slight modifications, the same as those which existed before 1st August 1971. The remaining ground—lack of consent—probably made the marriage void before that date, although this is a matter of some doubt.[4] If this was the effect of lack of consent, marriages affected by it and celebrated before 1st August 1971 will, of course, still be void.

Two of the grounds, inability to consummate the marriage and wilful refusal to do so, are so closely related that it will be convenient to deal with them together. We shall then consider the other four grounds in turn.

The unconsummated marriage

Even in canon law a marriage was not always finally and irrevocably indissoluble if it had not been consummated by the sexual act. If at the time of the ceremony either spouse was incapable of consummating it, he or she was regarded as lacking the physical capacity (as distinct from the legal capacity) to contract a valid marriage and the union could therefore be annulled. If, on the other hand, the marriage remained unconsummated because of one party's refusal to have sexual intercourse, canon law offered no relief because the ground of complaint was conduct following the ceremony.[5] Despite this, decrees were probably in fact given in some cases in reliance on the presumption that, if the marriage had not been consummated after three years' cohabitation through no fault of the petitioner, the respondent must

---

[1] Law Com No 53 (Report on Solemnisation of Marriage in England and Wales), 1973, Annex, para 121.
[2] Ibid, paras 121–133. For their proposals relating to formalities of marriage, see ante, pp 57–58.
[3] Re-enacting the Nullity of Marriage Act 1971, s 2, which came into force on 1st August 1971.
[4] For a full discussion of the problem, see the fourth edition of this book, at pp 79–83.
[5] *Napier v Napier* [1915] P 184, CA.

be impotent.[6] The law was put on a more rational footing by the Matrimonial Causes Act 1937, which enacted that a marriage should be voidable if it had not been consummated owing to the respondent's wilful refusal to do so. This was frequently criticised because it offended against the principle that an impediment avoiding a marriage should exist at the time of the ceremony. The Law Commission, however, recommended that it should remain a ground for nullity; the most cogent reason they advanced was that the petitioner is often uncertain whether failure to consummate is due to the respondent's impotence or wilful refusal and in practice will then plead both grounds in the alternative.[7] Only the legal or theological purist will object to the principle's giving way to practical expediency. But it must be admitted that there is something highly artificial about the whole concept. The petitioner's real complaint is that he (or she) is being deprived of normal sexual relations because of the respondent's impotence or conduct. If intercourse takes place once (perhaps after great delay and difficulty), the petitioner's power to petition for nullity goes and his sole remedy lies in divorce if the respondent is unable or unwilling to have further sexual relations. In the case of impotence, this would mean having to wait for five years' separation if the respondent refuses to consent to a decree.

It must be emphasised that non-consummation *as such* does not make a marriage voidable. There are two separate grounds on which a party may petition: that the marriage has not been consummated owing to the incapacity of either party to consummate it or that it has not been consummated owing to the respondent's wilful refusal to do so.[8] Clearly, it would be wholly unjust to permit the petitioner to rely on his own wilful refusal.

Meaning of consummation

A marriage is said to be consummated as soon as the parties have sexual intercourse after the solemnization.[9] The distinction between the act of intercourse and the possibility of that act resulting in the birth of a child must be kept clear: once the parties have had intercourse the marriage is consummated even though one or both are sterile.[10] If this were not so, the marriage could never be consummated if, for example, the wife were beyond the age of child bearing. Conversely, if the spouses have not had intercourse, the birth of a child as the result of fecundation *ab extra* or artificial insemination will not amount to consummation.[11]

In order to amount to consummation, the intercourse must, in the words of Dr Lushington in *D——E v A——G*[12] be 'ordinary and complete, and not partial and imperfect'. Hence, as in *D——E v A——G*, there will be no

---

[6] *G v M* (1885) 10 App Cas 171, HL, at 189–190. Cf *S v S* (*orse W*) [1963] P 162, 171, [1962] 2 All ER 816, 818–819, CA. The petitioner did not have to rely on this presumption and could always allege impotence during the first three years of the marriage.
[7] Thus in the five years 1973–1977 of all petitions alleging impotence and wilful refusal 23% alleged impotence alone, 55% alleged wilful refusal alone, and 22% alleged both in the alternative. No separate figures for the last category have been published since 1977.
[8] See now the Matrimonial Causes Act 1973, s 12(a), (b).
[9] Not *before* the solemnization. Hence the marriage is not consummated by reason of the fact that the parties have had pre-marital intercourse: cf *Dredge v Dredge* [1947] 1 All ER 29.
[10] *D——E v A——G* (1845) 1 Rob Eccl 279; *Baxter v Baxter* [1948] AC 274, [1947] 2 All ER 886, HL.
[11] Cf *Clarke v Clarke* [1943] 2 All ER 540; *L v L* [1949] P 211, [1949] 1 All ER 141.
[12] (1845) 1 Rob Eccl 279, 298.

consummation if the husband does not achieve full penetration in the normal sense. The necessity of complete intercourse has raised difficulties where the spouses use some form of contraception. In 1945 the Court of Appeal held in *Cowen v Cowen*[13] that there had been no consummation where the husband had invariably either worn a contraceptive sheath or practised coitus interruptus,[14] but two years later the House of Lords in *Baxter v Baxter*[15] overruled at least the first part of the decision in *Cowen v Cowen* by holding that the marriage had been consummated notwithstanding the husband's use of a sheath. As Lord Jowitt LC pointed out, the possibility of conception is irrelevant to the question of consummation and when Parliament passed the Matrimonial Causes Act in 1937 (the statute on which the petition was based) it was common knowledge that many people, especially young married couples, used contraceptives and that in common parlance this would amount to consummation.[16] The House of Lords deliberately left open the question whether coitus interruptus would amount to consummation,[17] but it has since been held at first instance that neither branch of the decision in *Cowen v Cowen* can any longer be regarded as good law[18] and also that a marriage is consummated even though the husband is physically incapable of ejaculation after penetration,[19] but not if he is incapable of sustaining an erection for more than a very short period of time after penetration.[20] Perhaps inevitably the courts have tended to concentrate on the husband's role during intercourse,[1] and on the authority of these cases it is suggested that the marriage is consummated as soon as the husband achieves full penetration (unless this is only transient) and that ejaculation is irrelevant.

Inability to consummate

A marriage is voidable if it has not been consummated owing to the incapacity of either party to consummate it.[2]

Inability to consummate may be due to physiological or psychological causes and may be either general or merely quoad the particular spouse.[3] It will be seen that the statute re-enacts the common law rule that a petitioner may show that the marriage has not been consummated because of either spouse's incapacity and may therefore petition in reliance on his own impotence.[4] This follows from the premise that one of the objects in giving relief when the marriage cannot be consummated is to prevent the formation of

---

[13] [1946] P 36, [1945] 2 All ER 197, CA.

[14] Ie, deliberate withdrawal before ejaculation.

[15] [1948] AC 274, [1947] 2 All ER 886, HL.

[16] At 286 and 290, 890 and 892, respectively.

[17] At 283 and 888, respectively.

[18] *White v White* [1948] P 330, [1948] 2 All ER 151; *Cackett v Cackett* [1950] P 253, [1950] 1 All ER 677. But it was held that coitus interruptus does not amount to consummation in *Grimes v Grimes* [1948] P 323, [1948] 2 All ER 147.

[19] *R v R* [1952] 1 All ER 1194.

[20] *W (otherwise K) v W* [1967] 3 All ER 178n.

[1] Thus there can be consummation even though the wife's vagina has been artificially extended (or, perhaps, wholly constructed): *S v S (otherwise W) (No 2)* [1963] P 37, [1962] 3 All ER 55, CA. But she must be biologically female to begin with: *Corbett v Corbett* [1971] P 83, [1970] 2 All ER 33. See, however, Taitz 15 Anglo-American LR 141.

[2] Matrimonial Causes Act 1973, s 12(a).

[3] Impotence from psychological causes must amount to invincible repugnance and not merely unwillingness or reluctance: *Singh v Singh* [1971] P 226, [1971] 2 All ER 828, CA.

[4] This rule was finally established in *Harthan v Harthan* [1949] P 115, [1948] 2 All ER 639, CA.

an adulterous union[5] and the recognition of the fact that a spouse may be impotent quoad the other but be perfectly capable of having normal sexual intercourse with others.[6]

At common law it was said that relief would be granted only if the impotence was incurable and the term 'incapacity' presumably still imports this element. In this context, however, 'incurable' has received a very extended meaning and impotence will be considered incurable not only if it is wholly incapable of any remedy but also if it can be cured only by an operation attended by danger or, in any event, if it is improbable that the operation will be successful or the party refuses to undergo it.[7] But where the petitioner relies upon her own impotence, it is submitted that the court might well take the view that she should not be allowed to complain of the situation if the impediment could be removed without danger to herself.[8]

The petitioner's knowledge of the *respondent's* impotence before marriage is not necessarily a bar to the petition,[9] although if he knew that impotence was a ground for nullity, his marrying the respondent in the circumstances might amount to such conduct as would entitle the latter to invoke the statutory bar that has replaced approbation.[10] But if the petitioner relied upon *his own* impotence, he failed at common law if he was aware of it beforehand and deceived the respondent, who could then plead the suppressio veri as a bar, or apparently in any case if at the time of the marriage he knew that the respondent was also impotent.[11] It is not clear whether these restrictions survive under the Act. If they are regarded as bars, they appear to have been swept away along with all the other common law bars;[12] it is possible to argue, however, that the absence of these conditions was a prerequisite to the petitioner's being able to bring proceedings at common law,[13] in which case they will have survived. The balance of authorities indicates that the latter view is correct.

At common law impotence was a ground for avoiding the marriage only if it existed at the time of the solemnization and there was still no practical possibility of the marriage being consummated at the date of the hearing.[14]

---

[5] See *D——E v A——G* (1845) 1 Rob Eccl 279, 299.

[6] See *C v C* [1921] P 399. Hence if each is impotent quoad the other, either may petition: *G v G* [1912] P 173.

[7] *S v S (orse C)* [1956] P 1, 11, [1954] 3 All ER 736, 741; *M v M* [1957] P 139, [1956] 3 All ER 769. Cf *L v L* (1882) 7 PD 16; *G v G* (1908) 25 TLR 328.

[8] A wilful refusal to take treatment in such a case might amount to wilful refusal to consummate the marriage: *S v S (orse C)* [1956] P 1 at 15–16, [1954] 3 All ER 736 at 743–744.

[9] *Nash v Nash* [1940] P 60, 64–65, [1940] 1 All ER 206, 209; *J v J* [1947] P 158, 163, [1947] 2 All ER 43, 44, CA, (overruled on another point by *Baxter v Baxter* (ante)).

[10] See post, p 98.

[11] *Harthan v Harthan* [1949] P 115, 129, [1948] 2 All ER 639, 644, CA. In the latter case therefore he should petition on the ground of the respondent's impotence for the knowledge will not necessarily bar him. See Bevan *Limitations on the Right of an Impotent Spouse to Petition for Nullity* 76 LQR 267.

[12] By the Nullity of Marriage Act 1971, s 3(4). See post, p 96.

[13] See the cases cited in Jackson *Formation and Annulment of Marriage* (2nd Edn) pp 352–354; Bevan loc cit.

[14] *Napier v Napier* [1915] P 184, CA; *S v S (orse W)* [1963] P 162, [1962] 2 All ER 816, CA, approving *S v S (orse C)* [1956] P 1, [1954] 3 All ER 736. For if the party is cured or curable at the time of the hearing, he or she could not have been incurably incapable at the time of the solemnization. In Scotland, it has been held that the party must have been incurable at all times since the solemnization: *M v W* 1966 SLT 25. This is a logical extension of the rule.

Consequently, if a party was capable of having sexual intercourse at the time of the ceremony but became impotent before the marriage was consummated (for example, as the result of an injury), it is highly doubtful whether a petition for nullity could have succeeded. The Act, however, makes no reference to incapacity at the time of the marriage and it therefore seems that a petition would now succeed in these circumstances.

Wilful refusal to consummate

A marriage will be voidable if it has not been consummated owing to the *respondent's* wilful refusal to do so.[15] (As the petitioner is complaining of marital misconduct, he may not of course rely on his own refusal.) Wilful refusal connotes 'a settled and definite decision come to without just excuse', and the whole history of the marriage must be looked at.[16] Thus in *Kaur v Singh*[17] the parties, who were both Sikhs, married in a register office on the understanding that they should not cohabit until they had gone through a religious ceremony of marriage in a Sikh temple, and it was held that in the circumstances the husband's refusal without excuse to make arrangements for such a ceremony amounted to wilful refusal to consummate the marriage.

Refusal to have intercourse in any form will clearly come within the statute, and so may wilful refusal to take treatment (attended by no danger) to remove a physical or psychological impediment to consummation.[18] Similarly, if there has been no opportunity to consummate the marriage (for example, because one party is in prison), an indication by one of them that he will not consummate it at any time in the future has been held to entitle the other to petition forthwith: the latter is not bound to wait to see whether the respondent changes his mind when the opportunity arises.[19] As we have seen, there will not be a wilful refusal to consummate if one spouse insists upon the use of contraceptives or, probably, of coitus interruptus. But *Baxter v Baxter*[20] has raised a difficulty which cannot be easily solved. Suppose the marriage is never consummated because the husband, H, refuses to use a contraceptive and the wife, W, refuses to let him have intercourse unless he does. It is difficult to see how either of them can be said to have refused to consummate, for W has been prepared to do so within the meaning given to the term by *Baxter v Baxter*, and H has expressed his willingness to have intercourse in the natural way.

---

[15] Matrimonial Causes Act 1973, s 12(b), re-enacting provisions going back to the Matrimonial Causes Act 1937.

[16] Per Lord Jowitt LC in *Horton v Horton* [1947] 2 All ER 871, 874, HL. He left open the question whether the petitioner could succeed if he had originally refused to consummate but then changed his mind by which time the respondent had changed her mind and refused to let the petitioner have intercourse. Cf *Potter v Potter* (1975) 5 Fam Law 161, CA (husband's refusal due to loss of sexual ardour for wife in similar circumstances not wilful).

[17] [1972] 1 All ER 292, CA, following *Jodla v Jodla* [1960] 1 All ER 625. See also *A v J* [1989] 1 FLR 110, and cf *Boggins v Boggins* [1966] CLY 4041 (husband who deserted wife before consummating marriage held to have wilfully refused to do so).

[18] *S v S (orse C)* [1956] P 1, 15–16, [1954] 3 All ER 736, 743–744.

[19] *Ford v Ford* [1987] Fam Law 232. The result is socially desirable, but it is difficult to see how the respondent's conduct comes within the wording of the Act (the marriage *has not been* consummated, not *will not be* consummated).

[20] Ante, p 87. For a contrary view, see Gower *Baxter v Baxter in Perspective* 11 MLR 176, particularly at 186–187.

Once the marriage has been consummated, it will not be voidable if one spouse subsequently refuses to continue to have intercourse. In such a case, as in the case of the use of contraceptives or the practice of coitus interruptus against the other spouse's will, the latter's only remedy lies in divorce.

Lack of consent

Section 12(c) of the Matrimonial Causes Act 1973 provides that a marriage shall be voidable if either party did not validly consent to it, whether in consequence of duress, mistake, unsoundness of mind or otherwise. Marriage is a contract and consequently absence of consent will invalidate the ceremony. But a contract of marriage is not quite on the same footing as other contracts in this respect because some facts which may vitiate a commercial contract (for example, fraud) did not affect a marriage at all at common law and the Act does not appear to have extended the grounds on which it can be annulled.

As has already been pointed out, lack of consent probably made the marriage void at common law.[1] The reason for making such a marriage voidable is that the parties themselves may wish to ratify it when true consent can be given and consequently third parties should not be able to impeach it.[2]

It will be seen that the petitioner may rely on the fact that the respondent did not consent to the marriage even though the petitioner himself was responsible for this state of affairs, for example by inducing a mistake or uttering threats. Whilst this logically followed when lack of consent made the marriage void, it may leave a respondent who wishes to adopt the marriage with a legitimate sense of grievance in such circumstances. Nevertheless, he will have no defence to the petition unless he can plead one of the statutory bars.[3]

We must now consider what facts will be regarded in law as vitiating consent.[4]

Unsoundness of mind

This will affect a marriage if, as a consequence, *at the time of the ceremony* either party was unable to understand the nature of the contract he was entering into. There is a presumption that he was capable of doing so and the burden of proof therefore lies upon the party impeaching the validity of

---

[1] In which case a marriage affected by lack of consent will still be void if it was contracted before 1st August 1971.

[2] See Law Com No 33, paras 11–15.

[3] See post, pp 96–100.

[4] The following discussion may not be exhaustive. To take a further example, if one of the parties to a marriage contracted abroad was so young at the time of the ceremony that he (or she) could not be said to have given full and free consent, the marriage may be voidable by English law unless he ratified it after attaining an age when he was capable of understanding the nature of the contract. See Poulter *Ethnic Minority Customs, English Law and Human Rights* 36 ICLQ 589 at 610–611.

the marriage.[5] The test to be applied was thus formulated by Singleton LJ in *In the Estate of Park*:[6]

'Was the [person] . . . capable of understanding the nature of the contract into which he was entering, or was his mental condition such that he was incapable of understanding it? To ascertain the nature of the contract of marriage a man must be mentally capable of appreciating that it involves the responsibilities normally attaching to marriage. Without that degree of mentality, it cannot be said that he understands the nature of the contract.'

Drunkenness and the effect of drugs

In the absence of any binding English authority, it is submitted that the effect of drunkenness and drugs will be the same as that of unsoundness of mind. Consequently the marriage will be voidable if, as a result of either, one of the parties was incapable of understanding the nature of the contract into which he was entering.[7]

Mistake

A mistake will affect the marriage in two cases only. First, a mistake as to the identity of the other contracting party will make the marriage voidable if this results in one party's failing to marry the individual whom he or she intends to marry. In the New Zealand case of *C v C*[8] W married H in the erroneous belief that he was a well known boxer called Miller. It was held that the marriage was not invalidated by the mistake because she married the very individual she meant to marry. Secondly, the marriage will be voidable if one of the parties is mistaken as to the nature of the ceremony and does not appreciate that he is contracting a marriage. In *Valier v Valier*[9] the husband, who was an Italian and whose knowledge of the English language was poor, was taken to a register office by the wife and there went through the usual form of marriage. He did not understand what was happening at the time, the parties never cohabited and the marriage was never consummated. It was held that he was entitled to a decree of nullity.

But if each party appreciates that he is going through a form of marriage with the other, no other type of mistake apparently can affect the contract.[10] Thus, it has been held that the marriage will not be invalidated by a mistake

---

[5] *Harrod v Harrod* (1854) 1 K & J 4, 9. But if the person is proved to have been generally insane, there will be a presumption that he was insane at the time of the marriage and the burden of proof will consequently shift on to the party seeking to uphold its validity: *Turner v Meyers* (1808) 1 Hag Con 414, 417.

[6] [1954] P 112, 127, [1953] 2 All ER 1411, 1430, CA. Cf Karminski J (in the Div Court) [1954] P 89, 99, [1953] 2 All ER 408, 414; Birkett LJ at 134–135 and 1434; Hodson LJ at 137 and 1436–1437 respectively; *Hunter v Edney* (1881) 10 PD 93, 95; *Durham v Durham* (1885) 10 PD 80, 82.

[7] Cf *Legey v O'Brien* (1834) Milw 325; *Sullivan v Sullivan* (1818) 2 Hag Con 238, 246 (per Sir W Scott).

[8] [1942] NZLR 356. But if A becomes engaged to B, whom she has never seen before, by correspondence, and C successfully personates B at the wedding, the marriage would be voidable because A intends to marry B and nobody else: ibid, p 359. It would be void if the personation invalidated the publication of banns: see ante, pp 46–47.

[9] (1925) 133 LT 830. See also *Ford v Stier* [1896] P 1, and *Kelly v Kelly* (1932) 49 TLR 99 (mistaken belief that ceremony was formal betrothal); *Mehta v Mehta* [1945] 2 All ER 690 (mistaken belief that Hindu marriage ceremony was ceremony of religious conversion).

[10] *Moss v Moss* [1897] P 263, 271–273; *Kenward v Kenward* [1950] P 71, 79, [1949] 2 All ER 959, 963 (per Hodson J), [1951] P 124, 133–134, [1950] 2 All ER 297, 302, CA (per Evershed MR).

as to the monogamous or polygamous nature of the union,[11] the other party's fortune,[12] the woman's chastity,[13] or the recognition of the union by the religious denomination of the parties.[14]

Fraud and misrepresentation

Unlike the case of a commercial contract, neither a fraudulent nor an innocent misrepresentation will of itself affect the validity of a marriage.[15] But if the misrepresentation induces an operative mistake (eg, as to the nature of the ceremony), the marriage will be made voidable by the latter.[16]

Fear and duress

If, owing to fear or threats, one of the parties is induced to enter into a marriage which, in the absence of compulsion, he would never have contracted, the marriage will be voidable.

The fear may be due to a number of causes. In *Buckland v Buckland*,[17] for example, the petitioner, a youth aged 20 resident in Malta, was groundlessly charged with defiling the respondent, a girl of 15. Although he protested his innocence, he was twice advised that he stood no chance of an acquittal but would probably be sent to prison for a period of up to two years unless he married her. He did so and it was held that he was entitled to a decree of nullity. Nor is it necessary that the fear should have been inspired by any acts on the other party's part: a number of recent cases, for example, have dealt with arranged marriages amongst members of immigrant communities.[18] A particularly horrifying example of duress imposed ab extra is to be seen in *Szechter v Szechter*.[19] The petitioner was a Polish national who had been arrested by the security police in Warsaw. After 14 months' interrogation and detention in appalling conditions she was sentenced to three years' imprisonment for 'anti-state activities'. Her health, which had always been poor, deteriorated rapidly and she came to the conclusion that she would not survive the sentence; if she did come out of prison alive, she believed that she was likely to be re-arrested and in any case would be unable to get any job other than one of a menial nature. The respondent was a distinguished Polish historian of Jewish origin whose presence in Poland was something of an embarrassment to the authorities and whom they were prepared to allow to emigrate. In order to effect the petitioner's release he

---

[11] *Kassim v Kassim* [1962] P 224, [1962] 3 All ER 426.

[12] *Wakefield v Mackay* (1807) 1 Hag Con 394, 398.

[13] Even though she is pregnant per alium: *Moss v Moss* (supra).

[14] *Ussher v Ussher* [1912] 2 IR 445.

[15] *Swift v Kelly* (1835) 3 Knapp 257, 293; *Moss v Moss* (supra) at p 266.

[16] *Moss v Moss* (supra), at 268–269.

[17] [1968] P 296, [1967] 2 All ER 300. See also *Scott v Sebright* (1886) 12 PD 21 (threats to make petitioner bankrupt, to denounce her and finally to shoot her); *Griffith v Griffith* [1944] IR 35 (fear of prosecution for unlawful carnal knowledge); Poulter *The Definition of Marriage in English Law* 42 MLR 409, 410–418. All the earlier cases are collected and exhaustively discussed by Manchester *Marriage or Prison: the Case of the Reluctant Bridegroom* 29 MLR 622.

[18] See *Singh v Kaur, Singh v Singh* and *Hirani v Hirani* post, p 94.

[19] [1971] P 286, [1970] 3 All ER 905. See also *H v H* [1954] P 258, [1953] 2 All ER 1229 (marriage contracted in Budapest to enable woman to escape from Hungary where she was likely to be sent to prison or concentration camp); *Parojcic v Parojcic* [1959] 1 All ER 1 (fear imposed by petitioner's father).

divorced his wife and went through a ceremony of marriage with the petitioner in prison. The scheme was successful, and eventually all the parties reached England, where the petitioner brought proceedings for nullity so that the respondent and his first wife could remarry. A decree was granted.

In *Szechter v Szechter* Simon P applied the following test:[20]

'It is, in my view, insufficient to invalidate an otherwise good marriage that a party has entered into it in order to escape from a disagreeable situation, such as penury or social degradation. In order for the impediment of duress to vitiate an otherwise valid marriage, it must, in my judgment, be proved that the will of one of the parties thereto has been overborne by genuine and reasonably held fear caused by threat of immediate danger (for which the party is not himself responsible), to life, limb or liberty, so that the constraint destroys the reality of consent to ordinary wedlock.'

There may be rare cases where the party is so terrified that he (or she) does not know what he is doing at all: a marriage contracted in such circumstances must be voidable as there is no consent whatever. In other cases the reference to the party's will being overborne has been criticised on the ground that he does in fact consciously choose to enter into marriage rather than accept the alternative presented to him.[1] The court must then decide whether the circumstances were such that it would be socially more objectionable to tie the party to the union than to permit him to repudiate it: the need to uphold the institution of marriage must be balanced against the need to do justice to the individual. This must depend on what he perceived to be the probable consequences of refusing to enter into the marriage and his capacity to resist the pressure brought to bear on him. If he is more susceptible to this pressure than another might be, the marriage should still be annulled even though a person of ordinary courage and resilience would not have yielded to it.[2]

Applying this test, it may be doubted whether the three limitations which Simon P placed upon the operation of duress as a ground for nullity are desirable or supported by earlier authorities. First, if the condition that the fear must be reasonably held means that the marriage will be voidable only if a reasonable person, placed in the position of the petitioner, would have concluded that the threats would have been implemented if the marriage had not taken place, it is directly contrary to the view stated earlier by Butt J in *Scott v Sebright*[3] and it is submitted that the latter is to be preferred. If a person is in a mental state in which he is no longer capable of offering resistance to threats, it seems immaterial that it would be obvious to a reasonable person, similarly placed, that the other has no intention of carrying them out at all.[4] Secondly, although Scarman J's decision in *Buckland v*

---

[20] At 297–298 and 915, respectively.

[1] Ingman and Grant *Duress in the Law of Nullity* [1984] Fam Law 92, citing Atiyah 98 LQR 197 and *DPP for Northern Ireland v Lynch* [1975] AC 653, [1975] 1 All ER 913, HL.

[2] *Scott v Sebright* (1886) 12 PD 21, 24; *Cooper v Crane* [1891] P 369, 376.

[3] (1886) 12 PD 21, 24. But Simon P's views are supported by *Buckland v Buckland* [1968] P 296, 301, [1967] 2 All ER 300, 302 (per Scarman J) and *H v H* [1954] P 258, 269, [1953] 2 All ER 1229, 1234 (per Karminski J).

[4] This is the view of the Law Commission in Law Com No 33, at p 27. Professor Davies *Duress and Nullity of Marriage* 88 LQR 549, suggests that the rule that the fear must be reasonably entertained applies only when it is imposed by someone other than the respondent or his agent. This is ingenious but it is not the basis of any reported case and could work injustice. In *Parojcic v Parojcic* (supra), for example, the petitioner entered into the marriage because her father threatened to send her back to Jugoslavia if she did not do so; why should she be tied to the marriage if a reasonable woman in her position would have realised that he had no intention of implementing his threat?

Buckland is clear authority for the proposition that the fear must arise from some external circumstances for which the party is not himself responsible, it is doubtful whether this rule is correctly expressed. In that case the petitioner succeeded because his fear arose from the false charge preferred against him; presumably he would have failed had he actually been guilty of defiling the respondent. Originally it was said that the fear must be unjustly imposed;[5] and whilst it could not be justly imposed if the party was not responsible for the events which had given rise to the threat, it does not follow that it will be justly imposed if he was responsible. If a man is threatened with maintenance proceedings unless he marries the woman allegedly carrying his child, it seems proper that he should be able to petition for nullity if he is not the father but that he should not be able to do so if the child is his. If, however, the woman's father threatens to shoot him if he does not marry her or, to take a different situation, if an employer threatens to prosecute a clerk for theft if he does not marry his daughter, one feels that the marriage should be voidable in both cases whether or not the man in question is responsible for the pregnancy or has committed the theft. The distinction is that it is reasonable to face a man with the choice between marriage and maintenance proceedings but not to face him with the choice between marriage and death or prosecution for theft.

More problematical is whether Simon P's third condition can be regarded as correct, namely the fear must be caused by 'threat of immediate danger to life, limb or liberty'. The Court of Appeal applied it in *Singh v Singh*[6] and *Singh v Kaur*,[7] but only a year after the latter case Ormrod LJ, delivering the leading judgment of the court in *Hirani v Hirani*,[8] denied the need for such threats and stated that the question is 'whether the pressure ... is such as to destroy the reality of consent and overbears the will of the individual'. The Court of Appeal is now free to apply either test[9] and it is strongly urged that it should apply the less stringent. The threat of financial or social ruin may work as strongly as the threat of physical violence on some minds,[10] and in some immigrant communities failure to comply with parental wishes in this regard may lead to ostracism and a complete break with the family.[11] If any of these facts have deprived a person of the effective power of refusing to enter into a marriage, he or she should be able to resile from it.[12]

It is therefore submitted that the only limitation on duress or fear as a ground for nullity is that a marriage will not be voidable if the fear is justly imposed in the sense that the party is responsible for the state of affairs which

---

[5] *Griffith v Griffith* [1944] IR 35, 43–44.
[6] [1971] P 226, [1971] 2 All ER 828, CA.
[7] (1981) 11 Fam Law 152, CA.
[8] (1982) 4 FLR 232, CA. Ormrod LJ had also given the leading judgment in *Singh v Kaur*.
[9] *Young v Bristol Aeroplane Co Ltd* [1944] KB 718, [1944] 2 All ER 293, CA.
[10] Cf *Scott v Sebright* (1886) 12 PD 21, where the respondent's threats to see that bankruptcy proceedings were taken against the petitioner and to 'accuse her to her mother and in every drawing-room in London of having been seduced by him' were apparently regarded as grounds (along with a threat to shoot her) for annulling the marriage.
[11] This was the threat in *Hirani v Hirani*.
[12] See further Davies loc cit at p 552; Ingman and Grant loc cit; Poulter *English Law and Ethnic Minority Customs*, 2.19–2.24; Bradney *Arranged Marriages and Duress* [1984] JSWL 278; Pearl [1971] CLJ 206; Bates 130 New LJ 1035 and the Australian cases there cited; Bradley 46 MLR 499.

has given rise to the threat and it is reasonable to face him with the choice between marriage and the implementation of the threat.[13]

'Sham marriages'

Cases like *Szechter v Szechter* raise a further question: is a 'sham marriage'— that is, where the parties go through the form of marriage purely for the purpose of representing themselves as married to the outside world with no intention of cohabiting—to be regarded in law as a nullity? This problem is more likely to arise with restrictive immigration laws: for example, a woman who is a citizen of state X may go through a form of marriage with a citizen of state Y merely in order to enter or remain in Y on the strength of her husband's nationality or passport.

Since the decision of the House of Lords in *Vervaeke v Smith*[14] there can be no doubt that such marriages are perfectly valid provided that the parties freely consented to contracting them. In that case a Belgian prostitute went through a ceremony of marriage with a British subject so that she could apply for British citizenship and thus escape deportation. The parties had no intention of living together and saw each other again on only one or two occasions. The majority of the House considered it indisputable that the marriage was valid.

Mental disorder

A marriage is voidable if, at the time of the ceremony, *either party*, though capable of giving a valid consent, was suffering (whether continuously or intermittently) from mental disorder within the meaning of the Mental Health Act 1983 of such a kind or to such an extent as to be unfitted for marriage.[15] 'Unfitted for marriage' in this context has been defined as 'incapable of carrying out the ordinary duties and obligations of marriage'.[16]

This must be distinguished from a ground for nullity that we have already considered: mental illness producing lack of consent. In the case of mental disorder it is presumed that the party was capable of giving a valid consent to the marriage but that the general state of his mental health at the time of the ceremony was such that it is right that the marriage should be annulled. It will be observed that the petitioner does not have to rely on the respondent's mental disorder but may rely on his own. This is necessary to enable a party to withdraw from a marriage if he entered into it in ignorance of the existence or extent of his illness or the effect which it would have upon his married life.

---

[13] See also Law Com No 33, paras 63–66 (to which Scarman J, as chairman, was a party): Davies loc cit.
[14] [1983] 1 AC 145, [1982] 2 All ER 144, per Lord Hailsham LC at 151–152 and 148, and Lord Simon at 162 and 156. Lord Brandon agreed with both speeches. See also *Silver v Silver* [1955] 2 All ER 614; *Puttick v A-G* [1980] Fam 1, [1979] 3 All ER 463; Rogers *Sham Marriages* 4 Fam Law 4; Wade *Limited Purpose Marriages* 45 MLR 159, particularly at 169–170.
[15] Matrimonial Causes Act 1973, s 12(d). This ground and the next two go back to the Matrimonial Causes Act 1937. For the meaning of 'mental disorder', see the Mental Health Act 1983, s 1(2).
[16] *Bennett v Bennett* [1969] 1 All ER 539.

Venereal disease

A marriage is voidable if at the time of the ceremony *the respondent* was suffering from venereal disease in a communicable form.[17] 'Venereal disease' is not defined in the Act: an important question today is whether it includes AIDS. Whilst this may be sexually transmitted, it can also be transmitted in other ways. It is clearly socially desirable to release a person from marriage to an infected spouse and it would be unreasonable to limit relief to a petitioner who could show that the respondent had acquired it as the result of sexual intercourse, a burden which many would be unable to discharge. It is submitted that to regard AIDS as a venereal disease for this purpose would suppress the mischief and advance the remedy that Parliament has provided,[18] but it is by no means certain that a court would adopt this construction.

Pregnancy per alium

A husband may petition for nullity if at the time of the marriage *the respondent wife* was pregnant by someone other than himself.[19]

2. BARS TO RELIEF

As in the case of any other voidable contract, at common law a party to a voidable marriage might effectively put it out of his own power to obtain a decree of nullity by his own conduct. In addition to specific limitations attached to the statutory grounds for nullity, there were two bars of general application: approbation and collusion. We shall consider the nature of approbation shortly; the essence of collusion was that the initiation or conduct of the suit had been in some measure procured or determined by an agreement or bargain between the parties, and the reason that it was a bar was that the existence of such an agreement raised doubts whether the decree would be granted on the merits at all. This did not prevent the presentation of a false case in an undefended suit, however, and withholding a decree for collusion was open to the objection that it implied that 'the sanctity of marriage is maintained by insisting that people should remain married as a punishment for their misbehaviour'.[20] Consequently on the recommendation of the Law Commission collusion was abolished as a bar by the Nullity of Marriage Act 1971 and all the others were replaced by statutory bars which are now the only ones applicable. There are three.[1]

Petitioner's conduct

Section 13(1) of the Matrimonial Causes Act 1973 provides:

'The court shall not ... grant a decree of nullity on the ground that the marriage is voidable if the respondent satisfies the court—

[17] Matrimonial Causes Act 1973, s 12(e).
[18] See *Heydon's Case* (1584) 3 Co Rep 7a for this principle of construction.
[19] Ibid, s 12(f).
[20] Law Com No 33, para 37.
[1] Nullity of Marriage Act 1971, ss 3 and 6(1); Matrimonial Causes Act 1973, s 13. These provisions implement the recommendations of the Law Commission: Law Com No 33, paras 36–45 and 76–86.

(a) that the petitioner, with knowledge that it was open to him to have the marriage avoided, so conducted himself in relation to the respondent as to lead the respondent reasonably to believe that he would not seek to do so; and

(b) that it would be unjust to the respondent to grant the decree.'

This replaces the former bar of approbation (or lack of sincerity, as it was called in the older cases). The principle underlying this bar was thus summarised by Lord Watson:[2]

'In a suit for nullity of marriage there may be facts and circumstances proved which so plainly imply, on the part of the complaining spouse, a recognition of the existence and validity of the marriage, as to render it most inequitable and contrary to public policy that he or she should be permitted to go on to challenge it with effect.'

It is clear that the same principle underlies the statutory bar and consequently much of the old law remains unaltered although there have been some changes in detail and some doubts have been resolved. Before we examine the question of the petitioner's conduct in more detail, however, three preliminary points must be made. First, the court will be bound to apply the bar only if the respondent satisfies it that the statutory conditions are fulfilled. Not only does this mean that the burden of proof is on the respondent, but if he chooses not to raise the bar at all, the court must grant a decree if a ground has been made out even if it is clear from the facts that these conditions are satisfied:[3] the bar no longer rests on public policy.[4] Secondly, no conduct on the petitioner's part can raise the bar unless he knew at the time that it was open to him to have the marriage avoided. This means that he must have been aware not only of the facts upon which the petition is based (for example, that he is not the father of the child that the respondent was carrying at the time of the marriage) but also that these facts would entitle him to petition for a decree of nullity.[5] Any act or omission when he was ignorant of either of these matters must be disregarded.[6] Thirdly, only conduct in relation to the petitioner can act as a bar.

Positive acts

It is clear that any positive act by the petitioner may raise the bar if a reasonable person in the respondent's position would have concluded that the petitioner intended to treat the marriage as valid and the respondent in fact drew this conclusion. An example of this is to be seen in *D v D*.[7] The parties adopted two children at a time when the husband knew that he could have the marriage annulled because of his wife's wilful refusal to consummate it. He later brought nullity proceedings. It was held that by agreeing to the adoption he had so conducted himself in relation to the wife as to lead her to believe that he would not seek to do so.

[2] *G v M* (1885) 10 App Cas 171, 197–198, HL.
[3] This point was not taken in *D v D* [1979] Fam 70, [1979] 3 All ER 337, where the wife, having raised the defence, then elected not to pursue it. Dunn J, however, held that in such circumstances it could not be said to be unjust to grant the decree.
[4] *D v D* (supra).
[5] The respondent is presumed to know the law and the burden is on him to prove that he did not: *W v W* [1952] P 152, 162, [1952] 1 All ER 858, 863, CA.
[6] This re-enacts the common law rule: see *G v M* (supra), at p 186.
[7] [1979] Fam 70, [1979] 3 All ER 337.

In some cases spouses may well resort to adoption or artificial insemination if one of them is impotent so that a child cannot be conceived in the normal way, and the same principle will apply. If by consenting to the act the petitioner admits that the marriage is never likely to be consummated and also implies that any child which may be conceived will be born into a normal family where the husband and wife are validly married, the respondent may well infer that he will not thereafter petition for nullity. Nor can it make any difference if the petitioner gives consent in the hope that the adoption or birth of the child will remove a psychological impediment. If, however, he has made the position clear to the respondent, he can still petition if his purpose fails and the marriage remains unconsummated, because nothing he has done will have led the respondent to believe that he will not seek to have the marriage annulled. But he may not later rely on a mental reservation 'locked in his bosom and not declared' to the respondent if the reasonable conclusion from his acts and declared intentions is that he is waiving his power to bring proceedings.[8]

In some circumstances the mere fact that the petitioner has married the respondent at all may reasonably lead the latter to believe that the former will not subsequently petition for nullity. If a man marries a woman knowing that one of them is impotent or suffering from mental disorder and knowing also that this is a ground for nullity, she may reasonably conclude that he intends to treat the marriage as valid and thus raise the marriage itself as a bar if he does petition. For the same reason a party who has deprived the other of the power of consenting freely to the marriage by inducing a mistake or uttering threats may not be able to petition. A similar case arises if the parties entered into an agreement before marriage that they would not have sexual intercourse. Although this is regarded as contrary to public policy and is therefore not binding on them,[9] it may preclude either of them from obtaining a decree of nullity if the marriage is in fact never consummated and the agreement led the respondent to believe that the petitioner would not bring proceedings.[10] If one of the parties is old, infirm or seriously crippled, the marriage may well have been on this understanding, express or implied. A fortiori an agreement between the spouses that the petitioner will not institute proceedings for nullity will be a good defence to a petition.[11]

Although estoppel in the strict sense of the term cannot apply if the marriage is voidable, a party who brings other matrimonial proceedings with the knowledge that it is open to him to have the marriage annulled may thereby bar himself from petitioning for nullity later if the other spouse draws the conclusion that he does not intend to do so. Thus a wife who knows that her marriage is voidable because of her husband's impotence may lose her power to petition for nullity if she brings proceedings for an order in a magistrates' court based on his desertion.[12] Her husband might likewise lose his power to petition if he took part in the proceedings without indicating that he reserved the right to have the marriage avoided later.

---

[8] Cf *W v W* [1952] P 152, 168, [1952] 1 All ER 858, 866, CA.
[9] Cf *Brodie v Brodie* [1917] P 271.
[10] Cf *Morgan v Morgan* [1959] P 92, [1959] 1 All ER 539; *Scott v Scott* [1959] P 103n, [1959] 1 All ER 531.
[11] Cf *Aldridge v Aldridge* (1888) 13 PD 210.
[12] Cf *Tindall v Tindall* [1953] P 63, [1953] 1 All ER 139, CA. Similarly, a wife might bar herself if she continued to accept income from a trust in the wife's favour in a marriage settlement.

Delay

Just as some active step on the petitioner's part may bar him from bringing proceedings for nullity, delay in bringing them may equally bar him if he knows that it is open to him to have the marriage avoided and the delay has led the respondent reasonably to believe that he does not intend to do so. Obviously this will depend inter alia on the length of the delay and whether the petitioner has made it reasonably clear that he intends to bring proceedings, or at least may do so at a not too remote time in the future. The question must be one of fact: did the petitioner lull the respondent into a false sense of security or a false belief that he would not petition?

Injustice of decree

As we have seen, it is not sufficient that the petitioner has led the respondent to believe that he will not seek to have the marriage avoided, the latter must also show that it would be unjust to him (or her) to grant the decree. As in the case of divorce, justice will rarely be served by refusing to set aside a marriage that is already dead, particularly when the petitioner will usually be able to obtain a divorce after five years' separation; but there will undoubtedly be some cases when it would be manifestly unjust to grant a decree against an unwilling respondent. For example, a respondent in the position of the wife in *D v D*[13] might satisfy the court that it would be unjust to her to annul the marriage because she would be left with two adopted children. The defence is perhaps most likely to succeed if the petitioner relies on his own impotence (or mental disorder) for consideration must necessarily be given to the respondent's attitude and reaction to a situation for which he is in no way responsible.[14] Among the matters which the court should take into account in deciding whether to grant a decree are the length of time the marriage has lasted, the existence of any children of the family, any religious or other personal objections that the respondent has to the decree, and the financial loss that he (or she) might suffer as a result of nullity (for example, the loss of pension rights or Social Security benefits).

Lapse of time

In all cases except those based on impotence or wilful refusal to consummate, a decree of nullity must normally be refused if the proceedings were not instituted within three years of the date of the marriage.[15] This is independent of the bar last considered, and even if the petition is brought within three years, the respondent may still raise the petitioner's delay or other conduct as a bar if it reasonably led him to conclude that the petitioner would not seek to have the marriage annulled.

The reason for this further bar is to ensure that the parties' status is not

[13] For the facts see ante, p 97. In this case it was held not to be unjust to grant the decree because the respondent did not pursue the defence.

[14] Cf *Pettit v Pettit* [1963] P 177, [1962] 3 All ER 37, CA. The husband did not discover that he could petition on the ground of his own impotence for more than 20 years after the marriage and after the birth of a child as the result of *fecundatio ab extra*. Under the old law of approbation the court refused to grant the decree because it would have been inequitable to do so. If the husband had known all along that he could petition, it is submitted that the decision would be the same today.

[15] Matrimonial Causes Act 1973, s 13(2).

left in doubt for too long: consequently there is no power to extend the period even though the petitioner was unaware of the facts or that they made the marriage voidable. This may well work injustice, however. The Law Commission concluded that hardship was most likely to arise if the complaining party was mentally disordered. They had in mind two problems in particular: old and lonely people not fully in possession of their faculties may well become the object of attention of fortune hunters, and a petition may have to be presented by the party's next friend who may not become aware of all the facts during the first three years of the marriage.[16] The Commission's recommendation for an extension of the statutory period was implemented in section 2 of the Matrimonial and Family Proceedings Act 1984,[17] which enables the court to grant leave for the presentation of a petition based on any ground, notwithstanding that more than three years have elapsed since the date of the marriage, provided that the petitioner has suffered from mental disorder within the meaning of the Mental Health Act 1983 at any time during the first three years of the marriage and that the court considers that it would be just to do so. Whilst this provision will overcome some difficulties experienced in the past, it is regrettable that it was limited to this one case. If, for example, the husband does not discover for more than three years that he is not the father of the child which his wife was carrying at the time of the marriage, he cannot claim any matrimonial relief at all as he cannot base a petition for divorce on her pre-marital sexual intercourse.[18]

Lapse of time is not a bar in the case of inability or wilful refusal to consummate the marriage because the petitioner may properly try to overcome the impediment or aversion for a longer period than three years.[19]

Petitioner's knowledge

If the petition is based on the respondent's venereal disease or pregnancy per alium, the decree must be refused unless the court was satisfied that the petitioner was ignorant of the facts alleged at the time of the marriage.[20] This bar applies to no other ground although, as we have seen, the fact that the petitioner knew of the existence of the ground and that he could petition for nullity might enable the respondent to argue that he was led to believe that the petitioner did not intend to have the marriage annulled.

3. EFFECT OF DECREE

Although a decree has always been necessary to annul a voidable marriage, at common law (as in the case of a void marriage) it pronounced the marriage 'to have been and to be absolutely null and void to all intents and purposes

---

[16] See Law Com No 116 (Time Restrictions on Presentation of Divorce and Nullity Petitions), Pt III.

[17] Amending s 13 of the Matrimonial Causes Act 1973. Note that the petition does not have to be based on the petitioner's mental disorder.

[18] See post, pp 195 and 207.

[19] See Law Com No 33, paras 79–85. Until 1971 there was a bar of one year in the case of petitions based on mental disorder, venereal disease and pregnancy per alium. The provisions of the Matrimonial Causes Act implement the recommendations of the Law Commission.

[20] Matrimonial Causes Act 1973, s 13(3). This replaces similar legislation going back to the Matrimonial Causes Act 1937.

in the law whatsoever'. The consequence was that before the decree the parties were regarded as husband and wife both in law and in fact but after the decree absolute they were deemed in law never to have been married at all. The logical application of this anomalous doctrine produced some startling results. The children of a voidable marriage were automatically bastardised by the decree; the trusts under a marriage settlement all failed and the interest of the person entitled before the solemnization of the marriage revived; and if a widow remarried and the second marriage was annulled, she reverted to the status of her first husband's widow and could therefore claim an annuity payable to her dum vidua.[1] Some of these anomalies were swept away by statute—for example, children of a voidable marriage retained their legitimacy—and after the Second World War there was an increasing tendency for the judges to regard decrees of nullity in respect of voidable marriages more like decrees of divorce.[2] This doctrine was never consistently applied, however, and by 1971 it was becoming increasingly difficult to predict in any given case whether the court would apply the strict logic of the old common law principle or follow the more realistic approach of some of the more recent cases.

The Nullity of Marriage Act sought to sweep away the remaining anomalies and to clarify the law. It is now provided:[3]

'A decree of nullity granted after 31st July 1971 in respect of a voidable marriage shall operate to annul the marriage only as respects any time after the decree has been made absolute, and the marriage shall, notwithstanding the decree, be treated as if it had existed up to that time.'

Unfortunately the effect of this obscurely worded section is far from clear. It leaves no doubt that the parties must now be regarded as having been married throughout the whole period between the celebration of a voidable marriage and the decree absolute. Two examples will illustrate the operation of this part of the provision:

If H marries W, then marries X, and then obtains a decree of nullity of the first marriage on the ground of W's impotence, the marriage to X will still be void because H was married to W when he contracted it.

If a pension is payable to W, the widow of A, until she remarries and she then contracts a voidable marriage with H which is later annulled, she cannot reclaim her pension because she is still regarded as having remarried.[4]

What is not clear is the effect of the decree on the parties' status after it has been made absolute. The Act expressly states that it shall operate to *annul* the marriage, not to *terminate* it. This implies that the effect is different from that of a decree of dissolution and it is arguable that the parties revert to their previous status. Thus in the second example given above W would once

---

[1] *Re Wombwell's Settlement* [1922] 2 Ch 298 (marriage settlement); *Re d'Altroy's Will Trusts* [1968] 1 All ER 181 (widow's annuity). See also *Newbould v A-G* [1931] P 75, and *Re Rodwell* [1970] Ch 726, [1969] 3 All ER 1363 (parties regarded as never having been married).

[2] *R v Algar* [1954] 1 QB 279, [1953] 2 All ER 1381, CCA (wife remained incompetent to give evidence against husband); *Wiggins v Wiggins* [1958] 2 All ER 555 (second marriage contracted during subsistence of voidable marriage remained void notwithstanding annulment of the first).

[3] Matrimonial Causes Act 1973, s 16, re-enacting the Nullity of Marriage Act 1971, s 5, and implementing the recommendations of the Law Commission: Law Com No 33, paras 21–22 and 25. Quaere whether this provision also applies to foreign decrees. On principle it should not do so: see Graveson *Conflict of Laws* (7th Edn) p 345; North *The Private International Law of Matrimonial Causes* p 267.

[4] *Ward v Secretary of State for Social Services* [1990] 1 FLR 119.

more be regarded as the widow of A even though she is also regarded as having been married to H; consequently although she could not claim a pension payable until remarriage, she could claim it if it were payable during her widowhood. It is difficult to believe that Parliament really intended such a Gilbertian situation and, despite the infelicitous wording of the Act, it is submitted that the consequences of the annulment of a voidable marriage must be the same as those of the dissolution of a valid one.

The section has effect only if the decree absolute was granted on or after 1 August 1971 (when the Nullity of Marriage Act came into operation). In the case of a decree pronounced before this date it may still be necessary to consider the law as it was before the Act was passed.[5] In this connection it should particularly be noted that concluded transactions would never be reopened—a rule that will be of equal importance whenever the decree was pronounced if, contrary to the above submission, the parties still revert to their previous status. Before the marriage was annulled money might have been paid and property distributed on the assumption (valid at the time) that the parties to the marriage were husband and wife. To attempt to set these transactions aside might not only produce chaos but also work substantial injustice, so that the rule was evolved that 'transactions which have been concluded, things which have been done, during the period [of the voidable marriage] on the footing of the existence of that status, cannot be undone or reopened'.[6] Thus, in *Re Eaves*[7] property was bequeathed to the testator's son subject to a life interest in favour of the plaintiff so long as she remained the testator's widow. Six years after the testator's death the widow remarried, and on the eve of her second marriage she permitted the son to sell the property and to use the proceeds for his own purposes on the assumption that her own interest would cease. The second marriage was subsequently annulled on the grounds of the husband's impotence, and the widow then claimed a life interest in the proceeds of the sale. It was held that she must fail, for the sale was a concluded transaction carried out on the footing that the second marriage was valid.

It is not clear what 'transactions and things' are included in this category, but it is submitted that any out and out payment of money (whether capital or income) or assignment of property would come within the exception.

D. Estoppel

If it is alleged that a marriage is void, the court is usually bound to find in favour of the party making the allegation if one of the grounds considered above is established, whether he is petitioning for nullity or the question of the validity of the marriage has arisen in some other proceedings. The question arises, however, whether a party can ever be estopped from asserting the invalidity of the marriage even though he could prove that it is void. Two illustrations will indicate the sort of problem that can arise. If a married man

---

[5] See the 4th Edition of this book, pp 69–71.
[6] Per Clauson LJ in *Re Eaves* [1940] Ch 109, 117, [1939] 4 All ER 260, CA.
[7] [1940] Ch 109, [1939] 4 All ER 260, CA, following *Dodworth v Dale* [1936] 2 KB 503. This case is complicated by the fact that the widow, having acquiesced in the sale of the property, could not be permitted in equity to go back on the transaction.

goes through a form of marriage with a woman after representing to her that he is a bachelor or a widower and then leaves her unsupported, may he raise the nullity of this marriage as a defence to any action brought by her for maintenance? Alternatively, if previous matrimonial proceedings have been brought between the same parties on the assumption that the marriage is valid, may either subsequently petition for nullity or put the validity of the marriage in issue in later proceedings?

It is submitted that a distinction must be drawn between estoppel by conduct and estoppel per rem judicatam for this purpose. In the former case the better view seems to be that the parties by their own conduct cannot prevent the court from enquiring into the real state of affairs and declaring what their true status is. In *Miles v Chilton*,[8] where the husband petitioned for nullity on the ground that the wife was already married at the time of the ceremony in question, Dr Lushington held that the wife's averment that the husband had deceived her into believing that she had already been divorced by her first husband was no answer to the petition. The position with respect to estoppel per rem judicatam is more complicated. Decrees of nullity, divorce and judicial separation are all judgments in rem and bind not only the parties but the whole world. Hence nobody can assert the validity of a marriage after a decree of nullity has been pronounced or, it seems, deny its validity after a decree of judicial separation.[9] If a petition for nullity, divorce or judicial separation is dismissed, this will create an estoppel inter partes only. If, for example, H unsuccessfully petitions for a decree of nullity on the ground that the other party to the marriage, W, was married to another man at the time of the ceremony, neither H nor W can now assert that the marriage is void for this reason, although a third person who was not a party to the proceedings or privy to them could still do so.[10] If the outcome of any other proceedings between the parties in the High Court rests on the validity of their marriage, this will presumably also create an estoppel inter partes, so that neither of them could assert that the marriage was void if, for example, successful proceedings for maintenance had been previously brought under section 27 of the Matrimonial Causes Act.[11] It has been held that proceedings before magistrates cannot create an estoppel in the High Court[12] or, presumably, in a county court. Although non-matrimonial proceedings in a county court have been held to create an estoppel in a magistrates' court, it has been stated obiter that they cannot bind the High Court in matrimonial proceedings.[13]

---

[8] (1849) 1 Rob Eccl 684. The contrary view stated *obiter* by the Divisional Court in *Bullock v Bullock* [1960] 2 All ER 307, at 309 and 313, does not seem to be supported by the authorities there cited.

[9] See Tolstoy *Marriage by Estoppel* 84 LQR 245, and the authorities there cited, particularly *Woodland v Woodland* [1928] P 169.

[10] The problem arose in an acute form in *Wilkins v Wilkins* [1896] P 108, CA. On the wife's petition for divorce the respondent husband's answer had been that the marriage was void because the wife's first husband was alive at the time of his marriage to the petitioner. This fact was expressly found against him. The first husband later returned to England and the second husband then petitioned for nullity. It was held that the first judgment estopped him from doing so, but the Court of Appeal solved the problem by giving him leave to apply for a new trial on that issue.

[11] See post, p 692.

[12] *Hayward v Hayward* [1961] P 152, 161, [1961] 1 All ER 236, 243.

[13] *Whittaker v Whittaker* [1939] 3 All ER 833, 837. Presumably matrimonial proceedings in a

When questions of status are involved, estoppel inevitably creates difficulties. There may be little justification for permitting either party to assert the invalidity of a marriage when he or she has already had an opportunity of doing so but, as Phillimore J said in *Hayward v Hayward*,[14] public policy demands that, when status is in issues, the courts should declare the truth unencumbered by technical rules. If the statement of law above is correct, a man may be validly married to one woman but estopped from denying that he is also married to a second: a result no less absurd than the fact that a stranger may be able to show that a marriage is void whilst, as between themselves, the parties are prevented from doing so. For this reason the doctrine of estoppel should be applied as narrowly as possible in matrimonial causes. It is submitted that it should be limited to cases where the issue has already been expressly litigated: hence earlier proceedings for maintenance should not prevent either party from alleging that the marriage is void if that question was never before the court. It may also be possible for a party to reopen an issue which has been the subject of a finding in previous proceedings if further relevant evidence, which he could not have adduced with reasonable diligence in those proceedings, has since become available to him.[15]

In any event estoppel should be confined to cases where the marriage in question is alleged to be void and not extended to those where it is voidable. Now that a voidable marriage is to be treated as having existed up to the decree absolute, there is nothing inconsistent in an earlier decision based on the assumption that the marriage is valid and a later decree declaring the marriage to be voidable. If, say, the wife obtains a decree of judicial separation during the first three years of marriage, this should not *as such* preclude the husband from subsequently petitioning for a decree of nullity on the ground that she was at the time of the marriage pregnant by another man. His failure to cross-petition for nullity when she petitioned for judicial separation might amount to such conduct on his part as to lead her reasonably to believe that he would not seek a decree of nullity, but this would enable her to raise a statutory bar and not an estoppel. The former would succeed only if the husband knew at the time of the earlier proceedings that it was open to him to have the marriage annulled and if it would be unjust to the wife to grant the decree. Estoppel, if it were relevant, would operate automatically: it is submitted that it cannot apply at all.

---

county court will raise an estoppel in all courts; they have been held to create an estoppel in non-matrimonial proceedings in the High Court: *Razelos v Razelos* [1969] 3 All ER 929.
[14] [1961] P 152, 158–159, [1961] 1 All ER 236, 241–242; approved obiter in *Rowe v Rowe* [1980] Fam 47 at 53 and 58, [1979] 2 All ER 1123, at 1127 and 1131, CA, and by Lord Hailsham LC in *Vervaeke v Smith* [1983] 1 AC 145, 157, [1982] 2 All ER 144, 152, HL. It is submitted, however, that Phillimore J did not sufficiently differentiate between estoppels per rem judicatam and estoppels in pais. In *Taylor v Taylor* [1967] P 25, 29, [1965] 1 All ER 872, 875, it was conceded that no estoppel of any kind would bind the court but the point was not argued.
[15] Cf *Mills v Cooper* [1967] 2 QB 459, 468–469, [1967] 2 All ER 100, 104, CA, per Diplock LJ.

Chapter 4

The effects of marriage

A. Introductory

The principal effect of marriage at common law was that for many purposes it fused the legal personalities of husband and wife into one. The clearest exposition of this doctrine of unity of husband and wife is probably that of Blackstone, who said:[1]

'By marriage, the husband and wife are one person in law; that is, the very being or legal existence of the woman is suspended during the marriage, or at least is incorporated and consolidated into that of the husband; under whose wing, protection, and *cover*, she performs everything; and is therefore called in our law-French a *feme-covert, femina viro co-operta*; is said to be *covert-baron*, or under the protection and influence of her husband, her *baron*, or lord; and her condition during marriage is called her *coverture*. Upon this principle of a union of person in husband and wife, depend almost all the legal rights, duties, and disabilities, that either of them acquire by the marriage.'

The principle was enunciated in the *Dialogus de Scaccario* in the twelfth century and has been repeated by every leading common law writer since.[2] But it may be doubted whether this doctrine was ever a firmly established rule of the common law. One or two examples will suffice to show that it was but imperfectly applied. Thus it operated to prevent any action at common law between the spouses, but if a tort was committed either by or against a married woman both she and her husband were correctly joined as co-defendants or co-plaintiffs to the action, and notwithstanding the maxim *actio personalis moritur cum persona*, if the husband predeceased the wife, she could still be sued or sue in person. A woman on marriage ipso facto acquired her husband's domicile but not his nationality. Similar inconsistencies were to be found in the law relating to the interest taken by a husband in his wife's property. He acquired an absolute interest in her chattels, a similar interest in her choses in action but only provided that they were reduced into possession, a power to dispose of her leasehold interests during his lifetime but no power to dispose of them by will, and no more than an interest for his life in her inheritable estates of freehold. It is difficult to see on what single principle the common law could logically arrive at all these conclusions.

Neither equity nor the ecclesiastical law accepted this doctrine of unity of personality, and both gave married women access to their courts and even permitted actions between spouses. But it was not until 1870 that the Married

---

[1] *Commentaries*, i, 442.
[2] See Williams *Legal Unity of Husband and Wife* 10 MLR 16 at pp 16–18, and the exhaustive judgment of Oliver J in *Midland Bank Trust Co Ltd v Green (No 3)* [1979] Ch 496, [1979] 2 All ER 193.

Women's Property Act of that year gave a wife an extremely limited right to maintain an action in her own name in the courts of common law.[3] Whilst a series of statutes extending over 65 years and culminating in the Law Reform (Married Women and Tortfeasors) Act of 1935 to a very large extent put a married woman in the same legal position as her unmarried sister, they were typical of so much English legislative reform in that they created extensive exceptions to the old rules without abolishing outright the fundamental principle on which the anomalies were based. They did not give the wife the legal status of a feme sole except in certain clearly defined and limited fields, and even these exceptions were construed, if not narrowly, at least inconsistently. As Lush put it:[4]

'It is untraversable that a married woman's position in law is anomalous and enigmatic....
    The rule of unity ... still prevails as a rule in those matters wherein it was established at common law and has not been abrogated by statute. The rule at the present day lifts its head hydra-like and is on occasions applied with surprising results.'

The rule was doubtless biblical in origin[5] but in time, as the quotation from Blackstone shows, it became the legal justification for subordinating the wife's will and acts to those of her husband. Neither approach can be defended today. Any privilege or incapacity conferred on the parties by marriage must now be justified by reference to public policy. This could be based, for example, on the need to protect one spouse from undue pressure from the other or to ensure that neither is forced to act in a way which most people would regard as repugnant to the whole relationship of husband and wife. It is difficult to believe that the view that marriage as such creates a legal unity of personalities, irrespective of the social implications, has survived the decision of the Court of Appeal in *Midland Bank Trustee Co Ltd v Green (No 3)*.[6] A husband and wife were sued for conspiracy; it was argued that they could not be liable on the ground that they were one person in law and therefore could not conspire with each other. This defence failed. At first instance Oliver J concluded a long and erudite judgment, in which he reviewed the history and implications of the doctrine, with these words:[7]

'Unless I am compelled by authority to do so—and I do not conceive that I am—I decline to apply, as a policy of the law, a mediaeval axiom which was never wholly accurate and which appears to me now to be as ill-adapted to the society in which we live as it is repugnant to common sense.'

The same sentiments were expressed in the Court of Appeal, where Oliver J's judgment was affirmed. Lord Denning MR expressed himself in these words:[8]

'Nowadays, both in law and in fact, husband and wife are two persons, not one ...

---

[3] But a woman judicially separated from her husband could sue and be sued as if she were a feme sole by the Matrimonial Causes Act 1857, s 26.

[4] *Husband and Wife* (4th Edn) pp 21 and 58. See generally the whole of the first chapter of that work; Williams *Legal Unity of Husband and Wife* 10 MLR 16; Kahn-Freund *Inconsistencies and Injustices in the Law of Husband and Wife* 15 MLR 133, 16 MLR 34, 148; *A Century of Family Law* (ed Graveson and Crane).

[5] Genesis 2, 24; Genesis 3, 16. See Fortescue *De Laudibus Legum Anglie* c XLII.

[6] [1982] Ch 529, [1981] 3 All ER 744, CA.

[7] [1979] Ch 496, 527, [1979] 2 All ER 193, 220.

[8] At 538–539 and 748, respectively.

The severance in all respects is so complete that I would say that the doctrine of unity and its ramifications should be discarded altogether, except in so far as it is retained by judicial decision or by Act of Parliament.'

In more picturesque language Sir George Baker said that to hold that a husband and wife could not be liable in the tort of conspiracy because they were one person

'would ... be akin to basing a judgment on the proposition that the Earth is flat, because many believed that centuries ago. We now know that the Earth is not flat. We now know that husband and wife in the eyes of the law and in fact are equal.'[9]

These changes have of course affected the spouses' rights and obligations both vis-à-vis each other and vis-à-vis third persons. In this chapter we shall examine the scope of these rights and duties. We shall first discuss the right to consortium and the corresponding duty to cohabit that each spouse owes to the other. We shall then consider how far marriage affects rights and duties in contract and tort both as between the spouses themselves and between the spouses and third persons. Finally we shall examine two matters of public law: the problems created by the relationship of husband and wife in the criminal law and its relevance in the law of nationality. The effect of the relationship on rights in property and the duty of support will be considered in later chapters.[10]

Unmarried cohabitants

Unmarried cohabitants cannot of course claim any right to each other's consortium: this arises solely from marriage. But some of the consequences of cohabitation may obviously be of profound importance to them—for example, the protection of confidences—as will be the effect of cohabitation on their legal relationship with third persons. When looking at the legal consequences of consortium, therefore, we shall compare the legal position of spouses with that of unmarried cohabitants.

B. The right to consortium

1. THE NATURE OF CONSORTIUM

Mutual duty to cohabit

Consortium means living together as husband and wife with all the incidents that flow from that relationship. At one time it would have been said that the husband had the right to his wife's consortium whilst the latter had not so much a reciprocal right to her husband's consortium as a correlative duty to give him her society and her services—a view which was not entirely obsolete in the middle of the nineteenth century.[11] A clear illustration of the wife's legal subjection to her husband can be seen in the old common law rule that a woman who murdered her husband was guilty of petit treason, like the vassal who slew his lord or the servant who slew his master.[12]

---

[9] At 542 and 751, respectively.
[10] See post, chs 17 and 20.
[11] See the judgment of Coleridge J in *Re Cochrane* (1840) 8 Dowl 630.
[12] The distinction between petit treason and murder was abolished in 1828 by 9 Geo 4, c 31, s 2.

Whether a husband could enforce his right to consortium by physically confining his wife remained in doubt until the end of the nineteenth century. In 1852 the Court of Queen's Bench held that they would not force a wife to return to her husband against her will by enabling him to obtain custody of her by habeas corpus.[13] But this decision did not determine whether he could enforce his right extra-judicially by lawfully confining her once she was in his house. More than a century earlier the Court of King's Bench had held that he was entitled to restrain her only in order to protect his property or his honour, for example if she squandered his wealth or went 'into lewd company',[14] but in 1840 Coleridge J denied that there was any such limitation on the husband's powers.[15] It was eventually not until Parliament had accorded to a married woman a measure of financial independence of her husband by the Married Women's Property Act of 1882[16] that it was finally established that she had a similar right to her personal liberty by the decision of the Court of Appeal in *R v Jackson* in 1891.[17] In that case the wife had gone to live with relations whilst her husband was absent in New Zealand. After his return she refused to live with him again and failed to comply with a decree for restitution of conjugal rights. Consequently he arranged with two men that they should seize her as she came out of church one Sunday afternoon, and she was then put into a carriage and taken to her husband's residence, where she was allowed complete freedom of the house but was not permitted to leave the building. She then applied for a writ of habeas corpus and it was unanimously held by the Court of Appeal that it was no defence that the husband was merely confining her in order to enforce his right to her consortium. So ended the husband's right to treat his wife as he would a recalcitrant animal. In the words of McCardie J:[18]

'From the date of their decision the shackles of servitude fell from the limbs of married women and they were free to come and go at their own will.'

This principle was reinforced more recently by the Court of Appeal in *R v Reid*,[19] where it was held that a husband who steals, carries away or secretes his wife against her will is guilty of the common law offence of kidnapping her. As Cairns LJ said in delivering the judgment of the court:[20]

'The notion that a husband can, without incurring punishment, treat his wife, whether she be a separated wife or otherwise, with any kind of hostile force is obsolete.'

But it is important to remember that these cases have in no way altered the law relating to a husband's right to his wife's consortium; they merely decided that he is not entitled to resort to extra-judicial methods to enforce it. Hence it was still possible even fifty years ago to speak of the husband as the head of the family. But the movement for the equality of the rights of the sexes, which had begun in the middle of the nineteenth century and which had gained renewed impetus by women's work in the First World War, was

[13] *R v Leggatt* (1852) 18 QB 781.
[14] *R v Lister* (1721) 1 Stra 478. Cf Viner's *Abridgement*, Tit Baron and Feme, V a, 11.
[15] *Re Cochrane*, supra. See Lush *Husband and Wife* (4th Edn) pp 24 et seq.
[16] Post, p 561.
[17] [1891] 1 QB 671, CA.
[18] *Place v Searle* [1932] 2 KB 497, 500–501.
[19] [1973] QB 299, [1972] 2 All ER 1350, CA; Hall [1972A] CLJ 220.
[20] At 303 and 1353, respectively.

now to be felt in the home. The victory gained in the field of public law in the Sex Disqualification (Removal) Act of 1919 was carried into the field of private law. In 1923 Parliament equated the rights of the spouses to petition for divorce;[1] in 1925 it established the principle that they have equal rights with respect to their children;[2] and in 1967 it gave each of them the power to apply for an order regulating their rights to occupy the matrimonial home.[3] All these changes reflect the modern view that the wife is no longer the weaker partner subservient to the stronger but that both spouses are the joint, co-equal heads of the family. This is also the position today as regards consortium, so that it can be said: 'It seems to be clear that at the present day a husband has a right to the consortium of his wife, and the wife to the consortium of her husband',[4] and these rights must now be regarded as exactly reciprocal.

It follows, of course, that a wife has no greater right to force herself upon her husband than he has to compel her to cohabit with him. In *Nanda v Nanda*[5] a wife, whose husband had deserted her, installed herself against his will in the flat in which he was living with another woman and their two children. It was held that she had no right to trespass on her husband's property which had never been the matrimonial home and that he was entitled to an injunction to restrain her from doing so again in the future.

The incidents of consortium

As has already been stated, consortium primarily means living together as husband and wife. Normally this will involve sharing the common matrimonial home, but this is not absolutely essential. It may be possible for the spouses to cohabit only from time to time, as where the husband has to spend long periods away from home for reasons of business or where he is a member of the armed forces and consequently can live with his wife only when he is on leave.[6] So long as both spouses retain the intention of cohabiting whenever possible, the consortium is regarded as continuous and will come to an end only if one or both of them lose this intention.[7]

Consortium, then, connotes as far as possible the sharing of a common home and a common domestic life. It is difficult to go beyond this and to define with more precision the duties which the spouses owe to each other: this is, after all, a matter of common knowledge rather than a subject for legal analysis. The incidents of consortium are capable of considerable variation and clearly will depend upon such facts as the age, health, social position and financial circumstances of the spouses. Jurisprudentially, in a sense consortium resembles ownership, for husband and wife enjoy 'a bundle

[1] Post, p 183.
[2] Post, p 293.
[3] Post, p 613.
[4] Per Scrutton LJ in *Place v Searle* [1932] 2 KB 497, 512, CA.
[5] [1968] P 351, [1967] 3 All ER 401. The wife's position was, if anything, strengthened by her having obtained a decree for restitution of conjugal rights but this gave her no right to insist on cohabitation. Decrees for restitution of conjugal rights have now been abolished: see post, p 119.
[6] Cf *Huxtable v Huxtable* (1899) 68 LJP 83 (both spouses domestic servants residing with different families).
[7] *R v Creamer* [1919] 1 KB 564, CCA; *Santos v Santos* [1972] Fam 247, [1972] 2 All ER 246, CA. See further post, p 212.

of rights some hardly capable of precise definition'.[8] Nevertheless it may be worthwhile to examine in a little more detail one or two of these rights which have been directly or indirectly the subject of judicial decision.

Use of surname

An adult may use any surname he chooses provided that his intention is not to perpetrate a fraud.[9] Most wives assume their husbands' surnames on marriage, although they may continue to be known by their former names for professional or business purposes. Likewise a woman usually retains her former husband's name after the marriage has been terminated either by death or by divorce, and a man has no such property in his name as to entitle him to sue for an injunction to prevent his divorced wife from using it unless, at any rate, she is doing so for the purpose of defrauding him or some other right of his is being invaded.[10] Similarly an unmarried woman may use the surname of the man with whom she is living if she wishes, although she may be civilly or criminally liable if she does so for the purpose of defrauding another.

The matrimonial home

As we have already seen, it is the duty of the spouses to live together as far as their circumstances will permit. But differences may arise between them as to where the matrimonial home is to be. In accordance with the view that the husband was the head of the household, the earlier opinion was that he had the right to determine this and a judicial dictum to this effect is to be found as late as 1940.[11] Today, however, this, like other domestic matters of common concern, is something in which both spouses have a right to be heard and which they must settle by agreement—a view most clearly voiced by Denning LJ in *Dunn v Dunn*.[12] Such an agreement may be entered into before marriage[13] or after it, and will remain in force until a change of circumstances (for example, a change in the spouses' financial position or health or business interests) makes it necessary or desirable for them to change their home and thus come to a fresh agreement.

Where the spouses find it impossible to come to an agreement, neither of them has an absolute right to determine where the home is to be and all the circumstances must be taken into consideration. If the husband is the sole breadwinner, he may be entitled to the last word for the simple reason that

---

[8] Per Lord Reid in *Best v Samuel Fox & Co Ltd* [1952] AC 716, 736, [1952] 2 All ER 394, 401, HL.

[9] The execution and enrolment of a deed poll merely provide evidence of the executant's intention to be known by a different name and have no other legal significance.

[10] *Cowley v Cowley* [1900] P 305, CA; affirmed [1901] AC 450, HL. Cf *Du Boulay v Du Boulay* (1869) LR 2 PC 430, 441, PC. Thus, if she holds herself out as his wife after he has remarried, she may be guilty of libel or slander if the reasonable inference is that he is not legally married to his second wife.

[11] *Mansey v Mansey* [1940] P 139, 140, [1940] 2 All ER 424, 426. See also *King v King* [1942] P 1, 8; [1941] 2 All ER 103, 110.

[12] [1949] P 98, 103, [1948] 2 All ER 822, 823, CA. See also *McGowan v McGowan* [1948] 2 All ER 1032, 1035; *Walter v Walter* (1949) 65 TLR 680; *Hosegood v Hosegood* (1950) 66 (pt 1) TLR 735, 739, CA.

[13] *King v King* (supra). Cf *G v G* [1930] P 72.

he must be able to live near his place of work,[14] but if the wife is working and the husband is not, her considerations must come first.[15] Moreover, whatever arrangements one proposes must be reasonable from the other's point of view; the husband cannot, for example, insist upon the wife's living with his mother when the two women obviously will not be able to share the same house.[16] Similarly, if business requirements make it necessary for one spouse to move, the other will not be bound to go too if, say, the proposed removal would be liable to impair the latter's health or would be contrary to his or her own business interests.[17]

The practical importance of the question of the right to choose the matrimonial home lies in the fact that, if the spouses separate as a result of their inability to agree on where the home is to be, it is the spouse who is acting unreasonably who will be in desertion. Where both act unreasonably (or, at least, where it cannot be said that either clearly has right upon his side), it would seem that neither can allege that the other is in desertion.[18]

Sexual intercourse

We have already seen that each spouse owes the other a duty to consummate the marriage and that (with certain exceptions) the incapacity of either or the wilful refusal of the respondent to do so will entitle the petitioner to a decree of nullity.[19] This mutual right to intercourse continues after the marriage has been consummated provided that it is reasonably exercised; but one spouse is not bound to submit to the demands of the other if they are inordinate, perverted or otherwise unreasonable, or in any case if they are likely to lead to a breakdown in health.[20] Similarly a husband is not entitled to insist upon using contraceptives or practising coitus interruptus against the wife's will if it is unreasonable to deprive her of the opportunity of bearing children.

If one spouse insists upon intercourse in such circumstances or wilfully refuses to have intercourse at all, the other will be entitled to withdraw from cohabitation without being in desertion and may charge the guilty party with constructive desertion. A course of conduct of this sort would also enable the spouse suffering as a consequence to establish such behaviour that he (or she) could not reasonably be expected to live with the other for the purpose of divorce and proceedings under the Domestic Proceedings and Magistrates' Courts Act.[1] Supervening impotence, on the other hand, like any other deterioration in a spouse's health, would not on principle appear to be a ground for any sort of matrimonial relief at all.[2]

---

[14] Per Denning LJ in *Dunn v Dunn* (supra) at 103 and 823, respectively. Cf Hodson LJ in *W v W (No 2)* [1954] P 486, 515, [1954] 2 All ER 829, 840, CA.

[15] As in *King v King* (supra).

[16] *Millichamp v Millichamp* (1931) 146 LT 96; *Munro v Munro* [1950] 1 All ER 832, CA. Contrast *Jackson v Jackson* (1932) 146 LT 406.

[17] See *Walter v Walter* (1949) 65 TLR 680 (post, p 208).

[18] Post, p 208.

[19] Ante, pp 85–90.

[20] Either because of the state of the spouse's health or because of the manner in which the other insists upon intercourse (eg, coitus interruptus). Similarly, a husband may not insist upon intercourse if he knows himself to be suffering from a venereal disease: *Foster v Foster* [1921] P 438, CA.

[1] See post, pp 195 (behaviour) and 205 and 207 (desertion).

[2] But see post, pp 197–198.

At the end of the seventeenth century Hale wrote:[3]

'But the husband cannot be guilty of a rape committed by himself upon his lawful wife, for by their mutual matrimonial consent and contract the wife hath given up herself in this kind unto her husband which she cannot retract.'

Although Hale cited no authority for this view, it was generally regarded as a correct statement of the common law.[4] But the change in attitude towards the relationship of the spouses during the present century, coupled with the fact that today virtually everyone will find abhorrent the idea that a man can with impunity force his wife to have sexual intercourse with him against her will, led the courts to seek ways of limiting the scope of the husband's immunity, and they grafted exceptions on the rule by holding that her consent can be retracted following a court order or by the parties' agreement.[5] The husband's immunity from prosecution was further reduced by the decision in *R v Miller*[6] that, following *R v Jackson*[7] a husband could not insist on his right to have intercourse by force and that he could therefore be convicted of an assault on his wife even though he used no more force than necessary to achieve his aim.

The question of the husband's immunity from prosecution for rape was considered by the House of Lords in *R v R*[8] in 1991. The wife left the husband and told him that she intended to petition for divorce. Some three weeks later he broke into her parents' house, where she was living, and attempted to have sexual intercourse with her against her will. The trial judge ruled that the husband's immunity had been lost, whereupon he pleaded guilty to attempted rape. He then appealed to the Court of Appeal and, when his appeal was dismissed, to the House of Lords. Lord Keith, with whose speech the other members of the House agreed, maintained that the common law is capable of evolving in the light of changing social, economic and cultural developments. Marriage, he pointed out, 'is in modern times regarded as a partnership of equals and no longer one in which the wife must be the subservient chattel of the husband'. Consequently any reasonable person must now regard Hale's proposition as unacceptable.[9] The only obstacle to declaring that a husband now has no immunity was section 1 of the Sexual Offences (Amendment) Act 1976 which, for the first time, laid down a statutory definition of rape including the words '*unlawful* sexual intercourse'. This phrase usually connotes extra-marital intercourse[10] and consequently it

---

[3] 1 Hale PC 629. But he could be guilty of aiding and abetting another to rape her: *Lord Audley's Case* (1631) 3 State Tr 401, HL; *R v Leak* [1976] QB 217, [1975] 2 All ER 1059, CA.

[4] It was not until *R v Clarence* (1888) 22 QBD 23 that judicial doubts were expressed about its correctness.

[5] *R v Clarke* [1949] 2 All ER 448 (judicial separation); *R v O'Brien* [1974] 3 All ER 663 (decree nisi of divorce); *R v Steele* (1976) 65 Cr App Rep 22, CA (non-molestation injunction); *R v Roberts* [1986] Crim LR 188, CA (separation deed).

[6] [1954] 2 QB 282, [1954] 2 All ER 529. Although this decision is clearly consonant with changed social views, it is difficult to see how it can be supported logically. If the wife was deemed to have given an implied consent to intercourse, she ought also to have been considered to have given an implied consent to any acts connected therewith and this should have been a defence to a charge of assault. Cf *R v R* [1991] 4 All ER 481, 486, HL. See also *R v Kowalski* [1988] 1 FLR 447, CA (husband guilty of indecent assault by forcing wife to submit to fellatio before sexual intercourse).

[7] [1891] 1 QB 671, CA (ante, p 108).

[8] [1991] 4 All ER 481, HL.

[9] At pp 483–484.

[10] Cf *R v Chapman* [1959] 1 QB 100, [1958] 3 All ER 143, CCA.

could be argued that the Act had reintroduced the old common law rule by making it impossible for a husband to rape his wife in any circumstances. Lord Keith rejected this argument on the grounds that it was inconceivable that Parliament had this intention and that 'unlawful' in this context could not reasonably import the existing common law exceptions. The House therefore concluded that the word was mere surplusage and that 'in modern times the supposed marital exception in rape forms no part of the law of England'.[11]

Marital confidences

If a marriage breaks down, bitterness and vindictiveness may lead one spouse to break marital confidences and to broadcast information imparted and received on the shared understanding that it would go no further. Does the law offer the other any remedy in such circumstances?

As a general principle it now seems settled that, in the absence of a contract, three elements are required if an action for breach of confidence is to succeed: the information must have 'the necessary quality of confidence about it'; it must have been imparted in circumstances importing an obligation of confidence; and there must be an unauthorised use of that information to the detriment of the party communicating it.[12] It is clear that the relationship of husband and wife will satisfy the second condition. As Ungoed-Thomas J said in *Argyll v Argyll*:[13]

'There could hardly be anything more intimate or confidential than is involved in that relationship, or than in the mutual trust and confidences which are shared between husband and wife. The confidential nature of the relationship is of its very essence and so obviously and necessarily implicit in it that there is no need for it to be expressed.'

It is more difficult to predict whether the information in question will have 'the necessary quality of confidence' to satisfy the first condition. Information about the parties' sexual conduct will be protected;[14] to this might be added information about their health, financial matters or any other matter publication of which was not contemplated at the time it was imparted.

It is also probable that equity will assist the plaintiff only if he or she comes to the court with clean hands. An attempt to raise this defence was made in the *Argyll* case. Some two years after divorcing the plaintiff on the ground of her adultery, the defendant wrote a series of articles for a newspaper, some of which contained information relating to the plaintiff's 'private life, personal affairs and private conduct communicated to the defendant in confidence during the subsistence of the marriage'. The defendant argued

---

[11] At p 489. This brings English law into line with that of Scotland: *S v HM Advocate* 1989 SLT 469. See further Law Com Working Paper No 116 (Rape within Marriage). The total abolition of the old common law rule has not been universally regarded as desirable. See the 15th Report of the Criminal Law Revision Committee (Sexual Offences), Cmnd 9213, paras 2.57 et seq. A narrow majority of the committee opposed the suggestion because they considered that investigation and proof might be difficult and that, once the wife had made a complaint, she could not stop investigation by the police and this might prevent a future reconciliation or impair one that had already occurred.

[12] See *Coco v A N Clark (Engineers) Ltd* [1969] RPC 41, 47, applying *Saltman Engineering Co, Ltd v Campbell Engineering Co, Ltd* (1948) [1963] 3 All ER 413n, CA, and followed in *Stephens v Avery* [1988] Ch 449, [1988] 2 All ER 477.

[13] [1967] Ch 302, 322, [1965] 1 All ER 611, 619.

[14] *Stephens v Avery* (supra).

that the court should refuse to grant an injunction on the grounds that she had herself published articles disclosing matrimonial secrets and that her own view of marriage, as exemplified by her adultery, could only be described as immoral. Ungoed-Thomas J held that this defence failed, first because the defendant proposed to disclose much more intimate confidences so that his breaches would have been 'of an altogether different order of perfidy', and secondly because, however reprehensible the plaintiff's own adultery may have been, her subsequent conduct could only undermine confidence for the future and not retrospectively release the defendant from his duty to keep confidences already disclosed. The learned judge therefore granted an injunction to prevent the defendant from divulging the confidences in question and the newspaper from publishing them.

Unmarried cohabitants

In *Stephens v Avery*[15] Sir Nicolas Browne-Wilkinson V-C held that an injunction could be granted to prevent the defendant from disclosing to a newspaper details of the plaintiff's homosexual relationship with a third person which had been communicated and received expressly in confidence. He left open the question whether the relationship of unmarried sexual partners in itself creates a duty of confidentiality (so as to satisfy the second element necessary for a successful action for breach of confidence without an express undertaking)[16] or whether an earlier case, in which it had been held that a homosexual relationship did not raise such a duty,[17] was correctly decided. As the relationship of a man and woman cohabiting outside marriage can be as intimate and confidential as that of a married couple, it is submitted that confidences exchanged between them should be entitled to the same protection as similar confidences between husband and wife.

Evidence in legal proceedings

When one considers the question of testimony in legal proceedings, however, two principles of public policy may come into conflict. The first is the need to protect marital confidences and, more generally, to protect a person from having to give evidence against his or her spouse. The second is that in any proceedings, civil or criminal, no evidence should be excluded if it will help the court or the jury to arrive at the truth. There are three separate but related issues: competence, compellability and privilege.

Competence

At common law neither the parties nor their spouses were competent witnesses in civil proceedings or (with very few exceptions) in criminal proceedings. A spouse's evidence was excluded for a number of reasons: the fact that it might be untrustworthy, the wish to preserve marital harmony and to protect marital confidences, and the undesirability of having a witness giving evidence against his or her spouse and the consequent unfairness of permitting

---

[15] [1988] Ch 449, [1988] 2 All ER 477.
[16] At 454 and 481 respectively.
[17] *M and N v Kelvin MacKenzie and News Group Newspapers Ltd* (1988) (unreported) cited in *Stephens v Avery* (supra) at 456 and 482–483 respectively.

evidence to be given for the spouse. In civil proceedings this rule was abolished by the Evidence Amendment Act 1853 and spouses became competent to give evidence for any party.[18] In criminal proceedings, however, the common law rule lasted till the passing of the Criminal Evidence Act 1898, which also for the first time made the accused generally competent to give evidence on his or her own behalf. This Act enabled a spouse to give evidence for the defence subject to some qualifications; various statutes also made the spouse a competent witness for the prosecution in the case of certain crimes, mainly of a sexual nature or against children. This position could scarcely be justified today, however,[19] and section 80 of the Police and Criminal Evidence Act 1984 has made the accused's spouse a competent witness for the prosecution, the accused and any co-accused in all cases unless the husband and wife are charged jointly, in which case neither is competent to give evidence *for the prosecution* so long as he or she is liable to be convicted.[20] Consequently, if one of them pleads guilty, he can do so because he cannot then be jeopardised by his own evidence.

Compellability

Once spouses became competent in civil proceedings, the main reason for their not being compelled to give evidence disappeared. The Evidence Amendment Act 1853 accordingly made them compellable as well as competent.

The arguments against forcing a person to give evidence against his or her spouse in criminal proceedings are, however, much more cogent. The Police and Criminal Evidence Act has struck a compromise.[1] For the first time the spouse is made a compellable witness for the accused in all cases unless the spouses are charged jointly. But he or she may be compelled to give evidence for the prosecution or a person jointly charged with the accused in only three cases.[2] These are:

(a) If the offence charged involves an assault on, or injury or a threat of injury to, the spouse or a person under the age of 16. The ambit of this provision is not clear. It obviously covers offences which necessarily involve an assault or injury (which need not be violent) on the person concerned, for example, wounding, administering poison or sending a letter threatening to murder. But the word 'involves' is wide enough to cover any offence the commission of which happened in the particular circumstances to involve injury. Suppose, for example, that a husband is charged with inciting his wife to steal and he did so by threatening her with violence if she failed to carry out his wishes: the offence charged clearly involves (in the wide sense) a threat

---

[18] S 1. But they were not competent to give evidence in proceedings instituted in consequence of adultery until 1869: Evidence Further Amendment Act 1869, s 3.

[19] See the Eleventh Report of the Criminal Law Revision Committee 1972, Cmnd 4991, para 148.

[20] This applies even though the evidence relates to events which occurred before the section came into force: see *R v Cruttenden* [1991] 2 QB 66, [1991] 3 All ER 242, CA. The prosecution may not comment on a spouse's failure to give evidence: Police and Criminal Evidence Act 1984, s 80(8).

[1] Implementing Cmnd 4991, paras 149–153. For a discussion of some of the difficulties this provision gives rise to, particularly if the accused is charged with some offences which fall within the exceptions and others which do not, or is jointly charged with another, see Creighton *Spouse Competence and Compellability* [1990] Crim LR 34.

[2] S 80(2), (3), (4). The co-accused must be jointly charged and not merely jointly indicted: *R v Woolgar* [1991] Crim LR 545, CA. A spouse is not compellable if jointly charged.

of injury to the accused's wife. Bearing in mind that making a spouse a compellable witness is a radical departure from a long and deeply held principle of English law, it is submitted that the word should be construed in the narrower sense and that the prosecution should not be able to call the wife against her will.

(b) If the offence charged is a sexual offence[3] against a person under the age of 16.

(c) If the offence charged consists of attempting or conspiring to commit any of the above offences or of aiding, abetting, counselling, procuring or inciting their commission.

However repugnant it may seem to force a person to give evidence against his or her spouse facing a criminal charge, in these cases the principle is outweighed by the need to enable the prosecution to produce evidence without which it would often be impossible to prove the offence. This will be effective, however, only if the witness is prepared to give evidence, and there is no doubt that a number of prosecutions, particularly of offences involving assault, are not brought because of the victim's unwillingness to testify, whether from fear or some other cause.[4]

If a spouse is a competent but not compellable witness, it should be made clear to him—if necessary by the judge—before he takes the oath that he need not give evidence if he does not wish to do so.[5]

Privilege

The objection that making a spouse a competent witness would force the disclosure of marital confidences led the Common Law Commissioners (on whose recommendation the Evidence Amendment Act of 1853 was passed) to recommend that communications between spouses should be privileged because, as they said, 'so much of the happiness of human life may fairly be said to depend on the inviolability of domestic confidence'. This recommendation was followed in the Acts making spouses competent witnesses, but a curious twist was given to it because the privilege was given to the spouse *to whom* the statement was made and not to the maker of it.[6] Hence if the statement in question was made by the husband to the wife, *he* might be compelled to disclose it although the wife might not; but if she waived her privilege he had no power to stop her from breaking his confidence. This was illogical and indefensible in civil proceedings but was even more anomalous in criminal proceedings; if the accused's wife gave evidence and was asked whether her husband had admitted his guilt to her, she alone decided whether to preserve his confidence. Consequently the privilege has now been abolished in both civil[7] and criminal[8] proceedings.

---

[3] As defined in s 80(7).
[4] See Edwards 139 New LJ 691.
[5] *R v Pitt* [1983] QB 25, [1982] 3 All ER 63, CA.
[6] Evidence Amendment Act 1853, s 3 (civil proceedings); Criminal Evidence Act 1898, s 1(d) (criminal proceedings).
[7] Civil Evidence Act 1968, s 16(3), implementing the recommendations of the Law Reform Committee contained in their 16th Report, Cmnd 3472. The Committee was of the opinion that the judge's discretion to exclude evidence gave sufficient protection: see paras 42–43.
[8] Police and Criminal Evidence Act 1984, s 80(9). See the 11th Report of the Criminal Law Revision Committee: Cmnd 4991, para 173.

It must be emphasised that the privilege was that of the witness and that the communication as such is not protected at all. Consequently it has always been possible for the prosecution to put in evidence a statement made by the accused to his spouse if they could prove it without calling either as a witness. This occurred in *Rumping v DPP.*[9] The police intercepted a letter written by the accused, who was charged with murder, to his wife and containing a virtual confession of guilt. It was held by the House of Lords that it had been properly admitted in evidence. This rule will still be of importance if the spouse refuses to give evidence.

A married witness may, however, claim certain other privileges in *civil* proceedings. The rule that a witness may not be compelled to answer any question or produce any document that tends to expose him to criminal proceedings has now been extended to questions and documents that might incriminate his or her spouse.[10] An arguably more important example of privilege attaches to statements made by either spouse to the other or to a third person with a view to effecting a reconciliation. The basis of this is the public interest in trying to secure a reconciliation rather than a divorce and the recognition that complete frankness will not be obtained if the parties have at the back of their mind the fear that whatever is said may be given in evidence if the attempt at reconciliation fails. Such statements have been judicially regarded as made without prejudice, which means that the mediator will be required to give evidence if the parties waive the privilege.[11] This may inhibit the mediator and it has been suggested that they should be covered by public interest immunity so that neither the parties nor the mediator would be able to waive it.[12] It is not clear that a similar privilege would attach to statements made in the course of conciliation; as it is in the public interest that parties should reach an agreed solution to matters in dispute between them, it is urged that statements made to a conciliator should be covered by a similar privilege.[13]

Former spouses

At common law the incompetence of a witness to give evidence for or against a spouse continued in respect of matters which occurred during the marriage even though the marriage had subsequently been dissolved or, if it was voidable, annulled.[14] This rule has been expressly abolished with respect to

---

[9] [1964] AC 814, [1962] 3 All ER 256, HL. The only protection given to the accused is the general discretion vested in the court to exclude prejudicial evidence improperly obtained.

[10] Civil Evidence Act 1968, s 14.

[11] *Theodoropoulas v Theodoropoulas* [1964] P 311, [1963] 2 All ER 772, and the cases there cited; *Pais v Pais* [1971] P 119, [1970] 3 All ER 491. It is immaterial whether the initiative was taken by one of the spouses or by a third person: *Henley v Henley* [1955] P 202, [1955] 1 All ER 590 n. See also the Domestic Proceedings and Magistrates' Courts Act 1978, s 12(7); McCrory *Confidentiality in Mediation of Matrimonial Disputes* 51 MLR 442.

[12] McCrory loc cit.

[13] McCrory loc cit. See also the Report of the Matrimonial Causes Procedure Committee, para 4.60; Law Com No 192 (Ground for Divorce) paras 5.43–5.48; Report of the Conciliation Project Unit, paras 5.78–5.84. Statements made in a conciliation appointment under the scheme in operation in the Principal Registry are privileged: *Practice Direction* [1992] 1 All ER 421. For conciliation, see post, pp 224–230.

[14] *Monroe v Twistleton* (1802) Peake Add Cas 219; *R v Algar* [1954] 1 QB 279, [1953] 2 All ER 1381, CCA.

criminal proceedings[15] but not with respect to civil proceedings. It was justified on the ground that the witness must not be put in a position where he might be forced to break confidences entrusted to him during the marriage.[16] As this principle no longer applies whilst the marriage is still subsisting, it can scarcely apply when it has been dissolved. It would be manifestly absurd if divorce placed a former spouse under an incompetence which did not exist before.[17]

Cohabitants

At common law the rules relating to the incompetence of spouses to give evidence did not apply to the parties to a void marriage[18] or a fortiori to cohabitants who had been through no form of marriage at all. Today the social justification for not forcing a witness to give evidence against a spouse accused of a criminal offence or to answer a question that might incriminate the latter in civil proceedings might be considered to apply with equal force to those living together outside marriage. In view of the current move to bring spouses more into line with other witnesses, however, it is highly unlikely that the remaining exceptional rules would be extended to cohabitants.

2. LOSS OF THE RIGHT TO CONSORTIUM

The right to consortium can be lost, broadly speaking, in four ways.

First, if the spouses agree to live apart, the agreement divests each of them of the right to the other's consortium. But once the agreement comes to an end, the right will revive. Hence, if, say, the husband entirely repudiates his obligations under the agreement, the wife will be entitled to treat it as at an end and, if she does so, may demand that the husband should resume cohabitation.

Secondly, a decree of judicial separation relieves the spouse obtaining the order from the duty of cohabiting with the other, so that, as long as the order is in force, the right to consortium ceases to exist. This topic will be discussed in greater detail in chapter 5. Although an order excluding one spouse from the matrimonial home does not specifically suspend the right to consortium, its practical effect is of course the same.[19]

Thirdly, although a marriage is not legally terminated until a decree of divorce (or of nullity in the case of a voidable marriage) is made absolute, the duty to cohabit will come to an end once the decree nisi is pronounced. At this stage the marriage is dead in fact and clearly neither party can now call on the other to cohabit.

Finally, matrimonial misconduct will also deprive the spouse misconducting himself of the right to the other's consortium. Clearly this term is sufficiently wide to include any conduct which would afford a defence to a

---

[15] Police and Criminal Evidence Act 1984, s 80(5). This applies even though the evidence relates to events which occurred before the section came into force: *R v Cruttenden* [1991] 2 QB 66, [1991] 3 All ER 242, CA.

[16] *Monroe v Twistleton* (supra); *O'Connor v Marjoribanks* (1842) 4 Man & G 435.

[17] See Cross *Evidence* (7th Edn) pp 218–219.

[18] *Batthews v Galindo* (1828) 4 Bing 610; *R v Khan* (1986) 84 Cr App Rep 44, CA.

[19] See further post, pp 160 et seq.

charge of desertion brought against the other spouse: it would obviously be absurd to say in the same breath that the latter owes a duty to cohabit and yet is not in desertion if he breaks off cohabitation.[20] It must not be forgotten that this duty is mutual, and, as Jeune P put it:[1]

> 'Neither party to a marriage can, I think, insist on cohabitation unless she or he is willing to perform a marital duty inseparable from it.'

Moreover, it would seem that a matrimonial offence committed by one spouse will deprive him of the right to the other's consortium whatever be the other's own conduct. Hence, a husband is not bound to cohabit with his wife if she has committed adultery, even though he has committed adultery too.[2]

3. BREACH OF THE DUTY TO COHABIT

Although the right to consortium has been likened to the rights attached to ownership, in one important respect this analogy breaks down, for as between the spouses the duty to cohabit is legally completely unenforceable. The doctrine of unity of personality prevented either spouse from suing the other at common law, and consequently the only remedy that a deserted spouse had was to petition for a decree for restitution of conjugal rights. Petitions were originally brought in the ecclesiastical courts; they were transferred to the Divorce Court in 1858 and finally to the High Court in 1875. The decree called upon a spouse in desertion to resume cohabitation with the petitioner. If it was disobeyed, the respondent could originally be excommunicated, but the power to excommunicate on this ground was abolished by statute in 1813 and was replaced by a power to commit for contempt.[3] This was in turn abolished by the Matrimonial Causes Act of 1884, after which there was no direct sanction for failure to comply with the decree at all. The Act of 1884 compensated for this by enacting that disobedience to a decree for restitution should give the other spouse an immediate right to petition for judicial separation or, until 1923 in the case of a wife, for divorce if the husband had also committed adultery. For many years petitions were still brought by wives who wanted to take advantage of the court's power to make ancillary orders, particularly orders for maintenance, but the need to use this machinery was largely removed by the Law Reform (Miscellaneous Provisions) Act 1949, which gave a wife power to petition for maintenance in the High Court without bringing any other proceedings. The decree for restitution had obviously become a complete anomaly and it was eventually abolished by section 20 of the Matrimonial Proceedings and Property Act 1970.[4]

Although the duty to cohabit is not specifically enforceable, a breach of it may lead to other consequences. If there is a total breach, the spouse in default will be in desertion, and this will in turn enable the other to petition

---

[20] For good cause for separation, see post, pp 205–206.
[1] *Synge v Synge* [1900] P 180, 195.
[2] *Brooking-Phillips v Brooking-Phillips* [1913] P 80, CA.
[3] Ecclesiastical Courts Act 1813.
[4] During the years 1965–1969 there were on the average 29 petitions for restitution a year and nine decrees. The courts still give *indirect* support to the right to consortium, eg by declaring void any condition attached to a bequest providing an incentive for the beneficiary to live apart from his or her spouse or to obtain a divorce: see *Re Johnson's Will Trusts* [1967] Ch 387, [1967] 1 All ER 553, and the cases there cited.

for divorce or judicial separation at the end of two years or to make an application immediately for an order under the Domestic Proceedings and Magistrates' Courts Act. If there is only a partial breach of the mutual duties that the spouses owe each other, this may in itself give the innocent party the right to petition for divorce, judicial separation or nullity if it is sufficiently serious (for example, behaviour such that the other spouse cannot reasonably be expected to live with him or wilful refusal to consummate the marriage). If the conduct is something less than this, it may nevertheless still entitle the other to break off cohabitation completely without being in desertion (or even so as to put the defaulting spouse in constructive desertion) if it is such as to make married life together virtually impossible.[5]

C. Remedies for interference with the right to consortium

The problem to be considered here is this: if as a result of D's act one spouse (say, the husband) loses the consortium of the other, can he recover damages for this loss from D? Two situations must be examined. The first is where the husband already has a cause of action against D, either in contract or in tort, and claims that D's wrongful act has led to the loss of consortium—for example, that he has been so disfigured as the result of D's negligent car driving that his wife has left him. The second is where the husband's sole ground for complaint is that D's act has deprived him of his wife's services or society—for example, that his wife has had to spend a considerable time in hospital because of D's negligence causing her injury.

Loss of consortium due to breach of contract

If as a result of breach of a contractual duty owed by the defendant to the plaintiff, the latter loses the consortium of his spouse, he may recover for this loss by way of damages for breach of contract provided that it was likely to result from the breach and was therefore not too remote a consequence of the breach. Thus in *Jackson v Watson & Sons*,[6] where the plaintiff's wife died from food poisoning as a result of eating salmon which the defendant had sold to the plaintiff, the Court of Appeal held that he could recover for the loss of her services.

Loss of consortium due to the defendant's tort

The same principle applies if the loss of consortium is due to a tort committed by the defendant against the plaintiff, provided that the plaintiff would have had a cause of action even if his spouse had not left him and the loss is not too remote a consequence. In *Oakley v Walker*[7] the plaintiff's wife left him because of a change in his personality due to an accident caused by the defendant's negligence. It was held that, as this was a foreseeable consequence of the latter's act, the plaintiff could recover for his loss. It would seem,

[5] Eg, conduct inducing a belief that he had committed adultery. See post, p 206.
[6] [1909] 2 KB 193, CA.
[7] (1977) 121 Sol Jo 619. Cf *Lynch v Knight* (1861) 9 HL Cas 577, HL; *Lampert v Eastern National Omnibus Co Ltd* [1954] 2 All ER 719n.

however, that a husband cannot now recover if the tort is actionable only on proof of special damage and the sole injury he has suffered is the loss of his wife's consortium. Section 2 of the Administration of Justice Act 1982 provides: 'No person shall be liable in tort ... to a husband on the ground only of his having deprived him of the services or society of his wife'. Hence if a wife leaves her husband as the result of the defendant's slandering him in words not actionable per se, the Act apparently leaves him without a remedy.

Where the breakdown of the marriage has led to divorce, the Court of Appeal held in *Pritchard v J H Cobden Ltd*[8] that the husband could not throw his financial loss (for example, to pay the wife a lump sum) on to the tortfeasor. When the divorce court makes an order for financial relief, it redistributes the spouses' total assets and it is inept to use the word 'loss' in this context. Admitting the plaintiff's claim would also produce a vicious circle, for the damages would depend on the order and this in turn would depend on the husband's assets, including the damages. It could also cause procedural difficulties: if the action for damages came on first, the court would have to make an estimate of what order the divorce court would make, and if the application for financial relief were heard first, the tortfeasor could legitimately claim that he should be heard in these proceedings. Notwithstanding the force of this last point, it is submitted that a claim for additional capital expenditure should be admitted. Liability to make periodic payments (or a lump sum payment in satisfaction of future payments) clearly should not be recoverable from the defendant because the plaintiff would otherwise have had to make them out of future income and he can thus meet any claim out of compensation received for loss of future earnings. But if the divorce results in his having to provide a separate home for himself or for his former wife and children, there seems no reason why this should not be regarded as a recoverable loss provided that the cost can be quantified.

Actions by wives

As will be seen below, the husband's action largely reflected the quasi-proprietary interest he had in his wife's services at common law. This raises the question whether a wife may include a claim for damages for loss of consortium in an action for breach of contract or in tort. The House of Lords were divided on this point in *Lynch v Knight*,[9] but it is submitted that the sole question is whether loss of consortium is too remote a consequence of the defendant's breach of duty and consequently it must be immaterial whether the plaintiff is a man or woman. This was the view of Hilbery J in *Lampert v Eastern National Omnibus Co Ltd*[10] where he held that the plaintiff, who had been badly disfigured in an accident for which the defendant's

---

[8] [1988] Fam 22, [1987] 1 All ER 300, CA. The court declined to follow an earlier decision of the Court of Appeal to the opposite effect in *Jones v Jones* [1985] QB 704, [1984] 3 All ER 1003, on the ground that it did not constitute a precedent because the principle had been conceded by the defendant and was not argued before the court.

[9] (1861) 9 HL Cas 577, HL. In *Best v Samuel Fox & Co Ltd* [1952] AC 716, 732–733, [1952] 2 All ER 394, 399, HL, Lord Goddard's speech (in which Lord Oaksey and Lord Reid concurred on this point) is sufficiently wide to preclude any action by a wife for loss of consortium, but in that case the tort had been committed against the husband.

[10] [1954] 2 All ER 719n. But if the tort is not actionable per se, and the *only* damage that the wife can show is the loss of her husband's consortium quaere whether she can succeed. See further Fridman *Consortium as an 'Interest' in the Law of Torts* 32 Can Bar Rev 1065.

servant was partly to blame, could have recovered for the loss of her hus-band's consortium had she been able to prove that the disfigurement was the cause of his leaving her.[11]

Actions by cohabitants

If the sole question is one of remoteness, the same principle should apply if the plaintiff was not married to the person whose companionship he or she has lost. The need for a remedy is even stronger if the plaintiff is left unsupported as a result because he (or, more likely, she) will have no claim for maintenance against his former partner. The risk that the latter might have left the plaintiff unsupported in any event could be reflected in the damages awarded. On the other hand, such a claim, it is believed, would be a novel one and considerations of policy could lead the courts to take the view that the risk of extending the principle of cases like *Lampert v Eastern National Omnibus Co Ltd*[12] to a multitude of situations (which would not be confined to cohabiting couples) could have such far reaching and undesirable consequences that one must accept that this is another example of the special legal consequences that flow from the relationship of husband and wife. One hopes that they would not feel compelled to accept this conclusion.

Independent actions for loss of consortium

Because the husband was regarded as having a quasi-proprietary interest in the wife and her services at common law, he could obtain damages against anyone who interfered with his right. This could take the form of enticement (a tort also available to a wife),[13] harbouring the wife,[14] or adultery. The last began as the common law action for criminal conversation (or crim con) by which the husband could obtain compensation for the loss of his wife's comfort and society as the result of the adulterer's wrongful act. Crim con was abolished by the Matrimonial Causes Act of 1857 and replaced by a statutory claim for damages in the divorce court which was almost always made on a petition for divorce. In addition, if the husband lost his wife's services as the result of a tort committed against *her*, he could maintain a separate and independent action against the tortfeasor. This served a useful purpose: if, for example, the wife was seriously injured as the result of the defendant's negligence, it provided a means by which the husband could recover the expenses to which he had been put, such as for medical and nursing care, the provision of help to look after himself and the children, and visiting her whilst she was in hospital. Although a wife might be put to similar expenses if her husband was injured, the action was not available to her.[15]

After the Second World War actions for enticement were rarely brought and even the claim for damages for adultery was becoming uncommon. It

---

[11] In fact she failed because the spouses had been getting on badly together for a long time and the husband had merely used his wife's disfigurement as an excuse for leaving her.

[12] [1954] 2 All ER 719n. See further supra.

[13] *Gray v Gee* (1923) 39 TLR 429. This replaced an earlier writ of ravishment or trespass vi et armis de uxore rapta et abducta available only to the husband.

[14] This was probably obsolete before it was formally abolished: see the judgment of Devlin J in *Winchester v Fleming* [1958] 1 QB 259, [1957] 3 All ER 711.

[15] *Best v Samuel Fox & Co Ltd* [1952] AC 716, [1952] 2 All ER 394, HL.

was doubtful whether it was any longer socially desirable to give either spouse a remedy if the loss of the other's consortium was due to the latter's voluntary act, even though the defendant had induced or encouraged it. Consequently the Law Reform (Miscellaneous Provisions) Act of 1970 abolished actions for enticement and harbouring and the right to claim damages for adultery.[16] Even the action based on the defendant's tort against the wife was regarded as anachronistic, and there was no justification for refusing a similar cause of action to the wife. Bodies concerned with law reform recommended various changes in the law, including the abolition of the husband's claim.[17] It was this view which prevailed and the action was abolished by section 2 of the Administration of Justice Act 1982.[18]

This change had been made possible by the development of a much more rational approach to the problem of compensating a spouse for the loss he or she suffers as the result of a tort committed against the other. The leading decision is that of the Court of Appeal in *Cunningham v Harrison*,[19] which must be read with the judgment of a different division of the court in *Donnelly v Joyce*[20] delivered on the following day, which deals with the allied question of compensating parents for loss suffered as a result of the defendant's tortiously injuring their child. In *Cunningham v Harrison* the plaintiff was permanently paralysed in a road accident caused by the defendant's negligence. His wife looked after him at home for 15 months until her own death just before the trial. She devoted the whole of her day to him and normally had to get up in the night as well. On legal advice he entered into an agreement with her to pay her £2,000 a year for nursing him and then claimed compensation for this from the defendant. It was held that he could properly recover the value of the additional services rendered to him as a part of *his* damages: it was not necessary to create a legal obligation to pay the wife by entering into a contract with her. In the second case of *Donnelly v Joyce* the plaintiff, aged six years, sustained serious injuries to his leg as the result of the defendant's negligence. He was in hospital for three months and then had to attend daily as an out-patient. The leg required special bathing and dressing twice a day and consequently his mother gave up her job in order to be able to take him to hospital and to carry out the necessary treatment. As in the earlier case it was held that the child could recover the mother's loss of earnings as part of *his* damages.

The basis of the decision in *Donnelly v Joyce* was explained by Megaw LJ in the following words (which apply equally to the facts of *Cunningham v Harrison*):[1]

'The plaintiff's loss ... is not the expenditure of money ... to pay for the nursing attention. His loss is the existence of the need ... for those nursing services, the value of which for the purpose of damages—for the purpose of the ascertainment

---

[16] Ss 4 and 5(a) and (c). This implemented the recommendations of the Law Commission: Law Com No 25, paras 99–102.

[17] See the 11th Report of the Law Revision Committee (Loss of Services, etc) 1963, Cmnd 2017; Law Com No 56, Report on Personal Injury Litigation—Assessment of Damages 1973, paras 115–161; Report of the Royal Commission on Civil Liability and Compensation for Personal Injury (the Pearson Commission) 1978, Cmnd 7054, paras 343–351 and 445–447.

[18] For the wording, see ante, p 121.

[19] [1973] QB 942, [1973] 3 All ER 463, CA.

[20] [1974] QB 454, [1973] 3 All ER 475, CA. Followed in *Taylor v Bristol Omnibus Co Ltd* [1975] 2 All ER 1107, CA. See also *Croke v Wiseman* [1981] 3 All ER 852, CA.

[1] At 462 and 480, respectively.

of the amount of his loss—is the proper and reasonable cost of supplying those needs.'

It therefore seems immaterial who provides the services and the same principle must apply whether it is a spouse, unmarried cohabitant, parent or other relative who gives up work to look after the injured plaintiff.

If professional services are hired, the measure of damages will be their cost. The Court of Appeal, however, has not been prepared to permit damages to be recovered on the same scale when the plaintiff has been looked after by a spouse or parent. A major element in the claim in such cases is usually the loss of the latter's earnings and these can be recovered in full provided that they do not exceed the cost of hiring professional services.[2] Similarly it was held in *Donnelly v Joyce* that the plaintiff could recover the value of goods which had to be specially provided for him (in that case socks and boots) even though his parents had paid for them. In other cases the sum to be awarded is what is sufficient to enable the plaintiff to make reasonable recompense to the person concerned;[3] whilst the court must have regard to commercial rates, in practice they award substantially less to take account of the fact that the person performing the services is suffering no financial loss and is acting out of love or duty.[4] Any agreement to pay a relative for gratuitous services rendered out of love (such as that entered into in *Cunningham v Harrison*), designed to increase the damages awarded, is likely to be regarded as a sham and ignored.[5]

In *Cunningham v Harrison* it was suggested by Lord Denning MR that the plaintiff should hold any damages recovered for services rendered and expenses incurred by another on trust for that person.[6] In *Housecroft v Burnett*,[7] however, it was pointed out that this statement was *obiter* and is inconsistent with the ratio decidendi of *Donnelly v Joyce*: if the plaintiff is recovering for his own loss and does not have to show any legal obligation to reimburse the person who has provided services or goods for him, the latter has no claim for their value even though the sums involved are large.

Fatal Accidents Act

Since the decision of Lord Ellenborough CJ in *Baker v Bolton*[8] it has been the accepted rule in tort that 'the death of a human being could not be complained of as an injury'. Consequently the dependants of a person who had been killed as the result of another's negligence might be left penniless and without recourse against the tortfeasor. The problem became much more serious with the introduction of heavy machinery and the invention of the railway in the early nineteenth century. Parliament eventually ameliorated

---

[2] See eg *Donnelly v Joyce* (supra); *Daly v General Steam Navigation Co Ltd* [1980] 3 All ER 696, CA; *Housecroft v Burnett* [1986] 1 All ER 332, CA. In *Croke v Wiseman* [1981] 3 All ER 852, CA, the court took into account not only the plaintiff's mother's loss of earnings but also the loss of her pension rights. The plaintiff cannot recover more than the commercial rates on the principle of having to mitigate his loss.
[3] *Housecroft v Burnett* (supra) at 343.
[4] *Davies v Tenby Corpn* [1974] 2 Lloyd's Rep 469, at 473, 476 and 479, CA; *Housecroft v Burnett* (supra).
[5] *Housecroft v Burnett* (supra) at 343.
[6] [1973] QB 942, 952, [1973] 3 All ER 463, 469, CA.
[7] [1986] 1 All ER 332, 343, CA.
[8] (1808) 1 Camp 493. The principle was affirmed by the House of Lords in *Admiralty Comrs v SS Amerika (owners)* [1917] AC 38.

the position by passing in 1846 the Fatal Accidents Act (commonly called Lord Campbell's Act). This permitted certain dependants of a person killed as the result of the defendant's wrongful act, neglect or default to recover the financial loss suffered as a result of the death. The Act was extensively amended in the course of the next 100 years, and all the relevant statutes were repealed and their provisions consolidated in the Fatal Accidents Act of 1976. This in turn has been amended by section 3 of the Administration of Justice Act 1982.

For whose benefit the action will lie

The action will not lie on behalf of everyone who was dependent on the deceased but only on behalf of the following:[9]

(1) The deceased's wife or husband.

(2) A former wife or husband of the deceased, that is a person whose marriage to the deceased has been dissolved, annulled or declared void.

(3) Anyone who was living with the deceased in the same household immediately before the latter's death and had been so living for not less than two years as his or her wife or husband. The meaning of this expression has already been discussed.[10]

(4) A child or other descendant of the deceased.

(5) Anyone who was treated by the deceased as a child of the family in relation to *any* marriage to which the deceased was a party. The meaning of 'child of the family' will be discussed later.[11]

(6) A parent or other ascendant of the deceased.

(7) Anyone whom the deceased had treated as his parent. This is the correlative of class (5) above.

(8) The deceased's brother, sister, uncle or aunt or the issue of any of them.

In deducing any of the above relationships:

'(a) any relationship by affinity shall be treated as a relationship by consanguinity, any relationship of the half blood as a relationship of the whole blood, and the stepchild of a person as his child, and

(b) an illegitimate person shall be treated as the legitimate child of his mother and reputed father.'

It will be seen that those coming within classes (1), (2) and (5) and a child in class (4) would all have had a claim or potential claim for maintenance against the deceased had he survived. With respect to class (3) it may be assumed that, if the survivor had been financially dependent on the deceased, that dependency would have continued: this class recognises that extramarital relationships may be as firm and enduring as that of husband and wife. All the other cases consist of comparatively close relations who in certain circumstances might have received financial support from the deceased. (The only exception is class (7) which contemplates a similar de facto relationship.) If a person cannot bring himself within any of these relationships, however, he has no claim even though he was financially dependent on the deceased.

---

[9] Fatal Accidents Act 1976, s 1, as substituted by the Administration of Justice Act 1982, s 3(1).
[10] Ante, pp 7–8.
[11] Post, pp 368–369.

Thus no action will lie on behalf of an elderly friend who was being supported by the deceased.

The possibility of a vast number of claims is ruled out because, in addition to showing that he comes within one of the statutory classes, a claimant must also have suffered some pecuniary loss as a result of the death.[12] Hence, if the wife had parted from her husband before his death, she could claim nothing under the Act if she could have obtained no maintenance from him and there was no reasonable or substantial expectation of their resuming cohabitation.[13] Nor could a former spouse recover anything if a claim for financial relief had already been dismissed. If the claimant was wholly or partly dependent on the deceased before his death, pecuniary loss is obviously easy to prove as, for example, in the case of a wife who has been supported by her husband, a child supported by his parent, or an old person supported by a relative. Benefits in kind are sufficient for this purpose provided that their value is capable of being assessed.[14] But even though the deceased had made no contribution to the claimant's support before his death, an action will lie under the Act provided that the latter had a reasonable expectation of pecuniary advantage in the future if the other had survived.[15] This is particularly important in the case of a child who could have looked to the deceased to pay for his education or, conversely, of a parent who had reasonable hopes of being supported by his child in his old age.[16] In any case the financial benefit that the claimant has lost as a result of the death must derive from the relationship and must not be a mere business loss.[17]

The action must be brought by the personal representatives of the deceased on behalf of the dependants.[18]

Against whom the action may be brought

An action under the Fatal Accidents Act will lie against any person whom

---

[12] *Duckworth v Johnson* (1859) 4 H & N 653.

[13] *Davies v Taylor* [1974] AC 207, [1972] 3 All ER 836, HL. A mere speculative possibility of a reconciliation is not enough.

[14] *Berry v Humm & Co* [1915] 1 KB 627 (wife's domestic services); *Dalton v South Eastern Rly Co* (1858) 4 CBNS 296 (presents of food); *Franklin v South Eastern Rly Co* (1858) 3 H & N 211 (gratuitous performance of services by son for which claimants had been paid).

[15] There must be more than a 'mere speculative possibility of benefit' (per McCardie J in *Barnett v Cohen* [1921] 2 KB 461, 471) or a 'bare chance of receiving some slight pecuniary help' (per Stephen J in *Stimpson v Wood* (1888) 57 LJQB 484, 486).

[16] *Taff Vale Rly Co v Jenkins* [1913] AC 1, HL; *Kandalla v British Airways Board* [1981] QB 158, [1980] 1 All ER 341; *Wathen v Vernon* [1970] RTR 471, CA; Fleming [1973] CLJ 17.

[17] *Burgess v Florence Nightingale Hospital for Gentlewomen* [1955] 1 QB 349, [1955] 1 All ER 511 (no claim for loss of income due to death of plaintiff's wife who had been his professional dancing partner). Contrast *Malyon v Plummer* [1964] 1 QB 330, [1963] 2 All ER 344, CA (wife could recover for loss of value of directorship in company in which she and her deceased husband had been co-directors because her appointment was due to the relationship of husband and wife).

[18] Fatal Accidents Act 1976, s 2 (as substituted by the Administration of Justice Act 1982, s 3(1)). If there are no personal representatives or the personal representatives do not bring proceedings within six months of the death, the action may be brought by all or any of the dependants. Only one action may be brought, but if a dependant has been improperly excluded, he may have an action against the personal representatives or other plaintiffs: per Lord Atkin in *Avery v London and North Eastern Rly Co* [1938] AC 606, 613, [1938] 2 All ER 592, 595, HL.

the deceased could himself have sued in respect of the fatal injury had he not died.[19]

Assessment of damages

Generally speaking, damages are to be measured solely by reference to the material loss which the dependants have suffered as a result of the death. In particular, if an action is brought on behalf of a person who had been living with the deceased as his wife or her husband, the court is required to take into account the fact that the claimant had no enforceable right to be maintained by the deceased.[20] Damages may also be awarded for bereavement to the deceased's wife or husband or, if he was a minor who had never been married, to his parents.[1] Apart from this, however, no compensation may be claimed for wounded feelings, mental suffering or loss of love or a happy home.[2] A dependant may also recover any funeral expenses he has incurred.[3]

For the detailed way in which damages are assessed, reference should be made to textbooks on the law of torts.

Carriage by railway and air

Special statutory provisions relate to fatal accidents arising from the operation of a railway or an aircraft.[4]

D. Contract

At common law a married woman possessed no contractual capacity at all and neither she nor her husband could sue or be sued on any contract made by her except as his agent.[5] Equity did not take the same strict view, and if a wife had separate property, she could bind this by contract although she

---

[19] Hence no action will lie if the deceased had already sued for his own injuries, if he had received full compensation in his lifetime (*Read v Great Eastern Rly Co* (1868) LR 3 QB 555), or usually if his own claim was statute barred (Limitation Act 1980, ss 12(1) and 33).

[20] Fatal Accidents Act 1976, s 3(4), as substituted by the Administration of Justice Act 1982, s 3(1).

[1] Ibid, s 1A, as substituted. If the child was illegitimate, only his mother may claim. If both parents of a legitimate child claim, the sum awarded is to be divided between them equally. It is not necessary for the claimants to show that they have suffered any financial loss: see s 3(1), as substituted. Damages for bereavement are limited to £7,500: Damages for Bereavement (Variation of Sum) (England and Wales) Order 1990.

[2] *Blake v Midland Rly Co* (1852) 18 QB 93.

[3] Fatal Accidents Act 1976, s 3(5), as substituted. These may be recovered even though the claimant cannot prove financial dependency, but they must be reasonable: *Stanton v Ewart F Youldon Ltd* [1960] 1 All ER 429; *Hart v Griffith-Jones* [1948] 2 All ER 729 (claim for embalming body of child allowed but not for a monument to place over grave).

[4] See the International Transport Conventions Act 1983 and the Carriage by Air Act 1961 (as amended).

[5] See further Morrison in *A Century of Family Law* (ed Graveson and Crane) ch 6. Even if she expressly contracted as a feme sole, she was not estopped from pleading that she was a married woman for capacity cannot be created by estoppel: *Cannam v Farmer* (1849) 3 Exch 698. This rule applied even though she was engaging in trade on her own account except by custom in the City of London: *Clayton v Adams* (1796) 6 Term Rep 604, and see *La Vie v Phillips* (1765) 3 Burr 1776.

could not render herself *personally* liable on any agreement. On marriage the benefit of all contracts already made by the wife vested in the husband and both could be sued on them;[6] and any ante-nuptial contracts made between the spouses were automatically discharged.

The first statutory inroad of general application was made by the Married Women's Property Act of 1870, which enacted that a married woman's wages and earnings should be regarded as her separate property and gave her a power to maintain an action to recover them in her own name.[7] The Married Women's Property Act of 1882 (which provided that all property acquired by a wife after 1882 should remain her separate property)[8] gave her full contractual capacity and enacted that every contract entered into by her otherwise than as an agent should be deemed to be a contract with respect to her separate property and should bind it.[9] This Act also retained the principle introduced in 1874[10] that a husband should be liable for his wife's ante-nuptial debts and contracts only to the extent of property belonging to her which he acquired or to which he became entitled jure mariti. Section 1 of the Law Reform (Married Women and Tortfeasors) Act of 1935 now provides that a married woman shall be capable of rendering herself and being rendered liable in respect of any contract, debt or obligation, and of suing and being sued in contract, and also that she shall be subject to the law relating to bankruptcy and the enforcement of judgments and orders as if she were a feme sole.[11]

It is thus obvious that she now has full power to enter into a contract either with a stranger or with her own husband.[12] But the law relating to the contracts between spouses is subject to one important qualification. Whilst an agreement between them will clearly be enforceable if it represents a business arrangement, the courts are not prepared to interfere in the running of the home by giving legal effect to the sort of arrangements that spouses living together make every day in order to regularise their domestic affairs. The leading case in this field is still that of *Balfour v Balfour*[13] where the Court of Appeal held that an agreement, under which the husband, who was about to go abroad, promised to pay the wife £30 a month in consideration of her not looking to him for further maintenance, was unenforceable because

[6] Judgment was entered against both and the wife could be called upon to satisfy it if she had separate property.

[7] Ss 1 and 11. See further post, p 560. The Matrimonial Causes Act 1857, s 26, had already provided that, so long as a decree of judicial separation was in force, a married woman should be regarded as a feme sole for the purpose inter alia of the making and enforcement of contracts.

[8] See post, p 561.

[9] As amended by the Married Women's Property Act 1893. As the contract bound only a married woman's estate, she could not be made personally liable on it; consequently she could not be committed under a judgment summons (*Scott v Morley* (1887) 20 QBD 120, CA) or made bankrupt if she failed to satisfy a judgment debt unless she was carrying on trade separately from her husband (*Ex p Jones* (1879) 12 Ch D 484, CA; Married Women's Property Act 1882, s 1(5)).

[10] By the Married Women's Property Act (1870) Amendment Act 1874. This Act was passed to remedy an injustice caused by the Married Women's Property Act 1870, s 12, which entirely abolished the husband's common law liability for his wife's ante-nuptial contracts and so left her creditors without a remedy if she had no separate property.

[11] For the effects of this Act on married women's property, see post, p 562.

[12] She had power to contract with her husband under the Act of 1882: *Butler v Butler* (1885) 14 QBD 831 (Wills J); affirmed 16 QBD 374, CA.

[13] [1919] 2 KB 571, CA. See also *Spellman v Spellman* [1961] 2 All ER 498, CA (agreement as to ownership of car unenforceable).

there was no intention to enter into legal relations. If the spouses are cohabit-ing when they enter into the agreement, there is a presumption that they do not intend to be legally bound.[14] Although public policy obviously demands that the courts should not be compelled to adjudicate on matters of domestic convenience, this principle can work injustice in the situation of which *Balfour v Balfour* itself is typical, where the spouses subsequently separate and the wife takes no steps to obtain a maintenance order in reliance on her husband's promise to make her periodical payments. Consequently its application should be strictly limited. The presumption does not operate if the parties have separated or are at arm's length and about to separate: in these cir-cumstances their intention becomes a question of fact to be inferred from all the evidence.[15] In most cases of this sort, where the agreement relates to financial arrangements, it will be almost impossible to conclude that they did not intend to be legally bound by the terms.

The Act of 1935 has entirely abolished the husband's liability for his wife's contracts entered into before marriage, since he now acquires no property out of which he can meet her debts.[16] The only problem that remains is whether marriage automatically discharges executory contracts already entered into between the spouses, since the old common law rule has never been expressly abolished. In *Butler v Butler*[17] Wills J held that under the Act of 1882 the common law position still obtained. His interpretation of the relevant sections seems to be very narrow, and in any event the unambiguous wording of the 1935 Act suggests that today the spouses may mutually enforce any ante-nuptial contract notwithstanding the marriage.[18] Thus, if a man and woman enter into articles of partnership, it is scarcely credible that the contract will be automatically discharged if they later intermarry. But just as some agreements entered into by the spouses after marriage will be unenforceable because there is no intention to create legal relations, contracts of the same nature entered into beforehand may well be discharged on marriage (or even if the parties start to cohabit) by a tacit agreement because it cannot be the parties' intention that the obligations created by them should any longer be enforceable by the courts.

The wife as her husband's agent

At common law a married woman could always act as an agent since the latter does not require to have any contractual capacity. The fact that the agent happens to be the principal's spouse is clearly immaterial if the other party to the contract relies upon an express authorisation or a presumed

[14] This appears to be the view of the majority of the Court of Appeal in *Gould v Gould* [1970] 1 QB 275, [1969] 3 All ER 728. An agreement made when the spouses 'were not living together in amity' was held to be legally binding in *Re Windle* [1975] 3 All ER 987.

[15] In *Merritt v Merritt* [1970] 2 All ER 760, CA, Lord Denning MR was of the opinion that there was a presumption that they intend to be bound; Widgery LJ went no further than saying that there was no presumption that they did not intend to be bound; Karminski LJ regarded the question simply as one of fact.

[16] S 3.

[17] Supra. There was no appeal against this part of the decision and the Court of Appeal expressed no opinion on it.

[18] See Chitty *Contracts* (26th Edn) i, p 611; Kahn-Freund 15 MLR 138–140. The Court of Appeal upheld the validity of such a contract in *Re Kendrew* [1953] Ch 291, [1953] 1 All ER 551, CA, but the point was not argued and the contract was made in contemplation of marriage.

authority arising from a business relationship or a ratification by the principal of the other's acts.[19] But the relationship of husband and wife presents two particular problems: the wife's presumed agency arising from cohabitation and a particular example of agency by holding out.[20]

Presumption of agency from cohabitation

If a married woman is cohabiting with her husband, there is a presumption that she has his authority to pledge his credit for necessary goods and services which belong to those departments of the household which are normally under her control.[1] Coming within this category are such contracts as those for the purchase of food, clothing for the wife and children, domestic utensils and small articles of furniture, contracts for the hire of domestic help, contracts for repairs and probably also contracts for the education of children.

This presumption was obviously of much greater importance in times when a married woman had no contractual capacity than it is today; for as she is the person who normally makes such contracts, tradesmen would have had no remedy at all had she not been acting as her husband's agent. As it was, they had a prima facie cause of action against him if the goods supplied were necessaries. Today it may still be necessary to rely on the presumption if the wife has no property and is therefore not worth suing. In other cases the question will be whether the tradesman can properly hold the husband or the wife liable for the price of the goods (or services) supplied, for the husband cannot be made liable if the tradesman has given credit exclusively to the wife and has treated her throughout as the principal.[2] If he has in fact supplied the goods on the husband's credit, he may still rely on the presumption that the wife had her husband's authority to pledge it, and if the husband rebuts this, the wife will then be personally liable on her implied warranty of authority to bind him.[3]

The burden of proving that the goods (or services) supplied were necessaries is on the plaintiff.[4] The term 'necessaries' in this context bears the same meaning as it does in other branches of the law of contract, that is, goods (or services) which are suitable to the wife's condition of life and to her actual

[19] As in *West v Wheeler* (1849) 2 Car & Kir 714.
[20] Until 1970 the wife also had an agency of necessity: see post, p 650.
[1] *Debenham v Mellon* (1880) 6 App Cas 24, HL; *Phillipson v Hayter* (1870) LR 6 CP 38. Cf *Gregory v Parker* (1808) 1 Camp 394 (acknowledgement by the wife of a debt incurred by her in purchasing goods deemed to be an acknowledgement by the husband's agent for the purpose of the Statute of Limitations). In *Debenham v Mellon* where the spouses lived in an hotel as manager and manageress, Lord Selborne LC expressed doubts whether there was a sufficient matrimonial establishment to raise the presumption at all (at 33). Sed quaere? There is no presumption of authority after the spouses have separated and an actual authority must then be proved: *Wallis v Biddick* (1873) 22 WR 76.
[2] *Miss Gray Ltd v Cathcart* (1922) 38 TLR 562; *Callot v Nash* (1923) 39 TLR 292.
[3] For an agent's warranty of authority, see Bowstead *Agency* (15th Edn) pp 457–469; Fridman, *Agency* (5th Edn) pp 218 et seq. The fact that the goods are supplied on the order of a wife cohabiting with her husband raises no presumption of joint liability: *Morel Bros & Co Ltd v Westmorland* [1904] AC 11, HL. If a tradesman signs judgment against the wife, this amounts to an election to treat her as personally liable: ibid; contrast *C Christopher (Hove) Ltd v Williams* [1936] 3 All ER 68, CA (obtaining liberty to sign judgment against her not such a conclusive election).
[4] *Callot v Nash* (supra).

requirements at the time they are sold and delivered (or rendered).[5] Hence articles of mere luxury can never be necessaries. If the goods (or services) could be classed as necessary but are of an expensive variety, for example an expensive dress, they can be necessaries only if they are not extravagant when tested against the husband's ostensible standard of living and that which he permitted his wife to adopt;[6] and if they were extravagant by this test[7] or if the wife is already adequately supplied with goods of this kind,[8] the action against the husband must fail.

As McCardie J emphasised in *Miss Gray Ltd v Cathcart*,[9] this presumption is rebuttable. In addition to proving that the contract was not one for necessaries or of a sort which one could expect the husband to have given his wife authority to make, the husband may rebut it in any one of three different ways:

(1) By showing that he had already forbidden the plaintiff to give the wife credit.[10]

(2) By proving that he had forbidden his wife to pledge his credit. After considerable judicial controversy it was finally settled by the House of Lords in *Debenham v Mellon*[11] that such a prohibition is effective even though the plaintiff was unaware of it, although of course in such a case the husband may be liable by holding out.[12]

(3) By showing that the wife had an adequate allowance out of which she could herself have paid for the goods or services.[13] In fact the payment of a *fixed* sum (whether it is adequate or not) will usually carry with it an implied prohibition against pledging the husband's credit further and thus defeat the plaintiff.[14] Whether the presumption is raised if the wife has an adequate income of her own, so that she has no need to rely on her husband for money to buy necessaries, is more doubtful; in the absence of an agreement between the spouses that the wife alone shall be liable for necessaries bought by herself (which will of course have the effect of an implied prohibition),[15] the question must be regarded as an open one, but it would probably be more in keeping with modern social opinion to hold that the wife was contracting as principal, at least if the goods were for her own use.[16]

---

[5] Cf the Sale of Goods Act 1979, s 3(3), and see Cheshire, Fifoot and Furmston *Contract* (12th Edn) pp 428–430.

[6] *Morgan v Chetwynd* (1865) 4 F & F 451; *Phillipson v Hayter* (1870) LR 6 CP 38; *Seymour v Kingscote* (1922) 38 TLR 586.

[7] *Miss Gray Ltd v Cathcart* (infra).

[8] *Reneaux v Teakle* (1853) 8 Exch 680; *Miss Gray Ltd v Cathcart* (infra).

[9] (1922) 38 TLR 562.

[10] *Miss Gray Ltd v Cathcart* (supra).

[11] (1880) 6 App Cas 24, HL, following *Jolly v Rees* (1864) 15 CBNS 628.

[12] See infra.

[13] Even though the plaintiff was unaware of this: *Morel Bros & Co Ltd v Westmorland* [1904] AC 11, HL; *Slater v Parker* (1908) 24 TLR 621.

[14] *Remmington v Broadwood* (1902) 18 TLR 270, CA; *Miss Gray Ltd v Cathcart* (supra). The question whether a mere agreement to pay a fixed allowance would have the same effect was left open in *Remmington v Broadwood*. If the husband opens an account on which he permits the wife to draw, this will not amount to an implied prohibition against pledging his credit if the arrangement is merely for his own convenience: *Goodyear v Part* (1897) 13 TLR 395.

[15] See *Seymour v Kingscote* (1922) 38 TLR 586 at 587–588.

[16] Her income was stated to be immaterial in *Callot v Nash* (1923) 39 TLR 292, 293, and *Seymour v Kingscote* (supra), at 587. In *Biberfeld v Berens* [1952] 2 QB 770, 782, [1952] 2 All ER 237, 243, CA, these dicta were criticised by Denning LJ but that case was concerned with the wife's agency of necessity (based on the husband's duty to maintain her) where the principle involved

Agency by estoppel

If a husband has in the past paid for goods supplied by his wife in such circumstances as to lead the tradesman with whom she has been dealing to conclude that he has given her an authority to buy goods on his credit, he will then be estopped from denying that she had any such authority and will consequently be liable for any further goods sold to her by that particular tradesman.[17] The importance of this rule lies in the fact that the husband's merely forbidding his wife to pledge his credit will not relieve him of liability for debts contracted by her if he has held her out in the past to have such an authority and does not inform those tradesmen with whom she has been dealing that it has been revoked.[18]

What will amount to a sufficient holding out for this purpose must necessarily depend upon the facts of each case. Repeated paying of bills will doubtless create an estoppel, as may taking an active part in selecting the goods and directing the performance of the contract.[19] But a husband does not hold out his wife as having authority to pledge his credit merely by accompanying her when she shops,[20] or by giving her a cheque to pay her debts;[1] nor does his having paid for goods delivered to the matrimonial home in the past make him liable to pay for those subsequently ordered by his wife to be sent elsewhere.[2]

Presumably the general law of agency will apply in the case of contracts made by the wife after the husband's death so that his personal representatives will not be estopped from denying the wife's power to render the estate liable.[3] Whilst the general rule is that an agency is terminated by the principal's insanity (whether or not the agent or person dealing with him was aware of this fact), it was held by the Court of Appeal in *Drew v Nunn*[4] that a husband who had held out his wife as having his authority remained liable to a tradesman who had supplied her with goods in ignorance of his insanity.

Cohabitants

The old common law rules relating to the wife's contractual incapacity, the husband's liability for her debts contracted before marriage, and the discharge of contracts made between the spouses before marriage obviously never applied between cohabiting couples who were not married to each other. Cohabitation, however, may be relevant in the law of contract in three ways.

First, if an agreement between spouses were to be held to be a mere domestic arrangement giving rise to no intention to be legally bound, as in

---

was essentially different. On agency arising from cohabitation generally, see Bowstead *Agency* (15th Edn) pp 121–125.

[17] *Drew v Nunn* (1879) 4 QBD 661, CA; *Filmer v Lynn* (1835) 1 Har & W 59.

[18] See *Debenham v Mellon* (1880) 6 App Cas 24, HL, at 34, 36–37. Similarly he may be estopped from denying her authority even after they have ceased to live together: *Wallis v Biddick* (1873) 22 WR 76, 77.

[19] *Jetley v Hill* (1884) Cab & El 239 (contract for the supply of furniture and for the decoration of the matrimonial home).

[20] *Seymour v Kingscote* (1922) 38 TLR 586, 588; *Callott v Nash* (1923) 39 TLR 292, 294.

[1] *Durrant v Holdsworth* (1886) 2 TLR 763.

[2] *Swan & Edgar Ltd v Mathieson* (1910) 103 LT 832.

[3] Cf *Blades v Free* (1829) 9 B & C 167.

[4] (1879) 4 QBD 661, CA. Hanbury *Agency* (2nd Edn) p 37 submits that this result, though practically convenient, is inconsistent; Powell *Agency* (2nd Edn) pp 403–404 doubts the correctness of the case but admits that sometimes it may work justice.

Balfour v Balfour[5] a similar agreement made between a cohabiting couple would presumably be equally unenforceable. Secondly, the presumption of agency arising from cohabitation applies when a woman is living with a man as his wife even though they are not married to each other. The cases suggest that this principle may operate only if they hold themselves out as married,[6] and the presumption will not apply, of course, once they separate.[7] Finally, as agency by estoppel arises from one person's having held out another as having his authority to enter into contracts on his behalf, it can arise whether the parties are married or not.[8]

E. Torts

The fiction of legal unity produced two separate rules in tort:

(1) If a tort was committed by or against a married woman, her husband had to be joined as a party to the action and failure to do so could be pleaded in abatement.

(2) No liability in tort could arise between spouses and no action in tort could be brought by either of them against the other.

We must now consider how far these rules still apply.

Torts committed by or against the wife

At common law the husband had to be joined as a party to any action brought by or against the wife in respect of any tort whether committed before or after marriage.[9] A married woman was given the power to maintain an action in her own name to recover her separate property by the Married Women's Property Act of 1870[10] and a full power to sue in respect of any tort committed against her by the Married Women's Property Act of 1882.[11] As in the case of contract, the Acts of 1874 and 1882 limited the husband's liability for her ante-nuptial torts to the extent of her property which he acquired or became entitled to,[12] but, whilst the latter Act made the wife personally liable for all her torts, neither Act affected his liability for torts committed by her during marriage.[13] The retention of the common law rule

---

[5] Ante, p 128.
[6] *Munro v De Chemant* (1815) 4 Camp 215; *Blades v Free* (1829) 9 B & C 167. But in *Watson v Threlkeld* (1798) 2 Esp 637, it was held that the tradesman could recover even though he was aware of all the facts, and in *Debenham v Mellon* (1880) 6 App Cas 24, 33, HL, Lord Selborne LC stated obiter that the presumption arises if the woman lives with the man whether or not she assumes the name of his wife.
[7] *Munro v De Chemant* (supra). A fortiori the presumption will not arise if they have never cohabited at all even though the man permits the woman to use his name: *Gomme v Franklin* (1859) 1 F & F 465.
[8] *Ryan v Sams* (1848) 12 QB 460.
[9] If the wife died before judgment, the action abated; if the husband died, the cause of action survived against the widow or for her benefit. There was no liability for a tort committed by the wife *during marriage* if the cause of action was substantially contractual: *Liverpool Adelphi Loan Association v Fairhurst* (1854) 9 Exch 422; *Edwards v Porter* [1925] AC 1, HL (obtaining loans by fraud). Cf the law relating to minors' contracts.
[10] S 11.
[11] See now the Law Reform (Married Women and Tortfeasors) Act 1935, s 1(c).
[12] See ante, p 128. His liability for ante-nuptial torts was not affected by the Act of 1870 at all.
[13] *Edwards v Porter* (supra).

may have been justified in 1882, because few married women then would have had any property on which a successful plaintiff could execute judgment, but the passage of years rendered absurd the anomaly that the husband could be sued for her torts although he acquired none of her property jure mariti.[14] This was eventually removed by the Law Reform (Married Women and Tortfeasors) Act 1935, which has abolished his liability *as husband* for all her torts whenever committed.[15] But he may of course still be vicariously liable on other grounds, for example because he has authorised the commission of the particular act or because his wife was his servant acting in the course of her employment.

Actions between spouses

After the passing of the Married Women's Property Act of 1870 a wife could maintain an action to recover her separate property against her husband,[16] but with this and one other[17] exception no action could be brought in tort between spouses. This produced both anomalies and injustice. It was anomalous that a husband could not sue his wife for damage to his property, however maliciously caused, or that, even though the spouses were living at arm's length, one could slander the other with impunity. It was unjust that third parties' rights could be affected if the tortfeasor and his victim happened to be married to each other. For example, if the driver of a motor car negligently injured his wife, his insurance company was relieved from its duty to compensate her, for the husband was under no liability; for the same reason, if the wife was injured as the result of the combined negligence of her husband and a third person, the latter had to bear the whole loss and could claim no contribution from the other.[18]

This situation has been remedied by section 1 of the Law Reform (Husband and Wife) Act 1962,[19] which provides that each spouse shall have the same right of action against the other in tort as though they were not married. This applies equally to an action brought after the marriage has been dissolved (or presumably annulled) in respect of a tort committed during matrimony,[20] but in one respect the law here is different, for if the action is brought during the subsistence of the marriage, the court has a discretion to stay the action in two cases. First, it may do so if it appears that no substantial benefit would accrue to either party from the continuation of the proceedings. This is designed to prevent trivial actions brought in bitterness to air matrimonial grievances;[1] consequently it is not contemplated that the power would be exercised if the parties were no longer living together as an economic unit

---

[14] See the observations of Swift J in *Newton v Hardy* (1933) 149 LT 165, 168 (an enticement case and therefore more absurd than most).

[15] S 3.

[16] S 11. Re-enacted in principle by the Married Women's Property Act 1882, s 12, and the Law Reform (Married Women and Tortfeasors) Act 1935, s 1.

[17] Under s 26 of the Matrimonial Causes Act 1857 either spouse could sue the other in tort if a judicial separation was in force.

[18] *Drinkwater v Kimber* [1952] 2 QB 281, [1952] 1 All ER 701, CA. But a master was vicariously liable if a servant in the course of employment tortiously injured his or her spouse: *Broom v Morgan* [1953] 1 QB 597, [1953] 1 All ER 849, CA.

[19] Passed as a result of the Ninth Report of the Law Reform Committee 1961, Cmnd 1268. See Stone, 24 MLR 481; Kahn-Freund 25 MLR 695.

[20] S 3(3).

[1] See Cmnd 1268, paras 10–13.

and the damage was real, or if the spouse was a purely nominal defendant and the real purpose of the action was to recover damages from a source outside the family. Such would be the case, for example, if the driver of a car wished to claim an indemnity from his insurance company.[2] Secondly, the court may stay the action if it relates to property and the questions in issue could more conveniently be disposed of by an application under section 17 of the Married Women's Property Act 1882. As we shall see,[3] the court has much more extensive powers under that section than it has in a common law action in tort. Consequently if the case raises complex questions of the spouses' rights in matrimonial assets or if a just solution is likely to demand an order for the sale or division of property, it is submitted that it should be dealt with under section 17.[4] On the other hand, if there is no dispute over title and damages or an injunction is the appropriate remedy, the case should proceed as an action in tort.

It must be remembered that, quite apart from the provisions of section 17 of the Married Women's Property Act, other proceedings are also open to a husband or wife in respect of a tortious act committed by the other. In practice these are most important in the case of molestation and interference with the right to occupy the matrimonial home and are considered more fully elsewhere in this book.[5]

Rationale of the present law

Whatever the theoretical basis of the old law may have been, any privileges that still exist can now be justified only on the ground of public policy. It is clear from the decision of the Court of Appeal in *Midland Bank Trust Co Ltd v Green (No 3)*[6] that the doctrine of unity no longer has any place in the law of tort. The plaintiff sued his parents for damages for conspiracy to defraud him; the defence relied on the argument that, as the doctrine of unity apparently prevented the spouses from being prosecuted alone for criminal conspiracy,[7] the same principle must apply to the tort (although it was accepted that they could both be sued for conspiring together with a third person). The court held that the doctrine had no place in the tort of conspiracy and refused to apply what Oliver J described at first instance as 'the primitive and inaccurate maxim that spouses are one person'.[8] Whatever immunity exists must be based on public policy and there is no overriding principle

---

[2] For presumably the court would look at all the facts and not stay the action merely because no substantial benefit would arise from the defendant's satisfying the judgment. But suppose the wife were to be injured by her husband and a third person and the latter were to claim contribution from the husband who was not insured. Could the husband then argue that an action between the spouses would have been stayed on the ground that no substantial benefit would accrue to either of them and that consequently he cannot be made to contribute because he is not a person 'whose liability could be established in an action brought against him' for the purpose of the Civil Liability (Contribution) Act 1978, s 1?

[3] Post, p 568.

[4] See Cmnd 1268, para 14. In an action for damages the court may exercise any power that it has under s 17 or direct that any question should be dealt with under that section: Law Reform (Husband and Wife) Act 1962, s 1(2).

[5] See post, pp 160 et seq.

[6] [1982] Ch 529, [1981] 3 All ER 744, CA, affirming [1979] Ch 496, [1979] 2 All ER 193 (Oliver J). By the time the case came to trial all three parties had died and the action was carried on by and against their personal representatives.

[7] See post, p 138.

[8] At 525 and 218, respectively.

protecting spouses from liability for injury which, acting in concert, they have deliberately inflicted on the plaintiff.

The same approach can be seen in two nineteenth century cases of libel. In *Wenman v Ash*[9] it was held that the publication by the defendant to the plaintiff's spouse of a statement defamatory of the plaintiff is actionable. In *Wennhak v Morgan*[10] on the other hand communication by one spouse to the other of a statement defamatory of a third person was held not to constitute a publication of that statement for the purpose of the law of libel and slander.[11] The second case reflects the principle that communications between spouses should be privileged; in *Wenman v Ash*, however, there was no reason why the normal rule should not apply: indeed publication of a defamatory statement to the spouse of the person defamed may do him a greater injury than publication to a stranger.

F. Criminal law

The doctrine of unity has never applied generally in the criminal law so as to make a husband vicariously liable for his wife's crimes or to prevent either of them from being liable in most cases for a crime committed against the other. But it has made a number of periodical and inconsistent appearances which must be considered seriatim.

Marital coercion

There was a rule of common law that if a married woman committed certain offences in the presence of her husband, this raised a presumption (which was rebuttable)[12] that she had committed the crime under his coercion and consequently he and not she was prima facie liable to be convicted. Both the origin[13] and the extent of this rule are uncertain, but it seems to have applied to all misdemeanours[14] and most felonies, but not to grave felonies such as murder or to treason.[15] It had in any event become anomalous by the twentieth century and it was finally abolished by section 47 of the Criminal Justice Act of 1925 which replaced it by the following statutory defence:

'On a charge against a wife for any offence other than treason or murder it shall be a good defence to prove that the offence was committed in the presence of, and under the coercion of, the husband.'

It will be observed that this section effects two changes in the law. First,

[9] (1853) 13 CB 836. See also *Theaker v Richardson* [1962] 1 All ER 229, CA (letter addressed to the plaintiff and opened by her husband held to be actionable).
[10] (1888) 20 QBD 635.
[11] Huddleston B and Manisty J both agreed that publication was precluded by the doctrine of unity. Manisty J alone rested his decision on the further ground of public policy.
[12] *R v Smith* (1916) 12 Cr App Rep 42, CCA; *R v Torpey* (1871) 12 Cox CC 45.
[13] Stephen saw in it a method of circumventing the rule that a woman could not plead benefit of clergy: *History of Criminal Law*, ii, 105. Turner thought it more likely that it originated at a time when the wife was considered to have no will of her own and was entirely sub virga viri sui: Kenny *Criminal Law* (19th Edn) p 69.
[14] *R v Torpey* (supra). *R v Smith* (supra) was also a case of a misdemeanour. For the contrary view, see *R v Cruse* (1838) 8 C & P 541.
[15] Kenny op cit, p 68.

the burden of proof is now upon the wife to prove the coercion; secondly, it would seem to apply to all offences, both indictable and summary, except for the two named. It is not clear, however, what is meant by 'coercion' in this context. It presumably means something more than a threat of physical violence, which is a defence available to anyone charged with a criminal offence except murder and, perhaps, treason. It will probably be sufficient for the wife to show that her will was overborne either by her husband's conduct (for example, a threat to keep her or their children short of money) or merely by his dominating personality.[16]

This defence must be strictly construed. Hence it is not available to a woman living with a man as his wife if they are not in fact married to each other[17] or to a woman who mistakenly believes that she is married to the man applying coercion.[18]

Impeding a spouse's arrest

The generally accepted view is that at common law a wife could not become an accessory after the fact to her husband's felony or a principal to his treason by receiving him, because she was bound in law to do so.[19] The offence of being an accessory after the fact to a felony has now been abolished,[20] but by section 4 of the Criminal Law Act 1967 it is now an offence for any person, knowing or believing that another has committed an arrestable offence, to do any act with intent to impede his arrest or prosecution without lawful authority or reasonable excuse. It is arguable that the old law relating to accessories survives to give a wife a lawful authority for harbouring her husband or, alternatively, that either spouse (and, perhaps, an unmarried cohabitant) now has a reasonable excuse for harbouring the other by virtue of their marital relationship. But even under the old law the courts were apparently reluctant to permit the wife to raise the defence and they are

---

[16] *R v Pierce* (1941) 5 JCL 124; *R v Richman* [1982] Crim LR 507. See further Williams *Criminal Law: The General Part* (2nd Edn) p 249; Smith and Hogan *Criminal Law* (6th Edn) pp 238–240; Edwards *Compulsion, Coercion and Criminal Responsibility* 14 MLR 297. The Law Commission has recommended that a wife (like anyone else) should be able to rely only on duress and that consequently the defence of marital coercion should be abolished: Law Com No 83, paras 3.1–3.9.

[17] *R v Court* (1912) 7 Cr App Rep 127, CCA.

[18] *R v Ditta* [1988] Crim LR 43, CA. The court also questioned obiter whether a wife could raise the defence if the marriage was polygamous. Removing her immunity on this ground would be inconsistent with the general recognition of polygamous marriages in this country (see ante, p 61), and some women coming from countries where polygamy is practised are more likely to be coerced by their husbands than those born here.

[19] But in *R v Holley* [1963] 1 All ER 106, CCA, the Court of Criminal Appeal were of the opinion that the rule was merely a particular application of the rule of marital coercion and had therefore been abolished by the Criminal Justice Act 1925, s 47 (supra), in the absence of actual coercion. Sed quaere? In *R v Holley* the actual decision was that, if a wife assisted her husband and another together, she might be an accessory after the fact to the *latter's* felony. It was also formerly said that a wife could not be an accessory after the fact by concealing a felon jointly with her husband. Curiously enough, the husband was not bound to shelter his wife and might therefore by so doing become an accessory after the fact to her felony.

[20] By s 1 of the Criminal Law Act 1967 which abolished the distinction between felonies and misdemeanours and enacted that the law relating to misdemeanours should apply to all indictable offences.

probably even less likely to let either spouse do so under the new statutory provision.[1]

Conspiracy

It is now provided by statute that a husband and wife may not be convicted of conspiring together, and it is generally believed that this was the position at common law.[2] But this does not prevent them from being convicted of conspiring with the other and a third person.[3]

Theft

Under the doctrine of unity husband and wife were deemed to have unity of possession so that neither could be guilty of stealing the other's property. But once the concept of separate property had been extended by the Married Women's Property Act of 1882, it was obvious that the fiction once more worked an anomaly. Accordingly the Act modified the rule by providing, broadly speaking, that either could be guilty of stealing the other's property if they were not living together.[4] This effected a compromise between the rule of public policy which militates against criminal proceedings being instituted by one spouse against the other and the desirability of protecting interests in property by the sanctions of the criminal law.

These provisions have been repealed by the Theft Act 1968 which has produced a different sort of compromise. For the purposes of that Act and the Theft Act 1978 a husband and wife are to be regarded as separate persons and each can now be convicted of theft of the other's property, obtaining it be deception and so forth.[5] But neither the spouse nor a third person may institute proceedings against anyone for any offence of stealing or doing unlawful damage to property which at the time belongs to the accused's spouse, or for any attempt, incitement or conspiracy to commit such an offence, without the consent of the Director of Public Prosecutions. The purpose of this provision is to reduce the risk of a prosecution which might prejudice a continuation of married life. Consequently there are two exceptions where such a risk is minimal. The Director's consent is not required, first, if at the time of the offence the accused and his or her spouse were not bound to cohabit by virtue of a judicial decree or order[6] or, secondly, if the accused is charged with committing the offence jointly with the spouse.[7] The second exception is ambiguous. At first sight it seems to apply if, say, the wife pawned property belonging to her and the spouses then jointly took it back without the pawnbroker's consent. The difficulty inherent in this

---

[1] See *R v Holley* (supra). In any event the offence may be prosecuted only with the consent of the Director of Public Prosecutions: Criminal Law Act 1967, s 4(4). See further Pace *Impeding Arrest* [1978] Crim LR 82.

[2] Criminal Law Act 1977, s 2(2)(a); *Mawji v R* [1957] AC 126, [1957] 1 All ER 385, PC. But see Williams *Legal Unity of Husband and Wife* 10 MLR 20–24. Either spouse may be convicted of inciting the other to commit a crime.

[3] *R v Chrastny* [1992] 1 All ER 189, CA.

[4] Married Women's Property Act 1882, s 12, later replaced by the Larceny Act 1916, s 36.

[5] Theft Act 1968, s 30(1); Theft Act 1978, s 5(2). Either of them can also be guilty of the theft of property belonging to them both jointly.

[6] This includes an injunction restraining one spouse from molesting the other and debarring him from the matrimonial home: *Woodley v Woodley* [1978] Crim LR 629.

[7] Theft Act 1968, s 30(4).

interpretation of the proviso is that for the purpose of the Theft Act the property would be regarded as belonging to the pawnbroker and the policy underlying the Act does not require consent in this situation. An alternative interpretation is that it applies if two persons, A and B, jointly steal or damage the property of A's spouse, in which case apparently consent would not have to be obtained to prosecute B, although it would still be required to prosecute A. As B is outside the ambit of the section anyway, this makes the proviso redundant.[8]

Institution of proceedings

Save in the cases just noticed either spouse now has the same power to institute criminal proceedings against the other as though they were not married.[9]

G. Citizenship and the right to live in the United Kingdom

Although at first sight the question of citizenship appears to have little to do with family law, in fact it has close connections with it for a number of reasons. In the first place, a person's right of abode in the United Kingdom may be valueless to him if other members of his family do not share it and, as we shall see, the *right* to live in this country is now virtually confined to British citizens. In turn the acquisition of British citizenship depends in most cases upon the possession of such citizenship by at least one parent. Finally, the rules relating to the naturalisation of the spouse of a British citizen are less stringent than those relating to the naturalisation of other persons.

British citizenship

Since the Second World War the concept of British nationality has been radically changed. The emergence of independent countries within the Commonwealth led to a demand that each should determine locally who would qualify for its own citizenship, possession of which would give the holder British nationality and thus the right to live in the United Kingdom. In accordance with this policy the British Nationality Act of 1948 created the new status of Citizen of the United Kingdom and Colonies. Within little more than a decade of the passing of this Act, however, the problems presented by the large scale immigration of Commonwealth citizens into this country led to statutory controls, with the result that citizens of independent Commonwealth countries and many citizens of the United Kingdom and Colonies ceased to have an automatic right to enter and stay in this country. The latest Act, the Immigration Act 1971, in its original form, provided that the right of abode in this country was to be confined to those citizens of the United Kingdom and Colonies who satisfied certain conditions together with

---

[8] See further Smith *Law of Theft* (6th Edn) paras 464–468. An offence of theft would include robbery. The subsection does not prevent the arrest of the thief except by his or her spouse or on an information laid by the spouse: ibid, s 30(5) (added by the Criminal Jurisdiction Act 1975, Sch 5).
[9] Theft Act 1968, s 30(2).

women who were Commonwealth citizens and were or had been married to men with a right of abode.[10]

The resulting confusion between citizenship and the right of abode caused misunderstanding and endless difficulties. One of the chief objects of the British Nationality Act of 1981 was to bring the two concepts back into line. Consequently it has created three new categories of citizens: British citizens, British Dependent Territories citizens and British Overseas citizens. Qualification for British citizenship resembles qualification for the right of abode under the Immigration Act although there are significant differences between them. A British Dependent Territories citizen is one who has similar links with a Dependent Territory. Anyone who was a citizen of the United Kingdom and Colonies when the Act came into force (1st January 1983) and did not become a British citizen or a British Dependent Territories citizen became a British Overseas citizen.[11]

A citizen of the United Kingdom and Colonies who had the right of abode in this country at the commencement of the British Nationality Act 1981 automatically became a British citizen.[12] There were also complex transitional provisions enabling persons to be registered as British citizens if they were in the process of acquiring citizenship of the United Kingdom and Colonies by residence or would have been entitled to register as such citizens with the right of abode in this country.[13] There are five ways in which a person can now acquire British citizenship: by birth, adoption, descent, registration and naturalisation.

Birth

The Act has made a fundamental departure from the common law rule that birth in this country automatically confers British nationality. Now a person will be a British citizen by virtue of birth here only if one of his parents (or, if he is illegitimate, his mother) is at the time a British citizen or settled in this country, that is ordinarily resident in the United Kingdom without being in breach of the immigration laws or subject to any restriction on the period for which he or she may remain.[14] If a person born here is not a British citizen

[10] For details see the sixth edition of this book at pp 162–163. In one exceptional case a Commonwealth citizen, who was not a citizen of the United Kingdom and Colonies, could acquire a right of abode. As originally enacted, the Immigration Act used the word 'patrial' to describe those with the right of abode. This term is not used in the British Nationality Act.

[11] For details of British Dependent Territories citizenship and British Overseas citizenship, see the British Nationality Act 1981, Pts II and III and Sch 6 (which lists the Dependent Territories). See also the British Nationality (Falkland Islands) Act 1983. A residual category of British subjects without citizenship is retained by Pt IV. For a critical discussion of the Act generally, see Blake 45 MLR 179.

[12] S 11(1). There is an exception of very limited application to some persons born stateless contained in s 11(2), and s 11(3) extends citizenship to a very small number of people born in other Commonwealth countries.

[13] See ss 7–10.

[14] Ss 1(1) and 50(2)–(5), (9). He will not be regarded as settled, however, if he has been specially exempt from the immigration laws or his exemption flows from his being a member of a Commonwealth or foreign force or, generally speaking, of a diplomatic mission. A newly born infant found abandoned in this country will be presumed to be a British citizen unless the contrary is shown: s 1(2). A posthumous legitimate child will be a British citizen if his father had such citizenship or was settled at his death: s 48. The new law is bound to give rise to considerable difficulties; for example, the question whether a parent was settled may be raised many years after his death. See Blake loc cit, pp 184–187.

at birth, he is entitled to be registered as one during his minority if either of his parents (or his mother if he is illegitimate) becomes a British citizen or settled in this country.[15]

There is an obvious danger that these rules, taken alone, will increase the number of stateless people, because there is no guarantee that other children born in this country will acquire their parents' nationality. There are other provisions in the Act designed to reduce statelessness but they are of limited application.[16] Consequently it is further provided that any other person born in this country may be registered as a British citizen if during each of the first ten years of his life he was not absent from the United Kingdom for more than 90 days.[17] This is aimed at limiting the extension to children who can be said to have a real link with this country and who have not spent a substantial part of their early childhood in, for example, their parents' homeland.

Adoption

A minor (of whatever nationality) adopted by an order made by a court in the United Kingdom will become a British citizen if one of the adopters is a British citizen.[18]

Descent

At common law children not born within British territory acquired British nationality only in very limited circumstances (for example, if they were the children of a British ambassador).[19] Legislation during the eighteenth century conferred the status of a British subject on anyone born abroad whose father or paternal grandfather was a natural-born British subject.[20] The Naturalization Act of 1870 extended British nationality to the children of naturalised subjects provided that they resided in this country during their minority,[1] and the same Act also provided that, if his parents lost British nationality by naturalisation in a foreign country, a minor residing in that country would also lose his British nationality.[2] These rules were considerably modified by the British Nationality and Status of Aliens Acts and again underwent complete revision in the British Nationality Act of 1948. Under that Act a legitimate child born outside the United Kingdom and Colonies would generally be a citizen thereof only if his father was such a citizen otherwise than by descent. Save in exceptional circumstances citizenship was

---

[15] S 1(3).

[16] See Sch 2.

[17] S 1(4). In special circumstances the Secretary of State may permit registration even though the applicant has been absent for more than 90 days in any one or more years: s 1(7).

[18] S 1(5). He will retain British citizenship even though the adoption order ceases to have effect for any reason: s 1(6).

[19] Jones *British Nationality* (1947 Edn) pp 34 et seq.

[20] Foreign Protestants (Naturalization) Act 1708; British Nationality Acts 1730 and 1772. See Jones op cit, pp 69–72. Another remarkable example of nationality by descent is to be found in the provisions of 4 Anne, c 16, 1705 (now repealed), under which all the issue of Princess Sophia, the mother of King George I, other than Roman Catholics, who were born before 1949, are British subjects: *A-G v Prince Ernest Augustus of Hanover* [1957] AC 436, [1957] 1 All ER 49, HL.

[1] S 10(5). See Jones op cit, 101–103.

[2] S 10(3).

thus conferred only on the first generation born abroad and not on two generations, as it was under the earlier Acts, but it was possible to transmit citizenship for another generation by registering the birth at a United Kingdom consulate.[3]

Under the British Nationality Act of 1981 a person born outside the United Kingdom is a British citizen if at the time of his birth either of his parents (or his mother, if he is illegitimate) is a British citizen otherwise than by descent or is a British citizen in service under the Crown or a European Community institution or in some similar designated service.[4] This has had the effect of considerably reducing the number of children to whom citizenship by descent can be transmitted for two generations; on the other hand it has extended the ability to transmit it for one generation to illegitimate children and to legitimate children claiming through one parent only.

The severity of the new law has been partly mitigated by two provisions designed to protect a child of a citizen by descent with a substantial connection with this country. First, if the latter was in the United Kingdom during some period of three years preceding the child's birth and one of the parent's own parents was a British citizen otherwise than by descent, the child is entitled to be registered as a British citizen within twelve months of his birth, even though this event occurred abroad.[5] (It will be seen that this limits transmission by this means to the second generation.) Secondly, if either parent is a citizen by descent and the child and *both* his parents have been in the United Kingdom for three years since his birth, he may be registered as a British citizen provided that he is still a minor and both his parents consent.[6]

Registration

One further case of acquisition of citizenship by registration should be noted. Any British Dependent Territories citizen, British Overseas citizen, British subject under the Act,[7] or British protected person, who has been in the United Kingdom for five years, is entitled to be registered as a British citizen provided that he was not in breach of the immigration laws during any part of that period and that during the last twelve months he was not subject at any time under those laws to any restriction on the period for which he might remain in this country.[8]

[3] For details, see the sixth edition of this book, p 333.

[4] Ss 2 (qv for further details) and 50(9). For the full definition of 'citizen by descent', see s 14, and for the position of posthumous children, see s 48. See also the transitional provisions in s 9 and Sch 8, para 3.

[5] S 3(2), (3). Absences totalling no more than 270 days during the period of three years are to be disregarded. In special circumstances the Secretary of State may accept an application for registration up to six years after the child's birth: s 3(4).

[6] S 3(5), (6). Absences totalling not more than 270 days are to be disregarded in each case. Only one parent need satisfy these conditions if the other has died or their marriage has been terminated or they are legally separated. If the child is illegitimate, his mother must satisfy them.

[7] See ss 30–32. The main categories are British subjects without citizenship and certain citizens of Eire who are also British subjects. See also the Hong Kong Act 1985, Sch, para 2, and the Hong Kong (British Nationality) Order, SI 1986/948, which confer the status of British National (Overseas) on certain persons who are British Dependent Territories citizens by virtue of their connection with Hong Kong.

[8] S 4(1)–(4), as amended by the Hong Kong (British Nationality) Order 1986. Absences totalling not more than 450 days in all and not more than 90 days in the last twelve months are to be disregarded. The Secretary of State has power to waive any of the conditions. For British subjects without citizenship, see Pt IV of the Act. There is a discretionary power to register

Naturalisation: British citizens' spouses

A general discretionary power to naturalise any applicant of full age and capacity who satisfies the statutory conditions is preserved by the Act.[9] Naturalisation of a parent does not confer citizenship on his children but the Secretary of State has a general discretionary power to register any minor as a British citizen in these circumstances.[10]

The position of a British citizen's spouse requires fuller consideration. Strangely enough, the doctrine of unity had no application at common law with respect to nationality. A foreign woman did not acquire British nationality by marrying a British subject, and a woman who was a British subject did not lose her status by marrying a foreigner.[11] Although this rule was completely reversed by legislation during the nineteenth century,[12] a series of statutes passed since 1914 reflected the change in status of married women by reverting to the common law principles.[13]

Whilst this meant that a woman who was not a citizen of the United Kingdom and Colonies did not become such a citizen by marrying a man who possessed citizenship, she was nevertheless entitled to acquire it by registration.[14] One of the more radical changes made by the British Nationality Act of 1981 was the removal of this entitlement. At the same time it has put both husbands and wives of citizens on the same footing. Now, if a man (or woman), who is not a British citizen, marries a citizen and wishes to acquire citizenship himself, he must apply for naturalisation unless he qualifies to be registered as a citizen in one of the ways already considered. The conditions for naturalisation that have to be fulfilled by the spouse of a British citizen, however, are less stringent than those imposed on others: in particular he (or she) need have been in the United Kingdom for only three years (and not five years) and does not have to have any knowledge of English, Welsh or Scottish Gaelic. He must be of good character and not subject to any restriction under the immigration laws on the period for which he may remain here.[15] It will be appreciated, however, that acquisition of

---

any British Dependent Territories citizen etc as a British citizen if he has been in Crown or similar service: see s 4(5), (6). The effect of s 5 is to give inhabitants of Gibraltar the right to be registered as British citizens without fulfilling any conditions at all.

[9] S 6(1) and Sch 1, paras 1 and 2.

[10] Under s 3(1).

[11] Jones *British Nationality*, p 72; Parry *British Nationality*, p 36. But see Baty *The Nationality of a Married Woman at Common Law* 52 LQR 247.

[12] Aliens Act 1844, s 16; Naturalization Act 1870, s 10(1).

[13] Status of Aliens Act 1914, s10; British Nationality and Status of Aliens Act 1918, s 2(5); British Nationality and Status of Aliens Act 1933, s 1(1). These Acts provided that a British woman marrying a foreigner should not lose her British nationality if she did not acquire that of her husband, that the status of the wife of a man who acquired or lost British nationality after the marriage should not automatically follow that of her husband but that she should be given the option of doing likewise, and that a woman who was a British subject at birth should be entitled to resume British nationality if the state of which her husband was a subject was at war with this country. The same principles were applied to citizenship of the United Kingdom and Colonies under the British Nationality Act 1948.

[14] Registration required the approval of the Secretary of State in certain circumstances (see the British Nationality Act 1948, s 6(2), (3)), and might also be refused on the ground of public policy.

[15] S 6(2) and Sch 1, paras 3 and 4. Absences may be disregarded if they total no more than 270 days of which no more than 90 days may have been in the last twelve months. The applicant must not have been in breach of the immigration laws at any time during the three years.

citizenship by naturalisation is a matter of discretion and not of right, as was registration by a wife under the 1948 Act.

A woman who is a British citizen no longer loses her citizenship on marrying an alien although, if she acquires her husband's nationality, she may divest herself of British citizenship by registering a declaration of renunciation like anyone else possessing dual nationality.[16]

Right of abode

'All those who have the right of abode in the United Kingdom ... shall be free to live in, and to come and go into and from, the United Kingdom without let or hindrance' except for the need to establish their right.[17] It is possessed by all British citizens and those Commonwealth citizens who had the right before 1st January 1983, when the British Nationality Act 1981 came into force.[18] Persons coming from the Channel Islands, the Isle of Man and the Republic of Ireland are generally exempt from immigration control and certain restrictions do not apply to European Community nationals and members of their families, but except for them and one or two other special cases,[19] all other persons, whatever their citizenship or nationality, may enter this country and stay here only if they are permitted to do so under the Immigration Rules made by the Home Secretary.[20] Permission may be unconditional or, if the individual is here for a particular purpose (for example, as a student or to take up employment), it may be given for a limited period of time and made subject to other conditions such as registration with the police.[1]

It has already been pointed out that, from the point of view of family law, the most important question is whether an individual who has the right or permission to stay in this country may be joined by his family. Three points must be made at the outset. First, a person with the right of abode has no *right* to be accompanied by members of his family: they must obtain entry clearance or leave to enter or remain.[2] Secondly, under the Immigration Rules no one is to be regarded as the husband or wife of another if he or she is under the age of 16.[3] Thirdly, because problems were apparently being caused by men entering the country with two or more wives, a woman, W,

---

[16] See now the British Nationality Act 1981, s 12. The Secretary of State may withhold registration during wartime.

[17] Immigration Act 1971, s 1(1).

[18] Ibid, s 2 (as substituted by the British Nationality Act 1981, s 39(2)). The exercise of the right is subject to the Home Secretary's power to make an exclusion order under Part II of the Prevention of Terrorism (Temporary Provisions) Act 1989. For the right before 1983, see the sixth edition of this book, pp 162–163.

[19] See ibid, ss 1(3), 8 and 9 and Sch 4, as amended by the British Nationality Act 1981, s 39(4) and Sch 4; Immigration Act 1988, s 7; HC 251 (1990), paras 68–74 and 146–154.

[20] The current rules are to be found in the Statement of Changes in Immigration Rules HC 251 (1990). 'They are not to be construed with all the strictness applicable to the construction of a statute or statutory instrument. They must be construed sensibly according to the natural meaning of the language which is employed': per Lord Roskill in *Alexander v Immigration Appeal Tribunal* [1982] 2 All ER 766, 770, HL.

[1] Immigration Act 1971, ss 1(2), (4) and 3, as amended by the British Nationality Act 1981, Sch 4.

[2] *R v Secretary of State for the Home Department, ex p Rofathullah* [1989] QB 219, [1988] 3 All ER 1, CA. Under s 2(2) of the Immigration Act 1971 as originally enacted the wife or former wife of a man with the right of abode automatically possessed it herself.

[3] HC 251, para 2.

will no longer be given permission to enter or stay here as the wife of a man, H, if (a) her marriage is de facto polygamous (even though the husband had no other wife when she married him) and (b) another wife of H has been in the United Kingdom since her marriage or has been granted entry clearance to enter this country as H's wife, unless W has been lawfully in this country otherwise than as a visitor at a time when there was no such wife satisfying condition (b).[4]

Under the current rules, the wife and children under the age of 18 of a person who has been given permission to enter the country for a limited period as a student will usually be given leave to enter for the same period if they can be maintained and accommodated without recourse to public funds.[5] Similar rules apply to the wife *or husband* and minor children of a person admitted to seek or take up employment or as a businessman, self-employed person or a person of independent means.[6] If a person of either sex is present and settled in the United Kingdom[7] or is admitted for settlement, his or her spouse will be granted entry clearance provided that the marriage was not entered into primarily to obtain permission to enter the United Kingdom and the parties have met and intend to live together permanently as husband and wife.[8] The restrictions are imposed because of the belief that in the past some men (particularly from India) were obtaining entry into this country by contracting arranged marriages, sometimes by proxy, to women (or possibly young girls) whom they had never met. It must also be shown that the parties and their dependants can be maintained without recourse to public funds in accommodation of their own or which they occupy.[9] The spouse will be admitted initially for no more than 12 months: this provides a probationary period at the end of which the time limit may be removed provided that the marriage has not been terminated and each party still has the intention of living permanently with the other as his or her spouse.[10]

A child born in the United Kingdom who is not a British citizen will be given leave to remain here for the same period (which may be indefinite) as his parents.[11] Other unmarried children under the age of 18 will be admitted for settlement (a) if both parents are settled here or admitted for settlement, or (b) if one parent only is settled here or admitted for settlement and either he (or she) has had the sole responsibility for the child's upbringing[12] or the other parent is dead, or (c) if one parent or another relative is settled here or

---

[4] Ibid, paras 3–5. This restriction does not apply if W has been in the United Kingdom before 1 August 1988 and she came for settlement as H's wife. See also the Immigration Act 1988, s 2, which applies to women who had the right of abode under s 2(2) of the Immigration Act 1971 as originally enacted (see n 2, supra).

[5] HC 251, paras 31, 32 and 116. Note that this does not include a student's husband.

[6] Ibid, paras 46, 122–124 and 127–129.

[7] Ie if he is here lawfully, is ordinarily resident here and is free from any restriction on the period for which he may remain: ibid, para 1.

[8] For the meaning of 'met', see post, p 146, n 19. For the interrelationship of these conditions, see *R v Immigration Appeal Tribunal, ex p Kumar* [1987] 1 FLR 444, CA.

[9] HC 251, para 50.

[10] Ibid, paras 51 and 132.

[11] Ibid, paras 133–137.

[12] This will depend inter alia on the source and degree of financial support of the child and whether there is cogent evidence of genuine interest and affection so that it can fairly be said that the parent has remained ultimately in sole control of the child's upbringing for a substantial period of time although not necessarily for the whole of the child's life: *R v Immigration Appeal Tribunal, ex p Sajid Mahmood* [1988] Imm AR 121, 126–127.

accepted for settlement and there are serious and compelling family or other considerations making exclusion undesirable and suitable arrangements have been made for the child's care.[13] Children over the age of 18 must qualify for settlement in their own right unless there are the most exceptional compassionate circumstances, but special consideration may be given to fully dependent unmarried daughters under the age of 21 who formed part of the family unit overseas and have no close relatives to turn to at home.[14] Widowed mothers, widowed fathers over the age of 65, and both parents together if one is over the age of 65 may be admitted for settlement if they are wholly or mainly dependent[15] on sons or daughters settled in the United Kingdom and have no close relatives to turn to at home.[16] Other parents, grandparents, sons, daughters, brothers, sisters, uncles and aunts may be admitted only if they are living alone and there are most exceptional compassionate circumstances.[17] In all cases the person to whom the applicant is related must show that the latter can be adequately housed in accommodation which that person owns or occupies himself and that he is able and willing to maintain the applicant adequately, in each case without recourse to public funds. If the applicant is someone other than a child, the sponsor must also show that he has the means to maintain any other relatives who would be admissible as the applicant's dependants and has adequate accommodation for them.[18]

A man or woman seeking admission to the United Kingdom to marry a person who is present and settled in this country or who is admitted for settlement on the same occasion must hold entry clearance granted for this purpose. This will be issued only if conditions are satisfied similar to those applicable to spouses: it must not be the primary purpose of the intended marriage to enable the fiancé or fiancée to obtain admission to this country, the parties must have met and intend to live together permanently as husband and wife,[19] and maintenance and accommodation must be available both before and after the marriage. The applicant will be admitted for six months in the first instance, and if the marriage does not take place within this time,

---

[13] HC 251, para 53. 'Parent' includes (a) a step-parent if the original parent is dead, (b) the father and mother of an illegitimate child, and (c) an adoptive parent (including one who has adopted another de facto: *R v Immigration Appeal Tribunal, ex p Tohur Ali* [1988] 2 FLR 523, CA) if there has been a genuine transfer of parental responsibility because the natural parent is unable to care for the child and the adoption is not one of convenience to facilitate the child's admission. An example of a compelling reason making exclusion undesirable would be the other parent's inability to look after the child. Special rules relate to children if one parent is given only limited leave to enter the country and to children born in the United Kingdom who are not British citizens: ibid, paras 54 and 61–67. There is no provision in the Rules for a child to be brought into the United Kingdom for adoption here, but the Home Secretary may exceptionally exercise his discretion and permit a child to enter for this purpose: *R v Secretary of State for the Home Department, ex p Khan* [1985] 1 All ER 40, CA. See Macdonald *Immigration Law and Practice* (2nd Edn) 250–253.

[14] Ibid, para 55.

[15] Including emotional dependence: *R v Immigration Appeal Tribunal, ex p Khatun* [1989] Imm AR 482.

[16] Ie to turn to in case of financial or other need (eg the problems of living alone): *R v Immigration Appeal Tribunal, ex p Swaran Singh* [1987] 3 All ER 690, CA.

[17] HC 251, paras 56–57. A parent or grandparent who has remarried should not be admitted unless he or she cannot look to his or her spouse or children of the second marriage for support.

[18] Ibid, paras 52 and 56–57.

[19] 'Met' means 'made each other's acquaintance' and not merely physically met: *Raj v Entry Clearance Officer* [1985] Imm AR 151.

an extension will be granted only if good cause is shown for the delay, there is satisfactory evidence that the marriage will take place at any early date, and the maintenance and accommodation requirements will continue to be met. If the marriage takes place within the initial or extended period, permission to stay in this country will be extended for a further 12 months; the time limit will then be removed in the same circumstances as apply to other spouses seeking permission to stay here.[20]

If a person who is not a British citizen is deported, his or her minor children and, if the person deported is a man, his wife and her minor children are liable to be deported too.[1] In deciding whether to order the deportation of members of the family, the Home Secretary will take all the facts into account including their length of residence in this country, other ties they may have with the United Kingdom, whether they can be maintained without becoming a charge on public funds, any compassionate or other special circumstances and any representations made on their behalf. He will not normally order the deportation of a wife if she has qualified for settlement in her own right or if she has been living apart from her husband. Children will not normally be deported if they have spent some years in the United Kingdom and are nearly 18, if they have left home and are financially independent, or if they are married. If a child is still at school, the Home Secretary will take into account the effect deportation would have on his education as well as plans for his care and maintenance if he stays here.[2]

---

[20] HC 251, paras 47, 48 and 130–132. These provisions also apply to other persons admitted temporarily who then marry a person settled here.
[1] Immigration Act 1971, ss 3(5) and 5, as amended by the British Nationality Act 1981, Sch 4, and Immigration Act 1988, Sch.
[2] HC 251, paras 169–171. For readmission, see para 172.

Chapter 5

Physical protection

A. Introductory[1]

Violence in the home is no new phenomenon. Although Hale had denied that a husband had a legal power to administer corporal punishment to his wife,[2] it was stated in Bacon's Abridgment in 1736 that a husband might beat his wife (but not in a violent or cruel manner) and confine her.[3] Blackstone, writing some 30 years later, maintained that, whilst the practice had become obsolete in polite society, 'the lower rank of people, who were always fond of the old common law, still claim and exert their ancient privilege'.[4] Little was heard of the problem for another century until Parliament intervened in 1878 following a campaign drawing attention to the brutal treatment of many working-class women.[5] The Matrimonial Causes Act of that year gave a criminal court, before which a man was convicted of aggravated assault on his wife, the power to make a separation and maintenance order in her favour and to vest in her the legal custody of the children of the marriage under the age of ten years if it felt that her future safety was in peril.[6]

Almost another 100 years passed before the question became one of public concern again. Publicity was given to it by the setting up of women's aid refuges[7] and was maintained by the feminist movement. This in turn led to the establishment of a Select Committee of the House of Commons which heavily criticised the effectiveness of the existing remedies open to women who were the victims of violence at the hands of their husbands or the men with whom they were cohabiting and made a number of proposals for reform.[8] One of the most important of these was embodied in the provisions of the Domestic Violence and Matrimonial Proceedings Act of 1976. A report of the Law Commission, which appeared shortly afterwards,[9] also addressed the problem and recommended that magistrates be given greatly extended powers to deal with domestic violence. Effect was given to these proposals

[1] See generally Law Com Working Paper No 113 and Law Com No 207, 1992 (Domestic Violence and Occupation of the Matrimonial Home).
[2] *Lord Leigh's Case* (1674) 3 Keb 422, where he said that *castigatio* meant no more than admonition and confinement.
[3] Tit Baron and Feme (B).
[4] *Commentaries* i 455.
[5] See Frances Power Cobbe *Wife Torture in England* (1878).
[6] S 4.
[7] Particularly by Erin Pizzey in Chiswick. See her *Scream Quietly or the Neighbours will Hear*, and also *Violence in the Family* (ed Borland), and Borkowski, Murch and Walker *Marital Violence*. For a comprehensive discussion of the social and legal problems see Freeman *Violence in the Family* and Hoggett and Pearl *The Family, Law and Society* (3rd Edn) ch 9.
[8] See the Report of the Select Committee on Violence in Marriage HC 553 (1974–75). See also Maidment *The Law's Response to Marital Violence in England and the USA* 26 ICLQ 403.
[9] Law Com No 77 (Report on Matrimonial Proceedings in Magistrates' Courts).

in sections 16, 17 and 18 of the Domestic Proceedings and Magistrates' Court Act 1978.

Although the references above have all been to the ill-treatment of wives, it must not be overlooked that a husband (or male cohabitant) may also be the object of his wife's or partner's violence.[10] A more urgent social problem (in the sense that the victim may be unable to do anything for himself) is created by abuse of children. In some cases the only protection that can be afforded to a child is to remove him from the family by means of a care order: this will be considered more fully in chapter 16, post. In other cases the obvious remedy is to ensure that the child is removed from the physical care of the offending parent and given such protection from violence as the law can afford: this will often involve giving protection to the parent with whom he is living as well. It will be necessary, therefore, to consider the position of spouses, cohabitants and children together in this chapter.

Often the only action that the victim can take immediately is to leave home. She (for the spouse in danger will usually be the wife) may be able to obtain shelter, at least temporarily, with a relative or friend. If she cannot, the question facing her is how she is to obtain accommodation and maintenance. The duty cast on local authorities to house homeless persons will be considered in the next section. Her immediate financial problems may be eased by applying for income support: this will be considered in chapter 20, post. We must also examine the legal remedies available to the victim of domestic violence. These can be broadly divided into two groups. First, with respect to past acts, she (or he) may institute criminal proceedings. She may also bring an action for damages in tort for battery, but in the vast majority of cases this is of no importance for the simple reason that the other party would not be able to satisfy any judgment awarded. Secondly, she may take steps to obtain an order to prevent further violence or annoyance in the future and, if necessary, to exclude her husband or partner from the home. In practice, the second type of remedy is much more important than the first.

B. Emergency accommodation

Part III of the Housing Act 1985, which contains provisions originally enacted in the Housing (Homeless Persons) Act 1977, imposes a duty on all housing authorities[11] to help anyone applying to them for accommodation or for assistance in obtaining accommodation if they have reason to believe that he is homeless or threatened with homelessness.

A person is homeless for the purpose of the Act if there is no accommodation in Great Britain which he, together with any other person who normally resides with him as a member of his family or in circumstances in which it is reasonable for that person to reside with him:

'(a) is entitled to occupy by virtue of an interest in it or by virtue of an order of a court, or

[10] See Borkowski et al op cit, particularly ch 2; Freeman op cit ch 9.
[11] Ie district councils and London borough councils: Housing Act 1985, s 1.

(b) has ... an express or implied licence to occupy ..., or
(c) occupies as a residence by virtue of any enactment or rule of law giving him the right to remain in occupation or restricting the right of another person to recover possession.'

He is also homeless if he has such accommodation but:

'(a) he cannot secure entry to it, or
(b) it is probable that occupation of it will lead to violence from some other person residing in it or to threats of violence from some other person residing in it and likely to carry out the threats.'[12]

The word 'family' is not defined for the purpose of this Part of the Act and it is submitted that it should be interpreted broadly. It should include persons related by blood or marriage, children adopted de jure or de facto, and persons living together as husband and wife.[13]

If one spouse is the sole owner or tenant of the matrimonial home, this fact alone will not bring the other within the first limb of the definition because the latter will have a statutory right to remain in occupation under the Matrimonial Homes Act.[14] Conversely, a person will be regarded as homeless if his or her partner changes the locks so that he cannot get into the house. It will also be noticed that paragraph (b) of the second limb does not require that violence or threats of violence will probably be offered to the person seeking accommodation: a wife, for example, will be homeless if she or a child living with her are likely to be treated with violence if they return.

The accommodation must be such that it is reasonable for the person concerned to continue to occupy it.[15] This does not refer simply to its quality:[16] the housing authority is also bound to take into consideration the physical and mental needs of the applicant. Thus in *R v Broxbourne Borough Council, ex p Willmoth*[17] it was held that the authority should take into account the fact that the man with whom the applicant had been living violently and brutally assaulted her and seized their child in the street.

A person is to be regarded as threatened with homelessness if it is likely that he will become homeless within 28 days.[18]

'Accommodation' in this context means settled accommodation and consequently a person who has become homeless and is living in temporary accommodation is still homeless for the purpose of the Act. As Hodgson J pointed out in *R v Ealing London Borough Council, ex p Sidhu*,[19] if this were not so, a woman temporarily housed in a refuge could not call on the housing authority for assistance. To enable her to do so, the refuge would have to

[12] S 58.
[13] Cf the definition for the purpose of Part IV (succession to a secure tenancy): s 113 (post, p 848).
[14] See post, p 613. Similarly spouses of statutory tenants and secure tenants are entitled to remain in occupation by virtue of the Rent Act 1977 and the Housing Acts 1985 and 1988: see post, pp 631, 633 and 640.
[15] S 58(2A), (2B), added by the Housing and Planning Act 1986, s 14(2).
[16] See eg *R v South Herefordshire District Council, ex p Miles* (1984) 17 HLR 82 (rat infested hut); *Gloucester City Council v Miles* [1985] FLR 1043, CA (house rendered uninhabitable by vandalism).
[17] (1989) 22 HLR 118, CA, following *R v Kensington and Chelsea Royal London Borough Council, ex p Hammell* [1989] QB 518, [1989] 1 All ER 1202, CA. See also *R v Brent London Borough Council, ex p Omar* (1991) 23 HLR 446.
[18] S 58(4).
[19] (1982) 3 FLR 438. Cf *R v Purbeck District Council, ex p Cadney* [1986] 2 FLR 158 (wife, who had left home voluntarily and was then required to leave temporary accommodation, not homeless).

give her 28 days' notice so that she would be 'threatened with homelessness': a procedure which would merely pile stress on stress unnecessarily.

The housing authority must make appropriate inquiries in all cases and must give every applicant advice and assistance to secure accommodation.[20] Their obligations are much more extensive if they are satisfied that the applicant has a priority need. Persons with a priority need include inter alia:

(a) those with dependent children who reside with them or who might reasonably be expected to reside with them,[1]

(b) persons who are vulnerable as a result of old age, mental illness or handicap, physical disability or other reason, or who reside with or might reasonably be expected to reside with someone coming within this category, and

(c) pregnant women.[2]

The authority's duty to such a person depends on whether or not they are satisfied that he became homeless (or threatened with homelessness) intentionally. If they are not so satisfied, they must take reasonable steps to secure that accommodation becomes available for his occupation (or, in the case of a person threatened with homelessness, that it does not cease to be available). If they are so satisfied, they are bound only to secure accommodation for his occupation for such period as they consider will give him a reasonable opportunity of securing accommodation for himself.[3] Consequently the distinction between those who became homeless intentionally and those who did not is vital because in the former case the authority merely has a duty to provide temporary accommodation whilst in the latter the applicant will immediately get priority over all others on the authority's housing list.[4]

A person is to be regarded as becoming homeless intentionally if, after consideration of all the relevant facts known to him, he deliberately does or fails to do something as a result of which he ceases to occupy accommodation which is available for his occupation and which it would have been reasonable for him to continue to occupy.[5] Thus a tenant will become homeless intentionally if he loses possession of premises as a result of *wilfully* failing to pay rent or breaking some other covenant in his lease: there is no need to prove

---

[20] Ss 62 and 65(4).

[1] The child need not be wholly and exclusively dependent on the applicant or reside solely with him: *R v London Borough of Lambeth, ex p Vagliviello* (1990) 22 HLR 392, CA (applicant could have priority need although child residing with him only $3\frac{1}{2}$ days a week).

[2] S 59, qv for the full definition.

[3] Ss 63, 65(2), (3) and 69(1). In the former case the housing authority is under no duty to secure accommodation if neither the applicant nor any person who might reasonably be expected to reside with him has a local connection with their area provided that one of them has a local connection with another housing authority's area. If the first authority notifies the second of the facts, the duty to secure accommodation is cast on the latter: ss 67 and 68. Local connection is normally based on residence, employment or family associations: s 61 qv for the full definition. There is no power to transfer the duty in this way if the applicant or any person who might reasonably be expected to reside with him will run the risk of domestic violence in the second authority's area: s 67(2)(c), (3).

[4] If the applicant unreasonably refuses to take appropriate accommodation offered to him, the authority is not bound to make any further offers: *R v Westminster City Council, ex p Chambers* (1982) 4 FLR 487.

[5] S 60; *Devenport v Salford City Council* (1983) 4 FLR 744, CA.

that he intended to become homeless. If another member of the family encourages or acquiesces in conduct which results in the tenant's becoming homeless intentionally (for example, a wife who turns a blind eye or does nothing to prevent her husband from dissipating his earnings instead of paying the rent), that person will be regarded as intentionally homeless as well. The housing authority is entitled to assume acquiescence unless the evidence indicates the contrary;[6] but it is bound to give separate consideration to the position of each resident and in the absence of acquiescence it will be obliged to secure accommodation for the person at fault if he resides with one who has not become homeless intentionally.[7]

It will be observed that the question is whether the tenant *became* homeless intentionally, not whether he is now homeless intentionally. Consequently if, as in *Din v Wandsworth London Borough Council*[8] the applicant deliberately left available accommodation, he will be considered to have become homeless intentionally even though he would probably have been evicted later and thus have become homeless unintentionally. Conversely, if, as in *Gloucester City Council v Miles*,[9] the applicant became homeless because her husband had vandalised her home to such an extent that it became uninhabitable, she will not be homeless intentionally even though, had she stayed there, she would probably have become so through non-payment of rent. As the occupation of temporary accommodation is to be disregarded, it also follows that if someone, who became homeless unintentionally, subsequently does some deliberate act which leads to his eviction from temporary accommodation, he will not thereby become intentionally homeless.[10]

The same test is to be applied mutatis mutandis to determine whether a person is threatened with homelessness intentionally.[11]

We may now apply these principles to a person forced to leave home as the result of his or her spouse's or partner's violence. It will be assumed that a wife is driven out of the matrimonial home by her husband, but it will be appreciated that the same principles apply if a wife forces her husband to leave or if the parties are unmarried.[12]

If the husband locks the wife out of the home or occupation of it will probably lead to violence or threats of violence which the husband is likely to carry out, she becomes homeless for the purpose of the Act. She may well seek temporary shelter with relations, friends or in a refuge but, as we have seen, this will not affect her status as a homeless person. The housing authority is therefore, at the least, bound to give her advice and appropriate assistance in securing accommodation. She will have a priority need for accommodation if she is pregnant or vulnerable or has dependent children who are residing with her or who might reasonably be expected to reside with her if she obtained suitable accommodation. At one time housing authorities refused

---

[6] *R v North Devon District Council, ex p Lewis* [1981] 1 All ER 27. If the spouse acts in good faith in ignorance of a relevant fact, she will not be regarded as having acquiesced and therefore will not be intentionally homeless: *R v Mole Valley District Council, ex p Burton* (1988) 20 HLR 479.

[7] *R v Mole Valley District Council, ex p Burton* (supra); *R v London Borough of Ealing, ex p Salmons* (1990) 23 HLR 272.

[8] [1983] 1 AC 657, [1981] 3 All ER 881, HL.

[9] [1985] FLR 1043, CA.

[10] *R v East Hertfordshire District Council, ex p Hunt* [1986] 1 FLR 431.

[11] S 60(2); *Dyson v Kerrier District Council* [1980] 3 All ER, 313, CA.

[12] See generally Thornton *Homelessness through Relationship Breakdown* [1989] JSWL 67.

to regard women with children as having a priority need unless they first obtained a custody order for fear that, having 'jumped the queue' on this ground, they would then lose custody. But, as Hodgson J pointed out in *R v Ealing London Borough Council, ex p Sidhu*,[13] there is nothing in the Act to justify this practice, which should not be followed. The Code of Guidance issued by the Secretary of State under section 71 of the Act in fact recommends authorities to provide accommodation for *all* women in danger of violence. Although authorities are bound to have regard to the Code in exercising their functions, it has no statutory authority: they are free to depart from it in any particular case and may well do so if there are a large number of deserving cases waiting for housing in their area.[14]

If the wife has been forced to leave home because of her husband's violent behaviour towards her or their children, she has obviously not become homeless intentionally. Consequently, if she has a priority need, the housing authority is under a duty to secure accommodation for her. If she has been locked out, it is submitted that the authority should look at the reason for the husband's act and if this has been caused by her conduct—for example, by her own violent behaviour—it should be attributed to her and she would be regarded as intentionally homeless.[15]

The duty to house homeless persons has placed an almost intolerable burden on many authorities. Some have taken the view that, if the need to provide accommodation for a married woman arises from her husband's behaviour, it is not unreasonable to expect her to ease the strain by obtaining an ouster injunction and thus solving the problem herself.[16] Like the practice, mentioned earlier, of requiring her to obtain a custody order when she claimed that dependent children residing with her gave her a priority need, there is nothing in the Act justifying the authority's putting pressure on the wife in this way and their doing so was roundly condemned by the Court of Appeal in *Warwick v Warwick*.[17] Ormrod LJ said:[18]

'I think it would be an abuse of the process of the court to use the court's very extensive powers in dealing with the occupation of matrimonial homes during the stress of divorce proceedings to allow those powers to be used in order to play the obscure housing policy games of local authorities.'

These words scarcely do justice to the authorities' attempts to deal with an often insoluble problem and were admittedly spoken in the course of a judgment allowing an appeal from an order requiring the husband to leave a house in an area to which the wife had no intention of returning because she feared further interference from him. Nevertheless, whilst it might be proper to encourage the wife to take proceedings in an appropriate case, it

---

[13] (1982) 3 FLR 438. The authorities' requirement also overlooked the fact that, even if the husband obtained custody, the wife might still have care and control.
[14] See *De Falco v Crawley Borough Council* [1980] QB 460, [1980] 1 All ER 913, CA.
[15] Cf *R v Wandsworth London Borough Council, ex p Nimako-Boateng* [1984] FLR 192. If she has children living with her, an application cannot be made on their behalf, even though they are not homeless intentionally: *R v Bexley London Borough Council, ex p B* (1992) Times, 20 April.
[16] See Thornton loc cit 71–73 and 81.
[17] (1981) 3 FLR 393, CA. See Wright 138 New LJ 594.
[18] At 395.

cannot be right to put pressure on her if she is reluctant to do so.[19]

C. Protection afforded by the criminal law

Either spouse (or cohabitant) may be prosecuted for assaulting the other (whether for common assault or an assault occasioning actual bodily harm) or for committing one of the more serious offences of wounding or causing grievous bodily harm.[1] In practice, however, the criminal law is little used by victims of domestic violence. The reasons are numerous: the emotional strain that a prosecution would put on the victim (whom we will assume for the sake of illustration to be the wife) and her children, the financial loss she would suffer if prosecution led to her husband's losing his job, and the fear of reprisals if he were released on bail pending his trial or, in any case, after his ultimate release. Most women also find the police unhelpful and ineffective. In most forces there has been an established attitude that the home is beyond police surveillance and a fear that a prosecution, once launched, may fail because of the wife's reluctance to proceed because of a reconciliation or because of one of the reasons mentioned above.[2] The fact that the accused's spouse is now a compellable witness for the prosecution in cases of asault[3] may ease the position, and current guide-lines set out by the Home Office recommend the police to deal with domestic violence in the same way as violence between strangers.[4]

Compensation for injury

Originally the criminal injuries compensation scheme excluded virtually all cases of domestic violence. There were a number of reasons for this: it was feared that it would be difficult to establish the facts; there would be a large number of claims, many of them trivial; if the parties were subsequently reconciled, any compensation awarded would increase the family assets as a whole and consequently the offender would benefit from his own wrong.[5] It was obvious, however, that many seriously injured women were being prevented from making genuine claims. Consequently the scheme was modified

[19] Insofar as the views expressed by Woolf J in *R v Wandsworth London Borough Council, ex p Nimako-Boateng* [1984] FLR 192, 196, are inconsistent with the passage cited from Ormrod LJ's judgment, it is submitted that they should not be followed. It is not clear that *Warwick v Warwick* was brought to the learned judge's notice. See further Bryan *Domestic Violence: A Question of Housing?* [1984] JSWL 195; Pearl in *Essays in Family Law 1985* p 20.
[1] For details of these offences see Smith and Hogan *Criminal Law* (6th Edn) pp 375 et seq. See also Edwards and Halpern *Protection for the Victim of Domestic Violence* [1991] JSWL 94.
[2] The reasons are discussed in greater detail in the Report of the Select Committee on Domestic Violence (supra), para 43; Hoggett and Pearl op cit pp 383–389; Freeman op cit pp 184 et seq; Borkowski et al *Marital Violence* ch 8 and p 127; Maidment loc cit pp 406–413 and *The Relevance of the Criminal Law to Domestic Violence* [1980] JSWL 26; Pahl *Police Response to Battered Women* [1982] JSWL 337. See also the evidence given to the Select Committee by the Metropolitan Police.
[3] See ante, p 115.
[4] Home Office Circular No 60/1990, which also points out that research has shown that withdrawal of complaints is less common than has been supposed. See Hoggett and Pearl op cit pp 387–389; Keevely [1990] Fam Law 418; Brownlee *Compellability and Contempt in Domestic Violence Cases* [1990] JSWL 107.
[5] See Freeman op cit p 182.

in 1979, although it will be seen that account is still taken of the fears mentioned above.

Under the scheme now in force if at the time of the injury the victim and any person responsible for it were living in the same household as members of the same family, compensation can be claimed only if the following three conditions are satisfied.[6]

(a) The person responsible for the injury must have been prosecuted for the offence unless the Criminal Injuries Compensation Board considers that there are practical, technical or other good reasons for there having been no prosecution.

(b) In the case of violence between adults in the family, the victim and the person responsible must have stopped living together in the same household before the application for compensation was made and it must seem unlikely that they will live together again.

(c) If the victim is a minor, the Board must be satisfied that it would not be against his interest to make a full or reduced award.

For the purpose of the scheme a man and woman living together as husband and wife are to be regarded as members of the same family. The phrase 'living in the same household' is the same as that used in the Matrimonial Causes Act,[7] and it would therefore seem that, if a husband and wife would be regarded as separated for the purpose of the law of divorce, either of them should be able to apply for compensation if she (or he) suffered a criminal injury at the hands of the other. This was certainly not the position under the original scheme where the test was simply whether the victim and the offender were living together as members of the same family. In *R v Criminal Injuries Compensation Board, exp Staten*[8] the Divisional Court declined to apply the niceties of the divorce law and held that the Board had properly refused compensation to a woman who had been injured by her husband when they were living in the same accommodation, even though it was argued that a divorce court would have regarded them as living apart. It remains to be seen whether the courts will interpret the modified wording in the same way. As fraudulent claims are hardly likely to be made by victims who are separated for the purposes of the law of divorce, it is submitted that they should be able to apply in these circumstances. The same argument would apply mutatis mutandis to unmarried cohabitants. But difficulties would obviously arise in the case of children to whom this test could not be applied unless they were living entirely with one parent to the complete exclusion of the other. Because the criminal injuries scheme does not deal solely with injuries to spouses or unmarried cohabitants, courts may continue to apply the simpler test of, in effect, whether the parties were living under the same roof laid down in *Exp Staten*.

The Board may withhold or reduce compensation if (a) all reasonable steps have not been taken promptly to inform the police; (b) the applicant has failed to give reasonable assistance to the Board; or (c) having regard to the applicant's criminal convictions and unlawful conduct or his (or her) character and way of life, it is inappropriate to make a full (or any) award.

[6] See the 26th Report of the Criminal Injuries Compensation Board, Cm 1365, 1990, App C, para 8.
[7] See post, pp 211–212.
[8] [1972] 1 All ER 1034.

If the victim dies in consequence of the injury, the Board will entertain an application from any person who is a dependant for the purpose of the Fatal Accidents Act.[9]

Under the Criminal Justice Act 1988[10] the present scheme is to be replaced by a statutory scheme, although its introduction has been indefinitely postponed. The main difference between the two is that, whereas under the present scheme payments are technically ex gratia, under the new one a victim will be able to make a claim as of right. The principle underlying claims resulting from domestic violence remains unchanged, but the following differences of detail should be noted.[11]

(1) Limitations are imposed if the victim is over the age of 18 and was living in the same household as the person or persons responsible for the injury. The omission of the words 'as members of the same family' does not appear to effect any change.

(2) The person responsible must have been prosecuted unless there is a *sufficient* reason why he had not. Again, the change of wording seems immaterial.

(3) *Unless circumstances prevent him (or her) from doing so*, the victim must have ceased to live in the same household as the person responsible *and must not intend to do so again*.

(4) A dependant will be able to claim compensation even though the victim's death was not the result of the injury.

D. Proceedings to give future protection

We must now consider the various steps which a spouse or cohabitant may take to secure protection for the future.

1. JUDICIAL SEPARATION

The classic means by which a spouse could obtain protection was by the decree of divorce a mensa et thoro pronounced in the ecclesiastical courts. The Matrimonial Causes Act of 1857 abolished that decree and replaced it by the decree of judicial separation. One of the advantages of the decree was that the court could order financial provision for the wife; consequently as long as the grounds for divorce were limited, judicial separation provided her with a degree of both financial and physical protection. But alternative ways of obtaining maintenance, the relative ease with which divorce can now be obtained, and the possibility of obtaining an injunction by much speedier proceedings have all tended to discourage spouses from seeking the remedy.

Nevertheless judicial separation can still serve a practical purpose, as is demonstrated by the enormouse increase in the number of petitions since 1972. In that year there were 330. The number rose steadily to 7,480 in 1982,

---

[9] Cm 1365, App C, para 15. For the meaning of dependant under the Fatal Accidents Act, see ante, p 125.

[10] Ss 108–116 and Schs 6 and 7.

[11] Ss 110(5) and 111(1)(b) and (11). See also s 112 (power to withhold or reduce compensation and withholding an award from a minor unless it is in his interest to make it).

but a fall to 6,098 in 1984 was followed by a further dramatic fall to 3,479 in 1985.[12] (These figures should be compared with the drop in the number of applications for magistrates' orders in the same period.[13] The two may well be connected and reflect some practitioners' preference for county courts.)[14] The reason for this sharp increase in the popularity of judicial separation apparently lies largely in the extension, in 1971, of the court's power to grant the same financial relief on judicial separation as it can on divorce. Many wives may wish to invoke this power (as well as the power to make orders in relation to children and to grant an injunction against domestic violence all in the same proceedings) without petitioning for divorce. In some cases, the reluctance to start divorce proceedings will be due to religious conviction; in others the wife, intending to petition for divorce later, may start with a petition for judicial separation for tactical reasons.[15] Some petitioners still hope for an ultimate reconciliation but, by obtaining a decree of judicial separation, they gain an immediate remedy whilst leaving the way open for divorce on the ground on which the decree was granted if this hope is not fulfilled.[16] Decrees were also formerly sought by spouses who had not been married for three years and consequently could petition for divorce only in exceptional circumstances; the fall in the number of petitions for judicial separation by over 40 per cent in 1985 (the first full year in which all spouses were able to petition for divorce after the first year of marriage) suggests that this change in the laws will produce a permanent significant reduction. The number has now levelled out at just short of 3,000 a year, of which about 90 per cent are presented by wives.[17]

The Law Commission have concluded that judicial separation (which they would prefer to term a separation order) should remain as an alternative for spouses who wish to obtain the financial relief available but do not seek divorce for reasons of conscience or because they could not be compensated for the loss of pension rights or other benefits which they would suffer. As judicial separation marks the de facto end of the marriage for many, they recommend that the ground should be the same as for divorce and that either spouse should be able to apply to convert it into a divorce.[18]

Jurisdiction

The Act of 1857 vested the power of granting decrees of judicial separation in the Divorce Court, from which it was transferred to the High Court in

---

[12] The ratio of petitions in 1982 to petitions in 1971 was 35:1. In the same period the number of divorce petitions increased by only 50%. Since 1972 over 60% of all petitions for judicial separation each year have been based on the respondent's behaviour.

[13] See ante, p 15, n 17.

[14] See Garlick *Judicial Separation: A Research Study* 46 MLR 719, 727–731.

[15] Eg a husband wishing to remarry may offer his wife apparently reasonable financial terms if she will petition for divorce. It may be inadvisable for her to accept the offer until she has obtained discovery of his means, which she can do in proceedings for judicial separation.

[16] See post, p 187.

[17] Separate statistics for petitions brought by husbands and wives were not published in 1990. For the reasons why petitioners seek judicial separation, see Maidment *Judicial Separation*; Garlick ubi supra. The need for ancillary relief, procedural tactics and later petitions for divorce account for the fact that until 1980 fewer than 50% of petitions for judicial separation were followed by decrees.

[18] See Law Com No 192 (Ground for Divorce), paras 4.2–4.19 and 5.86–5.87. For the Commission's recommendations relating to the ground for divorce, see post, pp 243–244.

1875. Now every petition must be presented to a divorce county court (including the Principal Registry of the Family Division in London). Proceedings may be transferred to the High Court; if the petition is undefended, the decree will normally be granted under the special procedure in the county court.[19]

Jurisdiction was originally based on the parties' residence (the basis of jurisdiction in the ecclesiastical courts) or domicile in this country. When proposing changes in the law relating to jurisdiction in divorce, however, the Law Commission pointed out that judicial separation declares the parties' marital status, affects their mutual obligations, and enables the court to make the same orders in relation to financial relief and the children of the family as it can make on divorce. They therefore recommended that jurisdiction to pronounce both decrees should be the same.[20] Effect was given to these proposals in the Domicile and Matrimonial Proceedings Act 1973, and the court now has jurisdiction to entertain a petition for judicial separation if (and only if) (a) either of the parties is domiciled in England or Wales when the proceedings are begun or has been habitually resident there throughout the period of one year ending with that date, or (b) proceedings for divorce, nullity or judicial separation, over which the court has jurisdiction, have already begun.[1] The latter provisions means, for example, that if a husband brings a petition for divorce, which the court has jurisdiction to hear solely by virtue of his habitual residence in England, and he then ceases to be resident here, the wife can cross-petition for judicial separation notwithstanding that at the time of her cross-petition neither of the spouses is domiciled or resident in this country. There are no obligatory stays in proceedings for judicial separation (as there are in divorce) but the law relating to discretionary stays, their removal and their effect on ancillary orders is exactly the same as in divorce.[2] The court should usually stay a petition for judicial separation if proceedings for nullity or divorce are being brought elsewhere so that the question of the validity or subsistence of the marriage may be determined first.

Choice of law

The Act does not provide for the choice of the substantive law to be applied. In the past it was always assumed that English law would be applied and this is undoubtedly still true.[3]

Grounds for judicial separation

A decree of divorce *a mensa et thoro* could be pronounced on the ground of the respondent's adultery or cruelty or, if the wife were the petitioner, on the ground that the husband had committed (or possibly attempted to commit)

---

[19] Matrimonial and Family Proceedings Act 1984, ss 33, 39 and 42; County Courts Act 1984, s 41; Family Proceedings Rules 1991, r 2.24(3). See further ante, pp 13–14 and post, p 235.

[20] Law Com No 48 (Report on Jurisdiction in Matrimonial Causes), paras 63–66. For jurisdiction in divorce, see post, p 230.

[1] S 5(2), (5). This change deprives spouses of a remedy which they formerly had if both are resident in this country but neither satisfies the statutory requirements. See Hartley and Karsten 37 MLR 179, at p 184.

[2] See post, pp 231–233.

[3] See Law Com No 48, para 105.

rape or an unnatural offence. The Matrimonial Causes Act of 1857 preserved all these as grounds for judicial separation, and over the years were added the respondent's desertion,[4] failure to comply with a decree for restitution of conjugal rights[5] and incurable insanity.[6]

Under the old law the main grounds for a judicial separation were the same as the grounds for divorce. Given that the law of divorce was based essentially on the commission of a matrimonial offence by the respondent, this is not surprising. There is, however, another good reason for keeping the grounds the same. For spouses who have a conscientious objection to divorce a decree of judicial separation may mark the de facto end of the marriage, and it is arguable that they should be able to obtain a decree only in similar circumstances to those who wish to bring their marriage to a de jure end by a decree of divorce. The principle was adopted by the Divorce Reform Act 1969. All the former grounds for a decree of judicial separation were abolished and it is now provided that the five facts on which a petitioner can rely to establish irretrievable breakdown of the marriage as the ground for divorce shall be *grounds* for judicial separation.[7] As these are much more important in connection with divorce, we shall defer a detailed consideration of them until we deal with that subject.[8]

As the decree does not dissolve the marriage bond but can in fact be rescinded, the court is not concerned with whether or not the marriage has irretrievably broken down; if any of the grounds is made out, the court must grant a decree provided that the provisions of section 41 of the Matrimonial Causes Act 1973 (relating to children) are complied with.[9] Furthermore, sections 5 and 10 of that Act do not apply to judicial separation:[10] they are both inappropriate because the decree is not irreversible and does not affect the parties' status. On the other hand, the provisions in the Act relating to reconciliation do apply; and the court may adjourn the proceedings, the petitioner's solicitor must provide his certificate, and periods of cohabitation not exceeding six months may be ignored just as in proceedings for divorce.[11]

Unlike a divorce, a petition for judicial separation may be presented within the first year of the marriage.

The decree and its effects

Since a decree of judicial separation effects no change of status and may in certain circumstances subsequently be discharged, it is not made in two stages like a decree of divorce or nullity but takes effect immediately it is pronounced.

---

[4] For two years under the Matrimonial Causes Act 1857; for three years under the Matrimonial Causes Act 1937.
[5] Matrimonial Causes Act 1884.
[6] Matrimonial Causes Act 1937.
[7] See now the Matrimonial Causes Act 1973, s 17(1).
[8] Post, pp 187 et seq.
[9] See post, pp 366–369. But if one party petitions for divorce and the other petitions for judicial separation, the court should not grant the latter if it pronounces a decree nisi of divorce: *Lawry v Lawry* [1967] 2 All ER 1131, CA.
[10] These permit a respondent in certain circumstances to oppose a decree nisi of divorce on the ground of hardship, to have a decree nisi rescinded if his consent was obtained by a misrepresentation, or to delay its being made absolute pending suitable financial provision. See post, pp 213 and 214–220.
[11] See post, pp 221–223.

The principal effect of the decree is that it relieves the petitioner from the duty of cohabiting with the respondent.[12] This means that so long as it is in force neither spouse can be in desertion.[13] In addition the court has power to make a number of orders relating to the children of the family and to financial relief.[14] The decree will also affect the devolution of a spouse's property if he or she dies intestate.[15] But it must be remembered that for all other purposes the spouses remain husband and wife; neither of them is at liberty to remarry, for example, and such of the common law disabilities arising from marriage as remain will continue in force.[16]

Discharge of decrees

The ground on which either party is most likely to apply for the discharge of a decree of judicial separation is that the spouses have resumed cohabitation. The court clearly has power to order a discharge in such circumstances[17] and there is at least one dictum that the decree will be automatically discharged in such a case.[18] In addition there is probably a residual power to rescind the decree whenever common sense and justice demand it, at least provided both spouses consent.[19]

2. NON-MOLESTATION AND EXCLUSION ORDERS

It is obvious that a much speedier and more effective remedy is necessary than that afforded by judicial separation (which is in any event not available to unmarried cohabitants). That usually sought today is an order restraining one party from molesting the other and any children, coupled, if necessary, with a further order excluding the defendant from the parties' home. (In an appropriate case the latter order may be obtained without the former.) An order obtained in the High Court or a county court will usually be in the form of an injunction (often referred to as a non-molestation or ouster injunction). Alternatively, the court may accept an undertaking from the offending party, which is as binding and effective as an order made by the court.[20] As we shall see in the next section, magistrates' courts also have a more limited power to make orders for the protection of a spouse (but not a cohabitant) and children of the family.

---

[12] Matrimonial Causes Act 1973, s 18(1).

[13] Post, p 204.

[14] See post, pp 366–369 (children) and ch 21 (financial relief).

[15] See post, p 817.

[16] Cf *Moss v Moss* [1963] 2 QB 799, [1963] 2 All ER 829 (one spouse remained incompetent to give evidence on the prosecution of the other).

[17] *Oram v Oram* (1923) 129 LT 159.

[18] Per AL Smith J in *Haddon v Haddon* (1887) 18 QBD 778, 782–783. The correctness of this decision is of vital importance if it is alleged that desertion has started to run after a resumption of cohabitation following a decree.

[19] *Schlesinger v Schlesinger* (1966) Times, 22 June, where a decree was discharged to enable the wife (who was not domiciled in this country) to obtain a divorce in South Africa.

[20] *Hussain v Hussain* [1986] Fam 134, [1986] 1 All ER 961, CA.

To understand fully the law relating to ouster injunctions, it is necessary to understand the rights which parties have to occupy the home. Some readers may therefore find it convenient to familiarise themselves with the relevant law first.[21]

For the sake of illustration, it will be assumed that the party seeking protection is the wife or female cohabitant. It must be borne in mind, however, that the same principles apply if a husband or male cohabitant seeks an order.

Injunctions in other proceedings

Non-molestation injunctions

If other proceedings are pending between the parties (whether in the High Court or a county court), the most effective way of obtaining protection will be by seeking an injunction in those proceedings restraining the husband or cohabitant from molesting, assaulting or otherwise interfering with the applicant and the children. Such an injunction can apparently be granted in proceedings for an order under the Children Act 1989 if it is necessary for the child's protection, and the court has similar powers if the child is a ward of court.[22] An injunction may also be obtained in an action in tort, for example for assault or trespass.[1] But an injunction may be granted only to support an existing legal or equitable right.[2] In this connection it must be remembered that English law knows of no tort of molestation or harassment as such, and in *Patel v Patel*[3] the Court of Appeal held that the judge had correctly discharged so much of an injunction as restrained the defendant from approaching within 50 yards of his father-in-law's house on the ground that this would not constitute any actionable wrong. An injunction could be obtained, however, if the conduct complained of amounted to another tort, for example trespass, nuisance or any conduct calculated to impair the plaintiff's health and having this effect.[4] Thus in *Burnett v George*[5] the plaintiff had been granted an injunction prohibiting the defendant from assaulting, molesting or otherwise interfering with her. The defendant appealed on the ground that molestation and interference were not actionable wrongs. The Court of Appeal accepted this argument but, as there was evidence that the plaintiff's health had been impaired by threats made by the defendant over the telephone, they continued the injunction after limiting it to assaulting or otherwise interfering with her by doing acts calculated to cause her harm.

---

[21] See post, pp 612 et seq.

[22] *Re W (a minor)* [1981] 3 All ER 401, CA (Guardianship of Minors Act); *Re V* (1979) 123 Sol Jo 201 (wardship). See further post, p 473, and Douglas 45 MLR 468.

[1] *Egan v Egan* [1975] Ch 218, [1975] 2 All ER 167 (trespass to land); *Bush v Green* [1985] 3 All ER 721, CA (trespass to goods).

[2] See *Richards v Richards* [1984] AC 174, [1983] 2 All ER 807, HL, per Lord Hailsham LC at 200 and 813, Lord Scarman at 212 and 822, and Lord Brandon at 218 and 827. Lord Diplock and Lord Bridge concurred.

[3] [1988] 2 FLR 179, CA.

[4] See *Wilkinson v Downton* [1897] 2 QB 57; *Janvier v Sweeney* [1919] 2 KB 316, CA.

[5] [1992] 1 FLR 525, CA. See further Fricker *Personal Molestation or Harassment* [1992] Fam Law 158.

As between husband and wife, however, it seems to be accepted law that a non-molestation injunction can always be granted.[6]

If the parties are married, other matrimonial proceedings may be pending between them, in which case an injunction is most commonly sought in those proceedings. Orders always cover molestation if this is necessary to protect the applicant or children. The court has a general power to grant an injunction in any cause or matter before it, and in a case of urgency the petitioner may apply for such relief before presenting the petition.[7] The injunction must 'bear some sensible relationship to the cause of action'.[8] Consequently a court could properly order one spouse not to molest the other or a child of the family in proceedings for divorce or judicial separation, because the decree, if granted, would terminate the petitioner's duty to cohabit with the respondent; on the other hand it would not do so if the petitioner was bringing proceedings for financial provision under section 27 of the Matrimonial Causes Act 1973.[9] The order, once made, remains in force and can be continued after the final decree has been pronounced,[10] but there is some doubt about the extent of the court's powers to grant a fresh injunction after a decree absolute of divorce or nullity or a decree of judicial separation. It is clear that, so long as ancillary proceedings are pending, the court is still seised of the cause and may therefore grant an injunction provided that it has some connection with the ancillary relief sought. Thus if an application or order relating to children is in existence, an injunction could be granted prohibiting the husband from molesting both them and the wife, because molestation of her will usually affect the children living with her.[11] This would not apply, however, if the only outstanding matter was the wife's application for periodical payments. In such a case—and a fortiori if there are no ancillary proceedings at all—the court is no longer seised of any relevant matter and consequently appears to have lost its powers to grant an injunction. The Court of Appeal was inclined to the opposite view in *Webb v Webb,*[12] but this opinion must be treated with reserve.[13] It is in line with decisions at first

---

[6] See *Robinson v Robinson* [1965] P 39, 42, [1963] 3 All ER 813, 814, where Karminski J was of the opinion that the wife could apply to the Queen's Bench Division or Chancery Division for a non-molestation injunction, and *Montgomery v Montgomery* [1965] P 46, 51, [1964] 2 All ER 22, 24, where Ormrod J said that the wife had a *right* not to be molested.

[7] Supreme Court Act 1981, s 37; County Courts Act 1984, s 38; RSC Ord 29, r 1; CCR Ord 13, r 6. If proceedings have not begun, the court will put the petitioner on terms providing for the presentation of the petition within a given time.

[8] Per Finer J in *McGibbon v McGibbon* [1973] Fam 170, 173, [1973] 2 All ER 836, 838.

[9] *Des Salles d'Epinoix v Des Salles d'Epinoix* [1967] 2 All ER 539, CA. Cf *Andrew v Andrew* [1990] 2 FLR 376 (no jurisdiction to grant injunction in proceedings under the Inheritance (Provision for Family and Dependants) Act 1975). But an injunction might be granted if one party's conduct was calculated to deter the other from pursuing the action (ibid 377).

[10] *Robinson v Robinson* [1965] P 39, [1963] 3 All ER 813. Cf *Vaughan v Vaughan* [1973] 3 All ER 449, CA.

[11] *Quinn v Quinn* (1983) 4 FLR 394, CA. In this connection it should be remembered that orders relating to children are made 'from time to time' and therefore will remain in force until the child's eighteenth birthday.

[12] [1986] 1 FLR 541, CA.

[13] The appeal was from an ex parte application and the court indicated that the jurisdiction point could be fully argued at the inter partes hearing: see further *Wilde v Wilde* [1988] 2 FLR 83, 86, CA. The view that the court has no jurisdiction if no relevant proceedings are pending is supported by an unreported decision that an injunction cannot be granted after a petition has been dismissed: *Pickering v Pickering* (1959) CA, cited in Rayden and Jackson *Divorce* (16th Edn) 891.

instance[14] and is practically expedient and obviates the need to start fresh proceedings (for example, for assault), but it is difficult to support it in logic. It is scarcely reasonable to say that the wife could return to the court 20 or 30 years after the decree absolute, and one of the difficulties raised by the case is to see where the line is to be drawn.

Ouster injunctions

Until 1983 injunctions excluding a party from the home were frequently sought and granted in other proceedings, particularly divorce proceedings and proceedings relating to children. In that year, however, Lord Brandon, delivering the leading speech in the House of Lords in *Richards v Richards*,[15] pointed out that by what is now section 1 of the Matrimonial Homes Act 1983 a spouse with the statutory rights of occupation given by that section may not be evicted or excluded from the matrimonial home except with the leave of the court *given by an order under that section*. He added that it must follow that the owner of the property can be evicted only under a like order, and presumably the same argument would apply if both had a legal estate in the land. Consequently, if the parties are married, an ouster injunction can be granted only in proceedings taken under that Act or, in the case of actual or threatened domestic violence, under the Domestic Violence and Matrimonial Proceedings Act 1976.[16] If other matrimonial proceedings are on foot between the parties, however, an application under the Matrimonial Homes Act may be made in those proceedings.[17]

If the parties are unmarried, the Matrimonial Homes Act has no application. It may be possible to take proceedings under the Domestic Violence and Matrimonial Proceedings Act, but if this is not available (for example because they have ceased to live with each other in the same household as husband and wife) the position is less clear. The court has a general power to grant an injunction[18] but, as we have seen, this can be exercised only in support of an existing legal or equitable right. Hence if only one party has a legal or beneficial interest in the property and the other has no licence or other right to remain in occupation, the former may obtain an ouster injunction because the latter would be a trespasser.[19] The position would be the same if the applicant had an exclusive right to occupation.[20] It must be remembered in this connection that a spouse loses her (or his) common law and statutory rights to occupy the other's house after a decree absolute of divorce. Consequently, if, say, the husband is the sole legal and beneficial owner, he may obtain an order against his former wife unless the court has ordered that the statutory rights should continue.[1] If, on the other hand,

---

[14] *Montgomery v Montgomery* [1965] P 46, [1964] 2 All ER 22; *Ruddell v Ruddell* (1967) 111 Sol Jo 497. In *Lucas v Lucas* [1992] 2 FLR 53, CA (where the application was for an ouster injunction) the court assumed jurisdiction two months after decree absolute, pointing out that it would have been possible to do so in any case by giving the applicant formal leave to start fresh proceedings. But it should be noted that relevant proceedings (an application for financial relief including a property adjustment order) were still on foot.

[15] [1984] AC 174, [1983] 2 All ER 807, HL; Hall [1984] CJL 38.

[16] See infra.

[17] Family Proceedings Rules 1991, r 3.9(3).

[18] Under the Supreme Court Act 1981, s 37, and the County Courts Act 1984, s 38.

[19] *Lucas v Lucas* (supra).

[20] As, for example, the defendant had in *Tanner v Tanner* [1975] 3 All ER 776, CA (post, p 619).

[1] *Vaughan v Vaughan* [1953] 1 QB 762, [1953] 1 All ER 209, CA (common law rights); Matrimonial Homes Act 1983, ss 1(10) and 2(4) (statutory rights). See post, p 614.

both parties have a beneficial interest in the property, neither has a right to evict the other and therefore prima facie cannot obtain an ouster injunction against him.[2] The court may, however, be able to grant such an injunction ancillary to a non-molestation injunction if this is necessary to give effect to the latter.[3]

There are conflicting decisions of the Court of Appeal concerning the court's power to grant an ouster injunction in proceedings relating to children. In *Ainsbury v Millington*[4] the applicant and respondent (who were not married) were joint tenants of a council house. Shortly after the birth of their child the respondent was sentenced to 18 months' imprisonment and while he was in prison the applicant married another man who moved into the house with her. On the respondent's release the applicant and her husband left the house and she then brought proceedings under the Guardianship of Minors Act seeking custody, care and control of the child and an order that the respondent should vacate the house so that she could return there with her husband. The Court of Appeal held that there was no jurisdiction to grant an ouster order under that Act and that there was no other statutory jurisdiction to do so because the applicant had no right to occupy the property to the exclusion of the other joint tenant. *Ainsbury v Millington* was followed in *M v M*,[5] where both parties were living in the former matrimonial home after the dissolution of their marriage. The Court of Appeal held that it had no power to grant an ouster order against the former husband under its inherent jurisdiction to protect the children because the mother had no proprietary interest in the house. The father was admittedly the sole owner of the property, but this does not affect the wider principle for which the case is apparently an authority, namely that property rights cannot be overridden solely on the ground that this is in the children's interest. In *Wilde v Wilde*,[6] however, the court reached the opposite conclusion. Both parties continued to live in the former matrimonial home, of which they were joint tenants, after a decree absolute of divorce. The wife had been given care and control of their children, aged eight and six. Some seven months after the decree absolute she applied for an ouster injunction which the county court judge granted as the house was needed as a home for the children and it was impossible for her to return there so long as the husband was in occupation. The Court of Appeal upheld the decision on the ground that the court has an inherent jurisdiction to ensure the protection of children.[7] Neither *Ainsbury v Millington* nor *M v M* was cited.

Wilde v Wilde is clearly inconsistent with these two cases. Following the re-affirmation of the principle that an injunction can be granted only in

---

[2] Cf *Waugh v Waugh* (1981) 3 FLR 375, CA.

[3] *Ainsbury v Millington* [1986] 1 All ER 73, 77, CA (per Croom-Johnson LJ). If one party evicts the other by force, the latter could obtain an order that she be permitted to enter and remain on the premises, but in the absence of a non-molestation order the court could not restrain the defendant from entering.

[4] [1986] 1 All ER 73, CA. The court distinguished the earlier case of *Re W* [1981] 3 All ER 401, CA, on the ground that in that case the claimant was the sole owner of the property in question and also that a non-molestation order has been made, while in *Ainsbury v Millington* the applicant was trying to keep the respondent out of property of which he was joint tenant.

[5] [1988] 1 FLR 225, CA.

[6] [1988] 2 FLR 83, CA.

[7] The court said that it was bound by *Quinn v Quinn* (1983) 4 FLR 394, CA, without considering whether this case could still be regarded as good law after *Richards v Richards*.

support of an existing right,[8] the issue is whether a parent with care and control of a child can be said to have such a right. It is submitted that she does not and that the ratio decidendi of *Ainsbury v Millington* and *M v M* is to be preferred. One parent can look to the other for maintenance but the latter is not bound to provide accommodation for his child on specific premises. It follows that the court has no power to grant an ouster injunction in proceedings under the Children Act. It has also been suggested that there is an inherent jurisdiction to exclude a parent from the home in wardship proceedings,[9] but there is no firm authority for this view and it is equally inconsistent with the majority opinion in *Richards v Richards*.[10]

The position therefore seems to be that after decree absolute a party to a marriage that has been dissolved who is not the sole owner of the former matrimonial home but is seeking sole occupation of it must apply in the divorce proceedings for a property adjustment order or an order transferring a protected, statutory, assured or secure tenancy to her.[11] A former unmarried cohabitant in this position is remediless unless she has a child of whom the other party is the father when she can apply under the Children Act for a settlement or transfer of the parties' former home for the benefit of the child.[12]

Domestic Violence and Matrimonial Proceedings Act 1976

The inadequacy of these remedies, particularly for an unmarried cohabitant who cannot take matrimonial proceedings, led the Select Committee on Violence in Marriage to make the recommendations later embodied in the Domestic Violence and Matrimonial Proceedings Act. The main object of the Act is to give a county court power to grant an injunction to prevent the applicant's spouse or unmarried partner molesting her (or him) or a child living with her and to protect her occupation of the parties' home even though the applicant does not seek any other relief.

An application may be made by either party to a marriage (whether or not they are living together) or by either of two cohabitants who are living with each other in the same household as husband and wife.[13] The phrase 'living in the same household' has caused some difficulty. Obviously the Act does not apply to an unmarried couple who have never lived together, even though they have a child;[14] conversely, parties living at arm's length under the same roof will still be regarded as living in the same household unless they are living entirely separately.[15] But the literal interpretation of the phrase could nullify the effect of the section because in many cases a woman will be forced to leave home before she can take any legal action. To overcome this difficulty a series of cases in the Court of Appeal has laid down the rule that the parties satisfy the conditions if they were living with each other at the time of the

---

[8] In *Richards v Richards* [1984] AC 174, [1983] 2 All ER 807, HL. See ante, p 161.
[9] Per Lord Scarman in *Richards v Richards* (supra) at 207 and 818 respectively.
[10] It was held that there was no such power in *Re D* (1982) 13 Fam Law 111.
[11] This assumes that the court has not ordered that the spouse's statutory rights of occupation under the Matrimonial Homes Act shall continue after the termination of the marriage. See further post, pp 614 (continuation of occupation rights), 736–738 (property adjustment orders) and 637 and 640 (transfer of tenancies).
[12] See post, p 583.
[13] Section 1(2). For the meaning of 'living together as husband and wife', see ante, p 7.
[14] *Tuck v Nicholls* [1989] 1 FLR 283, CA.
[15] *Adeoso v Adeoso* [1981] 1 All ER 107, CA.

violence or other incident which led the applicant to leave.[16] There must come a time when it will be impossible to regard them as still living together at all, and in *Harrison v Lewis*[17] it was held that the court had no jurisdiction under the Act when the defendant assaulted the applicant nine months after they had stopped cohabiting. In many cases a long separation will itself indicate that the applicant no longer needs the court's protection, and as Ormrod LJ observed in *McLean v Nugent*,[18] the longer the lapse of time between the cessation of the parties' relationship and the commencement of proceedings, the more difficult it will be for the applicant to bring herself within the section.

A divorced person clearly does not come within the ambit of the Act even though the former spouses are still living together[19] (unless of course they have resumed cohabitation in the full sense and are living with each other in the same household as husband and wife). Hence a divorced wife will usually have to seek such ancillary relief as is available to her in the divorce proceedings. Nor does the Act apply, for example, if the parties are parent and child, brother and sister, or other members of the same family, or a homosexual couple.

Under section 1 of the Act a county court may grant an injunction containing one or more of the following provisions:

(a) restraining the other party from molesting the applicant;
(b) restraining him from molesting a child living with the applicant;
(c) excluding him from any part of the matrimonial home or from a specified area in which the matrimonial home is included;
(d) requiring him to permit the applicant to enter and remain in the matrimonial home.

In the case of an unmarried couple the term 'matrimonial home' is to be construed as though they were married.[20]

Three aspects of these provisions need special comment. First, the word 'molest' has a wide meaning. There must be an intention to cause distress or harm[1] but, given this, it includes pestering, causing trouble, vexing, annoying and putting to inconvenience.[2] It will cover any form of assault and physical interference and such other activities as inflicting one's society on the other party, lying in wait for her, following her about, shouting obscenities at her, sending her abusive letters,[3] repeatedly telephoning her, or any other form of harassment that calls for the intervention of the court.[4] Secondly, the

---

[16] See particularly *O'Neill v Williams* [1984] FLR 1, 9, CA. Earlier decisions to the same effect are to be found in *Davis v Johnson* [1979] AC 264, [1978] 1 All ER 841, CA; *McLean v Nugent* (1980) 1 FLR 26, CA; *McLean v Burke* (1982) 3 FLR 70, CA; and *White v White* [1983] Fam 54, [1983] 2 All ER 51, CA. These cases were not considered in *M v M* [1988] 1 FLR 225, where the court gave no reason for holding that the Act did not apply even though the parties (who were divorced) had both been living in the former matrimonial home a month before the hearing.
[17] [1988] 2 FLR 339, CA.
[18] (1980) 1 FLR 26, 32, CA. Cited and followed in *O'Neill v Williams* (supra) at p 10.
[19] *White v White* (supra).
[20] Section 1(2).
[1] *Johnson v Walton* [1990] 1 FLR 350, 352, CA.
[2] See *Vaughan v Vaughan* [1973] 3 All ER 449, CA.
[3] *George v George* [1986] 2 FLR 347, CA.
[4] As in *Horner v Horner* [1982] Fam 90, [1982] 2 All ER 495, CA (intercepting wife and handing her threatening letters).

defendant may be restrained from molesting *any* child living with the applicant.[5] The Act does not define 'child', and the term probably includes anyone under the age of 18. He obviously does not have to be the child of both spouses or even of either of them, nor need he have ever lived with the defendant. What is less certain is whether the court has power under the Act to make an order with respect to an adult who is a child (in the sense of a son or daughter) of the applicant or, perhaps, of the defendant. If, say, the husband is assaulting or pestering his 20 year old daughter, she needs the same protection as her younger sister, and it would be regrettable if the Act were to be interpreted so as to prevent the court from affording it to her. Thirdly, although the court has no express power to grant an injunction with respect to the contents of the house, it is submitted that any attempt by the respondent to remove them against the applicant's will could well amount to molestation of the latter.

Despite the short title of the Act, the court has jurisdiction even though the defendant has not offered violence to the applicant provided that there has been a real threat of violence or disturbance.[6]

If the parties are unmarried, the Act gives the court a power to vest in the applicant a *right* to occupy the home that she (or he) might not otherwise have. In *Davis v Johnson*[7] the House of Lords held that its purpose, which is to protect cohabitants against homelessness as well as molestation, would be defeated if a party had to rely on a proprietary right to invoke its jurisdiction. Consequently an applicant who is only a bare licensee can obtain an order excluding the other party from the home. This will not affect any other proprietary right of the respondent who could therefore dispose of the property but it will suspend his right to occupy the premises so long as it is in force.

Applications to the High Court

Section 1 of the Act confers jurisdiction only on county courts. The High Court's practice has been changed so that it may now grant an injunction containing any of the provisions mentioned above even though no other relief is sought.[8] It would seem, however, that this would not enable that court to grant an injunction excluding an unmarried cohabitant from the parties' home if the applicant had no legal or equitable right in the property to be protected.

---

[5] Hence if the child normally resides with, say, a grandparent and not with the applicant, the latter may not be able to obtain an injunction under the Domestic Violence and Matrimonial Proceedings Act even though the child spends part of his time with her. Presumably a child continues to live with the applicant during a temporary absence (eg in hospital or at a boarding school): cf Adoption Act 1976, s 72(1A) (post, p 443).

[6] *Galan v Galan* [1985] FLR 905, 914, CA (per Purchas LJ). Quarrelling, recrimination and tension between the parties are apparently not enough: *Wilde v Wilde* [1988] 2 FLR 83, at 87 and 93, CA. It is immaterial that the defendant's acts were involuntary (eg owing to epilepsy): *Wooton v Wooton* [1984] FLR 871, CA.

[7] [1979] AC 264, [1978] 1 All ER 1132, HL.

[8] See now Family Proceedings Rules 1991, r 3.9(2).

Matrimonial Homes Act 1983

This Act is not available to unmarried cohabitants and deals solely with the occupation of the matrimonial home. Its provisions will be dealt with more fully later;[9] suffice it to say for the present that, if one spouse has a statutory right to occupy the matrimonial home given by section 1(1) of the Act,[10] the High Court or a county court may make an order:

(a) declaring, enforcing, restricting or terminating that right; or
(b) prohibiting, suspending or restricting the exercise by either spouse of the right to occupy the home; or
(c) requiring either spouse to permit the other to exercise that right.[11]

If both spouses are entitled to occupy a dwelling house which is or has been their matrimonial home by virtue of a legal estate vested in them jointly or by virtue of a contract or any enactment (so that rights of occupation will not be conferred by section 1(1)), either of them may apply for an order prohibiting, suspending or restricting the other's right to occupy the home or requiring the latter to permit the applicant to exercise her or his own right.[12]

In either case the court may restrict either spouse's right to the occupation of certain parts of the home only, and in particular may exclude him or her from any part of it used wholly or mainly for the other's trade, business or profession. Hence, if the husband is a medical practitioner, the wife might be forbidden to enter his surgery or garage; conversely, his right to enter the house could be restricted to those parts. Entry may be restricted to certain times or for certain purposes, for example to enable the excluded spouse to have contact with children. The court may also order the spouse occupying the house or any part of it by virtue of an order made under the Act to pay the other an occupation rent and may impose on either of them obligations to repair and maintain the house and to pay other outgoings (for example, rates or mortgage repayments).[13] Orders may be for a limited period of time and the court may make an interim order to last, say, until the hearing of divorce proceedings or until the wife finds suitable alternative accommodation.[14]

Exercise of the power to grant a non-molestation injunction

As failure to comply with an injunction may result in the committal of the party in default, an order should be made (whether under the Domestic Violence and Matrimonial Proceedings Act or by way of ancillary relief in other proceedings) only in really serious cases where there is some evidence of molestation in the past[15] and it is necessary to protect the applicant. Thus an injunction has been refused to a husband who, pending divorce proceedings, was living under the same roof as his wife and could afford to

[9] See post, pp 613–618.
[10] See post, p 613.
[11] S 1(2), (9). An order under the Act cannot be made against third persons: *Kalsi v Kalsi* [1992] 1 FLR 511, CA.
[12] S 9. A mortgagee's right to possession is to be disregarded.
[13] Ss 1(3) and 9(2).
[14] Ss 1(4) and 9(2); *Baynham v Baynham* [1969] 1 All ER 305, CA.
[15] *Spindlow v Spindlow* [1979] Fam 52, [1979] 1 All ER 169, CA.

move elsewhere,[16] and a county court has refused to grant an injunction to a wife who intended to continue to cohabit with her husband but claimed that she needed an injunction to protect her when he was drunk.[17] If a party applies for an order ex parte, the court should exercise its jurisdiction even more sparingly and only when it is necessary to act quickly to avert a real and immediate danger of serious injury or irreparable damage.[18]

Injunctions restraining a spouse from coming within a specified distance of the matrimonial home will be granted when this is the only way of giving effective protection to the applicant or a child.[19]

Exercise of the power to make an exclusion order

By 1983 two distinct and inconsistent lines of cases were to be seen. One placed the main emphasis on the parties' conduct and relationship: the question to be asked was whether the wife was reasonable in refusing to return to the home if the husband was there.[20] The other emphasised the welfare of the children: an injunction would be granted in favour of the mother if she needed the home for accommodation for them, irrespective of her reason for living apart from her husband.[1] It became necessary to decide between these two principles in *Richards v Richards*.[2] Whilst still living with her husband, the wife presented a petition for divorce based on allegations of his behaviour which the husband denied and the judge described as 'rubbishy'. The wife then left the house which the spouses occupied and, after living with a friend for a short time, she sought an injunction in the divorce proceedings to exclude her husband from the home. The trial judge found that she had no reasonable grounds for refusing to live with her husband but as she would not do so he felt compelled to grant the injunction to give the children somewhere to live, despite the fact that this was unjust to the husband. The Court of Appeal dismissed the husband's appeal but a furher appeal to the House of Lords was successful.[3] Having held that the proceedings should have been brought under what is now the Matrimonial Homes Act 1983,[4] the majority of the House held that the court must apply the criteria set out in section 1(3) of the Act. This provides:

> 'On an application for an order under this section, the court may make such an order as it thinks just and reasonable having regard to the conduct of the spouses in relation to each other and otherwise, to their respective needs and financial resources, to the needs of any children and to all the circumstances of the case ...'

[16] *Freedman v Freedman* [1967] 2 All ER 680n.
[17] *F v F* [1989] 2 FLR 451. This decision has been criticised on the ground that it defeats Parliament's object to protect an applicant from violence within the family (see *Butterworths Family Law Service*, para B[38]), but it seems scarcely reasonable to expect one party to live with the other under threat of committal proceedings if he misbehaves. An injunction should not be granted if the defendant is incapable of understanding its nature and consequences: *Wookey v Wookey* [1991] Fam 121, [1991] 3 All ER 365, CA.
[18] *Ansah v Ansah* [1977] Fam 138, [1977] 2 All ER 628, CA; *Practice Note* [1978] 2 All ER 919.
[19] Eg if the defendant repeatedly follows the applicant about, tries to keep her out of the matrimonial home or would otherwise live in the same block of flats.
[20] *Elsworth v Elsworth* (1978) 1 FLR 245, CA; *Myers v Myers* [1982] 1 All ER 776, CA.
[1] *Bassett v Bassett* [1975] Fam 76, [1975] 1 All ER 513, CA; *Walker v Walker* [1978] 3 All ER 141, CA; *Samson v Samson* [1982] 1 All ER 780, CA.
[2] [1984] AC 174, [1983] 2 All ER 807, HL.
[3] It should be added that by the time the case got to the House of Lords the parties had reached a compromise by which the children lived in the house for the whole time and the wife lived there during the week and the husband at weekends.
[4] See Pearl in *Essays and Family Law 1985* (ed Freeman) pp 23 et seq.

In particular the principle of the paramountcy of the child's welfare, which the court is required to take into account in deciding questions relating to the upbringing of a child and the administration of his property,[5] applies only to those questions and not to the question of the occupation of the matrimonial home.

Lord Brandon, with whom Lord Diplock and Lord Bridge agreed, further stated that the same criteria must be applied if proceedings are brought under the Domestic Violence and Matrimonial Proceedings Act.[6] Although the Matrimonial Homes Act does not apply to unmarried cohabitants, the Court of Appeal has since held that the same criteria should be adopted in disputes between them.[7] We must now consider these in a little more detail.

The parties' conduct

Richards v Richards has clearly reinstated the need to take into account the relationship of the parties and the reasonableness of the applicant in refusing to live with the respondent. The husband's physically assaulting the wife or children[8] or threatening to do so[9] will obviously justify her in refusing to live with him; on the other hand, mere tension, unpleasantness and inconvenience are not enough.[10] It is submitted that conduct becomes critical if it makes the position impossible or intolerable, and if the applicant has lived with the respondent and tolerated his conduct for a long time, this may indicate that the court's protection is not needed.[11] The Court of Appeal has repeatedly pointed out that to evict a man from his own home is a 'Draconian order' which should not be made lightly.[12] The result has been to place more emphasis on the parties' conduct which has now in practice become the dominant consideration in most cases.[13]

The parties' needs and financial resources

What is particularly important is the parties' ability to find other accommodation. This will depend in part on their financial situation; alternatively one of them may be able to live with parents or other relations. The court must also take into account the claims of each to be rehoused by the housing authority.[14] If there is no practical alternative to permitting the parent looking

---

[5] See now Children Act 1989, s 1(1), post, p 336.

[6] At 222 and 829 respectively. But see Parkinson *The Domestic Violence Act* [1986] Fam Law 70.

[7] *Lee v Lee* [1984] FLR 243, CA.

[8] Even if involuntary: *Wooton v Wooton* [1984] FLR 871, [1985] Fam Law 31 CA (violence due to epilepsy).

[9] *Baggott v Baggott* [1986] 1 FLR 377, CA.

[10] Cf *Richards v Richards* (supra); *Wiseman v Simpson* [1988] 1 All ER 245, CA. Contrast *Scott v Scott* [1992] 1 FLR 529, CA, where it was held that the husband might properly be excluded if this was the only way to prevent him breaking a non-molestation injunction even though there was no evidence of violence.

[11] As in *Wooton v Wooton* (supra).

[12] *Summers v Summers* [1986] 1 FLR 343, CA; *Wiseman v Simpson* (supra); *Tuck v Nicholls* [1989] 1 FLR 283, CA.

[13] Cf *Blackstock v Blackstock* [1991] 2 FLR 308, CA, where the Court of Appeal upheld a county court's refusal to grant the wife an ouster order after an incident in which the wife's arm had been broken on the ground that it would be manifestly unjust to exclude the husband (who had suffered a broken cheekbone) if she caused the situation.

[14] *Wooton v Wooton* (supra); *Thurley v Smith* [1984] FLR 875, CA.

after the children to occupy the matrimonial home with them, such an order must be made even though the other will find it difficult to find other accommodation.[15]

The children's needs

Although these are no longer the paramount consideration in all cases, in some they may be so clamant as to become so.[16] Difficulty arises if the mother unreasonably refuses to live with the father and he is unable to look after the children himself. The effect that compelling parties to live together may have on the children must be considered,[17] and other things being equal, the children's needs must still predominate.[18] In *Lee v Lee*[19] the parties (who were not married) had had a stormy relationship which culminated in the applicant's taking a large overdose of pills. As little weight could be placed on the conduct of either party in the circumstances, the children's need for a home led the Court of Appeal to make an order excluding the man from the home so that the children could live there with their mother.

Other considerations

The court may refuse to make an ouster order if there is a real possibility of reconciliation. Similarly, if the parties have been living apart for some time before the application, this may indicate that there is no need for an injunction, at least as a short term remedy.[20] Nor is it a proper use of the jurisdiction to make an order 'to allow the dust to settle'[1] or to bring the respondent to his senses.[2] If the house is owned jointly with a third person, the court must also take into account the effect of an order on the relationship between the applicant and other persons entitled to occupy the premises and may refuse to grant an injunction if this would produce an impossible position.[3]

If other matrimonial proceedings are pending, the court will tend to retain the status quo and may exclude the husband if it considers that the wife is entitled to remain in the matrimonial home until the hearing of the petition and that she will not be able to do so if he is there[4] or if he unlawfully tries to evict her or to deal with the property in a way which might prejudice her right of occupation.[5]

[15] *Re T* [1987] 1 FLR 181, CA.
[16] Per Lord Hailsham LC in *Richards v Richards* (supra) at 204 and 816 respectively.
[17] *Wiseman v Simpson* (supra).
[18] This means that, if the court has before it questions of both the care and control of children and occupation of the matrimonial home, the former must be resolved first: *Re T* (supra). But see *Scott v Scott* (supra). The court may make an order under s 8 of the Children Act 1989 in any proceedings brought under the Domestic Violence and Matrimonial Proceedings Act and s 1 of the Matrimonial Homes Act: see post, p 364.
[19] [1984] FLR 243, CA.
[20] *O'Neill v Williams* [1984] FLR 1, CA.
[1] *Summers v Summers* (supra).
[2] *Burke v Burke* [1987] 2 FLR 71, CA.
[3] *Chaudhry v Chaudhry* [1987] 1 FLR 347, CA.
[4] *Jones v Jones* [1971] 2 All ER 737, CA (husband ordered to leave house with his mistress whom he had installed there). Secus if the wife will ultimately have to surrender possession to the husband whatever the outcome of the proceedings: *Murcutt v Murcutt* [1952] P 266, [1952] 2 All ER 427. See also *Boyt v Boyt* [1948] 2 All ER 436, CA.
[5] *Halden v Halden* [1966] 3 All ER 412, CA. Cf *Pinckney v Pinckney* [1966] 1 All ER 121n (husband ordered to remove mistress whom he had installed in the matrimonial home).

Duration of orders

Non-molestation orders may be of indefinite duration. Exclusion orders, on the other hand, are intended to provide a short term remedy and consequently any order made should take effect as soon as possible after giving the respondent a reasonable time to find other accommodation[6] and should last only so long as is reasonably necessary to enable the applicant to find alternative accommodation or to take other proceedings.[7] There is a danger that an injunction could become an instrument of oppression,[8] and normally the court should impose a limit of three months on its operation in the first place.[9] It will always be open to the applicant to apply for an extension or for the respondent to apply for a discharge. But if the respondent repeatedly returns after injunctions cease to have effect and thus compels the applicant to return to the court for further relief, it will be proper to grant an injunction to run indefinitely until further order.[10]

Enforcement of injunctions

The usual means of enforcing an injunction is to apply to the court to have the party in default committed to prison for contempt.[11] This will normally take a number of days and in the meantime the wife may be at risk from a violent husband. Consequently section 2 of the Domestic Violence and Matrimonial Proceedings Act 1976 affords a much more effective weapon. If a judge grants an injunction (in whatever terms)[12] restraining the other party to the marriage from using violence against the applicant or a child living with the applicant or excluding the other party from the matrimonial home or a specified area in which the matrimonial home is included, he may attach to it a power of arrest. Two points should be noted about this power. First, it exists whenever such an injunction is granted and is not confined to injunctions granted under section 1 of the Act.[13] Secondly, as in the case of section 1, the term 'parties to a marriage' includes a man and woman living with each other in the same household as husband and wife.[14] But the court has no jurisdiction to attach a power of arrest save in the circumstances laid down by the Act: hence, for example, it may not do so to support an order forbidding a father from removing a child from the mother's care and

---

[6] *Dunsire v Dunsire* [1991] 2 FLR 314, CA.
[7] *Davis v Johnson* [1979] AC 264, [1978] 1 All ER 1132, HL. A fortiori if the injunction is granted ex parte: *G v G* [1990] 1 FLR 395, CA.
[8] *Hopper v Hopper* [1979] 1 All ER 181, CA.
[9] *Practice Note* [1978] 2 All ER 1056.
[10] *Spencer v Camacho* (1983) 4 FLR 662, CA; *Galan v Galan* [1985] FLR 905, CA.
[11] The other methods of enforcing an injunction are by a fine or (in the High Court) writ of sequestration. As a minor under the age of 17 cannot be imprisoned for contempt, an injunction will be ineffectual and should not be granted unless he has an income so that even a small fine might have a salutary effect: *Wookey v Wookey* [1991] Fam 121, [1991] 3 All ER 365, CA.
[12] But there must be an injunction and there is no power to attach a power of arrest if the defendant gives an undertaking: *Carpenter v Carpenter* [1988] 1 FLR 121, CA. It is doubtful whether a power of arrest can be attached if the proceedings are taken under the Matrimonial Homes Act 1983 because the court technically makes an order and does not grant an injunction.
[13] *Lewis v Lewis* [1978] Fam 60, [1978] 1 All ER 729, CA.
[14] Section 2(2). See further ante, pp 165–166.

control[15] or if the injunction was granted in divorce proceedings after the decree absolute had been pronounced.[16]

Some of the provisions of section 2 are different from those of section 1. A power of arrest can be attached only to an injunction restraining the defendant from using violence (and not to other forms of molestation) and on a literal interpretation cannot be attached to an injunction excluding him from part of the matrimonial home.[17] Furthermore, the court may exercise this power only if the defendant has caused actual bodily harm to the applicant or the child concerned and considers that he is likely to do so again. Actual bodily harm is not confined to physical assault and has been said to include 'any hurt or injury calculated to interfere with the health or comfort' of another: hence it would seem sufficient that the defendant's conduct has caused nervous shock or other injury to the other's state of mind.[18] In *Kendrick v Kendrick*,[19] however, the Court of Appeal held that, for the purpose of section 2 of the Domestic Violence and Matrimonial Proceedings Act at least, it must be shown that the applicant suffered real psychological damage and that there was 'a real change in [her] psychological condition'. Hence there was no jurisdiction to attach a power of arrest when all the wife showed was that she was afraid that her husband would return home so that she could not return there herself. Presumably the decision would have been otherwise if his conduct had engendered real terror.

If a power of arrest is attached to an injunction, any constable may arrest the defendant if he has reasonable cause for suspecting that he is in breach of any provision mentioned above. This gives immediate protection to the party obtaining the injunction because she may invoke the assistance of the police without having to take proceedings to have the defendant committed. To assist her, a copy of the injunction must be delivered to the officer in charge of the police station for her address.[20] Once arrested, the defendant must be brought before a judge within 24 hours (disregarding Sundays, Christmas Day and Good Friday) but may not be released within that time except on a judge's direction.[1]

As Ormrod LJ observed, a power of arrest 'is a very useful remedy in exceptional cases where men or women persistently disobey injunctions and make a nuisance of themselves to the other party and to others concerned'.[2] Because of the potential threat to the defendant's liberty it has been described as a 'Draconian remedy'[3] and should not be used indiscriminately or regarded as a routine addition to an order and normally should not be attached for more than three months.[4]

[15] *Re G (Wardship)* (1982) 4 FLR 538, CA.
[16] *White v White* [1983] Fam 54, [1983] 2 All ER 51, CA; *Duo v Duo* [1992] 3 All ER 121, 130, 131, CA.
[17] Presumably because the court would not make such an order if the defendant is likely to treat the applicant with violence (which would justify it in attaching a power of arrest).
[18] See *R v Miller* [1954] 2 QB 282, 292, [1954] 2 All ER 529, 534 (per Lynskey J).
[19] [1990] 2 FLR 107, CA.
[20] Family Proceedings Rules 1991, r 3.9(6), (7).
[1] Section 2(3)–(5), as amended by the Domestic Proceedings and Magistrates' Courts Act 1978, Sch 2.
[2] *Lewis v Lewis* (supra) at 63 and 731 respectively.
[3] Per Sheldon J in *Harrison v Lewis* [1988] 2 FLR 339, 343, CA.
[4] *Lewis v Lewis* (supra); *Practice Note* [1981] 1 All ER 224, where it is pointed out that the police are rarely called on to take action on an injunction which is more than three months old. For a startling use of the power, see *Boylan v Boylan* (1980) 11 Fam Law 76, CA.

3. PROCEEDINGS IN MAGISTRATES' COURTS

Orders for personal protection

As we have already seen,[5] the power formerly possessed by magistrates to make a separation order was abolished on the recommendation of the Law Commission who proposed that it should be replaced by a power to make an order forbidding either spouse to use violence against the other or a child and, if necessary, excluding him from the matrimonial home. They considered that such proceedings would not be made redundant by the powers given to county courts by the Domestic Violence and Matrimonial Proceedings Act but would complement them by affording summary, local and inexpensive relief.[6] Their proposals are now substantially embodied in the provisions of sections 16, 17 and 18 of the Domestic Proceedings and Magistrates' Courts Act 1978. Only a party to a marriage may apply for an order: these proceedings are not available to a divorced person or to a man or woman cohabiting outside marriage.

On the application of either spouse, a magistrates' court may make an order that the other spouse shall not use or threaten to use violence against the person of the applicant or the person of a child of the family. The court must be satisfied that the respondent has already used or threatened to use such violence and that the order is necessary for the protection of the applicant or a child. In addition it may include a further provision that the respondent shall not incite or assist any other person to use or threaten to use violence; this power may prove very valuable when it is believed that a husband might instigate a friend or relation to use violence.[7]

A comparison of these provisions with those contained in section 1 of the Domestic Violence and Matrimonial Proceedings Act 1976 will show that magistrates' powers are more limited in three respects. First, even though they are convinced that there is a real danger that the respondent will use violence, they cannot make an order, for example, if he has used violence against another person but has not done so or threatened to do so against the applicant or a child of the family. Secondly, the order may only prohibit violence *against the person*: magistrates have no power to forbid the respondent from carrying out psychological warfare on the applicant or a child or from indulging in any other form of molestation.[8] Thirdly, the order may relate only to the applicant or a child *of the family*: on the other hand, the child need not be living with the applicant and may apparently be of any age.[9]

Magistrates have also been given a power to exclude a spouse from the matrimonial home and they may make an order requiring the respondent to leave the home, prohibiting him from entering it, and requiring him to permit

---

[5] Ante, p 15.

[6] Law Com No 77 (Report on Matrimonial Proceedings in Magistrates' Courts), paras. 3.15–3.17.

[7] S 16(1), (2), (10). The court has jurisdiction whether or not the application is coupled with an application for any other order under the Act.

[8] The Law Commission justified this on the ground that allegations of psychological damage might involve the difficult task of assessing expert evidence given by psychiatrists. This overlooks the fact that the applicant would probably be advised not to commence proceedings in a magistrates' court if such evidence was likely to be adduced and that in any case magistrates had been trying cases of mental cruelty since 1895.

[9] For the meaning of 'child of the family', see post, pp 368–369.

the applicant to enter and remain there. In order to ensure that the power will be exercised only where there is substantial evidence that the respondent is likely to resort to violence, much more stringent conditions must be fulfilled. The court must be satisfied, first, that the applicant or a child of the family is in danger of being physically injured by the respondent (or would be in such danger if they were to enter the matrimonial home)[10] and, secondly, that the respondent

(a) has already used violence against the person of the applicant or a child of the family; or
(b) has threatened to do so and has actually used violence against another person; or
(c) has threatened to do so in contravention of an order previously made under this section.[11]

Although the court is not given an express power to restrict a spouse's right to part only of the home, it has been suggested that the power to make an order 'subject to such exceptions and conditions as may be specified' permits it to do so.[12]

If it is essential that the application should be heard without delay, some of the requirements relating to the constitution of family proceedings courts may be waived.[13] If there is imminent danger of physical injury to the applicant or a child of the family, the court has a power to make an *expedited order* forbidding the respondent to use violence (but not an order excluding him from the matrimonial home) which may not remain in force for more than 28 days (although a further expedited order may then be made).[14] Subject to this, magistrates have an unlimited power to determine the length of time for which an order shall remain in force and to attach such exceptions or conditions as they think fit.[15] Either spouse may apply to have any order varied or revoked.[16]

Magistrates must obviously exercise their powers in the same way as the High Court or a county court does when asked to grant a non-molestation injunction and should make an order only in a really serious case when it is necessary for the protection of the applicant or a child of the family. Similarly, although Lord Brandon did not specifically state in *Richards v Richards*[17] that the criteria set out in section 1(3) of the Matrimonial Homes Act

[10] It need not be an *immediate* danger: *McCartney v McCartney* [1981] Fam 59, [1981] 1 All ER 597.
[11] S 1(3), (4). An order has no further effect on any estate or interest in the matrimonial home possessed by the respondent or any other person: s 17(4).
[12] S 16(9). See *Butterworths Family Law Service* para B[93].
[13] See s 16(5).
[14] In particular an order may be made even though the respondent has not been given due notice of the proceedings: ie, this is akin to an ex parte injunction. An expedited order will also come to an end if the hearing of the complaint begins within 28 days. See ss 16(6) (as amended by the Courts and Legal Services Act 1990, Sch 18) and (8) and 17(3).
[15] S 16(9). Thus the court might attach a condition that the respondent should not interfere with the contents of the home.
[16] S 17(1). The High Court or a divorce county court may direct that the order shall cease to have effect in any subsequent matrimonial proceedings. If either spouse applies for an order relating to the occupation of the matrimonial home (or former matrimonial home) under s 1(2) or 9 of the Matrimonial Homes Act 1983, the court hearing that application may discharge an order relating to the occupation of the home made under the Domestic Proceedings and Magistrates' Courts Act: ibid, s 28.
[17] [1984] AC 174, [1983] 2 All ER 807, HL. See ante, p 169.

1983 must be applied in proceedings under the Domestic Proceedings and Magistrates' Courts Act, they obviously must be. The outcome of litigation should not depend on the court in which the applicant chooses to bring the action.

Enforcement of orders

Like judges under the Domestic Violence and Matrimonial Proceedings Act magistrates may attach a power of arrest to an order, but the details differ considerably. Magistrates may do this only if the order forbids the respondent to use violence against the person of the applicant or a child of the family or to enter the matrimonial home, and the court must be satisfied that the respondent has already physically injured one of them and is likely to do so again.[18] Like the High Court or a county court, magistrates should attach a power of arrest only if it is essential for the efficacy or the order.[19] As in the case of a power of arrest attached to an injunction, a constable may arrest anyone whom he has reasonable cause for suspecting of being in breach of such an order and must then bring him before a magistrate within 24 hours (excluding Sundays, Christmas Day and Good Friday).[20] It will therefore be seen that a constable cannot exercise this power if he has reason to believe that the respondent has merely threatened to use violence (but has not actually used it) or is refusing to leave the matrimonial home or to permit the applicant to enter it.

If no power of arrest is attached, an applicant may apply for a warrant for the arrest of a respondent alleged to have disobeyed an order.[1] A person guilty of disobedience may be fined up to £2,000 or committed to prison for not more than two months for each breach.[2]

Concurrent orders

A spouse may wish to apply for an order in a county court (or the High Court) even though she has already obtained one in a magistrates' court. This could occur, for example, if a husband, who had previously used violence against his wife, is now molesting her in some other way; similarly, if she commences divorce proceedings, it is usually convenient to have all orders made in the same court. The existence of a magistrates' order does not preclude an application to a county court but it is undesirable that two orders should be in existence simultaneously. Consequently the county court should grant an injunction only on the applicant's undertaking to have the magistrates' order discharged.[3]

In *O'Brien v O'Brien*[4] the Court of Appeal held that the fact that a

---

[18] Physical injury may not include psychological harm and thus may be narrower than 'actual bodily harm' required by the Domestic Violence and Matrimonial Proceedings Act (ante, p 173).

[19] *Widdowson v Widdowson* (1982) 4 FLR 121, 125.

[20] S 18(1)–(3).

[1] S 18(4), (5). The effect (probably unintended) of these provisions is that a respondent who disobeys an order by *threatening* to use violence or by refusing to leave the matrimonial home or to permit the applicant to enter it may be arrested on a warrant if no power of arrest is attached but may not be arrested at all if one is attached.

[2] Magistrates' Courts Act 1980, s 63(3). In the event of two or more breaches, however, consecutive periods of imprisonment may not be imposed: *Head v Head* [1982] 3 All ER 14.

[3] *Horner v Horner* [1982] Fam 90, [1982] 2 All ER 495, CA.

[4] [1985] FLR 801, CA.

magistrates' court has declined to make an order does not prevent a county court judge from doing so even though the applicant relies on the same evidence in both cases. Unfortunately the court did not give reasons for its decision. As the husband had treated the applicant with violence, the magistrates clearly had jurisdiction, and it seems scarcely relevant that the county court judge apparently granted the injunction in custody proceedings and not under the Domestic Violence and Matrimonial Proceedings Act. The decision could be justified as an example of the principle that proceedings before magistrates cannot create an estoppel in a county court;[5] one trusts that it will not encourage unsuccessful applicants before magistrates to take hopeless cases to a county court.

Binding over to be of good behaviour

If no other proceedings are open to the victim of molestation or harassment, his or her sole remedy is to apply to a magistrates' court for an order requiring the other party to be of good behaviour towards the complainant. If the latter fails to comply with the order he can be committed to prison for a period of six months or until he does comply with it, whichever is the shorter.[6]

4. PROPOSALS FOR REFORM

Nearly a decade ago Lord Scarman observed:[7]

'The statutory provision is a hotchpotch of enactments of limited scope passed into law to meet specific situations or to strengthen the powers of specified courts. The sooner the range, scope and effect of these powers are rationalised into a coherent and comprehensive body of statute law, the better.'

Reviewing the present state of the law in their Report on Domestic Violence and Occupation of the Family Home,[8] the Law Commission identified a number of inconsistencies and anomalies: the scope of the remedies offered by the various courts differs; the criteria they apply in exercising their discretion when deciding whether to make an ouster order are outdated and fail to take account of the different situations with which the courts have to deal; no protection is given to former cohabitants and others falling outside specific categories except for the often inadequate remedies offered by the law of torts; and the courts have no means of adjusting cohabitants' rights of occupation apart from their limited powers under the Domestic Violence and Matrimonial Proceedings Act.[9]

With respect to non-molestation orders the Commission propose that these shortcomings should be dealt with by giving all courts power to make an order whenever it is just and reasonable to do so having regard to all the circumstances including the need to secure the health, safety and well-being

---

[5] See ante, p 103.
[6] Magistrates' Courts Act 1980, s 115. The defendant may also be required to find sureties. See Parker 9 Fam Law 76.
[7] *Richards v Richards* [1984] AC 174, 206–207, [1983] 2 All ER 807, 818, HL.
[8] Law Com No 207, 1992, following Law Com Working Paper No 113 (Domestic Violence and Occupation of the Matrimonial Home).
[9] See further ibid, Part II.

of the applicant and any relevant child,[10] whether or not there has been physical violence. They recommend extending the power to apply for an order to anyone who could be broadly described as associated with the respondent by virtue of a family or similar relationship, as they believe that 'when problems arise in close family relationships, the strength of emotions involved can cause unique reactions which may at times be irrational or obsessive'[11] and thus give rise to molestation, harassment and violence. Specifically, those entitled to apply would include spouses and former spouses, cohabitants (that is, persons living with each other as husband and wife) and former cohabitants, other persons living in the same household,[12] specified relations,[13] engaged couples and former engaged couples, persons who have had a sexual relationship with each other (not necessarily involving sexual intercourse),[14] and parents and others who have or have had parental responsibility for a child.

The Commission's proposals respecting orders relating to occupation of the home (which they term 'occupation orders') are equally radical. If the applicant is entitled to occupy property by virtue of a beneficial interest, contract or statutory right,[15] they propose that she (or he) should be able to obtain an occupation order if the property has at any time been the home of both parties. They recommend that she should be able to obtain an order against anyone against whom she could obtain a non-molestation order: they justify this extension on the ground that an occupation order will frequently be necessary to support a non-molestation order. They envisage the extension of the principle in *Davis v Johnson*[16] by proposing that an applicant who is not entitled to occupy the property should be able to apply for an order against a former spouse, cohabitant or former cohabitant, which would resolve the difficulty exemplified by *Ainsbury v Millington.*[17] The court would have the same powers that it now has under the Matrimonial Homes Act (including that of making ancillary orders) and also a power to exclude the respondent from a defined area in which the home is situated. The Commission would also empower the court to make an order with respect to property which the parties intended should be their home but which never became so. All courts would have power to make occupation orders, but magistrates would have to decline jurisdiction or transfer a case to a county court if it were necessary to determine the parties' right to occupy the home. The Commission suggest criteria (which would be more stringent in the case of ex parte applications) to be applied uniformly before an order were made.

---

[10] Ie any child who is living or might reasonably be expected to live with either party, any child with respect to whom an order under the Children Act 1989 or the Adoption Act 1976 is in question in the proceedings, and any other child whose interests are relevant.

[11] Law Com No 207, para 3.17.

[12] But excluding employees, tenants, lodgers and boarders, as the Commission wish to exclude harassment at work and from landlords. This fails to take account of the fact that many lodgers and boarders are fully integrated into the family with whom they are living and that it may be a matter of chance whether a person is excluded. (For example, two people sharing accommodation may be joint tenants or one may be the sub-tenant of the other.)

[13] Thus closing the gap seen in *Patel v Patel* (ante, p 161).

[14] The Commission cited the boyfriend and girlfriend in a romantic relationship (para 3.24) but the category clearly includes homosexual couples. The vagueness of the term may make the proposal controversial.

[15] Including the spouse's statutory rights of occupation under the Matrimonial Homes Act 1983.

[16] Ante, p 167.

[17] Ante, p 164.

The Commission also recommend improving cohabitants' rights by extending the court's existing power to transfer a tenancy from one spouse to the other on divorce, nullity or judicial separation[18] to transferring a tenancy from one cohabitant to the other on the breakdown of their relationship. They also propose that the court should be empowered to order the transferee to compensate the transferor.

The Commission would further strengthen powers of arrest, in particular by making it obligatory for the court to attach a power whenever there has been violence or threatened violence unless the applicant or any child involved would be adequately protected without it. What will doubtless prove to be their most controversial recommendation is that the police should have power to apply for a civil remedy on behalf of the victim if they have been involved in an incident of molestation or actual or threatened violence. They would first be obliged to consult the victim (just as the court would have to take account of her views), but the police could proceed and the court could make an order without her consent if they considered this appropriate. The Commission believe this power is desirable to protect a woman who is so cowed that she is unable to take the initiative herself; it would also reduce the threat of intimidation and help the police to prevent further violence. Against this must be balanced the objection of involving the police in the civil law and of permitting one person to take proceedings in another's name against her will.[19] It remains to be seen whether the Commission's proposals, however laudable, will be politically acceptable.

[18] See post, pp 637 and 640.
[19] See further paras 5.18–5.23.

Chapter 6

The termination of marriage

In English law a valid marriage may be terminated only by the death of one of the parties or by a decree of dissolution or divorce pronounced by a court of competent jurisdiction.

A. Death and presumption of death

Death

The death of either party ipso facto brings the marriage to an end.

Decree of presumption of death and dissolution of marriage

Before 1938 the disappearance of one of the spouses presented an insurmountable difficulty. If H's wife, W, disappeared in such circumstances as to lead to the reasonable inference that she was dead (although her death could not be proved), H could remarry without committing the crime of bigamy and his second marriage would be *presumptively* valid. But if it were later proved that W was in fact alive when H remarried, then, of course, the second marriage would be *conclusively* void with all the legal consequences that that entailed. In order to meet this situation, section 19 of the Matrimonial Causes Act 1973 permits the court to make a decree of presumption of death and of dissolution of the marriage if it is satisfied that there are reasonable grounds for supposing that the petitioner's spouse is dead.[1] The general presumption of death which may be raised by seven years' absence is specifically applied to these proceedings by the provision that

'... the fact that for a period of seven years or more the other party to the marriage has been continually absent from the petitioner and the petitioner has no reason to believe that the other party has been living within that time shall be evidence that the other party is dead until the contrary is proved.'[2]

The petitioner is not bound to rely on this period of absence. The court may accept any satisfactory evidence from which it may be presumed that the spouse is dead:[3] the inference to be drawn from the seven years' absence is of particular importance when there is no evidence at all of what has happened since. It will be observed that the statutory presumption is different from that which arises at common law after seven years' absence. What is important under the statute is the petitioner's belief. In *Thompson*

---

[1] The power was originally given by the Matrimonial Causes Act 1937. Proceedings must be commenced in a divorce county court but should normally be transferred to the High Court. Matrimonial and Family Proceedings Act 1984, s 33(3); *Practice Direction (Family Division: Distribution of Business)* [1992] 3 All ER 151.

[2] Matrimonial Causes Act 1973, s 19(3).

[3] Eg, the otherwise inexplicable disappearance of an explorer.

v Thompson[4] Sachs J held that nothing must have happened during the period of seven years from which the petitioner, as a reasonable person, would conclude that the other spouse was still alive. Although the point was left open in *Thompson v Thompson*,[5] the court is hardly likely to accept that the belief is reasonably held unless the petitioner has made all appropriate enquiries. The jurisdiction is discretionary; consequently, even if the petitioner can claim the benefit of the presumption, the court will not pronounce a decree, contrary to the justice of the case, where there is a probability that the other party is still alive. This might occur, for example, if an explorer had announced his intention of spending more than seven years in a country with which communication is impracticable.[6]

A decree nisi must be rescinded if the other spouse is found to be still alive.[7] Once it has been made absolute, however, it dissolves the marriage irrevocably even though the other subsequently reappears.[8]

As in the case of divorce, the court has jurisdiction if the petitioner is domiciled in England when the proceedings are begun or has been habitually resident here throughout the period of one year ending with that date.[9]

Now that a spouse may seek a divorce after five years' separation, proceedings for presumption of death and dissolution are of less importance than they were formerly.[10] In some cases he might succeed in reliance on five years' separation although he would certainly fail if he asked the court to presume that the other spouse was dead. On the other hand, he will have to petition for presumption of death if he wishes to have the marriage dissolved within five years of the other's disappearance or of his own decision to bring consortium to an end.

B. Divorce

1. HISTORICAL INTRODUCTION[11]

We have seen that the doctrine of the indissolubility of marriage was accepted by the English ecclesiastical courts after the Reformation, so that

[4] [1956] P 414, [1956] 1 All ER 603. A pure speculation is insufficient. The petitioner must give evidence: *Parkinson v Parkinson* [1939] P 346, [1939] 3 All ER 108. (It was also held in this case that the fact that the spouses parted under a separation agreement is no bar to the proceedings.) For the common law presumption, see ante, pp 68–70.
[5] At 421 and 605, respectively.
[6] *Thompson v Thompson* (supra), at 424–425 and 608, respectively.
[7] *Manser v Manser* [1940] P 224, [1940] 4 All ER 238. Presumably the decree would also have to be rescinded if the petitioner relied on the presumption and it was proved that the other spouse had been alive at some time during the previous seven years, even though it was not known whether he was still alive.
[8] But in that case the court has power to make orders for financial relief: *Deacock v Deacock* [1958] P 230, [1958] 2 All ER 633, CA. The Court of Appeal was unimpressed by the argument that the Matrimonial Causes Act draws a distinction between these proceedings and divorce and empowers the court to order financial relief only on divorce.
[9] Domicile and Matrimonial Proceedings Act 1973, s 5(4), implementing the recommendations of the Law Commission: Law Com No 48 (Report on Jurisdiction in Matrimonial Causes), paras 71–74.
[10] Cf the Report of the Matrimonial Cause Procedure Committee (1985) para 4.123, where it is stated that in most circumstances petitioners prefer to petition for divorce relying on five years' separation.
[11] For an eminently readable brief account of the history of divorce, see the Report of the Committee on One-parent Families, Cmnd 5629, Pt 4, Ss 2 and 3.

these courts had no power to pronounce a decree of divorce a vinculo matrimonii which would permit the parties to remarry.[12] In addition to decrees of nullity and jactitation of marriage, they could pronounce decrees of restitution of conjugal rights and divorce a mensa et thoro. The former called on a deserting spouse to resume cohabitation with the petitioner, and the latter (which was granted on the grounds of adultery, cruelty or the commission of an unnatural offence) relieved the petitioner from the duty of cohabiting with the respondent without severing the marriage tie.[13] The only way in which an aggrieved party could obtain a divorce a vinculo matrimonii was by Act of Parliament, the expense of which was sufficient to put relief beyond the hope of most. In addition, by the end of the eighteenth century, the practice of the House of Lords was to give a reading to a bill introduced on behalf of the husband only on the ground of adultery and then only after he had obtained a divorce a mensa et thoro in an ecclesiastical court and had successfully sued the adulterer for damages in the old common law action of criminal conversion. Adultery alone would not suffice in the case of a bill presented on behalf of the wife, who had to show that the adultery was aggravated (for example, bigamous or incestuous) or that her husband had committed an unnatural offence.[14]

The Matrimonial Causes Act 1857

This Act was passed to give effect to the report of a royal commission which had been appointed in 1850 to enquire into the law relating to matrimonial offences. In addition to vesting the existing jurisdiction of the ecclesiastical courts in a new statutory Divorce Court (from which it was transferred to the High Court in 1875)[15] the Act for the first time in English law permitted divorce a vinculo matrimonii by judicial process. The term 'divorce' was henceforth confined to this decree, whilst that of divorce a mensa et thoro was renamed 'judicial separation'. But the distinction between the position of the husband and that of the wife was retained, for a husband could petition for divorce on the ground of adultery alone (provided that he joined the alleged adulterer as a co-respondent instead of suing him at common law in criminal conversion), whilst a wife had to prove either adultery coupled with incest, bigamy, cruelty or two years' desertion, or, alternatively, rape or an unnatural offence.[16]

It will be seen that the purpose of the Act was primarily to change the process by which a divorce was obtained from a legislative one to a judicial one: adultery remained the one matrimonial offence which would justify the dissolution of the marriage bond. Here, too, one sees reflected the mid-Victorian attitude to sexual morality: whilst one act of adultery by a wife was considered unforgivable and gave the husband the power to petition for divorce without more, she could not even rely on a series of associations

---

[12] Ante, p 72.

[13] Readers unfamiliar with ecclesiastical reports before 1858 are warned of the confusing terminology. The word 'divorce' simpliciter almost always means divorce a mensa et thoro; if 'divorce a vinculo matrimonii' is used, it always means nullity.

[14] There were on the average fewer than two divorces by statute a year on the husband's petition and only a total of four on the wife's petition. See generally Jackson *Formation and Annulment of Marriage* (2nd Edn) pp 27–40, and the authorities there cited.

[15] By the Judicature Acts of 1873 and 1875.

[16] Matrimonial Causes Act 1857, s 27.

by him unless the adultery was 'aggravated'.[17] The principle that divorce was a remedy for a matrimonial wrong was further applied in provisions absolutely precluding the court from pronouncing a decree if the petitioner had been guilty of connivance or condonation of if the parties had entered into a collusive agreement concerning the prosecution of the suit. The court was also given a discretionary power to refuse a decree in certain circumstances, in particular if the petitioner had himself been guilty of adultery.[18]

Extension of the grounds for divorce

The law remained in this state until 1923, when the Matrimonial Causes Act of that year put the husband and wife in the same position by permitting the latter to petition on the grounds of adultery simpliciter.[19] A P Herbert's Matrimonial Causes Act 1937 further extended the grounds for divorce by permitting either spouse to base his or her petition on the other's cruelty, desertion for three years, or (subject to certain other conditions) supervening incurable insanity.[20] This last provision shows an important departure from the principles underlying the law of divorce, for whereas before 1938 it had always been necessary for the petitioner to show that the respondent had committed a matrimonial offence, a petition based upon the respondent's insanity disclosed a state of affairs in no way due to his fault which nevertheless made it socially undesirable that the petitioner should still be tied to the respondent by marriage.

The movement for reform

The enormous social changes following the Second World War led to much public discussion of the whole basis of the law of divorce and a radical reappraisal of the principles underlying it. There had been a vast increase in the number of divorces,[1] and although this must in some measure reflect an increase in the number of marriages that had broken down, other factors came into play. Legal aid had opened the doors of the divorce court to

---

[17] One reason for the distinction was the fear that the wife might try to palm illegitimate children upon the husband. If the wife left the husband in consequence of his adultery, this would put him in constructive desertion, so that in theory the effect of the legislation was merely to delay the wife's remedy for two years. In practice, however, she would usually not be able to afford to do so; the only way in which she could obtain maintenance from him by a court order was by obtaining a judicial separation based on his adultery, which would automatically prevent desertion from running.

[18] Matrimonial Causes Act 1857, ss 30 and 31.

[19] Matrimonial Causes Act 1923, s 1. It did not strictly equate the spouses' rights for the wife could still petition on the grounds of the husband's rape or unnatural offence, while there was no corresponding basis for the husband's petition.

[20] Matrimonial Causes Act 1937, ss 2 and 3. This Act very largely gave effect to the recommendations of the majority of the members of a Royal Commission appointed in 1909 (the Gorell Commission, Cd 6478). For a lively account of the history of the passage of this bill through Parliament, see Sir Alan Herbert's *The Ayes have it* (1937).

[1] In 1938 (following AP Herbert's Act) there were 9,970 petitions; the figure rose steadily during and immediately after the Second World War reaching a peak in 1947 with 47,041. Following the introduction of legal aid, the figure rose from 29,096 in 1950 to 37,637 in 1951. After another decline the figures again rose steadily from 1959 until 1985, since when they have been level. In 1970 (the last year before the Divorce Reform Act came into force) there were 70,575 petitions; in 1990 there were 191,615.

many who could not previously have afforded it; the attitude of society towards divorced spouses (particularly 'guilty' spouses) had changed; and many religious bodies were taking a far less rigid attitude.[2] More than 90% of all petitions were undefended and some of these undoubtedly amounted to divorce by consent. The law could be abused by the husband's providing his wife with evidence of adultery committed on one occasion in a hotel bedroom.[3] In other cases both spouses were guilty and cross-petitions were launched purely to give the parties an advantage when it came to the question of financial provision.

Consequently the idea that the purpose of divorce was to provide a remedy available only to the 'innocent' spouse for a matrimonial wrong committed by the other seemed to many to be a singularly outdated concept which obscured the true social function of divorce. Essentially this exists to enable the spouses to enter into a fresh legal union if they wish to do so. At the same time the court must give such protection as it can to the children of the family affected by the breakdown and adjust financial and property rights in view of the possibility of remarriage. There should also be machinery to facilitate a reconciliation if there is still any possibility of this being successful.[4] Hence, it was argued, divorce should be available to either spouse when the marriage has irretrievably broken down: to insist on the commission of a matrimonial offence lays stress upon the symptoms of breakdown rather than on the breakdown itself. The introduction of this principle would have the effect of reducing the number of stable illicit unions where there was no foreseeable chance of the parties being able to marry or of their children being legitimated because the spouse of one of them refused to release his or her partner on account of religious or moral scruple, financial advantage or vindictiveness. Some people, on the other hand, regarded the idea as fundamentally unjust in that it would enable a party to take advantage of his own wrong and obtain a divorce against the will of an innocent spouse, who might have a conscientious objection to divorce, and that a wife in particular might suffer serious financial hardship as a consequence of the decree.

A Royal Commission (the Morton Commission), appointed to enquire into the law of England and Scotland concerning marriage and divorce, published its report in 1956.[5] Of the nineteen members only one was in favour of totally scrapping the matrimonial offence as the basis of our divorce law, but nine of the rest would have introduced the breakdown of the marriage as evidenced by separation for seven years as an alternative ground. But apart from one unsuccessful attempt to change the law in a private member's bill in the House of Commons,[6] little was done until two major publications appeared in 1966. In the first, *Putting Asunder*, a group appointed by the Archbishop of Canterbury to consider the law of divorce in contemporary society came down in favour of the breakdown theory.

---

[2] The courts also took a less restrictive attitude by widening the concept of cruelty.
[3] The judges have always viewed such evidence with suspicion but there can be no doubt that many such 'arranged' petitions were successful.
[4] See Law Commission *Reform of the Grounds of Divorce: the Field of Choice* Cmnd 3123, paras 13 et seq.
[5] Cmd 9678.
[6] Introduced by Mr Leo Abse MP. By withdrawing the controversial clauses, he enabled the rest of the bill to get on the statute book as the Matrimonial Causes Act of 1963.

Logically they argued that this must be the sole ground of divorce and that possible abuse must be guarded against by a judicial inquest in each case. They further recommended that a decree should be refused if it would be unjust because of the petitioner's conduct or because the financial provision proposed was inadequate. *Putting Asunder* was referred to the Law Commission who in turn reported in *Reform of the Grounds of Divorce: the Field of Choice*.[7] They concluded that the Archbishop's group's proposals were impracticable and put forward a number of possible alternatives based on the fundamental assumption that the aims of a good divorce law are 'to buttress, rather than undermine, the stability of marriage, and when, regrettably, a marriage has irretrievably broken down, to enable the empty legal shell to be destroyed with the maximum fairness and the minimum bitterness, distress and humiliation'. Their own preference was for introducing as an additional ground for divorce the breakdown of the marriage as evidenced by a period of separation which should be shorter if the respondent consented than if he did not.

The Divorce Reform Act

The consequence was the passing of the Divorce Reform Act 1969. It represented a compromise between the views put forward by the Archbishop's group and the Law Commission. All the old grounds for divorce were abolished and replaced by one ground, that the marriage has irretrievably broken down. This, however, may be established only by proof of one or more of five facts set out in the Act. Three of these are akin to, but not identical with, the old grounds of adultery, cruelty and desertion, and therefore impute fault to the respondent. The other two are periods of separation: two years if the respondent consents to the granting of the decree and five years if he does not. The old bars to divorce, both absolute (like the petitioner's connivance and condonation) and discretionary (like the petitioner's own adultery), were abolished, but various safeguards are to be found to give financial protection to the respondent if the petitioner relies on a period of separation. In both cases the respondent may apply for the decree not to be made absolute until adequate financial provision is made for him (or her), and in the case of five years' separation the respondent may oppose the grant of a decree nisi on the ground that divorce will result in grave financial or other hardship to him. Other provisions are designed to encourage reconciliation and to ensure that spouses are not prejudiced if their attempts are unsuccessful.

Because of the fears expressed that parties (particularly wives) divorced against their will could well suffer financial hardship, the Act did not come into force until 1st January 1971. This enabled Parliament to pass the Matrimonial Proceedings and Property Act of 1970, which reformed the whole law relating to the powers of the High Court and divorce county courts to grant financial relief for the protection of the spouses and the children of the family.[8]

---

[7] Cmnd 3123. See further MacKenna, *Divorce by Consent and Divorce for Breakdown of Marriage* 30 MLR 121; Kahn-Freund 30 MLR 180.

[8] For a critical examination of the provisions of the Divorce Reform Act 1969, see Passingham, *The Divorce Reform Act 1969*; Levin 33 MLR 632; Freeman *The Search for a Rational Divorce Law*, Current Legal Problems 1971, 178. For comparison with other legislation in

The Matrimonial Causes Act 1973

This Act repealed and replaced the statutory provisions relating to matrimonial causes administered in the High Court and divorce county courts
to be found mainly in the two Acts mentioned in the last two paragraphs
together with the Matrimonial Causes Act 1965 and the Nullity of Marriage
Act 1971.[9] It is essentially a consolidating statute and made only minor
changes in the existing law.

2. PETITIONS DURING THE FIRST YEAR OF MARRIAGE

When the grounds for divorce were extended in 1937, a counterbalancing
restriction was imposed. No petition might be presented during the first
three years of the marriage unless leave was obtained on the ground that
the case was one of exceptional hardship suffered by the petitioner or of
exceptional depravity on the part of the respondent.[10] When this restriction
came under the scrutiny of the Law Commission, the evidence they received
indicated that, so far from fulfilling the aims of a good divorce law, it
actually caused bitterness, distress and humiliation by forcing petitioners
to wash their dirty linen in public. The resulting embarrassment prevented
some spouses from applying for leave to petition; others were led to
exaggerate allegations with the result that any hope of the parties' reaching
a settlement was jeopardised.[11] The Commission was nonetheless of the
opinion that 'a restriction is a useful safeguard against irresponsible or trial
marriages and a valuable external buttress to the stability of marriages
during the difficult first years'; they further stated that they would not like
'to contribute to an attitude of mind in which divorce comes to be regarded,
not as the last resort, but as the obvious way out when things go wrong'.[12]
They therefore concluded that a balance had to be struck between imposing
unnecessary hardship on a spouse and making divorce 'so rapidly available
that marriage becomes a merely transient state capable of being repudiated
at whim'.[13] As they pointed out, an absolute bar has the advantages of
certainty and consistency and, acknowledging that any period would be
arbitrary, they came down in favour of replacing the discretionary bar by
an absolute bar of one year.

   This recommendation was implemented by section 1 of the Matrimonial
and Family Proceedings Act 1984.[14] No petition for divorce may now be
presented before the expiration of one year from the date of the marriage.[15]

---

the Commonwealth, see Selby, *The Development of Divorce Law in Australia* 29 MLR 473;
Holden *Divorce in the Commonwealth*, 20 ICLQ 58.
[9] Isolated sections had to be kept alive because they affect other branches of the law (eg,
matrimonial property).
[10] Matrimonial Causes Act 1937, s 1.
[11] See Law Com No 116 (Time Restrictions on Presentation of Divorce and Nullity Petitions),
paras 2.5–2.8.
[12] Ibid, paras 2.14 and 2.15.
[13] Ibid, para 2.29.
[14] Substituting a new s 3 of the Matrimonial Causes Act 1973.
[15] If a petition is presented within a year, the proceedings (including decree absolute) will be
void: *Butler v Butler* [1990] 1 FLR 114.

This, however, does not prevent a spouse from later basing a petition on facts which occurred during the first year of marriage.

3. DIVORCE AFTER PREVIOUS PROCEEDINGS

One of the provisions of the Matrimonial Causes Act of 1973 is designed to help the possibility of reconciliation without slamming the door to divorce if the attempt fails. If a husband, say, commits adultery or deserts his wife, she may wish for some form of matrimonial relief less than divorce in the hope of a reconciliation; on the other hand, there would be a danger that, if this hope were not realised, she might later be unable to obtain a divorce because of the difficulty of proving the alleged offence or, in the case of desertion, because she had consented to the separation by obtaining a judicial separation. Consequently, it is provided that on a petition for divorce the court *may* treat any previous decree of judicial separation or any order made in domestic proceedings in a magistrates' court as sufficient evidence of the ground on which it was granted provided that the petitioner gives evidence in the later divorce proceedings.[16] The special application of these provisions when the petition is based upon desertion will be considered below.[17]

C. The ground for divorce

By section 1(1) of the Matrimonial Causes Act 1973 there is only one ground for divorce, that the marriage has broken down irretrievably. Irretrievable breakdown, however, may be established only by proving one of the five facts set out in section 1(2). If none of these is made out, the court may not pronounce a decree even though it is convinced that the marriage is at an end.[18] If any one of the facts is proved, the court must pronounce a decree nisi (subject to one exception)[19] unless it is satisfied that the marriage has not broken down irretrievably.[20] Hence proof of any of the facts raises a presumption of breakdown: it must be stressed, however, that the breakdown need not be the result of the fact relied on, even though this imputes misconduct to the respondent.[1] Although it is the duty of the court 'to inquire, so far as it reasonably can, into the facts alleged' by both parties,[2] in practical terms the burden on the petitioner is solely to establish

---

[16] Matrimonial Causes Act 1973, s 4, as amended by the Domestic Proceedings and Magistrates' Courts Act 1978, Sch 2. But the court is not bound to treat the previous finding as conclusive. If previous proceedings have been brought in the High Court, the parties are generally bound by any findings of facts in issue *provided that they have been the subject of investigation and adjudication*. This applies in any subsequent proceedings in the High Court or in an inferior court, but proceedings in a magistrates' court will apparently not estop a party from alleging or denying the same facts later in the High Court. Nor does an estoppel bind the court, which is under a statutory duty to investigate the facts alleged by each party. See ante, p 103, and *Thoday v Thoday* [1964] P 181, [1964] 1 All ER 341, CA and the cases there cited.

[17] Post, pp 204–205.

[18] As in *Richards v Richards* [1972] 3 All ER 695 (post, pp 196–197).

[19] Ie, grave hardship to the respondent if the petitioner relies on five years' separation: see post, pp 214–218.

[20] Matrimonial Causes Act 1973, s 1(4).

[1] *Stevens v Stevens* [1979] 1 WLR 885; *Buffery v Buffery* [1988] 2 FLR 365, CA.

[2] Matrimonial Causes Act 1973, s 1(3).

one of the facts and it is for the respondent in a defended suit to show, if he wishes, that the marriage has not broken down irretrievably. The petitioner's assertions, though clearly highly relevant, cannot be conclusive,[3] but there can be very few cases indeed where there is still any chance of a reconciliation by the time the case has got as far as the hearing,[4] and if the decree is granted under the special procedure (as will usually be the case) the petitioner's statement will in fact be conclusive.[5]

We must now examine the five facts set out in the Act.

1. THE RESPONDENT'S ADULTERY

The first fact on which the petitioner may rely is that the respondent has committed adultery and that the petitioner finds it intolerable to live with him.[6] It will be seen that there are two limbs. Adultery by itself is no longer sufficient: Parliament has accepted that infidelity may be a symptom of breakdown rather than a cause of it and that an isolated act of adultery may not even be a symptom.

Adultery

Adultery may be defined as sexual intercourse between two persons of whom one or both are married but who are not married to each other.[7]

Nature of the act

There need not be full penetration to constitute adultery,[8] but, as the Court of Appeal held in *Dennis v Dennis*,[9] there must be some penetration of the female by the male organ, although, as in the case of rape, any degree of

---

[3] *Ash v Ash* [1972] Fam 135, 141, [1972] 1 All ER 582, 586; *Katz v Katz* [1972] 3 All ER 219, 223.

[4] It must be shown that the marriage has irretrievably broken down at the date of the hearing (and not at the date of the petition). Any other interpretation of the Act would make nonsense of the provisions empowering the court to adjourn the proceedings to enable the parties to attempt a reconciliation (see post, p 221): *Pheasant v Pheasant* [1972] Fam 202, 206, [1972] 1 All ER 587, 589.

[5] For the special procedure, see post, p 235.

[6] Matrimonial Causes Act 1973, s 1(2)(a). It will be observed that, unlike previous statutes, the Act does not require the adultery to have been committed since the celebration of the marriage. It is inconceivable, however, that the courts will construe this as enabling a petitioner to rely on pre-marital adultery (to which he could have been a party). Cf the rule that pre-marital conduct cannot justify desertion, post, p 206.

[7] The Family Proceedings Rules 1991, r 2.7(1), provides that the petitioner is not bound to name the person with whom it is alleged that the respondent has committed adultery, but if he (or she) does so, the person named must be joined as a co-respondent unless the court otherwise directs. But quaere whether this is not ultra vires s 49 of the Matrimonial Causes Act 1973, which appears to require the petitioner to name the person unless excused by the court for special reason. A finding of adultery in matrimonial proceedings in the High Court or a county court is prima facie evidence (which may be rebutted) of its commission in any subsequent civil proceedings: Civil Evidence Act 1968, s 12. Hence if A obtains a decree of divorce alleging his wife's adultery with B, B's wife could use this as evidence of B's adultery if she were to bring divorce proceedings.

[8] *Rutherford v Richardson* [1923] AC 1, HL; *Thompson v Thompson* [1938] P 162, [1938] 2 All ER 727; *Sapsford v Sapsford* [1954] P 394, [1954] 2 All ER 373.

[9] [1955] P 153, [1955] 2 All ER 51, CA.

penetration, however slight, will suffice. Hence it seems that a woman who has herself artificially inseminated with another man's seed does not thereby commit adultery.[10]

Act must be voluntary

In order to be guilty of adultery, a person must have had sexual intercourse voluntarily.[11] Hence if a married woman is raped, she does not commit adultery.[12] The principle applies equally if a woman's consent is negatived by force or fear; a more difficult problem arises if either party alleges that his act was not voluntary because he was suffering from mental disorder at the time that he committed it. The moral turpitude of a person who commits a matrimonial offence resulted in a tendency to regard adultery and cruelty as similar in character to criminal offences and therefore to apply the *M'Naghten* rules to them.[13] Consequently insanity was held to be a defence if the party alleged to have committed adultery was so insane as not to know the nature and quality of his act, or, if he did, that he did not know that what he was doing was wrong in the sense of morally blameworthy or culpable.[14] Although it was subsequently held that insanity was not necessarily a defence to a charge of cruelty,[15] it is submitted that it should remain so in the case of adultery, at least if its effect was that the party could not be said to have consented to the act at all. The effect of drink or drugs raises a much more difficult question. It has been held that a wife is not guilty of adultery if she has consented to the act because of drink taken in excusable circumstances:[16] what circumstances, however, will be considered excusable? The House of Lords has laid down the principle that self-induced intoxication is no defence to a criminal charge when no specific intent has to be proved, because there is no justification for giving a person in this position a protection that he would otherwise not have.[17] It is submitted that this should apply to adultery for the same reason; consequently, a wife should be excused, for example, if unknown to her her drinks had been 'laced' but not if she was entirely responsible for her own situation.[18]

---

[10] Artificial insemination has been held not to amount to adultery in Scotland: *Maclennan v Maclennan* 1958 SLT 12. See also Bartholomew *Legal Implications of Artificial Insemination* 21 MLR 236, at 251 et seq. For the contrary view see Tallin *Artificial Insemination* 34 Can Bar Rev 1, 166. But her husband might be able to present a petition based on her behaviour if she were inseminated without his consent.

[11] *Clarkson v Clarkson* (1930) 143 LT 775. Cf *N v N* (1963) 107 Sol Jo 1025.

[12] *Clarkson v Clarkson* (supra). The fact that the man would not be guilty of a criminal offence because he believed that the woman was consenting is irrelevant, but as the question whether or not she consented is peculiarly within her knowledge, the burden of proving lack of consent is on her: *Redpath v Redpath* [1950] 1 All ER 600, CA.

[13] *R v M'Naghten* (1843) 10 Cl & Fin 200, HL. See Smith and Hogan *Criminal Law* (6th Edn) pp 185 et seq.

[14] *Yarrow v Yarrow* [1892] P 92; *Hanbury v Hanbury* (1892) 8 TLR 559, CA; *S v S* [1962] P 133, [1961] 3 All ER 133.

[15] *Williams v Williams* [1964] AC 698, [1963] 2 All ER 994, HL.

[16] *Goshawk v Goshawk* (1965) 109 Sol Jo 290.

[17] *DPP v Majewski* [1977] AC 443, [1976] 2 All ER 142, HL.

[18] In any case, even though force, fraud, insanity, etc, will exculpate one party, the party acting voluntarily will be guilty of adultery: see *Barnett v Barnett* [1957] P 78, [1957] 1 All ER 388; *S v S* (supra). See further Fridman *Mental Incompetency* 80 LQR 84, pp 96–98.

Standard of proof

There has been considerable judicial controversy over the standard of proof required when there is an allegation of adultery. As the proceedings are civil, one would expect it to be sufficient to show that the party was guilty on the balance of probabilities; confusion has arisen because of the tendency (seen above in connection with insanity) to treat adultery as akin to a criminal offence and therefore to require proof beyond reasonable doubt. In *Blyth v Blyth*[19] the House of Lords were divided in their obiter views about the correct test. The problem has been further complicated by the rule at common law that the presumption of legitimacy could be rebutted only by evidence putting the matter beyond reasonable doubt; if a husband's evidence of his wife's adultery was the birth of a child of which he alleged he could not be the father, the courts declined to be forced into a position in which they might have to hold that the wife had committed adultery but that the child was legitimate.[20] By enacting that 'any presumption of law as to the legitimacy ... of any person may ... be rebutted by evidence which shows that it is more probable than not that [he] is illegitimate', section 26 of the Family Law Reform Act of 1969 appears to have replaced the common law standard of proof by that of the balance of probability. If this is so, the courts must now accept the same standard of proof in the case of adultery: otherwise, in the situation outlined above, they might have to hold that the wife had not committed adultery but that the child was illegitimate—an even more absurd result than the opposite. Nevertheless in *Serio v Serio*[1] the Court of Appeal declined to accept that the standard of proof referred to in the section was 'a mere balance of probability' but must indicate 'a standard commensurate with the seriousness of the issue involved'. This decision seems to have put a gloss on the express wording of the Act; it has also left considerable doubt over the precise test to be applied.[2]

Intolerability

Whether or not the petitioner finds it intolerable to live with the respondent is clearly a question of fact and the test is subjective: did *this* petitioner find it intolerable to live with *this* respondent?[3] If the court is satisfied of this, it is quite irrelevant that the petitioner's attitude is wholly unreasonable, but he may be required to give some explanation or justification for his attitude so that its genuineness may be tested.[4]

It will be observed that the Act does not require any causal connection

---

[19] [1966] AC 643, [1966] 1 All ER 524, HL.

[20] *F v F* [1968] P 506, [1968] 1 All ER 242, following dicta in *Preston-Jones v Preston-Jones* [1951] AC 391, [1951] 1 All ER 124, HL where the same situation had arisen.

[1] (1983) 4 FLR 756, CA at 763 and 765, applying the test formulated by Denning LJ in *Bater v Bater* [1951] P 35, 37, [1950] 2 All ER 458, 459, CA. This had been previously applied in *Bastable v Bastable* [1968] 3 All ER 701, 704, CA. See further post, p 272.

[2] In *Bastable v Bastable* (supra) Edmund Davies LJ referred to 'the almost metaphysical difference between such varying standards of proof' and doubted whether such a distinction could effectively be made (at 707).

[3] *Goodrich v Goodrich* [1971] 2 All ER 1340, 1342; *Pheasant v Pheasant* [1972] Fam 202, 207, [1972] 1 All ER 587, 590.

[4] *Goodrich v Goodrich* (supra), at 1342; *Roper v Roper* [1972] 3 All ER 668, 670; *Cleary v Cleary* [1974] 1 All ER 498 at 501 and 503, CA.

between the two limbs. After some initial doubts, when it was suggested that the petitioner should be able to allege that he found it intolerable to live with the respondent only if this was in consequence of the adultery, the Court of Appeal held in *Cleary v Cleary*[5] that the statute must be interpreted literally and that the petitioner may therefore rely not only on the adultery but also on any other matter to show that further cohabitation would be intolerable to him. In that case the husband took the wife back after she had committed adultery, but she continued to correspond with the man in question, went out at night and finally left him to live with her mother. The husband stated in evidence that he could no longer live with her because 'there was no future for the marriage at all'. The court held that he had established irretrievable breakdown of the marriage notwithstanding that he found life with her intolerable not on account of her adultery but on account of her subsequent conduct. In other cases a decree has been granted when the petitioner found life with the respondent intolerable because of the latter's refusal to consider a reconciliation[6] and because of his treatment of the parties' children.[7]

Cleary v Cleary has not passed without judicial criticism[8] and it may yet be overruled by the House of Lords. It is difficult to reconcile this interpretation with the provision that cohabitation for a period not exceeding six months after the petitioner discovers the respondent's adultery shall be disregarded in determining whether he finds it intolerable to live with the respondent,[9] which implies that it must be the discovery of the adultery that makes cohabitation intolerable. More substantial criticism may be levelled against it when one considers some of the anomalies that it produces. If the petitioner finds life with the respondent intolerable because of the latter's personal habits, it is not immediately apparent why the commission of adultery (which may be purely fortuitous) should forthwith give him the power to petition for divorce. Nor, indeed, need the petitioner find it intolerable to live with the respondent because of the latter's conduct at all. If the reason is that he has fallen in love with another woman, there is no logical reason why he should not establish irretrievable breakdown of his marriage.[10] *Cleary v Cleary* also opens the door to divorce based on adultery at which the petitioner has connived. He clearly could not be heard to say that he found life with the respondent intolerable because of such an act, but if he finds it intolerable for some other reason, the express abolition of all the old bars indicates that he could now obtain a divorce by persuading the respondent to commit adultery.[11] One feels that the judges would hesitate to assist him in achieving this end, but it is difficult to see how they could avoid doing so.

[5] [1974] 1 All ER 498, CA. See Rudd 5 Fam Law 176.
[6] *Goodrich v Goodrich* (supra).
[7] *Carr v Carr* [1974] 1 All ER 1193, CA.
[8] See *Carr v Carr* (supra). For a contrary view, see Eekelaar 90 LQR 292.
[9] Matrimonial Causes Act 1973, s 2(2). See post, p 222.
[10] This runs counter to the view expressed by Lord Denning MR in *Cleary v Cleary* (supra) at p 76, where he denied that the petitioner would be able to show irretrievable breakdown in these circumstances. The inference from this obiter dictum is that he can say that he finds life with the respondent intolerable only if this is the result of the latter's own conduct. Sed quaere? Now that the Court of Appeal has adopted the literal interpretation of the Act, no further gloss should be put on it.
[11] Cf Simon P's Riddell Lecture, printed in *Rayden on Divorce* (11th Edn) p 3234.

2. THE RESPONDENT'S BEHAVIOUR

The petitioner may establish that the marriage has irretrievably broken down by showing that the respondent has behaved in such a way that the petitioner cannot reasonably be expected to live with him.[12]

It is unfortunate that this is frequently abbreviated to 'unreasonable behaviour'.[13] This suggests that all one has to look at is the quality of the respondent's behaviour, whereas in fact what is important is the effect of that conduct upon the petitioner.

Nature of the test to be applied

Whether the respondent's behaviour has been such that the petitioner can no longer reasonably be expected[14] to live with him is essentially a question of fact. It is neither desirable nor possible to categorise conduct as guilty or blameless in the abstract. But one point must be stressed at the outset. As we have seen, the question whether the petitioner finds it intolerable to live with the respondent must be answered subjectively: whether his attitude is reasonable is irrelevant. In dealing with behaviour, however, the question is whether the petitioner can *reasonably* be expected to live with the respondent and it is for the court, and not the petitioner, to answer it.[15] The test is thus objective, but this is not the same as asking whether a hypothetical reasonable spouse in the petitioner's position would continue to live with the respondent. The court must have regard to the personalities of the individuals before it, however far these may be removed from some theoretical norm, and it must assess the impact of the respondent's conduct on the particular petitioner in the light of the whole history of the marriage and their relationship. The test generally accepted is that formulated by Dunn J in *Livingstone-Stallard v Livingstone-Stallard*[16] and adopted by the majority of the Court of Appeal in *O'Neill v O'Neill:*[17]

> 'Would any right-thinking person come to the conclusion that *this* husband has behaved in such a way that *this* wife cannot reasonably be expected to live with him, taking into account the whole of the circumstances and the characters and personalities of the parties?'

This was spelled out rather more fully by Bagnall J in *Ash v Ash:*[18]

> 'I have to consider not only the behaviour of the respondent ... but the character,

---

[12] Matrimonial Causes Act 1973, s 1(2)(b). This fact is also a ground on which a magistrates' court can make a maintenance order: see post, p 671.

[13] Described as a 'linguistic trap' by Ormrod LJ in *Bannister v Bannister* (1980) 10 Fam Law 240, CA.

[14] Ie required: *Pheasant v Pheasant* [1972] 10 Fam 202, 207, [1972] 1 All ER 587, 590. The word 'expected' is not used in an anticipatory sense.

[15] See *Ash v Ash* [1972] Fam 135, 139–140, [1972] 1 All ER 582, 585; *Pheasant v Pheasant* (supra) at 207–208 and 590, respectively; *Katz v Katz* [1972] 3 All ER 219, 223; *Richards v Richards* [1972] 3 All ER 695, 699; *Thurlow v Thurlow* [1976] Fam 32, 46, [1976] 2 All ER 979, 988; *O'Neill v O'Neill* [1975] 3 All ER 289, 292, CA.

[16] [1974] Fam 47, 54, [1974] 2 All ER 766, 771. Italics supplied. See also *Ash v Ash* (supra) at 140 and 585, respectively.

[17] [1975] 3 All ER 289, 295 (per Roskill LJ with whom Browne LJ agreed). See also *Bergin v Bergin* [1983] 1 All ER 905 at 908 and 909; *Buffery v Buffery* [1988] 2 FLR 365, CA; *Birch v Birch* [1992] 1 FLR 564, CA, where Cazalet J surprisingly referred to the test as subjective.

[18] [1972] Fam 135, 140, [1972] 1 All ER 582, 585.

personality, disposition and behaviour of the petitioner. The general question may be expanded thus: can this petitioner, with his or her character and personality, with his or her faults and other attributes, good and bad, and having regard to his or her behaviour during the marriage, reasonably be expected to live with this respondent?'

Consequently the respondent's behaviour must be looked at not in isolation but in relation to all the relevant circumstances.

Respondent's conduct

Clearly one must start by looking at the respondent's conduct. Essentially this fact has replaced the old ground of cruelty, where the courts used to apply the same test as they did in desertion: there had to be 'such grave and weighty conduct as renders the continuance of matrimonial cohabitation virtually impossible'.[19] In *Buffery v Buffery*,[20] however, the Court of Appeal agreed with Dunn J in *Livingstone-Stallard v Livingstone-Stallard*[1] that it was not helpful to import notions of constructive desertion into this new fact or to analyse the degree of gravity of conduct required to enable a petitioner to succeed in reliance on it. The question is one of fact. Thus a wife has obtained a decree against a husband who has treated her with violence,[2] who persisted in a course of conduct designed to drive her from the matrimonial home,[3] whose domineering manner led him to belittle her and level abuse and unwarranted criticism at her,[4] and who made the matrimonial home virtually uninhabitable for months by carrying out building operations (which he was not qualified to do) as well as quite unjustifiably alleging that the two children of the marriage were not his.[5] Similarly, a husband has successfully relied on his wife's association with another man stopping short of adultery.[6] From this it follows that the petitioner could complain of the respondent's adultery under this head without also having to show that he found life with the other intolerable, although he could scarcely do so if he had connived at the adultery in question or there was some other conduct on his part (for example, his own adulterous association) which might lead the court to conclude that he could reasonably be expected to live with the respondent notwithstanding the latter's adultery.[7]

A more difficult problem arises if the parties are immigrants or members of an ethnic minority group to the majority of whom the respondent's behaviour might be acceptable, although it would be regarded as intolerable by the community at large. Whether the other can reasonably be expected to live with him must depend in part upon how long the parties have lived in this country and how well they have become integrated into English

---

[19] *Young v Young* [1964] P 152, [1962] 3 All ER 120; *Ogden v Ogden* [1969] 3 All ER 1055, CA.
[20] [1988] 2 FLR 365, 367, CA.
[1] [1974] Fam 47, 54, [1974] 2 All ER 766, 771. But see Hall [1974] CLJ 219.
[2] *Ash v Ash* (supra). See also *Bergin v Bergin* (supra).
[3] *Stevens v Stevens* [1979] 1 WLR 885.
[4] *Livingstone-Stallard v Livingstone-Stallard* (supra).
[5] *O'Neill v O'Neill* [1975] 3 All ER 289, CA.
[6] *Wachtel v Wachtel* (1972) Times, 1 August.
[7] Cf *Poon v Tan* (1973) 4 Fam Law 161, CA (bigamy). The significance of this will be appreciated more fully when we consider the consequences of cohabitation for more than six months after the discovery of the adultery (post, pp 222–223). See Levin 33 MLR 632, 640–641.

society. In *Quoraishi v Quoraishi*,[8] for example, the fact that the parties were both educated and had lived in this country for nine years was highly relevant in deciding that the wife was not in desertion when she left her husband after he took a second wife against her will; this implies that she could herself have based a petition on his behaviour. But even newly arrived immigrants must be expected to conform to the basic standards of conduct of the community in which they have chosen to live and, to take extreme examples, a court could not be expected to accept as a defence the fact that in the country from which they have come it is usual for a husband to treat his wife with violence or confine her to the house.

On the other hand the petition must amount to more than a complaint that the parties are incompatible, that they no longer have anything in common and cannot communicate,[9] or that one of them is bored with the marriage.[10] In *Pheasant v Pheasant*, Ormrod J dismissed the petition of a husband whose sole charge against the wife was that she was unable to give him the demonstrative affection for which he craved whereas, as the learned judge found, she had given him all the affection she could and nothing in her behaviour could be regarded as a breach of any of the obligations of marriage. Similarly in *Stringfellow v Stringfellow*[11] the Court of Appeal held that simple desertion on the part of the respondent cannot found a petition based on this fact. The reason given was that any other conclusion would make the third fact on which a petitioner can rely—two years' desertion—wholly redundant. An equally valid argument would be that, as a petitioner is bound to accept an offer to resume cohabitation made by a deserting spouse,[12] desertion alone cannot possibly justify a claim that he cannot reasonably be expected to live with the respondent.

It must be stressed, however, that behaviour implies some form of conduct and not merely a state of mind. As Baker P put it in *Katz v Katz*:[13]

'Behaviour is something more than a mere state of affairs or a state of mind, such as for example a repugnance to sexual intercourse, or a feeling that the wife is not reciprocating the husband's love, or not being as demonstrative as he thinks she should be. Behaviour in this context is action or conduct by one which affects the other. Such conduct may either take the form of acts or omissions or may be a course of conduct, and, in my view, it must have some reference to the marriage.'

To take examples of positive acts from the old law of cruelty, behaviour could consist of sexual perversion and homosexual activities,[14] insistence on coitus interruptus knowing that it was affecting the wife's health,[15] persistent

---

[8] [1985] FLR 780, CA. See further ante, p 64.
[9] As in *Buffery v Buffery* (supra).
[10] As in *Kisala v Kisala* (1973) 117 Sol Jo 664.
[11] [1976] 2 All ER 539, CA. Contrast *Shears v Shears* (1972) 117 Sol Jo 33, where a decree was granted to a husband whose wife had obtained an injunction ordering him to leave the matrimonial home on grounds which subsequently proved to be baseless and then persistently and unreasonably refused him access to their children. Her conduct would have justified him in leaving her, however anxious she might have been to resume cohabitation later.
[12] See post, pp 209–210.
[13] [1972] 3 All ER 219, 223.
[14] *Arthur v Arthur* (1964) 108 Sol Jo 317, CA (husband respondent); *Coffer v Coffer* (1964) 108 Sol Jo 465 (wife respondent).
[15] *Knott v Knott* [1955] P 249, [1955] 2 All ER 305.

drunkenness, addiction to gambling, commission of criminal offences (particularly of a sexual character),[16] threats, insults, nagging, persistent dishonesty causing embarrassment,[17] maliciously taking matrimonial proceedings,[18] and obsessional conduct of various kinds.[19] It is equally clear that behaviour may be negative. In practice it may be more difficult for a petition to succeed in reliance on negative behaviour because a spouse may often be expected to tolerate more in the way of inactivity than of violent conduct,[20] but neglect, indifference, meanness and failure to provide maintenance have all been held to constitute cruelty in the past.[1] But when the petitioner is relying on an omission, it is submitted that it must be wilful: it is difficult to see how an involuntary failure to act can ever amount to 'behaviour'. This has caused difficulty in the past when the basic trouble between the spouses has been sexual. As Baker P pointed out in the passage quoted above, repugnance to sexual intercourse is not behaviour; but refusal of intercourse clearly will be if it is wilful.[2] It has been held, however, that a wife could not rely on this fact when she had been made unhappy by infrequent and unsatisfactory intercourse due to the husband's low sexual drive;[3] a fortiori involuntary abstinence due to supervening impotence cannot be behaviour on the part of a spouse who may be desperately anxious to have normal sexual relations.

Obviously the whole history of the marriage must be looked at: the cumulative effect of a series of acts might well amount to behaviour which the petitioner cannot reasonably be expected to put up with, even though each of them taken separately might be too trivial.[4] Conduct which has occurred since cohabitation came to an end may also be relied on, for example assaults or pestering telephone calls.[5] On the other hand, by analogy with the law of desertion, the petitioner probably cannot complain of the respondent's behaviour before the marriage.[6]

---

[16] *H v H* (1964) 108 Sol Jo 544. Contrast *Boushall v Boushall* (1964) Times, 7 November.

[17] *Stanwick v Stanwick* [1971] P 124, [1970] 3 All ER 983, CA.

[18] *Buxton v Buxton* [1967] P 48, [1965] 3 All ER 150.

[19] *Williams v Williams* [1964] AC 698, [1963] 2 All ER 994, HL (constant accusations of infidelity and searching for wife's lovers); *Howell v Howell* (1964) Times, 10 June (obsessional cleaning of house all night); *Crump v Crump* [1965] 2 All ER 980 (ritual wiping of everything to kill 'cancer germs').

[20] Per Rees J in *Thurlow v Thurlow* [1976] Fam 32, 46, [1975] 2 All ER 979, 988.

[1] *Gollins v Gollins* [1964] AC 644, [1963] 2 All ER 966, HL. See also *Carter-Fea v Carter-Fea* [1987] Fam Law 131, CA (financial irresponsibility affecting wife and children).

[2] *Sheldon v Sheldon* [1966] P 62, [1966] 2 All ER 257, CA (cruelty).

[3] *Dowden v Dowden* (1977) 8 Fam Law 106, CA. Cf *B(L) v B(R)* [1965] 3 All ER 263, CA; *P v P* [1964] 3 All ER 919. But in *P(D) v P(J)* [1965] 2 All ER 456, it was held that a wife was guilty of cruelty by refusing to have intercourse even though this was due to an invincible fear of conception and childbirth. By approving these decisions, the Court of Appeal in *Sheldon v Sheldon* (supra) appeared to be demanding different standards of sexual participation from husbands and wives. This seems to be quite out of keeping with modern views of the spouses' roles in the sexual side of their marriage, and *Dowden v Dowden* should be applied whichever spouse is the petitioner.

[4] *Stevens v Stevens* [1979] 1 WLR 885. As Henn Collins J put it in relation to cruelty, 'Dropping water wears the stone': *Atkins v Atkins* [1942] 2 All ER 637, 638.

[5] Cf *Britt v Britt* [1955] 3 All ER 769, CA (cruelty).

[6] *Sullivan v Sullivan* [1970] 2 All ER 168, CA, post, p 207.

The respondent's knowledge, belief, motive and intention

In 1963 the House of Lords decisively rejected the view that cruelty necessarily connotes any intention on the respondent's part and they held that, if his conduct could fairly be called cruel, it does not matter whether it springs from a desire to hurt or from selfishness or sheer indifference.[7] Obviously this principle must apply even more strongly to the new fact of behaviour. But this does not mean that the state of the respondent's mind will be irrelevant in every case. Admittedly it is likely to be so when the effect of his conduct on the petitioner is physical. If a husband makes a savage attack on his wife, his motive is immaterial. But in other cases his knowledge of the probable consequences of his acts could be decisive. If he buys a cat as a pet, for example, this will not normally be behaviour on his part which will enable the wife to allege that she cannot reasonably be expected to live with him, but she might be able to do so if he knows that she is made physically ill by cats and a fortiori if he introduces it into the house with the intention of injuring her health. If the effect of the respondent's conduct is psychological, these matters will frequently be most important, particularly if the petitioner's complaint is that she has been neglected, and in doubtful cases they will be decisive. In the words of Lord Pearce:[8]

> 'Whereas a blow speaks for itself, insults, humiliations, meannesses, impositions, deprivations, and the like may need the interpretation of underlying intention for an assessment of their fullest significance.'

Effect of the respondent's mental illness

In *Williams v Williams*[9] the House of Lords laid down the rule that the respondent's mental illness was not necessarily a defence to a charge of cruelty but was one of the matters to be taken into account along with the parties' temperaments and other circumstances. The tendency has been to follow that case when dealing with the respondent's behaviour under the new law. In *Katz v Katz*[10] and *Richards v Richards*[11] Baker P and Rees J independently adapted the test propounded by Lord Reid in the following words:[12]

> 'In my judgment, decree should be pronounced against such abnormal person ... simply because the facts are such that, after making all allowances for his disabilities and for the temperaments of both parties, it must be held that the character and gravity of his behaviour was such that the petitioner cannot reasonably be expected to live with him.'

A wife may reasonably be expected to nurse a sick husband and to tolerate some degree of abnormal behaviour on his part: the question in each case is whether this particular husband's conduct has become so abnormal that she can no longer reasonably be expected to live with him. Thus in *Richards*

---

[7] *Gollins v Gollins* (supra).
[8] *Gollins v Gollins* (supra) at 690 and 989, respectively.
[9] [1964] AC 698, particularly at 731 and 762, [1963] 2 All ER 994, particularly at 1009 and 1029, HL.
[10] [1972] 3 All ER 219, 224.
[11] [1972] 3 All ER 695, 700. See also *Thurlow v Thurlow* [1976] Fam 32, 44, [1975] 2 All ER 979, 987.
[12] At 723 and 1004, respectively.

v Richards the petition was dismissed when the wife's only substantial complaint was that the husband, whose illness made him moody and taciturn and caused him to disturb his wife at night when he got up because of insomnia, had on one occasion lost his temper and struck her on the head four or five times without causing her injury. In *Katz v Katz*, however, the wife was granted a decree where the husband, who was a manic depressive and had spent some time in a mental hospital, constantly made her feel small before visitors, called her a slut before their children, and produced in her such a severe state of anxiety that she made a determined attempt to commit suicide.

The later decision of Rees J in *Thurlow v Thurlow*,[13] however, appears to have gone much further. As a result of mental disease the wife became progressively less able to perform any domestic duties. She threw things at her mother-in-law (with whom their circumstances obliged the spouses to live), burnt articles on the electric heater and wandered into the street, causing her husband stress and worry. Eventually she became bedridden and incontinent and was admitted to hospital when her husband could no longer cope with the situation. There was no reasonable hope that her condition would improve and the husband petitioned for divorce alleging that her behaviour was such that he could no longer reasonably be expected to live with her. Rees J granted him a decree.

The learned judge stated explicitly that, if the behaviour in question stems from misfortune, such as mental or physical illness or an accident, the court must take full account of all the obligations of the married state including the normal duty to accept and share the burdens imposed by the respondent's ill-health. But it must also consider the length of time the petitioner has had to bear them, the effect upon his health and his capacity to bear the stresses imposed, and in the end must decide whether he can fairly be required to live with the respondent.[14] This, however, overlooks the real problem: how far can one regard as 'behaviour' conduct over which the respondent has no control? There can be no doubt that acts can amount to behaviour if they are genuinely voluntary even though they are the consequences of derangement like the wife's throwing things and wandering in the street in *Thurlow v Thurlow*. To take an extreme case, a wife could not reasonably be expected to live with a husband who attacked her with a knife in the insane belief that she was about to murder him. But could the same be said if he struck her during an epileptic fit or was found in the street whilst sleep-walking? These cannot be regarded as his acts at all. The same principle applies if the alleged behaviour is negative in nature. Although Rees J left the point open, a person who is rendered permanently comatose or turned into a 'human vegetable' as the result of a road accident cannot be said to be 'behaving' in any sense of the word. Why should the result be legally different if he is gradually reduced to this state as a result of mental deterioration?[15] No social purpose would be served in keeping

---

[13] [1976] Fam 32, [1975] 2 All ER 979. See Hall, [1975] CLJ 207.

[14] At 44 and 987, respectively.

[15] In *Smith v Smith* (1973) 118 Sol Jo 184, a decree was refused when the wife's inertia and cabbage-like existence was due solely to presenile dementia: her actions were involuntary and 'her mind did not go with her body'. This followed *Priday v Priday* [1970] 3 All ER 554, where Cumming-Bruce J held that such a person could no more be regarded as cruel than one who had been physically paralysed by a stroke, even though the petitioner was worn down as a result. In *Thurlow v Thurlow* Rees J expressly disagreed with *Smith v Smith*

the marriage alive in cases like *Thurlow v Thurlow* and it is urged that the petitioner should be granted a decree whenever possible, but once the respondent ceases to have any control whatever over his conduct, the courts are compelled to withhold relief because he is not 'behaving'. It is for Parliament, not the judges, to amend the Act.[16]

The petitioner's health, temperament and conduct

Although it has been repeatedly said that the judges are no longer required to pass judgment on the parties but merely to consider the impact of the respondent's conduct on the petitioner, it is obvious that the latter's temperament and behaviour cannot be ignored. The court must consider the particular petitioner's capacity to endure the respondent's behaviour and how far that capacity was or ought to have been known to the respondent. Thus, if a wife is pregnant or in a poor state of health, she is entitled to more considerate treatment from her husband.[17] Conversely, acts which appear on the face to be unpardonable may in the particular circumstances be, if not justified, at least excused by the petitioner's own conduct and the amount of provocation she offered to the respondent.[18]

The petitioner's acquiescence in the respondent's behaviour in the past will also be relevant in determining whether he can reasonably be expected to live with the latter in the future. In *Archard v Archard*[19] both parties were devout Roman Catholics at the time of their marriage. The wife was later advised on medical grounds that she should not conceive for another two years and, having lost her faith, insisted on the use of contraceptives. The husband was then told by his priest that he should stop sleeping with his wife and his resulting dilemma caused great unhappiness to both spouses. Wrangham J held that in the circumstances there was a conflict of two reasonable attitudes and that the wife had failed to establish behaviour on the part of her husband such that she could not reasonably be expected to live with him. Having entered into marriage on the understanding that they would not use artificial means of birth control because of the husband's religious beliefs, the wife could not complain if he refused to change his views. Equally, it is submitted, he could not have complained at his wife's refusal to have intercourse in view of her medical condition. But the fact that the petitioner tolerated earlier conduct does not automatically debar her from saying that she cannot reasonably be expected to live with the respondent in the light of later behaviour: each incident must be put in context. In *Bergin v Bergin*,[20] for example, the wife 'accepted as part of married life' three serious physical attacks by her husband. Six months after the last, when she was two months pregnant, she left in fear when her husband started throwing the furniture about. It was held that she was

---

and distinguished *Priday v Priday* on the ground that it was dealing solely with cruelty (at 43–44 and 986, respectively).
[16] But see Eekelaar, 92 LQR 10.
[17] Cf *Lauder v Lauder* [1949] P 277, [1949] 1 All ER 76, CA (cruelty).
[18] Cf *King v King* [1953] AC 124, [1952] 2 All ER 584, HL (cruelty) and see *Ash v Ash* [1972] Fam 135, 140, [1972] 1 All ER 582, 585–586.
[19] (1972) Times, 20 April. (This report does not appear in all editions of the newspaper.)
[20] [1983] 1 All ER 905.

justified in alleging that she could not reasonably be expected to live with him after this last incident notwithstanding that she had tolerated the first three.

In any event, submission to behaviour must be voluntary if it is to be called acquiescence, and if the petitioner has virtually no option but to submit, he will not be precluded from petitioning in reliance on these acts.[1] Again, as we shall see later, no account may be taken of the fact that the parties have lived with each other for a period or periods not exceeding six months since the occurrence of the final incident relied on. If the petitioner has lived with the respondent for a longer period, this must necessarily be strong evidence to negative an allegation that he or she cannot reasonably be expected to do so. It is not conclusive, however, and will not stand in the way of a decree if it can be explained away on other grounds.[2]

Probability of recurrence of behaviour

A question that could be important in some cases is whether the petitioner is entitled to obtain a decree in reliance on the respondent's behaviour if there is no probability that it will recur. This might occur, for example, if it has been the result of mental illness that is now cured. It is submitted that the answer must depend on all the facts and, in particular, on the nature of the conduct which has occurred. If, say, the respondent has committed savage physical attacks on the petitioner, it might be unreasonable to expect her to resume cohabitation with him in any circumstances, and as the Act provides that the petitioner must establish that the respondent *has behaved* in such a way that she *cannot* reasonably be expected to live with him, the fact is made out. If, on the other hand, less serious conduct has had a milder effect (for example if constant nagging in the home has caused the petitioner to become depressed), the court might well conclude that she cannot say that she cannot reasonably be expected to live with him once the cause of the conduct has been removed.

3. THE RESPONDENT'S DESERTION

The petitioner may show that the marriage has irretrievably broken down by proving that the respondent has deserted the petitioner for a continuous period of at least two years immediately preceding the presentation of the petition.[3]

This fact is relied on comparatively rarely because the petition will usually be based on two years' separation if the respondent consents.[4] A petitioner may wish to use it, however, if the respondent is in desertion and refuses to consent to a decree; and even after five years' separation (when the respondent's consent is not required) it avoids the possibility that the

[1] Cf *Meacher v Meacher* [1946] P 216, [1946] 2 All ER 307, CA (wife obtained decree on ground of cruelty based on husband's assaulting her for visiting her sister notwithstanding that she could have avoided assaults by giving in to his unreasonable demands); *T v T* [1964] P 85, [1963] 2 All ER 746, CA (submission to sodomy).
[2] See post, pp 222–223.
[3] Matrimonial Causes Act 1973, s 1(2)(c). For the computation of the period of two years, see *Warr v Warr* [1975] Fam 25, [1975] 1 All ER 85.
[4] In the four years 1986–1989 fourteen times as many petitions were based on two years' separation and consent as on desertion. The figures for 1990 were not published.

respondent will use section 5 or 10 of the Matrimonial Causes Act to oppose or delay the granting of the decree absolute.[5]

Desertion consists of the unjustifiable withdrawal from cohabitation without the consent of the other spouse and with the intention of remaining separated permanently. It therefore follows that four elements must be present before desertion can be proved:

(a) The de facto separation of the spouses;
(b) The animus deserendi—ie, the intention on the part of the spouse in desertion to remain separated permanently;
(c) The absence of consent on the part of the deserted spouse; and
(d) The absence of any reasonable cause for withdrawing from cohabitation on the part of the deserting spouse.

These four conditions will shortly be considered in turn.

It must not be thought that it is the party who takes the physical step of leaving the matrimonial home or otherwise withdrawing from cohabitation who is necessarily the deserting spouse. In cases of simple desertion this is so, but where one spouse virtually drives the other from the home or behaves in such a way that the latter can no longer reasonably be expected to live with him or her, then it may be the spouse remaining in the matrimonial home and not the spouse who departs from it who is in desertion. Such a case is known as 'constructive desertion' and will have to be considered separately.

Desertion for two years

The requirement that the respondent must have deserted the petitioner for a continuous period immediately preceding the presentation of the petition means that, subject to a statutory exception which will be mentioned later,[6] two or more periods cannot be added together so as to give a period of two years in the aggregate. Consequently if, say, a husband deserts his wife for a year, resumes cohabitation for a period of eight months and then deserts her again, the two years' period must be calculated from the date on which he left her for the second time. Moreover the desertion must still be running when the proceedings are commenced. A rigid application of this principle might work hardship if the petitioner had previously obtained a judicial separation and consequently, as we shall see, an exception has also been provided to this rule too.[7]

Separation

There can be no desertion unless there is a de facto separation between the spouses. It is not sufficient for this purpose that one of them has abandoned some of the obligations of matrimony or refused to perform isolated duties (eg, refused to have sexual intercourse);[8] there must be a rejection of all the obligations of marriage,[9] in other words, there must be a complete cessation of cohabitation.

[5] See post, pp 214–220. Desertion (with no minimum period of time) is also a ground on which a magistrates' court may make a maintenance order.
[6] See post, p 223.
[7] See post, pp 204–205.
[8] *Weatherley v Weatherley* [1947] AC 628, [1947] 1 All ER 563, HL.
[9] Per Evershed MR in *Perry v Perry* [1952] P 203, 215, [1952] 1 All ER 1076, 1082, CA.

This state of affairs is normally brought about by one spouse's leaving the matrimonial home. But it may be impossible for the spouse wishing to leave to find accommodation elsewhere, and the situation may arise where the spouses continue to live under the same roof but where one shuts himself off from the other so that they are living as two units rather than one. Although there is a presumption that in such a case there is no de facto separation sufficient to constitute desertion,[10] this is rebuttable, for 'desertion is not the withdrawal from a place, but from a state of things'.[11] Hence, if there has been a total cessation of cohabitation, there can be desertion just as effectively as if the husband and wife were living in two separate houses.

The correct test to be applied in such a case is: Are the spouses living as two households or as one?[12] This must be strictly construed. Cohabitation must have entirely ceased; there cannot be desertion if any matrimonial services are performed even though these are isolated and intermittent.[13] Each case must turn upon its own facts. In *Naylor v Naylor*[14] the wife performed no marital duties, the husband stopped giving her housekeeping money and, although they continued to reside under the same roof, they lived separately without any communal or family life. The Divisional Court held that in the circumstances there was a sufficient separation to sustain a finding by magistrates that the wife was in desertion. In *Hopes v Hopes*,[15] on the other hand, when the husband had for the most part shared a common table and to some extent a common life with the rest of the family so that to an outsider the situation would not have appeared abnormal, the Court of Appeal held that there was not sufficient separation to amount to desertion. It will be seen, therefore, that all matrimonial services and any form of common life must entirely cease.

Since all that must be proved is the factum of separation, it is irrelevant for this purpose that the spouses are forced to live apart, for example if one of them is in prison.[16] The opposite situation will arise if one of them cannot afford to leave their existing accommodation. If the house is large enough for them to live independently, the fact that they are obliged to share living accommodation to a certain extent should not prove fatal;[17] if, on the other hand, they are sharing a small flat, it may be impossible for them to avoid living in the same household,[18] in which case neither apparently could be in desertion.

[10] *Bull v Bull* [1953] P 224, at 226, 228, [1953] 2 All ER 601 at 602, 603, CA.
[11] Per Lord Merrivale P in *Pulford v Pulford* [1923] P 18, 21. Cf the meaning of 'living apart', post, pp 211–213.
[12] *Hopes v Hopes* [1949] P 227, at 231, 236, [1948] 2 All ER 920 at 922, 925, CA; *Bull v Bull* (supra) at 226, 230 and 602, 604, respectively; *Walker v Walker* [1952] 2 All ER 138, CA; *Baker v Baker* [1952] 2 All ER 248, CA.
[13] But the mere fact that the husband pays his wife maintenance will not prevent there being a de facto separation: *Smith v Smith* [1940] P 49, [1939] 4 All ER 533.
[14] [1962] P 253, [1961] 2 All ER 129, where the earlier cases are fully explained.
[15] [1949] P 227, [1948] 2 All ER 920, CA. Cf *Littlewood v Littlewood* [1943] P 11, [1942] 2 All ER 515; *Le Brocq v Le Brocq* [1964] 3 All ER 464, CA.
[16] *Beeken v Beeken* [1948] P 302, CA (parties sent to different Japanese prison camps during the Second World War).
[17] Cf Lord Merriman P in *Everitt v Everitt* [1949] P 374, 387–388, [1949] 1 All ER 908, 917–918, CA.
[18] As in *Adeoso v Adeoso* [1981] 1 All ER 107, CA.

The animus deserendi

Even though there is a de facto separation, there will be no desertion unless the guilty spouse has the intention of remaining permanently separated from the other. There will be no question of desertion if one spouse is temporarily absent on holiday or for reasons of business or health;[19] nor prima facie will there be desertion if the absence is involuntary, for example owing to service in the armed forces or imprisonment. But in these cases there will be desertion if the intention can be specifically proved, for example if the respondent makes it clear that he wishes to have nothing more to do with the petitioner.[20]

Normally the animus deserendi will be present when one spouse leaves the other, so that the desertion will commence immediately on separation. But if, when the original separation took place, the parties intended to return to each other, and one of them later resolves not to resume cohabitation, desertion begins as soon as the animus is formed.[1]

If the party alleged to be in desertion suffers from mental illness, it is a question of fact whether he is capable of forming the necessary animus. In *Perry v Perry*[2] the wife left her husband because she suffered from the insane delusion (quite unfounded in reason) that he was trying to murder her. Lloyd-Jones J held that her conduct must be judged as though her belief was true and in these circumstances it was clear that there could be no desertion because she believed that she had good cause for leaving her husband.[3] Hardship might face a spouse if the other party, already in desertion, developed mental illness because desertion could continue only if he retained the animus deserendi,[4] and he might also lack the capacity to consent to a divorce after two years' separation. Consequently section 2(4) of the Matrimonial Causes Act provides that the court may treat the desertion as continuing in such circumstances.[5]

Lack of consent

Historically desertion is a matrimonial offence; consequently there can be no desertion if the separation is by consent.[6]

Whether consent has been given is a question of fact. It may be expressly given as a simple licence to go or be embodied in a separation agreement;[7]

---

[19] See *G v G* [1964] P 133, [1964] 1 All ER 129.

[20] *Beeken v Beeken* (supra). Contrast *Townsend v Townsend* (1873) LR 3 P & D 129 (husband in prison—no animus deserendi).

[1] *Pulford v Pulford* [1923] P 18; *Pardy v Pardy* [1939] P 288, [1939] 3 All ER 779, CA. There can be desertion even though the parties have never cohabited at all: *De Laubenque v De Laubenque* [1899] P 42; *Shaw v Shaw* [1939] P 269, [1939] 2 All ER 381.

[2] [1963] 3 All ER 766. Cf *Brannan v Brannan* [1973] Fam 120, [1973] 1 All ER 38. Contrast *Kaczmarz v Kaczmarz* [1967] 1 All ER 416 (wife, who believed husband to be guilty of grave sin—apparently by having sexual intercourse with her—not amounting to a matrimonial offence, held to be in desertion when she refused to cohabit with him as a consequence).

[3] For good cause for separation, see post, pp 205 et seq.

[4] *Crowther v Crowther* [1951] AC 723, [1951] 1 All ER 1131, HL.

[5] This subsection comes into play only if desertion has already begun: it has no application to cases like *Perry v Perry*.

[6] *Pardy v Pardy* [1939] P 288, [1939] 3 All ER 779, CA.

[7] Where it is alleged that the consent has been embodied in a separation agreement, it is a question of construction whether the agreement binds the parties to live apart. Thus, in

alternatively, it may be implied by the party's conduct. For example, in *Joseph v Joseph*[8] the wife persuaded the husband to grant her a *get* which by Jewish law effects a divorce; although this would not dissolve the marriage by English law, nevertheless it was held by the Court of Appeal that the wife had thereby shown her consent to living apart from her husband and could therefore no longer assert that he was in desertion.

Two points, however, must be borne in mind. First, there must in fact be an agreement to live apart; if there is no such agreement, it is irrelevant that one spouse was glad to see the other go. In the words of Buckley LJ in *Harriman v Harriman*:[9]

> 'Desertion does not necessarily involve that the wife desires her husband to remain with her. She may be thankful that he has gone, but he may nevertheless have deserted her.'

Secondly, the consent must have been freely given and if, for example, it is extorted under duress, it will not prevent desertion from running.[10]

If consent to the separation is withdrawn, desertion will automatically begin provided that the other conditions are satisfied.[11] If the separation was originally intended to be purely temporary (for example, for a holiday or business trip or until the husband obtained a job near the matrimonial home), the consent will lapse at the end of this time, and if one spouse then unjustifiably refuses to resume cohabitation, he will be in desertion.[12] If during that period either of them decides not to return to the other at all, desertion will begin as soon as the latter becomes aware of the animus deserendi; if he is unaware of it, there can be no desertion because the separation will still be with his consent.[13] If the agreement is to last indefinitely, either spouse can resile from it and if the other unjustifiably rejects an offer to resume cohabitation, he will be in desertion. There must, however, be a genuine offer and not merely an exploratory approach or a

---

Crabtree v Crabtree [1953] 2 All ER 56, CA, it was held that a husband's promise to pay his wife £2 a week 'if they shall so long live separate and apart from each other' did not amount to a consent by the wife to his leaving her, for the words merely defined the duration of the husband's financial liability; a similar conclusion was reached in *Bosley v Bosley* [1958] 2 All ER 167, CA. See further Blom-Cooper *Separation Agreements and Grounds for Divorce* 19 MLR 638, where Australian and New Zealand cases are also discussed.

[8] [1953] 2 All ER 710, CA. Distinguished on the facts in *Corbett v Corbett* [1957] 1 All ER 621.

[9] [1909] P 123, 148, CA. See also *Kinnane v Kinnane* [1954] P 41, [1953] 2 All ER 1144, and cf *Beigan v Beigan* [1956] P 313, [1956] 2 All ER 630, CA; *Pizey v Pizey* [1961] P 101, [1961] 2 All ER 658, CA. The same principle could apply if the spouses resume cohabitation in an attempt to effect a reconciliation after a period of desertion. If they then live apart again after agreeing that the attempt has been unsuccessful, it would be more realistic to regard desertion as beginning again: cf *Morgan v Morgan* (1973) 117 Sol Jo 223.

[10] *Holroyd v Holroyd* (1920) 36 TLR 479 (wife virtually forced by husband to sign separation agreement because she thought that this was the only means of obtaining maintenance from him: husband held to be in desertion).

[11] *Pardy v Pardy* [1939] P 288, 303, [1939] 3 All ER 779, 783, CA. The burden of proof is on the spouse alleging that the other is in desertion: *Pizey v Pizey* [1961] P 101, 110, [1961] 2 All ER 658, 664, CA.

[12] *Shaw v Shaw* [1939] P 269, [1939] 2 All ER 381 (separation until the husband was earning enough to set up a home for himself and his wife).

[13] *Nutley v Nutley* [1970] 1 All ER 410, CA.

preliminary enquiry. Furthermore, if the party making the offer has been guilty in the past of conduct which would have justified the other in leaving anyway, he must also give a credible assurance that it will not be repeated in the future; and in any event there must be no unreasonable conditions attached.[14] But the spouse to whom an offer is addressed is bound to consider it, and as the Court of Appeal held in *Gallagher v Gallagher*,[15] if he fails to do so and rejects it out of hand, he will be in desertion whether it is reasonable or not.

The spouses may have intended the agreement to last for their joint lives rather than for an indefinite period. If necessary, the court must infer their intention from the terms of the agreement and the circumstances of their parting, but it will not readily conclude that the agreement is to last for ever if this is not stated expressly. As Pearce LJ said in *Bosley v Bosley*:[16]

'Often in the rather haphazard parting of husband and wife, the fact of a mutual agreement to separate has to be deduced from things done and things said in emotion and temper. The court should, I think, be slow to decide that there is imported a term that the separation shall be for ever and that there shall be no opportunity for any unilateral change of mind, no right to ask the other party to return to cohabitation.'

If the agreement is to last for their joint lives, it will normally be terminated (like any other contract) only by the consent of both spouses or by a breach by one accepted by the other as ending his own obligations.[17]

Effect of other matrimonial proceedings

If the deserted spouse obtains a judicial separation, he cannot allege that the other is in desertion, because the decree relieves the petitioner from the duty of cohabiting with the respondent and thus puts it out of the latter's power to return.[18] This argument applies with equal force to a deserted spouse who obtains an injunction or order excluding the other from the matrimonial home. It will thus be seen that, by obtaining short-term relief, a spouse might effectively lose the power to obtain a divorce based on desertion. Consequently, it is now provided that, if a decree of judicial separation is in force, a spouse petitioning for divorce may rely on the fact that the respondent had been in desertion for a continuous period of two years immediately preceding the institution of the earlier proceedings provided that the decree has been in force continuously and that the parties

---

[14] *Fraser v Fraser* [1969] 3 All ER 654.
[15] [1965] 2 All ER 967, CA.
[16] [1958] 2 All ER 167, 173, CA; followed in *Hall v Hall* [1960] 1 All ER 91.
[17] There is no need for the other party to inform the party in breach that he elects to treat himself as discharged; it is sufficient that he makes no attempt to insist on performance and is in fact willing to resume cohabitation: *Pardy v Pardy* [1939] P 288, [1939] 3 All ER 779, CA. But if he enforces the agreement and so refuses to accept the repudiation, desertion will not begin: *Clark v Clark (No 2)* [1939] P 257, [1939] 2 All ER 392.
[18] *Harriman v Harriman* [1909] P 123, CA. This also applied if the deserted spouse obtained a magistrates' order containing a non-cohabitation clause because this had the same effect as a judicial separation. (Magistrates ceased to have power to make such orders in 1981: see ante, p 15.)

have not resumed cohabitation since it was granted.[19] Similarly the court may treat the respondent as having been in desertion during any period in which there was in force an injunction or order excluding him from the matrimonial home (or former matrimonial home).[20]

Want of reasonable cause

If one spouse has a reasonable cause or excuse for leaving the other, then there will be no unjustifiable separation and consequently he will not be in desertion. Whether a particular excuse is sufficient in law is often a question of great difficulty, but it should be noted at the outset that it may be due either to the other spouse's misconduct or to circumstances (for example, illness) connected with the spouse who would otherwise be in desertion.[1]

The petitioner's behaviour

It has always been recognised that one spouse's conduct may be such that the other is justified in breaking off cohabitation and, if he does so, he will not be in desertion. The test to determine whether the conduct has reached this pitch has been formulated in various ways. The best known and most frequently cited is that of Lord Penzance who said that the conduct must be 'grave and weighty';[2] this was expanded by Simon P to conduct amounting to 'such a grave and weighty matter as renders the continuance of the matrimonial cohabitation virtually impossible'.[3] On the other hand it has been said that 'the ordinary wear and tear of conjugal life does not in itself suffice'.[4]

It has already been noticed that the same test used to be applied to cruelty.[5] This suggests that the application of a different test to determine whether a spouse's behaviour has been such that the other cannot reasonably be expected to live with him has indirectly changed the test for desertion. The two must obviously be kept in line; otherwise, as Ormrod LJ indicated in *Pheasant v Pheasant*,[6] a petitioner, who would be in desertion if he left the respondent, might nevertheless be able to obtain a divorce based on the latter's behaviour. Facts held to justify separation in the past would now support a petition based on the respondent's behaviour, for example that the latter has committed adultery,[7] has made unfounded charges of

---

[19] Matrimonial Causes Act 1973, s 4(3). This also applies to a magistrates' order containing a non-cohabitation clause, and the respondent may be treated as having been in desertion during *any* period in which such an order was in force: ibid, s 4(5) (added by the Domestic Proceedings and Magistrates' Courts Act 1978, s 62).

[20] Ibid, s 4(4) (added by s 62 of the 1978 Act). Presumably the other constituent elements of desertion must all be present. In practice this provision is likely to be relied on comparatively rarely because the respondent's conduct which led to the making of the order would usually be such that the petitioner could not reasonably be expected to live with him and thus itself provide the ground for divorce.

[1] See Irvine *'Reasonable Cause' and 'Reasonable Excuse' as Justification for Separation* 30 MLR 659.

[2] *Yeatman v Yeatman* (1868) LR 1 P & D 489, 494.

[3] *Young v Young* [1964] P 152, 158, [1962] 3 All ER 120, 124. Cf *Dyson v Dyson* [1954] P 198, 206, [1953] 2 All ER 1511, 1514; and *Oldroyd v Oldroyd* [1896] P 175, 184 ('practically impossible for the spouses to live properly together').

[4] Per Asquith LJ in *Buchler v Buchler* [1947] P 25, 45–46, [1947] 1 All ER 319, 326, CA.

[5] Ante, p 193.

[6] [1972] Fam 202, 208, [1972] 1 All ER 587, 591. Cf *Stringfellow v Stringfellow* ante, p 194.

[7] Cf *Glenister v Glenister* [1945] P 30, [1945] 1 All ER 513.

adultery or homosexual conduct,[8] or is overbearing and domineering and always insists on having his own way[9] but not by want of attention or affection alone.[10] The conduct complained of need not be culpable, and physical or mental illness will justify separation if it is likely to jeopardise the health or safety of the other spouse or their children.[11] It has also been held that a spouse will not be in desertion if he leaves as the result of a reasonable but mistaken belief that the other has given him good grounds for doing so provided that the belief is based on the other spouse's own acts.[12]

It must be stressed that no conduct can be regarded as a good cause for separation unless it in fact led to it. Hence, if a wife leaves her husband after he has committed adultery, she will none the less be in desertion if she did not know of his offence or was indifferent to it and intended to leave anyway.[13] Furthermore, as in the case of constructive desertion,[14] the other spouse's conduct presumably cannot be a good cause for separation unless it occurred during the marriage. If this is so, discovery after marriage of the other spouse's pre-marital activities can never be a defence to desertion.

The respondent's circumstances

The most obvious example of his own circumstances on which a spouse might rely to justify a separation is an enforced absence due to illness or business. In such cases it will almost always be temporary and for this reason could not amount to desertion. If he is advised to remain away from the other for a good medical reason, it would seem on principle that he ought to be able to defeat a charge of desertion on the further ground that he has good cause for remaining apart, even though the separation may be for ever. This reasoning, however, does not seem to have commended itself to the Court of Appeal in *Lilley v Lilley*.[15] Owing to mental illness the wife developed an invincible and apparently incurable repugnance to her husband. After being discharged from a mental hospital, she refused to return to him and made it clear that she never would do so. This was a rational decision in the sense that she was capable of forming an animus deserendi and the Court of Appeal accordingly held that she was in desertion. But this entirely overlooks the possible adverse effect of a return

[8] *Marsden v Marsden* [1968] P 544, [1967] 1 All ER 967 (adultery); *Russell v Russell* [1895] P 315, CA (homosexuality).
[9] *Timmins v Timmins* [1953] 2 All ER 187, CA. For the problems presented if the parties are members of an ethnic minority community, cf ante, pp 193–194.
[10] *Buchler v Buchler* (supra).
[11] *G v G* [1964] P 133, [1964] 1 All ER 129.
[12] *Glenister v Glenister* (supra) (wife's conduct leading husband to believe that she had committed adultery). Contrast *Elliot v Elliot* [1956] P 160, [1956] 1 All ER 122, CA (husband not justified in leaving wife after his mother had told him that the wife had committed adultery). But he cannot justify living apart if he ceases to have reasonable cause for believing the other has committed an offence (eg if the latter produces an innocent explanation of the conduct): *Forbes v Forbes* [1954] 3 All ER 461; *Beer v Beer* [1948] P 10, 14, [1947] 2 All ER 711, 713. See further Bevan *Belief in the other Spouse's Adultery* 73 LQR 225.
[13] *Herod v Herod* [1939] P 11, [1938] 3 All ER 722; *Day v Day* [1957] P 202, [1957] 1 All ER 848. But there is a presumption that the offence has induced the defendant to leave the complainant, so that the burden of proving ignorance or indifference is on the latter: *Earnshaw v Earnshaw* [1939] 2 All ER 698, CA.
[14] See post p 207.
[15] [1960] P 158, [1959] 3 All ER 283, CA.

upon her mental health. The injustice of branding such a spouse as a deserter is manifest, and the case was applied with obvious reluctance in *Tickle v Tickle*,[16] where a Divisional Court was compelled to hold a mentally ill husband to be in desertion in similar circumstances even though the medical evidence indicated that a return to his wife would almost certainly result in his having to go back to hospital.

Constructive desertion

It is not necessarily the spouse who takes the physical step of leaving the matrimonial home who will be in desertion. As early as 1864 it was recognised that, where one spouse behaves in such a way that the other is virtually compelled to leave, the former may be in law the deserter and is said to be in constructive desertion.[17] This may take the form of a physical eviction (or locking the other spouse out) or an order to leave. Much more commonly, however, the deserted spouse leaves because the other's conduct has made further life together impossible. The test to determine whether the offender is in constructive desertion is the same as that used to determine whether the other is in simple desertion.[18] It has already been argued that this should be the same as applied to behaviour as a fact on which a spouse can base a petition for divorce.[19] Consequently, a spouse petitioning for divorce will rarely, if ever, have to rely on constructive desertion because he can base his petition on the respondent's conduct alone. Conversely, if the respondent successfully defends a petition based on behaviour by showing that his conduct is not such that the petitioner cannot reasonably be expected to live with him, the latter cannot subsequently rely on the same facts in a petition based on constructive desertion, for he will be estopped from alleging that the respondent's conduct is sufficiently grave.[20]

The conduct complained of must have taken place during the marriage. In *Sullivan v Sullivan*[1] a husband left his wife immediately after discovering that she was pregnant per alium at the time of the marriage but failed to take any steps to have the marriage annulled. He later petitioned for divorce on the ground of his wife's desertion. The Court of Appeal held that he must fail because he was in fact complaining of her physical state at the time of the marriage: the conduct which had given rise to it had occurred beforehand. This decision is regrettable because it implies that a husband who leaves his wife in such circumstances is in desertion himself and has no immediate remedy if he does not discover the facts within three years (as might happen if he thought he was the father himself). A more desirable solution would have been to hold that pre-marital conduct can give rise to

---

[16] [1968] 2 All ER 154.

[17] *Graves v Graves* (1864) 3 Sw & Tr 350.

[18] *Hall v Hall* [1962] 3 All ER 518, CA; *Saunders v Saunders* [1965] P 499, [1965] 1 All ER 838.

[19] Ante, p 205.

[20] Cf the rule that an unsuccessful case of cruelty could not succeed as a case of constructive desertion: *Ogden v Ogden* [1969] 3 All ER 1055, CA, and the cases there cited. If the respondent's conduct does not of itself justify the petitioner in leaving, the latter cannot put the other in constructive desertion by presenting him with an ultimatum: *Buchler v Buchler* [1947] P 25, 44–45, [1947] 1 All ER 319, 325, CA; *Bartholomew v Bartholomew* [1952] 2 All ER 1035, CA.

[1] [1970] 2 All ER 168, CA.

constructive desertion if (as in this case) it is bound to have an effect on the parties' relationship after marriage.

Mutual desertion

A question that has been canvassed is whether it is possible for both spouses to be in desertion simultaneously. The problem arises when one spouse is obliged to go away for reasons of business or health and the other cannot or will not go too. This happened in *Walter v Walter*,[2] where the husband and wife were both working in different parts of London. The husband moved to be nearer his place of work and the wife remained in the former matrimonial home to be near hers. Neither consented to the separation. It was held by Willmer J that in such circumstances neither of them could succeed on petitions based upon desertion because neither could prove that the separation was due to the other's fault.

This decision was criticised by Lord Denning who expressed the obiter view that in such a case both spouses are in desertion.[3] But this opinion can itself be attacked on two grounds. It has been suggested that each spouse has a duty to compromise in such circumstances:[4] in that case, if either rejects a genuine and reasonable compromise put forward by the other, he will be in desertion. But if neither will even propose a compromise or no reasonable compromise is possible in the circumstances, it seems contrary to principle to permit either to allege that the other is in desertion, because neither could show that the other has brought about the separation. Secondly, it has been doubted whether mutual desertion is legally possible.[5] It is submitted, however, that there is no logical basis for this view, even if the facts which could give rise to it are not likely to occur very often. Suppose that a husband, whilst in hospital, decides not to return to his wife and, on his discharge, does not go back to the matrimonial home. His wife in the meantime has decided to leave him and, unbeknown to him, has already gone to live elsewhere. There is a de facto separation, each has the animus deserendi, each has acted in ignorance of the other's decision and therefore cannot have consented to his or her withdrawal from separation; consequently if neither has any jusification for his action, both have satisfied all the conditions for simple desertion.[6] It remains to be seen, however, whether the courts will accept this argument.

---

[2] (1949) 65 TLR 680. For choice of the matrimonial home, see ante, pp 110–111.

[3] *Hosegood v Hosegood* (1950) 66 (pt 1) TLR 735, 740, CA; *Beigan v Beigan* [1956] P 313, 320, [1956] 2 All ER 630, 632, CA.

[4] Irvine *Mutual Desertion* 30 MLR 46.

[5] *Simpson v Simpson* [1951] P 320, 330, [1951] 1 All ER 955, 960 (per Lord Merriman P); *Lang v Lang* (1953) Times, 7 July, CA (per Jenkins and Hodson L JJ); *Crossley v Crossley* (1962) 106 Sol Jo 223 (per Simon P). In *Price v Price* [1970] 2 All ER 497, CA, Davies LJ left the question open (at 498) and Sachs LJ was inclined to follow the dicta in *Lang v Lang* (at 501).

[6] See Denning LJ in *Beigan v Beigan* (supra); Irvine loc cit. On similar facts to these Wrangham J found both spouses in desertion in *Price v Price* [1968] 3 All ER 543, but this was reversed by the Court of Appeal (supra) on the further ground that the wife, having discovered that her husband had gone elsewhere, never put her plan into effect and consequently the husband alone was in desertion. This seems to lay undue weight on the question of which of them took the technical step of leaving the home and, insofar as the wife would have left herself if the husband had come back, makes desertion turn on a question of chance (which it ought not to do). If, as Phillimore LJ stated at 502, it is necessary for a party, having formed the intention to desert, to leave the other *in pursuance of it*, the case is inconsistent with the

Termination of desertion

As the petitioner must show that the desertion has been continuous for a period of two years, its termination is of the same importance as its commencement. All four conditions must be present in order to constitute the offence, so that desertion will terminate if any one or more of these conditions cease to be satisfied.

Resumption of cohabitation

If the spouses resume cohabitation, there will then be no de facto separation and therefore no desertion. Just as desertion is 'the withdrawal from a state of things', so, in the words of Lord Merriman P in *Mummery v Mummery*:[7]

'A resumption of cohabitation must mean resuming a state of things, that is to say, setting up a matrimonial home together, and that involves a bilateral intention on the part of both spouses so to do.'

Hence, whilst there is a presumption that desertion will have come to an end if the spouses reside under the same roof again, this will be rebutted if it can be shown that they had no intention of living together as husband and wife.[8] Both spouses must have this intention, and desertion will continue if only one spouse possessed it.[9]

As we shall see later, in order not to impede a possible reconciliation, any period or periods not exceeding six months in which the spouses have lived together in the same household are to be disregarded.[10]

Loss of animus deserendi

Desertion will come to an end if the party in desertion loses the animus deserendi. But it is not sufficient in this case for him mentally to resolve to return to the other spouse; he must communicate his intention by offering to return.[11] In the case of simple desertion all that is necessary is for the guilty spouse to make the offer: his motive for doing so is irrelevant. Provided that the offer is genuine, the other is bound to accept it.[12] If he fails to do so, he himself will be in desertion.[13]

But if the deserting spouse has been guilty of behaviour which entitles

---

earlier decision of the Court of Appeal in *Pardy v Pardy*, ante, p 202, n 1. See Irvine 34 MLR 194.

[7] [1942] P 107, 110, [1942] 1 All ER 553, 555.

[8] *Bartram v Bartram* [1950] P 1, [1949] 2 All ER 270, CA (no resumption of cohabitation when wife joined husband in his mother's house but performed no wifely duties and treated him like a lodger whom she disliked). See also *Watson v Tuckwell* (1947) 63 TLR 634 and contrast *Bull v Bull* [1953] P 224, [1953] 2 All ER 601, CA. A resumption of cohabitation can take place elsewhere than in the matrimonial home: *Abercrombie v Abercrombie* [1943] 2 All ER 465 (desertion terminated when spouses spent a weekend together in a hotel on a 'second honeymoon').

[9] *Mummery v Mummery* (supra). Cf *Perry v Perry* [1952] P 203, [1952] 1 All ER 1076, CA (desertion not terminated even though a child was born as a result of intercourse).

[10] Matrimonial Causes Act 1973, s 2(5). See post, p 223.

[11] *Williams v Williams* [1939] P 365, 369, [1939] 3 All ER 825, 828, CA.

[12] *Dyson v Dyson* [1954] P 198, [1953] 2 All ER 1511; *Price v Price* [1951] P 413, [1951] 2 All ER 580n; *Irvin v Irvin* [1968] 1 All ER 271.

[13] 'The tables are turned': *Pratt v Pratt* [1939] AC 417, [1939] 3 All ER 437, HL; *Thomas v Thomas* [1946] 1 All ER 170; *Everitt v Everitt* [1949] P 374, [1949] 1 All ER 908, CA.

the other to stay away, a simple offer to return need not necessarily be accepted. If he has been guilty of adultery, the innocent spouse is never bound to take him back;[14] in other cases the offending spouse must give the other a credible assurance that the conduct complained of will not be repeated in the future. The amends that the guilty spouse must make is a question of degree; the more reprehensible his conduct has been in the past, the stronger must his assurances be for the future, and some conduct may be so gross that the innocent spouse is not bound to accept the offer at all.[15]

The offer must be genuine in the sense that the spouse making it must be prepared to implement it if it is accepted. Where there is real doubt about this, the correct way of resolving it may be by accepting the offer,[16] but this is not necessary if the evidence clearly points to the contrary. Thus in *Dunn v Dunn*[17] it was held that a husband was entitled to reject an offer made by his wife (who had previously ordered him to leave the matrimonial home) in view of the fact that she had ordered him out before, had refused to let him have a key to the house, was bringing unjustified charges of cruelty against him, and had sent the invitation, couched in affectionate terms, by registered post. Moreover, a spouse is bound only to accept an offer to resume cohabitation in the full sense of the word and not one with unreasonable conditions attached.[18]

Supervening consent

If the deserted spouse subsequently consents to living apart, the desertion will automatically come to an end.[19] Whether or not he has done so is a question of fact: clearly a spouse can no longer allege that the other is in desertion if he obtains a judicial separation or enters into a separation agreement.

[14] *Everitt v Everitt* (supra) at 381–386 and 913–916, respectively. This applies equally if the innocent spouse has reasonable grounds for believing that the other has committed adultery even though he has not in fact done so: *Everitt v Everitt* at 379–381 and 911–913.

[15] *Edwards v Edwards* [1948] P 268, 272, [1948] 1 All ER 157, 160. See also *Thomas v Thomas* [1924] P 194, CA; *Theobald v Theobald* [1962] 2 All ER 863. Tiley *Desertion and the Bona Fide Offer to Return* 83 LQR 89, argues forcefully that, even though the innocent spouse can never be bound to accept an offer to resume cohabitation made by a spouse who has committed adultery, this will nevertheless terminate the offeror's desertion if it is made in good faith. The logic of this is unassailable if one assumes that the animus deserendi must always be present in the subjective sense. But the cases all indicate that the criterion for the *continuation* of desertion is whether the deserted spouse is justified in refusing to resume cohabitation: see Irvine 83 LQR 338, 29 MLR 331.

[16] *Dunn v Dunn* [1967] P 217, at 226, 228–229, [1965] 1 All ER 1043 at 1048, 1049.

[17] [1967] P 217, [1965] 1 All ER 1043. See also *Thomas v Thomas* [1924] P 194, CA; *W v W (No 2)* [1954] P 486, [1954] 2 All ER 829, CA.

[18] It has been held that a wife was not bound to accept offers to resume cohabitation in the following circumstances: *Hutchinson v Hutchinson* [1963] 1 All ER 1, CA (on condition that parties did not have sexual intercourse); *Barrett v Barrett* [1948] P 277, CA (on condition that parties' daughters did not come with her); *Fletcher v Fletcher* [1945] 1 All ER 582 (to join husband in a community devoted to service in retreat and believing in the communal ownership of property). Except where the spouse alleged to be in desertion becomes insane (see ante, p 202), he is presumed to retain the animus, so that the burden is upon him to prove that desertion has come to an end: *Bowron v Bowron* [1925] P 187, 195, CA; *W v W (No 2)* (supra) at 502 and 832–833, respectively; *Coulter v Coulter* [1962] NI 145.

[19] Desertion is presumed to continue, so that the complainant does not have to show that he was at all times ready and willing to take the defendant back: *Sifton v Sifton* [1939] P 221, [1939] 1 All ER 109.

Good cause for separation supervening

If the deserted spouse commits some act which would justify the other in refusing to live with him any longer, the desertion will come to an end unless it can be shown that this act did not alter the other's intention to live apart. Prima facie, therefore, the desertion will cease, and the burden is upon the spouse originally deserted to prove that his conduct did not affect the other's mind.[20] Thus, in *Richards v Richards*[1] the wife committed adultery two years after her husband had deserted her, and it was held that this brought the existing desertion to an end, because she failed to show that her act had not impeded any possible reconciliation. Conversely, as in *Brewer v Brewer*,[2] even if the deserted spouse communicates to the other the clear intention of not having him or her back, this will not bring the desertion to an end if the evidence shows that this did not effectively prevent the deserter from taking steps to bring about a reconciliation.

4. TWO YEARS' SEPARATION

The petitioner may establish that the marriage has broken down irretrievably by showing that the spouses have lived apart for a continuous period of at least two years immediately preceding the presentation of the petition *and* that the respondent consents to the decree being granted.[3] This was one of the most controversial provisions of the Divorce Reform Act because it introduced, albeit to a limited extent, divorce by consent.

Living apart

The Matrimonial Causes Act provides that spouses are to be treated as living apart unless they are living with each other in the same household.[4] On this base the courts have built up two principles. First, if the spouses are living under the same roof, they can be regarded as living apart only if they are living in two households: in other words there must be the same degree of separation as is necessary to constitute desertion.[5] Hence they will not be living apart if they share their meals and living accommodation, even though they sleep in separate rooms, no longer have sexual intercourse and largely live their own lives.[6] Conversely, they will be treated as still living apart if the wife, having left her husband for another man, sub-

---

[20] *Herod v Herod* [1939] P 11, [1938] 3 All ER 722. Obviously it cannot affect the other's intention if he is unaware of the commission of the act: cf ante, p 206.

[1] [1952] P 307, [1952] 1 All ER 1384, CA.

[2] [1962] P 69, [1961] 3 All ER 957, CA. See also *Bevan v Bevan* [1955] 3 All ER 332; *Church v Church* [1952] P 313, [1952] 2 All ER 441 (subsequent adultery); *Pardy v Pardy* [1939] P 288, [1939] 3 All ER 779, CA (subsequent adultery of which the respondent was unaware). But if the deserted spouse communicates his or her intention of not taking the other back at or near the beginning of the separation, this may be evidence of consensual separation and thus negative desertion: per Holroyd Pearce LJ in *Brewer v Brewer* at 89 and 967, respectively.

[3] Matrimonial Causes Act 1973, s 1(2)(d).

[4] Ibid, s 2(6).

[5] *Mouncer v Mouncer* [1972] 1 All ER 289. See ante, pp 200–201.

[6] *Mouncer v Mouncer* (supra). Cf *Hopes v Hopes* (ante, p 201).

sequently takes him in as a lodger because he is ill and has nowhere else to go.[7]

But even if the spouses are physically separated, it does not follow that they are living apart for the purpose of the Act. The second principle, formulated by the Court of Appeal in *Santos v Santos*,[8] is that they will not be so treated unless consortium has come to an end. So long as both spouses intend to share a home when circumstances permit them to do so, consortium is regarded as continuing;[9] consequently before they can be said to be living apart, one of them at least must regard the marriage as finished. If they agree to separate or one deserts the other, it will be obvious to both that consortium is at an end; if the separation is temporary or enforced (for example, because of a business trip or treatment in hospital), consortium will usually continue, but it will come to an end if either spouse decides not to return to the other. In the latter case the Court of Appeal in *Santos v Santos* further held that it is not necessary for that spouse to communicate his or her decision to the other and the statutory period can begin to run immediately. Suppose, for example, that a husband is serving a long term of imprisonment and his wife stands by him and regularly visits him; one of them resolves not to live with the other again but says nothing and the visits continue as before. Two years after making this decision he (or she) may petition for divorce with the other's consent. At first sight this seems surprising,[10] but in fact it accords with the policy of the Act. The period of separation is designed to provide evidence that the marriage has broken down irretrievably and this of itself justifies a restrictive interpretation of the words 'living apart' by requiring evidence that consortium was at an end during the whole of the period. Otherwise the following situation could arise: a husband, who has been abroad for more than two years, has a bitter quarrel with his wife on his first day home and so much heat is engendered that they agree to a divorce forthwith although neither up to that time had considered the marriage to be on the rocks. It cannot have been the intention of Parliament to permit divorce by consent in a case like this; some sort of cooling-off period is not only desirable but essential. Given this policy, however, the fact that one spouse has regarded the marriage as dead for at least two years must normally be pretty clear evidence that it has broken down irretrievably whether or not the other knew of this.[11] Despite the

---

[7] *Fuller v Fuller* [1973] 2 All ER 650, CA. Cf *Bartram v Bartram* (ante, p 209, n 8). Would the parties be regarded as living apart if the husband never moved out but merely changed places with the lodger? They would no more be living with each other than the spouses in *Fuller v Fuller*, but the courts may be less ready to infer that separation has begun than to hold that, once begun, it is continuing.

[8] [1972] Fam 247, [1972] 2 All ER 246, CA. See Bromley 88 LQR 328. The decision is in line with the interpretation of similar statutory provisions in other common law jurisdictions within the Commonwealth: see particularly *Sullivan v Sullivan* [1958] NZLR 912. For the interpretation of a similar provision in the Family Law Act in Australia, see Finlay *The Grounds for Divorce: the Australian Experience* 6 Oxford Journal of Legal Studies 368, 380 et seq.

[9] See ante, p 109.

[10] It may seem even more surprising that at the end of five years he could launch divorce proceedings without the other's consent: see post, p 214.

[11] Presumably one spouse need not have categorically decided never to resume cohabitation. If the parties agree that, if they live apart for a period, they may be able to live together again amicably in the future but their expectations are not fulfilled, the total time for which

suggestion[12] that it must be the petitioner who has formed the intention to break off consortium, it is submitted that it should be sufficient to show that either of them did so. The evidence that the marriage has broken down is equally strong in either case, and such a limitation would give a wholly unwarranted advantage to the spouse who made the decision not to return.

Respondent's consent

The respondent must affirmatively consent to the decree: it is not sufficient that he does not oppose it.[13] It follows that a petitioner cannot seek a decree relying on this fact if the respondent cannot be found or cannot give a valid consent because of mental illness. The mental capacity required to give a consent to dissolution of a marriage is the same as that required for its formation: did the respondent understand the nature and consequences of what he was doing?[14] He must be given such information as will enable him to understand the effect of the decree being granted.[15] He may withdraw his consent at any time before a decree nisi is pronounced, and if he does so (or does not give his consent in the first place) and two years' separation is the only fact alleged by the petitioner, the proceedings must be stayed.[16]

After decree nisi the respondent has only a qualified power to withdraw his consent and to attempt to prevent the decree being made absolute. If the court grants a decree solely on the fact of two years' separation coupled with the respondent's consent, the latter may apply to have the decree nisi rescinded on the ground that the petitioner misled him (whether intentionally or unintentionally) about any matter which he took into account in deciding to give his consent.[17] The court is not bound to rescind the decree; presumably it will order a rescission only if the respondent has been seriously misled. A change of mind after the decree has been made absolute will, of course, be too late.

---

they have been separated ought to indicate whether or not the marriage has broken down irretrievably and therefore should count towards the statutory period: see *Macrae v Macrae* (1967) 9 FLR 441, 464.

[12] Made obiter in *Beales v Beales* [1972] Fam 210, 218, [1972] 2 All ER 667, 671, allegedly following *Santos v Santos*. See further Bromley loc cit.

[13] *McG v R* [1972] 1 All ER 362. The usual way of proving consent is by producing the completed acknowledgement of service stating that the respondent consents to the decree, which must be signed by him personally: see Family Proceedings Rules 1991, r 2.10 and Form M6.

[14] *Mason v Mason* [1972] Fam 302, [1972] 3 All ER 315.

[15] Matrimonial Causes Act 1973, s 2(7). This is printed on the Notice of Proceedings served on the respondent: Family Proceedings Rules 1991, r 2.6(6) and Form M5.

[16] Family Proceedings Rules 1991, r 2.10(2). In *Beales v Beales* (supra) at 222 and 674, respectively, Baker P left open the question whether a respondent could ever be estopped from withdrawing a consent once given if the petitioner had acted on it to her detriment, for example by vacating the matrimonial home. With respect to the learned President, this cannot be a true case of estoppel because the representation would be to future conduct; nor could it be a form of quasi-estoppel because the petitioner is not using it as a shield. The real question must be whether a respondent can bind himself by contract not to withdraw his consent. Insofar as the Act implies that the respondent must be a consenting party at the time of the trial, it is submitted that his consent cannot be made irrevocable by being given by deed or for valuable consideration.

[17] Matrimonial Causes Act 1973, s 10(1). The matters on which a respondent is most likely to be misled are those relating to financial provisions.

5. FIVE YEARS' SEPARATION

The last fact on which a petitioner may rely is that the spouses have lived apart for a continuous period of at least five years immediately preceding the presentation of the petition.[18] This provision was even more controversial than the last because it enables the marriage to be dissolved against the will of a spouse who has committed no matrimonial offence and who has not been responsible for the breakdown of the marriage. On the one hand it was hailed as a measure that would bring relief to hundreds of couples who would otherwise live in stable illicit unions unable to marry because one or both of them could not secure release from another union; on the other hand it was castigated as a 'Casanova's charter'.

This fact is identical with the last except that the period of separation is five years and the respondent's consent is not required. It will thus be seen that a decree could be granted even though the respondent is incurably insane. If five years' separation is established, a decree can still be refused if it would cause the respondent grave financial or other hardship.[19]

D. Divorce: protection of the respondent and children

1. PROTECTION OF THE RESPONDENT

Two provisions of the Matrimonial Causes Act are designed to give protection to the respondent when the petitioner relies on two or five years' separation—in other words when the petition does not disclose any fault or breach of matrimonial obligation on the respondent's part.

Hardship to the respondent

If the petitioner relies on *five years'* separation, section 5 of the Act permits the respondent to oppose the grant of a decree nisi on the ground that the dissolution of the marriage will result in grave financial or other hardship to him *and* that it would be wrong in all the circumstances to dissolve the marriage. If the court finds that the petitioner has established five years' separation and makes no such finding as to any other fact from which irretrievable breakdown of the marriage could be inferred, it must dismiss the petition if it is satisfied that the respondent's allegations are true.

In the vast majority of cases the wife is much more likely to suffer hardship, particularly financial hardship, from the granting of a decree than the husband.[20] Consequently in the following discussion it will be assumed that the wife is resisting the husband's petition. It must be remembered, however, that precisely the same principles will apply if the respondent is the husband.

The hardship must result from the dissolution of the marriage: it is not enough for the respondent to show that hardship would result if the divorce were based on five years' separation. In *Grenfell v Grenfell*[1] the wife

---

[18] Matrimonial Causes Act 1973, s 1(2)(e).
[19] See infra.
[20] In every reported case in which grave hardship has been alleged the wife has been the respondent.
[1] [1978] Fam 128, [1978] 1 All ER 561, CA.

presented a petition for divorce based on her husband's behaviour. He cross-petitioned on the basis of five years' separation, and in her reply the wife pleaded that, as she was a practising member of the Greek Orthodox Church, her conscience would be affronted if the marriage were to be dissolved 'otherwise than on grounds of substance'. It was held that, as she was seeking a divorce herself, she could not argue that she would suffer hardship if the marriage were to be dissolved and so her reply was struck out. Furthermore, the hardship must be the result of dissolution and not of the breakdown of the marriage.[2] Hence the fact that the husband will be supporting two families will be irrelevant if he is already living with the woman he wishes to marry and has children by her. Whether it be financial or other hardship, it must also be grave.[3] Whether or not there would be grave hardship must be considered 'subjectively in relation to the particular marriage and the circumstances in which the parties lived while it subsisted',[4] but what matters is not whether the respondent feels that she would suffer (which she would in most cases) but whether sensible people knowing all the facts would think so.[5] It has been said that one must look at the situation through the eyes of the respondent and then judge objectively the reality of the apprehension.[6] It would clearly be wrong to deprive the petitioner of relief because of the respondent's ill-founded fears, and the objective test of whether the reasonable man would agree that the particular wife would suffer grave hardship must be the only one that the court can apply.

Divorce will frequently cause financial hardship to a wife (particularly if she has children), but the courts are slow to find that this will be grave. Hardship includes the loss of the chance of acquiring any benefit which the respondent might acquire if the marriage were not dissolved.[7] We have already seen that, if the husband has already set up another home, divorce will not make the slightest difference to his current financial obligations and therefore could not cause the wife any further hardship.[8] Likewise, the potential loss of rights on the husband's intestacy will usually be immaterial because he will presumably be advised to make a will in favour of other beneficiaries: whether the marriage is dissolved or not, the wife will have a claim under the Inheritance (Provision for Family and Dependants) Act 1975.[9] In practice grave hardship will be due to one (or both) of two causes.

[2] *Talbot v Talbot* (1971) 115 Sol Jo 870.
[3] 'Grave' qualifies both 'financial' and 'other hardship': *Rukat v Rukat* [1975] Fam 63, [1975] 1 All ER 343, CA.
[4] Per Dunn J in *Talbot v Talbot* (supra), cited with apparent approval by Karminski LJ in *Mathias v Mathias* [1972] Fam 287, 299, [1972] 3 All ER 1, 6, CA.
[5] Per Lawton LJ in *Rukat v Rukat* (supra) at 73 and 351, respectively. To quote his example: 'The rich gourmet who because of financial stringency has to drink vin ordinaire with his grouse may well think he is suffering hardship; but sensible people would say he was not.'
[6] *Balraj v Balraj* (1980) 11 Fam Law 110, CA. See also *Rukat v Rukat* (supra) at 72 and 75, and 350 and 353 respectively. But how does one judge the reality of an apprehension that one will be damned in the next world if one dies divorced?
[7] Matrimonial Causes Act 1973, s 5(3).
[8] This means that the husband will suffer if he and the other woman are not prepared to live with each other unless they marry, because divorce will affect his obligations.
[9] See post, pp 821 et seq. It is equally irrelevant for the wife to complain that the amount being paid by the husband under an existing order is too little; this has nothing to do with the consequences of dissolution and the wife's remedy is to apply for a variation of the order: *Dorrell v Dorrell* [1972] 3 All ER 343, 347.

First, the wife will no longer be able to claim Social Security benefits (such as a widow's pension and a retirement pension) by virtue of her husband's contributions. This does not apply if she is over the age of 60 at the time of the divorce because she will then be entitled to benefits as though her husband had died,[10] but in other cases the Court of Appeal in *Rieterbund v Rieterbund*[11] laid down the principle that the court must not ignore the claims she has to income support. There is no stigma attached to its receipt and it can make no difference to the wife which public fund the money comes from. If, therefore, the amount she would receive from income support is not substantially less than what she would receive from the contributory benefit, she will suffer no hardship as a result of the divorce. If, on the other hand, she is likely to be earning a wage after her husband's death or retirement, she might receive considerably more from the contributory benefit because her earnings will not reduce it as they would reduce the sum she received by way of income support. Each case must turn on its own facts: in *Reiterbund v Reiterbund* the wife could not rely on the potential loss of a widow's pension as grave financial hardship because she was likely to remain incapable of earning her own living and would therefore still be partially dependent on income suport whether she received a widow's pension or not.

The other likely cause of grave financial hardship will be the potential loss of pension rights (other than those payable under the Social Security Act) accruing to an employee's widow. It will be necessary to make a reasonable assessment of the possible loss and the wife will not be able to argue that this amounts to grave financial hardship if it is too remote a contingency. In this connection it must be remembered that some funds are held on discretionary trusts under which the trustees may pay a pension to a woman with whom the husband has been living to the exclusion of his widow. Similarly, a middle-aged wife is more likely to be affected than a young one, and it will be unusual for a young, able-bodied wife, capable of earning her own living, to be able to make out a case of grave financial hardship.[12] Although it has been held that the loss can be offset if the husband purchases an annuity or secures the payment of premiums of an insurance policy of equal value,[13] this may be worth little in days of inflation, particularly if the pension is index-linked and so subject to periodical revision to keep pace with inflation. The courts are obviously loth to keep alive a marriage that has irretrievably broken down and in *Le Marchant v Le Marchant*[14] the Court of Appeal held that the husband's offer to transfer the matrimonial home (worth about £5,000) to the wife, to pay her a further £5,000 on his retirement and to take out an insurance on his own life for £5,000, which would be payable to her if she survived him, offset an index-linked widow's pension then worth £1,300 a year. One wonders what the real value of this settlement proved to be. It is clear, however, that a

---

[10] See the Social Security (Widow's Benefit and Retirement Pensions) Regulations, SI 1979 No 642, regs 8 and 12.
[11] [1975] Fam 99, [1975] 1 All ER 280, CA; affirming the judgment of Finer J [1974] 2 All ER 455; Bissett-Johnson and Pollard 38 MLR 449; Lowe 6 Fam Law 24, 59; Snaith 126 New LJ 341.
[12] Per Stephenson LJ in *Mathias v Mathias* (supra) at pp 301–302 and 8, respectively.
[13] *Parker v Parker* [1972] Fam 116, [1972] 1 All ER 410. Cf post, p 784.
[14] [1977] 3 All ER 610, CA.

husband will be at a disadvantage if he has neither the capital nor the income to offer some real compensation to his wife: in *Julian v Julian*,[15] for example, the difference between a pension of £790 a year (which the respondent could claim as the petitioner's widow) and an annuity of £215 a year (which was all the husband could afford to purchase) was held to be so great as to cause the wife grave financial hardship, and the petition was dismissed.

The position of the children may also be relevant in determining whether the respondent would suffer financial hardship. In *Lee v Lee*[16] the wife needed accommodation to look after her son who was then in hospital but who would require constant attention during the day time on his discharge. As the husband's proposal to sell the matrimonial home and give her half the proceeds of sale would not have enabled her to buy a flat for this purpose, the petition was dismissed.[17]

The Court of Appeal has refused to define what 'other grave hardship' could comprise,[18] but in all the cases reported up to now the respondent has alleged that the divorce would be anathema to her on religious grounds or would result in social ostracism.[19] In most of them the wife has come from overseas and has sought to have the petition dismissed because of the effect that a divorce would have on her standing amongst her own community. A typical example is to be found in *Banik v Banik*,[20] where the wife was a Hindu still living in India. It was held by the Court of Appeal that it was not sufficient that the divorce would cause her distress and unhappiness or that she personally would regard it as immoral or contrary to the rules of her community; she must establish that shame, disgrace or degra-

---

[15] (1972) 116 Sol Jo 763. Grave financial hardship was also found in *Brickell v Brickell* [1974] Fam 31, [1973] 3 All ER 508, CA (potential loss of pension of £232 a year) and *Johnson v Johnson* (1981) 12 Fam Law 116 (potential loss of index linked pension worth £2,000 a year). See further Vickers 123 New LJ 240.

[16] (1973) 117 Sol Jo 616. (On appeal a decree was granted because regrettably the son had died in the meantime: 5 Fam Law 48, CA.)

[17] Obviously in many cases the wife's allegation will involve a detailed examination of the parties' financial position before decree nisi, thus anticipating the similar enquiry that will have to be made if the decree is granted and the wife claims financial relief (as she presumably will). Consequently the judge should reserve this question to himself to avoid unnecessary waste of time and costs. If the petitioner has misled the respondent about his financial position or about the terms he proposes for her provision, with the result that the respondent has consented to the petition which she would otherwise have opposed, she may have the decree nisi rescinded: *Parkes v Parkes* [1971] 3 All ER 870, CA. Quaere whether she could still do so if the decree has already been made absolute: presumably this would be in the court's discretion. See generally Cretney 122 New LJ 48.

[18] *Banik v Banik* [1973] 3 All ER 45, 48, CA.

[19] Cf the opinion of Ormrod LJ in *Rukat v Rukat* [1975] Fam 63, 75, [1975] 1 All ER 343, 352, CA. It has been suggested that an orthodox Jewish wife could oppose the grant of a decree if her husband refused to grant her a *get*, without which she could not remarry by Jewish law: Maidment *The Legal Effect of Religious Divorces* 37 MLR 611, 621. Sed quaere? She would not be alleging that the dissolution of the marriage would cause her grave hardship.

[20] [1973] 3 All ER 45, CA. The court remitted the case for rehearing and a decree was later pronounced because the wife's statement that she would become a social outcast could be discounted and it would not be wrong to dissolve the marriage: 117 Sol Jo 874. See also *Parghi v Parghi* (1973) 117 Sol Jo 582 (Hindu wife resident in Bombay); *Rukat v Rukat* (supra) (Roman Catholic wife with family in Sicily); *Balraj v Balraj* (1980) 11 Fam Law 110, CA (wife resident in a Kshatriya community in India; divorce would also reduce daughter's marriage prospects).

dation would fall on her. Whether this would amount to grave hardship if it were established is a question of fact and degree: the defence has not been successful in any reported case.

Even if the respondent does prove that the decree would cause her grave hardship, the court must still pronounce a decree unless it is also of the opinion that it would be wrong to do so. The use of 'wrong' in this context is unusual and its meaning is ambiguous and obscure; in *Brickell v Brickell*[1] Davies LJ was of the opinion that it meant 'unjust or not right in all the circumstances of the case'. The court must take into account specifically the conduct and interests of the parties and the interests of any children and other persons concerned (for example, the person whom the petitioner wishes to marry),[2] and in the end will have to balance those interests against the hardship that a divorce would cause the respondent.[3] The latter's age, earning capacity and intention to remarry and the length of time that the parties have cohabited are all highly relevant, and in practice the courts are not likely to refuse a decree if the wife is young, healthy and capable of earning her own living or if the marriage has lasted for only a short time or has been dead for many years.[4] The respondent's conduct may likewise be a vital fact, and in *Brickell v Brickell* a decree was pronounced against a wife who had deserted her husband and broken up his business by her conduct even though the potential loss of a pension caused her grave financial hardship. Although the children's interests must be considered, the Court of Appeal in *Mathias v Mathias*[5] apparently paid no regard to the wife's argument that the husband's remarriage (which would be possible only if he were granted a divorce) could cause financial hardship to their child. The husband's father had left half his residuary estate (which was worth £20,000) to the husband's legitimate children in equal shares, and by remarrying the husband might have further legitimate children and thus reduce the existing child's interest. No reason was given for disregarding this: but it is submitted that it would have been unjust to the petitioner to keep the marriage on foot merely to prevent the birth of further legitimate children.

---

[1] [1974] Fam 31, 37, [1973] 3 All ER 508, 511, CA.
[2] Matrimonial Causes Act 1973, s 5(2). 'Children' includes children over the age of 18: *Allan v Allan* (1973) 4 Fam Law 83.
[3] See *Rukat v Rukat* (supra) at pp 75 and 352, respectively. In *Mathias v Mathias* [1972] Fam 287, 299, [1972] 3 All ER 1, 7, CA, Karminski LJ adopted the words of Dunn J in *Talbot v Talbot* (1971) 115 Sol Jo 870 that 'regard had to be had to the circumstances of the persons involved, including the children, and also to the balance which had to be maintained between upholding the sanctity of marriage and the desirability of ending "empty" tries'. The reference to upholding the sanctity of marriage seems scarcely relevant to a case where ex hypothesi the marriage has irretrievably broken down.
[4] *Mathias v Mathias* (supra) at 301–302 and 8, respectively; *Rukat v Rukat* (supra) at 76 and 353, respectively.
[5] [1972] Fam 287, [1972] 3 All ER 1, CA. It was further held that the potential loss of state and army pensions was not grave financial hardship to a wife of 32 and that it would be wrong not to dissolve the marriage when the parties had cohabited for less than three years out of ten. In *Balraj v Balraj* (supra) the court held that the daughter's position could be ameliorated by the petitioner's paying her a sum to compensate her for the loss of her reputation.

Financial protection for the respondent

If a decree nisi is granted solely on the basis of *two or five years' separation*, the respondent may apply for it not to be made absolute unless the court is satisfied (a) that the petitioner should not be required to make financial provision for the respondent *or* (b) that the financial provision made by the petitioner for the respondent is reasonable and fair or the best that can be made in the circumstances. If the court is not so satisified, it *must* withhold the decree.[6]

It should be noticed that the latter condition is satisfied only if the provision is *made*; it is not sufficient for the petitioner to make proposals which would be satisfactory if they were carried out. Thus, if the court approves the payment of a lump sum, the decree should not be made absolute until the sum is actually paid in order to prevent the petitioner from frustrating the purpose of the provision by obtaining his decree and then failing to carry out his undertaking.[7]

This provision is designed to afford further protection to the respondent by giving her another weapon that can be used against the petitioner. The threat to delay the latter's remarriage by holding up the decree absolute may be perfectly proper if the petitioner is deliberately evading his financial responsibilities. In *Hardy v Hardy*,[8] for example, the petitioner, who was the son of a very rich bookmaker and racehorse trainer, was employed by his father as an assistant trainer at the minimum salary payable under union arrangements. He could obviously have earned much more elsewhere and had considerable future expectations which might result in the making of a substantial lump sum order at a later date. In these circumstances the Court of Appeal was of the opinion that the decree should not have been made absolute until reasonable and fair provision was made for the wife, if necessary by a voluntary payment, even though the court was not in a position to make an order for the immediate payment of a lump sum. Similarly, the court may withhold the decree absolute until the petitioner has remedied his failure to make payments for a child of the family under an existing separation agreement, even though there is no continuing obligation, if non-payment in the past leaves the respondent at a financial disadvantage and there is no other ready way of enforcing the petitioner's obligation.[9] On the other hand the statute can obviously be abused. Consequently, even though the court finds that the petitioner has not made such financial provision as he should have made, it may nevertheless make the decree absolute if it appears that there are circumstances making it desirable that this should not be delayed *and* the court has obtained a satisfactory undertaking from the petitioner that he will make such financial provision for the respondent as the court may approve.[10] This does not mean that the court can accept a blanket undertaking which would leave

---

[6] Matrimonial Causes Act 1973, s 10(2), (3). Failure to comply with this provision makes the decree absolute voidable, not void: *Wright v Wright* [1976] Fam 114, [1976] 1 All ER 796.

[7] *Wilson v Wilson* [1973] 2 All ER 17, CA. This would apply equally to the transfer or settlement of property and to securing periodical payments. How can it apply to unsecured periodical payments, which create a continuing obligation? It is necessary to obtain a court order before the decree is made absolute?

[8] (1981) 2 FLR 321, CA.

[9] *Garcia v Garcia* [1991] 3 All ER 451, CA.

[10] Matrimonial Causes Act 1973, s 10(4).

the petitioner ignorant of what he is to do and the respondent ignorant of what she is to get. The petitioner must give an outline of what he proposes and the court should not make the decree absolute until it is satisfied that these proposals are reasonable and fair or the best that can be made.[11]

In deciding what financial provision (if any) the respondent ought to make for the petitioner, the Act requires the court to consider all the circumstances including specifically the age, health, conduct, earning capacity, financial resources and financial obligations of each of the spouses, and also the probable financial position of the respondent if the marriage is dissolved and the petitioner dies first.[12] Generally speaking, the court should take into account the same matters as it considers when assessing financial provision.[13] Thus in *Krystman v Krystman*[14] it was held that the petitioner should not be required to make any provision for his wife when the parties had cohabited for only a fortnight at the beginning of the marriage, which had taken place 26 years before, and the wife (whose income exceeded the husband's) had previously made no financial claim on him at all.

A comparison of this provision with that contained in section 5 shows three important differences between them. First, it applies to both two and five years' separation whilst section 5 applies only to five years' separation. In practice, however, it is unlikely that a respondent will invoke this provision in the case of two years' separation because she (or he) will consent to the decree only if she is satisfied that she will receive the best financial provision possible in the circumstances and, if she has been misled, she can apply to have the decree nisi rescinded.[15] Secondly, section 5 applies to grave financial or other hardship (and is therefore not confined to financial matters) whilst the provision we have just considered refers at the highest to reasonable and fair financial provision. Finally, reflecting the second point of difference, it merely enables the respondent to delay the decree absolute, whilst section 5 enables her to oppose the making of the decree nisi in limine and is therefore a much more powerful weapon.

2. PROTECTION OF CHILDREN

In exceptional circumstances the court may direct that the decree is not to be made absolute until further order if it is of the opinion that it is likely to have to exercise its powers under the Children Act with respect to certain children of the family and it needs to give further consideration to the case.[16] This provision will be discussed in detail later,[17] but it should be noted that it differs from those we have been considering in two respects: it applies to all cases, on whatever fact the petition is based, and the court acts on its own initiative and not on the application of the respondent.

---

[11] *Grigson v Grigson* [1974] 1 All ER 478, CA.
[12] Matrimonial Causes Act 1973, s 10(3).
[13] *Lombardi v Lombardi* [1973] 3 All ER 625, 629, CA. See post, pp 771 et seq.
[14] [1973] 3 All ER 247, CA. See further post, p 777.
[15] For rescission of decree nisi, see ante, p 213.
[16] Matrimonial Causes Act 1973, s 41, as substituted by the Children Act 1989, Sch 12, para 31.
[17] Post, pp 361–365.

E. Divorce: reconciliation and conciliation

1. RECONCILIATION

The emphasis of the Divorce Reform Act was on irretrievable breakdown and therefore on the possibility of reconciliation. A number of provisions now contained in the Matrimonial Causes Act are designed to promote this.[18]

Adjournment of proceedings

If at any stage it appears that there is a reasonable possibility of a reconciliation between the parties, the court may adjourn the proceedings for such period as it thinks fit to enable attempts at reconciliation to be made.[19] This is of no practical importance at all. If an undefended case is dealt with under the special procedure, the court will have no opportunity of judging whether reconciliation is possible; and once a defended case has come to trial, any attempts to achieve it are likely to be successful only in the most exceptional circumstances.[20]

Solicitor's certificate

If the petitioner instructs a solicitor to act for him, the latter is required to certify whether or not he has discussed with the petitioner the possibility of a reconciliation and given him the names and addresses of persons qualified to help effect a reconciliation between estranged spouses.[21] The object of this provision is 'to ensure that parties know where to seek guidance when there is a sincere desire for a reconciliation, and it is important that reference to a marriage guidance counsellor or a probation officer should not be regarded as a formal step which must be taken in all cases irrespective of whether or not there is any prospect of reconciliation'.[1] It is highly doubtful, however, whether it is of any value. Many petitioners do not instruct a solicitor,[2] and many solicitors may treat the certificate as a formality unlikely to lead to any real attempt to resume married life. In any event, no sanction follows if the solicitor states that he has not discussed the possibility of a reconciliation.[3] It is not surprising that the Booth Committee saw no useful purpose in retaining the requirement and recommended its abolition.[4] There is, however, some evidence that there is a possibility of reconciliation in a number of marriages that are currently

---

[18] For a critical appraisal of these provisions, see Griew *Marital Reconciliation—Context of Meanings* [1972A] CLJ 294.
[19] Matrimonial Causes Act 1973, s 6(2).
[20] See Griew loc cit pp 308–310. For the special procedure, see post, pp 235–236.
[21] Matrimonial Causes Act 1973, s 6(1); Family Proceedings Rules 1991, r 2.6(3) and Form M3.
[1] *Practice Direction* [1972] 3 All ER 768. See Griew loc cit pp 307–308.
[2] See post, p 234.
[3] Shortly after the Divorce Reform Act came into force it was judicially stated that, if there had been no discussion, the court might feel bound in some cases to exercise its power to adjourn the proceedings to see whether a reconciliation could be effected: *Goodrich v Goodrich* [1971] 2 All ER 1340. It is highly unlikely that any court would do so today.
[4] Report of the Matrimonial Causes Procedure Committee (1985) paras 4.42–4.43.

dissolved,[5] and solicitors should be aware that they may have a greater role to play in encouraging parties to seek reconciliation than some of them apparently realise.

Cohabitation

Certain provisions of the Matrimonial Causes Act are designed to enable the spouses to try to effect a reconciliation by resuming cohabitation for a limited period without prejudicing their right to petition for divorce if the attempt fails.

Adultery

If the parties live with each other in the same household for any period or periods not exceeding six months in all after the petitioner discovered that the respondent had committed adultery, their living together for this time is to be disregarded in determining whether the petitioner finds it intolerable to live with the respondent. But if they live with each other for more than six months, the petitioner cannot rely on the adultery at all.[6] 'Living with each other in the same household' has the same meaning as it has in relation to two or five years' separation as a fact establishing irretrievable breakdown of the marriage,[7] so that time will not run against the petitioner if the spouses are living under the same roof as two separate households. Conversely, if they are living apart but both treat the marriage as still on foot notwithstanding the adultery, they will be regarded as living with each other for this purpose.

Respondent's behaviour

A similar rule applies if the petitioner relies on the respondent's behaviour. If the parties have lived with each other in the same household for a period or periods not exceeding six months in all after the date of the final incident relied on by the petitioner, this is to be disregarded in determining whether he can reasonably be expected to live with the respondent.[8] But in this case the Act does not expressly state what the position is to be if they cohabit for more than six months. This is obviously strong evidence that the petitioner can be expected to live with the other spouse, but the deliberate omission of any express enactment (as appears in the case of adultery) indicates that it is not to be conclusive. In most cases it will be difficult for the court to resist the inference that the petitioner can be expected to live with the respondent or even that the marriage has not irretrievably broken down,[9] but it may do so if the petitioner can show some other reason for his or her actions, for example if he or she was cowed into remaining with

---

[5] Davis and Murch, *Grounds for Divorce*, ch 4.

[6] Matrimonial Causes Act 1973, s 2(1), (2), (6). The fact that the parties have lived with each other for more than six months will not stop the petitioner from relying on further adultery committed since they separated even though this is a continuation of the same adulterous association: *Carr v Carr* [1974] 1 All ER 1193, CA. It is highly doubtful whether the period is long enough to effect a reconciliation in many cases or whether the attempt is likely to be successful if the petitioner has to keep his eye on the calendar: see Griew loc cit, pp 313–314.

[7] See ante, pp 211–212.

[8] Matrimonial Causes Act 1973, s 2(3), (6).

[9] *Katz v Katz* [1972] 3 All ER 219, 224.

the respondent[10] or cohabited for the protection of the children or because there was nowhere else to live.[11]

Desertion and separation

In determining whether the period of two years' desertion or two or five years' separation has been continuous, the court must similarly disregard any period or periods not exceeding six months in all in which the parties have lived together in the same household. In these cases, however, the periods of cohabitation must be ignored in calculating the length of time the parties have been apart.[12] Hence if the husband leaves his wife, they then live together for four months, and he then leaves her again, she will not be able to petition for divorce alleging desertion or separation until two years and four months have elapsed from his first leaving her. This is the only exception to the rule that two or more periods of desertion or separation cannot be added together to give a period of two or five years in the aggregate.

Cohabitation after decree nisi

Although the decree is pronounced in two stages, it is nonetheless a single decree, and consequently cohabitation between decree nisi and decree absolute is to be treated in the same way as cohabitation before decree nisi. Hence if the parties live together for more than six months after a decree nisi based on adultery, this must lead to its rescission,[13] and a decree based on the respondent's behaviour will not be made absolute if the subsequent cohabitation shows that the court was wrong in finding that the petitioner could not reasonably be expected to live with the respondent *at the time of the decree nisi.*[14] It is immaterial that, at the time of the hearing, the court is convinced that the marriage has broken down irretrievably so that a second petition will succeed.[15] Whilst this may appear to invite unnecessary proliferation of legal proceedings, it must be remembered that one party should not be permitted to hold the threat of divorce over the other's head after a reconciliation. This suggests that the same rule should be applied if the petition is based on two years' desertion or two or five years' separation, even though the Act requires that the period in question should immediately precede the presentation of the petition: in all cases it could be argued that the court was wrong in finding that the marriage had broken down irretrievably when it pronounced the decree nisi.[16]

The court must, of course, disregard any periods of cohabitation which it would have had to leave out of account had they occurred before decree

[10] *Court v Court* [1982] Fam 105, [1981] 2 All ER 531.
[11] *Bradley v Bradley* [1973] 3 All ER 750, CA.
[12] Matrimonial Causes Act 1973, s 2(5), (6). It is doubtful whether the period is long enough: cf p 222, n 6, ante.
[13] *Biggs v Biggs* [1977] Fam 1, [1977] 1 All ER 20.
[14] *Savage v Savage* [1982] Fam 100, [1982] 3 All ER 49. Contrast *Court v Court* (supra).
[15] *Savage v Savage* (supra).
[16] Unless one spouse applies to have the decree nisi rescinded, in practice cohabitation after decree nisi is likely to come to light only if the application to have the decree made absolute is made more than 12 months after the decree nisi was pronounced. In such a case the spouse making the application is bound to lodge an explanation for the delay giving inter alia details of any cohabitation since the decree nisi: Family Proceedings Rules 1991, r 2.49.

nisi, but any period of cohabitation preceding the decree nisi must obviously be added to any period following it.

2. CONCILIATION[17]

The ineffectiveness of the provisions in the Matrimonial Causes Act encouraging attempts at reconciliation has led to the belief that conciliation is much more likely to be successful. A clear lead was given by the Committee on One-Parent Families, which defined conciliation as 'assisting the parties to deal with the consequences of the established breakdown of their marriage, whether resulting in a divorce or a separation, by reaching agreements or giving assents or reducing the area of conflict upon custody, support, access to and education of the children, financial provision, disposition of the matrimonial home, lawyers' fees, and every other matter arising from the breakdown which calls for a decision on future arrangements'.[18] Conciliation thus has two main objects: to define the matters on which the parties are in dispute, and to encourage them to come to an agreed solution. The conciliator must be—and must be seen to be—neutral: he may clarify issues and propose possible solutions, but he must not seek to impose any of them on the parties.[19]

The growth of interest in conciliation reflects the changed attitude towards divorce generally and the shift of emphasis from the fact of dissolution to its financial consequences and especially its effect on the children of the marriage. Research suggests that the children find emotional adjustment more difficult if the parents' relationship is hostile and conflict between them continues after divorce or separation, particularly if contact with one parent is not maintained.[20] One of the strongest arguments in favour of conciliation is that the possibility of bitterness will be reduced and the prospects of both spouses continuing to play an active role as parents will be enhanced if they can reach agreement. The adversarial procedure of the courts, on the other hand, may well exacerbate antagonism.[1] Conciliation enables the parties to retain control of their own affairs rather than have a solution imposed on them.

Two types of conciliation have developed: 'in-court' and 'out-of-court'.

---

[17] There is a mass of periodical literature on this subject, some of which is referred to in the following notes. See generally Parkinson *Conciliation in Separation and Divorce*; Fisher (ed) *Family Conciliation within the UK*; Report of the Conciliation Project Unit, 1989.

[18] Cmnd 5629, para 4.288. See also Parkinson op cit p 52. For further discussion of the aims of conciliation, see Davis *Mediation in Divorce* [1983] JSWL 139; Bottomley *Resolving Family Disputes* and Gerard *Conciliation; present and future* both in Freeman (ed) *The State, the Law and the Family*.

[19] This distinguishes a conciliator from an adjudicator (who has the power to impose a solution), an arbitrator (by whose decision the parties have agreed to be bound) and a negotiator (who acts on behalf of one party only).

[20] See Rutter *Maternal Deprivation Re-assessed*; Wallerstein and Kelly *Surviving the Break Up*; Wallerstein and Blakelee *Second Chances: Men, Women and Children a Decade after Divorce*; Lund [1984] Fam Law 199.

[1] See eg the Report of the Inter-departmental Committee on Conciliation 1983, para 1.13; Parkinson op cit p 69 and 13 Fam Law 22; Murch *Justice and Welfare in Divorce* 210; the Family Law Sub-committee of the Law Society *A Better Way out*, para 15.

In-court conciliation

This can be said to have begun in 1971, when machinery was set up which enabled the court to refer a case to the court welfare officer when it considered that there were ancillary proceedings in which conciliation might serve a useful propose.[2] In 1977 a scheme was launched in the Bristol county court which at first dealt only with defended divorce proceedings but was extended two years later to cover disputes over custody and access. The parties and their solicitors attend an appointment for directions before the district judge; if the issues are essentially issues of law or fact, the district judge can assist by pointing the way towards a possible resolution, but if they are 'emotional or involve children, the parties withdraw ... with a welfare officer who adopts a combination of conciliatory and investigatory techniques'.[3] If agreement is reached, the district judge can make the necessary consent orders. Many other county courts have since set up similar schemes,[4] and some encourage conciliation outside the court premises. In 1979 the Principal Registry in London set up a system of pre-trial reviews to try to settle defended cases and extended it to property adjustment and lump sum applications in the following year.[5] Unfortunately, it proved to be a failure[6] and was abandoned after only 14 months. In 1983, however, the Principal Registry introduced a new pilot scheme based on the Bristol model which has been extended to cover all applications for orders under section 8 of the Children Act 1989 (including those arising in wardship proceedings), the consideration of arrangements under section 41 of the Matrimonial Causes Act 1973, and wardship summonses. Both parties and their legal advisers are required to attend a conciliation appointment; they must be accompanied by any children over the age of nine because it will sometimes be appropriate for them to be seen by the district judge or welfare officer. Parties are given an opportunity of retiring to a private room with a welfare officer, and if conciliation is successful, the district judge will make such orders as are appropriate.[7] If the parties cannot reach an agreement, the welfare officer acting as conciliator may subsequently be asked to make a report to the court, but it is now accepted that these two roles cannot be combined and that the same officer should not carry out both functions.[8]

---

[2] *Practice Direction* [1971] 1 All ER 894.
[3] Parmiter 78 LS Gaz 196, qv for further details of the scheme.
[4] See the Report of the Inter-departmental Committee on Conciliation, para 3.14; Report of the Conciliation Project Unit, paras 8.5–8.17. For the way in which some operate, see Rose and Gellis [1991] Fam Law 92; Davis [1991] Fam Law 130.
[5] *Practice Direction* [1979] 1 All ER 112; *Practice Direction* [1980] 1 All ER 592.
[6] See Davis and Bader 80 LS Gaz 627, 679. The main reasons for the failure seemed to be the half-hearted way in which it was run and solicitors' lack of support for it.
[7] *Practice Directions* [1982] 3 All ER 988, [1984] 3 All ER 800 and [1992] 1 All ER 421. If the application for a s 8 order is for a residence or contact order, the application must be referred for conciliation. The district judge has a discretion to direct a conciliation appointment in proceedings under s 41 of the Matrimonial Causes Act 1973 or in a wardship summons.
[8] *Re H* [1986] 1 FLR 476; *Practice Direction* [1986] 2 FLR 171. See also the Report of the Matrimonial Causes Procedure Committee, paras 4.61–4.63; Taylor [1984] Fam Law 302; Pugsley et al [1986] Fam Law 164. But a welfare officer may encourage conciliation: Fisher and Coates [1989] Fam Law 96. For the difficulty that can arise when the roles are confused, see *Scott v Scott* [1986] 2 FLR 320, CA. See further post, p 380.

There is some evidence that the parties feel under pressure to reach a decision in as short a time as possible and some complain of crude arm-twisting and a search for a compromise regardless of the justice of the case. District judges and welfare officers may try to impose their own solution on the parties, and so far from leading them to reach their own agreement, the procedure may come to resemble that of a contested court appearance.[9]

Out-of-court conciliation

Out-of-court conciliation is independent of the court in the sense that parties are not referred to it by the court and a conciliator's services are available to them before they embark on litigation. It began in 1978, also in Bristol, as the result of the initiative of a group committed to taking action following the publication of the Report of the Committee on One-Parent Families. The conciliators are qualified social workers or marriage guidance counsellors, and most couples are referred by solicitors or refer themselves. A number of other independent schemes have since been set up in other parts of the country.[10]

The chances of success of out-of-court conciliation are said to be greater because the parties are more likely to resort to it before they take up entrenched positions. It has weaknesses, however. There is no guarantee that full and accurate information will be available about the parties' financial position,[11] and if one party is more dominant than the other, the weaker may be pressed to agree to disadvantageous terms. It is therefore imperative that the parties' solicitors should accompany them to give advice and, if necessary, approve proposals put forward.[12]

The future of conciliation

In 1982 an inter-departmental committee was set up to report on the nature, scope and effects of existing conciliation services and 'to consider whether those or further facilities should be promoted or developed and, if so, how this could best be done within existing resource planning'. The committee were of the opinion that there is a role for conciliation but that out-of-court schemes do not save money and appear to be more expensive than in-court schemes. They therefore concluded that Government funding of out-of-court schemes was not justified and that conciliation should be provided by in-court schemes.

Their report met with considerable criticism.[13] The Advisory Committee on Legal Aid argued that there are grounds for supporting out-of-court schemes from public funds.[14] The Matrimonial Causes Procedure Committee

[9] See Davis and Bader [1985] Fam Law 42, 82; Davis op cit 138; Roberts *Mediation in Family Disputes* 46 MLR 538, 556.
[10] See generally Roberts loc cit; Report of the Inter-departmental Committee on Conciliation, App 6; Report of the Conciliation Project Unit, paras 8.13–8.38. The scheme set up by the Family Law Bar Association under which parties can apply for a recommendation of appropriate terms of settlement of a financial dispute (see [1985] Fam Law 284) is really a form of arbitration rather than conciliation.
[11] See further, post, p 229.
[12] Parkinson 12 Fam Law 13; Gerard op cit 285.
[13] See Davis and Westcott 47 MLR 215; Yates [1983] JSWL 339, 133 New LJ 994 and [1984] Fam Law 48.
[14] See 34th Annual Report, para 121.

in 1985 and the Law Commission in 1990 also gave the strongest support for the availability of conciliation in matrimonial proceedings and argued that it should be extended beyond the residence and contact issues to which in-court conciliation is at present limited. As the success of conciliation depends on the parties' co-operation and agreement, both rejected a suggestion that conciliation should be compulsory, although they were of the opinion that every encouragement should be given to the parties to make use of the service. They therefore concluded that the parties should be encouraged to seek conciliation and that the court should be able to refer them to a conciliator and adjourn the case for conciliation, but the parties themselves must decide whether they will take part.[15]

The Inter-Departmental Committee on Conciliation recommended that a research unit should be established to monitor different types of in-court conciliation. As a result a Conciliation Project Unit, based on the University of Newcastle-on-Tyne, was set up with wider terms of reference to include an examination of the costs and effectiveness of out-of-court schemes as well. Its report, published in 1989, is in some respects disappointingly inconclusive. The Unit challenged accepted wisdom relating to the cost of conciliation, that is the resource cost less the saving in legal costs flowing from the tendency for conciliation to lead to speedier or more durable (and therefore less costly) settlements. They concluded that court-based conciliation adds on average about £150 to the cost of settling a dispute, of which £25 to £30 is borne by the parties themselves. Out-of-court conciliation is more costly, and the net effect of conciliation is probably to add about £250 to the overall cost of settling a disputed child issue in the county court, of which some £40 is borne by the parties. At the same time the Unit considered that conciliation generates important social benefits. They concluded that, to be most effective, it should be a recognised alternative to legal procedures for the resolution of disputes but should not be mandatory and should not focus entirely on issues relating to children. They recommended the establishment of a national service, which would be part of a network of local services covering both conciliation and counselling and would be independent of the courts and the probation service. After assessment an individual or couple would be channelled into the appropriate service. If legal proceedings have already begun, the parties (with solicitors if they so wish) should be requested to attend a conference with a district judge and a court welfare officer, which could investigate the nature of the issues in dispute between the parties and provide them with information about the options available for their resolution. If one or both of the parties declined to attempt conciliation, disputes would have to be resolved by traditional processes.

The development of conciliation reflects the change in legislative and judicial policy observable over the past 30 years. So long as divorce was regarded as a remedy for a matrimonial wrong, public policy demanded that the sanctity of marriage should be upheld by rigorous proof that the statutory conditions for the grant of a decree were satisfied. Hence it was felt that 'when the parties ... are acting in complete concert, the Court ...

[15] Report of the Matrimonial Causes Procedure Committee, paras 3.10–3.13 and 4.53–4.65; Law Com No 192 (Ground for Divorce) paras 5.29–5.39. For further details of the Committee's and Commission's proposals, see post, pp 241–244.

is rendered unable to pronounce a decree ... with sufficient confidence in its justice',[16] and the petition would have to be dismissed if it was proved that the conduct of the suit had been determined by agreement. The danger of collusion was equally high in respect of ancillary matters, for an unscrupulous spouse might, for example, be prepared to petition for divorce or not to defend a petition only on the other's undertaking to pay a disproportionately high sum by way of maintenance or not to oppose an application for care and control of the children. Denning J maintained in 1945 that agreements could be made with perfect propriety provided they were entered into in good faith,[17] but it was not until 1963 that collusion became a discretionary (as distinct from an absolute) bar to divorce[18] and not until 1969 that it ceased to be a bar altogether.[19] Even stronger legislative approval of this reversal of public policy is to be seen in the principle of the Children Act that the court should make an order under that Act only if it considers that this is better than making no order at all.[20] Given this emphasis on the desirability of the parties' reaching an agreed solution to the issues over which they are in dispute,[1] it is inevitable that conciliation must be regarded as an acceptable—and in many cases preferable—alternative method of resolving them.

This makes it essential that any system adopted should contain safeguards to ensure that agreements are fair and freely negotiated. The following are some of the problems that have to be faced.

Communications made in the course of conciliation

Conciliation is unlikely to be successful if there is a danger that a statement made by one party in the course of negotiations may later be put in evidence by the other if they fail to arrive at an agreement. It has already been urged that such statements should be absolutely privileged.[2]

Binding nature of agreements

No agreement between the parties can oust the jurisdiction of the court,[3] so that any terms on which they agree in the course of conciliation will be binding only when approved by the court. This raises some difficult questions.

First, it is not clear whether a respondent can be bound by an agreement not to defend. In *N v N*[4] after the wife had presented a petition based on the husband's behaviour, the parties entered into an agreement in which the wife undertook not to proceed with the suit for five months in order that they could explore the possibility of a reconciliation. If at the end of

---

[16] Per Jeune J in *Churchward v Churchward* [1895] P 7, 30.
[17] *Emanuel v Emanuel* [1946] P 115, [1945] 2 All ER 494.
[18] Matrimonial Causes Act 1963, s 4.
[19] Divorce Reform Act 1969, which repealed the relevant subsection of the Matrimonial Causes Act 1965.
[20] Section 1(5). See post, p 345.
[1] But this principle is not applied uniformly. Cf the rule that the parties cannot by agreement restrict the right of either of them to apply to a court for financial relief (post, pp 657–658).
[2] See ante, p 117. Statements made at a conciliation appointment under the scheme in operation in the Principal Registry are privileged: *Practice Direction* [1992] 1 All ER 421.
[3] See post, p 657 (financial agreements).
[4] [1992] 1 FLR 266.

this period she decided that the attempt had failed, the husband agreed not to defend the petition. At the end of the five months the wife decided that the reconciliation had not been a success and proceeded with the petition, whereupon the husband sought leave to file an answer out of time. Ewbank J held that he was bound by his agreement. The objection to this decision is that the court is bound to enquire into the facts alleged by both parties[5] and shutting out the respondent appears to fetter the court's ability to perform its statutory duty. Ewbank J emphasised that the purpose of the agreement in this case had been to promote reconciliation and admitted that the position would have been different if the respondent had agreed to allow a false case to be put to the court. Nevertheless, without necessarily suggesting that the petitioner is deliberately misleading the court, the respondent, by defending, denies the validity of her allegations. If, as in *N v N*, the defence is virtually certain to fail and the respondent will embitter relations by pursuing it, it is clearly desirable to hold him to his agreement. In many cases, however, it may not be possible to reach this conclusion without hearing his case in full. The decision must therefore be treated with reserve.[6]

Another problem that may arise from an agreement freely entered into between the parties is that the court may take the view that it should give effect to a clause in it relating to financial provision even though it would have made a more generous award.[7] Although a party could resile from an agreement if he or she had been misled, it would obviously be imprudent to accept an offer in ignorance of the other's income and assets. This presents no problem in in-court conciliation because, if either party is seeking financial relief, each is required to furnish an affidavit of means and may request further information from the other.[8] Some parties engaged in out-of-court conciliation will already know enough about each other's financial position to enable them to reach a fair settlement, but in other cases the chances of success will be slim because of the inability of one party to ensure that he or she has a full picture of the other's assets. There is clearly no way of solving this difficulty because it is impossible to invoke the court's powers.

Legal liability of conciliator

The influence a conciliator may have on the parties raises the question whether he could be liable if, at his suggestion, one of them agrees to terms which are clearly disadvantageous compared with what a court is likely to award. This is likely to occur only if the party concerned acted without legal advice in out-of-court conciliation, but in this situation a conciliator, having placed himself in a position where he knows that it is very likely that that party will rely on his advice in deciding whether to accept an offer

---

[5] Matrimonial Causes Act 1973, s 1(3).
[6] In *N v N* the respondent had to apply for leave to file an answer out of time because of the five months' delay. The second (and much less controversial) ground for the decision was that leave in the circumstances would be refused. But this question would not arise if the petition was not presented until after the agreement was made.
[7] See post, p 745.
[8] Family Proceedings Rules 1991, rr 2.58 and 2.63. This is not necessary if the parties apply for a consent order before affidavits have been filed (which will occur if they reach an agreement before proceedings are begun): ibid, r 2.61.

made by the other, can be expected to anticipate that he (or she) will do so. This satisfies the essential conditions for liability in negligence if the conciliator fails to take reasonable care to ensure that the advice, if followed, will produce a fair settlement.[9] On the other hand, a duty of care will be laid on a defendant only if it is just and reasonable to do so.[10] For this reason a court might be slow to impose liability on a conciliator who has acted in good faith because this could defeat the public interest in encouraging conciliation.[11] It is possible that an action would be more likely to succeed if it were based on a specific statement rather than on a general recommendation or encouragement, for example if the conciliator were to say: 'A court would not give you more'.

At present the outcome of any action against a conciliator is doubtful, but the possibility of success is a matter of which conciliators should be aware.

F. Divorce procedure

1. JURISDICTION OF ENGLISH COURTS

Jurisdiction was originally based solely on domicile and a court could pronounce a decree only if the husband (and therefore the wife) was domiciled in England when the petition was presented.[12] Had domicile retained its original meaning of a person's home, this might have been a satisfactory principle; but the technical meaning that it acquired produced many anomalies. One of the most glaring flowed from the wife's inability to acquire a separate domicile, so that, even though she had always been resident in this country, she could not obtain relief here if her husband was domiciled abroad. Two statutory bases of jurisdiction were introduced to meet this case, and a wife was able to petition (a) if her husband had deserted her or had been deported and had been domiciled in England immediately before the desertion or deportation, or (b) if she had been ordinarily resident in this country for three years immediately preceding the presentation of the petition and her husband was not domiciled in any other part of the United Kingdom or in the Channel Islands or the Isle of Man.[13]

Nevertheless hardship remained. A man habitually resident in this country but domiciled abroad could never obtain a divorce here. A woman in this

---

[9] See *Caparo Industries plc v Dickman* [1990] 2 AC 605, 620, [1990] 1 All ER 568, 576, HL (per Lord Bridge).

[10] *Governors of the Peabody Donation Fund v Sir Lindsay Parkinson & Co Ltd* [1985] AC 210, [1984] 3 All ER 529, HL; *Caparo Industries Plc v Dickman* (supra) at pp 618 and 574 respectively (per Lord Bridge).

[11] The House of Lords has also indicated that the law is now attaching greater significance to traditional categories of distinct and recognisable situations as a guide to the existence, scope and limits of a duty of care: *Caparo Industries Plc v Dickman* (supra) at pp 618 and 574 (per Lord Bridge), 628 and 582 (per Lord Roskill), 635 and 587 (per Lord Oliver). If a duty of care were held to exist, the standard expected of the defendant would undoubtedly be higher if he were legally qualified.

[12] *Le Mesurier v Le Mesurier* [1895] AC 517, PC.

[13] The first exception was introduced by the Matrimonial Causes Act 1937, s 13, and the second by the Law Reform (Miscellaneous Provisions) Act 1949, s 1.

position could do so if she could bring herself within one of the statutory exceptions, and it was anomalous that she alone could rely on three years' residence here. If the parties were British subjects domiciled in a country which based its divorce jurisdiction on nationality, they could get a divorce in neither country. Consequently the Law Commission recommended that jurisdiction should be extended to enable either spouse to petition if he or she had been habitually resident in this country for a year.[14] This recommendation (together with a modification of the original principle necessitated by the wife's ability to acquire a separate domicile) was implemented by the Domicile and Matrimonial Proceedings Act 1973, which also swept away the former statutory bases of jurisdiction.

Jurisdiction

The court now has jurisdiction if (and only if) either of the parties (a) is domiciled in England and Wales on the date when the proceedings are begun *or* (b) was habitually resident here throughout the period of one year ending with that date.[15] In addition, once proceedings for divorce, nullity or judicial separation, over which the court has jurisdiction, are pending, it may entertain other proceedings with respect to the marriage falling into any of these three categories even though it would not otherwise have jurisdiction when the second proceedings were begun.[16] Suppose, for example, that a wife petitions for judicial separation and that the only fact giving the court jurisdiction is that she has been habitually resident here for a year. She then ceases to be resident in this country and the husband cross-petitions for divorce. The court will have jurisdiction to hear the divorce petition even though neither party is then domiciled or resident in this country.

Discretionary stays

One of the consequences of this increased jurisdiction is the greater likelihood that other matrimonial proceedings will be brought simultaneously in another country. If, for example, the husband starts divorce proceedings elsewhere, the wife may be tempted to petition in this country in the belief that she is likely to obtain better financial provision. To prevent the embarrassment that might ensue, the court has a discretionary power to stay any matrimonial proceedings in this country if before the beginning of the trial (or first trial)[17] it appears that any proceedings in respect of the marriage in question or capable of affecting its validity or subsistence are continuing in any country outside England or Wales. The court may order a stay only if the balance of fairness (including convenience) is such that it is appropriate that the other proceedings should be disposed of first, and in deciding this the court must have regard to all relevant facts at the time including the convenience of the parties and witnesses and any delay or expense that might otherwise result. In *de Dampierre v de Dampierre*[18] the

[14] Law Com No 48 (Report on Jurisdiction in Matrimonial Causes) 1972.
[15] Domicile and Matrimonial Proceedings Act 1973, s 5(2).
[16] Ibid, s 5(5).
[17] Ie trial of the suit or any issue (except as to jurisdiction). A stay may be granted notwithstanding that the court has already heard an application for ancillary relief: *Thyssen-Bornemisza v Thyssen-Bornemisza* [1986] Fam 1, [1985] 1 All ER 328, CA.
[18] [1988] AC 92, [1987] 2 All ER 1, HL.

House of Lords held that the essential question is whether the facts connect the matrimonial dispute more closely with another forum; if so, the court should not be deterred from remitting the case to that forum simply because that would deprive one party of a juridical advantage provided that substantial justice will still be done. In *de Dampierre v de Dampierre* both parties were French nationals and had spent their early married life in France. Although they had resided in England, the husband's family and business interests were based in France and the wife had severed her connections with this country and now lived in New York. The husband began divorce proceedings in France and the wife then petitioned in England. Her sole reason for doing so was that under French law she might recover no maintenance for herself if the court concluded that she had been exclusively responsible for the breakdown of the marriage. In these circumstances the House of Lords held that the English proceedings should be stayed. The facts indicated a strong connection with France and practically none with England, and although the wife's claim for maintenance might fail in France, the principle applied by the French court was acceptable 'in a highly civilised country with which this country has very close ties of friendship'[19] and it was impossible to conclude that injustice would be done if the wife was compelled to pursue her remedy there.

The court may act on its own initiative. To ensure that it has before it all the necessary information the petitioner and, if the respondent cross-petitions, the respondent are bound to furnish particulars of all such proceedings that they know to be pending: if they fail to do so, the court may order a stay even after the trial has begun.[20]

Obligatory stays

Because of their proximity, conflicts between jurisdictions within the British Isles are likely to occur more often and to be more embarrassing than conflicts with other countries. Factors other than the country with which the marriage is most closely connected will not affect the court's judgment in deciding in which jurisdiction the proceedings should be permitted to continue, and clear rules are desirable for the guidance of the parties' advisers and to ensure uniform decisions within the United Kingdom. Consequently if proceedings for divorce or nullity (which may have the effect of altering the parties' status) are also being brought in Scotland, Northern Ireland, the Channel Islands or the Isle of Man, the court is *bound* to order a stay on the application of either of the parties provided that, to ensure that proceedings are continued in the appropriate jurisdiction, three further conditions are also satisfied: (i) the parties must have resided together since the celebration of the marriage; (ii) the place where they last resided together (or where they were residing together when the English proceedings were begun) must have been in the other jurisdiction; and (iii) one of the parties must have been habitually resident in the other jurisdiction

---

[19] Per Lord Goff at 110 and 12 respectively. The court must also consider the question of the children of the marriage: *Shemshadfard v Shemshadfard* [1981] 1 All ER 726; *Thyssen-Bornemisza v Thyssen-Bornemisza* (supra).

[20] Domicile and Matrimonial Proceedings Act 1973, s 5(6) and Sch 1, paras 7 and 9.

throughout the year ending with the date on which they last resided together.[1]

Removal of stay

Once the court has made an order staying proceedings (whether discretionary or obligatory), it may remove the stay on the application of either party if the proceedings in the other country have been concluded or stayed or if a party to those proceedings has been guilty of unreasonable delay in prosecuting them.[2]

Ancillary orders

If the court orders a stay on the ground that proceedings are being brought outside the British Isles, it has a complete discretion with respect to ancillary orders. When the proceedings are being brought in Scotland, Northern Ireland, the Channel Islands or the Isle of Man, however, detailed rules are laid down to ensure that all matters are dealt with by the same court. Essentially no ancillary orders may be made and any order already made will cease to have effect three months after a stay (discretionary or obligatory) is imposed unless an order is necessary because a matter needs to be dealt with urgently. If the other court makes an order for periodical payments for a spouse or child or a section 8 order under the Children Act, the English court has no further power at all to make an order dealing with the same matters and any such order already made will cease to have effect.[3]

Choice of law

Strangely enough, the Act does not expressly provide rules for the choice of law to be applied. In the case of the former statutory exceptions it was assumed that this was to be English law even though this was not the parties' *lex domicilii*,[4] and this principle was confirmed by later legislation.[5] It is generally accepted that this rule still applies:[6] any other would produce insuperable difficulties if the parties were domiciled in different countries or if their *lex domicilii* did not permit divorce at all.

---

[1] Ibid, Sch 1, para 8.
[2] Ibid, Sch 1, para 10. An obligatory stay, once removed, cannot be reimposed.
[3] Ibid, Sch 1, para 11, as amended by the Matrimonial Homes and Property Act 1981, s 8(3), and the Children Act 1989, Schs 13 and 15. For s 8 orders, see post, ch 11. Nor may the court make an order for the payment of a lump sum to a child if the other court has made an order for periodical payments for the child. Cf post, pp 375–376 (jurisdiction to stay custody proceedings).
[4] *Zanelli v Zanelli* (1948) 64 TLR 556, CA.
[5] See the Matrimonial Causes Act 1950, s 18(3), and subsequent legislation re-enacting it.
[6] *Quoraishi v Quoraishi* (1983) 4 FLR 706, affd [1985] FLR 780, CA; Dicey and Morris, *Conflict of Laws*, 4th Supp to 11th Edn, 85–86; Cheshire and North, *Private International Law*, 11th Edn, 632–635; Law Com No 48, paras 103–108.

2. PETITIONS

All suits for divorce are commenced by a petition presented to a divorce county court.[7] The information which the petition must contain is set out in the Family Proceedings Rules 1991.[8] It must be accompanied by a statement of arrangements proposed for the minor children of the family under the age of 16 or in receipt of education and training.[9]

In order to reduce the enormous claims that divorce proceedings were making on the legal aid fund, legal aid was withdrawn from virtually all undefended proceedings for divorce and judicial separation when the special procedure was extended to petitions based on any of the five facts in 1977, although it can still be obtained to make or oppose an application for an injunction, financial relief or an order in relation to children.[10] This means that the petitioner must now draft the petition and take all further steps himself or pay to have these done professionally out of his own pocket. If, however, his disposable capital and income do not exceed the sums fixed by the relevant regulations, he may apply for legal advice and assistance under the Green Form Scheme to which, depending on his disposable income and capital, he may have to contribute part of the costs.[11] Under this scheme a solicitor may give advice on drafting the petition and taking procedural steps;[12] printed forms of petition are available from law stationers and, if the petitioner is not in receipt of advice, the court staff will give assistance.

Appropriate cases may be transferred to the High Court.[13]

3. TRIAL OF CAUSES: THE SPECIAL PROCEDURE

Defended causes

When the petition is served on the respondent, there must also be served on him two forms.[14] The first sets out the steps which he must take and the consequences of the granting of a decree. The second is a form of acknowledgement of service, which asks him inter alia whether he intends to defend the proceedings. If he wishes to do so, however, it is not sufficient to return the form: he must also file an answer within 29 days of receiving the notice.[15] A defended cause is ultimately tried in open court in the normal way.

---

[7] Matrimonial and Family Proceedings Act 1984, s 33; Family Proceedings Rules 1991, r 2.6.
[8] See r 2.3 and App 2.
[9] Ibid, r 2.2.
[10] But not to make an application in relation to children if there is no reason to believe that it will be opposed.
[11] For details see *Butterworths Family Law Service*, paras A[249]–[253].
[12] But as the solicitor is not 'acting for' the petitioner, he is not required to file a certificate with regard to reconciliation (ante, p 221).
[13] See ante, p 14.
[14] Family Proceedings Rules 1991, r 2.6(6) and Forms M5 and M6.
[15] Ibid, r 2.12 and Form M5, para 3. An answer may not be filed without leave after directions for trial have been given: r 2.14.

The validity of an agreement not to defend a petition has already been discussed.[16]

Undefended causes: the special procedure

Before 1973 in almost every undefended case a decree was granted following the uncontested evidence in open court of the petitioner and any other witness necessary to support his case. Appearance in court often led to considerable anxiety for the petitioner and to costs which, whether borne by the parties or the legal aid fund, were not insignificant. It also involved a great deal of judicial time. Consequently in 1973 there was introduced a 'special procedure' to dispense with the need to give evidence in court if the case was not defended. Originally it applied only to petitions based on two years' separation, but since 1977 all undefended petitions for divorce or judicial separation (but not for nullity) are dealt with under this procedure (which is no longer 'special' but normal).

If the respondent does not defend the petition, the petitioner must make a written application for directions for trial. This must be accompanied by an affidavit verifying the contents of the petition and the statement of arrangements for the children and giving certain other information and also by any corroborative evidence on which the petitioner intends to rely. The district judge then enters the cause in the special procedure list.[17] If he is satisfied that the petitioner has proved his case and is entitled to a decree, he makes and files a certificate to this effect and a day is fixed on which a judge or district judge will pronounce the decree nisi in open court. Neither party need be present when this is done.[18]

Confusion arises because respondents acting without advice do not always appreciate the need to file an answer if they have stated that they propose to defend. The petitioner does not have to give the respondent notice of his intention to apply for directions and the application 'starts the ball rolling which inevitably ends in a decree nisi ... unless an answer is filed'.[19] Once the district judge has made the certificate, the decree nisi must be pronounced unless the respondent obtains leave to have it set aside, and this will not be granted unless (a) the respondent was not served with the petition or knew nothing about the proceedings because of a deception or mistake for which he was not responsible,[20] or (b) there are substantial grounds for believing that the decree would be contrary to the justice of the case, or (c) owing to ignorance of the law or lack of full advice the respondent was unaware of the need to file an answer in time *and* the court

---

[16] Ante, pp 228–229.

[17] Ibid, r 2.24 and Forms M7 (a)–(e). If the petition is based on two years' separation, the respondent must also have given notice that he consents to the granting of the decree. Adultery may be proved by an admission made by the respondent on the form of acknowledgement of service.

[18] Ibid, r 2.36; *Practice Direction* [1977] 1 All ER 845. If the district judge is not satisfied that the petitioner has proved his case, he may give him an opportunity to file further evidence or remove the cause from the special procedure list. The same procedure applies mutatis mutandis if the case goes undefended on a cross-prayer contained in the respondent's answer.

[19] Per Ormrod LJ in *Sandholm v Sandholm* (1979) 1 FLR 359, 361.

[20] See *Cahill v Cahill* [1986] Fam Law 102, CA.

is satisfied that, if the case he wishes to put forward were accepted, it might well lead to a different result.[21]

4. DECREES

The decree is made in two stages: the decree nisi, followed by the decree absolute. Subject to the provisions of section 10 of the Matrimonial Causes Act, which gives financial protection to the respondent when the petition is based on two or five years' separation, and section 41, when children are involved,[1] the petitioner may apply for the decree to be made absolute at any time after the expiration of six weeks from the granting of the decree nisi unless the court fixes a shorter time in the particular case; if the petitioner fails to apply for a decree absolute, the respondent may make the application at any time after the expiration of three months from the earliest date on which the petitioner could have applied.[2] There are a number of reasons for the delay: in particular an unsuccessful respondent may appeal against the granting of the decree nisi, the Queen's Proctor or any other person may intervene to show cause why the decree should not be made absolute, and the court may set aside or rescind the decree nisi in certain other circumstances.[3]

Whether the decree is one of divorce or presumption of death and dissolution, the marriage ceases as soon as the decree is made absolute[4] and either spouse is then free to remarry.[5] The decree nisi does not have

[21] *Mitchell v Mitchell* [1984] Fam 1, [1983] 3 All ER 621, CA. See also *Day v Day* [1980] Fam 29, [1979] 2 All ER 187, CA; *Back v Back* (1979) 1 FLR 355, CA. As the respondent must be notified of the day on which the decree nisi is to be pronounced, he may well appear to oppose it without notifying the petitioner; if he does so, the court must not grant leave to set aside the district judge's certificate without giving the petitioner an opportunity of opposing the application: *Sims v Sims* (1979) 1 FLR 351, 353, CA.

[1] See ante, pp 219–220 and post, pp 366–369.

[2] Matrimonial Causes Act 1973, ss 1(5) and 9(2); Matrimonial Causes (Decree Absolute) General Order 1972. It should rarely be necessary for the court to reduce the period: *Practice Direction* [1977] 2 All ER 714. This is particularly true if the petition is based on two or five years' separation because the respondent may then lose the financial protection afforded by s 10 of the Matrimonial Causes Act 1973, as happened in *Dryden v Dryden* [1973] Fam 217, [1973] 3 All ER 526. For a case where the period was reduced, see *Torok v Torok* [1973] 3 All ER 101 (decree expedited to prevent a Hungarian court from dissolving the marriage, which would have left the wife with no effective claim for financial provision). If the application is made more than twelve months after the decree nisi, the applicant must account for the delay: Family Proceedings Rules 1991, r 2.49(2).

[3] See the Report of Matrimonial Causes Procedure Committee, para 4.103. Interventions by the Queen's Proctor are now very rare. During the years 1972–1975 (the last year for which statistics were published) there were only eight a year on the average. The Queen's Proctor's assistance may be invoked by the court itself, eg if an undefended suit presents a difficult point of law which counsel briefed by him can then argue. See the Matrimonial Causes Act 1973, ss 8 and 9(1), and the Report of the Morton Commission, Cmd 9678, paras 947–968.

[4] The decree dissolves the marriage *status* and not the marriage *ceremony*: *Thynne v Thynne* [1955] P 272, [1955] 3 All ER 129, CA. In the wife's petition for divorce and the decrees made thereon the particulars of a second void ceremony were inserted. It was held that the decree nisi and the decree absolute could be amended so as to make it clear that the parties' marriage had been dissolved. If it is doubtful which of two ceremonies was valid, the court should determine the question so that the valid one is named in the decree: *Amadasun v Amadasun* [1992] 1FLR 585.

[5] No clergyman of the Church of England or the Church in Wales can be compelled to marry any divorced person during the lifetime of his or her former spouse or to permit his church or chapel to be used for the solemnization of such a marriage: Matrimonial Causes Act 1965, s 8(2).

this effect, and if either party remarries before it is made absolute, the second marriage will be void. If there has been a fundamental procedural irregularity—for example, if the petition is presented within the first year of the marriage[6] or is never served on the respondent[7]—the decree will be void and may be rescinded even though it has been made absolute.[8] If either party has remarried in the meantime, the second marriage will automatically become void ab initio.[9]

G. Criticism of the modern law and proposals for reform[10]

1. THE GROUND FOR DIVORCE

The main criticism that can be levelled against the new divorce law is that it is a compromise between the old law based on matrimonial fault and the new concept of irretrievable breakdown which perpetuates many of the defects of the former without necessarily producing the advantages of the latter. The necessity of establishing one of the five facts set out in section 1(2) of the Matrimonial Causes Act is largely designed to ensure that the technically 'innocent' spouse shall not be divorced against his or her will until the parties have been separated for five years. This has produced the inevitable consequence that, however the Act is worded, practitioners still tend to think in terms of five grounds for divorce. Furthermore, it is no credit to a legal system, which makes irretrievable breakdown the sole ground for divorce, that judges are compelled to dismiss a petition because none of the facts has been established even though they are satisfied that the marriage has broken down irretrievably.

One of the advantages of adopting the irretrievable breakdown theory is that the decree should merely recite a state of affairs without attributing blame or passing any sort of moral judgment, and much of the bitterness should be taken out of the proceedings if one party were not to be labelled as technically innocent and the other as technically guilty when in many cases the conduct of both has contributed to the collapse of their marriage. But this is precisely what the court still has to do if any of the first three facts is alleged. We now have a 'dual system' in which matrimonial offences and separation (attributing fault to neither party) stand side by side as, in

[6] *Butler v Butler* [1990] 1 FLR 114.
[7] *Ebrahim v Ali* [1983] 3 All ER 615; *Purse v Purse* [1981] Fam 143, [1981] 2 All ER 465, CA (where the decree was rescinded after the petitioner's death).
[8] But a decree absolute will not be rescinded in any other circumstances, for example on the ground that it has been obtained by fraud: *Callaghan v Hanson-Fox* [1992] Fam 1, [1992] 1 All ER 56.
[9] *Rogers v Rogers* [1962] CLY 1045.
[10] For criticisms of the present law see particularly Mortlock *The Inside of Divorce* (written before the introduction of the special procedure); Eekelaar *Family Security and Family Breakdown* pp 230–249, *Family Law and Social Policy* (2nd Edn) pp 27–63 and *The Place of Divorce in Family Law's New Role* 38 MLR 241; Davis and Murch *Grounds for Divorce*; Finlay *Reluctant but Inevitable the Retreat of Matrimonial Fault* 38 MLR 153 and the other authorities there cited; Elston, Fuller and Murch *Judicial Hearings of Undefenced Divorce Petitions* 38 MLR 609 (an informative study of petitioners' attitudes); Murch *Justice and Welfare in Divorce* and *The Role of Solicitors in Divorce Proceedings* 40 MLR 625, 41 MLR 25.

effect, grounds for divorce.[11] If the petitioner (whom we will assume to be the wife) alleges that the respondent is in desertion or has behaved in such a way that she cannot reasonably be expected to live with him, the court must still make a value judgment about the parties' conduct towards each other. It becomes even more difficult to justify the present position when one recalls that a spouse can base a petition on the 'offence' fact of behaviour which attributes no fault to the respondent at all.[12] If the petitioner wants a divorce (or is prepared to accede to the respondent's request for one) without having to wait for two years' separation, she is compelled to rely on his adultery or behaviour and is thus forced to allege a breach of his matrimonial obligations.

The following analysis of the facts on which petitions were based in 1989 is instructive:[13]

| | Petitions filed by | | |
	Husbands	Wives	Total
Adultery	19,920	31,730	51,650
Behaviour	12,460	76,590	89,050
Desertion	650	1,390	2,040
Two years' separation (with consent)	11,460	19,150	30,610
Five years' separation	4,670	5,430	10,100
Adultery and behaviour	210	620	830
Adultery and desertion	50	50	100
Behaviour and desertion	70	90	160
Other combinations	20	50	70
Total	49,510	135,100	184,610

It will be seen that over 75% of all petitions alleged only adultery or behaviour (or both): in other words it was unnecessary for the petitioner to wait for two years' separation. This certainly lends support to the contention that many petitioners rely on the first two facts to give the parties an immediate divorce. When one adds in the petitions alleging desertion, an 'offence' fact was relied on by nearly 80% of all petitioners. It is clear that the hope that the new law would enable a large number of marriages to be brought to an end without recriminatory allegations has not been fulfilled.

Examining the problem in 1990, the Law Commission drew attention to many other criticisms of the existing law.[14] A petitioner not wishing to wait two years for a divorce may exaggerate trivial incidents to give a passable impression of 'unreasonable behaviour', and this practice tends to provoke unnecessary bitterness and hostility between the parties.[15] This in turn may affect their relationship with their children and destroy any possibility of reconciliation. The need for couples not wishing to apportion blame to live apart for two years discriminates against those with lower incomes because separation may be impossible without substantial resources or a court order. If one party alone is able to petition, this puts him or her in a strong

---

[11] Eekelaar *Family Law and Social Policy* (2nd Edn) ch 3.
[12] See ante, pp 196–198. Cf Eekelaar op cit, p 44.
[13] This analysis was not made in the statistics for 1990. Except for the grand total the figures are deduced from samples and rounded to the nearest 10.
[14] Law Com No 192 (Ground for Divorce), Part II.
[15] See also Eekelaar op cit pp 43–48.

position when it comes to discussing the future of the children and financial arrangements and so distorts the parties' bargaining position. It is obvious that the present law has failed in its object to enable the marriage to be brought to an end with the minimum bitterness, distress and humiliation, and reform is urgently needed. The Commission's own proposals are considered later.[16]

2. PROCEDURE

The special procedure

We have already seen that the special procedure was introduced with three objects in mind: to reduce costs, to save judicial time, and to relieve petitioners of the anxiety and embarrassment of giving evidence. Whilst it has been partially successful in these respects,[17] its results have arguably not been entirely beneficial. Whereas judges would permit the amendment of a technically defective petition at the trial without the need to re-serve it if the respondent would not be prejudiced, district judges inevitably reject all defective documents with resultant delay.[18] As the petitioner is under no obligation to inform the respondent that he is applying for directions for trial, the latter does not know when the registrar will make and file his certificate.[19] Judges have virtually lost all control over undefended cases and the actual adjudication is made by the district judge. It is impossible for the court to discharge its statutory duty 'to inquire, so far as it reasonably can, into the facts alleged by the petitioner',[20] or to heed earlier warnings that it should not necessarily accept the petitioner's assertions.[1] On the other hand, in practice judges trying undefended suits in open court could do little more than accept the evidence that petitioners chose to put before them and they tended not to assume an inquisitorial role:[2] it was probably no more difficult to satisfy most judges then than it is to satisfy a district judge today.[3] Although it is impossible to test the hypothesis, one cannot help suspecting that a number of decrees are granted on grounds that are legally insufficient, and the fact that petitioners no longer have to give oral evidence may tempt some to commit a flagrant act of perjury. For many the special procedure must have all the appearances of obtaining divorce by post and it is doubtful whether this can be regarded as fulfilling the object of 'buttressing, rather then undermining, the stability of marriage'.[4]

[16] Post, pp 243–244.
[17] It seems that the proportion of parties going to a solicitor for help has not been significantly reduced. In one survey it was discovered that over 90% of parties *with children* had consulted a solicitor: Davis, Macleod and Murch *Special Procedure in Divorce* 12 Fam Law 39.
[18] See Westcott 8 Fam Law 209.
[19] See ante, p 235.
[20] Matrimonial Causes Act 1973, ss 1(3) (divorce) and 17(2) (judicial separation). Hence the Matrimonial Causes Procedure Committee recommended that the provisions should be repealed: Report, para 2.18.
[1] See ante, p 188.
[2] See Elston, Fuller and Murch *Judicial Hearings of Undefended Divorce Petitions* 38 MLR 609, 622, where they point out that the judge asked questions concerning the breakdown of the marriage in only a quarter of the cases they observed.
[3] Cf Law Com No 116 (Time Restrictions on Divorce), para 2.21.
[4] See ante, p 185.

Whilst manipulation of the divorce law is to be deplored, these changes reflect a much more profound shift in the whole nature of the divorce process. In the words of one distinguished writer in this field:[5]

'Rapidly changing social values concerning marriage, the status of women and the role of the family in society profoundly affect the character of divorce proceedings. In recent years emphasis has moved away from preoccupation with the history of a broken marriage towards a greater concern for the family's future.... This is better than apportioning guilt and innocence. Modern divorce is about the division of money and property and the future care of the children.'

The result is that procedure—particularly the means by which decisions relating to finance, property and children are arrived at—is now of much greater practical importance than the law relating to the ground for divorce. It is difficult to disagree with the conclusion that the special procedure 'makes the complexity of the substantive law ... seem unnecessary and irrelevant'.[6]

Defended petitions

In 1970, the last full year in which the old law was in operation, over 95% of petitions were undefended. In some cases cross-petitions were filed: in other words, both spouses were anxious to have the marriage dissolved but each wished the other to appear as the guilty party on the record. The usual reason for this was that a guilty wife was in a worse position than a technically innocent one when it came to the question of the award of maintenance, but now that the innocence or guilt of the parties will no longer affect the award of financial relief, there is less incentive to oppose the making of a decree.

In 1989 fewer than 1% of petitions were defended but in the majority of these cases a decree was granted to the respondent on a cross-petition. There are a number of reasons for this. Some parties still consider that a stigma attaches to divorce, at least so far as the 'guilty' spouse is concerned, and consequently will try to avoid having this label attached to them.[7] The petitioner will inevitably be advised to make out the strongest possible case in the petition and details of the parties' marital history may be so exaggerated and cause such deep resentment that the respondent insists on defending, and perhaps cross-petitioning, in order, as he sees it, to put the record straight.[8] If the petitioner pleads that the respondent has been guilty of gross misconduct and the latter does not defend, he may find himself faced with an estoppel in ancillary proceedings relating to financial provision.[9] Against this must be weighed the emotional and financial demands that a defended cause can make on the parties, the harmful consequences

---

[5] Murch *Justice and Welfare in Divorce* p 3.

[6] Cretney *Principles of Family Law* (3rd Edn) p 163.

[7] The courts have recognised the legitimacy of this attitude by permitting a respondent to file an answer out of time when the petition is based on the respondent's behaviour and the latter wishes to cross-petition for divorce based on the petitioner's own adultery, but not when it is based on five years' separation: *Rogers v Rogers* [1974] 2 All ER 361, CA; *Collins v Collins* [1972] 2 All ER 658, CA.

[8] See Davis, Macleod and Murch *Special Procedure in Divorce* 12 Fam Law 39, 42.

[9] But see post, pp 783–784. Quite apart from the question of estoppel, it may be necessary for the court to have a clear picture of the cause of the breakdown when dealing with ancillary matters: *Mustafa v Mustafa* [1975] 3 All ER 355.

for their children, and the sheer futility of defending a petition when the marriage clearly has broken down irretrievably,[10] for whatever may be the respondent's motive, defended proceedings will generally still be attended by bitterness, distress and even humiliation. Consequently every attempt should be made to discourage suits from being defended when this would serve no purpose. The courts themselves try to do this; for example, if the respondent admits the petitioner's allegations (thus admitting that a ground for divorce has been made out), the court will not hear a cross-petition filed for the purpose of obtaining a decree on allegations made against the petitioner.[11] In some cases conciliation might enable the parties to agree to the presentation of an undefended petition by one of them.

The Matrimonial Causes Procedure Committee

This changed approach clearly demanded a complete reappraisal of divorce procedure.[12] Consequently in 1982 Lord Hailsham LC set up a Committee under the chairmanship of Booth J to examine the whole question of matrimonial procedure and in particular to recommend reforms (a) to mitigate the intensity of disputes, (b) to encourage settlements, and (c) to provide further for the welfare of the children of the family. With regard to proceedings leading up to the decree, the main thrust of their Report, published in 1985, was that bitterness between the parties might be reduced if unnecessary acrimonious allegations were eliminated and defended suits kept to a minimum; furthermore parties should be encouraged and helped to settle financial matters and questions relating to children themselves with the benefit of legal advice and, if necessary, the assistance of conciliators. They said:[13]

'On the evidence presented to us we are satisfied that the bitterness and unhappiness of divorcing couples is frequently exacerbated and prolonged by the fault element in divorce and that this is particularly so where the fact relied on is behaviour, whether or not the suit is defended. Great hostility and resentment may be generated by the recital in the petition of allegations of behaviour, often exaggerated and sometimes stretching back over many years, to the extent that no discussion can take place between the parties or any agreement be reached on any matter relating to their marriage or to their children.'

They therefore proposed that it should be possible for the parties to make a joint application[14] for divorce if they so wished and that it should no longer be necessary to name the person with whom it is alleged that the respondent has committed adultery or to give particulars of behaviour when the application is based on this fact. The Committee believed that this would reduce hostility between the parties and remove the desire to defend the petition in many cases. Particulars of behaviour would have to be given if the respondent sought them or if the suit were defended and in the latter case the alleged adulterer (if known) would have to be served and given an opportunity to intervene if he or she wished to do so.[15]

[10] See the Report of the Matrimonial Causes Procedure Committee (1985), para 2.16.
[11] *Grenfell v Grenfell* [1978] Fam 128, [1978] 1 All ER 561, CA.
[12] Murch op cit p 3.
[13] Report para 2.10. Cf Murch op cit p 210.
[14] The word 'application' would replace 'petition': ibid, paras 4.2–4.4.
[15] Ibid, para 4.12–4.26.

The next major change proposed by the Committee is that there should be an initial hearing within about ten weeks of filing the application in every case involving children to whom section 41 of the Matrimonial Causes Act applies[16] and also in cases where the respondent has stated an intention to oppose the grant of the decree. Both parties would be required to attend together with their legal advisers if desired.

'The purpose of the hearing will be to make orders in respect of agreed matters, including the decree, to refer the parties to conciliation where appropriate, to define the issues remaining between them and to give directions.'[17]

The Committee hoped that as many agreed orders could be made as possible, including orders relating to children and financial relief, a view later shared by the Law Commission.[18] If the application for divorce were unopposed, a provisional decree would be granted by the district judge at this hearing, thus doing away with the pointless formal pronouncement of the decree nisi in open court.[19] If there were no children to whom section 41 applied and the respondent did not oppose the decree (so that no initial hearing would be required), a modified special procedure would be retained leading to the granting of a provisional decree by the district judge.[20]

The fact that the decree is pronounced in two stages apparently confuses some parties who do not realise that one of them has to apply for it to be made absolute before the marriage is dissolved. Consequently the Committee recommended that the existing terms 'decree nisi' and 'decree absolute' should be replaced by 'provisional decree' and 'final decree' and that the latter should normally issue automatically four weeks after the grant of the former. To protect a party where this would work hardship (for example, because no order had been made for financial relief) the court would be given a power to delay the final decree in appropriate cases.[1] In accordance with the general proposal that details likely to inflame the parties' relationship should be kept to a minimum, the Committee also recommended that the decree should merely state that their marriage had irretrievably broken down and had been dissolved without disclosing the fact on which the application was based.[2]

The Committee's specific recommendations relating to conciliation and children are considered in more detail elsewhere.[3]

Insofar as the recommendations are designed to reduce the emotional strain involved in divorce proceedings, they are to be warmly welcomed. In particular one must applaud the emphasis on conciliation. The initial hearing would counter any impression that divorce is obtainable by post for those who are required to attend, although it remains to be seen whether compelling both parties to meet would necessarily encourage co-operation in all cases. One of the main objections is that the proposed abolition of the need to serve particulars of adultery and behaviour might open the

---

[16] For the children to whom this section applies see post, pp 368–369.

[17] Report, para 3.5.

[18] See ante, p 227.

[19] Ibid, paras 3.5–3.9 and 4.53–4.90. A list of the provisional decrees granted would be posted in the precincts of the court: para 4.106.

[20] Ibid, paras 4.92–4.94.

[1] Ibid, paras 4.103–4.112.

[2] Ibid, para 4.107.

[3] See ante, pp 226–227 (conciliation), and post, p 366 (children).

door even wider to divorce by consent. The Committee answered this by pointing out that we effectively have divorce by consent now if the parties are agreed on the incidents of behaviour to be set out in the petition and consequently their recommendations would not substantially alter the position.[4] This may be so, but agreements of this kind are probably rare and at present the petitioner has at least to swear to the truth of the particulars pleaded from which the registrar must himself determine whether the fact is made out.

3. THE LAW COMMISSION'S PROPOSALS

In their report on the ground for divorce,[5] the Law Commission concluded that irretrievable breakdown of the marriage should remain the sole ground for divorce but for the reasons set out earlier[6] they rejected proof of breakdown by facts based on fault or separation. Instead they recommended that divorce should no longer be seen as a single event but should be granted only after a process continuing for a period of time. This would demonstrate that the breakdown is irretrievable, give the parties the opportunity of facing up to the consequences of divorce and enable the practical problems to be resolved.

The process they contemplate would begin by either (or preferably) both of the parties lodging at a court a sworn statement that he or she (or both) believes that the marriage has broken down. Each party would then be given a comprehensive information pack explaining inter alia the purpose of the period of consideration and reflection, the effects of divorce and separation, the powers of the court, and the nature and purpose of counselling, reconciliation, conciliation and mediation. After eleven months either or both of them (irrespective of which lodged the initial statement) would be able to apply for an order for divorce or separation[7] on making a declaration that the maker (or makers) believe that the breakdown of their marriage is irreparable. In the intervening period the parties could be offered counselling or conciliation and the court should make orders relating to children, financial provision and property adjustment. This means that these orders would be made before the order for divorce was pronounced (and not, as now, after the decree nisi) and reflects the principle that the practical consequences of divorce should be settled before the marriage is dissolved. If the parties wished to attempt a reconciliation and they jointly notified the court, the period would be suspended until one of them stated that he or she wished it to start running again: if the attempt were successful, they could jointly withdraw the statement of marital breakdown, when the process would automatically come to an end. The court would normally make an order for divorce or separation a month after the application (giving a minimum period of 12 months from the lodging of the initial

---

[4] Report, para 4.24. In undefended proceedings the petitioner is no longer obliged to name the person with whom it is alleged the respondent has committed adultery: see ante, p 188, n 7.

[5] Law Com No 192.

[6] See ante, pp 238–239.

[7] A separation order would replace a decree of judicial separation. The ground for each would be the same and a decision about which order was preferred could be left until the application was made. See further ante, p 157.

statement). As at present, however, it should be able to postpone the order in exceptional circumstances if this were necessary to enable it to consider whether it should exercise any of its powers under the Children Act in respect of any children of the family or to make any proper financial arrangements. The court would also be able to refuse an order for divorce if this would result in grave financial or other hardship to one of the parties and it would be wrong in the circumstances to dissolve the marriage.[8]

These recommendations, if implemented, would introduce a wholly new basis for dissolution of marriage. They would meet the principal criticisms of the present law—that it is unjust and arbitrary and can engender bitterness and discriminate against poorer spouses—and by enabling either or both spouses to initiate the process would remove any implication that either was responsible for the breakdown. Their main departure from the principles underlying English divorce law for nearly 150 years is that it would no longer be necessary to rely on acts (whether behaviour or separation) that have already occurred. There is an inevitable danger that lodging the statement of marital breakdown, which is designed to start the period of consideration and reflection, could be used as a warning shot or even regarded as a sort of insurance policy, at least if the parties had no children. Whether these proposals are adopted by Parliament is now a political issue, but it is at least significant that a substantial number of people interviewed in a public opinion survey conducted for the Commission supported them.[9]

[8] See Law Com No 192, Part V.
[9] Ibid, App D.

Part II

The law relating to children

Summary of contents

Chapter 7

The Children Act 1989

A. Introduction and background to the Act

1991 was a landmark year for child law for it was on 14 October 1991 that the Children Act 1989 was fully implemented.[1] The 1989 Act brought about the most fundamental change in our child law and has been fairly described by Lord Mackay LC as: 'the most comprehensive and far reaching reform of child law which has come before Parliament in living memory.'[2]

1. THE GENESIS OF THE ACT

(a) The Child Care Review

The Act is the product of a long and thorough consultation process during the course of which virtually the whole of English child law was subjected to detailed review.[3] The process began with the Review of Child Care Law set up in 1984 (in response to a recommendation of the House of Commons Social Services Select Committee[4]) by the then Department of Health and Social Services and assisted by the Family Law team at the Law Commission. That review produced twelve informal consultation papers during 1984 and 1985 and a Report to Ministers in September 1985 which was published as a further consultation paper.[5] The review's recommendations were essentially accepted by the government in their White Paper: 'The Law on Child Care and Family Services'.[6]

The Review of Child Care Law was concerned with the public law relating to children and in particular the local authority services to be provided for children and their families and the procedures to protect children where families fail.

(b) Review of private law

At the same time as the review was investigating child care law the Law Commission undertook a full-scale review of the private law. That process began with a review of the law dealing with the consequences of birth

---

[1] Save for ss 5(11) and (12), discussed post, p 400, which were not implemented until 1 February 1992: Children Act 1989 (Commencement No 2 Amendment and Transitional Provisions) Order 1991, art 2. It might also be noted that a few provisions had been implemented earlier.
[2] 502 HL Official Report (5th series) col 488.
[3] The outstanding exception was adoption law, which itself became the subject of review in 1990: see ch 13.
[4] Second Report 1983–1984 on *Children in Care* HC 360–361 (the Short Report).
[5] *Review of Child Care Law* (DHSS, 1985).
[6] 1987 Cm 62.

outside marriage[7] and the resulting legislation, the Family Law Reform Act 1987, removed most of the remaining differences between children whose parents were married to each other and those who were not.[8] Against this background the Commission examined most of the remaining aspects of the private law publishing Working Papers on *Guardianship,*[9] *Custody,*[10] *Care, Supervision and Interim Orders in Custody Proceedings*[11] and *Wards of Court.*[12] The first three of these working papers resulted in the Commission's Report on *Guardianship and Custody,* published in 1988.[13] Annexed to that Report was a Bill to give effect not only to the Law Commission's recommendations but also to show how an integrated scheme of court orders might look. That Bill was taken up by the government and expanded into what eventually became the Children Act 1989.

(c) Other important influences

(i) The Cleveland and other Child Abuse Inquiry Reports

Important though the reviews of both the public and private law were, it was the 'Cleveland crisis' that provided the final impetus for reform. As Lord Mackay LC said, it was a coincidence of the two reviews together with the Cleveland Report[14] which provided: 'an historic opportunity to reform English law into a single rationalised system as it applies to the care and upbringing of children'.[15]

The Cleveland Report was concerned with the removal of scores of children from their families because of alleged sexual abuse. In those cases the concern was that the authority had acted too precipitately but in a number of other inquiries, notably those investigating the deaths of Jasmine Beckford,[16] Heidi Kosela,[17] Tyra Henry,[18] Kimberly Carlile[19] and Doreen Aston,[20] all of whom either were or had been in local authority care, the concern was that the local authority had not acted quickly enough. However, all these reports were influential in the final shaping of the 1989 Act and, in the words of one commentator,[21] 'contributed much to a balanced view

---

[7] Law Com No 118, *Illegitimacy* (1982) and Law Com No 157, *Illegitimacy* (1986).

[8] Discussed in ch 8.

[9] 1985, Working Paper No 91.

[10] 1985, Working Paper No 96.

[11] 1987, Working Paper No 100.

[12] 1987, Working Paper No 101.

[13] Law Com No 172. It might also be mentioned that various procedural aspects of child law were examined in the *Report of the Matrimonial Causes Procedure Committee* (the 'Booth Committee') HMSO 1985 and further explored in the Lord Chancellor's Department's Consultative Paper: *Improvements in the Arrangements for Care Proceedings,* 1988.

[14] *Report of the Inquiry into Child Abuse in Cleveland 1987* (the 'Butler-Sloss Report'), 1988 Cm 412.

[15] *The Child: A View Across the Tweed* (1988) Denning LJ 89, 93.

[16] *A Child in Trust: Report of the Panel of Inquiry Investigating the Circumstances Surrounding the death of Jasmine Beckford,* London Borough of Brent, 1985.

[17] 1986.

[18] *Whose Child? The Report of the Public Inquiry into the death of Tyra Henry,* London Borough of Lambeth, 1987.

[19] *A Child in Mind: Protection of Children in a Responsible Society, Report of the Inquiry into the Circumstances surrounding the death of Kimberley Carlile,* London Borough of Greenwich, 1989.

[20] *Report to the Area Review Committee for Lambeth, Lewisham and Southwark London Boroughs,* 1989.

[21] Brenda Hoggett in her introduction to White, Carr and Lowe *A Guide to the Children Act 1989* (1990).

of the procedures needed to protect children, especially in the early stages where abuse is suspected'.

Although the Cleveland crisis undoubtedly prompted speedy reform, the Act is far from a categorical endorsement of the Butler-Sloss recommendations[1]. For example the recommendation that there should be an 'Office of Child Protection' which was further explored by a Lord Chancellor's consultation paper,[2] was not taken up. Similarly, the recommendation to maintain the role of wardship in child care cases was not accepted. Indeed quite the contrary line is taken by the 1989 Act with result that effectively local authorities can no longer look to wardship at all as a means of obtaining a care order.[3] This had not been specifically recommended either by the Law Commission or the Child Care Review but was a decision made by the government itself.[4]

(ii) The European Convention on Human Rights

An important influence on the final shape of the 1989 Act was the European Convention on Human Rights. There had been pressure from Europe for reform of English law to give effect to the fundamental rights of parents and children especially in relation to family life as protected by Article 8. In particular there had been much concern about the then inability of parents to challenge local authority decisions restricting parental access to children in care.[5] As Andrew Bainham says, 'Undoubtedly many of the reforms relating to care procedures, (and in particular those giving parents and others the right to challenge contact decisions by local authorities)[6] have been inspired, if not positively mandated, by the [United Kingdom's] obligations under the Convention.'

(iii) The Gillick decision

Another influence on the 1989 Act was that of the House of Lords' decision in *Gillick v West Norfolk and Wisbech Area Health Authority*[7] which was concerned with an older child's capacity to consent to medical treatment in cases where he has sufficient understanding to make up his own mind. The Act recognises in several places the importance of ascertaining and taking into account the child's own wishes to an extent commensurate with his age and understanding. The question of whether the preferences of a mature child should not only be taken into account but be *determinative* of the matter in question provoked considerable debate during the passage of the Bill.[8] In general, however, save in certain specified instances,[9] the Act does not give mature children the rights to act independently of those

---

[1] See Bainham *Children, The New Law, The Children Act 1989*, p 4.
[2] *Improvements in the Arrangements for Care Proceedings*, 1988.
[3] Under s 100—discussed in ch 14.
[4] As Lord Mackay LC explained in his *Joseph Jackson Memorial Lecture* (1989) 139 NLJ 505, 507, the government's decision to restrict its use was taken late in the day.
[5] See eg *R v United Kingdom* [1988] 2 FLR 445, E Ct HR, *O v United Kingdom; H v United Kingdom* (1987) Series A, No 120, E Ct HR and *W v United Kingdom; B v United Kingdom* (1987) Series A, No 121, E Ct HR.
[6] Ie under s 34 of the 1989 Act, discussed in ch 16.
[7] [1986] AC 112, [1985] 3 All ER 402, HL, discussed post, pp 295–296 and 306–309.
[8] See Bainham *Children, The New Law, The Children Act 1989*, p 5.
[9] Viz under ss 38(6), 43(8) and 44(7), discussed post, pp 526, 536 and 540.

with parental responsibility. On the other hand the effect of its promotion of the child's own views and in particular of provisions allowing the child himself to apply for leave to seek certain orders,[10] should not be underestimated.

2. THE NEED TO RATIONALISE AND SIMPLIFY THE PREVIOUS LAW

It has been said[11] that the 1989 Act has two main aims, namely, 'to gather together in one place, and (it is hoped) one coherent whole, all the law relating to the care and upbringing of children and the provision of social services for them, and to provide a consistent set of legal remedies which will be available in all courts and in all proceedings'. To appreciate the significance of such apparently simple aims it is necessary to say something of the old law.

Before the Children Act 1989, child law, like so much of English law, had developed upon an ad hoc basis through both statute and case law and predominantly in terms of remedies rather than rights. In the result the law had become complicated and technical and had no underlying general philosophy. Remedies and procedure varied according to the jurisdiction invoked and the court involved. There were, for example, separate statutes conferring different powers on the courts to make orders relating to children in divorce proceedings,[12] in proceedings for financial relief before magistrates[13] and in so-called free standing proceedings, namely those solely concerned with disputes about children.[14]

Within this complicated framework there were in fact two distinct systems, namely that dealing with private law and that governing public law. Broadly speaking 'public orders' involved local authorities whereas 'private orders' did not. Each of these systems developed and operated independently of the other with the anomalous result, for example, that, whereas children could be committed to local authority care in private law proceedings, private law orders were not available in care proceedings.

Furthermore the interrelationship between the two sets of orders was uncertain, for example, did a custody order override a care order in every case? Another oddity of the pre-1989 Act law was that whereas the higher courts, principally the divorce county court, were generally involved in private law disputes, the predominant court dealing with local authority applications to remove children from their families was the magistrates' juvenile court.[15]

Even in this brief résumé of the position before the Children Act 1989 mention must be made of the High Court's wardship jurisdiction,[16] which

[10] Under s 10(2)(b), (8), discussed post, p 359.
[11] See Brenda Hoggett *The Children Bill: The Aim* [1989] Fam Law 217.
[12] See the Matrimonial Causes Act 1973, ss 41–44, discussed in the seventh edition of this work at pp 294–298.
[13] See the Domestic Proceedings and Magistrates' Courts Act 1978, ss 8–11, 14, 34 discussed in the seventh edition of this work at pp 305–306.
[14] See the Guardianship of Minors Act 1971 discussed in the seventh edition of this work at pp 307–308. There was also the further jurisdiction under the Children Act 1975 to grant custodianship to those other than parents, discussed in ch 11 of the seventh edition.
[15] Though the county court and High Court each had powers to commit children to care in matrimonial proceedings, as the High Court also had in wardship proceedings, see further below.
[16] For a full discussion of this jurisdiction see ch 14.

straddled the divide between private and public law. Under this ancient jurisdiction the court had wide powers to protect children including a statutory power to commit children into care.[17] Because of its width and flexibility, wardship was increasingly used to deal with difficult or complex cases. The jurisdiction was chiefly invoked by local authorities who had been encouraged to use it as a means of obtaining committal to care orders in circumstances where the statutory scheme would otherwise have been unavailable, inconvenient or unsuitable.[18] It could even be used in cases where previous applications under the statutory scheme had failed.

The ability of local authorities to use wardship rather than the statutory scheme not only called into question the standing of the latter but highlighted another anomaly, namely, the differing criteria justifying the child's removal from his family into local authority care. For example, whereas in care proceedings under the Children and Young Persons Act 1969 relatively precise child-centred grounds had first to be satisfied, under the Child Care Act 1980 the assumption of parental rights had to be justified by the *parents'* conduct. In wardship and matrimonial proceedings, on the other hand, although technically committals to care could only be made in exceptional circumstances where it was impracticable or undesirable for the child to be placed in the care of his parents or other individuals,[19] in practice, the matter was resolved upon what was considered best for the child.

The not inconsiderable achievement of the Children Act is to have rid the law of most of the complications and anomalies of the old law and to draw together both the private and public law under a single statutory scheme. As one commentator has observed of the Act it is 'remarkable that, at least in terms of volume, so much has been replaced by so little'.[20]

B. The ambit and scope of the 1989 Act

The 1989 Act has a wide ambit covering both the private and public law relating to the care and upbringing of children and the provision of services to them and their families. Under the Act there is a unified structure both of law and jurisdiction. In general all courts have the same powers when dealing with children.[1] For the first time, for example, there is concurrent jurisdiction at all levels to hear care proceedings.[2] Similarly, for the first time proceedings can be transferred from a magistrates' court to a county court and vice versa, as well as between county courts and the High Court.

In providing a uniform set of powers the Act replaces much of the

---

[17] Under s 7(2) of the Family Law Reform Act 1969.
[18] See generally Lowe *The Role of Wardship in Child Care Cases* [1989] Fam Law 38.
[19] See eg Family Law Reform Act 1969, s 7(2), Matrimonial Causes Act 1973, s 43(1), Guardianship Act 1973, s 2 and the Domestic Proceedings and Magistrates' Courts Act 1978, s 10.
[20] Bainham, op cit, p 6.
[1] An important exception, however, is in respect of the powers to make financial orders under Sch 1 of the 1989 Act, discussed in ch 20. Note also that only the High Court has jurisdiction to deal with international child abduction cases: see post, ch 15.
[2] Under the Children (Allocation of Proceedings) Order 1991, however, proceedings must normally be stated in the magistrates' court; see post, p 257.

previous legislation. For example, the Guardianship of Minors Acts 1971 and 1973, the Children Act 1975, the Child Care Act 1980 and the Children and Young Persons (Amendment) Act 1986 have been repealed together with those provisions of the Children and Young Persons Act 1969 dealing with care and supervision orders in civil proceedings and those under the Family Law Reform Act 1969 conferring statutory powers in wardship proceedings. Furthermore the Matrimonial Causes Act 1973 and the Domestic Proceedings and Magistrates' Courts Act 1978 have been so amended as to ensure that the powers to make orders relating to children in those proceedings are governed by the Children Act 1989.

Apart from providing for new orders in both the private and public law field, the Act also completely re-writes the law relating to:

(a) the provision of services for children and families by local authorities,[3]
(b) community and voluntary homes[4] and
(c) private fostering and child minding.[5]

Hence, statutes such as the Nurseries and Child-Minders Regulation Act 1948, the Foster Children Act 1980 and the Children's Homes Act 1982 have been repealed.

The scope of the Act goes beyond even this. For example both substantative and consequential amendments are made to adoption law[6] and a number of other statutes notably those dealing with child abduction have also been substantially amended to bring them into line with the 1989 Act. Also the power to make the new section 8 orders in any 'family proceedings', which for these purposes includes both adoption and domestic violence proceedings,[7] further extends the impact of the Act to areas not primarily governed by it.

It is important to appreciate, however, that wide though the Act is, it is by no means the only Act governing child law. Indeed there are some areas, notably those dealing with the child's status, surrogacy and the question of who is a parent, upon which the 1989 has little or no impact.[8] Other areas not primarily governed by the 1989 Act are adoption,[9] child abduction[10] and financial orders in divorce or matrimonial proceedings.[11]

Even in those areas where the wide sweeping reforms have been made, previous case law has not necessarily been rendered otiose. For example, the established case law on the ambit and application of the welfare principle,[12] on resolving disputes between parents about who should look after the children[13] and on the function and role of welfare officers,[14] still provides a useful starting point when interpreting the 1989 Act.

---

[3] Under Part III and Sch 2 of the 1989 Act.
[4] Under Parts VI–VIII.
[5] Under Parts IX and X.
[6] By Sch 10 of the 1989 Act, see post, ch 13.
[7] See s 8(3), discussed post, p 364.
[8] See ch 8 for a detailed discussion.
[9] See ch 13.
[10] See ch 15.
[11] See chs 20 and 21.
[12] Discussed in ch 10.
[13] Discussed post, pp 384 et seq.
[14] Discussed post, pp 377 et seq.

C. Some key changes

1. NEW CONCEPTS

In producing what the Department of Health's *Introduction to the Children Act 1989*[15] describes as a 'practical and consistent code' the 1989 Act embodies three fundamental changes of concept, namely, parenthood replacing guardianship as the primary concept, 'parental responsibility' replacing the concept of parental rights and duties and new powers to make residence orders rather than custody orders.

With regard to the first, as the Law Commission had observed,[16] before the Children Act the law had no coherent legal concept of parenthood as such. Instead rights and duties were based upon the concept of guardianship, rather than parenthood, and although its significance had diminished it was still the case immediately before the 1989 Act that the father was, during his lifetime, the *sole* guardian of his legitimate child. The 1989 Act has now abolished the concept of parental guardianship[17] and the term 'guardian' is now reserved for those formally appointed to take the place of parents upon their death.[18]

The introduction of the new concept of 'parental responsibility' is of particular importance under the Act. As Professor Hoggett has said:[19]

'The [Act] assumes that bringing up children is the responsibility of their parents and that the State's principal role is to help rather than to interfere. To emphasise the practical reality that bringing up children is a serious responsibility, rather than a matter of legal rights, the conceptual building block used throughout the [Act] is "parental responsibility". This covers the whole bundle of duties towards the child, with their concomitant powers and authority over him, together with some procedural rights to protection against interference... It therefore represents the fundamental status of parents.'

The meaning and scope of this vital concept is discussed in chapter 9.

The third change is the provision through section 8 of a new set of powers replacing the former powers to make custody and access orders. These new powers[20] are more flexible than the former and are intended to be less emotive. To this end they are drafted in clear and simple terms designed to settle practical questions (principally with whom the child is to live and whom the child can see) and not to confer abstract rights. In this way it is hoped that the symbolism of victory[1] that had come to be attached to custody and related orders will not be associated with these new section 8 orders.

These section 8 orders provide the 'basic menu' of the Act in that they can be made, either upon application or by the court acting on its own motion, in any 'family proceedings' including therefore proceedings brought by individuals or by local authorities. Moreover, the Act adopts an 'open

[15] HMSO, 1989, Foreword.
[16] Law Com No 172 *Guardianship and Custody*, 1988, para 2.2.
[17] See s 2(4) of the 1989 Act, discussed further post, p 293.
[18] Guardianship is discussed in ch 12.
[19] *The Children Bill: The Aim* [1989] Fam Law 217.
[20] Discussed in detail in ch 11.
[1] See King *Playing the Symbols—Custody and the Law Commission* [1987] Fam Law 186.

door' policy by allowing anyone (not otherwise entitled to seek an order) to seek the court's leave to apply for a section 8 order.[2]

2. CHANGES IN PUBLIC LAW

(a) Services for children and families[3]

The Act provides a comprehensive statement of the social services to be provided by local authorities for families and children.[4] For the first time services for handicapped and disabled children are brought under the same umbrella as those for other children in need.

An important object of the Act is to promote these services as positive help for children in need. Emphasis is placed on the need for local authorities and families to work in partnership and often upon the basis of written agreements. Authorities are under a positive duty to consult the parents and children, and to promote contact between the child and his parents, family and friends. Even if compulsory measures are taken, the authorities remain under the positive duty to promote contact.

The Act ends the local authorities' former powers to assume parental rights by administrative means. Instead, if compulsory measures are thought necessary, the authority must apply for a court order. Unless and until such an order is made, those with parental responsibility can remove the child from accommodation.[5]

(b) A new threshold for state care and supervision[6]

The Act creates a single statutory route into compulsory care. Only if the statutory threshold under section 31 can be satisfied, can the court make a care or supervision order. Consistent with this policy is the ending of the courts' powers in matrimonial and wardship proceedings to commit children into care of their own motion.[7]

The underlying philosophy of the new threshold was explained by Lord Mackay LC in his Joseph Jackson Memorial Lecture:[8]

> 'the integrity and independence of the family is the basic building block of a free and democratic society and the need to defend it should be clearly perceivable in the law. Accordingly, unless there is evidence that a child is being or is likely to be positively harmed because of a failure in the family, the state, whether in the guise of a local authority or a court, should not interfere.'

It is important to appreciate that section 31 provides the minimum criteria that have to be satisfied before a care or supervision order may be granted.

---

[2] Under s 10 of the 1989 Act, discussed post, p 359.
[3] For a useful résumé see Hoggett *The Children Bill: The Aim* [1989] Fam Law 217, 218. For further discussion see ch 16.
[4] To this end the child care services provided by the Child Care Act 1980 and the services for the handicapped and disabled under the National Assistance Act 1948 and the National Health Service Act 1977 have been replaced.
[5] Under s 20(8) of the 1989 Act, discussed post, p 504.
[6] For a brief résumé see Hoggett, op cit at p 221. Discussed in detail in ch 16.
[7] Though note the powers under s 37, discussed post, p 374.
[8] (1989) 139 NLJ 505 at p 508.

However, satisfaction of section 31 alone by no means guarantees an order since the court must still be satisfied that making an order is better for the child than making no order[9] and that there are no other suitable alternative orders.[10] For this reason section 31 is generally referred to as providing 'threshold provisions' rather than 'grounds' for a care or supervision order.

3. GENERAL PRINCIPLES[11]

Section 1 of the 1989 Act sets out a number of basic principles intended to be of general application both in the private law and public law context. The basic controlling principle in all cases where a *court* is considering what order, if any, to make is that under section 1(1) the child's welfare is the paramount consideration. Under section 1(2) the court is directed to have regard to the general principle that delay in determining questions about a child's upbringing is 'likely to prejudice the welfare of the child'. To avoid delay the court is given for the first time the power to impose timetables for proceedings.[12]

Under section 1(5) the court is directed not to make an order 'unless it considers that doing so would be better for the child than making no order at all'.[13] This provision is said to embody the so-called 'non-intervention' principle, the effect of which is to require *in every case* justification of why it is in the child's interests that an order be made. It is no longer sufficient that each party consents to an order being made, though the court is not prevented from making an order in such circumstances. Section 1(5) is intended to reinforce rather than undermine parental responsibility.[14]

D. Procedural changes

Accompanying the substantive changes brought about by the 1989 Act are equally important procedural changes some of which are provided for in the Act itself but others result from the many rules and regulations issued in association with the new legislation. For example, fundamental changes have been made to the court structure creating in effect a specialist division at every level. Important changes too have been made to court procedure, rules of evidence and to the very function and role of the courts when dealing with children.

---

[9] Pursuant to s 1(5).
[10] Eg under s 8.
[11] Discussed generally in ch 10.
[12] Under ss 11(1) and 32(1), discussed below.
[13] Discussed in detail, post, pp 345–347.
[14] See Hoggett, op cit, at p 218.

1. CHANGES IN COURT STRUCTURE

(a) County court

Under the Children (Allocation of Proceedings) Order 1991 there are, for the purpose of hearing cases involving children, the following classes of county court, namely, divorce county courts, family hearing centres and care centres.[15] These classes are in addition to non-designated county courts which have jurisdiction to hear domestic violence proceedings even when involving children.

Family hearing centres and care centres are new and are in effect specialist courts with exclusive jurisdiction to hear respectively contested section 8 cases and public law cases involving local authorities. Only 'designated family judges' and 'nominated care judges'[16] have jurisdiction to hear cases at these centres.

The thinking behind this development[17] is that the concentration of family work in the centres ensures that specialist judges can be effectively employed to ensure that cases are dealt with expeditiously and that continuous hearings can be assured thus avoiding the need for lengthy adjournments.

The general jurisdictional scheme is that all cases involving children initiated in the county court (with the sole exception of domestic violence application) must be started in a divorce county court but in *all* cases any contested section 8 application must be transferred to a family hearing centre.[18] Family hearing centres, however, are not competent to hear care and related proceedings transferred from the magistrates' courts. Instead such applications have to be heard in a care centre.[19]

(b) Magistrates' courts

Magistrates' courts have also been reorganised with the creation of 'family proceedings courts'.[20] These courts, which are staffed by magistrates drawn from the 'family panel'[1] replace the former domestic courts and have sole jurisdiction to hear civil proceedings concerning children.[2] As in the higher courts the object of these changes is to have specially trained magistrates hearing children cases.[3]

---

[15] Many courts combine all these functions including the Principal Registry in London, see art 19 of the Children (Allocation of Proceedings) Order 1991.

[16] Ie circuit judges specified by the Lord Chancellor under the Courts and Legal Services Act 1990, s 9 and *Practice Direction (Family Proceedings: Allocation to Judiciary)* [1991] 4 All ER 764, who have undertaken specialist training.

[17] See Harris and Scanlan *The Children Act 1989, A Procedural Handbook* para 9.10.

[18] Art 16 of the Allocation Order 1991.

[19] Art 18. For the provision for transfer of cases see further below.

[20] Children Act 1989, s 92(1).

[1] See Family Proceedings (Constitution) Rules 1991 and Family Proceedings Courts (Constitution) (Metropolitan Area) Rules 1991.

[2] Formerly care proceedings were heard by the juvenile court. This court (now known as the Youth Court) is now exclusively concerned with juvenile crime.

[3] See the Department of Health's *Introduction to the Children Act 1989* HMSO, 1989, para 1.49.

(c) New committees[4]

In addition to the changes to the courts two new committees have been created. The first is the Family Court Business Committee which is concerned with availability of resources, priorities in relation to other litigation and sound practice in transferring cases between courts. The second is the Family Court Services Committee whose main purpose is to provide a forum for professional concerns about issues arising under the 1989 Act and the conduct of the various agencies and professions in safeguarding children's welfare. In each case the committees are chaired by the designated family judge and serviced by the court administrator. The Business Committee's membership comprises a district judge, a representative of justices' clerks from courts operating family panels, a representative from a local authority's social services and legal departments, a manager of a local guardian ad litem panel and a local representative from the Legal Aid Board. The Services Committees have a wider membership comprising inter alia a barrister, a solicitor in private practice, a solicitor from the local authority legal department, a probation officer, an area health authority representative, a number of the medical profession, a police representative, a social worker, a guardian ad litem, a justices' clerk and a district judge.

It might also be noted that the overall operation of the Children Act 1989 is monitored by the Children Act Advisory Committee, currently chaired by Booth J.

2. ALLOCATION OF PROCEEDINGS

(a) Commencement of proceedings

The allocation of proceedings concerning children is principally governed by the Children (Allocation of Proceedings) Order 1991. By article 3 certain 'specified proceedings', namely those concerning local authorities (including principally care and related proceedings) must be started in the magistrates' court.[5] Apart from these proceedings the 1991 Order does not regulate the court level at which other proceedings must be started. However, many other cases will be 'self regulating' in the sense that those concerning children in divorce cases must be made, in the first instance, to the divorce county court, while those concerning children in maintenance applications under the Domestic Proceedings and Magistrates' Courts Act 1978 must be made to the magistrates' courts. There is no formal regulation[6] on the initial court allocation of free standing applications for section 8 orders or orders under Part 1 of the 1989 Act.

---

[4] See generally Harris and Scanlan, op cit, paras 9.11–9.15.
[5] It might be noted that the former requirement that the applicant be resident in the relevant local area has been dropped. Applicants can therefore bring proceedings in any magistrates' court they wish.
[6] Informal pressure is, however, exerted by the Legal Aid Boards in the sense that in applications for legal aid reasons for choosing a higher court have to be given, effectively forcing applicants to justify why applications should not be made to the magistrates' court: see Application for Legal Aid Form CLA5.

(b) Transfer of proceedings

The transfer of proceedings is solely controlled by the Children (Allocation of Proceedings) Order 1991[7]. Under this Order proceedings can for the first time be transferred sideways, that is, for example, from one magistrates' court to another.[8] This transfer would be justified, for example, if a case could be heard more quickly. Proceedings can also be transferred from one court level to another, including for the first time, from a magistrates' court to a county court and vice versa.[9]

Detailed rules govern the transfer of care and related proceedings[10] but the basic scheme in the initial allocation is determined by the justices' clerk who can allocate the case to his own or another magistrates' court or to a care centre. Any party who disagrees with the initial allocation is entitled to apply to a nominated district judge ('the gate keeper') for a fresh allocation. At this stage, cases can be allocated to a care centre or to the High Court or back to a magistrates' court. An appeal against the district judge's decision is only possible if he refers the case back.[11]

3. PROCEDURE AND EVIDENCE

Procedure is governed by the rules which, like the substantive law, have been entirely rewritten. There are two sets of rules, namely, the Family Proceedings Rules 1991,[12] which govern procedure in the High Court and county court and the Family Proceedings Courts (Children Act 1989) Rules 1991 which govern procedure in the magistrates' courts. In line with the principle of unity of jurisdiction between the courts and of facilitating easy transfer from one level to another applications and orders are made on a common set of forms, copies of which are set out at the end of each set of rules. At all court levels proceedings are commenced by application[13] either on a prescribed form or, where there is no form, in writing.

One consequence of the new common procedure is that in the higher courts written evidence is no longer submitted in the form of sworn affidavits.[14] Instead written evidence is submitted in the form of signed statements. The greatest impact of the changes, however, is with respect to procedure in the magistrates' courts where for the first time (in line with the other courts) there is a requirement for advance disclosure of written evidence[15] and a

---

[7] Ie ss 38 and 39 of the Matrimonial and Family Proceedings Act 1984 (discussed ante at p 14) do not apply: art 5 of the Allocation Order 1991.

[8] Arts 6 and 10.

[9] Arts 7 and 8. The transfer between the High Court and county is governed by arts 12 and 13.

[10] Arts 7–11.

[11] Pursuant to the Children (Allocation of Proceedings) (Appeals) Order 1991.

[12] Part 4 of which governs applications under the Children Act 1989.

[13] This means that proceedings in magistrates' courts are no longer started by complaint. One consequence of this has been the introduction from 1 April 1992 of application fees in that court: Magistrates' Courts Fees (Amendment) Order 1992.

[14] Though this remains the procedure in wardship and child abduction proceedings.

[15] Family Proceedings Courts (Children Act 1989) Rules 1991, r 17, and Family Proceedings Rules 1991, r 4.17, discussed inter alia in *Clarke Hall and Morrison on Children* at 1[243] and in Harris and Scanlan, op cit, at paras 5.11–5.13. It might also be noted that hearsay evidence is admissible under the Children (Admissibility of Hearsay Evidence) Order 1991.

general expectation that magistrates will have read the papers in advance of the hearing.

At all levels (including magistrates' courts) the court must state any findings of fact and give reasons for its decision.[16] This is the first time that magistrates have been obliged to give reasons for their decision other than where an appeal has been lodged.

4. ROLE OF THE COURTS

An important result of the many procedural changes is that the courts' role will have changed. For example all courts will have a greater managerial role consequent upon the duty to impose timetables and to give directions to adhere to that timetable. This is the first time that the courts themselves have been placed under a *duty* to ensure the speedy disposal of cases.

All courts are expected to take a more active role in proceedings. As the Department of Health's *Introduction to the Children Act 1989* puts it:[17]

'Under the Act the courts have an independent duty to do what is best for the child. If the courts are to discharge that duty often they will have to take an active part in the proceedings rather than simply acting as umpires between the contending parties.'

Further encouragement to take an active role is the general requirement (adverted to above) of advance disclosure of evidence and the greater powers of the court to control what further evidence should be adduced.

The net result of this more active involvement is that court proceedings are likely to be more inquisitorial and rather less adversarial than in the past. This approach, coupled with a requirement of more openness particularly on the part of local authorities,[18] seems much better suited to determining what options are best for the child and reinforces the view that in these cases the child's welfare should be the sole concern and not whether one party or the other 'wins or loses'.

---

[16] Family Proceedings Rules 1991, r 4.21(4) and Family Proceedings Courts (Children Act 1989) Rules 1991, r 21(6).
[17] HMSO 1989, para 1.51.
[18] *R v Hampshire County Council, ex p K* [1990] 2 QB 71, [1990] 2 All ER 129 (in which the authority sought to withhold medical records) should no longer arise.

Chapter 8

Parents and children

A. Who are the parents of a child?

1. INTRODUCTION

Until relatively recently it would have gone without saying that the person
who gave birth to the child was the mother and the person by whom she
conceived was the father. Indeed traditionally the law has taken the blood
tie or genetic link as the test of parenthood.[1] However, with the advance
of medical science and in particular with the advent of human assisted
reproduction the position has now become more complicated. Indeed these
advances have called into question the appropriateness of having legal
parentage solely based on a genetic link.

Reflecting these advances and following detailed inquiry into the whole
subject by the Warnock Committee on Human Fertilisation and Embryology,[2] there is now comprehensive legislation in the form of the Human
Fertilisation and Embryology Act 1990 governing issues arising from
assisted reproduction, including, inter alia, the question of who is to be
regarded as a parent.

Before discussing who in law are regarded as parents of a child it is
helpful to say a little about the different techniques of assisted reproduction.

2. TECHNIQUES OF HUMAN ASSISTED REPRODUCTION[3]

(a) Artificial insemination

Artificial insemination refers to the placing of semen into a woman's vagina,
cervix or uterus (ie womb) by means other than sexual intercourse. If the
woman's husband's sperm is used the process is referred to as artificial
insemination by husband or AIH. If someone else's sperm is used it is
known as artificial insemination by donor or AID. It has been estimated
that some 1,700 children a year are born in the UK as a result of AID.[4]

---

[1] Hence the use of blood tests to determine parentage, see post, p 274. For the legal significance
of being a parent see post, p 278.
[2] Report of the Committee of Inquiry into Human Fertilisation and Embryology (1984) Cmnd
9314 whose recommendations were essentially accepted in the government's White Paper
Human Fertilisation and Embryology: A Framework for Legislation (1987) Cm 259.
[3] See generally Douglas *Law, Fertility and Reproduction* (1991) ch 6 and the Warnock Report,
op cit, chs 3–7. The various techniques are neatly summarised in *Legislation on Human
Infertility Services and Embryology Research: A Consultation Paper* (1986) Cm 46 upon which
the text heavily relies.
[4] See the 1986 Consultation Paper, para 7. The first documented use of AID was in 1884, see
Douglas, op cit, at p 109.

(b) In vitro fertilisation (IVF)

The technique of in vitro fertilisation is to take a ripe egg from the woman's ovary just before ovulation (ie when the egg would have been released naturally). It is then mixed with sperm in a dish (in vitro) so that fertilisation can occur. If the egg is fertilised, it is returned to the uterus, where it may implant, and then develop as normal. This technique, first perfected in 1978 by Robert Edwards and Patrick Steptoe, has about a 15 per cent success rate and it is thought that about 1,000 children a year are born in the UK as a result of the treatment.

A variant of IVF is that known as gamete intra-fallopian transfer or GIFT for short. Here the ova and sperm are mixed together in a drop of fluid and then placed back in the fallopian tube. In other words no attempt is made to produce an embryo[5] outside the body.

(c) Egg and embryo donation

Egg collection technology coupled with IVF make it possible to obtain an egg from a donor for transfer to another woman having been fertilised with either the husband's or a donor's sperm in vitro. Of course where the donor's gametes[6] are used, that person will be the child's genetic parent. It will be appreciated that IVF treatment has created the possibility that the woman who gives birth to a child may not be the genetic mother. In the case of embryo transfer neither the woman nor her partner (unless his sperm is used), will be genetically related to the child.

(d) Surrogacy

Surrogacy[7] involves one woman carrying a child for another with the intention that the child be handed over. It is not to be confused with the techniques for human assisted reproduction just described though the surrogate may well have conceived by one of those methods. We will discuss the effect and regulation of surrogacy agreements later in this chapter.[8]

3. WHO IS THE LEGAL MOTHER?

Until the advent of in vitro fertilisation, provided the fact of the birth could be proved there could be no doubt that the woman giving birth must in law be the child's mother. As Lord Simon was able to say as recently as 1976 in *The Ampthill Peerage*[9]: 'Motherhood, although also a legal relationship, is based on a fact, being proved demonstrably by parturition.'

There can still be no doubt where the woman has conceived by artificial insemination or by in vitro fertilisation of her ovum that she is the legal mother. The difficulty arises where the person giving birth is not the child's

---

[5] Ie a live human embryo where fertilisation is complete: s 1(1)(a) of the Human Fertilisation and Embryology Act 1990.
[6] Ie eggs in the case of a woman, sperm in the case of a man.
[7] See the definition in the Surrogacy Arrangements Act 1985, s 1(2).
[8] Post, p 267.
[9] [1977] AC 547, 577, [1976] 2 All ER 411, 424, HL.

genetic mother but is the carrying mother as a result of egg or embryo donation in in vitro fertilisation. As Scott Baker J said in *Re W (Minors) (Surrogacy)*[10] 'The advent of IVF presented the law with a dilemma: whom should the law regard as the mother?'. Arguments can be led either way. On the one hand given the biological connection it could be argued that the genetic mother should be regarded as the child's legal mother. On the other hand because of the bizarre consequences that would follow if the genetic mother is unknown (for example, the child's birth would have to be registered with the name of the mother unknown) there would seem a strong case for considering the carrying mother the legal mother.[11] An alternative approach altogether is to hold the *intending* parent the legal parent.[12]

The position at common law has still to be determined. The matter was raised in *Re W (Minors) (Surrogacy)*[13] but left open, upon an undertaking by the 'commissioning' genetic parents that[14] they would apply for a 'section 30 order'[15] as soon as the provision was implemented. However, adopting the Warnock Committee's recommendation,[16] section 27(1) of the Human Fertilisation and Embryology Act 1990 provides:

'The woman who is carrying or has carried a child as a result of the placing in her of an embryo or of sperm and eggs, and no other woman, is to be treated as the mother of the child.'

Where this provision applies then in all cases the woman giving birth and no other woman will, unless the child is subsequently adopted[17] or a section 30 order[18] is subsequently made, be treated as the legal mother regardless of genetic connection. Section 27, however, does *not* have retrospective effect[19] and only applies in relation to children carried by women as a result of the placing in them of embryos or of sperm and eggs, or of their artificial insemination on or after 1 August 1991.[20] For this reason it may still be necessary to resolve the position at common law. On the other hand the section applies regardless of whether the woman was in the United Kingdom or elsewhere at the time of the placing in her of the embryo or the sperm and eggs.[1]

[10] [1991] 1 FLR 385, 386.
[11] See Bromley *Aided Conception—the Alternative to Adoption* in *Adoption, Essays in Social Policy, Law and Sociology* (Ed Bean) ch 11 at pp 189–190.
[12] As mooted by Douglas, op cit at p 129.
[13] Supra.
[14] The genetic mother had no womb but was able to produce the eggs which were taken from her medically and fertilised in vitro by her husband's sperm. Two resultant embryos were implanted in the surrogate host mother who gave birth to the twins who had lived with the 'commissioning couple' ever since.
[15] Discussed post, p 265.
[16] Op cit, at para 6.8.
[17] S 28(2).
[18] S 30 orders are discussed post, p 265.
[19] S 49(3).
[20] The date on which s 27 came into force, by SI 1991/1400.
[1] S 27(3). But there is no domicile requirement, nor is there a requirement that the child be born in England and Wales but the provisions can only apply where, by the conflict of law rules, English law is held to be the applicable law.

4. WHO IS THE LEGAL FATHER?

The position regarding who is the legal father is more complicated than that of the mother for while in general the genetic father (ie the man whose sperm fertilised the egg) is regarded as the legal father, this is subject to two exceptions. Conversely there are occasions when, notwithstanding the absence of any genetic link, a man will be treated as the legal father.

(a) When genetic fathers are not legal fathers

There are two exceptions to the general rule that the genetic father is the legal father provided by section 28(6) of the Human Fertilisation and Embryology Act 1990.[2] These are (a) where he is a donor whose sperm is used for 'licensed treatment'[3] and whose consent to the use of his sperm has been obtained in accordance with the requirements of Schedule 3 to the 1990 Act; and (b) where his sperm is used after his death. One incidental but important effect of these exceptions is that there will be occasions when a child has no legal father.[4]

(b) Where non-genetic 'fathers' are treated as legal fathers

At common law only genetic fathers could be regarded as legal fathers. The strictness of this position, however, made no allowance for the use of the various techniques of assisted reproduction, the only object of which is for childless couples to have children that they could regard as their own. A good example is the AID child conceived by a wife because her husband was sterile or sub-fertile or because he was the possible carrier of an inheritable disease, but whom (as usually will be the case) the couple wish to treat as though he were the husband's.[5] Although the absence of legal fatherhood made little difference to the legal relationship between him and the child because his treating the child as his own made the latter a child of the family[6] and, since the sperm donor's identity would not normally be divulged, there was virtually no risk of legal claims arising between the donor and the child.[7] Nevertheless there were potentially a number of longer-term problems. For example, the child had no entitlement to the husband's estate, if the latter died intestate[8] nor any claim if any of his mother's relatives died intestate or if property was held on trust for the husband's children or the wife's legitimate children. If the child made such

---

[2] Which only applies to children carried by women as a result of the placing in them of embryos or of sperm or eggs, or of their artificial insemination on or after 1 August 1991: s 49(3).
[3] Ie treatment requiring those who offer it to be licensed under the 1990 Act, Sch 2. See generally: Douglas, op cit, pp 110 et seq.
[4] Eg in those cases where such children are born to a woman who has no partner who is deemed to be the legal father under s 28(2) and (3), discussed below.
[5] They might even register the husband as the father. If the husband is known not to be the father, the person registering the birth will commit an offence under the Perjury Act 1911, s 4.
[6] Unless the spouses separated before the child's birth. See post, p 368.
[7] Before the 1990 Act good clinical practice required the doctor carrying out the insemination not to divulge the donor's identity.
[8] Although he would have a claim to provision under the Inheritance (Provision for Family and Dependants) Act 1975 as a child of the family. See post, p 823.

a claim and the spouses knew that the husband was not the father, they had either to connive at the deception or be forced to disclose facts which they had wished to keep secret.

Following pressure to change the law[9] section 27 of the Family Law Reform Act 1987 provided that in relation to a child born in England and Wales after implementation of the provisions (viz 4 April 1988) as the result of the artificial insemination of a woman, who at the time of the insemination was a party to a marriage,[10] and was artificially inseminated with the semen of someone other than the other party to the marriage, that child 'shall not be treated as the child of any person other than the parties to that marriage' unless it is proved to the court's satisfaction that the other party to the marriage did not consent to the insemination. In other words, under this provision, an AID child born to a married couple is presumptively the child of both the parties, and the presumption can be rebutted only by showing[11] that the husband did not consent to the artificial insemination of his wife.

Section 27 only applied to AID children and not to those born as a result of using other forms of assisted reproduction. Section 28 of the Human Fertilisation and Embryology Act 1990, however, makes provision for other forms of assisted reproduction, as well as artificial insemination.[12] Specifically section 28(2) provides that where a married woman[13] is carrying or has carried a child as the result of the placing in her of an embryo, or sperm and eggs, or of her insemination, then notwithstanding that the sperm was not donated by her husband, he and no other person[14] is treated as the father of the child unless it is shown that he did not consent to his wife's treatment. This provision is, however, subject to section 28(5)(a) by which the common law presumption of legitimacy based on marriage[15] takes priority over the requirement of the husband's consent. What this seems to mean[16] is that the husband will be regarded as the father unless the issue is raised when, if he did not consent, the presumption will have to be rebutted usually by means of blood tests.

The 1990 Act goes further by enacting, in section 28(3), that where donated sperm is used for a woman in the course of licensed 'treatment

---

[9] Both the Law Commission (Law Com No 118, paras 12.9, 12.11) and the Warnock Committee (ibid at para 4.17) had recommended change.

[10] Being a marriage not at the time annulled or dissolved, but including a void marriage if, at the time of the insemination, both or either of the parties reasonably believed that the marriage was valid. It is presumed, unless the contrary is shown, that one of the parties did so believe: s 27(2). It will be noted that the problem about whether a mistake of law can support a reasonable belief (discussed post at p 281) would appear to be relevant in this context.

[11] Presumably, upon the balance of probabilities.

[12] Note, however, that this provision is *not* retrospective; s 49(3). This means that s 27 of the Family Law Reform Act 1987 will continue to apply to AID children born on or after 1 April 1988 but before the commencement of s 28 (viz 1 August 1991): s 49(4).

[13] For these purposes, marriage includes a void marriage if, as is presumed until the contrary is shown, at the time of the treatment resulting in the child's birth, one of the parties reasonably believed that the marriage was valid: s 28(7)(b), but it does not include the case where a judicial separation was in force: s 28(7)(a).

[14] S 28(4).

[15] See post, p 270.

[16] See Douglas, op cit, at p 129.

services'[17] provided for her and a man together then that man, and no other person, shall be treated as the father of the child if section 28(2) does not apply (for example where the woman is not married or where there is a judicial separation order in force). Commonly this will mean that the male cohabitant of the treated woman will be treated as the legal father but there is no necessity to prove cohabitation.

5. SECTION 30 ORDERS[18]

Under section 30(1) of the Human Fertilisation and Embryology Act 1990 the court[19] is empowered to make an order providing for a child to be treated in law as the child of the parties to a marriage in circumstances where the child has been carried by a woman other than the wife as a result of the placing in her of an embryo or sperm and eggs or her artificial fertilisation following the use of gametes of one or both of the spouses.[20] This power is subject to a number of conditions, as follows.

Applications can only be made by a husband and wife, both of whom must be at least 18 and at least one of whom must be domiciled in part of the United Kingdom or the Channel Islands or Isle of Man.[21]

The application must be made within six months of the child's birth.[1]

At the time of application the child's home must be with the husband and wife.[2]

Before any order can be made, the court must be satisfied that the carrying woman and the father (including her husband if he is the father by virtue of section 28(2)) have freely and with full understanding of what is involved, agreed unconditionally to the making of an *order*[3]: in this regard the surrogate mother's agreement is ineffective if given less than six weeks after the child's birth.[4] No agreement is required if a person who cannot be found or is incapable of giving an agreement.[5]

The court must also be satisfied that no money or other benefit has been given, paid or received by the spouses in connection with the making of the order, the giving of agreement, the handing over of the child or the making of any arrangements with a view to the making of the order.[6]

This prohibition does not apply to payment of reasonable expenses which presumably will cover such things as the surrogate's expenses for maternity

[17] Ie those covered in Sch 2 to the 1990 Act.
[18] See generally Douglas *Law, Fertility and Reproduction* 158–161. See also Morgan and Lee *Human Fertilisation and Embryology Act 1990*, pp 153–4. This section was a late addition to the legislation prompted by the much publicised 'Cumbria' case, subsequently reported as *Re W (Minors) (Surrogacy)* [1991] 1 FLR 385, discussed ante at p 262.
[19] Ie High Court, county court or magistrates' court: HFEA 1990, s 30(8)(a).
[20] S 30 does *not* apply if the child was conceived as the result of normal intercourse between the husband and the surrogate mother, as occurred in *Re Adoption Application (Payment for Adoption)* [1987] Fam 81, [1987] 2 All ER 826.
[21] HFEA 1990, s 30(2), (3)(a) and (4).
[1] S 30(2). Special retrospective provision was made for children born before the Act, permitting applications to be within six months of the coming into force of the Act.
[2] S 30(3)(a).
[3] Ie not to the *application*: s 30(5).
[4] S 30(6). A similar provision is made in adoption; see post, p 425.
[5] S 30(6). 'Cannot be found' and 'incapable of giving agreement' presumably have the same meaning as in adoption, see post, p 427.
[6] S 30(7).

clothes, travel for AID or IVF treatment and for ante-natal check ups and possibly for her loss of earnings consequent on giving up work to have the baby. Further payments or benefits may be authorised by the court. The point has been well made[7] that since the court will only become apprised of the matter when the application is made, to be effective, authorisation will have to be retrospective. However following the interpretation of the similar provisions in the adoption legislation[8] it seems likely that section 30(7) will be regarded as giving the courts power retrospectively to authorise payments.

Section 30 bears the hallmarks of hurried legislation and there are a number of uncertainties. For example although section 30(8)(a) makes it clear that proceedings under this section are to be regarded as 'family proceedings' for the purposes of the Children Act 1989, it is not beyond argument[9] that in deciding whether to make a section 30 order the court is bound to treat the child's welfare as its paramount consideration. The better view is, however, that it is so bound.[10]

One result of making section 30 proceedings 'family proceedings' is that as well as making or refusing an order the court is also empowered to make a section 8 order[11] or to give a section 37 direction inviting the local authority to investigate the circumstances of the case,[12] whether or not such an application is made.[13]

Although the obvious intention of the Act is that the effect of the order is to make the applicants the child's *sole* legal parents there is no specific provision extinguishing the former parentage.[14] Even if such extinguishment is regarded as implicit, there is no formal provision, as there is in adoption, for the section 30 parents to register the child as 'theirs' nor are there any provisions dealing with rules of consanguinity.

The wisdom of requiring the surrogate's (and, where appropriate, her husband's) consent to the making of the order rather than to the making of the application may also be questioned, since a late withdrawal of consent after the child has been placed with the applicants will bar the court from making a section 30 order (though not a section 8 order) regardless of the child's welfare.

It may finally be noted that under section 30(9)(a) regulations may extend with modification enactments about adoption to section 30 proceedings. As has been pointed out,[15] the dilemma is that if such regulations are made prospective 'commissioning parents' may attempt to by-pass controls, but

---

[7] By Douglas, op cit, at pp 159–160.
[8] Cf *Re An Adoption Application* [1992] 1 FLR 341, per Hollings J and *Re Adoption Application (Payment for Adoption)* [1987] Fam 81, [1987] 2 All ER 826, per Latey J. See also post, p 447, n 12.
[9] See eg Hogg *Surrogacy—Nobody's Child* [1991] Fam Law 276.
[10] See Douglas, op cit at p 160 n 65 who considers it doubtful whether a court would hold that the matter concerned only the status of the child and so exclude the application of s 1(1) of the Children Act 1989 applying the reasoning of *S v McC, W v W* [1972] AC 24, [1970] 3 All ER 107, HL, discussed post, p 343. The court is definitely bound to apply the paramountcy principle when deciding whether or not to make a s 8 order. See post, p 342.
[11] Discussed post, pp 351 et seq.
[12] S 37 is discussed post, p 374.
[13] See s 10(1)(b) of the 1989 Act, discussed post, p 365.
[14] See Hogg, op cit at p 277.
[15] Douglas, op cit, p 160.

if they are not then there is a risk that section 30 orders 'will amount to no more than rubber-stamping in which case their whole rationale might be queried'. At the time of writing no such regulations have been made.

6. SURROGACY AGREEMENTS[16]

Although the precise arrangements may differ, a surrogacy agreement is basically one by which a woman ('the carrying mother') agrees to bear a child for someone else ('the commissioning parents'). For the purposes of the Surrogacy Arrangements Act 1985, a 'surrogacy arrangement' is one made before the woman began to carry the child 'with a view to any child carried in pursuance of it being handed over to, and parental responsibility being met (so far as practicable) by another person or persons'.[17] It is the essence of such agreements that the carrying mother agrees to hand over the baby at birth to the commissioning parents and not to exercise any parental responsibility that she may have in respect of the child. Such agreements came into prominence as a result of the much publicised 'Baby Cotton' case,[18] which is believed to be the first case in the United Kingdom of a commercially arranged surrogacy agreement.[19]

The 'Baby Cotton' case aroused much public debate about the desirability of such agreements in general and of commercial surrogacy in particular. Although the Warnock Committee stated that their evidence suggested that the weight of public opinion was against the practice of surrogacy,[20] they nevertheless did not recommend imposing a complete ban. Instead they recommended that it be a criminal offence for a person to be involved in negotiating or making a surrogacy arrangement on a commercial basis.[1] Adopting this recommendation section 2(1) of the Surrogacy Arrangements Act 1985 provides:

'No person shall on a commercial basis do any of the following acts in the United Kingdom, that is—

    (a) initiate or take part in any negotiations with a view to the making of a surrogacy arrangement,
    (b) offer or agree to negotiate the making of a surrogacy arrangement, or
    (c) compile any information with a view to its use in making, or negotiating the making, of surrogacy arrangements

and no person shall in the United Kingdom knowingly cause another to do any of those acts on a commercial basis.'

[16] See generally Douglas *Law, Fertility and Reproduction* ch 7, Bromley 'The Legal Aspects of Surrogacy Agreements' in *Children and The Law* (ed Freestone) p 1 and the Report of the Committee of Inquiry into Human Fertilisation and Embryology (the Warnock Report) Cmnd 9314, ch 8. See also Wright *Surrogacy and Adoption: Problems and Possibilities* [1986] Fam Law 129, Harding *The Debate on Surrogate Motherhood* [1987] JSWL 37. and Montgomery *Surrogacy and the Best Interests of the Child* [1986] Fam Law 59.
[17] S 1(2) as amended by the Children Act 1989, Sch 13, para 56.
[18] Reported as *Re C (A Minor) (Wardship: Surrogacy)* [1985] FLR 846.
[19] But it was not the first surrogacy agreement to come before the court: see *A v C* [1985] FLR 445, CA (decided in 1978).
[20] Cmnd 9314 at para 8.10.
[1] Ibid at para 8.18.

Section 3 also prohibits the advertising of such services.[2]

To constitute an offence the arrangement must be made before the surrogate mother begins to carry the child and it must be made with a view to the child being handed over to, and the parental responsibility being exercised (so far as practicable) by, another person or persons. It is to be noted that the surrogate mother and the 'commissioning' parents are excluded from liability for their participation in the arrangements (though they can be liable for the advertising offence). It is also to be noted that it is only an offence knowingly to assist in the negotiations for a commercial surrogacy arrangement.[3]

Although the participating individuals might not have been committing an offence under the 1985 Act in cases where the arrangement was expressly made with a view to the child's adoption by the commissioning parents the contracting parties committed an offence under the adoption legislation.[4] Now, however, as we have seen, section 30 of the Human Fertilisation and Embryology Act 1990 permits a court to order that a child born as a result of surrogacy be treated as that of the commissioning parents if a number of conditions are met. Hence, provided arrangements do not infringe the Surrogacy Arrangements Act 1985, those made in contemplation of a section 30 order cannot be held illegal.

The availability of a section 30 order does not however solve all problems about enforceability. What, for example, is the position if the surrogate mother refuses to hand over the child or if the commissioning parents refuse to accept the child? In its original form, notwithstanding the recommendation of the Warnock Committee[5] the 1985 Act was silent on whether surrogacy arrangements were enforceable although the generally accepted view was that they were not. The matter now has been put beyond doubt, for following an amendment introduced by the Human Fertilisation and Embryology Act 1990,[6] section 1A of the Surrogacy Arrangements Act 1985 now unequivocally states that 'No surrogacy arrangement is enforceable by or against any of the persons making it'.

Given that such arrangements are unenforceable, what then happens to the child? If there is no dispute between the parties, there is no compulsion to go to court. However, given that the surrogate mother will be treated as the child's legal mother even if she is not the genetic mother,[7] it would

---

[2] The penalty for involvement in a surrogacy arrangement is imprisonment for up to 3 months and a fine not exceeding level five and for unlawful advertising a fine not exceeding that level. The consent of the Director of Prosecutions is necessary for prosecution. The offences are triable summarily and an information can be laid up to 2 years after the commission of the offence instead of the usual period of 6 months.

[3] Ie it is not an offence to help in carrying out the arrangement after it has been made. An unsuccessful attempt was made to change this in the Surrogacy Arrangements (Amendment) Bill 1986.

[4] Viz Adoption Act 1976, s 57 though the court could subsequently authorise payment; see eg *Re An Adoption Application* [1992] 1 FLR 341 and *Re Adoption Application (Payment for Adoption)* [1987] Fam 81, [1987] 2 All ER 826.

[5] Cmnd 9314 at para 8.19.

[6] S 36(1).

[7] Under s 27 of the Human Fertilisation and Embryology Act 1990 discussed ante at p 262. Furthermore if she is married and conception has resulted from assisted reproduction methods (commonly surrogacy agreements take the form of the woman agreeing to be artificially inseminated with the commissioning man's semen) her husband may be treated as the legal father pursuant to s 28 of the 1990 Act, discussed ante, p 264.

seem advisable for the commissioning parents to seek a section 30 order. If they are unable to do this because, for example, the surrogate mother has withdrawn her consent or has refused to hand over the child the commissioning parents can still seek a section 8 order[8] under the Children Act 1989. In this event it is clear that in resolving any disputes the court is bound to treat the child's welfare as its paramount consideration.[9] Another possibility, provided the child is handed over, is for the commissioning parents to apply to adopt the child. This might be thought appropriate, for example, where the child is born as a result of normal intercourse so that section 30 cannot apply.[10]

B. Proof of parentage

1. MOTHERS

Normally proving who the mother is presents no difficulties, because the fact of birth and identity can be established by the evidence of the doctor or other persons present at the birth and, as Lord Simon said in the *Ampthill Peerage* case,[11] motherhood is proved demonstrably by parturition: mater est quam gestatio demonstrat. However, it is not unknown for mothers to be given the wrong children in maternity hospitals and there have been cases where parents have attempted to pass off a supposititious child as their own, usually in order to defraud others who would be entitled to property in default of children of the marriage.[12]

Difficult problems of proof may also arise in the context of immigration where first-hand evidence of the birth may be absent.[13]

2. FATHERS

(a) Use of presumptions

(i) Presumption that the mother's husband is the father

Before the advent of blood tests and more recently DNA testing paternity could normally be inferred only from the fact that the alleged father had sexual intercourse with the mother about the time when the child must have been conceived. Consequently, if two men had intercourse with her during the relevant period, it would be impossible to prove affirmatively

---

[8] Discussed in ch 11.
[9] S 1(1) of the Children Act 1989. Nevertheless it seems likely that if the carrying mother wishes to keep the child and is in a position to give the child a loving and caring home, she will be allowed to do so—cf *A v C* [1985] FLR 445, CA and *Re P (Minors) (Wardship: Surrogacy)* [1987] 2 FLR 421.
[10] Adoption is discussed in ch 13.
[11] [1977] AC 547, 577, [1976] 2 All ER 411, 424, HL.
[12] Eg *Slingsby v A-G* (1916) 33 TLR 120, HL where the wife deceived her own husband. Cf the popular belief, current at the time, that the son born to James II's consort was smuggled into the queen's room in a warming-pan in order to prevent the descent of the Crown to James's Protestant daughters.
[13] See eg the case of Mrs Sabah referred to in [1986] Fam Law 66.

which is the father. Moreover, the fact that intercourse took place can in most cases be proved only by the evidence of the parties themselves or circumstantially from their conduct and the opportunities which were presented to them.

The impossibility of proving affirmatively the paternity of the child led at least as early as the twelfth century to the adoption of civil law maxim 'Pater est quem nuptiae demonstrant', that is, if a child is born to a married woman, her husband is presumed to be his father until the contrary is proved.[14] This means that if it is alleged that the husband is not the father, the burden of rebutting the presumption is cast on the asserter. This presumption applies even though the child is born so soon after the marriage that he must have been conceived beforehand[15] and, in the case of a posthumous child, if he was born within the normal period of gestation after the husband's death.[16] Difficulty arises, however, if the birth takes place an abnormally long time afterwards. In *Preston-Jones v Preston-Jones*[17] the House of Lords agreed that judicial notice could be taken of the fact that there is a normal period of gestation (although the period is variously given as 270 to 280 days or as nine months),[18] but Lord Mac-Dermott added that judicial notice must also be taken of the fact that the normal period is not always followed. It would seem, however, that the longer the period deviates from the normal, the more easily will the presumption be rebutted, until there comes a time when it is not raised at all, although it is difficult to say where the line is to be drawn.[19]

It seems that the presumption applies equally in the case of a child born after a decree of divorce. In *Knowles v Knowles*[20] the child could have been conceived before or after the decree absolute. Wrangham J held that the presumption of legitimacy operated in favour of presuming that conception took place whilst the marriage was still subsisting and that the husband was the father although, as he pointed out, in such circumstances it may be rebutted much more easily.

Conflicting presumptions arise if the child must have been conceived during the subsistence of a marriage since terminated by the husband's death or divorce and the mother has remarried before the birth. It is submitted, however, that in the absence of evidence to the contrary the first husband should be presumed to be the father since it ought to be presumed that the mother had not committed adultery.[1] If, however, the child must have been conceived when the husband and wife were living apart under a

[14] Glanvil, book 7, ch 12. See also Bracton, fol 6; Co Litt 373; Blackstone's *Commentaries i*, 457, Nicolas *Adulterine Bastardy*; and Lord Simon who said in the *Ampthill Peerage* Case [1977] AC 547, [1976] 2 All ER 411 at 577 and 424 respectively 'Fatherhood ... is a presumption.'
[15] See *Gardner v Gardner* (1877) 2 App Cas 723, HL. *R v Luffe* (1807) 8 East 193; *Anon v Anon* (1856) 23 Beav 273; *Turnock v Turnock* (1867) 36 LJP & M 85.
[16] *Re Heath* [1945] Ch 417, 421–422, per Cohen J.
[17] [1951] AC 391, [1951] 1 All ER 124, HL. See further, post, p 273, n 16.
[18] Per Lord Simonds at 401 and 127, Lord Morton at 413 and 136, Lord MacDermott at 419 and 139–140, respectively.
[19] See ibid, at 402, 403, 407, 413–414 and 128, 130, 132, 135–136, respectively.
[20] [1962] P 161, [1962] 1 All ER 659, cf *Re Leman's Will Trusts* (1945) 115 LJ Ch 89. It is submitted that the dictum to the contrary in *Re Bromage* [1935] Ch 605, 609, cannot be supported.
[1] See *Re Overbury* [1955] Ch 122, [1954] 3 All ER 308, where Harman J found in favour of the first husband's paternity on the facts.

decree of judicial separation there is no presumption that the husband is the father since it is presumed that the spouses observed the decree and did not have intercourse.[2]

Former proceedings may also raise an estoppel as to paternity. For example, if the issue of the child's parentage has been determined in divorce proceedings, the finding will bind the spouses *as between themselves* but it cannot bind either of them as against a third person nor can it bind the child or any other person who was not a party to the proceedings.[3] On the other hand it is now provided[4] that where a person has been found to be the father in any relevant proceedings[5] before any court in the United Kingdom, that is prima facie evidence of paternity in any subsequent proceedings.

(ii) No presumption where child is born to an unmarried mother

Where a child is born to an unmarried mother there is no presumption of paternity, not even where the child is born to a cohabiting couple. However, entry of a man's name as that of the father on the registration of the child's birth is prima facie evidence of paternity.[6] It is a nice point whether the making of a parental responsibility agreement[7] will be regarded as prima facie evidence of paternity. In other cases the burden for establishing paternity will lie on the asserter, though no doubt strong inferences may be drawn from the fact of cohabitation. In proving paternity, it has been held[8] that the irrebuttable presumption in criminal law that a boy under the age of 14 is incapable of rape does not import a similar presumption against his paternity in civil proceedings.

Whether there should be a presumption of paternity in the case of cohabiting couples, as there is in some Commonwealth jurisdictions,[9] was

[2] *Hetherington v Hetherington* (1887) 12 PD 112; *Ettenfield v Ettenfield* [1940] P 96, 110, [1940] 1 All ER 293, 301, CA. The reason is hardly satisfactory because the decree relieves the petitioner from the duty of cohabiting with the respondent; it does not forbid cohabitation, let alone sexual intercourse. The same rule applied to magistrates' separation orders when they had power to make them, but the presumption would not be displaced if there was in force a maintenance order but no separation order: *Bowen v Norman* [1938] 1 KB 689, [1938] 2 All ER 776. In any event the reasoning has no application to *voluntary* separation: cf *Ettenfield v Ettenfield* (supra), but the presumption may be rebutted more easily: *Knowles v Knowles* [1962] P 161, 168, [1962] 1 All ER 659, 661.
[3] *B v A-G* [1965] P 278, [1965] 1 All ER 62. But the husband's failure to deny that a child is a child of the family in undefended proceedings will not raise an estoppel because to permit it to do so might invite unnecessary litigation: *Rowe v Rowe* [1980] Fam 47, [1979] 2 All ER 1123, CA.
[4] Civil Evidence Act 1968, s 12, as amended by the Family Law Reform Act 1987, s 29.
[5] Defined to mean National Assistance Act 1948, s 42; Social Security Act 1986, s 26; proceedings under the Children Act 1989; and proceedings which would have been relevant proceedings for the purposes of section 12 of the Civil Evidence Act 1968 in the form in which it was in force before the passing of the Children Act 1989 (viz Family Law Reform Act 1969, s 6; Guardianship of Minors Act 1971; Children Act 1975, s 34(1)(a), (b) or (c); Child Care Act 1980, s 47; Family Law Reform Act 1987, s 4 and proceedings for revocation of a custodianship order under the Children Act 1975, s 35): Civil Evidence Act 1968, s 12(5) as amended by the Courts and Legal Services Act 1990, s 116, Sch 16, para 2.
[6] *Brierley v Brierley* [1918] P 257.
[7] Discussed post, p 323.
[8] *Kane v Littlefair* [1985] FLR 859.
[9] Eg Tasmania, New South Wales and Ontario: see Law Com No 118 at para 10.53, n 120.

considered but rejected by the Law Commission[10] on the basis that unlike marriage, which requires no further evidence, cohabitation is not so easy to prove. It is submitted, however, that there is no reason why there should not be a presumption of paternity in cases where a couple have made a parental responsibility agreement.

(iii) Rebutting the presumption

Standard of proof
At common law the generally accepted view was that the presumption could only be rebutted by evidence establishing beyond reasonable doubt that the husband could not be the father. However the Family Law Reform Act 1969, section 26, now states that the presumption may be rebutted upon the balance of probabilities.[11] The effect of this change is not altogether clear.[12] In *S v McC, W v W*[13] Lord Reid thought that it meant that even weak evidence must prevail if there is no other evidence to counterbalance it. On the other hand in *Serio v Serio*[14] it was held that the standard of proof required was not simply that needed in an ordinary civil action but that commensurate with the seriousness of the matter at issue. Given the certainty of their results, this difference of view will make no difference in cases where DNA tests have been carried out but in cases where such tests have not been or could not be carried out (for example where one or more of the persons concerned is dead) it could be crucial. For example, if the sole evidence is that the mother and the alleged father had made a parental responsibility agreement, that would seem to satisfy Lord Reid's test but it may not satisfy the *Serio* test.

What has to be rebutted
The husband's paternity is based on the twofold presumption that the husband and wife had sexual intercourse and that the child is the issue of the intercourse. Before the advent of blood tests it was by rebutting the former presumption (for example, by showing that, at the time when the child must have been conceived, the husband was either permanently impotent, at least quoad the wife, or temporarily impotent, whether from illness or any other cause)[15] that the husband was most likely to prove that he was not the father. However, the presumption could also be rebutted

---

[10] Ibid, at para 10.54.
[11] This implements the recommendations of the Law Commission: see Law Com No 16, Blood Tests and the Proof of Paternity in Civil Proceedings, para 15. In criminal proceedings apparently the presumption must still be rebutted by evidence placing the matter beyond reasonable doubt. Can therefore a man be convicted of incest with a girl who is presumed to be his daughter but whom he would not be compelled to maintain in civil proceedings?
[12] See Bradney *Blood Tests, Paternity and the Double Helix* [1986] Fam Law 378.
[13] [1972] AC 24, 41, [1970] 3 All ER 107, 109, HL.
[14] (1983) 4 FLR 756, 763, CA per Sir David Cairns. See also *Re JS (A Minor) (Declaration of Paternity)* [1981] Fam 22, [1980] 1 All ER 1061, CA and *W v K (Proof of Paternity)* [1988] 1 FLR 86. See further ante, p 190.
[15] *The Banbury Peerage Case* (1811) 1 Sim & St 153, HL, for a full account of which see Nicolas, op cit, 291 et seq. While impotence would generally suffice to show that he is not the father it must be remembered that the wife could have been pregnant as a result of AIH (as in *REL v EL* [1949] P 211, [1949] 1 All ER 141) or of fecundatio ab extra (as in *Clarke v Clarke* [1943] 2 All ER 540). It is submitted, however, that once it has been shown that the wife could not have conceived as a result of intercourse in the usual way, there can no longer be a presumption of paternity.

by showing that the husband could not have had intercourse with his wife because of his absence at the relevant time[16] or even by showing that intercourse was so unlikely that it can be concluded on the balance of probability that it did not take place.[17]

Once it is established that the spouses had intercourse at the relevant time the husband must show that the child is not the issue of that intercourse to rebut the presumption of paternity. This normally implies that the wife has committed adultery. It is established, however, that the fact the wife has committed adultery does not per se[18] rebut the presumption because this merely shows that the husband or the adulterer could be the father.[19] Although, as we shall see,[20] the most common way to rebut the presumption is by the use of blood tests, it is possible to do so in other ways, for example, by reference to common physical characteristics. In the past the courts were slow to admit evidence suggesting that the child had inherited some physical characteristics from a particular man and must therefore be his child and on a number of occasions excluded evidence of facial resemblance on the ground that it was too vague.[1] This is obviously a matter of degree, however; it would clearly be wrong to exclude such evidence in all cases (particularly in view of the changed standard of proof) and it was admitted in *C v C*.[2] In many cases little weight should be attached to it, but in others it should put the matter well beyond the balance of probabilities. Other evidence—for example that of race[3] or genetic characteristics[4]—is much more cogent. If both spouses are white but the child and the alleged adulterer is black, can it be doubted that the adulterer is the father?

---

[16] This would be difficult to prove in cases where the husband had been absent for a relatively short time and it is sought to show that the child must have been conceived during that period. In that situation regard is to be had to *Preston-Jones v Preston-Jones* [1951] AC 391, [1951] 1 All ER 124, HL where the husband did not have access to his wife for a period of 360 days to 186 days before the child's birth, and it was held that the evidence adduced was sufficient to rebut the presumption that he was the father.

[17] See, eg, the *Aylesford Peerage Case* (1885) 11 App Cas 1, HL; *Morris v Davies* (1837) 5 Cl & Fin 163, HL. In *Smith v May* (1969) 113 Sol Jo 1000, the presumption was rebutted even though the parties admitted sharing the same bed.

[18] Aliter if the husband can be shown to be sterile.

[19] It was formerly held that this was so even though the husband invariably used a contraceptive (*Francis v Francis* [1960] P 17, [1959] 3 All ER 206) but this might now rebut the presumption on the balance of probability if the other man did not use one. Similarly, if the presumption is raised by the wife's pregnancy at the time of the marriage, it cannot be rebutted merely by showing that she had intercourse with another man before her marriage: *Gardner v Gardner* (1877) 2 App Cas 723, HL.

[20] Post, p 270.

[1] *Slingsby v A-G* (1916) 33 TLR 120 at 122, 123, HL; *Plowes v Bossey* (1862) 31 LJ Ch 681, 683.

[2] [1972] 3 All ER 577.

[3] Such evidence was apparently admissible even before the standard of proof was changed; *Slingsby v A-G* (supra), at 122.

[4] Eg webbed toes. In some countries 'anthropological tests', as they are known, can be ordered by the courts in cases where blood tests are inconclusive. The Law Commission (Law Com No 16 *Blood Tests and the Proof of Paternity in Civil Proceedings*, para 16), however, did not recommend the introduction of such tests in England because of the then doubts about their medical validity.

(b) The use of blood and DNA tests to establish parentage[5]

(i) The nature of the tests

In cases where parentage (usually paternity) is in issue the most cogent
evidence is likely to be obtained by blood tests in general and DNA tests
in particular. Such tests may be used either to rebut the presumption or
allegation of paternity or to establish parentage.

Until DNA tests became publicly available[6] reliance was placed on blood
tests. Based on the fact that certain characteristics of a person's blood are
inherited and that if the mother's blood does not possess a characteristic
possessed by the child, he must have inherited it from the father, blood
tests could go some way in resolving issues of paternity. The great drawback
of such tests, however, is that although they can definitely show that a
man cannot be the father, they can only show with varying degrees of
probability that he is the father.[7] In contrast DNA tests (or genetic
fingerprinting as it is sometimes referred to) can, by matching the alleged
father's DNA bands with that of the child's (having excluded these bands
that match the mother's) make positive findings of paternity with virtual
certainty.[8]

Although DNA tests can be made from a variety of bodily samples
because courts are only permitted to order blood tests[9], they are commonly
made from blood samples.

(ii) The power to order blood tests

The power to order blood tests is governed by section 20 of the Family
Law Reform Act 1969.[10] This provides that any court may direct blood
tests to be used in any *civil* proceedings in which the paternity of any person
is to be determined. The purpose of the tests must be to show whether *a
party to the proceedings* is or is not the father. Consequently no order may
be made, for example, in administration proceedings if the question is
whether a claimant is the child of a deceased parent, information about
whose blood happens to be available. Similarly, there is no power to order
a test if paternity is not in issue.[11]

It is important to appreciate that section 20 does not inhibit the giving

---

[5] See generally Grubb and Pearl *Blood Testing, Aids and DNA Profiling* (1990) ch 6.

[6] 1 June 1987—cf *Re J (A Minor) (Wardship)* [1988] 1 FLR 65.

[7] Though as these tests were being perfected, the degree of probability could be very high, in
some cases over 99.8 per cent, see the scales referred to in *Armitage v Nanchen* (1983) 4
FLR 293. See also *Serio v Serio* supra.

[8] See Yaxley *Genetic Fingerprinting* [1988] Fam Law 403, Grubb and Pearl, op cit, p 161 et
seq and Bradney *Blood Tests, Paternity and the Double Helix* [1986] Fam Law 378.

[9] S 23 of the Family Law Reform Act 1987, which makes provision for 'scientific tests', has
not been implemented and is unlikely to be so; see Home Office Circular 91/1989, discussed
by Grubb and Pearl, op cit at p 173.

[10] For the common law position see *S v S; W v Official Solicitor* [1972] AC 24, [1970] 3 All
ER 107, HL, discussed in the seventh edition of this work at p 248 and the Law Commission
Report on Blood Tests and the Proof of Paternity in Civil Proceedings (1968), Law Com
No 16.

[11] See *Hodgkiss v Hodgkiss* [1985] Fam Law 87 where it was held in divorce proceedings that
there was no power to order a test to satisfy the husband's curiosity since no issue as to
paternity had been raised in the proceedings and the husband had conceded that the children
were 'children of the family'. But see the comment at [1985] Fam Law 87.

of evidence. If all the parties agree, they do not have to obtain the court's consent before having a test carried out. What the Act does is to give the court a discretion to direct a test if they do not agree. In *S v S* the House of Lords indicated that the discretion had to be judicially exercised, but they refused to lay down any guidelines. So far as blood tests of children are concerned, it is submitted that the courts should continue to follow *S v S* itself. All the members of the House were of the opinion that a test should usually be ordered; but the court has a duty to protect a child and the general rule would be displaced if the test 'would be against the child's interests'[12] if, 'having regard to the facts and circumstances of a particular case, his interests are such that their protection necessitates the withholding from a court of evidence which may be very material'[13] or if 'it would be unjust to order a test for a collateral reason to assist a litigant in his or her claim'.[14] The House of Lords refused to accept that the mere fact that a test could establish conclusively that the child was illegitimate was sufficiently against his interest to withhold consent even though, as in *W v Official Solicitor*, this would leave him with no known father at all. This danger is far outweighed by the demands of public policy that all relevant evidence should be made available. Furthermore the suppression of evidence would not encourage the mother's husband, whose suspicions would be unallayed, to accept the child as his, whereas he might be prepared to do so if a test did not exclude his paternity; and the child himself in later life might resent the fact that a full investigation was not conducted at the time. It will usually be in the child's interest—as well as in the public interest—that the truth should out,[15] and in divorce proceedings, at least, a direction is usually given.[16]

As the Court of Appeal stressed in *Re JS (A Minor)*,[17] however, a paternity issue should be pursued only if it has a material bearing on some other issue which has to be tried, and a blood test should be directed only when this condition is satisfied. In that case the mother of a child, who was admittedly illegitimate, lived with X. Either X or Y could have been the child's father. Y made the child a ward of court and sought to establish paternity in the hope of being able to see the child. The court refused to let him pursue the paternity issue because he would not be granted an order to see the child in any event and it was not in the child's interest to disturb his relationship with X.

Similarly there is little doubt that a court would refuse to direct a test if the husband sought it solely in the hope of acquiring evidence of his wife's adultery.[18]

---

[12] Per Lord Reid [1972] AC 24 at 45, [1970] 3 All ER 107 at 113.

[13] Per Lord Morris at 53 and 120, respectively.

[14] Per Lord Hodson at 58 and 124, respectively.

[15] *S v S* (supra), at 45 and 113 (per Lord Reid) 55–56 and 122 (per Lord Morris), 59 and 124, respectively (per Lord Hodson).

[16] *Practice Direction (Paternity: Guardian ad litem)* [1975] 1 All ER 223, qv for the circumstances in which a guardian ad litem should be appointed for the child.

[17] [1981] Fam 22, [1980] 1 All ER 1061, CA.

[18] See *M(D) v M(S) and G (M(DA) Intervening)* [1969] 2 All ER 243, CA. See also *Re F (Minor: Paternity Tests)* (1992) Times, 31 July, but cf *T v T* (1992) Times, 31 July, CA.

(iii) The need for consent

There is no compulsion attached to the direction. Except in the case of a person suffering from mental disorder, samples may not be taken without his consent if he is over 16 or without the consent of the person having the care and control of him if he is under that age.[19] But the court may draw such inferences as appear proper from a person's failure to give consent or to take steps to give effect to the direction, and if he is a party claiming relief in reliance on the presumption of legitimacy, the court may dismiss his claim even though there is no evidence to rebut the presumption.[20] The last provision would apply, for example, to a wife claiming maintenance for a child which she alleges is her husband's who refuses to have herself and the child tested. To bar the claimant from relief in such circumstances appears on the face of it to be reasonable: the difficulty is that an adverse inference drawn against an adult party might also be adverse to the child. It is questionable whether the Act was right to give a court power to refuse to make an order for maintenance because the mother declines to submit a blood test when it could have made submission compulsory; what one must guard against is drawing the wholly illogical conclusion that the child cannot be that of the husband.

(iv) Procedure[1]

Under section 20(1A) of the 1969 Act[2] a person applying for a direction for blood tests must specify who is to carry out the tests. This allows the applicant to choose the tester and therefore effectively the type of test.[3] This matter, however, is not entirely left in the applicant's hands because the court can decline to make the direction if it considers that it would be inappropriate to specify the person named in the application.[4]

The person responsible for carrying out the tests must make a report of the results to the court.[5] Such a request is received as evidence[6] and must be in prescribed form stating inter alia whether or not any party is excluded by the tests as being the father.[7]

3. LEGAL PROCEDURES FOR ESTABLISHING PARENTAGE

There are basically two ways in which the issue of parentage may be determined by the court. First the court may have to make a specific finding of parentage before the action may proceed. For example it is a prerequisite

---

[19] S 21. For persons suffering from mental disorder, s 21(4).
[20] S 23. For an example of a husband reasonably refusing to submit to a blood test, see *B v B and E (B Intervening)* [1969] 3 All ER 1106, CA.
[1] See generally Blood Tests (Evidence of Paternity) Regulations 1971.
[2] Added by the Children Act 1989, s 89, substituted by the Courts and Legal Services Act 1990, s 116, Sch 16, para 3.
[3] Ie, since DNA tests are more expensive, whether they are prepared to pay the higher price.
[4] S 20(1B)(b), added by the Children Act 1989, s 89, substituted by the Courts and Legal Services Act 1990, s 116, Sch 16, para 3. The chosen tester must be on the Home Secretary's approval list: Home Office Circular 91/1989.
[5] S 20(2).
[6] S 20(3). It should rarely be necessary to call persons conducting tests to give oral evidence.
[7] S 20(4).

of an application for a parental responsibility order under section 4 of the Children Act 1989[8] that the applicant is the father and if it is in dispute it will have to be proved to the court's satisfaction before the application can proceed.[9] Similarly, an application for financial relief against an unmarried father is dependent upon the respondent being the father.[10] The second procedure for establishing parentage is by means of a declaration, under section 56 of the Family Law Act 1986, which we discuss later in this chapter.[11]

4. REGISTRATION OF BIRTHS

As we have seen[12] inclusion of the father's name in the register of births is prima facie evidence of his paternity. Under the Births and Deaths Registration Act 1953, section 2, the child's married parents are obliged to register the birth within 42 days. In contrast the unmarried father has no obligation to register himself as the father and indeed does not have a general right to do so. The unmarried father's name may however be entered on the register in the following circumstances namely:[13]

(i) at the joint request of the mother and the father, in which case both must sign the register;
(ii) at the mother's request upon production of a declaration by her and the father to the effect that he is the father;
(iii) at the father's request upon production of a declaration by him and the mother to the effect that he is the father; or
(iv) at the written request of either the mother or the father upon the production of a copy of a parental responsibility agreement, a parental responsibility order or an order requiring him to make financial provision for the child.

If the child's birth has been registered with no father named, it may be re-registered showing the father's name if one of these conditions has been satisfied.[14]

5. DISCOVERING GENETIC PARENTAGE

Children may of course consult the birth register to discover who their registered parents are. In addition, following the recommendations of the Warnock Committee[15] that a child should have a right, when 18, to basic

[8] Discussed post at pp 324 et seq.
[9] See, by way of analogy, *Re O (A Minor: Access)* [1985] FLR 716.
[10] Applications for financial relief are discussed in ch 20.
[11] Post, p 284.
[12] Ante, p 271.
[13] Births and Deaths Registration Act 1953, s 10 as substituted by the Family Law Reform Act 1987, s 24 and amended by the Children Act 1989, Sch 12, para 6.
[14] Births and Deaths Registration Act 1953, s 10A, as substituted by the Family Law Reform Act 1987, s 25 and amended by the Children Act 1989, Sch 12, para 6. Re-registration can also be made following declaration of parentage: s 14(A) of the 1953 Act, added by the Family Law Reform Act 1987, s 26. It will be noted, however, that re-registration is *not* possible following the making of a s 30 order under the Human Fertilisation and Embryology Act 1990, discussed ante at p 265. Why not?
[15] Report of the Committee of Inquiry into Human Fertilisation and Embryology (1984) Cmnd 9314, para 4.21.

information about ethnic and genetic origins, section 31(4) of the Human Fertilisation and Embryology Act 1990 provides that an adult[16] having been given a suitable opportunity to receive proper counselling[17] may apply to the Human Fertilisation and Embryology Authority to give him notice stating whether or not the information contained in the Authority's register shows that but for sections 27–29 of the 1990 Act some other person would or might be his parent. If it does, the Authority must give the applicant such information as is permitted by the regulations, about the person concerned or about whether a person specified in the request as a person whom the applicant proposes to marry would or might be related.

C. The legal significance of parentage

Like a number of other legal systems, English common law refused to accept that the mere fact of parenthood gave rise to a legally recognised relationship between parent and child. Instead it chose to recognise only the legal relationship between parent and legitimate child. We will discuss the concept and significance of legitimacy when considering the child's position (see below). Suffice to say here that, although the significance of status has declined, English law continues to distinguish parents, and in particular fathers, whose children have been born in lawful wedlock from those whose children have not. Hence while all mothers automatically have parental responsibility only fathers whose children are legitimate automatically have such responsibility.[18] That, however, is not to say that parenthood per se has no legal significance. For example each parent is liable to maintain his child and an action for maintenance can be brought both under the Social Security Act 1986 and, for example, under the Children Act 1989, Schedule 1.[19] Rights of succession automatically flow from the parent-child relationship[20] as do the rules on prohibited degrees of marriage[1] and incest. All parents have a right to apply without leave for a section 8 order under the Children Act 1989[2] and there is a presumption that a child in local authority care should have reasonable contact with each parent.[3]

D. The meaning of 'child'

At common law a child attained his majority at the age of 21 but following the Latey Committee's recommendation[4] the age of majority, as enacted by section 1(1) of the Family Law Reform Act 1969, is now 18. A 'child'

[16] A person under the age of 18 has a more limited right to request information about a person he proposes to marry: ibid, s 31(6)(b) and (7).
[17] S 31(3) of the Human Fertilisation and Embryology Act 1990.
[18] Children Act 1989, s 2(1) and (2), discussed post, p 322.
[19] See ch 20.
[20] See ch 22.
[1] See ante, p 36.
[2] See post, p 358.
[3] Children Act 1989, s 34, discussed post, p 530.
[4] Committee on the Age of Majority 1967, Cmnd 3342, para 134.

(which term is now preferred to 'minor' and 'infant') may therefore be said to be a person under the age of 18.[5]

E. The child's status

1. INTRODUCTION

Most systems of jurisprudence have drawn a distinction between the legal position of a child born of a legally recognised union and that of a child born of an illicit union or as a result of a casual act of intercourse. Children born in the latter circumstances are commonly accorded an inferior legal status and have markedly less rights than those born in former circumstances. This was certainly true of the common law, which like Roman law and the modern systems based on it,[6] adhered rigidly to the rule that no child could be legitimate unless he was born or conceived in wedlock.[7] At common law an illegitimate child had no legal relationship with his father or, initially, with his mother. However, as a result of successive Acts of Parliament, the harshness of this position has now been significantly mitigated: the concept of legitimacy has been widened; children born illegitimate may now be legitimated if their parents subsequently intermarry and, most important, the legal disadvantages attached to illegitimacy have nearly all been removed.[8] As a result of these changes the question whether a child is legitimate or illegitimate has become markedly less important. Nevertheless unlike some systems such as that in New Zealand,[9] and despite the Law Commission's one time suggestion that the concept should be abolished here,[10] the basic status of legitimacy and illegitimacy remains and is to some extent still relevant in determining the legal relationship between a child and his parents.

---

[5] This is the definition of 'child' under s 105(1) of the Children Act 1989. As Cretney and Masson op cit at 463 point out, however, not all laws relating to children are linked to the age of majority. In fact there is little consistency in the age below which legislation concerning children applies. For a helpful summary see eg the Consumers Association's *Children, Parents and the Law* pp 156–161.

[6] But this was not the only criterion accepted in Western Europe. See further, Wolff *Private International Law* (2nd Edn) p 385, and the *American Restatement of the Conflict of Laws* s 137 and Comment, where it is pointed out that in some legal systems a person may be the legitimate child of one parent but not of the other.

[7] Though it has always been possible for the legislature to legitimate a person illegitimate at common law.

[8] For the drawing of an interesting parallel between the decline in importance of legitimacy and the decline of the great landed families for whom the protection of patrilineal descent was crucial, see Eekelaar *Family Security and Family Breakdown* pp 13–15.

[9] Where as a result of the Status of the Children Act 1969, s 3(1), no distinction is drawn between the status of children born to married parents and those born to unmarried parents: *Butterworth's (NZ) Family Law Guide* (2nd Edn) 6.71, and Bromley and Webb *Family Law* pp 429–439. The New Zealand enactment has served as a model for other legislation in parts of Australia and Canada: see Eekelaar *Family Law and Social Policy* (2nd Edn) p 139. Soviet law, which in 1918 abolished the distinction between legitimate and illegitimate children, nevertheless found it necessary for certain purposes in 1944 to draw a distinction between those born to parents who had registered their marriage and others: see the comments of Gsovski *Soviet Civil Law* vol 1 pp 111, 121–122. See also Butler *Soviet Law* pp 192 et seq, and Lapenna *The Illegitimate Child in Soviet Law* 25 ICLQ, 156.

[10] Law Com Working Paper No 74 Illegitimacy; see further post, p 286.

2. THE CONCEPT OF LEGITIMACY

(a) The position at common law

At common law a child is legitimate if his parents were married at the time of his conception or at the time of his birth.[11] Commonly, legitimate children are both conceived and born in wedlock but a similar status is accorded to other classes of children, namely (a) those whose parents were married when they were born even though they must have been conceived before the marriage;[12] and (b) those whose parents were married at the time of their conception, even though the marriage was terminated before their birth. Consequently, a posthumous child will be legitimate, as will be the child whose parents' marriage was terminated by divorce between the time of his conception and his birth.[13]

In the absence of authority it is thought that a child, conceived as a result of pre-marital intercourse whose parents then marry but whose father dies before his birth, is legitimate. Had the father survived, the child would certainly have been legitimate,[14] and, as we have seen, the common law does not bastardise a child merely because he is born posthumously.

It seems beyond argument that a child conceived during the marriage as a result of artificial insemination with the husband's own semen (AIH) is legitimate and, conversely, at common law, the child conceived as a result of artificial insemination by the semen of a donor other than the husband (AID), is illegitimate. What, however, is the child's status if the wife conceives by AIH after her husband's death? At common law,[15] such a child must surely be illegitimate for were the position otherwise children conceived by the parties *after* their divorce would also have to be regarded as legitimate.[16] The common law has still to determine the status of a child born to a host mother but genetically of commissioning parents.[17]

(b) Statutory changes

(i) Legitimacy of children of void marriages

Since a void marriage is a marriage neither in fact nor in law, children of such a marriage were necessarily illegitimate at common law. However following the recommendation of the Morton Commission on Marriage

---

[11] Blackstone's *Commentaries* i 446, 454–457. For a full account of the common law relating to legitimacy and a detailed examination of the cases before 1836, see Nicolas *Adulterine Bastardy*.

[12] Co Litt 244 a; Blackstone's *Commentaries* i 454. See also Nicolas, op cit, and the cases cited ante, p 270.

[13] *Knowles v Knowles* [1962] P 161, [1962] 1 All ER 659.

[14] Similarly, if the child was born to a mother who is 'brain dead' but kept alive on a life support machine until the child's birth.

[15] The common law is still relevant where the artificial insemination took place before 1 August 1991. After that the position is governed by the Human Fertilisation and Embryology Act 1990, discussed on this point, ante at p 263.

[16] See Bromley *Aided Conception: The Alternative to Adoption* in *Adoption, Essays in Social Policy, Law and Sociology* (Ed Bean) 174 at 175.

[17] Again the common law remains relevant in cases where the in vitro fertilisation took place before 1 August 1991. After that the position is governed by the Human Fertilisation and Embryology Act 1990, discussed ante, p 262.

and Divorce,[18] the law was changed by the Legitimacy Act 1959 which itself has since been replaced by the Legitimacy Act 1976. Section 1(1) now provides:[19]

'The child of a void marriage, whenever born, shall ... be treated as the legitimate child of his parents if at the time of the insemination resulting in the birth or, where there is no such insemination, the child's conception (or the time of the celebration of marriage if later) both or either of the parties reasonably believed that the marriage was valid.'

In common with other provisions relating to status, section 1(2) provides that the section only applies if the child's father was domiciled in England and Wales at the time of the child's birth or, if he died before the birth, immediately before his death.[20]

It has been held by the Court of Appeal in *Re Spence*[1] that section 1(1) does not apply to a child *born*[2] before his parents entered into a void marriage.

As originally worded, the Act seemed to lay the burden of proof upon the person asserting the legitimacy, a burden which might be difficult to discharge particularly if the issue is raised many years later. However, section 1(4) now provides[3] that, in relation to any child born on or after 4 April 1988,[4] it is to be presumed, unless the contrary is shown, that one of the parties reasonably believed, at the relevant time, that the marriage was valid. Another problem with the provision is the meaning of 'reasonably believed'. It seems to be established that this imports an objective test, that is, the belief must be one that a reasonable man would have held in the circumstances.[5] This test led to doubts whether the mistake of law would support a reasonable belief. However, following the Law Commission's recommendations[6] section 1(3)[7] now provides that such a mistake can support a reasonable belief.

(ii) Legitimacy of children of voidable marriages

At common law a decree of nullity, where the marriage was voidable, had retrospective effect and automatically bastardised the issue of the marriage.[8] When the grounds for nullity were extended by the Matrimonial Causes Act 1937, it was appreciated that this rule might work hardship in those cases where the marriage was annulled because the respondent was of

---

[18] Cmnd 9768, paras 1184–1186. This recommendation was intended to reflect the position in Scottish common law and many other jurisdictions which recognised the harshness of declaring as illegitimate children of parents whose marriage turned out to be void, at least where one, if not both, of the parents was ignorant of the invalidity.

[19] As amended by the Family Law Reform Act 1987, s 28(1).

[20] Cf the provisions relating to legitimatio per subsequens matrimonium, post, p 282.

[1] [1990] Ch 652, [1990] 2 All ER 827, CA. Douglas: 1990 2 Journal of Child Law 56 (comment on the first instance decision subsequently upheld by CA).

[2] *Aliter* if *conceived* before but born after the putative ceremony.

[3] Added by s 28(2) of the Family Law Reform Act 1987 following the Law Commission's recommendation at Law Com No 118 *Illegitimacy* at para 10.51.

[4] Ie the date on which the amendment came into force.

[5] *Hawkins v A-G* [1966] 1 All ER 392, 397. See Samuels 29 MLR and note the criticisms of this test by Bevan *Children* p 247.

[6] Law Com No 118, para 10.52.

[7] Added by the Family Law Reform Act 1987, s 28(2).

[8] See ante, at p 101.

unsound mind or epileptic or was suffering from a venereal disease in a communicable form, since the wife might conceive before the petitioner discovered the existence of the impediment. Consequently, the 1937 Act provided that in these two cases any child born of the marriage should be legitimate notwithstanding the annulment of the marriage.[9] Where the respondent was pregnant by a man other than the petitioner, the question of the legitimacy of the child did not arise, and apparently the legislature did not foresee that any child would be born if the marriage had not been consummated. Since then, however, cases concerning children born as a result of pre-marital intercourse,[10] of fecundatio ab extra[11] and of artificial insemination have come before the courts.[12]

This anomaly was removed by section 4(1) of the Law Reform (Miscellaneous Provisions) Act 1949, which provided that *any* child who would have been the legitimate child of the parties to a voidable marriage had it not been annulled should be deemed to be their legitimate child.[13] The same result is now reached by section 16 of the Matrimonial Causes Act 1973 which, by enacting that a voidable marriage shall be treated as if it had existed up to the date of the decree absolute, must necessarily preserve the legitimacy of any child born or conceived between the date of the marriage and the date of the decree as well as any child legitimated by the marriage.[14]

(iii) Legitimation

Canon law adopted the Roman law rule that a bastard would become legitimate if his parents subsequently intermarried, provided that they had been free to marry each other at the time of the child's birth. But the importance of establishing the identity of the heir at law, to whom descended the valuable private rights and important public duties of the ownership of an inheritable estate of freehold land in the Middle Ages, led the common law to reject this doctrine of legitimatio per subsequens matrimonium, and an attempt to introduce it by the Statute of Merton in 1235 was successfully resisted by the temporal peers.[15] Consequently, no form of legitimation was

---

[9] S 7(2).

[10] As in *Dredge v Dredge* [1947] 1 All ER 29.

[11] As in *Clarke v Clarke* [1943] 2 All ER 540.

[12] As in *REL v EL* [1949] P 211, [1949] 1 All ER 141.

[13] This provision, however, did not have retrospective effect. Consequently, except in those cases provided for in section 7(2) of the Matrimonial Causes Act 1937, the children of voidable marriages annulled before 16 December 1949, remain illegitimate: *Re Adams* [1951] Ch 716, [1951] 1 All ER 1037.

[14] For s 16, see ante, p 101. The section will not legitimate a child who never was legitimate (eg, because the husband was not the father): *Re Adams*, supra. Quaere whether the section operates if the parties are not domiciled in England and the decree bastardises the child by the lex domicilii. The wording suggests that it will continue to be regarded as legitimate in this country.

[15] But under the curious doctrine of bastard eigne and mulier puisne, if the parents of an illegitimate child (the bastard eigne) married and had a legitimate child (the mulier puisne) and the bastard entered on the father's freehold land after his death and himself died seised so that it descended to his (the bastard's) issue, this gave the bastard's heirs an indefeasible right to the land and the rights of the mulier puisne and all other heirs were completely barred: Jackson, *Formation and Annulment of Marriage* (2nd Edn) pp 46–48, and the authorities there cited.

recognised by English municipal law until the passing of the Legitimacy Act 1926, by which time the property legislation of 1925 had rendered it almost wholly unnecessary to establish the identity of the heir save in the case of the descent of an unbarred entailed interest.

The Legitimacy Act 1926 provided that a child should be legitimated by the subsequent marriage of his parents. But it also adopted the Canon Law rule that legitimation was impossible if either parent was married to any other person at the time of the child's birth.[16] However, a child conceived whilst one of his parents was married could still be legitimated if this marriage was terminated before his birth, and in many cases decrees of divorce were expedited for this reason. The Legitimacy Act 1959 extended these provisions to children born when either or both of their parents were married.[17] These Acts have now been repealed and their provisions re-enacted in the Legitimacy Act 1976. Section 2 provides:

> '... where the parents of an illegitimate person marry one another, the marriage shall, if the father of the illegitimate person is at the date of the marriage domiciled in England and Wales, render that person, if living, legitimate from the date of the marriage.'

A person will be legitimated by this section only if *his father* was domiciled in England and Wales *at the time of the marriage*. Legitimation does not have retrospective effect, so that no one can be legitimated unless he is still alive when his parents marry (or, if they were married before the date on which the Act by virtue of which he was legitimated came into force, on that date).[18] The fact that an adopted child is to be regarded as the child of the adoptive parent and of no other person does not prevent an illegitimate child from being legitimated if he has been adopted *solely* by one of his parents who then marries the other parent.[19]

3. DECLARATIONS OF PARENTAGE AND STATUS[20]

The question of a child's status may be put in issue in a number of ways, for example, if he claims an interest in property or if in divorce proceedings the husband relies upon the fact of his birth as evidence of his mother's adultery. Normally, however, any judicial decision will be a judgment in personam and consequently will bind only the parties to it and their privies, that is, persons claiming through them. The desirability of some sort of procedure to enable a disputed question of legitimacy to be settled once for all led to the passing of the Legitimacy Declaration Act 1858, which was repealed and substantially re-enacted in the Matrimonial Causes Act 1973, section 45. Under section 45, any person could petition for a decree that he was legitimate or that he or his parents or grandparents were validly

[16] S 1(2).
[17] S 1.
[18] Legitimacy Act 1926, s 1(1); Legitimacy Act 1959, s 1(2); Legitimacy Act 1976, Sch 1, para 1. But if the parents had married before the relevant Act came into force, the children could be legitimated on that date, even though one or both *parents* had already died: *Re Lowe* [1929] 2 Ch 210.
[19] Legitimacy Act 1976, s 4. For the effect of adoption, see post, pp 455–456.
[20] For declarations in other family matters, see ante, pp 70–71.

married. But a petitioner could not obtain a declaration of legitimacy of anyone other than himself,[1] nor was there any power to declare anyone illegitimate[2] or to make a declaration of paternity of any illegitimate child.[3]

Following a review by the Law Commission,[4] particularly in the light of changes in the law relating to legitimacy, section 45 was repealed and replaced by fresh provisions in the Family Law Act 1986 and amended by the Family Law Reform Act 1987.

Under section 56 of the 1986[5] Act the following declarations may be sought: (1) that the person named in the application is the father or the mother, or that particular persons are the parents of the applicant; (2) that the applicant is the legitimate child of his parents; and (3) that the applicant has become or has not become a legitimated person. Such applications can be made either in the High Court or county court.[6]

It will be noted that unlike the old law an *unmarried* person can be declared to be a parent but it remains the case that it is not possible to obtain a declaration of illegitimacy.[7] Furthermore, as before, an applicant can only seek a declaration about his own status and not that of anyone else (though in determining his own status the marital status of the alleged parents[8] may also be put in issue).

These provisions are subject to a number of safeguards, reflecting the Law Commission's concern that bare declarations could be abused. Hence, as before, no application can be made unless the applicant is domiciled or has been habitually resident for one year in England and Wales at the date of the application.[9] There is power, at any stage of the proceedings, to send the papers to the Attorney-General and, whether or not such papers are sent, the Attorney-General can intervene in the proceedings.[10]

Where the truth of the proposition to be declared has been proved to the court's satisfaction, the court shall make that declaration 'unless to do so would be manifestly contrary to public policy'.[11] If a declaration is made, it is binding upon the Crown and all other persons,[12] and the Registrar General will be informed.[13] If the declaration is refused, the court cannot grant a declaration that has not been applied for.[14]

[1] *Aldrich v A-G* [1968] P 281, [1968] 1 All ER 345.
[2] *B v A-G* [1966] 2 All ER 145n.
[3] *Re JS* [1981] Fam 22, [1980] 1 All ER 1061, CA.
[4] See Law Com No 118, paras 10.1–10.27 and Law Com No 132, *Declarations in Family Matters*, paras 3.9–3.14.
[5] As substituted by the Family Law Reform Act 1987, s 22.
[6] Family Law Act 1986, s 63. The procedure is governed by Family Proceedings Rules 1991, r 3.13 for declarations of parentage and r 3.14 for declarations of legitimacy and legitimation.
[7] Ibid, s 58(5)(b).
[8] But not grandparents, as previously.
[9] Family Law Act 1986, s 56(4).
[10] Ibid, s 59.
[11] S 58(1). This proviso seems to put into statutory form the power exercised in *Puttick v A-G* [1980] Fam 1, [1979] 3 All ER 463; see ante, pp 70–71.
[12] S 58(2).
[13] S 56(5) as added by the Family Law Reform Act 1987.
[14] S 58(3).

4. THE SIGNIFICANCE OF THE CHILD'S STATUS

At common law the illegitimate child being filius nullius had no legal relationship with (originally) either of his parents and consequently had no rights, for example, to receive maintenance,[15] to succeed to their property or to other benefits normally accruing from the relationship of parent and child. Many of these disabilities subsisted until well after the Second World War but more recently have been whittled away. For example, following the reforms of the Family Law Reform Acts of 1969 and 1987 children whose parents are not married now have full rights of intestate succession.[16] They can also succeed as an heir to an entailed estate.[17] Such children can now make claims as dependants both under the Inheritance (Provision for Family and Dependants) Act 1975 and the Fatal Accidents legislation.[18] Substantial improvements have been made to the right of support. Indeed under the Children Act 1989, Schedule 1 either parent can be ordered to pay to the other or to the child secured or unsecured periodic payments, lump sum payments or make property transfers.[19]

Despite these important changes it cannot yet be said that children whose parents are unmarried are in exactly the same legal position as those whose parents are married. There remain two areas of discrimination, namely with regard to citizenship and succession to a title of honour. For the purposes of claiming citizenship an illegitimate child is regarded as the child of his mother and not his father.[1] Although the Law Commission could see no reason in principle why this rule should not be changed, they felt unable to make definite proposals since, being a United Kingdom matter, it was outside their terms of reference.[2] It is however, surely a matter of regret that the government felt unable to change the rule. As one commentator has pointed out,[3] with the advent of DNA fingerprinting by which it has become significantly easier to establish parentage, it is now particularly hard to justify the retention of this discriminatory rule.

With regard to titles of honour, section 19(4) of the 1987 Act makes it clear that despite the new construction of the term 'heir' children of unmarried parents will not be able to succeed to property which is limited to devolve along with a dignity or title of honour. However, this should not be read as meaning that such children will never be able to succeed since that will depend upon the terms of the letters patent issued under the

---

[15] But see Cretney: *Principles of Family Law* (4th Edn) p 594.
[16] Post, pp 646 et seq.
[17] Family Law Reform Act 1987, s 19(2); discussed post, p 646.
[18] Fatal Accidents Act 1976 as substituted by the Administration of Justice Act 1982: discussed ante at p 124.
[19] Discussed post at pp 696–697.
[1] British Nationality Act 1981, s 50(9). See further ante, pp 140–142.
[2] See Law Com No 118 para 11.9. The Scottish Law Commission came to a similar conclusion: see Scot Law Com No 82, paras 8.3–8.5.
[3] Cretney [1987] Fam Law 404.

Great Seal. At the moment they are in a form[4] which limits succession to the 'heirs ... of his body lawfully begotten' which is enough to show a contrary intention against devolvement to children whose parents are unmarried. However, if in the future the form 'to X and the heirs of his body' were used then any child could succeed under the terms of section 19(2).

Apart from these two substantive differences there is also the important distinction that whereas parties seeking a divorce must necessarily have their plans for their child's future scrutinised by the court,[5] there is no similar compulsion in cases where unmarried parents separate.

With regard to a *legitimated* child it is expressly provided that such a person shall have the same rights and obligations in respect of the maintenance and support of himself and other persons as if he had been born legitimate, and any legal claim for damages, compensation, allowances, etc, by or in respect of a legitimate child shall apply in the case of one legitimated.[6] Similarly, for the purpose of determining whether he is a British citizen he is to be treated as being born legitimate as from the date of his parents' marriage and is able to claim through his father or his mother.[7] Subject to what is said later with respect to rights in property[8] a legitimated person is in the same position as if he had been born legitimate. On the other hand a legitimated person is not entitled to succeed to a title of honour.[9]

5. SHOULD REFERENCE NOW BE MADE TO LEGITIMACY AND ILLEGITIMACY?

(a) Background to the Family Law Reform Act 1987

At one time the Law Commission favoured the radical plan that the status of illegitimacy should be abolished altogether.[10] They argued that since the label was itself discriminatory, true equality demanded not simply the removal of the remaining areas of legal discrimination but the abolition of the very status. Indeed so strongly were they committed to this view, that they were prepared to countenance the necessary corollary of their recommendations that all fathers should be treated equally. The overwhelming response, however, was against giving all fathers automatic rights[11] and accordingly, in their full report on Illegitimacy,[12] the Law Commission did not advocate abolition of status but recommended instead a change in terminology with the terms 'marital' and 'non marital' replacing so far as possible 'legitimate' and 'illegitimate'.

[4] See the discussion in Law Com No 118, at para 8.26.
[5] Under s 41 of the Matrimonial Causes Act 1973, discussed post, p 366.
[6] Legitimacy Act 1976, s 8.
[7] British Nationality Act 1981, s 47(1).
[8] See post, pp 646 and 818–820.
[9] Legitimacy Act 1976, Sch 1, para 4(2). A similar disability attaches to children who are treated in law as the child of both the mother and her husband in cases where the child had been carried by a woman as a result of the placing in her of an embryo or of sperm and eggs or her artificial insemination.
[10] For a convincing argument against giving all fathers automatic rights see Hayes (1980) 43 MLR 299, though Eekelaar *Second Thoughts on Illegitimacy Reform* [1985] Fam Law 261 argued that the status could have been abolished without giving all fathers equal rights.
[11] See their Working Paper No 74 on Illegitimacy published in 1979.
[12] Law Com No 118 (1982), particularly at Part IV.

Before these recommendations were acted upon, the issue was examined by the Scottish Law Commission.[13] They observed[14] that 'so long as marriage exists and children are born there will be children born out of marriage. In some cases of children born out of marriage, the parents will marry each other after the birth: in others they will not. These are facts and, short of abolishing marriage, there is nothing the law can do about them.' Like the English Law Commission they did not recommend abolishing the status of illegitimacy, but unlike that body the Scots could see no merit in introducing the new terms 'marital' and 'non marital'. As they said[15] that 'was just another way of labelling children, and experience in other areas, such as mental illness, suggests that new labels can rapidly take on old connotations'. They concluded that they did not wish to see 'a discriminatory concept of "non-maritality" gradually replace a discriminatory concept of "illegitimacy"'. Accordingly they recommended that the terms 'legitimate' and 'illegitimate' as applied to people, should wherever possible cease to be used in legislation. To achieve this, they recommended that, where distinctions based on marriage were necessary, future legislation should distinguish between fathers rather than children. Where it was thought necessary to distinguish people on the basis of whether or not their parents were married to each other at any relevant time (which they hoped would be a 'very rare exception') it should be done expressly in those terms. The Scottish Law Commission's proposals were enacted in the Law Reform (Parent and Child) (Scotland) Act 1986.

Following these developments, the English Law Commission reconsidered its proposals and in a second report, published in October 1986,[16] advocated reform along the Scottish lines. Their recommendations were enacted by the Family Law Reform Act 1987.

(b) The Family Law Reform Act 1987

Apart from making important changes to the status of some children born as a result of AID and amending the provision dealing with children of void marriages, the 1987 Act has left untouched the basic concept of legitimacy. However, implementing the strategy of reducing the need to refer to the concept, in cases where it is still necessary to distinguish between children born within marriage and those born without, the Act has introduced the important change that reference be made to the parents, rather than to the children, and whether or not they are married to each other. This general approach is set out by section 1 of the 1987 Act.

Section 1(1) provides that references in the 1987 Act and any succeeding Act or statutory instrument to 'mothers' or 'fathers' or 'parents' refers, unless the contrary intention appears, to all such persons regardless of whether they have or had been married to each other at any time. The clarity of this opening provision is immediately obscured by definitional provisions designed to distinguish (in simple terms) parents (primarily fathers) of legitimate from those of illegitimate children. To avoid using the words 'legitimate' or 'illegitimate', section 1(2) refers instead to a person

[13] Scot Law Com No 82 (1984).
[14] Ibid, at para 9.1.
[15] Ibid, at para 9.2.
[16] Law Com No 157.

whose parents were not married to each other at the time of the child's birth. However, it was recognised that this shorthand definition was insufficient by itself because a child can be legitimate even though his parents were not married at the time of his birth. Accordingly section 1(2) is made subject to section 1(3) so that references to 'a person whose father and mother were not married to each other at the time of the child's birth'[17] do not include (and correspondingly, references to a person whose parents were married to each other at the time of his birth do include) cases where the child is (a) rendered legitimate by section 1 of the Legitimacy Act 1976 even though his parents' marriage is void, (b) legitimated by reason of his parents' subsequent marriage, (c) adopted and (d) 'otherwise treated in law as legitimate'.[18] For example, as will be seen,[19] section 2(1) of the Children Act 1989 states that: 'where a child's father and mother were married to each other at the time of his birth, they shall each have parental responsibility for the child' whereas according to section 2(2) if they were not so married then only the mother and not the father has such responsibility. The unsuspecting reader might think that these provisions mean what they say and conclude that parental responsibility is only automatically vested in a father if he is married to the mother at the time of the child's birth. In fact, however, he will also have responsibility if for example he subsequently marries the mother or conversely if he had divorced his wife at the time of the child's birth.

Whether the law needed to have been so complex is debatable.[20] It might have been less confusing, for example, simply to have referred to the *parents* being legitimate or illegitimate. Despite its resulting complexity, in deference to the clear spirit of the 1987 Act, we shall avoid, where possible, labelling children and as a matter of shorthand convenience will refer to mothers or fathers as 'unmarried' when referring to parents of a child whose mother and father are not and have not been married to each other.

F. The changing nature of the parent-child relationship

1. INTRODUCTION

Like society's views about the role of the family and of the individual members within the unit, the legal attitude towards the parent-child relationship has not remained static. The principle catalyst for legal change in the past has been the rise of individualism, first with respect to women and

---

[17] By s 1(4) a child's birth is to be taken to include the period beginning with insemination resulting in his birth or, where there was no such insemination, his conception, and ends with his birth.

[18] This covers the case, for example, where the child is conceived through the placing in the woman of an embryo or sperm and eggs or of her artificial insemination and born to a married woman and who therefore, by virtue of ss 27–29 of the Human Fertilisation and Embryology Act 1990, is treated in law as being the child of the woman and her husband.

[19] Post, p 322.

[20] See eg Lowe *The Family Reform Act 1987—Useful Reform but an Unhappy Compromise?* (1988) Denning LJ 77.

then, perhaps even more important, with respect to children.[1] With regard to the former, the growing calls for women's rights during the nineteenth century led in the end to the fundamental change that, whereas formerly parental rights were vested in the father (at any rate in respect of legitimate children) they are now shared between the father and the mother. The growing acceptance that a child is a person in his own right[2] led first to concern about his welfare and protection and, more recently, to the recognition that in limited circumstances at least, he might have rights of his own. This in turn has led to a fundamental change in the nature of parental authority. In the past it was accurate to think of the parental position in terms of rights and duties, for at common law fathers had almost complete autonomy over their legitimate children and their interest was akin to a proprietorial one;[3] by the 1980s, however, the emphasis had clearly shifted towards parental responsibility,[4] which position is now firmly entrenched in the Children Act 1989.[5]

2. THE INITIAL STRENGTH OF THE FATHER'S POSITION WITH RESPECT TO LEGITIMATE CHILDREN

Common law recognised the natural duties of protecting and maintaining one's legitimate minor children, and although the machinery for enforcing these duties was almost wholly ineffective, nevertheless they could properly be regarded as unenforceable legal obligations.[6] Moreover, it is obvious that, at any rate in early law, these duties could be performed only if the parent actually had the custody of the child, and in many cases the father would be the only member of the family who would be physically capable of carrying them out. Consequently it is not surprising to discover that his duty to protect carried with it the correlative right to the custody of all minor children and that this right was absolute even against the mother except in the rare cases where the father's conduct was such as gravely to imperil the children's life, health or morals. Custody carried with it many rights and powers in addition to care and control. A father was entitled to the services of his children in his custody and to correct them by administering reasonable corporal punishment. He alone might determine the form of their religious and secular education. Whilst his powers were never as wide as those of the paterfamilias in Roman law, the same fundamental approach

[1] The legal and social background to these developments is well summarised by Maidment *Child Custody and Divorce* chs 4 and 5.

[2] There are those who maintain that until the seventeenth century the concept of childhood did not exist: see eg Aries *Centuries of Childhood*, though this view has not escaped criticism. See the references in Maidment, op cit, at 91–92.

[3] See further below. Ironically the common law has not been entirely immutable: see, for instance, *R v D* [1984] AC 778, [1984] 2 All ER 449, HL, where, in holding that even a father could be guilty of the common law offence of kidnapping his own child, Lord Brandon said (at pp 805 and 456 respectively): 'The common law, however, while generally immutable in its principles ... is not immutable in the way it adapts those principles in a radically changing world and against the background of radically changed social conventions and conditions.'

[4] See eg Woolf J in *Gillick v West Norfolk and Wisbech Area Health Authority* [1984] QB 581, 596, [1984] 1 All ER 365, 373, who said that the interests of parents are more accurately described as responsibilities and duties.

[5] See ch 9.

[6] For a more detailed account see *A Century of Family Law* (eds Graveson and Crane) ch 4 'Parental Control and Guardianship' by Pettit.

is apparent. Physical control represented the kernel of this rights; without it the others could not be enforced, and the procedural machinery of the common law was such that only his right could be specifically enforced by the writ of habeas corpus.

At common law, therefore the father was entitled to the legal custody of his legitimate children until they reached the age of 21,[7] but his rights could be lost, if to enforce them would probably lead to the physical or moral harm of the child[8] or if his claim was not made bona fide.[9] After his death, the mother was entitled to the legal custody of her minor children for nurture,[10] but even this right was superseded after 1660 if the father appointed a testamentary guardian under the provisions of the Tenures Abolition Act.[11] Common law accorded no other right to the mother as such, and so absolute against her were the father's rights that he could lawfully claim from her possession even of a child at the breast.[12]

The common law position was tempered by the intervention of equity. The jurisdiction of equity to intervene between parent and child is derived from the prerogative power of the Crown as parens patriae to interfere to protect any person within the jurisdiction not fully sui juris. This power was naturally exercised by the Lord Chancellor, and although it fell into abeyance when the Court of Wards was set up in 1540, successive Chancellors began to use their powers more and more extensively when this court was abolished in 1660.[13] From the Court of Chancery the jurisdiction passed to the High Court under the Judicature Acts of 1873 and 1875.

One advantage that equity had over the common law was that its procedure was much better adapted to deal with disputes concerning children. Common law, limited as it was to the issue of a writ of habeas corpus, could only enforce the right to physical control; equity, on the other hand, acts in personam, so that it could not only make orders concerning, for example, the child's education, but also effectively ensure that they were carried out. A further step that could be taken was to have the child made a ward of court. This procedure had a number of advantages. Not only could the person to whom care and control was given always turn to the court for advice, but the ward remained under the permanent control of the court during minority, so that any dereliction of duty on the part of the former and any interference with the latter were punishable as a contempt of court. Furthermore, the court could give care and control of the child to his own parent, which meant that the child would remain in the latter's possession whilst the court could ensure that the parental powers were exercised in his best interests.

At first the intervention of equity scarcely had any impact upon the father's position. It left untouched the common law duties of a parent and indeed gave prima facie effect to the father's right to custody of his legitimate

---

[7] *Thomasset v Thomasset* [1894] P 295, CA; *Re Agar-Ellis* (1883) 24 Ch D 317, CA.
[8] Eg apprehension of cruelty or grossly immoral or profligate conduct: *Re Andrews* (1873) LR 8 QB 153, 158.
[9] Eg, if his purpose was to hand the child over to another: cf *Re Turner* (1872) 41 LJQB 142.
[10] *R v Clarke* (1857) 7 E & B 186, 200.
[11] See the seventh edition of this work at p 350.
[12] *R v De Manneville* (1804) 5 East 221.
[13] Holdsworth *History of English Law*, vi 648. The Court of Wards was set up by the 32 Hen 8, c 46, and abolished by the Tenures Abolition Act 1660.

children unless he had forfeited them by his immoral or cruel conduct or was seeking to enforce them capriciously or arbitrarily. As Cotton LJ said in *Re Agar-Ellis*:[14]

'This court holds this principle—that when, by birth, a child is subject to a father, it is for the general interest of families, and for the general interest of children, and really for the interest of the particular infant, that the Court should not, except in very extreme cases, interfere with the discretion of the father, but leave to him the responsibility of exercising that power which nature has given him by the birth of the child.'

On the other hand there was a growing view, which ultimately prevailed, that the welfare of the child was the first consideration and equity would not hesitate to deprive a father of his rights if it would clearly be contrary to the child's interests to give effect to them. In the words of Lord Esher MR in *R v Gyngall*:[15]

'The court is placed in a position by reason of the prerogative of the Crown to act as supreme parent of the child, and must exercise that jurisdiction in the manner in which a wise, affectionate, and careful parent would act for the welfare of the child. The natural parent in the particular case may be affectionate, and may be intending to act for the child's good, but may be unwise, and may not be doing what a wise, affectionate, and careful parent would do. The Court may say in such a case that, although they can find no misconduct on the part of the parent, they will not permit that to be done with the child which a wise, affectionate, and careful parent would not do. The court must, of course, be very cautious in regard to the circumstances under which they will interfere with the parental right... The court must exercise this jurisdiction with great care, and can only act when it is shown that either the conduct of the parent, or the description of the person he is, or the position in which he is placed, is such as to render it not merely better, but—I will not say 'essential', but—clearly right for the welfare of the child in some very serious and important respect that the parent's rights should be suspended or superseded; but ... where it is so shown, the Court will exercise its jurisdiction accordingly.'

Hence, although originally equity interfered with the father's rights hardly less readily than the common law, by the end of the nineteenth century it would do so if there was any threat of physical or moral harm to the child; and if a father once abandoned or abdicated his right, he would not be allowed to reassert it arbitrarily if this would be contrary to the child's interests.[16]

As in other fields, equity ensured that where its own rules were in conflict with those of common law, the former should prevail. It would not only grant an injunction to restrain a person from applying for a writ of habeas corpus to obtain the custody of a child[17] but would also prevent a person who had already obtained the writ from interfering with the child if this was not in his interests.[18] As in the case of other conflicts between law and equity, the Judicature Act of 1873 expressly provided that the rules of equity relating to the custody and education of minors should prevail over

---

[14] (1883) 24 Ch D 317, 334, CA.
[15] [1893] 2 QB 232, 241–242, CA. See also *Re O'Hara* [1900] 2 IR 232, CA; *Official Solicitor v K* [1965] AC 201, [1963] 3 All ER 191, HL.
[16] See *Re O'Hara* [1900] 2 IR 232, 240–241; *Re Fynn* (1848) 2 De G & Sm 457, 474–475.
[17] Per Lindley LJ in *R v Barnado, Jones's Case* [1891] 1 QB 194, 210, CA.
[18] *Andrews v Salt* (1873) 8 Ch App 622.

those of common law.[19] But even before this the common law courts recognised the superiority of the jurisdiction of the Court of Chancery to this extent, that, if proceedings were pending in the latter court, an application for habeas corpus would be stayed until the decision of Chancery was known.[20] Since the rules of equity are now bound to prevail, the circumstances in which common law would refuse a father custody are now of historical interest only.

3. THE POSITION WITH REGARD TO ILLEGITIMATE CHILDREN

At common law a bastard was filius nullius and consequently none of the legal powers or duties which flowed from the relationship of parent and legitimate child was accorded him or his parents.[1] This meant, inter alia, that the father could not claim custody.[2] Eventually it became accepted that the right of control vested in the mother.

Although as we have seen,[3] most of the legal disabilities attached to illegitimacy have now been removed by statute, it remains the case that unless he subsequently acquires it by order or by agreement, parental responsibility is vested in the mother to the exclusion of the father even though the latter's paternity is not in doubt.[4]

4. THE STRENGTHENING OF THE MOTHER'S POSITION

The inevitable corollary of the strength of the father's position was the weakness of the mother's in respect of legitimate children. However, during the nineteenth century Parliament intervened in a series of statutes, the effect of which was to whittle down the father's rights further and also to give the mother positive rights to custody which even equity did not accord to her. The history of this change in attitude can best be seen by a brief examination of the principal provisions of each statute.

(a) Talfourd's Act 1839

This Act marks a decisive point in the history of family law for it empowered the Court of Chancery to give the mother custody of her children until they reached the age of seven and access to them until they came of age. But the Act specifically provided that no order was to be made if the mother had been guilty of adultery.

(b) Custody of Infants Act 1873

This extended the principle of Talfourd's Act by empowering the court to give the mother custody until the child reached the age of 16. It did not, however, repeat the proviso relating to her adultery. Section 2 introduced

---

[19] See now the Supreme Court Act 1981, s 49.
[20] *Wellesley v Duke of Beaufort* (1827) 2 Russ 1, 25–26; *R v Isley* (1836) 5 Ad & El 441.
[1] Blackstone *Commentaries* i, 458–459.
[2] See eg *R v Moses Soper* (1793) 5 Term Rep 278.
[3] Ante, p 285.
[4] See now the Children Act 1989, s 2(1) and (2), discussed post, p 322.

a further reform, which had long been overdue, by enacting that arrangements as to custody or control in separation deeds (which had formerly been void as contrary to public policy) should be enforceable so long as they were for the child's benefit.

(c) Guardianship of Infants Act 1886

It will be noted that neither of these two Acts gave mothers rights as such, but were concerned to extend the court's discretion to grant orders in the mother's favour. However, a third Act, the Guardianship of Infants Act 1886, not only extended judicial discretion by empowering the court to give the mother custody of her children until they reached the age of 21, but also stopped the father from defeating the mother's right after his death by appointing a testamentary guardian and enacted that the mother was to act jointly with any guardian so appointed. Furthermore, for the first time it gave limited powers to a mother to appoint testamentary guardians.

(d) Twentieth century developments

Although, as we shall see, the move to establish maternal rights proved to be of passing significance, with attention becoming more focussed on the child's welfare, the process of equalising parental rights continued in the present century. The Guardianship of Infants Act 1925 provided that in any proceedings before any court[5] neither the father nor the mother should be regarded as having a claim superior to the other in respect of the custody or upbringing of the child. It also gave the mother the same right to appoint testamentary guardians as the father. The Guardianship Act 1973 gave each parent (of a legitimate child) equal and separately exercisable rights. Finally, with the abolition of the archaic rule that during his lifetime the father was the *sole* guardian of his legitimate child by section 2(4) of the Children Act 1989, it can now be said that the legal position of married parents with respect to their child are equal.

G. Do children have independent rights?

1. THE EVOLUTION AND DEVELOPMENT OF THE WELFARE PRINCIPLE[6]

A striking feature of the early law was its apparent lack of concern for the child. By the end of the last century, however, there seemed to be a growing awareness of the child's welfare, possibly triggered by the movement in the mid-nineteenth century that children should have a right to basic education and the general rise of individualism. For example, under the Custody of Infants Act 1873 parental agreements about custody could not be enforced if the court did not think that it was for the child's benefit. Further, the

---

[5] Jurisdiction to make orders relating to custody etc which had formerly been exercisable only by the High Court and (since 1886) by county courts was extended (subject to certain exceptions) to magistrates' courts.
[6] See generally Maidment *Child Custody and Divorce* ch 4. See also Hall *The Waning of Parental Rights* [1972B] CLJ 248.

Guardianship of Infants Act 1886 directed the court to have regard to the child's welfare as well as to the conduct and wishes of the parents, when deciding custody applications. The most obviously child-centred statute was the Custody of Children Act 1891 which was passed as the direct result of a number of cases in which parents had succeeded in recovering from Dr Barnardo children whom they had placed in his now famous 'homes' or whom they had abandoned and he had taken in. It provided that if a parent had abandoned or deserted his child or allowed him to be brought up by, and at the expense of, another person, school, institution or local authority, in such circumstances as to show that he was unmindful of his parental duties, he had to prove that he was fit to have custody of the child claimed.

The more enduring development, however, was judicially inspired. We have already noted[7] equity's changing attitude during the last century, beginning with a marked reluctance to interfere with a father's right to custody and ending with its increasing readiness to interfere if it was in the child's interests to do so.[8] It is evident that during the early part of this century still more weight was being placed upon the child's welfare. Some argue, and indeed it has been judicially stated,[9] that by 1925 the Chancery Division already regarded the child's welfare as the paramount consideration. Whether the courts consistently applied such a test may be doubted but at any rate, as one commentator said,[10] by 1925 'the tide was flowing strongly in favour of the welfare of the child as the predominating consideration'. In any event the Guardianship of Infants Act 1925 provided, inter alia, that in deciding issues concerning the custody or upbringing of a child all courts were to regard the child's welfare as the *first and paramount consideration*. The striking difference between this Act and that of 1886 with regard to the weight to be placed on the child's welfare is evidence of quite a remarkable change of thought within a short period. Whether the 1925 Act was intended to do anything more than further the process of equalising parental rights whilst at the same time extending the courts' discretionary power to override the absolute rights of the father in custody cases is perhaps debatable.[11]

Nevertheless the lasting effect has proved to be the unequivocal establishment of the paramountcy of the child's welfare which now forms the cornerstone of the current law when dealing with the upbringing of children. The paramountcy principle was re-enacted in the Guardianship of Minors Act 1971. It is now embodied in section 1(1) in Children Act 1989.[12]

2. CHILDREN'S ABILITY TO MAKE DECISIONS FOR THEMSELVES

As we shall see, the application of the welfare principle effectively overrides any other person's rights in respect of the child once the issue comes before

[7] Ante, p 291.
[8] Maidment, op cit, at pp 99–100 argues that this readiness was promoted by the provisions of the Guardianship of Infants Act 1886.
[9] By Lord Guest in *J v C* [1970] AC 668, 697, [1969] 1 All ER 788, 809, HL.
[10] Hall, op cit, at p 248.
[11] In *A v Liverpool City Council* [1982] AC 363, 371, [1981] 2 All ER 385, 387, HL, Lord Wilberforce described the provision as a 'sex equality' enactment.
[12] Discussed in ch 10.

the court.[13] This obviously dilutes parental authority but it does not in itself give a child rights as such.[14] Indeed until the issue comes before the court, parents still generally have considerable authority over their children. It is in this latter respect that the decision in *Gillick v West Norfolk and Wisbech Area Health Authority*[15] is important. That case concerned a Government Circular in which doctors were advised that in 'most unusual circumstances' it would be proper for them to give contraceptive advice and treatment to a girl under the age of sixteen without her parents' knowledge or consent. The applicant sought a declaration that this was unlawful because it infringed her parental *right* to be informed and to veto any medical treatment of her children at any rate until they were sixteen.[16]

Mrs Gillick's action failed and her contention about parental rights was rejected. The majority view was that parental authority exists for the benefit of the child and not for the parent. It therefore lasts only as long as a child needs protection. It will end therefore when the child is sufficiently mature to make the decision for himself. As Lord Scarman put it:

> 'The underlying principle of the law ... is that parental right yields to the child's right to make his own decisions when he reaches a sufficient understanding and intelligence to be capable of making up his own mind on the matter requiring decisions.'

Although the *Gillick* decision can simply be seen as a further (albeit important) example of the diminution of parental authority in the eyes of English law, potentially it is of much greater significance. In apparently[17] establishing that parental authority ends in respect of any decision that the child is mature and intelligent enough to decide for himself, it seems to acknowledge that the child himself has the power to make his own decisions. If this is how the decision will be interpreted[18] then it might fairly be described as a landmark of children's rights.[19]

The early indicators are however that *Gillick* might be interpreted narrowly. In *Re R (A Minor) (Wardship: Medical Treatment)*[20] Lord Donaldson MR did not consider that it established that 'Gillick competent' children (as he referred to children competent to make informal decisions) had a right to veto medical treatment.

It has also been commented,[1] however, that despite Lord Mackay LC's assertion that the Children Act 1989 does nothing to change the underlying principle of the *Gillick* decision, essentially the Act takes a narrow view of

---

[13] Post, pp 340–342.

[14] On the question of whether children should be given rights, see Freeman *The Rights and Wrongs of Children*, particularly ch 2. See also Justice *Parental Rights & Duties and Custody Suits* which suggested that a Children's Ombudsman should be created.

[15] [1986] AC 112, [1985] 3 All ER 402, HL, discussed further post, pp 306 et seq.

[16] Ie until s 8 of the Family Law Reform Act 1969, discussed post, p 306, gave them a right to consent for themselves.

[17] But note the reservation expressed by Eekelaar at 102 LQR 4, 7.

[18] But see Bainham *The Balance of Power in Family Decisions* [1986] CLJ 262, 273 who argues that the decision stops well short of recognising general rights of young people to make major decisions for themselves. See also Eekelaar: 'The Emergence of Children's Rights' [1986] 6 OJLS 161.

[19] See, for example, the discussion by Cretney *All ER Annual Review 1985*, 184 and by Lowe and White *Wards of Court* (2nd Edn) at 12–16.

[20] [1992] Fam 11, [1991] 4 All ER 177, CA, Douglas (1992) 55 MLR 569. See also *Re J (A Minor) (Inherent Jurisdiction: Consent to Treatment)* (1992) Times, 15 July, CA. Discussed post, pp 308–309.

[1] Cretney and Masson, op cit, at p 475.

the decision. Hence mature children may make some decisions which are essentially personal (for example, to veto a medical examination and assessment), but where others are involved the decision is left to the carers whose action may be controlled by the courts. In any event even if the *Gillick* decision were to be interpreted widely, in practice the central issue will be whether the child is mature enough to take the decision in question. This is bound to place third parties in a difficult position. However, it seems unlikely that a judge would accept that a child is mature if the latter is advocating a course of action that the judge considers harmful to the child. These two considerations are likely to limit the practical effects of the decision in *Gillick's* case.

Chapter 9

Parental responsibility

A. Introduction

1. THE LAW COMMISSION'S PROPOSALS

As we saw in chapter 8 over the last 150 years the legal attitude towards the parent-child relationship has undergone profound change. Originally, emphasis was placed on father's rights. Then, for a short period attention was paid to improving the mother's position. Finally, the position was reached where the primary focus was on the child. Despite these important developments, before the Children Act 1989 statutes still referred to 'parental rights and duties' or 'parental powers and duties' or the 'rights and authority' of a parent. Not only were these terms inconsistent with one another but as the Law Commission had earlier commented:[1] 'It can be cogently argued that to talk of "parental rights" is not only inaccurate as a matter of juristic analysis but also a misleading use of ordinary language'. In their Report on Guardianship and Custody[2] the Commission was concerned that because of the continued use of such terms the law did not adequately recognise that parenthood is a matter of responsibility rather than of rights. Accordingly they recommended the introduction of the concept of 'parental responsibility' to replace all the ambiguous and misleading terms previously employed in statutes. In the Commission's view, 'responsibility' 'would reflect the everyday reality of being a parent and emphasise the responsibility of all who are in that position.'[3]

The government accepted the Commission's recommendation and 'parental responsibility' has now become a pivotal concept of the 1989 Act.

2. THE DUAL MEANING OF RESPONSIBILITY

As one leading commentator has observed,[4] parental responsibility can represent two ideas: one, that parents must behave dutifully towards their children; the other, that responsibility for child care belongs to parents, not the state. Both these ideas are important and both are embodied in the Act. The former idea is well summed up first by Lord Mackay LC, who said[5] when introducing the Bill, the concept of 'parental responsibility':

'emphasises that the days when a child should be regarded as a possession of his

[1] Law Com No 118, *Illegitimacy*, 1982, para 4.18.
[2] Law Com No 172, 1988.
[3] Ibid at para 2.4.
[4] Eekelaar 'Parental responsibility: State of Nature or Nature of the State?' [1991] JSW & FL 37.
[5] 502 HL Official Report (5th series) col 490.

parents, indeed when in the past they had a right to his services and to sue on their loss, are now buried forever. The overwhelming purpose of parenthood is the responsibility for caring for and raising the child to be a properly developed adult both physically and morally.'

This comment is echoed by the Department of Health's introductory guide to the Children Act[6] which states that parental responsibility:

'emphasises that the duty to care for the child and to raise him to moral, physical and emotional health is the fundamental task of parenthood and the only justification for the authority that it confers.'

Both these comments reflect in turn the earlier landmark decision of *Gillick v West Norfolk and Wisbech Area Health Authority*[7] in which, at any rate, Lords Fraser and Scarman emphasised that parental power to control a child exists not for the benefit of the parent but for the benefit of the child.

How far the change of terminology from rights and duties to responsibility makes a change in substance to the law is arguable[8] though its effect upon lay persons should not be underestimated, for saying a parent has responsibilities rather than rights in itself conveys a quite different message. In any event there is more to the notion of parental responsibility than just a change in name, for as section 2 makes clear not only can more than one person have parental responsibility at the same time but perhaps more important a person does not cease to have responsibility because someone else acquires it.[9] Furthermore each holder of responsibility can continue to exercise it by himself or herself without the need to consult any other holder subject only to the overriding condition that he or she must not act incompatibly with any existing court order.[10] In the words of one learned commentator[11] these detailed provisions 'create a scheme which does give effect to a coherent general philosophy much more consistent with a "responsibility" based framework then with "rights" based notions.'

It is the enduring nature of responsibility particularly when allied with the presumption of non intervention under section 1(5)[12] that encapsulates the second idea referred to above, namely that responsibility for child care belongs to parents rather than the state. As one commentator has put it[13] by providing that responsibility should continue despite, for example, a court order that the child should live with one of them, parents 'are to understand that the state will not relieve them of their responsibilities'. This is further underscored by the fact that responsibility cannot be voluntarily surrendered to a public body[14] and that even where a care order is made compulsorily placing the child in local authority care the parents still retain

---

[6] 'Introduction to the Children Act 1989' (HMSO, 1989) para 1.4.
[7] [1986] AC 112, [1985] 3 All ER 402, HL, discussed at pp 295 and 306.
[8] The Law Commission itself, Law Com No 172, 1988, at para 2.4 thought that it would make 'little difference in substance.'
[9] S 2(5) and (6) discussed post at p 332.
[10] S 2(7) and (8) discussed post at p 333.
[11] S M Cretney 'Defining the Limits of State Intervention: The Child and Courts' in *Children and the Law* (ed Freestone, 1990) 58 at p 67.
[12] Discussed post at p 345.
[13] Cretney, op cit.
[14] Ie when the child is 'accommodated' by a local authority under s 20, discussed in ch 16, parental responsibility is not acquired by the authority; see the discussion by Eekelaar, op cit at pp 40–42.

their responsibility.[15] In short the 1989 Act through the concept of parental responsibility emphasises the idea that 'once a parent always a parent' and that prima facie the primary responsibility for deciding what should happen to their children even upon their separation should rest with the parents themselves.[16]

3. CONSISTENT USE OF THE RESPONSIBILITY CONCEPT

Apart from providing a change in terminology an inestimable advantage of the 1989 Act is its consistent use of the concept of parental responsibility. Hence, besides parents others, such as those granted residence orders, guardians and local authorities in whose care or emergency care children have been placed, each have parental responsibility (though this is not necessarily as extensive as that of the parents).[17] Furthermore existing statutes, notably the Adoption Act 1976, the child abduction legislation, and statutes dealing with the obligations of those looking after children to protect and educate them, have been amended to bring them into line with the 1989 Act.

It remains now to consider the meaning and scope of parental responsibility; who has parental responsibility; in respect of whom there is responsibility; the duration of responsibility; the position of those sharing responsibility; and the position of those caring for children without parental responsibility.

B. The meaning and scope of 'parental responsibility'

1. LACK OF A COMPREHENSIVE DEFINITION

Important though the concept is, the 1989 Act does not contain a comprehensive definition of what 'parental responsibility' comprises. Instead section 3(1) states that 'parental responsibility' means 'all the rights, duties, powers, responsibility and authority which by law a parent of a child has in relation to the child and his property'.

In so defining responsibility the Act implements the strategy recommended by the Law Commission. The Commission did not consider[18] it practicable to provide a statutory list of factors that are comprised in parental responsibility pointing out that such a list would have to change from time to time to meet differing needs and circumstances and, in the light of *Gillick v West Norfolk and Wisbech Area Health Authority*,[19] would have to vary with the age and maturity of the child and circumstances of the case. The wisdom of this strategy can be debated. Some have deprecated it[20] while others[1] have agreed with the Law Commission pointing out that the law

---

[15] The effect of care orders is discussed post, pp 523 et seq.
[16] Cf the Matrimonial Causes Procedure Committee (the 'Booth Committee') 1985, para 3.2.
[17] See post, p 300.
[18] Law Com No 172, para 2.6.
[19] [1986] AC 112, [1985] 3 All ER 402, HL.
[20] See eg Jones (1989) 139 NLJ 728, Lyon [1989] Fam Law 49, 50 and Scot Law Com No 135, Report on Family Law, 1992, para 2.18.
[1] White, Carr and Lowe *A Guide to the Children Act 1989*, para 2.6.

before the Children Act had worked reasonably well without a list and to have produced one might simply have caused unprofitable debate. Whatever one's views, the fact remains that it is necessary to explore more precisely what parental responsibility means not only to determine what those who have it are entitled and bound to do but also to determine the ambit of the court's powers to make specific issue and prohibited steps orders under section 8.[2]

2. SOME PRELIMINARY OBSERVATIONS

Before examining some of the more important aspects of parental responsibility some preliminary observations may be made. First, although the broad definition under section 3(1) necessarily refers to the pre-1989 Act position,[3] it must do so subject to the change of emphasis from *rights* to *responsibilities*. One problem in particular is deciding whether a former 'right' attaches only to a parent or to anyone with parental responsibilities.[4] As the Law Commission themselves commented,[5] the incidents of parenthood with which they were concerned were those that related to the care and upbringing of a child and not specifically incidents that attached to parents *qua* parents.

Secondly, the exercise of parental responsibility may be qualified by agreement of the parties (for example, the father agreeing that the child is to live with the mother) or by order of the court. In the latter instance the extent to which responsibility can be asserted is effectively limited by the paramountcy of the child's welfare which principle the court is bound to apply in any proceedings concerning his upbringing or the administration of his property.[6]

Thirdly, the older the child the less extensive and important parental responsibility may become. As Lord Denning MR so eloquently put it in respect of custody:[7]

'... it is a dwindling right which the court will hesitate to enforce against the wishes of the child, the older he is. It starts with the right of control and ends with little more than advice.'

In any event, as we have said, according to the decision in *Gillick v West Norfolk and Wisbech Area Health Authority*,[8] parental authority may cease in respect of any decision that the child is mature and intelligent enough to make himself though this has now been put in doubt by Lord Donaldson MR's judgment in *Re R (A Minor) (Wardship: Medical Treatment)*[9].

Fourthly, the ambit of responsibility varies. It is widest when enjoyed by parents or guardians but less extensive when vested in others by means of a residence order or in local authorities by reason of a care order.[10] It is narrowest when vested in those who have obtained an emergency protection order.[11]

---

[2] See post, p 355.
[3] For which see Eekelaar *What are Parental Rights?* 89 LQR 210; Hall *The Waning of Parental Rights* [1972B] CLJ 248; Maidment *The Fragmentation of Parental Rights* [1981] CLJ 135 and Law Com Working Paper No 91 Guardianship paras 2.25 et seq.
[4] For example the right to bury or cremate a deceased child. See post, p 311.
[5] Law Com No 172, 1988, para 2.7.
[6] Discussed post, ch 10.
[7] *Hewer v Bryant* [1970] 1 QB 357, 369, [1969] 3 All ER 578, 582, CA.
[8] [1986] AC 112, [1985] 3 All ER 402, HL.
[9] [1992] Fam 11 [1991] 4 All ER 177, discussed ante at p 295.
[10] See post at pp 328 and 523 respectively.
[11] See post, p 539.

Fifthly, the absence of responsibility does not necessarily mean that a person has no obligation towards the child. 'It does not make him a parent or relative of the child in law, for example, to give him rights of inheritance, or to place him under a statutory duty to maintain the child.' Conversely, as the Department of Health's *Introduction* to the Children Act 1989, observes[12]: 'the effect of having parental responsibility is to empower a person to take most decisions in the child's life'. It is to be noted that unmarried fathers have a statutory duty to maintain their children regardless of whether they also have parental responsibility.

3. WHAT PARENTAL RESPONSIBILITY COMPRISES

In the absence of an agreed list it is suggested that parental responsibility comprises at least the following:

a. Providing a home for the child.
b. Having contact with the child.
c. Determining and providing for the child's education.
d. Determining the child's religion.
e. Disciplining the child.
f. Consenting to the child's medical treatment.
g. Consenting to the child's marriage.
h. Agreeing to the child's adoption.
i. Vetoing the issue of a child's passport.
j. Taking the child outside the United Kingdom and consenting to the child's emigration.
k. Administering the child's property.
l. Protecting and maintaining the child.
m. Agreeing to change the child's surname.
n. Representing the child in legal proceedings.
o. Burying or cremating a deceased child.
p. Appointing a guardian for the child.

Consenting to a child's marriage was considered in chapter 2. Appointment of a testamentary guardian and agreeing to a child being adopted or freed for adoption are discussed in chapters 12 and 13. Maintenance and rights over the child's property are discussed in chapters 19 and 20. We shall now discuss the remaining important legal aspects of parental responsibility.

(a) Providing a home for the child

A key aspect of parental responsibility is that of looking after and bringing up the child. Based upon the common law right of a person to possession of his child, it now seems better to say that those with responsibility have a prima facie right to provide a home for the child and the power to determine where the child should live. The right is protected by the criminal law to the extent that persons without responsibility commit the crime of child abduction if they remove the child without lawful authority.[13] As between individuals with parental responsibility the right is qualified to the

---

[12] Para 2.4.
[13] Child Abduction Act 1984, s 2: discussed post, p 319.

extent that removal of a child outside the United Kingdom without the consent of other individuals with parental responsibility can amount to a crime.[14] Associated with providing a home is the necessary accompanying power inter alia physically to control children at any rate until the years of discretion. As Lord Lane CJ once commented, restraint of a child's movement is usually well within the realms of reasonable parental discipline.[15] It is also established that responsibility includes the power to control the child's movements whilst in someone else's care.[16] On the other hand it is also established that a parent and therefore presumably any other person with parental responsibility can commit the common law crime of kidnapping[17] or unlawful imprisonment[18] if a child (old enough to make up his own mind) is forcibly taken or detained against *his* will.

The point has been well made[19] that although even a parent with parental responsibility may effectively lose the right to look after his child to an individual who cares for him for a prolonged period,[20] such a parent will nevertheless retain the right at any time to remove the child accommodated by a local authority.[1]

(b) Contact with the child

Prima facie parental responsibility encompasses seeing or otherwise having contact with the child. While not an absolute right since in any litigation it will be contingent upon the child's welfare, nevertheless as Lord Oliver said in *Re KD (A Minor) (Ward: Termination of Access)*:[2] 'As a general proposition a natural parent has a claim to [contact with] his or her child to which the court will pay regard and it would not I think, be inappropriate to describe such a claim as a "right"'. This 'right' is protected to the extent that there is a statutory presumption of reasonable contact between a child in local authority care or under emergency protection and, inter alios, those with parental responsibility.[3] It has been argued[4] that since it is a normal assumption that a child will benefit from continued contact with both

[14] Under the Child Abduction Act 1984, s 1 (as amended by the Children Act 1989). Note the defences, however, under s 1(5).
[15] *R v Rahman* (1985) 81 Cr App Rep 349, 353, CA. See also *Hewer v Bryant* [1970] 1 QB 357, 373, [1969] 3 All ER 578, 585, CA, per Sachs LJ.
[16] *Fleming v Pratt* (1823) 1 LJ (OS) KB 194.
[17] *R v D* [1984] AC 778, [1984] 2 All ER 449, HL: see Lowe 134 NLJ 995.
[18] *R v Rahman* (supra). See Khan [1986] Fam Law 69.
[19] Cretney and Masson, *Principles of Family Law* at 487.
[20] Cf *J v C* [1970] AC 668, [1969] 1 All ER 788, HL, discussed post, p 340. A person with whom the child has had his home for three years will not need to seek leave to commence proceedings for a residence order: Children Act 1989, s 10(5), (10) discussed post, p 359. In such an application the court is bound to apply the welfare principle, see post, p 342. It is established that a parent has no right of action or remedy in damages against a stranger who interferes with the parent's right in respect of his relationship with his children: *F v Wirral Metropolitan Borough Council* [1991] Fam 69, [1991] 2 All ER 648, CA.
[1] Under s 20(7) of the Children Act 1989, discussed post, p 504.
[2] [1988] AC 806, 827, [1988] 1 All ER 577, 590, HL.
[3] Children Act 1989, ss 34(1), 44(13) discussed at pp 530 and 539 respectively. As Cretney and Masson observe, op cit, at p 492: 'although parental responsibility does not give an absolute right to contact with a child those with such power ... do have a right to a court adjudication of restriction of contact'.
[4] See Clarke Hall and Morrison, op cit, at para 1[63].

parents,[5] it may be that parental *responsibility* properly encompasses the prima facie duty to allow the child to have contact with either or both parents.

If parental responsibility encompasses the power to control the child's movements it would also seem to follow that it includes the power to restrict those with whom the child may have contact, though this has yet to be authoritatively established. Resolution of this issue may be of particular importance in determining the ambit of the courts' power to make prohibited steps orders under s 8 of the 1989 Act.[6]

(c) Education

Although at common law parental rights included the right to determine what education the child should receive[7] there was no enforceable duty upon parents to see that their children were educated.[8] Now, under the Education Act 1944, the parent of every child between the ages of five and sixteen[9] must ensure that he receives 'efficient full-time education suitable to his age, ability and aptitude either by regular attendance at school or otherwise'.[10]

'Parent' for these purposes includes any person who is not a parent but who has parental responsibility for the child or who has care of the child.[11] Failure to perform this duty can result in a criminal prosecution[12] and the child may be subject to an education supervision order.[13]

Those with parental responsibility or who have care of children can discharge their duty by ensuring that they attend independent rather than state schools or even by educating them at home, provided in this latter instance the local education authority is satisfied that the child is receiving efficient and full-time education suitable to his age etc. Where state education is relied upon, education authorities are required to comply with 'parental' wishes as to choice of school so far as it is compatible with the provision of efficient instruction and training and the avoidance of unreasonable public expenditure.[14] To enable a reasoned choice to be made 'parents' must

---

[5] See eg Lord Oliver in *Re KD* supra at pp 827 and 590 respectively and *M v M (Child: Access)* [1973] 2 All ER 81, per Wrangham J at p 85 and per Latey J at p 88.

[6] Discussed post, p 355.

[7] For a striking example see *Tremain's* case (1719) 1 Stra 167, discussed by Cretney and Masson op cit at p 487. See also *Andrews v Salt* (1873) 8 Ch App 622—father's wishes to be respected after his death.

[8] *Hodges v Hodges* (1796) Peake Add Cas 79.

[9] If the child's sixteenth birthday falls between 1 September and 31 January inclusive, he remains of compulsory school age until the end of the spring term; in other cases until the end of May: Education Act 1962, s 9; Education (School-leaving Dates) Act 1976, s 1.

[10] Education Act 1944, ss 35 and 36; Raising of the School Leaving Age Order 1972, SI 1972 No 444. If the child is living with both parents, the statutory duty is cast on both of them: *Plunkett v Alker* [1954] 1 QB 420, [1954] 1 All ER 396.

[11] Education Act 1944, s 114(1D).

[12] Ibid, ss 37, 39, 40. Parents can now be fined but not imprisoned for a breach of a school attendance order.

[13] Children Act 1989, s 36.

[14] Education Act 1944, s 76; Education Act 1980, s 6; it will be noted therefore that education authorities are *not* under an absolute duty to comply with parental wishes.

be given information about the availability of primary and secondary education available[15] and inter alia the curriculum and subject choice.[16]

(d) Religious upbringing[17]

A person with parental responsibility has a right to determine the child's religious education, though there is no duty to give a child a religious upbringing. This right to the child's religious education is protected to the extent that a local authority cannot cause a child in their care 'to be brought up in any religious persuasion other than that in which he would have been brought up if the order had not been made'.[18] Adoption agencies are also required, when placing a child for adoption, to have regard, so far as practicable, to any wishes of the child's parent or guardian as to the child's religious upbringing.[19] Parents with parental responsibility additionally can require a child's exclusion from religious studies lessons and school assembly.[20]

(e) Discipline

A person with parental responsibility[1] may lawfully inflict moderate and reasonable corporal punishment for the purpose of correcting a child or punishing an offence.[2] Whether or not the punishment is reasonable must depend upon all the facts of the case, and in particular the age and strength of the child and the nature and degree of the punishment. If it goes beyond what is reasonable, it is unlawful and would therefore render the individual criminally liable for assault.[3]

Most school authorities and community houses can no longer administer corporal punishment[4] even if those with parental responsibility approve.[5]

---

[15] Education Act 1980, s 8 as amended by the Education Reform Act 1988, s 31.
[16] Education (School Information) Regulations 1981, SI 1981/630 as amended.
[17] See generally Bevan *Child Law* paras 11.02–11.16 and Yates (1989) 1 JCL 89.
[18] Children Act 1989, s 34(6)(a).
[19] Adoption Act 1976, s 7.
[20] Education Reform Act 1988, s 9.
[1] But not someone who is not in *loco parentis*: see *R v Woods* (1921) 85 JP 272 in which it was held to be unlawful for an elder brother to administer corporal punishment where both sons were living with their father and consequently the older could not be considered as being in *loco parentis* to the younger.
[2] *R v Hopley* (1860) 2 F & F 202; *R v Woods*, supra. Restraint of a child's movement is usually well within the realms of reasonable parental discipline: per Lord Lane CJ in *R v Rahman* (1985) 81 Cr App Rep 349, 353, CA.
[3] *R v Derriviere* (1969) 53 Cr App Rep 637, CA. If the child died, the parent could be guilty of manslaughter or even murder: see post, p 313. An unreasonable restraint of a child's movement can render a parent guilty of unlawful imprisonment: *R v Rahman*, supra.
[4] Education (No 2) Act 1986, s 47 extended to grant maintained schools by the Education Reform Act 1988, Sch 12 and to some independent schools by SI 1989/1233 and SI 1989/1825, and Children's Homes (Control and Discipline) Regulations 1990, SI 1990/87.
[5] Corporal punishment without parental consent was held to be in breach of the European Convention on Human Rights see *Re Campbell and Cosans* (1982) 4 EHRR 293, European Court of Human Rights, discussed by Douglas (1988) 2 Int J Law and Fam 76.

(f) Consent to medical treatment[6]

Prima facie anyone with parental responsibility (including a local authority),[7] can give a valid consent to the child's surgical, medical or dental treatment. This prima facie position, however, is subject to some limitations and uncertainty. For example, the absence of consent does not necessarily mean that the treatment is unlawful nor conversely is it clearly established that the power of consent extends to all forms of treatment for whatever reason. A further complication arises when the child is able to give consent himself or herself.

(i) Where the child cannot consent for himself

Unless the child is 16 or over or is of sufficient age and understanding to consent for himself (see below) the consent of a person with parental responsibility will normally be required for any treatment. In most cases there can be little doubt that such consent is effective to give the medical practitioner protection against any possible criminal charges or action in tort.[8] Such exoneration may not, however, be given if the treatment is clearly against the child's interests though even then there might be some situations where sanction can properly be given. For example the transplant of a child's kidney to a twin may not be in the donor's medical interests but if, having been properly guided by medical advice, a reasonable person with parental responsibility, weighing the risks to the donor against the advantage to the other, would give his consent, all concerned should be given legal protection.[9]

Whether there are limits to the types of treatment to which those with parental responsibility can consent has yet to be resolved. According to Lord Templeman in *Re B (A Minor) (Wardship: Sterilisation)*[10] sterilisation of a girl under the age of 18 can only be lawfully carried out with leave of a High Court judge. However, Lord Templeman was the only Law Lord to say this and the precise legal basis for his assertion remains uncertain.[11] It has since been held[12] that High Court leave is not required for an operation the inevitable effect of which is to sterilise the child provided its object is for therapeutic reasons[13] to relieve the child of a medical condition.

Absence of consent does not automatically mean that the treatment is unlawful. Practitioners have long been advised that in an emergency treatment may be given if the well-being of the child could suffer by delay

---

[6] See generally Kennedy and Grubb *Medical Law: Text and Materials* ch 4.

[7] See *R v Kirklees Metropolitan Borough Council, ex p C (A Minor)* [1992] 2 FLR 117.

[8] Failure to obtain the necessary consent could lay the medical practitioner open to a prosecution for battery upon the child or for one of the graver forms of assault. It may also give rise to a claim in tort for trespass for which the practitioner may be liable for loss regardless of fault. See for example *Re R (A Minor) (Wardship: Medical Treatment)* [1992] Fam 11, 22, [1991] 4 All ER 177, 184, CA per Lord Donaldson MR.

[9] For a discussion of this problem see Kennedy and Grubb *Medical Law: Text and Materials* 300 et seq.

[10] [1988] AC 199, 205, [1987] 2 All ER 206, 214, HL, discussed by A Grubb and D Pearl 'Sterilisation and the Courts' [1987] CLJ 439. A similar conclusion was reached by the Australian High Court in *Department of Health v JWB and SMB* (1992) 66 ALJR 300.

[11] Furthermore if he is right, to what other treatment does the embargo extend?

[12] *Re E (A Minor) (Medical Treatment)* [1991] 2 FLR 585 per Sir Stephen Brown P.

[13] It should be noted that in *Re B* supra, the Law Lords rejected the notion of a non-therapeutic sterilisation.

caused in obtaining consent.[14] There is also some authority[15] for saying that consent is not required if those with parental responsibility have abandoned or, possibly, neglected the child. In cases of doubt, however, a ruling can be sought from the court because it is well established that the High Court can override either the giving or the refusal to give consent. For example in *Re D (A Minor) (Wardship: Sterilisation)*[16] a gynaecologist intended permanently to sterilise a mentally handicapped girl aged eleven (with her parent's consent) to prevent the possibility of her having children in the future. An educational psychologist concerned with the case then made the child a ward of court. Heilbron J concluded that there was no foreseeable risk of an unwanted pregnancy and that as the girl would have sufficient understanding to be able to make up her own mind on the matter when she was older, the operation should not take place. In *Re B (A Minor) (Wardship: Medical Treatment)*[17] the court sanctioned, contrary to the parents' wishes, a life saving operation for a newly born mongol child.

Although the absence of any consent can lay the practitioner open to an action by or on behalf of the child,[18] apart from seeking an injunction to prevent the proposed treatment it is difficult to see what other legal action a person with parental responsibility could bring in his own right.[19]

(ii) Where the child is 16 or 17 or 'Gillick competent'[20]

The Family Law Reform Act 1969, section 8 provides that a minor over the age of 16 may effectively consent to any surgical, medical or dental treatment without his parent's or guardian's concurrence.[1] It might reasonably have been inferred from this provision that a child below the age of 16 could not give such consent. However, section 8(3) states that 'Nothing in this section shall be construed as making ineffective any consent which would have been effective if this section had not been enacted'. It is authoritatively established by *Gillick v West Norfolk and Wisbech Area Health Authority*[2] that a child below the age of 16 has the capacity to consent to treatment provided he has sufficient understanding and intelligence to understand what is proposed. In that case the applicant, a mother of four daughters under the age of 16, sought a declaration that a circular issued by the DHSS, in which doctors were advised that in 'most unusual

---

[14] Upon the basis of the common law defence of necessity: cf Ministry of Health Circular F/19/113 1967 and Home Office Circular 63/1968.

[15] *Gillick v West Norfolk and Wisbech Area Health Authority* [1986] AC 112, [1985] 3 All ER 402, HL per Lord Scarman at 189 and 424 and Lord Templeman at 204 and 435.

[16] [1976] Fam 185, [1976] 1 All ER 326.

[17] [1981] 1 WLR 1421, CA. See also more recently *Re B (Wardship: Abortion)* [1991] 2 FLR 426 in which the court overrode a mother's wishes and gave permission for the 12 year old daughter to have an abortion.

[18] See p 305, n 8 above.

[19] Parents no longer have the right to sue for the loss of his child's services: see below. It should be added that practitioners who ignore the guidelines in *Gillick* could be subject to disciplinary action by their professional body.

[20] The phrase used by Lord Donaldson MR in *Re R (A Minor) (Wardship: Medical Treatment)* [1992] Fam 11, [1991] 4 All ER 177, CA to refer to child under the age of 16 who has sufficient age and understanding to give a valid consent to medical treatment.

[1] See also the Mental Health Act 1983, s 131(2).

[2] [1986] AC 112, [1985] 3 All ER 402, HL.

circumstances' it would be proper for them to give contraceptive advice and treatment to a girl under the age of 16 without her parent's knowledge or consent, was unlawful. The application failed[3] because it was held that the law does not recognise any rule of absolute parental authority until a fixed age and that even with regard to contraceptive treatment a girl of sufficient maturity and understanding could give a valid consent.

Whether a child has sufficient understanding is a question of fact to be determined in each case. Clearly, the degree of understanding required varies according to the nature of the proposed treatment. It does not, for example, require much intelligence to appreciate that a broken leg needs mending[4] whereas, as *Gillick* itself shows, considerable understanding is required before a child under 16 can validly consent to the prescription of contraceptive treatment. Whether there is an age below which a child will be assumed not to have the capacity to consent, no matter how obvious the illness and how simple the treatment, has yet to be determined, though it seems unlikely that the court would want to give definitive guidance.[5] Another issue not fully resolved is the degree of understanding a child must have to be able to give a valid consent. In the context of agreeing to contraceptive treatment, Lord Scarman at least, seemed to expect considerable understanding. He said:[6]

'It is not enough that she should understand the advice which is being given: she must also have sufficient maturity to understand what is involved. There are moral and family questions, especially her relationship with her parents; long-term problems associated with the emotional impact of pregnancy and its termination; and there are risks to health of sexual intercourse at her age, risks which contraception may diminish but cannot eliminate.'

With respect to Lord Scarman this looks suspiciously like importing into this area of law the doctrine of informed consent, which, in the context of the tort of negligence at least, the House of Lords have rejected.[7] It may indeed be doubted whether any adult—let alone a child under the age of 16—could validly consent to contraceptive treatment under Lord Scarman's test. In practice it seems likely that consideration will only be given to whether the child has sufficient maturity to understand the advice.[8] Even this, however, will not be easy for a practitioner to judge.

Another problem not adverted to in *Gillick* is where the child's mental state fluctuates. If during a lucid period the child is fully able to understand the advice is that sufficient to make him or her '*Gillick* competent'? It was

---

[3] For a trenchant criticism of the acceptance that Mrs Gillick had locus standi to apply for the declaration, see Harlow 49 MLR 768.

[4] In *Gillick*, supra, at 201 and 432 respectively Lord Templeman said a doctor could safely remove tonsils or a troublesome appendix if an intelligent child of 15 had consented.

[5] Cf *R v D* [1984] AC 778, 806, [1984] 2 All ER 449, 457, HL, where, in the context of the common law offence of kidnapping to which the child's consent is a defence (see p 319), Lord Brandon said that while it was a matter for a jury in every case, 'I should not expect a jury to find at all frequently that a child under the age of 14 had sufficient understanding and intelligence to give its consent'.

[6] In *Gillick v West Norfolk and Wisbech Area Health Authority*, supra, at 189 and 424 respectively.

[7] In *Sidaway v Board of Governors of the Bethlehem Royal Hospital and the Maudsley Hospital* AC 871, [1985] 1 All ER 643, HL. See also Cretney All ER Annual Review 1985 at 175.

[8] Which is all Lord Fraser seemed to require: see *Gillick v West Norfolk and Wisbech Area Health Authority*, supra, at 174 and 413 respectively.

held in *Re R (A Minor) (Wardship: Medical Treatment)*[9] that it did not. Competence to consent is not to be assessed at a particular moment in time but in conjunction with the child's whole medical history and background.[10] In other words it is established that *Gillick* competence cannot fluctuate on a day-to-day basis so that a child is one day regarded as competent but not on another.

It might have been supposed that once it is established that a '*Gillick* competent' child has consented to the proposed treatment, no further inquiry need be made and the continued involvement of the parent can be ignored. It seems evident, however, that the *Gillick* decision does not go so far. In particular it does not give doctors a carte blanche to prescribe contraceptives to girls under the age of 16. According to Lord Fraser[11] as well as being satisfied that the girl understands his advice the doctor must also be satisfied that he cannot persuade her to allow him to inform her parents, that she is very likely to begin or continue to have sexual intercourse with or without contraceptive treatment, that without the advice or treatment her health is likely to suffer and that her best interests require him to give the advice, treatment or both without parental consent. Even with respect to simpler treatment Lord Fraser seemed to contemplate some parental involvement. Hence while he did not doubt the capacity of a 15 year old to consent to having a broken arm set he added that 'of course the consent of the parents should normally be asked'.[12] Whether the subsequent obtaining of parental consent in this latter example is a legal necessity may be doubted but it is clearly prudent for a medical practitioner even after the *Gillick* decision to obtain the consent of a person with parental responsibility wherever possible.

It might have been supposed that the inevitable corollary of holding that a '*Gillick* competent' child can give a valid consent is that such a child can similarly refuse consent. However, this has been said not to be the case. According to Lord Donaldson MR in *Re R (A Minor) (Wardship: Medical Treatment)*,[13] all that *Gillick* decided was that a competent child could consent but not that he could *determine* whether or not he should receive medical treatment. In his view both the parents (and now presumably any person with parental responsibility) *and* the court retain the power to give consent for treatment even of a '*Gillick* competent' child notwithstanding that that child has refused consent. The same would be true of a child aged 16 or 17. In Lord Donaldson's view there are concurrent powers to consent (which he described as being 'keys which unlock a door') and only if all the 'keyholders' fail or refuse to consent will a veto be created.

In holding that parents retain the power to consent to their child's medical treatment notwithstanding that the child is '*Gillick* competent' (or even aged 16 or 17), Lord Donaldson MR went further than either of the other two judges. Staughton LJ, however, agreed with him that the High

---

[9] [1992] Fam 11, [1991] 4 All ER 177, CA: Douglas (1992) 55 MLR 569 and Masson [1991] Fam Law 528.

[10] Per Lord Donaldson MR at pp 25–26 and 187 respectively and Farquaharson LJ at pp 31 and 191 respectively.

[11] *Gillick* case, supra, at 174 and 413 respectively. It must be a matter of doubt whether in practice a medical practitioner will always be so thorough as Lord Fraser's test demands.

[12] Ibid at 169 and 409 respectively.

[13] [1992] Fam 11 at 23, [1991] 4 All ER 177 at 185. For a criticism of this approach see Douglas (1992) 55 MLR 569.

Court under its wardship jurisdiction[14] had the power to override a '*Gillick* competent' child's refusal to consent. In reaching this latter decision both their Lordships accepted that the wardship jurisdiction vested wider powers in the court than those vested in parents (or those with parental responsibility) so as in effect to protect children against themselves.[15] In the subsequent case of *Re J (A Minor) (Inherent Jurisdiction: Consent to Treatment)*[16] the Court of Appeal held that notwithstanding section 8 of the Family Law Reform Act 1969, the court acting under its inherent jurisdiction could overrule a 16 year old anorexic child's refusal to consent to medical treatment.

These decisions, particularly that of Lord Donaldson MR in *Re R* are both important and controversial. It remains to be seen how the law will develop but if Lord Donaldson's approach is accepted[17] (though with respect his distinction between *consenting* to and *determining* treatment is difficult to follow) the implications go far beyond the issue of consent.[18] In this respect, however, no matter how the decision is developed it cannot take away the *statutory* right under the Children Act 1989 for children of sufficient age and understanding to make an informed decision to refuse to submit to medical examinations or assessments contained in court directions in emergency protection or child assessment orders.[19]

(g) Vetoing the issue of a passport

The normal practice of the Passport Agency is to require the consent of a parent with parental responsibility to an application by a child for a passport (other than a one year British Visitor's Passport).[20] However, as is expressly stated on the face of a contact or residence order: '*Any* person with parental responsibility may ask the United Kingdom Passport Agency ... not to issue a passport allowing the child to go abroad without the knowledge of that person'.[1] Objections to the issue of a passport will also be considered if the police have notified the Agency of an intention to exercise their power of arrest under the Child Abduction Act 1984.[2]

(h) Taking the child outside the United Kingdom and arranging for the child's emigration

Parents with parental responsibility acting in unison have the power to take their child outside the United Kingdom and can therefore arrange for his emigration. Neither parent has the *unilateral* right, if the other parent has parental responsibility, to take or remove the child, under the age of 16

---

[14] The wardship jurisdiction is discussed in ch 14.

[15] See the arguments in Lowe and White *Wards of Court* (2nd Edn), para 6.55 and Bainham *The Balance of Power in Family Decisions* [1986] CLJ 262, 274–5. Cf Eekelaar *The Eclipse of Parental Rights* 102 LQR 4, 6–8.

[16] (1992) Times, 15 July, CA. See also *Re E* (21 September 1990, unreported), in which Ward J overrode a 15 year old's religious objection to having a life-saving blood transfusion.

[17] Ironically, since it was unanimously ruled that the child was not '*Gillick* competent', Lord Donaldson MR's remarks about the parents' and the courts' powers were obiter.

[18] Not least, for example, for the duration of parental responsibility as well as for the children's *rights*. See ante, pp 295–296.

[19] Children Act 1989, ss 43(7) and 44(6).

[20] See *Clarke Hall and Morrison on Children*, para 1[82].

[1] Form CHA 7. Emphasis added.

[2] Discussed further post, p 484.

from the United Kingdom without the other's consent[3] since to do so is an offence under the Child Abduction Act 1984, s 1(1). In the case of children whose parents are not married, the mother has an unfettered power of removal unless the father has parental responsibility in which case his consent is required.[4] The father, on the other hand, will always require the mother's consent to remove the child save where he has a residence order in his favour, in which case he may remove the child without anyone's consent for any period of less than one month. Guardians are similarly empowered to remove the child from the United Kingdom unless there are other persons with parental responsibility in which case their consent is also required.

The powers of removal are further fettered in the event of the making of a residence or care order. A person in whose favour a residence order is made is thereby entitled to remove the child from the United Kingdom for a period of less than one month without anyone's permission[5] but can only remove the child for a period in excess of one month with the written consent of every person having parental responsibility or with leave of the court.[6] The making of a care order prevents any person from removing the child from the United Kingdom without the written consent of every person with parental responsibility[7] or leave of the court though the local authority themselves can arrange for the child's removal for a period of less than one month without anyone's permission[8] and, with approval of the court, may make arrangements for the child in their care to live outside England and Wales.[9]

The net result of these provisions is that anyone who has parental responsibility must consent to the child's removal from the United Kingdom for more than one month while those with sole responsibility and those with joint responsibility acting in unison can arrange for the child's removal from the United Kingdom for any period.

(i) Child's name

By convention a child born to married parents takes his father's surname though it would seem that the father cannot insist upon this. A child whose parents are not married normally takes his mother's surname but he may be known by the father's.

Once the child's name has been registered neither married parent may

---

[3] It is a defence under s 1(5) of the Child Abduction Act 1984 if the child is removed (a) in the belief that the other person has consented or would have done had he been aware of all the relevant circumstances, (b) after taking all reasonable steps to communicate with the other person the accused had been unable to do so or (c) the other person has unreasonably refused to consent. Section 1(5)(c) does *not* apply if the person who refused consent had a residence or custody order in his favour: s 1(5A), added by the Children Act 1989, Sch 12, para 37(3). In cases where there is sufficient evidence to raise the application of s 1(5) the burden is on the prosecution to show that s 1(5) does not apply: s 1(6).
[4] Child Abduction Act 1984, s 1(3)(a)(ii).
[5] Children Act 1989, s 13(2).
[6] Ibid, s 13(1).
[7] Ibid, s 33(7)(b).
[8] Ibid, s 33(8)(a).
[9] Ibid, s 33(8)(b) and Sch 2, para 19.

change it without the other's consent save where that other parent is dead.[10] The granting of a residence order does not entitle that person to change the child's surname without the written consent of every person who has parental responsibility for the child or the leave of the court.[11] Similarly the making of a care order does not entitle a local authority to cause the child to be known by a new surname without the written consent of every person with parental responsibility or the leave of the court.[12]

There is no requirement to execute a formal deed for change of surname, since a person may call himself what he likes. However, the execution and enrolment of a deed may be useful for evidential purposes.[13] There is no formal provision for changing a forename.

(j) Representation

In general (see below) a child can only bring legal proceedings, at any rate in the High Court and county court, by his 'next friend'.[14] Similarly if civil proceedings are brought against him he must be represented by a guardian ad litem.[15] Parents have long been regarded as having the prima facie[16] entitlement to act in each of those capacities and it must now be accepted that anyone with parental responsibility is in the same position. It should be noted that with respect to proceedings under the Children Act 1989 and under the High Court's inherent jurisdiction special rules apply so that children may not need to act through a next friend or guardian ad litem[17].

(k) Burying or cremating a deceased child

It is established that a parent who has the means to do so, is bound to provide for the burial of his deceased child.[18] Such a duty may therefore properly be considered to be an aspect of parental responsibility. However in *R v Gwynedd County Council*[19] it was held that as the local authority's responsibility towards a child in care ceased upon the child's death, the right to bury the child vested in the parent rather than the foster parent. Put into the language of the 1989 Act it can be said that as the local authority's responsibility ended upon the child's death, the right to bury

---

[10] According to *Re T* [1963] Ch 238, 241, [1962] 3 All ER 970, 971 a child of tender years has no power to change his own name. Quaere the legal position of the older child?

[11] Children Act 1989, s 13(1), discussed further at p 362.

[12] Ibid, s 33(7).

[13] See the enrolment of Deeds (Change of Name) Regulations 1983, SI 1983/680.

[14] RSC Ord 80, r 2(1), CCR Ord 10.

[15] RSC Ord 80, r 2(2). It should be noted that RSC Ord 80 and CCR Ord 10 *only* applies to proceedings before the High Court and county court. The better view is that in absence of any express restrictions children are entitled to conduct their own proceedings before *magistrates'* courts.

[16] *Woolf v Pemberton* (1877) 6 Ch D 19. Note there is a power of removal if a proper case is made out: *Re Taylor's Application* [1972] 2 QB 369, [1972] 2 All ER 873 (successful application to remove a parent who refused to accept compromise of thalidomide application, though decision to remove the particular parent was reversed on appeal).

[17] Family Proceedings Rules 1991, r 9.2A, added by the Family Proceedings (Amendment) Rules 1992, r 6.

[18] *R v Vann* (1851) 2 Den 325, 15 JP 802, approved by Lord Alverstone LJ in *Clark v London General Omnibus Co Ltd* [1906] 2 KB 648, at 659, CA and recently followed in *R v Gwynedd County Council, ex p B* [1992] 3 All ER 317, CA. Presumably this duty can be discharged by cremating the child.

[19] Supra.

the child vested exclusively in the parents with parental responsibility.[20] Similarly, those who have parental responsibility by means of a residence order will lose it upon the child's death. Accordingly the right to bury a deceased child seems exclusively to be vested in parents with parental responsibility and guardians.

(l) Child's services

Formerly, persons with parental rights were entitled, at common law, to the domestic services of their unmarried children under the age of 18 actually living with them as part of the family. While the legal enforcement of this right was impossible, its former significance lay in the fact that it provided the parent with his only common law remedy against a stranger for interference with parental rights.[1] However, insofar as the loss of service is due to a tort committed against the child, the parents' cause of action has been abolished by the Administration of Justice Act 1982, section 2(b). Furthermore it has recently been held[2] that there is no cause of action against a stranger for interference with parental rights in respect of the relationship with their children. For practical purposes therefore parental responsibility cannot be said to include a right to domestic services.[3]

(m) Protection

(i) Physical protection

Although it is correct to say that anyone with parental responsibility is under a prima facie duty to afford physical protection to the child, at common law such a prima facie duty is owed by anyone who willingly undertakes to look after another who is incapable of looking after himself. Hence the duty can be owed to a step-child or foster child[4] and can continue after the child reaches his majority if he is unable to look after himself owing to some physical or mental disability.[5] Whether the duty exists in any given case depends inter alia upon the necessity of protection. A crippled mother, for example, would not be under any duty to protect a healthy son aged 17. In *R v Shepherd*,[6] where a girl aged 18, who normally lived away in service but returned home from time to time, died there in childbirth, it was held that her mother was under no duty to send for a midwife because the girl was beyond the age of childhood and was entirely emancipated.

---

[20] It should be noted, however, that local authorities have permissive powers to arrange for the child's burial or cremation should the parents not wish or be able to exercise their rights: Children Act 1989, Sch 2, para 20.

[1] Discussed *in extenso* in the sixth edition of this work at pp 329 et seq.

[2] *F v Wirral Metropolitan Borough Council* [1991] Fam 69, [1991] 2 All ER 648. Cf *Donnelly v Joyce* [1974] QB 454, [1973] 3 All ER 475, CA, discussed ante, pp 123–124, on the question of damages.

[3] See post, p 642 and Cretney and Masson, op cit, at pp 489–490 for discussion as to whether parents can claim all or part of their children's wages as contribution towards their upkeep.

[4] *R v Bubb* (1850) 4 Cox CC 455; *R v Gibbins and Proctor* (1918) 13 Cr App Rep 134, CCA.

[5] *R v Chattaway* (1922) 17 Cr App Rep 7, CCA (starvation of a helpless daughter aged 25).

[6] (1862) Le & Ca 147. (The age of majority was then 21.)

Common law liability

If a child's death is caused or accelerated by a breach of the duty to protect, the person owing the duty may be guilty of manslaughter. In this respect, however, whereas in the case of an act of commission it is sufficient to establish an unlawful act (so that a parent will be guilty of manslaughter if he beats the child so severely that he dies)[7] in the case of omission it was held in *R v Lowe*[8] that the accused will not be guilty unless he has shown a degree of negligence amounting to recklessness. It must be proved that he was indifferent to an obvious risk of injury to the child's health, welfare or safety or that he actually foresaw the risk but determined to run it.[9] In that case the father, whose intelligence was below average, failed to ensure that the child received proper medical attention with the result that the latter died. The jury expressly found that he had not been reckless and the Court of Appeal accordingly quashed a conviction for manslaughter.[10]

If the act or omission is intended to cause the child's death (for example by intentional starvation) then the accused will be guilty of murder, and the same is true if the conduct is so intrinsically likely to do so that a jury can infer that the death must have been contemplated.[11]

Although a person will be criminally liable for assault if he inflicts physical injury on a child or puts him in fear that he will do so, where the breach of the duty to protect the child takes the form of neglect, abandonment or some other omission, the common law criminal sanctions are wholly inadequate to ensure the child's protection.[12] In *R v Friend*[13] it was said to be an indictable misdemeanour at common law for a person under a duty to provide for an infant of tender years to neglect to do so and thereby injure his health. Few indictments appear to have been preferred, and in any case no offence was committed unless the child's health actually suffered as a result. In 1889 Parliament passed the first Prevention of Cruelty to, and Protection of, Children Act.[14] The principles underlying this Act were considerably extended by later statutes, and the modern law is largely contained in the Children and Young Persons Acts 1933 to 1969.[15]

---

[7] *R v Griffin* (1869) 11 Cox CC 402.

[8] [1973] QB 702, [1973] 1 All ER 805, CA.

[9] Cf *R v Stone* [1977] QB 354, [1977] 2 All ER 341, CA.

[10] For cases where parents have been found guilty of manslaughter by neglect, see *R v Walters* (1841) Car & M 164 (exposure); *R v Bubb* (supra) (failure to provide food and clothing); *R v Downes* (1875) 1 QBD 25 (failure to call in medical advice).

[11] *R v Walters* (supra); *R v Bubb* (supra); *R v Handley* (1874) 13 Cox CC 79; *R v Gibbins and Proctor* (supra).

[12] Note, however, the specific statutory offence of an aggravated assault upon a boy under the age of 14 or upon any female, as well as the more serious offence of unlawfully and maliciously wounding or inflicting grievous bodily harm: Offences against the Person Act 1861, ss 20 and 43. For criminal assault generally: see Smith and Hogan *Criminal Law* (6th Edn) ch 12.

[13] (1802) Russ & Ry 20. See also *R v Hogan* (1851) 2 Den 277.

[14] Earlier statutory intervention (more limited in its scope) is to be seen in the Poor Law Amendment Act 1868, s 37.

[15] Children and Young Persons Act 1933; Children and Young Persons (Amendment) Act 1952; Children and Young Persons Act 1963; Children and Young Persons Act 1969 as amended by the Children Act 1989, Schs 12 and 13.

Liability under the Children and Young Persons Act 1933

Section 1(1) of the 1933 Act provides:

'If any person[16] who has attained the age of sixteen years and has responsibility for any child or young person under that age, wilfully assaults, ill-treats, neglects, abandons, or exposes him, or causes or procures him to be assaulted, ill-treated, neglected, abandoned, or exposed, in a manner likely to cause him unnecessary suffering or injury to health (including injury to or loss of sight, or hearing, or limb, or organ of the body, and any mental derangement), that person shall be guilty of [an offence]...'[17]

By section 17 of the Act the following are liable under section 1:[18]

'(a) any person who—

(i) has parental responsibility for him (within the meaning of the Children Act 1989); or
(ii) is otherwise legally liable to maintain him; and

(b) any person who has care of him.'

This wording is extremely wide and would cover, for example, a school teacher and anyone over the age of 16 acting as a baby sitter.

As can be seen the object of the Act is to make criminal any wilful course of conduct likely to cause physical or mental injury to the child. The Act itself specifies that neglect shall include failure to provide adequate food, clothing, medical aid[19] or lodging or, if the parent or guardian is unable to provide any of them, failing to take steps to procure them through the Department of Social Security.[20] But clearly many other types of cruelty and neglect are covered, such as beating a child, locking him up alone, leaving him in an otherwise deserted house or shutting him out in inclement weather, if such acts are likely to cause the child concerned suffering or ill-health. A person will be liable, however, only if his act is *wilful*: hence he must either know that his conduct might cause suffering or injury to health or not care whether this results or not.[1] Consequently an ignorant parent who does not know that the child's health is at risk will not be guilty of an offence if he fails to summon medical aid even though a reasonable person would be aware of this fact: if he does know this, however, he will presumably be guilty even though he has some religious or other reason for refusing to provide assistance.[2]

Parents (and others having responsibility for children) may also be criminally liable for causing the death of a child under the age of three by overlying it in bed whilst drunk,[3] for allowing a child under the age of 12

---

[16] There can be joint liability: see *R v Gibson and Gibson* [1984] Crim LR 615, CA.

[17] The phrase 'in a manner likely to cause ... injury to health' governs the whole of the preceding phrase 'wilfully assaults ... abandoned, or exposed': *R v Hatton* [1925] 2 KB 322, CCA. The section has virtually superseded the Offences against the Person Act 1861, s 27, which relates to the abandonment and exposure of children under two years of age.

[18] The Act says 'presumed to be liable', but the presumption is apparently irrebuttable: *Brooks v Blount* [1923] 1 KB 257.

[19] Unreasonable refusal to permit a surgical operation may amount to wilful neglect: *Oakey v Jackson* [1914] 1 KB 216.

[20] Children and Young Persons Act 1933, s 1(2)(a).

[1] *R v Sheppard* [1981] AC 394, [1980] 3 All ER 899, HL.

[2] As in *R v Senior* [1899] 1 QB 283 (religious objection to calling in medical aid), which appears to have been approved on its facts in *R v Sheppard* (supra).

[3] Children and Young Persons Act 1933, s 1(2)(b).

to be in a room containing an unguarded fire or other heating appliance with the result that the child is killed or seriously injured,[4] or for permitting children under the age of 16 (subject to certain exceptions) to take part in or train for dangerous performances.[5]

Orders forbidding molestation and violence

The courts' powers to protect the interests of children by granting non-molestation orders is discussed in chapter 5.

(ii) Moral protection

Although there was no positive method either at common law or in equity of ensuring that parents took adequate steps to secure their child's moral welfare, as a result of statutory intervention there is at least a partial obligation to afford moral protection. An attempt has been made to prevent the acquisition of sexually depraved habits by making it an offence inter alia for anyone with parental responsibility to cause or encourage the seduction or prostitution of his daughter under the age of 16, or to permit a child between the ages of four and 16 to be in a brothel.[6] Similarly it is an offence to allow a child under the age of 16 to beg,[7] and penalties are imposed upon parents who permit children to take part in entertainments or to go abroad for the purpose of performing for profit except under stringent conditions.[8]

(iii) Civil liability

Up to now only the criminal sanctions for a breach of the duty to protect have been discussed. It remains to consider, however, whether any civil action will lie. The liability of a parent (or others having responsibility or even care of the child) may be relevant if he is insured (as in the case of a car driver) or if another defendant wishes to join the parent as a third party (for example, if the driver of a car which has injured the child wishes to claim contribution from a parent who has let him stray on the road). It is also conceivable that a child might sue his own parent if the natural ties which would normally prevent his doing so have been severed by the breaking up of the family as a whole. However so far as English cases are concerned the context in which liability has so far been discussed is in relation to alleged breaches of duty by foster parents.

It seems clear that the only possible action (apart from assault) is a common law action for damages for negligence. The child must therefore prove that he has been injured as a result of the other's breach of duty to take care to avoid such acts or omissions as are foreseeably likely to injure him.

[4] Ibid, s 11, as amended by the Children and Young Persons (Amendment) Act 1952, s 8.
[5] Ibid, ss 23 and 24; Children and Young Persons Act 1963, s 41 and Schs 3 and 5.
[6] Sexual Offences Act 1956, s 28 (as amended by the Children Act 1989); Children and Young Persons Act 1933, s 3 (as amended by the Children Act 1989). These provisions also apply to anyone having the care of the child.
[7] Children and Young Persons Act 1933, s 4.
[8] Ibid, s 25; Children and Young Persons Act 1963, ss 37–40 and 42.

Independent duty of care
Where a duty of care exists independently so that, had the injured person been a stranger, he could have recovered from the tortfeasor, the relationship of parent and child should not *ipso facto* bar the action. An obvious example would occur if a child, who is a passenger in his father's car, is injured as a result of the latter's negligent driving. The father's duty of care similarly extends to an unborn child whereas the mother's duty to an unborn child arises only when she is driving a motor vehicle.[9]

No independent duty
Where there is no independent duty, so that the child has to rely solely on the common law duty to protect owed to him by his parent or other person having parental responsibility or of those simply looking after him, the position is less clear. In *Surtees v Kingston-Upon-Thames Borough Council*[10] whilst in foster care the plaintiff, when aged 2, had an accident in which she sustained serious injuries to her foot. The injuries were caused by immersion in water hot enough to cause third degree burns. Although the precise circumstances were disputed, the court accepted the foster parents' explanation that whilst the foster mother was out of the bathroom the plaintiff somehow placed her foot in the wash basin and switched on the hot water tap. The foster mother took the plaintiff immediately to a doctor who treated her daily. It was held that on these facts the action for negligence should fail.[11] With respect to the foster parents it was held that, in the domestic circumstances in which the foster mother was performing her normal household duties, the kind of injury sustained by the plaintiff was not foreseeable. In reaching this decision both Stocker LJ and Browne-Wilkinson VC were mindful of the danger of imposing an impossibly high standard of care in domestic situations. It was expressly accepted that for this purpose the duty owed by foster parents was exactly the same as that owed by a parent. Browne-Wilkinson VC further observed:[12]

> 'There are very real public policy considerations to be taken into account if the conflicts inherent in legal proceedings are to be brought into family relationships... The studied realm of the Royal Courts of Justice ... is light years away from the circumstances prevailing in the average home. The mother is looking after a fast-moving toddler at the same time as cooking the meal, doing the housework, answering the telephone, looking after the other children and doing all the other things that the average mother has to cope with simultaneously, or in quick succession, in the normal household. We should be slow to characterise as negligent the care which ordinary loving and careful mothers are able to give to individual children, given the rough-and-tumble of home life.'

The reluctance to impose too high a standard of care upon those looking after children should not be taken to imply that such carers will never be

[9] The Congenital Disabilities (Civil Liability) Act 1976, s 2. Liability can only accrue provided the child is born alive: s 4(2)(a).
[10] [1991] 2 FLR 559, CA.
[11] It was conceded that the authority could not be liable if the foster parents were exonerated for blame though in any event Stocker LJ considered *obiter* that as a matter of causation the claim against the authority was bound to fail unless the injuries were deliberately inflicted. For a criticism of this observation see Douglas [1991] Fam Law 426–427. It is established that foster parents are *not* agents of the local authority: *S v Walsall Metropolitan Borough Council* [1986] 1 FLR 397, CA.
[12] [1991] 2 FLR at 583–4. But cf Beldam LJ who dissented.

held to be negligent. An instructive decision is that of the New Zealand Court of Appeal in *McCallion v Dodd*.[13] In that case parents alighted from a bus at night with their two children and started to walk along the road in the dark. The mother, who was deaf and, as the father knew, was not wearing her hearing aid, took the plaintiff, aged four, by the hand and the father carried the baby in his arms. A car driven by the defendant hit the mother and the plaintiff, killing the mother and severely injuring the boy. The plaintiff sued the defendant in negligence and the defendant claimed contribution from the father on the ground that he had also broken a duty of care owed to the plaintiff. The jury found that the defendant had been negligent and also found that the father had been negligent in permitting the boy to walk in the road on the wrong side and in the path of oncoming traffic. On appeal it was unanimously held that, even though the boy was under the immediate control of his mother, the father continued to be under a special duty because of her deafness. Turner and McCarthy JJ thought that no duty of care was created purely by the relationship of parent and child but that it arose from the fact that the father had taken the boy on to the road,[14] although admittedly the relationship is evidence of the fact that the parent has undertaken the duty to supervise and control the child's conduct.[15] North P however, thought that, although a stranger would be liable in negligence only if he had assumed or accepted the care of the child, parents 'at all times *while present* are under a legal duty to exercise reasonable care to protect their children from foreseeable dangers' and that duty cannot be shed by a parent who is present.[16] In most cases it will make little difference which view is correct but the wider rule formulated by North P is to be preferred. Indeed, it is submitted that it should be even more broadly based. If a parent leaves a child in the care of one known to be unreliable and the child comes to harm as the result of the latter's irresponsibility, the parent should be civilly liable.

It was unanimously held in *McCallion v Dodd* that there was no question of the plaintiff's damages being reduced as the result of the father's negligence. Here the court followed *Oliver v Birmingham and Midland Omnibus Co Ltd*.[17] The plaintiff, aged four, was crossing a road with his grandfather, who was holding his hand, when an omnibus bore down on them. The grandfather let go of the plaintiff's hand and jumped to safety; the plaintiff was struck by the omnibus owing to the driver's negligence and was injured. It was held that his action for damages against the omnibus company was not affected by his grandfather's contributory negligence.

4. LIABILITY FOR CHILDREN'S ACTS

Hitherto we have been concerned with what responsibility comprises but another not unimportant issue is the potential liability of those having parental responsibility.

[13] [1966] NZLR 710. See Mathieson 30 MLR 96. See also *S v Walsall Metropolitan Borough Council*, supra, where damages were awarded against foster parents in respect of injuries suffered by a child whilst in their care.
[14] At 725 and 728.
[15] Per McCarthy J at 729.
[16] At 721 (Italics supplied).
[17] [1933] 1 KB 35.

(a) Contracts

It is established that a parent (and therefore any person with parental responsibility) will never be liable as such for any contract made by the child.[18] Such persons may however be liable on the ordinary principles of agency if they have authorised the child to make the contract or, in the case of unauthorised contracts, by estoppel or ratification.[19]

(b) Torts

As in the case of contracts, neither parents nor others with parental responsibility will be liable as such for a child's tort unless they have authorised its commission.

A parent or someone with parental responsibility may also be personally liable if he himself has been negligent by affording the child an opportunity of injuring another. This is a particular application of the tort of negligence, and the test is therefore: did the parent by his act or omission cause or permit his child to do an act which was foreseeably likely to harm the person injured and against which a reasonably prudent parent would have guarded? If so, he will be liable. In *Newton v Edgerley*[20] the defendant permitted his twelve-year-old son to have possession of a shotgun but did not instruct him how to handle it when others were present. Although the defendant had forbidden his son to use the gun when other children were near he was nonetheless held personally liable in negligence for the injury to a child who was accidentally shot by his son because he ought to have foreseen that his son would succumb to temptation and consequently should either have forbidden him to use the gun at all or have instructed him how to handle it in the presence of others. On the other hand in *Donaldson v McNiven*[1] the defendant had let his son aged 13 buy an airgun. He forbade him to fire it outside the house and the boy gave his word that he would not do so. He always fired it in a cellar under the house until one day he took it outside, fired it and in so doing put out the plaintiff's eye. It was held that the father was not liable, for he had taken all reasonable precautions to ensure that the gun was fired in a safe place and no damage would have resulted but for the son's disobedience, unfaithfulness and folly which the defendant could not reasonably have foreseen.

Although these cases both deal with liability for permitting a child to have a dangerous toy or weapon, there is no reason why it should be restricted to this field. Thus if an adult in charge of a young child on a busy road negligently lets him run out into the traffic with the result that the driver of a car, in swerving to avoid the child, injures himself or another, that adult must on principle be liable for the damage.[2]

---

[18] *Mortimore v Wright* (1840) 6 M & W 482.

[19] See generally works on the law of contract and agency.

[20] [1959] 3 All ER 337. See also *Bebee v Sales* (1916) 32 TLR 413.

[1] [1952] 2 All ER 691, CA. See also *Jauffir v Akhbar* (1984) Times, 10 February; *Gorely v Codd* [1966] 3 All ER 891.

[2] Cf *Carmarthenshire County Council v Lewis* [1955] AC 549, [1955] 1 All ER 565, HL, where a school authority was liable in similar circumstances for negligently letting a child run out of the school premises on to a road with the result that a lorry driver was killed. See further Waller *Visiting the Sins of the Children* 4 Melbourne ULR 17.

(c) Crimes

At common law a parent was not liable for his child's crimes unless he himself was guilty of aiding and abetting. But the fact that a child's criminal propensities may be due to bad home influence or a lack of parental supervision has now been recognised by statute. If a court imposes a fine or costs or makes a compensation order for the commission of an offence by a child under the age of 17, it may order that these be paid by the child's parent or guardian (but not other persons even if they have parental responsibility) unless the latter cannot be found or the court is satisfied that he has not conduced to the commission of the offence by neglecting to exercise due care or control of the child.[3]

5. LIABILITY FOR INTERFERENCE WITH PARENT'S AND CHILDREN'S RIGHTS

(a) Criminal liability

Although the contrary view was once held,[4] there is apparently no common law offence of taking a child against his parents' will.[5] A number of statutory offences have been created, however. They are now principally contained in section 2 of the Child Abduction Act 1984 and sections 19 to 21 of the Sexual Offences Act 1956 (which repealed and consolidated earlier legislation on the subject). Three distinct cases must be considered.

(i) Children under the age of 16 years

Under the Child Abduction Act 1984, section 2, it is an offence for a person 'unconnected' with the child[6] to take or detain, without lawful authority or reasonable excuse, a child under the age of 16 so as to remove him from or to keep him out of the lawful control of any person having or entitled to lawful control of him.[7] The offence may be committed in respect of a

---

[3] Children and Young Persons Act 1933, s 55; Children and Young Persons Act 1969, s 3(6) and Schs 5 and 6; Administration of Justice Act 1970, Sch 11; Criminal Justice 1972, Sch 5. The court *must* exercise this power if the child is under 14. A local authority having parental responsibility for a child or young person who is in their care or who is being provided with accommodation by them is regarded as a parent or guardian for these purposes: Children and Young Persons Act 1933, s 55(5) (added by the Criminal Justice Act 1991, s 57(2)), reversing *Leeds City Council v West Yorkshire Metropolitan Police* [1983] 1 AC 29, [1982] 1 All ER 274, HL. Where a local authority allows a child to be under the charge or control of a parent or guardian that person can be liable though it is a question of fact whether the arrangements made between the parties constitute a transfer of control: *Leeds City Council v West Yorkshire Metropolitan Police*, supra. See Samuel 98 LQR 358. See also the Criminal Law Act 1977, s 36 (liability of parent or guardian for unpaid fine).

[4] East *Pleas of the Crown*, 429–430.

[5] Ie the removal must be against the child's will: *R v Hale* [1974] QB 819, [1974] 1 All ER 1107. It is now established that a parent can be guilty of the common law offence of kidnapping his own child: *R v D* [1984] AC 778, [1984] 2 All ER 449, HL, and see Lowe 134 NLJ 995; and of unlawfully imprisoning his own child: *R v Rahman* (1985) 81 Cr App Rep 349, CA; see Khan [1986] Fam Law 69. For a discussion of the statutory offence under s 1 of the Child Abduction Act 1984 see ante, p 308.

[6] Ie who is not a parent or guardian and has no residence or custody order in his favour: s 1(2) of the Child Abduction Act 1984.

[7] This provision implements with some modification the recommendations of the Criminal Law Revision Committee in their 14th Report, Offences Against the Person, 1980 Cmnd 7844, paras 239–249. The offence carries a maximum penalty of seven years' imprisonment: Child Abduction Act 1984. s 4.

child of either sex, and regardless of whether the interference is permanent or temporary.[8] There is no need to prove force or fraud so it can be an offence to persuade a child to leave his parents. Under this Act a person is regarded as 'taking' a child if he causes or induces the child to accompany him or any other person or causes the child to be taken.[9] It is a defence if the accused can show that he reasonably believed that the child was 16 or, in the case of an unmarried father, that he was or reasonably believed himself to be the child's father.[10]

(ii) Girls under the age of 16 years

It is an offence for a person acting without lawful authority or excuse to take an unmarried girl (but not a boy) under the age of 16 out of the possession[11] of her parent or other person having the parental responsibility for or care of her against his will.[12] Neither force nor fraud is necessary:[13] mere persuasion to leave home is sufficient. If she leaves without any persuasion or force on the part of the accused, no offence is committed, even though he subsequently acquiesces in her suggestion that they should stay together and takes no steps to send her home; but if he takes the active step of suggesting that she should leave her parents, he will be liable.[14] Since the original object of the section was to protect the parents' rights, it is established the consent of the girl is irrelevant.[15]

A person may be guilty even though he did not intend to deprive the parent of lawful control permanently. The offence is committed once the accused puts the girl in a situation which is inconsistent with her parent's physical care of her. In *R v Timmins*[16] it was held that there was a sufficient taking where the accused took a girl to London for three days for the purpose of sleeping with her and at the end of that time told her to return to her father. On the other hand, a mere temporary absence will not suffice if it is not inconsistent with the relationship of parent and daughter.

The accused will have a good defence if he neither knew nor ought to have known that the girl was in anyone's lawful control, for then there will

---

[8] There is no requirement of substantial interference which ought to obviate the problems created by *R v Jones* [1973] Crim LR 621, infra, n 11.
[9] Child Abduction Act 1984, s 3(a). There is a similar definition of 'detain' under s 3(c).
[10] Ibid, s 2(2).
[11] Therefore taking a girl for a walk will not constitute an offence under this section: *R v Jones*, supra.
[12] Sexual Offences Act 1956, s 20. The importance of this provision has been considerably lessened since the Criminal Law Amendment Act 1885 made it an offence to have unlawful sexual intercourse with a girl under the age of 16.
[13] But taking a girl by either of these means will of course amount to the commission of the offence: *R v Hopkins* (1842) Car & M 254, where the accused fraudulently induced the parent to let him take the girl away.
[14] *R v Jarvis* (1903) 20 Cox CC 249; *R v Olifier* (1866) 10 Cox CC 402. But it is to be inferred from the earlier cases that if the accused and the girl leave her house together, he will be liable whoever made the suggestion: *R v Robins* (1844) 1 Car & Kir 456; *R v Biswell* (1847) 2 Cox CC 279.
[15] *R v Manktelow* (1853) 6 Cox CC 143. But see Eekelaar 89 LQR at 215. The parent's having previously permitted the girl to lead an immoral life may be evidence that her leaving was not against his will: *R v Primelt* (1858) 1 F & F 50; *R v Frazer and Norman* (1861) 8 Cox CC 446.
[16] (1860) 8 Cox CC 401.

be no mens rea at all.[17] But if he knows that he is interfering with parental control, it will be no defence that he thought that the girl was over the age of 16.[18] Similarly it will be a good defence that the accused honestly believed that he had a right to the girl's lawful control;[19] but no other motives, for example religious or philanthropic, will excuse his conduct.[20]

(iii) Girls under the age of 18 years

It is an offence to abduct any unmarried girl under the age of 18 with the intention that she should have unlawful sexual intercourse.[1] The offence is the same as the case of a girl under the age of 16 except that the prosecution must also prove the accused's intent.[2] It is also a defence that the accused had reasonable cause to believe that the girl was over the age of 18.

(b) Civil liability

(i) Damages for loss of services

The former tort of wrongfully depriving a parent of his child's services has now been abolished by the Administration of Justice Act 1982.[3]

(ii) Damages for interference with parental responsibility

There is no known tort of interference with parental rights nor therefore with parental responsibility. This was recently established in the leading case, *F v Wirral Metropolitan Borough Council*[4]. The facts were complex but basically involved a complaint by the parents that what was originally understood by them to be a short-term placement with foster parents to which arrangement they had agreed, ended by becoming a long-term arrangement to which they had not agreed and that this therefore constituted a wrongful interference with their rights. In support of this argument they prayed in aid the European Convention on Human Rights and the European Court's decision in *R v United Kingdom*[5] as recognising a right of consortium between parent and child as one of the 'fundamental elements of family life'.[6] After an exhaustive review of the cases the Court of Appeal unanimously concluded in Purchas LJ's words: 'neither under the old common law, apart from the action *per quod servitium amisit*, nor under modern authority is

---

[17] *R v Hibbert* (1869) LR 1 CCR 184. But the number of cases today where the accused would not have constructive knowledge must be negligible.

[18] *R v Prince* (1875) LR 2 CCR 154.

[19] *R v Tinkler* (1859) 1 F & F 513.

[20] *R v Booth* (1872) 12 Cox CC 231.

[1] Sexual Offences Act 1956, ss 19 and 21. (The maximum punishment in either case is 2 years' imprisonment.) 'Unlawful' sexual intercourse means intercourse outside the marriage bond: *R v Chapman* [1959] 1 QB 100, [1958] 3 All ER 143, CCA. Hence no offence will be committed if the accused takes the girl away from her parents with the honest and bona fide intention of marrying her.

[2] *R v Henkers* (1886) 16 Cox CC 257.

[3] S 2(b). But see *Donnelly v Joyce* [1974] QB 454, [1973] 3 All ER 475, CA on the question of damages in an action brought by the child, ante, p 123.

[4] [1991] Fam 69, [1991] 2 All ER 648, CA. Bainham (1990) 3 Journal of Child Law 3 and Cretney [1991] Fam Law 301.

[5] [1988] 2 FLR 445.

[6] Pursuant to art 8 of the Convention.

there a parental right necessary to found a cause of action against a stranger upon which the common law would grant a remedy in damages.'

(iii) The Fatal Accidents Act

We have already seen that parents and children come within the category of dependants for the purposes of the Fatal Accidents Act, so that either may sue any person who has unlawfully caused the death of the other for compensation for percuniary loss resulting from the death.[7]

C. Who has parental responsibility

1. MARRIED PARENTS

Section 2(1) of the 1989 Act provides that where the father and mother of the child were married to each other at the time of the child's birth they *each* have parental responsibility. The phrase 'married to each other at the time of the child's birth' has to be interpreted in accordance with s 1 of the Family Law Reform Act 1987.[8] Stated simply this means that both the father and the mother automatically each have parental responsibility in respect of their legitimate children.[9] A similar position obtains with respect to parents of adopted children.[10]

2. UNMARRIED PARENTS

(a) The position at the child's birth

Where the father and mother of the child were not married to each other at the time of the child's birth (effectively meaning where the child is illegitimate) then section 2(2) of the Children Act 1989 provides that the mother but not the father has parental responsibility for the child.

(b) Subsequent acquisition of parental responsibility by the unmarried father[11]

Although the unmarried father does not automatically have parental responsibility, as section 2(2)(b) states, he can subsequently acquire it in accordance with the provisions of the 1989 Act. He can acquire responsibility in the following ways:

(1) by subsequently marrying the child's mother;
(2) upon taking office as a formally appointed guardian of the child;
(3) by making a parental responsibility *agreement* with the mother;

[7] See ante, p 124.
[8] S 2(3) of the Children Act 1989.
[9] See ante p 280 for a discussion of the circumstances in which children are regarded as 'legitimate'. For a discussion of the legal position of the man whose wife makes a parental responsibility agreement with another man, see post, p 326.
[10] See s 1(3)(c) of the Family Law Reform Act 1987.
[11] See generally: Doggett *Unmarried fathers and section 4 before and after the Children Act 1989* (1992) 4 JCL 39.

(4) by obtaining a parental responsibility *order*;

(5) by obtaining a residence order in which case a separate parental responsibility order *must* be made.

(i) Subsequent marriage

By subsequently marrying the mother, the father brings himself within section 2(1) of the 1989 Act and, provided the child was a minor (ie under the age of 18) at the time,[12] will therefore automatically have parental responsibility. Because conferment of responsibility is an *automatic* consequence, although the Act does not expressly say so, the parents' subsequent marriage must be regarded as overriding any prior parental responsibility order or agreement.[13]

(ii) Guardianship

To become a guardian, the father must formally have been appointed as such by the child's mother, or by the court in accordance with the terms set out in section 5 of the 1989 Act (discussed in chapter 12). Such an appointment can only take effect after the mother's death.

(iii) Parental responsibility agreements

Pursuant to section 4(1)(b) the father and mother may by a parental responsibility agreement provide for the father to have parental responsibility for the child. Such agreements, however, only have effect if they are made in prescribed form and recorded in the prescribed manner.[14] Both the prescribed form and manner of recording are provided for by the Parental Responsibility Agreement Regulations 1991.[15]

This new power to make parental responsibility agreements implements the recommendation of the Law Commission. As the Commission pointed out,[16] although the father could apply for what was then a parental rights and duties order under section 4 of the Family Law Reform Act 1987, the need to resort to judicial proceedings to obtain parental responsibility seemed 'unduly elaborate, expensive and unnecessary unless the child's mother object[ed]'. On the other hand, in recommending this new power, the Commission was also aware of the dangers of undue pressure being exerted upon mothers to make such agreements.[17] Accordingly, they recommended a relatively formal procedure whereby, in order to be binding, the agreement would have to be in a prescribed form and checked by the county court, to ensure that the parents were fully aware of the importance

---

[12] It is therefore possible for a child to be legitimated by his parents' subsequent marriage yet for the father not to have or have had parental responsibility.

[13] The significance of this is that, unlike responsibility acquired by orders or agreements, responsibility acquired through marriage cannot be ended upon a court order other than adoption—see post, p 332.

[14] S 4(2). However as Masson *The Children Act 1989, Text and Commentary* points out at 41–17 an informal agreement could still operate as a delegation of responsibility under s 2(9), discussed post at p 334.

[15] SI 1991/1478.

[16] Law Com No 172, para 2.18.

[17] Indeed, it was because of the potential pressure, that the Law Commission did not originally recommend the power to make binding agreements—see Law Com No 118, *Illegitimacy*, 1982, para 4.39.

and effect of what they were doing[18]. However, this proposal did not find its way into the final version of the Act and the only formal requirements under the 1991 Regulations are that the agreement in prescribed form should be signed by both parents and witnesses and subsequently filed in the Principal Registry of the Family Division. For this latter purpose the agreement and two copies must be taken or posted to the Principal Registry. Sealed copies will be returned to the mother and the father, while the record is open to public inspection.

It can be seen therefore that the formalities are minimal and that in particular there is no investigation of whether the agreement is in the child's best interests or of why the parents are entering into it. Indeed there is no effective check on whether, for example, the man is the father of the child concerned. The Agreement Form contains the express warning:

'The making of this agreement will seriously affect the legal position of both parents. You should both seek legal advice before completing this form.'

Whether such warnings are sufficient to allay the fears, expressed both by the Law Commission and during the passage of the Bill,[19] that mothers may be bullied into conferring rights upon the fathers at a time when they are particularly vulnerable to pressure, may be open to doubt.[20]

(iv) Parental responsibility orders

Replacing the former power order under section 4 of the Family Reform Act 1987 to make parental rights and duties orders, section 4(1)(a) of the 1989 Act now provides that the court[1] may, upon the application by an unmarried father (ie *not* upon its own motion), order that he shall have parental responsibility for the child. If the applicant's paternity is in doubt and *a fortiori* if it is disputed, it will have to be proved before the action may proceed.[2]

In deciding whether or not to make a parental responsibility order the court must, in line with the general principles of the Act, treat the child's welfare as its paramount consideration[3] and be satisfied that making the order would be better for the child than making no order at all.[4] In *Re H (Minors) (Adoption: Putative Father's Rights) (No 3)*[5], a decision on parental rights and duties orders under section 4 of the Family Law Reform Act 1987, Balcombe LJ commented that in deciding whether or not to make an order:

---

[18] Which was argued to be unworkable anyway by Cretney: see 'Defining the Limits of State Intervention: The Child and the Court' in *Children and the Law* (ed Freestone) at pp 65–66.

[19] See particularly Lord Banks, 502 HL Official Report (5th series) cols 1180–82 and 503 HL Official Report col 1319.

[20] See eg Doggett, op cit at p 40.

[1] Ie High Court, county court or magistrates' court: s 92(7).

[2] Cf *Re O (A Minor: Access)* [1985] FLR 716, CA, and *Re W (A Minor) (Interim Custody)* [1990] 2 FLR 86, CA.

[3] Ie pursuant to s 1(1), discussed post at p 336.

[4] Ie pursuant to s 1(5), discussed post at p 345. However in White, Carr and Lowe 'A Guide to the Children Act 1989' para 2.21 it was pointed out that it could be argued that s 1(5) does *not* apply since a parental responsibility order relates to the *parent* and not the child. The authors considered, however, that such an argument was likely to be rejected.

[5] [1991] Fam 151, [1991] 2 All ER 185, 189, CA.

'... the court will have to take into account a number of factors of which the following will undoubtedly be material (although there may well be others as the list is not intended to be exhaustive): (1) the degree of commitment which the father has shown towards the child; (2) the degree of attachment which exists between the father and the child; (3) the reasons of the father for applying for the order.'[6]

In *Re C (Minors)*[7] Mustill LJ stated the basic test to be:

'... was the association between the parties sufficiently enduring; and has the father by his conduct during and since the application shown sufficient commitment to the children, to justify giving the father a legal status equivalent to that which he would have enjoyed if the parties had married?'

The overall tenor of the decisions on the 1987 Act, which is likely to be followed with respect to the 1989 Act, is that provided the father can show that he has established a meaningful relationship with the child a court should be slow to refuse an order. Furthermore it has been held that section 4 orders can be made notwithstanding that the child is in local authority care,[8] or is about to be freed for adoption[9] and the father's inability to enforce most of his 'rights' is not necessarily decisive.[10] On the other hand it has been said that violence against the child is a factor that should always lead to a rejection of the father's application.[11]

It may be noted that the restriction under section 9(6) which prevents the court from making a section 8 order in respect of a child aged 16 or over save in 'exceptional circumstances'[12] does *not* apply to the making of section 4 orders. Similarly, there is no *enjoinder* to have regard to the check-list set out by section 1(3)[13] though there is nothing to prevent the court from considering them if it so wishes. This means that the court is not *obliged* to have regard to older children's wishes yet, as has been pointed out,[14] given that, if the father applies instead for a residence order which is opposed by the mother, the court *must* have regard to the child's wishes, it is difficult to see why the check-list should not apply at the very least to contested section 4 applications.

(v) Residence orders

If a court grants an unmarried father a residence order (discussed in chapter 11) then by section 12(1) the court is also bound to make a *separate* section 4 order. The importance of the section 4 order being made separately is that it will not automatically come to an end if the residence order is ended but will require an express order ending it, if the child is still a minor.

[6] The application form for a parental responsibility order, specifically asks the applicant to state his reasons for making the application: Family Proceedings Rules 1991, Form CHA1.
[7] [1992] 2 All ER 86, 93.
[8] *D v Hereford and Worcester County Council* [1991] Fam 14, [1991] 2 All ER 177.
[9] *Re H (Minors) (Adoption: Putative Father's Rights) (No 3)*, supra. Freeing for adoption is discussed post at p 436.
[10] *Re C (Minors)* supra.
[11] Per Ward J in *D v Hereford and Worcester County Council*, supra. It has also been commented that abuse of the mother might be just as damaging to the father's claims, see Doggett, op cit at p 41.
[12] Discussed post, p 356.
[13] Discussed post, p 338.
[14] By Doggett op cit at p 41. See also *Clarke Hall and Morrison on Children*, Vol 1, para 1[103].

(vi) The effect of parental responsibility orders and agreements

The effect of a court order or a properly recorded agreement is the same, namely, it confers parental responsibility upon the unmarried father. In most cases he will share responsibility jointly with the mother, or if the mother is dead, with any formally appointed guardian. He could also share responsibility with some other person in whose favour a residence order has been made. The legal position of a husband whose wife makes a parental responsibility agreement with another man is not clear. Prima facie that agreement confers responsibility on that other man yet because of the presumption of paternity[15] the woman's husband could also be regarded as having responsibility. Of course once the issue is before the court the conundrum can be solved by a finding of paternity, but what is the position before that? Although there is no objection in principle to two men having parental responsibility in relation to a child, because only one man can actually be the child's father only one of them can be regarded as having responsibility. Although the making of an agreement is some evidence that the husband might not be the father it seems unlikely that the court would regard an agreement alone as sufficient to rebut the presumption of the husband's paternity. One cannot shut one's eyes to the possibility that both the mother and the other man might know that the husband is or could be the father but want to shut him out if the other man is prepared to accept the child is his. In many cases, however, there is likely to be other evidence, for example that before the birth the woman had left her husband to live with the other man.[16]

Although in general terms it is correct to say[17] that an unmarried father with parental responsibility is in the same legal position with regard to the child as if he had married the mother, the effect should be neither over-estimated nor underestimated. Even without responsibility the father is regarded as a 'parent' for the purposes of the Children Act 1989.[18] He therefore, for example, has the right to apply to the court for a section 8 order[19] and is entitled to reasonable contact with a child in local authority care.[20] Furthermore the lack of parental responsibility, as we have seen,[1] does not mean that such fathers have no statutory duty to maintain their children. On the other hand conferring parental responsibility upon unmarried fathers does not alter the status of the child. Hence the child will still not take British citizenship through the parents, nor will he be able to succeed to a title of honour through his parents.[2] How then does the legal position of an unmarried father change upon being vested with parental responsibility? The principal effects are:

(1) he becomes a 'parent' for the purposes of the adoption legislation

---

[15] Discussed ante, pp 269 et seq.
[16] It is also relevant to know who is registered as the father.
[17] See eg Department of Health's Guidance and Regulations, Vol 1, 'Court Orders', para 2.5.
[18] See ante, p 287.
[19] Under s 10(4), discussed post, p 358.
[20] Under s 34, discussed post at p 530.
[1] Ante at p 301.
[2] See ante, p 285.

and can therefore withhold his agreement to a proposed adoption or order freeing the child for adoption;[3]

(2) he becomes entitled to remove his child from local authority accommodation if he is willing and able to provide accommodation or to arrange for accommodation to be provided for his child;[4]

(3) he can appoint a guardian;[5]

(4) he can give a valid consent to his child's medical treatment;[6]

(5) he has the power to consent to his child's marriage;[7]

(6) he is empowered to express a preference as to the school at which he wishes his child's education to be provided;[8]

(7) the mother will need to obtain his consent to take the child (under the age of 16) outside the United Kingdom.[9]

In *Re C (Minors) (Parental Rights)*[10] Waite J commented that upon being vested with parental responsibility the father assumes 'an immediately enforceable burden' to maintain the child. However, as we have said,[11] a father is liable to maintain his child irrespective of whether he also has parental responsibility and in any event a court order will be needed to enforce his obligation whether or not he has responsibility.

(vii) Ending parental responsibility orders or agreements

Parental responsibility orders and agreements remain effective notwithstanding that the couple live together or subsequently separate. They will, however, automatically end once the child attains his majority[12] and, as we have discussed,[13] if the father subsequently marries the mother during the child's minority. Apart from these instances parental responsibility may be brought to an end only upon a court order to that effect. Such an order may be made upon the application (ie not of the court's own motion) of:

(1) any person who has parental responsibility for the child (this will include the father himself) or,

(2) with leave of the court, the child himself.[14]

In the latter case, the court may grant leave only if it is satisfied that the child has sufficient understanding to make the proposed application.[15] The court may not end a section 4 order while a residence order in favour of the unmarried father remains in force.[16]

In deciding whether to end a section 4 order or agreement, the court must regard the child's welfare as its paramount consideration and be

---

[3] Adoption Act 1976, s 72(1); see post, p 423.
[4] Children Act 1989, s 20(7); discussed at p 504.
[5] Ibid, s 5(3).
[6] See ante, p 305.
[7] Marriage Act 1949, s 3(1A)(a)(i); see ante, p 44.
[8] Education Act 1981, s 6, see *Clarke Hall and Morrison on Children* Vol 2, F [651]–[675].
[9] Child Abduction Act 1984, s 1(3)(a)(ii); see ante, p 285.
[10] [1992] 1 FLR 1 at p 9.
[11] Ante at p 301.
[12] Children Act 1989, s 91(7) and (8).
[13] Ante at p 323.
[14] S 4(3).
[15] S 4(4).
[16] S 11(4).

satisfied that discharging the order is better than making no order at all.[17] Nevertheless, it is submitted that the court should be slow to make such an order particularly when the court made a section 4 order in the first place. The position might be different following an agreement, where for example, it could be shown that the mother had been subjected to undue pressure to sign. It should be borne in mind that parental responsibility vested in the married father may be ended only upon the child's adoption, so that the ending of a residence order in the father's favour should not automatically mean that parental responsibility should also come to an end. In any event, a separate order expressly ending the section 4 order will be required to end the father's parental responsibility.

3. THE POSITION OF NON-PARENTS

Those who are not parents do not have parental responsibility automatically but they can acquire it. For example, any person taking office as a guardian has parental responsibility for the child concerned.[18] Similarly any person (who is not a parent or guardian) in whose favour a residence order has been made has parental responsibility for the duration of the order[19] though this will not entitle such a person to consent to an order freeing the child for adoption or an adoption order nor may he appoint a guardian.[20] An individual also acquires parental responsibility upon being granted an emergency protection order though this will only entitle him to take 'such action in meeting his responsibility for the child as is reasonably required to safeguard or promote the welfare of the child (having regard in particular to the duration of the order)'.[1]

Local authorities can also acquire parental responsibility. They will do so primarily on the making of a care order[2] when they will share responsibility with any parent or guardian. If they are satisfied that it is necessary to do so to safeguard or promote the child's welfare, however, they may determine the extent to which a parent or guardian of the child may meet his parental responsibility for him.[3] In no event, however, will a local authority be empowered to change the child's religion, to consent to an order freeing him for adoption, to agree to his adoption or to appoint a guardian.[4] Local authorities also acquire parental responsibility to the same limited extent as individuals upon being granted an emergency protection order.

---

[17] Pursuant to s 1(1) and 1(5).
[18] S 5(6).
[19] S 12(2).
[20] S 12(3).
[1] Children Act 1989, ss 44(4)(c) and 44(5)(b). Emergency protection orders are discussed post at pp 534 et seq.
[2] S 33(3)(a). Care orders are discussed post, pp 507 et seq.
[3] S 33(3)(b), (4).
[4] S 33(6).

4. SHOULD THE ALLOCATION OF PARENTAL RESPONSIBILITY BE MODIFIED?

Parental responsibility is not automatically vested in any person other than each married parent or the unmarried mother. Should it be? One candidate is the unmarried father particularly if he is living with the mother in a stable union and is sharing the upbringing of the child. As we have seen,[5] the Law Commission at one stage proposed abolishing the concept of illegitimacy altogether with the consequence that all fathers would be in the same legal position with regard to their child.[6] That suggestion, however, met with little favour[7] and it was not recommended. The Law Commission also rejected any compromise solution by which automatic responsibility could be vested in so-called 'meritorious' fathers principally because no adequate definition of such men could be found. The system operating in New Zealand,[8] under which parental rights are vested jointly in both parents provided that they are living together as man and wife at the time of the child's birth, was rejected inter alia because it was both arbitrary and difficult to operate and it was thought it would not necessarily promote the welfare of children.[9] Instead the Law Commission favoured the proposal first implemented in the Family Law Reform Act 1987 and now enacted in the Children Act 1989 that unmarried fathers should be able to apply to a court to obtain full parental status.

In their later review of the law the Commission considered[10] that the issue of giving unmarried fathers automatic parental status had been fully canvassed and rejected though, as we have seen, their new recommendation, since implemented by the 1989 Act, was that unmarried fathers and mothers should be able to make binding agreements conferring parental responsibility on fathers. The Scottish Law Commission went through a not dissimilar process and also rejected the idea of conferring an automatic status on the unmarried father.[11] However in their latest review they have not only reopened the question[12] but have recommended that[13] 'in the absence of any court order regulating the position, those parents of the child should have parental responsibilities and rights whether or not they are or have been named to each other'.

Whether in the light of this the English Law Commission could be persuaded to re-open the issue remains to be seen.

Another person for whom a case for vesting automatic responsibility can be made is the step-parent who marries one of the child's parents and shares in day-to-day care.[14] Indeed now that it is clear that even the

---

[5] Ante, p 286.
[6] Working Paper No 74 on Illegitimacy.
[7] For a summary of the criticism see Law Commission No 118 (1st Report on Illegitimacy) para 4.26 and Hayes 43 MLR 299.
[8] Under the Guardianship Act 1968 (as amended), s 6.
[9] See ibid, paras 4.23–4.36. Other suggestions, eg that parental rights should be based on voluntary acknowledgment of paternity were also rejected: see paras 4.37–4.40.
[10] Law Com No 172, para 2.17.
[11] Scot Law Com No 82 (1984), paras 2.2–2.5; see Law Reform (Parent and Child) (Scotland) Act 1986, s 2(1).
[12] Discussion Paper No 99 (1990), paras 2.23 et seq.
[13] Report on Family Law (Sco Law Com No 135, 1992), para 2.50.
[14] One advocate for this change is Masson: see her arguments inter alia in *Old families into new: a status for step-parents* in *State, Law and the Family* (ed Freeman) ch 14 pp 237 et seq.

absent parent will not lose parental responsibility if a step-parent sub-sequently acquires it by obtaining a residence order there would seem less objection in principle to vesting it automatically in the latter.[15] If, however, it is felt that as with unmarried fathers the law should vest responsibility only in those non-parents who positively seek it, consideration might still be given to enabling the parents and step-parent to make a tripartite parental responsibility agreement.[16]

D. In respect of whom there is responsibility

Parental responsibility exists in respect of a 'child', that is, a person under the age of 18.[17] It is a moot point as to whether responsibility exists for a married child.[18]

1. THE POSITION WITH REGARD TO UNBORN CHILDREN[19]

The 1989 Act is silent on when parental responsibility begins but in the absence of any indication to the contrary it is suggested that references to 'child' in the Act mean a live child.[20] Accordingly, it is submitted that no one has parental responsibility until the child is born and that therefore the parents' position with regard to their unborn child is unaffected by the 1989 Act.[1]

It would appear that fathers have no rights over foetuses. At any rate this was the reasoning of Sir George Baker P in *Paton v British Pregnancy Advisory Service Trustees*[2] when he refused a husband's application for an injunction to prevent his wife from having an abortion. An unmarried father was similarly refused an injunction in *C v S*.[3] In *Paton's* case strong *obiter* doubts were also expressed as to whether the court should interfere even though the medical practitioners involved had not acted in good faith in issuing the certificate required by the Abortion Act 1967 and there was an obvious attempt to commit a crime: it is not for the civil courts to interfere with the exercise of doctors' discretion under the Act. This view

---

[15] Cf Law Com Working Paper No 91, *Guardianship*, paras 4.15 to 4.19 which canvassed views about the possibility of step-parents acquiring responsibility by administrative rather than judicial means but did not pursue the point because it attracted little support at the time: Law Com No 172, *Guardianship and Custody*, para 2.22.

[16] See *Report on Pathways to Adoption Research Project* by Murch, Lowe, Borkowski, Copner and Griew (Bristol University) p 217.

[17] Children Act 1989, s 105(1).

[18] See post, p 332.

[19] See generally Douglas *Law, Fertility and Reproduction* pp 82–83, 187–189.

[20] For a similar interpretation of the meaning of 'child' under the Children and Young Persons Act 1969, s 70(1) see *D (A Minor) v Berkshire County Council* [1987] AC 317, [1987] 1 All ER 20, HL.

[1] If Parliament had intended to make a change it would surely have expressly done so.

[2] [1979] QB 276, [1978] 2 All ER 987. See further Kennedy 42 MLR 324; Phillips 95 LQR 332; Lowe 96 LQR 29 and Lowe and White *Wards of Court* (2nd Edn), paras 2–3. The husband also failed before the European Commission of Human Rights which ruled that although he had *locus standi* to bring the complaint, there had been no breach of the Convention since the abortion was certified as being necessary for the wife's health: (1980) 3 EHRR 408.

[3] [1988] QB 135, [1987] 1 All ER 1230, CA.

may appear to have been weakened by the fact that both Heilbron J and the Court of Appeal in *C v S* were prepared to hear argument that the proposed abortion was contrary to the provisions of the Infant Life (Preservation) Act 1929, section 1. However, Sir John Donaldson MR commented that even if a breach of the 1929 Act could have been proved, 'strong consideration' would still have been paid to Sir George Baker P's comment that the matter would be better left to the Director of Public Prosecutions who could then consider whether prosecutions should be brought. It is submitted that even if the abortion were ex facie illegal the father still could not obtain an injunction to prevent the commission of the proposed criminal act once it is accepted that he has no right which would be affected.[4]

Re F (In Utero)[5] unequivocally establishes that there is no power to ward an unborn child though interestingly the principal reason for so holding was the unacceptable clash between the unborn child's interests and those of the mother that the exercise of wardship would inevitably entail, rather than the foetus's having no rights of its own to protect.

2. THE POSITION WITH REGARD TO EMBRYOS[6]

As one commentator has said:[7] 'The advent of assisted reproduction and the ability to fertilise an ovum *in vitro* and to maintain the resulting embryo for a number of days has required the law to work out whether, and how, to protect such an embryo'. The legal framework is now provided for by the Human Fertilisation and Embryology Act 1990 which in turn is based upon the recommendations of the Warnock Report.[8] Detailed consideration of this Act lies outside the scope of this work,[9] nevertheless it is worth noting that in contradistinction to his position with regard to a foetus, the father (as well as the mother) does have rights with respect to an embryo in vitro whilst outside the womb. Whilst stopping short of providing for ownership, the 1990 Act nevertheless provides that embryos can only be used, stored or disposed of with the consent of the *persons* whose gametes were used to create the embryo in vitro.[10]

---

[4] Cf *Gouriet v Union of Post Office Workers* [1978] AC 435, [1977] 3 All ER 70, HL. But see Kennedy, loc cit.

[5] [1988] Fam 122, [1988] 2 All ER 193, CA. Lowe *The Limits of Wardship Jurisdiction* (1988) 1 Journal of Child Law 6 and Fortin *Can You Ward a Foetus?* (1988) 51 MLR 768. For further discussion of this case see post, ch 14.

[6] See Douglas, op cit, ch 3 and Kennedy and Grubb *Medical Law: Text and Materials* 655 et seq.

[7] Douglas, op cit at p 33.

[8] Report of the Committee of Inquiry into Human Fertilisation and Embryology (1984) Cmnd 9314.

[9] For more detailed reading, see eg Morgan and Lee *The Human Fertilisation and Embryology Act 1990* Douglas *Law, Fertility and Reproduction* [1991] Fam Law 110.

[10] Sch 3.

E. Duration of parental responsibility

One of the important aspects of parental responsibility under the Children Act 1989 is its enduring nature and that in particular it is not lost merely because someone else acquires it. Nevertheless responsibility does not have an unlimited duration. As we have said it can only exist in respect of a 'child'.

In all cases therefore parental responsibility ends upon the child attaining his majority. It will clearly end upon the child's death.[11] Those other than parents who have responsibility by reason of a care order and anyone who has responsibility by reason of an emergency protection order only have responsibility for the duration of the order.[12]

Apart from the above-mentioned circumstances there is uncertainty as to whether other events can end parental responsibility. Before the Children Act 1989 there was authority for saying that the right of custody ended upon the child's marriage[13] and that it was suspended whilst the child was serving in the armed forces[14] but it remains to be seen whether a similar position will be taken with regard to parental responsibility. There is also conflicting opinion as to whether responsibility ceases in respect of any aspect of a child's upbringing about which the child himself is sufficiently mature to make his own decisions.[15] Perhaps the better view in each of these situations is that parental responsibility does not end but that the scope for its exercise is limited.

F. Sharing parental responsibility for a child and the right of independent action

Although self-evident, given the position of married parents under section 2(1) of the Children Act 1989, section 2(5) nevertheless expressly provides that more than one person may have parental responsibility for the same child at the same time. Section 2(6) further provides that a person with parental responsibility does not cease to have it solely because some other person subsequently acquires it. This latter provision which, in the words of one commentator,[16] 'encapsulates the ethos of continuing parental responsibility' means, for example, that a parent will not lose responsibility because someone else such as a step-parent, grandparent, foster parent or even, most remarkably, a local authority acquires it. Section 2(6) should

---

[11] It is established however that even if the child had been in care the parent retains the right to bury the child: *R v Gwynedd County Council, ex p B* [1992] 3 All ER 317, CA.

[12] See respectively ss 12(2), 33(3) and 44(4)(c).

[13] See eg *Hewer v Bryant* [1970] 1 QB 357, 373, [1969] 3 All ER 578, 585, CA per Sachs LJ; *R v Wilmington Inhabitants* (1822) 5 B & Ald 525, 526 and *Lough v Ward* [1945] 2 All ER 338, 348.

[14] *R v Rotherfield Greys Inhabitants* (1823) 1 B & C 345, 349–350.

[15] Cf the comment of Lord Scarman in *Gillick v West Norfolk and Wisbech Area Health Authority* [1986] AC 112, 186, [1985] 3 All ER 402, 421–422, which suggests it does, but which was specifically rejected by Lord Donaldson MR in *Re R (A Minor) (Wardship: Medical Treatment)* [1992] Fam 11, 23 [1991] 4 All ER 177, 185, discussed ante at p 308, which suggests it does not. See also Eekelaar 102 LQR 4, but cf Bainham [1986] CLJ 262.

[16] Bainham *Children, The New Law, The Children Act 1989* para 2.18.

not however be read as meaning that a court order can never end a parent's responsibility. An adoption order clearly does because the statute expressly says so.[17]

Where parental responsibility is shared then, as section 2(7) provides, each person in whom it is vested 'may act alone and without the other (or others) in meeting that responsibility' except where a statute expressly requires the consent of more than one person in a matter affecting the child. This power to act independently, however, is subject to the important limitation under section 2(8), namely, that a person with parental responsibility is not entitled to act in any way that could be incompatible with a court order.[18]

The impact of section 2 with regard to the married parents of a child is as follows: under section 2(1) each parent has parental responsibility and by section 2(7) each may act independently and without the other, subject only to express statutory provisions to the contrary. This latter qualification preserves, for example, the embargo imposed by section 1 of the Child Abduction Act 1984, against one parent taking the child outside the United Kingdom without the other's consent and maintains the need to obtain each parent's agreement to an adoption order as laid down by section 16 of the Adoption Act 1976. This ability to act independently means of course not simply that neither parent has a right of veto but also that there is no legal duty upon parents to consult each other.[19] Accordingly, where there is a disagreement between the parents, the burden will be on the one seeking, for example, to prevent a step which the other is proposing, to take the issue to court. According to the Law Commission[20] the independence of each parent should be seen 'as part of the general aim of encouraging both parents to feel concerned and responsible for the welfare of their children'.[1]

When the parents separate or are divorced, each continues to have parental responsibility even if a residence order has been made in favour of one of them. A parent whose child does not live with him should still be regarded in law as a parent and should be treated as such by, for example, schools and therefore be given information and an opportunity to take decisions about his child's education. Where that parent has the child with him, then subject to his not acting in a way that is incompatible with any court order, he will be able to exercise his responsibilities to the full. In other words, even where a residence order has been granted in one parent's favour, *each* will still be able to exercise his or her responsibilities without having to consult the other, and neither will have the right of veto

---

[17] Adoption Act 1976, s 12(3)(a), discussed post, p 455. As Lord Mackay LC said during the Debates on the Children Bill (588 HL Official Report (5th series) col 1175) the word 'solely' is used advisedly in s 2(6), ie an adoption order deprives a parent of responsibility not *solely* because adoptive parents acquire it but because the 1976 Act expressly extinguishes it.

[18] The absence of a court order, however, does not necessarily mean that parental responsibility may be exercised without qualification. For example since ultimate responsibility for a ward of court rests with the court (see post, p 460), the warding of a child must immediately operate at least to limit freedom of action.

[19] This resolved the uncertainty of the former law which seemed to impose no duty to consult but did confer a power of veto, see Law Com Working Paper No 96, *Custody*, para 2.34 et seq.

[20] Law Com No 172, para 2.10.

[1] Though for a critique of this position see Bainham [1990] Fam Law, 192, 193, discussed below.

over the other's action. The wisdom of so providing has been criticised at any rate with respect to serious or long-term decisions affecting children on the grounds that by failing to provide for consultation and a right of objection the Act while in form appearing to favour joint parenting following breakdown, 'in substance reinforces the already superior *de facto* position of the person with physical care'.[2] In theory the embargo against acting incompatibly with a court order covers not only express prohibitions but implicit restrictions as well. For example, as the Law Commission instanced,[3] where a child has to live with one parent and go to school nearby, it would be incompatible for the other parent to arrange for him to have his hair done in a way which will exclude him from the school. It would not, however, be incompatible for that parent to take him to a particular sporting occasion over the weekend, no matter how much the parent with whom the child lived might disapprove. However, the point has been well made[4] that the courts might well be reluctant to find that an order has been broken without a clear indication of what the order permits.

As section 2(6) makes clear neither parent loses parental responsibility solely because someone else has acquired it through a court order. This means, for example, that upon divorce a father does not lose responsibility even if a step-father also acquires it under a residence order made in his favour.[5] In this situation the mother, step-father and father all share responsibility for the child and subject to not acting incompatibly with a court order, all three can exercise their responsibility independently of the others. A similar situation arises if grandparents or other relations or foster parents have residence orders made in their favour.

G. Delegation of parental responsibility

As under the common law, section 2(9) provides that a person with parental responsibility cannot surrender or transfer any part of his responsibility to another. Section 2(9), however, recognises for the first time the power of a person with responsibility to 'arrange for some or all of it to be met by one or more persons acting on his behalf'. Such delegation can be made to another person who already has parental responsibility[6] or to those who have not, such as schools or holiday camps. The aim of this provision is to encourage parents (regardless of whether or not they are separated) to agree among themselves on what they believe to be the best arrangements for their children. Section 2(9) provides that delegation will not absolve a person with parental responsibility from any liability for failure on his part to discharge his responsibilities to the child, for example not to neglect,

---

[2] Bainham [1990] Fam Law at p 193. As Cretney and Masson *Principles of Family Law* (5th Edn) more cryptically observe at p 514: 'The fact that two or more estranged parties have parental responsibility for the child is likely to increase the opportunities for dispute rather than resolve problems'.
[3] Law Com No 172, para 2.11.
[4] See Cretney and Masson, op cit, 514 n 1a.
[5] It will be noted that step-parents may acquire parental responsibility only through a residence order or upon being appointed a guardian. They do not acquire responsibility simply by marrying the child's parent.
[6] S 2(10).

abandon, expose or cause or procure a child under the age of 16 to be assaulted or ill-treated under sections 1 and 17 of the Children and Young Persons Act 1933.[7]

H. The position of those caring for a child who do not have parental responsibility

Resolving the confusion of the pre-1989 Act law[8] the Children Act clarifies the legal position of those who are caring for a child but who do not have parental responsibility, by providing that they 'may (subject to the provisions of this Act) do what is reasonable in all the circumstances for the purpose of safeguarding or promoting the child's welfare'. As is observed in the Department of Health's *Guidance and Regulations*,[9] what is reasonable 'will depend upon the urgency and gravity of what is required and the extent to which it is practicable to consult a person with parental responsibility'. Prima facie while a carer may be able to consent to the child's medical treatment in the event of an accident, he will not be able to consent to major elective surgery. Indeed, as has been observed,[10] it may also be difficult for the carer to convince a doctor that he has sufficient authority to consent to medical treatment which may be desirable but not essential. Anyone who cares for a child is obliged not to assault, ill-treat, neglect, abandon or expose the child in a manner likely to cause unnecessary suffering or injury to health.[11]

[7] See ante, p 314.
[8] See Law Com No 172, para 2.16.
[9] Vol 1, Court Orders, para 2.11.
[10] Cretney and Masson, op cit at 515.
[11] Children and Young Persons Act 1933, s 1.

Chapter 10

General principles under the Children Act 1989

A. The paramountcy of the child's welfare

As we saw in chapter 8 English law progressed in a remarkably short time from virtually having no regard to the child's welfare to treating it as being the first and paramount consideration. In similar but not exactly the same vein section 1(1) of the Children Act 1989 lays down the cardinal principle that:

'When any court determines any question with respect to:

(a) the upbringing of the child; or
(b) the administration of the child's property or the application of any income arising from it,

the child's welfare shall be the court's paramount consideration.'

It should be noted that whereas formerly courts were directed[1] to treat the child's welfare as their *first and* paramount consideration, section 1(1) of the 1989 Act simply directs the court to treat the child's welfare as its paramount consideration. However, it is neither contemplated nor intended that the omitted words will lead to a change of practice.[2] Although in the past 'first' had, in the words of the Law Commission,[3] 'led some courts to balance other considerations *against* the child's welfare rather than to consider what light they shed upon it', that view has long ceased to be the law. As Lord MacDermott put it, in the case of *J v C,*[4] the paramountcy principle connotes:

'... a process whereby, when all the relevant facts, relationships, claims and wishes of parents, risks, choices and other circumstances are taken into account and weighed, the course to be followed will be that which is most in the interests of the child's welfare as that term is now to be understood. That is the first consideration because of its first importance and the paramount consideration because it rules upon or determines the course to be followed.'

In this sense, therefore, the 1989 Act's paramountcy formulation simply reflects the previous well established position that the child's welfare is the court's sole concern and other factors are relevant only to the extent that they can assist the court in ascertaining the best solution for the child.

---

[1] Ie under s 1 of the Guardianship of Minors Act 1971.
[2] See *C v C (A Minor) (Custody: Appeal)* [1991] 1 FLR 223, CA in which Balcombe LJ commented (at p 230) that it seemed to him that the new wording would not make 'any material difference' to the law.
[3] Law Com No 172 *Review of Child Law, Guardianship and Custody*, 1988, para 3.13, citing *Re L (Infants)* [1962] 3 All ER 1, CA and *Re F (An Infant)* [1969] 2 Ch 238, 241.
[4] [1970] AC 668, 710–711, [1969] 1 All ER 788, 820–821, HL.

In choosing the paramountcy formulation, the Government rejected the Law Commission's recommendation,[5] that 'when determining any question under the Act the welfare of *any child likely to be affected* shall be the court's *only* concern'. The Commission were unhappy with a pure paramountcy formulation, being concerned inter alia[6] that litigants might still be tempted to introduce evidence that had no relevance to the child in the hope of persuading the court to balance one against the other. Even if this fear had been justified (which was doubtful given that the paramountcy formulation had been well tested before the Act and seemed to produce the right balance both in terms of the evidence submitted and the weight put on it) the Law Commission's own formulation carried the equally undesirable risk of courts refusing to hear evidence unless it directly addressed the question of what is best for the child.

More serious objections against the Commission's proposals could be made with respect to the requirement to consider the welfare of any child. First, as has been pointed out,[7] such a requirement could lead to wide and speculative enquiries which ultimately could blur the court's view and duty towards the welfare of the child before it. Under such a test the court might have had to compromise between the interests of two or more children.[8] In any event once the enjoinder to consider the welfare of the particular child before the court is departed from there seems no reason to stop at the welfare of other children. A plausible case could be made out to include the welfare of others, for example, an adult but disabled sibling who is still living with the family or an infirm parent or grandparent, each of whom could be argued to have claim for consideration equal with other children. However, any such broadening might have had the effect of weakening the protection of children which the Law Commission itself was not prepared to contemplate.[9]

1. THE MEANING OF 'WELFARE'

The term 'welfare' as such is not defined in the 1989 Act and although the welfare principle had been the cornerstone of child law for some considerable time before the new legislation it is surprisingly difficult to find judicial articulation of its meaning. One of the few statements is that of Lindley LJ who, in 1893, said:[10]

'... the welfare of the child is not to be measured by money alone nor by physical comfort only. The word welfare must be taken in its widest sense. The moral and religious welfare must be considered as well as its physical well-being. Nor can the ties of affection be disregarded.'

[5] Clause 1(2) of the Draft Bill published in Law Com No 172.
[6] See ibid, para 3.14.
[7] White, Carr and Lowe *A Guide to the Children Act 1989* para 1.6.
[8] But it is not always possible even under the paramountcy test to treat *each* child's welfare as the paramount consideration, see eg *Clarke-Hunt v Newcombe* (1982) 4 FLR 482, CA discussed post at p 387.
[9] Law Com No 172 at para 3.12.
[10] *Re McGrath (Infants)* [1893] 1 Ch 143, 148.

Perhaps the best modern statement of the meaning of 'welfare' is that made in a New Zealand case by Hardy Boys J who said:[11]

'"Welfare" is an all-encompassing word. It includes material welfare, both in the sense of an adequacy of resources to provide a pleasant home and a comfortable standard of living and in the sense of an adequacy of care to ensure that good health and due personal pride are maintained. However, while material considerations have their place, they are secondary matters. More important are the stability and the security, the loving and understanding care and guidance, the warm and compassionate relationships, that are essential for the full development of the child's own character, personality and talents.'

Ideally, the court should be concerned to promote the child's long-term future.[12] However, while there are cases where the court has clearly anticipated future contingencies such as parental acquisition of employment and remarriage[13] or where regard has been had to furthering the child's education and general prospects,[14] inevitably the court will tend to concentrate on the immediate ties and environment of the child.

It is sometimes said that in applying the welfare principle the court must act in the child's best interests. However, this may put an unduly sanguine gloss on the court's functions: it should be appreciated that a judge is not dealing with what is ideal for the child but simply with what is the best that can be done in the circumstances. Perhaps not untypical of the dilemmas faced by the court is that described by Cumming-Bruce LJ as being before the trial judge in *Clarke-Hunt v Newcombe*,[15] namely:

'There was not really a right solution; there were two alternative wrong solutions. The problem for the judge was to appreciate the factors in each direction and to decide which of the two bad solutions was the least dangerous, having regard to the long-term interests of the children...'

2. THE CHECK-LIST

Although the 1989 Act does not define 'welfare' it has introduced a check-list of relevant factors to which in certain circumstances (discussed below) the court must have regard, when deciding what, if any, order to make. The introduction of a check-list had been recommended by the Law Commission[16] both as 'a means of providing greater consistency and clarity in the law' and 'as a major step towards a more systematic approach to decisions concerning children'.

In other words the object is not to redefine what is meant by 'welfare' but to provide a means by which greater homogeneity can be achieved in

[11] In *Walker v Walker and Harrison*, noted in [1981] NZ Recent Law 257 and cited by the Law Commission, Working Paper No 96, *Custody* (1985), para 6.10.
[12] Unless perhaps where the short-term disadvantages are so overwhelming as to rule out the long-term option: see eg *Thompson v Thompson* [1987] Fam Law 89, CA.
[13] See respectively *Re DW (A Minor) (Custody)* [1984] Fam Law 17, CA and *S(BD) v S(DJ)* [1977] Fam 109, [1977] 1 All ER 656, CA.
[14] See *May v May* [1986] 1 FLR 325, CA (order made in favour of father who was more academic than the mother) and cf *Re DW*, supra and *Re O (Infants)* [1962] 2 All ER 10, CA (boy's long-term future better in Sudan, girl's in England).
[15] (1983) 4 FLR 482, CA. A good example of the operating of the 'least detrimental' alternative is *Re P (A Minor) (Custody)* (1983) 4 FLR 401, CA discussed post, p 384, n 10.
[16] Law Com No 172, paras 3.17 et seq.

exercising the undoubtedly wide discretion in determining what is best for the child. The inestimable advantage of a list is that it enables everyone from the judge to the litigant, the advocate to the welfare officer, to focus on the same issues at the same time.

(a) The contents of the 'list'

The check-list, which is contained in section 1(3) is as follows:

'(a) the ascertainable wishes and feelings of the child concerned (considered in the light of his age and understanding);
(b) his physical, emotional and educational needs;
(c) the likely effect on him of any change in his circumstances;
(d) his age, sex, background and any characteristics of his which the court considers relevant;
(e) any harm which he has suffered or is at risk of suffering;
(f) how capable each of his parents, and any other person in relation to whom the court considers the question to be relevant, is of meeting his needs;
(g) the range of powers available to the court under this Act in the proceedings in question.'

We shall consider later[17] in more detail how the check-list applies in particular cases but at this stage it is relevant to make the following observations.

First, the check-list is not exhaustive and indeed might properly be regarded as the minimum that will be considered by the court. It is always open to the court to specify other matters which it would like to see included in the welfare officer's report.[18]

Secondly, the contents of the check-list follows that recommended by the Law Commission save for the addition of that under section 1(3)(g), the purpose of which is to emphasise the court's duty to consider not only whether the order being sought is the best for the child but also to consider the alternatives that the Act makes available. This, as we shall see,[19] has particular application in care proceedings in which it is incumbent upon the court to consider not just whether or not to make the care order but whether, for example, a residence order under section 8 would better serve the child's interests.

Thirdly, although a statutory check-list is new, with the exception of section 1(3)(g), the factors themselves are drawn from and build upon previous practice. Nevertheless it is to be noted that as a result of section 1(3)(a) the courts are directed for the first time to have regard to the child's own wishes both in the context of private disputes over children following their parents' separation or divorce and in care proceedings.[20] It will be noted however, that the child's view is *not* expressed to be determinative,[1] though clearly the older the child the more persuasive his views will be.

[17] See post, pp 385 et seq.
[18] See post, p 379.
[19] Post, p 517.
[20] Cf adoption, where it has long been a statutory requirement: Adoption Act 1976, s 6, discussed post at p 417.
[1] See Lord Mackay's comments at 502 HL Official Report (5th series) col 1135.

(b) When the check-list applies

Section 1(4) directs the courts to have regard to the check-list in *contested* section 8 applications and *all* proceedings under Part IV of the 1989 Act including therefore all applications for care and supervision orders. There is, however, nothing to prevent the courts from considering the factors in other proceedings if they so choose and indeed particularly in contested applications under sections 4[2] and 5[3] it would seem prudent to do so.

The reason for restricting the application of section 1(3) to *contested* section 8 cases is that in many family proceedings such as divorce there is often no choice as to where and with whom the child should live. If section 1(3) applied to all section 8 cases courts might feel compelled to investigate even these cases in depth.[4] Such an investigation would not only be a waste of resources but also, arguably, an unwarranted intrusion into family autonomy.

Although section 1(3) specifically directs *the court* to have regard to the check-list it will clearly be useful to legal advisers and their clients both in preparing and in arguing their case. The Law Commission envisaged[5] that the list would enable parties to prepare relevant evidence and that focussing clients' minds on the real issues might help to promote settlements.

3. THE MEANING OF 'PARAMOUNT'

As we said earlier in this chapter even before the implementation of the Children Act 1989 it had been established that the child's welfare was so overwhelmingly important as effectively to be the sole consideration.

The effect of the paramountcy of the child's welfare is strikingly illustrated by the leading case, *J v C*.[6] In that case a Spanish couple came to England looking for work. Whilst here the mother gave birth to a boy but because she was ill the baby went to live with English foster parents. When the couple later returned to Spain they took the boy with them but whilst they were in Spain the boy's health deteriorated and he went back to the foster parents. The parents meanwhile went to West Germany to look for work and having successfully improved their economic position returned to Spain. They then sought their son's return. Unfortunately, litigation was protracted and it took a further five years for the case to reach the House of Lords. By that time the boy, who had spent all but eighteen months of his ten years with the foster parents in England, had become well integrated into the family. Moreover, he had been brought up as an English boy, spoke little Spanish and scarcely knew his parents. The House of Lords held that even assuming the parents to be 'unimpeachable' nevertheless their interests could be, and were in this case, outweighed by the child's welfare. They therefore refused to interfere with the trial judge's order that care and control should be given to the English foster parents and not to the natural parents since the latter 'would be quite unable to cope with the problems of adjustment or with the consequential maladjustment and suffering and

---

[2] Discussed ante at p 324.
[3] Discussed post at p 404.
[4] See Law Com No 172 at para 3.19.
[5] Ibid at para 3.18.
[6] [1970] AC 668, 710, [1969] 1 All ER 788, 820–821, HL.

the father's character would inflame the difficulties'.

The significance of *J v C* cannot be over-emphasised: it unequivocally established that the child's welfare is so overwhelmingly important that it can outweigh the interests of even unimpeachable parents in seeking to look after their own child against a stranger. A fortiori it is the dominant consideration in disputes between parents. Perhaps even more significant than this is the fact that in their first assessment of the application of the welfare principle the Law Lords were so committed to and appreciative of the child's welfare. Thus *J v C* set the pattern of development for the following decades and must be still regarded as the locus classicus on the application of the welfare principle under the Children Act 1989.

A good example of the influence of *J v C* and a further illustration of the significance of the paramountcy of the welfare principle is in relation to the parties' conduct. During the nineteenth century it was the practice of the Divorce Court not to give care and control to a mother who had committed adultery[7] and it was not until the turn of the century that the courts were prepared to concede that this should not automatically deprive her of custody.[8] Even as late as 1962 the Court of Appeal was of the opinion that, however rare it was for one person to be solely responsible for marital breakdown, when this occurred the 'unimpeachable' parent's wishes must be given special consideration.[9] In *S(BD) v S(DJ) (Children: Care and Control)*,[10] however, the Court of Appeal held that the earlier decisions were inconsistent with *J v C* and that, if the welfare of the child so demands, care and control must be left with the 'guilty' party, however unjust the other will believe the decision to be.[11] In other words the interests of justice between the parents do not outweigh the welfare principle.

It is now established that matrimonial misconduct is relevant only insofar as it reflects on that person as a parent. The court is not concerned to punish the adult for his conduct[12] but only with doing what is best for the child. Indeed in *S(BD) v S(DJ)* the use of the term 'unimpeachable' parent was deprecated at any rate in the context of an inter-parental dispute.[13] As Ormrod LJ said:[14]

'I have never known and still do not know what it means. It cannot mean a parent who is above criticism because there is no such thing. It might mean a parent against whom no matrimonial offence has been proved. If so it adds

---

[7] See eg *Clout v Clout* (1861) 2 Sw & Tr 391. Cf the provisions of Talfourd's Act, ante at p 292. But custody was not refused to an adulterous father in the absence of some further factor likely to lead to the child's corruption.

[8] *Re A and B (Infants)* [1897] 1 Ch 786, CA.

[9] *Re L (Infants)* [1962] 3 All ER 1, CA.

[10] [1977] Fam 109, [1977] 1 All ER 656, CA, followed in *Re K (Wardship: Care and Control)* [1977] Fam 179, [1977] 1 All ER 647, CA. See Hall [1977] CLJ 252.

[11] As in *Re K*, supra, where the father (a clergyman) was prepared to go to any lengths to effect a reconciliation with his wife and to avoid his children being brought up in a house in which she would be living in adultery with her lover. See further Berkovits 10 Fam Law 164.

[12] See *Re L (Minors) (Wardship: Jurisdiction)* [1974] 1 All ER 913, 926, CA, per Buckley LJ.

[13] It may still have some relevance in the context of a dispute between parents and third parties.

[14] Ibid at 115–116 and 661 respectively. See also *Re R (Minors) (Wardship: Jurisdiction)* (1981) 2 FLR 416, 425 where Ormrod LJ referred to the 'unimpeachable parent' as being in 'forensic limbo'.

nothing to the record which is before the court and in any event is now outmoded. I think in truth it is really an advocate's phrase.'

Whether the paramountcy principle has in fact been diluted by another of the general principles laid down by section 1 of the 1989 Act, namely, that of non-intervention, will be discussed later.[15]

4. WHEN THE PARAMOUNTCY PRINCIPLE APPLIES

The paramountcy principle has a wide though not unlimited application. As section 1(1) states, it applies whenever a court is called upon to determine any question about the child's upbringing or the administration of his property. *J v C*[16] establishes that the principle applies equally to disputes between parents and other individuals as well as to disputes between parents[17] and, as the Department of Health's Guidance on the 1989 Act states,[18] it applies *whenever* a court is considering whether to make a section 8 order (ie regardless of who the parties are or in which proceedings the issue is raised).

Not all proceedings directly affecting the child's upbringing or property are governed by the paramountcy principle. For example, it is expressly excluded by section 105(1) from applications for maintenance for a child. Furthermore although in general terms the principle applies to proceedings under Parts IV and V it will only come into play provided the applicant can satisfy the court that the preconditions for a care order or for an emergency protection have been made out.[19] As Andrew Bainham has pointed out,[20] 'The more limited application of the welfare principle in care proceedings reflects the need to set limits to the power of the state to intervene in the family, by defining more specifically the circumstances in which this is permissible.'

In other areas statutory law puts a different weighting on the child's welfare. For example in deciding whether to make an adoption order[21] the court is directed to treat the child's welfare as its *first* consideration.[1] The child's welfare is similarly to be given first consideration in proceedings relating to the adjustment of property and financial matters on divorce.[2]

In applications to oust an adult from the matrimonial home following the ruling in *Richards v Richards*,[3] applying section 1(3) of the Matrimonial Homes Act 1983, the child's welfare whilst a relevant factor is not to be elevated above other factors such as the conduct of the adult parties. As one commentator has pointed out,[4] this differing weighting of the child's welfare is 'the mechanism whereby Parliament stipulates the relative importance

---

[15] Post, p 346.
[16] [1970] AC 668, [1969] 1 All ER 788, HL, discussed supra.
[17] Though this is not to say that parents and non parents stand on exactly the same footing, see post, p 388.
[18] *Guidance and Regulations*, Vol 1, Court Orders, para 2.57.
[19] See post, ch 16.
[20] *Children: The New Law*, p 11.
[21] *Aliter* if in those proceedings the court is deciding whether to make a s 8 order.
[1] Adoption Act 1976, s 6 discussed post at p 417.
[2] Matrimonial Causes Act 1973, s 25(1), discussed post at p 758.
[3] [1984] AC 174, [1983] 2 All ER 807, HL, discussed ante at p 169.
[4] Bainham, op cit, at p 11.

to be attached to the often conflicting interests of children and adults'. In this respect it is to be noted that in divorce proceedings the child's welfare is not thought to be relevant *at all* on the question of whether the decree itself should be granted.

The respective interests of adults and children, however, are not the only reason for curbing the application of the paramountcy principle. In the past, for example, the courts have refused to apply the welfare principle so as to interfere with the discretionary power clearly vested by Parliament in another body or court. On this basis it has been held that local authority decisions about children in their care[5] and immigration authorities' decisions about children[6] are generally immune from review on the merits. Similarly it has been held that there are no special rules governing appeals against lower courts' decisions about children.[7] The courts had also previously developed the policy[8] that unless the child's upbringing was *directly* in issue the paramountcy principle did not apply. On this basis it had been held that what was then section 1 of the Guardianship of Minors Act 1971 (the predecessor to section 1(1) of the 1989 Act) did not apply to the question of whether to direct a blood test to establish paternity,[9] or to the issue of whether to exclude a spouse from the matrimonial home,[10] or when deciding whether to prevent publication of a book alleged to be harmful to a ward of court[11] or in determining whether to grant permission to use evidence admitted in wardship proceedings in subsequent criminal proceedings.[12] Adopting a similar line of reasoning it has been held that the paramountcy principle has no application to the question of whether to grant leave to apply for a section 8 order under section 10.[12A]

It may be noted that the inapplicability of section 1(1) does not necessarily mean that the court has no powers for it seems that the higher courts, at least, have an inherent *protective* jurisdiction.[13] Under this jurisdiction the child's welfare, though still important, is not the paramount consideration and must be weighed against any other competing interests.[14]

The paramountcy principle only applies, if at all, in the course of litigation. As one commentator has pointed out,[15] it does not apply, for example, to the statutory obligations of local authorities towards children being looked after by them[16] nor can it be said to apply to parents (or

[5] *A v Liverpool City Council* [1982] AC 363, [1981] 2 All ER 385, HL, discussed further, post, p 545.
[6] *Re Mohamed Arif (An Infant)* [1968] Ch 643, [1968] 2 All ER 145, CA, discussed further post, p 474.
[7] *G v G* [1985] 2 All ER 225, HL, discussed further post, p 383.
[8] Upon which see generally Lowe and White *Wards of Court* (2nd Edn) paras 7–5 et seq.
[9] *S v McC, W v W* [1972] AC 24, [1970] 3 All ER 107, HL, discussed ante at p 275.
[10] *Richards v Richards*, supra, discussed ante at p 169.
[11] *Re X (A Minor) (Wardship: Jurisdiction)* [1975] Fam 47, [1975] 1 All ER 697, CA. See also *Re M and N (Minors) (Wardship: Publication of Information)* [1990] Fam 211, [1990] 1 All ER 205, CA and *Re W (Wardship: Publication of Information)* [1992], CA, discussed post, p 476.
[12] *Re S (Minors) (Wardship: Police Investigation)* [1987] Fam 199, [1987] 3 All ER 1076.
[12A] *Re A & W (Minors) (Residence Order: leave to apply)* [1992] 2 FLR 154, CA per Balcombe LJ.
[13] See ch 14.
[14] Compare *Re X*, supra, with *X County Council v AB* [1985] 1 All ER 53 and *Re M and N (Minors) (Wardship: Publication of Information)* [1990] Fam 211 at p 223 per Butler-Sloss LJ, discussed post, p 476.
[15] Bainham, op cit, p 10.
[16] Ie s 22(3) of the Children Act 1989 which obliges them to safeguard and promote such children but not to regard their welfare as the paramount consideration.

those with parental responsibility) save to the extent that decisions which conflict with the child's welfare can be reviewed by the courts.[17]

B. Delay prima facie prejudicial to child's welfare

Section 1(2) enjoins the court, in any proceedings in which any question with respect to a child's upbringing arises, 'to have regard to the general principle that any delay in determining the question is likely to prejudice the welfare of the child'. It will be noted that this principle applies to all proceedings concerning a child's upbringing[18] and is not therefore confined to proceedings under the 1989 Act but applies equally for example to adoption proceedings and to proceedings under the High Court's inherent jurisdiction.[19]

The case for making some provision about the deleterious effect of delay was cogently argued by the Law Commission.[20] They pointed out that 'prolonged litigation about their future is deeply damaging to children, not only because of the uncertainty it brings for them, but also because of the harm it does to the relationship between the parents and their capacity to co-operate with one another in the future'. They also commented that in most cases it is to the advantage of one of the parties to delay proceedings as long as possible. Despite section 1(2) it should not be thought that delay is *always* detrimental to the child's welfare. On occasions it will be beneficial for time to be allowed to settle things down.[1] What section 1(2) aims to prevent is unnecessary and unplanned delay for reasons that have nothing to do with the child's welfare.

The principal effect of section 1(2) is to place the onus upon the courts to ensure that all proceedings concerning children are conducted as expeditiously as possible. To this end the courts are directed[2] both in applications for section 8 orders and for orders under Part IV to draw up a timetable and to give appropriate directions for adhering to that timetable. The procedure for the timetable of proceedings is governed by the Rules,[3] the general strategy of which is that until the application is finally disposed of, a definite return *date* must be fixed before the end of any directions appointment or other hearing of the case.[4] Once the time has been fixed it

---

[17] See Cretney and Masson *Principles of Family Law* (5th Edn) 519. Cf Dickens *The Modern Function and Limits of Parental Rights* 97 LQR 462, 471 who asserts, correctly it is submitted, that parental [responsibility] is not to do positive good, but to avoid harm. See the similar thesis by Thomson in his inaugural lecture: *Shades of the Prison-Home Conception in Scots Law* at pp 9 et seq.

[18] Note, however, the exclusion of maintenance from the definition of 'upbringing' under s 105(1).

[19] However the timetabling provisions do not apply to proceedings other than those under the Children Act.

[20] Law Com No 172, para 4.55.

[1] See, for example, *S v S (Minors) (Custody)* [1992] Fam Law 148 (temporary order made to allow a 'volatile family situation' involving young children to settle down).

[2] By ss 11(1) and 32(1).

[3] Ie the Family Proceedings Rules 1991, which govern proceedings in the High Court and county court, and the Family Proceedings Courts (Children Act 1989) Rules 1991 which govern proceedings in the magistrates' courts.

[4] Family Proceedings Rules 1991, r 4.4(2); Family Proceedings Courts (Children Act 1989) Rules 1991, r 4(2), for details of which see eg *Clarke Hall and Morrison on Children* 1[53].

cannot be extended save by leave of the court.[5] Among the possible sanctions against practitioners for failing to comply with the timetable are being personally penalised in costs, being held guilty of professional misconduct[6] or ultimately being held guilty of contempt of court.

C. The non-intervention principle

One of the most innovative and potentially influential principles of the Act is that laid down by section 1(5), namely, that whenever a court is considering whether to make one or more orders under the 1989 Act with respect to a child, it 'shall not make the order or any of the orders unless it considers that doing so would be better for the child than making no order at all'.

1. UNDERLYING PHILOSOPHY

This provision reflects a basic philosophy of the 1989 Act, namely, that of non-intervention which in turn rests 'on the belief that children are generally best looked after within the family with both parents playing a full part and without resort to legal proceedings'.[7] This basic non-interventionist standpoint has been memorably described as 'privatising the family',[8] though perhaps more accurately by others as a policy of deregulation.[9]

Respect for family autonomy, which in any event is encouraged by Article 8 of the European Convention on Human Rights,[10] is not new to English law. Indeed, historically, the family was largely left unregulated[11] and has generally remained so where the family unit is healthy. During the past century, however, English law has become increasingly interventionist over the protection of children.[12] Where the 1989 Act breaks new ground, or at any rate marks a new turning point, is that even where the family unit has broken down, the non-interventionist principle still applies.

2. IMPACT OF SECTION 1(5)

Though applying to all applications for orders under the 1989 Act, section 1(5) was intended to have most impact in the so-called private law context and in particular in proceedings following divorce or separation. In that context the Law Commission were concerned[13] that under the pre-1989 Act law, many orders relating to children were merely 'part of the divorce

---

[5] Family Proceedings Rules 1991, r 4.15(1); Family Proceedings Courts (Children Act 1989) Rules 1991, r 15(5).
[6] Cf *Re M* (1989) Times, 29 December, CA.
[7] *Introduction to the Children Act 1989* (HMSO 1989) para 1.3.
[8] Inter alia by Cretney *Privatising the Family: The Reform of Child Law* (1989) Denning LJ 15 and Bainham *The Privatisation of the Public Interest in Children* (1990) 53 MLR 206.
[9] See eg Douglas *Family Law under the Thatcher Government* 1990 17 JLS 411, 425, n 17.
[10] Which provides for 'respect for family life', see ante, p 18.
[11] See, for example, Eekelaar *What is Critical Family Law?* (1989) 105 LQR 244.
[12] For arguments for and against intervention see eg Freeman *The Rights and Wrongs of Children* ch 7.
[13] Law Com No 172 at para 3.2.

package'. They accepted that, while sometimes orders might bring stability and certainty even in uncontested cases, there was a risk that in other cases orders could polarise the parent's role and perhaps alienate the child from one or other of the parents. Section 1(5) is intended to focus the court's attention on whether *any* order is necessary. As will be seen[14] this new standpoint has led to profound changes being made to the courts' duty under section 41 of the Matrimonial Causes Act 1973 in deciding whether to delay the granting of a decree absolute of divorce.

We shall consider the application of section 1(5) in particular proceedings in due course[15] but lest its impact is misunderstood it should be said that what the section demands is that *in every case* the court will need to be satisfied that it is for the child's welfare that an order be made. It does *not* say that if the parties are agreed no order can be made though obviously in these circumstances the court will need to be especially convinced that it is *in the child's interests* for an order to be made.

Although local authorities have always had to justify why a child should be removed from the family into their care, section 1(5) is not without new significance in this context. Because it requires the court to be satisfied *before* making an order that it is better for the child to make an order rather than no order, unlike the position before the 1989 Act, local authorities are required to explain to the court when applying for a care order what their plans are for the child if they obtain the order.[16]

3. THE INTER-RELATIONSHIP OF THE WELFARE PRINCIPLE AND THE NON-INTERVENTION PRINCIPLE

As Andrew Bainham has pointed out,[17] 'the relationship between the welfare principle and the non-intervention principle is problematical since there must exist a degree of tension between the two. The former, by making the best interests of children 'paramount' prioritises those interests over the interests of adults, the latter ... which ... accords primacy to the wishes and interests of adults, usually parents'. It is his contention that the welfare principle has in reality been 'hijacked by non interventionism'[18] because, as he says, the non-interventionist stance taken in the 1989 Act means that parental wishes, especially where both parents are in agreement, will determine an increasing number of issues affecting children.

While it is difficult to gainsay these arguments it may nevertheless be asked whether the pre-1989 Act law was so very different.[19] Under the

---

[14] See post, p 366.

[15] See post, p 376.

[16] See eg Cretney 'Defining the Limits of State Intervention: The Child and the Courts' in *Children and The Law* (ed Freestone) 58, 64. See further ch 15.

[17] *The Children Act 1989, Welfare and Non-Interventionism* [1990] Fam Law 143, 145.

[18] *Privatisation of the Public Interests in Children* (1990) 53 MLR 206, 221.

[19] In any event it can be questioned whether the welfare principle itself is truly child-centred. As Maidment commented the 'welfare principle, ostensibly child-centred, has also been and probably always will be a code for decisions based on religious, moral, social and perhaps now social science-based beliefs about child-rearing...' but she adds that: 'these decisions were in the past and are for the present made by adults for adults about adults. When a court makes a custody decision it may attempt to heed the child's needs, but it is essentially making a decision as to which available adult ... is to care for the child...': *Child Custody and Divorce* p 149.

former law the courts were generally reluctant to interfere with arrangements agreed between the parents. Under the 1989 Act the difference may simply be that the court may make no order at all rather than an order reflecting the parents' agreement. Furthermore the Act does allow for children themselves, at any rate those of sufficient understanding, to apply for leave to seek a section 8 order[20] and, as we have seen,[1] the child's wishes are expressly included in the check-list to which the court must have regard at least in contested section 8 and all care proceedings. If anything, therefore, under the 1989 Act there is more rather than less regard for the child's own wishes to be taken into account.

[20] Under s 10(8), discussed post, p 359.
[1] Ante at p 339.

Chapter 11

The court's powers to make orders under Part II of the Children Act 1989

A. Introduction and background

In this chapter consideration is given to the courts' powers under Part II of the Children Act 1989 to make orders (other than financial orders which are discussed in chapter 20) in what are termed 'family proceedings'.

Part II is based on the Law Commission's recommendations contained in its *Report on Guardianship and Custody*.[1] The Commission commented[2] that while the main principles of the pre-1989 Act law were reasonably clear and well accepted, the details were complicated and confusing with the result that it was 'undoubtedly unintelligible to ordinary people, including the families involved' and on occasion may have prevented families or the courts from 'finding' the best solution for their children.

Three major difficulties with the old law were identified by the Commission.[3]

First, the courts' powers differed according to the proceedings brought. For example whereas divorce courts could allocate custody, care and control and access in any way they thought fit, other courts acting under the Guardianship of Minors Act 1971 or the Domestic Proceedings and Magistrates' Courts Act 1978 could only make legal custody orders or access orders. One consequence of this difference was that whereas the divorce courts could make joint custody orders, other courts could not, though they could specify what rights (other than actual custody) should be retained by a person not awarded legal custody.[4] There were also wide variations in the courts' powers to make orders in favour of third parties[5] and even as to the ability of third parties to intervene in existing proceedings.[6]

Second, there was confusion as to the precise effect of orders and in particular, following *Dipper v Dipper*[7] about the legal effect of a sole custody as opposed to a joint custody order. It certainly was not immediately

---

[1] Law Com No 172, 1988.
[2] Ibid at para 1.1.
[3] Ibid at paras 4.2 et seq.
[4] This latter power was rarely, if ever, exercised.
[5] Under the Matrimonial Causes Act 1973, courts could make custody or care and control orders whereas under the Guardianship of Minors Act 1971 and the Domestic Proceedings and Magistrates' Courts Act 1978 they could make custodianship orders.
[6] Third parties, for example, could not intervene in proceedings under the 1971 or 1978 Act even though orders could be made in their favour. For a detailed account of the position of grandparents under the old law see Douglas and Lowe *Grandparents and the Legal Process* [1990] JSWL 89.
[7] [1981] Fam 31, [1980] 2 All ER 722, CA discussed *in extenso* in the 7th edition of this work at pp 295 and 302.

obvious (especially to the parents concerned),[8] for example, that a sole custody order did not put the custodial parent in sole control, nor that a joint custody order technically gave the parent without care and control a right of veto over the custodial parent's long-term plans for the child.

Third, the law was applied inconsistently. For example, the Law Commission's supplemental study[9] found that in one busy court only 2 per cent of the custody orders made were joint custody orders but in another court nearly 33.8 per cent were joint.

Complexity and technicality were not, however, in the Commission's view, the only things wrong with the law relating to custody. The Commission was also concerned that the law made the stakes too high. As they pointed out,[10] all the research evidence[11] shows that children who fare best after their parents' separation are those who are able to maintain a good relationship with both parents. While recognising the obvious limitation that law cannot make people co-operate, the Commission argued that at least it should not stand in their way. Hence, if the parties can co-operate with each other, the law should intervene as little as possible, but if they cannot, the law should at least try to 'lower the stakes' and avoid the impression that the 'loser loses all'.

With the above considerations in mind and with the general aim of making the law 'clear, simpler and, we hope, fairer for families and children alike' the Law Commission recommended that the differing powers of the various courts should be replaced by a new set of powers common to all courts and which are designed to be less emotive and more flexible.

1. THE GENERAL STRATEGY

The courts' previous statutory powers[12] to make custody, care and control, custodianship and access orders have been removed.[13] Instead, the courts are empowered to make a range of new orders, collectively known as 'section 8 orders', namely residence orders, contact orders, prohibited steps orders and specific issue orders. While the first two roughly equate (although they are not the same) to custody and access orders, the other two orders are new. They are modelled on the wardship jurisdiction and implement the Law Commission's recommendation[14] to incorporate the most valuable features of the prerogative jurisdiction into the statutory jurisdiction. Overall, the section 8 powers are intended to concentrate both the court's and the parties' minds on the practical issues which generally arise with respect to children, rather than on the allocation of theoretical rights and duties.

[8] Nor apparently to legal practitioners: see Priest and Whybrow *Custody Law and Practice in Domestic and Domestic Courts* (1986) (Supplement to Law Com Working Paper No 96).
[9] Priest and Whybrow, ibid.
[10] Law Com No 172, para 4.5.
[11] Notably that of Wallerstein and Kelly *Surviving the Breakup*. See also Wallerstein and Blakeslee *Second Chances: Men, Women and Children a Decade After Divorce*.
[12] Viz under the Matrimonial Causes Act 1973, s 42(1) and (2); the Domestic Proceedings and Magistrates' Courts Act 1978, s 8(2) and 14; the Guardianship of Minors Act 1971, ss 9, 10, 11 and 14A; the Children Act 1975, ss 33(1) and 34(1); and the Adoption Act 1976, s 25.
[13] By Sch 15 to the 1989 Act.
[14] Law Com No 172, para 1.4. Wardship is discussed in ch 14.

As well as providing a new range of powers, Part II also provides a clear plan governing who can apply for an order. The basic scheme (under section 10) is that some people, for example parents or guardians, are entitled to apply for a section 8 order, while others, for example, relatives, will be able to seek the court's leave either to intervene in existing family proceedings or to initiate their own proceedings to seek a section 8 order.

Another important change under the 1989 Act is the removal of the court's power in matrimonial and other private law proceedings concerning children to make committal to care or supervision orders.[15] Instead under section 37 the courts are empowered only to invite the local authority to investigate the circumstances and to decide whether to apply for a care or supervision order. However in place of these former powers is a new power under section 16 to make 'family assistance' orders, the object of which is to provide short-term help for the family.

2. THE IMPACT OF THE 1989 ACT ON EXISTING PRIVATE LAW ORDERS

It is not proposed to give a detailed account of the transitional provisions under the Children Act 1989.[16] Nevertheless it is important to appreciate that existing orders dealing with custody, care and control, custodianship and access remain in force notwithstanding the implementation of the 1989 Act.

In general such orders remain in force according to the terms of the original order[17] subject to the following:

(i) Any declaration of unfitness to have custody ceases to have effect;[18]
(ii) No matter what form the original order took, 'married' parents will *each* be regarded as having parental responsibility;[19]
(iii) Those persons who are not parents who have been granted custody, custodianship, or care and control have parental responsibility for the duration of the order;[20]
(iv) Those persons who are not parents who have been granted access do *not* have parental responsibility but nevertheless for the duration of the order, such persons will be entitled, without leave, to apply for a contact order under section 8;[1]
(iv) Applications to vary or discharge an existing order may be made under the 1989 Act;[2] and

---

[15] For details see pp 297–298, 306, 308 and 369 of the 7th edition of this work.
[16] For a comprehensive summary see Douglas *The Children Act 1989 Transitional Arrangements Guide*. See also Burrows [1991] Fam Law 437; Bracewell J [1991] Fam Law 457 and *Children Act 1989 Transitional Provisions* [1991] Fam Law 496.
[17] Ie they remain in force until the child reaches his majority or until such time as specified in the order. Any embargo against taking the child out of England and Wales made in divorce court custody orders also remains in force.
[18] Sch 14, para 3.
[19] Sch 14, para 6(1), (2), (3). This also applies to custodianship orders which means that parents' rights ceased to be superseded on 14 October 1991. For a discussion of custodianship see ch 11 of the 7th edition of this work.
[20] Sch 14, para 7. Therefore such persons do not require leave to apply for a s 8 order: Sch 14, para 7(3)(b).
[1] Sch 14, para 9.
[2] Discharge and variations are discussed post, p 371.

(v) Existing custody and care and control orders may be enforceable under section 14 of the 1989 Act.[3]

B. Section 8 orders

1. THE POWERS

The expression 'a section 8 order' means any of the orders mentioned in section 8(1), that is, a contact order, a prohibited steps order, a residence order and a specific issue order. It also includes any order varying or discharging a section 8 order.[4]

In making any section 8 order the court has further supplemental powers (designed to ensure maximum flexibility) under section 11(7) to: (a) include directions as to how the order is to be carried out; (b) impose conditions to be complied with by any person in whose favour the order has been made or any parent or other person who has parental responsibility, or any parent with whom the child is living; (c) specify the period for which the order or any provision in it is to have effect; and (d) make such incidental, supplemental or consequential provision as the court thinks fit.

(a) Residence orders

A residence order 'means an order settling the arrangements to be made as to the person with whom the child is to live'.

Insofar as they determine where the child is to live, residence orders are similar to care and control orders which they replace. There are, however, some important differences. First, based on the fundamental principle[5] that changes in the child's residence should interfere as little as possible with his relationship with both parents, *each* parent retains full parental responsibility and with it the power to act independently unless the latter is incompatible with the court's order, regardless of who has a residence order.[6] Second, it is intended that the new order should be flexible enough to accommodate a wider range of situations than previously. Third, because the order is spelt out in clear and simple terms[7] meaning what it says but no more than what it says, it should be seen for what it is, namely, an order resolving a real (and of course an important) issue between the parties but nothing else. In particular therefore it is hoped that the symbolism of victory that had come to be attached to custody orders[8] will not be associated with residence orders.

In its simplest form the order need do no more than name the person with whom the child will live. However both the phrase 'settling the

---

[3] See post, p 370.
[4] S 8(2).
[5] Law Com No 172, para 4.16.
[6] See ante at p 333.
[7] Cf Bainham *Children The New Law* (1990) para 3.6 who says that the order is deceptively simple principally because s 8 does not spell out its full consequences vis-à-vis parental responsibility.
[8] Highlighted by the many disputes under the pre-1989 Act law as to whether the court should make a sole or joint custody order, when all the real issues, namely who was to look after the child and the amount of contact there should be, had been agreed between the parties.

arrangements' and the power under section 11(7) to add directions and conditions, give the court considerable scope to set out more detailed provisions.[9] For example a residence order may be made on condition that the parent does not remove the child from the United Kingdom,[10] or that the parent does not move to another town.[11] Conditions may also be made to ensure that the child will receive any necessary blood transfusions or medical treatment notwithstanding the objections of the 'residential parent'.[12] Although the precise limits of these additional powers have still to be determined, they clearly should only be made where it is necessary to protect the child's welfare.[13] The Law Commission did not expect the supplemental powers under section 11(7) to be used at all frequently.[14] However, it may reasonably be expected that additional conditions are more likely to be made in the context of care proceedings.[15]

Although residence orders are said to settle the arrangements to be made as to *the person* with whom the child is to live, because of the general presumption under the Interpretation Act 1978, section 6(c) that words appearing in a statute in the singular include the plural, residence orders may be made in favour of more than one person, for example, parent and step-parent, grandparents or foster parents.[16] Furthermore joint residence orders may be made in favour of two or more persons who do not live together.[17] It is within the court's powers to make a joint residence order in favour of *both* parents *and* their respective new partners.

Joint residence orders may be made to accommodate shared care arrangements between parents, for example that the child spends weekdays with one parent and weekends with the other or term time with one parent and school holidays with the other. In each of these examples it is equally open to the court to sanction the arrangement by making a residence order in favour of the other. However, if it can be shown that a joint residence order would reduce the hostility between the parents it would seem to be in the interests of the child's welfare to make that type of order.

Joint orders can also be made that a child spend alternate weeks with each parent. In this respect the position established by *Riley v Riley*[18] that shared care and control *cannot* be granted, must be taken to be reversed.

---

[9] It may sometimes be a moot point whether such additional provisions are technically within the court's powers under s 8 or s 11(7).

[10] Without such express restriction, the 'residential parent' can remove the child from the United Kingdom for any period or periods of less than one month under s 13(2), discussed post, p 362.

[11] Per Lord Mackay 505, HL Official Report (5th series) Col 345.

[12] Cf *Jane v Jane* (1983) 4 FLR 712 in which effectively the father was given the power to consent to medical treatment but the mother (a Jehovah's Witness) looked after the child.

[13] Cf *B v B (Custody: Conditions)* (1979) 1 FLR 385, CA where the Court of Appeal struck out a condition of a custody order that the children aged four and two had until they were the age of six to be put to bed by 6.30 pm and that if the mother went out after that hour, they were to be left with the father, his mother or some other person approved by him.

[14] Law Com No 172, para 4.21.

[15] Discussed further in ch 16 at p 523.

[16] In theory there is nothing to stop the court making an order in favour of more than two people, although in practice it is rarely likely to do so.

[17] S 11(4).

[18] [1986] 2 FLR 429, CA. Cf, however, *J v J (A Minor) (Joint Care and Control)* [1991] 2 FLR 385, where the court was satisfied that in the 'exceptional circumstances' of the case it was in the five-year-old child's interests to be subject to a joint care and control order.

In that case, the Court of Appeal commented that a divorce court order, approving an arrangement by which a child was to spend alternate weeks with each of her parents, should never have been made in the first place, even though the arrangement had been working well for three years before the original order. However, as the Law Commission observed,[19] it is not the intention of these provisions that children *have* to spend their time more or less equally between their parents. The argument that a child needs a single settled home will be a strong one in most cases. As the Department of Health's *Guidance and Regulations* states:[1]

'... it is not expected that it will become a common form of order because most children will still need the stability of a single home, and partly because in the cases where shared care is appropriate there is less likely to be a need for the court to make any order at all. However, a shared care order has the advantage of being more realistic in those cases where the child is to spend considerable amounts of time with both parents, [and] brings with it certain other benefits (including the right to remove the child from accommodation provided by a local authority under section 20), and removes any impression that one parent is good and responsible whereas the other parent is not.'

Where a residence order is made in favour of two persons who do not live together, then, under section 11(4), the order may specify the periods during which the child is to live in the different households concerned. Such directions may be general rather than specific and in some cases may not be needed at all.

Given that under a joint residence order neither carer is obliged to consult the other unless this is specified in the order, it is important that the order is clear on such points as schooling which are fundamental to the success of the arrangement.[2]

Where as a result of a residence order 'the child lives, or is to live, with one of two parents who each have parental responsibility for him', that order will cease to have effect if the parents live together for a continuous period of more than six months.[3]

Under section 11(3) the court can make, inter alia, a residence order 'even though it is not in a position to dispose finally of those proceedings'. Furthermore under section 11(7)(c) such orders can have effect for a specified period. By these provisions the court can make interim provision by way of a residence order for a limited period. It should be noted, however, that the Act makes no distinction between a final residence order and one made as an interim measure. Hence *all* such orders will have the same effect and will, for example, discharge any existing care order.[4]

(b) Contact orders

A contact order requires 'the person with whom the child lives, or is to live, to allow the child to visit or stay with the person named in the order, or for that person and the child otherwise to have contact with each other'.

Although contact orders are similar to access orders, which they replace,

[19] Law Com No 172, para 4.12.
[1] Volume 1, Court Orders, para 2.28.
[2] Cretney and Masson *Principles of Family Law*, (5th Edn) at p 547.
[3] S 11(5).
[4] S 91(1), see post, p 357. It has been held that application can be made ex parte: *Re B (Minor) (Residence Order)* [1992] 3 WLR 113, CA.

the form of the order is different in that rather than provide for the parent to have access to the child, it provides for the *child* to visit or stay with the person named in the order. The emphasis therefore, is on the child rather than the parent.[5] It should also be appreciated that while the child is with the parent, that parent may exercise his parental responsibility subject to not acting incompatibly with a court order.[6] As the words 'otherwise to have contact with each other' make clear contact orders embrace both physical and non-physical contact and may therefore range from long or short visits to contact by letter or telephone.

Orders may provide for the child to have contact with any person (including, where appropriate, a sibling) and more than one contact order may be made in respect of a child. A contact order can be the sole order made even between parents and is likely to be so where there is no dispute as to the person with whom the child is to live. By analogy with case law on access, courts may make orders permitting contact orders to take place abroad.[7]

It is widely expected that the usual order will be for reasonable contact but where that is the sole order between parents, having regard to the non-intervention principle under section 1(5)[8] one may question the need to make the order at all. The position would be different where the court thinks it appropriate to make a residence order, or where the applicant is not a parent, for example a grandparent, and an order might be valuable if the person with whom the child lives is likely to prevent contact. Where restricted or supervised contact is thought appropriate the court may attach any directions or conditions under section 11(7). However, as the Department of Health's *Guidance and Regulations* points out 'a section 8 contact order is a positive order in the sense that it requires contact to be allowed between an individual and a child and *cannot be used to deny contact*. This would require a prohibited steps order'. [Emphasis added.] Like any other section 8 order a contact order can be made subject to directions or conditions under section 11(7). One example is that the child is not to have contact with a parent's new partner.[9]

Like residence orders, contact orders requiring one parent to allow the child to visit the other parent will automatically lapse if the parents subsequently live together for a continuous period of more than six months.[10]

Section 8 contact orders should not be confused with 'care contact orders' under section 34. The former exclusively control contact between individuals and cannot be made in favour of a local authority or while the child is in care.[11] The latter exclusively control contact with a child in local authority care.[12]

---

[5] This is more in keeping with the views expressed by Wrangham J in *M v M (Child: Access)* [1973] 2 All ER 81 that access is properly to be regarded as a right of the child rather than a right of the parent.
[6] See ante, p 333.
[7] *Re F (A Minor) (Access Out of Jurisdiction)* [1973] Fam 198, [1973] 3 All ER 493.
[8] Discussed ante at p 345.
[9] See eg *G v G* (1981) 11 Fam Law 148 (transsexual not to be accompanied with his male friend).
[10] S 11(6).
[11] S 9, discussed post, p 357.
[12] Discussed post, p 530.

(c) Prohibited steps orders and specific issue orders

These two new orders, which are modelled on the wardship jurisdiction, are intended to broaden all the court's powers when dealing with children.

A prohibited steps order 'means an order that no step which could be taken by a parent in meeting his parental responsibility for a child, and which is of a kind specified in the order, shall be taken by any person without the consent of the court'. It empowers a court to place a *specific* embargo upon the exercise of parental responsibility. This is in contrast to the vague requirement in wardship that 'no important step' in the child's life be taken without the court's prior consent.[13] The Law Commission instanced[14] as an example an embargo that the child should not be removed from the United Kingdom which they said might be useful in cases where no residence order had been made so that the automatic restrictions against removal under section 13[15] do not apply. But there are many other examples, as for instance prohibiting contact with a parent or someone else, restraining a particular medical operation, preventing repeated removal of children outside the United Kingdom for periods of less than one month by the residential parent and preventing the child's removal from his home before the court has had time to decide what order, if any, should be made.

Although the order *itself* must relate to parental responsibility it is clear that it can be made against *anyone* regardless of whether he has parental responsibility. Hence orders can be made against an unmarried father whether or not he has responsibility and similarly against a third party, for example restraining an individual or group from associating with the child.[16]

A specific issue order 'means an order giving directions for the purpose of determining a specific question which has arisen, or which may arise, in connection with any aspect of parental responsibility for a child'. These orders enable a specific question relating to the child to be brought before the court, the aim of which is not to give one parent or the other a general 'right' to make decisions in a particular respect but to enable a particular dispute to be resolved.[17] Orders may be made either in conjunction with another section 8 order or on their own. Disputes as to the child's education[18] or medical treatment are examples of the type of issues that could be resolved with such an order, including where necessary, the giving of detailed directions. Another example of the use of a specific issue order is to order the child's return as, for example, where one parent has wrongfully kept the child abroad.[19] It is also contemplated that the court could, in resolving the dispute, attach a condition to a residence or contact order that decisions may not be taken without informing the other person or giving the other the opportunity to object.[20]

---

[13] Wardship is discussed in ch 14. It is assumed that an order as vague as prohibiting *any* important step could not be made as a prohibited steps order.

[14] Law Com No 172, para 4.20.

[15] Though note the operation of the Child Abduction Act 1984, s 1, discussed ante at p 310.

[16] To be enforceable, however, the person against whom the order is to be made should be joined as a party. See *Clarke Hall and Morrison on Children* Vol 1, 1[221].

[17] Department of Health's *Guidance and Regulations*, Vol 1, Court Orders, para 2.32.

[18] See eg *Re P (A Minor) (Education)* [1992] 1 FLR 316, CA.

[19] See *Re D (A Minor) (Child Removal From Jurisdiction)* [1992] 1 All ER 892, CA.

[20] Law Com No 172, para 4.18.

Both a prohibited steps and a specific issue order may be made against someone who is abroad, provided at any rate, there is some utility in the order.[1] Furthermore to facilitate emergency applications it is expressly provided by the rules that applications for both orders may be made ex parte.[2]

Limitations on specific issue and prohibited steps orders

An important limitation both on prohibited and specific issue orders is that they must concern an aspect of parental responsibility. The court may not, therefore, make a prohibited steps order restricting, nor a specific issue order sanctioning, publicity about the child, since that has nothing to do with parental responsibility.[3] Similarly, it cannot make a specific issue order compelling a local authority to provide support services. Whether a prohibited steps order could be made effectively ousting a parent from the matrimonial home by forbidding contact with the child particularly if that person owns the house in question is problematic. It may therefore be advisable whenever possible to pursue such a remedy under the domestic violence legislation.[4]

Neither a prohibited steps nor a specific issue order should be made with a view to achieving a result which (a) could be achieved by a residence or contact order, or (b) which the High Court could not achieve in the exercise of its inherent jurisdiction.[5] The former embargo is to guard against the slight risk, particularly in uncontested cases, that the orders might be used to achieve the same practical results as residence or contact orders but without the same legal effects.[6] The latter embargo prevents local authorities applying for a prohibited steps or specific issue order as a way of obtaining the care or supervision of a child, an order that the child be accommodated by them or any aspect of parental responsibility.[7] Accordingly, a prohibited steps order cannot be made restraining a parent from objecting to his child being accommodated by a local authority or from removing the child from accommodation pursuant to the rights conferred by section 20(7) and (8).[8]

2. RESTRICTIONS ON MAKING SECTION 8 ORDERS

(a) Children aged 16 or over

Implementing the Law Commission's recommendation[9] and effectively confirming the former practice with respect to custody orders, section 9(7) and (6) respectively provide that a section 8 order (other than a variation or

---

[1] *Re D (A Minor) (Child: Removal From Jurisdiction)*, supra.
[2] Family Proceedings Rules 1991, r 4.4(4); Family Proceedings Courts (Children Act 1989) Rules 1991, r 4(4). Notwithstanding that the Rules only make express provision for ex parte applications for prohibited steps and specific issue orders it has been held that an application for a residence order can be made ex parte: *Re B (Minors) (Residence Order)* [1992] 3 WLR 113, CA.
[3] See Department of Health's *Guidance and Regulations*, op cit, at para 2.31.
[4] Discussed in ch 5.
[5] S 9(5). The High Court's inherent jurisdiction is discussed in ch 14.
[6] Law Com No 172, para 4.19. Department of Health's *Guidance and Regulations*, op cit, para 2.34.
[7] Department of Health's *Guidance and Regulations*, para 2.33.
[8] Discussed post at p 504.
[9] Law Com No 172, para 3.25.

discharge) should not be made in respect of a child who has attained the age of sixteen, nor should any order be expressed to have effect beyond a child's sixteenth birthday, unless the court is satisfied that the 'circumstances of the case are exceptional'. Orders not expressed to extend beyond the child's sixteenth birthday automatically end when he reaches sixteen.[10] Where a direction is made, the order will cease to have effect when the child reaches the age of eighteen.[11]

There is no definition of what is meant by 'exceptional circumstances' in this context. The Law Commission instanced the need to protect an older child from the consequences of immaturity, though a more obvious example is the mentally or physically handicapped child aged over 16.[12] The Law Commission had no doubt, however, that such appropriate cases would be 'rare' and that 'the court will no doubt always wish to make the child a party before doing so'.

(b) Children in local authority care

Section 9(1) prevents the court from making a section 8 order other than a residence order, with respect to a child who is already the subject of a local authority care order. This embargo is based on the well established principle,[13] endorsed both by the *Review of Child Care Law*[14] and the Law Commission[15] that in general the court's 'private law' powers should not be used to interfere with local authorities' exercise of their statutory parental responsibility.

Residence orders are different from the other section 8 orders, since their whole purpose is to determine with whom the child is to live. Hence, such orders may be made even though the child is in care. Obviously, if the court thinks the child ought to be living with someone else (who will also have parental responsibility), it is inconsistent with the continuation of the care order. The Law Commission[16] thought that in principle, just as care orders may supersede whatever previous arrangements for the child's upbringing have been made, so should residence orders. Accordingly, section 91(1) provides that the making of a residence order discharges any existing care order.

Applications for residence orders in respect of a child in care operate, therefore, as applications to discharge care orders. For those with parental responsibility this remedy provides an alternative to seeking a discharge under section 39[17] and would be useful in cases where the parents are divorced or separated. For others, for example, fathers who do not have parental responsibility and relatives, an application for a residence order is the only means open to them to seek a discharge of a care order.[18]

One effect of the embargo under section 9(1) is that the court cannot

---

[10] Children Act 1989, s 91(10).
[11] S 91(11).
[12] See Department of Health's *Guidance and Regulations*, Vol 1, Court Orders, para 2.49.
[13] See *A v Liverpool CC* [1982] AC 363, [1981] 2 All ER 385, HL, discussed post at p 545.
[14] DHSS, 1985, paras 8.2–8.10.
[15] Law Com No 172, para 4.52.
[16] Ibid at 4.53.
[17] Discussed post at p 528.
[18] This new scheme reverses *Re M and H (Minors) (Local Authority: Parental Rights)* [1990] 1 AC 686, [1988] 3 All ER 5, HL. See *Re A and W (Minors) (Residence Order: Leave to Apply)* [1992] 2 FLR 154, 161, CA per Balcombe LJ.

make a care order *and* a section 8 order. However, because the embargo only applies where a child is subject to a care order there is nothing to prevent a court making a *supervision* order *and* a section 8 order, nor will section 9(1) apply where the child is being 'accommodated' by a local authority under section 20.[19] Furthermore, even if the child is initially the subject of a care order, once a residence order has been made, since that discharges the care order, *any* other section 8 order can *then* be made.

(c) Restrictions in the case of local authorities

Section 9(2) prevents local authorities from applying for and the courts from granting them a residence or contact order.[20] The embargo is intended to prevent local authorities from obtaining parental responsibility other than by a care order under section 31. If local authorities wish to restrict contact to a child accommodated by them, they must seek a care order and have the matter dealt with in those proceedings. The combined effect of section 9(1) and (2) is that where a child is in care, a local authority cannot apply for *any* section 8 order. On the other hand, authorities may seek leave to obtain a prohibited steps or specific issue order in respect of a child accommodated by them, though this provision may not be used as a disguised route to seeking a residence or contact order.[1]

3. WHO MAY APPLY FOR SECTION 8 ORDERS?

The Act adopts what may be described as an 'open door' policy whereby some are entitled to apply, while others can, with leave of the court, apply for section 8 orders either by intervening in existing 'family proceedings' or by initiating their own proceedings.

The detailed scheme, set out by section 10 (which governs both initiating and intervening in family proceedings) is as follows:

(a) Persons entitled to apply without leave

Parents, guardians and those with a residence order in their favour are entitled to apply for *any* section order.[2] As Andrew Bainham points out[3] this group of people have such a close connection with the child that it would be inappropriate to present them with the additional hurdle of applying for leave to obtain a court hearing.

Following the Family Law Reform Act 1987 the expression 'parent' clearly includes the unmarried father.[4] It has even been argued[5] that the expression includes the natural parents of a child freed for adoption though this seems unlikely.[6]

---

[19] Discussed post at p 503.
[20] Though query whether an authority could apply for a residence order in favour of someone else? See post p 361.
[1] S 9(5), discussed ante at p 356.
[2] S 10(4).
[3] *Children, The New Law,* para 3.36.
[4] For a discussion of the 1989 Act on this point, see ante p 287. It is understood that some courts are (wrongly) insisting that only those with parental responsibility are entitled to apply.
[5] Hersham and McFarlane [1990] Fam Law 322–323.
[6] See the discussion at p 440.

In addition to the above, certain other persons are entitled to apply for a residence order or contact order without leave, namely:[7]

(a) any party to a marriage (whether or not subsisting) in relation to whom the child is a 'child of the family';
(b) any person with whom the child has lived for a period of at least three years (this period need not be continuous but must not have begun more than five years before, or end more than three months before the making of the application);[8]
(c) any person having the consent of:
   (i)   each of the persons in whose favour a residence order is in force;
   (ii) the local authority, if the child is subject to a care order; or
   (iii) in any other case, each of the persons who have parental responsibility for the child.

Group (a) primarily refers to step-parents though to qualify the child in question must be a 'child of the family'.[9]

Those not otherwise included in the above mentioned categories will nevertheless be entitled to apply for a variation or discharge of a section 8 order if either the order in question was made on his application or, in the case of a contact order, he is named in that order. Furthermore, section 10(7) reserves the power of rules of court to prescribe additional categories of people who may make applications without prior leave.[10]

(b) Persons entitled to apply with leave

The general scheme is that *anyone*, including the child himself and any body, authority or organisation professionally concerned with children, who is not otherwise entitled to apply, can seek leave of the court to apply for *any* section 8 order.[11] The only exception to this scheme is any person 'who is, or was at any time during the last six months, a local authority foster parent' who must have the consent of the local authority to apply for the court's leave unless he is a relative of the child or the child has been living with him for at least three years preceding the application.[12] This latter period need not be continuous but must not have been more than five years before the making of the application.[13]

The purpose of this last restriction is to prevent premature applications, unduly interfering with the local authority's plans for the child and so undermine their efforts to bring stability to the child's life.[14] It is also intended to guard against the risk of deterring parents from voluntarily using the fostering services provided by local authorities which, it is argued, could easily happen if the restrictions were relaxed. However, despite the

[7] See s 10(5).
[8] S 10(10).
[9] For the meaning of which see post p 368.
[10] One category of potential applicants for whom the rule might change are grandparents: see further below.
[11] S 10(1)(a)(ii). Local authorities are subject to the restrictions in s 9 discussed ante p 358.
[12] S 9(3).
[13] S 9(4).
[14] See Lord Mackay LC in 502 HL Official Report (5th Series), cols 1221–1222. This provision had *not* been recommended by the Law Commission.

importance of these objections the restriction lies at odds with that in adoption where foster parents can apply for an order after providing a home for the child for twelve months[1] and many might agree with the observation that having to obtain local authority consent *and* leave of the court is one hurdle too many.[2]

It is to be noted that because of the different wording of sections 9(4) and 10(10) there could be occasions, viz where foster parents provided a home for the child for three years but not within three months preceding the application, where consent of a local authority is not required but leave of the court is.

(c) The leave criteria

When considering whether to grant leave the court is directed by section 10(9) to consider:

(a) the nature of the proposed application for the section 8 order;

(b) the applicant's connection with the child;

(c) any risk there might be of that proposed application disrupting the child's life to such an extent that he would be harmed by it; and

(d) where the child is being looked after by a local authority—
    (i)   the authority's plans for the child's future, and
    (ii) the wishes and feelings of the child's parents.[3]

It has been held by the Court of Appeal in *Re A and W (Minors) (Residence Order: Leave to Apply)*[4] that when deciding whether to grant leave the paramountcy of the child's welfare principle under section 1(1) has no application.

The court may only grant leave to a child to seek a section 8 application provided it is satisfied that he has sufficient understanding to make the proposed application.[5]

The requirement of leave is intended to act as a filter to protect the child and his family against unwarranted interference with their comfort and security, whilst ensuring that the child's interests are properly respected. It is expected that the more tenuous the applicant's connection with the child the harder it will be to obtain leave.[6] Conversely, the closer the connection the more readily leave should be given. Where parents are divorcing, it is expected, for example, that grandparents will readily obtain leave. As the Law Commission put it,[7] the requirement of leave will 'scarcely be a hurdle

---

[1] Adoption Act 1976, s 13(1) and (2), discussed post p 442.
[2] Lord Meston in 502 HL Official Report (5th Series) col 1221.
[3] Though not, as Bainham points out, ibid at para 3.43, the wishes and feelings of the child.
[4] [1992] 2 FLR 154, CA.
[5] S 10(8). The child may apply for leave without a 'next friend': Family Proceedings Rules 1991, r 9.2A, added by the Family Proceedings (Amendment) Rules 1992.
[6] Any person seeking leave must file a written request setting out the reasons for the application and a draft of the application for making of which leave is sought: Family Proceedings Rules 1991, r 4.3(1), Family Proceedings Courts (Children Act 1989) Rules 1991, r 3(1). Leave can be granted with or without a hearing: ibid r 4.3(2) and r 3(2) respectively.
[7] Law Com No 172, para 4.41. For a discussion of the legal position of grandparents under the 1989 Act see generally *The Children Act 1989—What's in it for Grandparents?* (Grandparents' Federation, 1991). For a study of the grandparents' position before the Act see generally: Douglas and Lowe *Grandparents and the Legal Process* [1990] JSWL 90 and Kaganas and Piper *Grandparents and the Limits of the Law* (1990) 4 Int J of Law and Family 27.

at all to close relatives such as grandparents ... who wish to care for or visit the child'. In fact the position of grandparents attracted considerable debate during the passage of the Children Bill and a number of attempts were made to give them an entitlement to apply for a residence or contact order. The Government's response to each of those attempts was that the legislation strikes the right balance. As Lord Mackay LC commented:[8]

> '[t]here is often a close bond ... between a grandparent and a grandchild ... and in such cases leave, if needed, will no doubt be granted. Indeed, in many cases it will be a formality; but we would be naive if we did not accept that not all interest shown by a grandparent in a child's life is necessarily benign, even if well intentioned. Arguably, at least until we have some experience of wider rights of application, the law should provide some protection to children and their parents against unwarranted applications by grandparents when they occur'.

(d) Applying for orders in favour of someone else

The Act is silent on whether applications may be made for a section 8 order in favour of someone else. However, implicit in the ability of a child to obtain leave for such orders is that he, at least, can seek a residence order in favour of another person. Of more significance, however, is whether a local authority could apply for a residence order to be made on someone else's behalf, for example, in favour of grandparents who, though capable, are reluctant to apply themselves, or in favour of a parent but subject to conditions.

This in turn will depend upon the interpretation of section 9(2) which provides:

> 'No application may be made by a local authority for a residence order or contact order *and* no court shall make such an order in favour of a local authority'. [Emphasis added.]

If the word 'and' is read disjunctively then local authorities cannot apply in any circumstances for a residence or contact order but if it is read conjunctively it can be argued that all that section 9(2) prevents is local authorities from applying for a residence or contact on their own behalf.

4. EFFECT OF RESIDENCE ORDERS

(a) Parental responsibility

Whilst in force residence orders confer parental responsibility on those in whose favour they are made such as grandparents or other relatives, or foster parents who would not otherwise have that responsibility.[9] In the case of 'unmarried fathers' however, upon making a residence order in their favour, the court is *bound* to make a separate parental responsibility order under section 4.[10]

---

[8] 503 HL Official Report (5th Series), col 1342.
[9] S 12(2). Note the restrictions on that responsibility under s 12(3) discussed ante at p 328.
[10] S 12(1), discussed ante at p 325.

(b) Change of child's surname

Under section 13(1)(a), it is an automatic condition of all residence orders that no person may cause the child to be known by a new surname without either the written consent of every person who has parental responsibility or leave of the court. This implements the Law Commission's recommendation, following their comment[11] that a child's surname is an important symbol of his identity and relationship with his parents and that while it may be in his interests for it to be changed, it was not a matter on which a parent with whom the child lives should be able to take unilateral action.

It will be noted that it is not a statutory requirement to have the *child's* consent to the change of his surname. However, if the child objects he may seek leave to apply for a prohibited steps order to prevent the change.[12]

The issue could come before the court either as a formal application for leave[13] to change the name or as an application to restrain a change or threatened change. However in *all* instances the court must treat the child's welfare as its paramount consideration, pursuant to section 1(1). Before the Children Act 1989 there had been two marked differences of approach: one was that a change of name was an important matter which should be permitted only where the child's welfare so demanded;[14] the other that the issue was relatively unimportant and that fathers were tending to lay too much emphasis on it when the purpose was to avoid embarrassment and there was no intention of destroying their links with their children.[15] However in *W v A*[16] the Court of Appeal, recognising this irreconcilable difference, came down decisively in favour of the former view that a change of name was an important matter. In that case the Court of Appeal refused to reverse a decision declining to permit a change of name even though the child was emigrating to Australia with his mother and stepfather. It was certainly the Law Commission's intention that this should be the line followed after the Children Act. Consequently, it will be relatively difficult to obtain leave to change the name save perhaps where the father has disappeared from the scene entirely or if, for example, the name had notorious associations owing to the father's conduct. Ironically, however, a mother who changes the child's surname unlawfully may gain an advantage because, if it has been used for some time, it may not be for the child's welfare to change it back again.[17]

(c) Removal of child from the United Kingdom

Under section 13(1)(b), where a residence order is in force, no person may remove the child from the United Kingdom (ie England and Wales, Scotland and Northern Ireland), without either the written consent of every person who has parental responsibility or leave of the court. Under section 13(2), however, a person in whose favour a residence order has been made can remove the child for a period of less than one month without anyone's

---

[11] Law Com No 172, para 4.14.
[12] See Lord Mackay LC, 502 HL Official Report (5th series), col 1264.
[13] See application form CHA 11.
[14] *Re T* [1963] Ch 238, [1962] 3 All ER 970; *Y v Y* [1973] Fam 147, [1973] 2 All ER 574: *Re WG* (1976) 6 Fam Law 210, CA.
[15] *R (BM) v R (DN)* [1978] 2 All ER 33; CA, *D v B* [1979] Fam 38, [1979] 1 All ER 92, CA.
[16] [1981] Fam 14, [1981] 1 All ER 100, CA, following *L v F* (1978) Times, 1 August.
[17] As in *Y v Y* supra.

permission. This latter provision places those with a residence order in a special position for, as we have seen,[18] it is normally an offence under the Child Abduction Act 1984 to remove a child under the age of 16 without the other parent's consent.

These provisions implement the Law Commission's recommendations[19] and are intended to provide simple and clear rules which can be remembered and observed. Permitting unrestricted temporary removals is intended to allow a person in whose favour a residence order has been made to make arrangements for holidays without having to seek the permission of the 'non-residential' parent or parents, and without even having to give notice. This principle presumably extends to each person in whose favour a joint residence order is made. It might also be noted that there is no limit on the number of temporary removals permitted. In cases of dispute, however, parents are entitled to seek a prohibited steps order to curtail the right or to apply for a restriction of the right to be added to the residence order, pursuant to the court's powers to add conditions under section 11(7).[20]

Where permission is sought to take the child out of the country for more than one month specific application for leave must be made to the court. Under section 13(3), the court may grant leave either generally or for specified purposes. In deciding whether to grant leave the court must apply the principle of the paramountcy of the child's welfare under section 1(1). The most extreme of the problems likely to come before the court in this context is where the 'residential' parent wishes to emigrate and seeks leave to take the child out of the country but is opposed by the other parent upon the basis that he will thereby effectively be deprived of further contact. The test generally applied by the courts is that, provided the request is reasonable and bona fide, leave will be granted unless it can be shown to be against the child's interests.[1] In the case of very young children it will be difficult to show harm but in the case of older children factors such as education and the relationship with the 'non-residential' parent are likely to be of more weight. In *Tyler v Tyler*[2] the father who had enjoyed frequent contact with his two boys now aged 9 and 6 successfully opposed the mother's request for leave to emigrate to Australia to join her family. It was found in that case, however, that the mother's dominant motive was bitterness towards her husband and that furthermore she would be able to cope with the disappointment if permission were refused.

---

[18] Ante at p 309.

[19] Law Com No 172, para 4.15.

[20] See eg Department of Health's *Guidance and Regulations*, Vol 1, Court Orders, para 2.27 and Lord Mackay LC, 503 HL Official Report (5th series), col 1354.

[1] See eg *M v M (Minors) (Removal from Jurisdiction)* [1992] Fam Law 291, CA; *Re F (A Ward) (Leave to Remove Ward Out of the Jurisdiction)* [1988] 2 FLR 116; *Belton v Belton* [1987] 2 FLR 343, CA; *Lonslow v Henning (Formerly Lonslow)* [1986] 2 FLR 378, CA; *Chamberlain v de la Mare* (1982) 4 FLR 434, CA and *P (LM) v P (GE)* [1970] 3 All ER 659, CA.

[2] [1989] 2 FLR 158, CA, this was the first reported instance of permission to emigrate with the children being refused. But note the criticisms of this case at [1989] Fam Law 316–317. See also *M v M*, supra, where the case was remitted for a re-hearing because the court had not applied the right test.

5. WHEN SECTION 8 ORDERS CAN BE MADE

(a) Family proceedings

Under section 10(1) the court[3] is empowered to make a section 8 order 'in any family proceedings in which a question arises with respect to the welfare of any child'.

The term 'family proceedings' is defined by section 8(3) as meaning any proceedings 'under the inherent jurisdiction of the High Court in relation to children' or under the enactments listed in section 8(4). With regard to the former, which principally, though not exclusively,[4] refers to wardship proceedings, it is expressly added that the term does not refer to applications for leave by local authorities to invoke the High Court's inherent jurisdiction.

The enactments listed in section 8(4) are as follows:

Parts I, II and IV of the 1989 Act;
the Matrimonial Causes Act 1973,
the Domestic Violence and Matrimonial Proceedings Act 1976,
the Adoption Act 1976,
the Domestic Proceedings and Magistrates' Courts Act 1978,
the Matrimonial Homes Act 1983, sections 1 and 9, and
the Matrimonial and Family Proceedings Act 1984, Part III.

Applications under section 30 of the Human Fertilisation and Embryology Act 1990 also rank as 'family proceedings'.[5]

The introduction of the concept of 'family proceedings' implements the Law Commission's recommendation[6] and is intended to rationalise, harmonise and, in some cases, expand the courts' powers. It should be appreciated that before the 1989 Act the courts' powers not only varied from level to level but also from proceedings to proceedings. There was frequently no logic behind the differences. For example, whereas magistrates' courts could, under the Domestic Proceedings and Magistrates' Courts Act 1978, make orders about children regardless of whether the application for financial relief was successful, the higher courts could only make such orders on an application for financial provision under section 27 of the Matrimonial Causes Act 1973[7] if an order for financial relief was made. In other proceedings, namely variation of maintenance agreements or financial relief after a foreign divorce, the court had no powers over the children at all. Similarly, the court had no powers over the children in domestic violence cases, yet, as the Law Commission pointed out, the needs of the children are frequently an important factor in determining the relief sought. Indeed, it seemed to the Commission 'highly artificial' for the court to be able to exclude one person from the matrimonial home, at least in part for the children's sake, yet not to be able to order that the child should live with

---

[3] Ie the High Court, county court or magistrates' court: s 92(7).
[4] See ch 14.
[5] Human Fertilisation and Embryology Act 1990, s 30(8). For a discussion of s 30, see ante, p 265.
[6] Law Com No 172, para 4.37.
[7] Discussed post, p 692.

the parent remaining in the home. Happily, the 1989 Act has eliminated these variations and restrictions.[8]

The wide ambit of the definition of 'family proceedings' should be appreciated. As well as covering domestic violence proceedings it also includes both care and adoption proceedings. The reason for including these proceedings is that by extending the range of options the court will be able best to meet the child's needs.[9] Wide though the definition is, however, it does *not* include proceedings under Part V of the 1989 Act. This means that in applications for emergency protection orders and child assessment orders the court *cannot* made a section 8 order.

The inclusion of wardship proceedings under 'family proceedings' furthers[10] the policy of reducing the need to resort to the jurisdiction, because there will be less incentive to use it if the outcome is likely to be the same as in other proceedings. Furthermore, where an application is made the expectation is that, where appropriate, the court will make a section 8 order and discharge the wardship.

(b) Any child

Section 10(1) allows an order to be made in respect of 'any child'. In other words the court's powers are not limited to 'children of the family'[11] or to the biological children of the parties.

(c) Upon application or upon the court's own motion

Section 10(1) provides that section 8 orders can be made either upon application or, once proceedings have begun, by the court itself whenever it 'considers that the order should be made *even though no such application has been made*' [emphasis added]. Although the Law Commission expected[12] that orders would normally be made upon application the significance of the courts' ability to make section 8 orders on their own motion should not be overlooked. It effectively means that in many cases[13] once litigation on a family matter is on foot there is at least a risk that the court might choose to make a section 8 order in respect of the child regardless of the parties' wishes. This may be so even though the litigation is not primarily about the child[14] as, for example, where a spouse petitions for divorce, nullity or judicial separation or where a spouse or cohabitant seeks relief against his or her partner's violence.

In this respect, however, a distinction needs to be drawn between proceedings where the court is merely empowered to make orders and those

---

[8] It might be noted, however, that whereas the court is obliged to consider the children in applications for financial relief under the Domestic Proceedings and Magistrates' Courts Act 1978 (see post, p 370) there is no such duty in an application under s 27 of the Matrimonial Causes Act 1973.

[9] The impact of these options is discussed respectively in chapters 13 (adoption) and 16 (care proceedings.)

[10] Law Com No 172, para 4.35. Wardship is discussed in ch 14.

[11] The meaning of which is discussed post, p 368 and note the restrictions under s 9(6) ante, p 356.

[12] Law Com No 172, para 4.38.

[13] Though of course not all, for example, proceedings under Part V of the 1989 Act, proceedings under the Family Law Act 1986 (discussed ante at p 283) and the Child Abduction and Custody Act 1985 (discussed post pp 487 et seq) do not rank as 'family proceedings'.

[14] Or where it concerns just one aspect, as for example where a spouse or cohabitant seeks a maintenance order in respect of the child.

where it is bound to consider whether to make an order. Although the court is never bound to make an order (indeed, as we have seen,[15] pursuant to section 1(5), there is a presumption against doing so) clearly it is more likely to do so in cases where it is obliged to consider the children.[16] Proceedings falling under this latter category are divorce, nullity and judicial separation proceedings under the Matrimonial Causes Act 1973 and proceedings for financial relief under the Domestic Proceedings and Magistrates' Courts Act 1978. It is these proceedings that we shall now consider.

6. THE COURT'S DUTY IN DIVORCE, NULLITY AND JUDICIAL SEPARATION PROCEEDINGS

(a) The section 41 duty[17]

Before the Children Act 1989, pursuant to section 41 of the Matrimonial Causes Act 1973, no decree of divorce or nullity could be made absolute until the court had declared that it was satisfied that the arrangements for the welfare of any child of the family were 'satisfactory' or 'the best that can be devised in the circumstances' or that 'it is impractical for the party or parties appearing before the court to make any such arrangements'. The aims of this provision and the accompanying 'section 41 hearing' were to ensure that divorcing parents made the best possible arrangements for their children and to identify cases of particular concern where protective measures might be necessary.

The effectiveness of the section 41 machinery was well researched and much criticised.[18] The Booth Committee[19] had earlier recommended that the procedure be retained but improved so that, for example, fuller information would have to be filed and the respondent encouraged either to file a statement jointly with the applicant or to send in his own. The Law Commission, however, felt that the procedure was not truly successful in achieving either of its basic objectives.[20] Moreover, the court's former duty, in effect, to approve proposed arrangements lay uneasily alongside a policy of non-intervention. Accordingly, they recommended that the former duty be replaced with the more modest one namely to *consider* the proposed arrangements for the children in order to decide what, if any, order to make and that only in exceptional circumstances should the court delay the granting of the decree absolute.

---

[15] Ante at p 346.

[16] Conversely, of course, if the court is not obliged to consider the children it is unlikely in most cases to make a s 8 order. The Law Commission refrained from recommending that the court should be obliged to consider children in domestic violence proceedings pointing out (ibid at para 4.34) that often the case is far too urgent for that.

[17] For the background and history of this provision see Hall 'Children and Divorce' in *Children and the Law* (ed Freestone) 201.

[18] Davies, MacLeod and Murch *Undefended Divorce: Should Section 41 of the Matrimonial Causes Act 1973 be Repealed?*; Maidment *Theoretical and Empirical Considerations in State, Law and the Family Critical Perspectives* (ed Freeman), and Freeman *The Rights and Wrongs of Children* ch 6. The pros and cons of such appointments are excellently summarised in Law Com Working Paper No 96 (*Custody*) paras 4.8–4.10.

[19] Report of the Matrimonial Causes Procedure Committee, paras 4.35, 4.37, 4.51, 4.69 and 4.75.

[20] Law Com No 172, para 3.6.

Following the Law Commission's recommendations section 41 has been rewritten[1] and now directs the court in divorce, nullity or judicial separation proceedings to consider:

'(a) whether there are any children of the family to whom this section applies; and

(b) where there are any such children, whether (in the light of the arrangements which have been, or are proposed to be, made for their upbringing and welfare) it should exercise any of its powers under the Children Act 1989 with respect to any of them.'

Reflecting the Law Commission's view that there would still be exceptional circumstances[2] where the court should delay the granting of a decree absolute, section 41(2) provides:

'Where in any case to which this section applies, it appears to the court that—

(a) the circumstances of the case require it, or are likely to require it, to exercise any of its powers under the Act of 1989 with respect to any such child;

(b) it is not in a position to exercise that power or (as the case may be) those powers without giving further consideration to the case *and* [emphasis added]

(c) there are exceptional circumstances which make it desirable in the interests of the child that the court should give a direction under this section,

it may direct that the decree of divorce or nullity is not to be made absolute, or that the decree of judicial separation is not to be granted, until the court orders otherwise.'

The clear intention of section 41(2) is that a decree should be delayed only in exceptional circumstances and not therefore simply where the court feels it should exercise its powers under the 1989 Act. However, it is understood that following the advice given in the Official Guidance to Listing Officers the practice in some courts is to delay the granting of the decree absolute until all outstanding matters under the Children Act 1989 have been resolved.[3]

(b) The section 41 procedure

Accompanying the important substantive change has been the equally significant change in procedure. Before the 1989 Act the divorce courts generally discharged their section 41 duties by means of a formal appointment conducted by the judge. The current procedure is that consideration of the arrangements for the children is undertaken by the district judge by means of examining the detailed Statement of Arrangements for Children Form[4] which must accompany the divorce petition.[5] If, having examined this form, the district judge is satisfied that the court need not exercise its powers under the 1989 Act, he should certify accordingly.[6] If he is not so

---

[1] By Sch 12, para 31 of the 1989 Act.

[2] Eg where the parties are refusing to consider how best to meet their parental responsibility in the changed circumstances.

[3] Even if the argument is about the duration of contact. Although this is a possible interpretation of Family Proceedings Rules 1991, r 2.39(2) it is inconsistent with s 41(2) and is therefore surely wrong.

[4] Form M4.

[5] Family Proceedings Rules 1991, r 2.2(2). This form must be signed by the petitioner personally and if possible agreed with by the respondent.

[6] Family Proceedings Rules 1991, r 2.39(2).

satisfied then he can direct[7] that (a) further evidence be filed, (b) a welfare report be ordered or (c) that one or more of the parties attend before him. In other words in most cases, like the special procedure in divorce, the initial scrutiny of the proposed arrangements for the children is a 'paper exercise' conducted without any of the parties being present.

(c) To whom section 41 applies

(i) Children under the age of 16

In line with the court's powers to make section 8 orders, the duty under section 41 applies only to children under the age of sixteen, save where the court expressly directs otherwise,[8] as for example, in the case of a handicapped child.

(ii) Child of the family

Section 41 applies only to a 'child of the family', that is, in relation to the parties to a marriage:[9]

> '(a) a child of both of those parties; and
> (b) any other child, not being a child who is placed with those parties as foster parents by a local authority or voluntary organisation,[10] who has been treated by both of those parties as a child of the family.'

Category (a) refers to any child, including an adopted child, who is treated in law as being a child of the spouses. Subject to the exceptions mentioned above category (b) includes any child (including one *privately* fostered) regardless of parentage whom both parties have treated as a member of the family. Whether a child has been so treated is a question of fact. Common sense excludes some children, for example, young lodgers, au pair girls, and relatives who are being looked after during their parents' temporary absence. In all cases, however, the test is an objective one.[11] It has been held, for instance, that a child can be a 'child of the family' even though a maintenance order against the natural father in respect of the child remains in force,[12] nor will the fact that the husband mistakenly believed the child to be his own prevent the child being a child of the family if the husband treated him as such.[13]

---

[7] Family Proceedings Rules 1991, r 2.39(3).

[8] Matrimonial Causes Act 1973, s 41(3).

[9] See Matrimonial Causes Act 1973, s 52 as amended by the Children Act 1989, Sch 12, para 33.

[10] This is in line with the general policy of limiting the right of foster parents to apply for orders vesting some control over the child so as not to discourage parents from allowing their child to be fostered.

[11] See *Teeling v Teeling* [1984] FLR 808, 809, CA, per Ormrod LJ, and *D v D (Child of the Family)* (1981) 2 FLR 93, CA.

[12] See *Carron v Carron* [1984] FLR 805, CA, where, following their marriage, the mother and stepfather took the mother's two children into their household and lived together for four years. That, according to Ormrod LJ, made it inevitable that there should be a finding that the two children were children of the family. In the case of private foster parents, the fact that a child is still being maintained by the natural parents could well indicate that the child was not a child of the foster parents' family, but it will not be decisive: see Law Com No 25 (Report on Financial Provision in Matrimonial Proceedings) paras 23–32.

[13] See *W(RJ) v W(SJ)* [1972] Fam 152, [1971] 3 All ER 303.

There are two sets of circumstances in which it may be legally impossible for a child to be treated as a child of the family. First there must be a family of which the child may be treated as a member; consequently a child may not become a child of the family if the unit never existed in the first place[14] or if it has ceased to exist. In the latter regard, if, for instance, the wife has a child by another man after her husband has left her, but the husband agrees to treat the child as his own even though they continue to live apart, such a child cannot be a child of the family.[15] Once a family has been shown to exist, however, a child can be a child of the family even if the spouses have lived together for an extremely short period.[16] Secondly, there is authority for the proposition that a child cannot be treated as a child of the family before he is born. In *A v A (Family: Unborn Child)*[17] the husband had married the wife knowing her to be pregnant and believing himself to be the father. Six days after the marriage the wife left him. When the child was born five months later, she was obviously not the husband's child but the daughter of a Pakistani with whom the mother had also had intercourse before the marriage. The only evidence that the husband had treated the child as his own was the fact that he had married the mother, but Bagnall J held that 'treatment' involved behaviour towards the child who must be in existence. This seems a narrow and technical interpretation which is capable of working injustice since it would prevent the court from making an order even though the husband knew all along that he was not the father[18] and it is urged that it ought not to be followed.[19]

It is submitted that a child of the parties who has been adopted by someone else or has been freed for adoption cannot normally be a 'child of the family'. An adopted child ceases in law to be a child of the parties and therefore falls outside the first part of the definition in section 52 and the provisions about treating a child cannot refer to conduct before the adoption. The position with regard to a freeing order is less clear since its effect is confined to extinguishing parental responsibility[20] but it is submitted that while the order is in force the child will not be regarded as a child of his natural parents' family.[1]

A husband's failure to deny that a child is a child of the family in undefended divorce proceedings does not estop him from asserting otherwise in subsequent proceedings.[2]

---

[14] Cf *W v W (Child of the Family)* [1984] FLR 796, CA.

[15] *M v M (Child of the Family)* (1981) 2 FLR 39, CA. Aliter if the parties resume living together: see *Teeling v Teeling*, supra.

[16] See *W v W (Child of the Family)*, supra, where the man spent barely a fortnight with his wife and child.

[17] [1974] Fam 6, [1974] 1 All ER 755.

[18] This may be particularly harsh with regard to family provision after death where the same definition is used under the Inheritance (Provision for Family and Dependants) Act 1975, s 1(1)(d).

[19] However, the decision has since been approved by Sheldon J, sitting in the Court of Appeal, in *W v W (Child of the Family)*, supra. See also *Re Leach Decd* [1986] Ch 226, 223, [1985] 2 All ER 754, 758, CA, per Slade LJ.

[20] For the effect of adoption orders and freeing orders, see ch 13.

[1] The Law Commission Working Paper No 96, *Custody*, at para 2.15, draws attention to the fact that once a child *has been treated* as a child of the family, jurisdiction appears to exist whether or not the treatment continues.

[2] *Rowe v Rowe* [1980] Fam 47, [1979] 2 All ER 1123, CA. See also *Healey v Healey* [1984] Fam 111, [1984] 3 All ER 1040.

7. THE COURT'S DUTY IN APPLICATIONS FOR FINANCIAL RELIEF UNDER THE DOMESTIC PROCEEDINGS AND MAGISTRATES' COURTS ACT 1978

The court has a duty to consider the children even though the application does not directly concern their upbringing, where one spouse applies for financial relief against the other under the Domestic Proceedings and Magistrates' Court Act 1978.[3] Section 8 of the 1978 Act provides that where such application is made:

'... if there is a child of the family who is under the age of eighteen, the court shall not dismiss or make a final order on the application until it has decided whether to exercise any of its powers under the Children Act 1989 with respect to the child.'

'Child of the family' has the same meaning as under the Matrimonial Causes Act 1973.[4] It will be noted, however, that unlike the divorce courts, in these proceedings magistrates have a general duty to consider all children of the family under the age of 18.[5]

8. ENFORCING SECTION 8 ORDERS[6]

Where a person is required by a section 8 order to give up a child to another person and the court that made the order is satisfied that the child has not been given up, it may make another authorising an officer of the court or a constable to take charge of the child and deliver him to that other person.[7] Apart from this important power which is available to any court, more general powers of enforcement are, in the case of the High Court and county court, provided by the law of contempt of court, and in the case of magistrates' courts, by section 63(3) of the Magistrates' Courts Act 1980.

As far as the two higher courts are concerned the breaking of a court order constitutes a contempt of court the sanction for which can be imprisonment (or committal), fine or having the contemnor's assets frozen (sequestration). Although sequestration can be useful where the contemnor has gone abroad[8] the major sanction for breaking a section 8 order is likely to be committal. Before any committal order may be made the court has to be satisfied beyond reasonable doubt[9] that the defendant knowingly broke the order. Furthermore it is a requirement[10] that a penal notice (that is a notice formally warning the person against whom the order is made that failure to obey it constitutes a contempt of court for which the offender may be sent to prison) must have been attached to the order in question.

---

[3] Under s 2, 6 or 7, discussed in ch 20.

[4] Domestic Proceedings and Magistrates' Courts Act 1978, s 88(1), as amended.

[5] Cf Matrimonial Causes Act 1973, s 41(3), which limits the court's duty to children under the age of 16 unless the court expressly directs otherwise; see ante, p 368.

[6] See generally Lowe (1992) 4 Journal of Child Law 26.

[7] Family Law Act 1986, s 34.

[8] Particularly therefore in child abduction cases: see post, p 485.

[9] See eg *Dean v Dean* [1987] 1 FLR 517, CA, and *Re Bramblevale* [1970] Ch 128, [1969] 3 All ER 1062, CA.

[10] RSC Ord 45 r 7(4) and see Supreme Court Practice 45/1/7 for forms (High Court); CCR Ord 29, r 1(3) (county court).

It is also established[11] that penal notices can only be attached to orders that are injunctions or injunctive in form. In other words mere directions are not prima facie enforceable.[12] It is a moot point whether a residence order in itself is enforceable since it is not in injunctive form.[13]

With regard to magistrates' powers, section 14 of the 1989 Act makes express provision for the enforcement of residence orders under section 63(3) of the Magistrates' Courts Act 1980. At first sight this special provision might be thought to mean that the other section 8 orders are not enforceable in the magistrates' court. However, the reason for making such provision for residence orders is that they might otherwise be thought declaratory only and therefore not enforceable.[14] No such difficulty attends the other section 8 orders which accordingly are enforceable under section 63(3). Section 63(3) of the 1980 Act, which empowers magistrates to fine or imprison offenders for breaking orders, is not happily worded and seems more apt to deal with continuing breaches. Nevertheless the provision can be interpreted[15] as empowering magistrates to punish *past* breaches though this point has still to be authoritatively resolved.

Even if the court is satisfied that an order has been knowingly broken by the defendant it should regard the enforcement powers both for contempt and under the 1980 Act to imprison or fine as remedies of the last resort. As Ormrod LJ commented in *Ansah v Ansah,*[16] 'Committal orders are remedies of the last resort; in family cases they should be the very last.' Accordingly applications to attach penal notices and for committal orders should not be seen as normal ways of bringing enforcement problems before the court. Careful thought needs to be given to the provocative and emotional effect that such applications can have in themselves. Furthermore it is always important not to lose sight of the *child's* welfare in these types of dispute.[17]

Nevertheless in appropriate cases it will be right to imprison an offender.[18]

9. VARYING AND DISCHARGING ORDERS

(a) Section 8 orders

All section 8 orders may subsequently be varied or discharged. Indeed this is one of the important distinguishing features between these orders and adoption.[19]

---

[11] *Re P (Minors) (Custody Order: Penal Notice)* [1990] 1 WLR 613, CA, and *D v D (Access: Contempt: Committal)* [1991] 2 FLR 34, CA.
[12] Eg those forbidding a change of surname and removal from the UK under s 13 of the 1989 Act, cf *Re P* supra.
[13] See the arguments of Lowe, op cit, at p 27. This would seem to be the raison d'être for s 14 in relation to enforcing orders in the magistrates' court. See below.
[14] Following *Webster v Southwark London Borough Council* [1983] QB 698, [1983] 2 WLR 217.
[15] See *P v W (Access Order: Breach)* [1984] Fam 32, 40 per Wood J.
[16] [1977] Fam 138, 143, [1977] 2 All ER 638, 643, CA.
[17] See eg *I v D (Access Order: Enforcement)* [1988] 2 FLR 286, where a parent failed to comply with an access order, in which Sheldon J commented that the court should be concerned with what is best for the child and consider how to get the access order working rather than with punishment of the parent. See also Ormrod LJ's trenchant comments in *Churchard v Churchard* [1984] FLR 635, 638, CA.
[18] See eg *C v C (Access Order: Enforcement)* [1990] 1 FLR 462, CA (mother imprisoned for seven days).
[19] Adoption is discussed in ch 13.

All the substantive and procedural requirements for the making of a section 8 order apply to their subsequent variation or discharge.[20]

(b) 'Existing orders'

Applications to vary or discharge 'existing orders', that is, custody, care and control, custodianship, access orders and orders determining any aspect with respect to a child's education and upbringing made under various statutes[1] before the Children Act 1989 are governed by the 1989 Act.[2] The general scheme is that separate applications can be made to discharge an 'existing order'.[3] Alternatively a variation can be effected by a section 8 order. In the latter case if the court makes a residence order, any 'existing order' is automatically discharged,[4] but the making of any other section 8 order operates merely to modify the existing order.[5] For example a custody or care and control order would be modified by the making of a contact or prohibited steps order.

C. Other powers

1. FAMILY ASSISTANCE ORDERS

Section 16 of the 1989 Act empowers the court to make a 'family assistance order'. Such an order requires either a probation officer to be made available or the local authority[6] to make an officer of the authority available 'to advise, assist and (where appropriate) befriend any person named in the order'.[7] Those who may be named in the order are: any parent (which includes the unmarried father) or guardian of the child, any person with whom the child is living or in whose favour a contact order is in force with respect to the child, and the child himself.[8]

This new power replaces the former power to make supervision orders in private law proceedings which, according to the Law Commission,[9] failed to reflect the different purposes for which supervision orders were made, namely, those in favour of local authorities where the main concern was child protection, and those in favour of a welfare or probation officer which were aimed at giving short-term help to the family. Family assistance orders simply have the latter function.

As the Department of Health's *Guidance and Regulations* puts it:[10] 'A

---

[20] S 8(2) which provides that 'a section 8 order means inter alia, any order varying or discharging such an order'.

[1] As listed by Sch 14, para 5(2). It will be noted that orders not made under statute, ie those made under the wardship jurisdiction, are *not* affected by these transitional provisions. See also ante, p 350.

[2] See generally Douglas *Children Act 1989 Transitional Arrangements Guide.*

[3] Sch 14, para 11(3).

[4] Sch 14, para 11(1).

[5] Sch 14, para 11(2).

[6] Subject to s 16(7); see below.

[7] S 16(1).

[8] S 16(2).

[9] Law Com No 172, para 5.12.

[10] Vol 1, Court Orders, para 2.50. See also Law Com No 172, para 5.19.

supervision order is designed for the more serious cases, in which there is an element of child protection involved. By contrast, a family assistance order aims simply to provide short-term help to a family, to overcome the problems and conflicts associated with their separation or divorce. Help may well be focussed more on the adult than the child.'

(a) When orders may be made

Family assistance orders may be made in any 'family proceedings' whether or not any other order has been made.[11] The power may be exercised only by the court acting upon its own motion though there is nothing to stop parties requesting the court to make such an order during the course of family proceedings. However, the lack of the right to apply for such an order would seem to prevent parties from applying to the court *solely* for a family assistance order.

Before any order can be made, the court must be satisfied that 'the circumstances of the case are exceptional'.[12] Precisely what is meant by 'exceptional circumstances' in this context has yet to be determined by the courts. In general, however, it seems clear that the order should not be made as a matter of routine. The Department of Health's *Guidance* also points out that[13] 'it will be particularly important in all orders for the court to make plain at the outset why family assistance is needed and what it is hoped to achieve by it'.

As well as having to be satisfied that the circumstances are exceptional, the court must also be satisfied that the consent of every person named in the order, other than the child, has been obtained.[14] There is, therefore, no formal requirement that the child himself should consent, nor is there a statutory requirement to ascertain the child's own wishes and feelings about such an order since the enjoinder to do so under section 1(4) does not apply to making section 16 orders.[15]

A family assistance order may not be made requiring a local authority to make one of its officers available unless the authority agrees or the child concerned lives or will live in its area.[16]

Where an order requires a probation officer to be made available, that officer must be selected in accordance with arrangements made by the probation committee for the area in which the child lives or will live.[17] If the probation officer selected is unable to carry out his duties, another probation officer must be selected in the same manner.[18]

---

[11] S 16(1).
[12] S 16(3)(a).
[13] Ibid at para 2.52.
[14] S 16(3)(b).
[15] See ante p 340. Nevertheless as White, Carr and Lowe *A Guide to the Children Act 1989*, para 3.54 argue, there is nothing to prevent the court from discovering the child's views and, indeed, in the light of *Gillick v West Norfolk and Wisbech Area Health Authority* [1986] AC 112, [1985] 3 All ER 402, HL, the court may take the view that the child's own wishes ought to be taken into account (at least where the child is mature enough to make his own decisions).
[16] S 16(7).
[17] S 16(8).
[18] S 16(9).

(b) Effect and duration of order

Section 16 gives no guidance as to which officers should be appointed but in the private law context the most appropriate appointee will usually be the welfare officer who has compiled the welfare report for the court, while in care proceedings, the obvious candidate is the social worker attached to the particular case. It is not possible to appoint a guardian ad litem (even where that person has made a report to the court) since such a person will be neither a probation officer nor an officer of the local authority and will therefore be outside the terms of section 16(1)(a) and (b).

Under section 16(4), a family assistance order may direct the person named in the order or such of the persons so named as may be specified 'to take such steps as may be specified in the order with a view to enabling the officer to be kept informed of the address of any person named in the order and to be allowed to visit each person'. If a section 8 order is also in force, the officer is empowered to refer to the court the question of whether a section 8 order should be varied or discharged.[19]

A family assistance order is intended to be only a short-term remedy. Hence, section 16(5) provides that unless a shorter period is specified the order will have effect only for six months from the day on which it is made. However, there is no restriction on making any further order.[20]

2. SECTION 37 DIRECTIONS

Before the Children Act 1989 courts could in exceptional circumstances upon their own motion commit children into local authority care or make supervision orders in private law proceedings.[1] This power, however, runs counter to the policy under the 1989 Act to have just one route into care. Accordingly, it has been abolished. Under section 37, however, if in any family proceedings, 'it appears to the court that it may be appropriate for a care or supervision order to be made ... the court may direct the appropriate authority to undertake an investigation of the child's circumstances'. Pending this investigation the court can make an interim care order under section 38.[2]

When undertaking the investigation following a section 37 direction the authority must consider inter alia whether they should apply for a care or supervision order.[3] If they decide to apply for an order, then contrary to the normal rule,[4] they must apply to the court that made the direction.[5] If they decide not to apply for an order they must nevertheless inform the

---

[19] S 16(6).
[20] Cf Department of Health's *Guidance and Regulations*, op cit, at para 2.52.
[1] See the 7th edition of this work at pp 297–298, 306 and 308.
[2] Discussed post, p 525.
[3] S 37(2).
[4] Applications for care orders must normally be commenced in the magistrates' courts: Children (Allocation of Proceedings) Order 1991, art 3.
[5] At any rate where that court is the High Court or a care centre otherwise 'in such care centre as the court which directs the investigation may order': Children (Allocation of Proceedings) Order 1991, art 3(2).

court within eight weeks[6] of their reason for so deciding.[7] The court, however, has no further power to commit a child into care.

D. General jurisdictional rules under the Family Law Act 1986

Part I of the Family Law Act 1986[8] governs jurisdiction to make inter alia section 8 orders under the Children Act 1989 (but not to vary or discharge them).[9] The general aim of the Act is to avoid conflicts of jurisdiction[10] arising within the United Kingdom.[11] To this end the Act provides for uniform jurisdictional rules when making 'Part I orders' the scheme of which is:

(a) jurisdiction is prima facie vested in the UK court in which divorce, nullity or judicial separation proceedings are continuing, but

(b) if there are no such proceedings, jurisdiction is vested in the UK court of the jurisdiction in which the child is habitually resident, and

(c) where neither (a) nor (b) applies, jurisdiction is vested in the UK court of the place where the child is physically present.

In more detail the effect of the 1986 Act is as follows: where there are divorce or nullity proceedings under the Matrimonial Causes Act 1973 (where jurisdiction is based on a *spouse's* domicile or habitual residence for one year)[12] the court can make a section 8 order in relation to children of the family[13] while such proceedings are continuing.[14] Proceedings are continuing for this purpose until the child reaches 18, unless they have been dismissed.[15] Even if the proceedings have been dismissed there is still jurisdiction to make a section 8 order if it is made forthwith or where an application had been made on or before the dismissal.[16] A similar position obtains in respect of judicial separation proceedings save that there is no jurisdiction to make a section 8 order if divorce or nullity proceedings are 'continuing' in Scotland,[17] Northern Ireland or the Isle of Man.[18] Even if the court has jurisdiction, where it considers it more appropriate for matters

---

[6] S 37(4), unless the court directs otherwise.

[7] S 37(3).

[8] This Part implements the recommendations of the English and Scottish Law Commissions in their Report, *Custody of Children—Jurisdiction and Enforcement within the United Kingdom* (Law Com No 138, Scot Law Com No 91, 1985).

[9] S 1(1)(a). The Act also governs the High Court's inherent jurisdiction to make certain other orders, post, p 479.

[10] Though this has not prevented *all* such conflicts: see eg *T v T (Custody: Jurisdiction)* [1992] 1 FLR 43.

[11] Ie England and Wales, Scotland and Northern Ireland: s 42. The Act also applies to the Isle of Man: Family Law Act 1986 (Dependent Territories) Order 1991, SI 1991/1723. References to the UK court also includes the Isle of Man court.

[12] Ante, p 230.

[13] Defined by s 42(4)(a) in line with the definition in s 105(1) of the Children Act 1989, discussed ante at p 368.

[14] Ss 2 and 2A(1).

[15] S 42(2).

[16] S 2A(1)(c).

[17] Proceedings are 'continuing' in Scotland only until the child reaches 16: s 42(3).

[18] S 2A(2).

relating to the child to be determined outside England and Wales, it can direct that no section 8 order be made by any court in or in connection with these matrimonial proceedings.[19]

In the case of 'non-matrimonial proceedings' that is, proceedings for financial relief under section 27 of the Matrimonial Causes Act 1973,[20] sections 2, 6 and 7 of the Domestic Proceedings and Magistrates' Courts Act 1978[1], and Schedule 1 to the Children Act 1989[2] and in respect of free standing applications concerning children under section 10 of the Children Act 1989,[3] jurisdiction to make section 8 orders is confined[4] to children who are at the date of application habitually resident in England and Wales or who are present here and not habitually resident in Scotland, Northern Ireland or the Isle of Man. Jurisdiction on either basis, however, is excluded[5] if divorce, nullity or judicial separation proceedings are 'continuing' in Scotland, Northern Ireland or the Isle of Man and the child is a 'child of the family'.[6]

In all cases the court has a discretion to refuse an application if the matter has already been dealt with outside England and Wales or to stay the application if proceedings are continuing outside England and Wales.[7]

E. Deciding what orders, if any, to make

1. PRINCIPLES TO BE APPLIED

As we discussed in chapter 10, the controlling principle in deciding whether or not to make an order under Part II of the 1989 Act is the paramountcy of the child's welfare.[8] In applying this principle the court's first task is to decide whether to make an order at all since under section 1(5) the court is directed[9] not to make an order under the 1989 Act 'unless it considers that doing so would be better for the child than making no order at all'.

How this principle will operate in the context of Part II applications is, until practice becomes settled, a matter of speculation. The basic principle is that in each case the court will require to be convinced of the benefit to the particular child of any order sought. Clearly this will be easier to satisfy in cases of dispute but it by no means automatically follows that no order can be granted if the parties are agreed. According to the Department of Health's *Guidance* on the 1989 Act:[10]

'There are several situations where the court is likely to consider it better for the child to make an order than not. If the court has had to resolve a dispute between the parents, it is likely to be better for the child to make an order about it. Even

[19] S 2A(4).
[20] Discussed at p 692.
[1] Discussed at p 670.
[2] Discussed at p 694.
[3] Discussed at p 364.
[4] By ss 2(2) and 3 of the Family Law Act 1986.
[5] By s 3(2).
[6] See s 42(4).
[7] By s 5. See *Re H* (1992) Times, 5 March.
[8] S 1(1) of the Children Act 1989 discussed ante at pp 336 et seq.
[9] Ie it is mandatory for the court to consider the question.
[10] Vol 1, Court Orders, para 2.56.

if there is no dispute, the child's need for stability and security may
served by making an order. There may also be specific legal advantag
so. One example is where abduction of the child is a possibility, si...
order is necessary for enforcement proceedings in other parts of the Uniteu
Kingdom under the Family Law Act 1986, and under the European Convention
and under the Hague Convention an order will be necessary if the aggrieved party
is, for example, an unmarried father or a relative who would not otherwise have
'rights of custody'. An advantage of having a residence order is that the child
may be taken out of the country for periods of less than one month without the
permission of other persons with parental authority or the court, whereas without
an order this could amount to an offence under the Child Abduction Act 1984.
Also if a person has a sole residence order in his favour and appoints a
[testamentary] guardian for the child, the appointment will take effect immediately
on that person's death, even where there is a surviving parent. Depending on the
circumstances of the case, the court might therefore be persuaded that an order
would be in the child's interest.'

How far the court will be prepared to make orders on the basis of the need
for security remains to be seen but it is clear that if section 1(5) is to have
any meaning it cannot do so as a matter of routine. Similarly, since it can
be argued *in every case* that the holder of a residence order can remove the
child from the United Kingdom for periods of less than one month and
that any guardianship appointment comes into force on the residence
holder's death, the court will surely require some especial justification for
making an order on that basis.

One circumstance not mentioned in the *Guidance* which would seem to
justify the order is where it can be shown that without an order the person
looking after the child will not be accorded priority on a local authority
housing list. Another circumstance justifying an order could be where the
applicant, for example, an unmarried father or relative, who has no parental
responsibility, is seeking a contact order. Even if the parties are agreed, the
making of a contact order would seem justified since in the absence of any
order the applicant has no legal standing with regard to the child.

If the court decides to make no order because it feels that it is in the
best interests of the child that no order should be made, an order to that
effect must be prepared.[11]

2. OBTAINING EVIDENCE

(a) Welfare reports[12]

Although the parties themselves will give evidence and are free to call
witnesses when presenting their case[13] it is important both in contested cases
and those in which the proposed arrangements are not thought to be
satisfactory, that the court has an independent assessment of the facts. In

---

[11] See Form CHA 57. The court must also give its reasons: Family Proceedings Rules 1991,
r 4.21(4), Family Proceedings Courts (Children Act 1989) Rules 1991, r 21(6).

[12] For a general account of a welfare officer's work see Murch *Justice and Welfare in Divorce
Part 2*; Maidment *Child Custody and Divorce* 73–78; Hoggett and Pearl *The Family, Law
and Society* (3rd Edn) 551–555 and James and Wilson *Reports for the court: The Work of
the Divorce Court Welfare Officer* [1984] JSWL 89; Gibbons *A framework for court welfare
reports* [1989] Fam Law 60.

[13] But note the restrictions on the use of expert evidence connected with medical or psychiatric
examinations of the child, discussed below at p 382.

private law cases this vitally important role is normally played by court welfare officers.[14]

Court welfare officers are qualified probation workers. In London there is a permanent staff attached to the Supreme Court undertaking solely civil work, and in the provinces too there is increasing specialisation in divorce court work.[15]

Section 7(1) of the 1989 Act empowers any court, when considering *any* question with respect to a child under the 1989 Act, to ask a probation officer or a local authority to report to the court 'on such matters relating to the welfare of that child as are required to be dealt with in the report'. The power to ask for a report in relation to any issue under the 1989 Act means that welfare reports may be ordered in care proceedings. However, as we discuss in chapter 16, this independent role is usually undertaken by guardians ad litem who, unlike welfare officers, represent the child in the proceedings. Nevertheless on occasion it might be necessary for the court welfare officer to act in care cases to save time and resources. Indeed, in some cases such an officer may have already done so, for example, in family proceedings where the court decides, after hearing the evidence, that it should exercise its powers under section 37 and invite the local authority to investigate the case with a view to the authority applying for a care or supervision order.[16]

It will be noted that section 7 empowers the courts to ask a local authority to report rather than court welfare officers.[17] However it is not intended or expected that local authorities will be asked as a matter of routine but only in those cases where there is an obvious connection with the case.[18] Under section 7(5) it is the duty of the local authority or probation officer to comply with any court request for a welfare report. However, where the court decides to ask the local authority to report, it can ask them to arrange for this to be done either by one of their officers or 'such other person (other than a probation officer) as the authority consider appropriate'.[19]

It is doubtful whether a court can appoint an independent social worker to prepare a report, at least without the other party's consent,[20] and it should not in any event do so merely because a party is dissatisfied with a welfare officer's conduct.[1] It should be appreciated that a welfare officer is an officer of the court and as such has an independent role being neither the child's representative nor a witness for either party.

[14] But note the power (discussed below) of courts to ask local authorities to report.
[15] Whether welfare officers should continue to be drawn from the probation service rather than from a specialised family court service is discussed by Murch, op cit, chs 9 and 10.
[16] Discussed ante at p 374.
[17] So far as the divorce courts are concerned this is new but magistrates had such powers before the Children Act 1989.
[18] See Law Com No 172, para 6.17.
[19] This is intended to cover the situation where, as a result of close co-operation, the NSPCC, for example, acting on behalf of the local authority, is seen to be the key worker for the particular child: see White, Carr and Lowe *A Guide to the Children Act 1989*, para 8.6.
[20] *Cadman v Cadman* (1981) 3 FLR 275, 12 Fam Law 82, CA. But there is nothing to stop a party from calling a social worker to give expert evidence.
[1] Where a party is dissatisfied the proper course is to invite the court to appoint another welfare officer: *Cadman v Cadman*, supra.

(i) When reports should be ordered

The court is not bound to order welfare reports in every case. Indeed as the Law Commission said[2] the court has to be moderate when exercising its powers. Welfare officers' time is limited and must be spent on cases where it will be most valuable. It must also be acknowledged that reports can be a source of delay[3] and, mindful of the court's general duty under section 1(2) to be aware of the likelihood of delay prejudicing the child's welfare, the court might have to balance the advantages to be gained from a report against the disadvantage of the time it takes to obtain it.[4] Further, in deciding whether to call for a report, the court must have regard to its duty under section 1(5) to make orders only where to do so is better for the child than making no order. Nevertheless the expectation is that some sort of report will be required in most contested cases.[5]

Reports can be ordered at any stage of the proceedings,[6] though they will usually be asked for at a directions hearing.[7] Once appointed welfare officers must be notified by the court of any decisions made during the course of the proceedings and of the dates for hearings.[8]

(ii) The role and function of welfare officers

Once appointed, welfare officers are generally expected to investigate the circumstances of the child or children concerned and the important figures in their lives with a view to providing the court with factual information on which to make a decision.[9] The report may be made in writing or orally as the court requires.[10] To save time the court can specify upon what matters the report is to be made.[11] Although there are no formal guidelines on how an officer should prepare his report, it is expected that he will visit and interview the various parties, including the child, at their respective homes, and if necessary, to extend enquiries to the wider family, school, family doctor and other persons whose observations may be helpful. It has been said that without these investigations the report is useless and

---

[2] Law Com No 172, para 6.15.

[3] Before the Children Act 1989 such delays could be considerable: see eg *Plant v Plant* (1982) 4 FLR 305, 12 Fam Law 179, CA—a delay of nine months; *Elder v Elder* [1986] 1 FLR 610, [1986] Fam Law 190, CA—eight months' delay; and *Re H (Conciliation: Welfare Reports)* [1986] 1 FLR 476—a delay of over five months said to be unacceptable in the case of a baby. See also Murch *Justice and Welfare in Divorce* pp 135 et seq.

[4] See eg *Re H (Minors) (Welfare Reports)* [1990] 2 FLR 172, CA.

[5] Per Lord Mackay LC, 502 HL Official Report (5th series), col 1203. Nevertheless before the 1989 Act there was a sharp variation in the use of reports. For a succinct account of the various research findings see Maidment *Child Custody and Divorce* pp 73–74. See also Priest and Whybrow Supplement to Law Com Working Paper No 96, para 4.18.

[6] In the case of proceedings before magistrates a single justice can order the report: Family Proceedings Courts (Children Act 1989) Rules 1991, r 2(5)(c).

[7] See Harris and Scanlan *The Children Act 1989, A Procedural Handbook* para 5.16.

[8] Family Proceedings Rules 1991, r 4.5, Family Proceedings Courts (Children Act 1989) Rules 1991, r 5.

[9] Per Dillon LJ in *Scott v Scott* [1986] 2 FLR 320, 322, CA.

[10] S 7(3). The normal expectation is that the report will be written.

[11] But in the absence of a direction welfare officers should produce a general background report. Under s 7(2) the Lord Chancellor 'may make regulations specifying matters which, unless the court orders otherwise, must be dealt with in any report'. No such regulations, however, have been made.

unacceptable[12] nor is a court likely to derive much assistance from a report, at any rate in contested cases, if the officer has not seen each party with the child. In *Re W (A Minor) (Custody)*[13] for instance, where the officer had not seen the children with their mother because they only lived with her at weekends, Cumming-Bruce LJ commented:[14]

'Where a welfare officer is charged with the responsibility of reporting in a welfare report to a judge for the purpose of helping the judge in a disputed custody case … it is of the utmost importance, particularly where children are small, that the welfare officer finds a way of getting to know the child or children in both homes and observing the relationships between the child, the grown-ups and everybody else in both homes.'

At one stage some welfare officers appeared not to have undertaken an investigative role even though they had been asked to produce a report for the court. This was because they confused another role of theirs, namely, to effect conciliation between the parties. It has been emphasised, however, that the reporting and conciliation roles are quite distinct and to some extent incompatible. Hence, an officer who has been involved in conciliation with the parties should not be appointed to produce a report and all officers appointed to produce a report are expected to undertake the investigations outlined above and not to assume a conciliation role.[15]

It is inevitable that to some extent a welfare officer will rely on hearsay evidence. Indeed it has been said that in the nature of things such officers could not do what is required of them and comply with the hearsay rule.[16] However, although section 7(4) provides that, regardless of any rule of law which would otherwise prevent it from doing so, the court may take into account any statement contained in, or evidence given in respect of matters referred to, in the report, regard should still be had to *Thompson v Thompson*.[17] In that case it was said that on controversial issues, for example making adverse findings against a party, if an officer is constrained to pass on second-hand evidence he should endeavour to make this explicit and indicate his source of information and his reasons, if he has any, for agreeing with such an opinion.

The welfare officer must file his report either as directed by the court or in the absence of a direction, at least five days before the hearing at which it will be given or considered, and, as soon as practicable, the court must serve a copy of the report on the parties and any guardians ad litem.[18] The report is a confidential document which should not be disclosed to anyone

---

[12] Per Ewbank J in *Re H (Conciliation: Welfare Reports)* [1986] 1 FLR 476.
[13] (1983) 4 FLR 492, CA. See also *Edwards v Edwards* [1986] 1 FLR 187, affd at [1986] 1 FLR 205, CA and *Re R (Minors) (Custody)* [1986] 1 FLR 6, CA.
[14] *Re W (A Minor) (Custody)*, supra, at 501.
[15] See *Scott v Scott* [1986] 2 FLR 320, CA, and *Re H (Conciliation: Welfare Reports)* [1986] 1 FLR 476. The Booth Committee (Report of the Matrimonial Causes Procedure Committee, 1985) at para 4.63 had already recommended that the same officer should not both conciliate and later report in the same case. See also Sir J Arnold's letter in [1986] Fam Law 197 and Latham *Welfare Reports and Conciliation* [1986] Fam Law 195 and Maidment *Divorce Court Welfare Service* 136 NLJ 438. But cf Pugsley's letter [1986] Fam Law 338. See also the discussion ante, p 225.
[16] Per O'Connor LJ in *Webb v Webb* [1986] 1 FLR 462, 463, CA.
[17] [1986] 1 FLR 212, 216–217, CA. See also *Edwards v Edwards* [1986] 1 FLR 187, and *H v H (A Minor), K v K* [1990] Fam 86, [1989] 3 All ER 740, CA.
[18] Family Proceedings Rules 1991, r 4.13(2), Family Proceedings Courts (Children Act 1989) Rules 1991, r 13(2).

other than a party, his legal representative, the guardian ad litem and the Legal Aid Board, without the leave of the court.[19]

Unless excused by the court, the welfare officer must attend the hearing if the court gives him notice that his report will be given or considered then. Any party may question the welfare officer about his report at such a hearing.[20] Although the major purpose of the investigation is to provide factual background information, quite frequently in weighing the options open to the court, the report contains recommendations by the welfare officer,[1] or if it does not, the court will sometimes ask the officer at the hearing for his views. However, it is established practice that, save in exceptional circumstances, the judge (and *a fortiori* the justices) should not discuss the case privately with the welfare officer in the absence of the parties.[2] Such recommendations are not binding upon the court, nevertheless it says a lot about the general esteem with which the welfare service is held that if a court departs from a welfare officer's recommendation it should state the reasons for so doing.[3] Although there are several reported examples of the court not following a recommendation,[4] in practice the welfare officer's view commands great respect and it should be appreciated that in most cases he is the most influential figure in the decision-making process.[5]

(b) Obtaining evidence from children

As children are not normally parties to the proceedings[6] the court will commonly learn the child's view through the welfare report.[7] Indeed it has been said that it is important that an independent welfare officer should see the child to ascertain his view.[8] In addition it was established before implementation of the Children Act 1989 that the High Court and county court, but not the magistrates' court,[9] have the power to interview the child in private.[10] In the absence of specific rules governing the courts' powers to interview children in private it is assumed that this practice will continue to apply under the 1989 Act. While such private interviews can be helpful, much will depend upon the age, ability and temperament of the child and the skill of the judge, and the decision whether or not to see the

---

[19] Family Proceedings Rules 1991, r 4.23(1), Family Proceedings Courts (Children Act 1989) Rules 1991, r 23(1).
[20] Family Proceedings Rules 1991, r 4.13(1), Family Proceedings Courts (Children Act 1989) Rules 1991, r 13(1).
[1] In one study, carried out by Eekelaar and Clive with Clarke and Raikes *Custody after Divorce* (1977), 70 per cent of reports were found to contain a recommendation.
[2] *Re C (A Minor) (Irregularity of Practice)* [1991] 2 FLR 438, CA.
[3] See *W v W (Custody of Child)* [1988] 2 FLR 505, CA; *Stephenson v Stephenson* [1985] FLR 1140, [1985] Fam Law 253, CA; and *Dickinson v Dickinson* (1982) 13 Fam Law 174, CA.
[4] See eg *Re W (A Minor) (Custody)* (1983) 4 FLR 492, 13 Fam Law 47, CA; *Leete v Leete and Stevens* [1984] Fam Law 21 and *H v H* [1984] Fam Law 112, CA.
[5] See eg Murch, op cit, ch 8.
[6] Though there is power to join the child as a party in the High Court and county court and to order that the child be separately represented: Family Proceedings Rules 1991, r 9.5.
[7] For the relevance of such views see post, p 385.
[8] Per Dunn J in *Re A (Minors) (Wardship: Child in Care)* (1979) 1 FLR 100.
[9] See *Re T (An Infant)* (1974) 4 Fam Law 48; *Re T (A Minor) (Welfare Report Recommendation)* (1977) 1 FLR 59 and *Re W (Minors)* (1980) 10 Fam Law 120.
[10] There is, however, no power to see the parent separately in private: see *C v C* (1981) 11 Fam Law 147.

child is entirely a matter for the latter. As Ormrod LJ said:[11]

> 'If ever a matter was a personal matter for a judge it is the question of seeing or not seeing children. It is a highly sensitive decision both for the child and the judge himself and a judge, in my judgment, is fully entitled to make up his own mind ... about whether or not to see children. It is a very delicate situation indeed in my experience and it can be extremely embarrassing to a judge when he can see already the likelihood that he will come to a decision which is adverse to the wishes of the child.'

If a judge does decide to see a child in private it is wrong to promise not to divulge confidences vouchsafed to him.[12]

(c) Expert evidence—examination of the child

It is expressly provided by the rules[13] that before a child may be medically or psychiatrically examined or otherwise assessed for the purpose of preparing expert evidence for use in family proceedings, leave of the court must first be obtained.

F. Appeals

ROUTES OF APPEAL

There is right of appeal against the making or the refusal to make any order under the Children Act including section 8 orders. Appeals from magistrates' decisions lie to the High Court,[14] those from county courts and the High Court lie to the Court of Appeal.[15] Leave to appeal to the Court of Appeal is not required where the residence, education or welfare of the child is concerned[16] or where the applicant has been refused *all* contact.[17]

It is desirable in all cases concerning children that appeals should be heard as speedily as possible but it is particularly important in cases where a transfer of residence has been ordered. In *Re W (Minors)*[18] it was stated that in such cases appeals should be *heard* within 28 days of the decision.[19]

---

[11] In *D v D* (1979) 2 FLR 74, 10 Fam Law 53, CA. See also *Clarke-Hunt v Newcombe* (1982) 4 FLR 482, 485, CA, per Butler-Sloss J.

[12] See *Elder v Elder* [1986] 1 FLR 610, CA; *Dickinson v Dickinson* (1982) 13 Fam Law 174; and *H v H (Child: Judicial Interview)* [1974] 1 All ER 1145, CA.

[13] Family Proceedings Rules 1991, r 4.18(1), Family Proceedings Courts (Children Act 1989) Rules 1991, r 18(1). It may be noted that what is restricted is actual examination or assessment, but not experts' views on the findings of such examinations etc.

[14] Children Act 1989, s 94.

[15] County Courts Act 1984, s 77(1); Supreme Court Act 1981, s 16.

[16] Supreme Court Act 1981, s 18(1)(h)(i).

[17] Ibid, s 18(1)(h)(ii).

[18] [1984] 3 All ER 58n, [1984] 1 WLR 1125, CA. See also *Ridgway v Ridgway* [1986] Fam Law 363, CA, which stressed the need for legal aid to be granted quickly.

[19] Failure by barristers (or solicitors) to exercise the greatest possible diligence in complying with the time limits imposed by the courts for the preparation of appeals may be regarded as professional misconduct: *Re M (A Minor)* (1989) Times, 29 December, CA.

(a) The position pending appeal

Under the general powers to impose directions and conditions under section 11(7) of the Children Act 1989[20] any court can postpone the operation of any section 8 order pending an appeal or can make any other interim arrangement.[1]

(b) The powers of appellate courts

An appellate court may grant or dismiss the appeal. Alternatively, if it is satisfied that the original order was wrong but it is unsure upon the evidence what orders should be made, it can remit the case for a rehearing and in the meantime give directions as to care and control. Exceptionally, the appellate court can hear fresh evidence to resolve its doubts about the original decision.[2]

In deciding what order the appellate court should make, it is now well established that there are no special rules governing appeals in cases involving children. The leading case is *G v G*,[3] in which the House of Lords unequivocally held that an appellate court cannot overturn a first instance decision merely upon the basis that it disagrees with it. An appellate court has no power simply to substitute its own view. Instead it has to be satisfied that either the judge has erred as a matter of law (ie he applied the wrong principle) or that he relied upon evidence that he should have ignored or ignored evidence that he should have taken into account or that the decision was so 'plainly wrong' that the only legitimate conclusion was that the judge had erred in the exercise of his discretion.

Although this latter ground gives scope for argument in any particular case,[4] it is to be emphasised that the test is difficult to satisfy.[5]

Whether the law should be so restrictive on appeal is debatable.[6] In *G v G* the House of Lords took the view that there is desirability in putting an end to litigation particularly as in many cases there is no obviously right answer.[7] They also endorsed the view that an appellate court should be

---

[20] Discussed ante, p 351.

[1] It is expected that stays will not normally be granted for more than 14 days: cf *Hereford and Worcester County Council v EH* [1985] FLR 975, 977, per Wood J.

[2] Per Lord Scarman in *B v W (Wardship: Appeal)* [1979] 3 All ER 83, 95–96, HL. The admission of fresh evidence is at the court's discretion: see *A v A (Custody Appeal: Role of Appellate Court)* [1988] 1 FLR 193, CA; *M v M (Minor: Custody Appeal)* [1987] 1 WLR 404, CA, *Re C (A Minor) (Wardship Proceedings)* [1984] FLR 419, CA, and *Ladd v Marshall* [1954] 3 All ER 745. The admission of fresh evidence may justify upholding the original decision even though it has been held plainly wrong: *M v M (Minor: Custody Appeal)*, supra. Appeals concerning children do not however automatically call for an up-to-date welfare report: *M v M (Welfare Report)* [1989] 2 FLR 354, CA.

[3] [1985] 2 All ER 225, HL. See Eekelaar 48 MLR 704 and Robinson [1985] Fam Law 330.

[4] For a discussion of the law prior to *G v G* see Maidment *Child Custody and Divorce* pp 54–59.

[5] See eg *May v May* [1986] 1 FLR 325, CA. In *Re T (A Minor)* [1986] Fam Law 189, CA, it was stated that legal aid should not be granted for hopeless appeals, while in *Re G (A Minor) (Role of the Appellate Court)* [1987] 1 FLR 164, CA, it was said that where appeals, which were unarguable in the light of *G v G*, were brought by legally aided parties, the court might have to consider whether appropriate orders costs ought to be made to ensure that public money was not wasted.

[6] See the excellent critique by Eekelaar 48 MLR 704.

[7] See Lord Fraser [1985] 2 All ER at 228 referring to *Clarke-Hunt v Newcombe* (1982) 4 FLR 482, 488, CA, per Cumming Bruce LJ.

chary of overruling a decision particularly in cases concerning the upbringing of children where it is so important to have seen the parties and witnesses.[8]

G. Applying the welfare principle in particular cases

1. GENERAL CONSIDERATIONS

As we discussed in chapter 10, pursuant to section 1(4) it is mandatory for the court, in a contested application for a section 8 order, to have regard to the statutory check-list. However, before discussing the application of the check-list it is important to stress that the role of this list is to aid the court to determine what is best for the child, not to provide *rules* for so determining. It remains the case that beyond saying that the child's welfare is the paramount consideration there are no *rules* for determining disputes over children. As Dunn LJ put it in *Pountney v Morris:*[9]

> 'There is only one rule; that rule is that in a consideration of the future of the child the interests and welfare of the child are the ... paramount consideration. But within that rule, the circumstances of each individual case are so infinitely varied that it is unwise to rely upon any rule of thumb, or any formula to try to resolve the difficult problem which arises on the facts of each individual case.'

Another key to understanding the decision-making process is to appreciate that essentially the court's function is to determine which of the options set before it best accommodates or, at any rate, is least detrimental to the child's interests. It is one thing, for example, to have to determine which of two loving and caring parents should look after the child but quite another whether the child should live with a third party[10] rather than a parent. As we shall see, although the welfare principle applies to each type of dispute the courts have developed the idea that even in private law disputes denying a parent an order looking after his child in favour of a third party requires special justification.[11]

Among the most agonising cases are those where the court has to decide which of two capable, loving and caring parents should look after the child. It is in these cases where the check-list that we are about to discuss come most prominently into play. Of course it is in the nature of a finely balanced case that some facts will weigh heavily on the side of one claimant while others will favour the other but it is clear that in reaching its conclusion the court should consider all the circumstances of the case, and in the light of the evidence adduced, make the best decision it can. As Megarry J pointed

---

[8] See eg *Re F (A Minor) (Wardship: Appeal)* [1976] Fam 238, [1976] 1 All ER 417, CA.

[9] [1984] FLR 381, 384, CA.

[10] *A fortiori* if the realistic choice is between a parent and local authority care: cf *Re P (A Minor) (Custody)* (1983) 4 FLR 401, CA where faced with a choice of making an order in favour of a lesbian mother or committing the child into care (the father having objected to his child living in a lesbian household without seeking an order for himself) the court, with some anxiety, made an order in favour of the mother. (This was the first reported example of a lesbian mother being granted custody: cf post, p 392.)

[11] See *Re K (A Minor) (Ward: Care and Control)* [1990] 3 All ER 795, CA, and *Re K (A Minor) (Wardship: Adoption)* [1991] 1 FLR 57, CA as explained by *Re H (A Minor) (Custody) (Interim Care and Control)* [1991] 2 FLR 109, CA, discussed post, p 388.

out in *Re F (An Infant)*[12] the problem cannot be solved arithmetically or quantitatively by using some sort of 'points system'.

2. THE STATUTORY CHECK-LIST

Although the *statutory* check-list is new, most of the considerations themselves are drawn from and build upon previous practice. For this reason to illustrate their possible application we will refer to pre Children Act case law.

(a) The ascertainable wishes and feelings of the child concerned (considered in the light of his age and understanding)[13]

Although it is only since the 1989 Act that the courts have become obliged in private law cases other than adoption to consider the child's own views and wishes, in practice the courts have long done so. As Butler-Sloss LJ said in *Re P (A Minor) (Education)*,[14] shortly before implementation of the 1989 Act:

'The courts, over the last few years, have become increasingly aware of the importance of listening to the views of older children and taking into account what children say, not necessarily agreeing with what they want nor, indeed, doing what they want, but paying proper respect to older children who are of an age and the maturity to make their minds up as to what they think is best for them, bearing in mind that older children very often have an appreciation of their own situation which is worthy of consideration by, and the respect of, the adults, and particularly including the courts.'

Clearly the older the child the more relevant and persuasive his views.[15] Nevertheless as Butler-Sloss LJ indicated, the court's obligation is to consider the child's wishes and feelings, not to give effect to them, but to be the better able to judge what is for his welfare. It must be remembered that the child may have been coached by one parent and that sometimes the child's own wishes are so contrary to his long-term welfare that the court may feel justified in ignoring them altogether.[16] In other words even the views of an older or mature child is but one of the factors to be considered in deciding what order, if any, to make.

(b) The child's physical, emotional and educational needs

To speak of needs may be simply a way of expressing an adult's preference in an apparently child-centred way. As Maidment wrote:[17] 'when a court makes a ... decision it may attempt to heed the child's needs but it is essentially making a decision as to which available adult ... is to care for the child ...'.

---

[12] [1969] 2 Ch 238, 241, [1969] 2 All ER 766, 768.
[13] See Law Com No 172, paras 3.22 et seq.
[14] [1992] 1 FLR 316, 321, CA.
[15] For examples of where the child's wishes have proved decisive see eg *Marsh v Marsh* (1977) 8 Fam Law 103; *Clarke-Hunt v Newcombe* (1982) 4 FLR 482, CA; *Williamson v Williamson* [1986] 2 FLR 146, [1986] Fam Law 217, CA; and *Re P (A Minor) (Education)* supra.
[16] See *Re S (Infants)* [1967] 1 All ER 202, 210; *Doncheff v Doncheff* (1978) 8 Fam Law 208, CA; *Guery v Guery* (1982) 12 Fam Law 184, CA and *Re DW (A Minor) (Custody)* [1984] Fam Law 17, CA.
[17] *Child Custody and Divorce*, p 149.

A wide variety of 'needs' can be relevant under this consideration though in the absence of post-1989 Act case law it is a matter of speculation as to whether certain 'needs' will be examined under this heading rather than under those relating to the age of the child or the capability of the parents.

(i) Physical needs

Physical needs *can* include the need for adequate accommodation but, as Wood J said in *Stephenson v Stephenson*,[18] in most cases 'disadvantages of a material sort must be of little weight'. The court's major concern is for the child's security and happiness not his material prospects. Any other approach would automatically put a poor parent at a disadvantage. Nevertheless, a party's financial position cannot be entirely ignored: for example, if he is so poor that he cannot even provide a home, this in itself might be sufficient to refuse him a residence order.[19] Even in a less extreme case a parent who can offer a child good accommodation must, other things being equal, have the edge over the one who cannot.[1] But again the quality of the home life that the child will have must not be measured in purely material terms: the amount of time and energy that a parent can devote to his care and upbringing is of considerable importance. This may mean that a mother who can spend the whole of her time with her children will have an advantage over a father who will be out at work all day, whatever alternative arrangements he can make to have them looked after.[2] In this respect it might be noted that in *B v B (Custody of Children)*[3] where an unemployed father was successfully looking after his child, it was held that the judge had erred in law in putting in the balance as a determining factor the man's moral duty to find work and not to rely upon the benefits provided by the welfare state.[4]

(ii) Emotional needs

Among the child's emotional needs is that of attachment perhaps to a particular parent or to a sibling or even to a family. Before the 1989 Act these respective needs played an important role and can be expected to do so after the Act. With regard to attachment to a particular parent one influential notion in the past at any rate has been that young children need their mothers.[5] However even under the old law such a need was a consideration and not a presumption and this is the position after the 1989 Act. As Butler-Sloss LJ put it in *Re S (A Minor) (Custody)*:[6]

[18] [1985] FLR 1140, 1148, CA.
[19] Although as Cretney and Masson, op cit at p 531 point out, for the purposes of the Housing Act 1985 a person caring for a child who is homeless has a priority need.
[1] *Re F* [1969] 2 Ch 238, [1969] 2 All ER 766.
[2] See *Re K* [1977] Fam 179, [1977] 1 All ER 647, CA; *S (BD) v S (DJ)* [1977] Fam 109, [1977] 1 All ER 656, CA.
[3] [1985] FLR 166, CA.
[4] Nevertheless there seems some judicial suspicion about a man giving up work to look after his children: See eg *B v B (Custody of Child)* [1985] FLR 462, CA (father became unemployed after being granted custody and pending the appeal). Heilbron J commented (at 465) that this was not a case in which the father 'has deliberately given up work in order to go on social security'. See also Sir John Arnold P's comment at 466.
[5] This maternal preference was undoubtedly influenced by Bowlby's and others' theories of maternal deprivation: see the discussion in Maidment's *Child, Custody and Divorce* at pp 182–184. See further the discussion in the 7th edition of this work pp 323–326.
[6] [1991] 2 FLR 388, 390, CA.

'There are dicta ... to the effect that it is likely that a young child, particularly perhaps a little girl, would be expected to be with her mother, but that is subject to the overriding factor that the welfare of the child is the paramount consideration. When there is a dispute between parents as to which parent should take the responsibility of the care of the child on a day-to-day basis, it is for the justices or for the judge to decide which of those parents would be the better parent for the child, who cannot have the best situation since they are together caring for her. I would just add that it is natural for young children to be with mothers but where it is in dispute, it is a consideration but not a presumption.'

In the subsequent case of *Re A (A Minor) (Custody)*[7] Butler-Sloss LJ said:

'In cases where the child has remained throughout with the mother and is young, particularly with a baby or a toddler, the unbroken relationship of the mother and child is one which it would be very difficult to displace unless the mother was unsuitable to care for the child. But where the mother and child have separated, and the mother seeks the return of the child, other considerations apply, and there is no starting-point that the mother should be preferred to the father and only displaced by a preponderance of evidence to the contrary.'

In short, maternal preference remains an important consideration particularly where she has continuously looked after the child in question. However as with each of the statutory considerations it has to be weighed in the balance with all the others.

Another consideration which can be said to be a 'need' is that of sibling support. In general the courts dislike separating children. As Purchas LJ said in the leading case of *C v C (Minors: Custody)*:[8]

'It is really beyond argument that unless there are strong features indicating a contrary arrangement ... brothers and sisters should wherever possible, be brought up together, so that they are an emotional support to each other in the stormy waters of the destruction of their family.'

Occasionally this consideration can be decisive. In *Adams v Adams*[9] for example, the mother sought an order to look after her daughter but not her son but her application failed because it was held preferable to keep the two children together. In *Clarke-Hunt v Newcombe*[10] it was held that, as it was in the younger boy's interests to be with his mother and it was inappropriate to separate the brothers, both boys should live with her, even though it was against the elder boy's wishes and possibly slightly detrimental to his interests. However influential this consideration may be, it is of course not a rule.[11]

---

[7] [1991] 2 FLR 394, 400, CA. There is, however, said to be a rebuttable presumption that a baby's interests are best served by being with the mother: *Re W (A Minor)* (1992) Times, 22 May, CA.

[8] [1988] 2 FLR 291, 302, CA. See also *Adams v Adams* [1984] FLR 768, 772, CA, where Dunn LJ said: 'All these cases depend upon their own facts, but it is undesirable, other things being equal, that children should be split when they are close together in age and obviously fond of one another... Children do ... support one another and give themselves mutual comfort, perhaps more than they can derive from either of their parents.' But the disapproval of splitting siblings is not new: see *Re Besant* (1879) 11 Ch D 508, 512, CA, per Jessel MR.

[9] Supra.

[10] (1982) 4 FLR 482, CA.

[11] For example the children's own wishes must be a factor, cf *Re B (Minors) (Custody)* [1991] 1 FLR 137, CA. For another example of the separation of children see *Re O (Infants)* [1962] 2 All ER 10, CA (boy's long-term future thought to be better served by being with his father in the Sudan whereas the girl's was with her mother in England). Cf *C v C* (1981) 11 Fam Law 147, CA, where Ormrod LJ commented that to produce so complete a separation requires very cogent reasons.

Another aspect of emotional need is that of attachment to the family. Clearly this will come into play where the dispute is between parents and third parties. In *Re K (A Minor) (Wardship: Adoption)*[12] Butler-Sloss LJ went as far as to say[13] that in a dispute between a mother and applicants for adoption:

'The question is not: would the child be better off with the plaintiff? but is the family so unsuitable that the welfare of the child positively demanded the displacement of ... the parental responsibility'.

However, she later said in *Re H (A Minor) (Custody: Interim Care and Control)*[14] comments such as those in *Re K* must be read subject to the overriding paramountcy of the child's welfare and as Lord Donaldson MR put it in the same case:[15]

'... of course there is a strong supposition that, other things being equal, it is in the interests of the child that it shall remain with its natural parents. But that has to give way to particular needs in particular situations.'

(iii) Educational needs

Education is an important aspect of a child's upbringing and the question of whether a child at school is a relevant factor in deciding who should look after the child. Occasionally, parental attitude to education can be a significant factor. In *May v May*[16] care and control was granted to the father inter alia because he laid greater emphasis on academic achievements in contrast to the freer and easier attitude of the mother and her cohabitant to the time the children (aged 8 and 6) should be working.

(c) The likely effect on the child of any change in his circumstances

Before the Children Act 1989 this consideration would have been referred to[17] as the continuity of care or status quo factor. It has long been recognised that removing a child from a home that he has known can have damaging long-term consequences.[18] As Ormrod LJ said:[19]

'... it is generally accepted by those who are professionally concerned with children that, particularly in the early years, continuity of care is a most important part of a child's sense of security and that disruption of established bonds are to be avoided whenever it is possible to do so.'

The previous practice of having to adduce good reasons to justify moving a child from a well established home is expected to apply with equal force under the 1989 Act. Similarly it is expected that the courts will continue to be reluctant to move a child even as an interim measure in the absence of

---

[12] [1991] 1 FLR 57, 62, CA.
[13] Adapting an earlier comment of Fox LJ in *Re K (A Minor) (Custody)* [1990] 2 FLR 64, 67, CA.
[14] [1991] 2 FLR 109, 111.
[15] Ibid at p 113.
[16] [1986] 1 FLR 325, CA.
[17] See eg the 7th edition of this work at p 326.
[18] Cf *Re Thain* [1926] Ch 676 in which the trauma of being moved were dismissed as being merely transitory.
[19] *Dicocco v Milne* (1983) 4 FLR 247, 259, CA.

a welfare report[1] and should not do so if there is a doubt about the capability of the person with whom the child is to live.[2]

Clearly, the status quo argument becomes stronger the longer the child has been with one party and is especially powerful if the other has lost contact with the child. On the other hand, if, as in *Allington v Allington*,[3] the parties have only been separated for a few weeks and the absent parent has maintained regular contact with the child there can effectively be no status quo argument at all. In assessing what the status quo is the court should examine the whole history of the case and not simply the position immediately before the hearing. Hence, where a parent has 'snatched' a child from the other, the court may properly regard the status quo as being the position before the snatch.[4]

Empirical evidence showed that before the Children Act 1989 the courts normally made orders confirming the situation and only rarely ordered that the child be moved.[5] A similar reluctance to make orders moving the child is likely to continue under the 1989 Act. Nevertheless as Ormrod LJ pointed out:[6]

'... the status quo argument depends for its strength wholly and entirely on whether the status quo is satisfactory or not. The more satisfactory the status quo, the stronger the argument for not interfering. The less satisfactory the status quo, the less one requires before deciding to change.'

In any event it is important to remember that the status quo argument is only one factor and the court may well think that the child's welfare in any particular case might be better served by his being moved.

Under its general powers under section 11(7) a court can postpone the operation of any section 8 order pending an appeal or make any other interim arrangement. If the practice before the Act continues, then in cases where the child's move has been ordered, the court will normally grant a stay upon a party's application on the ground that he intends to appeal.[7] Such stays, however, should only be granted for a short period until the notice of appeal can be filed. Any further continuation of the stay can then be considered by the court hearing the appeal.[8] It is generally expected that

---

[1] See eg *Elder v Elder* [1986] 1 FLR 610, CA. In *Re H (A Minor)* (1991) Times, 1 February, CA it was held that a transfer of custody should be made only in exceptional circumstances upon an ex parte application.

[2] As in *Re W; Re L (Minors) (Interim Custody)* [1987] Fam Law 130, CA, where the mother had a drink and anxiety problem.

[3] [1985] FLR 586, CA.

[4] As in *Edwards v Edwards* [1986] 1 FLR 187, Fam Law 99, affd, [1986] 1 FLR 205, CA. There is however, no rule that the child should be returned in snatching cases. The only principle is that the child's welfare is the paramount consideration: *Re J (A Minor) (Interim Custody: Appeal)* [1989] 2 FLR 304, CA.

[5] In less than 1 per cent of the cases studied by Eekelaar, Clive, Raikes and Clarke *Custody in Divorce* (1977) paras 13.14 and 13.29.

[6] In *S v W* (1980) 11 Fam Law 81, 82, CA.

[7] See the 7th edition of this work at pp 327–328. Stays can be granted by courts acting upon their own motion but courts should not normally do so unless asked to by a party: *S v S (Custody Order: Stay of Execution)* [1986] 1 FLR 492, [1986] Fam Law 67. The party intending to appeal would, however, be well advised to seek a stay: cf *Elder v Elder* [1986] 1 FLR 610, CA.

[8] See *Townson v Mahon* [1984] FLR 690, 697, CA per Stephen Brown LJ, and *S v S (Custody Order: Stay of Execution)*, supra.

appeals against the transfer of custody should be heard within 28 days.[9]

(d) The child's age, sex, background and any characteristics of his which the court considers relevant

Consideration of the child's age is obviously linked to other matters such as the child's wishes and when combined with sex can be relevant to the choice of parents. As a matter of law, however, it is clear, as Butler-Sloss LJ said in *Re S (A Minor) (Custody)*[10] that 'there is no presumption that one parent should be preferred to another parent at a particular age [of the child]'. Furthermore although it seems divorce affects children differently according to their age,[11] there is no scientific basis for thinking for example, that young children benefit most from a maternal upbringing[12] or indeed that the child's well-being is affected by the sex of the parent with whom he is living.[13] Nevertheless it is probably true that given the choice between two caring parents, both of whom can provide satisfactory homes and neither of whom has lost contact with their young children, the courts are likely to choose the mother. In *Re W (A Minor) (Custody)*,[14] for example, Cumming Bruce LJ having rejected as an unwise generalisation the proposition that normally a young child should be with his mother, said:

'... if all ... factors are nicely balanced, then probably it is right for a child of tender years to be brought up by his or her natural mother.'

The child's background can include his religious upbringing. In the past this was of crucial significance but today this consideration is of much less importance. It is inconceivable, for instance, that a parent would be refused a residence order on the ground of atheism.[15] In the case of a very young child (or probably any child of no fixed religious beliefs) the question of religious upbringing will have little bearing on the outcome of the case.[16] On the other hand, if the child has already had religious instruction, its continuation will be of vital importance if a break in it would produce emotional disturbance.[17] Occasionally the limitations imposed by a particular sect on the child's activities may be relevant. The fact that membership of the Exclusive Brethren would deprive the child of normal social

[9] *Re W (Minors)* [1984] 3 All ER 58n. See also *Ridgway v Ridgway* [1986] Fam Law 363, CA, which stressed the need for legal aid to be granted quickly. Failure by barristers and solicitors to exercise the greatest possible diligence in complying with the court imposed time limits for preparation of the appeal may be regarded as professional misconduct: *Re M (A Minor)* (1989) Times, 29 December, CA.
[10] [1991] 2 FLR 388, 390, CA. Cf *Re W (A Minor)* (1992) Times, 22 May, CA (held to be a rebuttable presumption that *babies'* interests are best served by being with their mother.
[11] See eg Wallerstein and Kelly *Surviving the Breakup* chs 10 and 13.
[12] See the summary of various research findings in Maidment *Child Custody and Divorce* pp 182–186. See also King *Maternal Love, Fact or Myth?* 4 Fam Law 61.
[13] See eg Chambers *Rethinking the Substantive Rules for Custody Disputes in Divorce* [1984–85] Michigan Law Review 477, 524–527 and by Cretney and Masson, op cit, at p 533.
[14] (1982) 4 FLR, 492, 504, CA. See also Butler-Sloss LJ's comment in *Re S (A Minor) (Custody)*, ibid at p 390 that 'it is natural for young children to be with their mother' cited and discussed ante at pp 386–387.
[15] Cf *Shelley v Westbrooke* (1817) Jac 266n in which the poet Shelley was denied custody on this ground.
[16] Cf *Re C (MA) (An Infant)* [1966] 1 All ER 838, at 856 and 864–865, CA.
[17] This certainly influenced Willmer LJ in *Re M (Infants)* [1967] 3 All ER 1071, 1074, CA.

contacts and limit his opportunities for further education has influenced
the court in its decision to vest custody in the parent who does not profess
these views,[18] though, as was emphasised in *Re T (Minors) (Custody:
Religious Upbringing)*,[19] it is not for the court to pass judgment on parental
beliefs where they are socially acceptable and consistent with devout and
respectable life. In other words being a Jehovah's Witness, for example,
does not ipso facto mean that that parent should not be granted a residence
order,[20] but membership of an extreme sect could have this consequence.
In *Re B and G (Minors) (Custody)*[1] the decisive factor in denying a father
and stepmother an order to look after the children which they had been
doing for five years was that they were scientologists and so held views
which were found to be 'immoral and obnoxious'. In appropriate cases, for
example, where the care-giver has a different religion from that of the child
it would be open to the court to make a residence order on condition that
the child's religious upbringing will be continued.[2] On the other hand it
could be a condition of an order that the adult does not involve a child in
his religion.[3]

Racial origin, cultural background and linguistic background[4] are issues
that can be considered under this head and are likely on occasion to prove
important particularly in the context of care proceedings[5] but are less likely
to influence decisions in inter-parental disputes.

(e) Any harm which the child has suffered or is at risk of suffering

The 'harm' referred to in this consideration has the same meaning as it
does for the purposes of care proceedings[6] and accordingly means both ill-
treatment and the impairment of health or development. It clearly covers
both physical and psychological trauma. It also covers sexual abuse which,
if proved,[7] is obviously likely to be a significant consideration but even so
may not inevitably mean that the abuser should not, for example, be
allowed contact.[8]

[18] *Hewison v Hewison* (1977) 7 Fam Law 207, CA. See Bradney 9 Fam Law 139. Contrast *Re H (A Minor) (Custody: Religious Upbringing)* (1980) 2 FLR 253.

[19] (1975) 2 FLR 239, CA.

[20] Although parties are sometimes asked to undertake not to involve their children, for example, in the house-to-house visiting in connection with the work as a Jehovah's Witness: see eg *Re C (Minors) (Wardship: Jurisdiction)* [1978] Fam 105, [1978] 2 All ER 230, CA.

[1] [1985] FLR 493, CA. The court felt that it could not rely on the father's undertaking to remove the children from 'the evil forces of scientology'.

[2] In the past, however, the court has been content to accept undertakings to this effect, see eg *Re E (An Infant)* [1963] 3 All ER 874, where a Jewish couple were required to bring up a ward of court as a Roman Catholic and *J v C* [1970] AC 668, [1969] 1 All ER 788, HL where protestants gave a similar undertaking to bring up a child as a Roman Catholic. Contrast *Roughley v Roughley* (1973) 4 Fam Law 91, CA.

[3] Cf *Re C (Minors) (Wardship: Jurisdiction)*, supra.

[4] Considerations to which local authorities must have specific regard under s 22(5)(c), see post, p 506.

[5] Cf *Re P (A Minor) (Transracial Placement)* [1990] 1 FLR 96, CA and *Re N (A Minor) (Adoption)* [1990] 1 FLR 58.

[6] S 105(1) provides that 'harm' has the same meaning as in s 31(9), discussed further post, p 513.

[7] For the standard of proof cf *Re G (A Minor) (Child Abuse: Standard of Proof)* [1987] 1 WLR 1461.

[8] See *H v H (Child Abuse: Access)* [1989] 1 FLR 212, CA; *L v L (Child Abuse: Access)* [1989] 2 FLR 16, CA, and *C v C (A Minor) (Child Abuse: Evidence)* [1988] 1 FLR 462. Cf *Re R (A Minor) (Access)* [1988] 1 FLR 206, CA.

(f) How capable each of the child's parents, and any other person in relation to whom the court considers the question to be relevant, is of meeting his needs

A wide variety of circumstances can be brought into this heading ranging from the parents' medical condition to their lifestyle. As has been pointed out[9] capacity to act as a good parent should not be seen as predetermined so for example, while it is established that lesbianism is a factor to be taken into account, it should not be regarded as *ipso facto* rendering the mother unfit to look after her child.[10]

It is to be noted that as well as parents the capability of any other person in relation to whom the court considers the question to be relevant must also be examined. This will clearly include any new partner of the parent.[11]

3. CONSIDERATIONS WHEN PROHIBITING CONTACT BY PARENTS

The statutory check-list is of course equally relevant to the issue of whether or not to make a contact order. Nevertheless it is to be borne in mind that when considering contact the court is less concerned with a person's overall ability to look after the child and hence might more readily grant contact than a residence order.

As with all issues directly concerning the child's upbringing the controlling principle in deciding whether or not to make a contact order is the paramountcy of the child's welfare.[12] Furthermore the principle applies regardless of whether the child's parents are married to each other[13] and whether it is sought to end or reintroduce contact.[14] Bearing this principle in mind it would be wrong to say that as a matter of law there is a *presumption* that a parent should be permitted contact.[15] Nevertheless it has been repeatedly said that the court should be slow to deny contact between a child and his parent. In *Re H (Minors) (Access)*[16] Balcombe LJ expressly approved *M v M (Child: Access)*[17] the headnote of which reads:

'No court should deprive a child of [contact with] either parent unless it was wholly satisfied that it was in the interests of that child that [contact] should cease, and that was a conclusion at which the court should be extremely slow to arrive. [Contact] was to be regarded as a basic right of the child rather than a basic right of the parent. Save in exceptional circumstances to deprive a parent of [contact] was to deprive a child of an important contribution to his emotional and material growing up in the long-term.'

According to Balcombe LJ the correct test in these types of cases is to ask whether there are cogent reasons why a child should be denied contact with

[9] Cretney and Masson, op cit at p 534.
[10] *C v C (Custody of Child)* [1991] 1 FLR 223, CA. See also *B v B (Custody, Care and Control)* [1991] Fam Law 174. For an account of some empirical evidence on this issue see Tasker and Golombok *Children Raised By Lesbian Mothers* [1991] Fam Law 184.
[11] See eg *Scott v Scott* [1986] 2 FLR 320, CA (mother's cohabitant found to have committed acts of indecency against the child).
[12] See generally *Re KD (A Minor) (Ward: Termination of Access)* [1988] AC 806, [1988] 1 All ER 577, HL.
[13] *S v O (Illegitimate Child: Access)* (1977) 3 FLR 15.
[14] *Re H (Minors) (Access)* [1992] 1 FLR 148, CA.
[15] See Ormrod LJ in *A v C* [1985] FLR 445, 455–456, CA. See also *Re W (A Minor: Access)* [1989] 1 FLR 163.
[16] [1992] 1 FLR 148, 150, CA. See also *Re M (Minors)* (1990) Times, 22 February, CA.
[17] [1973] 2 All ER 81.

his parent rather than to ask whether any positive advantages are to be gained by continuing or resuming contact. In that case the court ordered visiting contact for an introductory period pending a full welfare report notwithstanding that the father had not seen his children for over three years.[18] In *Re B (Minors) (Access)*[19] a father's eccentric and bizarre but not violent behaviour was held not to justify refusing contact. It has also been held[20] that there is no *principle* of law that a parent who has sexually abused his child should ipso facto be prevented from seeing the child and on occasion contact has been allowed to continue.[1]

Although courts seem predisposed to preserve contact with both parents wherever possible, there are obviously occasions when it is not in the child's interests to do so. Examples in the past have included cases where the parent had sexually abused his child[2] and where continued contact was shown to be directly harmful to the child either physically[3] or emotionally in the sense of undermining the child's security.[4] Contact may also be refused on the ground of indirect harm as, for example, where the effect on the care-giving parent is so adverse as to impair that parent's care of the child. Normally this factor is only likely to justify prohibiting contact where the non-care-giving parent's conduct causes genuine and justified anxiety about the child's well-being.[5] However, the implacable hostility of the care-giving parent to the making of a contact order with respect to the other parent is a factor to be taken into account and might in itself justify a refusal.[6] Similarly, the child's own opposition will be a highly significant factor.[7] More unusual cases include *A v C*[8] and *Re C (A Minor) (Access)*.[9] In the former case a man paid a woman to have his child by artificial insemination, the plan being that she would hand over the baby to the man and his wife (who could no longer have children). In the event the mother reneged on the agreement and kept the baby. The father failed both in his application to look after the child and to see it. The latter was refused on the grounds that the father's relationship was wholly artificial and there was no sense in perpetuating it. The latter case concerned a stepfather of a child of the family. Following divorce from the stepfather the mother

---

[18] Cf *Re C (Minors) (Access)* [1985] FLR 804, CA and *Starling v Starling* (1979) 4 FLR 135, CA.
[19] [1992] 1 FLR 140, CA.
[20] *H v H (Child Abuse: Access)* [1989] 1 FLR 212, CA.
[1] *H v H*, supra and *C v C (Child Abuse: Evidence)* [1988] 1 FLR 462.
[2] See eg *S v S* [1988] Fam Law 128, CA and *Re R (A Minor) (Child Abuse)* [1988] Fam Law 129.
[3] As in *Geapin v Geapin* (1974) 4 Fam Law 188, CA where a boy suffered serious asthmatic attacks when in contact with his father.
[4] See eg *Re C (Minors) (Access)* [1985] FLR 804, CA; *Williams v Williams* [1985] FLR 509, CA (though the children were being indoctrinated against the father); and *Wright v Wright* (1980) 2 FLR 276, CA.
[5] See *Re BC (A Minor) (Access)* [1985] FLR 639, CA and *M v J (Illegitimate Child: Access)* (1982) 3 FLR 19. See also *Wright v Wright* (1980) 2 FLR 276, CA, where the mother feared that her husband, a Jehovah's Witness, would 'indoctrinate' her children.
[6] As in *Re B (A Minor: Access)* [1984] FLR 648, CA.
[7] Cf *Re N (A Minor) (Access: Penal Notice)* [1992] 1 FLR 134, CA, and *Churchard v Churchard* [1984] FLR 635.
[8] [1985] FLR 445, CA (decided in 1978).
[9] [1992] 1 FLR 309, CA.

resumed cohabitation with the child's natural father but then left to cohabit with another man. The child, who was still living with the mother, had discovered the identity of her natural father. It was held that notwithstanding the long period that the child had lived with the applicant it was not in her interests to continue to have contact with him, given his intensity of feelings and her current situation vis-à-vis the mother's new cohabitant and her natural father.

Chapter 12

Guardianship

A. Introduction

The term 'guardian' has a variety of meanings[1] but the specific concern of this chapter is the institution of legal guardianship over children during their minority. Formerly, the concept of guardianship was a complex one and it was well described[2] as a formula used to attribute powers over a child's upbringing to a particular individual or individuals. However, following its reform by the Children Act 1989 guardianship can now be said to be the legal process by which a person is given parental responsibility for a child on the death of one or both of the child's parents. In short a 'guardian' is someone who has been formally appointed to take the place of the child's deceased parent.

DISTINGUISHING GUARDIANS FROM PARENTS, FOSTER PARENTS AND 'CO-PARENTS'

(a) Parents

Following the Children Act 1989 reforms the concepts of parenthood and guardianship are now legally distinct: parents are no longer regarded as guardians and apart from exceptional cases in which an unmarried father is appointed guardian instead of being given parental responsibility under section 4 of the 1989 Act,[3] no guardians will be parents.

(b) Foster parents

A guardian must be distinguished from a foster parent, who has de facto care of a child without being the legal guardian. If a parent is dead or is unfit to exercise his responsibilities, it is clearly essential for someone else to stand in loco parentis to a child; but by English law parental responsibility will not vest in a guardian unless he has been formally appointed as such either by a deceased parent or by a court order. In a large number of cases, of course, this never happens; and if both parents die, a child's grandparents or other near relations will assume de facto control of the child without

---

[1] See, for example, the use of 'guardianship' under the Mental Health Act 1983 with which we are not concerned. It might also be noted, that some statutes, for example the Education Act 1944, s 114(1D), give an extended meaning to the term 'guardian' so as to impose duties upon those having de facto care of children as well as upon those who have a legal relationship with them; see further below. For the meaning and role of guardians ad litem, see pp 519–521.
[2] Cretney *Principles of Family Law* (4th Edn, 1984) p 296.
[3] Discussed ante at pp 323–328.

taking steps to have themselves appointed legal guardians at all. Although such persons do not have parental responsibility, that does not mean that they have no obligations towards the child. Indeed, as we have seen,[4] under s 3(5) of the 1989 Act such persons 'may (subject to the provisions of this Act) do what is reasonable in all the circumstances for the purpose of safeguarding or promoting the children's welfare'. There is also, both at common law and under the Children and Young Persons Act 1933, a duty to afford protection.[5] Furthermore anyone who cares for a child will be criminally liable under the 1933 Act[6] if he wilfully fails to provide the child with adequate food, clothing, medical aid or lodging. Similarly, the Education Act 1944 places such a person under a duty to see that the child receives full-time education.[7]

Despite the absence of any formal legal status the de facto care-giver may still be subject to public scrutiny and regulation. If a child is deemed to be privately fostered then the carers will be subject to the provisions of Part IX of the Children Act 1989, the purpose of which is to ensure that the child is visited periodically by local authority officers who must satisfy themselves that the child's welfare is being satisfactorily safeguarded and who must give any necessary advice to the foster parents.[8]

A privately fostered child is a child, under the age of 16, who is cared for and accommodated (whether for reward or not) by someone *other* than his parent,[9] a person having parental responsibility for the child or a relative[10] for a period or intended period of 28 days or more.[11] However, to ensure that normal domestic arrangements are not within the scope of these provisions and that placements which are more appropriately controlled by other provisions are excluded, Part IX is subject to a number of exceptions under Schedule 8. Hence the provisions do not apply if the child lives in the same premises as a parent or a person having parental responsibility for the child or a relative who has assumed responsibility for him. Similarly, the provisions are excluded where the child is being looked after by a local authority or lives in accommodation provided by a voluntary organisation, or in a school in which he is receiving full-time education,[12] hospital, nursing or mental nursing home, or is subject to a supervision order. As these provisions are complementary to those relating to protected children under the Adoption Act 1976, they do not apply to such children either.[13]

[4] Ante at p 335.
[5] Ante at pp 312 et seq.
[6] Ss 1 and 17.
[7] Ss 36 and 114(1D).
[8] Children Act 1989, s 67(1) and the Children (Private Arrangements for Fostering) Regulations 1991 (SI 1991/2050). For a discussion of private fostering under the Children Act see Vol 8 of the Department of Health's *Guidance and Regulations* and *Clarke Hall and Morrison on Children* Vol 1, 2-[401]–[500].
[9] Including the unmarried father.
[10] Defined by s 105(1) of the 1989 Act as 'a grandparent, brother, sister, uncle or aunt (whether of the full blood or half blood or by affinity) or a step-parent'.
[11] Children Act 1989, s 66. An intention to look after a child for more than 28 days may be inferred from the facts: cf *Surrey County Council v Battersby* [1965] 2 QB 194, [1965] 1 All ER 273.
[12] Note that children under 16 who are pupils at a school which is not maintained by a local education authority are treated as privately fostered if they live at the school during school holidays for more than two weeks: Sch 8, para 9.
[13] Sch 8, para 5. For protected children see post, p 444.

Where a child is (or it is proposed that he be) fostered privately then the person arranging the fostering, the person proposing the fostering and the foster parents must give notice to the local authority.[14] Furthermore parents and those with parental responsibility for the child must also give prior notice of a proposed private fostering arrangement (provided they are aware that the child is to be fostered and whether or not they are involved in the arrangement). These notice requirements enable local authorities to investigate in advance the suitability of the proposed foster parents and the placement.

In addition to empowering its officers to inspect premises a local authority may impose conditions inter alia upon the number, age and sex of the children that may reside there and the accommodation, equipment and medical arrangements to be provided for them.[15] It may forbid a person to keep foster children (or a particular child) or to use premises for that purpose.[16] Certain persons, whose previous history or connections indicate that they are not fit to have the care of foster children, are forbidden to maintain foster children unless they first obtain the local authority's written consent.[17] In each of these cases there is provision for appeals to be made to the court.[18]

Fostering also occurs when a child in the care of a local authority or in the charge of a voluntary organisation is boarded out. As we have seen, Part IX does not apply to such foster parents; their selection and supervision are largely governed by the Foster Placement (Children) Regulations 1991. We shall consider the problems that can arise when the authority or organisation wishes to remove the child against the foster parent's will when we discuss children in care.[19]

(c) Persons other than parents with residence orders in their favour

The legal position of guardians may also be compared with that of a person, other than a parent, who has a residence order in his favour. As we have seen,[20] the effect of a residence order is to vest parental responsibility in the person named in the order for the duration of the order but unlike a guardian[1] such a person is not empowered to appoint a guardian himself nor to agree to the child's adoption.[2] Furthermore although the process of granting residence orders to third parties bears some resemblance to the court process of appointing guardians the resulting orders are conceptually different, in that the guardian replaces the deceased parent or parents whereas a person will normally be granted a residence order whilst the child's parents are alive and will therefore share parental responsibility with them. It is not possible for parents to make a private arrangement formally conferring parental responsibility on a third person.[3]

[14] Children (Private Arrangements for Fostering) Regulations 1991 (SI 1991/2050).
[15] Children Act 1989, Sch 8, para 6.
[16] S 69.
[17] S 68.
[18] Applications should be made to a magistrates' court: the Children (Allocation of Proceedings) Order 1991, art 3(1)(g), see Sch 8, para 8.
[19] See ch 16.
[20] Ante, p 361.
[1] See post, p 405.
[2] Children Act 1989, s 12(3).
[3] Children Act 1989, s 2(9), discussed ante at p 334.

B. The position of guardians before the Children Act 1989

Guardianship has had a long history and, before its reform by the Children Act 1989, had become a complicated product of common law, equity and statute.[4] Its early history was succinctly described by the Law Commission as follows:[5]

'The institution of guardianship was originally of concern only to those who had property. It began as a lucrative incident of feudal tenure and developed as a means of safe-guarding a family's property and securing its transmission from one generation to another. Subsequently it became the instrument for maintaining the authority of the father over the upbringing of his children.'

The position that obtained before the Children Act 1989 was briefly as follows. The law recognised both parental and non-parental guardianship. With regard to the former notwithstanding the general equalisation of mothers' and fathers' rights it remained the case that during his lifetime the father was the *sole* guardian of all his legitimate children. It was only upon his death that the mother became a guardian either alone or jointly with any other guardians appointed by the father. The common law made no provision for guardianship of illegitimate children and even though the mother was eventually recognised[6] as having exclusive parental rights and duties she was not formally regarded as a guardian.[7] With regard to non-parental guardianship, statute eventually conferred[8] equal rights on mothers and fathers to appoint a testamentary guardian in respect of legitimate children with the mother having the exclusive right to do so with respect to her illegitimate children. Testamentary appointments took effect upon the death of the appointing parent even if the other parent was still alive. However if the latter objected, he could apply to the court to prevent the appointee from acting. A guardian could also apply to that court if he considered the parent unfit to have custody and the court had various powers to resolve such disputes.[9]

The courts also had power to appoint guardians. For the most part these powers had become statutory and were contained in the Guardianship of Minors Acts 1971 and 1973. Under this legislation a magistrates' court, county court or High Court all had power to make appointments following the death of either or both parents.[10] In addition it was generally thought that the High Court retained an inherent jurisdiction to appoint guardians.[11]

---

[4] For an excellent summary of the history see the Law Commission Working Paper No 91 on *Guardianship* (1985), Part II. For a detailed history see eg Holdsworth *History of English Law* (7th edn, 1966) Vol III. See also Bevan *Child Law* ch 4 and ch 10 of the 7th edition of this work.

[5] In their Working Paper No 91 at para 3.1.

[6] Children Act 1975, s 85(1).

[7] Though in *Re A* (1940) 164 LT 230 it was held that the Guardianship of Infants Act 1925 had given the mother the right to appoint a testamentary guardian for her illegitimate child.

[8] Restricted rights were first conferred by the Guardianship of Infants Act 1886 and equal rights by the Guardianship of Infants Act 1925 which was then consolidated by the Guardianship of Minors Act 1971.

[9] See pp 352–3 of the 7th edition of this work.

[10] For a discussion of these powers see pp 353–355 of the 7th edition of this work.

[11] Though this had been doubted by *Re C (Minors) (Adoption by Relatives)* [1989] 1 All ER 395, CA. In fact the Guardianship Act 1973, s 7(2) expressly preserved the High Court's inherent power to appoint a guardian of the estate.

Historically the law recognised two separate functions of guardians, namely the protection of the person and the protection of the property of the ward, and these functions could be vested in two entirely different sets of people: guardians of the person, with no right to control the ward's property, and guardians of the estate, with no right to control the ward's person.[12] Although the 1925 property legislation had virtually rendered the latter type of guardianship obsolete, it remained useful to appoint the Official Solicitor, for example, to administer an award made to the child by the Criminal Injuries Compensation Board in respect of injuries caused by the parents.[13]

Although in broad terms guardians (unless of the estate only) had similar rights and duties with respect to the child as a parent,[14] they were not in exactly the same position.[15] For example, unlike parents, guardians could not be made liable to maintain their wards nor could they appoint a guardian themselves. On the other hand they probably had wider powers than parents in respect of the child's property. There was uncertainty as to whether a guardian had a right of access to the child nor was the position entirely clear as to who had the right to care and control of the child where the parent was still alive. Indeed overall the Law Commission concluded[16] that the inter-relationship was obscure particularly where the parent was also described as a guardian.

C. The need for reform

As the Law Commission commented,[17] the notion of parental guardianship confused the separate legal concepts of parenthood and guardianship. In their view it was both sensible and practical to regard parenthood as the primary concept and to distinguish it from the role of a guardian who acts in loco parentis. Accordingly they recommended the abolition of the archaic rule under which parents, who for all practical purposes had the same rights and authority, were sometimes guardians and sometimes not.[18]

On the other hand, although relatively little was known about the frequency of guardianship appointments,[19] the Law Commission considered[20] that the law should provide some means of supplying a person or persons who could step into the shoes of a parent or parents who have died. Following consultation the Commission found unanimous support

---

[12] If there was no separate guardian of a minor's estate, a guardian appointed by a deceased parent or by the court under the Guardianship of Minors Act 1971 had all the rights, powers and duties of a guardian of the estate in addition to being guardian of the person: Guardianship Act 1973, s 7.
[13] See Law Commission Working Paper No 91, note 95.
[14] For example both had a statutory right to consent to the marriage of a child under the age of 18 and to agree to the child's adoption.
[15] For a detailed analysis of the former position see Law Commission Working Paper No 91, para 2.24–2.35 and pp 355–360 of the 7th edition of this work.
[16] Working Paper No 91, para 2.35.
[17] Law Com Working Paper No 91, para 3.2.
[18] Law Com Report No 172 on *Guardianship and Custody* (1988) para 2.2.
[19] Though they did commission a small study undertaken by Mrs Priest in the North East of England—see Appendix B of Working Paper No 91.
[20] Working Paper No 91, para 3.17.

for the power both of the parents and courts to appoint guardians.[1] However although it found no evidence of abuse or irresponsibility on the part of the parents, the Commission did canvas opinion as to whether there should be some form of public control of guardians appointed by parents, for example, by subjecting non-related guardians to the same provisions as private foster parents.[2] In the event, however, these suggestions were not pursued[3] nor were the suggestions for extending guardianship to permit *inter vivos* appointments.[4] A number of other suggestions for reform[5] were, however, recommended, namely, vesting full parental responsibility in guardians, simplifying the method by which parents can appoint a guardian, providing in general that parental appointments come into force only upon the death of the surviving parent and changing and clarifying the courts' powers both to appoint and remove guardians. As will be seen, all these recommendations have been enacted in the Children Act 1989. One recommendation, however, has not been adopted, namely the abolition of guardians of the estate.[6]

D. The modern law

The law of guardianship has been refashioned and is now exclusively controlled by sections 5 and 6 of the Children Act 1989. Following the Law Commission's recommendation the concept of parental guardianship has been abolished[7] and, save for the exceptional case where the unmarried father becomes a guardian the status is now confined to those formally appointed to take the place of a deceased parent or parents. With one exception it is no longer possible to appoint different types of guardians. This one exception is the High Court's inherent power to appoint a guardian of a child's estate which has been preserved by section 5(11) and (12). As has been said, the Law Commission recommended the abolition of this power arguing[8] that trusteeship would adequately and more appropriately fill any gap. In the event the government disagreed and in a late amendment made provision to preserve the High Court's power. That power is heavily circumscribed by the rules[9] in that only the Official Solicitor can be so appointed and even then only when the consent of the persons with parental responsibility has been signified to the court or when, in the court's opinion, such consent cannot be obtained or may be dispensed with.[10] Furthermore appointments may be made only in certain defined circumstances, for example, when the Criminal Injuries Compensation Board has made or intends to make an award to the child, when payment to the child has been ordered by a foreign court or tribunal or when the child is entitled to the

[1] Law Com No 172, para 2.2.
[2] Law Com Working Paper No 91, paras 3.23 et seq.
[3] Law Com No 172, para 2.32.
[4] Discussed in Working Paper No 91 paras 4.19 et seq.
[5] See Law Com No 172, paras 2.23–2.31.
[6] Law Com No 172, para 2.24—see further below.
[7] Following the express abolition of the rule of law that a father is the natural guardian of his legitimate children by s 2(4) of the Children Act 1989 and the repeal (by Sch 15) of s 3 of the Guardianship of Minors Act 1971 which provided that upon the death of one parent the other became the guardian of any legitimate child.
[8] Law Com No 172, para 2.24.
[9] Viz RSC Ord 80, r 13.
[10] Ord 80, r 13(1).

proceeds of a pension fund, and in each case only where such an appointment seems desirable to the court.[11] In practice the number of such appointments is likely to remain small and confined to cases where the parents are dead or where it is unsuitable for them to be involved (for example where they had caused the injuries to the child).

Guardians of the estate apart, all guardians have parental responsibility for the child,[12] which effectively places them in the same legal position as parents at least so far as the care and upbringing of the child is concerned. The conferment of full parental responsibility was central to the role of guardians as envisaged by the Law Commission. As they put it:[13]

'The power to control a child's upbringing should go hand in hand with the responsibility to look after him or at least to see that he is properly looked after. Consultation confirmed our impression that it is now generally expected that guardians will take over any responsibility for the care and upbringing of a child if the parents die. If so, it is right that full legal responsibility should also be placed upon them.'

One consequence of having parental responsibility is that guardians can themselves appoint guardians.

1. APPOINTMENT OF GUARDIANS

(a) Private appointment of guardians

Any parent with parental responsibility (ie not an unmarried father without such responsibility) and any guardian may appoint an individual to be the child's guardian.[14] Although reference is made to '*an* individual', it is clear that more than one person may be appointed as a guardian.[15] Furthermore an additional guardian or guardians can be appointed at a later date.[16] There is nothing to prevent an appointment being made by two or more persons jointly.[17]

There is no restriction or control on who may be appointed nor are there any means of scrutinising an appointment unless a dispute or issue is subsequently brought before the court.[18] Appointments can be made only in respect of children under the age of 18.[19]

A valid appointment must be made in writing, dated and signed by the person making it.[20] It is hoped that this simple method of appointment will encourage parents (particularly young parents who are notoriously reluctant to make wills) to appoint guardians.[1] This will not preclude appointments

[11] Ord 80, r 13(2).
[12] Children Act 1989, s 5(6).
[13] Law Com No 172, para 2.23.
[14] Ss 5(3) and 5(4).
[15] This is implicit in s 6(1) which refers to 'an additional guardian'. In any event under the Interpretation Act 1978, s 6(c) unless there is a contrary intention, words in the singular in a statute presumptively include the plural. But 'individual' does not include a 'body', see post, p 404.
[16] S 6(1).
[17] S 5(10).
[18] See post, p 406 for discussion of the courts' powers to remove a guardian.
[19] S 105(1). Query whether an appointment would take effect once the child is married.
[20] S 5(3).
[1] See Law Com No 172, para 2.29.

being made in a will since such means will satisfy the minimum requirements. In the case of an appointment made by will which is not signed by the testator, it will be valid if it is signed at the direction of the testator in accordance with the Wills Act 1837, section 9.[2] An appointment will also be valid in any other case provided it is signed at the direction of the person making the appointment, in his presence and in the presence of two witnesses who each attest the signature.[3] These latter provisions cater for the blind or physically disabled persons who cannot write.[4]

(i) Revoking an appointment

Section 6 of the Children Act 1989 provides that a later appointment revokes an earlier appointment (including one made in an unrevoked will or codicil) made by the same person in respect of the same child, unless it is clear that the purpose of the later appointment is to appoint an additional guardian. It is also open to the person who made the appointment (including one made in an unrevoked will or codicil) expressly to revoke it in a signed written and dated instrument.[5] Section 6(4) further provides than an appointment made in a will or codicil is revoked if the will or codicil is revoked. An appointment, other than one made by will or codicil, will also be revoked if the person making it destroys the document with the intention of revoking the appointment.[6]

(ii) When the appointment takes effect

An appointment no longer automatically takes effect upon the death of the appointing parent. Instead, the appointment can normally take effect only upon the death of the sole remaining parent with parental responsibility.[7] Of course if the appointing person already is the sole parent with parental responsibility then the appointment will take effect immediately upon his death,[8] but, if not, it will not take effect until the death of the surviving parent. The exception to this position, provided by section 5(7)(b) of the 1989 Act, is that the appointment takes effect immediately upon the death of the appointing person if there was a *sole*[9] residence order in his favour at the time of his death.

The rationale of delaying the operation of a guardianship appointment is to avoid unnecessary conflict between a surviving parent and a guardian appointed by the deceased parent. As the Law Commission said,[10] there seems little reason why the surviving parent should have to share parental responsibility with a guardian who almost invariably will not be living in the same household. In effect the law protects the surviving parent from interference by an outsider though of course if that parent wishes informally

---

[2] S 5(5)(a).
[3] S 5(5)(b).
[4] But not for those who are mentally incapacitated: cf Department of Health's Children Act 1989: *Guidance and Regulations,* Vol 1, Court Orders, para 2.18.
[5] S 6(2).
[6] S 6(3).
[7] S 5(8).
[8] S 5(7)(a).
[9] *Aliter,* if a residence order had also been made in favour of a surviving parent: s 5(9).
[10] Law Com No 172, para 2.28.

to seek the help of the appointee he can also do so without jeopardising his parental status. On the other hand if the appointee wishes to challenge this position he will need to seek the court's leave to obtain a section 8 order.

While this basic stand-point seems right where the child was living with both parents in a united family before the death of one of them, different considerations apply where the parents are divorced or separated. Endorsing the Law Commission's view,[11] the law takes the position that if there was a court order that the child should live with the parent who had died, that parent should be able to provide for the child's upbringing in the event of his death. This position, as one commentator has put it,[12] effectively means that a parent in whose favour a residence order has been made is able to exclude the other parent from the physical care of the child in the event of his death.[13] This position has been criticised from two points of view. First, the Scottish Law Commission have commented[14] that the exception makes no provision for the position where the spouses are separated, or even divorced but where there is no residence order. The father, for example, may simply have abandoned his family. As they say: 'In many of these cases it might well be desirable for an appointment of a guardian to be capable of coming into operation, even though there is a surviving parent somewhere.' Bainham[15] on the other hand, questions the very rationale of the exception commenting:

'The survivor will, of course, have joint parental responsibility with the guardian but will have the onus of bringing the child's position before the court in the event of a disagreement between them.[16] This is not very easy to reconcile with the ethos of continuing parental responsibility following divorce. It casts the non-residential parent in the role of an outsider who is liable to interfere with the child rather than that of a concerned parent who is anxious to step in to the breach left by the deceased'.

(iii) Disclaiming the appointment

Section 6(5) of the Children Act 1989 provides for a formal right to disclaim an appointment. This new right[17] must be exercised 'within a reasonable time of his first knowing that the appointment has taken effect'. Furthermore, it must be disclaimed by an instrument in writing, signed by the appointee. There is provision to make regulations for the recording of such disclaimers (which would then be ineffective unless recorded)[18] but at the time of writing no regulations have been made.

---

[11] Ibid at para 2.28.
[12] Bainham *Children: The New Law,* para 2.40.
[13] For the issue of whether this ability would justify making a residence order see ante, p 377.
[14] Discussion Paper No 88, *Parental Responsibilities and Rights, Guardianship and the Administration of Children's Property* (1990) para 3.11.
[15] *Children: The New Law,* para 2.40.
[16] Eg under s 6(7) he can seek a court order to end the appointment: see further below.
[17] Which only applies to persons appointed by a parent or guardian and not to those appointed by the court since they would have consented to the appointment.
[18] Under s 6(6).

(b) The court's power to appoint guardians

(i) When the power may be exercised

Under section 5(1) of the 1989 Act the High Court, a county court or a magistrates' court[19] may appoint an 'individual' to be a child's guardian if:

'(a) the child has no parent with parental responsibility for him; or
(b) a residence order has been made with respect to the child in favour of a parent or guardian of his who has died while the order was in force.'

Confining the power to the appointment of an individual means that a court cannot appoint a *body* such as a local authority to be a guardian.[20] On the other hand applying the Interpretation Act 1978, section 6(c)[1] the court may appoint more than one guardian.

It will be noted that the court's power arises only (1) where the child has no parent with parental responsibility or, (2) upon the death of a parent or guardian in whose favour a residence order[2] was in force. It can, therefore, make an order even though the child has a *guardian* (other than the child's unmarried father), or is the subject of a residence order in favour of a non-parent. It can also make an order if the child's unmarried father is still alive, provided he has not obtained parental responsibility.

The court's powers may be exercised in any family proceedings[3] either upon application (of the person wishing to be appointed) or 'if the court considers that the order should be made even though no application has been made for it'.[4]

(ii) Who may apply?

Any individual[5] may apply to be appointed. There is no requirement that leave of the court must first be obtained. On the other hand an application can only be made under section 5 by an individual himself wishing to be a guardian. However, since under section 5(2), the court has power in any family proceedings to make an appointment of its own motion, once proceedings are in train there would seem nothing to stop any other interested person, including the child himself, from applying to seek the appointment of another individual to be a guardian.

(iii) In respect of whom may applications be made?

An application may be made only in respect of a 'child', that is, a person under the age of 18.[6] There is no express embargo against making an appointment in respect of a married child, although it remains to be seen whether in practice the courts would be prepared to make an appointment in such a case.

[19] See s 92(7).
[20] This is contrary to the recommendation made in the Government White Paper *The Law on Child Care and Family Services* (Cm 62, 1987).
[1] See ante, p 401 n 15.
[2] Unless a residence order was also made in favour of the surviving parent: s 5(9).
[3] Discussed ante at pp 364 et seq.
[4] S 5(2).
[5] But not a 'body' such as a local authority.
[6] S 105(1).

(iv) The courts' power

In accordance with the general principles under section 1, when deciding whether to make an appointment, the court is enjoined to regard the child's welfare as the paramount consideration and to be satisfied that making an order is better than making no order at all. It is not, however, *obliged* to have specific regard to the circumstances set out in section 1(3), though the court is free to do so if it so wishes. There is no restriction comparable to that under section 9(6) with respect to section 8 orders that appointments with respect to 16- or 17-year-olds should only be made in 'exceptional circumstances'.

Since section 5 proceedings rank as 'family proceedings' the court can make, either upon application or upon its own motion, any section 8 order in addition to or instead of appointing a guardian.[7]

2. EFFECT OF BEING APPOINTED A GUARDIAN

Apart from where the Official Solicitor is appointed guardian of a child's estate,[8] *all* persons appointed as guardians, whether by private appointment or by the court, have parental responsibility for the child.[9] The effect of this is to place guardians in virtually the same legal position as parents with parental responsibility. The key difference is that, unlike a parent, a guardian is not a 'liable relative' under the Social Security Act 1986, section 26[10] nor may orders for financial relief be made against him.[11] This means that although guardians are under a duty to see that the child is provided with adequate food, clothing, medical aid and lodging[12] and to educate the child properly,[13] no financial orders can be made against them. The absence of any legal liability on guardians to maintain their children might seem at odds with the general policy of awarding them full parental responsibility. The Law Commission, however, considered[14] that apart from representing a major change of policy the imposition of financial liability upon guardians might 'act as a serious deterrent to appointments being made or accepted'. It should also be added that guardians have no rights of succession upon the child's death, nor can a child take British citizenship from his guardian.

On the other hand a guardian is in a stronger legal position than a non parent in whose favour a residence order has been made in that, unlike the latter,[15] a guardian has a right to consent to or withhold consent from an application to free a child for adoption, to agree to or withhold agreement from the child's adoption and to appoint a guardian.

---

[7] S 10(1).
[8] For an account of the legal position of a guardian of the estate see Law Com Working Paper No 91, para 2.23.
[9] S 5(6).
[10] Discussed post at p 666.
[11] Ie under the powers provided for by s 15 and Sch 1 of the 1989 Act, discussed post at pp 694–700.
[12] Ie pursuant to the Children and Young Persons Act 1933, s 1(2)(a); see ante, p 314.
[13] Ie pursuant to the Education Act 1944, ss 36 and 114(1D), see ante, p 303.
[14] Law Com No 172 at para 2.25.
[15] See s 12(3) discussed ante at p 328.

3. TERMINATION OF GUARDIANSHIP

(a) Automatic termination

The guardian's duties clearly cease if the child dies,[16] and automatically end when he attains the age of 18.[17] Whether the guardian's powers cease upon the child's marriage is perhaps debatable for, while section 5 imposes no such express limitation, it may well be held that there is no scope for the operation of guardianship, save perhaps in respect of the child's property. In any event, it seems unlikely that a guardian would be permitted to interfere with the activities of a married child even if the guardianship continues. Guardianship also ends upon the death of a sole guardian, unless, pursuant to the powers vested by section 5(4), the guardian has appointed another individual to be the child's guardian in his place. If a guardian dies leaving others in office, the survivors continue to be guardians.

(b) Removal by the court

Under section 6(7) of the Children Act 1989 a court[18] can make an order bringing *any* appointment made under section 5 to an end. Such an order can be made at any time upon the application of:

(1) any person who has parental responsibility including the guardian; or
(2) the child himself, with leave of the court; or
(3) upon the court's own motion in any family proceedings, if the court considers that the appointment should be brought to an end.

In deciding whether to end the guardianship, the court must be guided by the welfare principle, pursuant to section 1(1) of the 1989 Act. If, for example, the guardian expresses his unwillingness to continue the court is unlikely to consider it to be for the child's welfare that the appointment should continue. But the power to end the appointment is not confined to cases where the guardian wishes to be released. In the past appointments have been brought to an end because of actual or threatened misconduct of the guardian (for the court will attempt to avert a possible danger to the ward rather than wait for it to happen),[19] the abandonment of his rights for such a length of time that it would not be in the child's interest to permit him to reassert them,[20] or merely because of a change of circumstances which rendered it for some reason better for the child to have a new guardian.[1] If it decides to end the guardianship the court may appoint another individual to take the former guardian's place. It is also open to the court to make a section 8 order. Indeed, as one commentator has pointed out[2] where the court orders a guardian's removal it may have to consider the

---

[16] Though query whether a guardian has a duty to bury or cremate the child: cf *R v Gwynedd County Council, ex p B* [1992] 3 All ER 317, CA, discussed ante at p 311.
[17] Ss 91(7) and 91(8).
[18] Ie the High Court, county court or a magistrates' court: s 92(7).
[19] *Beaufort v Berty* (1721) 1 P Wms 703, 704–705; *Re X* [1899] 1 Ch 526, 531, CA.
[20] *Andrews v Salt* (1873) 8 Ch App 622.
[1] *Re X* (supra) at pp 535–536; *F v F* [1902] 1 Ch 688, where a guardian who had become a Roman Catholic was removed although she had made no attempt to influence her ward, a Protestant.
[2] Bainham, op cit, at para 2.43.

appointment of a new guardian to prevent a hiatus in parental responsibility for the child.

Following the reforms of the Children Act 1989 guardianship now has the clearly defined role of facilitating the replacement of a deceased parent by another person in whom is vested parental responsibility. Furthermore by simplifying the procedure for making private appointments the law has arguably done all that it can to encourage the making of such appointments. Whether more use of guardianship will be made remains to be seen. However as has been commented elsewhere,[3] the complete absence of control on private appointments is striking and is in marked contrast, for example, with the plethora of controls on adoption and even private fostering. This absence of control could be justified on the basis that parents are in a better position than either the courts or local authorities to decide who is best able to care for their children after their death. In any event there remains the safeguard of the local authority's investigative powers to protect children in need or at risk. In practice, little is known about the operation of private guardianships.[4] Research is needed, for example, to discover how common such appointments are; how many are made without even the appointee's knowledge or consent; how many such appointments are disclaimed; and most important, whether there is any evidence to suggest that children may be at risk of abuse by guardians.

---

[3] Douglas and Lowe 'Becoming a Parent in English Law' (1992) 108 LQR 414.
[4] Apart from the valuable but small scale study by J Priest appended to Law Com Working Paper No 91. See also Scot Law Com, Discussion Paper No 88, para 3.2.

Chapter 13

Adoption[1]

A. Introduction

1. THE NATURE OF ADOPTION, BACKGROUND TO THE LEGISLATION AND FURTHER REFORM

In English law adoption refers to the process by which a child's legal parentage is entirely and irrevocably transferred from one set of adults, usually the birth parents, and vested in other adults, namely the adoptive parents.[2] As the Houghton Committee's report[3] put it, adoption involves: 'the complete severance of the legal relationship between parents and child and the establishment of a new one between the child and the adoptive parent'. Adoption is the only means by which parental responsibility can be entirely transferred during the parents' lifetime.

Adoption can only be effected through a court process and the jurisdiction is entirely statutory. This is because at common law parental rights and duties were held to be inalienable.[4] Hence, no change of status comparable to the adoptio or adrogatio of Roman law could be recognised. The absence of such a mechanism generated considerable dissatisfaction both from spouses who were probably childless and anxious to bring up another's child as their own but who hesitated to do so because of the lack of safeguards and from those who had effected a de facto adoption but who felt vulnerable to the very real risk of the parents later turning up and taking the child back.[5]

---

[1] For general reference see Richards *Adoption*, Hoggett and Pearl *The Family, Law and Society* (3rd Edn) pp 637 et seq. For a detailed account of the law as it stood before the Children Act see Bevan *Child Law* ch 5. For a collection of articles on contemporary issues in adoption law and practice see (1991) Adoption and Fostering Vol 15 No 4. For an earlier collection of multidisciplinary essays and articles, see *Adoption: essays in social policy and sociology* (ed Bean) and *Child Adoption* (ABAFA, 1979).

[2] In lay terms 'adoption' can have a wider meaning. For example, it is sometimes said that a person, particularly a stranger in blood, who looks after a child in the event of parental death or abandonment, has 'adopted' him. This relationship is described as foster parenthood in this book, and its legal consequences are discussed in ch 12. For the meaning of 'adoption' for the purposes of the Immigration Rules see *R v Immigration Appeal Tribunal, ex p Tohur Ali* [1988] 2 FLR 523, CA (ante, p 146).

[3] Cmnd 5107, 1972, at para 14. See also The Inter-Departmental Review of Adoption Law, Discussion Paper No 1, *The Nature and Effect of Adoption* (1990), para 2, which describes adoption as the process by which the legal relationship between a child and his or her birth parents is severed and an analogous relationship between the child and the adoptive parents is established.

[4] *Vansittart v Vansittart* (1858) 2 De G & J 249; *Walrond v Walrond* (1858) John 18 and *Humphrys v Polak* [1901] 2 KB 385, CA.

[5] The Report of the Committee on Child Adoption ('The Hopkinson Report') (1921) Cmnd 1254, para 13 commented that it was not unknown for parents who had previously rejected the child to reclaim him once he had reached the age when he could work and earn wages.

Although there were a variety of factors[6] that contributed to the increased pressures for reform, the main catalyst was the substantial increase in the number of orphans following the First World War which in turn led to a large increase in de facto adoptions. The resulting demand for reform led eventually to the passing of the Adoption of Children Act 1926.[7]

The 1926 Act was extensively amended in the light of subsequent experience and criticisms, and all earlier legislation was repealed and consolidated by the Adoption Act 1958. Further dissatisfaction with various aspects of the law and procedure led to the appointment of a Departmental Committee, the 'Houghton Committee', whose report was published in 1972.[8] Most of their recommendations (some of them in modified form) were accepted and incorporated into the Children Act 1975. However, because some of the provisions, notably those concerned with the establishment of an 'adoption service' (discussed below), involved extensive administrative reorganisation and considerable expenditure of public money, the Act was not immediately fully implemented. The law was immediately consolidated by the Adoption Act 1976, which came into force on 1 January 1988 when all the provisions of the 1975 Act were implemented. The 1976 Act has itself since been amended by Schedule 10 to the Children Act 1989.[9] Although many of the changes resulting from these amendments were consequential upon the changes of concepts, terminology and philosophy introduced by the 1989 Act, there were a number of unrelated substantive changes. These were not based on any specific report but advantage was taken of the opportunity to make some helpful but piecemeal changes apparently[10] to meet the needs of particular groups.

As we said in chapter 7,[11] adoption was the one area of child law not to be reviewed during the 1980s. However, after the enactment of the Children Act 1989, a full scale review of adoption law was instigated. This review has been carried out by an Inter-Departmental Committee under the aegis of the Department of Health. At the time of writing the Review has published four Discussion Papers[12] and three Background Papers,[13] but has not produced its final report.

---

[6] Neatly summarised by Cretney *Principles of Family Law* (4th Edn) p 420. See also the fifth edition (by Cretney and Masson) at pp 661–662 and Discussion Paper No 1, op cit at para 2.

[7] Passed following the 'Hopkinson Report', supra, and two Reports of the Child Adoption Committee, Cmnd 2401 and 2469 (1925).

[8] Cmnd 5107. The original chairman of the committee was Sir William Houghton but after his death the chair was taken by Judge Stockdale. On this report generally see Stockdale 3 Fam Law 15, Davies 36 MLR 245 and Samuels 36 MLR 278.

[9] See generally White, Carr and Lowe *A Guide to the Children Act 1989* ch 11 and the Department of Health's *Guidance and Regulations* on the Children Act 1989, Vol 9, *Adoption Issues*.

[10] As explained by David Mellor when introducing the new Schedule: HC Official Report, SC B, 6 June 1989, col 380.

[11] Ante, p 247.

[12] Viz *The Nature and Effect of Adoption* (No 1, 1990), *Agreement and Freeing* (No 2, 1991), *The Adoption Process* (No 3, 1991) and *Intercountry Adoption* (No 4, 1992).

[13] Viz *International Perspectives* (No 1, 1990), *Review of Research Relating to Adoption* (No 2, 1990) and *Intercountry Adoption* (No 3, 1992).

2. A COMPARISON OF ADOPTION WITH OTHER RELATIONSHIPS AND ORDERS

As we have said, an adoption order completely severs the legal relationship between the child and his natural parents and vests full parental responsibility exclusively in the adopters.[14] The result in brief is that for all legal purposes the adopters step into the shoes of the child's natural parents; by 'parents' in other words is now meant not the child's natural parents; but his adoptive parents.[15] Such a relationship is thus distinguishable from that of a married parent and child, unmarried father and child, and guardian and ward. It resembles most closely the first, for, although there need be no blood relationship between the parties, the legal consequences are almost the same. It differs most markedly from the second for the law does not automatically vest parental responsibility by reason of the blood relationship: adoption in fact creates virtually the converse situation. It resembles the third in that the adoptive parents, like guardians, stand in loco parentis to the child to whom they are not necessarily related in blood, but differs from it in that the relationship of guardian and ward does not make the child a member of the guardian's family, for example, for the purposes of the devolution and acquisition of property.

An adoption order is distinguishable from a residence order under section 8 of the Children Act 1989 because it severs the legal ties between the child and his natural parent whereas the latter does not. Furthermore, whereas the former order is permanent (ie the child remains a member of the adoptive family even after he attains his majority), the latter can subsequently be varied and, in any event, ceases to have effect once the child reaches the age of 18. Finally, as we discuss later, a different weight is placed upon the child's welfare in adoption proceedings, in that it is the *first* consideration, rather than the paramount consideration as in section 8 proceedings.

It is perhaps permanence rather than severance that is the more significant feature of an adoption order. At any rate the psychological importance of having the security of a permanent order has been stressed by the courts[16] and, as one leading expert has put it,[17] 'Although no one can guarantee what the future will hold, a permanent placement is one that is *intended* to last and which is given the legal security to make this possible. A permanent home provides the child with the basis for his healthy emotional development.'

3. THE CHANGING PATTERN OF ADOPTION

Since the 1960s there has been a dramatic reduction in the number of adoptions; from a peak of 24,831 orders made in England and Wales in

---

[14] See the Adoption Act 1976, s 12.

[15] The effects of an adoption order are discussed more fully post, p 455.

[16] See eg *Re F (A Minor) (Adoption: Parental Agreement)* [1982] 1 All ER 321, 326, CA per Ormrod LJ with Bridge LJ in *Re SMH and RAH* [1979] CA Transcript 103.

[17] Adcock *Alternatives to Adoption* (1984) Adoption and Fostering, Vol 8, No 1, 12. Cf Triseliotis *Permanency Planning* (1991) Adoption and Fostering, Vol 15, No 4.

1968 there were just 7,044 orders in 1989.[18] One of the main reasons for this decline is the reduction in the number of babies available for adoption. In 1970, for instance, out of a total 8,649 children adopted before the age of one by non-parents 7,449 children were born to unmarried mothers (the traditional source of babies for adoption). Figures since then show a continuous drop in the overall total of adoptions of children under the age of one declining from, for example, 4,548 in 1975 to 1,115 in 1989.[19] This decline in the number of babies available for adoption was noted in 1972 by the Houghton Committee[20] and was then thought to be accounted for by the reduction of the number of unwanted babies because of the increased availability of contraception and abortion. Furthermore, more unmarried mothers tend to keep their children because of the changing attitudes to illegitimacy and the availability of state benefit and 'reasonable employment prospects and in some areas day care provision'. Today one would add that an increasing number of children are born to unmarried couples living together in a stable union. A second major reason for the overall decline in adoption was a change in the law consequent upon the Houghton Committee's recommendation[1] aimed at discouraging joint adoptions by natural parents and step-parents. In 1971 10,751 step-parent adoption orders were made. In 1983 there were 2,872 such orders, which represented 31.8 per cent of the total number of orders made.[2]

Against this fall in overall numbers there have also been changes in adoption practice; in particular local authorities have increasingly seen and used adoption as the means by which they can best secure the long-term welfare not just of babies but also of older children[3] and handicapped children in care. The figures for the number of children adopted from care rose from 1,488 in 1979 to 2,605 in 1990.[4] Further, as the House of Commons' Second Report on the Children Act 1975[5] noted, there has also been an increase in the number of adoptions in which parental agreement

---

[18] Office of Population Censuses and Surveys (series Fm 2) marriage and divorce statistics (HMSO) (1990); see Adoption Review, Discussion Paper No 3, op cit at pp 6 et seq. A comprehensive table of statistics of orders made from 1927 to 1971 is included in Appendix B of the Houghton Report. An analysis of the adoption orders made in 1975–1983 can be found in the *Children Act 1975 Second Report to Parliament* (HMSO 1984). Annual analyses can be found in Office of Population Censuses and Surveys Monitor (OPCS) series FM2.

[19] OPCS, Marriage and Divorce Statistics 1989 (1990), Table 6.2. Nevertheless the placement of babies for adoption is still an important element of adoption agencies' work. In the Bristol study 37 per cent of adoptions by non-relatives were of children under the age of one: Lowe and Murch with Borkowski, Copner and Griew *Pathways to Adoption*, Bristol University (1991), Table 3.10. For a summary of this research see Lowe [1992] Fam Law 52.

[20] Op cit at para 20.

[1] Op cit at para 115 and discussed in detail below at p 420.

[2] In the Bristol study, step-parent adoptions accounted for 34 per cent of the overall sample: *Pathways to Adoption*, op cit, Table 2.3.

[3] The current trend is for an increasing proportion of adoption orders to be made in respect of older children eg 8 per cent were aged 10 or over in non-parental adoptions in 1975 compared with 16 per cent in 1983 and 27 per cent in 1986: (1987) Adoption and Fostering, Vol 11, No 4, 48–49.

[4] See Adoption Review, Discussion Paper No 3, op cit, para 9. 5.8 per cent of children who left care in the year ending March 1985 were adopted: (1988) Adoption and Fostering, Vol 12, No 2, 55. This proportion for the year end March 1988 rose to 7.4 per cent, see Adoption Law Review, Discussion Paper No 1, para 56.

[5] HMSO, 1984.

has been dispensed with[6] which 'may reflect the greater willingness of agencies, acting on the welfare principle, to consider adoption in spite of parental opposition'. This change of attitude by Social Services departments has been accompanied by a much more determined effort to secure adoption placements for children hard to place to the extent of having extensive publicity campaigns, one of the best known being the 'Be My Parent' scheme organised by the British Agencies for Adoption and Fostering (BAAF).[7]

Sir Roger Ormrod said:[8] 'Instinctively we all see adoption as the process of amputating a baby from the mother and grafting it into another family, all contact with the natural mother being cut off so that a child is a child of the new family.' As the foregoing discussion shows, however, while such 'conventional' orders are still important they are no longer the norm. However, there are those, Sir Roger included, who believe that the legislation was not only originally but still is essentially designed for such 'conventional' orders. In particular it is felt that adoption is not well suited to deal with older children since the severing of links with his natural family becomes something of a legal fiction to a child well able to remember his origins and not always appropriate if he has worthwhile links with his siblings or grandparents.[9] The appropriateness of having a unitary concept of adoption to deal both with young and old children alike is one of the issues addressed by the Adoption Law Review.[10]

4. SOME CURRENT ISSUES

(a) Open adoption[11]

Traditionally adoption has been a secretive process designed not simply to facilitate the irrevocable transfer of parentage but to protect unmarried mothers and the children from excessive stigma and to enable childless couples to avoid the oppressive taint of infertility.[12] Hence law and practice were designed so that the birth parents would have nothing to do with the process of selecting adopters: on the contrary they would generally have no knowledge of the adopters and of course they would have no further contact with their child. Similarly adopters would not know of the birth parents' identity. One result of this secrecy was that adopters were generally reluctant to tell their children that they were adopted.

Law and practice have moved on from this traditional view. Impetus for change was first given by studies in the 1960s and 1970s demonstrating the

---

[6] For a discussion on dispensing with parental agreement, see post, pp 426 et seq.
[7] Under which written profiles with photographs, and most recently, video profiles of individual (but unidentified) children are widely circulated. There have also been television campaigns from time to time.
[8] *Child Care Law: a personal perspective* (1983) Adoption and Fostering, Vol 7, No 4, 10, 15.
[9] But for the court's ability to provide for continuing contact where an adoption is made, see post, p 447.
[10] See Discussion Paper, No 1, op cit, Part E, discussed post, pp 456–457.
[11] See generally: *Open Adoption—The Philosophy and the Practice* (ed A Mullender); *Openness in Adoption* (1991) Adoption and Fostering, Vol 15, No 4, 81–115 and the Adoption Law Review, Discussion Paper No 1, op cit, Part C and paras 98–109.
[12] See Triseliotis 'Open adoption' in *Open Adoption—The Philosophy and the Practice*, p 19.

deleterious effect upon adopted children of not knowing of their own identities.[13] Eventually the law was changed permitting adopted children, when they were 18, to have access to their birth records and to pursue the possibility of establishing contact with their birth family.[14] Today it would be regarded as bad practice for adopters to hide the fact that their child is adopted.[15]

A second impetus for change resulted from the practice of placing older children for adoption when it came to be realized that the automatic termination of contact between the child and his natural family was not necessarily in the child's interests.[16] In turn the courts have accepted that it is not inconsistent with adoption for the child to have continued contact with his family.[17]

A further stage of 'open adoption' is to involve the birth parents in the process of selecting adopters and there are some agencies that actively encourage this. How far the law should be further changed to promote openness is another of the issues addressed by the Adoption Law Review.[18]

(b) Inter-country adoptions[19]

A matter of growing concern is the practice of inter-country adoptions, that is, where applicants deliberately seek a child from overseas and bring him back to this county and apply to adopt him. These children usually come from a poor country, often from Latin America, though most recently from Romania. There are no reliable statistics for inter-country adoption in the United Kingdom though they were thought to number about 100–120 a year before adoption from Romania began.[20] However, during 1990 over 400 children from Romania alone have been brought here for adoption.[1]

Inter-country adoptions raise a number of fundamental issues such as the obvious dangers of exploiting vulnerable birth parents, the desirability of transracial adoptions and the difficulty of international control. Against this is the need of the adopters themselves who are often desperate to have children but who are too old to be considered by adoption agencies, at any rate to adopt babies, and not least, the desperate plight of at least some of the children as, for example, the Romanian orphans.

It is by no means easy to balance these needs though practicality suggests that attempting to control inter-country adoption is probably better than attempting to outlaw it. However, it is a hotly disputed issue as to whether

[13] See McWhinnie *Adopted Children: How They Grow Up* (1967) and Triseliotis *In Search of Origins* (1973).
[14] Discussed post, p 452.
[15] This, however, is not an enforceable obligation see eg *Re S (A Minor) (Adoption by Step-parents)* [1988] 1 FLR 418, CA.
[16] See eg Triseliotis *Adoption with Contact* (1985) Adoption and Fostering, Vol 9, No 4, 19 and Fratter *Family Placement and Access.*
[17] Ie courts can expressly make provision for continuing contact in an adoption order, see post, p 447.
[18] See Discussion Paper No 1, paras 98–109.
[19] See generally Adoption Law Review, Discussion Paper No 4 and Background Paper No 3.
[20] See Adoption Law Review, Discussion Paper No 4, para 27.
[1] Adoption Law Review, ibid, para 27.

it is desirable to have transracial adoptions at all.[2] Many agencies are against placing black children with white adopters though a rigid policy to this effect is almost entirely open to judicial review.[3]

Another issue of current concern, particularly to immigrant communities is that of adoption and immigration and in particular the use of adoption to acquire British citizenship.[4]

5. THE RESPONSIBILITY FOR PLACING CHILDREN FOR ADOPTION

(a) Prohibition of private placements

The selection of potential adopters and the placement of the child with them is clearly a crucial step in the adoption process. From the child's point of view it is obviously important that the placement is a success so that every effort needs to be made, before the placement, to ensure as far as possible that the applicants will provide the particular child with a loving and secure home. Surprisingly, however, until 1982[5] there was no restriction on individuals[6] placing children for adoption. Although commonly such private arrangements were made through doctors or even solicitors, there was, as the Houghton Committee pointed out,[7] nothing to prevent a mother making a placement with a casual acquaintance such as someone she met at the launderette. This lack of control had obvious dangers: if the potential adopters were unsuitable (a not unlikely consequence, given the inexperience of the placers) the placement could be disastrous for the child; it could also lead to improper pressure being brought upon the mother.[8]

Following the Houghton Committee's recommendation[9] it is now[10] unlawful for a person other than an adoption agency to place a child for adoption unless the proposed adopter is a relative of the child or he is acting pursuant to a High Court order. Those contravening these provisions are liable to a maximum of three months' imprisonment and a fine not exceeding Level 5 on the standard scale.[11]

'Placement', for these purposes, refers to the single act of transfer rather than to a continuous state of looking after the child. Hence because section

[2] See inter alia Gill and Jackson *Adoption and race: black, Asian and mixed race children in white families* (1983).

[3] See eg *Re J K (Adoption: Transracial Placement)* [1991] 2 FLR 340, *Re P (A Minor) (Adoption)* [1990] 1 FLR 96, CA and *Re N (Minors) (Adoption)* [1990] 1 FLR 58.

[4] Space forbids doing justice to this subject but for an excellent review of the issues, see Khan *Adoption and Immigration* (1986) 130 Sol Jo 213 and inter alia *Re W (A Minor) (Adoption: Non-Patrial)* [1986] Fam 54, [1985] 3 All ER 449, CA and *Re H (A Minor) (Adoption: Non-Patrial)* [1982] Fam 121, [1982] 3 All ER 84.

[5] When s 28 of the Children Act 1975 was brought into force.

[6] It had previously been illegal for any 'body of persons' other than an adoption agency to make arrangements for adoption, see the unamended s 29 of the Adoption Act 1958.

[7] Op cit at para 81.

[8] It is illegal to give or receive any payment or reward in consideration of an adoption; Adoption Act 1976, s 57, discussed post, p 447.

[9] Op cit at para 92.

[10] Adoption Act 1976, s 11(1) and (3).

[11] Adoption Act 1976, s 11(3), as amended by the Criminal Justice Act 1982. It is an offence both to arrange private placements *and* to receive a child unlawfully placed. In the latter instance, however, it must be proved that the placement was unlawful and that the accused knew of the purpose of the placement: *Gatehouse v Robinson* [1986] 1 WLR 18.

11 has no extra-territorial effect a private placement abroad is no offence even if the couple then bring the child to the United Kingdom for adoption.[12] On the other hand an offence will be committed if, as in *Re A (Adoption: Placement)*,[13] the child is handed over to the couple in the United Kingdom, or even if one of the couple brings the child from abroad and joins his spouse with the child in this country.[14]

It remains lawful to make private arrangements for the adoption of the child by a relative,[15] and it is not an offence to make a private placement in pursuance of a High Court order. An unlawful placement does not per se prevent an adoption order from being made, though in such cases it will be necessary to obtain High Court dispensation.[16] The above provisions do not prevent private *fostering* placements being made[17] nor is there anything to prevent such foster parents from subsequently applying for adoption. However, if it is clear that the foster arrangement is a mere subterfuge and that both the placer and the recipient intended that the child should be adopted, both will be guilty of an offence.[18]

(b) Adoption agencies

The principal burden both of selecting potential adopters and for placing children for adoption rests with adoption agencies, that is, approved adoption societies and local authorities.[19]

Voluntary societies have long helped to facilitate adoptions. Some societies, for example, the Catholic Children's Society and Church of England Children's Society, aim primarily to serve particular denominational interests. Some, for example, Barnados, are national organisations; others are local. Formerly control of such societies was through a local system of registration, but following the Houghton Committee's recommendations[20] there is now a central controlling system. Any voluntary society wishing to act or to continue to act as an adoption agency must apply to the Secretary of State for Social Services for approval.[1] Applicants must be incorporated non-profit making bodies.[2] Approval is contingent upon the Secretary of State's satisfaction that the applicant is likely to make an effective contribution to the adoption service. Regard is specifically to be had to the applicant's adoption programme, including its ability to make provision for

[12] As in *Re Adoption Applications 8605489/99* (1988) Adoption and Fostering, Vol 12, No 2, p 58.
[13] [1988] 1 WLR 229.
[14] *Re An Adoption Application* [1992] 1 FLR 341.
[15] Adoption Act 1976, s 11(1)(a). 'Relative' is defined in the Adoption Act 1976, s 72(1) as grandparent, brother, sister, uncle and aunt whether of the full blood or half blood or by affinity and regardless of whether the child is legitimate or illegitimate. The unmarried father is specifically included in the definition. Great aunts and uncles are not 'relatives' for these purposes; see *Re S (Arrangements For Adoption)* [1985] FLR 579, CA. See also *Re C (Minors) (Wardship: Adoption)* [1989] 1 All ER 395, CA.
[16] Adoption Act 1976, s 11(1)(b).
[17] Private foster parents are required to notify the local authority under the Children Act 1989, Sch 8, para 7.
[18] *Gatehouse v Robinson*, supra.
[19] Adoption Act 1976, ss 1(4), 72(1).
[20] Op cit at para 61.
[1] Adoption Act 1976, s 3.
[2] See the Health and Social Services and Social Security Adjudications Act 1983, s 9 and Sch 2, para 22, and Adoption Agencies Regulations 1983, r 2(2).

children who are free for adoption; the number and qualifications of its staff; its financial resources and the organisation and control of its operations.[3] Approval only lasts for three years and the Secretary of State is in any event empowered to withdraw approval.[4]

The functions and duties of adoption agencies are tightly controlled by the Adoption Agency Regulations 1983.[5] Under these regulations the agency is obliged to set up an adoption panel[6] whose function with regard to every child referred to it is, inter alia, to consider and make recommendations as to whether adoption is in the child's best interests and whether the prospective adopter is a suitable person to adopt the child.[7] The agency itself has a duty whenever it is considering adoption to explain to the child, having regard to his age and understanding, and to parents, inter alia the implications of adoption.[8] A similar duty is owed to the prospective adopters to whom there must in addition be offered a counselling service.[9] The agency also has a duty to collect and collate information about the child and his parents, to make arrangements for medical examinations, to provide background information about the child to the prospective adopters, to visit the child after placement, and generally to provide advice and assistance.[10]

It will be seen therefore that through these provisions most children are only placed for adoption with applicants who have been carefully screened by professional and experienced bodies.

6. ADOPTION SERVICE

Although numerous adoption agencies had existed for some time, the Houghton Committee was concerned that a comprehensive service might not be available throughout the country. Accordingly, the Committee recommended[11] that it should be mandatory for every local authority to provide an adoption service as part of their general child care and family casework provision and to ensure in co-operation with voluntary services that a comprehensive adoption service is available throughout their area. These recommendations are now embodied in the Adoption Act 1976, sections 1 and 2.[12]

---

[3] Adoption Act 1976, s 3(3).

[4] Adoption Act 1976, ss 3(7) and 4. For a full list and location of agencies, see *Adopting a Child* published annually by BAAF.

[5] For a helpful explanation of the Regulations, see Local Authority Circular LAC (84)3.

[6] Reg 5.

[7] Reg 10.

[8] Reg 7.

[9] Reg 8.

[10] Regs 6, 11 and 12. Failure to comply with these regulations does not necessarily vitiate the adoption, see *Re T (A Minor) (Adoption: Validity of Order)* [1986] Fam 160, sub nom *Re T (A Minor) (Adoption: Parental Consent)* [1986] 1 All ER 817, CA.

[11] Op cit, ch 3.

[12] As amended by the Children Act 1989, Sch 11, para 1. For an explanation of what services should be available and how authorities and voluntary societies should co-ordinate their efforts, see DHSS Circular LAC 87(8).

7. THE WEIGHTING OF THE CHILD'S WELFARE[13]

Although the courts have always had to be satisfied that an adoption order would be for the child's benefit, until the implementation of the Children Act 1975, there was no specific guidance on the weighting to be accorded to the child's welfare during the various stages of the adoption process. The guiding principle is now provided by the Adoption Act 1976, section 6, which states:

'In reaching any decision relating to the adoption of a child a court or adoption agency shall have regard to all the circumstances, first consideration being given to the need to safeguard and promote the welfare of the child throughout his childhood; and shall so far as practicable ascertain the wishes and feelings of the child regarding the decision and give due consideration to them, having regard to his age and understanding.'

It will be noticed that the section falls short of making the child's welfare the *paramount* consideration as under the Children Act 1989, section 1. Indeed it was apparently felt[14] that the irrevocable severance of family ties involved in adoption justified giving less weight to the child's welfare than in other cases concerning the child's upbringing.[15] In point of fact, however, it is hard to state with precision what difference there is between 'first' and 'paramount'.[16] Perhaps the most authoritative guidance is that given by Lord Simon when he said:[17] 'In adoption proceedings the welfare of the child is not the paramount consideration (ie outweighing all others), but it is first consideration (ie outweighing any other).' In short while the child's welfare remains the single most important factor it does not necessarily outweigh all other considerations. As we shall see, when one takes this in conjunction with the requirement to obtain or dispense with parental agreement there is marked difference in the weighting of the child's welfare in adoption cases compared with those under section 8 by the Children Act 1989.

It should be noted that section 6 applies to adoption agencies as well as to the courts.

B. The making of adoption orders

1. WHO MAY BE ADOPTED

An adoption order may be made only in respect of a person who is under

---

[13] See generally Bevan and Parry *Children Act 1975* ch 3 and Bennion *First Consideration: A Cautionary Tale* 126 NLJ 1237. For the application of s 6 see post, p 447.
[14] See Bevan and Parry, op cit, para 33.
[15] A similar weighting is given under the Matrimonial Causes Act 1973, s 25(1), as amended by the Matrimonial and Family Proceedings Act 1984, s 3; see post, p 758.
[16] In *Re W (A Minor) (Adoption)* [1984] FLR 402, 404, CA Cumming Bruce LJ described the difference as 'manifestly an extremely fine distinction'. *Re W* is an unusual example of a judge expressly but erroneously applying the paramountcy test in adoption.
[17] In *Re D (An Infant) (Adoption: Parent's Consent)* [1977] AC 602, 638, HL.

the age of 18 and has never been married. An adopted child may be readopted.[18]

2. WHO MAY APPLY FOR ADOPTION

(a) Age, health, domicile and status of applicant

Immediately before the Children Act 1989 the law prevented *anyone* under the age of 21 from applying to adopt.[19] However, the 1989 Act has amended the uniform minimum age requirement to the limited extent of permitting a joint application by a married couple where one spouse is the mother or father of the child and aged at least 18 and the other spouse is at least 21.[20] Although there is no prescribed maximum age, it should be appreciated that in practice adoption agencies are unlikely to consider applicants aged over 40 (and often over 35) at any rate as potential adopters for healthy babies.[1] Obviously age, for example in the case of grandparent applicants, can be a factor that the court can take into account when deciding whether an adoption order would be for the child's benefit. Whether upper age limits should be made more explicit either in legislation or guidance has been raised by the Adoption Law Review.[2]

Although there are no statutory requirements in respect of the health of adopters, as the Adoption Law Review points out,[3] adoption agencies are required in the regulations to obtain a report on the prospective adopters' health.[4] The Review is seeking views as to whether there should be central guidelines on this issue.

A single applicant, or, in the case of a joint application, one of the

---

[18] Adoption Act 1976, ss 12(5), (7) and 72(1) (definition of 'child') and see *Re D (A Minor) (Adoption Order: Validity)* [1991] Fam 137, 144, [1991] 3 All ER 461, 465, CA per Balcombe LJ. The child's domicile does not affect jurisdiction: *Re B (S) (Infant)* [1968] Ch 204, [1967] 3 All ER 629 but see post, p 447, n 13.

[19] Adoption Act 1976, ss 14(1) and 15(1). Under the Adoption Act 1958, as originally enacted, a sole applicant and at least one of joint applicants had to be aged 25 unless he or she was a parent or relative of the child. The Houghton Committee (at paras 70–78) recommended the introduction of a uniform age because there was some evidence that the minimum age of 25 was preventing some suitable couples from adopting and a minimum age of 21 would give an opportunity of testing the strength of a teenage marriage. For the present law see Adoption Act 1976, ss 14(1), (1A), (1B) and 15(1) (as amended by the 1989 Act, Sch 10, para 4).

[20] Adoption Act 1976, s 14(1B) added by the Children Act 1989, Sch 10, para 4. Ironically, following this change the Adoption Law Review, Discussion Paper No 3, ibid at para 39, asks whether there is a case for standardising the minimum age. The room for manoeuvre, however, is limited in this respect by Art 7 of the European Convention on the Adoption of Children which specifies that an adoption order should only be made if the adopter is between 21 and 35 save where the applicant is a parent or there are exceptional circumstances.

[1] See the discussion in the Adoption Law Review, Discussion Paper No 3, at paras 40 et seq. These conditions may be relaxed where application is made to adopt older children or those with disabilities: see para 43.

[2] Ibid at para 44.

[3] Ibid at para 46.

[4] Adoption Agencies Regulations 1983, reg 8(2)(c). These matters include personal and family history and the current state of health, it also includes consumption of tobacco and alcohol. See also *R v Secretary of State for Health, ex p Luff* [1992] 1 FLR 59, where the court refused to quash a Department of Health's recommendation to the Home Office that the adoptive applicants in respect of two Romanian children were unsuitable, because of the male applicant's health following a heart by-pass operation.

applicants must be domiciled in a part of the United Kingdom,[5] Channel Islands or Isle of Man, unless the application is for a Convention Order[6] or for an order permitting the applicants to adopt the child abroad.[7]

The Act permits both joint and single applications. In the former case, an order may not be made upon the application of more than one person unless the applicants are married to each other.[8] This means, for example, that brothers and sisters and cohabiting couples cannot jointly apply for adoption. The embargo on cohabitants is in line with the prohibition under Article 6(1) of the European Adoption Convention. Nevertheless given the increasing incidence of children born to parents who are not married but who are living together in stable unions the justification for this restriction may well be open to question.[9] As adoption agencies usually place a child with a married couple[10] a sole applicant is likely to be a relative or an unmarried parent of the child.[11] An order may not be made on the sole application of a married person unless his spouse cannot be found or is by reason of ill health, whether physical or mental, incapable of making an application for an adoption order[12] or, alternatively, if the spouses have separated and are living apart and the separation is likely to be permanent.[13] This is of course designed to avoid the highly artificial situation of a child being adopted by one of two married persons living together, the other of whom refuses to apply for an order. If the sole applicant is the mother or father[14] of the child no order can be made unless the court is satisfied that the other natural parent is dead or cannot be found or there is some other reason justifying the other natural parent's exclusion.[15] The reason for the exclusion has to be recorded.[16]

---

[5] Ie England, Wales, Scotland and Northern Ireland: Interpretation Act 1978, Sch 1.

[6] Adoption Act 1976, ss 14(2), 15(2). 'Convention Orders' are discussed below at p 453.

[7] Adoption Act 1976, s 55.

[8] Adoption Act 1976, s 14. If joint applicants are not married to each other, the order is voidable and not void: *Re F (Infants) (Adoption Order: Validity)* [1977] Fam 165, [1977] 2 All ER 777, CA; cf *Re RA* (1974) 4 Fam Law 182.

[9] Cf Adoption Law Review, op cit, at paras 51 et seq.

[10] Placements with a single applicant living with a partner, however, are by no means unknown. For the propriety of this practice cf Adoption Law Review, ibid, at para 55 et seq.

[11] Or, possibly, in the case of a child originally boarded out with foster parents, by a single foster parent. In 1983 and 1984 there were respectively only 82 and 81 orders made in favour of single applicants.

[12] What does this provision contemplate? It is easy to see that a person's mental health may be such that he is incapable of making an application but difficult to see how his physical health can have this effect. Does it envisage a spouse whose health is such that no court would make an order? If so, this might in any case lead the court to conclude that the applicant's home is such that it would not be for the child's benefit to make such an order in his favour.

[13] Adoption Act 1976, s 15(1)(b).

[14] Notwithstanding the definition of 'parent' as including only those with parental responsibility, it is thought that *this* reference includes the unmarried father, cf Bevan and Parry, op cit, at para 97 and Bevan *Child Law* (1989) para 5.57.

[15] The burden of proof is a heavy one, see *Re C (Minor) (Adoption by Parent)* [1986] Fam Law 360. This is in line with the Houghton Committee's recommendations, at paras 98–102, on which the provision is based. The Committee was afraid that adoption was being used simply as a means of cutting out the other natural parent rather than to promote the child's welfare.

[16] Adoption Act 1976, s 15(3).

(b) Step-parent adoptions[17]

In the ensuing discussion the expression 'step-parent adoption' refers to the case where a parent, usually the mother, and a spouse who is not the parent jointly apply to adopt the child. Commonly this occurs following divorce and remarriage (the 'post-divorce' step-parent adoption) but it also occurs following a parent's death and the surviving parent's remarriage ('post-death' step-parent adoption) or where the mother was not married in the first place ('illegitimate' step-parent adoption). Until the Children Act 1975, there were no formal restrictions on any type of step-parent adoption application. The Houghton Committee,[18] however, was concerned about the growing number of adoptions involving step-parents, which by 1970 exceeded 10,000. They were particularly concerned with 'post-divorce' step-parent adoptions which they felt were an inappropriate use of the jurisdiction and, given the consequential extinguishment of the legal links with half his family, potentially damaging to the child.[19] The Committee felt that the preferable alternative was to extend the provisions enabling a step-parent to apply to become a guardian.

Although the reform did not take the exact form recommended by the Houghton Committee nevertheless following their recommendations courts were consequentially directed to dismiss 'post-divorce' step-parent adoption applications if they considered the matter would be better dealt with by an application to the divorce court for what was then a custody order.[20]

This direction was at first taken to be a clear expression of a policy to discourage adoptions by parents and step-parents.[1] Indeed the appellate courts initially interpreted the section as requiring the applicant to prove that adoption was better than a joint custody order made by the divorce court.[2] This meant, as Ormrod LJ acknowledged,[3] that given the child would be living with the applicants regardless of the outcome of the application, they would have to rely on the intangible advantages of adoption. However, in an apparent volte face, the Court of Appeal held in

---

[17] For a full study of the law and practice before the Children Act 1989 see Masson, Norbury and Chatterton *Mine, Yours or Ours*, summarised in (1982) Adoption and Fostering. Vol 5, No 2, 7 and for further analysis see Priest *Step-parent Adoptions: What is the Law?* [1982] JSWL 285 and Rawlings *Law Reform with Tears* 45 MLR 637. See also the Adoption Law Review Discussion Paper No 1, paras 29–46 and 125–134 and Discussion Paper No 3, paras 26–33.

[18] Op cit at paras 103–110.

[19] Inter alia because it might inhibit open and frank recognition of the true situation and could make it more difficult for the child to come to terms with his origins. In point of fact the Committee had little available research on such adoptions, see the criticisms, inter alia, of Maidment *Step-parents and Step Children, Legal Relationships in Serial Unions* in *Marriage and Cohabitation in Contemporary Societies* Eekelaar and Katz (eds).

[20] Adoption Act 1976, s 14(3), in cases where the application was made jointly by a parent and step-parent, and s 15(4) where the application was by the step-parent alone.

[1] See, for example, Local Authority Circular LAC (76) 22 at para 10(ii) which stated, inter alia, that a parent and step-parent of a child 'will not normally be able to get an adoption order if the parent has custody of the child ... following ... divorce proceedings'. In 1977, the first full year of the operation of the provision, the number of applications fell by 42 per cent to 4,545.

[2] See eg *Re S (Infants) (Adoption by Parent)* [1977] Fam 173, [1977] 3 All ER 671, CA, and for a striking dismissal of an application, see *Re W v W (A Minor)* (1976) Times, 26 November. The impact of these decisions on the lower courts was by no means consistent: see the research findings of Masson et al, op cit.

[3] In *Re S*, supra.

Re D (Minors) (Adoption by Step-Parent)[4] that the section required the dismissal of the application only if it could be shown that the matter could be better dealt with by a joint custody order. This approach, as the Adoption Law Review put it, was more in accord with the actual wording of the provision but did not reflect the original intentions of the Houghton Committee.

In the case of 'post-death' or 'illegitimate' step-parent adoption applications a more tortuously worded provision[5] directed the court in cases where parental agreement to the adoption had been given or dispensed with, that it should nevertheless treat the application as one for custodianship[6] rather than adoption where the child's welfare would not be better safeguarded by an adoption order than it would by a custodianship order. This provision too was eventually interpreted as meaning that, unless the court was satisfied that a custodianship order would offer the child a greater benefit than the adoption order, the court should not consider the question of custodianship further.[7]

It can be seen that these legislative attempts to restrict step-parent applications essentially failed and that long before the Children Act 1989 they had in fact become a dead letter. That is not to say that step-parent applications were automatically granted for as with all applications the court had to be satisfied that adoption was in the child's interests[8] and that parental agreement had either been given or should be dispensed with.[9]

The Children Act 1989 has now formally repealed the provisions intended to restrict step-parent adoption applications.[10] Indeed by specifically enacting that a parent aged at least 18 can jointly apply with a spouse aged at least 21 to adopt his or her child the 1989 Act could be seen as giving tacit approval to such applications.[11] Whether in fact the new legislation will make any difference to practice has yet to be established. However while the repeals per se are not significant, the fact that under the 1989 Act adoption proceedings rank as 'family proceedings' thereby giving the court the option of making section 8 orders in general and residence orders in particular, could be more important.[12] It is also to be noted that the whole issue of step-parent adoption has again been raised by the Adoption Law Review, opinion being canvassed, for example, as to whether there should be some administrative method of step-parents acquiring parental responsibility.[13]

---

[4] (1980) 2 FLR 102, CA.
[5] S 37 of the Children Act 1975, discussed in the seventh edition of this work at p 372.
[6] The meaning of which is discussed, post, p 422.
[7] See *Re S (A Minor) (Adoption or Custodianship)* [1987] Fam 98, [1987] 2 All ER 99, CA.
[8] See eg *Re P (Minors) (Adoption)* [1989] 1 FLR 1, CA, where an application to adopt two out of three step-children was refused.
[9] Cretney and Masson *Principles of Family Law* (5th Edn) argue at p 558 that in such cases courts might be less prepared to dispense with a parent's agreement. Nevertheless the Bristol study found that in 80 per cent of their sample of step-parent applications an order was granted: *Pathways to Adoption*, op cit, Table 2.9.
[10] Adoption Act 1976, ss 14(3) and 15(4) and the Children Act 1975 are repealed by the Children Act 1989, Sch 15.
[11] See ante, p 418.
[12] See further the discussion, post, p 448.
[13] See Discussion Paper No 1, op cit, paras 130 et seq. See also Discussion Paper No 3, op cit, para 26, et seq.

(c) Adoption by relatives[14]

Although there are no formal restrictions against relatives applying to adopt the courts have long had reservations about granting adoption to such applicants fearing, inter alia, that an order would distort the natural relationships particularly in the case of adoption by grandparents.[15] It was also felt that the severance of legal ties with the birth parents fits uneasily with an adoption within the family. Another concern in the case of grandparent applicants could be their age.[16] It was accepted, however, that there remained circumstances where an adoption order could be justified.[17]

The Houghton Committee reiterated concern about such adoptions fearing the consequential dangers of hiding the real circumstances from the child.[18] They considered that an application for guardianship would normally be preferable. As a result of the Committee's recommendations, a new jurisdiction, custodianship, was created by which applicants could seek orders vesting in them parental rights and duties but which did not extinguish the legal relationship between the child and his birth parents.[19] It was hoped and expected that relatives would use this option rather than adoption.[20] In any event even if they applied for adoption the court was empowered[1] to treat the application as if it were for custodianship provided the requirements for adoption had been satisfied and that such an order was thought more appropriate than adoption. The evidence showed that in fact grandparents were beginning to apply for custodianship[2] but that a custodianship order on an adoption application was rarely made.[3]

The Children Act 1989 has now abolished custodianship but in its place has provided the section 8 alternative in that, subject to obtaining court leave, relatives can apply for a residence order. Furthermore since adoption proceedings rank as 'family proceedings', the court can of its own motion make a section 8 order upon an adoption application. Since the conditions to be satisfied before a section 8 order can be made are simpler than for custodianship[4] it can reasonably be expected that relatives will generally look to that rather than to adoption. Nevertheless it should not be assumed that adoption orders will never be thought appropriate for relatives. It was noticeable that although the overall number of adoptions by relatives was

---

[14] See generally the Adoption Law Review, Discussion Paper No 1, paras 47–49 and 135 and Discussion Paper No 3, paras 26–33.

[15] As Vaisey J said in *Re DX (An Infant)* [1949] Ch 320, 321 'The ostensible relationship of sisters between those who are in fact mother and child is unnatural and its creation might sow the seeds of grievous unhappiness for them both...' but courts now seem much less concerned about this theoretical consequence. See further below.

[16] See eg *Re W (A Minor) (Adoption by Grandparents)* (1980) 2 FLR 161, CA.

[17] See eg *Re DX*, supra; *Re G (DM) (An Infant)* [1962] 2 All ER 546, and *Re B (MF) (An Infant)* [1972] 1 All ER 898, CA. In the latter case an order was granted even though *continued* contact between the siblings (only one of whom was adopted) was envisaged.

[18] Ibid at para 111.

[19] Discussed in ch 11 of the seventh edition of this work.

[20] See pp 375–376 of the seventh edition of this work.

[1] Children Act 1975, s 37.

[2] In their study for the Department of Health, Bullard, Malos and Parker found that more than half of custodianship applications were by grandparents: *Custodianship. Caring for other people's children* (HMSO, 1991) Tables 24–28.

[3] Only 2 such cases were found in the Bristol study: *Pathways to Adoption*, op cit, Table 2.10.

[4] In particular there is no requirement that the child has had his home with the applicant.

small,[5] in the few reported cases on the issue the courts still made adoption rather than custodianship orders.[6] It has also been noticeable that the courts have become less concerned with the argument that an adoption order distorts the natural relationship.[7] Given that adoption has the advantage of permanence it is likely that, even with a section 8 alternative, an adoption order will still be thought appropriate in cases, where, for example, relatives have been the sole care-givers for some time, especially if the parents are virtual strangers to the child.[8]

3. AGREEMENT TO THE MAKING OF AN ORDER

It is a fundamental requirement[9] that before an adoption order may be made each parent or guardian must either agree to the order or have had his agreement dispensed with. It is by this means that the law recognises and seeks to protect the parental interest. Indeed so important is the right to refuse agreement regarded, that it is not lost even if others, including a local authority, acquire parental responsibility.[10]

(a) Whose agreement is required?

The Act requires the agreement of each parent or guardian. By 'parent' is meant a parent with parental responsibility. It does *not* therefore include the unmarried father[11] unless he has parental responsibility through an order or agreement.[12] In the case of an adopted child, 'parent' refers to *each* adoptive parent. 'Guardian' refers to any person formally appointed by an individual or by a court. Although his agreement is not required, an unmarried father who does not have parental responsibility is nevertheless entitled to be heard on the merits of the application if he is contributing

---

[5] In the Bristol study only 7 per cent of the overall sample were applications by relatives: *Pathways to Adoption*, op cit, Table 2.3.

[6] Eg *Re S (A Minor) (Adoption: Custodianship)* [1987] Fam 98, [1987] 2 All ER 99, CA, and *Re W (A Minor) (Adoption: Custodianship)* [1992] Fam Law 64, CA. For earlier examples of such orders see eg *Re O (A Minor) (Adoption by Grandparents)* [1985] FLR 546, where paternal grandparents had looked after the child for four years following abandonment of the mother, and *Re M (A Minor) (Adoption: Parental Agreement)* [1985] FLR 664, where the child had been with grandparents since he was 11 weeks old and had had virtually no contact with his mother.

[7] See eg *Re C (A Minor) (Adoption Order: Condition)* [1989] AC 1, [1988] 1 All ER 705, 713, HL where Lord Ackner dismissed the contention that an adoption order should be refused because the child would be devastated to learn that her natural brother would no longer be in law her brother as being 'quite unreal'. See also *Re W (A Minor) (Adoption: Custodianship)*, supra.

[8] Cf *Re W (A Minor) (Adoption by Grandparents)* (1980) 2 FLR 161 where an adoption order was granted as the court considered that it would be in the child's interests for the grandparents to be able to appoint testamentary guardians in the event of their death.

[9] Adoption Act 1976, s 16(1)(b).

[10] Cf Children Act 1989, ss 12(3) and 33(6)(b).

[11] See *Re M (An Infant)* [1955] 2 QB 479, [1955] 2 All ER 911, CA, and *Re L (A Minor) (Adoption: Procedure)* [1991] 1 FLR 171, CA.

[12] Adoption Act 1976, s 72(1), definition of 'parent' as amended by the Children Act 1989, Sch 10, para 30(7).

to the child's maintenance.[13] The courts in any event have a general discretion to add any person[14] or body as a respondent and this may include the unmarried father if he has contact or has expressed interest in attending the hearing.[15]

An entitlement to be heard on the merits of the application is not as strong a right as being able to withhold agreement but a more effective option to oppose adoption is for the unmarried father to apply for a residence order under section 8 of the Children Act 1989.[16] In that event the issue will be whether the court should grant a residence order or make the adoption order. To arrive at a proper conclusion and enable all the parties to be heard, the court should hear both applications at the same time and not give judgment on one until it has heard the other.[17] As with all section 8 order applications, the problem must be resolved by reference to what is best for the child's welfare, and even though the father may be entitled to special consideration, if the welfare of the child demands it, an adoption order will be made.[18]

The child's agreement is not required.[19] However, in deciding whether an adoption order will be for the child's welfare the court and adoption agency are bound[20] so far as practicable to ascertain the child's wishes and feelings about the proposed adoption and 'give due regard to them, having regard to his age and understanding'.

(b) Form of the agreement

If the agreement is to be effective, the court must be satisfied that it was

---

[13] When he must be joined as a respondent, see Adoption Rules 1984, r 15(2)(h) (applicable to High Court and county court). The rules governing magistrates' courts, the Magistrates' Courts (Adoption) Rules 1984, largely follow the same wording and numbering and will not hereafter be separately cited.

[14] With the exception of the child, who can only be a party in High Court proceedings, see the Adoption Rules, rr 4(2)(g) and 4(3).

[15] The court will learn of this through reports made to the court pursuant to the requirements under the Adoption Rules, Sch 2. There is, however, no requirement to name the father in an application unless his agreement is required and a judge has no authority to order an agency to interview him: *Re L (A Minor) (Adoption: Procedure)* [1991] 1 FLR 171, CA, but see the comments at [1991] Fam Law 270. It would also appear that no one is under an obligation to 'seek out the unmarried father'—see *Re Adoption Application (No 2) No 41/61* [1964] Ch 48, 58, [1963] 2 All ER 1082, 1088 per Wilberforce J.

[16] Alternatively an application for a parental responsibility order under s 4 would delay any adoption application.

[17] *Re O (An Infant)* [1965] Ch 23, [1964] 1 All ER 786, CA. Ideally, therefore both applications should be heard in the same court, see *Re Adoption Application 41/61* [1963] Ch 315, [1962] 3 All ER 553 but cf *Re Adoption Application (No 2) 41/61* [1964] Ch 48, [1963] 2 All ER 1082. It has been held that a similar position obtains if the unmarried father's application is for contact; see *Re G (A Minor) (Adoption and Access Applications)* (1979) 1 FLR 109. This has more recently been said to be not a rigid rule: *Re G (A Minor) (Adoption and Access Applications)* [1992] 1 FLR 642, CA, where a father made an application for interim access.

[18] As in *Re O*, supra, *Re Adoption Application (No 2) 41/61*, supra; *Re NWAM* Adoption and Fostering Vol 99 No 1 of 1980, 62, CA, and *Re B* Adoption and Fostering Vol 100 No 2 of 1980, CA. Cf *Re C (MA) (An Infant)* [1966] 1 All ER 838, CA, which, it is submitted, should no longer be regarded as good law.

[19] In some other jurisdictions older children's agreement is required, see eg Adoption Law Review, Background Paper No 1, paras 116–120.

[20] Adoption Act 1976, s 6.

given freely and with a full understanding of what is involved.[1] Agreements must also be unconditional and may be given without knowing the applicant's identity.[2] It is no longer possible to make an agreement conditional on the child being brought up in a particular religion. Instead, when placing a child for adoption, adoption agencies are required to have regard, so far as practicable, to any wishes of the child's parent or guardian as to the religious upbringing of the child.[3]

Agreement to the making of an adoption order may be given before or at the time of the hearing; in the former event, documentary evidence of the giving of the agreement is admissible and there is no need for the parent to attend the hearing.[4] The mother cannot give an effective agreement until the child is six weeks old.[5] The agreement must be operative when the order is made and can therefore be withdrawn at any time before that.[6] It should be appreciated, however, that as soon as agreement is given, then as Ormrod LJ put it 'time begins to run against the parent'.[7] In other words the longer the agreement has been effective the more likely it will be regarded as 'unreasonable' subsequently to withhold agreement.

Another important consequence of agreeing to the making of an adoption order is that thereafter that parent or guardian cannot, while the application is pending, remove the child against the will of the person with whom the child has his home, save with the court's leave.[8] Although at one time it was thought that this restriction operated only upon the formal signing of the agreement, it has been held[9] that the embargo can apply to an oral agreement, though clearly cogent evidence of such an agreement will be required.

---

[1] There is some support for saying that a parent must know all the material facts before his agreement should be regarded as having been given: cf *Re M (Minors) (Adoption)* [1991] 1 FLR 458, CA (order set aside where father agreed to adoption by mother and step-father in ignorance that his wife, who died three months later, was terminally ill), and *Re An Adoption Application* [1992] 1 FLR 341 (mother's agreement, given in ignorance that male applicant was involved in criminal proceedings, not to be relied upon).

[2] Adoption Act 1976 s 16(b)(i). Applicants not infrequently opt for anonymity, in which case they should apply, before commencing proceedings, for a serial number to be assigned to them: Adoption Rules 1984, r 14. Thereafter proceedings must be conducted so that the applicants' identity is not revealed to *any* respondent who is not already aware of the identity: r 23(3). According to the Adoption Law Review, Discussion Paper No 3, at para 221 the use of serial numbers may cause problems in practice outside the High Court and the suggestion has been made that the procedure be tightened by, for example, having to obtain leave to make a serial number application.

[3] Adoption Act 1976, s 7.

[4] Ibid, s 61. Written agreements should be witnessed by a Reporting Officer: see Adoption Act 1976, s 65. See also the Adoption Rules 1984, r 17.

[5] Adoption Act 1976, s 16(4). This condition is clearly designed to prevent the mother from being persuaded to give her agreement before she has recovered from the child's birth.

[6] *Re F (An Infant)* [1957] 1 All ER 819 and *Re K (An Infant)* [1953] 1 QB 117, [1952] 2 All ER 877, CA.

[7] In *Re H (Infants) (Adoption: Parental Consent)* [1977] 2 All ER 339, 340, CA, post, p 430.

[8] Adoption Act 1976, s 27(1). See also Adoption Law Review, Discussion Paper No 3, para 147.

[9] By *Re T (A Minor) (Adoption: Parental Agreement)* [1986] Fam 160, [1986] 1 All ER 817, CA.

4. DISPENSING WITH AGREEMENT[10]

The court's power to dispense with agreement is the means by which the law attempts to balance the parental interest with the child's welfare. It should be appreciated at the outset, however, that because agreements can only be dispensed with on certain specified grounds (outlined below), an adoption order cannot necessarily be made merely because it is for the child's welfare. This therefore distinguishes adoption from residence orders under section 8 of the Children Act 1989, the reason being that in adoption the very parent-child relationship is at stake. Whether it is justifiable to subordinate a child's welfare to parental interests may be questioned and should in any event be borne in mind during the ensuing discussion.[11]

Although there are relatively few contested adoptions they are no longer the rarity that they once were.[12] In 1978, for example, 773 orders (representing 6.3 per cent of all orders) were made without parental agreement, while in 1983 the figure was 956, representing 11 per cent.[13] In a sample of cases decided between 1986 and 1988 the Bristol research study found that 19 per cent of applications to adopt were made without the mother's agreement.[14]

Before we examine the grounds upon which agreement can be dispensed with, two preliminary points should be mentioned. First, although section 6 of the Adoption Act 1976 states that in reaching any decision relating to adoption the court should treat the child's welfare as the first consideration, it has been held by the Court of Appeal in *Re P (An Infant) (Adoption: Parental Agreement)*,[15] that the section has no application to the issue of dispensing with agreement. Although, as will be seen, this decision is not as significant as it would appear,[16] it nevertheless seems a questionable interpretation.[17] The second problem relates to the order in which the issues should be heard in cases where agreement is withheld. It has been held[18] that the court must first decide whether it is for the child's welfare to be adopted before deciding whether the agreement should be dispensed with

---

[10] See generally Adoption Law Review, Discussion Paper No 2, paras 31 et seq. See also Sachs *Agreement to adoption—some recent cases* 1991 3 Journal of Child Law 57, *Agreement to Adoption* [1985] Fam Law 203 and *Adoption and Dispensing with Parental Agreement* (1983) 13 Fam Law 26.

[11] On this see Adoption Law Review, Discussion Paper No 1, Part D.

[12] Commenting upon the practice of the 1960s, Rowe, Hundleby, Paul and Keane said (Adoption and Fostering, Vol 103, No 1 of 1981, 23, 24) that adoption agencies seldom advised prospective adopters to resist a parent who changed her mind.

[13] See respectively Children Act 1975, First Report to Parliament, HC 266, Table D and the Second Report, HMSO 1984, Table B.

[14] *Pathways to Adoption*, op cit, Table 2.11.

[15] [1977] Fam 25, [1977] 1 All ER 182, CA.

[16] Because in relation to the most common dispensing ground, unreasonableness, it is well established that a reasonable parent will have the interests of his child at heart, see post at p 423.

[17] As is pointed out, obiter, by Lord Simon in *Re D (An Infant) (Adoption: Parental Agreement)* [1977] AC 602, 641, [1977] 1 All ER, 145, 163, HL. Leave to appeal to the House of Lords on this point was refused in *Re M (A Minor)* [1980] CLY 1801. See also *Re H; Re W* (1983) 4 FLR 614, 624, CA, per Purchas LJ, discussed by Waterhouse J in *Re BA (Wardship: Adoption)* [1985] FLR 1008, 1031.

[18] *Re D (A Minor) (Adoption: Freeing Order)* [1991] 1 FLR 48, CA, and *Re R (A Minor) (Adoption: Parental Agreement)* [1987] 1 FLR 391n, CA.

but that as a matter of procedure it is preferable that the two issues be heard together.[19]

Pursuant to section 16 the court may dispense with agreement in the circumstances set out below.

(a) Cannot be found or incapable of signing agreement

If the parent or guardian *cannot be found or is incapable of giving agreement*, agreement may be dispensed with. Agreement will not lightly be dispensed with on this ground. In *Re F (R) (An Infant)*,[20] for instance, it was held that before agreement could be dispensed with on the ground that the parent 'could not be found' it had to be shown that all reasonable and proper steps had been taken. In that case it was held that all such steps had not been taken since in their search for the birth mother the applicants had failed to get in touch with the father with whom the mother was still in contact. 'Incapable of giving agreement' normally refers to those who are mentally incapable but in *Re R (Adoption)*,[1] where the parents were living in a totalitarian country, it was held that their agreement could be dispensed with on the grounds that (a) they could not be found since there were no practical means of communicating with them and (b) they were incapable of giving their agreement to a proposal of which they were ignorant and could not practically be made aware.

(b) Unreasonably withholding agreement

If the parent or guardian *is withholding his agreement unreasonably*, agreement may be dispensed with. This in practice is a common ground[2] for applying to the court to dispense with agreement and gives rise to the most difficulty. Whether or not agreement is unreasonably withheld is a question of fact in each case and 'reasonableness' is to be judged at the date of the hearing.[3]

(i) Reasonableness—the Re W test

The leading case is *Re W (An Infant)*[4] in which the House of Lords resolved an earlier conflict of opinion by unanimously rejecting the contention that as a matter of principle unreasonableness connoted culpability. The Law Lords all agreed that the test is objective: would a reasonable parent, placed in the situation of the particular parent, withhold agreement? As Lord Hailsham LC put it:[5]

---

[19] *Re K (A Minor) (Adoption: Procedure)* [1986] 1 FLR 295, CA. Ultimately, however, the court retains a discretion and separate hearings could be justified in serial number cases in courts where it might be difficult to maintain the applicants' anonymity; *Re LS (A Minor) (Adoption: Procedure)* [1986] 1 FLR 302, CA.

[20] [1970] 1 QB 385, [1969] 3 All ER 1101, CA.

[1] [1966] 3 All ER 613. Applied in *Re An Adoption Application* [1992] 1 FLR 341.

[2] In the Bristol Research Study, it was found to be the *sole* ground for 45 per cent of birth mothers and 63 per cent of birth fathers, see Adoption Law Review, op cit at para 37.

[3] See eg *Re L (A Minor) (Adoption: Statutory Criteria)* [1990] 1 FLR 305, CA; *Re S (An Infant)* [1973] 3 All ER 88, CA, and *Re W (Adoption: Parental Agreement)* (1981) 3 FLR 75, CA. Cf *Re C (Minors) (Adoption)* [1992] 1 FLR 115, 132, in which Balcombe LJ commented 'it does not follow that a parent who starts by reasonably refusing agreement becomes unreasonable because of the delay [in hearing the application]'.

[4] [1971] AC 682, [1971] 2 All ER 49, HL.

[5] Ibid at 699 and 56, respectively.

'... the test is reasonableness and not anything else. It is not culpability. It is not indifference. It is not failure to discharge parental duties. It is reasonableness in the context of the totality of the circumstances.'

Obviously unreasonableness can include culpability; it can also include callous indifference and '(when carried to excess) sentimentality, romanticism, bigotry, wild prejudice, caprice, fatuousness or excessive lack of common sense'.[6] In many cases it will be easy to say whether, looked at objectively, the parent is acting reasonably or not, but in others one reasonable parent might withhold his agreement whilst another might not do so. In the latter type of case the court must respect the particular parent's decision to refuse to agree and must not substitute its own view. As Lord Hailsham LC said:[7]

'The question in any given case is whether a parental veto comes within the band of possible reasonable decisions and not whether it is right or mistaken. Not every reasonable exercise of judgment is right, and not every mistaken exercise of judgment is unreasonable.'

All the facts must be looked at but obviously the reasonable parent will give the greatest weight to the child's welfare. As Lord Hailsham LC said:[8]

'But, although welfare per se is not the test, the fact that a reasonable parent does pay regard to the welfare of his child must enter into the question of reasonableness as a relevant factor. It is relevant in all cases if and to the extent that a reasonable parent would take it into account. It is decisive in those cases where a reasonable parent must so regard it...'

Although it is not necessary to show a prognosis of lasting damage if an order is not made, there must be some really serious factor justifying the use of the guillotine:[9] it was said in Re W that agreement may be dispensed with if the parent has ignored or disregarded some appreciable ill or risk or some substantial benefit likely to be avoided or to accrue if the child were adopted.[10] A reasonable parent must clearly take account of financial and educational prospects, but of much greater importance, of course, is the child's future happiness and stability of his home life. Although little weight should be given to the parent's vacillation under stress or to the pain that the loss of the child will inevitably cause the applicants,[11] it must be appreciated that to tear the child away from those whom he has come to regard as his parents may have disastrous consequences. This in itself may force the reasonable parent to agree to the adoption; and the longer the child has been with the applicants, the greater is the danger to be guarded against. In Re W itself the child had been placed with the applicants when he was a week old and had remained there for 18 months. He had settled down well. The mother, who was unmarried and who later withdrew her agreement, already had two other children by different fathers; there was a grave risk of more (which would reduce her prospects of marriage); there was no man in the household; and it was doubtful whether she had

[6] Per Lord Hailsham LC, ibid, at 700 and 56 respectively.
[7] Ibid at 700 and 56 respectively.
[8] Ibid at 700 and 56 respectively.
[9] Per Cumming-Bruce J in Re B (Adoption By Parent) [1975] Fam 127, 143, [1975] 2 All ER 449, 462, cited with approval in Re D (An Infant) (Adoption: Parent's Consent) [1977] AC 602 at 632 and 644, [1977] 1 All ER 145 at 155 and 166, HL.
[10] Re W, supra, per Lord Hailsham LC at 700 and 56 and Lord MacDermott at 709 and 64.
[11] Per Lord Hailsham LC, ibid at 700 and 56–7, respectively.

the capacity to bring up three children. In these circumstances the House of Lords held that there was ample evidence to support the finding that the mother was unreasonably withholding her agreement.

Re W marked an important shift in favour of the child's interests though falling short (as it was bound to do) of holding that the child's welfare is of paramount importance. It is submitted that in principle the decision draws the fairest balance between the interests of the child and those of the parents and adoptive applicants that can be achieved under the current legislation. In practice, however, the *Re W* test can be difficult to apply. As Lord Wilberforce said in *Re D (An Infant) (Adoption: Parent's Consent)*[12] it involves considering how a parent in the circumstances of the actual parent 'but (hypothetically) endowed with a mind and temperament capable of making reasonable decisions would approach a complex question involving a judgment as to the present and the future, and the probable impact of these on the child'. *Re D* involved a father who was a practising homosexual. His wife had divorced him and remarried and the child of the marriage, a boy aged seven, was living with her and her second husband who now wished to adopt him. If the father were to continue to have access, the boy was bound to come into contact with other men of his own predilections sooner or later. At first instance the county court judge concluded: 'A reasonable man would say "I must protect my boy even if this means parting from him for ever so that he can be free of this danger." ... The father has nothing to offer his son at any time in the future'. In view of this finding, the House of Lords held that he had correctly concluded that the father was withholding his agreement unreasonably. It must be emphasised, however, that each case will turn upon its own facts: the parent's homosexuality will not of itself mean that his refusal to agree to the adoption will be unreasonable if this presents no danger to the child.[13]

Clearly the suitability of the parents to look after their child is an important factor in assessing reasonableness. If, for example, adoption is opposed on the basis that the child should be returned but the parents cannot offer a stable home that in itself must go a long way to showing 'unreasonableness'.[14] However, even if the parent is in a position to offer a stable home (or to resume contact) that does not ipso facto make the

---

[12] [1977] AC 602, 625, [1977] 1 All ER 145, 150, HL. In *Re W (Adoption: Parental Agreement)* (1981) 3 FLR 75, 79, CA, Ormrod LJ described it as a 'rather difficult concept—perhaps a sophisticated concept', while in *Re S (An Infant)* [1973] 3 All ER 88, 91, CA, Davies LJ pointed out that it 'is very difficult to decide what a reasonable mother would do; it is very difficult for a mother ... where ties of blood and emotional matters are involved to be reasonable at all'. See also Balcombe LJ's similar comments in *Re L (A Minor)* [1990] 1 FLR at p 314. For a case where the judge erroneously applied a simple subjective test, see *Re R (A Minor: Adoption) (Parental Agreement)* [1987] 1 FLR 391, CA.

[13] See ibid at pp 629, 640, 641–642 and 153, 162, 163 and 168 respectively.

[14] See eg *O'Connor v A and B* [1971] 2 All ER 1230, HL, where both parents were thought to be unstable; *Re W (Adoption: Parental Agreement)* (1981) 3 FLR 75, CA, where, inter alia, the court doubted the mother's capacity to look after both the child in question and her other child in overcrowded accommodation; *Re V (Adoption: Parental Agreement)* [1985] FLR 45, CA, where young parents had no clear plans for looking after the child and *Re M* (1988) Adoption and Fostering, Vol 12, No 3, 49, CA, where extensive efforts to rehabilitate children with mother failed because of her inability to look after them, Sheldon J commenting 'Children are not guinea pigs to be used in teaching adults parenting skills, nor are they objects on which parents, however devoted, can practise indefinitely until they can achieve some acceptable standard'.

refusal reasonable. Other considerations, notably the child's welfare and the interests of the applicants, must be taken into account. The relative importance of these considerations may well vary according to the context in which the issue arises. At any rate it is important to distinguish the situation where the parent at first agrees to the adoption and allows the child to be placed but then withdraws that agreement, from that where the child has been placed as a foster child and the foster parents apply to adopt. Special considerations may also apply to adoptions within the family. Another crucial fact in all cases is the age of the child: loss of contact with a baby, even for a short time, is more significant than a temporary loss of contact with an older child.

(ii) The 'vacillating parent'

Although in *Re W* the House of Lords accepted that vacillation is not in itself unreasonable, nevertheless the fact that a parent has allowed the child to be placed for adoption cannot be ignored if agreement is subsequently withdrawn. As Lord Reid put it in *O'Connor v A and B*,[15] if it was the parent's action that first brought the adopting family in, they ought not to be displaced without good reason. The crucial factor, however, is the child's welfare. If the child has become settled with the applicants then the longer that is allowed to continue the more unlikely it is that a parent will be reasonable in withholding agreement. As Ormrod LJ said in *Re H (Infants) (Adoption: Parental Consent)*:[16]

> 'the relative importance of the welfare of the children is increasing rather than diminishing in relation to dispensing with [agreement].[17] That being so it ought to be recognised by all concerned with adoption cases that once the formal [agreement] has been given or perhaps once the child has been placed with the adopters, time begins to run against the mother and, as time goes on, it gets progressively more and more difficult for her to show that the withdrawal of [agreement] is reasonable.'

'Vacillating parents' are commonly young mothers[18] who have to make a difficult decision in traumatic circumstances, yet as Ormrod LJ said:[19] 'Although it is easy to understand the difficulties of the mother as a young woman, it is equally easy to be over-indulgent in approaching her problems because, once she takes the step of initiating adoption proceedings, she starts a chain reaction which can only be stopped with great damage to some people'. If a mother changes her mind it is imperative that she should

---

[15] [1971] 2 All ER 1230, 1232, HL. In *Re P (Adoption: Parental Agreement)* [1985] FLR 635, 637, CA, Griffiths LJ commented: 'just because the mother changes her mind in the course of the agonising decision as to whether or not her child should be adopted must not be held against her as conclusive evidence that she is being unreasonable. But ... it is a factor to be borne in mind, bearing the long-term welfare of the child, because the longer the mother vacillates the more difficult it becomes for any bond to be forged with her again, and it is a factor which may show that the mother does not make the judgment of a reasonable parent, which is the test that the judge ultimately has to apply'.

[16] [1977] 2 All ER 339n, 340. See also his similar comments in *Re W (Adoption: Parental Agreement)* (1981) 3 FLR 75, 82, CA.

[17] But note the observations of Purchas LJ in *Re H; Re W (Adoption: Parental Agreement)* (1983) 4 FLR 614 at 624, CA, set out below at p 432.

[18] But see *Re W (Adoption: Parental Agreement)* [1984] FLR 880, CA.

[19] In *Re W (Adoption: Parental Agreement)* (1982) 3 FLR 75 at 81. See also *Re G (A Minor) (Adoption: Parental Agreement)* [1990] 2 FLR 429, CA.

act quickly and be in a position to offer a secure and loving home for the child if the withholding of agreement is to be regarded as reasonable.[20]

(iii) The parent who has never agreed to the adoption

In contrast to the 'vacillating' parent is the parent who has never agreed to the adoption, for example, where the child is in local authority care. Indeed in the Bristol study 81 per cent of all adoptions by non-relatives were of children who had previously been looked after by a local authority.[1] In *Re F (A Minor) (Adoption: Parental Agreement)*[2] a two year old child was taken into care after being ill treated and was immediately placed with foster parents with whom the child remained for the next three years. The local authority considered that rehabilitation with his mother was not feasible and that it was in the child's interests to be adopted by the foster parents who then applied for an order. The mother, who had not even seen her child for two years, opposed the adoption, but it was held that she was unreasonably withholding her agreement since no reasonable mother could have thought that continued contact[3] with her would have been of benefit to the child. It was held that in the circumstances the mother was acting unreasonably because adoption best secured the child's home with the foster parents since, relying on Bridge LJ in *Re SMH and RAH:*[4]

'Unless the adoptive parents are put in the legal position of being in a full sense parents of [the child] they are never in the position, and never will be in the position, to give [the child] the reassurance which the sense of security required by [this child] is surely going to need.'

A more striking decision is *Re H.*[5] A six week old child was removed from a mother who had a history of mental illness and was taken into care through wardship proceedings. At first the court made an order allowing the mother to see her child but this was ended at a subsequent hearing in which the local authority received strong encouragement to place the child for adoption. Shortly afterwards, however, the mother was divorced and subsequently remarried since when she made a miraculous recovery. She renewed her efforts to obtain contact. The authority, however, without

---

[20] In *Re PA (An Infant)* [1971] 3 All ER 522, CA, a young mother was 'badgered' into agreeing, withdrew the agreement within three weeks, and, at the date of the hearing, had become engaged to a 'thoroughly reliable young man': her withholding of agreement was held reasonable. Cf *Re H* Adoption and Fostering, Vol 99, No 1 of 1980, 59, CA; *Re V (Adoption: Parental Agreement)* [1985] FLR 45, CA; and *Re J (A Minor) (Wardship: Adoption: Custodianship)* [1987] 1 FLR 455, where it was held inter alia that a West Indian mother was entitled to take into account the fact that the applicants were white and were Jehovah's Witnesses. The child, however, remained with the foster parents with access to the mother for two days each year.

[1] This figure comprised 33 per cent in voluntary care and 48 per cent in compulsory care: *Pathways to Adoption*, op cit, Table 4.3.

[2] [1982] 1 All ER 321, CA.

[3] The evidence established beyond doubt that it was essential for the child to remain with the foster parents for the rest of his dependent life. Even access was regarded as a remote possibility.

[4] [1979] CA Transcript 103, cited by Ormrod LJ, ibid at p 326 and 108, respectively.

[5] Adoption and Fostering, Vol 105, No 3 of 1981, 62, CA. In *Re El-G (Minors) (Wardship and Adoption)* (1983) 4 FLR 589, CA, a mother who, because of ill health had only looked after her children for a total of five weeks in four years, was held to be unreasonably withholding agreement even though her health was fully restored. See also *Re H (Adoption: Parental Agreement)* (1981) 3 FLR 386, CA.

telling the mother, placed the child for adoption. The application was not finally heard for some 18 months, in part because of the authority's delay in filing evidence. It was held that while the authority's action could be criticised[6] the mother was nevertheless withholding her agreement unreasonably since the child was a relative stranger to her and a complete stranger to her husband, while on the other hand the child had established strong bonds with the adopters.

The above cases illustrate how crucial the child's welfare had become in judging reasonableness. This shift of emphasis was noted in *Re H; Re W (Adoption: Parental Agreement)*,[7] but the Court of Appeal thought that there had to be some limit to it. Purchas LJ pointed out that there was 'room for the reasonable withholding of [agreement] by the natural parent even if those responsible for the child's welfare, who are normally professionals, hold an acceptable view that the child's welfare demands adoption'. He continued:

'Where the natural parent presents himself at the time of the hearing as someone capable of caring for the child, this is a factor which even the hypothetical, reasonable parent should take into account together with the other circumstances of the case including, of course, the ultimate welfare of the child. Where there is an inherent defect likely to persist in the natural parent ... this is clearly an important factor; but where the unsuitability of the parent can only be related to past history, ... unless the past history is likely to influence the future position, ... then it should carry little weight in the mind of the hypothetical, reasonable parent. The chances of a successful reintroduction to, or continuance of contact with, the natural parent is a critical factor in assessing the reaction of the hypothetical reasonable parent...'

Of the two appeals, *Re W* is the more striking. It concerned a boy who had been taken into care when he was just under two years old. The mother's marriage had broken down and she had become an alcoholic and suffered depression. Subsequently, however, her marriage was dissolved, she made a complete recovery, and following her remarriage she sought, some five years after she had last seen her son, to re-establish contact. The local authority began to make arrangements for the mother to see her son but these were never implemented because the mother was sent to prison for fraud. At that point the authority decided to support the foster parents, with whom the child had been for the last nine years, in their adoption application. The Court of Appeal, however, upheld the decision that the mother's refusal to agree to the adoption was reasonable, based principally upon the belief that there was at least a chance of future successful contact with the child.

Re H, Re W has been criticised[8] as looking too subjectively at the parent's attitude and minimising the effect of past conduct towards the child. In *Re W* it is hard to see how contact could have been anything but speculative. Nevertheless it has to be remembered that in reaching its decision the Court of Appeal was deliberately attempting to reduce the importance of the child's welfare when judging reasonableness, at any rate in the context of

[6] Whether a bona fide and reasonable sense of injustice might be a relevant factor in the mind of a reasonable parent is discussed below at p 434.
[7] (1983) 4 FLR 614, CA.
[8] By *Butterworths Family Law Service* Division E [2630].

foster parent applications.[9] Subsequent case law, however, provides little evidence that *Re H, Re W* has led to a consistent marked change of attitude. Rather decisions have continued to oscillate between concern for the child's welfare and protection of the parent's interest. In retrospect *Re H, Re W* can simply be seen as being an extreme example of a decision based on the parent's wishes. It remains the case that there are relatively few reported decisions in which a parent's refusal to agree to the adoption has been upheld by the court and research has shown that in practice it is unusual for an adoption application to be refused.[10]

Where a refusal to agree to the adoption order has been upheld, the parent has commonly, at the time of the hearing,[11] either currently been seeing his child or has had contact in the recent past.[12] Indeed in *Re C (Minors) (Adoption)*[13] Balcombe LJ commented that where children were in local authority care and enjoying beneficial contact with their parents it was premature for the local authority to apply to free the children for adoption.[14] In *Re E (A Minor) (Adoption)*[15] it was held reasonable for the mother to take into account the benefit of contact with siblings or other near relatives.[16] On the other hand complete absence of contact for some years continues to be a telling factor against the parent especially if the child is well settled with the applicants and it can be shown that any change would be damaging to the child. In *Re B (A Minor) (Adoption: Parental Agreement)*,[17] following a history of neglect and inadequate parenting a boy and his sister were taken into care and eventually placed with long-term foster parents. Over the next four years the mother continued to see the children and was still seeking to have them back. The local authority then decided to end contact for a trial period to see how the children would respond but it was later restored in a compromise reached with the mother. At this stage, however, there was a marked difference in the children's attitudes. The girl, who had failed to settle with the foster-parents, wanted to see her mother and eventually she went back to live with her. The boy had settled well with the foster parents and he was no longer interested in seeing his mother. Subsequently, the foster parents applied to adopt the boy. At this stage the boy was 11 years old and had lived with the applicants for 7 years and was entirely integrated with that family. He wanted to be adopted. Overturning the first instance decision, the Court of Appeal

[9] Purchas LJ, ibid at 620, expressly distinguished placements with adopters with parental agreement from the conversion of an 'ordinary fostering arrangement' into adoption.

[10] *Pathways to Adoption*, op cit, Table 2.9, discussed further, post, p 450.

[11] As in *Re H (A Minor) (Adoption)* [1985] FLR 519, CA, *Re M (A Minor) (Adoption Order: Access)* [1986] 1 FLR 51, CA, and *Re V (A Minor) (Adoption: Consent)* [1987] Fam 57, [1986] 1 All ER 752, CA.

[12] As in *Re BA (Wardship and Adoption)* [1985] FLR 1008.

[13] [1992] 1 FLR 115, CA.

[14] Freeing for adoption is discussed below, p 436.

[15] [1989] 1 FLR 126, CA.

[16] Cf *Re C (A Minor) (Adoption Order: Conditions)* [1989] AC 1, [1988] 1 All ER 705, HL (discussed post at p 448), where the House of Lords dispensed with the mother's agreement and made an adoption order with a condition for access to continue with a sibling. This option was not open to the court in *Re E* as it was a freeing case. Query whether *Re E* would now be decided the same given the new powers to made a contact order under section 8 of the Children Act 1989? See post, p 449.

[17] [1990] 2 FLR 383, CA. See also *Re GB (Minors) (Adoption Parental Agreement)* [1985] FLR 719.

dispensed with the mother's agreement and granted the adoption.

In reaching this decision the Court of Appeal, mindful that the applicants with an order would not seek to prevent future contact between the boy and his mother and sister, considered the granting of the order offered the best chance of preserving such contact. On the other hand they held that the judge at first instance had misdirected himself by taking into account the mother's sense of injustice (stemming from the local authority's termination of contact). In *Re E (Minors) (Adoption: Parental Agreement)*,[18] however, a sense of grievance was held to be relevant. In that case, two children had been placed with long-term foster parents with a view to adoption and parental access was terminated. The mother applied to a magistrate's court for an order that she should see the children but this application was adjourned pending the outcome of the local authority's application to free the children for adoption. In the event the freeing hearing was not heard for some months by which time the guardian ad litem changed her mind about continuing contact with the parents which had previously been regarded as beneficial. It was held in these circumstances that the mother's withholding of agreement could not be said to be unreasonable since, notwithstanding that the evidence pointed to the children's welfare being served by adoption, the hypothetical reasonable parent was entitled to have regard to the circumstances leading to that state of affairs and to say that she did not have a proper opportunity to demonstrate that continued contact would be beneficial.

The majority decision[19] in *Re E* is clearly reminiscent of that in *Re H, Re W*[20] and provides continuing evidence of the oscillating approaches to this difficult and sensitive question. As the Adoption Law Review observes[1] the Children Act 1989 goes some way to improving the position in the sense that local authorities are obliged to arrange reasonable contact between children in care and their families[2] unless the court allows them to refuse it. Furthermore the 1989 Act gives the court more options, for example, to make a contact order as well as an order freeing the child for adoption or to make a residence order instead of adoption.[3] Nevertheless as the Review tellingly puts it:[4]

> 'the basic problem will remain, that the birth parents' theoretical right to withhold agreement may be rendered worthless by the way the professionals have decided to handle the case. Clearly, for many children in care, adoption may be the right solution, but this should be the result of a fair assessment of the situation, not as a result of shortcomings in practice.'

(iv) Adoptions within the family

A third context in which the question of unreasonable withholding of agreement arises is with respect to adoption applications from within the

---

[18] [1990] 2 FLR 397, CA.
[19] Dillon LJ dissented, stressing that the test of reasonableness was to be applied at the date of the hearing.
[20] Supra. See the comment on *Re E* at [1990] Fam Law 345–6.
[1] Discussion Paper No 2, op cit, para 78.
[2] Under s 34 of the Children Act 1989, discussed post, p 530.
[3] Discussed post, p 448.
[4] Ibid at para 78.

family. As we have seen,[5] the courts themselves have been reluctant to grant adoption to relatives and, until recently, there have been statutory restrictions on step-parent applications.

Assuming, however, that adoption is thought appropriate, parental agreement must still be obtained or dispensed with. Given that in most cases the child will remain with applicants regardless of the outcome of the application there is a strong analogy with the foster parent cases. However as the Adoption Law Review has observed, there may be perceived differences in public and private law cases. Where parents separate or divorce, it is generally assumed to be for the benefit of the child to maintain links with both parents. In these cases the court is less concerned with the parent's overall ability to look after the child.[6] Hence, if there is continued contact with the child the parent is unlikely to be held unreasonable in withholding agreement. On the other hand if there has been little or no contact and the parent has nothing else to offer, the withholding of agreement is likely to be held unreasonable.[7]

(c) Other grounds for dispensing with agreement

Another ground exists if the parent or guardian *has persistently failed without reasonable cause to discharge the parental duties in relation to the child.* This does not merely include the legal obligations towards the child (for example, to maintain him) but also the natural and moral duty to show affection, care and interest.[8] But the failure must be culpable and 'of such gravity, so complete, so convincingly proved that there can be no advantage to the child in keeping continuous contact with the natural parent who has so abrogated his duties that he for his part should be deprived of his own child against his wishes'.[9] In *Re D (Minors) (Adoption by Parent)*[10] the court refused to dispense with the father's agreement solely on the ground that he failed to provide for his daughter or see her for a year. As Baker P pointed out, when a marriage breaks down, the husband will often withdraw or drift apart from the family temporarily, particularly when, as in that case, he is living with another woman.

Other grounds are as follows:

If the parent or guardian has *abandoned or neglected the child.*[11]

If he *has persistently ill-treated the child.*[12]

If he *has seriously ill-treated the child* and (whether because of the ill-

---

[5] Ante at p 422.

[6] Discussion Paper No 2, op cit, para 70.

[7] See eg *Re M (Adoption: Parental Agreement)* [1985] FLR 664.

[8] *Re P (Infants)* [1962] 3 All ER 789, *Re B(S) (An Infant)* [1968] Ch 204, [1967] 3 All ER 629.

[9] Per Baker J in *Re D (Minors) (Adoption By Parent)* [1973] Fam 209, 214, [1973] 3 All ER 1001, 1005. It might be noted that this draconian interpretation has meant that virtually no applications are now made on this ground.

[10] Supra. See also *Re H (Minors)* (1974) Times, 26 November and *Re M (Adoption: Parental Agreement)*, [1985] FLR 664, 665.

[11] 'Abandoned' and 'neglected' connote conduct which would render the parent or guardian liable to criminal proceedings under the Children and Young Persons Act 1933, s 1 (ante at p 314): *Watson v Nickolaisen* [1955] 2 QB 286, [1955] 2 All ER 427; *Re W* (unreported), cited in *Re P (Infants)*, supra, and *Re M (Adoption: Parental Agreement)*, supra.

[12] 'Persistent' implies a series of acts: in *Re A (A Minor) (Adoption: Dispensing with Agreement)* (1979) 2 FLR 173, CA, it was held that severe and repeated assaults over a period of three weeks sufficed.

treatment or for some other reason) the rehabilitation of the child within the parent's or guardian's household is unlikely. This ground was first introduced in the Children Act 1975 following the recommendations of the Houghton Committee.[13] It was intended to cover even a single act of violence. The requirement that rehabilitation is unlikely[14] provides an important limitation on the power to dispense with an agreement on this ground although it should be noted that the unlikelihood of rehabilitation does not to have stem from the ill-treatment.[15]

It will be appreciated that these last for grounds are fault-based. In practice they are relied upon only in a minority of cases.[16]

(d) Are the current grounds satisfactory?

The Adoption Law Review considered the present position to be 'clearly unsatisfactory'.[17] Assuming that the court's power to dispense with agreement should be retained, the Review canvasses[18] a number of options for reform, namely:

1. Given their relatively infrequent use, should the fault-based grounds be repealed?
2. Should the unpredictable 'reasonableness' test be replaced by, for example, the statutory threshold criteria applicable to care orders?
3. If not, should there be introduced a statutory check-list of facts to be taken into account?

The Review also points out[19] that with the greater flexibility of orders available under the Children Act 1989, 'it is important that all concerned give careful consideration to the alternatives and that these are not ruled out as a result of decisions taken too early in the process. It may be, for example, that adoption agencies should prepare parents for the possibility that adoption may not be the all-or-nothing order that they might have anticipated.'

5. FREEING THE CHILD FOR ADOPTION[20]

A former weakness in the law was that there was no procedure whereby parental agreement could be made binding before the final adoption hearing.

---

[13] Op cit at paras 219–220.
[14] Adoption Act 1976, s 16(5).
[15] Eg rehabilitation could be unlikely because the parent has been imprisoned for an unrelated offence or because the child is in care. It has been held that the question of rehabilitation should be interpreted in the light of s 6, ie first consideration being given to the need to promote the child's welfare: *Re PB (A Minor) (Application to Free for Adoption)* [1985] FLR 394, 405, per Sheldon J.
[16] See the discussion in Adoption Law Review, Discussion Paper No 2, op cit, at paras 34 and 37.
[17] Discussion Paper No 2, op cit, para 85.
[18] Ibid, paras 85–96.
[19] Ibid at para 95.
[20] See generally *Adoption Law Review*, Discussion Paper No 2, Part 2; Lowe *Freeing for Adoption: The Experience of the 1980s* [1990] JSWL 220, the Bristol Research Study *Report of the Research into the Use and Practice of the Freeing for Adoption Provisions* (1991) and the study in Scotland, Lambert, Buist, Triseliotis and Hull *Freeing Children for Adoption* summarised in (1990) Adoption and Fostering, Vol 14, No 1, 36.

The possibility that a parent might change his mind about the adoption was an understandable source of fear to applicants and agencies alike and the attendant uncertainty was hardly conducive to the child's interests. Moreover some felt that the law itself encouraged parental indecision.[1] To overcome such difficulties a procedure, known as 'freeing the child for adoption' has been introduced,[2] under which parental agreement can be bindingly given or finally dispensed with at an earlier stage of the adoption process.

(a) Applying for an order

Only an adoption agency can apply for a freeing order. Furthermore, following changes made by the Children Act 1989, unless at least one parent with parental responsibility[3] or a guardian consents to the making of the freeing *application*, an agency cannot apply to free the child for adoption, unless the child is in local authority care under a care order.[4] It has been argued[5] that this change restricts local authorities' ability to plan for some children's long-term future since in the absence of agreement they are forced to obtain a care order before even applying for a freeing order. This is bound to delay the process and in some cases, for example, where a handicapped child has been accommodated[6] from birth and the parents are unwilling rather than unable to provide a home for him, might thwart the plan altogether, since the authority might not be able to obtain a care order.[7]

As with adoption, application for a freeing order may not be made in respect of a child who is or has been married but may be made notwithstanding that the child has previously been adopted.[8]

(b) Agreement to the making of an order

No freeing *order* may be made unless the persons whose agreement is required to an adoption order freely and with full understanding of what is involved agree generally[9] and unconditionally to the child being adopted

---

[1] See the Houghton Report, op cit, at para 168.

[2] Under ss 18–20 of the Adoption Act 1976 and based on but not exactly following the Houghton Committee's recommendations, op cit, paras 173–186, discussed by Lowe *Freeing for Adoption: The Experience of the 1980s*, loc cit, at pp 220–221.

[3] Ie not an unmarried father without parental responsibility.

[4] Adoption Act 1976, s 18(2), (2A) as amended by the Children Act 1989, Sch 10, para 6. Previously no consent seemed to be required if the child was in (what would now be termed) local authority accommodation. This change is in line with the general philosophy of the Children Act 1989 that 'accommodation', being a voluntary service provided by local authorities, is not to be undermined by the possibility of parents being unable to remove their children, save where an authority can satisfy the 'threshold' requirements for a care order under s 31; see post, p 511.

[5] Lowe, [1990] JSWL 220, 232.

[6] 'Accommodation' is discussed post, p 503.

[7] Because the threshold criteria under s 31 of the Children Act 1989 (discussed post, p 511) may be not satisfied.

[8] Adoption Act 1976, s 18(8), as substituted by the Children Act 1989, Sch 10, para 6(3).

[9] Ie unlike an adoption application the agreement is not given with a specific application in mind. The mother's agreement is ineffective if given within six weeks of the child's birth: Adoption Act 1976, s 18(4). A parent does not have to attend the hearing: Adoption Act 1976, s 66(3).

or their agreement is dispensed with on one of the grounds enabling the court to dispense with it when making an adoption order.[10] Furthermore before making a freeing order, the court must be satisfied that an unmarried father who does not have parental responsibility has no intention of applying for a parental responsibility order under section 4 of the Children Act 1989 or a residence order under section 10 of that Act or, if he were to make any such application, it would be likely to be refused.[11] In cases where the father has shown a real commitment to the child it might be difficult to show that a section 4 application would fail. In *Re H (Minors) (Adoption: Putative Fathers' Rights) (No 3)*,[12] for example, a section 4 order was made even though the court had no doubt that the father's agreement to the freeing order should be dispensed with on the ground that it was being unreasonably withheld. Where section 18(7) of the Adoption Act cannot be satisfied, the freeing application cannot be decided until the other issue has been settled. If a section 4 order is made or a residence order is granted, the father will then have parental responsibility[13] and his agreement to the freeing order will be required or have to be dispensed with. However, as *Re H* shows, it by no means follows that the granting of a section 4 order alone[14] will automatically mean that the court will not then dispense with the father's agreement to a freeing order.

Where it is sought to dispense with agreement, if the child is not already placed for adoption, the court must be satisfied that the child is likely to be so placed.[15] In practice this provision seems relatively easy to satisfy. As Sheldon J has pointed out in *Re PB (A Minor)*[16] there is no need for the local authority to have any particular candidates in mind before commencing proceedings to free for adoption since the court need only be satisfied that it is 'likely that the child will be placed for adoption—*a likelihood which may be thought to be beyond doubt in the case of most young children*' [emphasis added].

As with adoption it is established that the court must decide in a freeing application whether adoption is in the interests of the child before considering whether to dispense with the agreement of the parent.[17] Although the grounds for dispensing with agreement are the same as for adoption applications it had been suggested[18] that it would be harder to show that a parent is being 'unreasonable' in withholding agreement if the child has not yet been placed. There are, however, no reported cases in which an application has been dismissed on this ground. Indeed in *Re E (A Minor) (Adoption)*[19] Balcombe LJ commented that:

---

[10] Adoption Act 1976, s 18(1).
[11] Ibid, s 18(7), as substituted by the Children Act 1989, Sch 10, para 6(3).
[12] [1991] Fam 151, [1991] 2 All ER 185, CA, discussed ante, p 324.
[13] Under s 12(1) of the Children Act 1989 the court is bound upon granting the unmarried father a residence order to make a s 4 order. Fathers with parental responsibility are 'parents' under the Adoption Act 1976, s 72(1) as amended by Sch 10, para 30(7) of the 1989 Act.
[14] Aliter if a residence order is granted.
[15] Adoption Act 1976, s 18(3).
[16] [1985] FLR 394, 403.
[17] *Re D (A Minor) (Adoption: Freeing Order)* [1991] 1 FLR 48, CA referred to ante, p 426.
[18] See eg the seventh edition of this work at p 403.
[19] [1989] 1 FLR 126, 133. But note the comments by the Adoption Law Review, Discussion Paper No 2, at para 110. For reported instances of contested freeing applications being granted where the child had not yet been placed for adoption see eg *Re D (A Minor)*

'... the hypothetical reasonable mother could also take into account—*although I doubt whether she could properly place much weight on this factor*—that the choice lay between the family unit, with all its known deficiencies, with which [the child] had never lost contact and a new and untried (although carefully vetted) placement with adopters.' [Emphasis added.]

Perhaps predictably, given that a freeing application comes at an earlier stage and is more likely to be contested than an adoption application,[20] the recently reported cases in which the withholding of agreement has been held to be reasonable have all been freeing applications.[1] Nevertheless research has shown that a refusal of a freeing application is unusual.[2]

(c) The effect of an order

(i) Transfer of parental responsibility

The raison d'être of a freeing order is to end the parental interest in the child. To this end section 18(5) of the Adoption Act 1976, as amended,[3] provides that upon making the order 'parental responsibility for the child is given to the adoption agency' and any parental responsibility which any person had for the child before the order was made is extinguished.[4]

(ii) Revocation of freeing orders

Before making a freeing order the court must be satisfied that each parent or guardian who agrees to the adoption has been given the opportunity of making, if he so wishes, a declaration that he prefers not to be involved in future questions concerning the adoption of the child. Any such declaration must be recorded by the court.[5] Notwithstanding the transfer of parental responsibility the Act provides that unless a parent makes such a declaration, the agency must, within fourteen days following the date twelve months after the making of a freeing order, inform him whether the child has been adopted or placed for adoption and must thereafter give him notice whenever the child is placed or ceases to have his home with a person with whom he has been placed, until an adoption order is made.[6] Once this initial period of twelve months has elapsed, the former parent or guardian may apply for the freeing order to be revoked provided that the child has not been adopted and does not have his home with a person with whom

---

(Adoption: Freeing Order) supra; *Re C (A Minor)* (1987) Times, 16 October and *Re L (A Minor)*, *Re K (A Minor)* (1988) Adoption and Fostering, Vol 12, No 4, 55.

[20] See below at p 436.

[1] Eg *Re C (Minors) (Adoption)* [1992] 1 FLR 115, CA, *Re E (Minors) (Adoption: Parental Agreement)* [1990] 2 FLR 397, CA and *Re E (A Minor) (Adoption)* [1989] 1 FLR 126, CA.

[2] In the Bristol study only 1 per cent of freeing applications were refused: *Pathways to Adoption*, op cit, Table 2.9.

[3] By Sch 10, para 6(2) of the Children Act 1989.

[4] S 18(5) of the Adoption Act 1976 applying s 12(2) to freeing orders.

[5] Adoption Act 1976, s 18(6). In practice declarations are made in a minority of cases. The Bristol Study found they were made in 17 per cent of their sample: see their Freeing Report, op cit, Table 3.45. Failure to observe s 18(6) does not invalidate a freeing order: *Re C (Minors) (Adoption)* [1992] 1 FLR 115, 130, CA per Balcombe LJ.

[6] Adoption Act 1976, s 19. In *R v Derbyshire County Council ex p T* [1990] Fam 164, [1990] 1 All ER 792 it was held the obligation to inform the parent arises when the agency decides to end the placement for adoption and not when the child is physically moved.

he has been placed for adoption.[7] Once an application for revocation is pending the adoption agency cannot place the child for adoption without a court order.[8] In deciding whether to revoke the order the court must have regard to all the circumstances, first consideration being given to the need to safeguard and promote the welfare of the child throughout his childhood.[9] The revocation of a freeing order extinguishes the parental responsibility given to the adoption agency and gives it to the parent or parents who previously had parental responsibility, or a guardian whose appointment was extinguished by the freeing order.[10] A revocation, on the other hand, does not revive a section 8 or care order previously made under the Children Act 1989, nor does it revive a duty to make payments for the child arising from a court order or agreement that has been extinguished by a freeing order.[11]

If an application to revoke is refused, the agency ceases to be under any obligation to give notice of the child's progress and the former parent or guardian making the application cannot make a further application for revocation of the order without leave of the court.[12]

(iii) The status of the freed child

As the Adoption Law Review says[13] the status of a freed child is 'unclear and might best be described as a legal limbo'. There is thought to be[14] uncertainty, for example, as to the ensuing succession rights.

One former uncertainty, with regard to the position of a freed child vis-à-vis the local authority, has been resolved by the Children Act 1989, namely is that of being 'looked after'.[15]

(iv) The status of the former parent

It has been argued[16] that although a freeing order extinguishes parental responsibility it does not mean that the birth parents cease to be 'parents' for the purposes of the Children Act 1989. In consequence it is said that they have standing to apply for section 8 orders under the Children Act 1989 *as of right* notwithstanding that a freeing order has been made. Against

---

[7] Adoption Act 1976, s 20.
[8] Adoption Act 1976, s 20(2).
[9] Ie Adoption Act 1976, s 6 applies, see s 20(4). See generally Bellamy *Revocation of Freeing Orders* [1990] Fam Law 352.
[10] Adoption Act 1976, s 20(3), as substituted by Sch 10, para 8(2) to the Children Act 1989. For further discussion on this change see White, Carr and Lowe *A Guide to the Children Act 1989*, para 11.16 et seq.
[11] Adoption Act 1976, s 20(3A)(a), added by Sch 10, para 8(2) to the Children Act 1989. Section 20(3A)(b) makes it clear that a revocation order does not affect any person's parental responsibility insofar as it relates to the period between the making and revocation of the freeing order.
[12] Adoption Act 1976, s 20(4). Leave shall not be given unless it appears to the court that, owing to a change of circumstances or for any other reason, it is proper to allow the application to be made: s 20(5).
[13] Discussion Paper No 2, para 134.
[14] See Discussion Paper No 2, paras 137–138.
[15] See s 22 of the Children Act 1989 as discussed by Discussion Paper No 2, para 135. The concept of being 'looked after' by a local authority is discussed post, p 505.
[16] Hershman and McFarlane *The Children Act 1989: access or contact with a child freed for adoption* [1990] Fam Law 322–323.

this it has been argued[17] that the Adoption Act 1976 qualifies their status by the term 'former parent' and that such an interpretation would deny the logic of a freeing order, which is that such parents no longer have rights in relation to the care and upbringing of the child, apart from those in relation to revocation. On this argument, former parents would need the court's leave to apply for a section 8 order, which it is suggested would rarely be given.

(d) The use of freeing orders

Although there is no compulsion upon agencies to apply to free children for adoption,[18] most people envisaged, and the Houghton Committee certainly intended, that it would be commonly used not least because that is what the natural parents (particularly mothers) would wish.[19] In practice the frequency of use varies from agency to agency with some not using it at all and others using it in a minority of cases up to a maximum of one case in three.[20] One of the main reasons for its relatively infrequent use is that, instead of being the speedy process that it was intended to be, it has proved in practice to be a lengthy process riddled with delay.[1] The Bristol Study found that on average it took just over nine months from the time of application to obtain a freeing order with a third of cases taking in excess of nine months and 5 per cent in excess of 18 months.[2]

Although it was expected that the procedure would be useful where a parent might withhold agreement, the general assumption at the time of implementation was that freeing would be mainly a consensual process. Its principal use, however, is in contested or otherwise difficult cases with as many as 75 per cent of applications being contested.[3] Another unintended and controversial use of the process is to free children already placed with prospective adopters.[4] The agency's motive in using the freeing process even where the child has been placed for adoption is to shield the would-be adopters from the stress of taking on the contest with the birth parents. Not everyone agrees that this is a legitimate use of the jurisdiction[5] and in any event it is possible for the court to join the adoptive applicants as

---

[17] See the Bristol Study's Freeing Report, at p 69, summarised by the Adoption Law Review, Discussion Paper No 2, para 140.

[18] See Sheldon J in *Re PB (A Minor) (Application to Free for Adoption)* [1985] FLR 394, 404 explaining Cumming-Bruce LJ's remarks which suggested otherwise in *Re M (A Minor) (Wardship: Jurisdiction)* [1985] Fam 60, 71, CA.

[19] See eg Hayes and Williams *Adoption of Babies, Agreeing and Freeing* 12 Fam Law 233, 236.

[20] See the Bristol Study's Freeing Report, sections 2.2 and 3.2.1 summarised by the Adoption Law Review, Discussion Paper No 2, paras 146 et seq.

[1] The courts themselves have been critical of delay. In *Re PB* supra, for instance, where there was a delay of over a year, Sheldon J commented that with reasonable expedition it should be possible to fix a date within three months. See also *Re C (A Minor)* (1987) Times, 16 October, where 18 months elapsed between the institution of the application and the date of the judgment.

[2] Tables 3.6–3.8 of the Bristol Study Freeing Report.

[3] See the Bristol Study Freeing Report, op cit, Tables 3.19–3.22.

[4] The Bristol Study found this to be the case in 21 per cent of cases with a further 9 per cent so placed during the pendency of the application: ibid, Table 3.36.

[5] See eg White *Freeing or placement: the dilemma for adoption agencies* (1989) Journal of Child Law, Vol 1, No 2, p 41.

parties.[6] It is established, however, that the potential adopters are not barred from subsequently applying to adopt if the freeing application fails.[7]

(e) The future of freeing

As the Adoption Law Review puts it, judged by the Houghton Committee's criteria, freeing has failed.[8] The question remains, should the procedure be scrapped or retained but improved. The Review clearly signposts the former option.[9] As it points out there is a general desire to limit the number of court proceedings in which the child is involved and that it is illogical that the procedure is only used in some but not all cases and that the local authorities may or may not have prospective adopters in mind. More damningly it is pointed out that what arguments there are for freeing favour the agency and prospective adopters. There is little evidence to suggest that freeing is beneficial to the children.

Among the alternative options being canvassed is to replace freeing with an application *by the local authority* to dispense with parental agreement to adoption, coupled with an application by the prospective adopters for a provisional order.[10] Another option is to provide that, where agreement has been given before the adoption hearing, it should become irrevocable after a prescribed period.[11]

C. Procedure for the making of adoption orders

1. CHILD MUST LIVE WITH THE APPLICANTS BEFORE THE MAKING OF AN ORDER

To ensure as far as possible that the adopters are suitable people to bring the child up it is provided that in all cases the child must have had his home with applicants for a certain prescribed period before the court hearing. In the case of agency placements[12] or applications by parents, step-parents or relatives, no order can be made unless the child is at least 19 weeks old and at all times during the preceding 13 weeks has had his home with the applicants or one of them. In other cases, that is where the child was originally fostered,[13] the child must be at least 12 months old and at all times during the preceding 12 months have had his home with the

---

[6] Adoption Rules 1984, r 4(3). Indeed in contested cases it has been said that it is desirable that they should be made parties, per Balcombe LJ in *Re C (Minors) (Adoption)* [1992] 1 FLR 115, 129, CA.

[7] Ie the principle of res judicata does not apply: per Eastham J in *Re B* (1990) Adoption and Fostering, Vol 14, No 1, 62.

[8] Discussion Paper No 2, para 176. For a similar conclusion see the Bristol Study's Freeing Report, op cit at 5.4. See also the conclusion of the Scottish study.

[9] See para 180. Both the Bristol and the Scottish studies were in favour of its retention subject to improvements being made.

[10] See para 182. The advantage of this is that the agency rather than the adoptive applicants would take on the contest with the birth parents.

[11] See para 82. This is the position in Australia, see the discussion at paras 25–26.

[12] Or placements made in pursuance of a High Court order.

[13] It will be recalled that 'private' placements for adoption are unlawful, see ante, pp 414–415. A nominal fostering arrangement made with the intention that the child will be adopted is also an offence; see *Gatehouse v Robinson* [1986] 1 WLR 18, discussed ante, p 414.

applicants or one of them.[14] It will be noted, that these provisions prescribe the minimum period before which an *order* may be made but an adoption *application* may be made at any time.[15]

In determining with what person a child has his home, any absence at a hospital or boarding school and any other temporary absence,[16] is disregarded.[17] The possibility that the whole period could be spent away from the applicants' home is guarded against by the further provision that the agency placing him, or the local authority in non-agency placements, must have sufficient opportunities to see the child with the applicant or, in the case of a joint application, both applicants together in the home environment.[18] It has been held[19] that though difficult to define with precision, 'home' must comprise some element of regular occupation (whether past, present, or intended for the future, even if intermittent) with some degree of permanency, based on some right of occupation whenever it is required; it is where you find the fixed comforts of home; the fixed residence of a family or household. Though ultimately a question of fact to be decided in each case, a house that is merely visited by members of the family is unlikely to constitute a home for these purposes. In all non-agency placements the 'home' must be in England or Wales[20] though this does not mean that the applicants should be living or resident there at any particular time provided the local authority is given sufficient opportunity to see the child in his 'home environment'.[1]

2. NOTICE TO LOCAL AUTHORITY MUST BE GIVEN IN NON-AGENCY PLACEMENTS

Formerly, it was a requirement in all cases where the child was below the upper limit of compulsory school age that applicants other than parents notified the local authority of their intention to apply for adoption. The purpose of such notice was to ensure the proper supervision of children placed for adoption, as it was the local authority's responsibility to visit the child and to satisfy itself as to his well-being. The Houghton Committee,[2] however, felt that where the placement had been made by an adoption agency the child's welfare could best be supervised by that agency. Following their recommendations it is now only necessary to notify the local authority in cases where the child has not been placed for adoption by an adoption

---

[14] Adoption Act 1976, s 13(1) and (2).
[15] The Adoption Law Review, Discussion Paper No 3, asks whether instead a minimum period should be prescribed before an *application* should be made. If so, what period? See the discussion at paras 23, 141–143.
[16] Quaere whether this would include allowing the child to spend time with his parents; cf *Re CSC (An Infant)* [1960] 1 All ER 711 and *Re B (An Infant)* [1964] Ch 1, [1963] 3 All ER 125.
[17] Adoption Act 1976, s 72(1A) added by the Children Act 1989, Sch 10, para 30(a).
[18] Adoption Act 1976, s 13(3). The wording is regrettably vague. Presumably the agency or authority must have significant opportunity to see whether the proposed adoption is likely to be for the child's welfare, but cf *Re Y (Minors) (Adoption: Jurisdiction)* [1985] Fam 136, [1985] 3 All ER 33 where Sheldon J in effect refused to lay down how many visits may be necessary.
[19] *Re Y (Minors) (Adoption: Jurisdiction)*, supra.
[20] In order to satisfy Adoption Act 1976, ss 13(3)(b) and 22(1).
[1] See *Re Y* supra.
[2] At paras 237–239.

agency. In such cases the applicant must, not more than two years or less than three months before the order, give written[3] notice to the local authority, within whose area the child has his home, of the intention to apply for an adoption order.[4] Immediately notice is given the child becomes a 'protected child' and the local authority is under a duty to visit the child and to satisfy itself as to the child's well-being and to give such advice as to care and maintenance as may appear to be needed.[5]

Upon receipt of such notice the local authority must investigate the matter, in particular the suitability of the applicants, any other matter relevant to the child's long-term welfare and whether the placement was unlawful, and submit a report to the court.[6]

3. THE APPOINTMENT OF A REPORTING OFFICER OR GUARDIAN AD LITEM[7]

As soon as practicable after the making of an application, or at any subsequent stage, the court must appoint a reporting officer in cases where it appears that a parent or guardian is willing to agree to the adoption.[8] The reporting officers' duties are, inter alia:[9] (1) to ensure that any parental agreement has been given freely and with a full understanding of what is involved;[10] (2) to witness the signature of the written agreement to the making of the order; (3) to investigate all the circumstances relevant to that agreement; and (4) in the case of freeing applications, to confirm that opportunity has been given to the parent to make a declaration that he no longer wishes to be involved in future questions about the child's adoption. The reporting officer, must, on completion of his investigations, make a written report to the court drawing attention to any matters that may be of assistance. This report is confidential.

The court must appoint a guardian ad litem in cases where it appears that the parent or guardian is unwilling to agree to the adoption; it may do so if there are special reasons and it seems that the child's welfare requires it.[11] It therefore follows that if one parent agrees to the adoption but the other does not, both officers should be appointed. It also means

---

[3] See the definition of 'notice' in the Adoption Act 1976, s 72(1).

[4] Adoption Act 1976, s 22(1) and (1A) as added by the Children Act 1989, Sch 10, para 10(1). The two-year requirement is new and is in line with the new provision under s 32(4) as to when a child ceases to be 'protected'.

[5] Adoption Act 1976, ss 32 and 33. A child ceases to be 'protected' in the circumstances set out by s 32(4) (as amended by the Children Act 1989, Sch 10, para 18(4)).

[6] Adoption Act 1976, ss 22(2), (3). Adoption agencies are under a similar obligation in respect of agency placements, s 23. If an agency wishes to remove a protected child it should apply for an emergency protection order under Part V of the Children Act 1989, discussed post, p 536.

[7] See generally Monro and Forrester *The Guardian ad Litem*, ch 16.

[8] Adoption Rules 1984, rr 5 (freeing) and 17. Appointments are made from a panel established under the Guardians Ad Litem and Reporting Officers (Panels) Regulations 1991 (issued pursuant to s 65A of the Adoption Act 1976, added by the Children Act 1989, Sch 10, para 29). They must not be employees of the agency involved in the proceedings: Adoption Act 1976, s 65(2).

[9] Adoption Rules, rr 5(4), 17(4).

[10] This might be thought to import an obligation to inform and advise on the nature and consequences of an adoption order.

[11] Adoption Rules, rr 6, 18.

that if a parent at first agrees but later changes his mind or vice versa, both officers will have had to be appointed. The same person can act as a reporting officer and as a guardian.[12] Like reporting officers, guardians ad litem are generally selected from a panel, though in High Court proceedings the Official Solicitor may assume that role.[13]

The overall role of the guardian is to safeguard the child's interests before the court. His specific duties are,[14] inter alia, to investigate the matters alleged in the application, any report made by the agency or local authority, any statement of facts on which the case for dispensing with agreement is based and any other matters that he considers relevant. When these extensive duties are completed he must submit a confidential[15] report to the court. The guardian also has to advise on whether the child should be present at the hearing and to perform such other duties as appear to him to be necessary or as the court may direct.

4. THE APPLICANTS' POSITION PENDING AN APPLICATION[16]

Once a parent has agreed to the making of an order he cannot, without leave of the court, remove the child against the applicants' will during the pendency of the application.[17] Similarly an adoption agency may not remove a child it has placed for adoption.[18] In the case of a freeing application, if the child is in the care of a local authority adoption agency making the application,[19] the parent is barred from removing the child even if he has not consented to the application.[20]

Greater protection is given to applicants with whom the child has had his home for *five years*; in such a case *no-one* is entitled to remove the child from the applicants' home against their will without the court's leave once an application has been made or for three months after notice has been given to the local authority of an intention to apply.[1] This provision was designed particularly to protect foster parents by preventing parents from seeking the return of their child merely to stop the adoption.[2] Even a local authority in whose care the child is cannot remove the child once an application is pending. However, if the applicants' sole purpose is to prevent

---

[12] Adoption Rules, rr 6(3), 18(3).
[13] He will not normally be involved in cases where the application is proceeding with the consent of the natural parents: *Practice Direction* [1986] 2 All ER 832.
[14] Pursuant to Adoption Rules, rr 6(6), 18(6).
[15] It is a matter for judicial discretion whether the report is disclosed to a party; see *Re PA (An Infant)* [1971] 3 All ER 522, CA, though normally adverse findings are disclosed; see *Re C (Adoption Application: Hearing)* (1981) 3 FLR 95, CA; *Re T (Confidential Report: Disclosure)* (1982) 3 FLR 183, CA, and *Re B (A Minor)* (1983) Times, 21 October, CA.
[16] See generally *Adoption Law Review*, Discussion Paper No 3, Part 8.
[17] Adoption Act 1976, s 27(1). It will be noted that the prospective adopters can agree to the child's return, but see the criticism in Bevan and Parry *Children Act 1975* para 132.
[18] Adoption Act 1976, ss 30(1)(b), (2).
[19] Ibid, s 27(2) and 27(2A) added by the Children Act 1989, Sch 10, para 14.
[20] Adoption Act 1976, s 27(2).
[1] Ibid, s 28.
[2] See the Houghton Report, at paras 139–147 and 161–164. The Committee abandoned their original proposal that after five years foster parents should be able to apply for adoption with the local authority's agreement (but without the parents' agreement) because this might have led foster parents to weaken links between parent and child, caused anxiety to parents, and inhibited them from placing children in care as a consequence.

the authority from removing the child, an adoption order is unlikely to be made.[3]

D. Jurisdiction, functions and powers of the court

1. JURISDICTION

An adoption order or an order freeing the child for adoption may be made by the High Court, a county court or a magistrates' court.[4] In general therefore applicants can choose the level of court in which they wish to proceed.[5] In practice most orders are made by county courts.[6] Proceedings can be transferred from one county court to another and from a county court to the High Court and vice versa.[7] Applications started in a magistrates' court are heard by the family proceedings court[8] and under the Children (Allocation of Proceedings) Order 1991 there is power to transfer cases to the county court.[9]

2. FUNCTIONS OF THE COURT

The court must be satisfied about three things:[10] that the order, if made, will be for the child's welfare,[11] that every parent or guardian of the child freely, and with full understanding of what is involved, agrees unconditionally to the making of the order (unless his agreement has been

[3] See *Re H (A Minor) (Adoption)* [1985] FLR 519, CA, and see the comments thereon in [1985] JSWL at 364, [1985] Fam Law at 135 and Adoption and Fostering, Vol 9, No 1 at 59.

[4] Adoption Act 1976, s 62. Only the High Court has jurisdiction: (i) if the child is not in Great Britain when the application is made: Adoption Act 1976, s 62(3), (ii) if the application is for a Convention Adoption Order (discussed post, p 453): ibid, s 62(4) or (iii) if the placement would otherwise be unlawful: see ibid, s 11(1)(b); *Re A (Adoption: Placement)* [1988] 1 WLR 229. It would also seem advisable to apply to the High Court in cases where illegal payments have been made; cf *Re Adoption Application (Payment for Adoption)* [1987] Fam 81, [1987] 2 All ER 826; and *Re An Adoption Application* [1992] 1 FLR 341.

[5] Though note the restrictions mentioned in footnote 4 above. It has been said, per Sheldon J in *Re PB (A Minor) (Application to Free for Adoption)* [1985] FLR 394, 396, that a magistrates' court might be thought to be the least suitable tribunal to hear long-contested cases. A magistrates' court must refuse to make an order if it considers the matter would be more conveniently dealt with by the High Court: Adoption Act 1976, s 63(3).

[6] Under the Children (Allocation of Proceedings) Order 1991, arts 14 and 17, applications commenced at the county court now start in the divorce county court and must be transferred to a family hearing centre if the application is opposed. In 1986 82 per cent of orders were made by county courts, 15 per cent by magistrates and 3 per cent by the High Court (OPCS Monitor, FM 3 87(1). Applications to the High Court have increased eight-fold over the last 10 years, which is mainly attributable to the growth of wardship: see the Adoption Law Review, Discussion Paper No 3, para 191.

[7] Arts 10 and 12. The High Court similarly has power to transfer cases to the county court: art 13.

[8] Children Act 1989, s 92.

[9] Art 8. This power of transfer between magistrates' courts and the county court is new.

[10] Adoption Act 1976, ss 6, 16 and 24(2).

[11] This is the first point that must be decided. See *Re D (A Minor) (Adoption: Freeing Order)* [1991] 1 FLR 48, CA, discussed ante at p 426.

dispensed with), and that no unauthorised payments or rewards for the adoption have been made or agreed upon.[12]

In reaching its decision, the court relies heavily (though not exclusively) on the adoption agency's or local authority's report and that of the reporting officer or guardian ad litem. The main benefit that the child is likely to receive is the long-term security of having new parents who can show real care and affection in substitution for those who are unable or unwilling to perform their parental duties. But 'welfare' is a sufficiently wide term to include material benefit as well.[13]

In any case, there must be a genuine intention that the applicants should stand in loco parentis to the child. An order will be refused where it is clear, for example, that the real motive for the application is to enable the child (particularly, if he has nearly attained his majority) to acquire British citizenship rather than to promote his welfare.[14] Notwithstanding that an order can only be made in respect of a 'child' and that under section 6 of the Adoption Act 1976 the court's first consideration in making an adoption order is the child's welfare *throughout his childhood*, (a) a benefit during minority is *not* a condition precedent to the making of an order and (b) a benefit accruing after majority[15] is a relevant factor to be taken into account when deciding whether to make an order.[16]

3. THE COURT'S POWERS

(a) The power to add terms and conditions

Under section 12(6) of the Adoption Act 1976 an adoption order (but not a freeing order)[17] 'may contain such terms and conditions as the court thinks fit'. A number of cases have considered the meaning and ambit of this provision with regard to continuing contact but the leading case is now *Re C (A Minor) (Adoption Order: Conditions)*.[18] That case concerned a

---

[12] Ie that there have been no payments or promise of payment contrary to the Adoption Act 1976, s 57. It is, however, lawful for adoption agencies to pay an allowance to adopters: Adoption Act 1976, s 57A, added by the Children Act 1989, Sch 10, para 57A and see the Adoption Allowance Regulations 1991. See generally the Department of Health's *Guidance and Regulations*, Vol 9, Adoption Issues, ch 2. The court can also retrospectively 'authorise' payments: *Re Adoption Application (Payment for Adoption)* [1987] Fam 81, [1987] 2 All ER 826; and *Re An Adoption Application* [1992] 1 FLR 341.

[13] *Re A (An Infant)* [1963] 1 All ER 531, 534. If the child has a substantial connection with a foreign country (for example, if he is domiciled there or is a foreign national), one of the matters to be taken into account in deciding whether the order will be for his benefit is whether it will be recognised in that country: *Re B(S) (An Infant)* [1968] Ch 204, [1967] 3 All ER 629.

[14] *Re W (A Minor)* [1986] Fam 54, [1985] 3 All ER 449, CA. See also *Re H (A Minor) (Adoption: Non-Patrial)* [1982] Fam 121, [1982] 3 All ER 84 and *Re A (An Infant)* [1963] 1 All ER 531. Cf *Re R (Adoption)* [1966] 3 All ER 613. Where a UK citizen proposes to adopt a foreign child notice should be given to the Home Office so that the Secretary of State may, if he so wishes, be added as a party: see *Re W*, supra at p 62 and p 454 respectively; and *R v Secretary of State for Health, ex p Luff* [1992] 1 FLR 59.

[15] For example, the benefit of having a secure home and status which could be particularly important, if as in *Re D*, the child is mentally handicapped.

[16] *Re D (A Minor) (Adoption Order: Validity)* [1991] Fam 137, [1991] 3 All ER 461, CA.

[17] See the definition of 'adoption order' in s 72(1) of the Adoption Act 1976 and see *Re C (Minors) (Adoption)* [1992] 1 FLR 115, 129, CA per Balcombe LJ.

[18] [1989] AC 1, [1988] 1 All ER 705, HL.

child who was in long-term care. The mother refused to agree to her daughter's adoption on the ground that it would weaken the child's relationship with her brother. The judge held that the relationship between the siblings should be preserved and refused to make the order. The applicants appealed and sought a condition attached to the adoption that the brother should have continuing access to his sister. Overruling the Court of Appeal, the House of Lords held that the court had power under section 12(6) to attach such a condition where it was clearly in the child's interests to do so, and that such an order would be enforceable by committal for contempt. In reaching this decision Lord Ackner stressed that to safeguard and promote the child's welfare it was important that the court should retain 'the maximum flexibility given to it by the Act'. However, he added:[19]

> 'The cases rightly stress that in normal circumstances it is desirable that there should be a complete break, but that each case has to be considered on its own particular facts. No doubt the court will not, except in exceptional cases, impose terms or conditions as to access to members of the child's natural family to which the adopting parents do not agree... Where no agreement is forthcoming the court will, with very rare exceptions, have to choose between making an adoption order without terms or conditions as to access, or to refuse to make such an order and seek to safeguard access through some other machinery, such as wardship. To do otherwise would be merely inviting future and almost immediate litigation.'

Lord Ackner further observed that a distinction could properly be drawn between contact with natural parents and contact with other relatives, the former being harder to justify than the latter, if an adoption order is to be made.

The ambit of section 12(6) has been further considered in *Re D (A Minor) (Adoption Order: Validity)*.[20] In that case the Court of Appeal held that courts can limit or impose conditions upon the parental responsibility that would otherwise vest in the adopters[1] or might otherwise be extinguished in the natural parents[2] but they cannot thereby impose terms that would grant to adopters more extensive rights than the natural parents would have had. Hence they held that they could not under section 12(6) grant an injunction restraining grandparents from having further contact with the child. However, as we discuss below, this distinction drawn in *Re D* may not prove of lasting importance as the court can now exercise its section 8 powers under the Children Act 1989.

(b) The power to make section 8 orders under the Children Act 1989[3]

Proceedings under the Adoption Act 1976 are designated 'family pro-

---

[19] Ibid at pp 17–18 and 712–713 respectively. See also the comments of the Adoption Law Review, Discussion Paper No 1, paras 71–72.1

[20] [1991] Fam 137, [1991] 3 All ER 461, CA.

[1] For example that the child be brought up in a particular religion. Maidment *Access and Family Adoptions* (1977) 40 MLR 293 argues that that is what the statutory provision was *solely* designed for.

[2] *Re C (A Minor) (Adoption Order: Condition)* [1986] 1 FLR 315, CA, in which it was held to be inconsistent with an adoption order to impose a condition that the adoptive parents inform the natural father of the child's progress. Sed quaere?

[3] See generally *Adoption Law Review*, Discussion Paper No 1, paras 57 et seq and White, Carr and Lowe *A Guide to the Children Act 1989*, paras 11.20–11.22.

ceedings' for the purposes of the Children Act 1989[4] with the consequence
that courts are empowered, either upon application, or upon their own
motion, to make section 8 orders.[5] It is generally accepted that section 8
orders may be made instead of or in addition to an adoption or freeing
order.[6] Unlike adoption, in deciding whether to make a section 8 order
courts are bound to treat the child's welfare as the *paramount* (not first)
consideration pursuant to section 1(1) of the 1989 Act.

(i) As alternative orders

It is a moot point whether the courts have a *duty* in adoption and freeing
applications to consider making alternative orders under section 8 (in
particular a residence order).[7] Nevertheless these alternatives are readily
available and, being more straightforward than the previous alternative of
custodianship,[8] can be expected to be used more often. In particular it is
thought likely that residence orders will more often be considered an
appropriate alternative to adoption by step-parents or relatives.[9]

(ii) As additional orders

The availability of section 8 orders as an additional power means that the
courts can make contact, prohibited steps and specific issue orders[10] as well
as an adoption or a freeing order. In the case of an adoption order courts
can therefore use either section 12(6) of the Adoption Act 1976 or its section
8 powers to make additional orders. One suspects, however, that the section
8 alternative will generally be preferred since the court's powers are more
clearly defined. In the case of freeing applications courts can only look to
section 8 to make any additional orders since, as we have seen,[11] section
12(6) does not apply.

Apart from the important consequence that courts can now make both
a freeing order and a contact order[12] it is not expected that the new power
to make a contact order will lead to a dramatic change of policy and that

[4] Children Act 1989, s 8(4)(d).
[5] Ibid, s 10(1)(b), discussed ante, p 365.
[6] S 12(3)(aa) of the Adoption Act 1976 (added by the Children Act 1989, Sch 10, para 3(3))
provides that an adoption order extinguishes 'any order under the Children Act 1989' but
this presumably operates to extinguish any *previous* order: White, Carr and Lowe, op cit at
para 11.22 and the *Adoption Law Review*, Discussion Paper No 1, note 111.
[7] Cf White, Carr and Lowe, op cit, at 11.20 who argue that there is, and the Adoption Law
Review, Discussion Paper No 1, at para 63, which states that there is no duty. If, however,
the child is subject to a care order, it could be argued that since an adoption (or freeing)
order would discharge that order, a duty to consider s 8 alternatives arises because such
proceedings fall under s 1(4)(b) of the 1989 Act in which the statutory check-list under
s 1(4) (and in particular s 1(3)(g) which obliges the court to consider its alternative powers)
has to be considered.
[8] Under the tortuous provision of s 37 of the Children Act 1975, discussed in the seventh
edition of this work at pp 372–373.
[9] See the Adoption Law Review, Discussion Paper No 1, at para 64. Note also the observation
at para 113 that a residence order can be made more permanent by an additional order
under s 91(14) that a named person be prevented from applying for an order under the 1989
Act without court leave.
[10] But not a residence order as this would be inconsistent with an adoption or freeing order.
[11] Ante, p 447.
[12] Query therefore whether *Re E (A Minor) (Adoption)* [1989] 1 FLR 126, CA, discussed ante,
p 433, would now be decided the same way.

Re C[13] will continue to be the leading authority. The availability of a prohibited steps order, however, means that the distinction drawn in *Re D*[14] between limiting the responsibility and granting adopters more extensive rights, may now no longer be relevant since it would seem open to the court to make a prohibited steps order preventing others from having contact with the child.

(c) Interim orders[15]

Instead of making the order applied for, the court may make an interim order to last for not more than two years, the effect of which is to give parental responsibility of the child to the applicant upon such terms for the maintenance of the child and otherwise as the court thinks fit.[16] The purpose of an interim order is to enable the adopters to act for a probationary period, and it is thus a useful compromise when the court is genuinely unable to make up its mind whether the applicants will make good adopters. It has also been used when the court was uncertain whether the child should be adopted or go to live with a parent,[17] although it must be rarely desirable for interim orders to be made in such circumstances because of the uncertainty which they produce. The section requires the court to be satisfied that the parents' or guardians' agreement has been given or dispensed with and, if the child was not placed by an adoption agency, three months' notice must have been given to the local authority. By implication no other conditions have to be satisfied and it would therefore seem that, for example, an interim order could be made even though the 'home' requirements set out under section 13 of the Adoption Act 1976 have not been satisfied.

(d) Refusal to make an order[18]

Adoption and freeing applications are rarely refused. 96 per cent of adoption applications by non-relatives sampled in the Bristol Study resulted in an order being made. No orders were actually refused, the remaining 4 per cent were withdrawn or adjourned.[19]

If the court refuses to make any order at all (or if at any stage the application is withdrawn) and the child was placed for adoption by an adoption agency, he must be returned to that body within seven days.[20]

---

[13] Discussed ante, p 447.

[14] Discussed ante, p 448.

[15] See generally *Adoption Law Review*, Discussion Paper No 3, paras 196–199.

[16] Adoption Act 1976, s 25(1) as amended by the Children Act 1989, Sch 10, para 11. By s 25(2) the period laid down in the original order may be extended provided that the total period is not greater than two years.

[17] *S v Huddersfield Borough Council* [1975] Fam 113, [1974] 3 All ER 296, CA.

[18] See generally *Adoption Law Review*, Discussion Paper No 3, op cit, paras 169–199.

[19] 81 per cent of step-parent applications resulted in an order and none was refused. Perhaps more strikingly, given that they are more often contested, 84 per cent of freeing applications were successful with only two applications (1 per cent) being refused: *Pathways to Adoption*, op cit, 2.9. More strikingly still it was found that it made no difference to the outcome whether the application was contested or not, see the Freeing Report, op cit, Table 3.43.

[20] Adoption Act 1976, s 30(3). This also applies if an interim order expires without a full order being made. The court may extend the time for returning the child for a period not exceeding six weeks: ibid, s 30(6). This power might be exercised, eg if unsuccessful applicants wished to appeal.

There is no statutory obligation to return the child in other cases.[1] The reason for the difference is this: in the first case the body concerned must obviously try to find other suitable applicants, whereas in the second there may be good reasons for permitting the applicants to retain care and control even though an adoption order has not been made. This might occur, for example, if the court refuses to make the order because the child's mother withdraws her agreement; if she wishes to look after the child she will need to seek a residence order the outcome of which is dependent upon the welfare principle.[2]

The former power to make a supervision or care order upon a refusal to make an adoption order has been repealed.[3] Instead, as in other 'family proceedings', the court may, if it thinks it appropriate, direct a local authority to investigate the child's circumstances with a view to the authority's deciding whether or not to bring care proceedings.[4]

If the application for adoption is refused, the applicants may normally make a further application only if the court is satisfied that, because of a change of circumstances or for some other reason, this is proper.[5]

(e) Adoption of children abroad

Persons who are not domiciled in England and Wales, Scotland or Northern Ireland (in whose favour therefore a full adoption order cannot be made)[6] but who wish to remove a child out of the country to obtain an adoption order under their lex domicilii can apply to the High Court or county court for an order giving him parental responsibility for the child.[7] The court has jurisdiction to make such an order only if it would have had jurisdiction to make a full order had the applicant possessed the relevant domicile.[8] The order authorises the applicant to remove the child out of the country[9] but it does not affect devolution of property or the child's citizenship. The court has no power to make an interim order or an order freeing the child for adoption.[10]

(f) Revocation of adoption orders

It is specifically provided that an adoption order may be revoked if an illegitimate person, who has been adopted by his mother or father alone,

---

[1] Unless the child is in the care of a local authority and the authority demands his return: Adoption Act 1976, s 31(1).
[2] See ante, p 376.
[3] Adoption Act 1976, s 26, repealed by the Children Act 1989, Sch 15.
[4] Under s 37 of the Children Act 1989, discussed ante, p 374. This change is in line with the general policy of the 1989 Act that children should be committed into local authority care only if the threshold criteria laid down by the Children Act 1989, s 31 have been satisfied.
[5] Adoption Act 1976, s 24(1). A court can, however, stipulate that the provision does not apply, see *Re V (A Minor) (Adoption: Consent)* [1987] Fam 57, [1986] 1 All ER 752, CA.
[6] Unless they are domiciled in the Channel Islands or Isle of Man.
[7] Adoption Act 1976, s 55, as amended by the Children Act 1989, Sch 10, para 22.
[8] But if the applicant is a parent, a step-parent or relative, or if the child was placed by an adoption agency, the child must be 32 weeks old and have had his home with the applicants for the preceding 26 weeks: Adoption Act, s 55(2).
[9] Which is otherwise an offence: Adoption Act 1976, s 56. See *Re C (Minors) (Wardship: Adoption)* [1989] 1 All ER 395, CA.
[10] Adoption Act 1976, s 55(2).

is subsequently legitimated by his parents' marriage.[11] There is no further statutory provision for revoking an order although an appeal will, of course, lie from the making of or the refusal to make an adoption order.[12] In exceptional cases, however, former parents could seek to 'undo' an adoption order by making the child a ward of court and seeking care and control; before the court would investigate the full merits of such an application, the applicant had to have an extremely strong prima facie case.[13] Former parents can now also seek leave of the court to apply for a residence order but as in wardship leave is only likely to be given in exceptional cases.[14]

(g) Registration of adoption, the Adoption Contact Register and information about birth records[15]

The Registrar General is obliged to keep a separate register of adoptions.[16] Records are also kept enabling connections between entries in this register and the register of births to be traced, but these records may be searched only with the leave of the court.[17] There is one exception to this rule: any person over the age of 18 who has been adopted may obtain a copy of his birth certificate which means that he may be able to trace his natural parents.[18] There is no right of access to birth records for anyone under the age of 18, but any person under that age intending to marry in England and Wales may obtain information indicating whether or not the parties are likely to be related within the prohibited degrees.[19]

The right of access to birth records, which was introduced following the Houghton Committee's recommendations[20] is of course of no assistance to those who fail to discover that they are adopted or where no records exist. It may be of little assistance to those adopted a long time ago.

[11] Adoption Act 1976, s 52. The order may be revoked by the court that made it on the application of any of the parties concerned.
[12] Appeals from magistrates' courts lie to the High Court: Adoption Act 1976, s 63(2); in other cases to the Court of Appeal. An order made by a magistrates' or county court can be questioned by judicial review. On the question of revocation, see *Skinner v Carter* [1948] Ch 387, at 389, 395 and 397, [1948] 1 All ER 917, at 920 and 921, CA. See also *Re M (A Minor) (Adoption)* [1991] 1 FLR 458, where exceptionally leave to appeal was granted out of time and an adoption order set aside, the father having agreed to an adoption by his former wife and new husband not knowing that she was terminally ill.
[13] See *Re O (A Minor) (Wardship: Adopted Child)* [1978] Fam 196, [1978] 2 All ER 27, CA, where the application succeeded. Cf *Re C (A Minor) (Wardship: Adopted Child)* [1985] FLR 1114, CA.
[14] A more difficult issue is where leave is sought to apply for a contact order.
[15] See generally Adoption Law Review, Discussion Paper No 1, para 73–81 and the Department of Health's *Guidance and Regulations*, Vol 9, ch 3.
[16] Adoption Act 1976, s 50.
[17] Ibid, s 50 and Sch 1. The court for this purpose means the court making the adoption order, the High Court or the Westminster County Court. A search might be ordered, for example, if the child was entitled to a gift under a disposition taking effect before the adoption order but not vesting until after it had been made.
[18] Ibid, s 51. This, however, is not an absolute right, see *R v Registrar General, ex p Smith* [1991] 2 QB 393, [1991] 2 All ER 88, CA (access denied because of danger of birth mother being physically harmed by the applicant). 33,000 adopted children have so far taken advantage of this provision: Adoption Law Review, Discussion Paper No 1, note 140.
[19] Ibid, s 51(2).
[20] Para 303. Controversially this recommendation was introduced with retrospective effect. However those adopted before 12 November 1975 are required to see a counsellor before they can be given information: ibid, s 51(7)(b), as amended by the Children Act 1989, Sch 10, para 20(2).

Access to birth records enables some adopted persons to trace and make contact with their birth parents but until recently it was difficult to discover whether that contact would be welcome. In this regard the newly created Adoption Contact Register is important.[1] The purpose of the Register is 'to put adopted people and their birth parents or other relatives in touch with each other where this is what they both want. The Register provides a safe and confidential way for birth parents and other relatives to assure an adopted person that contact would be welcome and give a contact address.'[2] The Register comprises two parts:[3] Part I, upon which is maintained the name and address of any adopted person who is over 18 and has a copy of his birth certificate and who wishes to contact a relative and Part II upon which is entered, subject to certain prescribed conditions,[4] the current address and identifying details of a relative[5] who wishes to contact an adopted person.

Surprisingly there is no requirement for counselling nor is there a facility for exchanging limited information, such as medical information.

E. Convention adoption orders[6]

Whereas the traditional basis of jurisdiction to make adoption orders in English law is the applicants' domicile, in many foreign systems it is the parties' nationality. This has naturally caused difficulties in cases with a foreign element (for example, where the applicants are British subjects domiciled abroad) and the desire to produce a uniform law of jurisdiction and recognition led to the Hague Convention on the adoption of children in 1965.[7] The terms of the convention were embodied in the Adoption Act 1968 and so far as they relate to jurisdiction to make orders are now contained in the Adoption Act 1976, section 17. As it will be seen, the essential connecting links are the nationality and residence of the parties.

It will be convenient at the outset to define some of the technical terms used in the Acts. An adoption order made under section 17 is known as a *Convention adoption order*. A *Convention country* is any country outside British territory designated by the Secretary of State as a country in which the Convention is in force.[8] *British territory* means the United Kingdom, the Channel Islands, the Isle of Man and a colony, being a country designated for this purpose or, if no country is designated, any of those countries. A *United Kingdom* national is a citizen of the United Kingdom and colonies satisfying such conditions as the Secretary of State may

---

[1] Under the Adoption Act 1976, s 51A (added by the Children Act 1989, Sch 10, para 21) the Registrar General is required to maintain such a Register. In fact the Register is operated on behalf of the Registrar General by the Office of Population Censuses and Surveys.

[2] Department of Health's *Guidance and Regulations*, Vol 9, para 3.2.

[3] Adoption Act 1976, s 51A(2).

[4] Viz upon payment of a prescribed fee, that the applicant is aged 18 or over, that the Registrar General has either a record of the applicant's birth or sufficient information to obtain a certified copy of the record of the birth and that the applicant is a relative: s 51A(3)–(6).

[5] Ie 'any person (other than an adoptive relative) who is related to the adopted person by blood (including half-blood) or marriage': s 51A(13)(a).

[6] See generally the Adoption Law Review, Discussion Paper No 4, paras 51–52.

[7] Cmnd 2613.

[8] At present only Austria and Switzerland have been so designated: SI 1978, No 1431.

specify.[9] A stateless person is to be regarded as a national of the country in which he habitually resides.[10]

Only the High Court has power to make a Convention adoption order.[11] Subject to what is said below, the same law and procedure apply to applications for Convention orders as to applications for other orders.

1. WHO MAY BE ADOPTED

An adoption order may be made only in respect of a person who (i) is under the age of 18; (ii) has not been married; (iii) is a national of the United Kingdom or a Convention country; and (iv) habitually resides in British territory or a Convention country.[12]

2. WHO MAY APPLY FOR AN ORDER

A sole applicant must either (a) habitually reside in Great Britain *and* be a national of a Convention country, or (b) habitually reside in a British territory or a Convention country *and* be a United Kingdom national. A joint application may be made by a husband and wife, in which case both must satisfy either condition (a) or condition (b). No order may be made on the sole application of a married person except in the cases applicable to other adoptions set out in the Adoption Act.[13]

3. CONSENTS AND CONSULTATIONS

If the child is not a United Kingdom national, no order may be made unless the provisions relating to 'consents and consultations' of the internal law of the country of which he is a national are complied with. This does not, however, apply to consents by or consultations with the applicant and members of his family (including his or her spouse). If the child is a United Kingdom national, the law relating to the consent of parents and guardians seems to be the same as it is on other applications for adoption orders. If consent may be dispensed with under the relevant law, the body empowered to do this is the High Court in the case of any application made in England, whatever the child's nationality.[14]

4. RESTRICTIONS ON THE MAKING OF ORDERS

In two cases the court has no power to make a Convention order at all:

(1) If the applicant or applicants are not United Kingdom nationals and

---

[9] Adoption Act 1976, s 72(1). For details, see the Convention Adoption (Miscellaneous Provisions) Order, SI 1978 No 1432.
[10] Adoption Act 1976, s 70.
[11] Ibid, s 62(4).
[12] Ibid, ss 12(5), 17(2) and 72(1).
[13] Ibid, ss 17(4), (5). For sole applications by married persons, see ante, p 419.
[14] Ibid, ss 17(6), (7) and 71.

the order is prohibited by a specified provision of the internal law of the country of which they are nationals provided that, in the case of a joint application, they are nationals of the *same* Convention country.[15] Such a prohibition might relate, for example, to the relative ages of the child and the applicants or their blood relationship.

(2) If the applicant or applicants and the child are all United Kingdom nationals living in British territory.[16] The purpose here is clearly to restrict the operation of section 17 to adoptions with a foreign element. It will be seen that there is a gap, however, for if the above conditions are satisfied and the applicants are not domiciled in any part of the British Isles, there is no jurisdiction to make an order at all.

5. ANNULMENT OF ORDERS

There is a power to annul Convention adoption orders which does not apply to other orders. Provided that either the child or the adopters reside in Great Britain, the High Court may annul an order on the ground that the adoption was prohibited by the internal law of the country of which the adopters were nationals or that it contravened provisions relating to consents of the internal law of the country of which the child was national.[17] As in the case of other orders, a Convention adoption order may also be revoked if the child was adopted by his father or mother and has subsequently been legitimated by their marriage.

F. The legal consequences of the making of an adoption order[18]

The Adoption Act 1976, section 39, enacts in general terms:[19]

'(1) An adopted child shall be treated in law—

(a) where the adopters are a married couple, as if he had been born as a child of the marriage (whether or not he was in fact born after the marriage was solemnized);

(b) in any other case, as if he had been born to the adopter in wedlock (but not as a child of any actual marriage of the adopter).

(2) An adopted child shall be treated in law as if he were not the child of any other person other than the adopters or adopter....

(4) It is hereby declared that this paragraph prevents an adopted child from being illegitimate.'

[15] Ibid, s 17(4), (5), (8).
[16] Ibid, s 17(3). For other difficulties, see McClean and Patchett *English Jurisdiction in Adoption* 19 ICLQ 1; Blom *The Adoption Act 1968 and the Conflict of Laws* 22 ICLQ 109.
[17] Ibid, ss 53(1) as amended by the Domestic Proceedings and Magistrates' Courts Act 1978, s 74(2), and 54(2). S 53(1) also enables a Convention adoption order to be annulled on the ground that it could have been impugned on any other ground under English law. The order would then presumably be a nullity anyway.
[18] See generally Adoption Law Review, Discussion Paper No 1, Part A.
[19] See also *Secretary of State for Social Services v S* [1983] 3 All ER 173, CA (the mother who takes her natural son to live with her after his adoptive mother's death is not his 'parent' and is therefore entitled to a guardian's allowance).

It is expressly provided that adoption extinguishes any existing parental responsibility vested in a parent or guardian (other than one of the adopters) or in any other person by virtue of a court order and any duty to make payments for the child's maintenance by virtue of an order or agreement unless the agreement constitutes a trust or expressly provides to the contrary.[20] Similarly, adoption automatically discharges any order, including a care order, made under the Children Act 1989.[1]

So far as marriage is concerned, an adopted child and his adoptive parents are deemed to come within the prohibited degrees of consanguinity, so that they may not intermarry.[2] Adoption, however, does not prevent a marriage between the child and his adoptive sister (or brother) or with any other adoptive relative. Conversely, as the modern law bears some relation to genetics, the child may not marry any person who would have come within the prohibited degrees if no adoption had been made.[3] A child who is not a British citizen will acquire such citizenship on adoption if his adoptive parent possesses it.[4] On the other hand, an adopted child may continue to claim a pension which was being paid to him or for his benefit at the time of the adoption as though no order had been made,[5] and adoption does not affect the descent of any peerage or dignity or title of honour.[6] Nor will adoption of an illegitimate child by a natural parent as *sole* adoptive parent prevent his legitimation if the adopter later marries the other parent.[7]

For the purposes of all other statutes an adopted child is to be regarded as the child of his adopter or adopters, whenever the statute was passed and the adoption took place.[8] So, for example, an adopted child may claim under the Fatal Accidents Act 1976 as a dependant of his adoptive parent or other adoptive relative but not of his birth parent.[9] Similarly adoption bars the child's inheritance claims against the birth parents' estate under the Inheritance (Provision for Family and Dependants) Act 1975.[10]

An adopted child's right to claim property under any disposition or on an intestacy will be dealt with when we consider children's rights to claim property generally.

G. The future of adoption

In its first Discussion Paper the Adoption Law Review[11] canvassed opinion

---

[20] Adoption Act 1976, s 12(2), (3), (4) as amended by the Children Act 1989, Sch 10, para 3.
[1] Ibid, s 12(3)(aa), added by the Children Act 1989, Sch 10, para 3(3).
[2] Marriage Act 1949, Sch 1. This continues to apply if a subsequent adoption order is made, and the child may not marry a former adoptive parent.
[3] Adoption Act 1976, s 47(1). Nor does adoption affect the law relating to incest.
[4] British Nationality Act 1981, s 1(5). In the case of a joint adoption the child will acquire British citizenship if one of the adopters possesses it. He will retain British citizenship even if the order ceases to have effect for any reason: ibid, s 1(6).
[5] Adoption Act 1976, s 48. For the effect of adoption on certain policies of insurance, see ibid, s 49.
[6] Ibid, s 44(1).
[7] Legitimacy Act 1976, s 4. See ante, p 283.
[8] Adoption Act 1976, s 39(5), (6).
[9] Cf *Watson v Willmot* [1991] 1 QB 140, [1991] 1 All ER 473.
[10] See *Re Collins (decd)*[1990] Fam 56, [1990] 2 All ER 47 (post, pp 823–824).
[11] Op cit in Part E.

on a number of broad sweeping options for reform all of which are predicated on the basis that the fundamental purpose of adoption is to secure a permanent home for the child. As one commentator has put it:[12] 'In essence the question to be addressed is whether adoption should continue to be a unitary concept in which transfer and severance are integral parts or whether it can achieve the permanence objective in some other way.'

Option A contemplates the retention of the current law but with additional provisions to facilitate openness and flexibility. With regard to openness the Review notes changes in practice both here and in Australia and New Zealand but asks whether such changes should be practice led or be encouraged by changes in the legislation to promote it. Increased flexibility is thought to be provided by the powers to make section 8 orders but the Review canvasses views as to whether courts should be under a *duty* to consider these alternatives. Views are also canvassed as to whether some express provision should be made to allow in exceptional cases applications to revoke an adoption order.

Option B is more radical and, based on the French model, contemplates two types of adoption: the traditional existing type involving complete severance and a second less drastic order amounting in terms to an irrevocable residence order which would facilitate permanence yet still enable both birth and adoptive parents to share parental responsibility.

Option C comprises a basic form of adoption involving the permanent transfer of parental responsibility but with various options to accommodate individual circumstances. For example, orders could include the complete severance of existing familial relationships or provide for their continuation. Another optional feature could be a condition about continuing contact and where this is appropriate, provision could be made to encourage openness.

Option D concentrates on the appropriateness of adoption by step-parents and relatives and canvasses various alternatives including, for example, the acquisition of parental responsibility by administrative rather than judicial means.

Many of the suggestions in the various options overlap with one another and it may be that what will eventually emerge from the Review is some kind of combination. In the meantime there is considerable scope, following changes by the Children Act 1989, for the courts themselves to be more flexible and it may be that by the time any proposals for reform come before Parliament some of the changes advocated will have already been achieved.

---

[12] Bridge *Changing the nature and effect of adoption* (1990) 3 Journal of Child Law 37.

Chapter 14

Wardship and the inherent jurisdiction

A. Introduction

Unlike the jurisdictions dealing with children so far discussed, wardship is not based upon statute but upon an inherent power. Its origins[1] lie in feudal times when it was an incident of tenure by which, upon a tenant's death, the lord became guardian of the surviving infant heir's land and body. Although there was a protective element in the guardianship in that the lord was supposed to look after his ward, maintaining and educating him according to his station, the right was a valuable one since, inter alia, the lord was entitled to keep the profits of the land until the heir reached his majority. No one benefited more than the Crown (whose rights arose upon the death of a tenant-in-chief) and in 1540 the Court of Wards was created to enforce the sovereign's rights and the execution of his duties in connection with wardship. These rights, together with the Court of Wards, were abolished in 1660.[2] The wardship jurisdiction, however, survived in the hands of the Court of Chancery.

Jurisdiction was claimed upon the basis that the sovereign, as parens patriae, had a duty to protect his subjects, particularly those, such as infants,[3] who were unable to protect themselves, and that this duty had been delegated to the Lord Chancellor and through him to the Court of Chancery. Although there is some doubt about the historical validity of this claim, by the end of the nineteenth century (by which time jurisdiction had become vested in the Chancery Division of the High Court), it had become the authoritatively accepted basis of the jurisdiction.[4] Furthermore, it became established that the jurisdiction was not dependent upon the existence of property belonging to the infant.[5] At about the same time it had become established that decisions had to be based on what was best for the ward.[6]

Although by the turn of the century wardship had acquired most of the characteristics of the modern jurisdiction, it did not really begin to develop

[1] For a more detailed historical account see Lowe and White *Wards of Court* (2nd Edn) paras 1.1 et seq and the references there cited. See also *Re Eve* (1986) 31 DLR (4th) 1, Canadian Supreme Court.
[2] By the Tenures Abolition Act 1660.
[3] And, originally, lunatics. However, it is now accepted that there is no longer a parens patriae jurisdiction with regard to mentally handicapped adults: *Re F* [1990] 2 AC 1, [1989] 2 All ER 545, HL.
[4] *Johnstone v Beattie* (1843) 10 Cl & Fin 42, 120 per Lord Eldon LC, and *Hope v Hope* (1854) 4 De GM & G 328, 344–5 per Lord Cranworth LC.
[5] See *Re Spence* (1847) 2 Ph 247, 251 per Lord Cottenham LC. In point of fact, until 1949, it was common practice to begin wardship by making a nominal settlement upon the child and then commencing an action to administer the trusts of the settlement: see *Re D* [1943] Ch 305, 306 and *Re X's Settlement* [1945] Ch 44, 45.
[6] See eg *R v Gyngall* [1893] 2 QB 232, 248, CA per Kay LJ.

until the old procedural shackles were removed in 1949.[7] Further impetus to the use of wardship was given in 1971 when the jurisdiction was transferred to the newly created Family Division of the High Court[8] and thereby became available in the provinces (through the district registries) as well as in London (in the Principal Registry).

Until 1986 wardship had been an exclusively High Court jurisdiction but since then it has been possible, at any rate after the main issues have been resolved, to transfer cases to the county court.[9]

It is commonly said that in wardship the court exercises its inherent jurisdiction. However in the light of the changes made by the Children Act 1989[10] it is important to distinguish the well established wardship jurisdiction from the separate inherent jurisdiction of the High Court referred to in the 1989 Act. Although the existence of a parens patriae power to protect children independent of wardship had been expressly acknowledged by the court[11] before the 1989 Act there had been little cause to develop it, given the wide ranging nature of the wardship jurisdiction. However, in his Joseph Jackson Memorial Lecture,[12] Lord Mackay LC commented: 'in the government's view wardship is only one use of the High Court's inherent parens patriae jurisdiction. We believe, therefore, that is open to the High Court to make orders under its inherent jurisdiction in respect of children other than through wardship.' The Children Act 1989 is committed to this view and indeed, as we shall see, if a local authority wishes to obtain a High Court order in respect of a child already in care they must seek to invoke the inherent rather than the wardship jurisdiction.[13] In this chapter the two jurisdictions will be treated as separate. Consideration will first be given to wardship, which, though greatly affected by the Children Act 1989, nevertheless continues to exist.

B. Wardship[14]

1. CHARACTERISTICS OF THE WARDSHIP JURISDICTION

(a) Control vested in the court

A unique and fundamental characteristic of the jurisdiction is that through-

---

[7] By the Law Reform (Miscellaneous Provisions) Act 1949.
[8] Under the Administration of Justice Act 1970, s 1(2) and Schedule 1.
[9] Pursuant to s 38(2)(b) of the Matrimonial and Family Proceedings Act 1984.
[10] Discussed post, p 478.
[11] See eg *Re N (Infants)* [1967] Ch 512, [1967] 1 All ER 161, and *Re L (An Infant)* [1968] P 119, [1968] 1 All ER 20, CA, and note also the suggestion by Ewbank J in *R v North Yorkshire County Council, ex p M (No 3)* [1989] 2 FLR 82, that the High Court had an inherent power in other proceedings to make a child a ward of court.
[12] (1989) 139 NLJ 505, 507. See also the Department of Health's *Guidance and Regulations*, Vol 1, Court Orders, paras 3.98 et seq.
[13] See post, pp 478 and 482.
[14] For a detailed analysis of the jurisdiction before the Children Act 1989 see Lowe and White *Wards of Court* (2nd Edn) and Law Com Working Paper No 101 *Wards of Court*. For valuable accounts by (then) High Court judges, see Cross *Wards of Court* (1967) 93 LQR 200 and Balcombe *Wardship* (1981–2) Lit 223. See also Levy *Wardship Proceedings*; Pearce *Wardship, The Law and Practice*; and Lowe in *Wardship in the Law of England: The Child and the Courts* (eds Baxter and Edberts) pp 299–325. For discussion of the jurisdiction after the 1989 Act see *Clarke Hall and Morrison on Children* (10th Edn) 1 [651]–[744], White, Carr and Lowe *A Guide to the Children Act 1989*, ch 10 and Bainham *The Children Act 1989: The Future of Wardship* [1990] Fam Law 270.

out the wardship legal control over both the child's person and property is vested in the court. As Lord Scarman put it,[15] once a party persuades the court that it should make the child its ward 'the court takes over ultimate responsibility for the child'. In the past it has sometimes been said that the court becomes in effect the child's parent which, in post-Children Act 1989 terms, might now be expressed by saying the wardship vests the court with 'parental responsibility' over the child. Provided these notions are used in a loose sense there is something to be said for these analogies.[16] However, the court is not in the same position as a parent or other persons with parental responsibility in any strict sense. As Lord Donaldson MR has observed, it is clear that:

> '... the practical jurisdiction of the court is wider than that of parents. The court can, for example, forbid the publication of information about the ward or the ward's family circumstances. It is also clear that this jurisdiction is not derivative from the parents' rights and responsibilities, but derives from, or is, the delegated performance of the duties of the Crown to protect its subjects...'[17]

It might also be added that unlike a parent, the court is bound, when the child's upbringing is in issue, to treat the ward's welfare as its paramount consideration.[18]

(i) The effects of the court's control

Being under the court's protection does not of course mean that the ward is physically in the court's or judge's care but rather that the child and those with parental responsibility or otherwise having de facto care and control are subject to the court's control. This control is both an immediate and automatic consequence of wardship.[19] As Cross J put it,[20] once the child has been made a ward 'no important step in the child's life can be taken without the court's consent'. Failure to obtain the court's consent constitutes a contempt of court, for which the ultimate sanction is imprisonment and a fine.[1]

(ii) Extent of control

Despite the potential draconian sanction it is not easy to say precisely what constitutes an 'important step'.[2] It is well established that a ward may not marry[3] nor leave the jurisdiction without the court's consent. Formerly, the latter embargo meant that in all cases leave was required before a ward

---

[15] In *Re E (SA) (A Minor)* [1984] 1 All ER 289, 290, HL.

[16] Wardship is quite frequently referred to by the courts as a 'parental jurisdiction'.

[17] In *Re R (A Minor) (Wardship: Medical Treatment)* [1992] Fam 11, 24, [1991] 4 All ER 177, 186, CA. See also *Re J (A Minor) (Inherent Jurisdiction: Consent to Treatment)* (1992) Times, 15 July, CA. For a discussion of the court's powers over its wards, see post, pp 470 et seq.

[18] Ie pursuant to s 1(1) of the Children Act 1989, discussed further post, p 476.

[19] Ie the control begins as soon as the originating summons has been issued and without any specific court order. It ends when the wardship ends. Whether such immediate and automatic wide ranging protection can be justified has been questioned by the Law Commission: Law Com Working Paper No 101, paras 4.3 and 4.13.

[20] In *Re S (Infants)* [1967] 1 All ER 202, 209.

[1] See post, p 463.

[2] For a detailed discussion see Lowe and White, op cit, ch 5.

[3] See now the Marriage Act 1949, s 3(6).

could travel outside England and Wales. However, under the Family Law Act 1986, section 38, the automatic[4] embargo no longer prevents the child's removal to another part of the United Kingdom in which divorce or other matrimonial proceedings (in respect of the ward's parents) are continuing or in which the child is habitually resident.

Other 'steps' requiring prior court consent include:

Change of status: leave is necessary to commence proceedings to adopt a ward[5] and to 'free him for adoption'.[6]

Change of care-giver: the moving of a ward to new care-givers is likely to be regarded as an important step requiring court sanction.[7] An application for the compulsory admission to hospital of a mentally ill ward requires leave.[8] On the other hand there is no necessity to obtain leave to apply for an emergency protection order though the court should be informed as soon as possible.[9]

Change of whereabouts: any change of the ward's whereabouts must be notified to the court.[10]

Education: the notice of wardship issued with the originating summons states that there should be no 'material change in the arrangements' for the education of the ward without court leave.[11]

Medical matters: leave is *not* required for physical examinations, though it is required for psychiatric or psychological examinations.[12] Save in 'life or death' emergencies[13] any major medical treatment requires leave, for example, abortion,[14] sterilisation[15] and, possibly, any operation requiring a general anaesthetic.[16]

Blood tests with a view to establishing paternity: these probably require leave.[17]

---

[4] But the court can still make a specific order prohibiting the ward's removal from England and Wales.

[5] *F v S (Adoption: Ward)* [1973] Fam 203, [1973] 1 All ER 722, CA, and *Re F (Wardship: Adoption)* [1984] FLR 60, CA. Application can be made ex parte to a district judge: Family Proceedings Rules 1991, r 5.4(1)(a).

[6] *Practice Direction* [1985] 2 All ER 832. Application can be made ex parte to a district judge: Family Proceedings Rules 1991, r 5.4(1)(b).

[7] Cf *Re CB (A Minor) (Wardship: Local Authority)* [1981] 1 All ER 16, 24, CA per Ormrod LJ.

[8] Mental Health Act 1983, s 33.

[9] Cf *Re B (Wardship: Place of Safety Order)* (1979) 2 FLR 307.

[10] Family Proceedings Rules 1991, r 5.1(9). If this is a simple change of residence it is sufficient to inform the Registry.

[11] It has been suggested (see Clarke Hall and Morrison, op cit, para 1[655]) that taking steps to make a ward subject to a statement under the Education Act 1981 for the purposes of special education requires court leave.

[12] *Practice Direction* [1985] 3 All ER 576.

[13] Where the general practice is to operate regardless of consent, see ante, pp 305–306.

[14] *Re G-U (A Minor) (Wardship)* [1984] FLR 811.

[15] According to Lord Templeman in *Re B (A Minor) (Wardship: Sterilisation)* [1988] AC 199, 205, [1987] 2 All ER 206, 214, sterilisation of any girl under the age of 18 requires the sanction of the High Court in wardship proceedings. Sed quaere? Cf *Re E (A Minor) (Medical Treatment)* [1991] 2 FLR 585 in which it was held the court's consent was not required to perform an operation for therapeutic purposes even though a side effect is to sterilise the child.

[16] See Lowe and White, op cit, at para 5–22.

[17] See Lowe and White, op cit, at para 5–24. Cf *Re J (A Minor) (Wardship)* [1988] 1 FLR 65 where a mother of a ward of court was ordered to stay within the jurisdiction until a blood sample could be obtained from her.

Publicity: warding a child does not in itself impose a complete ban on publicity[18] but because court proceedings are confidential (unless judgment is given in open court) it is a contempt to publish any information relating to those proceedings.[19]

Involvement in criminal proceedings: leave is not required to call a ward as a witness in criminal proceedings, but it is required to interview a ward on behalf of a defendant in a criminal trial.[20] Similarly leave is not required for the police to interview a child who has been arrested merely because he happens to be a ward.[1] On the other hand the Crown Prosecution Service must obtain the court's consent before administering a caution to a ward.[2] Leave is also required to apply on a ward's behalf for compensation from the Criminal Injuries Compensation Board.[3]

(b) The special nature of the jurisdiction

Because legal control of the child vests in the court, wardship proceedings have always been regarded as special. For example, Viscount Haldane LC described[4] wardship as a 'parental and administrative' jurisdiction in which 'the disposal of controverted questions' was only an incidental function. In *Re B (JA) (An Infant)*[5] Cross J said:

> 'Wardship proceedings are not like ordinary civil proceedings. There is no "lis" between the parties. The plaintiffs are not asserting any rights; they are committing their child to the protection of the court and asking the court to make such order as it thinks is for the [ward's] benefit.'

In *Re E (SA) (A Minor) (Wardship)*[6] Lord Scarman commented that when exercising its wardship jurisdiction a court:

> '... must never lose sight of a fundamental feature of the jurisdiction, namely, that it is exercising a wardship, not an adversarial, jurisdiction. Its duty is not limited to the dispute between the parties: on the contrary, its duty is to act in the way best suited in its judgment to serve the true interest and welfare of the

---

[18] *Re L (A Minor: Freedom of Publication)* [1988] 1 All ER 418 and *Re W (Minors) (Wardship: Contempt)* [1989] 1 FLR 246.

[19] Administration of Justice Act 1960, s 12. The embargo covers not simply the actual proceedings but also any documents, for example, the Official Solicitor's report prepared for the case, see *Re F (Otherwise A) (A Minor)* [1977] Fam 58, [1977] 1 All ER 114, CA. This embargo extends to showing papers to an independent social worker, see *Practice Direction* [1983] 1 All ER 1097, and *Re C (Wardship: Independent Social Worker)* [1985] FLR 56; to medical officers: *Practice Direction* [1987] 3 All ER 640; to prospective adopters and their legal advisers: *Practice Direction* [1989] 1 All ER 169; and to using them in other proceedings; cf *Re R (MJ) (A Minor) (Publication of Transcript)* [1975] Fam 89, [1975] 2 All ER 749, CA; *Re J (A Minor) (Wardship)* [1984] FLR 535 and *Re S (Minors)* [1987] Fam 199, [1987] 3 All ER 1076.

[20] *Re R (Minors) (Wardship: Criminal Proceedings)* [1991] Fam 56, [1991] 2 All ER 193, CA.

[1] *Re R, Re G (Minors)* [1990] 2 All ER 633, though those having care and control should inform the wardship court at the earliest opportunity. See also *Re K (Minors) (Wardship: Criminal Proceedings)* [1988] Fam 1, [1988] 1 All ER 214.

[2] *Re A (A Minor) (Wardship: Police Caution)* [1989] Fam 103, sub nom *Re A (A Minor) (Wardship: Criminal Proceedings)* [1989] 3 All ER 610.

[3] *Practice Direction* [1988] 1 All ER 182, and *Re G (A Minor) (Ward: Criminal Injuries Compensation)* [1990] 3 All ER 102, CA.

[4] In *Scott v Scott* [1913] AC 417, 437, HL.

[5] [1965] Ch 1112, 1117.

[6] [1984] 1 All ER 289, 290, HL.

ward. In exercising wardship jurisdiction, the court is a true family court. Its paramount concern is the welfare of its ward.'

Though undoubtedly distinctive, wardship shares many of its characteristics with other child law jurisdictions. Indeed the trend has been to vest in all courts powers and procedure that were formerly unique to wardship.[7] For example, in all family proceedings hearsay evidence is admissible[8] and the court can make section 8 orders whether or not they have been applied for.[9] The paramountcy principle of course applies in all proceedings concerning a child's upbringing and, fostered by the Children Act, there has been a general move away from an adversarial approach in all children cases. Even so the peculiarity of the wardship jurisdiction cannot be ignored and indeed lies at the heart of the question[10] whether there is any difference between the court's powers in wardship and those under the general inherent jurisdiction outside wardship.

Another feature of the jurisdiction is that it is largely non-statutory. The general absence of such control has meant that wardship has been able to develop and adapt to changing conditions and values, the essential concern being to do what is best for its wards. The lack of formal restraint has resulted in the court having the widest (though not unlimited)[11] powers to protect its wards. Further, there are no statutory restrictions on who can invoke the jurisdiction.[12]

(c) Enforceability of orders and protection by contempt

As in any other court proceedings, orders and undertakings are enforceable on pain of contempt. In wardship, however, the court can also call upon the services of the Tipstaff[13] to enforce its orders.[14] For example, he can be directed to take the ward into his custody and deliver him to the person named in the order.[15]

In addition to the enforcement of court orders the contempt sanction can also be invoked in respect of the impairment of the court's special protective jurisdiction over its wards.[16]

[7] Indeed this is one of the underlying policies of the Children Act 1989: see Law Com No 172 *Custody and Guardianship* (1988) para 1–4.

[8] See the Children (Admissibility of Hearsay Evidence) Order 1991. In wardship hearsay evidence has always been admissible: *Re W (Minors) (Wardship: Evidence)* [1990] 1 FLR 203, CA. See now art 2 of the 1991 Order.

[9] Children Act 1989, s 10(1)(b), discussed ante, p 365. Cf *Re E (SA)*, supra.

[10] Discussed further post, p 480.

[11] See post, p 473.

[12] See below. Cf the Children Act 1989, s 10 under which leave is required, discussed ante, p 359.

[13] The Tipstaff is an officer attached to the Supreme Court.

[14] Pursuant to the Family Proceedings Rules 1991, r 5.2.

[15] See *G v L* [1891] 3 Ch 126. For other examples see Lowe and White, op cit, at para 6–65. This power is probably unique to wardship: see Law Com No 138, Scot Law Com No 91, 1985, para 6.36. However under the Family Law Act 1986, s 34 (discussed ante, p 370) any court making a 'Part I order' (ie any section 8 order, other than a variation or discharge or an order under the inherent jurisdiction giving care or providing for contact with or education of a child) 'can authorise an officer of the court or a constable to take charge of the child and deliver him to the person concerned'.

[16] As Cross LJ said in *Re B(JA) (An Infant)* [1965] Ch 1112 at 1117: 'Any action which tends to hamper the court in carrying out its duty [in protecting its ward] is an interference with the administration of justice and a criminal contempt of court'. For further details, see Lowe and White, op cit, ch 8.

2. WHO CAN BE WARDED[17]

(a) Child must be a minor

Only minors, that is persons under the age of 18,[18] may be warded. There is some doubt whether a married minor can be warded.[19] Although formerly a matter of speculation[1] it is now settled that a foetus cannot be made a ward of court.[2]

(b) The child must be subject to the jurisdiction

Under the inherent jurisdiction any minor who can be said to owe allegiance to the Crown may be warded.[3] In theory this means that any minor who is a British subject may be warded, regardless of his place of birth, domicile or residence.[4] However, as the Law Commissions have pointed out[5] there appears to be no reported case in which jurisdiction to ward has been based on the allegiance of a child who is neither present nor resident in England and Wales.

There is also jurisdiction to ward an alien minor who is physically present in England and Wales. This is because even aliens owe temporary allegiance whilst present in the jurisdiction.[6] In *Re P (GE) (An Infant)*[7] the Court of Appeal further held that there is jurisdiction to ward an alien child[8] who though not physically present is ordinarily resident in England and Wales at the time of the application. In that case the child had been taken to Israel by the father, during a contact visit, without the mother's consent or knowledge. It was held that in the circumstances the child remained ordinarily resident in England and that therefore there was jurisdiction.

[17] See generally Lowe *Who can be made a ward of court?* (1989) 1 Journal of Child Law 6.
[18] Family Law Reform Act 1969, s 1.
[19] *Re Elwes (No 2)* (1958) Times, 30 July, suggests there is jurisdiction, whereas cases on guardianship, eg *Mendes v Mendes* (1747) 1 Ves Sen 89, 91 per Lord Hardwicke LC, *R v Wilmington* (1822) 5 B & Ald 525, 526 per Abbot CJ and *Hewer v Bryant* [1973] 1 QB 357, 373 per Sachs LJ, suggest there is not. See Lowe and White, op cit, at paras 2.1 and 2.2.
[1] See eg Phillips (1979) 95 LQR 332 and Lyon and Bennett (1979) 9 Fam Law 35, 36 who argued that despite an apparent ruling to the contrary in *Paton v Trustee of British Pregnancy Advisory Service* [1979] QB 276, [1978] 2 All ER 987, per Sir George Baker P it was possible. Cf Lowe (1980) 96 LQR 29 and (1980) 131 NLJ 561.
[2] *Re F (In Utero)* [1988] Fam 122, [1988] 2 All ER 193, CA, Fortin *Legal Protection of the Unborn Child* (1988) 51 MLR 54 and Grubb and Pearl (1987) 103 LQR 340.
[3] See *Re P (GE) (An Infant)* [1965] Ch 568, 587 per Pearson LJ.
[4] See *Harben v Harben* [1957] 1 All ER 379, 381 per Sachs LJ.
[5] Law Com No 138, Scot Law Com No 91, 1985, at para 2.9. See further Lowe and White, op cit, at para 2.6, 7.
[6] See *Hope v Hope* (1854) 4 De G M & G 328, 346 per Lord Cranworth LC. For an extreme example see *Re C (An Infant) (1956) Times, 14 December*, child temporarily in England whilst en route from USA to USSR. See also *Johnstone v Beattie* (1843) 10 Cl & Fin 42 and *Re D (An Infant)* [1943] Ch 305, [1943] 2 All ER 411.
[7] [1965] Ch 568, [1964] 3 All ER 977. The decision has been followed in Canada, see eg *Nielson v Nielson* (1970) 16 DLR (3d) 321 and *Re Chester* (1975) 62 DLR (3d) 367 and in New Zealand, see *Scheffer v Scheffer* [1967] NZLR 466, but not in Scotland, see *Oludimu v Oludimu* 1967 SLT 105.
[8] The child was in fact stateless but it is submitted that this was not germane to the decision, see Lowe and White, op cit at para 2.11. However, Russell LJ, at 587, seemed prepared to extend jurisdiction to the case of a stateless person travelling abroad on a British travel document or a fortiori an alien holding a British passport. Quaere if this would now be accepted?

As an exception to the above rules it has been held that there is no jurisdiction to ward a child who is a member of the household of a parent entitled to diplomatic immunity.[9] It has also been doubted whether there is jurisdiction to ward an alien minor still present in the jurisdiction but who has been refused entry by immigration officials.[10]

(i) Limitations imposed by the Family Law Act 1986

Jurisdiction in wardship to make orders giving care of a child to any person or providing for contact with, or the education of, a child ('a section 1(1)(d) order')[11] is governed by sections 2(3) and 3 of the Family Law Act 1986. By these provisions jurisdiction is generally confined to those cases where, at the relevant date,[12] the child is either habitually resident in England and Wales or is present here and not habitually resident in another part of the United Kingdom or Isle of Man.[13] However, jurisdiction on either of the foregoing bases is normally excluded if, at the relevant date,[14] divorce, nullity or judicial separation proceedings are continuing[15] in another part of the United Kingdom or the Isle of Man. The latter rule does not apply where the High Court considers 'that the immediate exercise of its powers is necessary for [the child's] protection, in which case the child's physical presence will suffice'.[16] The initial burden of proof lies upon the person who invokes the jurisdiction to satisfy the court that it has jurisdiction. It has been held, however, that once it has been established[17] that the child's habitual residence[18] was in this country immediately before his departure, the burden of proof shifts to the other side to establish that the child was no longer habitually resident here at the time of application.

The intention of these provisions is principally to prevent conflicts of

---

[9] *Re C (An Infant)* [1959] Ch 363—discussed in detail in Lowe and White, op cit, at para 2.12 et seq.

[10] By Cross J in *Re Mohammed Arif (An Infant), Re Nirbhai Singh (An Infant)* [1968] Ch 643, but on appeal the point was left open. Nevertheless, wardship cannot in practice be used to challenge immigration decisions, see post, p 474, n 20.

[11] But excluding an order varying or revoking such an order: Family Law Act 1986, s 1(1)(d) as amended by the Children Act 1989, Sch 13, para 63(b).

[12] Ie where an application is made for a 's 1(1)(d) order', the date of the application or, where no such application has been made, the date of the order: s 3(6). This prevents the court having jurisdiction merely because the child has been warded in the past: see Law Com No 138, Scot Law Com No 91, para 4.28.

[13] Ss 2(3)(a) and 3(1).

[14] See n 12, above.

[15] Proceedings are treated as 'continuing' from the issue of the petition until (unless the proceedings have been dismissed) the child reaches 18 in Northern Ireland and the Isle of Man, or 16 in Scotland: s 42(2), as amended by the Family Law Act 1986 (Dependent Territories) Order 1991, s 42(3).

[16] S 2(3)(b), as amended by the Children Act 1989, Sch 13, para 64. Precisely what will trigger this 'emergency jurisdiction' is a matter of some doubt: see further Lowe and White, op cit, para 2-26.

[17] *Re E (A Minor)* (1991) unreported, CA.

[18] The meaning of which was explained in *F v S (Wardship: Jurisdiction)* [1991] 2 FLR 349. See also the discussion, post, p 489, on the meaning of 'habitual residence' for the purposes of the Hague Convention on International Child Abduction.

jurisdiction arising within the United Kingdom or the Isle of Man.[19] The Act nevertheless applies even where there is no potential conflict with another domestic court. As a result, it is no longer possible to make a 's 1(1)(d) order' in respect of a British subject who is neither present nor habitually resident in the jurisdiction.

Although in most cases an order within the meaning of section 1(1)(d) will be sought this will not always be so and in such cases the inherent basis of jurisdiction will be relevant. In *F v S (Wardship: Jurisdiction)*,[20] for example, Ward J held that the absence of jurisdiction under the 1986 Act did not preclude him from having jurisdiction to make an order requiring disclosure of the child's whereabouts. He refused, however, to order a parent to produce the child since that would have enabled the court then to have taken jurisdiction under section 2(3)(b) if that was necessary for the child's protection. As he pointed out,[1] such an order would have provided 'a devious entry to the court by the back door where Parliament have so firmly shut the front door to [section 1(1)(d)] orders being made'. In other words courts should not assume jurisdiction to make disguised section 1(1)(d) orders other than on the basis provided by the Family Law Act 1986.

(ii) Limitations imposed by the Child Abduction and Custody Act 1985

If an application has been made in an English court under the Hague or European Convention on international child abduction[2] for the return of a child the court is prevented from making orders in wardship.[3]

(c) The discretion to exercise jurisdiction

In cases where the court has jurisdiction it is nevertheless not bound to exercise it. The court generally refuses to exercise jurisdiction to review the exercise of discretionary powers vested in other bodies or tribunals such as local authorities[4] or the immigration service[5] or to interfere with the normal operation of criminal proceedings[6] or military law.[7] The court is naturally reluctant to exercise jurisdiction where the child's presence is merely a fleeting one, and in cases where the child has been abducted into this country it is established, in cases not governed by the abduction Conventions (see chapter 15), that the court must decide whether it is in the child's best interests to be returned immediately or to have the full merits of the case

---

[19] To this end it should be noted that under s 41 a child under the age of 16 who is habitually resident in one part of the UK or Isle of Man but who has been removed without the agreement of all persons having the right to determine where he should reside or in contravention of a court order, will be deemed to continue to be habitually resident in that part of the UK or the Isle of Man from where he was taken.

[20] [1991] 2 FLR 349.

[1] Ibid at p 356.

[2] These conventions are discussed in ch 15.

[3] The Child Abduction and Custody Act 1985, ss 9, 20, 27 and Sch 3.

[4] *A v Liverpool City Council* [1982] AC 363, [1981] 2 All ER 385, HL, discussed post, p 545.

[5] *Re Mohammed Arif (An Infant), Re Nirbhai Singh (An Infant)* [1968] Ch 643, [1968] 2 All ER 145, CA and *Re F (A Minor) (Immigration: Wardship)* [1990] Fam 125, [1989] 1 All ER 1155, CA. See further post, p 474, n 20.

[6] *Re K (A Minor) (Wardship: Criminal Proceedings)* [1988] Fam 1, [1987] 1 All ER 214.

[7] *Re JS (A Minor) (Wardship: Boy Soldier)* [1990] Fam 182, [1990] 2 All ER 861.

heard by the English court.[8] The court has a statutory power[9] to refuse to make orders or to stay proceedings if the matter has or is being dealt with in proceedings outside the United Kingdom.

3. PROCEDURE

(a) How to make a child a ward of court

Procedure for making a child a ward of court is now[10] governed by the Supreme Court Act 1981. Under section 41(1) no minor can be made a ward of court except by an order to that effect made by the High Court. Under section 41(2), however, a child (other than a child who is subject to a care order)[11] becomes a ward immediately an application for wardship is made (that is as soon as the originating summons is issued),[12] but he ceases to be one unless an application for an appointment to hear the summons has been made within 21 days.[13] A child does not otherwise cease to be a ward until either the court makes a specific order to that effect or until the child attains his majority.

Although a child does not become a ward until a summons is issued, in an emergency the court may make an order upon the applicant's undertaking to start proceedings at the earliest opportunity.[14] In the past this step has been taken to counter a threat to take a child out of the jurisdiction.

(b) The parties to the proceedings

Before the Children Act 1989 it was a unique feature of wardship that anyone with a sufficient interest in the child could seek to ward him. Indeed until 1967 there were no rules governing who could apply to ward a child. However, following *Re Dunhill*[15] where a night club owner warded one of his striptease artists purely for publicity purposes, certain rules were introduced.[16] Applicants must now[17] provide in the summons a brief description of their interest in, or relationship to, the minor and the particulars are then sent for recording in the register of wards.[18] If it appears that the application is an abuse of process, the summons may be dismissed. It is established, however, that any person having a proper interest may make a child a ward. In *Re D (A Minor) (Wardship: Sterilisation)*,[19] for example,

---

[8] *Re F (Minor: Abduction: Jurisdiction)* [1991] Fam 25, [1990] 3 All ER 97, CA, discussed post, p 487.
[9] Under the Family Law Act 1986, s 6. See *Re H (Minors)* (1992) Times, 5 March.
[10] For the former position, see Lowe and White, op cit, para 4.1.
[11] Supreme Court Act 1981, s 41(2A), added by the Children Act 1989, Sch 13, para 45(2).
[12] An originating summons may be issued by the Principal Registry or a district registry.
[13] Family Proceedings Rules 1991, r 5.3(1)(a).
[14] *Re N (Infants)* [1967] Ch 512. See also *L v L* [1969] P 25, [1969] 1 All ER 852. Insofar as *Re E (An Infant)* [1956] Ch 23, [1955] 3 All ER 174, indicates a contrary view, it is submitted that it is not good law. It is a contempt not to honour the undertaking to issue the summons; *Refson v Saggers* [1984] 3 All ER 111, CA.
[15] (1967) 111 Sol Jo 113—the summons was struck out as an abuse of process.
[16] By *Practice Direction* [1967] 1 All ER 828.
[17] Family Proceedings Rules 1991, r 5.1(6).
[18] Family Proceedings Rules 1991, r 5.1(4).
[19] [1976] Fam 185, [1976] 1 All ER 326. See also a case referred to in The Times on 21 May 1985 where the Brook Advisory Centre warded a child to authorise an abortion.

an educational psychologist attached to a local authority warded a child to prevent her being sterilised. It is also not unknown for a child himself to initiate proceedings.[20] It has been held[1] that the High Court has an inherent power to make a child a ward of court. On the other hand it appears that the Official Solicitor cannot ward on his own initiative[2] nor can a guardian ad litem *qua* guardian.[3] Formerly, local authorities could ward children but their ability to do so, at any rate where there is a care order, has effectively been ended by section 100 of the Children Act 1989.[4]

The rules are equally flexible as to who can be made defendants. Primarily the person against whom the order is sought is made the defendant but any other interested party can apply to be made a party.[5] Surprisingly, perhaps, the child is not automatically a party but is made one only in cases where it is thought appropriate.[6]

(c) Safeguarding the child's interests

As in other proceedings the court can call upon the court welfare service to provide a report upon the child's background.[7] A ward may, however, be ordered to be separately represented, in which case the Official Solicitor[8] will normally be appointed as guardian ad litem.[9]

Although not unique to wardship the services of the Official Solicitor are an important feature of the jurisdiction.[10] Unlike welfare officers, he represents the ward's interests, his main function being to give the child a voice in the proceedings. In the course of discharging that function he will make exhaustive inquiries with a view to preparing a detailed report on the child's position. Although neither the Official Solicitor nor any of his staff are trained social workers, the Office has acquired considerable skill in interviewing parties and over the years has become closely involved in the

---

[20] See Lowe and White, op cit, para 3.4. The ability of children now to seek leave to apply for a section 8 order, discussed ante, p 359, is however likely to assume more importance particularly as there is no necessity to be represented by a next friend.

[1] *R v North Yorkshire County Council, ex p M (No 3)* [1989] 2 FLR 82 per Ewbank J. See also the Mental Health Act 1983, s 96(1)(i).

[2] *Re D (A Minor) (Wardship: Sterilisation)*, supra, but see Lowe and White, op cit, at para 9.5.

[3] *Re T (Minors) (Wardship: Jurisdiction)* [1990] Fam 1, [1989] 1 All ER 297, CA, and *A v Berkshire County Council* [1989] 1 FLR 273, CA.

[4] Discussed post, p 478.

[5] In an application to restrain an undesirable relationship, discussed post, p 472, the person alleged to be undesirable should *not* be made a party; *Practice Direction* [1983] 2 All ER 672.

[6] See Family Proceedings Rules 1991, r 5.1(3), and *Practice Direction* [1982] 1 All ER 319, discussed below.

[7] For the welfare officer's role in wardship, see Lowe and White, op cit, ch 10.

[8] The Official Solicitor, who must be a solicitor of at least 10 years' standing, is appointed by the Lord Chancellor. His office is situated in London.

[9] The procedure is to name the child as a party and invite the Official Solicitor to act: *Re D (A Minor) (Wardship: Sterilisation)*, supra, at 197 per Heilbron J. It is established that the Official Solicitor should normally be the first person to be asked to represent the ward, *Re C (A Minor) (Wardship: Guardian Ad Litem)* [1984] FLR 419, CA; *Re ABCD (Minors) (Wardship: Guardian Ad Litem)* [1988] 2 FLR 500, and *Re JD (A Minor) (Wardship: Guardian Ad Litem)* [1984] FLR 359.

[10] For a general account of the Official Solicitor's role, see Evans (1966) 63 Law Soc Gaz 270–2, 335–7. For his role in wardship, see Turner (1977) Adoption and Fostering 30, Venables (1982) 3 Adoption and Fostering 45; Clarke Hall and Morrison, op cit, 1[822] et seq; and Lowe and White, op cit, ch 9.

welfare of wards.[11] His views and recommendations are treated with the greatest respect but of course they are not binding upon the court.

Valuable though the Official Solicitor's involvement in wardship is, his appointment is not to be regarded as a matter of routine. According to a *Practice Direction*[12] the joinder of the ward as a party and his representation by the Official Solicitor is only likely to be of assistance in exceptional circumstances. According to the present Official Solicitor[13] the cases where his appointment are commonly made are: where the child is old enough to express an independent view; the so-called 'teenage wardships', that is, where the parents are objecting to their child's association with some allegedly undesirable person; where the court requires some specific task, for example, a psychiatric examination of the ward or enquiry to be carried out; and those cases involving a difficult or novel point of law or some other difficulty, such as an international element.

4. COURT PROCEDURE

The initial appointment is heard by a district judge. He is empowered to make orders, principally, though not exclusively,[14] where they are agreed by the parties. He will determine what matters, if any, should be referred to the judge. District judges exercise considerable influence over the course of proceedings. They can, for example, be consulted over any matter arising during the wardship and can refer matters to the judge if there is resistance or delay.[15]

The main hearing is before the judge. Proceedings must initially be in the High Court although it is by no means uncommon for them to be before a deputy High Court judge appointed for the day.

Under the Matrimonial and Family Proceedings Act 1984, section 32(2)(b), wardship proceedings 'except applications for an order that a child be made, or cease to be, a ward of court' may be transferred to the county court. These provisions are intended to operate once the main issues have been decided.[16] According to a *Practice Direction*[17] unless the nature of the issues of fact or law make them more suitable for trial in the county court the following cases should not be transferred:

'... proceedings in relation to a ward of court; (i) in which the Official Solicitor is or becomes the guardian ad litem of the ward or of a party to the proceedings; (ii) in which a local authority is or becomes a party; (iii) in which an application

[11] As Ormrod LJ said in *Re G (A Minor) (Wardship: Costs)* [1982] 2 All ER 32 at 35 his assistance has enabled the court to solve many intractable welfare problems. For the various ways that he may become involved in wardship proceedings, see Lowe and White, op cit, at paras 9.4 et seq.
[12] [1982] 1 All ER 319.
[13] HDS Venables (1982) 3 Adoption and Fostering 45 at 46.
[14] Eg he can give leave for a ward's temporary removal from the jurisdiction unless it is opposed on the grounds that the child will not be returned: *Practice Direction* [1984] 2 All ER 407.
[15] See *Stockport Metropolitan Borough Council v B, Stockport Metropolitan Borough Council v L* [1986] 2 FLR 80, 82.
[16] See the Press Notice issued by the Lord Chancellor's Department, referred to by Clarke Hall and Morrison, op cit at 1[2704].
[17] [1992] 1 WLR 586.

for blood tests is made; (iv) in which an application is opposed on the grounds of want of jurisdiction; (v) in which there is a substantial foreign element; (vi) in which there is an opposed application for leave to take a child permanently out of the jurisdiction or where there is an application for temporary removal of a child from the jurisdiction and it is opposed on the ground that the child may not be duly returned; ...'

The above Direction leaves the court a discretion to transfer proceedings in any case though in respect of the matters outlined above it is clearly for the applicant to make out the case for such a transfer.

5. THE COURT'S POWERS

At the initial hearing the judge must first decide whether or not to continue the wardship. It is at this stage that issues of jurisdiction should be taken.[18] The wardship may be discharged if the court declines to exercise its jurisdiction, for example, because it considers the application spurious, because it declines to interfere with a decision of another body or tribunal or because it decides that wardship is of no further benefit to the child. In this last instance it has been held that the wardship should be discharged if there is no significant evidence on which to exercise the jurisdiction.[19]

Provided it is thought appropriate to exercise its jurisdiction the court has a wide range of powers at its disposal. Indeed before the Children Act 1989 it was its width of powers that made the jurisdiction especially attractive. However the 1989 Act, which implements a deliberate policy to reduce the need to invoke the jurisdiction,[20] both significantly narrows the wardship powers whilst at the same time expands the powers of other courts under other jurisdictions.[1]

(a) Section 8 orders

Since wardship proceedings rank as 'family proceedings'[2] the court is empowered to make section 8 orders under the Children Act 1989. Indeed the expectation is that the court will exercise section 8 powers in preference to its inherent powers wherever the two overlap.[3] Of course in considering whether or not to make a section 8 order the court will be bound not only to treat the ward's welfare as its paramount consideration, but pursuant to section 1(5), only make an order where it considers that making an order will be better for the child than making no order. In contested cases it will be bound to apply the statutory check-list.[4]

Although in the past it was thought to be inconsistent with the con-

---

[18] Particularly where the issue is one of discretion, see eg *Re D (A Minor)* (1978) 76 LGR 653.

[19] *Re F (Minors) (Wardship: Jurisdiction)* [1988] 2 FLR 123, CA. See also *Re Z (Minors) (Child Abuse: Evidence)* [1989] 2 FLR 3.

[20] Cf Law Commission Report No 172 on Guardianship and Custody at para 4.35.

[1] Principally by vesting in all courts in 'family proceedings' the power to make section 8 orders, see ante, p 364.

[2] Children Act 1989, s 8(3), discussed ante, p 364.

[3] See White, Carr and Lowe *A Guide to the Children Act 1989*, para 3.28.

[4] Ie the considerations listed in s 1(3) of the 1989 Act: s 1(4) discussed ante, p 339.

tinuation of wardship to make a custody order,[5] since a residence order only determines with whom the child is to live, it would seem to be consistent with the court's continuing control over its ward to make such an order.[6] In other words provided there is thought to be some benefit in continuing the wardship, the court can make a residence order and direct that the child continue to be a ward. In such cases the normal rules as to who has parental responsibility apply but anyone in whose favour a residence order is made will need to obtain the court's consent before taking any important steps in the ward's life.

The court's former wide powers to make access orders[7] are now accommodated by the power to make a section 8 contact order together with any directions or conditions under section 11(7).[8] Similarly, its powers to make orders about a ward's education or religious upbringing and many, though not all, of its powers to protect wards[9] can be made either as a prohibited steps or a specific issue order.

(b) Guardianship

It has been held to be inconsistent with the continuation of wardship for the court to appoint an individual to be a child's guardian.[10]

(c) Directing local authorities to investigate

The court's former powers both under statute and under the inherent jurisdiction to commit wards into local authority care and to make supervision orders have been respectively repealed and revoked.[11] Instead like any other court in family proceedings it can exercise its powers under section 37 of the Children Act 1989 and direct a local authority to undertake an investigation of the child's circumstances with a view to them considering whether or not to bring care proceedings. Pending this investigation the court has power under section 38 to make an interim care or supervision order.[12]

(d) Financial provision

The former powers to make maintenance orders for wards of court under section 6 of the Family Law Reform Act 1969 have been repealed.[13] Instead

---

[5] See *Re C B (A Minor) (Wardship: Local Authority)* [1981] 1 All ER 16, 24, CA, per Ormrod LJ discussed in the seventh edition of this work at p 429.

[6] See Clarke Hall and Morrison, op cit, para 1[694]. Cf *Re J (A Minor)* [1989] Fam 85, [1989] 3 All ER 590: court has power to determine ward's place of residence.

[7] See particularly *Re H (GJ) (An Infant)* [1966] 1 All ER 952, and *Re R(PM) (An Infant)* [1968] 1 All ER 691n. The power to deny contact must now be exercised as a prohibited steps order, see ante, p 354, but note the statutory power under the Children Act 1989, s 91(14), to provide that no further application be made without court leave; cf *Re N (Care and Control: Access)* (1982) 4 FLR 150, CA.

[8] Discussed ante, p 352.

[9] See further post, p 472.

[10] *Re C (Minors) (Wardship: Adoption)* [1989] 1 All ER 395, CA. However, there would be nothing to prevent the court from making a guardianship appointment and de-warding the child. The court's powers to appoint guardians are governed by s 5 of the Children Act 1989, discussed ante, pp 401 et seq.

[11] By the Children Act 1989, s 100(1) and (2), discussed further post, pp 478 and 481.

[12] See further post, p 525.

[13] By the Courts and Legal Services Act 1990, Sch 20.

statutory power[14] to make financial provision for wards of court is now governed by the Children Act 1989, Schedule 1, which is discussed in chapter 20.

(e) Property

The court has jurisdiction to resolve disputes over the ward's property. In the past wardship was very much concerned with administering property on the ward's behalf but the importance of this aspect of wardship has now declined. It nevertheless remains a useful jurisdiction both for administering a child's property and for resolving any disputes over it.

(f) Other powers to protect wards

Before the Children Act 1989 it was well established that the court had wide powers to protect its wards. For example, it could restrain the ward's marriage or his continued association with a named individual or group.[15] Third parties could be ordered not to communicate, harbour or even to attempt to discover the ward's whereabouts.[16] The court could also restrain the ward's removal from the jurisdiction, which power even extended to forbidding those who were not parties to assist the removal.[17] Conversely the court could sanction the ward's temporary or permanent removal from the jurisdiction. To the extent that these orders can be regarded as relating to aspects of parental responsibility they could now be made as prohibited steps orders though it remains to be seen whether such section 8 orders will be interpreted as giving quite such wide ranging powers. Other powers, such as the well established power to make specific restrictions on what may be published about a ward and his family,[18] which bind the world and not simply the parties,[19] do not relate to parental responsibility[20] and can only be made under the inherent power. Similarly, orders such as that made in *Re J (A Minor) (Wardship)*[1] preventing a mother leaving the jurisdiction before giving a blood sample can only be made under the inherent jurisdiction. There would also appear to be no section 8 power to make, as it

---

[14] It has been held that there is an inherent power to make financial provision: see eg *Calderdale Borough Council v H and P* [1991] 1 FLR 461 and *W v Avon County Council* (1979) 9 Fam Law 33 but see the criticism at [1991] Fam Law 220 and by Lowe and White, op cit, para 6.45.

[15] See eg *Re F (Otherwise A) (A Minor) (Publication of Information)* [1977] Fam 58, [1978] 3 All ER 274, CA, and *Iredell v Iredell* (1885) 1 TLR 260. Orders are usually made against the third party so as to avoid having to imprison the ward in the event of disobedience. For a case where a ward was imprisoned see *Re Crump (An Infant)* (1963) 107 Sol Jo 682.

[16] See eg *Re B (JA) (An Infant)* [1965] Ch 1112, [1965] 2 All ER 168; *Re R (PM)*, supra; and *Re B (A Minor) (Wardship: Child in Care)* [1975] Fam 36. In *Re JT (A Minor) (Wardship: Committal)* [1986] 2 FLR 107 the father was ordered not to attempt to remove his child from care.

[17] In *Re Harris (An Infant)* (1960) Times, 21 May, certain airlines were ordered not to carry a ward on any of their aircraft!

[18] See eg *Re M and N (Minors) (Wardship: Publication of Information)* [1990] Fam 211, [1990] 1 All ER 205, CA, *A v C* [1985] FLR 445, in which the court ordered that none of the parties should disclose to the child or anyone else the bizarre circumstances about the ward's birth, and *Re C (A Minor) (Wardship: Surrogacy)* [1985] FLR 846, in which the court ordered that there should be no publicity that might identify the 'commissioning parents'.

[19] *X County Council v A* [1985] 1 All ER 53.

[20] See ante, p 356.

[1] [1988] 1 FLR 65.

seems possible in wardship, non-molestation orders both in respect of the ward and those looking after him.[2] Even in wardship, however, there is some doubt as to whether there is power to make an ouster or exclusion order.[3]

The court has wide control over a ward's medical treatment. In *Re D (A Minor) (Wardship: Sterilisation)*,[4] for example, the court restrained the sterilisation of a ward even though her mother had consented to the operation. In *Re B (A Minor) (Wardship: Medical Treatment)*,[5] on the other hand, the court sanctioned, contrary to the parents' wishes, a life saving operation for a newly born mongol child. It has also been held[6] that as well as being able to override a parent's wishes it can also sanction medical treatment contrary to the wishes of a 'Gillick competent' child.

6. LIMITS OF THE COURT'S POWERS[7]

In broad terms the court's powers in wardship are limited to making orders that are of benefit to the ward.[8] Although there is some support for saying that there are no limits to the power to protect wards,[9] as Sir John Pennycuick said in *Re X (A Minor) (Wardship: Jurisdiction)*,[10] it is 'obvious that far-reaching limitations in principle on the exercise of this jurisdiction must exist'.

The courts themselves have been reluctant to define the legal limits of the jurisdiction, preferring instead to adopt the traditional English approach of simply resolving the particular issue before them. Nevertheless while the established limits have developed more as a result of practice rather than of strict legal restraint, there would appear to be some *de jure* as well as *de facto* limits. One accepted legal limit, for example, is that there is no

---

[2] See *Re V* (1979) 123 Sol Jo 201 and Lowe and White, op cit. There is no inherent power to attach a power of arrest, see *Re G (Wardship) (Jurisdiction: Power of Arrest)* (1983) 4 FLR 538, CA.

[3] Such an order was made in *Re V*, supra, but was refused in *Re D (Minors)* (1982) 13 Fam Law 111. It is a matter of speculation whether the child or applicant must have a proprietary interest in the property in question. Cf *Richards v Richards* [1984] AC 174, [1983] 1 All ER 1017, HL and *Ainsbury v Millington* [1986] 1 All ER 73, CA. But see *Wilde v Wilde* [1988] 2 FLR 83, CA. See further ante, pp 164–165.

[4] [1976] Fam 185, [1976] 1 All ER 326. Cf *Re B (A Minor) (Wardship: Sterilisation)* [1988] AC 199, [1987] 2 All ER 206, HL, where the sterilisation of a 17-year-old mentally incapable ward was sanctioned.

[5] [1990] 3 All ER 927, CA. See also *Re P (A Minor)* [1986] 1 FLR 272 and *Re B (Wardship: Abortion)* [1991] 2 FLR 426, where the court sanctioned an abortion in accordance respectively with a 15 and 12-year-old ward's wishes but contrary to those of the parents. In *Re C (A Minor) (Wardship: Medical Treatment)* [1990] Fam 26, [1989] 2 All ER 782, CA, the court directed that a terminally ill ward of court should receive treatment appropriate to her condition, that was to relieve her suffering rather than to prolong her life.

[6] *Re R (A Minor) (Wardship: Medical Treatment)* [1992] Fam 11, [1991] 4 All ER 177, CA, discussed ante, p 308. See also *Re J (A Minor) (Inherent Jurisdiction: Consent to Treatment)* (1992) Times, 15 July, CA, in which the court sanctioned treatment contrary to the wishes of a 16-year-old.

[7] See generally Lowe *The limits of the wardship jurisdiction, Part 2: The extent of the court's powers over a ward* (1989) 1 Journal of Child Law 44.

[8] See *Re V* (1979) 123 Sol Jo 201 where the court refused to hear a father's cross-application for an ouster order against his wife.

[9] See eg Wood J in *Re J (A Minor) (Wardship)* [1984] FLR 535, 539.

[10] [1975] Fam 47, 61, [1975] 1 All ER 697, 706, CA. See also *Re C (A Minor) (Wardship: Jurisdiction)* [1991] 2 FLR 168, 178 per Sir Stephen Brown P.

inherent power to make declarations of paternity.[11] Another is that there
is no inherent power to attach a power of arrest to a non-molestation
order.[12] It may be that both these decisions can best be explained by saying
that they are examples of the court's inability to make orders that are
unrelated, or at any rate only indirectly related, to the ward's interests.[13]
However, an alternative explanation of the latter decision is that there is
no inherent power to make orders that are purely statutory in origin.[14]

Another legal limit is that there is no inherent power to make orders that
are prohibited by statute. There is now, for example, no inherent power to
commit children into local authority care or to make supervision orders,
as this has been expressly revoked by section 100(2)(a) of the Children Act
1989.[15] As a general proposition, however, it would seem that the courts
should be slow to hold that an inherent power has been abrogated or
restricted by Parliament; they should only do so where it is clear that
Parliament so intended.[16] It was for this reason that in the past it has been
held that despite the statutory scheme dealing with children in local authority
care, the wardship jurisdiction had not thereby been ousted or abrogated
since the prerogative jurisdiction was neither expressly nor by necessary
implication so restricted.[17] Indeed in *theory*, it remains the case that the
court would exercise its inherent powers in respect of a child in care.[18]
However, it has become settled that as a matter of policy the court will not
interfere with the exercise of powers clearly vested in other bodies such as
local authorities[19] or the immigration service,[20] or in lower courts.[1] It is also
established that wardship cannot be used to interfere with the normal
criminal process[2] nor the normal operation of military law.[3]

[11] *Re JS (A Minor)* [1981] Fam 22, [1980] 1 All ER 1061, CA.
[12] *Re G (Wardship) (Jurisdiction: Power of Arrest)* (1982) 4 FLR 538.
[13] See the discussion by Lowe, op cit, at p 45.
[14] See Lowe, op cit, at p 46. It is a nice point whether the power to make maintenance orders
is a purely statutory power. Cf the Report of the Committee on the Age of Majority (the
Latey Committee) 1967 Cmnd 2342, para 250, which thought there was no inherent power
and *Calderdale Borough Council v H and P* [1991] 1 FLR 461 and *W v Avon County Council*
(1979) 9 Fam Law 33 in which it was held that there was an inherent power to make
maintenance orders.
[15] Discussed further post, pp 478 and 481.
[16] For a scholarly treatise on the whole topic of inherent powers see Jacob *The Inherent
Jurisdiction of the Court* (1970) 23 Current Legal Problems 23.
[17] See *Re M (An Infant)* [1961] Ch 328, 345, CA, per Lord Evershed MR and accepted by
the House of Lords in *A v Liverpool County Council* [1982] AC 363, [1981] 2 All ER 385,
HL. Cf *Re G (A Minor) (Witness Summons)* [1988] 2 FLR 396, (no power to set aside a
witness summons issued by the US authorities in connection with a Court Martial to be
held in England since, under the terms of the Visiting Forces Act 1952, the court martial
was a sovereign court vested with *exclusive* powers).
[18] See further post, p 482.
[19] See *A v Liverpool City Council*, supra, discussed post, p 545.
[20] See *Re Mohammed Arif (An Infant), Re Nirbhai Singh (An Infant)* [1968] Ch 643, [1968] 2
All ER 145, CA; *Re F (A Minor) (Immigration: Wardship)* [1990] Fam 125, [1989] 1 All
ER 1155, CA and *Re A (A Minor) (Wardship: Immigration)* [1992] 1 FLR 427, CA.
However, the wardship might be continued to safeguard the children where that would not
interfere with the immigration service's functions: *Re F*, supra and *Re K and S (Minors)
(Wardship: Immigration)* [1992] 1 FLR 432.
[1] See eg *Re A-H (Infants)* [1963] Ch 232; *Re S (Minors)* (1983) Times, 30 July, *Re K (KJS)
(An Infant)* [1966] 3 All ER 154; and *Re PJ (An Infant)* [1968] 1 WLR 1976.
[2] See eg *Re K (A Minor) (Wardship: Criminal Proceedings)* [1988] Fam 1, [1988] 1 All ER
214.
[3] See *Re JS (A Minor) (Wardship: Boy Soldier)* [1990] Fam 182, [1990] 2 All ER 861.

One issue that has exercised the court on a number of occasions is how far, if at all, the activities of those who are not in a family or personal relationship with the ward, can be restrained. This was first explored in *Re X*[4] in which the applicant warded his 14-year-old stepdaughter with a view to obtaining an injunction to restrain the publication of a book containing details about the ward's dead father's alleged sexual predilections. The stepfather maintained that the book's publication would be grossly damaging to his 'highly strung' stepdaughter. The application failed not because it was held that there was no such power but because in this instance it was felt that freedom of speech was more important than the ward's welfare, which was in any event only indirectly at risk. The implications of reaching a contrary decision would have been enormous since it would have meant that any activity that could be considered even indirectly harmful to a child might have been restrained by way of the wardship jurisdiction. Nevertheless *Re X* is not authority for saying that the independent activities of others can never be restrained to protect a ward or even that freedom of speech can never be curbed. Indeed in *X County Council v A*,[5] it was held that the press ought to be restrained from publishing details that could lead to the identity and whereabouts of the ward who was the child of a woman once convicted of manslaughter. In this latter case the restraint was on publicity directly referring to the ward and which would have been directly harmful. Subsequently restraining orders have been made, principally preventing identification of the children and their carers, it being established that to strike a proper balance between the welfare of children and freedom of speech injunctions ought to be no wider than necessary to protect the wards.[6] In *Re C (A Minor) (Wardship: Medical Treatment) (No 2)*[7] it was held that because publicity about the medical treatment of a terminally ill ward could affect the quality of care given to her, the court should issue an injunction prohibiting identification of the ward, the parents, the hospital at which she was being treated and the solicitor, notwithstanding that the ward herself was incapable of being affected by any publicity.[8]

Not all the cases seeking to control the activities of those unconnected with the ward have concerned publicity. In the extraordinary case of *Re C (A Minor) (Wardship: Jurisdiction)*[9] an independent day school run by a charity on orthodox Jewish principles admitted the son of Jewish parents on stringent conditions (including that the child should not live with his parents) but then indicated that the boy would be required to leave at the end of his first term. The local authority, concerned for the child's future, issued wardship proceedings seeking a mandatory injunction against the

---

[4] [1975] Fam 47, [1975] 1 All ER 697, CA.
[5] [1985] 1 All ER 53.
[6] See *Re M and N (Minors) (Wardship: Publication of Information)* [1990] Fam 211, [1990] 1 All ER 205, CA.
[7] [1990] Fam 39, [1989] 2 All ER 791, CA.
[8] Interestingly the injunction against identifying the parents was thought justified to protect the wardship jurisdiction since parents might refuse to make a child a ward of court if they thought that they might be identified and singled out for media attention. See also *Re X (Minors) (Wardship: Disclosure of Documents)* [1992] 2 All ER 595, in which Waite J refused to release wardship files for use in libel proceedings inter alia because the detrimental effect on the wardship jurisdiction would be substantial.
[9] [1991] 2 FLR 168, CA.

school requiring it to educate the boy. The Court of Appeal upheld the ruling that the order be refused. As Sir Stephen Brown P put it: 'If theoretically [the court] possesses such a power, I am clearly of the view that it is beyond the practical boundary of its wardship jurisdiction. This jurisdiction is not appropriate for use as an alternative to, or a cloak for, what appears, in fact, to be a claim for breach of contract by the parents against the school.'

What these cases in general and *Re C* in particular shows is that whilst the courts are reluctant to hold that there is no power to control the activities of those unconnected with a ward they will only exercise that power where it is essential to do so to protect the ward from direct harm.

7. THE PRINCIPLES UPON WHICH THE COURT ACTS

From time to time statements are made which suggest that the welfare of a ward is always the paramount consideration.[10] In the light of limits of the jurisdiction just adverted to, however, it is apparent that the individual ward's interests are not always thought to be overriding.[11] The best explanation for this seems to be that the paramountcy of the ward's welfare only applies when the court is called upon to exercise what used to be termed its custodial jurisdiction, and not where it is exercising a purely protective jurisdiction. In short the ward's welfare will only be the paramount consideration when section 1(1) of the Children Act 1989 applies, namely, where his upbringing or the administration of his property is directly in issue.[12]

Where the court is called upon to exercise a purely protective jurisdiction, that is where the issue falls outside the scope of section 1(1) of the 1989 Act and is not governed by other statutes, the ward's welfare is not accorded any specially weighted interest though it will remain an important consideration. Whether the court will protect a ward will depend on how seriously and how directly the child's interests may be harmed and how important any competing interests are. The operation of the protective jurisdiction is well illustrated by the contrasting decisions in *Re X* and *X County Council v A*.[13]

8. THE USE OF THE JURISDICTION

(a) The position before the Children Act 1989[14]

Before the Children Act 1989 the many and often unique characteristics of

---

[10] In *Re D (A Minor) (Justices' Decision: Review)* [1977] Fam 158, 163, Dunn J memorably referred to the 'golden thread' running through the wardship jurisdiction, namely, the welfare of the child 'which is considered in this court first, last and all the time'.

[11] See, for example, *Re M and N (Minors) (Wardship: Publication of Information)* [1990] Fam 211, 223, [1990] 1 All ER 205, 210, where Butler-Sloss LJ expressly said that in cases where restraint of publicity is sought 'the welfare of the ward is not the paramount consideration'.

[12] The scope of s 1(1) is discussed in ch 10.

[13] Discussed above at p 475.

[14] See generally Law Com Working Paper No 101 (1987) *Wards of Court*, Part III.

wardship proved useful to disparate applicants although the high costs[15] and lengthy delays in obtaining a court hearing militated against an even greater use. Nevertheless, as the following table[16] shows, there had been, particularly during the 1980s, a phenomenal rise in the number of wardships:

NO OF ORIGINATING SUMMONS

	Principal Registry	District Registries	Total
1951	74	Not applicable	74
1961	258	Not applicable	258
1971	622	Not applicable	622
1981	822	1081	1903
1985	965	1850	2815
1990	1146	3575	4721

The main reason for this growth was the use of wardship by local authorities, who for a variety of reasons, found it advantageous to use the prerogative jurisdiction rather than the statutory scheme to get children into care or to keep them there.[17] Local authority use of wardship increased considerably in the latter half of the 1980s accounting for between 32.5 per cent and 40 per cent of all applications in 1985, rising to 56 per cent in 1987 and 62 per cent in 1990.[18]

Another important use of wardship was by relatives who until 1985[19] had no other means of initiating court proceedings either to seek to look after the child or to have contact. In 1985 24 per cent of wardships involved relatives.[20]

Parents too used to look to wardship, particularly in relation to international child abduction where the immediacy of the prohibition against a ward's removal from the country together with the wide jurisdictional rules were an obvious advantage.[1] A more traditional use of the jurisdiction was the so-called 'teenage wardships', where parents warded their children to prevent their marriage to or continued association with someone was considered to be 'undesirable'.[2] Though occasionally useful, this declined

---

[15] The DHSS Child Care Review Costings Working Party (1986, para 5.21) estimated the average cost of an order confirming wardship to have been £5,960 in an uncontested case and £7,970 in a contested case.

[16] The 1951, 1961 and 1971 figures can be found in Cretney *Principles of Family Law* (1st Edn) p 289. The remaining statistics can be found in Judicial Statistics for each year.

[17] See Masson and Morton *The Use of Wardship by Local Authorities* (1989) 52 MLR 762 and Lowe *The Role of Wardship in Child Care Cases* [1989] Fam Law 38.

[18] Of 750 cases heard in 1985 by the Principal Registry analysed by the Law Commission, 32.5 per cent were found to be initiated by local authorities: Law Com Working Paper No 96 (1986) *Custody*, at para 5.38. The Costings Working Party, ibid, at 5.1, said that of 716 applications in the district registries in 1985, 40 per cent were found to involve local authorities: DHSS Review of Child Care Law Costings Working Party, 1986 para 5.12. The 1987 and 1990 proportions are given in the relevant Judicial Statistics. Curiously the 1990 figure is less than the 1989 when local authority use accounted for 66 per cent of the total.

[19] Ie until the implementation of the custodianship provisions; see ante, p 422.

[20] See Law Com Working Paper No 101 (1987) *Wardship* para 3.3. Grandparents were a particularly significant user of the jurisdiction: see Law Com Working Paper No 96 (1986) *Custody* para 5.38, n 92.

[1] See further ch 15.

[2] See Cross *Wards of Court* 83 LQR 200, 209 et seq; Turner *Wardship and the Official Solicitor* (1977) 2 Adoption and Fostering 30, 33 and Lowe and White, op cit, pp 12–1 et seq.

when the age of majority was reduced to 18, that use had declined long before implementation of the Children Act 1989.

In contrast to 'teenage wardships' was the use of wardship by children against their parents of which use there was some evidence.[3]

A further important role of wardship was its ability to handle novel cases, where the availability of High Court expertise, as well as the jurisdiction's wide powers, was clearly an advantage. A good example of this was in relation to determining the future of Britain's first and much publicised commercially arranged surrogate child.[4]

(b) The position after the Children Act 1989[5]

(i) Restrictions in public law cases

The major direct impact of the 1989 Act on the use of wardship is with respect to local authority use. The Act makes wardship and local authority care incompatible.[6] If a ward of court is committed to care the wardship ceases[7] and while a child is in care he cannot be made a ward of court.[8] Furthermore both the former statutory and inherent power to commit wards of court into local authority care and to make supervision orders have been respectively expressly repealed and revoked by section 100(1) and (2)(a).

As a result of the 1989 Act the use of wardship both by and against local authorities which, as we have seen, accounted for such a large proportion the cases, has been ended.

(ii) Private law cases

Although no express restraint is placed on the use of wardship by individuals by the 1989 Act, as the Department of Health's *Guidance and Regulations* puts it,[9] its impact will be considerable: 'By incorporating many of the beneficial aspects of wardship, such as the "open door" policy, and a flexible range of orders, the Act will substantially reduce the need to have recourse to the High Court.' Whether the advent of the 1989 Act will effectively end the use of wardship remains to be seen but there can be little doubt that applications will steeply decline.[10] Relatives, for example, will be generally better advised to seek, albeit with leave, section 8 orders in the lower courts, and in most cases it is difficult to see what advantages parents would gain from wardship, rather than pursuing remedies under the 1989 Act.

There remain, however, some distinctive features of the jurisdiction. One

---

[3] See the seventh edition of this work at p 434.

[4] *Re C (A Minor) (Wardship: Surrogacy)* [1985] FLR 846.

[5] See generally White, Carr and Lowe *A Guide to the Children Act 1989* ch 10 and Bainham *The Children Act 1989 The Future of Wardship* [1990] Fam Law 270.

[6] See the Department of Health's *Guidance and Regulations* on the Children Act 1989, Vol 1, Court Orders, para 3.99.

[7] Children Act 1989, s 91(4).

[8] Ibid, s 100(2)(c) and the Supreme Court Act 1981, s 41(2A), added by Sch 13, para 45(2), to the 1989 Act.

[9] Vol 1, Court Orders, para 3.98.

[10] Not least because legal aid is unlikely to be granted given, for the most part, the availability of adequate remedies in the lower courts.

remaining advantage is its immediacy: as soon as the originating summons is issued, the child becomes a ward and no important step may be taken without prior court sanction. The ability immediately to freeze the position might remain of some use, particularly in the context of child abduction.[11] It remains the case that the court's wardship powers are wider than those under section 8 and where advantage needs to be taken of this, it would be proper to ward. There will also be occasions where the court's overall control over a ward will be perceived as an advantage, for example, in the case of an abandoned child, where no-one looking after him has parental responsibility.[12] Finally, there will remain those extraordinary and novel cases in which wardship has proved uniquely useful.

Whether, even restrictively used, it is justified to retain wardship together with the generally comprehensive statutory scheme dealing with children, can be debated. However if wardships become unusual it seems unlikely that the Law Commission will consider it worthwhile to deliberate further about the jurisdiction's future.[13] In any event it is clearly for the benefit of children that there remains a residual jurisdiction to which recourse can be had when no other remedy is available. It would therefore seem prudent to retain the jurisdiction which, particularly in the recent past, has proved itself so able to safeguard and promote children's interests.

C. The inherent jurisdiction[14]

As we discussed at the beginning of this chapter, the Children Act 1989 is committed to the view that the High Court has an inherent jurisdiction to protect children quite apart from its wardship jurisdiction. It remains now to consider the scope of this general inherent jurisdiction though in the absence of developed practice the ensuing discussion is necessarily speculative.

1. JURISDICTION AND PROCEDURE

To invoke the inherent jurisdiction application must be made to the High Court.[15] Although no specific procedure is laid down by the Family Proceedings Rules 1991[16] in practice, like wardship, application is made by originating summons[17] with the plaintiff filing, unless otherwise directed, an affidavit in support of the application. Local authorities wishing to invoke the inherent jurisdiction must first obtain leave of the court.[18]

Jurisdiction to make orders giving the care of a child to any person or providing for contact, or the education of a child, is governed by the Family

[11] Though even here there is less need to obtain a court order: see ch 15.
[12] Discussed post, p 504.
[13] It technically remains under review.
[14] See generally Clarke Hall and Morrison, op cit, paras 1[732] et seq.
[15] Supreme Court Act 1981, Sch 1, para 3(b)(ii), as amended by the Children Act 1989, Sch 13, para 45(3).
[16] Part V specifically applies to wardship.
[17] A form has now been issued and is headed 'In the matter of the Supreme Court Act 1981'.
[18] Children Act 1989, s 100(3), discussed post, p 482.

Law Act 1986 and is co-extensive with the wardship jurisdiction.[19] It is assumed that jurisdiction to make orders outside the ambit of section 1(1)(d) is the same as in wardship.[20]

2. THE EFFECT OF INVOKING THE INHERENT JURISDICTION

Unlike wardship, the exercise of the inherent jurisdiction does *not* place the child under the ultimate responsibility of the court. This means that at no point will the child be subject to the rule obtaining in wardship that all important steps in the child's life have to be sanctioned by the court. This, at any rate, was the view of Lord Mackay LC who said, in his Joseph Jackson Memorial Lecture,[1] that under the scheme obtaining under the 1989 Act it was not thought 'appropriate or practicable for the responsibility for a child in the care of a public authority which is statutorily charged with looking after him to be subject to the detailed directions of another public authority, namely the courts.'

3. THE COURT'S POWERS

(a) The possible range and scope

Proceedings under the inherent jurisdiction rank as 'family proceedings' for the purposes of the Children Act 1989[2] so that in general terms the court is empowered either upon application or its own motion to make any section 8 order.[3] In practice, however, the major use of the jurisdiction is likely to be by local authorities in respect of children in their care.[4] In these cases, section 9(1) and (2) of the 1989 Act prevent the courts from making a section 8 order in a local authority's favour.[5] Recourse must therefore be had in these circumstances to the court's non-statutory powers. Precisely what powers these are remains a matter for speculation. At their widest the powers could be as extensive as those of wardship. This view could be justified on the basis that wardship is merely the machinery by which the court traditionally exercised its parens patriae powers to protect children but that it is not the only means by which these extensive powers could be exercised on behalf of the Crown.[6] Against this it could be argued that the wardship powers are wider because, unlike the inherent jurisdiction, ultimate responsibility for the child is vested in the court.[7] Furthermore it could be

---

[19] See ante, p 465.
[20] See Clarke Hall and Morrison, op cit, para 1[732]. For the position in wardship see ante, p 466.
[1] (1989) 139 NLJ 505 at 508.
[2] Children Act, s 8(3)(a).
[3] See ante, pp 365 et seq.
[4] See below.
[5] Discussed ante, p 358.
[6] A number of cases can be cited in support of this proposition, namely, *Re M and N (Wardship: Publication of Information)* [1990] Fam 211, [1990] 1 All ER 205, 210, CA per Butler Sloss LJ; *Re C (A Minor) (Wardship: Medical Treatment) (No 2)* [1990] Fam 39, 46, [1989] 2 All ER 791, 793, CA, per Lord Donaldson MR; *Re N (Infants)* [1967] Ch 512, [1967]; 1 All ER 161; and *Re L (An Infant)* [1968] P 119, [1967] 2 All ER 1110. Cf *Re E (An Infant)* [1956] Ch 23, [1955] 3 All ER 174.
[7] See Clarke Hall and Morrison, op cit, at para 1[734].

said that the inherent jurisdiction is co-extensive with that preserved by the Supreme Court Act 1981, section 37 which confers powers to grant injunctions only for the purposes of protecting legal or equitable rights.[8] *Re D (A Minor) (Adoption Order: Validity),*[9] in which the Court of Appeal held that it had no power under its inherent jurisdiction to impose an injunction restraining contact between an adopted child and his natural grandparents but did have such a power under its wardship jurisdiction, provides some support for a narrow application of the inherent jurisdiction.

However, in the first reported decision, *Re J (A Minor) (Inherent Jurisdiction: Consent to Treatment),*[10] on the application of the inherent jurisdiction since the Children Act 1989, it was held that the inherent powers are 'co-extensive with the powers traditionally exercised in wardship unless specifically limited'. In that case, the Court of Appeal specifically followed *Re R (A Minor) (Wardship: Medical Treatment)*[11] holding that under the inherent jurisdiction the court could sanction medical treatment of a 16 year old anorexic child contrary to her wishes.

(b) Express limitations

The Children Act 1989, section 100(2) expressly limits the exercise of the High Court's inherent jurisdiction by preventing (a) a child being placed in the care or put under the supervision of a local authority and (b) a child from being accommodated by or on behalf of a local authority. These embargoes are in line with the general policy of the Act to prevent the courts from making care or supervision orders other than under section 31.[12] Section 100(2)(d) also prevents the High Court from exercising its inherent jurisdiction:

'... for the purpose of conferring on any local authority power to determine any question which has arisen, or which may arise, in connection with any aspect of parental responsibility for the child.'

The none-too-clear result of this provision would appear to be that while the High Court may make orders under its inherent jurisdiction in respect of a child, in doing so, it may not confer on the local authority any degree of parental responsibility that it does not already have.[13] This is less likely to cause problems where the child is in care since the local authority will already be vested with parental responsibility.[14] Hence, the determination of a particular question by the court, for example, the sanctioning of specific medical treatment, will leave the local authority free to arrange for it to be carried out. Precisely how section 100(2)(d) operates upon a local authority's application in respect of a child who is not in their care and over whom they therefore have no responsibility remains to be seen.

---

[8] See *Richards v Richards* [1984] AC 174, [1983] 2 All ER 807, HL, discussed ante, p 169.
[9] [1991] Fam 137, [1991] 3 All ER 461, CA, discussed ante, p 448. The court did not exercise its wardship powers because the child was about to attain his majority. See also *Re C (A Minor) (Wardship: Jurisdiction)* [1991] 2 FLR 168, CA.
[10] (1992) Times, 15 July, CA.
[11] [1992] Fam 11, [1991] 4 All ER 177, CA, discussed ante, p 309.
[12] Discussed post, p 511.
[13] As it is expressed by the Department of Health's *Guidance and Regulations*, Vol 1, Court Orders, at para 3.102.
[14] See ante, p 328.

4. THE USE OF THE JURISDICTION

(a) By local authorities

The principal use of the inherent jurisdiction is expected to be by local authorities seeking to resolve specific questions about children being looked after by them. Indeed, if the child is subject to a care order, the inherent jurisdiction is the only means by which authorities can obtain further orders since, as we have seen, wardship has ceased to be an option and, because of the embargoes placed by section 9(1) and (2) of the 1989 Act, the court cannot make *any* section 8 order.

(i) The need to obtain leave

Before local authorities can invoke the inherent jurisdiction they must first obtain the court's leave.[15] The criteria for leave are set out in section 100(4) of the 1989 Act. Under section 100(4)(a) the court must be satisfied that the result sought to be achieved cannot be achieved under any statutory jurisdiction. This bar applies even where the statutory remedy is contingent upon the local authority having first to obtain leave before being able to seek an order.[16] This restriction will make it difficult for an authority to obtain leave for the exercise of the inherent jurisdiction in respect of a child not in their care, since in those circumstances they could seek to obtain a prohibited steps or specific issue order under section 8.[17] In these cases it will have to be shown that the remedy sought falls outside the scope of section 8. An order forbidding or restricting publicity or an order protecting an adult for the benefit of the child are examples that will satisfy this test.

Even if there is no alternative statutory remedy, under section 100(4)(b) the court must still be satisfied that: 'there is reasonable cause to believe that if the court's inherent jurisdiction is not exercised with respect to the child he is likely to suffer significant harm'. Although this provision is in line with the need to establish at least a likelihood of significant harm before the court is entitled to intervene to make a care or supervision order,[18] it may be questioned whether this ground for leave should be so narrow. It has been pointed out[19] that given that the local authority's objective cannot be the acquisition of parental responsibility, a less stringent test, such as the court having to be satisfied that the exercise of its inherent jurisdiction is necessary to secure the child's welfare, would not have upset the general philosophy of the 1989 Act and might have better served children's interests.

(ii) Circumstances in which the criteria for giving leave might be satisfied

It is not thought that local authorities will often be justified in having recourse to the inherent jurisdiction. Indeed the expectation is that, since they have parental responsibility, local authorities should make decisions themselves.[20] Nevertheless there will be occasions when recourse to the High

---

[15] Children Act 1989, s 100(3).
[16] Ibid, s 100(5)(b).
[17] See ante, p 355.
[18] Ie under s 31 of the 1989 Act, discussed post, p 511.
[19] By Eekelaar and Dingwall (1989) 139 NLJ 217. See also Lowe (1989) 139 NLJ 87.
[20] See the Department of Health's *Guidance and Regulations*, Vol 1, paras 3.100–3.101.

Court will be appropriate. In *Re J (A Minor)*,[1] for example, it was thought right to invoke the inherent jurisdiction to overcome a refusal of a 16 year old anorexic child in care to consent to medical treatment. Other examples might occur where irreversible medical treatment, such as abortion, sterilisation or life saving treatment is in issue.[2] As the Department of Health's *Guidance and Regulations*[3] say, these decisions are 'highly contentious and/or fall far outside the normal scope of decision-making for children in care'.

The above medical problems are extreme examples of situations when High Court intervention might be justified, but circumstances do not always have to be so extraordinary. For example, if a local authority wishes to obtain injunctions to prevent a violent father from discovering his child's whereabouts[4] or from molesting the child[5] or a social worker connected with the child,[6] or to restrain harmful publicity about the child,[7] then the inherent jurisdiction is the only means of obtaining the remedy and it should not be too difficult to satisfy the criteria for granting leave.

(b) By individuals

It is open to individuals to invoke the inherent jurisdiction but it is not expected that they will do so at all often. However one context where the remedy might be sought is in relation to challenging local authorities' decisions in relation to a child in their care. This issue will be discussed in chapter 16.

---

[1] (1992) Times, 15 July, CA.
[2] See the discussion in Clarke Hall and Morrison, op cit, at para 1[742].
[3] Vol 1, Court Orders, para 3.101.
[4] As in *Re JT (A Minor) (Wardship: Committal to Care)* [1986] 2 FLR 107.
[5] As in *Re B (A Minor) (Wardship: Child in Care)* [1975] Fam 36, [1974] 3 All ER 915.
[6] This is one example of the exercise of the inherent jurisdiction known to the authors.
[7] See eg *Re L (A Minor) (Wardship: Freedom of Speech)* [1988] 1 All ER 418 and other cases cited ante, p 472.

Chapter 15

International parental child abduction

A growing problem, particularly in the international context, is the removal of a child by one parent without the other's consent and often in breach of a court order.[1] Such removals are harrowing for the so-called 'innocent' parent and in any event are likely to put the child's welfare at risk. The problem becomes most acute where the child is taken out of the jurisdiction altogether since it then becomes much more difficult both to discover the child's whereabouts and to secure his return. It is estimated that four children a week are abducted and taken by their parents to another part of the United Kingdom and a further 200 a year are taken abroad.[2] Following legislative changes in the 1980s the chances both of foiling an attempted abduction and of recovering a child wrongfully taken have improved, but the resulting law is complex.

A. Preventing the child from being taken abroad

The best chance of recovering the child is to prevent him from leaving the jurisdiction in the first place. To this end the innocent party can invoke both the criminal and the civil law. Under the Child Abduction Act 1984[3] it is an offence even for a married parent to take his own child (under the age of 16) out of the United Kingdom without the requisite consents.[4] Although the principal object of the Act is to deter parents from abducting their children out of the country it also provides the means by which the innocent parents can seek to stop the abduction. Because it is an offence to *attempt* to take a child out of the United Kingdom, the police can arrest[5] anyone they reasonably suspect of attempting to take a child out of the country contrary to the provisions of the 1984 Act. Furthermore if the police decide to act they can, through their 'All Ports Warning System', effect a port stop whereby details of the child at risk of abduction are circulated by way of the police national computer broadcast facility to

---

[1] See generally *Clarke Hall & Morrison on Children*, paras 1 [932]–[1000]. See also Bevan *Child Law* (1989) 153–182, Cretney and Masson *Principles of Family Law* (5th Edn) 581–586, Lowe and White *Wards of Court* (2nd Edn) ch 17 and Sachs *Child Abduction* (1988). The court's attitude to abduction in the domestic context is discussed ante, p 389.

[2] See 130 Sol Jo 325. These are likely to be conservative estimates.

[3] Discussed at pp 309–310. Exceptionally the common law offences of child kidnapping or unlawful imprisonment might be relevant but these should not be prosecuted where the alleged offence is covered by the 1984 Act: *R v C (Kidnapping: Abduction)* [1991] 2 FLR 252, CA.

[4] An unmarried mother having sole parental responsibility does not require anyone's consent to remove the child but an unmarried father whether or not he has responsibility will need the mother's consent: Child Abduction Act 1984, s 1(3), discussed ante, p 310.

[5] Without a warrant, since it is an arrestable offence.

immigration officers at ports and airports throughout the country who will then assist the police in trying to prevent that child from leaving the country. As this is now[6] the only means of effecting a port alert any parent fearing that his child might be taken out of the country and wishing to take advantage of this facility must inform the police.[7] Before instituting a port alert the police must be convinced that the complaint is bona fide and the danger of removal real and imminent.[8] Although it is not necessary to have obtained a court order beforehand the existence of an order will be good evidence of the seriousness of the request for action from the police. Parties seeking police assistance should furnish as much information as possible inter alia about the child, the alleged abductor, the likely time of travel and the port of embarkation.[9]

Specific orders restraining a child's removal from the country can be obtained in civil proceedings. Principally this can be done by obtaining a prohibited steps order under section 8 of the Children Act 1989.[10] Such orders can restrain removal either from the United Kingdom as a whole or, in appropriate cases, England and Wales. As we have seen, an embargo against removal from the United Kingdom for any period in excess of one month is automatically included in any residence order.[11] Another means by which an embargo against the child's removal from the jurisdiction can be obtained is by making the child a ward of court.[12] The unique advantage of wardship is that the embargo automatically arises immediately the child is warded[13] and no other relief need be sought.

Apart from establishing the bona fides of a request to the police to activate a port alert, there are other advantages of invoking the civil process. First, a specific order prohibiting the child's removal can act as a deterrent in itself. Secondly, official assistance to trace the alleged abductor can be obtained.[14] Thirdly, if the order is broken the applicant can invoke the court's contempt powers[15] and can seek to enforce the order in other parts

---

[6] Formerly, there was a 'stop list' procedure operated by the Home Office which could only be activated if the child was a ward of court or if an injunction restraining the child's removal from the jurisdiction had been obtained.

[7] *Practice Direction (Child: Removal from Jurisdiction)* [1986] 1 All ER 983.

[8] Ie within 24–48 hours: *Practice Direction, supra.*

[9] *Practice Direction, supra.* If the police decide to use the port alert system, the child's name will remain on the stop list for four weeks. Quaere whether this is long enough.

[10] See, for example, *Re D (A Minor)* [1992] 1 All ER 892, CA. But even if a specific order is obtained, the port stop procedure must still be activated by the applicant.

[11] S 13(1)(b), (2) discussed ante, p 362. It might be noted however that such directions are not enforceable: *Re P (Minors) (Custody Order: Penal Notice)* [1990] 1 WLR 613, CA, discussed by Lowe in *Enforcing Orders Relating to Children* (1992) 4 Child Law 26.

[12] Wardship is discussed in ch 14.

[13] This *automatic* embargo (which at common law is enforceable irrespective of the defendant's knowledge of the wardship: *Re J (An Infant)* (1913) 108 LT 554 but cf *Re F (Otherwise A) (Publication of Information)* [1971] Fam 58, 88 per Lord Denning MR) normally prohibits the ward's removal from England and Wales without the court's leave. However, under the Family Law Act 1986, s 38, unless the court has directed otherwise, leave is not required to take the child to another part of the United Kingdom or the Isle of Man if divorce proceedings etc are continuing or if the child is habitually resident there. See also the discussion in [1992] Fam Law 94.

[14] Ie various government agencies will reveal the last known address of the alleged abductor: *Practice Direction* [1989] 1 All ER 765.

[15] These powers include committal to prison and sequestration (the freezing of the contemnor's assets) discussed ante, p 370. The latter remedy can be a useful lever against an abducting

of the United Kingdom[16] or in a country that is party to the European Convention on child abduction.[17] Fourthly, upon obtaining a prohibition against removal, steps can be taken to prevent the issue of a UK passport,[18] or if one has already been issued, to ask the court to order its surrender.[19]

Whatever means are used, speed is of the essence if an attempted abduction is to be foiled but even if all preventative measures have been taken in good time there is no guarantee that the child's removal will be stopped.

B. Dealing with abduction

Until the 1980s there was little international co-operation on parental child abduction and orders made in one jurisdiction were generally neither recognised nor enforceable in another. However, there are now two international conventions designed both to trace abducted children and to secure their return. In addition, under the Family Law Act 1986, certain orders relating to children made in one part of the United Kingdom or the Isle of Man can be enforced in another part of the United Kingdom or the Isle of Man. As a result of these developments there are different laws dealing with abduction depending on the country to or from which the child has been taken or brought.

1. CHILDREN TAKEN TO OR BROUGHT FROM A 'NON-CONVENTION COUNTRY' OUTSIDE THE UNITED KINGDOM

Once a child is removed outside the United Kingdom or the Isle of Man to a country that has implemented neither of the international conventions, the chances of recovering the child may be slim. Unless the abducting spouse returns voluntarily, the only legal means[20] is to institute appropriate civil proceedings in the country to which the child has been taken, if that is known, or, if the country in question has an extradition treaty with the United Kingdom, to try to have the abductor extradited for abduction and return the child.

---

parent who has left property in this country: see Lowe and White, op cit, paras 8–28 and 8–33 and note *Richardson v Richardson* [1989] Fam 95, [1989] 3 All ER 779, in which it was held that money raised by the sequestrators may be used to pay the innocent party's costs of instituting proceedings abroad to recover the child, and *Mir v Mir* [1992] Fam 79, [1992] 1 All ER 765 in which it was held that the court has power to order the sale of sequestered property.

[16] Pursuant to the provisions of the Family Law Act 1986, discussed post at pp 494–495.

[17] This convention is discussed post, pp 492 et seq.

[18] See the Home Office's revised leaflet, published at [1986] Fam Law 50 and *Clarke Hall and Morrison on Children* at para 1[82]. This procedure will not prevent a visitor's passport being issued at a post office and of course the procedure is inapplicable to foreign passport holders. If a solicitor agrees to hold a foreign passport he owes a duty of care to the other parent not to let it out of his possession: *Al–Kandari v JR Brown & Co* [1988] QB 665, [1988] 1 All ER 833, CA.

[19] Under the Family Law Act 1986, s 37. To prevent the re-issue of a passport the court should notify the Passport Office that it has ordered a surrender of a passport: *Practice Direction* [1983] 2 All ER 253.

[20] As opposed to taking the child back.

With regard to children brought into England and Wales from a non-convention country, the jurisdiction usually invoked by one of the parties is wardship. Under this jurisdiction it became established that the High Court would not regard itself as being bound by the order of a foreign court[1] and instead had to make its own independent judgment of the merits of the case.[2] At one time, the practice of the court was to make a 'summary' order for the child's return (ie there would be no full investigation into the merits of the case) unless a return could be shown to be harmful to the child.[3] In this way it was felt that the child's welfare was reasonably protected whilst the abduction was discouraged. That approach was held to be inconsistent with the welfare principle as applied by the House of Lords in *J v C*[4] and it became firmly established that the decision whether to make a summary order or to hear the full merits of the application must be determined according to the child's welfare.[5] In *Re F (Minor: Abduction: Jurisdiction)*,[6] however, the Court of Appeal emphasised that it was normally in the child's interests not to be abducted and that any decision about his upbringing was best decided by the court in the state in which he had hitherto been habitually resident. Accordingly, it was held that a return should be ordered provided the English court was satisfied that (a) the foreign court in question would apply principles acceptable to the English court and (b) there were no contra indications such as those referred to in Article 13 of the Hague Convention (discussed below). Although the obvious intention is to harmonise 'non-convention' law with 'convention law' the result seems reminiscent of the earlier approach which at one time seemed to have been rejected.

2. CHILDREN TAKEN TO OR BROUGHT FROM A 'CONVENTION COUNTRY'

The United Kingdom has implemented both the Hague Convention of 1980 on Civil Aspects of International Child Abduction and the European Convention of 1980 on Recognition and Enforcement of Decisions Concerning Custody of Children.[7] It has done this through the Child Abduction and Custody Act 1985.[8] Both conventions apply to children (under the age of 16) taken from the United Kingdom to another country that has

---

[1] Not even (before the implementation of the Family Law Act 1986) an order made in Scotland. For a notorious example see *Babington v Babington* 1955 SC 115.

[2] *Re B's Settlement* [1940] Ch 54, [1951] 1 All ER 949n and *McKee v McKee* [1951] AC 352, [1951] 1 All ER 942, PC.

[3] See *Re H (Infants)* [1966] 1 All ER 886, CA, and *Re E (D) (An Infant)* [1967] Ch 287, [1967] 1 All ER 329, CA.

[4] [1970] AC 668, [1969] 1 All ER, 788, HL, discussed ante, p 341.

[5] *Re L (Minors) (Wardship: Jurisdiction)* [1974] 1 All ER 913, CA, and *Re R (Minors) (Wardship: Jurisdiction)* (1981) 2 FLR 416, CA.

[6] [1991] Fam 25, [1990] 3 All ER 97, CA. See also *G v G (Minors) (Abduction)* [1991] 2 FLR 506, CA (decided in 1989) upon which the court relied in *Re F*.

[7] The full text together with explanation can be found in 1981 Cmnd 8155 (the European Convention) and in 1981 Cmnd 8281 (the Hague Convention). For general discussion of the Hague Convention, see Anton (1981) 30 ICLQ 357 and of the European Convention, see Jones (1981) 30 ICLQ 467.

[8] For a helpful explanation of the objectives of this Act see Lord Hailsham LC in 460 HL Official Report (5th series) cols 1248 et seq, 1985. The 1985 Act contains in its Schedules the texts of the two conventions as implemented by the UK.

implemented that convention (known as a 'Contracting State') and vice versa. At the time of writing 23 countries have implemented the Hague Convention and 13 the European Convention.[9] All but two of the signatories of the latter convention have also implemented the Hague Convention.[10] Unlike the European Convention, which is necessarily confined to Europe, the signatories of the Hague Convention include countries from North and South America, and Australasia as well as from Europe.

A key difference between the two conventions is that whereas the Hague Convention is concerned with the return of children wrongfully removed in breach of rights of custody or in breach of rights of access, the European Convention is concerned with the recognition and enforcement of custody *orders* and decisions relating to access. In other words whereas it is a prerequisite for the applicant to have a court order in his favour to invoke the European Convention it is not necessary to have such orders to invoke the Hague Convention. Nevertheless although their strategy is different, both conventions have the same basic aim, namely, to trace abducted children, to secure their prompt return and to organise or secure effective rights of access. Under each convention a Contracting State is bound to set up an administrative body known as the 'Central Authority' whose tasks are to collate and to send to appropriate agencies information about the child, and, if necessary to initiate judicial or administrative proceedings to attain the foregoing aims. These tasks are carried out mainly at the expense of each authority. In England and Wales the Central Authority is the Lord Chancellor.[11] However, when dealing with children brought to England and Wales from another Convention country, the Lord Chancellor has delegated some of his functions as the Central Authority to private firms of solicitors. The practice is that upon receiving an application in correct form, the Lord Chancellor's Department instructs a firm of solicitors on the client's behalf.[12] That firm must then immediately apply for legal aid which will be granted regardless of the applicant's means and which will not be subject to a merits test.[13] Once legal aid is granted the solicitor has sole responsibility for the conduct of the case. On the evidence to date this system seems to have been working well.

A second technique used by each convention is to curb the power of the domestic courts in each Contracting State to make an independent judgment of what is in the interests of a particular child so that a return will normally be ordered. This is certainly how the conventions have been interpreted in England, where the court rarely refuses to return an 'abducted child'.

(a) The Hague Convention[14]

(i) When the convention applies

This convention applies to any child, under the age of 16 and habitually

---

[9] See Appendix D for full list of Contracting States, post, p 856.
[10] Viz Belgium and Cyprus.
[11] Child Abduction and Custody Act 1985, ss 3 and 14.
[12] They are not instructed on the Department's behalf.
[13] Legal Aid (General) Regulations 1989, reg 14.
[14] See Everall *Hague Convention, The Children Act and other Recent Developments* [1992] Fam Law 164, Everall *Child Abduction after the Hague Convention* [1990] Fam Law 169; and Stanley *International Child Abduction The Hague and European Conventions* (1991) 3 Journal of Child Law 137.

resident in one Contracting State, who has wrongfully been removed or retained in another Contracting State.[15] The issue of the child's habitual residence is one of fact to be determined in the light of the particular circumstances but so far as the English courts are concerned it is established that it is the residence immediately before the wrongful removal or retention that is relevant.[16] It has also been held that there is a significant difference between ceasing to be habitually resident in one country and becoming habitually resident in another. As Lord Brandon said in *C v S (Minor: Abduction: Illegitimate Child)*[17] a person may cease to be habitually resident in country A in a single day whereas an appreciable period of time and a settled intention are necessary for someone to become habitually resident in Country B. Since it is a requirement to be habitually resident in a *Contracting* State it follows that the convention is not retrospective in the sense that the wrongful act must have taken place after the Contracting State has implemented the convention.[18]

For the purposes of this convention an act is 'wrongful' if it is in breach of rights of custody accorded to a person or institution or other body, either jointly or alone, by the law of the Contracting State in which the child is habitually resident and if at the time of removal or retention those rights were actually exercised either jointly or alone, or would have been so exercised but for the removal or retention.[19] In *C v S*[20] it was held that the unilateral removal of a child from Western Australia to England by an unmarried mother was not 'wrongful' because by the law of that state she alone had custody and guardianship and no restrictions had been placed on her with respect to taking her child abroad. For the purposes of English law, 'rights of custody' should be understood in the context of the Children Act 1989, namely, to refer to parental responsibility.[1]

Normally a wrongful removal or retention will be in breach of someone else's rights but it has been accepted by the English courts that a removal or retention is 'wrongful' if it is in breach of custody rights vested in a court[2] or of the defendant's own rights.[3] Wrongfulness can be established by reference to statute or case law[4] and it is no defence that the defendant did not know removal from the jurisdiction was prohibited.[5]

---

[15] Art 4.

[16] *Re S (A Minor) (Abduction)* [1991] 2 FLR 1, CA. See also *Re F (A Minor) (Child Abduction)* [1992] 1 FLR 548, CA.

[17] [1990] 2 All ER 961, 965, sub nom *Re J (A Minor) (Abduction: Custody Rights)* [1990] 2 AC 562, 578, HL.

[18] *Re H (Minors) (Abduction: Custody Rights), Re S (Minors) (Abduction: Custody Rights)* [1991] 2 AC 476, [1991] 3 All ER 430, HL. The convention has similarly been held in Scotland not to have retrospective effect: *Kilgour v Kilgour* 1987 SLT 568. For this reason the implementation dates (for which see Appendix D) are important.

[19] Art 3.

[20] Supra. Unmarried mothers are in a similar position under English law unless the father has acquired parental responsibility.

[1] The 1989 Act therefore makes no difference to the position of English parents under the convention: see Lord Mackay LC [1991] Fam Law 456–7.

[2] Eg where the child is a ward of court: see *Re J (Minor: Abduction: Ward of Court)* [1989] Fam 85, [1989] 3 All ER 590.

[3] *Re H (A Minor) (Abduction)* [1990] 2 FLR 439.

[4] Ie prohibition can be contained in an express court order as in *Re C (A Minor) (Abduction)* [1989] 1 FLR 403, CA or be implicit because of general case law: *C v C (Minors) (Child Abduction)* [1992] 1 FLR 163.

[5] *C v C (Minors) (Child Abduction)*, supra.

The convention refers both to wrongful *removal* and wrongful *retention*. It has been held by the House of Lords in *Re H, Re S*[6] that these are separate and mutually exclusive events both of which occur once and for all on a specific occasion. *Removal* occurs 'when a child, which has previously been in the state of its habitual residence, is taken away across the frontier of that state, whereas *retention* occurs where a child, which has previously been for a limited period of time outside the state of its habitual residence, is not returned on the expiry of such limited period'.[7] In each case removal or retention refers to removal or retention out of the jurisdiction of the courts of the state of the child's habitual residence. Wrongful removal or retention *within* the borders of the state of the child's habitual residence falls outside the scope of the convention.

(ii) Who can invoke the convention

Applicants must show either that they have 'rights of custody' which, for the purposes of the convention, includes rights relating to the care of the person of the child and, in particular, the right to determine the child's place of residence or that they have 'rights of access' by which is meant inter alia 'the right to take a child for a limited period of time to a place other than the child's habitual residence'.[8] It is important to appreciate therefore that it is not a necessary prerequisite to have obtained a court order to be able to invoke the Hague Convention.[9] In the case of a child taken from England and Wales, for instance, it is clear that anyone with parental responsibility for the child will have the necessary *locus standi* to apply,[10] and, as we have seen, such responsibility is automatically vested in married parents and unmarried mothers.[11] Nevertheless to assist an application for the recovery of a child taken out of England and Wales, an application can be made to the High Court for a declaration that the removal was 'wrongful'.[12]

Where a child has been wrongfully removed the applicant can apply for his child's return through a Central Authority.[13] Provided the application is accompanied by the appropriate documents[14] the Central Authority must, upon receiving it, take steps to discover the child's whereabouts and to seek his return.

(iii) The court's role

If in the course of securing the child's return the issue goes to a court, that court is forbidden by the convention to investigate the merits of the rights

---

[6] *Re H (Minors) (Abduction: Custody Rights), Re S (Minors) (Abduction: Custody Rights)* [1991] 2 AC 476, [1991] 3 All ER 230, HL.
[7] Per Lord Brandon *ibid* at p 240.
[8] Art 5.
[9] Cf the position under the European Convention, discussed post, p 492.
[10] See Lord Mackay LC [1991] Fam Law 457.
[11] Ante, p 322.
[12] Child Abduction and Custody Act 1985, s 8. For an example, see *Re J (Abduction: Ward of Court)* [1989] Fam 85, [1989] 3 All ER 590.
[13] The applicant can apply either to the Central Authority of the state in which the child is habitually resident or of the state to which it is thought that the child has been taken.
[14] Listed under Art 8; for details see Lowe and White, op cit, at para 17.35.

to custody.[15] By Article 12 the court is directed, if the application is brought within one year of the removal, to 'order the return of the child forthwith'. If more than a year has elapsed, the child should still be returned 'unless it is demonstrated that the child is now settled in its new environment'.[16]

Article 12 is subject to Article 13 under which a return can be refused if:

'(a) the person, institution or body having the care of the person of the child was not actually exercising the custody rights at the time of removal or retention, or had consented to or subsequently acquiesced in the removal or retention; or

(b) there is a grave risk that his or her return would expose the child to physical or psychological harm or otherwise place the child in an intolerable situation.

The judicial or administrative authority may also refuse to order the return of the child if it finds that the child objects to being returned and has attained an age and degree of maturity at which it is appropriate to take account of its views.

In considering the circumstances referred to in this Article, the judicial and administrative authorities shall take into account the information relating to the social background of the child provided by the Central Authority or other competent authority of the child's habitual residence.'

In each of the exceptions contained in Articles 12 and 13 the burden of proof lies on the applicant. Even if an exception is established the court still has a discretion to order the return under Article 18.

The English High Court, which has sole jurisdiction to hear convention applications with respect to children brought to England and Wales,[17] has interpreted these exceptions strictly. For example, it has been held that to establish that 'there is a grave risk that a return would expose the child to physical or psychological harm or otherwise place the child in an intolerable position' the risk must be more than an ordinary one and must be weighty and substantial and not trivial.[18] Placing the child in an intolerable situation has been held to envisage extreme and compelling matters which have to bear some similarity to the 'grave risk of harm' element.[19] The courts have not readily found there to be 'acquiescence'[20] nor accepted that a return

[15] Unless an application is not lodged within a reasonable time following receipt of notice: Art 16. Effectively this freezes any prior applications, including, in England and Wales, any residence order or wardship applications: ss 9 and 27 of the Child Abduction and Custody Act 1985.

[16] In *Re N (Minors) (Abduction)* [1991] 1 FLR 413 Bracewell J held that 'now' referred to the date of the commencement of proceedings and not the date of the hearing; that 'settled' involved both a physical element in the sense of relating to or being established in a community and an emotional constituent denoting security; and that 'new environment' encompassed place, home, school, people, friends, activities and opportunities but not, per se, the relationship with the parent.

[17] Child Abduction and Custody Act 1985, s 4.

[18] *Re A (A Minor) (Abduction)* [1988] 1 FLR 365, CA. See also *Re A (A Minor) (Wrongful Removal of a Child)* [1988] Fam Law 383; *Re E (A Minor) (Abduction)* [1989] 1 FLR 135, CA; and *C v C (Minor) (Abduction: Rights of Custody Abroad)* [1989] 2 All ER 465, CA.

[19] Per Bracewell J in *Re N (Minors) (Abduction)* [1991] 1 FLR 413.

[20] It has been said that acquiescence is a question of fact but the fact that the applicant applied for custody in the state of the child's habitual residence is a strong indication that there has been no acquiescence: *Re A (Minors: Abduction)* [1991] 2 FLR 241. On the other hand absence of court action does not necessarily indicate acquiescence: see *Re F (A Minor) (Child Abduction)* [1992] 1 FLR 548, CA. For an example of acquiescence see *Re A (Minors) (Abduction: Acquiescence)* [1992] 1 All ER 929, CA (father wrote to mother saying that although he knew the removal of his children was in breach of his rights he would not fight it). In this latter case it was held (Balcombe LJ dissenting) that acquiescence could not subsequently be withdrawn.

should be refused because of the child's objections.[1]

If a return is ordered then any other custody order ceases to have effect, but if a return is refused then the court can hear any other application upon its merits.[2]

(iv) Securing rights of access

Applications for organising or securing the effective exercise of rights of access can be presented to a Central Authority in the same way as an application for the child's return. For the purposes of English law a decision relating to access means a decision as to the contact which a child may or may not have with any person.[3] Under Article 21 the Authority is required to promote the peaceful enjoyment of access rights and to take steps to remove, as far as possible, all obstacles to their exercise, including taking proceedings to organise or protect access. If the child's return is not being sought then the court has power, at any rate where the child has become habitually resident in this country, to make fresh or amending orders for access under the convention. In making such orders the court must treat the child's welfare as its paramount consideration.[4]

(b) The European Convention

(i) When the convention applies

This convention applies to any child under the age of 16 who has been improperly removed. For these purposes 'improper removal' means the removal across an international boundary in breach of a decision relating to custody.[5] It is therefore a prerequisite under this convention that an applicant has an order in his favour, although under Article 12, if there is no enforceable decision at the time of the removal, an application can subsequently be made for a declaration that the removal is 'improper'.[6] Under Article 1(c) 'a decision relating to custody' means a decision of judicial or administrative authority insofar as it relates to the care of the person of the child including the right to decide on the place of his residence, or to the right of access to him. It is clear that a residence or contact order under section 8 of the Children Act 1989 will satisfy this requirement.

Unlike the Hague Convention it has been held, at any rate in England, that the European Convention has retrospective effect.[7] Hence, orders made before the state implemented the convention can be enforced at any rate in this country.

---

[1] It has been held, for instance that the court is not bound to adjourn the case to inquire into the nature of the child's objections and degree of maturity: *P v P (Minors) (Abduction)* [1992] 1 FLR 155. But for examples where a return was refused see *Re R (A Minor) (Abduction)* [1992] 1 FLR 105 (child aged 14 threatening suicide if returned) and *S v S (Child Abduction)* [1992] 2 FLR 311 (9-year-old's objections respected).
[2] Child Abduction and Custody Act 1985, s 25 and Art 16. 'Custody orders' include s 8 orders under the Children Act 1989: Child Abduction and Custody Act 1985, Sch 3.
[3] Ibid, s 27(4).
[4] *C v C (Minors) (Child Abduction)* [1992] 1 FLR 163. See also *B v B (Minors: Enforcement of Access Abroad)* [1988] 1 All ER 652.
[5] Art 1.
[6] In England and Wales such a declaration can be made in any custody proceedings: Child Abduction and Custody Act 1985, s 23(2).
[7] *Re L (A Minor) (Child Abduction)* 1991 Case No CA 1098/91 per Booth J.

(ii) Applying for the child's return

To secure the child's return, application should be made through a Central Authority together with the appropriate documents.[8] Upon receiving the application the Central Authority in the state addressed must, without delay, take appropriate steps, inter alia, to secure the recognition and enforcement of the custody order.[9] Recognition and enforcement is achieved by registering the court order in a court of the Contracting State to which the child has been taken. In England and Wales applications to register must be made in the High Court.[10] Once the order is registered the court has the same powers of enforcement as if it had made the original order[11] and in this way the child's return will be ordered.

Although a court can refuse to register the order it is generally expected that it will not. In any event the precise latitude for refusal depends upon whether the Contracting State has implemented Article 8. If it has, then provided the application is made within six months of the child's removal, registration is virtually mandatory. However, most Contracting States, including the United Kingdom, have not implemented that Article. In those states registration can, in all cases,[12] be refused within the terms of Article 10, which, inter alia, permits refusal 'where it is found that by reason of a change of circumstances including the passage of time but not including a mere change in the residence of the child after an improper removal, the effects of the original decision are manifestly no longer in accordance with the welfare of the child'. In line with the spirit of the convention the English courts have interpreted this to mean that the effects of the original decision must be manifestly incompatible with the child's welfare.[13] Another ground for refusing registration is that an application under the Hague Convention is pending.[14] In other words the former convention has precedence over the European Convention.

As under the Hague Convention, the domestic courts' powers to hear the merits of other custody proceedings are restricted during the pendency of an application for registration.[15] Upon registration all other custody orders cease to have effect[16] but if registration is refused other applications can be heard on their merits.[17]

---

[8] Art 4(2). The requisite documents are listed in Art 13.
[9] Art 5.
[10] Child Abduction and Custody Act 1985, s 16.
[11] Ibid, s 18.
[12] In Contracting States where Article 8 has been implemented, Art 10 only applies where the application is made more than six months after the removal. The UK did not implement Art 8 because it was felt to be too draconian and contrary to the provisions of the Hague Convention: see Lord Hailsham LC in 460 HL Official Report (5th Series) col 1253, 1985.
[13] Per Booth J in *Re G (A Minor) (Abduction: Enforcement)* [1990] 2 FLR 325. See also *Re K (A Minor) (Abduction)* [1990] 1 FLR 387. Cf *F v F (Minors) (Custody: Foreign Order)* [1989] Fam 1, [1988] 3 WLR 959 where registration was refused.
[14] Child Abduction and Custody Act 1985, s 16(4)(c).
[15] Ibid, s 20(1). For the exceptions see s 20(2).
[16] Ibid, s 25(1).
[17] Ibid, s 20(1).

(c) Choosing which convention to invoke

As we have said,[18] the Hague Convention has a wider application than the European since there are more signatories and applicants do not need to have a court order in their favour before they can invoke it. For applicants having a choice, that is, if they have rights of custody under an order made in one Contracting State and their child has been removed to another Contracting State both of which have implemented both conventions, there are two instances in which it might be preferable to invoke the European Convention. These are first, where the removal took place before implementation of the convention by one of the Contracting States in which case, as far as the English courts are concerned, it will only be possible to invoke the European Convention.[19] Second, if the child has been taken to a Contracting State that has implemented Article 8 of the European Convention, then provided an application under that convention is brought within six months a return is virtually mandatory. However, with regard to children brought to England and Wales, apart from the retroactivity point there is little to choose between the conventions, since the court normally orders the child's return in any event. If, however, an application is brought under both, precedence is given to the Hague Convention application.[20]

C. Children taken to or brought from another part of the United Kingdom

Until relatively recently orders relating to children made in one part of the United Kingdom were neither recognised nor enforceable in another part. This has now been changed by the Family Law Act 1986, which provides for a system of recognition and enforcement.[1]

Under section 25 any Part I order[2] made by a court in any part of the United Kingdom[3] or Dependent Territory[4] and in force in respect of a child under the age of 16, is to be recognised in any other part of the United Kingdom or Dependent Territory. Recognition does not itself mean that the order will be enforced.[5] Instead, application must be made to the court that made the original order for the order to be registered in another part

---

[18] Ante, p 488.
[19] Cf *Re H (Minors) (Abduction: Custody Rights), Re S (Minors) (Abduction: Custody Rights)* [1991] 2 AC 476, [1991] 3 All ER 230, HL, Hague Convention does not operate retrospectively and *Re L (A Minor) (Child Abduction)*, 1991 Case No CA 1098/91, European Convention does operate retrospectively.
[20] Child Abduction and Custody Act 1985, s 16(4)(c), discussed above.
[1] The Act is modelled on the Law Commission's proposals; see *Custody of Children—Jurisdiction and Enforcement within the United Kingdom* Law Com No 138 and Scot Law Com No 91, 1985. For further discussion, see Lowe and White *Wards of Court* (2nd Edn) paras 17.29 to 17.31.
[2] Elaborately defined by s 1 of the 1986 Act, see ante, pp 375 and 465.
[3] Ie England and Wales, Scotland and Northern Ireland: s 42 of the 1986 Act.
[4] Which at the time of writing only refers to the Isle of Man: Family Law Act 1986 (Dependent Territories) Order 1991, Sch 3.
[5] But it does mean, for instance, that a prohibition against the child's removal from any part of the United Kingdom will be effective throughout the United Kingdom.

of the United Kingdom or Dependent Territory.[6] Once the order is registered, the registering court has the same enforcement powers as it would have had, had it made the original application for enforcement. At the enforcement hearing, objections can be made by any interested party, for example upon the grounds that the original order was made without jurisdiction or because of changed circumstances the original order should be varied. The court has power either to enforce the order or to stay or to dismiss the application.[7] The general expectation is that the order will be enforced.[8]

It will be noted that as under the European Convention a prior court order is an essential prerequisite for action under the 1986 Act but unlike the conventions there is no administrative body to help with the applications. Furthermore the costs of enforcement fall upon the parties themselves. The enforcement system itself seems elaborate. Despite these criticisms the Act is nevertheless an important step forward in dealing with abduction within the United Kingdom.[9]

---

[6] Family Law Act 1986, s 27.
[7] Ibid, ss 30 and 31.
[8] It might be noted that the courts can only enforce Part I orders and not, for example, injunctions: see *Re K (Wards Jurisdiction: Interim Order)* [1991] 2 FLR 104, CA.
[9] Though problems of more than one court making a decision still arise: see for example *T v T (Custody: Jurisdiction)* [1992] 1 FLR 43.

Chapter 16

Children and local authorities

A. Introduction

There is a variety of reasons why parents cannot or should not be allowed
to look after their own children. They may be prevented from doing so by
illness or the child may be beyond their control. Alternatively, a parent
may be unwilling or unfit to bring up his own child, for example, he may
have abandoned the child or physically or sexually abused him or he may
have neglected him. The task of handling these difficult problems is delegated
to local authorities. For this purpose local authorities are non-metropolitan
counties, metropolitan districts and London Boroughs,[1] and by the Local
Authority Social Services Act of 1970 they are required to set up a single
social services committee responsible for all the services. The day to day
running of the authority's social services is under the control of the Director
of Social Services.[2]

1. THE DEVELOPMENT OF LOCAL AUTHORITY POWERS

The powers and duties of local authorities to protect and care for children
now derive from the Children Act 1989. In striking contrast to the previous
law, which had developed piecemeal, the 1989 Act provides a comprehensive
and unified scheme for dealing with children in need.

To put the 1989 Act in its context it is worth briefly adverting to the
earlier law. That law was based on two Acts, namely, the Child Care Act
1980 and the Children and Young Persons Act 1969. The former Act
consolidated earlier Acts, principally, the Children Act 1948 and parts of
the Children and Young Persons Act 1963 and the Children Act 1975. The
Children Act 1948 resulted from a report of the Curtis Committee[3] which
was set up to inquire into existing methods of providing for children
deprived of a normal home life and to consider what further steps should
be taken to ensure that they were brought up under conditions best
calculated to compensate for their lack of parental care. Reflecting the
concerns of the Committee the 1948 Act imposed on the local authority a
duty to receive a deprived child into care in certain circumstances and then
to bring him up according to his best interests. Wherever possible the
authority had to secure the discharge from care to parents, relatives or
friends as soon as may be.

During the 1950s there was an increasing awareness of the need to prevent
families breaking up and children being received into care. Social and

[1] Children Act 1989, s 105(1).
[2] Local Authority Social Services Act 1970, s 6.
[3] Cmnd 6922.

economic factors were seen to be important in family difficulties. Juvenile delinquency began to be attributed in many instances to 'deprivation' rather than 'depravity'. It was thought that intensive preventative work with families could help to solve the problems of offenders and non-offenders.

The Ingleby Committee,[4] set up in 1956, investigated these matters and subsequently the Children and Young Persons Act 1963 was enacted, under which all local authorities had as their first duty the power to give advice, guidance and assistance to diminish the need to receive children into care.

Prevention and rehabilitation became the keynote of much of the subsequent work of local authorities, and it was expected that this would lead to an improvement in the prevention of delinquency.

These principles were further emphasised in the Children and Young Persons Act 1969. Both offenders and non-offenders were to be dealt with in the same system, and the provisions were designed to discourage either coming before the courts. For both, the powers of the court were directed towards treatment. In fact the aim to reduce the relevance of criminal law by raising the age of criminal responsibility has never been implemented.

In the 1970s questions were again raised about the nature and efficiency of child care services. Difficulties were experienced as a result of changes in the structure of local authorities.[5] Children's departments, previously responsible for services to children and their families, were replaced by larger social services departments with responsibilities for the old, handicapped and mentally ill, as well as for children. The creation of a profession to manage all these inevitably lowered the level of child care expertise and raised the pressure of workloads. All this in a bureaucratic structure made it impossible in many instances for local authorities to provide the personalised services for children envisaged in the 1948 Act.

Lack of constructive long-term planning caused increasing concern. In spite of the apparent emphasis on returning children to their parents, it was considered that substantial numbers of children in care were unlikely ever to go back to their families and could not benefit from waiting in vain hope.[6]

There was a rising body of opinion that it was not necessarily in a child's interest to return to his natural parents. This was given philosophical expression in the book *Beyond the Best Interests of the Child*,[7] where the importance of 'psychological' parents was emphasised. The issue came into the public eye, however, in 1973 when Maria Colwell was killed by her stepfather after she had been removed from foster parents.[8] Inevitably, there was a demand for a curtailment of parental rights, so that children could be better protected from parental rejection, and plans could be made for their long-term welfare. However, there were contrary arguments, that it was often bad social work practice rather than parental failure which led to children languishing in care. Strengthening the powers of local authorities and third parties might serve to reinforce bad practice and lack of planning,

---

[4] Cmnd 1191.
[5] Under the Local Authority Social Services Act 1970.
[6] See Rowe and Lambert *Children Who Wait*.
[7] Goldstein, Freud and Solnit (Free Press).
[8] See the Report of the Committee of Inquiry into the Care and Supervision provided in relation to Maria Colwell (1974) HMSO.

and encourage foster parents, for example, to sabotage a parent's efforts to recover a child.

The trend towards greater recognition of the rights of a child as an individual could not be ignored. The resulting legislation, the Children Act 1975, attempted to balance his rights with those of his parents recognising that while most frequently they should coincide, they will at times conflict. This was reflected in the provision which required a local authority to give first consideration to the need to safeguard and promote the welfare of the child throughout his childhood.

Still different concerns were being voiced in the 1980s. Studies had raised awareness of the damage that local authority care (however well meaning) could do to family links[9] but this in turn 'encouraged local authorities to operate strong gate-keeping techniques to prevent children entering the system' with the result that care was denied to those who needed it. 'Social work thus became something which was done to clients rather than a way of helping families to help themselves'.[10] Yet another concern highlighted by the Cleveland crisis[11] was whether local authorities had become too powerful at the expense of family autonomy.

The Children Act 1989 attempts to take on board the lessons and experience of the past and to draw anew the balance between family autonomy and local authority powers to protect children.[12]

2. THE CURRENT LAW—SOME KEY CHANGES

(a) Non-intervention

One of the great achievements of the Children Act 1989 is to provide a single comprehensive code governing both private and public law. As we have seen in previous chapters one of the underlying philosophies of the Act is that of non-intervention and this basic standpoint is one of the key changes in the public law arena. As Lord Mackay said in his Joseph Jackson Memorial Lecture:[13]

'... the integrity and independence of the family is the basic building block of a free and democratic society and the need to defend it should be clearly perceivable in the law. Accordingly, unless there is evidence that a child is being or is likely to be positively harmed because of a failure in the family, the state, whether in the guise of a local authority or a court, should not interfere.'

This basic non-interventionist standpoint is emphasised by the fact that compulsory measures can only be taken following a court order and that no order may be made unless the basic threshold of 'significant harm' can be proved. Moreover the presumption under section 1(5)[14] that no order

[9] See eg Millham, Bullock, Hosie and Haak *Lost in Care* (1986) and *Social Work Decisions in Child Care* (DHSS, 1985).
[10] Cretney and Masson *Principles of Family Law* (5th Edn) p 593.
[11] Which was concerned with the scope of removal of children because of alleged sexual abuse, see ante, p 248.
[12] For the genesis of the Act, see ante, p 247.
[13] (1989) 139 NLJ 505, 507.
[14] Discussed in detail ante, p 345.

should be made at all unless it is for the child's welfare applies equally to proceedings involving local authorities. Even where an order is thought justified the court may still not make a care order if it thinks that an alternative section 8 order would be better.

(b) Working in partnership

A second key change allied both to the non-intervention principle and to the enduring nature of parental responsibility, is that local authorities must work in partnership with the parents. There is a strong enjoinder on authorities to make voluntary agreements with parents for the benefit of their children. As the Department of Health's *Guidance* puts it:[15]

> 'One of the key principles of the Children Act is that responsible authorities should work in partnership with the parents of a child who is being looked after and also with the child himself, where he is of sufficient understanding, provided that this approach will not jeopardise his welfare. A second, closely related principle is that parents and children should participate actively in the decision-making process. Partnership will only be achieved if parents are advised about and given explanations of the local authority's powers and duties and the actions of the local authority may need to take, for example, exchanges of information between relevant agencies... This new approach reflects the fact that parents always retain their parental responsibility. A local authority may limit parents' exercise of that responsibility when a child is looked after by a local authority as a result of a court order, but only if it is necessary to do so to safeguard and promote the child's welfare...
>
> The development of a successful working partnership between the responsible authorities and the parents and the child, where he is of sufficient understanding, should enable the placement to proceed positively so that the child's welfare is safeguarded and promoted.'

Not unrelated to the partnership ideal is that the services which under Part III of the Act local authorities are obliged to provide should be seen as a positive response to the needs of children and not as a mark of failure by the family or the professionals.

(c) Maintenance of links between the child and his family

In cases where it is necessary for children to live away from home either as a result of voluntary agreement or compulsory intervention stress is repeatedly placed on the importance of children maintaining links with their family. As *The Care of Children: Principles and Practice in Regulations and Guidance* puts it:[16]

> 'There are unique advantages for children in experiencing normal family life in their own birth family and every effort should be made to preserve the child's home and family links.'

To this end local authorities are under a general duty when safeguarding the welfare of children in need to promote the upbringing of children by the families[17] and, if they are looking after[18] the child, to endeavour to

---

[15] Vol 3, Family Placements, paras 2.10 and 2.11.
[16] (HMSO, 1989) p 8.
[17] Children Act 1989, s 17(1)(b).
[18] For the meaning of this see post, p 505.

promote contact between the child and his parents.[19] Even when in care or subject to an emergency protection order there is a presumption that the child will have reasonable contact with his family. Local authorities wishing to restrict this must obtain the prior sanction of the court.[20]

It remains now to consider the 1989 Act in more detail. We shall do this first by discussing the support services which under Part III local authorities are obliged to provide. Secondly, we shall discuss care and supervision orders under Part IV and thirdly, we shall examine the powers under Part V to protect children. Finally consideration is given to the various ways in which disputes with local authorities may be pursued.

B.   Local authority support for children and families[1]

Part III of the 1989 Act contains provisions on the services that a local authority must or may provide for children and their families. For the first time services for children in need and disabled children are brought together under one statute. The provisions are intended to enable authorities to support family life, although they may in certain circumstances charge for the service.

It is tempting for lawyers to overlook this part of the Act especially as it does not deal with 'court-based' law. Nevertheless it is not without relevance to the practising lawyer since the provision of such services both in the sense of past support to a particular family and what future support might be given, are important factors in deciding whether or not to make a care order.

1.   GENERAL DUTY TO CHILDREN IN NEED

Under section 17(1) every local authority has a general[2] duty:

'(a) to safeguard and promote the welfare of children in their area who are in need; and

(b) so far as is consistent with that duty to promote the upbringing of such children by their families,

by providing a range and level of services appropriate to those needs.'

A child[3] is defined as being 'in need' if:[4]

'(a) he is unlikely to achieve or maintain, or to have the opportunity of achieving or maintaining a reasonable standard of health or development without the

---

[19] Children Act 1989, Sch 2, para 15.
[20] Ibid, s 34, discussed post, p 530.
[1] See generally Department of Health's *Guidance and Regulations*, Vol 2, Family Support, Day Care and Educational Provision for Young Children. Part III is based on recommendation of the *Review of Child Care Law* (DHSS, 1985) and the Government's White Paper *The Law on Child Care and Family Services* (Cm 62, 1987).
[2] The inclusion of the word 'general' is intended to reverse *A-G (ex rel Tilley) v London Borough of Wandsworth* [1981] 1 All ER 1162, which had held under the old law that the welfare duty applied to individual children.
[3] Ie a person under the age of 18: Children Act 1989, s 105(1).
[4] S 17(10).

provision for him of services by a local authority under this Part;
(b) his health or development is likely to be significantly impaired or further impaired, without the provision for him of such services; or
(c) he is disabled.'

For these purposes 'health' means physical or mental health and 'development' means physical, intellectual, emotional, social or behavioural development.[5]

It will be appreciated that this definition is wide. Furthermore as the Department of Health's *Guidance* observes:[6]

'Sometimes the needs will be found to be intrinsic to the child, at other times however it may be that parenting skills and resources are depleted or under-developed and thus threaten the child's well-being.'

In discharging this general duty towards children in need, section 17(3) states that the services may be provided for the family of a particular child in need or for any member of his family, if they are provided with a view to safeguarding or promoting the child's welfare. For these purposes, 'family' includes any person who has parental responsibility for the child, and any other person with whom he has been living.[7] It is thus not limited to relatives.

The services provided under Part III may include giving assistance in kind or in exceptional circumstances in cash, unconditionally or conditionally as to repayment.[8] This removes the doubt which existed under the former law as to whether loans could be given. Authorities are required to have regard to the means of the child and each of his parents, although no person is liable for repayment at any time when he is in receipt of income support or family credit.[9] An authority may also contribute to the cost of looking after a child who is living with a person under a residence order, such as a relative or foster parent, except where that person is a parent or step-parent.[10]

Authorities are required to facilitate the provision of Part III services by other, in particular voluntary, organisations, and may make such arrangements as they see fit for others to provide such services (for example day care or fostering services).[11]

2. SPECIFIC POWERS AND DUTIES

In pursuance of the general duty, authorities have specific duties and powers which are set out in Schedule 2, Part I, among which are the following:

(a) Identification of children in need: Every local authority must take reasonable steps to identify the extent to which there are children in need in their area. They must also publish information about the services they provide.[12]

[5] S 17(11). This is the same definition as in s 31(9) in care proceedings, see post, p 513.
[6] Vol 2, para 2.5.
[7] S 17(10).
[8] S 17(6) and (7).
[9] S 17(8) and (9).
[10] Sch 1, para 15.
[11] S 17(5) and see further Department of Health's *Guidance and Regulations*, Vol 2, para 2.11.
[12] Sch 2, para 1.

(b) Promoting the upbringing of children by their families: Local authorities should make provision for advice, guidance, counselling and home help. This could include family aids or perhaps therapists who might advise on improving family dynamics. Occupational, social, cultural or recreational activities or assistance with holidays may be provided.[13] Where a child is being looked after by a local authority, the authority shall, unless it is not reasonably practicable or consistent with his welfare, endeavour to promote contact between the child and his family and shall ensure that they are kept informed of where he is being accommodated. However, the authority is not required to disclose the whereabouts of the child if he is in care and the authority has reasonable cause to believe that disclosure would prejudice the child's welfare.[14]

(c) Prevention of abuse and neglect: Every authority shall take reasonable steps through the provision of Part III services to prevent children in their area suffering ill-treatment or neglect. There is a duty to inform another authority if a child who the authority believe is likely to suffer harm, lives or proposes to live in the area of that authority.[15]

(d) Provision of accommodation by third party to protect children:Where it appears to an authority that a child is suffering or is likely to suffer ill-treatment at the hands of another person living at the same premises and that other person proposes to move from those premises, the authority may assist that other person to obtain alternative accommodation, including giving assistance in kind.[16] This provision is a response to concern expressed in the Cleveland Report[17] that children, who were allegedly sexually abused, were removed from the family home, when it might have been in their interests for the alleged abuser to have left, if he could have been provided with alternative accommodation. Under this provision local authorities can assist those who are willing to leave voluntarily but they have no power to order removal of a person from a child's household.

(e) Duty to consider racial groups: In making any arrangements either for the provision of day care under section 18 or designed to encourage persons to act as local authority foster parents, the authority shall have regard to the different racial groups to which children in need in their area belong.[18]

(f) Day care: Every local authority is required to provide such day care as is appropriate for children in need within their areas who are five and under and not yet attending school.[19] Day care is defined as any form of care or supervised activity provided for children during the day, whether or not on a regular basis.[20] The authority may provide day care for such children even though they are not in need.[1] They may also provide facilities including training, advice guidance and counselling for those who are caring for children in day care or who accompany children in day care.

[13] Sch 2, para 8.
[14] Sch 2, para 16.
[15] Sch 2, para 4.
[16] Sch 2, para 5.
[17] Cm 412, 1988.
[18] Sch 2, para 11.
[19] S 18(1). See generally Department of Health's *Guidance and Regulations*, Vol 2, paras 3.3 et seq.
[20] S 18(4).
[1] S 18(2).

3. ACCOMMODATING CHILDREN IN NEED

A key service under Part III of the 1989 Act is accommodation. Accommodation effectively replaces what was formerly known as 'voluntary care' but, reflecting the changes of philosophy under the Act, there are important differences between the two. Fundamentally, whereas voluntary care was perceived to be a mark of failure either on the part of the family or those professionals and others working to support them, accommodation is intended to be seen, in the words of the Government's White Paper:[2]

'... as part of the range of services a local authority can offer to parents and families in need of help with the care of their children. Such a service should, in appropriate circumstances, be seen as a positive response to the needs of families.'

An essential characteristic of this service is that it should be voluntary, that is, it should be based clearly on continuing parental agreement and operate as far as possible on a basis of partnership and co-operation between the local authority and parents.

Consistent with this philosophy, 'accommodated children' are not in local authority care nor do the authority thereby acquire parental responsibility. There are no formal restrictions on parents with parental responsibility removing their children out of accommodation[3] and the only means[4] that authorities have to take compulsory measures over the children is to apply for a formal care order or, in emergencies, an emergency protection order.[5] Another important innovation is the formal requirement to have written accommodation agreements between local authorities and the parents.

(a) The duty to accommodate

Under section 20(1) local authorities must provide accommodation where a child in need appears to require it as a result of:

'(a) there being no person who has parental responsibility for him;
(b) his being lost or abandoned; or
(c) the person who has been caring for him being prevented (whether or not permanently, and for whatever reason) from providing him with suitable accommodation or care.'

These criteria are virtually the same as under the old law for voluntary care, save for the words 'for whatever reason', which are said to make clear that accommodation may be provided because of the disability of the child as well as the disability of the parent.[6] Although technically this duty is owed to children under the age of 18[7] in relation to children aged 16 the duty to accommodate only arises where the local authority considers that

---

[2] *The Law on Child Care and Family Services* (Cm 62, 1987) para 21. The Government rejected the recommendation of the Review of Child Care Law that there should be a dual system of 'shared care' and 'respite care'.

[3] Under the former law once a child had been in voluntary care for 6 months or more 28 days' written notice of intended removal had to be given to the authority.

[4] Ie the former administrative mechanism by which local authorities could assume parental rights and duties (discussed at pp 446 et seq of the seventh edition of this work) has been abolished.

[5] Care orders and emergency protection orders are discussed post at pp 507 et seq and 536 et seq respectively.

[6] See Clarke Hall and Morrison *On Children*, para 2[51].

[7] Formerly the duty applied to children under the age of 17.

their welfare 'is likely to be seriously prejudiced' if they do not provide them with accommodation.[8]

How these criteria should be interpreted is largely a matter for the local authorities since, being the basis of voluntary agreement, they are unlikely to come before the courts.[9] Hence, although 'abandoned' has been interpreted under the adoption legislation as 'leaving the child to its fate'[10] it is by no means clear that this is how it should be interpreted in this context. It is also a matter for judgment whether in some cases the child's welfare requires a care order rather than an agreement for accommodation. It has been suggested that if there is no person with parental responsibility, accommodation should be a short-term solution.[11] However, given that there is a duty to accommodate such children if in need, it is by no means clear that the threshold criteria under section 31 (which must be satisfied before a care order can be made) could be satisfied since it might be hard to argue that being accommodated the child is suffering, or given the parents' absence is likely to suffer, significant harm.[12]

Before providing accommodation the authority must, as far as is reasonably practicable and consistent with the child's welfare, ascertain the child's wishes regarding the provision of accommodation and give due consideration to them having regard to his age and understanding.[13]

(b) Limits on providing accommodation

It is of the essence of the service that it is voluntary.[14] Hence the authority cannot provide accommodation if any person with parental responsibility for the child, who is willing and able to provide or arrange for accommodation, objects to the authority so doing.[15] Furthermore any person with parental responsibility may remove the child from accommodation at any time.[16] These provisions do not apply (a) where a child of 16 or over agrees to being provided with accommodation,[17] or (b) where the person agreeing has a residence order in his favour or has the care of the child by virtue of an order made under the High Court's inherent jurisdiction.[18]

One result of these provisions is that in the absence of a court order if one parent places the child in accommodation the other may remove him. Although it is clear that the court cannot make a specific issue or prohibited steps order requiring a local authority to provide accommodation against

---

[8] Children Act 1989, s 20(3). As Cretney and Masson, op cit, at p 599 say, it is not clear why such a restrictive approach was thought necessary in a duty which is in any event limited to children in need. The authority also has a *discretion* to provide accommodation for any person aged 16–21 if they consider that to do so would safeguard and promote the child's welfare: s 20(5).

[9] Conceivably these provisions could be tested in an action for judicial review (discussed post, p 548) on the basis that a local authority was refusing a service they were bound to provide.

[10] *Watson v Nikolaisen* [1955] 2 QB 286, [1955] 2 All ER 427.

[11] Clarke Hall and Morrison, op cit, para 2[52]

[12] The threshold criteria are discussed post, pp 511 et seq.

[13] Children Act 1989, s 20(6).

[14] Parental consent is not however necessarily required, since accommodation may be provided where the parents are dead or where they have abandoned the child.

[15] Children Act 1989, s 20(7).

[16] S 20(8).

[17] S 20(11).

[18] S 20(9).

the wishes of a parent,[19] it remains a moot point whether a parent could obtain a prohibited steps order preventing the other from objecting.[20]

Emphasising the voluntary nature of the service there is no longer any formal requirement that the parent has to give notice of an intention to remove the child. This, however, is a matter that should be covered in any accommodation agreement.

(c) Accommodation agreements[1]

It is central to the philosophy of the Act that an authority should seek to reach agreement with the parent or other person with parental responsibility on such matters as the purpose of accommodating the child and the period for which it might be provided, schooling and contact with the child.

Provision for making agreements is governed by the Arrangement for Placement of Children Regulations 1991, which as the Department of Health's *Guidance* explains:[2]

'... place a statutory duty on responsible authorities to draw up a plan in writing for a child whom they are proposing to look after or accommodate in consultation with the child, his parents and other important individuals and agencies in the child's life (regulation 3). Planning for the child should begin prior to placement. After placement, the plan should be scrutinised and adjusted (if necessary) at the first review four weeks after the date the child was first looked after and at subsequent reviews.'

4. LOCAL AUTHORITY DUTIES TOWARDS CHILDREN 'LOOKED AFTER' BY THEM[3]

The 1989 Act places a number of duties on the local authority in respect of children 'looked after' by them. The phrase 'looked after' refers *both* to children who are provided with accommodation (which is defined as accommodation for a continuous period of more than 24 hours)[4] *and* to those who are in care as a result of a care order.[5]

In relation to such a child the authority have a number of primary duties inter alia to:

(a) safeguard and promote his welfare and to make such use of services available for children cared for by their own parents as appears to the authority reasonable in the case of a particular child;[6]
(b) ascertain as far as practicable the wishes and feelings of the child, his parents, any other person who has parental responsibility and

---

[19] This would seem to be the result of s 9(5)(b).
[20] Query however whether the court in such circumstances would be prepared to make a residence order on the understanding that the child would in fact then be 'accommodated'.
[1] See generally Department of Health's *Guidance and Regulations*, Vol 3, Family Placements, paras 2.13 et seq, which is repeated in Vol 4, Residential Care, paras 2.13 et seq.
[2] See generally Department of Health's *Guidance and Regulations*, Vol 3, paras 2.17–2.74 and Vol 4, paras 2.17–2.74.
[3] See generally Department of Health's *Guidance and Regulations*, Vol 3, paras 2.17–2.74 and Vol 4, paras 2.17–2.74.
[4] Children Act 1989, s 22(2).
[5] S 22(1).
[6] S 22(3).

any other person the authority consider to be relevant, before making any decision with respect to a child they look after or propose to look after;[7]

(c) give due consideration, having regard to his age and understanding, to such wishes and feelings of the child as the authority have been able to ascertain, to his religious persuasion, racial origin and cultural and linguistic background and to the wishes and feelings of any person as mentioned in (b) above;[8]

(d) advise, assist and befriend him with a view to promoting his welfare when he ceases to be looked after by the authority.[9]

Underscoring the general duty to consider rehabilitation with the family, section 23(6) provides that unless to do so would not be reasonably practicable or consistent with the child's welfare the authority should make arrangements for the child to live with his family. In any event, under section 23(7) the local authority must, so far as is reasonably practicable and consistent with the child's welfare secure that the accommodation is near his home and that siblings are accommodated together.

Where an authority is 'looking after' a child they must provide him with accommodation while he is in their care and must maintain him. To this end they may place the child with a family, a relative of his or any other suitable person on such terms as to payment or otherwise as the authority determines.[10] Placement may also be made in a community home, a voluntary home or a registered children's home or by such other arrangements as seen appropriate to the authority.[11]

With regard to placements with the child's own family a distinction needs to be made between accommodated children and those in care. With regard to the former as there are no formal restrictions, he may simply be returned home in which case the child ceases to be accommodated.[12] With regard to the latter a child may only be placed with a parent, or other person who has parental responsibility for him, or a person who had a residence order in respect of the child immediately before the care order was made, provided a number of requirements, including consultation with certain prescribed persons and supervision and medical examination of the child, have been complied with.[13]

---

[7] S 22(4).

[8] S 22(5).

[9] S 24(1).

[10] S 23(2)(a).

[11] S 23(2)(b)–(d).

[12] Outside this circumstance, however, it is by no means clear when accommodation ceases in particular with regard to placements with relatives or friends.

[13] As laid down by the Children Act 1989, s 23(5) and Sch 2, para 13 and the Placement of Children with Parents Etc Regulations 1991.

C. Care and supervision proceedings

1. INTRODUCTION

As we have seen, the Children Act 1989 places considerable importance on local authorities working in partnership with families and the avoidance wherever possible of court proceedings. The expectation is[14] that voluntary arrangements through the provision of services to the child and his family should always be fully explored before compulsory powers are sought from the courts. Nevertheless voluntary arrangements will not solve all problems and, as under the previous law, the Children Act 1989 makes provision in the form of care and supervision orders, for compulsory measures to be taken to safeguard and promote children's welfare. Even so, as the Department of Health's *Guidance* emphasises,[15] where a care or supervision order is thought to be the appropriate remedy because control of the child's circumstances is necessary to promote his welfare 'applications in such proceedings should be part of a carefully planned process'.[16]

Although the scheme for compulsory intervention in the care and upbringing of a child under the Children Act 1989 shares some of the characteristics of the previous law (for example, that no child can be taken into care without a court order and that such an order can be made even if the parents are opposed to their child being in care), in many ways the new scheme is radically different from the old. Not least of the differences is that there is now only one route into care,[17] namely, as result of care order being made under section 31. Courts can no longer (save on a limited interim basis)[18] make care or supervision orders on their own motion. Instead such orders can only be made upon an application by a local authority or authorised person.[19] Local authorities, however, can no longer look to wardship as an alternative means of obtaining care orders.[20]

Among other key changes made by the 1989 Act are the following:

(1) the basis on which care or supervision orders can be made under section 31, the so-called 'threshold' provisions, is substantially different to the previous provisions;

(2) since care proceedings rank as 'family proceedings' for the purposes of section 8,[1] the court can make section 8 orders *whether or not* the threshold provisions under section 31 have been satisfied;

(3) in deciding what order to make, the court must apply the general principles under section 1. In particular it must treat the child's welfare as the paramount consideration and only make an order

---

[14] See the Department of Health's *Guidance and Regulations*, Vol 1, Court Orders, para 3.2.

[15] Ibid at para 3.2.

[16] Furthermore an application should proceed only after the child protection conference (discussed post, p 509) has concluded, having taken legal advice that no other course is open; see ibid, paras 3.10 and 3.12.

[17] Under the former law there were at least 12 different routes into compulsory care, see eg the *Review of Child Care Law*, Discussion Paper No 3, and the seventh edition of this work at pp 440 et seq.

[18] Pursuant to s 38 discussed post, p 525.

[19] Ie the NSPCC, see below.

[20] See ante, p 478. See also pp 466–468 of the seventh edition of this work for a discussion of how local authorities formerly used wardship.

[1] Children Act 1989, s 8(3), (4).

where that is thought better for the child than making no order;

(4) although care proceedings must normally[2] be commenced in the magistrates' family proceedings court, applications can be transferred to the county court or High Court, there being concurrent jurisdiction in all three levels of court;

(5) the proceedings themselves are more open and fair in that the child, his parents and others who are connected with the child can fully participate in them and, with the requirement of advance disclosure of evidence, parties will have due notice of the other's case;

(6) there is greater emphasis on representing the views, feelings and needs of the child;

(7) all parties, including the local authority, can appeal both against the making of, and the refusal to make, a care or supervision order;

(8) although a care order vests parental responsibility in the local authority, the parents do not thereby lose their responsibility; and

(9) there is a presumption that the child in care has a right of reasonable contact with a parent and other specified people. Furthermore parents and others have more extensive rights to litigate over contact disputes, including for the first time restrictions of contact.

2. INITIATING PROCEEDINGS

(a) Applicants

Under section 31(1) of the Children Act 1989 only a local authority or authorised person may apply for a care or supervision order. An 'authorised person' is defined by section 31(9) as the National Society for the Prevention of Cruelty to Children (NSPCC) and any of its officers or any other person authorised by the Secretary of State, of which there are none as yet. Where an authorised person proposes to make an application, he must, if it is reasonably practicable to do so and before making the application, consult the authority where the child is ordinarily resident.[3]

The police and local education authorities *no* longer apply for care or supervision orders, though the latter can apply for an education supervision order.[4] Parents or guardians have no rights to initiate proceedings themselves and the 1989 Act has no procedure equivalent to that under the former law[5] which enabled parents to force a local authority to take action in relation to a child beyond their control.[6]

(b) The responsibility for initiating proceedings

Although the NSPCC have an important role in child protection, it is the local authority that have the prime responsibility for initiating proceedings. They alone have a statutory duty (under section 47) both to investigate

---

[2] The exception is where a higher court makes a 'section 37' direction, discussed post, p 517.
[3] S 31(6). Note also the restrictions under s 31(7).
[4] Under s 36.
[5] Viz under the Children and Young Persons Act 1963, s 3 (as amended).
[6] As Masson: *The Children Act 1989, Text and Commentary* says (at pp 41–69) 'A parent who is unable to control his child can only request assistance from the local authority and make a complaint under s 26(3)(b) [discussed post, p 542] if it is refused.'

(either themselves or by an agency) all cases where they have reasonable cause to suspect that a child who lives or is found in their area is suffering or is likely to suffer significant harm and to determine inter alia whether to bring proceedings. The local authority is also obliged to investigate the child's circumstances following a court direction made under section 37 in other family proceedings[7] or upon being notified by a local education authority that a child has persistently failed to comply with a direction given in an education supervision order.[8]

In discharging this duty local authorities do not work alone. As the Department of Health's *Guidance* puts it:[9]

'The authority cannot expect to be sole repository of knowledge and wisdom about particular cases. Full inter-agency co-operation including sharing information and participating in decision-making is essential whenever a possible care or supervision case is identified.'

Facilitating inter-agency co-operation are two important bodies, namely, at the planning and policy level, Area Child Protection Committees and, at the local level, Child Protection Conferences.[10] The principal tasks of the former[11] include advice on, and the review of, local practice and procedure for inter-agency co-operation including training. The task of the latter is to decide what action should be taken in individual cases.

Membership of both the Area Child Protection Committees and the Child Protection Conferences comprises representatives from the various professions and agencies concerned with children, in particular, from the social services, the NSPCC, the police, education, the health authority, general medical practice, the health visiting service, the probation service and appropriate voluntary organisations. In the case of the Area Child Protection Committee membership is drawn from senior representatives of each of the agencies.

As *Working Together* emphasises:[12]

'The child protection conference is central to child protection procedures. It is not a forum for a formal decision that a person has abused a child. That is a matter for the courts. It brings together the family and the professionals concerned with child protection and provides them with the opportunity to exchange information and plan together. The conference symbolises the inter-agency nature of assessment, treatment and the management of child protection.'

There are two kinds of Child Protection Conference, the initial child protection conference and the child protection review. The purpose of the former, which should only be called after investigation has been made under section 47, is first to decide whether the child should be placed on the Child Protection Register[13] and secondly, to recommend a future plan for the child. If it is decided to place the child on the Register, the conference must appoint a named 'key worker' whose prime task is to fulfil the statutory

---

[7] See ante p 374.
[8] Children Act 1989, Sch 3, para 17.
[9] Vol 1, para 3.10.
[10] See generally *Working Together—Under the Children Act 1989* (HMSO, 1991). Area Child Protection Committees were formerly known as Area Review Committees and Child Protection Conferences as Case Conferences: see p 450 of the seventh edition of this work.
[11] See *Working Together*, para 2.12.
[12] Ibid, para 6.1.
[13] For a discussion of Protection Registers see *Working Together*, paras 6.36 et seq.

obligations of his agency to protect the child and to co-ordinate inter-agency co-operation.[14] The child and his family will therefore be placed under close scrutiny but the key worker must ensure that they are fully engaged in the child protection plan.[15]

The purpose of the child protection review is to review the arrangements for the protection of the child, examine the current level of risk and ensure that he continues to be adequately protected. The review must also consider whether inter-agency co-ordination is functioning effectively and generally to review the child protection plan. It must also consider whether the child's name should continue to be on the Register.[16]

Although there is no right for parents to attend the Child Protection Conference,[17] *Working Together* makes it clear their exclusion can be justified only in exceptional circumstances and that if they are excluded other means of communicating their views to the Conference are to be found.[18]

The Child Protection Conference's dual function of promoting the dissemination of information about a child among the various agencies and of co-ordinating the work of these services is crucial to the management of child protection. All too often in the past tragedies have resulted in cases where vital information about a child's circumstances has not been communicated to the local authority. Now, with properly co-ordinated services there is a better chance of spotting warning signs of abuse or neglect and of constructive action being taken before crisis points have been reached.

(c) In respect of whom applications may be made

As under the former law, no care or supervision order may be made with respect to a child who has reached the age of 17 (or 16 if he is married).[19] Now that it is no longer possible to invoke wardship[20] this means that in no circumstances can compulsory measures be taken in respect of such adolescents[1] although, as we have seen,[2] such persons may themselves approach the authority with a view to being provided with accommodation.

---

[14] See *Working Together*, paras 6.4 et seq.
[15] Ibid, para 6.7.
[16] Ibid, para 6.9.
[17] See *R v Harrow London Borough Council, ex p D* [1990] Fam 133, [1990] 3 All ER 12, CA.
[18] Ibid, para 6.9.
[19] Children Act 1989, s 31(3). Orders *can* still be made if the child is under 16 and validly married according to the laws of another country: Cf *Alhaji Mohamed v Knott* [1969] 1 QB 1, [1968] 2 All ER 563.
[20] See ante, p 478.
[1] Cf *Re SW (A Minor) (Wardship: Jurisdiction)* [1986] 1 FLR 24 where the High Court acting under its inherent jurisdiction committed a 17-year-old into care (which power is specifically abolished by s 100(2)(a)). For a criticism of this position see Lowe (1989) 139 NLJ 87 but cf Eekelaar and Dingwall 138 NLJ 217 and Bainham *Children: The New Law*, at para 5.7.
[2] Ante, p 504, n 8.

3. THE THRESHOLD CRITERIA[3]

(a) Some preliminary observations

No care or supervision order can be made unless the conditions set out by section 31(2) have been satisfied. These conditions have come to be known as the 'threshold criteria' to emphasise the point that they are not in themselves grounds or reasons for making a care or supervision order but rather the *minimum* pre-conditions for obtaining such orders. As Lord Mackay LC said in his Joseph Jackson Memorial Lecture:[4]

'Those conditions are the minimum circumstances which the government considers should always be found to exist before it can ever be justified for a court even to begin to contemplate whether the State should be enabled to intervene compulsorily in family life.'

Even if the criteria are satisfied the court must still decide that making any order is better for the child than making no order and that there are no suitable alternative orders under section 8.[5] If the criteria are not satisfied then in no circumstances can a care or supervision order be made. However this does not necessarily mean that the child will be returned to his parents since the court could still make a section 8 order.[6]

(b) The criteria

Section 31(2) provides that a court may only make a care or supervision order if it is satisfied:

'(a) the child concerned is suffering significant harm, or is likely to suffer significant harm; and
(b) the harm or likelihood of harm is attributable to—
    (i) the care given to the child, or likely to be given to him if the order were not made, not being what it would be reasonable to expect a parent to give to him; or
    (ii) the child's being beyond parental control.'

This wording[7] reflects the recommendations of the Child Care Review.[8] These criteria comprise two separate limbs *each* of which have to be satisfied. The first focuses on present or anticipated harm. The second is that the harm or likelihood of harm is attributable to the lack of reasonable parenting of the child or to the child's being beyond parental control. Unlike the former law, under which the grounds were more specific,[9] the basic criterion of 'significant harm', is relatively open-ended though stopping

---

[3] See generally Department of Health's *Guidance and Regulations*, Vol 1, Court Orders, paras 3.15 et seq; Freeman *Care After 1991* in *Children and the Law* (ed Freestone), pp 130 et seq; Cretney *Defining the Limits of State Intervention* in *Children and the Law*, ibid, pp 58, 68–71; Bainham *Children, the New Law*, paras 5.9 et seq. See also Clarke Hall and Morrison, op cit, paras 1[342] et seq and for a collection of multi-disciplinary papers see *Significant Harm* (Eds Adcock, White and Hollows).

[4] (1989) 139 NLJ 505, 506.

[5] Discussed post, p 522.

[6] See post, p 522.

[7] During its progress through Parliament a number of changes were made to the wording.

[8] *Review of Child Care Law* (DHSS, 1985), paras 15.12–15.27.

[9] Though, as we said, ante, p 251, the conditions were different according to which route was being invoked, being parent-centred under the Child Care Act 1980 or child-centred under the Children and Young Persons Act 1969.

well short of simply making the child's welfare the determining factor. The requirement in the second limb that the harm must be related either to the absence or potential absence of a reasonable degree of parental care or to the child being beyond parental control means, for example, that harm *solely* attributable to moving the child will not satisfy the criteria.[10]

One commentator has said[11] that each of the elements under section 31(2) 'will require considerable judicial exegesis. Almost every word will require interpretation and analysis.' However, how far the courts will be disposed to place strict interpretation on the criteria remains to be seen.[12] It needs to be borne in mind that, now there are no alternative means[13] of obtaining care or supervision orders, too strict an interpretation could leave a child at risk, while on the other hand even if the criteria are satisfied the court is *not* bound to make any order.

(c) Applying the criteria

(i) 'Is suffering or is likely to suffer'

This phrasing covers both present and future harm. The original Bill contained the words 'has suffered' rather than 'is suffering' but was changed to prevent an order being made 'on the basis of significant harm suffered several years previously and which is not likely to be repeated'.[14] Thus past harm is *not* in itself sufficient to satisfy the criteria, though it might be relevant to establishing future likelihood of harm. On the other hand while this present tense implies an existing condition, established case law such as *M v Westminster County Council*[15] on the application of the present tense under the Children and Young Persons Act 1969, suggests that this would not rule out proceedings where, because the local authority had taken action to prevent harm continuing, it had abated by the time of the hearing. As Butler-Sloss J said: 'A child's development is a continuing process. The present must be relevant in the context of what has happened in the past and it becomes a matter of how far in the past you go.' It is suggested, however, that in most cases arguments of this nature will be academic since it will normally be possible to satisfy the likelihood of harm test.[16]

The inclusion of the future element is an important innovation. Before the Children Act 1989 the failure to allow for purely anticipated harm in care proceedings led to local authorities resorting to wardship. The new test removes the objection under the old law that a care order could not be sought in the case of a child being looked after by the local authority

---

[10] Discussed post, p 515.
[11] Freeman, op cit, p 135.
[12] See the divergent views cited in White, Carr and Lowe *A Guide to the Children Act 1989*, op cit, para 6.7.
[13] Ie under wardship.
[14] Per David Mellor MP, HC Official Report, Sc B 23 May 1989, col 221.
[15] [1985] FLR 325, approved by the House of Lords in *D (A Minor) v Berkshire County Council* [1987] AC 317, [1987] 1 All ER 20.
[16] This would certainly have been so in *M v Westminster County Council*, supra, where the child's parents had a continuing drink problem and in *D (A Minor) v Berkshire County Council*, supra, where the parents had a continuing drug problem. See further below.

for any length of time.[17] It also allows proceedings to be considered to remove newborn babies, in particular the first child, where the parent has never been allowed to demonstrate parenting skills.[18] Most commentators[19] also believe that the inclusion of anticipatory harm would permit a care order to be made in the circumstances of *D (A Minor) v Berkshire County Council*[20] in which, under the old law, the House of Lords upheld a care order being made in respect of a baby born with a foetal drug syndrome derived from an addicted mother. One commentator has questioned this,[1] arguing that it would fail the second limb, namely, the lack of care given to the child since at the time of the harm, there was no 'child' but only a foetus.[2] But this argument overlooks the future element in section 31(2)(a), namely the lack of harm *likely to be given* which, given the parents' continued drug dependency in the *Berkshire* case, would clearly have been satisfied. Whatever the outcome might be in the *Berkshire* type of case, it is clear that no care proceedings can be taken to protect unborn children.[3]

Although the inclusion of the future element widens the former law, as the Department of Health's *Guidance* points out,[4] the conditions nevertheless are still intended 'to place a sufficiently difficult burden of proof upon the applicant as to prevent unwarranted intervention in cases where the child is not generally at risk'. For this reason judicial interpretation will be required to determine what is regarded as being 'likely' for the purposes of this provision.[5]

(ii) Harm

The central concept of the threshold criteria is harm. It is defined by section 31(9) to mean ill-treatment or the impairment of health or development. It seems clear that these are to be regarded as alternatives so that satisfaction of either is sufficient.[6]

Ill-treatment is defined by section 31(9) as including sexual abuse and forms of ill-treatment which are not physical. The inclusion of sexual abuse gives statutory recognition to the view that such abuse is by definition ill-treatment, though the Act neither defines the term nor indicates what comes

[17] Ie it reverses *Essex County Council v TLR and KBR* (1979) 9 Fam Law 15. See also Department of Health's *Guidance and Regulations*, op cit, para 3.22. But for problems that can arise under the second limb where children are being accommodated see post, p 515.

[18] For a past example in wardship see *Re B (A Minor)* (1982) Adoption and Fostering Vol 6, No 1, 50, CA discussed at p 466 of the seventh edition of this work. See also Freeman, op cit, at 136. For other examples of the possible application of the likelihood of harm see Department of Health's *Guidance and Regulations*, Vol 1, para 3.22.

[19] See eg Bainham, op cit at para 5.12, Masson, *The Children Act 1989, Text and Commentary*, pp 41–69, White, Carr and Lowe, op cit, para 6.10.

[20] Supra.

[1] Freeman, op cit, 136–138.

[2] Query whether even this argument would necessarily be accepted: The House of Lords 'got round' this argument under the old law and would no doubt continue to do so again.

[3] As Freeman, op cit, at p 158 correctly points out unborn children are not 'persons' under the age of 18. It has also been held by *Re F (In Utero)* [1988] Fam 122, [1988] 2 All ER 193, CA, discussed ante, p 459, that an unborn child cannot be warded.

[4] Ibid, para 3.22.

[5] See eg the discussion in Clarke Hall and Morrison, op cit, para 1[365].

[6] As the Department of Health's *Guidance and Regulations* points out, at para 3.19, this means that the child who is injured but who has made a complete recovery, could be demonstrated to have suffered 'harm' for the purposes of the proceedings.

within it.[7] Physical abuse is obviously ill-treatment (though even here fine lines might have to be drawn between reasonable corporal punishment by a parent and ill-treatment)[8] but the inclusion of other forms of abuse which are not physical is thought to include emotional abuse[9] and possibly, failure to obtain medical treatment.[10] However, the last two instances would also seem to amount to the 'impairment of health or development'.

Section 31(9) defines development as 'physical, intellectual, emotional, social or behavioural development' and health as 'physical or mental health'. This seems, as one commentator has said,[11] 'wide enough to cover any case of neglect—poor nutrition, low standards of hygiene, poor emotional care or through failure to seek treatment for an illness or condition'. It has been recently held[12] that truancy (formerly a specific ground for a care order) can cause a child 'harm' by the consequential impairment of intellectual or social development. It is also thought that 'harm' is generally wide enough to embrace 'moral danger' which was formerly a specific ground for making a care order.[13]

(iii) Is the harm 'significant'?[14]

Whatever the nature of the harm, the court has to consider whether the harm caused is 'significant'. Vital though this is to the application of the section it is not defined in the Act. A dictionary definition is that it should be 'considerable, noteworthy or important' and, reflecting the common sense view, the Department of Health's *Guidance* comments:[15]

> 'Minor shortcomings in health or minor deficits in physical, psychological or social development should not require compulsory intervention unless cumulatively they are having, or are likely to have, serious and lasting effects upon the child.'

Where the harm is due to ill-treatment no further guidance is given but in the case of impairment of health or development, reference must be made to section 31(10) which provides:

> 'Where the question of whether harm suffered by a child is significant turns on the child's health or development, his health or development shall be compared

---

[7] See, for example, *C v C (Child Abuse: Evidence)* [1988] 1 FLR 462, where the father was said to have indulged in 'vulgar and inappropriate horseplay' with his daughter. On this whole issue see the discussion by Freeman, op cit pp 140–142, who inter alia, asks whether exposing a child to pornographic material is sexual abuse?

[8] See Freeman, op cit, pp 142–146. Cf the Scottish Law Commission's proposals to make all corporal punishment an offence: Scot Law Com No 135, *Report on Family Law* (1992).

[9] See eg Clarke Hall and Morrison, op cit, para 1[352] and Freeman, op cit, p 140 both referring to *F v Suffolk County Council* (1981) 2 FLR 208 under the old law. Lord Mackay adverted to 'verbal abuse or unfairness' being encompassed by the definition: 503 HL Official Report col 342.

[10] See Freeman, op cit, p 141.

[11] Masson, op cit, pp 41–71.

[12] *Re O (A Minor) (Care Order: Education: Procedure)* [1992] 2 FLR 7 per Ewbank J. Though in most cases an education supervision order under s 36 is more likely to be sought.

[13] See eg Bainham, op cit, p 102 and Freeman op cit, pp 154–155 and 161. Both thought that the 13 year old Nigerian child in *Alhaji Mohamed v Knott* [1969] 1 QB 1, [1968] 2 All ER 563, validly married under her country's law would be thought to be suffering or likely to suffer significant harm by having intercourse before she reached puberty with her husband, a man twice her age with venereal disease.

[14] See generally *Significant Harm* (ed by Adcock, White and Hollows, 1992).

[15] Vol 1, para 3.21.

with that which could reasonably be expected of a similar child.'

Precisely what is meant by a 'similar child' in this context is hard to say and raises such basic questions as how far one should have regard to the child's background and whether the courts should apply different standards to children from different ethnic backgrounds.[16] Even if, as Lord Mackay suggested,[17] comparisons should be confined to physical (and presumably intellectual) attributes rather than background, there are still immense difficulties. For example, is a deaf child of deaf parents a 'similar child' to a deaf child of hearing parents?[18] The Department of Health's *Guidance* comments:[19]

> 'The meaning of "similar" in this context will require judicial interpretation, but may need to take account of environmental, social and cultural characteristics of the child. The need to use a standard appropriate for the child arises because some children have characteristics or handicaps which mean that they cannot be expected to be as healthy or well-developed as others. Equally if the child needs special care or attention (because, for example, he is unusually difficult to control) then this is to be expected for him. The standard should only be that which it is reasonable to expect for the particular child, rather than the best that could possibly be achieved; applying a "best" standard could open up the risk that a child might be removed from home simply because some other arrangement could cater better for his needs than care by his parents.

In the one decision so far reported on this provision, Ewbank J held[20] that in the case of a 15-year-old truant of average intelligence: ' "similar child" means a child of equivalent intellectual and social development, who has gone to school and not merely an average child who may or may not be at school'.

(iv) Is the harm attributable to the care given or likely to be given?

Having satisfied itself that the harm is significant, the court has also to be satisfied that it is attributable to the care given, or likely to be given, to the child not being what a reasonable parent would give to the child. The likely care complements the likely harm. Harm caused solely by a third party is therefore excluded, unless the parent has unreasonably failed to prevent it.[1] Equally clearly, harm *solely* attributable to moving the child will not satisfy the test. For this reason it is important to determine what is meant by 'care' in this context, a matter on which the Act is surprisingly silent. Although 'care' could simply be interpreted as referring to the day-to-day care given to the child by the person with whom the child is living, the better view is that it means more than this, connoting in addition, the love and affection that one would expect of reasonable parents.[2] Hence, in the case of a child being accommodated by a local authority but living with foster parents, the threshold criteria might still be satisfied notwithstanding

---

[16] For cases that have raised this issue under the old law see eg *Alhaji Mohamed v Knott*, supra and *Re H* [1987] 2 FLR 12.
[17] 503, HL Official Report, col 354.
[18] This is one of a number of examples that Freeman uses, op cit, pp 147–149 to highlight the difficulties of this test.
[19] Vol 1, para 3.20.
[20] In *Re O (A Minor) (Care Order: Education: Procedure)*, supra.
[1] See further Freeman, op cit, at p 150.
[2] See Clarke Hall and Morrison, op cit, at para 1[373] and Freeman, op cit, pp 150–151.

that the parents are now able to look after their child, if in the past they have not been visiting or keeping in touch.[3] On the other hand, if the parent has shown all the care and concern that a reasonable parent would show to a child living away from home for a time, then on either interpretation the criteria would not be satisfied. In such cases, however, the court would have to consider whether it would be preferable to make a residence order in favour of the foster parents.[4]

(v) Not being what it would be reasonable to expect a parent to give to him

This rather inelegant phrase imports an objective test. It is therefore no answer to say that the care given was to the best of the parents' limited abilities.[5] Parents cannot argue that they have particular problems, that they are feckless, unintelligent, irresponsible, alcoholic, drug abusers, poor or otherwise disadvantaged, which justifies them in providing a lower standard of care. It is no answer either that the care given was no different from that given by others in the same street or neighbourhood.[6] The Department of Health's *Guidance* suggests[7] that the court will wish to seek professional evidence on the standard of care which reasonable parents could be expected to provide with support from community-wide services as appropriate where the child's needs are complex or demanding, or the lack of reasonable care is not immediately obvious.

The focus of attention is on the care given or likely to be given to the child in question, not to an average child. If, for example, the child has particular difficulties in relation to his behaviour or handicap, the court will have to consider what a reasonable parent would provide for him. This could require a higher standard of care than for an average child.[8]

(vi) The child's being beyond parent control[9]

As the Department of Health's *Guidance* states,[10] this alternative causal condition was provided for in the previous legislation but was not linked with harm to the child. 'It provides for cases where, whatever the standard of care available to the child, he is not benefiting from it because of lack of parental control. *It is immaterial whether this is the fault of the parents or the child.*' [Emphasis added.]

In the one decision so far reported adverting to this issue,[11] Ewbank J commented that in respect of a 15-year-old truant:

---

[3] Hence in a case like *M v Wigan Borough Council* [1980] Fam 36, [1979] 2 All ER 958 where children were repeatedly looked after by the authority during the mother's difficult pregnancies but where the parents were repeatedly reluctant to take responsibility for them, the criteria would be satisfied. Similarly in a case like *W v Sunderland Borough Council* [1980] 2 All ER 514, where there was an unexplained failure over a long period to visit a child being looked after by the authority the criteria would also be satisfied.

[4] See post, p 522.

[5] Cf *O'Dare v South Glamorgan County Council* (1980) 3 FLR 1, CA.

[6] These matters may, however, be relevant to the question of whether an order should be made.

[7] Vol 1 at para 3.23.

[8] See the Department of Health's *Guidance and Regulations*, op cit, at para 3.25.

[9] See generally, Freeman, op cit, pp 156–157.

[10] Op cit at para 3.25.

[11] *Re O (A Minor) (Care Order: Education: Procedure)*, supra.

'... where a child is suffering harm in not going to school and is living at home it will follow that either the child is beyond her parents' control or that they are not giving the child the care that it would be reasonable to expect a parent to give.'

4. THE APPLICATION OF SECTION 1 PRINCIPLES

Having considered the threshold criteria it is incumbent upon the court in deciding what, if any, order to make to apply the general principles under section 1. This means that pursuant to section 1(1) the court must regard the welfare of the child as the paramount consideration.[12] It is also bound[13] to have regard to the statutory check-list contained in section 1(3).[14] Section 1(3)(g) directs the court to consider the range of powers available to it which means, because Part IV proceedings rank as 'family proceedings' for the purposes of section 8,[15] that the court must consider whether it should make a section 8 order. Even if the threshold criteria are satisfied the court may choose not to make a care order but make a section 8 order instead.[16]

Pursuant to section 1(5) the court must in any event consider whether it is better for the child to make any order than to make no order at all. To answer this question in the context of care proceedings the court will have to consider the plans which the authority is proposing for the child.[17] It will have to explore whether they are the best available plans for the child, and if so, whether an order is necessary for these plans.

The application of section 1 principles emphasises that satisfaction of the threshold criteria by no means guarantees that a care or supervision order will be made.

5. PROCEDURE AND EVIDENCE

(a) Making the application

Unless an application is being made following an investigation directed by section 37 (in which case the application should be made in the court that made the direction),[18] it should be made in the first instance to a magistrates' family proceedings court.[19] A separate application must be made for each child[20] on a prescribed form and a copy of the application must be served on all the parties.[1]

---

[12] Discussed ante, pp 336 et seq.

[13] See s 1(4)(b).

[14] Discussed ante, pp 385 et seq.

[15] S 8(3), (4).

[16] Discussed further post, p 522.

[17] It will be noted that the application form for a care or supervision order (Children Act Form CHA 19) requires the applicant to state the plans for the child.

[18] The Children (Allocation of Proceedings) Order 1991, art 3(2).

[19] Ibid, art 3(1). However, there is no requirement, as formerly, that the child resides in the petty sessional area.

[20] Family Proceedings Courts (Children Act 1989) Rules 1991, r 4(1)(a). As from 1 April 1992 fees are charged on all applications to the magistrates' courts: Magistrates' Courts Fees (Amendment) Order 1992.

[1] Ibid, r 4(1)(b).

Once an application has been made it can only be withdrawn with leave of the court.[2]

(b) Determining which court will hear the application

On receipt of the application, the magistrates' clerk will consider whether the proceedings should be transferred to a higher court or to another magistrates' court. The criteria for transfer are governed by the Children (Allocation of Proceedings) Order 1991. With regard to transferring proceedings from one magistrates' court to another the main criteria are accelerating the determination of the proceedings and to consolidate proceedings with other pending family proceedings,[3] but another reason might be the general convenience of the parties.

Under article 7 of the Allocation Rules cases can be transferred to a county court[4] either upon a party's application or upon the court's own motion. The three main criteria justifying a transfer are that (a) the proceedings are exceptionally grave, important or complex, (b) it is appropriate for the proceedings to be heard together with other pending family proceedings and (c) it would significantly accelerate the determination of the proceedings. The first of these criteria is spelt out in more detail and refers to (i) the complicated or conflicting evidence about the risks involved to the child's physical or mental well-being or about other matters relating to the welfare of the child, (ii) the number of parties, (iii) conflict with the law of another jurisdiction, (iv) some novel or difficult point of law, or (v) some question of general public interest. Although no mention is made of the length of proceedings the President of the Family Division has said in a case[5] in which the application was heard over eight separate days that a lengthy case inevitably causes problems for magistrates and could appropriately have been transferred. Such transfers are not bound to be accepted. It is within the district judge's powers to transfer the case to the High Court,[6] or to transfer the case back to the magistrates.[7]

If a transfer request is refused, under article 9 any party may apply for a transfer before the nominated district judge at the appropriate county court care centre. If he agrees to the request the district judge can transfer the case to his court, to another care centre or to the High Court.[8] Little guidance is given on whether to transfer a case to the High Court; article 9(3) merely states that the court must consider that the proceedings 'are appropriate for determination in the High Court' and that such a determination would be in the interests of the child. There is no appeal against the district judge's decision to allocate the case to a county court or the High Court.

It will be noted that as magistrates' clerks cannot allocate a case to the High Court, public law cases can only be heard at that level following a second allocation decision by the district judge.

[2] Ibid, r 5.
[3] The Children (Allocation of Proceedings) Order 1991, art 6.
[4] Ie a care centre, see ante, p 256.
[5] *J v Berkshire County Council* (1992), Times, 10 March.
[6] Under art 12. The criteria for transfer are the same as under art 9(3), discussed below.
[7] Art 11 and see the Family Proceedings Rules 1991 (as amended), r 4.6(6). An appeal may be made to a circuit judge against such a decision: the Children (Allocation of Proceedings) (Appeals) Order 1991.
[8] Art 9(2), (3) of the Allocation Rules and the Family Proceedings Rules 1991, r 4.6.

(c) Parties

Unlike the former law, which despite late improvements was anomalous in that parents were not automatically parties in the proceedings,[9] the current law is straightforward. The child and any person with parental responsibility all are automatically parties in care proceedings.[10] It is open to any other person to apply to be joined as a party and within the court's powers to direct that they be joined.[11]

(d) Representing the child[12]

One of the most important developments in care proceedings in the 1980s was the setting up of a system for the separate representation of children, by guardians ad litem. This highly successful system has been maintained under the Children Act 1989. Indeed under section 41 courts are required in specified proceedings[13] to appoint a guardian ad litem for the child 'unless satisfied that it is not necessary to do so in order to safeguard his interests'. This provision leaves courts less room for discretion than formerly[14] and appointments are expected to be the norm in care proceedings.[15] Such appointments should be made as soon as practicable after the commencement of proceedings.[16]

A guardian ad litem is an individual qualified in social work. The person appointed must be selected from a panel[17] but must not (a) be a member or officer or servant of the local authority or authorised person bringing the proceedings, or (b) have been at any time in the past an officer of the authority or voluntary organisation who has been directly concerned in that capacity in arrangements relating to the care or accommodation and welfare of the child, or (c) be a serving probation officer.[18] These provisions are designed to ensure that a guardian is independent of the parties. The independence of guardians has been held to be so important that it should not be compromised by any restriction placed directly or indirectly on the carrying of their duties. Hence in *R v Cornwall County*

---

[9] Discussed at pp 459–60 of the seventh edition of this work.

[10] Family Proceedings Courts (Children Act 1989) Rules 1991, r 7(1).

[11] For the procedure see ibid, r 7(2), (3). It may be noted that there are therefore no longer special rules applying to grandparents.

[12] See generally Department of Health's *Guidance and Regulations*, Vol 7, Guardians Ad Litem and other Court Related Issues, ch 2 and Monro and Forrester *The Guardian ad Litem* (1991).

[13] 'Specified proceedings' are defined by s 41(6) and include care and supervision proceedings, cases where a s 37 direction has been made, discharge applications, applications under Part V of the Children Act and contact in care proceedings under s 34.

[14] See eg *R v Plymouth Juvenile Court, ex p F and F* [1987] 1 FLR 169 and the discussion at p 461 of the seventh edition of this work. The new form of wording reflects that formerly applied to unopposed applications for discharge.

[15] During the debates on the Bill, David Mellor MP said on behalf of the Government, that guardians should be appointed in over 90 per cent of cases: HC Official Report, SC B, 23 May 1989, col 255.

[16] Family Proceedings Courts (Children Act 1989) Rules 1991, r 10(1); Family Proceedings Rules 1991, r 4.10(1). Though the court has power to make an appointment at any stage of the proceedings.

[17] Panels have to be set up by each local authority pursuant to the Guardians Ad Litem and Reporting Officers (Panels) Regulations 1991.

[18] Family Proceedings Courts (Children Act 1989) Rules 1991, r 10(7); Family Proceedings Rules 1991, r 4.10(7).

Council[19] an attempt by the local authority to lay down in advance the normal maximum time that should be spent on any particular case was quashed.

The guardian's general duty is to safeguard the interests of the child[20] and more specifically to advise on the following:

'(a) whether the child is of sufficient understanding for any purpose including the child's refusal to submit to a medical or psychiatric examination or other assessment that the court has power to require, direct or order;
(b) the wishes of the child in respect of any matter relevant to the proceedings, including his attendance at court;
(c) the appropriate forum for the proceedings;
(d) the appropriate timing of the proceedings or any part of them;
(e) the options available to the court in respect of the child and the suitability of each such option including what order should be made in determining the application;
(f) any other matter on which the court seeks his advice or about which he considers that the court should be informed.'[1]

In addition, since he will be appointed at an early stage of the proceedings the guardian should also be able to advise the court about the discharge of an emergency protection order, the making or extending of interim care or supervision orders and about directions in interim orders.

Unless one has already been appointed the guardian is required to appoint a solicitor to act for the child[2] but it is for the guardian to consider how the case should be presented in court on the child's behalf and to give instructions to the solicitor unless the latter considers the child wishes to give instructions that conflict with those of the guardian. Any solicitor so appointed must therefore work closely with the guardian ad litem. In a normal case he will take his instructions from the guardian. However, where the child wishes and is able to give instructions on his own behalf[3] which conflict with those of guardian, the solicitor must take his instructions from the child.[4] In that event the guardian continues with his duties save for instructing the solicitor.[5]

To carry out his duties the guardian must investigate all the circumstances including interviewing such persons as he thinks appropriate or as the court directs, inspect local authority records (see below), and bring to the court's attention such records and documents which in his opinion may be of assistance to the case. He may also obtain such professional assistance as

---

[19] [1992] 1 All ER 471, per Sir Stephen Brown P. For another case emphasising the independent role of guardians see eg *R v Birmingham Juvenile Court, ex p G* [1990] 2 QB 573, [1989] 3 All ER 336, CA.

[20] Children Act 1989, s 41(2)(b).

[1] Family Proceedings Courts (Children Act 1989) Rules 1991, r 11(4), Family Proceedings Rules 1991, r 4.11(4).

[2] Ibid, r 11(2) and 4.11(2) respectively.

[3] There is no definitive rule as to how old a child must be before he can be considered able to give instructions but as a rule of thumb, one might expect a child aged 10 and upwards as being capable. In *Re O (A Minor) (Care Order: Education: Supervision)* [1992] 2 FLR 7, discussed ante, p 515, a 15-year-old gave separate instructions to her solicitors.

[4] Family Proceedings Courts (Children Act 1989) Rules 1991, r 12(1) and Family Proceedings Rules 1991, r 4.12(1).

[5] He may, with leave, have legal representation: ibid, r 11(3) and 4.11(3) respectively.

he thinks appropriate or which the court directs him to obtain.[6] The 1989 Act now gives the guardian extensive rights to examine and take copies of any records of or held by a local authority in relation to a child including child protection conference minutes.[7]

At the end of these investigations the guardian produces a written report advising on the interests of the child, which, unless the court otherwise directs, should be filed with the court 7 days before the date fixed for the hearing. Copies are served by the court on the parties as soon as practicable thereafter.[8] As with court welfare reports the guardian's reports, though not binding, are very influential and there is general agreement that the system, particularly after implementation of the 1989 Act, is working well.

(e) Evidence[9]

Another important change made by the 1989 Act is with respect to the submission and treatment of evidence. Whereas before the 1989 Act evidence in care proceedings was oral, now at all court levels including, therefore, in the magistrates' courts, *written* statements of the substance of the oral evidence which the party intends to adduce has to be submitted in advance of the hearing.[10] Similarly, copies of any documents including expert's reports, on which a party intends to rely, have to be submitted in advance.[11] Furthermore further evidence or documents can only be brought in with the court's leave.[12] Subject to the court's directions, copies of the written evidence is served on the other parties also in advance of the hearing. Magistrates are expected to have read the written evidence ahead of the hearing.[13]

Special rules govern the use of expert evidence, in that no child can be medically examined or psychiatrically examined or otherwise assessed for the purpose of the preparation of expert evidence without leave of the court.[14]

The two-fold significance of the above-mentioned rules is that they ensure that the case is 'court driven' whilst at the same time providing for more open proceedings with advance disclosure of evidence to all the parties.[15]

Another change is in relation to hearsay. Under the Children (Admissibility of Hearsay Evidence) Order 1991 hearsay evidence is admiss-

---

[6] See r 11(a) and r 4.11(a) respectively. But note also r 18(1) and r 4.18 under which no medical or psychiatric examination of the child for the purpose of adducing evidence, should be carried out without leave of the court.

[7] Children Act 1989, s 42(1) as amended by the Courts and Legal Services Act 1990, Sch 16, para 18.

[8] Family Proceedings Courts (Children Act 1989) Rules, r 11(7) and Family Proceedings Rules 1991, r 4.11(7).

[9] See generally Clarke Hall and Morrison, op cit, paras 1[601] et seq.

[10] Family Proceedings Courts (Children Act 1989) Rules 1991, r 17(1)(a), Family Proceedings Rules 1991, r 4.17(1)(a).

[11] Ibid, r 17(1)(b), r 4.17(1)(b).

[12] Ibid, r 17(3), r 4.17(3).

[13] Family Proceedings Courts (Children Act 1989) Rules 1991, r 21(1). The Family Proceedings Rules 1991 do not make such express provision for the higher courts since advance reading of the documents is done as a matter of course.

[14] Ibid, r 18, r 4.18.

[15] Though even under the former law there was a move towards more openness, see in particular *R v Hampshire County Council, ex p K* [1990] 2 QB 71, [1990] 2 All ER 129 in which the local authority was condemned for withholding, pending the hearing, a medical report. See also *Re M (A Minor) (Disclosure of Material)* [1990] 2 FLR 36, CA.

ible in care and supervision proceedings before any court. This means, for example, that videos of child interviews are admissible in the magistrates courts as well as in the higher courts.[16]

6. COURT ORDERS

(a) Section 8 orders[17]

In care proceedings, as in any other proceedings under the Children Act 1989, the court must be satisfied that the making of an order is better for the child than making no order.[18] Assuming that the court concludes that some order should be made, consideration should first be given to the appropriateness of section 8 orders.[19]

Section 8 orders can be made whether or not they have been applied for[20] and irrespective of whether the threshold criteria have been satisfied.

If the threshold criteria under section 31 cannot be satisfied then although the court cannot make a care or supervision order it can still make a section 8 order.[1] One example might be where a child accommodated by a local authority has been happily fostered for some time, and the parent wishes to resume care. Section 31 may not be satisfied if the 'harm' can only be attributable to the move rather than to the standard of care that might be provided by the parent.[2] Nevertheless it may be appropriate to make a residence order in favour of the foster parents (perhaps with contact to the parent). Alternatively, depending on the merits of the case, for example, where the child has been accommodated following the mother's illness and the mother has now recovered, it may be right for the child eventually to live with his parents, but only following a phased return. The 1989 Act makes no express provision for ordering phased returns.[3] However, it may be possible to make a time limited residence order in favour of the foster parent[4] subject to the condition that there should be satisfactory rehabilitation followed by a residence order in favour of the parents.[5]

The ability to make a residence order in favour of third parties, even though the threshold provisions under section 31 cannot be satisfied, means that under the 1989 Act children can be removed or kept away from the care of their parents simply upon the welfare principle. However, immedi-

---

[16] But careful thought needs to be given as to their value. It is particularly important that those conducting the interviews have regard to the guidelines laid down in the Cleveland Report (1987, Cm 412) ch 12; see eg *Re E (A Minor) (Child Abuse: Evidence)* [1991] 1 FLR 420.

[17] See generally Lowe *The Application of Section 8 Orders to Care Proceedings* in *Child Protection* (Eds Adcock, White and Holloway) pp 43–52.

[18] Ie pursuant to s 1(5).

[19] This is because s 1(3)(g) directs the court to consider the range of powers available to it.

[20] Children Act 1989, s 10(1)(b). If, however, a court is minded to make an order not being sought it should give the parties an opportunity to address the court on the desirability of that option: *Croydon London Borough Council v A* [1992] 16 L S Gaz R 28.

[1] It can also make a family assistance order under s 16, discussed ante, p 372.

[2] See the discussion ante, p 515.

[3] Such an express provision had been recommended by the Review of Child Care Law, op cit, p 186. See further post, p 529.

[4] Assuming the foster parents are willing for the order to be made. Residence orders in favour of foster parents do not prevent a local authority from making contributions towards the cost of accommodation and maintenance of the child: Children Act 1989, Sch 1, para 15.

[5] For the power to add conditions see s 11(7), discussed ante, p 352.

ately before the 1989 Act it had been held that before depriving a parent of custody it had to be shown that the child's welfare positively demanded the displacement of the parent's care.[6] A similar approach may be expected under the 1989 Act.

Satisfaction of the threshold criteria does not inevitably mean that a care or supervision order will be made. It is within the court's powers, for example, to refuse to make a care order and make a section 8 order instead. One example may be where it is felt that though inadequate in the past, given sufficient support in the future, a parent could cope. A court could for instance grant a residence order to a parent on condition that she live at a mother and baby unit for some specified time.[7] In this type of case it is submitted that it is outside the court's power to make a specific issue order forcing the local authority to provide a particular service. Nevertheless notwithstanding the residence order the child may still qualify for services as a child in need.[8]

Another example where a care order might not be thought appropriate is where abuse has been proved but the perpetrator has since left, or is prepared to leave the home. In such a case a residence order might be made in favour of one parent perhaps with a condition that the other parent, or named person, is not invited back into the home, or with a prohibited steps order forbidding the other person from contacting the child.

A further example is where a parent has been proved inadequate, for example through alcohol or drug dependence, but there is a relative who could look after the child. In these circumstances a residence order in favour of the relative might be thought preferable to a care order.[9]

Provided the threshold criteria have been satisfied it is open to the court to make both a section 8 and a supervision order. The advantage of coupling a section 8 order with a supervision order is that the child's upbringing can be closely supervised and it may be that where it is thought right to make conditional residence orders it will generally also be appropriate to make a supervision order.[10]

It is to be emphasised that it is not open to the court to make both a section 8 order and a care order. The two are inconsistent.[11]

(b) Care orders

The making of a care order discharges *any* section 8 order, supervision order and a school attendance order. It also brings wardship to an end.[12]

As far as local authorities are concerned care orders have the twofold effect of (i) requiring them 'to receive the child into their care and to keep

[6] See *Re K (A Minor) (Ward: Care and Control)* [1990] 3 All ER, 795, CA, and *Re K (A Minor) (Wardship: Adoption)* [1991] 1 FLR 57, CA as explained by *Re H (A Minor) (Custody) (Interim Care and Control)* [1991] 2 FLR 109, CA, discussed ante, p 388.
[7] One problem still to be fully explored concerns the limits of the conditions that can be imposed on a residence order but the controlling principle must surely be that no condition that is fundamentally inconsistent with such an order may be made.
[8] Accordingly the local authority will be obliged to continue to so treat the child pursuant to the duties under s 17(1) and (10), see ante, p 510.
[9] In such a circumstance it seems unlikely that a court would wish to make an order in favour of the relative without first seeing that person.
[10] Cf the position on making an interim order under s 38(3) discussed post, p 526.
[11] See Children Act 1989, ss 9 and 91.
[12] Ibid, s 91(2)–(5).

him in their care while the order remains in force'[13] and (ii) vesting parental responsibility in the authority.[14]

The investing of parental responsibility in the local authority is in addition to and not at the expense of the parent's responsibility. In other words parents do not lose their responsibility upon the making of a care order.[15] However important and innovative though this notion of shared responsibility is, control very much rests with the local authority as is emphasised by section 33(3)(b) which provides that the authority has the power to determine the extent to which a parent or guardian may meet his parental responsibility insofar as it is necessary to do so to safeguard or promote the child's welfare. Nevertheless a parent or guardian who has care of the child is still entitled to do what is reasonable in all the circumstances of the case for the purpose of safeguarding or promoting the child's welfare[16] and retains any right, duty, power, responsibility or authority in relation to the child and his property under any other enactment.[17] These include the right to consent to the child's marriage, rights under the Education Act 1981 in relation to the child's special educational needs, financial responsibility for the child and some responsibility for his acts if he is in their charge and control.

The parental responsibility acquired by a local authority has some specific limitations. They are not allowed to cause the child to be brought up in any religious persuasion other than that in which he would have been brought up if no order had been made. They do not have the right to consent, or refuse to consent, to the making of an application for a freeing for adoption order or to agree, or to refuse to agree, to an adoption order or a proposed foreign adoption order, nor to appoint a guardian.[18] Furthermore while a care order is in force no person may cause the child to be known by a new surname without the written consent of every person with parental responsibility or by the leave of the court.[19] The same consents are required before a child may be removed from the United Kingdom except where removal is by the care authority for less than a month or the authority is arranging for a child to live outside England and Wales.[20]

It should be noted that once a care order is made the court cannot make any further directions.

(c) Supervision orders

A supervision order is an order putting the child under the supervision of a designated local authority or a probation officer.[1] It does not vest parental responsibility in the local authority. The court cannot make both a care order and supervision order.

While a supervision order is in force, the duty of a supervisor is:

---

[13] Ibid, s 33(1).
[14] Ibid, s 33(3)(a).
[15] Ibid, s 2(6). It will be noted however that persons other than parents who had parental responsibility by virtue of a residence order *will* lose it because a care order discharges the section 8 order.
[16] S 33(5).
[17] S 33(9).
[18] S 33(6).
[19] S 33(7).
[20] S 33(7) and (8). In the latter case the court's approval is required, see Sch 2, para 19.
[1] S 31(1)(b). See also Sch 3, para 9, with regard to the selection of a supervisor.

'(a) to advise, assist and befriend the supervised child;
(b) to take such steps as are reasonably necessary to give effect to the order; and
(c) where
  (i) the order is not wholly complied with; or
  (ii) the supervisor considers that the order may no longer be necessary, to consider whether or not to apply to the court for its variation or discharge'.[2]

A supervision order initially lasts for one year but it can be extended, upon an application by the supervisor, for up to a maximum of three years.[3]

An order can vest the supervisor with wide powers and may require the supervised child to comply with any directions given from time to time by the supervisor which require him to:

'(a) live at a place or places specified in the directions for a specified period or periods
(b) present himself to a specified person at a place and on a day specified
(c) participate in specified activities, such as education or training.'[4]

Furthermore, to help with compliance with these directions an order may include a requirement that, with the consent of a 'responsible person',[5] that person take all reasonable steps to ensure that the child complies with any direction given by the supervisor.[6]

The supervisor is not empowered to give directions as to the child's medical or psychiatric examination or treatment, but these can be made the subject of specific direction by the court, provided at any rate that where the child is of sufficient understanding to make an informed decision, he consents.[7]

(d) Interim orders[8]

The court has a wide range of powers to make interim orders, including, for the first time, interim supervision orders. It may also make a residence order or other section 8 orders for a limited period. As the Department of Health's *Guidance* says[9] the two main objectives of these powers are 'to enable the child to be suitably protected while proceedings are progressing where this is required, and to see that interim measures operate only for as long as necessary'.

Interim care or supervision orders may be made either following a section 37 direction by the court to a local authority to investigate the child's circumstances, or on an adjournment in care proceedings.[10] In each case

[2] S 35(1).
[3] Sch 3, para 6.
[4] Sch 3, para 2. Note that the original provision that such directions may only last for 90 days under Sch 3, para 7(1) has been repealed by the Courts and Legal Services Act 1990, Sch 16, para 27.
[5] Ie any person who has parental responsibility for the child and any other person with whom the child is living: Sch 3, para 1.
[6] Sch 3, para 3.
[7] Sch 3, para 4.
[8] See generally Department of Health's *Guidance and Regulations*, Vol 1, Court Orders, paras 3.35 et seq.
[9] Ibid at para 3.35.
[10] Children Act 1989, s 38(1). When considering adjourning the case the court should be mindful of the general principle that under s 1(2) delay is prima facie prejudicial to the child's welfare. Proceedings should not be adjourned simply because criminal proceedings are pending against the alleged abuser: *Re S (Child Abuse Cases: Management)* [1992] 1 FCR 31.

the court must be satisfied, *whether the proceedings are contested or not*, that there are reasonable grounds for believing that 'the circumstances with respect to the child are as mentioned in section 31(2)'.[11]

One of the key differences between a full and interim order is that in the latter case the court may give such directions as it considers appropriate with regard to medical or psychiatric examination or other assessment of the child and may direct that no examination or assessment is to take place at all or unless the court directs.[12] If the child is of sufficient understanding to make an informed decision he may refuse to submit to an examination or assessment.[13]

As the Department of Health's *Guidance* states,[14] the court is able to make a section 8 order as an interim measure, but if it makes a residence order it must also make an interim supervision order unless satisfied that the child's welfare will be satisfactorily safeguarded without one.[15]

The duration of interim care and supervision orders is governed by section 38(4) and (5) which are among the most obscure provisions of the whole of the 1989 Act. While it is clear that the *maximum* duration of an initial order is 8 weeks, there is less certainty about the length and number of subsequent orders that may be made. A good explanation can however be found in *Clarke Hall and Morrison on Children*, namely:[16]

'An interim care or supervision order may be made for such period as the court orders but may not last longer than eight weeks in the case of an initial order or the "the relevant period" in the case of a second or subsequent order: s 38(4). The relevant period is four weeks, or eight weeks from the date of the first order if that is longer. Thus, if the first order was made for two weeks, the second order could be made for six weeks. If the first two orders were made respectively for one week and two weeks, the third order could be made for five weeks. When deciding the period, the court must consider whether a party who was or might have been opposing the order was in a position to argue the case in full: s 38(10). There is no limit in principle to the number of interim orders which the court can make.'[17]

It should be added that the renewal of an interim order should not be regarded as a formality but requires separate consideration on its merits each time.[18]

7. APPEALS

Before the Children Act 1989 the law governing appeals in public law cases was complicated and anomalous. Some, but not all, parties could appeal

[11] S 38(2).
[12] S 38(6), (7).
[13] S 38(6).
[14] Vol 1, at para 3.41.
[15] S 38(3).
[16] At para 1[433].
[17] This latter interpretation is accepted by the Department of Health's *Guidance and Regulations*, Vol 1, which at para 3.46 says: 'Although there is no limit to the number of interim orders that can be made under the Act a balance will have to be struck between allowing sufficient time for enquiries, reports and statements, and risking allowing the child to continue in interim care or supervision for so long that the balance of advantage is distorted in favour of continued intervention.'
[18] Cf *R v Birmingham Juvenile Court, ex p P and S* [1984] FLR 343.

against the making of a care or supervision order but there was no general right of appeal against the refusal to make such orders. Where appeals did lie from magistrates' decisions they lay before the Crown Court and were by way of a full rehearing.[19] Under the Children Act 1989 the law is straightforward: anyone who was a party in the original proceedings may appeal against the making or refusal to make a care or supervision order (including an interim order). This means that like any other party local authorities now have full rights of appeal.

Appeals from magistrates' decisions lie to the High Court,[20] and from the county court and High Court to the Court of Appeal.[1] Although in each case the relevant rules[2] say that the appeal is by way of a rehearing this does not mean that it is a hearing de novo. As Hollings J said in *Croydon London Borough Council v A*[3] all that is meant by the term 'rehearing' is that the appeal court has 'a wide ranging power to consider and deal with the way in which the court below came to its decision but it is not empowered to hear evidence, except in certain exceptional circumstances.'

It is equally established[4] that these appeals are governed by the general principles laid down in *G v G*[5] namely, that before an appeal can succeed the first instance decision has to be shown to be wrong; it is not enough that the appellate court would have reached a different decision.

It has been held[6] that magistrates have no power to grant a stay of execution once a care order has been made, though acting under their inherent power, the county court and High Court have. On the other hand, section 40(1) and (2) of the Children Act 1989 specifically provide that a court may, if it *dismisses* an application for a care order and at the time of dismissal the child is the subject of an interim care or supervision order, make either a care or a supervision order, as the case may be, for a limited duration pending an appeal.[7] Similarly, upon granting a discharge, the court may order either that its decision is not to have effect or that the care or supervision order is to continue, pending the appeal.[8] In each case these orders may have effect only for the 'appeal period', that is, either between the lodging of an appeal and the determination of it, or the time during which an appeal may be made.[9]

---

[19] See generally, Bevan *Child Law*, paras 14.114–14.116.
[20] Children Act 1989, s 94(1) and the Family Proceedings Rules 1991, r 4.22. For the procedure see *Practice Direction* [1992] 1 All ER 864. Although this *Direction* directs that appeals will take place at the nearest convenient High Court Centre, it is subject to the availability of a suitable judge: cf *Oxfordshire County Council v R* [1992] 1 FLR 648.
[1] County Courts Act 1984, s 77(1) and Supreme Court Act 1981, s 16.
[2] Viz RSC Ord 55, r 3 and Ord 59, r 3.
[3] [1992] 16 L S Gaz R 28.
[4] See eg *Croydon London Borough Council v A* supra.
[5] [1985] 2 All ER 225, HL, discussed ante, p 383.
[6] *Re O (A Minor) (Care Order: Education: Procedure)* [1992] 2 FLR 7, per Ewbank J.
[7] Under the general powers to impose directions and conditions under s 11(7), any court can postpone the operation of any s 8 order pending an appeal or make any other interim arrangement.
[8] Children Act 1989, s 40(3).
[9] Ibid, s 40(4) and (6). The normal appeal period is 14 days in the case of a magistrates' decision: Family Proceedings Rules 1991, r 4.22(3)(a); but 7 days in the case of an interim care order: r 4.22(3)(b); and 4 weeks in the case of an appeal to the Court of Appeal: RSC Ord 59, r 4.

8. DISCHARGE OF CARE AND DISCHARGE AND VARIATION OF SUPERVISION ORDERS[10]

Section 39 of the Children Act 1989 makes provision for the discharge (but not a variation since that would interfere with the general principle that management of compulsory care is the local authority's responsibility)[11] of care orders and for the variation and discharge of supervision orders. These powers are not new but, following the recommendations of the *Review of Child Care Law*,[12] unlike the previous law, parents with parental responsibility now have an *independent* right to apply for a discharge[13] and the paramountcy of the child's welfare provides the clear basis for determining whether an order should be made.[14]

(a) Discharge of a care order

Under section 39(1) application for discharge of a care order may be made by any person who has parental responsibility, the child himself or the local authority. Since the making of a care order discharges any residence order[15] only mothers, married fathers, unmarried fathers having parental responsibility by virtue of a section 4 order or agreement,[16] and guardians can apply under section 39. Although this means that unmarried fathers without parental responsibility, relatives and foster parents cannot apply under section 39 they can seek to apply for a residence order under section 8 which, as we have seen,[17] operates to discharge a care order.[18] Unmarried fathers can apply as of right for a residence order but others will need first to apply for leave.[19] There is nothing to prevent those with parental responsibility from applying for a residence order rather than for a discharge under section 39 though unless there is a dispute between the applicants there would appear to be little advantage in doing so.[20]

In practice most applications for discharge of care orders are made by local authorities.[1] Indeed they are required by the Review of Children's Cases Regulations 1991[2] to consider at least at every statutory review of a case of a child in their care whether to apply for a discharge. Furthermore

---

[10] See generally the Department of Health's *Guidance and Regulations*, Vol 1, Court Orders, paras 3.54 et seq.

[11] Department of Health's *Guidance and Regulations*, op cit, para 3.54.

[12] (DHSS, 1985), ch 20.

[13] Previously they applied on the child's behalf and it was open to the guardian ad litem to seek a withdrawal: *R v Wandsworth West Juvenile Court, ex p S* [1984] FLR 713.

[14] The previous grounds were vague, see the seventh edition of this work at p 463.

[15] Children Act 1989, s 91(2).

[16] Discussed ante, p 326.

[17] Ante, p 357.

[18] Children Act 1989, s 91(1).

[19] See post, p 547 for discussion of foster parents' use of this provision.

[20] See ante p 357. Query whether s 40(4) operates to permit the court to substitute a supervision order and whether the automatic embargo against re-applying for six months without leave of the court under s 91(15) applies upon a section 8 application. In the latter case the court can use its powers under s 91(14) to provide that no further application may be made without leave.

[1] See Farmer and Parker *A Study of the Discharge of Care Orders* (1985) Table 4.

[2] Sch 2, para 1.

as part of each review the child has to be informed inter alia of steps he may take himself for the discharge of the order.[3]

Rather than grant the discharge simpliciter the court is empowered to substitute a supervision order.[4] In doing this there is no requirement that the threshold provisions under section 31(2) have to be proved again.[5] The controlling principle in all applications is the paramountcy of the child's welfare[6] and in reaching its decision the court is required to have regard to the statutory check-list under section 1(3).[7] This will mean that although parental fitness will be an important consideration in deciding what, if any, order to make, the primary focus will be on the child. Absence of a risk of harm to a child returning home may not in itself be enough to justify discharging the care order.[8] This means that parents (or the child) may have difficulty in establishing that a discharge is in the child's interests especially where there has been little contact.[9]

Contrary to the recommendation of the *Review of Child Care Law*[10] the 1989 Act makes no express provision to postpone the discharge of a care order to allow for a gradual or phased return of the child to his family. How far this can be done by other means is debatable. One possibility is for the court to control rehabilitation through its powers under section 34 to make care contact orders (see further, below). Alternatively, it may be possible to grant a residence order to the parents but to provide under section 11(7) that the child remains with its foster parents with increasing contact to the parents. However, neither of these options are without difficulty[11] and one wonders why provision for phased returns was not made.[12]

Once an application has been disposed of no further application without leave can be made within 6 months.[13]

(b) Discharge and variation of supervision orders

Under section 39(2) of the Children Act 1989 applications for discharge or variation of a supervision order may be made by any person who has parental responsibility for the child, the child himself or the supervisor. In addition, under section 39(3), a person who is not entitled to apply for a discharge but is a person with whom the child is living, can apply to vary

---

[3] Sch 1, para 5 to the 1991 Regulations.
[4] Children Act 1989, s 39(4).
[5] Ibid, s 39(5).
[6] Ibid, s 1(1).
[7] Discussed ante, p 340.
[8] See the *Review of Child Care Law*, op cit, para 20.17 and Bainham, op cit, para 5.76.
[9] See Cretney and Masson, op cit, at p 624.
[10] Op cit, para 20.26.
[11] Orders under s 34 can only be made upon express application, while it may be objected that it is inconsistent with a residence order to provide that the child lives with someone else. The alternative suggestion (see eg Masson *Children Act 1989 Text and Commentary*, pp 41–86) that an order can be postponed on conditions under s 40 seems only appropriate where appeals are lodged or at least anticipated. Query whether as White, Carr and Lowe *A Guide to the Children Act*, para 6.51 suggest, magistrates could use their powers under the Magistrates' Courts Act 1980, s 63(1).
[12] This was thought to be such a serious defect of the old law that in *Re J (A Minor) (Wardship: Jurisdiction)* [1984] 1 All ER 29 the Court of Appeal allowed a child to be warded as a rare exception to the so-called 'Liverpool principle', see post, p 546, n 20.
[13] Children Act 1989, s 91(15).

a requirement made upon him under the supervision order.[14]

As with applications for the discharge of care orders, in deciding what order to make the court must apply the principle of the paramountcy of the child's welfare. It cannot make a care order unless the criteria under section 31(2) have been satisfied.[15]

No application may be made without leave of the court within six months of the disposal of a previous application.[16]

9. CONTACT WITH CHILDREN IN CARE[17]

(a) Introduction

As we said earlier in this chapter[18] the Children Act 1989 places considerable importance on the active promotion by local authorities of contact between children being looked after by them and their families even to the extent of helping with the costs incurred in the visit.[19] This duty continues after a care order has been made and is underscored by the general provision under section 34(1) that there be reasonable contact between the child and inter alios his parents which can only be departed from by agreement or by court order.

Before examining section 34 in more detail the importance of the changes brought about by the 1989 Act should be appreciated. Before the Act, although emphasis was placed on the importance of maintaining contact between the child and his family,[20] the arrangements were mainly within the exclusive control of the local authorities. Only if contact was refused or terminated (but not therefore if restricted) was it possible for parents, guardians or custodians to challenge the decision in court.[1] Even this was an inadequate remedy since no application could be made until well after the termination or refusal[2] so that by the time the issue got to court, magistrates often had little choice but to uphold the local authority's decision.[3] Moreover it had been held[4] that once the termination or refusal had been upheld by the court there could be no further challenges.

---

[14] Ie a requirement made under Sch 3 of the 1989 Act, see ante, p 525.
[15] Ie there is no similar provision to that substituting a supervision order for a care order under s 39(5), discussed above.
[16] Children Act 1989, s 91(15).
[17] See generally the Department of Health's *Guidance and Regulations*, Vol 1, Court Orders paras 3.75 et seq and Vol 3, Family Placements, ch 6.
[18] Ante, p 499.
[19] Children Act 1989, Sch 2, para 16.
[20] In particular by the Code of Practice: Access to Children in Care, discussed in the seventh edition of this work at pp 469–70. The Code has been superseded by the 1989 Act, cf Department of Health's *Guidance and Regulations*, Vol 3, at para 6.5.
[1] Child Care Act 1980, s 12A–F, discussed in the seventh edition of this work at pp 481 et seq. It had become established that access decisions would not be 'reviewed' by the court in wardship (see post, p 546) though in cases of impropriety recourse could have been had to judicial review (discussed post, p 548).
[2] This was because notice of refusal or termination had first to be served by the local authority: Child Care Act 1980, s 12B.
[3] In a study carried out by Millham, Bullock, Hosie and Little *Access Disputes in Child Care* (1989) p 53, of 309 terminations notice only nine parents (3 per cent) re-established contact through legal proceedings.
[4] *R v West Glamorgan County Council, ex p T* [1990] 1 FLR 339.

Implementing the recommendations of the *Review of Child Care Law*,[5] section 34 effectively turns the previous law on its head by requiring the local authority to seek a court order *before* terminating or restricting reasonable contact. This fundamental change, arguably among the most significant changes introduced by the 1989 Act, means that parents and others have a more realistic chance of opposing local authority contact plans.

(b) The scheme under section 34

(i) The presumption of reasonable contact

The basic position is set out by section 34(1), namely that local authorities must normally allow the child reasonable contact with his parents (including the unmarried father regardless of whether he has parental responsibility) or guardians, a person in whose favour there was a residence order immediately before the making of the care order and a person who had the care of the child by virtue of an order under the High Court's inherent jurisdiction. Subject to any court order it is for the authority to decide what is 'reasonable' contact in the circumstances. The expectation is that the authority, child and any person concerned should as far as possible agree upon reasonable arrangements before the care order is made.[6] In any event local authorities are expected to provide details of the proposals for contact when applying for an interim or full care order.[7] Section 34(11) requires the court, before making a care order, to consider any contact arrangements that the authority have made or propose to make and to invite the parties to the proceedings to comment on those arrangements.

(ii) Departing from the general presumption

As an exception to the general presumption of reasonable contact, section 34(6) permits a local authority in matters of urgency to refuse contact for up to 7 days provided 'they are satisfied that it is necessary to do so in order to safeguard or promote the child's welfare'. In such cases the local authority is required to give written notice explaining the decision to the child if he is of sufficient understanding and to any person with whom there is a presumption of reasonable contact.[8]

Apart from this limited power it is incumbent upon the local authority to seek a court order restricting or denying contact,[9] if it wishes to depart from the general presumption of reasonable contact.[10]

---

[5] Ch 21. Cf the Second Report of the House of Commons Social Services Committee 1983–1984 (the 'Short Report') HC 360, paras 73 and 324 which expressed concern that local authority power had already been eroded too far by the access provisions under the Child Care Act 1980.

[6] See the Department of Health's *Guidance and Regulations*, Vol 1, para 3.76 and Vol 3, para 6.2.

[7] Ibid, Vol 3, para 6.2.

[8] Contact with Children Regulations 1991, reg 2.

[9] As it is entitled to do respectively under s 34(2) and (4).

[10] Once an order has been made it can be departed from by agreement, see further below.

(iii) The position of the child and other interested persons

A child in care has the right to make an application both for defined contact to be allowed with a named person and for an order authorising the authority to refuse to allow contact with any named person.[11] No doubt in most cases the authority will take the proceedings but where, for example, the authority are thought to be obstructive, the child may wish to take the initiative.

It is also open to those to whom the Act's presumption of reasonable contact applies,[12] and any other person who has obtained leave of the court,[13] to apply for an order about contact at any time if he is dissatisfied with the arrangements made or proposed for contact between the child and himself.[14]

(iv) The court's powers

The court is empowered both on making a care order and subsequently, either upon application[15] or acting upon its own motion,[16] to make such order as it considers appropriate as to the contact to be allowed,[17] to refuse contact with a named person[18] and in each case to impose such conditions as are considered appropriate.[19] The wording of these provisions is wide enough to permit the court to make interim orders. Although not defined it is thought that, as under a section 8 contact order (from which a section 34 order must generally be distinguished),[20] 'contact' under section 34 includes visiting, staying or other contact, for example by letter or telephone.[1]

In deciding what, if any, order to make the court must apply the general principles set out by section 1, namely, to regard the child's welfare as the paramount consideration, to consider the statutory check-list and to make an order only where it is in the child's interests to do so.

As will be appreciated these provisions give the court wide power to control the future direction of the case and although the court must always be mindful of what the local authority considers practicable it is not limited by what the authority thinks is reasonable. It is especially important when considering whether to refuse contact for the court to consider the long term plans of the local authority.[2]

---

[11] Children Act 1989, s 34(2) and (4).
[12] Viz those persons mentioned in s 34(1). See p 531, above.
[13] S 34(3)(b).
[14] S 34(3).
[15] See further below.
[16] Children Act 1989, s 34(5).
[17] S 34(2).
[18] S 34(4). Hence unlike a section 8 contact order, orders under s 34 can include denials of contact.
[19] S 34(7).
[20] If the child is in care no court may make a section 8 contact order: s 9(1), and any such order is discharged upon making a care order: s 91(2).
[1] See eg *Clarke Hall and Morrison* at para 1[464].
[2] Cf *Re S (Child in Care: Access)* [1991] 1 FLR 161, CA.

(v) Variation and discharge

Upon application by the local authority, child or any person named in the order, the court can vary or discharge any previous order made under section 34.[3] This means that a refusal of contact will no longer prevent a further application being made.[4] However under section 91(17) where an applicant has been refused contact he may not make another such application within 6 months without leave of the court. Although the Act is not specific on the point, the making of a residence order under section 8 must discharge a section 34 order since it is dependent upon the existence of a care order which is itself discharged by virtue of section 91(1).

It is not always incumbent for local authorities to seek court sanction to depart from the terms of a section 34 order since the Contact with Children Regulations 1991[5] allow this to be done by agreement between the authority and the person in relation to whom the order is made, subject inter alia to the agreement of the child if he is of sufficient understanding.[6] The idea behind this provision is to allow for flexibility and partnership in contact arrangements and to obviate the need to go back to court when all concerned agree to this arrangement.[7]

D. Powers under Part V

1. INTRODUCTION

Unlike Part IV of the Children Act 1989 which is primarily concerned with the promotion of children's interests in the mid- to long-term, Part V of the Act is concerned with short-term need to protect children at risk. As the Department of Health's *Guidance* puts it,[8] Part V is designed 'to ensure that effective protective action can be taken when this is necessary within a framework of proper safeguards and reasonable opportunity for parents and others connected with the child to challenge such actions before a court. The measures are short-term and time-limited, and may or may not lead to further action...'

In this section we shall be primarily concerned to discuss child assessment orders, emergency protection orders and the powers of the police to take a child into police protection. However, it should also be said that pursuant to section 47 local authorities have a positive duty to investigate cases of suspected child abuse and decide what action is appropriate.[9] As the

---

[3] S 34(9).
[4] Cf *R v West Glamorgan County Council, ex p T*, supra.
[5] Reg 3.
[6] It is also incumbent upon the authority to give written notification within 7 days to the child's parents or guardian, a person who had a residence order before the care order was made, a person who had care under an order made under the High Court's inherent jurisdiction and any other person whose wishes and feelings the authority considers relevant.
[7] See the Department of Health's *Guidance and Regulations*, Vol 3, para 6.31.
[8] Vol 1, Court Orders, para 4.1.
[9] For a detailed discussion of these duties see Department of Health's *Guidance and Regulations*, Vol 1, op cit, pars 4.78 et seq and *Clarke Hall and Morrison* paras [515] et seq.

Department of Health's *Guidance* points out,[10] action under section 47 'should be seen as the usual first step when a question of child protection arises...' Without such investigation the local authority is unlikely to succeed in any application for a child assessment or emergency protection order.

It may be that having investigated the matter the problems can be solved with the co-operation of the family. Indeed, as we have seen,[11] it is a basic tenet of the Act that the local authority work in partnership with the family and that intervention always has to be especially justified. This is no less true in so-called emergencies than at other times. Even if intervention is thought necessary it should always be done sensitively with a view to promoting the child's interests and, so far as it is consistent to do so, not to overlook the interests of the other members of the family. So-called 'dawn raids' (that is where children are removed from their families during the night), for example, should rarely be necessary.[12] In any event thought should always be given to whether the alleged abuser, rather than the child, should be removed from the family.[13]

2. CHILD ASSESSMENT ORDERS[14]

Described as 'a multi-disciplinary assessment in non-emergency situations'[15] a child assessment order is new with no parallel in the pre-1989 Act law. It was first proposed in the Kimberley Carlile Report[16] but the order was only included in the 1989 Act as a late amendment in response to a demand for a power to be able to see, examine and assess a child where there is concern as to his welfare, in the face of lack of co-operation from those responsible for him.[17]

(a) Application and criteria

Under section 43(1) the court may make a child assessment order on the application of a local authority or authorised person, if it is satisfied that;

'(a) the applicant has reasonable cause to suspect that the child is suffering or is likely to suffer significant harm;

---

[10] Para at 4.78.

[11] Ante, p 499.

[12] Such removals, for example in Orkney's and Rochdale's satanic child abuse cases (see respectively Brett *Orkney: aberration or symptom?* (1991) 3 Journal of Child Law 143 and *Rochdale Borough Council v A* [1991] 2 FLR 192), caused considerable public disquiet. It has recently been held that such removals should only be effected when there are clear grounds for believing significant harm would otherwise be caused to the children or vital evidence is only obtainable by such means: *Re A (Minors) (Child Abuse: Guidelines)* [1992] 1 All ER 153.

[13] For a detailed discussion of this issue see Cobley *Child abuse, child protection and the criminal law* (1992) 4 Journal of Child Law 78.

[14] See generally Department of Health's *Guidance and Regulations*, Vol 1, Court Orders, paras 4.6 et seq.

[15] By David Mellor 158 HC Official Report, col 596.

[16] *A Child in Mind—The Report of an Inquiry into the Death of Kimberley Carlile.*

[17] The government rejected the *alternative* proposal for a child protection notice inter alia because it would have allowed a local authority to take control of the situation by administrative action rather than by court order. See White, Carr and Lowe, op cit, para 7.10.

(b) an assessment of the state of the child's health or development, or of the way in which he has been treated, is required to enable the applicant to determine whether or not the child is suffering, or is likely to suffer, significant harm; and

(c) it is unlikely that such an assessment will be made, or be satisfactory, in the absence of a child assessment order.'

As with applications for care and supervision orders,[18] only the local authority and the NSPCC (as the only authorised person)[19] may apply for child assessment order. As the Department of Health's *Guidance* says:[20]

'The principal conditions are very specific. The order is for cases where there are suspicions, but no firm evidence, of actual or likely significant harm in circumstances which do not constitute an emergency; the applicant considers that a decisive step to obtain an assessment is needed to show whether the concern is well founded or further action is not required and that informal arrangements to have such an assessment carried out have failed.'.

It is to be emphasised that this order is not intended to be used in an emergency nor as a substitute for an emergency protection order. Indeed section 43(4) specifically enjoins the court not to make an assessment order if there are grounds for making an emergency protection order and the court thinks it ought to make such an order. The court is empowered to treat an application for an assessment order as an application for an emergency protection order.[1] The fact that these orders are not to be made in emergencies is further emphasised by the fact that applications are made on notice[2] and the hearing is inter partes.

Even if the court is satisfied as to the existence of the conditions it is not bound to make the order. As with other orders under the 1989 Act, the court must, pursuant to section 1(1) and (5), have regard to the paramountcy of the child's welfare and be satisfied that making the order would be better for the child than making no order at all. However, because these proceedings do *not* rank as 'family proceedings' for the purposes of section 8,[3] the court cannot make a section 8 order.

(b) Effect, commencement and duration of the order

A child assessment order has the twofold effect of placing a duty on any person who is in a position to do so to produce the child to the person named in the order to comply with such directions relating to his assessment as may be specified,[4] and of authorising any person carrying out the assessment, or any part of it, to do so in accordance with the order.[5]

The maximum period of the order is 7 days but this period runs from the date specified in the order and not from the date on which the order was made.[6]

[18] But cf emergency protection orders, discussed post, p 536.
[19] Children Act 1989, ss 31(9) and 43(13).
[20] Vol 1, para 4.8.
[1] Children Act 1989, s 43(3).
[2] S 43(11).
[3] See s 8(3) and (4), discussed ante, p 365.
[4] S 43(6).
[5] S 43(7).
[6] S 43(5). It is thought that the period must run continuously rather than, say, one day a week for 7 weeks, see *Clarke Hall and Morrison*, op cit, para 1[535].

Section 43(6) empowers the court to make directions on any matter relating to the assessment including directions as to the kind of assessment which is to take place and with what aim, by whom and where it will be carried out, and whether it will be subject to conditions, such as that the assessment should be a joint one involving experts appointed by the child's parents or the guardian ad litem as well as by the local authority. If an intrusive examination is to take place, such as a biopsy or genital examination, specific direction should be given. The order should include a direction as to whom the result of the assessment should be given.

Directions may also be made about whether, and if so, for how long, a child may be kept away from home.[7] Indeed since an assessment order does *not* confer parental responsibility the child may only be kept away from home in accordance with court directions. If the child is to be kept away from home, the order must contain such directions as the court thinks fit as to the contact the child is to be allowed to have with other persons.[8]

Notwithstanding any court directions if the child is of sufficient understanding to make an informed decision he may refuse to submit to a medical or psychiatric examination or other assessment.[9]

(c) Likely use of assessment orders

It is not expected that child assessment orders will be made frequently and it may be that they will be of most use where parents are ignorant or resistant to thinking about the possible harm to their child because of the state of his health or development. In many cases, the threat of the order may be sufficient to persuade parents to agree to an assessment, in which case there will be no need for an order. An assessment order cannot be made either where an emergency protection or a care order is made but in principle there is no reason why it cannot be made in respect of an accommodated child. Given the limited length of the order, any assessment of the child will necessarily be little more than an initial one (for this reason arrangements for the assessment need to be carefully planned). Nevertheless it is important to bear in mind that the whole purpose of the order is to obtain sufficient evidence either to allay fears about the child's well-being or to justify further action. Seven days should therefore give enough time to achieve this limited purpose.

3. EMERGENCY PROTECTION ORDERS[10]

(a) Introduction and background

The purpose of an emergency protection order is to provide for the immediate removal or retention of a child in a genuine emergency. Although it is not new to be able to sanction immediate action to protect a child, emergency protection orders differ in virtually every respect from place of safety orders which they replace.

---

[7] S 43(9).

[8] S 43(10).

[9] S 43(8). There is a similar provision in relation to emergency protection orders, see post, p 540.

[10] See generally the Department of Health's *Guidance and Regulations*, Vol 1, Court Orders, paras 4.28 et seq.

The new provisions are based on the recommendation of the *Review of Child Care Law*[11] and follows widespread criticism of place of safety orders: for example, that they were routinely used as a method of starting care proceedings rather than in genuine emergencies;[12] that they were granted too readily, often by a single justice in his own home on an ex parte application;[13] that they lasted too long[14] and that the grounds were not sufficiently focused on emergencies.[15] Furthermore the effects of an order were unclear and often misunderstood but were in any event inadequate in that the successful applicant had no clear responsibility for the child.[16]

(b) The grounds for an emergency protection order

Section 44(1) provides the first of three grounds upon which an emergency protection order may be made, namely, that on the application of any person the court is satisfied that there is reasonable cause to believe that the child is likely to suffer significant harm if the child: (i) is not removed to accommodation provided by or on behalf of the applicant; or (ii) does not remain in the place in which he is then being accommodated.

Although commonly the applicant will be the local authority or NSPCC, *any* person may apply under this provision, including even a parent or relative.[17] Where the applicant is not the relevant local authority, provision has been made for the authority, if they think it is in the child's best interests, to take over the order and therefore the powers and responsibilities for the child that go with it.[18] The court (and not the applicant) must be satisfied about likelihood of significant harm.[19] The ground itself is *prospective* so that evidence of past or even current harm is not sufficient unless it indicates that harm is likely to recur in the future. On the other hand this prospective test can be satisfied even though the harm has not yet occurred.[20]

Under section 44(1)(b) an order can be made upon application of a local authority where they are making enquiries under section 47(1)(b) because *they* (ie not the court) have reasonable cause to suspect that a child is suffering, or is likely to suffer, significant harm[1] and 'those enquiries are

---

[11] (DHSS, 1985), ch 13.
[12] See eg Norris and Parton *Administration of Place of Safety Orders* [1987] JSWL 1, 3. Research also showed that in many cases place of safety orders did not subsequently lead to compulsory care: Packman *Who Needs Care?*
[13] In Cleveland, for example, of 276 applications made between 1 January and 31 July 1987, 174 were granted by a single justice sitting at home: *Report of the Inquiry into Child Abuse in Cleveland in 1987*, (Cm 412, 1988), para 10.9.
[14] Viz up to 28 days—see the discussion in the *Review of Child Care Law*, paras 13.21 et seq.
[15] *Review of Child Care Law*, paras 13.8 et seq.
[16] Ibid, paras 13.12 et seq and the Cleveland Inquiry Report, para 10–8.
[17] This was also the case under the former law. However early experience of the 1989 Act suggests that application by individuals may not be as rare as expected. In such cases the local authority will also have to become involved because under s 47(1) they have a duty to investigate upon being informed of the existence of such an order. For the difficulties of individuals obtaining an extension, see post, p 540.
[18] See the Emergency Protection Order (Transfer of Responsibilities) Regulations 1991, discussed by the Department of Health's *Guidance and Regulations*, op cit, paras 4.32 et seq.
[19] The meaning of 'significant harm' is discussed ante, p 514, in relation to the 'threshold provisions' under s 31. See also ante, p 513, for discussion of 'likelihood'.
[20] Cf the former law where previous harm had to be shown.
[1] These duties under s 47 are also discussed at pp 508 et seq.

being frustrated by access to the child being unreasonably refused to a person authorised to seek access and that the applicant has reasonable cause to believe that access to the child is required as a matter of urgency'. Section 44(1)(c) provides for an application in the same circumstances by an authorised person (the NSPCC)[2] who has been making enquiries except that they must also satisfy the court as to their reasonable cause for suspicion.

Section 44(1)(b) and (c) are for use in emergency, that is, where enquiries cannot be completed because the child cannot be seen but there is enough cause to suspect the child is suffering or is likely to suffer significant harm. In cases where there is a need for further investigation of a child's health and development but he is thought to be safe from immediate danger, the proper order, if any, is a child assessment order.[3] The Department of Health's *Guidance and Regulations* puts the point well, commenting:[4] 'The hypothesis of the grounds at section 44(1)(b) and (c) is that this combination of factors is evidence of an emergency or the likelihood of an emergency.' It also makes the further point:

> 'The court will have to decide whether the refusal of access to the child was unreasonable in the circumstances. It might consider a refusal unreasonable if the person refusing had had explained to him the reason for the enquiries and the request for access, the request itself was reasonable, and he had failed to respond positively in some other suitable way—by arranging for the child to be seen immediately by his GP, for example. Refusal of a request to see a sleeping child in the middle of the night may not be unreasonable,[5] but refusal to allow access at a reasonable time without good reason could well be.'

Section 44(1) provides the minimum conditions that must be satisfied before an order can be made. However, it is not intended that upon being satisfied of the condition under section 44(1) the court should automatically make an order. The court must still consider both the welfare principle and the presumption of no order, pursuant to section 1(1) and 1(5). It may be added that because these proceedings are *not* 'family proceedings' as defined by section 8(3) and (4),[6] the court cannot make a section 8 order. On the other hand it can give directions about contact and medical or psychiatric examination or other assessment of the child.[7]

(c) Procedure

Unless arising from a section 37 direction to investigate[8] or there are proceedings pending in a higher court, an application for an emergency protection order must be made in the magistrates' family proceedings court and cannot be transferred to a higher court.[9] Application may, with leave of the clerk, be made ex parte[10] though hearings can be inter partes and indeed the court has the power to direct that the application be made inter

---

[2] Children Act 1989, s 31(9).
[3] Child assessment orders are discussed ante, p 534.
[4] Vol 1, op cit, para 4.39.
[5] Indeed removals in the middle of the night will require especial justification: cf *Re A (Minors) (Child Abuse: Guidelines)* [1992] 1 All ER 153, per Hollings J.
[6] Discussed ante, p 365.
[7] Children Act 1989, s 44(6), discussed below.
[8] Discussed ante, p 374.
[9] The Children (Allocation of Proceedings) Order 1991, arts 3 and 7(2).
[10] Family Proceedings Courts (Children Act 1989) Rules 1991, r 4(4).

partes.[11] An order can be made by a single justice.[12] However wherever possible the application, even on ex parte applications, should be made to a court.[13] A court hearing an application for an emergency protection order may take account of any statement contained in any report made to the court in the course of or in connection with the hearing or any evidence given during the hearing, which is in the opinion of the court relevant to the application.[14]

(d) The effects of an order

An emergency protection order authorises either the removal to or prevention of removal from accommodation provided by or on behalf of the applicant.[15] In the former instance the order operates as a direction to any person who is in a position to do so to comply with any request to produce the child to the applicant.[16] The court may also authorise an applicant to enter specified premises and search for a child and may include another child in the order if it believed there might be another child on the premises.[17]

The order gives the applicant parental responsibility for the child[18] but this is limited: the power to remove or to prevent removal can only be exercised to safeguard and promote the child's welfare.[19] Hence, for example, if the applicant gains access and finds that the child is neither harmed nor likely to be harmed, he may not remove the child.[20] In any event an applicant can exercise responsibility only insofar as it is reasonably required to safeguard or promote the child's welfare, having regard in particular to the duration of the order.[1] It would not therefore be appropriate to make any changes in the child's life which would have a long-lasting effect.

In the absence of a court direction the applicant must, during the subsistence of the order, allow the child reasonable contact with his parents, any other person with parental responsibility, any person with whom he was living immediately before the order, any person in whose favour there is a contact order in relation to him and any person acting on behalf of those persons.[2] The court, however, may give such directions as it considers appropriate about contact and may impose conditions.[3] It is expected that where the local authority is the applicant, the court will leave contact to

---

[11] Ibid, r 4(5).

[12] Ibid, r 2(5)(a).

[13] See the Department of Health's *Guidance and Regulations*, Vol 1, para 4.46 and following the recommendations of the Cleveland Inquiry Report, op cit, p 252.

[14] Children Act 1989, s 45(7).

[15] Ibid, s 44(4)(b).

[16] S 44(4)(a).

[17] S 48(3) and (4). This does not give the power to make a forced entry. If the applicant is refused or likely to be refused entry the court may issue a warrant authorising a constable to assist in the execution of the order using reasonable force if necessary: s 48(9).

[18] S 44(4)(c).

[19] S 44(5)(a). Removals should normally be at an agreed time following consultation with appropriate professionals. A proper explanation must be given to the child: Department of Health's *Guidance and Regulations*, Vol 1, para 4.58.

[20] Similarly, if a return appears safe, the child should be returned: s 44(10). In each case this might occur where the alleged abuser vacates the home.

[1] S 44(5)(b).

[2] S 44(13). This presumption of reasonable contact is in line with the general policy of the Act, see the discussion ante, p 530.

[3] S 44(6) and (8).

the authority's discretion or at any rate order that reasonable contact be negotiated.[4] If therefore the local authority wish to restrict contact it should seek a court direction to that effect.

Medical evidence is likely to be of importance in any future care proceedings so that early decisions or directions about examinations are crucial. For this reason although the parental responsibility acquired on the making of the order would permit the applicant to consent to the child's examination or assessment, it might be preferable to seek directions on the issue. Section 44(6)(b) empowers the court to make directions as to a medical or psychiatric examination or other assessment of the child, and under section 44(8) the court can direct that there be no such examination or assessment. In any event notwithstanding a court order the child can, if of sufficient understanding to make an informed decision, refuse to submit to an examination or other assessment.[5]

(e) Duration of the order

In the first instance an emergency protection order may be granted for up to 8 days.[6] Save where the applicant is an individual,[7] the court can, upon application, grant one period of extension[8] for a further seven days.[9]

There is no appeal against the making or refusal to make an emergency protection order.[10] However, an application to discharge the order may be made by the child, parent, any other person with parental responsibility or any person with whom the child was living before the order was made,[11] *except* where the person was given notice of and present at the original hearing.[12] No application for discharge can be heard before the expiry of 72 hours after the making of the order.[13]

4. POLICE PROTECTION[14]

As under the previous law[15] the police have limited but important powers to protect children. Section 46(1) of the 1989 Act enables a constable who has reasonable cause to believe that a child would otherwise be likely to suffer significant harm, either to remove him to suitable accommodation and keep him there or to 'take such steps as are reasonable to ensure that the child's removal from any hospital, or other place, in which he is then

---

[4] See the Department of Health's *Guidance and Regulations*, Vol 1, at para 4.62.
[5] S 44(7). This statutory right of veto is not thought to be affected by *Re R (A Minor) (Wardship: Medical Treatment)* [1992] Fam 11, [1991] 4 All ER 177, CA, discussed ante, p 309. See also *Re J (A Minor) (Inherent Jurisdiction: Medical Treatment)* (1992) Times, 15 July, CA.
[6] S 45(1). Cf the former place of safety orders which could be granted for up to 28 days.
[7] S 45(4) only permits application by those entitled to apply for a care order, viz a local authority or 'authorised person'.
[8] S 45(6).
[9] S 45(5).
[10] S 45(10).
[11] S 45(8).
[12] S 45(11).
[13] S 45(9).
[14] See generally Department of Health's *Guidance and Regulations*, Vol 1, paras 4.71 et seq and Cobley *Child abuse, child protection and the criminal law* (1992) 4 Journal of Child Law 78.
[15] Viz the Children and Young Persons Act 1969, s 28(2).

being accommodated, is prevented'. No child may be kept in police protection for more than 72 hours.[16]

As there is no power of search attached to this provision,[17] a child can
only be taken into police protection once the officer has found the child.
Commonly the power has been used to hold children such as runaways or
glue sniffers or those whose parents have abandoned them. It may also be
used where an officer attends a domestic dispute and finds a child living in
unhygienic conditions.[18]

Section 45(4) requires a constable taking a child into police protection
to inform, as soon as is reasonably practicable, relevant local authorities,
the child, his parents and other specified persons about the steps that have
been taken in relation to the child. The police do not acquire parental
responsibility but must do what is reasonable in all the circumstances of
the case for the purpose of safeguarding or promoting the child's welfare,
having regard in particular to the length of the period during which the
child will be in police protection.[19]

E. Disputing local authority decisions

1. INTRODUCTORY

Although, as the Department of Health's *Guidance* says,[20] the Children Act
1989 'envisages a high degree of co-operation between parents and authorities in negotiating and agreeing what form of action will best meet a
child's needs and promote his welfare' nevertheless the required co-operation
will not always be achieved or will break down. In any event other members
of the family may also be in dispute with the local authority; grandparents,
for instance, may feel that they should be able to take over the care of the
child. Disputes can also arise between foster parents and the authority. The
former, for instance, may wish to resist the latter's decision to remove a
child from their care.

In some cases the objection may be unfounded, while in others the
complaint will be of a relatively minor nature. Many such disputes can be
and are solved informally, often by patient counselling by social workers.
However not all such disputes will thereby be solved and, while no doubt
every effort is made to promote each child's welfare, serious mistakes are
sometimes made by local authorities in their management of the child.
There is little doubt too, that the interests of parents or of the wider family
or those of the foster parents are, on occasion, unjustly ignored. The
question therefore arises to what extent, and to whom, local authorities are
or should be accountable for their management of children in care.

Apart from applying for a discharge of a care order under section 39 or
challenging a decision about contact under section 34, which we have

---

[16] Children Act 1989, s 46(6).
[17] See Department of Health's *Guidance and Regulations*, op cit, para 4.71.
[18] Cf the powers to enter and search premises to save life or limb: s 17(1)(e) of the Police and
Criminal Evidence Act 1984.
[19] S 46(9).
[20] Vol 3, Family Placements, para 10.3.

already discussed,[1] there are a number of other ways in which a local authority decision may be challenged. Use can be made of the formal complaints or representation procedure which under the Children Act 1989 local authorities are bound to set up. Alternatively, applications may be made to the Secretary of State to use his default powers. Actions can be brought under, for example, the High Court's inherent jurisdiction or for judicial review or by seeking leave to apply for a residence order. A complaint can also be made to the 'local ombudsman'. Finally application can be made to the European Court of Human Rights.

We discuss each of these options in turn, but in the ensuing discussion, it might be borne in mind that the issue of reviewing local authorities' action is not simple. Although ideally one would wish to safeguard both the child's and the parents' (or other interested adults') interests it must be remembered that ultimately priority must be given to the child's welfare. A local authority may, for example, have acted improperly, yet a court may nevertheless be forced to uphold their decision, because it has become in the child's interests to do so. On the other hand while court scrutiny might be more effective if action has to be sanctioned by the court before it is carried out by the authority, such control might so fetter local authority action that the inevitable consequential delay would be to the general prejudice of children in care.

2. THE COMPLAINTS PROCEDURE[2]

As has been said, it is often possible to resolve problems informally and indeed some local authorities have appointed an officer specifically to support children and their representatives in participation in decision-making and in voicing their concerns.[3] Under section 26(3) of the Children Act 1989, however, it is now[4] mandatory for all local authorities to have a formal representation or complaints procedure. Furthermore to ensure that there is an independent element, section 26(4) provides that at least one person who is not a member or officer of the authority concerned must take part in the consideration of the complaint or representation and in any discussions held by the authority about the action to be taken. Under section 26(8) there is an obligation to publicise the complaints procedure. Rules governing the scope and procedure of the complaints scheme are provided by the Representations Procedure (Children) Regulations 1991.

(a) Who can complain

Under section 26(3) complaints may be made by:

(a) a child whom the local authority are looking after or who is not being looked after but is in need. This is intended both to ensure

---

[1] Ante at p 528 (discharge) and 530 (contact under s 34).
[2] See generally the Department of Health's *Guidance and Regulations,* Vol 3, Family Placements, ch 10 and for the background, *Review of Child Care Law* (DHSS, 1985), paras 220 et seq and Bainham *Children, The New Law,* paras 4.62 et seq.
[3] See the Department of Health's *Guidance and Regulations,* op cit at para 10.13.
[4] Before the 1989 Act although some local authorities had a complaints procedure they were not obliged to.

that children are consulted on decisions taken about them and to establish the system of complaints procedures for children the authority are looking after.[5] It may also assist a child who believes he should be accommodated where the authority are refusing to offer the service;

(b) a parent;[6]
(c) other person with parental responsibility;
(d) any local authority foster parent; or
(e) such other person as the authority considers has a sufficient interest in the child's welfare to warrant representations being considered by them.

In addition young people can complain if they consider that the local authority has not given them adequate preparation for leaving care or adequate after-care.[7]

Although section 26(3) permits a wide range of people, including foster parents, to use the procedure, those falling into the final category can only be heard at the local authority's discretion.[8] This has been criticised as being too restrictive in the case of representations being made by concerned members of the wider family.[9]

(b) What may be complained about

As section 26(3) says, the statutory complaints procedure caters for complaints about local authority support for families and their children under Part III of the 1989 Act. This, as the Department of Health's *Guidance* says,[10] 'will include complaints about day care, services to support children within their family home, accommodation of a child, after-care and decisions relating to the placement of a child or the handling of a child's case. The processes involved in decision making or the denial of a service must also be covered by the responsible authority's arrangements.'

Anything outside Part III (except decisions about the 'usual fostering limit')[11] including the placing of a child's name on the Child Protection Register and complaints by private foster parents on their own behalf do not have to be included in the scheme though, as the Department of Health's *Guidance* says, a responsible authority should consider what other matters might be appropriate to the procedures to meet the requirements of the Regulations.[12]

---

[5] According to the Department of Health's *Guidance and Regulations*, op cit at para 107, the responsible authority should always check with the child (subject to his understanding) that a complaint submitted on his behalf reflects his views and that he wishes the person submitting it to act on his behalf.

[6] Including the unmarried father.

[7] Children Act 1989, s 24(14), added by the Courts and Legal Services Act 1990, Sch 16, para 13.

[8] The procedure in these cases is governed by reg 4(4) of the Representations Procedure (Children) Regulations 1991.

[9] By Bainham, op cit, at p 86. Their principal form of redress will therefore be judicial review, see post, p 548.

[10] Op cit at para 10.8.

[11] Included under Representations Procedure (Children) Regulations 1991, reg 12(2).

[12] Ibid at para 10.9.

(c) Procedure and outcome

Upon receipt of a complaint from an eligible person, the responsible authority must acknowledge it and send a leaflet describing how the procedure works and giving the name of the officer responsible for co-ordinating the handling of complaints.[13] The authority and an independent person must consider the representation and formulate a response within 28 days.[14] Their written decision must be sent to the complainant, the child (if different) and to any other person whom the authority considers has a sufficient interest in the child. The letter must also remind the complainant of his right to have his complaint considered by a panel. If the claimant is dissatisfied with the responsible authority's response he has 28 days to request in writing that the complaint be heard by the panel,[15] which in turn must meet within 28 days after the receipt by the local authority of such a request.[16] The complainant and authority can each make written and oral submissions to the panel.[17] The panel must make a recommendation within 24 hours of its meeting and record it in writing[18] and give written notification of it to the responsible authority, the complainant, the independent person (if he is not a member of the panel) and any other interested person.[19] The responsible authority must consider what action, if any, should be taken in the light of the panel's findings[20] and, within 28 days of the panel's recommendation, notify inter alios the complainant and the child (if of sufficient understanding) of their decision and reasons for taking that decision.[1]

Although the procedure just described is clearly elaborate it is intended to be effective though, given that it is operated by the authority themselves, there must be some anxiety about the panel's objectivity and independence. However, although it is not expressly stated, if the authority ignore the panel's findings or fail to give satisfactory reasons, their action would seem amenable to judicial review.[2] It may also be observed that responsible authorities are required to monitor the operation and effectiveness of the procedure. To this end records of each complaint received and the outcome must be kept and an annual report dealing with the procedure's operation must be completed and presented to the Social Services Committee.[3]

---

[13] Department of Health's *Guidance and Regulations*, op cit, para 10.37.

[14] Reg 6 of the 1991 Regulations. The independent person can inter alia interview the child and, if different, the complainant: reg 8(1).

[15] Reg 8(2). The panel, which must include at least one independent person, is appointed by the local authority for this purpose: reg 8(2), (3). As the Department of Health's *Guidance and Regulations* at para 10.22 comments, this second stage of the procedure does not affect the complainant's right to complain about maladministration to the local ombudsman, discussed post, p 551, since the panel is not a decision-making body.

[16] Reg 8(4).

[17] Reg 8(5).

[18] Reg 9(1).

[19] Reg 9(2).

[20] Reg 9(3).

[1] Children Act 1989, s 26(7)(b).

[2] See Clarke Hall and Morrison, op cit, at para 2[108]. Cf Bainham, op cit, at para 4.68 who, before the Regulations were published, commented that the procedure lacked teeth in that it imposed no duty on the local authority to redress a grievance. Judicial review is discussed post, p 548.

[3] Reg 10.

3. DEFAULT POWERS OF THE SECRETARY OF STATE

Section 84 of the Children Act 1989 enables the Secretary of State to declare a local authority in default where he is satisfied that they have, without reasonable cause, failed to comply with a duty under the Act.[4] He may then give the necessary directions to the authority to ensure their compliance with the duty within a specified period. In the event of further default, these directions may be enforced by application to the High Court for judicial review.

In theory this provides another option for aggrieved individuals to pursue disputes against a local authority. It is not expected, however, that these powers will be exercised at all often,[5] still less that they will assist individuals, as it is more likely that the Secretary of State will exercise his powers, if at all, where an authority's failure to discharge its statutory duties affects a *class* as opposed to individual children.[6] It may be added that the existence of these default powers do not bar applications for judicial review.[7]

4. WARDSHIP AND THE INHERENT JURISDICTION

(a) The position before the Children Act 1989[8]

As we said in chapter 14,[9] before the Children Act 1989, local authorities, encouraged by the courts, frequently turned to wardship as a means of getting or keeping children in their care. In stark contrast, although it was accepted that the wardship jurisdiction had not been abrogated by the comprehensive statutory scheme governing local authority care,[10] the courts refused to allow their prerogative jurisdiction to be used as a means of challenging authorities' decision over children in care. The basic rationale for what became known as the '*Liverpool* principle' was that as Parliament had vouchsafed a wide discretion in local authorities over the management of children in care, it was not for the courts to subvert that intention by allowing parents and others a right of challenge through wardship and therefore outside the statutory system. As Lord Wilberforce said in *A v Liverpool City Council*:[11]

> 'In my opinion the court has no ... reviewing power. Parliament has by statute entrusted to the local authority the power and duty to make decisions as to the welfare of children without any reservation of reviewing power to the court.'

---

[4] Cf the similar power under the Education Act 1944, s 99.
[5] The default power under the Education Act 1944, s 99, is rarely used. See Logie *Enforcing statutory duties: the courts and default powers* [1988] JSWL 185.
[6] See HC Official Report S C 13 June 1989, col 492 per the Solicitor General and Bainham, op cit, para 7.78.
[7] *R v Secretary of State for the Environment, ex p Ward* [1984] 2 All ER 556.
[8] See generally Oliver *Challenging local authority decisions in relation to children in care—Part 1* (1988) 1 Journal of Child Law 26.
[9] Ante, p 477.
[10] See eg *Re M (An Infant)* [1961] Ch 328, 345, [1961] 1 All ER 788, CA per Lord Evershed MR, *Re B (Infants)* [1962] Ch 201, 223, CA, per Pearson LJ and *A v Liverpool City Council* [1982] AC 363, 373, [1981] 2 All ER 385, 388, HL per Lord Wilberforce.
[11] Ibid at 372 and 388 respectively. See Lowe 45 MLR 96 and Freeman 145 JPN 333 and 146 JPN 188, 202.

In the *Liverpool* case itself, the House of Lords refused to interfere with a local authority's decision to restrict a mother's contact with her child in care to a monthly supervised visit limited to one hour at a day nursery.[12]

In reaching this decision the House of Lords affirmed two earlier Court of Appeal decisions[13] in which it had been held that foster parents could not use wardship as a means of challenging a local authority's decision to remove children placed with them. The *Liverpool* principle was again applied by the House of Lords first in *Re W (A Minor)(Wardship: Jurisdiction)*[14] in which relatives unsuccessfully sought to use wardship to challenge a local authority's decision to place a child with a stranger (with a view to adoption) rather than with them[15] and then in *M v H*[16] in which an unmarried father failed in his application for custody of his child in local authority care.

The above cases successively barred wardship to foster parents, natural parents, relatives and unmarried fathers and there was little doubt that the '*Liverpool* principle' would equally have applied to any potential applicant, including a 'Gillick competent' child. However, not only was it established that the principle applied regardless of the applicant but it had also been held to apply both in relation to a child in care and where the local authority were actively contemplating taking proceedings.[17]

Despite the general principle of non-intervention there had nevertheless developed certain well defined instances when wardship could still be used, but these too had been whittled away. For example, in *Re W (A Minor)(Wardship: Jurisdiction)*[18] the House of Lords denied the existence of a residual category for intervention even in 'exceptional circumstances' while in *Re DM (A Minor)(Wardship: Jurisdiction)*[19] the Court of Appeal ruled that even if a local authority could be shown to have acted improperly, the proper action was judicial review and not wardship.

Effectively[20] therefore by the time the Children Act 1989 was implemented wardship could not be used as a means of challenging local authority decisions unless the authority itself chose to submit to the jurisdiction.[1]

---

[12] Under the law, as it then stood, local authorities had complete discretion over the amount of contact with a child in care.

[13] *Re M (An Infant)* [1961] Ch 328, [1961] 1 All ER 788, CA, and *Re T (AJJ) (An Infant)* [1970] Ch 688, [1970] 2 All ER 865, CA.

[14] [1985] AC 791, [1985] 2 All ER 301, HL. See Bainham 49 MLR 113.

[15] The birth parents had concealed from the rest of the family that they had asked the authority to take the child into care (they had agreed to an order freeing the child for adoption) and persuaded the authority, contrary to their normal practice, not to consult members of the wider family.

[16] [1990] 1 AC 686, [1988] 3 All ER 5, HL. See Hayes (1989) 1 Journal of Child Law 53. See also *Re TD (A Minor) (Wardship: Jurisdiction)* [1985] FLR 1150.

[17] See *Re E (Minors) (Wardship: Jurisdiction)* [1984] 1 All ER 21, CA; *W v Shropshire County Council* [1986] 1 FLR 359, CA and *W v Nottinghamshire County Council* [1986] 1 FLR 565, CA, discussed in the seventh edition of this work at p 474.

[18] [1985] AC 791, see particularly Lord Scarman at 797.

[19] [1986] 2 FLR 122, CA.

[20] Strictly it was still open to argue that the relevant body or court had inadequate powers to deal with the particular issue but that the court in wardship proceedings had the necessary powers which the child's welfare required to be used. However this so-called 'lacuna' argument rarely succeeded because the courts generally denied that there was an unintended gap in the relevant court's or body's powers. See the discussion in the seventh edition of this work at p 475.

[1] See, for example, *A v B and Hereford and Worcester County Council* [1986] 1 FLR 289.

(b) The position after the Children Act 1989[2]

As we discussed in chapter 14, under the Children Act 1989 wardship and local authority care are incompatible in the sense that a child cannot both be in care and a ward of court.[3] Accordingly, it is clear that individuals seeking to challenge a local authority's decision in respect of a child in care can no longer even attempt to do so by wardship and that consequently there can be no question of the local authority submitting to the jurisdiction. It is, however, possible for a challenge to be mounted under the High Court's inherent jurisdiction (which was discussed in chapter 14).[4] Although the point has yet to be directly tested it is thought that the '*Liverpool* principle' will operate.[5] A fortiori the '*Liverpool* principle' will apply in cases where a wardship application can still properly be made, that is, where the child is not subject to a care order. A foster parent looking after a child accommodated by a local authority can still in theory ward a child but if it is intended to challenge the authority's decision, for example, to remove the child, then the '*Liverpool* principle'[6] will surely be applied.

5. SEEKING LEAVE TO APPLY FOR A RESIDENCE ORDER

Mention has previously been made of the ability of parents and guardians to apply for a residence order as an alternative means of seeking a discharge of a care order.[7] However, it is open to any interested party to seek the court's leave to apply for a residence order, pursuant to section 10 of the Children Act 1989. This right offers a new means by which to challenge a local authority decision. This avenue was explored in *Re A and W (Minors)(Residence Order: Leave to Apply)*[8] in which a foster mother sought to challenge a local authority's decision that she should no longer be permitted to foster four children in their care. In the course of an action for judicial review, the applicant applied for leave to apply for a residence order. In refusing leave the Court of Appeal accepted that the ability of the court, pursuant to section 9(1), to make a residence order notwithstanding that the child is in care represented a fundamental change in the law and that to that extent the '*Liverpool* principle' had no direct application. However, that did not mean that on the application for leave the court should give no weight to the local authority's views. On the contrary section 10(9)(d)(i) expressly provides that the court is to have particular regard to the authority's plans for the future. Furthermore, given that under section 22(3) it is the authority's duty to safeguard and promote the welfare of any child in its care, it was held that the court should approach the application on the basis that the authority's plans for the child's future were designed for his welfare and that any departure from

---

[2] See generally Clarke Hall and Morrison, op cit, paras 1[743] et seq.
[3] Children Act 1989, ss 100(2)(c) and 91(4), discussed ante, p 478.
[4] Ante, pp 479 et seq.
[5] This was Balcombe LJ's view in *Re A and W (Minors) (Residence Order: Leave to Apply)* [1992] 2 FLR 154, CA, discussed further below.
[6] As extended inter alia by *Re E (Minors) (Wardship: Jurisdiction)*, supra and the other cases cited ante, p 546, n 17.
[7] Ante, p 357.
[8] Supra.

such plans might well be harmful to the child. In other words the court should, in these circumstances, be slow to grant leave.

6. JUDICIAL REVIEW[9]

Given that the High Court will not exercise its inherent powers then, unless it is appropriate to seek a residence order[10] the only means of obtaining an order to impugn a local authority's decision on the ground that they acted improperly, is by judicial review. In this context the two principal remedies sought will be that the original order be quashed, that is, that the court should grant certiorari, or, less commonly, that the local authority be ordered to comply with their statutory duty, for example, to provide some specific support service provided for in Part III and Schedule 2 of the 1989 Act,[11] that is, that the court should grant mandamus.

It is important to appreciate that judicial review is the standard administrative law remedy for correcting decisions[12] taken by inferior courts, tribunals and other bodies and as such no special rules apply in children cases.[13] The function of the court, as Scott Baker J neatly expressed it, is 'to consider in each case not whether the decision itself is right or fair but whether the manner in which the decision is made is fair'.[14]

(a) The requirements for judicial review

As a safeguard against frivolous, vexatious, or merely hopeless actions, applicants must obtain leave to apply for judicial review.[15] Applications must, inter alia, specify the grounds upon which the relief is sought and be accompanied by a affidavit verifying the facts relied upon.[16] Leave is not a formality for as Balcombe LJ said in *R v Lancashire County Council ex p M*[17] there must be a reasonable prospect of the court coming to the decision that the local authority's conclusion was so unreasonable that no reasonable local authority could ever have come to it. Bearing in mind that as far as individuals are concerned some information will be confidential,[18] having to establish even a prima facie case may be difficult. Yet it is only if the

---

[9] See generally Craig *Administrative Law* (2nd Edn), Evans and De Smith *Judicial Review of Administrative Action* and Wade *Administrative Law* (6th Edn).

[10] Ie where the applicant is seeking to have the child live with him.

[11] Cf *R v Bolton Metropolitan Borough Council, ex p B* [1985] FLR 343 where mandamus was sought to make the local authority comply with its duty to serve notice of a refusal or termination of access.

[12] There must be a reviewable 'decision': see *R v Devon County Council, ex p L* [1991] 2 FLR 541 (social worker informing applicant's cohabitant that he was suspected of sexual abuse, held not to be a 'decision').

[13] But this is not to say that in judging the reasonableness of a local authority's action in respect of children in their care attention should not be paid to the authority's duty to safeguard the child's interests. Cf *R v Harrow London Borough Council, ex p D* [1990] Fam 133, [1990] 3 All ER 12, CA, per Butler-Sloss LJ cited post, p 550.

[14] *R v Hereford and Worcester County Council, ex p D* [1992] 1 FLR 448, 457.

[15] Supreme Court Act 1981, s 31 and RSC, Ord 53, r 3.

[16] RSC, Ord 53, r 3(2). Applications should be brought promptly and normally within three months of the decision complained of: RSC, Ord 53, r 4.

[17] [1992] 1 FLR 109, 113, CA.

[18] Eg child protection conference records covered by the Foster Placement (Children) Regulations 1991, reg 14.

applicant can first negotiate this hurdle that the matter will be heard on its merits.

To substantiate a claim for judicial review, the applicant must be able to bring himself within the so-called *Wednesbury* principle[19] as interpreted by the House of Lords in *Council of Civil Service Unions v Minister for Civil Defence.*[20] According to Lord Diplock, in this case,[1] there are three main heads under which court intervention may be justified, namely, 'illegality', ie where there was an error of law in reaching the relevant decision; 'procedural impropriety', ie where the relevant rules have not been complied with; and 'irrationality', ie where a decision 'is so outrageous in its defiance of logic or of accepted moral standards that no sensible person who had applied his mind to the question to be decided could have arrived at it'.

(b) Circumstances in which judicial review has been sought

Actions for judicial review of local authority decisions have increased in recent years and there are now a number of reported cases. Complainants fall mainly into two groups, parents and foster parents, though applications have also been sought by guardians ad litem.[2] Complaints have been made about a variety of decisions including the placing of a child on a Child Protection Register,[3] deciding not to place the child at home on trial with the parents,[4] removing a child from foster parents,[5] removing a person from the list of approved adopters[6] and disclosing to others allegations of child abuse by a named person.[7]

By no means all of the above applications were successful but of those that were, it was commonly because the local authority failed to give the complainant an opportunity to put his side of the case or otherwise to explain their reasons. A striking example is *R v Norfolk County Council, ex p M*[8] which concerned a plumber working in a house where a teenage girl made allegations that she was sexually abused by him. She had twice previously been the victim of sexual abuse and a few days later made similar allegations against another man. After a case conference the plumber's name was entered in the Child Abuse Register as an abuser. His employers were informed and they suspended him pending a full enquiry. The first knowledge the plumber had of these allegations was the letter informing

---

[19] Ie following *Associated Provincial Picture Houses Ltd v Wednesbury Corpn* [1948] 1 KB 223, [1947] 2 All ER 680, CA.

[20] [1985] AC 374, [1984] 3 All ER 935, HL.

[1] Ibid at 410 and 950, respectively.

[2] See eg *R v Cornwall County Council* [1992] 2 All ER 471, in which the authority's attempt to prescribe maximum hours a guardian could work on a particular case without express authorisation from the council was successfully challenged; see ante, p 520.

[3] *R v Norfolk County Council, ex p M* [1989] QB 619, [1989] 2 All ER 359; *R v Harrow London Borough Council, ex p D* [1990] Fam 133, [1990] 3 All ER 12, CA, and *R v East Sussex County Council, ex p R* [1991] 2 FLR 358.

[4] *R v Bedfordshire County Council, ex p C* [1987] 1 FLR 239. Cf *R v Hertfordshire County Council, ex p B* [1987] 1 FLR 239 (child removed after being placed at home on trial).

[5] *R v Hereford and Worcester County Council, ex p R* [1992] 1 FLR 448 and *R v Lancashire County Council, ex p M* [1992] 1 FLR 109, CA.

[6] *R v London Borough of Wandsworth, ex p P* [1989] 1 FLR 387.

[7] *R v Devon County Council, ex p L* [1991] 2 FLR 541 and *R v Lewisham London Borough Council, ex p P* [1991] 3 All ER 529, [1991] 1 WLR 308.

[8] Supra. See also *R v Bedfordshire County Council, ex p C*, supra, *R v Hereford and Worcester City Council, ex p D*, supra, and *R v London of Wandsworth, ex p P*, supra.

him of the decision to place his name on the register. Waite J held that, given the serious consequences of registration for the plumber, the local authority had a duty to act fairly which they manifestly failed to do by not giving him an opportunity to meet the allegations.

The *Norfolk* case was clearly an exceptional one and, as Butler-Sloss LJ said in *R v Harrow London Borough Council, ex p D*,[9] recourse to judicial review in respect of placing a name on the Child Abuse Register ought to be rare. She further held that the court should not encourage applications to review case conference decisions or recommendations because it was important for those involved in this difficult area to 'be allowed to perform their task without having to look over their shoulder all the time for the possible intervention of the court'. Furthermore she pointed out that in 'balancing adequate protection for the child and the fairness to an adult, the interest of an adult may have to take second place to the needs of the child'.[10]

Although Butler-Sloss LJ's remarks specifically concerned case conference decisions and recommendations, her observations about the need to balance considerations have general application.[11] Indeed it can be said that in general, given the local authority's duty to safeguard the interests of children, in the absence of procedural irregularity it is hard to impugn a local authority decision. It is certainly not enough to question the wisdom of a decision. The applicant must discharge the heavy onus of showing that no reasonable local authority could have reached the particular decision complained of. In *R v Hertfordshire County Council, ex p B*[12] a mother's action for judicial review failed. In that case a child in care was allowed at home on trial with the mother but after three months the child was removed on the ground that rehabilitation had failed. A neighbour had asserted the mother had come home late one night and being drunk lay in the snow for some time with her child running about. In fact it was found that the authority had been concerned with wider considerations including the child's weight loss, his disruptive behaviour and hyperactivity. In dismissing the application Ewbank J commented:

'There were many cases where children were allowed home on trial and where the local authority had later to decide that it was not a success. Such a decision was well within the local authority's parental power and was not amenable to judicial review.'

---

[9] [1990] Fam 133, [1990] 3 All ER 12, CA.
[10] Ibid at pp 138 and 17 respectively. See also *R v London Borough of Wandsworth, ex p P*, supra, at 308 in which Ewbank J said: 'Foster-parents have to accept that their interests may have to be subordinated to the children they care for. Accordingly, provided the rules of fairness are complied with, the decision as to whether there is a risk or not, is one that has to be taken by the local authority. In the ordinary way, provided the rules of national justice are complied with the foster-parents have no redress.'
[11] See also *R v East Sussex County Council, ex p R*, supra; *R v Devon County Council, ex p L*, supra; and *R v Lewisham London Borough Council, ex p P*, supra.
[12] Supra. See also *R v East Sussex County Council, ex p R*, supra, *R v Devon County Council, ex p L*, supra; and *R v Lewisham London Borough Council, ex p P*, supra.

7. OTHER REMEDIES

(a) Applying to the 'local government ombudsman'[13]

Another procedure for questioning local authority decisions over children is to complain to the commissioner for local administration ('the local government ombudsman'). Under this procedure a local commissioner can investigate written complaints of 'maladministration'. Such complaints must first be directed to a local councillor of the authority concerned who may then refer the complaint to the commissioner. If the councillor refuses a request to refer the matter, the commissioner is nevertheless entitled to investigate the complaint.[14] The Court of Appeal has ruled[15] that it is not necessary for the complainant to spell out the particular maladministration which led to the injustice complained of; it is sufficient if he specifies the action alleged to be wrong.

To find the complaint justified the local commissioner must find that the authority has been guilty of 'maladministration'. This is generally taken to refer to the procedure by which the decision is made or put into action rather than to the merits of the particular decision itself.[16]

As a general mechanism for scrutinising administrative action, the procedure obviously has its merits but like judicial review it is of questionable use in the context of local authority decisions in respect of children in care. The main drawbacks are that the central concern is with procedural propriety and not the child's welfare; the commissioner may have no expertise in child matters; the investigation is itself a long process and will probably result in delaying implementation of plans for the child's long-term future,[17] and even if 'maladministration' is established there is no power to interfere with the decision taken by the authority.

(b) Applying to the European Court of Human Rights[18]

A local authority decision can occasionally be challenged as being in breach of the European Convention on Human Rights. To succeed the applicant must show that at least one of the Articles has been broken[19] the most relevant of which are in this context Article 8, under which there is 'the right to respect for ... private and family life' and Article 6, under which there is a right to be able to bring a civil matter before a court. In the past a number of applications successfully challenged the then inability of parents

---

[13] See Lowe and Rawlings 42 MLR 447 and (1979) 2 Adoption and Fostering 38 and Oliver *Challenging local authority decisions in relation to children in care—Part 2* (1989) 1 Journal of Child Law 58, 61.
[14] Local Government Act 1974, s 26.
[15] In *R v Local Comr for Administration for the North and East Area of England, ex p Bradford Metropolitan City Council* [1979] QB 287, [1979] 2 All ER 881, CA.
[16] See the *Bradford* case, supra.
[17] In the *Bradford* case, for example, where the claim of maladministration failed, the children were eventually adopted, see *Re SMH and RAH* [1979] CA Transcript 103, though their placement had been delayed pending the outcome of the Commission's investigations. Cf *Re BA (Wardship and Adoption)* [1985] FLR 1008, [1985] Fam Law 306.
[18] See generally Jacobs *The European Convention on Human Rights* (1975) 133, Douglas *The Family and the State under the European Convention on Human Rights* 2 Int Jo of Law and the Family 76 and ante, p 18.
[19] See eg *R v United Kingdom* [1988] 2 FLR 445, E Ct HR and *O v UK* (1987) 10 EHRR 82.

to challenge local authority decisions concerning contact with children in care and an authority's refusal to give access to the case records of a child in their care.[20] From the individual's point of view and certainly that of the child, however, such challenges are not an effective way of scrutinising individual decisions. An important drawback is that while the UK may be forced to change the domestic law and even to compensate the individual if the application is successful,[1] the local authority cannot be forced to change its decision. In any event by the time the case has been determined (which, given that it has to be ruled admissible by the commission and then heard by the court, can be measured in years) it is not very often likely to be in the child's interests to interfere with the original decision. Furthermore, the very delay can, if it impedes implementation of long-term plans, be seriously detrimental to the individual child.

[20] *Gaskin v United Kingdom* (1990) 12 EHRR 36.
[1] Pursuant to its obligations under Art 53—see ante, p 19.

Part III

Property and financial provision

Summary of contents

Chapter 17

Rights in property created and affected by the relationship of spouses and unmarried cohabitants

A. Husband and wife: historical introduction

During the last century legislation has considerably simplified the law of property as it is affected by the relationship of husband and wife. But since this branch of the law shows the development of the status of the wife from a subservient member of the family to the co-equal head of it more clearly than any other (except possibly the parents' rights with respect to their children), we shall start with a brief historical conspectus of the effects of marriage upon rights in property.[1]

1. COMMON LAW

Freeholds

The highly technical nature of the common law relating to real property is well reflected in the effects which marriage produced.

The husband's interest in his wife's freeholds

It was not unnatural that the medieval law should look to the husband rather than to the wife for the performance of the feudal dues which arose from freehold tenure. By marriage a husband gained seisin of all freehold lands which his wife held at the time of the marriage or acquired during coverture and was entitled to the rents and profits of them. If he predeceased the wife, she immediately resumed the right to all her freeholds; if she predeceased him, her estates of inheritance descended to her heir subject to the husband's right to retain seisin as tenant by the curtesy of England. This arose if the husband had issue born alive by the wife which was *capable* of inheriting her freeholds,[2] in which case he was entitled as tenant by the curtesy to an estate for his life in all her freeholds of inheritance to which on her death she was entitled in possession otherwise than as a joint tenant.

The wife had no power to dispose of her realty at all during marriage,[3]

[1] For further details and authorities reference must be made to the editions of standard works on real and personal property and equity published during the nineteenth and early twentieth centuries. The classic exposition of the common law position is to be found in Blackstone's *Commentaries*, vol ii. See also Dicey *Law and Opinion* (2nd Edn) pp 371–395.
[2] Hence if the wife were tenant in tail female, the birth of a son would not give the husband curtesy. Once the child was born alive, it was immaterial that it did not survive. See further Farrer *Tenant by the Curtesy of England* 43 LQR 87.
[3] But even at common law she could exercise a power of appointment given to her without her husband's concurrence.

and the husband alone could not dispose of it for more than his own interest. But together they could dispose of the whole estate. This was done by both spouses' levying a fine, when the court would examine the wife separately in order to ensure that her consent had been freely given. After the Fines and Recoveries Act 1833 the disposition was effected by deed which had to be separately acknowledged by the wife before a judge or commissioners who still had to examine her.[4]

The wife's interest in her husband's freeholds

During marriage the wife took no interest in her husband's realty at all, but, if she survived him, she became entitled by virtue of her dower to an estate for life in a third of all her husband's freeholds of inheritance of which he had been seised in possession (otherwise than as a joint tenant) *at any time during marriage* provided that she *could* have borne a child capable of inheriting, whether such a child was ever born or not.[5] Since dower created a legal estate, it attached even though the husband alienated the land; and it could be barred only by the wife's levying a fine. The practical inconvenience of this is obvious, so much so that the Statute of Uses enacted that dower could be barred by making a jointure in favour of the wife.[6] These difficulties were eventually obviated by the Dower Act of 1833, which provided that dower should not attach to any land which the husband disposed of during his lifetime or by will and that the wife's right to dower out of his estates of inheritance in respect of which he died intestate should be barred if he made a declaration to this effect by deed or will. As a quid pro quo the Act gave the wife dower in her husband's equitable freeholds in respect of which he died intestate, if he had not barred her right by declaration.

Tenancy by entireties

The doctrine of unity of legal personality produced another striking consequence in the law of property.[7] If land were granted to a husband and wife, they were said to take by entireties and received an interest which could not be turned into a tenancy in common by severance. Hence, unless they disposed of the estate during marriage, the survivor was bound to take the whole. Similarly, if land were granted to a husband, his wife and a third person, the spouses were regarded as one person and consequently they were entitled to only one half of the rent and profits and the third person was entitled to the other half.

---

[4] The necessity of acknowledgment was abolished by the Law of Property Act 1925, s 167.

[5] Hence if land were limited to H and the heirs of his body by his wife W, and after W's death H married X, X could not claim dower in the land since no child of hers could ever succeed to the tail special.

[6] If the jointure was settled before marriage, the dower was barred absolutely; if it was settled after marriage, the wife could elect between her jointure and her dower.

[7] Another consequence was that at common law there could be no conveyance between spouses. After the passing of the Statute of Uses in 1535, this difficulty was overcome by a grant to feoffees to the use of the other spouse.

Copyholds

As a general rule the law relating to copyholds was the same as that relating to freeholds. But the husband did not take as tenant by the curtesy unless there was a custom of the manor to that effect, and a widow's interest in her deceased husband's copyhold land was known as her freebench. The exact nature of this varied from place to place and sometimes gave her an interest in the whole of her husband's copyholds and sometimes only in a third. But it usually attached only to that land which he had neither devised nor alienated in his lifetime and consequently did not give rise to the same difficulties as dower. Freebench was unaffected by the Dower Act.

Leaseholds

The wife's leaseholds belonged to the husband during marriage and he therefore had the absolute power to dispose of them inter vivos. If the wife predeceased him, he took the whole of the balance of the term jure mariti; but if he predeceased the wife, her leaseholds automatically reverted to her and the husband had no power to dispose of them by will.

Pure personalty

All choses in possession belonging to the wife at the time of the marriage or acquired by her during coverture vested absolutely in the husband who therefore had the power to dispose of them inter vivos or by will. Even if he died intestate during the wife's life, they did not revert to her. The only exception to this rule applied to the wife's paraphernalia, that is those articles of apparel and personal ornament which were suitable to her rank and degree. Whilst the husband could dispose of these during his lifetime and the wife could alienate them neither inter vivos nor by will during marriage, the husband could not deprive her of them by bequest and on his death they became her property and did not form a part of his estate.[8]

The wife's choses in action belonged to the husband if he reduced them into possession or obtained judgment in respect of them during marriage. If he died before this was done, the right of action survived to the wife; if she predeceased him, he could sue by taking out letters of administration.[9] It follows that if the chose in action was reversionary, the husband would not be entitled to it if he died before it fell into possession leaving his wife surviving him.[10]

Fraud on the husband's marital rights

A contract to marry clearly gave the husband an expectant interest in all his wife's property—an interest in return for which he would of course on marriage be liable to maintain her and would be saddled with the liability for all her ante-nuptial torts and contracts.[11] Consequently the rule

---

[8] Unless the husband's estate was insolvent, in which case his creditors could take the wife's paraphernalia in satisfaction but not her necessary clothing.

[9] See ante, p 128.

[10] Hence it was impossible for them even jointly to make an absolute assignment of a reversionary interest before the passing of the Married Women's Reversionary Interests Act 1857 (Malins' Act).

[11] See ante, pp 128 and 133.

developed that any disposition made by an engaged woman without her fiancé's consent was voidable by him as a fraud on his marital rights. Since it was voidable only, it could not be set aside against a bona fide purchaser for value without notice of the engagement.

2. EQUITY

As a general rule equity followed the law. Thus the husband had the same rights over his wife's equitable freeholds and leaseholds and her equitable interests in pure personalty and the same power to dispose of them (subject to her concurrence in the case of her freeholds) as he had in respect of her legal estates and interests.[12] In only one case was there a marked difference: whilst the husband was entitled to a life interest in his deceased wife's equitable freeholds as a tenant by the curtesy, the wife was not entitled to dower in her deceased husband's equitable freeholds until the passing of the Dower Act in 1833.[13]

The husband's right to his wife's equitable interests in property was indefeasible once he had got possession of it, as would be the case, for example, if a trustee paid over the trust fund or an executor paid over a legacy. But if the husband was obliged to invoke the aid of Chancery to obtain the property, the court gave the wife an 'equity to a settlement'. It applied the maxim 'He who seeks equity must do equity' and, if the property was such that the husband would have an absolute power to dispose of it, it would lend him its assistance only on condition that he settled an adequate part of it on his wife and children for their maintenance.[14]

The wife's separate estate

But by far the most important contribution of equity to the law relating to a married woman's property was the development of the concept of the separate estate. By the end of the sixteenth century[15] it was established that if property was conveyed to trustees *to the separate use* of a married woman, she retained in equity the same right of holding and disposing of it as if she were a feme sole.[16] This applied whether the interest was in realty or personalty and whether it was in possession or reversion. She could therefore dispose of it inter vivos or by will and, like any other beneficiary of full age who was absolutely entitled, she could call upon her trustees to convey the legal estate. Only if she died intestate in respect of her separate estate did the husband obtain the same interest that he would have had in her equitable property had it not been settled to her separate use. Moreover it

---

[12] A power of appointment given to a married woman could be exercised without her husband's concurrence.

[13] But then only if he died intestate with respect to them and had not barred her dower: see ante, p 556.

[14] The wife could compromise her claim. Usually the husband would be ordered to settle half his interest, but this would clearly depend upon the wife's financial circumstances and on occasion he was ordered to settle the whole fund. The husband took the reversionary interest.

[15] See Holdsworth *History of English Law*, v, pp 310–315.

[16] If property were settled on an unmarried woman to her separate use, it also remained her separate estate after marriage. Hence, if an engaged woman settled her property on herself to her separate use without her fiancé's concurrence, he could have the settlement set aside as a fraud on his marital rights: see supra.

was finally held that not even the interposition of trustees was necessary, and if property were conveyed, devised or bequeathed to a married woman to her separate use so that the legal estate vested in the husband jure mariti, he was deemed in equity to hold it on trust for her and he acquired no greater interest in it than he would have done if it had been conveyed to trustees on similar terms.[17]

The restraint upon anticipation

Whilst separate estate in equity did much to mitigate the harshness of the common law rule, there was still one situation which it did not meet. For there was nothing to prevent a married woman from assigning her beneficial interest to her husband and thus vesting in him the interest which the separate use had sought to keep out of his hands, and the temptation presented to a grasping, spendthrift or insolvent husband was great. To circumvent this, equity developed about 1800 a second concept, complementary to the first, that of the restraint upon anticipation.[18] This could be imposed only if property was conveyed, devised or bequeathed to a woman's separate use, and, once it attached, it prevented her from anticipating and dealing with any income until it actually fell due. A restraint could be and usually was attached to the corpus too, in which case the whole fund became completely inalienable during marriage.

A restraint on anticipation could even be attached to the separate property of an unmarried woman. In this case she could deal with the property as if there were no restraint and could also totally remove the restraint by executing a deed poll to this effect. A woman to whose separate property a restraint had been attached before or during marriage could do the same after the marriage was terminated by her husband's death or by divorce. But in the absence of any such deed, as soon as she married or remarried, the restraint became operative as regards any property not alienated whilst she was a feme sole.

The restraint on anticipation was designed to protect not only the wife but also the members of her family who would be entitled to the property on her death.[19] Whilst it effectively kept the property out of the hands of the husband and his creditors, it had one obvious drawback. There might be a number of occasions on which it might be in the wife's interest to deal with property subject to a restraint, but nothing short of a private Act of Parliament could remove it. It was in order to overcome this difficulty that the Conveyancing Act 1881 gave the court power to bind her interest in such property provided that this was for her benefit.[20] But the court could only render a specific disposition binding and it had no general power to remove the restraint altogether.

---

[17] For the wife's power to bind her separate estate by contract, see ante, p 127.
[18] See Hart *The Origin of the Restraint upon Anticipation* 40 LQR 221.
[19] Kahn-Freund in *Matrimonial Property Law* (ed Friedmann) p 274. For the position in equity generally, see Dicey *Law and Opinion* (2nd Edn) pp 375–382.
[20] S 39, subsequently replaced by the Conveyancing Act 1911, s 7, and the Law of Property Act 1925, s 169.

3. MODERN LEGISLATION

By the middle of the nineteenth century it was clear that the old rules would have to be reformed. More and more women were earning incomes of their own, either in trade, or on the stage or by writing, and there were a number of scandalous cases of husbands' impounding their wives' earnings for the benefit of their own creditors or even mistresses. No relief could be obtained by the woman whose husband deserted her and took all her property with him. The separate use and restraint upon anticipation were clumsy creatures and were in practice unlikely to affect the property of any but the daughters of the rich who would have carefully drawn marriage settlements and would be the beneficiaries under complicated wills. Agitation for reform was discernible in many quarters and eventually produced a series of Acts of ever wider scope.[1]

The Matrimonial Causes Act 1857

So far as married women's property was concerned, this Act sought to remedy two existing defects in the law only. First, so long as a judicial separation was in force, the wife was now to be deemed to be a feme sole with respect to any property which she should acquire and thus for the first time in the history of English law she had the sole power to dispose of a legal interest either inter vivos or by will.[2] If the parties resumed cohabitation, all property so acquired was to be held for her separate use. Secondly, if a wife were deserted, she might obtain a protection order which would have the effect of protecting from seizure by her husband and his creditors any property and earnings to which she became entitled after the desertion and of vesting them in her as if she were a feme sole.[3]

The Married Women's Property Act 1870

As originally conceived, this Act was to anticipate the much wider provisions of the Act of 1882. But the Bill was so cut down in Parliament that in its final form the Act presented no more than a series of exceptions to the common law rule by providing that in a number of specified cases property acquired by the wife (for example, her earnings, deposits in savings banks, stocks and shares, and in very limited circumstances property devolving upon her on an intestacy) should be deemed to be held for her separate use. Moreover certain provisions applied only to women marrying after the passing of the Act. The whole Act was repealed by the Married Women's Property Act of 1882, but it remains of historical importance in that it gave a statutory extension to the existing equitable concept of the separate estate: the device that was later to be used in the Act of 1882.[4]

---

[1] See Dicey op cit pp 382–395.
[2] S 25.
[3] S 21.
[4] For the effect of the Act of 1870 on spouses' liability in contract and tort, see ante, pp 128 and 133.

The Married Women's Property Act 1882

Historically this Act is the most important of the whole series. It was of universal application, although it did not affect any rights which had vested by marriage before 1883. It provided that any woman marrying after 1882 should be entitled to retain all property owned by her at the time of the marriage as her separate property and that, whenever she was married, any property acquired by a married woman after 1882 should be held by her in the same way.[5] It also enacted that:

'A married woman shall ... be capable of acquiring, holding, and disposing by will or otherwise, of any real or personal property as her separate property, in the same manner as if she were a feme sole, without the intervention of any trustee'.[6]

It further provided that the law relating to restraint upon anticipation should remain unaffected.[7]

The sweeping nature of these changes is obvious. It now became impossible for a married man to acquire any further interest in his wife's property jure mariti by operation of law. No further tenancies by entireties could be created. A widower could claim an interest in his deceased's wife's property acquired after 1882 only if she died intestate with respect to it. The necessity of both spouses' joining in a conveyance of the wife's realty became obsolescent. But in one sense the changes were even more fundamental than these, for whilst the statute adapted the equitable concept of separate property,[8] it went further by vesting in the wife the *legal* interest in her property. The detailed provisions of the Act are too complex to be considered here,[9] but subject to the restraint on anticipation a married woman's capacity to hold and dispose of property was very nearly the same as that of a feme sole.

The property legislation of 1925

This legislation only incidentally affected rights in property of spouses as such. Its most important effect in this field lay in the changed rules of succession on an intestacy;[10] in particular dower and freebench[11] were abolished and the husband's right to his wife's freeholds as tenant by the curtesy is now virtually extinct.[12] Any remaining tenancies by entireties were

[5] Ss 2 and 5.
[6] S 1(1).
[7] S 19.
[8] Hence, for example, a married woman still could not be made bankrupt unless she came within the express provisions of s 1(5) by carrying on a trade separately from her husband.
[9] Amongst them are spouses' liability in contract (see ante, p 128), tort (ante, p 133) and criminal law (ante, p 138), policies of insurance in favour of a spouse or children (post, pp 581–582), and disputes over property arising between spouses (post, pp 567–569). The Act was modified in detail by the Married Women's Property Acts 1884, 1893, 1907 and 1908.
[10] See post, pp 814 et seq.
[11] Copyhold tenure was emancipated and converted into freehold tenure by the Law of Property Act 1922.
[12] It is limited to the case where the wife dies possessed of an unbarred entail: Administration of Estates Act 1925, s 45. There may also be curtesy in certain circumstances of the wife's determinable fee simple: Farrer *Tenant by the Curtesy of England* 43 LQR 87, at pp 100–102. Although this section does not apply to entailed interests, the Act repealed the Dower Act which gave the wife the right to dower in her husband's equitable freeholds. It thus entirely abolished dower, as a fee tail can now exist only as an equitable interest.

abolished, and a grant to a husband, his wife and a third person will now give each of them a third interest in the property.[13]

The Law Reform (Married Women and Tortfeasors) Act 1935

By 1935 almost all married women's property was owned by them as their separate property. To speak of 'separate property' therefore was becoming something of an anomaly, since married women in almost all cases had the same capacity to hold and dispose of it as a man or a feme sole. This was eventually recognised by Parliament in the Law Reform (Married Women and Tortfeasors) Act of that year which abolished the concept of the separate estate and gave to the wife the same rights and powers as were already possessed by other adults of full capacity. It provided:[14]

'... A married woman shall be capable of acquiring, holding, and disposing of, any property ... in all respects as if she were a feme sole.
 ... All property which—
(a) immediately before the passing of this Act was the separate property of a married woman or held for her separate use in equity; *or*
(b) belongs at the time of her marriage to a woman married after the passing of this Act; *or*
(c) after the passing of this Act is acquired by or devolves upon a married woman, shall belong to her in all respects as if she were a feme sole and may be disposed of accordingly.'

Although the Act did not affect any existing restraint on anticipation, it rendered void any attempted imposition of a restraint in any instrument executed after 1935 and in the will of any person dying after 1945, even though it was executed before 1936.[15]

The Married Women (Restraint upon Anticipation) Act 1949

Although after 1945 restraint upon anticipation was bound to disappear in the course of time, the Act of 1935 did not affect the validity of restraints already imposed. Whilst in 1882 it was apparently still necessary to protect a married woman's property in this way, the restraint could no longer be justified in the middle of the present century, when it served no further purpose but merely acted as an undue fetter on the wife's powers of alienation. Although the court could sanction individual dispositions if these were for her benefit,[16] the only way in which a restraint could be wholly removed was by a private Act of Parliament. It was the presentation of a bill for this purpose that ultimately led to the passing of the Married Women (Restraint upon Anticipation) Act in 1949, which removed all restraints whenever imposed and thus rendered the property to which they were attached freely alienable.

[13] Law of Property Act 1925, s 37. After 1882 the spouses could sever their half share as *between themselves* they took as ordinary joint tenants.
[14] Ss 1(a) and 2(1). The Act did not affect any rights in property accrued as the result of a marriage before 1883: s 4(1)(a).
[15] S 2.
[16] See ante, p 559. If the restraint were attached to land, the woman could sell the land under the provisions of the Settled Land Act 1925, but the restraint continued to attach to the capital.

B. Husband and wife: the modern law[17]

1. GENERAL PRINCIPLES

The effect of the Married Women's Property Acts

By extending the equitable principle of the separate estate, the Married Women's Property Acts replaced the total incapacity of a married woman to hold property at common law by a rigid doctrine of separate property. In the well known words of Dicey,[18] 'the rules of equity, framed for the daughters of the rich, have at last been extended to the daughters of the poor'. But, as Professor Kahn-Freund has shown,[19] the effects of the Acts were much wider than this. Spouses' property may be broadly divided into two types: that intended for common use and consumption in the matrimonial home and that intended for personal use and enjoyment. The latter is often in the form of investments or derived from the interest on investments, and it is obvious that, whilst in a poor family almost the whole of the property will fall into the first category, the richer the spouses the greater fraction of their property will fall into the second. Before 1883 the matrimonial home and its contents would almost invariably be vested in the husband to the exclusion of the wife, and the latter's separate property did little more than protect her investments. But, impelled by a movement which was ultimately to secure the almost complete legal equality of the sexes, Parliament extended the doctrine of separation to property forming the matrimonial home as well—a situation which the equitable concept was never intended to cover and with which it was ill adapted to deal.

This was inevitably bound to produce difficulties. But so long as the husband remained the bread winner, they were not acute, as it could still be argued that he retained the ownership of property bought out of his earnings. But during the Second World War most married women were wage earners as well, and what before 1939 had been something of an exception has now become the usual situation in most families. To apply the strict doctrine of separate property to matrimonial assets in such circumstances is manifestly absurd. As a result, judges have sought to adapt the principle by regarding both spouses as having an interest in the matrimonial home in many cases, even though the legal estate is vested solely in the husband. Legislation has also been passed to overcome some difficulties, particularly with respect to the occupation of the matrimonial home.

Doctrines effecting such radical changes are bound to bristle with difficulties. Marked differences of opinion amongst the judges have been reflected in confusing and sometimes contradictory decisions, and whilst clear patterns seem to emerge from time to time, they are liable to be suddenly obscured by a new case out of line with recent trends. In practice the most difficult problems arise when the marriage breaks down in the parties'

---

[17] See generally Miller *Family Property and Financial Provision*; Lesser, *The Acquisition of Inter Vivos Matrimonial Property Rights in English Law* 23 U of Toronto LJ 148.

[18] *Law and Opinion* (2nd Edn) p 395.

[19] In *Matrimonial Property Law* (ed Friedmann), pp 267 et seq. See also his article, *Recent Legislation on Matrimonial Property* 33 MLR 601.

lifetime, and as the Court of Appeal made clear in *Williams v Williams*,[20] whenever possible the parties should rely on the wide powers now possessed by the court to make orders for the transfer and settlement of property on divorce, nullity and judicial separation which largely remove the need to make an enquiry into the precise interest that each spouse has in the matrimonial home or other asset. It should not be thought, however, that the question of ownership is now merely academic.[1] Strict property rights are still of the greatest importance on the death or insolvency of one spouse because they alone will have to be applied to resolve any dispute between the other and the personal representatives or creditors. Furthermore, a spouse may not wish to take matrimonial proceedings or may not be able to apply for a property adjustment order because she (or he) has remarried.

The real trouble is that, except for family provision on death, such legislation as there has been during this century has sought to deal with isolated problems, and we need to complete the statutory overhaul of the whole field of matrimonial property law. Solutions adopted by other legal systems include community of property (under which the property belonging to both spouses is administered by the husband and divided between them or their personal representatives when the marriage comes to an end), community of gains (which limits community to property acquired during the marriage otherwise than by gift or inheritance), and deferred community (under which each spouse remains free to acquire and dispose of his or her own property but at the end of the marriage any net gain or surplus is divided equally between them). English courts already have a wide discretion to adjust rights by ordering the transfer and settlement of property following divorce, nullity and judicial separation. There are also extensive powers to order provision for members of the family and other dependants out of the estate of a deceased person. Bearing these points in mind, the Law Commission concluded in 1978 that it is not necessary to introduce any form of community of property in this country: most remaining hardship would be avoided if the spouses were co-owners of the matrimonial home, which is the most substantial asset in the majority of families. As it is, well over a half of all married couples who own their own homes own them jointly:[2] the Commission has recommended that this principle should be extended by statute to other spouses.[3]

---

[20] [1976] Ch 278, [1977] 1 All ER 28, CA. For the court's powers see post, pp 736–738.
[1] See *Kowalczuk v Kowalczuk* [1973] 2 All ER 1042, 1045, CA; *Griffiths v Griffiths* [1974] 1 All ER 932, 941, CA.
[2] See Todd and Jones *Matrimonial Property* (HMSO). Joint ownership is becoming much more popular than this figure suggests because the proportion of spouses buying a house in the decade 1962–71 and having it conveyed into joint names rose from 47% to 74%.
[3] Law Com No 86 (Third Report on Family Property). See also Law Commission Working Paper No 42 and Law Com No 52 (First Report on Family Property); Report of the Morton Commission, Cmd 9678, Pt IX; Simon *With all my Worldly Goods* ... (published by the Holdsworth Club of the University of Birmingham); Nevitt and Levin *Social Policy and the Matrimonial Home* 36 MLR 345; Baxter 37 MLR 175; Kahn-Freund *Matrimonial Property—Where do we go from here?* (Joseph Unger Memorial Lecture); Freeman *Towards a Rational Reconstruction of Family Property Law*, Current Legal Problems 1972, 84. For further criticisms particularly with respect to rented accommodation (including lettings by local authorities), see the Finer Report, Cmnd 5629, Pt 6. For discussion of some foreign systems, comparison with which is interesting and profitable, see *Matrimonial Property Law* (ed Friedmann); Milner *A Homestead Act for England* 22 MLR 458; Tarlo *Possession of the Matrimonial Home in Australia* 22 MLR 479; Górecki *Matrimonial Property in Poland* 26

What they envisaged is that spouses should be statutory co-owners of any property, freehold or leasehold, used as their matrimonial home unless they otherwise agreed or, in the case of a gift, the donor, settlor or testator otherwise stipulated.[4] Once the statutory trust attached to the land, neither would be able to dispose of it unless the other consented or the court dispensed with his or her consent.[5] The Commission rejected the possibility of introducing compulsory co-ownership of goods, partly because the value of used goods is so much less than half that of new goods that compensation in the form of half their actual value would not enable the loser to replace them. Instead they proposed that either spouse should be able to apply for an order concerning the use and enjoyment of 'household goods'.[6] In deciding whether to make such an order, the court should be guided particularly by the extent to which the applicant needed them to meet the normal requirements of his or her daily life and family responsibilities. If the other spouse contravened an order, the court could order him to pay the applicant such sum (which could be the replacement value) as it thought fair and reasonable by way of compensation.[7]

These proposals represent a compromise between the present English system of separate property and a comprehensive adoption of a system of community. They did not, however, command universal support and have never been implemented.[8] Ten years later the Commission considered the problem again in so far as it concerns pure personalty.[9] They highlighted a number of anomalies and inequalities in the law, including the rules relating to the acquisition of property out of a housekeeping allowance and the operation of the presumption of advancement.[10] They also pointed out that the law can work arbitrarily: for example, if the wife pays all the housekeeping bills out of her own earnings and the husband uses his to buy a car for the parties' joint use, the car will belong to him, whilst if they pool their earnings in a joint account, it will belong to them both.[11] The Commission have gone back on their earlier recommendation and now

---

MLR 156; Pedersen *Matrimonial Property Law in Denmark* 28 MLR 137; Johnson *Matrimonial Property in Soviet Law* 16 ICLQ 1106; Eekelaar *Family Security and Family Breakdown* pp 98 et seq.

[4] The Commission contemplated other exceptions. The most important was the ability of a spouse to exclude the house from co-ownership if he owned it at the time of the marriage.

[5] If one spouse's name did not appear on the title, she (or he) would be able to protect her interest by registering it as a land charge.

[6] Ie 'any goods, including a vehicle, which are or were available for use and enjoyment in or in connection with any home which the parties to the marriage have at any time during the marriage occupied as their matrimonial home'. Goods would be excepted if third parties had an interest in them, eg goods subject to hire, hire-purchase and conditional sale agreements.

[7] This would be in addition to the usual penalties for disobeying an order of the court. A person receiving the goods could also be ordered to pay compensation if he was aware of the order. In appropriate cases the party disposing of the goods could be ordered to pay compensation even though no order was in force.

[8] A bill to establish statutory co-ownership of the matrimonial home was introduced in the House of Lords in 1980 but it was made clear that government time would not be made available for it.

[9] Law Com No 175 (Matrimonial Property). Land was excluded from the Commission's recommendations because of its peculiar nature.

[10] See Law Com Working Paper No 90 (Transfer of Money between Spouses). See post, pp 572–573 (housekeeping allowances) and 574 (presumption of advancement).

[11] See post, p 571.

propose that, if one spouse acquires property intended wholly or mainly for the use or benefit of both, beneficial ownership should vest in both jointly. This would be subject to a contrary intention on the part of the purchaser or transferor provided that it was made known to the other at the time, and would not apply to property acquired by way of gift or inheritance or purchased or transferred wholly or mainly for the purpose of business.[12] The reason they propose that the property should be held jointly and not in equal shares is that they believe that this is what the parties themselves would wish and intend.

The implementation of this proposal would obviously lead to a considerable increase in the number of chattels jointly owned and thus in the risk that a purchaser from one party only would not acquire a good title. This risk, however, exists already: the buyer of a family car assumes that the seller is the absolute owner and does not enquire about the source of the funds with which it was originally bought. The Commission believe that the proposed change would introduce a fair rule and provide much greater certainty in this area of the law. It is certainly less complex than their earlier recommendations, but at present it seems no more likely to be implemented.

Issues between the spouses

Two questions arise here: in whom are the legal and equitable interests in the property vested and what rights short of ownership may one spouse have in the property of the other? So long as they are living amicably together, these questions rarely have to be answered, but they become vital if the marriage breaks down. This adds considerably to the difficulty, for the parties rarely contemplate the collapse of the marriage when they acquire property, and their respective rights in it are never discussed, let alone defined. Hence the courts are faced with the problem of having to infer an intention which the spouses never formulated at all.[13]

There are four different ways of solving disputes open to them.

Action for damages in tort

As we have already seen,[14] either spouse may now protect his or her interests in property by suing the other in tort, for example in trespass or conversion. Either may also bring an action against the other for the recovery of land. In this connection it should be remembered that if the spouses are jointly in possession of property or are jointly entitled to possession, one may be liable in trespass if he or she completely ousts the other or in conversion if he or she destroys the property or disposes of it.[15]

It will be recalled that the court may stay the action if the questions in issue could be disposed of more conveniently by an application under section 17 of the Married Women's Property Act 1882.[16]

---

[12] The Commission would also exclude policies of life assurance, which could mature many years after the termination of the parties' relationship.

[13] Cf *Re Rogers' Question* [1948] 1 All ER 328, CA; *Cobb v Cobb* [1955] 2 All ER 696, 699, CA.

[14] Ante, p 134.

[15] Torts (Interference with Goods) Act 1977, s 10; Salmond and Heuston *Law of Torts* (19th Edn) pp 56, 123.

[16] Ante, p 135. For proceedings under s 17, see infra.

Proceedings for an injunction

Either spouse may obtain an injunction to prevent the other from committing a continuing or threatened wrong against the plaintiff's property.[17] In practice this remedy is most frequently sought when the wife is trying to exclude the husband from entering the matrimonial home, and the particular problems that arise here are dealt with in chapter 5.[18]

Proceedings under section 17 of the Married Women's Property Act 1882

This section[19] provides that 'in any question between husband and wife as to the title to or possession of property'[20] either of them may apply for an order to the High Court or a county court and the judge 'may make such order with respect to the property in dispute ... as he thinks fit'.[1] These proceedings are of course usually invoked when the marriage has broken down. Disputes over rights in property may still be going on after the marriage has been legally terminated, and consequently section 17 has now been extended to enable former spouses to make an application for a period of three years after a decree absolute of divorce or nullity.[2] Similarly, engaged couples may well buy furniture and start to buy a house in contemplation of their marriage, and this may give them rights in property which are virtually indistinguishable from those acquired by married couples. The abolition of actions for damages for breach of promise of marriage deprived them of the means of recovering the expenses they had lost if the marriage did not take place. Consequently the summary procedure of section 17 has now been made available to the parties to an agreement to marry which has been terminated as well. An application must relate to property in which either or both of them had an interest while the agreement was in force and must be brought within three years of the termination of the agreement.[3]

---

[17] This may be done by bringing an action in tort under the Law Reform (Husband and Wife) Act 1962, in proceedings under the Domestic Violence and Matrimonial Proceedings Act 1976, or by way of ancillary relief in other matrimonial proceedings.

[18] Ante, pp 160 et seq.

[19] Replacing and extending the Married Women's Property Act 1870, s 9. The section has been amended by the Law Reform (Husband and Wife) Act 1962, Schedule (repealing s 23 of the Act of 1882) and the Statute Law (Repeals) Act 1969, Schedule, Pt III, which have taken away the power of a deceased wife's personal representatives and of banks, companies and other bodies to take proceedings under s 17, and by the Matrimonial and Family Proceedings Act 1984, s 43.

[20] Including choses in action (*Spellman v Spellman* [1961] 2 All ER 498, 501, CA) and property of which the claimant is a bare trustee and in which he has no beneficial interest at all (*Re Knight's Question* [1959] Ch 381, [1958] 1 All ER 812). The court may make an order with respect to property (including immovable property) situated abroad but will not do so if the order is likely to be ineffective (eg because a foreign court would disregard it) and the court has no means of enforcing it against the defendant in personam: *Razelos v Razelos (No 2)* [1970] 1 All ER 386n, approved in *Hamlin v Hamlin* [1986] Fam 11, [1985] 2 All ER 1037, CA. If there is no question as to title or possession but one spouse is, eg, seeking to enforce a trust for sale against the other, proceedings under s 17 are inappropriate and the same proceedings should be taken as would be taken between strangers: *Rawlings v Rawlings* [1964] P 398, [1964] 2 All ER 804, CA.

[1] Proceedings in the High Court are now assigned to the Family Division.

[2] Matrimonial Proceedings and Property Act 1970, s 39.

[3] Law Reform (Miscellaneous Provisions) Act 1970, s 2(2). For the abolition of actions for breach of promise, see ante, p 22, and also see generally Law Com No 26 (Breach of Promise of Marriage).

It will be seen that the court has jurisdiction to determine questions of title and possession. In order that it may do this, it was formerly held that there must be in existence specific property or a specific fund with respect to which the order might be made and that if the property or fund had ceased to exist, there was no power to make what would be in effect an order for damages for trespass, conversion or debt.[4] This clearly worked injustice if the defendant had already disposed of the property or fund in question; this has been remedied by section 7 of the Matrimonial Causes (Property and Maintenance) Act 1958, which has given the court power in such a case either to order the defendant to pay to the plaintiff such sum of money as represents the latter's interest in the property or fund or to make an order with respect to any other property which now represents the whole or part of the original.[5]

For some years there was considerable judicial controversy over the width of the powers which the wording of the section gave to the judges. It was, however, finally settled by the House of Lords in *Pettitt v Pettitt*[6] that the court has no jurisdiction under this section to vary existing titles and no wider power to transfer or create interests in property than it would have in any other type of proceedings. At the most it has, in the words of Lord Diplock, 'a wide discretion as to the enforcement of the proprietary or possessory rights of one spouse in any property against the other'.[7] Furthermore, the fact that the marriage has broken down, the circumstances of the breakdown and the conduct of the parties cannot affect title in the absence of an agreement between the spouses and are therefore all irrelevant to the outcome of proceedings brought under section 17.[8] But by using its powers to make different types of orders, the court may effectively control the way in which the property is used without departing from the principle that it cannot alter the title. Thus it may order a spouse to give up possession of a house, to deliver up chattels, to transfer shares and other choses in action or to pay over a specific fund, and it may even forbid him to dispossess the other spouse or to deal with the property in any way inconsistent with the other's rights.[9] Similarly the court may order the property to be sold and direct how the proceeds of sale are to be divided[10] or, if both spouses have an interest, it may order one of them to transfer his or her share to the other on the latter's paying the value of the property transferred.[11]

On the breakdown of a marriage one of the spouses will normally petition

---

[4] *Tunstall v Tunstall* [1953] 2 All ER 310, CA.

[5] But a specific property or fund must have been in existence originally and proceedings cannot be brought under s 17 for the recovery of a debt: *Crystall v Crystall* [1963] 2 All ER 330, CA. The Limitation Act has been held not to apply to such proceedings and consequently an order may be made even though the property was disposed of more than six years earlier: *Spoor v Spoor* [1966] 3 All ER 120.

[6] [1970] AC 777, [1969] 2 All ER 385, HL.

[7] At 820 and 411, respectively.

[8] *Pettitt v Pettitt* (supra).

[9] As in *Lee v Lee* [1952] 2 QB 489n, [1952] 1 All ER 1299, CA. In *Re Bettinson's Question* [1956] Ch 67, [1955] 3 All ER 296, it was held that an order could be made with respect to property which was subject to the doctrine of community of property under the law of the parties' domicile (California).

[10] Matrimonial Causes (Property and Maintenance) Act 1958, s 7(7).

[11] *Bothe v Amos* [1976] Fam 46, [1975] 2 All ER 321, CA.

for divorce, nullity or judicial separation and invoke the court's wider powers to make a property adjustment order under section 24 of the Matrimonial Causes Act. Consequently proceedings under section 17 are now comparatively rare and are likely only if the party seeking relief is unable or unwilling to take matrimonial proceedings or has remarried before applying for a property adjustment order.[12] Ironically, those whose engagement has been broken off now constitute a group of people for whom section 17 provides the best relief.

Proceedings under section 30 of the Law of Property Act 1925

If trustees for sale refuse to sell the trust property, this section enables any person interested to apply to the court for an order directing them to give effect to the trust, whereupon the court may make such order as it thinks fit. This power may be used to force the sale of the parties' home because if both have a beneficial interest in it, either as joint tenants or as tenants in common, this will automatically create a trust for sale. For the reasons stated in the last paragraph the future of a married couple's home will usually be settled by a property adjustment order rather than by proceedings under section 30.

Issues between one of the spouses and a stranger

The question to be considered here is how far rights in property created or affected by marriage can be enforced by one of the spouses against a third person. The latter may claim in one of a number of capacities, for example as a purchaser for value from the other spouse, as the other's creditor or trustee in bankruptcy, or as a beneficiary entitled to a deceased spouse's estate. It is essential to decide first what rights the claiming spouse has against the other spouse and then how far these rights are enforceable against the third person. This will depend upon the application of general principles of the law of property and in particular the nature of the latter's title. If he is, say, the husband's donee, the wife may enforce against him all those rights (other than purely personal rights) which she would have against her husband; if he is a purchaser of a legal estate or interest for value, he will take the property subject to the wife's legal rights but will not be bound by her equitable interests if he purchased in good faith and without notice of them.

2. PROPERTY ACQUIRED BY THE SPOUSES

Property owned by the spouses at the time of the marriage

Presumptively marriage will not affect the ownership of property vested in either of the spouses at the time. This will also be true of property which is used by them jointly in the matrimonial home (for example, furniture)

---

[12] See post, p 724.

in the absence of an express gift of a joint interest in law or in equity.[13]

Income

The income of either spouse, whether from earnings or from investments, will prima facie remain his or her own property.[14] But where the spouses pool their incomes and place them into a common fund, it seems that they both acquire a joint interest in the whole fund.

This occurred in *Jones v Maynard*.[15] In 1941 the husband, who was about to go abroad with the RAF, authorised his wife to draw on his bank account, which was thereafter treated as a joint account. Into this account were paid dividends on both the husband's and the wife's investments, the husband's pay and allowances and rent from the matrimonial home which was their joint property and which had been let during the War. The husband's contributions were greater than the wife's; the spouses had never agreed on what their rights in this fund were to be, but they regarded it as their joint savings to be invested from time to time. The husband withdrew money on a number of occasions and invested it in his own name, and finally, after the spouses had separated in 1946, he closed the account altogether. The marriage was later dissolved and the plaintiff sued her former husband for a half share in the account as it stood on the day it was closed and in the investments which he had previously purchased out of it. Vaisey J held that the claim must succeed. He said:[16]

'In my judgment, when there is a joint account between husband and wife, a common pool into which they put all their resources, it is not consistent with that conception that the account should thereafter ... be picked apart, and divided up proportionately to the respective contributions of husband and wife, the husband being credited with the whole of his earnings and the wife with the whole of her dividends. I do not believe that, when once the joint pool has been formed, it ought to be, and can be, dissected in any such manner. In my view a husband's earnings or salary, when the spouses have a common purse and pool their resources, are earnings made on behalf of both; and the idea that years afterwards the contents of the pool can be dissected by taking an elaborate account as to how much was paid in by the husband or the wife is quite inconsistent with the original fundamental idea of a joint purse or common pool.

In my view the money which goes into the pool becomes joint property. The husband, if he wants a suit of clothes, draws a cheque to pay for it. The wife, if she wants any housekeeping money, draws a cheque, and there is no disagreement about it.'

What, then, constitutes a 'common purse'? It would seem on principle

---

[13] Since the cases indicate that a joint interest will not be created unless both have contributed in some way to the purchase, in which case they will probably already own the property jointly before marriage: see post, p 588. For the effect of the subsequent acquisition of an English domicile by parties whose original lex domicilii imposed on them the doctrine of community of property, see *De Nicols v Curlier* [1900] AC 21, HL; for the converse case of the parties' acquiring a foreign domicile after the marriage, see *Re Egerton's Will Trusts* [1956] Ch 593, [1956] 2 All ER 817. See also Stone, *The Matrimonial Domicile and the Property Relations of Married Persons* 6 ICLQ 28; Goldberg *The Assignment of Property on Marriage* 19 ICLQ 557.

[14] Cf *Dixon v Dixon* (1878) 9 Ch D 587 (stock settled to the wife's separate use); *Barrack v M'Culloch* (1856) 3 K & J 110 (rents from houses settled to the wife's separate use); *Heseltine v Heseltine* [1971] 1 All ER 952 (income from wife's investments).

[15] [1951] Ch 572, [1951] 1 All ER 802.

[16] At 575 and 803, respectively.

to be essential that there must be a fund intended for the use of both spouses from which either may withdraw money and this will normally take the form of a joint bank account. Where they both contribute to this fund, as in *Jones v Maynard*, it is submitted that this intention will be imputed to the parties in the absence of any other agreement; where, however, the fund is derived from the income of one spouse alone, it is a question of fact whether this is to remain his or her exclusive property or whether there is an intention to establish a common fund. If the wife is the sole contributor to a joint account, she will prima facie take the whole beneficial interest.[17] On the other hand, if the husband is the sole contributor, the presumption of advancement will operate so as prima facie to give her an interest;[18] but this will be rebutted if, for example, it can be shown that the power to draw on the account was given for the husband's convenience by enabling the wife to draw cheques for the payment of housekeeping expenses.[19] Even though the beneficial interest in a joint account is initially vested in one spouse alone, his or her intention may change and it may be converted into a joint interest.[20] The courts will probably tend to find a joint beneficial interest today much more readily than they did in the past.

If either spouse withdraws money from the common purse, property bought with it will prima facie belong solely to that spouse if it is for his or her personal use (for example, clothes) but to both jointly if it is for their joint use (for example, a car). Investments purchased by means of the common purse will similarly belong to the purchaser unless it is clear that they are intended to represent the original fund. In *Re Bishop*[1] large sums had been withdrawn by both spouses to purchase investments in their separate names. In many cases blocks of shares were bought and half put in one name and the other half put in the other; other money was spent in taking up shares offered to the husband by virtue of rights which he possessed as an existing shareholder in the companies concerned. In these circumstances Stamp J had no difficulty in holding that the presumption could not be rebutted and that the spouse in whose name the shares had been purchased was entitled to the whole beneficial interest in them. He distinguished *Jones v Maynard* where Vaisey J had held that the husband was to be regarded as trustee for them both of investments which he had purchased, for in that case they had agreed that when there had been a sufficient accumulation the money should be invested and that that was to be their savings.

---

[17] *Heseltine v Heseltine* (supra) (houses purchased by husband out of joint account provided by wife's money held to belong to her absolutely). Contrast *Boydell v Gillespie* (1970) 210 Estates Gazette 1505 (wife's directing that property bought with her money should be conveyed into names of both spouses jointly held to give both an interest in it).

[18] *Re Figgis* [1969] 1 Ch 123, [1968] 1 All ER 999. Although the effect of these presumptions is considerably weaker today than it used to be (see post, p 574), they will still operate in a case like *Re Figgis* where both parties are dead and there is virtually no direct evidence of the parties' intentions at all.

[19] *Marshal v Crutwell* (1875) LR 20 Eq 328; *Hoddinott v Hoddinott* [1949] 2 KB 406, 413, CA; *Harrods Ltd v Tester* [1937] 2 All ER 236, CA (where the whole of the balance of a bank account opened by the husband in the wife's name was held to belong to the husband); *Simpson v Simpson* [1992] 1 FLR 601, 617 (transfer of money by husband into joint account intended only to ensure that wife could pay expenses during his final illness).

[20] *Re Figgis* (supra) at 145 and 1011, respectively.

[1] [1965] Ch 450, [1965] 1 All ER 249.

Like any other joint interest the balance of the fund will accrue to the survivor on the death of either spouse as it did in *Re Bishop*. It can of course be severed by agreement or assignment in the lifetime of both; in such a case or where, as in *Jones v Maynard*, the marriage breaks down and the court is asked to effect a partition, then, as we have seen from the passage of Vaisey J's judgment quoted above, the spouses will hold the balance of the fund as tenants in common in equal shares.[2]

Allowances for housekeeping and maintenance

This question is obviously closely allied to the last and originally the same principles were applied. Hence it was consistently held that if a husband supplied his wife with a housekeeping allowance out of his own income, any balance and any property bought with the allowance prima facie remained his property.[3] This might well work an injustice for it took no account of the fact that any savings from the housekeeping money were as much due to the wife's skill and economy as a housewife as to her husband's earning capacity.[4] It was to remedy this that the Married Women's Property Act 1964 was passed. Section 1 provides:

'If any question arises as to the right of a husband or wife to money derived from any allowance made by the husband for the expenses of the matrimonial home or for similar purposes, or to any property acquired out of such money, the money or property shall, in the absence of any agreement between them to the contrary, be treated as belonging to the husband and wife in equal shares.'

In the first place it should be noted that the Act applies only if the allowance is provided by the husband; it does not apply to the case where the wife goes out to work to support a husband who does the housekeeping. In such a case the allowance and any property bought with it presumably remain the wife's.[5] Secondly, it is not clear what the phrase 'expenses of the matrimonial home or similar purposes' covers. If, for example, a husband gives his wife money to pay off instalments of the mortgage on the matrimonial home, she may well be regarded as no more than his agent and thus acquire no interest in the house; but if he gives her a housekeeping allowance out of which it is intended that she should pay the instalments, it has been suggested that the effect of the section is to give her a half share in the fraction represented by each payment.[6] In the absence of any binding authority the words 'expenses of the matrimonial home' seem more apt to describe money spent in running it than in acquiring it.

If the allowance is made for this purpose, the rule applies not only to

---

[2] Cf post, p 589.

[3] *Blackwell v Blackwell* [1943] 2 All ER 579, CA; *Hoddinott v Hoddinott* [1949] 2 KB 406, CA.

[4] See the judgments of Denning LJ in *Hoddinott v Hoddinott* (supra), at 416, and *Rimmer v Rimmer* [1953] 1 QB 63, 74, [1952] 2 All ER 863, 868–869, CA.

[5] Earlier cases indicate that if the wife gives money to her husband for use in the home, she is deemed to give it to him as head of the family and the money therefore becomes his: see eg *Edward v Cheyne (No 2)* (1888) 13 App Cas 385, HL; *Re Young* (1913) 29 TLR 319 (where the presumption was rebutted on the facts). But it is very doubtful whether the courts would take such a view today. The Morton Commission recommended that the allowance should belong to both spouses equally, whichever of them provided it: Cmd 9678, para 701. See further Law Com Working Paper No 90 (Transfer of Money between Spouses).

[6] See the conflicting views in *Tymoszczuk v Tymoszczuk* (1964) 108 Sol Jo 676, and *Re Johns' Assignment Trusts* [1970] 2 All ER 210, 213.

the money but also to any property bought with it. Hence, if the wife were to buy furniture with the housekeeping savings, this would presumptively belong to her and her husband equally. This can be rebutted by proof of an express agreement between the spouses; what is not clear is whether the courts will be prepared to spell out an implied agreement when the circumstances demand it. If the wife uses part of the allowance to buy clothes for herself, it seems absurd that a half share of them should belong to the husband; can it not be argued that there must be a tacit agreement that the whole should belong to the wife?[7]

Two further weaknesses may be seen in the Act. First, the money or property is to be treated as belonging to the spouses in equal shares. Consequently on the death of one the whole beneficial interest will not automatically pass to the survivor (as it does in the case of the 'common purse')[8] but half will go to the personal representatives of the other. It is highly doubtful whether this is what the spouses will want or expect. In their desire to remedy the injustice caused by earlier cases where the marriage had broken down, the promoters of the Bill apparently overlooked the obvious fact that most marriages survive and that, whilst a joint interest can always be severed by the unilateral act of one party, it requires the conscious act of both to turn a tenancy in common into a joint tenancy. Neither this rule nor its consequences will be known to the vast majority of spouses and it is not inconceivable that a half share of furniture will inadvertently pass under a residuary bequest. Secondly, it is not clear whether the Act is to have retrospective effect. As there is no clear intention to affect vested rights, it is submitted that money and property belonging to the husband when the Act came into force[9] should remain his. Obviously in the course of time it will be forgotten when particular pieces of property were bought and it will become impossible to divide the balance of the fund into that which was provided before the operative date and that which was provided afterwards, so that the courts will probably be forced to hold that the Act does have retrospective effect.

Property purchased by one spouse

Any property purchased by one spouse with his or her own money will presumptively belong exclusively to the purchaser. Property bought out of money coming from the 'common purse' will also presumptively belong to the purchaser if it is for his or her own use.[10]

But this presumption is obviously rebuttable. Thus property bought by one spouse as a gift for the other will become the donee's. Hence if a husband buys clothes for his wife or gives her money to buy them for

---

[7] Perhaps a more difficult case would arise if the wife bought herself an expensive piece of jewellery. In the case of a 'common purse' contributed to by both the property would belong to the wife exclusively: see ante, p 571.

[8] See ante, p 572.

[9] 25th March 1964. This view seems to have commended itself to Goff J in *Re Johns' Assignment Trusts* (supra) at 213. The opposite view was taken by Master Jacob in *Tymoszczuk v Tymoszczuk* (supra), on the ground that the Act creates a presumption and therefore changes adjective law. For further difficulties that may arise, see Stone 27 MLR 576.

[10] See ante, p 571.

herself, they become her property,[11] and the same rule will prima facie apply in any other case where goods are bought for the other's personal use.[12]

Difficulties can arise if one spouse's money is used to buy property which is conveyed into the other's name or into joint names or, alternatively, if both spouses' money is used to buy property which is conveyed into the name of only one of them. The classic way of solving the problem is by applying two maxims of equity. If the wife alone provides the purchase money, there is a resulting trust in her favour and the husband (or the spouses jointly if the legal estate is vested in both) is presumed to hold the property on trust for her absolutely. On the other hand, if the husband provides the purchase money and has the property put into his wife's name or into joint names, he is presumed to intend a gift to his wife, and the presumption of advancement operates to give her prima facie the sole or a joint beneficial interest.[13] Precisely the same rules operate if both provide the money. If the property is conveyed into the husband's name alone, he will hold it on trust for them both and each will be entitled to a share proportionate to the contribution.[14] If the property is conveyed into the wife's name alone, the husband will be presumed to have made a gift of the whole of the property to her. These presumptions have always been rebuttable by evidence that the wife intended a gift in the first case or that the husband intended to keep the beneficial interest in the second.[15] But as the members of the House of Lords agreed in *Pettitt v Pettitt*,[16] they are much less strong today because some explanation of the parties' conduct will usually be available unless they are both dead. Lord Diplock went so far as to question whether they were still valid at all. As he observed, they are no more than a judicial inference of what the spouses' intention most probably was, drawn in cases relating to the propertied classes of the

---

[11] *Masson, Templier & Co v De Fries* [1909] 2 KB 831, CA. Contrast *Rondeau, Le Grand & Co v Marks* [1918] 1 KB 75, CA, where it had been agreed that they should remain the husband's property.

[12] *Re Whittaker* (1882) 21 Ch D 657 (piano). But cf *Windeler v Whitehall* [1990] 2 FLR 505, 517 (dressing table bought for unmarried cohabitant remained purchaser's property).

[13] *Mercier v Mercier* [1903] 2 Ch 98, CA (presumption of resulting trust for wife); *Silver v Silver* [1958] 1 All ER 523, CA (presumption of advancement). Hence if the husband had property conveyed to both spouses and a stranger, all three would hold on trust for the husband and wife jointly: *Re Eykyn's Trusts* (1877) 6 Ch D 115. There is a presumption of advancement even though the marriage is *voidable: Dunbar v Dunbar* [1909] 2 Ch 639; but not if the husband knows it to be *void*, for then there is to his knowledge no duty to maintain: *Soar v Foster* (1858) 4 K & J 152. Quaere if he does not know it is void. The presumption of advancement is also raised if a man has property conveyed into his fiancée's name: *Moate v Moate* [1948] 2 All ER 486.

[14] This could be relevant eg if furniture or a car were bought by the husband on hire purchase and both spouses contributed to the payment of the instalments. See Law Com Working Paper No 42, pp 131–134.

[15] The husband may not rebut the presumption by adducing evidence of his own fraudulent or unlawful intention: *Re Emery's Investment Trusts* [1959] Ch 410, [1959] 1 All ER 577 (evasion of tax in the USA); *Tinker v Tinker* [1970] P 136, [1970] 1 All ER 540, CA (defrauding creditors). The current tendency is to apply this principle only if not to do so would affront the public conscience: see *Tinsley v Milligan* [1992] 2 All ER 391, CA. Contrast *Griffiths v Griffiths* [1973] 3 All ER 1155 (fraudulent statements made after acquisition of interest held not to prevent husband's claiming it).

[16] [1970] AC 777, [1969] 2 All ER 385, HL; at 793 and 389 (per Lord Reid); 811 and 404 (per Lord Hodson); 814–815 and 406–407 (per Lord Upjohn); 824 and 414 (per Lord Diplock).

nineteenth and early twentieth century among whom marriage settlements were common and where the wife rarely contributed to the family income by her earnings. As such, they have little significance today when the parties may be legally aided, the wife is working, and their biggest asset, the matrimonial home, is being purchased by means of a mortgage.[17] The particular application of this problem to the purchase of the matrimonial home will be considered later.[18]

Gifts to spouses

Whether a gift belongs to one spouse alone or to both of them is a question of the donor's intention. In the case of wedding presents it is reasonable to assume in the absence of any evidence to the contrary that the husband's friends and relations intended to make the gift to him and the wife's to her.[19] There is no rule of law to this effect, however, and the court, exercising its discretion under section 17 of the Married Women's Property Act, may order the presents to be divided equally between them both.

3. TRANSACTIONS BETWEEN HUSBAND AND WIFE

Gifts between spouses

With the exceptions discussed below in the case of chattels, gifts between husband and wife are subject to the general law. In particular it should be noted that their relationship does not as such give rise to a presumption that either has exercised undue influence over the other.[20] This is somewhat surprising when one bears in mind the special treatment that equity accorded to married women in the past and the fact that spouses rarely take independent legal advice unless they are already at arm's length. A presumption can arise, however, if the circumstances show that one of them is particularly dependent on the other. This occurred in *Simpson v Simpson*,[1] where the husband's mental capacity had been reduced by a cerebral tumour and the effect of the transfer (which was out of character) was to defeat bequests to his children by a former marriage. It is also probably fair to say that the courts will look with particular care at any transaction entered into at the time of the breakdown of the marriage when both spouses are likely to be in an emotional state.[2] If its effect is to give one of them a considerable financial advantage with no counter-balancing advantage to the other, it will be set aside if the transferor is relatively poor and ignorant of the effects of property transactions in general and of the transaction in

---

[17] At 823–824 and 414, respectively. See also Lord Denning MR in *Falconer v Falconer* [1970] 3 All ER 449, 452, CA.
[18] Post, p 590.
[19] *Samson v Samson* [1960] 1 All ER 653, CA. Contrast *Kelner v Kelner* [1939] P 411, [1939] 3 All ER 957 (£1,000 deposited by the wife's father at the time of the marriage in a joint bank account in both spouses' names ordered to be divided equally between them). The spouses' subsequent conduct may turn a gift to one of them into joint property: *Samson v Samson*.
[20] *Howes v Bishop* [1909] 2 KB 390, CA; *MacKenzie v Royal Bank of Canada* [1934] AC 468, PC; *Bank of Credit and Commerce International SA v Aboody* [1990] 1 QB 923, 953, CA. Contrast *Bank of Montreal v Stuart* [1911] AC 120, PC, where undue influence was in fact exercised.
[1] [1992] 1 FLR 601.
[2] *Backhouse v Backhouse* [1978] 1 All ER 1158, 1166.

question in particular, and has neither received independent advice nor been urged to seek it.[3]

In order to perfect a gift of a chattel there must be an intention on the part of the donor to pass property to the donee and, in addition, either a deed executed by the former or a delivery of the chattel to the latter. Gifts by deed will be rare between spouses but, when they do occur, will again present no difficulties since the intention can be inferred from the execution of the deed. But a spouse who alleges that the other has effected a gift by delivery has to surmount two obstacles.[4] First, since spouses frequently use each other's property, an intention to make a gift cannot readily be inferred from permission to use the chattel in question, and consequently the burden of proof upon a spouse alleging a gift will probably be higher than upon a stranger.[5] Secondly, it may be wellnigh impossible in many cases to prove delivery. Where the goods are intended for the exclusive use of the donee (for example, clothes or jewellery), delivery will normally take place at the time the gift is made by a physical handing over and taking; but if the goods in question have already been used by both spouses in the home and will continue to be used in this way (for example, articles of furniture), there is not likely to be any apparent change of possession. There may indeed be an effective symbolic delivery of one chattel as representing the whole but spouses are hardly likely to carry out such an artificial act, the significance of which will not occur to them.[6] Where the possession of goods could be in one of two people (as will happen in the case of furniture used by both spouses in the matrimonial home), it is presumed to be in the owner, so that if ownership is changed by a deed of gift, the buyer or donee will be presumed to have taken possession as soon as the transaction is complete;[7] but this presumption cannot apply in the case of a gift by delivery since the delivery must be proved before a change in ownership can be established.[8] English courts have always been slow to infer a delivery of a chattel from one spouse to the other, doubtless because of the danger that they may fraudulently allege a prior gift of the husband's goods to the wife in order to keep them out of the hands of the former's creditors. An example of this reluctance can be seen in *Re Cole*.[9] In this case the husband

---

[3] *Backhouse v Backhouse* (supra), following *Cresswell v Potter* [1978] 1 WLR 255n. See Smith 123 Sol Jo 193. It is submitted that *Heseltine v Heseltine* [1971] 1 All ER 952, CA, must be incorrectly decided. The court imputed to the spouses an intention to create a trust 'for the benefit of the family' although their purpose could have been achieved only by an absolute gift to the husband. The court was obviously anxious to protect the wife after the marriage had broken down and took into account the husband's conduct, which cannot affect title. The wife's proper remedy now would be to apply for a property adjustment order in matrimonial proceedings.

[4] See Thornely *Transfer of Choses in Possession between Members of a Common Household* 11 CLJ 355; Diamond 27 MLR 357.

[5] Cf *Bashall v Bashall* (1894) 11 TLR 152, CA.

[6] *Lock v Heath* (1892) 8 TLR 295 (husband held to have given all his furniture to wife by symbolic delivery of chair); Thornely, loc cit, pp 357–358. For an effective constructive delivery by a father to his daughter, see *Kilpin v Ratley* [1892] 1 QB 582.

[7] *Ramsay v Margrett* [1894] 2 QB 18, CA; *French v Gething* [1922] 1 KB 236, CA.

[8] *Hislop v Hislop* [1950] WN 124, CA.

[9] [1964] Ch 175, [1963] 3 All ER 433, CA. Would the court have arrived at the same decision if, say, after the husband's death the question had arisen whether the goods belonged to the

completely furnished a new house before his wife set foot in it. When she arrived, he put his hands over her eyes, took her into the first room, uncovered her eyes and said 'Look'. She then went into all the other rooms and handled various articles; at the end the husband said to her: 'It's all yours'. The furniture nevertheless remained insured in his name. He subsequently became bankrupt and the question arose whether the trustee or wife was entitled to the goods in question. It was held that she had failed to establish an effective delivery and consequently the gift to her was never perfected. In the circumstances it would always seem wisest for a gift of goods used by both spouses to be made by means of a deed.[10]

Two statutory provisions should also be noticed. Under section 10 of the Married Women's Property Act 1882, a gift made by a husband to his wife may be avoided by his creditors if the property continues to be 'in the order and disposition or reputed ownership of the husband'. The Court of Appeal in *French v Gething*[11] has in effect rendered this section inapplicable to goods in the matrimonial home by holding that the maxim 'possession follows title' puts the goods outside the order and disposition or reputed ownership of the husband once the property has changed hands by the execution of a deed or by delivery;[12] but it will presumably apply to goods on, say, the husband's business premises of which the wife is never in apparent possession at all.[13] Secondly, a bill of sale will be void against the transferor's creditors with respect to goods in his possession or apparent possession seven days after the bill is executed, unless the bill is registered or the transferee obtains possession of the goods before the transferor becomes bankrupt or assigns his property for the benefit of his creditors generally or before an execution creditor levies execution.[14] A bill of sale is defined to include a number of documents by which property is transferred in goods capable of transfer by delivery.[15] But with respect to furniture and other goods used by both spouses in the matrimonial home and transferred by one of them to the other, *French v Gething* has made the provisions of the Bills of Sale Act as inapplicable as those of section 10 of the Married Women's Property Act, since the goods will be in the actual possession of the transferee and not in the apparent possession of the transferor.[16]

---

wife or to his personal representatives? See also *Bashall v Bashall* (supra); *Valier v Wright & Bull Ltd* (1917) 33 TLR 366.

[10] A similar difficulty would arise if one spouse pledged goods with the other. A mortgage would not create this problem, but it would have to comply with the Bills of Sale Acts: see Thornely, loc cit, pp 373–374.

[11] [1922] 1 KB 236, CA.

[12] This assumes, of course, that the delivery can be proved.

[13] Bankes LJ suggested in *French v Gething* at 244 that the operation of the Act might be limited to cases where the spouses were living on premises where the husband was carrying on business.

[14] Bills of Sale Act 1878, s 8.

[15] Ibid, s 4, qv.

[16] For the Act to apply the goods must in effect remain in the transferor's sole possession or apparent sole possession or be in premises solely occupied by him or be solely used or enjoyed by him: *Koppel v Koppel* [1966] 2 All ER 187, CA. See also *Ramsay v Margrett* (ante), and contrast *Hislop v Hislop* (ante). But the Act would apply in the case of a sale of goods if the property was not to pass immediately and the buyer's title depended on a written contract: Thornely, loc cit, p 371.

Improvements to property

If one spouse makes a substantial contribution to the improvement of any property in which the other has a beneficial interest, he (or she) is to be regarded as having thereby acquired an interest or a greater interest, as the case may be, in the property in question.[17] This provision is of particular importance in relation to the matrimonial home and will be considered in detail later.[18]

Voidable transactions

It is easy to see how transactions between husband and wife might be used as a means of defrauding creditors. To a man who is on the verge of bankruptcy or who is about to engage in a hazardous business operation there is a great temptation to settle the bulk of his property on trust for his wife and children and thus keep it out of the hands of his creditors and at the same time ensure that his family will be provided for. Parliament has sought to protect the creditors of the rogue who incidentally benefits his family whilst not prejudicing the members of the family of a man who settles property in good faith and then runs into financial difficulties. If, for example, a husband, fearing insolvency, transfers the matrimonial home or other property to his wife or children, his creditors or trustee in bankruptcy could seek to have the transfer set aside in the following circumstances.

Transactions defrauding creditors

Section 423 of the Insolvency Act 1986[19] is designed to protect the creditors of a person who has entered into a transaction at an undervalue with the intention of defeating their claims. This could take the form, for example, of disposing of property which would otherwise be available to satisfy a judgment debt or of dealing with property that has been charged in such a way as to deprive the creditor of the value of his security.

A 'transaction' for this purpose includes any gift, agreement or arrangement.[20] A transaction is deemed to be at an undervalue if the party entering into it (whom we will call the debtor) received no consideration, or the value he received was significantly less than the value he gave, or if he entered into it in consideration of marriage.[1] The court must be satisfied that the debtor's purpose in entering into the transaction which is being attacked was to put assets beyond the reach of a person who is making (or may at some time make) a claim against him or, alternatively, to prejudice the interests of such a person in some other way.[2] This may be inferred from the circumstances in which the transaction was entered into, for

---

[17] Matrimonial Proceedings and Property Act 1970, s 37.
[18] See post, pp 599–600.
[19] Replacing s 172 of the Law of Property Act 1925, which in turn replaced (with amendments) 13 Eliz 1, c 5.
[20] Insolvency Act 1986, s 436. Thus a lease may be set aside if a husband granted it to his wife with the intention of depriving the mortgagees of the land in question of the right to take vacant possession of it: *Lloyds Bank Ltd v Marcan* [1973] 3 All ER 754, CA.
[1] Insolvency Act 1986, s 423(1).
[2] Ibid, s 423(3). Presumably anyone prejudiced may apply for an order if the debtor's intention was to defraud any possible creditor in the future.

example from his being about to engage in a hazardous business undertaking[3] or from the fact that defrauding his creditors would be the natural and probable consequences of the transaction,[4] but any inference may be rebutted by other evidence.[5]

Proceedings may be brought by anyone prejudiced by the transaction or capable of being prejudiced by it (who is referred to as a 'victim of the transaction'). Presumably in the latter case he must establish that there is a very strong probability that he will be prejudiced in the future: it cannot have been Parliament's intention to permit anyone to apply to have a transaction set aside on the ground that he might possibly be prejudiced by it. Proceedings may also be brought by the debtor's trustee in bankruptcy or by the supervisor of a voluntary arrangement approved by his creditors.[6]

If the conditions set out above are satisfied, the court may make such order as it thinks fit to restore the position to what it would have been if the transaction had not been entered into and to protect victims' interests.[7] Its powers are extensive. In particular it may order a person (whether or not he was a party to the transaction) to transfer to another (either absolutely or for the benefit of all victims) any property in his hands transferred as part of the transaction (or any other property, including money,[8] representing the proceeds of sales of such property) and to account for any benefits received. It may also release or discharge the whole or part of any security given by the debtor.[9]

The transaction is voidable and not void; consequently no order can be made against anyone who was not a party to it if he acquired a benefit from it in good faith, for value and without notice of the circumstances by virtue of which an order could be made under section 423.[10] Hence if, say, the debtor gave property to his wife with intent to defraud a creditor and she then sold it to X, she could be made to account for the value of the benefit she had received but X could not if he was a bona fide purchaser without notice of the fraud.

Transactions at an undervalue entered into by a bankrupt

Section 339 of the Insolvency Act 1986[11] gives even wider protection to creditors. It is not necessary to prove any intent to defraud a creditor but the debtor must have been made bankrupt. The trustee of his estate may apply to the court for an order if the bankrupt entered into a transaction at an undervalue. He may attack any transaction effected not more than five years before the presentation of the petition on which the debtor was

---

[3] *Mackay v Douglas* (1872) LR 14 Eq 106; *Re Butterworth* (1882) 19 Ch D 588, CA.
[4] *Freeman v Pope* (1870) 5 Ch App 538.
[5] Cf *Re Wise* (1886) 17 QBD 290, CA.
[6] Insolvency Act 1986, ss 423(5) (definition of 'victim') and 424. Any application is to be treated as made on behalf of every victim of the transaction.
[7] Ibid, s 423(2). In *Re Maddever* (1884) 27 Ch D 523, CA, it was held (under earlier legislation) that a specialty creditor could have a conveyance set aside ten years after it had been executed and that the doctrine of laches had no application.
[8] See the definition of 'property' in s 436 of the Insolvency Act 1986.
[9] Ibid, s 425(1).
[10] Ibid, s 425(2), (3). Presumably constructive notice will deprive the transferee of protection: see (under s 172 of the Law of Property Act 1925) *Lloyds Bank Ltd v Marcan* [1973] 2 All ER 359 at 369.
[11] Replacing s 42 of the Bankruptcy Act 1914.

adjudged bankrupt, but if it was entered into more than two years before
that date, no order may be made unless at the time of the transaction the
bankrupt was insolvent or became insolvent in consequence of entering into
it. There is a rebuttable presumption that this condition is satisfied if the
transaction was entered into with 'an associate', including inter alios the
bankrupt's spouse, former spouse, reputed spouse, or relative.[12] The phrase
'reputed husband or wife' is unusual. It looks at first sight as though it is
intended to apply to transactions between parties living together as husband
and wife but, if this is so, the draftsman may largely have failed in his
purpose because the word 'reputed' implies that they must also be regarded
as married.[13]

The terms 'transaction' and 'at an undervalue' bear the same meaning
as they do under section 423.[14] It should also be noted that, in the absence
of consideration, a benefit is not protected merely because it was conferred
in pursuance of an order for financial provision made under section 24 of
the Matrimonial Causes Act 1973 on divorce, nullity or judicial separation.[15]
On the other hand, a party settling a compromised claim gives valuable
consideration: consequently if a consent order is made in pursuance of a
genuine compromise, the agreement will provide the consideration and the
property comprised in the order cannot be touched provided that the parties
acted in good faith.[16]

The court may make such order as it thinks fit to restore the position to
what it would have been had the bankrupt not entered into the transaction.
It has much the same powers as it has under section 423 except that
property has to be transferred to the trustee in bankruptcy. Similarly
property may be recovered from a third person into whose hands it has
come unless he is, or acquired it through, a bona fide purchaser for value
and without notice of the circumstances entitling the court to make an
order.[17] In addition the court may permit anyone adversely affected by the
order to prove in the bankruptcy for the loss he has suffered.[18]

---

[12] Insolvency Act 1986, ss 339, 341(1)(a), (2) and 435. There is a special period in the case of
a criminal bankruptcy: s 341(4), (5). A person is insolvent if he is unable to pay his debts
or his assets are less than his liabilities (including contingent and prospective liabilities):
s 341(3). 'Relative' means brother, sister, uncle, aunt, nephew, niece, lineal ancestor or lineal
descendant, including relations of the half blood and treating a person's illegitimate child,
stepchild and adopted child as his own child. 'Associate' also includes the spouse, former
spouse and reputed spouse of a relative and a relative of the bankrupt's spouse, former
spouse or reputed spouse: s 435(1), (2) and (8).
[13] This also begs the question: by whom must they have been regarded as husband and wife?
In the Scots law of presumption of marriage by cohabitation with habit and repute the
parties must be generally regarded as married amongst the circle in which they move: see
Clive Law of Husband and Wife in Scotland (2nd Edn) pp 64–65.
[14] Ibid, ss 339(3) and 436. See (under the Bankruptcy Act) Re Windle [1975] 3 All ER 987 at
994; Re A Debtor [1965] 3 All ER 453; Re Vansittart [1893] 1 QB 181; Re Ashcroft (1887)
19 QBD 186, CA.
[15] Matrimonial Causes Act 1973, s 39, as amended by the Insolvency Act 1985, Sch 8, and the
Insolvency Act 1986, Sch 14.
[16] Re Abbott [1983] Ch 45, [1982] 3 All ER 181.
[17] Insolvency Act 1986, s 342(2), (4).
[18] Ibid, s 342(1), (3).

Money lent by one spouse to the other

A loan by one spouse to the other usually raises no presumption of a gift by way of advancement, so that the lender will be able to recover the sum lent in the absence of evidence that a gift was intended.[19] This same principle has been applied to other transactions of a similar nature, for example the guarantee of the other's credit[20] and the fulfilling of the other's legal obligations;[1] in each case the spouse making the payment is prima facie entitled to recover it from the other.

If the borrower becomes bankrupt, his or her spouse is not entitled to any payment out of his estate until all other creditors have been paid in full.[2]

4. CONTRACTS OF INSURANCE

Insurable interests

Because of the relationship of husband and wife and their mutual rights and duties, each has an insurable interest in the life of the other. This means that if, say, a husband insures his wife's life up to any amount, he may recover the sum due on her death without proving any financial loss at all.[3] Each may also apparently insure any of the other's property which forms a part of the matrimonial home, as the use which he or she enjoys is sufficient to create an insurable interest.[4]

Life assurance policies in favour of the spouse or children of the assured

By section 11 of the Married Women's Property Act 1882, if either spouse effects a policy of assurance on his or her own life[5] expressed to be for the benefit of the assured's spouse or any or all of his or her own children[6] (or

---

[19] *Hall v Hall* [1911] 1 Ch 487 (mortgage of the wife's property to secure a loan to the husband). Contrast *Paget v Paget* [1898] 1 Ch 470, CA, where the facts indicated that a gift was intended. See further George *Disputes over the Matrimonial Home* 16 Conv 27, 31–33.

[20] *Re Salisbury-Jones* [1938] 3 All ER 459; *Anson v Anson* [1953] 1 QB 636, [1953] 1 All ER 867.

[1] *Outram v Hyde* (1875) 24 WR 268 (husband's discharging encumbrance on wife's realty); *Re McKerrell* [1912] 2 Ch 648 (wife's paying money due from husband on insurance policy). But if the husband purchases realty in the wife's name (thus raising a presumption of advancement) and raises the purchase money by a mortgage, sums paid on the mortgage will likewise be construed as a gift: *Moate v Moate* [1948] 2 All ER 486; cf *Silver v Silver* [1958] 1 All ER 523, CA.

[2] Insolvency Act 1986, s 329. This applies if the lender was the bankrupt's spouse at the commencement of the bankruptcy, whether or not they were married when the loan was made.

[3] *Reed v Royal Exchange Assurance Co* (1795) Peake Add Cas 70; *Griffiths v Fleming* [1909] 1 KB 805, CA; Married Women's Property Act 1882, s 11. Otherwise the policy would be void under the Life Assurance Act 1774. For joint policies taken out on both lives to be paid to the survivor on the death of either, see *Griffiths v Fleming*.

[4] *Goulstone v Royal Insurance Co* (1858) 1 F & F 276.

[5] This includes a policy providing for payment on death or disablement as the result of an accident provided that the sum is in fact paid on death (*Re Gladitz* [1937] Ch 588, [1937] 3 All ER 173) and an endowment policy payable on the earlier death of the assured (*Re Ioakimidis' Policy Trusts* [1925] Ch 403).

[6] This includes adopted children and, in the case of policies effected after 1969, children whose parents are not married to each other: Adoption Act 1976, s 39(1); Family Law Reform Act 1969, s 19(1), (3).

for the benefit of both the spouse and children), this creates a trust in favour of those persons. This has two important results. First, as objects of the trust they can enforce the policy even though there is no privity of contract between them and the insurance company. Secondly, as beneficiaries under a trust they are entitled to the whole of the sum assured notwithstanding the bankruptcy of the assured or the insolvency of his estate. In only one case will his or her creditors have any claim on the policy, for the Act specifically provides that if the policy was effected to defraud them, they shall be entitled to receive out of the money payable under the policy a sum equal to the premiums so paid.[7]

If the policy is taken out in favour of a *named* spouse or children, they take an immediate vested interest in equity. Thus in *Cousins v Sun Life Assurance Society*,[8] where the policy was issued for the benefit of Lilian Cousins, the assured's wife, who predeceased the life assured, it was held that the husband held the policy on trust for her personal representatives. But where the beneficiaries are merely designated as the husband, wife or children of the assured without being specifically named, this is construed as referring to those who fall into this category at the moment when the trust falls in, ie, at the assured's death, and before that time the spouse and existing children have only a contingent interest dependent upon their surviving the assured. In *Re Browne's Policy*[9] H, who was then married to W, took out a policy on his own life for the benefit of his wife and children. W predeceased H, who then married X. H was survived by X, five children of his first marriage and one child of his second. It was held that X and the six surviving children took a joint interest in the insurance money. If all the objects fail, there will be a resulting trust in favour of the assured's estate.[10]

Unless other trustees are appointed, the assured holds the policy as trustee, and as such must exercise options and otherwise deal with it in the way most favourable to the beneficiaries.[11] Similarly, after the death of a named object with a vested interest, the assured is presumed to continue to pay premiums to preserve the property for those entitled to the deceased beneficiary's estate and consequently may recover premiums paid after the death from the deceased's personal representatives.[12]

[7] S 11. This is particularly important in the case of a single premium policy.
[8] [1933] Ch 126, CA. See also *Re Smith's Estate* [1937] Ch 636, [1937] 3 All ER 472. If there are more beneficiaries than one, they take a joint interest: *Re Seyton* (1887) 34 Ch D 511. But the interest may of course be made expressly conditional upon the beneficiary's surviving the assured, in which case the former will have only a contingent interest during the assured's life: *Re Fleetwood's Policy* [1926] Ch 48.
[9] [1903] 1 Ch 188. See also *Re Parker's Policies* [1906] 1 Ch 526; *Re Seyton* (supra).
[10] *Re Collier* [1930] 2 Ch 37. Cf *Cleaver v Mutual Reserve Fund Life Association* [1892] 1 QB 147, CA.
[11] *Re Equitable Life Assurance Society of the United States* (1911) 27 TLR 213.
[12] *Re Smith's Estate* (supra). For a fuller discussion of the operation of the section and criticisms of the existing law, see Finlay '*Family' Life Insurance Problems* 2 MLR 266.

C. Unmarried cohabitants

The main distinction between the property rights of unmarried cohabitants and spouses is that property adjustment orders are not available to the former. Consequently disputes between cohabitants or former cohabitants over the ownership, occupation or use of property must be resolved, generally speaking, by applying the ordinary legal rules applicable to strangers. If, however, they have a child or children for whom one of them applies for financial provision, the court now has power inter alia to order the other to transfer property to the applicant and to order the settlement of property to which either of them is entitled, in each case for the benefit of the child.[13] As the Court of Appeal held in *K v K (Minors: Property Transfer)*,[14] 'benefit' in this context is not limited to a purely financial benefit. Consequently one of the ways in which this power can be exercised is by ordering the parties' former home to be transferred to whichever of them has the day to day care of the child. This comes within the statute because it gives the child the benefit of a home even though it also confers a benefit on the custodial parent. [15]

Income and housekeeping allowances

Cohabitants, like spouses, will be entitled to retain their own income. As the principle of the 'common purse'[16] rests not upon the relationship of the spouses but upon the purpose for which it was formed and the use to which it is put, it must apply equally to a joint account established by cohabitants.

If one cohabitant, say the man, provides the woman with whom he is living with a housekeeping allowance, the Married Women's Property Act of 1964 cannot apply. Prima facie, therefore, the common law rules are still relevant and any unspent balance will belong to him.[17] It is open to the courts to infer an intention that it should belong to them jointly: it remains to be seen whether they will do so readily.

Property purchased by a cohabitant

The main difference between cohabitants and spouses in this regard is that, as the presumption of advancement is raised by the husband's common law duty to maintain his wife, it does not apply if the parties are not married.[18] As we have seen, it is doubtful whether this makes any practical difference today.[19]

---

[13] Children Act 1989, s 15(1) and Sch 1, paras 1 and 2. See further post, pp 696–698.
[14] [1992] 2 All ER 727, CA.
[15] The Law Commission observed that few commentators considered this a valid objection: Law Com No 118 (Illegitimacy) para 6.6.
[16] See ante, pp 570–572; *Paul v Constance* [1977] 1 All ER 195, CA.
[17] See ante, p 572.
[18] Cf *Soar v Foster* (1858) 4 K & J 152 (void marriage).
[19] See ante, pp 574–575.

Transactions between cohabitants

The difficulty of proving the gift of a chattel from one spouse to the other is due to the need to establish delivery.[20] This is equally true in the case of unmarried cohabitants. The provisions of sections 339 and 423 of the Insolvency Act 1986 apply to an insolvent cohabitants as to any debtor or bankrupt.[1]

Contracts of insurance

Two doubts surround insurance contracts made by cohabitants.

First, does each have an insurable interest in the other's life so as to be able to recover the sum payable on the latter's death without proof of financial loss? In *Griffiths v Fleming*[2] the reason given by the majority of the Court of Appeal for the rule that a husband has an insurable interest in his wife's life was that he was not likely to indulge in 'mischievous gaming' on it, which brought the policy outside the mischief of the Life Insurance Act 1774. This argument applies with equal force to cohabitants. There must be some doubt about the conclusion that they are in the same position as spouses, however, because the courts may regard their relationship as less permanent and therefore not entitled to the protection given to married couples. If this is so, the survivor could recover on the policy only if he or she could establish an actual financial loss (for example, the loss of financial support or the value of housekeeping services).

Secondly, as section 11 of the Married Women's Property Act 1882[3] applies to contracts of insurance for the benefit of the assured's spouse or children, if one cohabitant insures his or her life for the benefit of the other (as distinct from a policy for the benefit of the assured's children), this will not create a trust in favour of the other partner. The latter may therefore have difficulty in enforcing it, and if the assured's estate is insolvent, the sum may be taken to pay the creditors.

---

[20] See ante, p 576.
[1] See ante, pp 578–580, and note the presumption that the conditions laid down by s 339 are satisfied if the bankrupt entered into the transaction with a reputed spouse.
[2] [1909] 1 KB 805, at 821, CA.
[3] See ante, pp 581–582.

Chapter 18

The matrimonial home

The critical importance of the home (whether the parties are married or not) requires that it be given separate treatment. Difficulty arises because it may have two functions. Its primary purpose is to provide shelter for the parties and their family. At the same time, if it is held in freehold or on a long lease, it will constitute the most valuable asset that most couples own and is thus an extremely valuable investment. If the relationship breaks down, these two aspects may come into conflict. Both parties may wish to continue in exclusive occupation (with or without children); alternatively, one may wish to do so while the other may wish to realise his or her investment. A party deprived of both the value of the home and the right to occupy it will often find it impossible to purchase other accommodation, and if the house is sold and the proceeds divided between them, both may face the same predicament. The problem may also arise if one party is insolvent, for a mortgagee may wish to realise his security or a trustee in bankruptcy may wish to sell the home to enlarge the assets available to the creditors. It will thus be seen that the interests of the creditors may come into direct conflict with those of the rest of the family who will still need a roof over their heads.

There are thus two distinct but interrelated problems: ownership and occupation. The first is concerned with the question, in whom are the legal and beneficial interests in the property vested? The second is concerned with the question, what rights of occupation does each party have in the home irrespective of ownership? After discussing these, we must consider the problems that arise if one of the parties is insolvent. Finally, we shall have to examine the additional security a party may enjoy if the property is leasehold and subject to statutory control.

A. Ownership

1. BENEFICIAL OWNERSHIP

Until the Second World War few working class families owned their own homes. In the vast majority of middle class families the husband would be the sole earner and, if the home was purchased, it would be conveyed into his name. Consequently, following the principle that property purchased with his own money presumptively belongs to the purchaser, the whole beneficial interest would vest in the husband to the exclusion of the wife.[1]

---

[1] *Re Sims' Question* [1946] 2 All ER 138. Hence rent received from a lodger was held to belong exclusively to the husband: *Montgomery v Blows* [1916] 1 KB 899, CA.

Now, however, many more families own their own homes,[2] and in most cases both spouses work, at least for a part of their married lives, and contribute to the common expenses of buying and running the home. The position has been further complicated by the steady increase in the value of most houses during the past 45 years. Suppose, for example, that a house was bought in the husband's name for £10,000, to which the wife contributed £2,000, and that it has been recently sold for £100,000. Assuming that the wife's contribution gives her some interest in the property, it is vital to determine whether she can recover no more than her £2,000, or a fifth of the present value (which will give her £20,000) or some other fraction of the price at which it was sold.

Accepted principles were obscured, at least temporarily, by the judges' desire to reward the wife on the breakdown of the marriage for her contribution to the family finances as a whole, as distinct from any direct contribution to the purchase of the home. As Lord Denning MR pointed out, it may be purely a matter of convenience which spouse pays off the mortgage and which pays other household expenses: they give no thought to the legal consequences of their acts (of which they are probably ignorant) and it is unjust to give the wife an interest in the house if she happens to pay the mortgage but not if she pays housekeeping bills instead.[3] The House of Lords, however, delivered a death blow to this attempt to adjust property rights to compensate the wife for her contribution to the welfare of the family in two cases decided within a year of each other, *Pettitt v Pettitt*[4] and *Gissing v Gissing*.[5] Two fundamental rules emerged. First, it is clear from *Pettitt v Pettitt* that English law knows of no doctrine of community of property or any separate rules of law applicable to family assets.[6] Consequently if one spouse buys property intended for common use with the other—whether it is a house, furniture or a car—this cannot per se give the latter any proprietary interest. From this follows the second principle, stated in *Gissing v Gissing*,[7] that if either of them seeks to establish a beneficial interest in property, the legal title to which is vested in the other, he or she can do so only by establishing that the legal owner holds the property on trust for the claimant.

The injustice which the courts sought to avoid was largely removed by the Matrimonial Proceedings and Property Act 1970, which gave the court a power to make property adjustment orders on pronouncing a decree of divorce, nullity or judicial separation and expressly required it to take into account inter alia 'the contributions which each of the parties has made ... to the welfare of the family'.[8] This makes it unnecessary to resort to other means to compensate the wife, and the power that the court has to take all relevant matters into account in making the fairest adjustment possible

---

[2] In 1989 66 per cent of households in Great Britain owned their own homes, of which 42 per cent were mortgaged: *General Household Survey 1989*, table 8.1.
[3] See, eg, *Fribance v Fribance* [1957] 1 All ER 357, 360, CA, and *Falconer v Falconer* [1970] 3 All ER 449, 452, CA.
[4] [1970] AC 777, [1969] 2 All ER 385, HL.
[5] [1971] AC 886, [1970] 2 All ER 780, HL.
[6] At 800–801 and 395 (per Lord Morris), 810 and 403 (per Lord Hodson), and 817 and 409 (per Lord Upjohn).
[7] At 896 and 782 (per Lord Reid), 900 and 785 (per Lord Dilhorne), and 904–905 and 789 (per Lord Diplock).
[8] See now the Matrimonial Causes Act 1973, ss 24 and 25(2)(f), post, pp 736 and 779.

on the breakdown of the marriage has led the Court of Appeal to deprecate a spouse's taking other proceedings to establish property rights when an application could be made for an order in matrimonial proceedings.[9] There are, however, at least four cases in which it will still be necessary to determine what interest in property a spouse has:[10]

(1) If she (or he) is unable or unwilling to take matrimonial proceedings.
(2) If she has remarried without applying for a property adjustment order in proceedings for divorce or nullity (when her power to do so will be barred).[11]
(3) It will have to be decided, on the death of one of the spouses, whether an interest forms part of his or her estate or vests in the survivor.
(4) It will have to be decided, on the insolvency of one of the spouses, what property is available for his or her creditors.

Unmarried cohabitants

The same principles must be applied to determine the property interests of unmarried couples. Their application, however, may not necessarily lead to the same results. The reason for this was explained by Griffiths LJ in *Bernard v Josephs*:[12]

'The legal principles to be applied are the same whether the dispute is between married or unmarried couples, but the nature of the relationship between the parties is a very important factor when considering what inferences should be drawn from the way they have conducted their affairs. There are many reasons why a man and a woman may decide to live together without marrying, and one of them is that each values his independence and does not wish to make the commitment of marriage; in such a case it will be misleading to make the assumptions and to draw the same inferences from their behaviour as in the case of a married couple. The judge must look most carefully at the nature of the relationship, and only if satisfied that it was intended to involve the same degree of commitment as marriage will it be legitimate to regard them as no different from a married couple.'

The significance of the reference to making assumptions and drawing inferences will be seen below. One point, however, must be stressed. As unmarried cohabitants are unable to petition for divorce or other matrimonial relief, neither can apply for a property adjustment order in matrimonial proceedings. Hence, unless they have children (when a property adjustment order can be made under the Children Act),[13] any claims they may have must be resolved solely by reference to the law of property. It is somewhat ironic that principles evolved to settle the property claims of spouses are now mainly relevant only to unmarried couples.

---

[9] *Williams v Williams* [1976] Ch 278, [1977] 1 All ER 28, CA; *Fielding v Fielding* [1978] 1 All ER 267, CA.
[10] To these the Law Commission would add that certainty of ownership may further stability in marriage: Law Com No 175 (Matrimonial Property), 1983, para 1.4.
[11] See post, p 724.
[12] [1982] Ch 391, 402, [1982] 3 All ER 162, 169, CA. See also *Gordon v Douce* [1983] 2 All ER 228, CA; *Burns v Burns* [1984] Ch 317, [1984] 1 All ER 244, CA; *Grant v Edwards* [1986] Ch 638, [1986] 2 All ER 426, CA.
[13] See ante, p 583.

Engaged couples

An engaged couple may well purchase their proposed matrimonial home
and begin to buy furniture before they marry and in this respect their
position may be little different from that of a newly married couple. For
this reason, if an agreement to marry is terminated, section 2(1) of the Law
Reform (Miscellaneous Provisions) Act 1970 extended the law relating to
the property rights of spouses to any property in which either of them had
a beneficial interest while the agreement was in force.[14] But now that it has
been settled that the ordinary principles of the law of trusts apply to the
property of married and unmarried couples alike, this provision is largely
otiose. One case in which it will apply is where one party contributes to
the improvement of the other's property, when it will bring section 37 of
the Matrimonial Proceedings and Property Act 1970 into play so as to give
the former an interest in the property.[15]

In the following discussion we shall refer to 'spouses' and 'the matrimonial
home'. Unless the contrary is stated, these terms must also be understood
to include cohabiting couples and their home.

The basic principle

The legal and equitable interests in property vest when it is acquired.
Consequently, unless these are subsequently changed by a conscious act of
the parties, the beneficial interests taken by spouses in the matrimonial
home depend on their intention *at the time of acquisition*. Difficulty arises
because spouses buying a house, furniture or other household goods
frequently give no thought to the question of ownership: they regard the
property as 'our house' or 'our washing machine'. To establish a claim to
it, however, it is not sufficient to show that it was purchased as a joint
venture or to be shared as a family home;[16] and in the event of a dispute,
a spouse who claims that the legal title does not reflect the beneficial
interests must show this from the parties' words and conduct. But as Lord
Diplock pointed out, a party's intention in this context must mean that
which his words and conduct lead the other to believe that he holds.[17]
Hence if the husband led the wife to believe that she would share a joint
beneficial interest in the house, this intention will be imputed to him even
though he actually proposed to take the whole interest himself. What the
parties said and did after the property was acquired is relevant only as
evidence of their common intention when it was bought.[18] As the majority
of the House of Lords held in *Pettitt v Pettitt*,[19] however, if the spouses
did not apply their minds to the question, the court cannot give effect to
some other agreement that they never entered into on the ground that that
would produce a just result, even though it is satisfied that they would have
made it had they thought about it. In other words, the court may have to

[14] See ante, pp 22–24.
[15] See post, pp 599–600.
[16] Per Lord Bridge in *Lloyds Bank plc v Rosset* [1991] 1 AC 107, 130, [1990] 1 All ER 1111,
1117, HL.
[17] *Gissing v Gissing* [1971] AC 886, 906, [1970] 2 All ER 780, 790, HL.
[18] *Gissing v Gissing* (supra) at 906 and 791 respectively; *Pettitt v Pettitt* [1970] AC 777, 816,
[1969] 2 All ER 385, 408, HL.
[19] [1970] AC 777, [1969] 2 All ER 385, HL, at 804 and 398 (per Lord Morris), 810 and 403
(per Lord Hodson), and 816 and 408 (per Lord Upjohn).

infer an intention the parties never articulated but it cannot impute to them an agreement they clearly did not make.

We shall now consider the various ways in which one spouse can establish a trust in his or her favour. It will be assumed that the claimant is the wife, as is normally the case; precisely the same principles apply if the claimant is the husband.

Declaration of beneficial interests

Prima facie effect must be given to the wording of the conveyance. As the Court of Appeal held in *Goodman v Gallant*,[20] if this expressly declares in whom not only the legal title but also the beneficial interests are to vest, it will be conclusive in the absence of fraud or mistake.[1] Hence if, as is common, the matrimonial home is conveyed to both spouses on express trust for sale for themselves as joint tenants in equity, this must give them a joint interest in the proceeds of sale, and if either of them severs the joint interest, they will become equitable tenants in common in equal shares.[2] If the conveyance declares they are to hold as tenants in common in equal shares or in some other proportion, they will be similarly bound by the wording. For this reason solicitors acting for parties buying their home should enquire what their intentions are and spell them out in the conveyance to prevent dispute in the future.[3]

Express intention

If the parties specifically agree what interest each is to take at the time the property is acquired, this will be conclusive evidence of their intention, at least in the absence of fraud or mistake.[4] A bare agreement, however, will not necessarily be legally effective if it is not reflected in the specific words of the conveyance. If the husband purchases the home entirely out of his own money and has it conveyed into his own name, an oral agreement between the spouses that the wife is to take a beneficial share will give her no interest. It will amount to no more than an imperfect gift, which equity will not perfect, or to a declaration of trust, which is required to be evidenced in writing.[5] Consequently, in the absence of written evidence, the

---

[20] [1986] Fam 106, [1986] 1 All ER 311, CA. Contrast *Re Gorman* [1990] 1 All ER 717, where the parties were not bound by the declaration because they had not signed the transfer. The transfer was nevertheless evidence (in the circumstances conclusive) of their common intention at the time the property was acquired.

[1] As in *Thames Guaranty Ltd v Campbell* [1985] QB 210, [1984] 2 All ER 585, CA. The spouses had agreed that the property should belong beneficially to the wife but that it should be conveyed into their joint names. The solicitor, assuming that they wished to take a joint beneficial interest, drafted the transfer to them as joint tenants in law *and equity*. It was held that the transfer could be rectified by deleting the words italicised, thus leaving both spouses as trustee for the wife alone.

[2] *Goodman v Gallant* (supra). The presentation of a divorce petition including a prayer for a property adjustment order does not effect a severance, so that if one spouse dies before the order is made, the whole interest will vest in the other by survivorship: *Harris v Goddard* [1983] 3 All ER 242, CA.

[3] Per Bagnall J in *Cowcher v Cowcher* [1972] 1 All ER 943, 959. See also *Bernard v Josephs* [1982] Ch 391, 403, [1982] 3 All ER 162, 170, CA; *Walker v Hall* [1984] FLR 126, 129, CA; *Marsh v von Sternberg* [1986] 1 FLR 526, 528.

[4] See *Re Gorman* (supra).

[5] Law of Property Act 1925, s 53(1)(b).

wife can claim a beneficial interest only if she acts on the agreement to her detriment so as to give rise to a constructive trust.[6]

Inferred intention: resulting trusts

The commonest way of inferring that the spouses intended that one of them should take an interest in the other's property is by applying the presumption of a resulting trust. As we have seen,[7] if a wife provides the whole of the purchase money for the matrimonial home and it is conveyed into her husband's name, the whole beneficial interest presumptively vests in her. If she provides part of the purchase money, she prima facie acquires a corresponding part of the beneficial interest. On the other hand, if a husband buys property and has it conveyed into his wife's name or into joint names, the presumption of advancement will operate and he will be presumed to intend to make her a gift of the interest conveyed to her. This also applies if a man buys property in his fiancée's name[8] but not if he has it conveyed into his unmarried partner's name. Although both presumptions are rebuttable and the presumption of advancement is unlikely to be applied today unless there is no other evidence of the parties' intention,[9] the concept of the resulting trust is frequently relied on to determine the beneficial ownership of the matrimonial home.

It is easy to infer the parties' intention if the house is paid for in cash. If, say, the price is £50,000, of which the husband provides £30,000 and the wife £20,000, and the conveyance is taken in the husband's name alone or in joint names, he will be entitled to three-fifths of the proceeds when it is sold and the wife to two-fifths.[10] A similar conclusion was reached in *Marsh v Von Sternberg*.[11] The parties jointly bought the leasehold reversion of a flat for £7,650 less than its market value because the respondent was a protected tenant. It was held that she must be regarded as having contributed this sum to the purchase, as she could have realised this benefit if she had bought the flat herself.

The same principle applies if (as is usually the case) part of the purchase price is raised by a loan. If in the above example the wife had provided £20,000 by a loan which she was solely responsible for repaying, this would be equivalent to the provision of the same sum in cash and she would still take a two-fifths interest. The same result follows if the loan is secured by a mortgage.[12] If *as between themselves* the parties agree that one of them alone shall be responsible for repaying the sum borrowed, he (or she) will be regarded as having provided it, and it will be presumed that they intended that he should take a corresponding interest in the property even though they are joint owners of the legal estate so that the other would have to be

---

[6] *Midland Bank plc v Dobson* [1986] 1 FLR 171, CA. See post, pp 591–595.
[7] Ante, p 574.
[8] *Moate v Moate* [1948] 2 All ER 486. Cf Law Reform (Miscellaneous Provisions) Act 1970, s 2(1).
[9] See ante, pp 574–575. It is submitted that, if property paid for by the wife is conveyed into joint names, this might be sufficient evidence today of her intention to confer a gift of a joint interest on the husband.
[10] *Pettitt v Pettitt* (supra) at 814 and 406 respectively; *Walker v Hall* (supra); *Burns v Burns* [1984] Ch 317, 344, [1984] 1 All ER 244, 264–265, CA.
[11] [1986] 1 FLR 526.
[12] See *Cowcher v Cowcher* [1972] 1 All ER 943, 949.

a party to the mortgage.[13] But if, as in *Marsh v Von Sternberg*, they agree that they are to be jointly responsible for repayment, they will be regarded as having provided the sum borrowed jointly even though in the event one of them repays the whole.[14]

Constructive trusts

Alternatively, a party may be able to establish a beneficial interest in the matrimonial home by showing that the other is a constructive trustee for her (or him). The claimant must show two things: (a) that the parties had a common intention that she should have a beneficial interest in the property acquired and (b) that she has acted to her detriment on the basis of, or in reliance on, that intention.[15] Equity will not allow the other party to deny that the claimant has an interest and will construct a trust to give effect to it.

It will be seen that most cases of a resulting trust would also take effect as a constructive trust, for one party will have contributed to the purchase of the matrimonial home on the basis of a common intention that she or he should have a beneficial interest in it. On the other hand the detriment suffered by the claimant need not be a financial one to establish a constructive trust.

The common intention

As in the case of a resulting trust, the common intention may have been expressed or it may have to be inferred from the parties' conduct, and what is important is what one party leads the other to believe that he intends, whether this represents his true intention or not. An express agreement may be rare, but it may be easy to spell out a common intention from discussions between the parties. Thus in *Eves v Eves*[16] it was held that the defendant's telling the plaintiff, who was a minor, that, had she been of full age, he would have put the house in their joint names gave rise to an understanding between them that she was to take an interest in the property. The same conclusion was reached in *Grant v Edwards*,[17] where the defendant told the plaintiff that her name was not going on to the title because that would

---

[13] See *Cowcher v Cowcher* (supra) at 950; *Bernard v Josephs* (supra) at 403 and 170 respectively; *Re Gorman* [1990] 1 All ER 717.

[14] Cf *Harwood v Harwood* [1991] 2 FLR 274, CA.

[15] *Grant v Edwards* [1986] Ch 638, [1986] 2 All ER 426, CA; *Maharaj v Chand* [1986] AC 898, [1986] 3 All ER 107, PC; *Lloyds Bank plc v Rosset* [1991] 1 AC 107, [1990] 1 All ER 1111, HL. The trust may attach to a legal or equitable interest or to an after-acquired estate or interest: *Stokes v Anderson* [1991] 1 FLR 391, 398, CA. See Hodkinson *Constructive Trusts* [1983] Conv 420; Montgomery *A Question of Intention?* [1987] Conv 16; Eekelaar *A Woman's Place* [1987] Conv 93; Clarke *The Family Home: Intention and Agreement* [1992] Fam Law 72.

[16] [1975] 3 All ER 768, CA. Cf *Midland Bank plc v Dobson* [1986] 1 FLR 171, CA (agreement 'to share everything'); *Ungurian v Lesnoff* [1990] Ch 206 (understanding that plaintiff would provide home for defendant); *Risch v McFee* [1991] 1 FLR 105, CA (defendant's saying that he would see that the plaintiff's name 'was on the paper about the ownership of the house'); *Stokes v Anderson* (supra) (plaintiff's saying that he 'would put [the defendant's] name on the deeds').

[17] [1986] Ch 638, [1986] 2 All ER 426, CA. For a clearer example of an expressed intention, see *Re Densham* [1975] 3 All ER 726, where the wife's name was omitted from the transfer owing to a misunderstanding.

prejudice her in the matrimonial proceedings pending between her and her husband.

If it is sought to establish an agreement from the parties' conduct, it is essential to distinguish conduct from which the existence of an agreement can be inferred from that relied on as the detriment giving rise to the trust.[18] If this is not done, there is a danger that any onerous task undertaken by one party will automatically give her (or him) an interest in the other's property. As the House of Lords held in *Lloyds Bank plc v Rosset*,[19] neither a common intention that the house is to be renovated as a joint venture nor a common intention that it is to be shared as the family home is sufficient to indicate that both parties are to take an interest; nor can such an inference be drawn from one party's undertaking work on the house if this can be explained on some other ground, for example to hurry things on so that the house will be ready for occupation sooner. The fact on which the claimant is most likely to rely is that she has contributed to the purchase of the home. There is no doubt that a *direct* contribution will satisfy the test, whether this is to the deposit, mortgage repayments or legal charges. This is implicit in all the speeches in *Gissing v Gissing* and was spelled out by Viscount Dilhorne and Lord Diplock.[20] The same will be true if payments are made out of a common fund to which both parties contribute. The position with respect to indirect payments has always been less certain. The problem will arise, for example, if both spouses are working and they agree that the easiest way to manage is for the husband to pay the instalments due on the mortgage and for the wife to pay household bills. It would be inequitable to say that he has the sole beneficial interest because the house is being paid for exclusively from his earnings. The truth is that both are contributing to the total cost of acquiring and running the home in the way that happens to be most convenient at the time, and title to property should not depend on the accident of temporary convenience, particularly when the parties have given no thought to the possible legal consequences of their agreement.

Gissing v Gissing left the law in an uncertain state. Lord Reid could see no reason for the distinction between direct and indirect contributions and thought that in many cases it would be unworkable.[1] Viscount Dilhorne took a diametrically opposed view.[2] Lord Diplock pointed out that, if the wife had made an initial contribution to the deposit or legal charges which indicated that she was to take some interest in the property, the court should also take account of her contribution to the mortgage instalments, even though these were indirect, because this would be consistent with a common intention that her payment of other household expenses would release the husband's money to pay off the mortgage and would thus be her contribution to the purchase of the home. But, he added, if the wife

---

[18] *Lloyds Bank plc v Rosset* (supra). See also *Grant v Edwards* [1986] Ch 638 at 648 and 652, [1986] 2 All ER 426 at 432–433 and 436, CA; Warburton [1986] Conv 291; Sufrin 50 MLR 94.

[19] [1991] 1 AC 107, 130, [1990] 1 All ER 1111, 1117, HL; Gardner 54 MLR 126.

[20] [1971] AC 886 at 900 and 907, [1970] 2 All ER 780 at 786 and 791–792, HL. See also Lord Bridge in *Lloyds Bank plc v Rosset* (supra) at 133 and 1119, respectively. All the other members of the House of Lords agreed with his speech.

[1] [1971] AC 886 at 896, [1970] 2 All ER 780 at 782, HL.

[2] At 901 and 786 respectively.

had made no initial contribution to the purchase, no direct contribution to
the repayment of the mortgage, and 'no adjustment to her contribution to
other expenses of the household which it can be inferred was referable to
the acquisition of the house', she cannot claim an interest in it 'merely
because she continued to contribute out of her own earnings or private
income to other expenses of the household'.[3] Lord Pearson similarly considered that there could be a contribution 'if by arrangement between the
spouses one of them by payment of the household expenses enables the
other to pay the mortgage instalments'.[4]

Griffiths LJ indicated the way the court should approach the problem in
Bernard v Josephs:[5]

> 'The fact that one party paid the mortgage may indicate that it was recognised
> by the couple that that party was solely responsible for providing the purchase
> price and therefore to be regarded as the sole beneficial owner. But often where
> a couple are living together and both are working and pooling their resources,
> which one of them pays the mortgage may be no more than a matter of internal
> accounting between them. In such a case the judge must look at the contributions
> of each to the "family" finances and determine as best he may what contribution
> each was making towards the purchase of the house. This is not to be carried
> out as a strictly mathematical exercise; for instance, if the man was ill for a time
> and out of work so that the woman temporarily contributed more, that temporary
> state of affairs should not increase her share, nor should her share be decreased
> if she was temporarily unable to work whilst having a baby. The contributions
> must be viewed broadly by the judge to guide him to the parties' unexpressed
> and probably unconsidered intentions as to the beneficial ownership of the house.'

Contribution to the expenses of the family as a whole, however, and a
fortiori the wife's contributions in kind by running the home and bringing
up the children, are not in themselves sufficient: there must be a substantial
contribution *to the acquisition of the home.*[6] Although as late as 1990 the
House of Lords expressed obiter doubts whether anything less than a direct
contribution would justify a court in inferring a common intention that the
wife would take an interest in the absence of an agreement or arrangement
to that effect,[7] it is submitted that the present state of the authorities
indicates that such an inference can be drawn if the wife can show that her
financial contributions freed the husband's own money and thus enabled
him to pay the deposit, legal charges or mortgage instalments.[8] Although
a substantial contribution to family expenses will no doubt suffice for this
purpose,[9] it is not always easy to predict whether a court will hold that
payments made by the wife will satisfy this test. Obviously the greater the
proportion that her contribution bears to the whole and the more limited
the family's finances, the more likely it will be that the parties intended
that she should take an interest in the home, and it seems to be easier to

[3] At 907–910 and 792–793 respectively.
[4] At 903 and 788 respectively.
[5] [1982] Ch 391, 403–404, [1982] 3 All ER 162, 170, CA.
[6] *Gissing v Gissing* (supra) at 901 and 786 (per Viscount Dilhorne) and 909 and 793 (per Lord Diplock); *Burns v Burns* [1984] Ch 317, [1984] 1 All ER 244, CA, at 331 and 254 (per Fox LJ) and 345 and 265 (per May LJ).
[7] *Lloyds Bank plc v Rosset* [1991] 1 AC 107, 133, [1990] 1 All ER 1111, 1119, HL.
[8] *Gissing v Gissing* (supra) at 903 and 788 (per Lord Pearson) and 908 and 792 (per Lord Diplock); *Burns v Burns* (supra) at 329 and 252 (per Fox LJ) and 344 and 265 (per May LJ).
[9] See *Burns v Burns* (supra) at 329 and 252 respectively.

infer an intention that her contributions will give her a beneficial interest if the legal estate is vested in both jointly. This occurred in *Crisp v Mullings*[10] and *Bernard v Josephs*:[11] in both cases the Court of Appeal held that the woman's working and contributing to the family finances gave her an interest in the proceeds of sale of the parties' home. On the other hand, in *Gissing v Gissing*[12] the wife's spending some £220 on furniture, laying a lawn and paying for her own and the parties' son's clothes gave her no interest in a house bought in the husband's name and paid for by a loan to him and a mortgage which he alone repaid. Similarly in *Burns v Burns*[13] the plaintiff failed to establish any beneficial interest in the defendant's house by decorating it, buying household goods, paying bills, bringing up their two children, and carrying out other domestic duties.

Acting on the intention

It is not sufficient for the claimant to prove that she acted to her detriment: she must have acted *on the basis of, or in reliance on*, the agreement, and there must be a link between the two.[14] If the agreement spelled out what she was to do to acquire an interest (for example, to contribute to mortgage payments), it will be easy to see whether this condition is satisfied. In most cases, however, it will be necessary to infer whether the claimant's conduct can reasonably be regarded as satisfying it. Direct and indirect contributions to the purchase price or mortgage repayments will obviously suffice,[15] but the detriment need not be financial. In *Grant v Edwards* Sir Nicolas Browne-Wilkinson V-C considered that the link could be established by 'any act done by her to her detriment relating to [the parties'] joint lives'.[16] Nourse LJ, however, referred more specifically to 'conduct on which the woman could not reasonably have been expected to embark unless she was to have an interest in the house',[17] and the latter view seems more in keeping with other decided cases. In *Midland Bank plc v Dobson*,[18] for example, it was held that the wife's using part of her income for household expenses, including the purchase of domestic equipment, and doing some ordinary periodic decorating, amounted to no more than 'the sort of work that members of a family do in a house' and did not give rise to a constructive trust in her favour in the absence of evidence that she acted in reliance upon an understanding that the house was to be owned jointly. In *Grant v Edwards* Sir Nicolas Browne-Wilkinson V-C and Nourse LJ agreed that a woman's going to live with a man or having a baby by him does not per se imply that she is to take an interest in the house because 'the law is not so cynical as to infer that a woman will only go to live with a man ... if

---

10 (1975) 239 Estates Gazette 119, CA.
11 [1982] Ch 391, [1982] 3 All ER 162, CA.
12 [1971] AC 886, [1970] 2 All ER 780, HL.
13 [1984] Ch 317, [1984] 1 All ER 244, CA.
14 *Grant v Edwards* (supra). But see Warburton [1986] Conv 291.
15 *Risch v McFee* [1991] 1 FLR 105, CA (direct contributions); *Grant v Edwards* (supra) (indirect contributions).
16 [1986] Ch 638, 657, [1986] 2 All ER 426, 439, CA. See also *Maharaj v Chand* [1986] AC 898, 907, [1986] 3 All ER 107, 112, PC.
17 At pp 648 and 433 respectively.
18 [1986] 1 FLR 171, 177, CA. Cf Purchas LJ in *Lloyds Bank plc v Rosset* [1989] Ch 350, 402, [1988] 3 All ER 915, 944, CA: '[The wife's] contribution must exceed that normally expected of a wife carrying out her normal matrimonial role.'

she understands that she is to have an interest in the home'[19] and her acts could be explained by natural love and affection. On the other side of the line it was held in *Cooke v Head*[20] that the claimant's helping the man with whom she was living to build the bungalow, which was to be their home, on land he had bought was sufficient to give her an interest in the property, and in *Eves v Eves*[1] a similar conclusion was reached when the woman had done a great deal of manual work (including demolition work and painting) on a dirty and dilapidated house which the man had bought. A different type of detriment can be seen in *Ungurian v Lesnoff*,[2] where it was held that the defendant, who had given up a promising academic career and her flat in Poland and had left her homeland on the understanding that the plaintiff would give her a home, had thereby acquired a life interest in the house that he had bought.

Proprietary estoppel

The essence of proprietary estoppel was thus described by Edward Nugee QC (sitting as a Deputy High Court Judge) in *Re Basham*:[3]

> 'Where one person, A, has acted to his detriment on the faith of a belief, which was known to and encouraged by another person, B, that he either has [been] or is going to be given a right in or over B's property, B cannot insist on his strict legal rights if to do so would be inconsistent with A's belief.'

To this should be added the requirement that B must know of the existence of his own right which is inconsistent with that claimed by A, for otherwise he is in the same position as A who will therefore acquire no prior equity.[4] If these conditions are established, B is bound to make good, as far as he can, the expectation he has encouraged.

The similarity to a constructive trust is immediately apparent in that in each case the person claiming the interest in property must have acted to his or her detriment, and it has been suggested that the principles underlying each should be assimilated.[5] The main point of distinction is that the claimant under a constructive trust must prove that she (or he) acted in reliance on a common intention that she should take an interest in the property, whereas an estoppel will arise if her acts result from her being misled by the other's conduct. A further distinction lies in the fact that, if the claimant adopts a detrimental course of conduct, there is a rebuttable

---

[19] Per Nourse LJ at pp 648 and 433 respectively. See Sir Nicolas Browne-Wilkinson V-C at pp 657 and 439 respectively.

[20] [1972] 2 All ER 38, CA. The work included demolishing a building, removing hard core and rubble, mixing cement, and painting.

[1] [1975] 3 All ER 768, CA.

[2] [1990] Ch 206. Cf *Hammond v Mitchell* [1992] 2 All ER 109 (partner's giving support to speculative venture which might have led to sale of property and loss of home).

[3] [1987] 1 All ER 405, 410. See generally Clarke *The Family Home: Intention and Agreement* [1992] Fam Law 72.

[4] *Coombes v Smith* [1986] 1 WLR 808. Estoppel can give the claimant an interest only in a specific piece of property and not in the other's assets generally: *Layton v Martin* [1986] 2 FLR 227, 239.

[5] See *Grant v Edwards* [1986] Ch 638, 656–657, [1986] 2 All ER 426, 439, CA (per Sir Nicolas Browne-Wilkinson V-C); *Austin v Keele* (1987) 72 ALR 579, 587, PC; *Lloyds Bank plc v Rosset* [1989] Ch 350, 387, [1988] 3 All ER 915, 933, CA (per Nicholls LJ); *Stokes v Anderson* [1991] 1 FLR 391, 399, CA (per Nourse LJ); Martin [1987] Conv 211; Hayton *Equitable Rights of Cohabitees* [1990] Conv 370.

presumption that she has done so in reliance on the assurances given to her.[6]

As with constructive trusts, the claimant may have acted to her detriment either by incurring expenditure or by prejudicing herself in some other way. In either case, however, her acts must have been induced by her mistaken belief.[7] So in *Coombes v Smith*[8] it was held that the plaintiff's leaving her husband, moving into a house provided by the defendant, having his child and looking after it could not found a proprietary estoppel because the reason for her conduct was that she preferred to live with the defendant and have his child rather than live with her husband. The owner of the property must also know of the claimant's mistake: he cannot encourage a belief of which he was ignorant.[9]

The principle can obviously be applied to give a proprietary interest to a spouse or a cohabitant: the facts in *Eves v Eves* and *Grant v Edwards*[10] could equally well have given rise to proprietary estoppel. In *Pascoe v Turner*[11] the plaintiff and defendant, who was his housekeeper, began to live together as husband and wife. After the relationship broke down, the plaintiff, who had moved out, told the defendant 'The house is yours and everything in it'. Relying on his statement, she spent money on redecoration, improvements and repairs. On his claim to possession of the house, the Court of Appeal held that, by encouraging or acquiescing in the defendant's belief that the house was hers, he was estopped from denying this and that the only way in which the equity could be satisfied was by compelling him to transfer the house to her.

Quantification of shares[12]

Up to now we have been discussing the circumstances in which a spouse may take a beneficial interest in the matrimonial home. We must now consider the further question: what is the size of the interest that each acquires?

There is no difficulty in quantifying the parties' shares if the conveyance spells out the beneficial interests or one of them acquires an interest by virtue of a resulting trust. In the former case the court must give effect to the conveyance.[13] If it vests the property in them jointly on an express trust for sale for themselves as joint tenants, they will become equitable tenants in common in equal shares if either of them severs the joint interest.[14]

---

[6] *Greasley v Cooke* [1980] 3 All ER 710, CA; *Coombes v Smith* (supra) at p 821.
[7] Hence there can be no estoppel if the claimant knew that the other reserved his right to change his mind or to revert to the original position: see *A-G of Hong Kong v Humphreys Estate (Queen's Gardens) Ltd* [1987] AC 114, [1987] 2 All ER 387, PC.
[8] [1986] 1 WLR 808. Cf the same principle applied to constructive trusts, ante, pp 594–595. The plaintiff also failed in *Coombes v Smith* because the defendant's statement that he would never see her without a roof over her head could not be construed as a promise that she could stay in the house against his wishes if their relationship broke down.
[9] *Brinnand v Ewens* (1987) 19 HLR 415, CA.
[10] Ante, p 591.
[11] [1979] 2 All ER 945, CA. See Sufrin 42 MLR 574.
[12] See Sparks *The Quantification of Beneficial Interests* 11 OJLS 39.
[13] Unless the conveyance can be rectified as the result of fraud or mistake: see ante, p 589.
[14] *Goodman v Gallant* [1986] Fam 106, [1986] 1 All ER 311, CA.

Similarly, if they take as tenants in common, the court must give effect to the trust thereby created and divide the proceeds in the proportions stated. If the circumstances in which the property was bought raise a resulting trust, the beneficial interests will be proportionate to the parties' contributions.[15]

Problems arise, however, in the case of constructive trusts.[16] In principle, the parties' interests must reflect their common intention when the property was acquired; in practice, as we have seen, an express agreement is rare and the court will have to infer their intention from their actions.[17] All the available evidence must be considered. In *Grant v Edwards*,[18] for example, both parties had made substantial contributions to the purchase of their home, the legal title to which was vested in the defendant and his brother (who was a purely nominal party with no beneficial interest). Following a fire at the house, the balance of the insurance money after the payment of repairs was put into a building society account in the joint names of the plaintiff and defendant. The Court of Appeal held that this was the best evidence of how they intended that the property should be shared and that each was entitled to a half interest.

Usually the best guide will be the parties' contributions, direct and indirect, to the purchase price and mortgage repayments.[19] In *Gissing v Gissing*[20] Lord Diplock saw:

> 'nothing inherently improbable in [the spouses'] acting on the understanding that the wife should be entitled to a share which was not to be quantified immediately upon the acquisition of the home but should be left to be determined when the mortgage was repaid or the property disposed of, on the basis of what would be fair having regard to the total contributions, direct or indirect, which each spouse had made by that date.'

Although this principle can be criticised as creating a 'wavering equity',[1] the Court of Appeal divided the parties' interests in proportion to their contributions in *Crisp v Mullings*[2] and *Walker v Hall*,[3] and it may be the only way of resolving an otherwise intractable problem. In *Passee v Passee*,[4] for example, the plaintiff, his aunt and his cousin together bought a house which was registered in the sole name of the plaintiff. They each provided cash sums of varying amounts and then contributed to a kitty out of which were paid all the outgoings including the repayment of the mortgage. The plaintiff later paid a substantial sum for capital improvements. The Court of Appeal concluded that the parties must have intended that their shares

---

[15] See ante, pp 590–591; *Cowcher v Cowcher* [1972] 1 All ER 943; *Marsh v Von Sternberg* [1986] 1 FLR 526.

[16] The same problems could equally well arise if the claimant establishes an estoppel.

[17] See ante, p 591, and Lord Diplock in *Gissing v Gissing* [1971] AC 886, 908, [1970] 2 All ER 780, 793, HL.

[18] [1986] Ch 638, [1986] 2 All ER 426, CA.

[19] See Griffiths LJ in *Bernard v Josephs* [1982] Ch 391, 404, [1982] 3 All ER 162, 170, CA, and the authorities there cited.

[20] [1971] AC 886, 909, [1970] 2 All ER 780, 793, HL.

[1] See *Marsh v Von Sternberg* [1986] 1 FLR 526, 533.

[2] (1975) 239 Estates Gazette 119, CA.

[3] [1984] FLR 126, CA. See also *Young v Young* [1984] FLR 375, CA; May LJ in *Burns v Burns* [1984] Ch 317, 344, [1984] 1 All ER 244, 264, CA, and Sir Nicolas Browne-Wilkinson VC in *Grant v Edwards* [1986] Ch 638, 655, [1986] 2 All ER 426, 437, CA.

[4] [1988] 1 FLR 263, CA.

should be arrived at by taking into account the total sum which each contributed, including the cost of the improvements.

In practice it may be wellnigh impossible to determine what proportion each party's contribution bore to the whole. An earlier method of approaching the problem, favoured by Lord Denning MR, proceeded on the basis that the court had a general power to do what is just and equitable in the circumstances and this frequently led to an equal division between the parties, at least if they were married. This received a decided check in *Gissing v Gissing* where it was held that the maxim 'Equality is equity' had been applied too often in this type of case. Nevertheless if both have made a substantial contribution but it is difficult to fix the proportions, the court may have to fall back on this principle.[5] Lord Diplock said further:[6]

> 'The same result ... may often be reached as an inference of fact. The instalments of a mortgage to a building society are generally repayable over a period of many years. During that period, as both must be aware, the ability of each spouse to contribute to the instalments out of their separate earnings is likely to alter, particularly in the case of the wife if any children are born of the marriage. If the contribution of the wife in the early part of the period of repayment is substantial but is not an identifiable and uniform proportion of each instalment, because her contributions are indirect or, if direct, are made irregularly, it may well be a reasonable inference that their common intention at the time of acquisition of the matrimonial home was that the beneficial interest should be held by them in equal shares and that each should contribute to the cost of its acquisition whatever amounts each could afford in the varying exigencies of family life to be expected during the period of repayment. In the social conditions of today this would be a natural enough common intention of a young couple who were both earning when the house was acquired but who contemplated having children whose birth and rearing in their infancy would necessarily affect the future earning capacity of the wife.'

It is understandable that 'an equitable knife must be used to sever the Gordian Knot' when the spouses' financial affairs have become so inextricably entangled that an equal division presents the only possible solution.[7] But at times the courts still go much further and fall back on the principle of dividing the property in such proportions as seem fair in the circumstances despite the criticisms against such a wide use of judicial discretion voiced by the House of Lords in *Pettitt v Pettitt*[8] and *Gissing v Gissing*.[9] In *Eves v Eves*,[10] where there was a clear understanding that the parties should take a joint interest, the Court of Appeal nevertheless awarded the plaintiff only a quarter share because, in the words of Lord Denning MR, 'one half would be too much'. Conversely in *Stokes v Anderson*,[11] where the house was worth over £100,000 and the defendant had provided at the most £14,500 towards buying out the half share owned by the plaintiff's former

---

[5] *Gissing v Gissing* (supra) at 903 and 788 (per Lord Pearson), 908 and 792–793 (per Lord Diplock). See also *Pettitt v Pettitt* [1970] AC 777, 804, [1969] 2 All ER 385, 397 (per Lord Morris of Borth-y-Gest).

[6] *Gissing v Gissing* (supra) at 908–909 and 793 respectively.

[7] See Lord Upjohn in *National Provincial Bank Ltd v Ainsworth* [1965] AC 1175, 1236, [1965] 2 All ER 472, 487, HL.

[8] [1970] AC 777, [1969] 2 All ER 385, HL.

[9] [1971] AC 886, [1970] 2 All ER 780, HL.

[10] [1975] 3 All ER 768, CA. For the facts, see ante, p 591. Brightman J would apparently have preferred an equal division and concurred in the result 'without great confidence' (at p 775).

[11] [1991] 1 FLR 391, 401, CA.

wife, the court made 'a broad approach' and took 'the fair view' that she was entitled to a quarter of the whole. Whether this approach produced a just solution is debatable; in any case it is to be deprecated as making it more difficult for the parties' advisers to negotiate a settlement.

Agreement to vary beneficial interests

It is of course always possible for the parties to agree to vary the size of their beneficial interests after the property has been bought. The variation is required to be in writing;[12] if it is not, it will be enforceable as a parol agreement of which equity will grant specific performance only if it is supported by valuable consideration.[13] Even if the parties did not enter into an express agreement, it might be possible to infer one from their conduct, for example by the use of a legacy to pay off the mortgage or by a permanent or substantial change in the contributions which they originally agreed or intended to make.[14]

Improvements to the matrimonial home

It may be argued that the parties' interests in the matrimonial home have been varied if, after purchase, one of them has been solely responsible for enhancing its value by extension or improvement (either by cash payments or by doing the work himself). Unlike a contribution to the purchase price, the mere fact that A does work on B's property does not of itself give A any interest in it. To establish such an interest, A must show that the expenditure was incurred or the work done in pursuance of an agreement or common intention that it should do so or, alternatively, that B has led A to believe that the improvement would confer an interest on him so as to give rise to a proprietary estoppel.[15]

So far as spouses and former engaged couples are concerned, the injustice that this could cause led to the passing of section 37 of the Matrimonial Proceedings and Property Act 1970.[16] This provides:

'... where a husband or wife contributes in money or money's worth to the improvement of real or personal property in which or in the proceeds of sale of which either or both of them has or have a beneficial interest, the husband or wife so contributing shall, if the contribution is of a substantial nature and subject to any agreement to the contrary express or implied, be treated as having then acquired by virtue of his or her contribution a share or an enlarged share, as the case may be, in that beneficial interest. ...'

It will be observed that this section (which refers to the improvement of any property and not merely to that of the matrimonial home) applies

---

[12] Law of Property Act 1925, s 53.
[13] *Cowcher v Cowcher* [1972] 1 All ER 943, 950.
[14] See *Gissing v Gissing* (supra) at 908 and 792 respectively; *Burns v Burns* (supra) at 344–345 and 265 respectively.
[15] *Pettitt v Pettitt* (supra), particularly at 818 and 409–410 respectively (per Lord Upjohn). See also *Thomas v Fuller-Brown* [1988] 1 FLR 237, CA; *Harwood v Harwood* [1991] 2 FLR 274, 294, CA.
[16] Enacted on the recommendation of the Law Commission: see Law Com No 25, paras 56–58 and pp 102–105. For difficulties arising under the section, see Oerton 120 New LJ 1008. It applies to engaged couples by virtue of s 2(1) of the Law Reform (Miscellaneous Provisions) Act 1970 (see ante, pp 22–23).

whether the contribution is in money or money's worth: in other words, it does not matter whether the spouse does the job himself or pays a contractor to do it. In the latter case, however, he must show that his contribution is identifiable with the improvement in question: a general contribution to the family's finances (like an indirect contribution to the price) will give him an interest in the home only if it is referable to the improvement.[17]

It will be seen that there are two limitations on the operation of the section. First, it will apply only if the contribution is of a substantial nature. Whether any particular improvement is sufficiently substantial to bring it within the ambit of the section is a question of fact: in *Re Nicholson*[18] the installation of central heating for £189 in premises worth £6,000 was regarded as a substantial contribution, but the purchase of a gas fire worth less than £23 was not. Secondly, the section applies 'subject to any agreement between the spouses to the contrary express or implied', so that if they agreed that the improvements should confer no interest on the party making them, this will be conclusive.

Section 37 applies in any proceedings including, for example, litigation between one spouse and a stranger claiming through the other. If the parties agreed on the size of the interest which the improvements were to confer on the spouse making them, the court must give effect to the agreement; in other cases it has power to make such order as appears just in all the circumstances. Normally this should reflect the amount by which the value of the property was increased at the time; if, for example, the wife puts the value of the husband's house up from £40,000 to £50,000, she should obtain one-fifth of the price when it is sold. The section also applies if both spouses have a beneficial interest in the property before the improvements are made: hence if in the above example the spouses were tenants in common of the house in equal shares when the wife made the improvements, she should now obtain three-fifths of the price.[19]

As section 37 does not apply to unmarried couples unless they are engaged to be married, one of them may claim an interest or enhanced interest in the matrimonial home as a consequence of improvement only by reference to the general law. The claimant may, of course, be able to prove or spell out an agreement between the parties that the work should have this effect; alternatively, it may be possible to infer from their conduct that this was their common intention. As in other cases of constructive trusts, however, the court will not be justified in drawing this conclusion unless the work is such that the party in question could be expected to carry it out only if he or she were to acquire an interest in the property as a result. In *Pettitt v Pettitt*[20] (where the parties were married) the husband alleged that as the result of doing work on the matrimonial home (which had been purchased by the wife out of her own money) he had increased its value by over £1,000. Most of the work consisted of redecorating the bungalow in question, but he had also made a garden, built a wall and

---

[17] *Harnett v Harnett* [1973] Fam 156, 167, [1973] 2 All ER 593, 603, per Bagnall J. (The question did not arise on appeal: [1974] 1 All ER 764, CA.)

[18] [1974] 2 All ER 386.

[19] *Re Nicholson* (supra).

[20] [1970] AC 777, [1969] 2 All ER 385, HL. The husband had to rely on the general law because the case was decided before the passing of the Matrimonial Proceedings and Property Act.

patio, and done other jobs outside. All the members of the House of Lords were agreed that he could claim nothing on the ground that, in the absence of an express agreement, he could acquire no interest by doing work of an ephemeral nature or 'do-it-yourself' jobs which any husband could be expected to do in his leisure hours.

The size of the interest so created will depend on the parties' common intention. In the absence of an express agreement it will presumably be calculated in the same way as an interest acquired by virtue of section 37 of the Matrimonial Proceedings and Property Act.[1]

Accounting for profits

The principle that a trustee must not take advantage of his position to make a personal profit for himself[2] applies when one spouse holds the matrimonial home or other property on trust for the other. In *Protheroe v Protheroe*[3] the husband owned the leasehold of the matrimonial home which he held for himself and his wife in equal shares. He later purchased the freehold reversion and it was held that he held this on the same trusts subject to his right to be repaid the price and legal costs incurred.

2. ENFORCING THE TRUST

If both spouses or cohabitants have a beneficial interest in the matrimonial home, their equitable joint tenancy or tenancy in common must take effect behind a trust for sale.[4] This is subject to an implied power to postpone the sale and, before exercising it, the legal owner is bound to consult the beneficiaries of full age interested in possession and 'as far as consistent with the general interest of the trust' give effect to their wishes.[5] If the parties cannot agree, either of them may call for an order that the trusts be executed, when section 30 of the Law of Property Act 1925 enables the court to make such order as it thinks fit.

So long as the parties are living together, they are likely to agree on the disposal of their home, so that there will be no question of an application to the court. If their relationship breaks down and they separate, one may well wish to remain in the former home and the other to have it sold so as to realise his capital. If the parties are married, the courts prefer to use their wide powers to make property adjustment orders under the Matrimonial Causes Act because they can then make a fair order after taking all relevant facts into account.[6] This can be done only if one of them petitions for divorce, nullity or judicial separation; consequently if no petition is presented and a fortiori if they are unmarried, this course is not open to them, and they will be compelled to invoke the court's powers under section 30.

[1] By analogy with the cases concerned with the acquisition of a beneficial interest by contribution to the purchase price.
[2] Ie the rule in *Keech v Sandford* (1726) 2 Eq Cas Abr 741.
[3] [1968] 1 All ER 1111, CA. For a criticism of the case, see Cretney *The Rationale of Keech v Sandford* 33 Conv 161.
[4] Law of Property Act 1925, ss 34 and 36; Settled Land Act 1925, s 36(4).
[5] Law of Property Act 1925, ss 25(1) and 26(3).
[6] See ante, p 586. For property adjustment orders, see post, pp 736 et seq.

The courts have consistently taken the view that if two people (whether married or not) buy property as a home for themselves (together with any children they may have), the underlying purpose of the trust is to provide a home and not an investment. Consequently, so long as that purpose subsists, the trust should not be executed and the property should not be sold.[7] But once that purpose is discharged, the court will order a sale.[8] The question that has to be answered therefore is: is the purpose of the trust still alive?

All the cases indicate that so long as one of the parties (usually the wife or mother) wishes to remain in the home *with dependent children*, she will be permitted to do so and the court will not order a sale.[9] In *Jones v Challenger*[10] the Court of Appeal ordered a sale when the marriage had broken down and the husband was living alone in the house; as it was no longer required as the matrimonial home, the primary object of the trust was now to provide the parties with an investment which had to be realised. On the other hand, Cumming-Bruce LJ, delivering the leading judgment of the Court of Appeal in *Chhokar v Chhokar*,[11] maintained that, although the rules are not inflexible, the court would not order a sale 'if the effect ... [would] be to prevent the beneficiaries or one of them from occupying the home as a matrimonial and/or family home' unless there were unusual circumstances. He pointed out that the children of the family were not themselves objects of the trust although their existence was one of the facts that the court had to take into account in deciding whether to make an order. It was not necessary for him to express the principle so widely because the wife was living in the house with two children and a sale was not ordered, and it is submitted that, as a general rule, a sale should be ordered if there are no children for the reasons stated in *Jones v Challenger*.

The court is bound to take all the relevant facts into account and these prima facie rules may be displaced by other facts which would make it unjust to order a sale.[12] In *Re Evers' Trust*[13] the mother's need for a home with her three children was no doubt the court's main reason for not ordering a sale, but it was also pointed out that the father had provided only one-fifth of the purchase money and had a secure home with his own mother. A sale may be postponed if one party needs time to find other accommodation[14] or if there is a reasonable chance of a reconciliation. A more striking example of a refusal to order a sale when it would be inequitable to do so can be seen in *Bedson v Bedson*,[15] where the wife had

---

[7] *Re Buchanan-Wollaston's Conveyance* [1939] Ch 738, [1939] 2 All ER 302, CA; *Williams v Williams* [1976] Ch 278, [1977] 1 All ER 28, CA; *Re Evers' Trust* [1980] 3 All ER 399, CA; *Bernard v Josephs* [1982] Ch 391, [1982] 3 All ER 162, CA; *Chhokar v Chhokar* [1984] FLR 313, CA.

[8] *Jones v Challenger* [1961] 1 QB 176, [1960] 1 All ER 785, CA. Miller *Family Property and Financial Provision* (2nd Edn) ch 7.

[9] See the cases cited in n 7, supra and Thompson *Overreaching after Boland* 6 LS 140.

[10] [1961] 1 QB 176, [1960] 1 All ER 785, CA. See also *Bernard v Josephs* (supra).

[11] [1984] FLR 313 at 327, CA. Reeve J agreed.

[12] See Schuz *Section 30 of the Law of Property Act 1925 and Unmarried Cohabitees* 12 Fam Law 108; Thompson *Cohabitation, Co-ownership and Section 30* [1984] Conv 103.

[13] [1980] 3 All ER 399, CA. Cf *Chhokar v Chhokar* (supra), where the court showed little sympathy for the owner of the house to whom the husband had sold it at an undervalue with the intention of evicting the wife.

[14] *Mayes v Mayes* (1969) 210 Estates Gazette 935 (husband temporarily unemployed and therefore finding it difficult to raise mortgage to buy another flat).

[15] [1965] 2 QB 666, [1965] 3 All ER 307, CA. See also *Hayward v Hayward* (1974) 237 Estates Gazette 577.

deserted her husband and the property in question (a draper's shop with a flat over it) had been bought out of the husband's savings and was his sole livelihood.

Another solution, which would do justice in some cases, would be to let the party in occupation remain in the house but to order her (or him) to pay the other the value of his share so that the latter could realise his capital. Under section 30 of the Law of Property Act the court has a power to attach conditions to an order for sale.[16] If it wishes to let one party buy the other out, therefore, it can proceed as the Court of Appeal did in *Bernard v Josephs*[17] and order the property to be sold but attach a condition that the order should not be enforced if one party pays the other the value of his share within a stated period.

A further example of the wide use the court can make of its discretionary powers under section 30 can be seen in *Re Evers' Trust*.[18] The judge at first instance had ordered that the parties' former home be sold but had deferred the execution of the order until the parties' child, who was living there with his mother, reached the age of 16. The Court of Appeal accepted that this was a proper exercise of the power; they pointed out, however, that circumstances might change unpredictably so that, in the event, it might not be appropriate to sell this house at that time or, alternatively, it might become appropriate to sell it much sooner. They therefore preferred to discharge the order and leave it to the father to re-apply at a more suitable time in the future. But it will be seen that the courts can use section 30 to make many of the orders in favour of an unmarried applicant that they can make in favour of a spouse under the Matrimonial Causes Act.[19]

Two particular points should be noted. First, on the death of one of the parties the other's share will become a part of his estate (unless the parties were joint tenants) and may not pass to the survivor. In this situation the court should take the same facts into account as it does when the parties separate during their joint lives and should not order a sale unless the property no longer serves the purpose of providing a family home for the survivor.[20] Secondly, if one party becomes insolvent, there may be a dispute between his creditors and the other party. The particular problems that this gives rise to will be considered later in this chapter.[1]

Distribution of assets after sale: equitable accounting

Even though the primary purpose of the trust comes to an end on the separation of the parties, the trust for sale nevertheless remains and the property in effect becomes an investment. This cannot affect the size of the beneficial interests, however; hence, as the Court of Appeal held in *Turton v Turton*,[2] if the parties hold as tenants in common in equal shares, each

---

[16] But this power exists only if an order is made: see *Dennis v McDonald* [1982] Fam 63, [1981] 2 All ER 632 (affirmed on other grounds [1982] Fam 63, [1982] 1 All ER 590, CA), followed by Kerr LJ in *Bernard v Josephs* (supra) at 410 and 175 respectively.

[17] [1982] Ch 391, [1982] 3 All ER 162, CA.

[18] [1980] 3 All ER 399, CA.

[19] See Thompson [1984] Conv 103.

[20] *Stott v Ratcliffe* (1982) 126 Sol Jo 310, CA.

[1] Post, pp 625–628.

[2] [1988] Ch 542, [1987] 2 All ER 641, CA, following *Walker v Hall* [1984] FLR 126, CA, and disapproving *Hall v Hall* (1981) 3 FLR 379, CA, where it had been held that in the case of unmarried cohabitants the home should be valued at the time of separation.

will be entitled to half the proceeds when the property is sold or, if one of them buys the other out, to half the value at the time of the transfer.[3]

Further accounting between the parties, however, may often be necessary. If one of them spends money on the property after they have separated, he will usually be entitled to call on the other to contribute to the expenditure if this preserves or enhances the value of the asset, because both will derive the benefit of the increased value when the investment is realised. In *Bernard v Josephs*,[4] for example, the proceeds of sale were divided between the parties only after the plaintiff had paid to the defendant the sum of £2,650 which the latter had spent on decorating the house and so increased the price obtained. The position regarding the payment of mortgage instalments is less clear. In *Cracknell v Cracknell*,[5] where the matrimonial home was owned jointly, the wife had left to live with another man. The husband continued to pay the instalments and the Court of Appeal held that she should compensate him for half the total payments he had made after their separation. In *Suttill v Graham*,[6] on the other hand, on virtually identical facts the Court of Appeal concluded that the wife should be required to compensate the husband only for the capital sum he had repaid, apparently on the ground that that alone increased the value of the equity. As we shall see below, the position may be complicated by the need to pay an occupation rent. Leaving this question aside, in the face of conflicting decisions of the Court of Appeal, that in *Cracknell v Cracknell* is to be preferred because, as was pointed out in *Re Gorman*,[7] the mortgagee will have a charge on the property for both unpaid interest and capital so that the value of the equity is increased by the payment of both.

A similar question that arises after separation is whether the party who has left the home is entitled to an occupation rent from the other. The answer can be given with more certainty following the decision of the Court of Appeal in *Dennis v McDonald*.[8] If the parties are co-owners, whether in law or equity, each is entitled to possession; consequently, if one leaves voluntarily, he or she is not entitled to any rent. If, however, one forces the other to leave, justice demands that he should pay rent to compensate the latter for the right she has lost and the need to pay for accommodation

---

[3] If the property is subject to a mortgage which, as between the parties, one alone is responsible for repaying, the unpaid debt should be debited to his share. Suppose that H and W buy a house for £50,000 of which W provides £25,000 in cash and H provides £25,000 borrowed from X. Each will get half the proceeds of sale but H will have to repay the loan out of his half. The same result should follow if the lender is a building society which takes a mortgage on the property. This principle was applied in *Cowcher v Cowcher* [1972] 1 All ER 943, 959, and *Re Densham* [1975] 3 All ER 726. See Sparkes *The Quantification of Beneficial Interests*, 11 OJLS 39, 46–52.

[4] [1982] Ch 391, [1982] 3 All ER 162, CA. Quaere whether the plaintiff should have had to pay only half of the expenditure, which is the extent to which the value of her half share had been increased. It was accepted that the wife should recover only half her expenditure in similar circumstances in *Re Gorman* [1990] 1 All ER 717.

[5] [1971] P 356, [1971] 3 All ER 552, CA. See also *Wilson v Wilson* [1963] 2 All ER 447, CA; *Davis v Vale* [1971] 2 All ER 1021, CA.

[6] [1977] 3 All ER 1117, CA. The Court of Appeal purported to follow *Leake v Bruzzi* [1974] 2 All ER 1196, CA, but see infra.

[7] [1990] 1 All ER 717. The court followed *Bernard v Josephs* [1982] Ch 391, [1982] 3 All ER 162, CA, where, however, *Suttill v Graham* was not cited.

[8] [1982] Fam 63, [1982] 1 All ER 590, CA. See Martin [1982] Conv 305; Webb 98 LQR 519; Schuz 12 Fam Law 108; Thompson [1984] Conv 103.

elsewhere: in *Dennis v McDonald* the sum ordered to be paid was one half of what would be a fair rent under the Rent Act.[9] What is not settled is what amounts to an 'ouster' in this context. *Dennis v McDonald* was a clear case because the plaintiff had left as the result of the defendant's violence: it is suggested that it is probably sufficient that one party's behaviour has been such that the other cannot reasonably be expected to live with him.[10]

If the party in occupation is bound to pay rent and is also paying mortgage instalments, it may be simpler to regard the payment of interest as equivalent to the payment of rent and thus avoid a double computation. In such circumstances it would be proper to order the party who has left to account for his or her proportionate part of the repayment of capital only. This occurred in *Leake v Bruzzi*[11] where the wife left the husband and obtained a divorce based on the fact that her husband's behaviour had been such that she could not reasonably be expected to live with him.

3. PROTECTION OF BENEFICIAL INTERESTS

The nature of the interests of joint tenants and tenants in common and the protection they are afforded against third parties were the subject of extensive review by the House of Lords in *City of London Building Society v Flegg*.[12] As Lord Oliver of Aylmerton (with whose speech all the other members of the House agreed) pointed out, a joint tenancy or tenancy in common must now take effect behind a trust for sale: the tenants' interests are in the proceeds of sale and in the net rents and profits of the land until sale.[13] Pending sale, a beneficiary may remain in occupation or possession of the property subject to the purpose for which the trust was created and to any agreement between the beneficiaries; if spouses or unmarried cohabitants are joint tenants or tenants in common of their home, each will clearly have a right to occupy it so long as they are living together. This, however, is no more than a means of enjoying the rents and profits in specie.[14] So far as practicable, the trustees must consult all beneficiaries of full age before dealing with the land.[15] If, however, the house is sold or mortgaged, the beneficiaries' equitable interests are overreached and a purchaser of a legal estate (including a legal mortgagee or chargee) is not bound by them even though he has notice of them provided that he pays the proceeds of sale or other capital money to two or more trustees (or a trust corporation).[16] Nor is he concerned to see that the beneficiaries have been consulted.[17] Hence once the property is sold and the beneficial interests

[9] Rent Act 1977, s 70(1), (2), and disregarding s 70(3).
[10] Cf *Leake v Bruzzi* (supra). For the facts, see below.
[11] [1974] 2 All ER 1196, CA. The wife was urged to adopt this solution in *Re Gorman* (supra). But this may not be the proper approach if little remains to be paid on the mortgage so that the interest element is low.
[12] [1988] AC 54, [1987] 3 All ER 435, HL. See Smith 103 LQR 520; Swadling [1987] Conv 451; Gardner 51 MLR 365; Harpum [1987] CLJ 392 and *Overreaching* [1990] CLJ 277; Thompson *Dispositions by Trustees for Sale* [1988] Conv 108; Sparkes [1988] Conv 141; Evans *Land Law: An Overview after Flegg* (1990) Lit 13.
[13] Law of Property Act 1925, ss 34–36.
[14] *City of London Building Society v Flegg* at pp 83 and 448 respectively.
[15] Law of Property Act 1925, s 26(3). See *Waller v Waller* [1967] 1 All ER 305.
[16] Ibid, s 27.
[17] Ibid, s 26(3).

overreached, the beneficiaries are no longer entitled to enjoy the rents and profits either in cash or in specie and cannot enforce any right of occupation or possession even though they were not parties to the conveyance. Similarly if the property is mortgaged by two or more trustees, the beneficiaries' interest shifts on to the equity of redemption, and whilst they will be able to remain in possession so long as the mortgage remains in existence, they cannot enforce any right to do so if the mortgagee exercises his statutory right of sale. In *City of London Building Society v Flegg* a husband, wife and the wife's parents agreed to buy a house in which all four could live. The property was conveyed to the husband and wife alone but the wife's parents, who had provided part of the purchase money, also had a beneficial interest. The husband and wife later mortgaged the property to the plaintiffs who sought possession of the premises when the spouses became insolvent. It was held that, although the wife's parents had a right to occupy the premises against their son-in-law and daughter, they had none whatever against the building society who were protected by having paid the sum borrowed to the two trustees.

The same conclusion would be reached if the husband and another were joint legal tenants of the matrimonial home in which the wife had a beneficial interest either under an express trust for sale or by virtue of a resulting or constructive trust. If the owners of the legal estate sold or mortgaged it, the wife's interest would be overreached and so unenforceable against the purchaser or mortgagee.[18]

In practice difficulty arises if the legal estate is vested in one spouse only (say, the husband) and the wife has a beneficial interest under a resulting or constructive trust. The husband should appoint another trustee (who would normally be the wife) but in many cases this will not be done, and if the husband sells or mortgages the house, the purchaser or mortgagee will deal with him alone. If the husband acts without the knowledge or consent of the wife, can she enforce her rights against the new legal owner if he seeks possession of the premises or takes steps to realise his security?

If the legal title is registered under the Land Registration Act 1925, any interest arising under a trust for sale is a minor interest which may be protected by lodging a caution.[19] In practice this may be of little use because the wife is unlikely to know the relevant law, although a caution might be lodged before the husband dealt with the land if she sought legal advice on the breakdown of her marriage. The wife is much more likely to be helped by the fact that her undivided share gives her an overriding interest. In *Williams and Glyn's Bank Ltd v Boland*[20] the husband was registered as the sole proprietor of the legal estate of the matrimonial home, but the wife had contributed a substantial sum towards the purchase and was admittedly an equitable tenant in common to the extent of her contribution. The husband later executed a legal mortgage to the appellant bank which made

---

[18] If the wife could raise a proprietary estoppel against the husband, it is not clear whether this would still be good against the purchaser or mortgagee: see Thompson [1988] Conv at 120. It would be anomalous if an estoppel gave her greater protection than an express trust.

[19] Land Registration Act 1925, ss 3(xv), 54 and 55; *Elias v Mitchell* [1972] Ch 652. The interest could also be protected by restriction if the husband deposited the land certificate at the registry.

[20] [1981] AC 487, [1980] 2 All ER 408, HL; Freeman 43 MLR 692 and 11 Fam Law 37; Smith 97 LQR 12; Murphy and Clark *The Family Home* ch 6.

no enquiries of the wife. When the husband failed to pay the sum secured, the bank started proceedings for possession of the house with a view to selling it under their powers as mortgagees. The wife resisted the action on the ground that her interest took priority over the bank's by virtue of section 20(1) of the Land Registration Act 1925. This provides that a disposition of registered land shall, when registered, confer on the transferee the estate expressed to be created subject to any overriding interests affecting it, and by section 70(1) of the Act:

'All registered land shall ... be deemed to be subject to such of the following overriding interests as may be for the time being subsisting in reference thereto ...:

(g) The rights of every person in actual occupation of the land or in receipt of the rents and profits thereof, save where the enquiry is made of such person and the rights are not disclosed.'

The House of Lords held that the wife's physical presence in the house coupled with the right to exclude others without a right to occupy clearly gave her actual occupation, and the fact that her husband (the owner of the legal estate) was also in actual occupation could not affect this. Furthermore, although the land was held on trust for sale, pending sale the wife had an interest subsisting in reference to the land itself.[1] Her claim must therefore succeed.

Williams and Glyn's Bank Ltd v Boland has created a number of difficulties for prospective purchasers (and particularly prospective mortgagees).[2] Some of these had to be considered by the House of Lords in *Abbey National Building Society v Cann*.[3] The respondent bought a house as a home for his mother and step-father. It was conveyed into his sole name and was paid for in part by the proceeds of sale of another house and in part (as his mother knew) by a mortgage, which the respondent negotiated with the appellant building society. He told the appellants that the property was being purchased for his sole occupation. The respondent and his step-father arrived on the premises about an hour before the transfer was completed and the charge created, and workmen began to lay the mother's carpets and bring in her furniture. The transfer and charge were not registered for another month, by which time the mother had moved into the premises herself. The appellants claimed possession of the property when the son fell behind with the payment of the mortgage; he did not resist the claim but his mother, relying on *Boland's* case, did so on the ground that she had an overriding interest by reason of her contribution to the purchase of the first home.

The House of Lords was primarily concerned with the effect of the mother's moving into actual occupation between the creation of the charge and its registration. There will inevitably be a delay between these two events; any inspection must obviously be made before the first but, as we have seen, section 20(1) of the Land Registration Act provides that the transferee or chargee will take subject to overriding interests subsisting *at*

---

[1] Ie the right to enjoy the rents and profits in specie: see ante, p 605.
[2] See Law Com No 115 (Implications of *Williams and Glyn's Bank Ltd v Boland*) 1982; Law Com No 188 (Overreaching: Beneficiaries in Occupation) 1989.
[3] [1991] 1 AC 56, [1990] 1 All ER 1085, HL.

registration. Taken literally, this produces the 'conveyancing absurdity'[4] that the purchaser, having made all possible enquiries and parted with his money, will be bound by an interest claimed by an occupant coming on to the land between completion and registration. To avoid this conclusion, the House held that, in order to assert an overriding interest against the purchaser, the claimant must be in occupation at the date of completion (and, presumably, also at the date of registration).[5] This reduces one of the hazards likely to arise following *Boland's* case, but there is clearly still a risk that the claimant will come into occupation during the delay between inspection and completion. If, as in *Cann's* case, the purchase of the property depends on the execution of a charge, the chargee would still appear to have priority because, as the House of Lords held, the two transactions are to be regarded as indivisible so that the purchaser acquires nothing but an equity of redemption to which the claimant's beneficial interest can attach. But if the owner of the legal estate mortgages it later, the owner of an overriding interest coming into occupation after the mortgagee has made enquiries but before the charge is created will be able to assert it against the mortgagee.

Another question that arose in *Abbey National Building Society v Cann* is the meaning of 'actual occupation'. It should be given its ordinary meaning of possession or presence on the land; 'actual' indicates physical possession as distinct from legal possession by receipt of rents and profits.[6] The term is apparently not synonymous with 'reside':[7] a person can obviously occupy one property and reside in another, and he can occupy premises by an agent, for example a caretaker.[8] The facts of *Lloyds Bank Plc v Rosset*[9] illustrate the difficulties that can arise. The husband purchased a semi-derelict house partly with the aid of a charge in favour of the appellant bank. The vendor let the husband and his wife into possession some six weeks before completion and the creation of the charge and during this time the wife spent almost every day on the premises directing building work and doing some decorating herself and occasionally slept there. The majority of the Court of Appeal held that the presence of the builders (who were agents of both parties) coupled with that of the wife amounted to actual occupation by her because 'there was ... physical presence on the property by the wife and her agent of the nature that one would expect of

---

[4] Per Lord Oliver of Aylmerton in *Abbey National Building Society v Cann* (supra) at 88 and 1097 respectively, citing Nicholls LJ in *Lloyds Bank plc v Rosset* [1989] Ch 350, 373, [1988] 3 All ER 915, 922, CA.

[5] Because, if he goes out of occupation before registration, his interest will cease to be an overriding interest. The beneficial interest must exist before completion; if it arises between completion and registration, the purchaser's equitable interest which arises by the payment or advance of money on completion will in any case take priority over it: see *Abbey National Building Society v Cann* (supra) at 87 and 1096 respectively.

[6] Per Lord Wilberforce in *Williams and Glyn's Bank Ltd v Boland* [1981] AC 487, 505, [1980] 2 All ER 408, 413, HL. For a detailed discussion of the difficulties this interpretation creates, see Sparkes *The Discoverability of Occupiers of Registered Land* [1989] Conv 342.

[7] See *Lloyds Bank plc v Rosset* [1989] Ch 350, [1988] 3 All ER 915, CA.

[8] *Lloyds Bank plc v Rosset* (supra); *Abbey National Building Society v Cann* (supra) at 93 and 1101 respectively (per Lord Oliver of Aylmerton).

[9] [1989] Ch 350, [1988] 3 All ER 915, CA. Having held that the wife acquired no beneficial interest (see ante, p 592), the House of Lords found it unnecessary to consider whether she was in actual occupation when the charge was created: [1991] 1 AC 107, [1990] 1 All ER 1111, HL.

an occupier having regard to the then state of the property'.[10] Mustill LJ, dissenting on this point, was of the opinion that the tradesmen's presence would not indicate to an enquirer that a person with a claim adverse to the owner's was in occupation: they were working on the site rather than in occupation of it, and the wife's activities were more in keeping with preparing the house for occupation than with occupation itself.[11] Bearing in mind that the statutory scheme replaces constructive notice in equity, this view is to be preferred. It certainly accords with that of the House of Lords in *Abbey National Building Society v Cann*,[12] where they held that the activities of the workmen laying carpets and carrying in furniture were no more than preparatory steps leading to the assumption of actual residential occupation later and that consequently the respondent's mother could not be said to be in actual occupation of the house when the charge was created. Like possession 'occupation' connotes some form of continuity rather than periodic visits and, it is submitted, should be unambiguous.

Temporary absence cannot bring occupation to an end, and the fact that a spouse's occupation may be intermittent presents a further hazard to the prospective purchaser. In *Kingsnorth Finance Co Ltd v Tizard*[13] the husband slept in the matrimonial home with the two children of the marriage; because the marriage was in difficulty the wife slept elsewhere but came to the house each day to feed the children. When the husband was away (as happened frequently) she slept there. The husband then applied for a loan from the plaintiffs to be secured by a mortgage of the house. It was held that the wife was in occupation, even though she was not there when the plaintiff's agent made his enquiries and the husband had temporarily removed all signs of her periodic visits.

If the land is unregistered, the position is more complex. The wife cannot register her interest under the Land Charges Act.[14] The basic principle was thus summarised by Lord Oliver of Aylmerton in *City of London Building Society v Flegg*:[15]

> 'The reason why a purchaser of the legal estate (whether by way of outright sale or by way of mortgage) from a single proprietor takes subject to the rights of the occupying spouse is ... because, having constructive notice of the trust as a result of the beneficiary's occupation, he steps into the shoes of the vendor or mortgagor and takes the estate subject to the same equities as those to which it was subject in the latter's hands, those equities and their accompanying incidents not having been overreached by the sale ...'

This implies that anyone dealing with the land will be protected only by the general equitable doctrine that a bona fide purchaser of a legal estate for value will take it free of any equitable interest of which he does not have actual or constructive notice.[16] Hence if he takes an equitable interest (for example, if a bank takes an equitable charge from the husband), the

---

[10] Per Nicholls LJ at 379 and 927 respectively.
[11] At 398–399 and 941–942 respectively.
[12] [1991] 1 AC 56, [1990] 1 All ER 1085, HL. For the facts, see ante, p 607.
[13] [1986] 2 All ER 54; Thompson [1986] Conv 283. The case dealt with unregistered land, but this can make no difference to this point.
[14] Interests arising under a trust for sale are expressly excluded from the definition of a general equitable charge: Land Charges Act 1972, s 2(4).
[15] [1988] AC 54, 83, [1987] 3 All ER 435, 448, HL.
[16] See Megarry and Wade *Real Property* (5th Edn) pp 404–405; Rudden *The Wife, the Husband and the Conveyancer* 27 Conv 51; Garner *A Single Trustee for Sale* 33 Conv 240.

wife must have priority. A purchaser of a legal estate will normally have constructive notice of the rights of any person in occupation of the land: this raises the question whether the fact that the wife is residing in the house will itself be sufficient notice of her interest to give her priority over the purchaser. In *Caunce v Caunce*[17] Stamp J held that it will not do so because her presence is not inconsistent with the husband's being the sole beneficial owner, but this case was doubted, although not expressly over-ruled, in *Williams and Glyn's Bank Ltd v Boland*.[18] One of the principal objections to holding that the wife's occupation gives the purchaser con-structive notice of her rights is that this compels him to make distasteful and embarrassing enquiries. In an earlier case dealing with the so-called 'deserted wife's equity', Upjohn J, refusing to cast upon a prospective purchaser or mortgagee the duty to enquire whether the owner of the property in question had deserted his wife, said:[19]

'If the law were otherwise it would mean that every intending purchaser or lender must inquire into the relationship of husband and wife and inquire into matters which are no concern of his and will bring thousands of business transactions into the area of domestic life and ties. That cannot be right.'

This applies with equal force to the problem we are considering here. It is doubtful, however, whether these cases can still be regarded as good law since the decisions in *Williams and Glyn's Bank Ltd v Boland* and *Abbey National Building Society v Cann*. Clearly nothing said in either case is binding in this context because both were concerned with registered land. But in *Boland's* case the House of Lords was obviously more concerned to protect the wife than the purchaser. In the words of Lord Wilberforce:[20]

'The extension of the risk area follows necessarily from the extension, beyond the paterfamilias, of rights of ownership, itself following from the diffusion of property and earning capacity. What is involved is a departure from an easy-going practice of dispensing with enquiries as to occupation beyond that of the vendor and accepting the risks of doing so. To substitute for this a practice of more careful enquiry as to the fact of occupation and, if necessary, as to the rights of occupiers cannot, in my view of the matter, be considered as unacceptable except at the price of overlooking the widespread development of shared interests in ownership.'

Although he was speaking only of conveyancing practice when the land is registered, precisely the same principles apply to unregistered land, as was pointed out in *Cann's case*;[1] and in *Kingsnorth Finance Co Ltd v Tizard*[2] the court declined to follow *Caunce v Caunce*. It is possible, however, that there is a difference between registered and unregistered land as regards the type of notice that binds a purchaser. In *City of London Building Society v Flegg* Lord Oliver of Aylmerton expressly approved an earlier dictum of Lord Wilberforce's to this effect.[3] Under the Land Registration Act it is

---

[17] [1969] 1 All ER 722.
[18] [1981] AC 487, 505, [1980] 2 All ER 408, 413 (per Lord Wilberforce, with whom three other members of the House agreed), ibid 511 and 418 respectively (per Lord Scarman).
[19] *Westminster Bank Ltd v Lee* [1956] Ch 7, 22, [1955] 2 All ER 883, 889. For the deserted wife's equity, see post, p 614.
[20] *Williams and Glyn's Bank v Boland* (supra) at 508–509 and 415–416 respectively.
[1] [1991] 1 AC 56, 87, [1990] 1 All ER 1085, 1096, HL.
[2] [1986] 2 All ER 54. See also *Hodgson v Marks* [1971] Ch 892, 934–935, [1971] 2 All ER 684, 690, CA (per Russell LJ).
[3] [1988] AC 54, 88, [1987] 3 All ER 435, 451, HL, citing *National Provincial Bank Ltd v Ainsworth* [1965] AC 1175, 1261, [1965] 2 All ER 472, 503, HL.

the fact of occupation that creates an overriding interest, whereas if the land is unregistered the intending purchaser probably has constructive notice only of matters that would have come to light had he made such enquiries or carried out such inspection as is reasonable in the circumstances. If he acts in this prudent fashion and does not find the wife in occupation or evidence which will give him notice of her occupation, he is protected; but if he does find such evidence and fails to make proper enquiries, the interest he acquires will be subject to hers.[4] A fortiori this must be so if the spouses have separated and the wife is living in the house alone.

If the wife consents to the transaction—and a fortiori if she is a party to the conveyance or mortgage—she cannot argue that any interest she may have in the property takes priority over the purchaser's or mortgagee's. Furthermore, if she knows that the house can be bought only with the help of a loan and supports the husband's proposal that this should be secured by a mortgage, then, as the Court of Appeal held in *Bristol and West Building Society v Henning*,[5] it must have been the spouses' common intention that the charge should take priority over both parties' beneficial interests. To secure his position the mortgagee may insist on the wife's being a party to the charge, and this will in any event be necessary if the legal estate is vested in both spouses jointly. He runs an obvious risk, however, if he leaves the husband to procure the wife's signature to the instrument. In practice, this is most likely to occur if the husband seeks a secured loan or overdraft to finance a business venture and the only security he can offer is that of the matrimonial home. If he knows that the wife may be unwilling to agree, he may resort to undue influence or misrepresentation to obtain her consent. This will not of itself affect the mortgagee but will do so in two cases. First, he will be in no better position than the husband and therefore cannot enforce the security against the wife, if the husband was acting as his agent in procuring her signature. As Dillon LJ put it in the leading judgment in the Court of Appeal in *Kingsnorth Trust Ltd v Bell*,[6] in this context the husband will be the mortgagee's agent 'if the creditor entrusts to the husband himself the task of obtaining the execution of the relevant document'. Hence the bank will take subject to the wife's interest if, as in that case, the husband was given the necessary documents to take home for the wife to sign, but not if he was merely left to tell her that the bank would grant a loan on the security of the house or, even, to obtain her agreement in principle.[7] Secondly, as the Court of Appeal held in *Bank of Credit and Commerce International SA v Aboody*,[8]

---

[4] *Kingsnorth Finance Co Ltd v Tizard* (supra) at 63–64.
[5] [1985] 2 All ER 606, CA (unregistered land). See also *Paddington Building Society v Mendelsohn* [1987] Fam Law 121, CA (registered land); *Equity & Law Home Loans Ltd v Prestidge* [1992] 1 All ER 909, CA (replacement mortgage). Had the House of Lords found in *Abbey National Building Society v Cann* (supra) that the respondent's mother had an overriding interest, they would have held that it would not have prevailed over the appellant's interest for the same reason. See also Thompson 49 MLR 245 and [1986] Conv 57.
[6] [1986] 1 All ER 423, 427, CA. In *Barclays Bank plc v Kennedy* [1989] 1 FLR 356, 364, CA, Purchas LJ referred to the bank's 'being content to leave it to the husband to obtain the wife's consent', but it is apparent from his judgment as a whole that he was applying the test laid down by Dillon LJ in *Kingsnorth Trust Ltd v Bell*.
[7] As in *Midland Bank plc v Perry* [1988] 1 FLR 161, CA.
[8] [1990] 1 QB 923, 973, CA. Although the bank had notice through its solicitor that the

the mortgage will not be enforceable against the wife if the creditor or his agent (for example, his solicitor) has notice of any misrepresentation made by the husband or of the circumstances which are alleged to constitute undue influence or from which any presumption of undue influence is alleged to arise.[9]

If the purchaser or mortgagee takes a legal estate subject to the wife's beneficial interest, the transaction will still have the effect of granting him whatever beneficial interest the husband has.[10] But even if he finds himself saddled with the wife's interest, it does not follow that she will be able to stay in occupation indefinitely. The purchaser will be entitled to take proceedings to enforce the trust for sale: in deciding whether to order the property to be sold, the court must take into account the same facts as it would if the proceedings had been brought by the husband, in whose shoes the purchaser now stands. If the husband is insolvent, the court may enforce a sale in bankruptcy proceedings and leave the wife to claim her share of the proceeds.[11]

B. Occupation

1. THE SPOUSES' RIGHT TO OCCUPY THE MATRIMONIAL HOME

If the spouses are joint tenants in law or if both of them have a beneficial interest in the matrimonial home, each will prima facie be entitled to occupy it as owner. If the legal and equitable title is vested in the husband alone, the wife can claim a right of occupation at common law not only by virtue of her right to her husband's consortium but also by virtue of her right to be maintained by him, for his duty to provide her with maintenance is primarily discharged by providing her with a home.[12] The right to consortium—and therefore the right to occupy the home—is forfeited if she commits a matrimonial offence.[13] Her right to her husband's consortium

husband had exercised undue influence over the wife, the action failed because the transaction was not to her manifest disadvantage. Contrast *Lloyds Bank plc v Egremont* [1990] 2 FLR 351, CA, where there was a misrepresentation but no agency or notice. Agency and notice are two separate grounds on which the creditor may be affected by the husband's conduct, and if he was acting as the creditor's agent, it is not necessary that the latter should also have notice of the misrepresentation or undue influence: *Bank of Credit and Commerce International SA v Aboody*, at p 972.

[9] The relationship of husband and wife does not of itself give rise to any presumption of undue influence: see ante, p 575.

[10] *Ahmed v Kendrick* [1988] 2 FLR 22, CA. In this case the husband and wife were joint tenants in law and equity. The husband sold the house to the defendant and forged the wife's signature on the transfer. It was held that, whilst this could not convey the legal estate, it severed the husband's joint tenancy in equity so that the spouses now held the property on trust for the wife and the defendant in equal shares. The court held that the decision to the contrary in *Cedar Holdings Ltd v Green* [1981] Ch 129, [1979] 3 All ER 117, CA, could not be regarded as authority since *Williams and Glyn's Bank Ltd v Boland* (supra).

[11] See post, pp 625–628.

[12] See *Price v Price* [1951] P 413 at 420–21, CA; *W v W (No 2)* [1954] P 486 at 515–516, [1954] 2 All ER 829 at 840, CA. She also has a right, within reason, to invite guests into the home: *Jolliffe v Willmett & Co* [1971] 1 All ER 478 at 483 (no right to authorise entry of enquiry agent seeking evidence of husband's adultery 13 years after the wife had left home).

[13] See *Chilton v Chilton* [1952] P 196 at 202, [1952] 1 All ER 1322 at 1325.

does not entitle her to occupy any other property belonging to him and he may obtain an injunction restraining her from entering it even though he has no justification for refusing to cohabit.[14]

If the wife is the sole legal and equitable owner of the matrimonial home, her duty to cohabit with her husband will give him a right at common law to use and occupy it. His right will be forfeited in the same circumstances as the wife's.[15]

The common law position has been of little practical importance since the spouses were given a statutory right to occupy the matrimonial home by the Matrimonial Homes Act of 1967. This Act was extensively amended during the next 15 years and its provisions are now consolidated in the Matrimonial Homes Act of 1983. By section 1(1) of the 1983 Act:

'Where one spouse is entitled to occupy a dwelling house by virtue of a beneficial estate or interest or contract or by virtue of any enactment giving him or her the right to remain in occupation, and the other spouse is not so entitled ... the spouse not so entitled shall have the following ... rights of occupation:

(a) if in occupation, a right not to be evicted or excluded from the dwelling house or any part thereof by the other spouse except with the leave of the court given by an order under this section;

(b) if not in occupation, a right with the leave of the court so given to enter into and occupy the dwelling house.'[16]

'Dwelling house' includes any building or part of a building (for example, a flat) occupied as a dwelling together with any yard, garden, garage or outhouse belonging to it and occupied with it.[17]

If the legal estate is vested in the husband alone but both spouses have a beneficial equitable interest, the subsection would not give the wife a statutory right of occupation because she would have a right to occupy by virtue of her beneficial interest. This would cause difficulties because she would be unable to register her right and thus lose the protection she would otherwise have against a purchaser from the husband. Consequently a spouse who has an equitable interest in a dwelling house or in the proceeds of sale is given a statutory right of occupation provided that he or she has no legal estate in the land either solely or jointly.[18]

It will be seen that section 1(1) applies, for example, if one spouse is a statutory tenant under the Rent Act 1977 or the Housing Act 1988 or a secure tenant under the Housing Act 1985 (because in each case he will be entitled to occupy the house by virtue of a statute) or if he goes into possession as a licensee or under a contract to take a lease or to purchase the freehold. Similarly if the spouses are living in the house of a third person, section 1(1) applies if the arrangement amounts to a contract with one of them (but not both). Hence if they are there, say, by virtue of a contract between the husband and his parents, he could not lawfully exclude

---

[14] *Nanda v Nanda* [1968] P 351, [1967] 3 All ER 401, ante, p 109.

[15] *Shipman v Shipman* [1924] 2 Ch 140 at 146, CA. This right extends to the husband's visitors as well (*Jolliffe v Willmett & Co*, supra) but not to one entering the house for the purpose of annoying the wife: *Weldon v De Bathe* (1884) 14 QBD 339, CA.

[16] A mortgagee's right to possession is to be disregarded in determining whether a spouse is entitled to occupy a dwelling house but this does not give the other spouse any greater rights if the mortgagee exercises his powers to realise his security: s 8(1).

[17] S 10 (1). In *Kinzler v Kinzler* [1985] Fam Law 26, CA, it was held that the whole of a hotel owned by the parties (and not just their living quarters) was the matrimonial home because there was only one door and one kitchen.

[18] S 1(11). For protection against a purchaser, see infra.

the wife although his parents could terminate her licence. But if one spouse (say, the husband) is a lessee or his right is contractual, the wife's position is necessarily more precarious because, if the husband's own breach of covenant or contract (for example, failing to pay rent or the purchase price) entitles the legal owner to recover possession, the wife's right will fall with the husband's.

The Act does not apply to any house which has never been the spouses' matrimonial home.[19] Consequently, a wife has no right to occupy any premises into which the husband has moved after leaving her. 'Matrimonial home' is not defined but presumably includes any house in which the parties have lived together as husband and wife.[20] The statutory rights continue only so long as the marriage subsists and will come to an end on the other spouse's death or on the dissolution or annulment of the marriage. But in the event of a matrimonial dispute or estrangement the court may order that the rights shall continue after the termination of the marriage (whether by death or a court order).[1] It may be advisable to seek such an order as the only way of protecting the wife if the home cannot be made the subject of a property adjustment order.[2]

The rights given by the Act are obviously purely personal. Common sense dictates that a spouse should be able to invite guests to come into the house (or that part of it which he is occupying), but it is very doubtful whether the right extends to permitting him to take in a lodger.[3]

The spouse's rights against third persons

If the wife is in sole occupation of the matrimonial home following a separation, the husband might attempt to evict her and realise his capital by selling the house to another. A series of cases decided between 1952 and 1965 had laid down the rule that a deserted wife could enforce her common law right to remain in the matrimonial home (of which her husband was the beneficial owner) not only against him but also against anyone claiming through him other than a bona fide purchaser for value of a legal or equitable estate or interest without notice of her claim. The validity of this so-called 'deserted wife's equity' was eventually considered by the House of Lords in *National Provincial Bank Ltd v Ainsworth*.[4] The husband had deserted his wife (the respondent) and left her and their children in the matrimonial home. He then conveyed the house to a company in which he

---

[19] S 1(10). Cf *Collins v Collins* (1973) 4 Fam Law 133, CA (separate flat in house owned by wife not part of matrimonial home).

[20] Thus it would not include a house in which the spouses had lived together before marriage because it would not have been their *matrimonial* home. But if they had been engaged to be married, the Law Reform (Miscellaneous Provisions) Act 1970, s 2(1), would appear to bring the Matrimonial Homes Act into play: see ante, pp 22–23.

[1] Ss 1(10) and 2(4). It is not clear what is meant by the expressions 'matrimonial dispute or estrangement': presumably they cover litigation and separation.

[2] See post, p 737.

[3] See further generally Crane *The Matrimonial Homes Act 1967* 32 Conv 148; Stone 31 MLR 305; Kahn-Freund *Recent Legislation on Matrimonial Property* 33 MLR 601, particularly at pp 609 et seq. For changes proposed by the Law Commission in 1978, see Law Com No 86, Book Two.

[4] [1965] AC 1175, [1965] 2 All ER 472, HL. For a detailed discussion of this decision, see Crane *After the Deserted Wife's Licence* 29 Conv 254 and 464. See also Bailey [1965] CLJ 216.

had a controlling interest and which in turn charged it to the appellant bank to secure a loan. This was not repaid and the bank, as mortgagee, claimed possession of the property charged. The wife set up her 'deserted wife's equity' but it was unanimously held that her defence must fail. The only case in which the wife's equity will avail her is where the sale by the husband is a completely sham transaction designed to enable him to obtain possession. Four of the members of the House of Lords in *Ainsworth's* case[5] considered that the earlier case of *Ferris v Weaven*[6] could still be justified on its special facts. In that case the husband, having deserted his wife and left her in the matrimonial home, sold the house to the plaintiff, his brother-in-law, for the sum of £30 which was never paid. The sole purpose of this conveyance was to enable the husband, who could not personally have obtained possession in the circumstances, to do so through the purchaser. It was held that the plaintiff could have no greater right than the husband and his claim must fail. The decision may still be of importance if the wife has not registered her right of occupation under the Matrimonial Homes Act,[7] although in many cases she could have the sale set aside as a transaction intended to defeat her claim for financial relief.[8]

The real problem is to balance the claims of the deserted wife against those of the husband's purchaser or (as is usually the case) his creditors either acting through his trustee in bankruptcy or seeking to realise their own security as mortgagees of the house in which the wife is living. Looked at from the conveyancing point of view, there are two fatal objections to the 'deserted wife's equity'. In the first place the wife's rights against the purchaser can clearly be no greater than they are against the husband himself. As against him she would lose her common law right to remain in the house if, for example, she were to commit adultery or the husband were to offer her suitable alternative accommodation. It is therefore transient and determinable and lacks the qualities of being definable, identifiable, permanent and stable which are essential if it is to be regarded as a right in property capable of binding the land in the hands of subsequent purchasers.[9] In the second place it must be possible for the prospective purchaser to discover precisely what rights exist in the land and these are of such a highly personal nature, known only to the spouses themselves, that he would be in an impossible position when he made enquiries.[10]

One of the main reasons for enacting the Matrimonial Homes Act of 1967 was to overcome these difficulties. For the sake of convenience in the following discussion it will again be assumed that the legal and beneficial interest in the home is vested in the husband to the exclusion of the wife,

---

[5] Lord Hodson (with whom Lord Guest concurred) at 1223 and 479; Lord Upjohn ('it may possibly be justified') at 1240 and 489; Lord Wilberforce at 1258 and 501, respectively.
[6] [1952] 2 All ER 233 (although the ratio decidendi is no longer good law). Megarry J concluded that the case was correctly decided on its facts in *Miles v Bull* [1969] 1 QB 258, [1968] 3 All ER 632, but as he pointed out (at 264 and 636, respectively) the fact that the price is low or not paid in full does not necessarily mean that the transaction is a sham. See further *Miles v Bull (No 2)* [1969] 3 All ER 1585.
[7] See infra.
[8] See post, p 801. Such an attempt failed in *Ainsworth's* case because the bank was a bona fide purchaser for value without notice of the husband's intention.
[9] *National Provincial Bank Ltd v Ainsworth* [1965] AC 1175, at 1224, 1233–1234, and 1248–1250, [1965] 2 All ER 472, at 479–480, 485–486, and 494–495, HL.
[10] Ibid, at 1234 and 1250, and 486 and 495–496, respectively.

but it must be remembered that exactly the same principles apply if it is vested in the wife to the exclusion of the husband. The way the Act seeks to protect both the wife and the purchaser is by providing that her right to occupy the matrimonial home (whether or not a court order has been made) shall be a charge on the husband's estate or interest in the property. The charge takes effect on the husband's acquisition of the property, the date of the marriage, or the commencement of the 1967 Act (1st January 1968) whichever last happens. It terminates on the husband's death or the dissolution or annulment of the marriage unless, in the event of a matrimonial dispute or estrangement, the court has previously made an order that it shall continue.[11]

If the right of occupation is a charge on a legal estate, it is registrable as a Class F land charge under the Land Charges Act 1972 or, in the case of registered land, by notice under the Land Registration Act 1925.[12] If the husband has only an equitable interest or is in occupation under, say, an agreement to lease (which will give him an equitable lease) or any other contract, the wife cannot register her charge for it is a charge on the husband's interest, not on the legal owner's estate. This could work injustice if the husband was a sole beneficiary under a trust of the house; in those circumstances, therefore, the wife can register her right of occupation against the trustees' estate or interest.[13] This could occur, for example, if the husband was the sole beneficiary under a deceased owner's will and the legal estate was still vested in the executors; by registering her right the wife will protect herself if they sell the house under their powers as personal representatives.

As a wife out of occupation may need even greater protection than a wife physically in the house (for example, if she has been constructively deserted), her charge may be registered even though she has not yet been given leave by the court to enter and occupy.[14]

The charge will bind any person deriving title under the husband except that it will be void against any purchaser of the land or any interest in it for value unless it is registered before completion.[15]

The wife is entitled to have only one charge registered under the Act. Consequently, if the spouses have two homes (for example, a town flat and a country cottage), she must make up her mind which occupation right she will register. If, after registering one, she registers another, the first registration must be cancelled.[16] Registration must also be cancelled if the court terminates the wife's right of occupation or when the marriage comes to an end unless the court has ordered that her right shall continue.[17] The wife

---

[11] Matrimonial Homes Act 1983, s 2(1) and (4).
[12] Ibid, s 2(8), (9), (11); Land Charges Act 1972, s 2(7).
[13] Ibid, s 2(2). There must be no one (born or unborn) other than the spouses who is or could be a beneficiary under the trust except under the potential exercise of a general power of appointment by either or both of the spouses alone: ibid, s 2(3).
[14] *Watts v Waller* [1973] QB 153, [1972] 3 All ER 257, CA. If she subsequently makes an unsuccessful application for leave, the registration will be cancelled.
[15] Land Charges Act 1972, ss 4(8) and 17(1). This also applies to anyone acquiring the husband's estate by surrender: Matrimonial Homes Act 1983, s 2(6).
[16] Matrimonial Homes Act 1983, s 3.
[17] Ibid, s 5. If the wife has an order continuing her right of occupation after the termination of the marriage, she must renew her registration (or register her charge if it was not registered before).

may release her right in whole or in part in writing and may agree in writing that another charge or interest shall take priority over it. If the charge is registered, the normal conveyancing procedure is for the wife to deliver to the purchaser on completion an application for the cancellation of the registration.[18]

In practice the wife has more to fear from a mortgagee than from a purchaser of the whole of the husband's estate. If he tries to sell the matrimonial home, she will usually be put on her guard by potential buyers' coming to view the premises; but if he mortgages the house to secure his overdraft, she may know nothing about the transaction until the bank tries to enforce its security. Ex hypothesi a solicitor will be acting for a husband alone when the matrimonial home is bought so there will be no one to advise her to register her right of occupation and in any event she will not contemplate the necessity of protecting her interest. When the marriage does break down, the property may already be mortgaged and her registration will come too late if she cannot pay the mortgage instalments and arrears herself. Clearly the Act will give effective protection to the wife only when an automatic registration of her right of occupation becomes a common practice.[19]

Decided cases have also shown that the Act can operate unfairly on the husband. The wife may not have told him that she has registered a charge and he may know nothing about it.[20] Again, a spiteful wife may refuse to have the registration cancelled even when the husband offers her other accommodation which it is unreasonable for her to refuse. The house may then become a useless asset which he can sell only after litigation between the spouses. In *Wroth v Tyler*,[1] for example, the wife, who was living in the matrimonial home with the husband, stood by whilst he was negotiating its sale and then registered her charge immediately the contract was entered into. As a result he was unable to make title and, because of the sharp increase in the price of houses at the time, the damages awarded against him for breach of contract probably caused him to become bankrupt.

The position of one who has purchased the premises in ignorance of the registration of the wife's charge is also not clear. By section 2(5) of the Act any registered order made under section 1 has the same effect against a person deriving title under the husband as it has against the husband himself. Hence if the wife has obtained an order prohibiting the husband from entering the home, this will likewise prohibit the purchaser from entering. The subsection then goes on to provide that subsections (2) to (8) of section 1 'shall apply in relation to any person deriving title under the [husband] ... and affected by the charge as they apply in relation to the [husband]'. Consequently, if no order has been obtained under the Act, the

---

[18] Ibid, ss 4 and 6.
[19] In which case the sheer bulk of registrations might make the system unworkable. See further Palley *Wives, Creditors and the Matrimonial Home* 20 NILQ 132.
[20] As in *Watts v Waller* (supra). But as the purpose of the Act is to protect rights of occupation, registration of a charge for any other purpose (eg to force a spouse wishing to sell the house to apply to the court and thus enable it to freeze the proceeds of sale) is an improper use of the Act and the court will set the charge aside: *Barnett v Hassett* [1982] 1 All ER 80.
[1] [1974] Ch 30, [1973] 1 All ER 897. See further Cretney 117 Sol Jo 475; Barnsley *Conveying the Matrimonial Home* Current Legal Problems, 1974, 76; Hayton *The Femme Fatale in Conveyancing Practice* 38 Conv 110.

purchaser may seek to evict the wife. As we have seen,[2] section 1(3) enjoins the court to take into account inter alia the spouses' needs and financial resources and all the circumstances of the case when deciding what order to make. On the face of it, in the situation we are considering, this subsection and section 2(5) read together require the court to consider the wife's *and the purchaser's* needs and resources, and the purchaser's position clearly comes within 'the circumstances of the case'. This argument was accepted by the majority of the Court of Appeal in *Kashmir Kaur v Gill*.[3] The wife, who had a young child and had been driven out of the matrimonial home by the husband's conduct, registered her right of occupation before the husband sold the house to the respondent, who was blind. Unfortunately the respondent's solicitors permitted him to complete the sale in ignorance of the registration, and the purchase money was entirely used in paying off two mortgages on the house. In the wife's proceedings for an order declaring her right to occupy the house and prohibiting the respondent from doing so, the county court judge held that he was entitled to consider the latter's position and in his discretion found in his favour. On the wife's appeal the majority of the Court of Appeal held that he had been correct to do so. Until the question is considered by the House of Lords this decision is binding. In a vigorous dissenting judgment, however, Sir Denys Buckley was of the opinion that, as a purchaser can be in no better position than the husband, the question the court must consider is whether the court would give the wife occupation against *him* and the purchaser's circumstances are therefore irrelevant. It would clearly frustrate the policy of the Act if a wife's unassailable claim against her husband could be defeated by his selling the house, however pitiful the purchaser's position might be. This is obviously right: moreover it is submitted that the outcome desired by Sir Denys Buckley can be achieved without doing violence to the language of the Act. One—and arguably the most compelling—circumstance is that the purchaser had constructive notice of the wife's rights[4] and consequently he should be able to oust her only if the other circumstances are most exceptional. This might occur if, for example, the purchaser (like the respondent in *Kashmir Kaur v Gill*) had acted in good faith and had a very strong claim to occupy the premises whilst the wife (unlike the wife in that case) had no particular need to stay there and had the financial resources to acquire other suitable accommodation.

2. UNMARRIED COHABITANTS' RIGHT TO OCCUPY THE HOME

As in the case of spouses, if both cohabitants have a legal or equitable interest in their home, each will have a right to occupy it. Unlike spouses, however, neither of them has a common law right to occupy the other's property and the provisions of the Matrimonial Homes Act do not apply to them.[5] Consequently if ownership is vested in one of them alone, the other's right to occupy the property must be found by reference to the

---

[2] Ante, pp 169–171.
[3] [1988] Fam 110, [1988] 2 All ER 288, CA.
[4] He would of course have a cause of action against his solicitor if the latter had been negligent.
[5] Unless they have been engaged to be married: see ante, p 614, n 20.

general law of property. In the following discussion we shall again assume for the purpose of illustration that the property is vested in the man.[6]

Contractual licence

If the woman has given up some existing right or suffered some other detriment to go and live with the man, it may be possible to regard this as consideration and thus give the woman a contractual licence. An illustration of this principle is to be seen in *Tanner v Tanner*.[7] The plaintiff bought a house for the defendant and their twin daughters and the defendant surrendered a rent-controlled tenancy to move into it. When the plaintiff later claimed possession of the house, it was held that, as the defendant had furnished consideration by giving up the security of her flat, the licence was a contractual one.

The facts of *Tanner v Tanner* were unusual in that the parties never lived in the house together. The problem more likely to arise is that facing a woman who, having set up home with a man in property belonging to him, is ordered to leave when their relationship breaks down. Even if she suffered a detriment, for example by giving up a secure tenancy like the defendant in *Tanner v Tanner*, it would usually be impossible to spell out any promise by the man that she could continue to reside in the house if he no longer wished to live with her. Any such undertaking is more likely to be given at the point of breakdown if the man leaves, but unless the woman suffers some fresh detriment (such as a reciprocal undertaking to pay rent or other outgoings), any consideration would be past and therefore ineffective to establish a contract.

Even if it is possible to spell out a contractual licence, it may well be difficult to infer the period for which the parties intended that the woman should be entitled to stay in the premises for, like spouses, cohabitants are apt not to contemplate the breakdown of their relationship. In *Tanner v Tanner* the Court of Appeal took the view that the defendant had a licence to remain in the house so long as the parties' children were of school age and it was reasonably required as a home for them and their mother. There is necessarily something arbitrary about terminating the licence when the children reached the age of 16 because they might continue in full-time education after that, but it was reasonable to imply that it should cease, say, if their mother married. The woman is likely to be less favourably treated if the children of the owner of the property are not living with her. In *Chandler v Kerley*[8] the defendant and her husband had sold their former matrimonial home to the plaintiff on the understanding that the defendant (who proposed to marry the plaintiff after her divorce) would continue to live there with him and the two children of her marriage. The relationship between the parties broke down very shortly afterwards and the plaintiff sought possession of the house. The Court of Appeal held that he could not have intended to assume the burden of housing the defendant and

---

[6] See generally Murphy and Clark op cit pp 102–123 and ch 7.
[7] [1975] 3 All ER 776, CA. Contrast *Horrocks v Forray* [1976] 1 All ER 737, CA.
[8] [1978] 2 All ER 942, CA. It is not clear what the consideration for the licence was; presumably it was the defendant's taking less than half the proceeds of sale because she was to continue to live in the house.

another man's children indefinitely and that the licence was terminable on her being given 12 months' notice which would enable her to find other accommodation.

There could be cases where the inference is that the woman should be permitted to stay in the property for life. The court should be slow to make such an order, however, because there is a danger that this could make her a tenant for life.[9] This would give her the right to sell the house provided that she complied with the provisions of the Settled Land Act 1925, which the parties could scarcely have contemplated.

Licence by estoppel

By analogy with proprietary estoppel, one party may claim a licence if the other has led her to believe (or has acquiesced in her belief) that she has, or will be given, permission to remain in the house and she acts to her detriment in reliance on this belief. A classic example of a licence of this sort is to be found in *Greasley v Cooke*.[10] The defendant had entered the service of a family as a maid. Later she and one of the sons cohabited in the family house for nearly 30 years; she looked after the family as a whole and in particular cared for the daughter who was mentally ill. She received no payment and asked for none because the members of the family had led her to believe that she would be entitled to remain in the house as long as she wished. In those circumstances, it was held that she should be able to do so and the plaintiffs' action for possession failed. As in other cases of proprietary estoppel it must be shown that the woman acted in reliance on the belief that she was to have a licence; the fact that she goes to live with the owner of the property and permits herself to become pregnant will not of itself give her any right to remain there.[11]

As the cases cited above show, the extent of the resulting equity is to make good the expectations which the owner has encouraged, insofar as fairness between the parties permits this to be done.[12]

Constructive trust

In one case, *Ungurian v Lesnoff*,[13] it was held that the facts established a trust rather than a licence. The defendant had left Poland and abandoned her career there in reliance on the parties' common intention that the plaintiff would buy a house where she could live with her children. In these circumstances Vinelott J held that full effect would not be given to this intention by inferring an irrevocable licence to occupy the house but that the plaintiff held it on trust to permit her to live there for the rest of her life.[14] While this must turn on the inference that the court drew from the parties' conduct, it is not immediately obvious why the judge reached this

[9] See *Dodsworth v Dodsworth* (1973) 228 Estates Gazette 1115, CA. But see post, p 621, n 17.
[10] [1980] 3 All ER 710, CA. See also *Maharaj v Chand* [1986] AC 898, [1986] 3 All ER 107, PC.
[11] *Coombes v Smith* [1986] 1 WLR 808.
[12] See *Re Basham* [1987] 1 All ER 405 at 417; Moriarty *Licences and Land Law* 100 LQR 376.
[13] [1990] Ch 206. See further ante, p 595.
[14] Unless and until the plaintiff sold the property with the defendant's consent and bought another residence for her in substitution for it.

conclusion for which he gave no reason. As we shall see, however, the distinction may be vital if the owner later sells the property without the occupant's consent.

Following two earlier decisions of the Court of Appeal,[15] Vinelott J went on to hold that, as the defendant was entitled to possession of the property for life, the land was limited in trust by way of succession and thus became settled land.[16] This gave her a life interest so that, as tenant for life, she could call for the legal estate and dispose of it under the powers conferred by the Settled Land Act 1925. This could scarcely have been contemplated by the parties and it is anomalous that a person who apparently has no more than a right to occupy the land should have greater powers in this respect than one who owns an undivided share. For this reason the court should be slow to reach such a conclusion.[17]

Bare licence

In other cases the woman will find herself no more than a bare licensee and the owner may recover possession of the premises after giving her reasonable notice to quit.[18] The period given must of course be sufficient to enable her to find accommodation for herself and any children living with her.

Settlement under the Children Act

Even though a cohabitant has only a bare licence or other limited right to remain in the parties' former home, she may be able to obtain an order under the Children Act 1989[19] enabling her to stay there if she has a child or children of whom the other is the father. In an appropriate case the court could order the parties' former home to be held on trust for the father subject to the mother's right to reside there until, say, all the children have completed their full-time education,[20] or even transfer it to her outright.[1]

Rights against third persons

Even though the owner of the parties' home or former home cannot evict the other party, the latter's position may become precarious if the former dies or disposes of the property.

If the occupant holds under a trust, a purchaser will be bound by her right of occupation in the same circumstances as he would be bound by a beneficial interest in the property itself, and her presence there will necessarily give him constructive notice of her rights.[2] In particular a volunteer

---

[15] *Bannister v Bannister* [1948] 2 All ER 133, CA; *Binions v Evans* [1972] Ch 359, [1972] 2 All ER 70, CA.

[16] By virtue of the Settled Land Act 1925, s 1(1)(i).

[17] See *Dodsworth v Dodsworth* (1973) 228 Estates Gazette 1115, CA. In *Binions v Evans* (supra) the court followed *Bannister v Bannister* (supra) with reluctance and the House of Lords may overrule these cases in the future.

[18] As in *Horrocks v Forray* [1976] 1 All ER 737, CA.

[19] Sch 1, para 1(2)(d). See post, p 697.

[20] Or 'until further order' to take account of the possibility of the mother's marrying or cohabiting with another man.

[1] As in *K v K (Minors: Property Transfer)* [1992] 2 All ER 727, CA. See ante, p 583.

[2] See ante, pp 606–611.

(for example, a devisee of the home) will take subject to them. A contractual licence, on the other hand, confers only a personal right on the licensee.[3] Consequently a cohabitant who has such a licence could enforce it against the other party's personal representatives, who are bound by his contractual obligations,[4] but not against a purchaser (even though he took with notice of it) unless the circumstances of the purchase make him a constructive trustee. A constructive trust will not be imposed in reliance on slender material:[5] the purchaser must have behaved in such a way as to make it unconscionable to permit him to deny the occupant's rights, for example by giving an express assurance that they would be respected[6] or paying a lower price because the land was subject to them.[7] The threat of litigation may be sufficient to deter a prospective purchaser but a vendor anxious to dispose of the property at the highest price is unlikely to impose terms which would create a trust.

A licence by estoppel may put the occupant in a stronger position because there is authority for the proposition that an estoppel binds the licensor's successors in title.[8] The position, however, is not clear. At the most, it is submitted, the requirement that the owner should satisfy the expectations raised by his conduct makes him in effect a constructive trustee; on the other hand the same facts could give rise to a contractual obligation or an estoppel and it would be anomalous if a person relying on the latter were in a stronger position than one given an express promise that she could remain in occupation.

3. EXCLUDING A PARTY FROM OCCUPATION

If, for example, one spouse or unmarried cohabitant is physically assaulting the other or their children, the latter's right to occupy the home will be valueless for she (or he) will not be able to enjoy it in any real sense so long as the assailant is there. Consequently, it may be necessary for the victim to seek an order excluding the other. The relevant law is discussed in chapter 5.[9]

4. USE OF FURNITURE

If the furniture in the parties' home is owned solely by, say, the husband or male cohabitant, prima facie he has the right to remove it from the home or dispose of it. In the case of a married couple this must be subject to the husband's common law duty to provide the wife with a home[10]

---

[3] *Ashburn Anstalt v Arnold* [1989] Ch 1, [1988] 2 All ER 147, CA.
[4] This was apparently assumed in *Horrocks v Forray* (supra) although the executors' claim for possession succeeded because it was held that the defendant did not have a contractual licence.
[5] *Ashburn Anstalt v Arnold* (supra) at 26 and 167 respectively.
[6] As in *Lyus v Prowsa* [1982] 2 All ER 953. The fact that the land is transferred expressly subject to the occupant's rights does not of itself create a constructive trust because this merely gives the transferee notice of their existence.
[7] As in *Binions v Evans* (supra).
[8] See Megarry and Wade *Real Property* (5th Edn) 806–808; Martin [1980] Conv 207; Hill 51 MLR 226.
[9] See ante, pp 160–177.
[10] See ante, p 612.

which, it is submitted, must include furniture and not just an empty house. In the only reported case dealing with the subject, *W v W*,[11] the furniture belonged partly to the husband and partly to the wife. After leaving his wife the husband claimed his portion of the goods, which included a table and chairs and the matrimonial bed. It was held that he was entitled to take his property because the wife could be expected to replace it in time, but Devlin J stated that he would not have been prepared to make this order if the husband had been acting vindictively or, in any case, if the wife would have been left with nothing but bare boards.

If the wife loses her right to be maintained at common law (for example, by committing adultery), she appears to have no claim on the husband's furniture and her sole remedy lies in a property adjustment order in matrimonial proceedings. The husband can lay no claim to the wife's furniture at all, as she is under no common law duty to maintain him. Unmarried cohabitants certainly have no right to each other's property. If, therefore, all the furniture belongs to the man and he manages to remove it, the woman's right to remain in their former home may prove to be valueless.

C. Insolvency and the matrimonial home

1. MORTGAGES AND CHARGES

If a spouse or unmarried cohabitant who is the sole legal owner of the matrimonial or quasi-matrimonial home mortgages it and later fails to pay the mortgage instalments, the mortgagee may wish to obtain vacant possession in order to realise his security. Even though the mortgagor has no defence to the claim, his or her spouse or partner may be protected if she or he did not concur in the mortgage, in which case of course the mortgagor will be able to remain in occupation as well. Again for the purpose of illustration it will be assumed that legal ownership is vested in the husband or male cohabitant.

We have already considered the circumstances in which a mortgagee will take subject to any beneficial interest which the wife or cohabitant has in the property.[12] Even if she has no such interest, a wife will be able to enforce her rights of occupation under the Matrimonial Homes Act provided that she registered them before the mortgage was taken.[13] In most cases this will be valueless because she will not have registered her rights if the home was mortgaged before the spouses went into possession and in practice she is unlikely to have done so even if she was in occupation when the husband charged the property. An unmarried cohabitant's position will similarly depend on whether a purchaser is bound by such right of occupation as she has.[14]

If a wife's or cohabitant's beneficial interest takes priority over a mortgage, the mortgagee, as a person interested, may bring proceedings to enforce

---

[11] [1951] 2 TLR 1135.

[12] See ante, pp 605–612.

[13] See ante, p 616. For the power to tack mortgages, see the Matrimonial Homes Act 1983, s 2(10).

[14] See ante, pp 621–622.

the trust for sale under section 30 of the Law of Property Act. On principle, the mortgagee should have no greater right than the husband. Hence if the wife and children are occupying the house as the family home, the primary object of the trust will still be in existence and the court should not order a sale. Conversely, it will normally do so if the spouses have separated and the wife is living in the house alone.[15] A more difficult problem arises if the spouses are living there together without children. Although the house will still be the family home, the right of the mortgagee to enforce his security cannot be entirely ignored, and there seems little justification for permitting the wife to remain when the husband has no defence against a claim for possession, particularly if the mortgagee could take bankruptcy proceedings when the court would almost certainly order the house to be sold.[16] Similar considerations would apply if the mortgagee brought proceedings to terminate the wife's or cohabitant's right of occupation.[17]

If the mortgagee is aware of the wife's or cohabitant's rights, he will insist on her agreeing that the charge shall take priority over them, and it would be prudent for him to give himself the maximum protection by insisting on her concurring in the mortgage in any event. Even if she does so, a wife (as distinct from an unmarried cohabitant) is still given a degree of protection by the Matrimonial Homes Act. This provides that, if a spouse entitled under the Act to occupy the whole or part of the matrimonial home makes any payment or tender in respect of rent, mortgage payments or other outgoings affecting the home, this shall be as effective as though it were made by the owner.[18] If the mortgagee brings proceedings to enforce his security, the court may stay or suspend the execution of any order made if the mortgagor is likely to be able to pay all sums due within a reasonable time.[19] The wife is given further protection by the requirement that the mortgagee must serve her with notice of proceedings if her right of occupation is registered; in any event she is generally entitled to be made a party if the court is satisfied that she may be expected to make such payments (or do anything else in satisfaction of the mortgagor's obligations) as might affect the outcome of the proceedings.[20] The difficulty is that the mortgagee is not bound to give her notice of the husband's default. As a result such massive arrears may have accumulated before she gets to hear of them that she will find it impossible to pay them off within a reasonable time even though she might have been able to pay each instalment as it fell due.

The provisions mentioned in the last paragraph do not apply to an unmarried cohabitant whose only hope of preserving her right would be to seek an agreement with the mortgagee that she should pay off the arrears.

---

[15] See ante, p 602.
[16] See post, pp 627–628.
[17] Cf ante, pp 614–618 and 621–622.
[18] Section 1(5).
[19] Administration of Justice Act 1970, s 36; Administration of Justice Act 1973, s 8; *Halifax Building Society v Clark* [1973] Ch 307, [1973] 2 All ER 33, CA; *Governor & Co of the Bank of Scotland v Grimes* [1985] QB 1179, [1985] 2 All ER 254, CA.
[20] Matrimonial Homes Act 1983, s 8(2)–(5).

Charging orders

If a judgment creditor obtains a charging order, this will have the same effect as an equitable charge created by the judgment debtor.[1] If it is imposed on the matrimonial home in which the wife has a beneficial interest, the judgment creditor will have to bring proceedings under section 30 like any other chargee and the court must apply the same criteria when deciding whether to order a sale. But the court's power to make a charging order is discretionary, and if the marriage has broken down and the wife is bringing divorce or other matrimonial proceedings, she may try to frustrate the judgment creditor by seeking to have the home transferred to her free of the charge by means of a property adjustment order under section 24 of the Matrimonial Causes Act 1973.[2] If the charging order has been made absolute before she commences matrimonial proceedings, the creditor's right to the order will prevail and any protection the wife has will be in section 30 proceedings. If she has already petitioned, the court should make the charging order absolute if it appears that after a sale enough money would be left to provide the wife and children with adequate alternative accommodation; if this is not so, the application should be transferred to the Family Division so that the same court can consider the position of both the wife and the judgment creditor. Normally the latter's right should not be extinguished completely: the most the court should do is impose a condition that the order should not be enforced so long as the wife is living in the house with children in full-time education.[3]

2. BANKRUPTCY

If the matrimonial home forms part of the assets of a bankrupt, his interest in it will vest in the trustee in bankruptcy immediately his appointment takes effect.[4] Hence if the bankrupt and his (or her) spouse or cohabitant are tenants in common,[5] the latter will retain her equitable share which will not be available for the other's creditors. Consequently, in bankruptcy the parties' interests in property will be of paramount importance.

The law relating to bankruptcy underwent extensive changes following the report of the Cork Committee and is now governed by the Insolvency Act 1986.[6]

---

[1] Charging Orders Act 1979, s 3(4).

[2] See post, p 736.

[3] Despite the court's reluctance to make a *Mesher* order: see post, pp 787–788. See *Harman v Glencross* [1986] Fam 81, [1986] 1 All ER 545, CA, and contrast *First National Securities Ltd v Hegerty* [1985] QB 850, [1984] 3 All ER 641, CA, where the court upheld a charging order absolute. See also Brown 55 MLR 284.

[4] Some tenancies protected by statute will not vest in the trustee unless he serves a notice on the bankrupt (as he might do, for example, if the tenancy had a saleable value): Insolvency Act 1986, ss 283(3A) and 308A (added by the Housing Act 1988, s 117).

[5] If they are equitable joint tenants, the joint tenancy will be severed when the property vests in the trustee and the trustee and the other party will become equitable tenants in common in equal shares.

[6] See the Report of the Review Committee on Insolvency Law and Practice (the Cork Committee), 1982, Cmnd 8558; Miller *The Family Home and the Insolvency Act 1985* [1986] Conv 391. The old law, governed by the Bankruptcy Act 1914, applies if the bankruptcy petition was presented before 29th December 1986.

Voidable transactions

The trustee may wish to have the spouse's or cohabitant's interest set aside under section 339 or 423 of the Insolvency Act, the details of which have already been discussed.[7] Homes recently purchased may well be caught by section 339. If within the period of two years preceding the presentation of the bankruptcy petition the husband had bought the matrimonial home with his own money and had it conveyed into the spouses' joint names as equitable beneficial owners, the trustee may claim the wife's beneficial interest as one obtained in a transaction at an undervalue. The same result would follow if the wife had contributed significantly less than the value of her equitable share or, in similar circumstances, if the house had been purchased more than two years but less than five years before the petition and the husband was then insolvent.

These provisions would also apply if the parties were not married.

Protection of members of the bankrupt's family

Whether the bankrupt (who, for the sake of example, will be assumed to be the husband) is the sole beneficial owner of the matrimonial home or has a limited beneficial interest, the trustee in bankruptcy will normally wish to sell it to increase the assets available for the creditors. This will bring their interests into direct conflict with those of the members of the bankrupt's family, who will wish to retain the property as a family home.

Section 336 of the Insolvency Act protects the occupation rights of the bankrupt's spouse. No rights of occupation under the Matrimonial Homes Act may be acquired in the period between the presentation of the petition and vesting of the bankrupt's property in the trustee, so that if the bankrupt marries during that period his wife will have no statutory rights. But existing rights of occupation under the Act will continue in force and bind the trustee, whether or not they are registered. The trustee has the same power to apply to the court to have these rights terminated, suspended or restricted as the husband would have had.[8] It will be observed that these provisions do not apply to an unmarried cohabitant.

Children are given protection by section 337, which applies when the bankrupt is entitled to occupy a dwelling house[9] by virtue of any estate or interest. If any person under the age of 18, who had his home with the bankrupt when the bankruptcy petition was presented *and* when the bankruptcy order was made, had at any time occupied that house with the bankrupt, the latter has the same rights of occupation against the trustee as a spouse under the Matrimonial Homes Act and cannot be evicted from the house without the leave of the court.[10] This protection is additional to that given by section 336 and is of importance if the children are living with the bankrupt but not with his wife (for example, because she is dead or the spouses are divorced) or if the mother is living with the bankrupt but is not married to him.

If the bankrupt and his spouse or former spouse are trustees for sale of a dwelling house, the trustee in bankruptcy may apply to the court for an

---

[7] See ante, pp 578–580.
[8] Insolvency Act 1986, s 336(1), (2).
[9] This is defined as in the Matrimonial Homes Act (ante, p 613): ibid, s 385(1).
[10] Ibid, s 337(1)–(4). Note that the children need not be the bankrupt's own children.

order to sell the property under section 30 of the Law of Property Act. Alternatively he may apply to have the occupation rights of the bankrupt's spouse or former spouse terminated. In either case the court must make such order as it thinks just and reasonable 'having regard to the interests of the creditors, to the conduct of the spouse or former spouse so far as contributing to the bankruptcy,[11] to the needs and financial resources of [that person], to the needs of any children and to all the circumstances of the case other than the needs of the bankrupt'.[12] If the application is made to terminate the bankrupt's own rights of occupation given by section 337, regard must be had to 'the interests of the creditors, the bankrupt's financial resources, the needs of the children and all the circumstances of the case other than the needs of the bankrupt'.[13] The court may make any order that it could make under section 1 of the Matrimonial Homes Act and so could permit the bankrupt to remain in occupation if he paid an occupation rent or other outgoings.[14] In either case, if the application is made more than a year after the property vested in the trustee, it is to be assumed that the creditors' interests outweigh all other considerations unless the circumstances are exceptional.[15]

In the absence of any reported cases it is difficult to predict how the courts will exercise their discretion if an application is made during the first year of the bankruptcy. The prime need of the wife and children is the provision of a home, and the different approach the court is required to make before and after this period implies that during the first year it should give much greater weight to the interests of the bankrupt's family than has been the practice in the past. Insolvency practitioners may well delay making any application under either section for a year so as to be able to take advantage of the more favourable provisions. This will effectively give the bankrupt and his spouse or partner a year in which to find other accommodation. After this period the Act gives statutory effect to the position under the old law when the creditors would always prevail unless the circumstances were exceptional.[16] The fact that the family will be rendered homeless is an inevitable consequence of the sale and is not exceptional:[17] and whilst the bankrupt or his wife would not be ordered to surrender possession until they had had reasonable time to make other arrangements,[18] there is only one reported case in which a sale was deferred for a longer period. In *Re Holliday*[19] the husband and wife were beneficial joint tenants of the matrimonial home. The husband presented a petition in his own bankruptcy to frustrate the wife's application for a property

---

[11] Eg her irresponsible prodigality, having regard to the bankrupt's financial position.

[12] Insolvency Act 1986, s 336(4).

[13] Ibid, s 337(5).

[14] The payment of outgoings will not give him any proprietary interest in the property: ibid, s 338.

[15] Ibid, ss 336(5) and 337(6).

[16] *Re Lowrie* [1981] 3 All ER 353, CA; *Re Citro* [1991] Ch 142, [1990] 3 All ER 952, CA; *Re Gorman* [1990] 1 All ER 717. See further Palley *Wives, Creditors and the Matrimonial Home* 20 NILQ 132; Hand *Bankruptcy and the Family Home* [1983] Conv 219; Miller 119 Sol Jo 582; Gravells 5 OJLS 132; Brown 55 MLR 284.

[17] *Re Lowrie* (supra) at 356.

[18] *Re Turner* [1975] 1 All ER 5; *Re McCarthy* [1975] 2 All ER 857. But immediate possession might be given to the trustee eg if the spouse was being obstructive: *Re McCarthy* at 859.

[19] [1981] Ch 405, [1980] 3 All ER 385, CA.

transfer order in divorce proceedings, and there was no evidence that any of his creditors would have petitioned. If an immediate sale had been ordered, the wife was unlikely to have been able to find alternative accommodation for herself and her three children in the neighbourhood so that their education would have been upset, and in the particular circumstances of the case a postponement would not have worked undue hardship on the creditors. The Court of Appeal held that in these exceptional circumstances 'the voice of the wife seeking to preserve a home for herself and the children ought in equity to prevail' and ordered that the house should not be sold for five years. There can be few cases in which creditors will not be prejudiced by a delay of more than a few months; consequently, if the trustee applies for an order after the first year, the court is likely to order an immediate sale unless the welfare of the children makes it imperative that they should stay in the matrimonial home, for example because they have reached a critical stage in their education.[20]

D. Statutory protection of leasehold property

The owners of many homes hold them on a lease (usually on a weekly, monthly or quarterly tenancy) and are given security of tenure principally by the Rent Act 1977 and various Housing Acts. We must now consider their position in the light of these statutory provisions.

1. THE PRIVATE SECTOR

Rent control is the outcome of the chronic shortage of rented property and began in this country in 1915 as the result of the shortage in the First World War. Until 1988 it was coupled with security of tenure on the ground that limiting the rent a landlord could charge gave no protection if he could evict the tenant, and security of tenure was valueless if the landlord could charge a rent which the tenant could not afford to pay. Rent control, however, itself produces a shortage of accommodation. Under the Rent Act 1977 either the landlord or the tenant of a *regulated tenancy* can apply to have a 'fair rent' determined, and once this is registered, it becomes the maximum rent that the landlord can charge under that or any subsequent regulated tenancy. 'Fair rent' is almost always less than that obtainable on the open market because no account is to be taken of any scarcity of similar rented accommodation in the locality. Consequently, when houses became vacant, many landlords preferred to sell rather than relet and there was no incentive for developers to build new property for letting. During the 1950s Conservative governments introduced legislation which decontrolled many tenancies and contemplated the eventual extinction of rent control altogether,[1] but within a decade a Labour government reversed this policy and extended control.[2] A renewed attempt to bring more rented accommodation on to the market was made by the Conservative government in the Housing

---

[20] See *Re Lowrie* (supra) at 356.
[1] Housing Repairs and Rents Act 1954; Rent Act 1957.
[2] Rent Act 1965; Rent Act 1968. See now s 1 of the Rent Act 1977 (a consolidating statute).

Act of 1980 which introduced two new types of tenancy: the *protected shorthold tenancy* and the *assured tenancy*. The former gave the landlord an unrestricted power to recover possession at the end of the term for which the lease was granted; the latter enabled bodies approved by the Secretary of State to let new buildings with much more limited security for the tenant.[3]

These innovations did not produce the results hoped for. A much more radical change was introduced by the Housing Act of 1988 which has largely divorced rent control from security of tenure. It has created a new type of *assured tenancy*, which is designed to replace the regulated tenancy, and an entirely new tenancy known as an *assured shorthold tenancy*. The former gives the tenant similar (but more limited) security to that given by the Rent Act to a tenant under a regulated tenancy. The tenant must, however, accept the rent agreed at the beginning of the tenancy and cannot apply to have a fair rent determined, although if the landlord of a periodic tenancy proposes an increased rent with which the tenant does not agree, the latter may refer the question to a rent assessment committee to determine a reasonable rent which will then become the new rent.[4] On the other hand, during the initial fixed term an assured shorthold tenant, like a protected shorthold tenant, may refer the agreed rent to a rent assessment committee[5] but he has no security.

Except for transitional provisions and two cases designed to protect existing tenants no new regulated tenancies may be created since the commencement of the 1988 Act (15th January 1989).[6] Existing regulated tenancies will ultimately be phased out or converted into assured tenancies,[7] but they are likely to constitute the largest number of tenancies subject to statutory control for many years.

It will be seen that the present state of the law is extremely complex. There are now three separate types of tenancy in the private sector governed by statute:

(1) Regulated tenancies, governed by the Rent Act 1977;
(2) Protected shorthold tenancies (now of diminishing importance) governed by the Housing Act 1980);
(3) Assured tenancies, governed by the Housing Act 1988.

In addition there are two types of tenancy and licence occupied by agricultural workers governed by statute:

(4) Protected agricultural occupancies, governed by the Rent (Agriculture) Act 1976;
(5) Assured agricultural occupancies, governed by the Housing Act 1988.

We must now examine the security given to each type of tenant or occupant and the members of his family.

---

[3] For details of assured tenancies under the Housing Act 1980, see ibid, ss 56–58; Housing and Planning Act 1986, ss 12–13.
[4] Housing Act 1988, ss 13 and 14. Unlike fair rent under the Rent Act, the rent must be that which the committee consider the landlord could be expected to obtain in the open market: s 14(1). This takes account of scarcity of similar accommodation.
[5] Ibid, s 22. Only one reference may be made.
[6] Ibid, s 34, qv for details.
[7] Some will be converted into assured tenancies on succession: see post, p 845.

Regulated tenancies

Regulated tenancies are still governed by the Rent Act 1977. This applies only to a house or part of a house let as a separate dwelling, a definition wide enough to include a flat.[8] Certain tenancies are not regulated; these include tenancies of premises let by the Crown, government departments, local authorities and certain other public bodies.[9] As the object of rent control is to protect the poorer tenant, it has always been limited to leases of premises of less than specified rateable values. Generally speaking, a tenancy will be regulated only if the rateable value of the premises did not exceed £1,500 in Greater London or £750 elsewhere on 1st April 1973 (or when the rateable value was first shown if this was later).[10]

Protected and statutory tenants

So long as a tenant is in occupation under a contractual lease, he is known as a *protected tenant* and is protected from arbitrary eviction by the terms of his contract. The Act goes much further by giving him a wide measure of protection after his lease ends. If he remains in possession after his contractual lease has been determined—for example, if his term has expired or he has been given notice to quit in accordance with the provisions of the lease—his tenancy becomes a *statutory tenancy*.[11] In certain circumstances a deceased tenant's spouse or cohabitant also becomes a statutory tenant.[12] A statutory tenant is generally speaking bound by all the terms and conditions in the original lease and entitled to the benefit of them.[13]

In order to claim the protection given by the Act against eviction, the statutory tenant must occupy the premises as his residence, for the policy of the Act is to protect the home and not to give the tenant any wider privileges.[14] A person may be in occupation of more than one home for this purpose simultaneously, as where he works in two places and has a home in each of them which he occupies when he is at that particular place:

---

[8] See Megarry *Rent Acts* (11th Edn) 84 et seq. For accommodation partly separate and partly shared, see the Rent Act 1977, s 22.

[9] For the full list of exceptions, see the Rent Act 1977, ss 5–16. Tenants of resident landlords and certain other tenants are given a more limited protection as parties to 'restricted contracts': see ibid ss 19 and 20 and Part V, as amended by the Housing Act 1980. Except for a transitional provision, no new restricted contract may be entered into after 14th January 1989: Housing Act 1988, s 36. This leaves tenants of resident landlords with no security. Tenants of business tenancies and of long tenancies at a low rent are given protection by the Landlord and Tenant Act 1954, as amended.

[10] For full details, see the Rent Act 1977, ss 4 and 25.

[11] Rent Act 1977, ss 1 and 2; Megarry, op cit, pp 224 et seq. If there were two or more joint contractual tenants but not all are in possession at the end of the contractual tenancy, those remaining become statutory tenants: *Lloyd v Sadler* [1978] QB 774, [1978] 2 All ER 529, CA. A husband's permitting his wife to remain in possession of the matrimonial home as a condition of paying a reduced sum under a maintenance order does not create the relationship of landlord and tenant so as to give the wife the protection of the Rent Act: *Bramwell v Bramwell* [1942] 1 KB 370, [1942] 1 All ER 137, CA. Cf *Marcroft Wagons Ltd v Smith* [1951] 2 KB 496, [1951] 2 All ER 271, CA (daughter permitted to remain in possession after her mother's death for a short time not protected by the Act).

[12] See post, p 842.

[13] Rent Act 1977, s 3.

[14] *Kavanagh v Lyroudias* [1985] 1 All ER 560, CA (tenant sleeping in one house but spending rest of time in another not in occupation of first house as his residence). See Brierley *The Rent Act 1977 and the Absent Tenant* [1991] Conv 345.

whether he can be said to occupy one as his second home is a question of fact and degree.[15] Likewise, a temporary absence will not suffice to bring his statutory tenancy to an end.[16] But he must retain both the corpus of possession and an animus revertendi. Thus it has been held that a wife who had gone away because of illness leaving her furniture in the house, in which her husband occasionally slept and to which she hoped to return as soon as her health improved, was still in occupation and was entitled to the protection of the Act.[17] But a mere animus without the corpus will not be sufficient, and consequently it has been held that a man who left his house deserted whilst serving a sentence of imprisonment ceased to be a statutory tenant.[18] He could have averted this result only 'by coupling and clothing his inward intention with some formal, outward, and visible sign of it', for example by installing a caretaker or relative to preserve the premises for his homecoming.[19] Conversely, if the tenant leaves the premises with no intention of ever returning there at all, he loses the status of a statutory tenant even though he leaves his furniture there with a caretaker or relative.[20]

But to this rule that the occupation must be personal is one important exception designed to protect the tenant's spouse—particularly the deserted wife. If one spouse is a protected or statutory tenant but the other is in occupation of the premises by virtue of his or her rights of occupation under the Matrimonial Homes Act, section 1(6) of that Act provides that this is to be regarded as possession by the tenant himself.[1] This is so even though the spouse in occupation has been deserted and is there against the tenant's will. This exception was originally grafted on to earlier Acts by the Court of Appeal and was based on the husband's common law obligation to maintain his wife and to provide her with accommodation.[2] Consequently she would lose this protection if she forfeited her right to be maintained and a husband's occupation could not be attributed to his wife. The Matrimonial Homes Act was clearly intended to give effect to this principle and to broaden it to cover both spouses, but the wording is unfortunately imprecise in its application to the requirement of the Rent Act that the tenant should occupy the premises *as his residence*.[3] Nevertheless, although

---

[15] See *Hampstead Way Investments Ltd v Lewis-Weare* [1985] 1 All ER 564, HL.

[16] Megarry, op cit, pp 245–249.

[17] *Wigley v Leigh* [1950] 2 KB 305, [1950] 1 All ER 73, CA.

[18] *Brown v Brash* [1948] 2 KB 247, [1948] 1 All ER 922, CA.

[19] Per Asquith LJ, ibid, at 254–255 and 926, respectively.

[20] *Skinner v Geary* [1931] 2 KB 546, CA (sister); *Robson v Headland* (1948) 64 TLR 596, CA (divorced wife and son); *Beck v Scholz* [1953] 1 QB 570, [1953] 1 All ER 814, CA (caretakers); *Colin Smith Music Ltd v Ridge* [1975] 1 All ER 290, CA (deserted cohabitant and their children); *Duke v Porter* (1986) 19 HLR 1, CA (nobody resident).

[1] Hence the tenancy will not have the protection of the Rent Act if it has never been the matrimonial home because neither the Matrimonial Homes Act (see ante, p 614) nor the case law carried forward from the earlier Acts will apply: *Hall v King* [1988] 1 FLR 376, CA. No order need have been made under the Act. A spouse (like a tenant) who is temporarily absent will remain in occupation for the purpose of the Act if he retains the corpus of possession and the animus revertendi: *Hoggett v Hoggett* (1979) 39 P & CR 121, CA.

[2] *Brown v Draper* [1944] KB 309, [1944] 1 All ER 246, CA; *Old Gate Estates Ltd v Alexander* [1950] 1 KB 311, [1949] 2 All ER 822, CA.

[3] The wording of the Matrimonial Homes Act goes back to the Matrimonial Homes Act of 1967. The requirement that the tenant should occupy the premises as his residence was specifically introduced by the Rent Act of 1968, but case law had similarly limited the application of the earlier Acts.

the matter is not entirely free from doubt, it is generally accepted that, so long as the tenant's spouse is occupying the premises as her (or his) residence, the protected or statutory tenancy will continue notwithstanding that the tenant is residing elsewhere.[4]

Recovery of possession

If a statutory tenant and his or her spouse both leave the premises, this automatically brings the tenancy to an end, and the landlord may retake possession or, if necessary, recover it by suing any trespasser on the property.[5] But so long as a protected or statutory tenancy is in existence, the landlord may obtain an order for possession only if the conditions laid down by the Rent Act are fulfilled. These are of two kinds.[6]

The first group comprises those cases in which the court may not make an order for possession unless it is satisfied that, having regard to all the circumstances, it is reasonable to do so. In addition the landlord must establish one or more of nine statutory grounds for possession. These include such diverse cases as the tenant's failure to pay rent or perform or observe other covenants; that the landlord reasonably requires the premises as a residence for himself or certain members of his family; and that suitable alternative accommodation is available to the tenant. The second group is mandatory in that the court is bound to make an order for possession if the landlord establishes one of the grounds. These mainly comprise claims by a landlord who requires the premises as a residence for himself and satisfies other stringent conditions.

The parties may not contract out of the Rent Act. Hence an agreement between the landlord and tenant that the latter shall surrender the premises (and a fortiori a notice by the tenant terminating the lease) will not give the landlord the right to recover possession.[7] Similarly there is no jurisdiction to make an order if the landlord rests his case on none of the statutory grounds even though the tenant does not defend the action.[8] But if the landlord alleges that a ground exists and the tenant does not contest this,

---

[4] See *Hall v King* (supra) and the judgment of Kerr LJ (with which Ewbank J agreed) in *Griffiths v Renfree* [1989] 2 FLR 167, 172–173. Once the landlord has obtained an order for possession and this has taken effect, the tenant is no longer entitled to remain in possession by virtue of the Rent Act and consequently the spouse loses the right of occupation under the Matrimonial Homes Act and becomes a trespasser, but she (or he) can still apply for the order to be suspended: Rent Act 1977, s 100, as amended by the Housing Act 1980, s 75(3).

[5] *Brown v Draper* [1944] KB 309, [1944] 1 All ER 246, CA; *Middleton v Baldock* [1950] 1 KB 657, 661–662, [1950] 1 All ER 708, 710, CA.

[6] Rent Act 1977, s 98 and Sch 15; Housing Act 1980, ss 66 and 67 and Sch 7; Rent (Amendment) Act 1985, s 1. See also the Rent Act 1977, s 101 (as substituted by the Housing (Consequential Provisions) Act 1985, Sch 2) and the Landlord and Tenant Act 1954, s 12(1). In the case of a contractual tenancy the landlord must also be able to claim possession apart from the Acts, eg by virtue of a forfeiture clause in the lease. For protection of sub-tenants, see the Rent Act 1977, s 137, as amended by the Housing Act 1988, Sch 18; *Leith Properties Ltd v Byrne* [1983] QB 433, [1982] 3 All ER 731, CA; *Smith's Charity v Willson* [1983] QB 316, [1983] 1 All ER 73, CA. See generally Megarry, op cit, chs 16 and 17.

[7] *Brown v Draper* (supra); *Middleton v Baldock* (supra); *Appleton v Aspin* [1988] 1 All ER 904, CA. But the fact that the tenant has given notice to quit and as a consequence the landlord has contracted to sell or let the premises or taken some other step as a result of which he would be seriously prejudiced if he could not obtain possession is itself a discretionary ground for giving possession. See Bridge *Surrender of Rent Act Tenancies* [1989] Conv 98.

[8] *Middleton v Baldock* (supra).

the court may make an order without enquiring into the truth of the allegation.[9]

Protected shorthold tenancies

A protected shorthold tenancy is one which satisfies the definition of a protected tenancy and is for a term certain of not less than one year nor more than five years and cannot be terminated by the landlord except for non-payment of rent or breach of any other covenant.[10] Protected shorthold tenancies were intended to induce more owners to lease property by virtually depriving the tenant of security at the end of the fixed term. This was done by giving the landlord the absolute right to recover possession of the premises at the end of the term.[11]

No new protected shorthold tenancies may be created since 15th January 1989. As presumably most landlords will wish to obtain possession at the end of the term, few tenancies are likely to be left after 1994.

Assured tenancies

Like a regulated tenancy, an assured tenancy under the Housing Act of 1988 must be of a dwelling house let as a separate dwelling with a rateable value not exceeding that applicable to regulated tenancies. It will be an assured tenancy, however, only if and so long as the tenant (or each of joint tenants) is an individual (and not a corporation) and the tenant or at least one of joint tenants occupies the dwelling house as his only or principal home.[12] As in the case of a regulated tenancy, a tenant who leaves the premises temporarily will presumably continue to occupy them so long as he retains the corpus of possession and the intention of returning, but if during his absence his principal residence is elsewhere, the tenancy will cease to be assured even though he leaves someone else (other than his spouse) in occupation. It will apparently become assured again if he returns,[13] but during his absence neither he nor the occupant can claim the benefit of security of tenure given by the Act (although if the tenancy is a contractual one, the landlord will be able to determine it only in accordance with the terms of the lease). One spouse's occupation is to be treated as that of the other.[14] Although, as in the case of protected and statutory tenancies under the Rent Act, the effect of this provision is not clear, the tenancy presumably remains assured if a sole tenant moves out leaving his

---

[9] *Middleton v Baldock* (supra) at 661, 669 and 710, 715, respectively.

[10] Housing Act 1980, ss 52 and 55(2), as amended by the Protected Shorthold Tenancies (Rent Registration) Order, SI 1987/265. The landlord must give the tenant a valid notice stating that the tenancy is to be a protected shorthold tenancy before the grant of the lease but the court may waive this requirement if it considers that it would be just and equitable to make an order for possession.

[11] For details, see ibid, ss 53–55. No assignment of the tenancy is permitted except under a property adjustment order made under s 24 of the Matrimonial Causes Act 1973.

[12] Housing Act 1988, s 1 and Sch 1. For accommodation partly shared with persons other than the landlord and the effect of sub-letting part of the premises, see ss 3 and 4.

[13] Cf *Crawley Borough Council v Sawyer* (1987) 20 HLR 98, 100, CA, where it was held that a dwelling house may remain the tenant's principal home notwithstanding an absence of several months.

[14] Matrimonial Homes Act 1983, s 1(6), as amended by the Housing Act 1988, Sch 17. See ante, pp 631–632.

or her spouse in occupation, at least so long as the dwelling house remains the latter's only or principal home.

Certain types of tenancy are not assured. These are similar to, but not identical with, tenancies excluded from protection under the Rent Act.[15] Assured tenancies created under the Housing Act of 1980 have been converted into assured tenancies under the 1988 Act.[16]

At the end of the fixed term an assured tenancy is converted into a statutory periodic tenancy on the same terms.[17] The landlord may bring a tenancy to an end only by obtaining a court order after serving two weeks' (or in certain cases two months') notice on the tenant.[18] The court may make an order only if one or more conditions are satisfied; like the conditions empowering a court to make an order for possession of a regulated tenancy under the Rent Act, some grounds are mandatory and some discretionary.[19] If one of the mandatory grounds is made out, the court must make an order for possession; they include, for example, three months' arrears of rent and, subject to certain restrictions, the landlord's requiring the premises as his or his spouse's home. The discretionary grounds include other rent arrears, the tenant's failure to perform or observe the covenants in the lease and the availability of suitable alternative accommodation; if the landlord establishes one of them, the court may make an order only if it thinks it reasonable to do so.[20]

Unlike a protected or statutory tenant, the tenant may terminate an assured tenancy by surrender or, if it is a periodic tenancy, by notice to quit. If there are two or more tenants, the consent of each is required to bring a contractual tenancy to an end before the term expires but the consent of all is required to continue a periodic tenancy. Consequently, if, say, husband and wife are joint tenants and one of them indicates to the landlord that he or she does not intend to renew the tenancy at the end of the current period, the other will lose her or his interest as well.[1]

Assured shorthold tenancies

An assured shorthold tenancy is a fixed term tenancy for a term of not less than six months, which the landlord cannot determine within the first six months except by a power of re-entry or forfeiture for breach of a term of

[15] Housing Act 1988, s 1(2) and Sch 1, qv for full details. In particular, certain temporary lettings made by private individuals to enable a local housing authority to fulfil its obligations to homeless persons under the Housing Act of 1985 are also excluded: ibid, s 1(6).

[16] Ibid, s 1(3)–(5).

[17] Other than a term giving the landlord power to determine the tenancy. For details, see ss 5 and 6.

[18] But the landlord of a fixed term tenancy may determine it if the lease gives him a power to do so for breach of any term or condition. The tenancy will then become a periodic one: ibid, ss 5, 8 and 45(4).

[19] In the case of a fixed term tenancy the terms of the tenancy must also enable the landlord to obtain possession on the ground in question: Housing Act 1988, s 7(6).

[20] For details, see ibid, s 7 and Sch 2. The court cannot make an order if the landlord bases his claim on none of the statutory grounds even though the tenant does not defend: cf ante, p 632. If possession is sought on a discretionary ground, the court may adjourn the proceedings, stay or suspend execution of the order and postpone the date of possession. The tenant's spouse or former spouse may apply for an adjournment, stay etc provided that she or he is in occupation of the premises and has rights of occupation under the Matrimonial Homes Act (see ante, p 613): ibid, s 9.

[1] *Hammersmith and Fulham London Borough Council v Monk* [1992] 1 AC 478, [1992] 1 All ER 1, HL.

the tenancy and in respect of which, before it is entered into, the landlord serves a notice stating that it is to be a shorthold tenancy. In addition, it must satisfy the definition of an assured tenancy given above.[2] Like other fixed term assured tenancies it is converted into a statutory periodic tenancy at the end of the fixed term. The peculiarity of an assured shorthold tenancy is that before the end of the fixed term the landlord can give the tenant two months' notice (to expire not earlier than the end of the term) that he requires possession of the dwelling house; once the tenancy has become a statutory periodic tenancy, he can give a similar notice, which must be for two months (or a period of the tenancy if this is longer) to expire at the end of a period. If these conditions are satisfied, the court is bound to make an order for possession. This mandatory ground is additional to the other grounds for possession applicable to all assured tenancies.[3]

Premises occupied by agricultural workers

Protected agricultural occupancies

Many agricultural workers were not protected by the Rent Act because they had merely a licence to occupy the premises (as distinct from a lease), or because the letting included board or attendance or the premises were let at a low rent or were comprised in an agricultural holding. In such cases a court was bound to make an order in favour of a farmer who brought proceedings to recover possession of 'tied accommodation' from a worker whose tenancy or licence had been lawfully terminated. This frequently caused hardship, particularly to retired workers and the members of the family of a deceased worker, and consequently the Rent (Agriculture) Act was passed in 1976 to extend security of tenure to farmworkers. Essentially this applies the provisions of the Rent Act to premises occupied by a whole-time agricultural worker (or former whole-time agricultural worker) by virtue of a licence or tenancy granted before 15th January 1989 by his employer (or former employer). In particular the grounds on which the owner can apply for possession are basically the same as those contained in the Rent Acts.[4]

Except for certain transitional cases no new protected occupancies can be entered into after 15th January 1989.[5]

Assured agricultural occupancies

The Housing Act of 1988 has replaced protected occupancies under the Rent (Agriculture) Act 1976 by assured agricultural occupancies. These comprise certain tenancies and licences occupied by an agricultural worker.

---

[2] Housing Act 1988, ss 20 and 45(4).
[3] Ibid, s 21.
[4] For details see the Rent (Agriculture) Act 1976, and for a full discussion of its provisions, see Clements *The 'Demise' of Tied Cottages* [1978] Conv 259. The Act does not apply to premises let by the Crown or the public bodies specified in the Rent Act or by a person occupying another dwelling in the same building as his own residence (s 5 and Sch 2, para 4). For details of the grounds on which the owner can apply for possession, which also apply to agricultural workers who are protected or statutory tenants under the Rent Act, see ibid, ss 6 and 7 and Sch 4, and the Rent Act 1977, s 99 and Sch 16.
[5] Housing Act 1988, s 34(4).

With certain exceptions they are to be treated as though they were assured tenancies.[6]

The position of the separated spouse

If the wife (or husband) of a tenant holding on a weekly or other periodic tenancy remains in the matrimonial home after the spouses separate and continues to pay the rent herself, a number of legal consequences follow. If the landlord is unaware of the separation and assumes that the husband is still in personal occupation of the premises, he will regard the wife as the husband's agent and the lease will still be vested in the husband. If the landlord is aware that the husband has left but continues to take the rent from the wife, it is a question of fact whether he treats the wife as her husband's agent (in which case the husband will remain the legal tenant) or whether he has accepted her as a new tenant (in which case she will become a new contractual tenant). The fact that the landlord accepts rent from the wife with full knowledge of the facts is not per se evidence of his having granted her a new lease for, as we shall see, he cannot evict her and consequently has no alternative to taking the rent from her.[7] But if no new tenancy is brought into existence, the original tenant, and not the spouse, continues to hold under the old tenancy.[8]

By enacting that the occupation of a spouse with rights of occupation is to be treated as occupation by the other spouse for the purpose of the Rent Act, the Matrimonial Homes Act 1983 gives the separated spouse of a protected or statutory tenant the same protection as the tenant himself. Unless the landlord can establish one of the statutory grounds, the wife cannot be evicted even though her husband wishes to terminate the tenancy. In *Middleton v Baldock*[9] the husband had deserted his wife and left her in the matrimonial home. The landlord served a notice to quit on the husband who acknowledged the landlord's right to the premises and offered to give him immediate possession. The landlord then brought separate actions against the spouses for possession, which the wife alone defended. Judgment was entered for the plaintiff in both actions, but both orders were reversed on the wife's appeal to the Court of Appeal. As the landlord's claim was based on none of the statutory grounds for obtaining possession, he could succeed only if the premises were vacated; and as the husband could not lawfully evict his wife, his acknowledgment of the landlord's right to enter could have no legal effect whatever. The landlord can obtain possession only if the husband obtains an order terminating the wife's rights of occupation. The husband remains liable for the rent,[10] but as non-payment

---

[6] For details see ibid, ss 24–26 and Sch 3.

[7] Cf *Morrison v Jacobs* [1945] KB 577, [1945] 2 All ER 430, CA. See also the alternative ground for the decision in *Wabe v Taylor* [1952] 2 QB 735, [1952] 2 All ER 420, CA, as explained in *SL Dando Ltd v Hitchcock* [1954] 2 QB 317, 324, [1954] 2 All ER 335, 337–338, CA, and *Cove v Flick* [1954] 2 QB 326n, 327, [1954] 2 All ER 441n, 442, CA. Payment of rent by the spouse in occupation is as good as if made by the tenant: Matrimonial Homes Act 1983, s 1(5).

[8] Hence a member of the spouse's family, who is not a member of the tenant's family, could not claim to have a regulated tenancy transmitted to him after her death: see post, p 843.

[9] [1950] 1 KB 657, [1950] 1 All ER 708, CA. See also *Brown v Draper* [1944] KB 309, [1944] 1 All ER 246, CA; *Old Gate Estates Ltd v Alexander* [1950] 1 KB 311, [1949] 2 All ER 822, CA.

[10] *Griffiths v Renfree* [1989] 2 FLR 167, CA (where the husband gave notice to the landlord).

of rent is one of the grounds on which the landlord may obtain possession, the wife may clearly have to pay it herself to secure her own occupation, in which case she may recover any sum paid from her husband.[11]

The same principles apply if the tenant is a protected occupier or statutory tenant under the Rent (Agriculture) Act. The position of the spouse of an assured tenant, however, is more precarious because, as we have seen, the tenant can terminate the tenancy by giving notice or surrendering it. If this occurs, the spouse loses her right to remain in occupation and can be evicted.[12]

Transfer of tenancies on divorce, nullity and judicial separation

If the marriage is dissolved or annulled, the tenant's spouse will lose the right to stay in occupation of the premises given by the Matrimonial Homes Act and consequently could be evicted.[13] To meet this difficulty, the court pronouncing a decree of divorce or nullity (or a decree of judicial separation) may make an order transferring a regulated or assured tenancy or an assured agricultural occupancy to the tenant's spouse. An order may be made at any time after decree nisi but cannot take effect until after decree absolute. (In the case of judicial separation it may be made and take effect at any time after the decree has been pronounced.) A spouse who has remarried cannot apply for an order.[14] The tenancy must still be in existence when the application for a transfer is made. Consequently, if the tenant (who we will assume is the husband) leaves the premises and gives notice to quit after a decree of divorce has been made absolute, the wife cannot apply for a transfer since her occupation is no longer attributed to her former husband and he has effectively terminated the tenancy.[15]

A transfer takes effect as a compulsory assignment, and the transferee takes subject to all the benefits and burdens of the covenants and the transferor ceases to be liable on them. This suggests that no transfer could be ordered if the lease contained an express covenant forbidding assignment; all the wife could do if the landlord refused to consent to the order would

[11] On the principle that if A discharges a legal obligation vested in B in order to preserve his (A's) own rights, B is under a quasi-contractual obligation to compensate A: see Cheshire, Fifoot and Furmston *Law of Contract* (12th Edn) pp 650–653. The possibility of the husband and landlord seeking to defeat the wife's right by collusively agreeing that the landlord shall falsely allege a ground for obtaining possession which the husband will not deny is averted only if the wife is joined as a party, when she can challenge the landlord herself. She should be joined as the person actually in possession: see Miller *Expenses of the Matrimonial Home* 35 Conv 332, 347–350. The husband must be joined as he is the statutory tenant: *Brown v Draper*, supra. See also Crane *After the Deserted Wife's Licence* 29 Conv 254, at 264–265.

[12] Cf *Hammersmith and Fulham London Borough Council v Monk* [1992] 1 AC 478, [1992] 1 All ER 1, HL.

[13] The court may make an order that the right of occupation shall continue after the termination of the marriage (see ante, p 614). If the tenant then gives notice of his intention to terminate the tenancy, it is arguable that the landlord can accept the notice and evict the wife because she is no longer a *spouse* entitled to occupy the dwelling house. But could it be said that the tenant has produced a merger of his tenancy with the reversion by surrender so as to give the wife the protection of s 2(6) of the Matrimonial Homes Act?

[14] Matrimonial Homes Act 1983, s 7 and Sch 1. The landlord must be given an opportunity of being heard.

[15] *Lewis v Lewis* [1985] AC 828, [1985] 2 All ER 449, HL. Quaere whether the wife could still apply if the husband had not given notice to quit: ibid at pp 834–835 and 452 respectively. It would seem that she could not because the tenancy has come to an end and a statutory tenancy cannot arise because neither the tenant nor his spouse will occupy the dwelling house.

be to apply to the court for a continuation of her rights of occupation.[16] In the case of a statutory tenancy the transferee becomes the statutory tenant in place of the transferor. If the spouses are joint tenants, the court has a similar power to extinguish the interest of one of them and vest the tenancy exclusively in the other.[17]

These provisions also apply to a statutory occupancy under the Rent (Agriculture) Act 1976. They do not apply to a contractual tenancy (or licence), which produces some anomalies for whether a tenancy is statutory may depend, for example, on whether the landlord has served a notice of increase in rent. It is not immediately apparent why the wife should be able to claim a transfer of the tenancy if this has occurred but not if it has not. In practice, a court is hardly likely to make an order if the husband is still employed by the landlord as an agricultural worker unless he is able to obtain suitable alternative accommodation.

2. PUBLIC SECTOR TENANTS

Secure tenancies

We have already seen that tenancies of premises let by various public authorities are not protected by other legislation so that tenants formerly lacked security. This gap was largely closed by the provisions of the Housing Act 1980, now consolidated in the Housing Act 1985, which created a new concept, that of the secure tenancy. This arises whenever the landlord is a local authority or one of certain other public bodies and the tenant is an individual occupying the dwelling house as his only or principal home (or, in the case of joint tenants, each of them is an individual and at least one of them satisfies this condition).[18] If the reversion ceases to be held by a public body, the tenancy becomes an assured one; if it is later held by a public body again, it will once more become a secure one.[19] A number of tenancies are excluded.[20]

Any purported assignment of a secure tenancy will be ineffective unless it is made (a) by way of exchange with another secure tenant,[1] (b) in pursuance of a property adjustment order made under section 24 of the Matrimonial Causes Act, or (c) to a person who could have been a qualified

---

[16] See ante, p 614. The wife would not be able to obtain a property transfer order under s 24 of the Matrimonial Causes Act 1973 because the husband could not make the assignment voluntarily: see post, p 737. (But this is possible in the case of a protected shorthold tenancy: see the Housing Act 1980, s 54(2).) It has been held in a county court that a transfer of a *statutory* tenancy under the Matrimonial Homes Act does not require the landlord's consent because otherwise he could thwart the operation of the section: see Hickman 129 New LJ 52.

[17] For the court's power to make orders with respect to liabilities and obligations arising before the order is made or takes effect, see Sch 1, para 5.

[18] For details, see the Housing Act, 1985, ss 79–81, as amended by the Housing and Planning Act 1986, Sch 5, and the Housing Act 1988, s 83 and Sch 18. For tenancies created since 15th January 1989, see the Housing Act 1988, s 35(4). As only one joint tenant has to occupy the dwelling house as his or her home, the tenancy will remain a secure tenancy even though the other is excluded by a court order.

[19] See also the Housing Act 1988, s 38.

[20] For the full list, see the Housing Act 1985, Sch 1, as amended.

[1] Or in certain circumstances with an assured tenant.

successor had the tenant died immediately before the assignment.[2] The tenancy will cease to be a secure tenancy if the tenant parts with possession of the dwelling house or sub-lets the whole of it or if it is vested or disposed of in the course of the administration of a deceased tenant's estate. Unless the tenancy passes to a qualified successor, once it has ceased to be a secure tenancy, it cannot become one again.[3] The provisions of the Act apply equally to a person occupying a dwelling house as a licensee if he would have had a secure tenancy had his licence been a lease.[4]

Periodic secure tenancies

So long as the tenant is in possession of premises by virtue of a lease for a term certain which has not expired, he has of course all the protection which his lease would afford to any other tenant.[5] Such leases are rare in the public sector but may arise. As in the private sector the need for protection arises under a short tenancy or when a longer lease expires. This is achieved by vesting in the tenant a periodic tenancy, the period being the same as that for which rent was last payable under the contractual lease. The terms of the new tenancy are the same as those of the original tenancy insofar as they are compatible with a periodic tenancy except that any provision for re-entry or forfeiture is disregarded.[6]

Recovery of possession

The landlord can bring a secure tenancy to an end only by obtaining an order for possession and the court cannot make such an order unless certain conditions are fulfilled. There are 17 grounds on which an order can be made including the non-payment of rent and the tenant's failure to perform or observe other covenants. In every case the court must be satisfied either that it is reasonable to make the order or that suitable accommodation will be available for the tenant when it takes effect; in some cases both these additional conditions must be satisfied.[7]

This applies only to termination by the landlord. A tenant, like an assured tenant, may terminate the tenancy by notice to quit or surrender.[8]

[2] Housing Act 1985, ss 91–92, as amended by the Local Government and Housing Act 1989, s 163. These restrictions do not apply to a tenancy for a term certain granted before 5th November 1982, but the tenancy will cease to be a secure one after the assignment except in the three exceptional cases mentioned in the text.

[3] Housing Act 1985, ss 90–93, as amended by the Local Government and Housing Act 1989, s 163. For the meaning of 'qualified successor', see post, p 848. If it is known that, when a deceased tenant's estate is disposed of, the tenancy will not be a secure tenancy (because it will not pass to a statutory successor), it ceases to be a secure tenancy at once.

[4] Except for certain licensees of almshouses and persons who entered the dwelling house or any other land as trespassers and to whom a licence was given as a temporary expedient: ibid, s 79(3), (4) and Sch 1, para 12.

[5] If the lease contains a provision for re-entry or forfeiture, the court may not make a possession order in pursuance of such a provision but instead shall make an order terminating the tenancy; when this takes effect, the tenancy becomes a periodic tenancy: ibid, ss 82(3) and 86. Hence the landlord can obtain possession only if he can also establish one of the statutory grounds for doing so (see infra). The same facts may satisfy both conditions, eg non-payment of rent.

[6] Ibid, s 86(2).

[7] Ibid, s 84 and Sch 2.

[8] For full details, see ibid, ss 83 and 84 and Sch 2, as amended by the Housing and Planning Act 1986, s 9, and the Housing Act 1988, s 83 and Sch 17.

Position of the separated spouse

If one spouse is a secure tenant and the other has a right to occupy the house by virtue of section 1 of the Matrimonial Homes Act 1983, the latter's occupation is treated as occupation by the tenant.[9] From this it follows that if the tenant (who, we will assume for the sake of argument, is the husband) and his wife separate and the latter continues to occupy the premises as her only or principal home, the tenancy remains a secure tenancy and the wife is entitled to the security which her husband would have been able to claim had he still been in occupation. Hence, as in the case of a private sector tenancy, the landlord cannot claim possession of the premises unless he can establish one of the statutory grounds on which he could obtain possession against the tenant. The wife must, of course, continue to pay the rent which, like the wife of a regulated or assured tenant, she could recover from her husband.[10]

If, however, the husband terminates the tenancy (or if the spouses are joint tenants and the husband refuses to renew a periodic tenancy) the wife will cease to be in occupation of premises held on a secure tenancy and may therefore be evicted.[11] If she wishes to remain in occupation, she must try to obtain a new tenancy from the landlord.[12]

Transfer of tenancies on divorce, nullity and judicial separation

The court has the same power to order the transfer of a secure tenancy to the tenant's spouse on divorce, nullity or judicial separation as it has in respect of private sector tenancies.[13]

3. UNMARRIED COHABITANTS

It will be seen that the special position of the spouse under the legislation we have been considering is not shared by the tenant's unmarried partner. If unmarried cohabitants are joint tenants, obviously each will be able to claim the benefits of security afforded to the tenant, but, as we have seen, if the tenancy is a periodic one, a notice to quit by one tenant determines the tenancy of both at the end of the current period.[14] If one of them (say, the man) is sole tenant and he temporarily leaves the premises with the intention of returning, the occupation of the other will enable the tenant to continue to enjoy the protection given by the various Acts (just as the occupation of a relative would) provided that, if he is an assured or secured tenant, he does not in the meantime establish his principal home elsewhere. If, on the other hand, he leaves permanently, his partner's occupation will not be attributed to him so that she will not have security of tenure: the

---

[9] Matrimonial Homes Act 1983, s 1(6), as amended by the Housing (Consequential Provisions) Act 1985, Sch 2.

[10] Cf ante, p 637.

[11] *Hammersmith and Fulham London Borough Council v Monk* [1992] 1 AC 478, [1992] 1 All ER 1, HL.

[12] She is more likely to succeed if she has a priority need and the landlord is the housing authority, because it will be bound to provide her with other accommodation: see ante, p 151.

[13] Matrimonial Homes Act 1983, s 7 and Sch 1, as amended by the Housing (Consequential Provisions) Act 1985, Sch 2.

[14] Ante, p 634.

landlord can terminate the lease as the premises will no longer be the tenant's home, and the court has no power to order an assignment if the relationship breaks down. An unmarried cohabitant considering applying for an ouster injunction should bear this in mind as a possible consequence of obtaining an order.

If the tenancy is secure, the cohabitant's position is stronger in one respect than if it were in the private sector: as she could be a qualified successor on the tenant's death, the latter can assign his tenancy to her so as to make her a secure tenant provided that he does so while they are still living together as husband and wife.[15] Otherwise, if she wishes to remain on the premises, she must try to persuade the landlord to terminate the lease and grant her a fresh tenancy.[16]

[15] See ante, pp 638–639.
[16] Note the comment made ante, p 640, n 12.

Chapter 19

Rights in property affected by the relationship of parent and child

A. General

Rights in property are not greatly affected by the relationship of parent and child. A parent, it seems, has no rights as such in the property of a child of any age; thus in the absence of any agreement he has no claim on a child's wages,[1] and even an arrangement by which the child promises to pay his father or mother a weekly sum for his board and lodging is probably unenforceable on the ground that the parties never intended to create any legally binding obligation.[2] Similarly, property bought by a child out of his income will remain exclusively his own.

In whom the ownership of gifts to a child vests is not so clear. The property in clothes and other articles of small value intended for immediate use by a young child would most probably be held to vest in the parent or parents (or other persons with parental responsibility for the child) who would therefore have the right to dispose of them. Similar goods bought for an older child presumably belong to the child: at what stage this transition is effected must be a question of fact in each case. If the gift is of greater value and the child is too young to have the necessary intention of receiving it, the legal interest will apparently vest in the parents. By section 3 of the Children Act 1989 'parental responsibility' includes 'the rights, powers and duties which a guardian of the child's estate ... would have had in relation to the child and his property' and 'in particular, the right ... to receive or recover in his own name, for the benefit of the child, property of whatever description and wherever situated which the child is entitled to receive or recover'.[3] This will then make the person with parental responsibility, like the former guardian of the estate, trustee for the child.

In practice, if a minor is entitled to property of any value, he will normally derive it under a settlement or will or on an intestacy, and the legal ownership will therefore usually vest in trustees.[4] His parents may be able to make a claim on the fund for his maintenance and education; the extent of this will depend on the terms of the instrument creating the interest and the provisions of the Trustee Act 1925 and the Administration of Estates Act 1925—matters which belong rather to the general law of property and impinge only indirectly upon family law.[5]

---

[1] Cf *Williams v Doulton* [1948] 1 All ER 603.
[2] Cf ante, pp 128–129. But if a child has a sufficient income to keep himself, a parent could not be guilty of failure to provide him with reasonable maintenance.
[3] S 3(2), (3).
[4] If a minor is absolutely entitled to property under a will or on an intestacy, the personal representatives may appoint trustees of the gift for the beneficiary and vest the property in them: Administration of Estates Act 1925, s 42(1).
[5] See generally works on equity and trusts.

Four subjects require particular attention.

Occupation of parent's house

A child of full age has no right to occupy his parent's home merely by virtue of their relationship, and in *Egan v Egan*[6] a mother obtained an injunction restraining her son, aged 19, from entering her house. This was admittedly a grave case of a son assaulting and maltreating his mother, stealing from her, and threatening to break in if she tried to exclude him, and in less serious cases the court may be slow to grant an injunction for this purpose.[7] It must be even more difficult to justify the exclusion of a minor child. There are, however, two possible courses of action that the parents might persuade the local authority to take: to provide accommodation for the child under section 20 of the Children Act 1989 because his conduct prevents them from providing him with accommodation or care or, if the child is under the age of 17, to take care proceedings under section 31 of that Act on the ground that he is likely to suffer significant harm because he is beyond parental control.[8] The difficulty they face is establishing that they cannot provide accommodation or care or that the child is likely to suffer significant harm, as the case may be. As parents cease to be under any criminal liability for neglecting or abandoning a child over the age of 16,[9] they can physically turn him out if he is over that age with impunity.

Presumption of advancement

If a father has property conveyed into the name of his legitimate child, this has always raised a presumption of advancement, so that, unless the presumption is rebutted, the child takes the whole beneficial interest and there will be no resulting trust in favour of the father.[10] The basis of this presumption is the recognition by equity of the father's obligation to provide for his children and to advance them, but it would seem to arise in every case of father and child and has even been applied where a father aged 92 transferred property to his son with whom he was living and who was looking after him.[11]

In other cases a resulting trust in favour of the purchaser will be presumed unless he has put himself in loco parentis to the child, that is, unless he has intentionally taken upon himself a father's duty to make provision for the other.[12] Whether or not one person is in loco parentis to another is a question of fact. Today little evidence will be required to establish the relationship between a mother and her child (particularly if the mother is widowed)[13] or between an unmarried parent and his or her child, and a

[6] [1975] Ch 218, [1975] 2 All ER 167.
[7] See *Waterhouse v Waterhouse* (1905) 94 LT 133 (injunction to exclude idle son aged 35 refused).
[8] See ante, pp 503 (provision of accommodation) and 511 (care proceedings).
[9] See ante, p 314.
[10] So held in a series of cases from *Dyer v Dyer* (1788) 2 Cox Eq Cas 92, to *Shephard v Cartwright* [1955] AC 431, [1954] 3 All ER 649, HL. On the question of the evidence admissible to rebut the presumption, see *Shephard v Cartwright*.
[11] *Hepworth v Hepworth* (1870) LR 11 Eq 10.
[12] Per Lord Cottenham LC in *Powys v Mansfield* (1837) 3 My & Cr 359, 367, and Jessel MR in *Bennet v Bennet* (1879) 10 Ch D 474, 477.
[13] *Bennet v Bennet* (supra), at 479–480. See also *Re Ashton* [1897] 2 Ch 574.

presumption of advancement would probably be raised automatically in such cases. The relationship may also arise, for example, between grandfather and grandchild,[14] uncle and nephew,[15] stepfather and stepchild,[16] and other strangers in blood, but it would have to be specifically established. If the child is living with his father, this may be evidence that another is not in loco parentis to him but it is by no means conclusive.[17]

Undue influence

If a transaction between parent (whether father or mother) and child or a transaction entered into by the child at the instance of either parent involves a sum so large that it cannot be reasonably accounted for on the ground of affection, there is a presumption that the parent has exercised undue influence over the other. Hence if the child later seeks to have such a contract or gift set aside for this reason, the burden shifts on to the party wishing to uphold it to prove that the child acted as the result of a free exercise of his will. The difficulty of discharging a negative burden is obvious: as was stated in *Re Pauling's Settlement Trusts*[18] it must be shown that the child acted spontaneously and with knowledge of his rights; it is desirable, though not essential, that he should have had independent advice given with knowledge of all the relevant circumstances and such as a competent and honest adviser would give if he were acting solely in the child's interest. The advice must be genuinely independent, and hence the burden is not discharged by showing that the child was advised by a solicitor who was acting for the parent or another interested party at the same time.[19]

The presumption of influence does not cease when the child comes of age or is 'emancipated' by marriage: there must be many cases when the natural influence which most parents are bound to have over their children continues after this. The question is purely one of fact, although the presumption will normally last for only a short time after the child attains his majority.[20] These points are well illustrated by *Lancashire Loans Ltd v Black*.[1] In this case a daughter, who had come of age and who had left her parental home on marriage, was persuaded by her mother to charge a reversionary interest under her grandfather's will in order to pay off the mother's debts. Later at the mother's instigation she signed a promissory

[14] *Ebrand v Dancer* (1680) 2 Cas in Ch 26.
[15] *Powys v Mansfield* (supra).
[16] *Re Paradise Motor Co Ltd* [1968] 2 All ER 625, CA.
[17] *Powys v Mansfield* (supra) at 368.
[18] [1964] Ch 303, 336, [1963] 3 All ER 1, 10, CA. See also *Lancashire Loans Ltd v Black* [1934] 1 KB 380, CA; *Powell v Powell* [1900] 1 Ch 243; and cf *Re Brocklehurst* [1978] Ch 14, [1978] 1 All ER 767, CA.
[19] *Lancashire Loans Ltd v Black* (supra); *Powell v Powell* (supra); *Bullock v Lloyds Bank Ltd* [1955] Ch 317, [1954] 3 All ER 726.
[20] *Re Pauling's Settlement Trusts* (supra) at 337 and 10, respectively. At the time this case was decided the age of majority was 21. Will the courts now accept that the reduction of the age of majority to 18 implies greater maturity and judgment on the part of a person over that age and give correspondingly less weight to the presumption?
[1] [1934] 1 KB 380, CA. See also *Bainbrigge v Browne* (1881) 18 Ch D 188, where the three children were all over the age of 21.

note for £775 plus interest at 85 per cent per annum and made a second charge on the reversion. The necessary instruments were drawn up by a solicitor who was also acting for the mother and the moneylenders concerned and who did not give the daughter a full explanation of the true nature and effect of the guarantee and the consequences of entering into it. It was held that the transactions must be set aside, as the moneylenders had full knowledge of all the facts from which undue influence could be inferred and could therefore be in no better position than the mother.

As in the case of all other transactions which are voidable in equity, the child will lose his power to have the contract or gift set aside by laches or by affirming the transaction after he has ceased to be under the parental influence. But, subject to this, it may be avoided against anyone save a bona fide purchaser for value without notice of the circumstances surrounding it.[2]

Family arrangements

Family arrangements are transactions which 'tend to the peace or security of the family, to the avoiding of family disputes and litigation, or to the preservation of family property'.[3] Common examples are agreements between members of the family to divide the property of a deceased member or to compromise claims under disputed wills. In arrangements of this sort the parents as heads of the family are bound to exercise some influence over the judgment of their children entering into the agreement, and consequently a strict application of the presumption of undue influence would make many such transactions voidable. A special rule has therefore been developed that family arrangements may be set aside on this ground only if a parent derives some benefit from the agreement which he did not formerly possess.[4] In addition it should be borne in mind that family arrangements are contracts uberrimae fidei and may therefore be avoided by any party on the ground that another party failed to disclose a material fact of which he was aware but of which the complaining party was ignorant.[5]

Life assurance policies in favour of children

As we have already seen, if either parent takes out a policy of assurance on his or her own life expressed to be for the benefit of any or all of his or her children, this will create a trust in favour of the child or children.[6]

---

[2] *Bainbrigge v Browne* (supra). In *Re Pauling's Settlement Trusts* (supra) it was held that children acting under parental influence could compel trustees to return money paid out in breach of trust when the latter knew (or ought to have known) of the undue influence.

[3] Per Romilly MR in *Hoghton v Hoghton* (1852) 15 Beav 278, 300.

[4] *Hoghton v Hoghton* (supra); *Hoblyn v Hoblyn* (1889) 41 Ch D 200, 206; *Turner v Collins* (1871) 7 Ch App 329 (where the son's action to have the deed set aside was in any case defeated by his own laches).

[5] *Gordon v Gordon* (1821) 3 Swan 400 (failure to disclose an earlier secret marriage between the parents, as a result of which the eldest son, believed to be illegitimate, was in fact legitimate); *Greenwood v Greenwood* (1863) 2 De G J & Sm 28 (failure to disclose the true value of property). Cf *Re Roberts* [1905] 1 Ch 704, CA (compromise effected on a false assumption of the party's rights).

[6] See ante, pp 581–582.

B. Dispositions in favour of children

The common law knew nothing of legitimation or adoption and regarded a bastard as filius nullius. Consequently it became settled law that the term 'children' in any instrument (whether testamentary or made inter vivos) prima facie must be construed as *legitimate* children. The same rule applied to any other relationship, and a bequest, for example, to the testator's nephews would normally confer a benefit only on the legitimate sons of his legitimate brothers and sisters.[7]

This was purely a rule of construction and the presumption could therefore be displaced if the instrument indicated a contrary intention on the part of the person executing it. It was rare for this to happen in the case of a deed, but in a number of reported decisions illegitimate children have succeeded in taking under a will. This occurred if the testator expressly included illegitimate children in his gift or if at the time of the execution of the will the legatees' parent had no legitimate children and was, to the testator's knowledge, dead,[8] or a woman beyond the age of child bearing,[9] or a man incurably impotent.[10]

This rule was relaxed by statute over the years. The Legitimacy Act of 1926 enabled legitimated children to take under a disposition taking effect after their legitimation,[11] and under the Children Act of 1975 they could claim under an instrument made on or after 1st January 1976 or a will taking effect on or after that date even though it came into operation before their parents' marriage.[12] The general presumption that 'children' prima facie means legitimate children was reversed by section 15 of the Family Law Reform Act 1969. This provided that in any disposition *made* on or after 1st January 1970, any reference to a child of any person should be construed as including an illegitimate child and any reference to a person related to another in some other manner should include an illegitimate person or one whose relationship is traced through an illegitimate person.[13] It did not, however, affect the construction of the word 'heir' or the devolution of an entailed interest.

Section 19 of the Family Law Reform Act of 1987 further amended the law in accordance with its policy to remove the legal disadvantages suffered by those born outside marriage. Its wording substantially follows that of the 1969 Act (except that it refers to persons whose parents have or had not been married to each other rather than to illegitimate persons). Like that Act it does not apply if a contrary intention is shown in the disposition

---

[7] See *Sydall v Castings Ltd* [1967] 1 QB 302, [1966] 3 All ER 770, CA (illegitimate daughter not a 'descendant' for the purpose of the trusts of a pension scheme).

[8] *Lord Woodehouselee v Dalrymple* (1817) 2 Mer 419.

[9] *Re Eve* [1909] 1 Ch 796. Contrast *Re Dicker* [1947] Ch 248, [1947] 1 All ER 317.

[10] *Re Herwin* [1953] Ch 701, [1953] 2 All ER 782, CA. See also *Hill v Crook* (1873) LR 6 HL 265, HL; *Dorin v Dorin* (1875) LR 7 HL 568, HL. As gifts tending to encourage or reward sexual immorality were regarded as contrary to public policy at common law, gifts to illegitimate children to be conceived after a deed or will took effect were also void: *Hill v Crook* (supra) at 278, 285–286; *Re Shaw* [1894] 2 Ch 573; *Occleston v Fullalove* (1874) 9 Ch App 147.

[11] Ss 1(3) and 3(1).

[12] Sch 1 Pt III, re-enacted in Legitimacy Act 1976, s 5(3).

[13] It also abolished the rule prohibiting an illegitimate child from claiming under a disposition if he was not in being when it took effect.

itself,[14] and it does not affect the devolution of property which (apart from that section) would devolve along with a title of honour. There is, however, one distinction: in any disposition whether inter vivos, by will or by codicil, *made* on or after 4th April 1988, the use of the word 'heir' is not to indicate an intention that a person whose parents have never been married to each other is not to take an interest and such a person can succeed to an entailed interest.[15]

The old law will still be relevant in the case of dispositions made or taking effect before the dates mentioned above. A fuller account of it will be found in the sixth edition of this book.

Adopted children

Under the Adoption of Children Act of 1926, an adopted child was not deemed to be the child of the adopters but remained the child of his natural parents for the purpose of the devolution of interests in property. This anomalous rule was altered by the Adoption of Children Act 1949 with respect to dispositions made after 1949 or, in the case of an intestacy, where the intestate died after 1949. Now as regards interests in property, the general principle is the same as that relating to personal rights and duties: ie, from the date of the adoption order an adopted child is deemed to become the child of the adopter or adopters and ceases to be regarded as the child of his natural parents or, if he has been previously adopted, of his former adopters, and therefore is no longer considered as related to any other person through his natural or former adoptive parents.

Earlier legislation followed the same principle as originally applied to legitimation and provided that an adopted person could claim as his adoptive parent's child only under a disposition of property made inter vivos after he was adopted or under a will or codicil of a person dying after that date.[16] As in the case of legitimation, this limitation was removed by the Children Act 1975 in the case of instruments made on or after 1st January 1976 or wills of testators dying on or after that date and, subject to any contrary indication, an adopted child may claim in such cases whether the disposition takes effect before or after the adoption. A disposition depending on the date of birth of a child of the adoptive parent or parents is to be construed as though the adopted child was born on the date of his adoption and two or more children adopted on the same day rank inter se in the order of their actual births. This provision, however, does not affect the operation of any condition depending on the child's reaching an actual age.[17] Thus, if there is a bequest in 1981 to K's eldest child at 18 and K adopts a child A and subsequently has a natural child B, A can claim when he reaches the age of 18 whether his adoption preceded or followed the testator's death.

The effect of an adoption on an interest which the child could have claimed had he not been adopted is not so clear. Suppose, for example,

---

[14] See s 1(1).

[15] For this purpose a disposition made by a will or codicil executed before 4th April 1988 is not to be treated as remade by a codicil executed on or after that date.

[16] But if a will or codicil was executed before 1st April 1959, this provision applied only if the adoption order was made before its *execution* unless it was confirmed by codicil after that date: Adoption Act 1958, s 17(2) and Sch 5, para 4(3).

[17] Adoption Act 1976, s 42. A disposition includes a power of appointment and the creation of an entailed interest: ibid, s 46(1), (2), (3), (5).

that there is a gift to X with remainder to his eldest son and that X's eldest son is S. If S has been adopted by someone other than X before the instrument creating the settlement takes effect, he can obviously claim nothing because he is no longer regarded as X's son at all. If X has died before S's adoption, so that S's interest has vested in possession, it is expressly preserved notwithstanding the adoption.[18] But what is the position if he is adopted after the disposition takes effect but before the interest vests in possession? A vested remainder is a present interest,[19] which suggests that on principle S should keep it. On the other hand, if one applies the maxim expressio unius exclusio alterius, the express preservation of an interest vested in possession implies that a vested remainder will be lost, and this is the solution the courts may well accept. If the interest is contingent and has not vested when the adoption takes place, it is presumably lost in any event. If, for example, the gift had been to X's eldest son at 18, S's adoption before that age must deprive him of all right to it because, when the condition is fulfilled, he is no longer regarded as X's son.

Notwithstanding the general rule there are various provisions designed to ensure that an illegitimate child *adopted by one of his parents as the sole adoptive parent* is not thereby deprived of an interest he could otherwise have taken. In the first place, such an adoption does not affect the child's entitlement to any property depending on his relationship to the adoptive parent.[20] Suppose, for example, that a testator, T, dying in 1981, makes a bequest in favour of his grandchildren alive at his death who reach the age of 18. His unmarried daughter, D, has a child, C, alive at T's death, whom she subsequently adopts as sole adoptive parent. C can still claim under the bequest. Moreover, if a disposition depends on the date of birth of an illegitimate child, neither his adoption by one of his parents as sole adopter nor his legitimation if he has been adopted will affect his entitlement.[21] Thus, if in the above example T had bequeathed a sum of money to his eldest grandchild when that child reached the age of 18 and C was his eldest grandchild, C could still claim even if he was adopted by D (or, having been adopted by D, he was legitimated by D's subsequent marriage to his father) after the birth of another grandchild.[1]

Unless the disposition otherwise provides, adoption does not affect the devolution of any property limited to devolve along with any peerage or dignity or title of honour (the descent of which will not be affected).[2] Trustees and personal representatives are not liable if they distribute property in ignorance of the making or revocation of an adoption order but beneficiaries may trace property into the hands of anyone other than a purchaser.[3]

---

[18] Ibid, s 42(4).
[19] Megarry and Wade *Law of Real Property* (5th Edn) pp 231–235.
[20] Adoption Act 1976, s 39(3).
[21] Ibid, s 43; Legitimacy Act 1976, s 6(2).
[1] Similarly, the revocation of an adoption order following the marriage of a child's parents will not affect any claim he could have made to property had the order remained in force: Legitimacy Act 1976, s 4(2). If he has been adopted and dies before his parents' marriage, he is deemed to be legitimated on that date for the purpose of preserving interests to be taken by or in succession to his spouse, children and remoter issue: Legitimacy Act 1976, s 5(6). For the effect of an adoption by a woman over 55 and the operation of the presumption that she is incapable of bearing children, see Adoption Act 1976, s 42(5).
[2] Adoption Act 1976, s 44.
[3] Ibid, s 45.

Chapter 20

Financial support for the members of the family

A. Introductory[1]

1. THE DUTY TO MAINTAIN A SPOUSE

(a) At common law

The common law rules relating to the maintenance of a spouse were the inevitable consequence of the doctrine of unity of legal personality. The wife, lacking the capacity to hold property and to contract, could neither own the bare necessities of life nor enter into a binding contract to buy them. Two principles followed. One of the essential obligations imposed upon a married man was to provide his wife with at least necessities, and a married woman could in no circumstances be held liable to maintain her husband. The common law rule that neither spouse could sue the other precluded her from enforcing her right by action if her husband failed to fulfil his duty to maintain her; this difficulty was overcome by giving the wife a power to pledge her husband's credit for the purchase of necessities if he did not supply her with them himself.

(i) Scope of the husband's duty

The husband's common law duty to provide his wife with the necessities of life was prima facie complied with if he provided a home for her.[2] She had no right to separate maintenance in a separate home unless she could justify living apart from him. Whilst the parties were cohabiting, the husband obviously had to provide his wife with food, clothing and other necessities. Conversely, provided that the wife was not in desertion, the husband's obligation remained even though the spouses were living apart, for example owing to the illness of one of them, the husband's own desertion,[3] or his irrational belief that she was going to kill him.[4]

The fact of marriage raised a presumption at common law that the husband was under a duty to maintain his wife. But her right to maintenance, generally speaking, was co-extensive with her right to her husband's

---

[1] See generally Miller *Family Property and Financial Provision* (2nd Edn) and Eekelaar and Maclean *Maintenance after Divorce* chs 1 and 2. For a fascinating study of how families generally organise their finances see Pahl *Money & Marriage*.

[2] See *Price v Price* [1951] P 413, 420–421, CA; *W v W (No 2)* [1954] P 486, 515–516, [1954] 2 All ER 829, 840, CA.

[3] *Holborn v Holborn* [1947] 1 All ER 32 (constructive desertion).

[4] *Brannan v Brannan* [1973] Fam 120, [1973] 1 All ER 38. But a reasonable though mistaken belief *induced by the wife's own conduct* relieved him from the duty of maintaining her just as it relieves him from the duty of cohabiting with her: *Chilton v Chilton* [1952] P 196, [1952] 1 All ER 1322, *West v West* [1954] P 444, [1954] 2 All ER 505, CA. See further ante, pp 205–207.

consortium, and if her conduct released him from the duty to cohabit with her, he automatically ceased to be under a duty to maintain her.[5] Thus a single act of adultery automatically deprived her of her right unless the husband connived at it or condoned it.[6] Similarly, she was not entitled to look to him for maintenance if she was in desertion, but whereas adultery terminated the right entirely (unless the husband condoned it), desertion merely suspended it and the right revived immediately the desertion came to an end.[7]

(ii) The agency of necessity

The power to pledge the husband's credit was termed the wife's agency of necessity. It extended to the purchase of necessaries both for herself and for the spouses' minor children, and the term 'necessaries' in this context included not only necessary goods such as food and clothing but also necessary services such as lodging, medical attention and education. Although the wife might divest herself of the right to be maintained by her own conduct, the husband could not revoke the authority by his unilateral act.

The agency of necessity was of great importance so long as the wife was generally incompetent to contract and own property at common law. Both these disabilities were removed by the Married Women's Property Act 1882, and by the end of the nineteenth century she could obtain maintenance from her husband not only in the High Court but also much more speedily in the magistrates' court. Consequently it became rare for a married woman to use her agency of necessity because tradesmen were naturally reluctant to give credit to a man who had deserted his wife and left her penniless. When it became possible for the wife to obtain immediate assistance from what was originally the Department of Health and Social Security and to claim the benefits of the National Health Act and the legal aid and advice scheme, the doctrine became an anachronism and was eventually abolished by the Matrimonial Proceedings and Property Act 1970.[8]

(b) The current position

The means by which maintenance can be claimed by a spouse are now entirely governed by statute. Unlike the common law it is open to either spouse to claim maintenance from the other. Furthermore since claims for maintenance no longer depend upon the duty to cohabit the commission of adultery or desertion are no longer automatic bars. The two statutes

[5] *Chilton v Chilton* (supra) at 202 and 1325, respectively.
[6] *Wright and Webb v Annandale* [1930] 2 KB 8, CA; *Wilson v Glossop* (1888) 20 QBD 354, CA (connivance); *Harris v Morris* (1801) 4 Esp 41 (condonation). If the wife had committed adultery, the husband's own conduct was irrelevant; *Govier v Hancock* (1796) 6 Term Rep 603 (husband guilty of adultery and cruelty to wife); *Stimpson v Wood & Sons* (1888) 57 LJQB 484 (husband guilty of adultery).
[7] *Jones v Newtown and Llanidloes Guardians* [1920] 3 KB 381. Hence if the wife was in simple desertion she could restore her right to maintenance by taking steps to effect a reconciliation: *Price v Price* (supra).
[8] S41. This followed the recommendations of the Law Commission: see Law Com No 25, paras 108–109 and Appendix II, paras 41–52 and 108. S41 was repealed by the Matrimonial Causes Act 1973, Sch 3, and not re-enacted. See further Diamond *Repeal and Desuetude of Statutes*, Current Legal Problems, 1975, 107, at pp 110–111.

governing maintenance between separated spouses are the Domestic Proceedings and Magistrates' Courts Act 1978 and the Matrimonial Causes Act 1973, section 27.

2. PARENTS' DUTY TO MAINTAIN CHILDREN BORN WITHIN THE MARRIAGE

At common law a father was under a duty to maintain only his legitimate minor children and to provide them with food, clothing, lodging and other necessities. But the duty was wholly unenforceable. A child has never had an agency of necessity[9] and a father is under no legal obligation to reimburse one who has supplied his child with necessaries. Unless he constituted the child his agent, the only way in which he could be compelled to fulfil his obligation was through the wife's agency of necessity, which extended to the purchase of necessaries for the children of the marriage as well as for herself.[10] With the abolition of the wife's agency of necessity, the common law position is now of purely historical interest.[11]

As with maintaining spouses the means by which financial provision can be claimed for children is entirely governed by statute. Where it is sought to obtain financial provision both for the spouse and the children recourse must be had to the Domestic Proceedings and Magistrates' Courts Act 1978 or the Matrimonial Causes Act 1973, section 27. If provision is sought only for children, application must be made under the Children Act 1989.

3. SUPPORT OBLIGATIONS OUTSIDE MARRIAGE

At common law a man had no duty to maintain anyone other than his wife and legitimate children. It remains the case that even between cohabiting adults there is no duty to maintain, although, as we shall see, in making orders for any children the court can include an element for the cost of the carer.[12] Furthermore where a parent is claiming income support for herself and her children, the Department of Social Security may seek recovery from the other parent of an amount to meet the claimant's income support allowance.[13]

So far as children born outside marriage are concerned the common law position was that neither the father nor the mother was liable for maintenance.[14] Although the Poor Law legislation cast upon the mother the obligation of maintaining her illegitimate child, she could still not recover the expenses of maintenance from the father in the absence of any

---

[9] *Mortimer v Wright* (1840) 6 M & W 482.

[10] *Bazeley v Forder* (1868) LR 3 QB 559.

[11] There is an old authority at nisi prius for the proposition that a father is also liable for necessaries supplied for the use of his children at the request of a servant who has charge of them: *Cooper v Phillips* (1831) 4 C & P 581. Today the courts might require proof of an ostensible authority.

[12] Post, p 698.

[13] Social Security Act 1986, s 24A, discussed post, p 667.

[14] *Ruttinger v Temple* (1863) 4 B & S 491. In *Hesketh v Gowing* (1804) 5 Esp 131, the father was held liable if he adopted the child as his own, but today it would probably be necessary to establish an authority to incur expenses on the child's behalf by the person seeking reimbursement.

contract to that effect between them.[15] A statute of 1576 empowered justices to make an order on the putative father for the maintenance of an illegitimate child charged on the parish,[16] but it was not until the Poor Law Amendment Act of 1844 that the mother was given the power to apply for an order for maintenance to be paid to herself. The law was amended and consolidated in the Bastardy Laws Amendment Act of 1872 and again in the Affiliation Proceedings Act 1957. Under this legislation the right of unmarried mothers to claim from alleged fathers was circumscribed. For example, applications could only be made to magistrates' courts, applicants had to be 'single' mothers, claims had to be brought within three years of the child's birth[17] and the mother's evidence had to be corroborated.[18] Happily, this procedure was substantially improved by the Family Law Reform Act 1987 and is now embodied in the Children Act 1989.

4. ENFORCEMENT OF THE DUTY TO MAINTAIN

(a) Maintenance agreements

Once it was accepted that separation agreements were not contrary to public policy, it became possible for a husband to enter into an enforceable contract to pay maintenance for his wife and his children. Now either spouse may covenant to pay maintenance to the other and either parent (whether married or not to each other) can covenant to pay maintenance for their children. Their rights are basically governed by the general principles of the law of contract but, as we shall see, some special rules apply to maintenance agreements.

(b) State support

Broadly speaking, anyone over the age of 18 whose income falls below the relevant sum laid down by the Social Security Act 1986 is entitled to apply to the Department of Social Security for income support. As any sum awarded is payable immediately, a spouse or unmarried partner without support will frequently turn to the Department before taking any other action. If support is given to a married person it is recoverable from that person's spouse and if support is given to any child under the age of 16 it is recoverable from either or both parents.[19]

(c) Maintenance in magistrates' courts

Until 1878 only the ecclesiastical courts or their successors, the Divorce Court and the High Court, could make orders for maintenance. That year saw an entirely new departure, for section 4 of the Matrimonial Causes Act enabled a criminal court, before which a married man had been convicted of an aggravated assault upon his wife, to make an order that she should no longer be bound to cohabit with him if it felt that her future safety was

---

[15] As to agreements to pay maintenance, see post, pp 656 et seq.
[16] 18 Eliz 1 c 3.
[17] Unless the father was voluntarily paying money for the child.
[18] See generally pp 640–641 of the seventh edition of this work.
[19] For discussion of income support and other benefits see post, p 665.

in peril. The court could also order a husband to pay maintenance to a wife in whose favour such a separation order was made and vest in her the legal custody of any children of the marriage under the age of ten years. In 1886 courts of summary jurisdiction were given a further power to make a maintenance order in favour of a woman whose husband had deserted her and was wilfully refusing or neglecting to maintain her.[1] Their jurisdiction to make orders on the application of married women was considerably increased by the Summary Jurisdiction (Married Women) Act of 1895, which in effect introduced a code of law relating to husband and wife to be administered in magistrates' courts. The success of that Act was reflected in the way in which its provisions were extended during the next half century in a series of Acts which became collectively known as the Summary Jurisdiction (Separation and Maintenance) Acts 1895 to 1949.[2] Magistrates' powers were again overhauled and widened by the Matrimonial Proceedings (Magistrates' Courts) Act 1960.

A striking feature of the early legislation was the absence of any action for child maintenance. The first such action was provided by the Married Women (Maintenance) Act 1920, under which, if legal custody of the child was granted to the applicant in proceedings under the Act, the court could order payment of a weekly sum not exceeding 10s (50p) for the child's maintenance.[3] There were still fixed limits both for orders for the spouse (£7.50) and the child (£3.50) under the Matrimonial Proceedings and Magistrates' Courts Act 1960. These limits were removed by the Maintenance Orders Act 1968.

The separate limits for spouse and child illustrate the earlier lack of recognition that their needs could not be divorced from one another.[4] However, a change of attitude was marked with the decision in *Northrop v Northrop*[5] in which it was held that where the parties separate by agreement[6] leaving the child with the wife, because of the latter's inevitable commitments to the child, the husband must be taken to have impliedly undertaken to maintain his wife. The inextricable link between the child's and care-giver's needs is now openly recognised so that, for example, rather than rigidly stipulating what each should receive, orders should be 'tax efficient' so as to maximise what the recipient household will receive.[7] Ironically, perhaps, the law has now come a full circle, since far from providing no remedy for child maintenance, it now provides, as a result of amendments introduced by the Matrimonial and Family Proceedings Act 1984, that in deciding what orders to make, magistrates must treat the welfare of any child of the family as the first consideration.

The main purpose of the Act of 1895 was to afford women of the working

[1] Married Women (Maintenance in Case of Desertion) Act 1886.
[2] These were: the Summary Jurisdiction (Married Women) Act 1895; the Licensing Act 1902, s 5; the Married Women (Maintenance) Act 1920; the Summary Jurisdiction (Separation and Maintenance) Act 1925; and the Married Women (Maintenance) Act 1949.
[3] A similar provision was later introduced under the Guardianship of Infants Act 1925, the weekly limit being £1.
[4] See also the discussion by Eekelaar and Maclean, op cit, pp 21–28.
[5] [1968] P 74, [1967] 2 All ER 961, CA.
[6] At that stage unless the husband had otherwise expressly or impliedly agreed he was not liable to maintain his wife upon consensual separation.
[7] See eg *Vasey v Vasey* [1985] FLR 596, CA. Since the Finance Act 1988 (discussed post, p 732) however, the scope for gaining tax advantages is now extremely limited.

and lower middle classes, who could not afford to take proceedings in the High Court, an opportunity to obtain matrimonial orders cheaply and speedily; and these advantages, together with the comparative informality and privacy of the proceedings, eventually brought to the courts many women in higher income groups. A parallel development is seen in the matrimonial relief to married men as well.[8] Under the Act of 1960 magistrates had jurisdiction to make three types of order: (a) to relieve the complainant from the duty of cohabiting with the defendant, the effect of which was, in almost all respects, the same as that of a judicial separation; (b) for the maintenance of one of the spouses; and (c) for the custody and maintenance of the children of the family. Except for orders relating to children, the court could not grant matrimonial relief unless the complainant established one of nine matrimonial offences, the law relating to some of which was highly technical and rigid. This meant that, after the introduction of the new divorce law in 1971, there was a wide divergence between the law administered in the divorce courts and that administered in magistrates' courts. In particular, there was a much greater emphasis laid on the parties' conduct in magistrates' courts and their powers were much less extensive. The Law Commission, reporting in 1976, considered that the function of magistrates' courts was 'to provide first aid in a marital casualty clearing station' and saw the objectives of their matrimonial jurisdiction as being:[9]

'(a) to deal with family relations during a period of breakdown, which is not necessarily permanent or irretrievable—
    (i) by relieving the financial need which such a breakdown can bring to the parties;
    (ii) by giving such protection to one or other of the parties as may be necessary;
    (iii) by providing for the welfare and support of the children; and
(b) to preserve the marriage in existence, where possible.'

So far as orders for the benefit of the wife or husband are concerned (as distinct from those for the benefit of the children), they first proposed the abolition of the power to make separation orders which, they concluded, served little purpose. They recommended that this jurisdiction should be replaced by a power to make much more effective orders for the physical protection of a spouse and the children of the family.[10] Secondly they proposed that the substantive law relating to maintenance should be brought more into line with the relief that a spouse can obtain on divorce and, in particular, that it should be simplified and that the grounds for application and the guidelines for the court should be the same whichever spouse applied.[11] These recommendations formed the basis of the provisions of Part I of the Domestic Proceedings and Magistrates' Courts Act 1978, which completely replaced the code set out in the Matrimonial Proceedings (Magistrates' Courts) Act 1960. Under the 1978 Act either spouse may apply for an order on any one of four grounds. In addition, magistrates' courts also have powers to make orders for payments which have been

[8] This was originally conferred by the Licensing Act 1902, s 5.
[9] Law Com No 77, Report on Matrimonial Proceedings in Magistrates' Courts, para 2.4.
[10] See the Domestic Proceedings and Magistrates' Courts Act 1978, ss 16–18, ante, pp 174 et seq. Separation orders made under the Matrimonial Proceedings (Magistrates' Courts) Act 1960 remain in force: ibid, Sch 1.
[11] See Law Com No 77, paras 2.1–2.14.

agreed by the parties as well as orders reflecting sums actually paid by one spouse to the other when they separate by agreement.

The 1978 Act has since been amended by the Matrimonial and Family Proceedings Act 1984, the principal effect of which is to provide that in deciding what order to make magistrates should give first consideration to the welfare of a child of the family under the age of 18, and to allow the payer to apply to the court for a consent order.

5. CONCURRENT ORDERS

The embarrassment which might result if two courts were seised of the question of maintenance simultaneously has led to the formulation of the rule that two orders should not be in force at the same time. A magistrates' court should normally refuse to deal with an application when proceedings are pending in a divorce court;[12] for the same reason a rule of practice was evolved that normally a divorce court would not make an order for maintenance so long as a magistrates' order was in force. Consequently, if the wife had previously obtained an order in a magistrates' court and then wished to apply for financial provision in a divorce court (as she might do if she later petitioned for divorce or wished to obtain security), she usually had to have the first order discharged and thus leave the way clear for relief in the divorce court.

This meant of course that she must run the risk of obtaining less than she was already getting and also that there might be a period before any order could be made in the divorce court, when she would be in receipt of nothing at all. The second difficulty has now been removed and in such a case the High Court or a divorce county court may direct that any order made under Part I of the Domestic Proceedings and Magistrates' Courts Act 1978 (other than for the payment of a lump sum) shall cease to have effect at any time.[13] This means that the court will normally discharge the first order from the date on which its own order is to come into force, but the wife still runs the risk of finishing up financially worse off than she was before, for the Act has not apparently altered the old rule of practice that she is not permitted to apply for a second order and then enforce the more favourable.[14]

A similar position obtains in relation to financial provision for children. As we shall see, a parent may obtain maintenance for a child in the High Court, a county court or a magistrates' court under the Children Act 1989 or in a magistrates' court under the Domestic Proceedings and Magistrates' Courts Act. If there is a later petition for divorce, the petitioner may wish to obtain an order for financial provision in the divorce court. That court itself can discharge an order made under the Domestic Proceedings and Magistrates' Courts Act.[15]

---

[12] See post, pp 672–673.
[13] Domestic Proceedings and Magistrates' Courts Act 1978, s 28.
[14] See *Ross v Ross* [1950] P 160, [1950] 1 All ER 654.
[15] Under s 28.

B. Maintenance agreements

1. BETWEEN SPOUSES

To be legally enforceable, a maintenance agreement must constitute a contract between the parties. Consequently, if it is not by deed[16] the party seeking to enforce a promise to pay maintenance must show that she (or he) has furnished consideration. This will normally not be difficult because the undertaking will be embodied in a separation agreement in which each party gives consideration by releasing the other from the duty to cohabit or will be part of a much more complicated financial transaction involving the division of property and the compromising of other claims. If there is no consideration at all, however, a promise not made by deed will be unenforceable.

Basically the parties' rights and duties are determined by the general law of contract. If the agreement is a maintenance agreement for the purpose of section 34 of the Matrimonial Causes Act 1973, however, two peculiar rules apply to it: certain provisions may be void by statute, and in certain circumstances either party may apply to have the agreement altered. The result is that in many cases the wife (who will usually be the party to whom payments are to be made) will have the best of both worlds because she can hold her husband to his covenant and also take other proceedings to obtain maintenance. Whilst the provisions of the Act are doubtless necessary to protect some wives who have been induced to accept unreasonably low terms, they may well have the undesirable effect of leading many legal advisers to dissuade husbands from settling financial provisions out of court.[17]

(a) Definition of maintenance agreement

To come within section 34 of the Matrimonial Causes Act 1973, an agreement must be *in writing* and made between spouses or former spouses. It must also be:

> '(a) an agreement containing financial arrangements, whether made during the continuance or after the dissolution or annulment of the marriage; or
> (b) a separation agreement *in writing* between the same parties containing such arrangements.'

From this it will be seen that an agreement entered into after a decree absolute of divorce or nullity can come within the statute only if it contains financial arrangements. An agreement containing no such arrangements can come within the statute only if it is a separation agreement made whilst the parties are still married to each other.

Financial arrangements are defined as:

> '... provisions governing the rights and liabilities towards one another when living separately of the parties to a marriage (including a marriage which has been

---

[16] For the meaning of which see now the Law of Property (Miscellaneous Provisions) Act 1989, s 1.
[17] See Passingham and Harmer *Law and Practice in Matrimonial Causes* (4th Edn) pp 149–153.

dissolved or annulled) in respect of the making or securing of payments or the disposition or use of any property, including such rights and liabilities with respect to the maintenance or education of any child, whether or not a child of the family.'[18]

There is some doubt whether an agreement comes within the section if someone other than the spouses is a party to it. In *Young v Young*[19] the spouses and the husband's brother had entered into an agreement in which the husband had covenanted to pay the wife £8 a week and the wife had been given the use of a house (which was the joint property of the husband and his brother) on her undertaking to keep it in reasonable repair. On the husband's application to have the agreement altered, it was held that it was not a maintenance agreement for the purpose of the Act because the brother was a party to it and the Act contemplated only agreements between husband and wife. Taken literally, this statement can scarcely be true: if the husband agrees to settle periodical payments on the wife, the agreement cannot fail to be a maintenance agreement solely because trustees are parties to it. There seems to be no objection to the alteration of the kind of agreement in *Young v Young* provided that the rights and obligations of third parties are not affected, and it is urged that it should not be followed.

(b) Void provisions

It was at one time fairly common in separation agreements for the husband to covenant to make periodical payments to the wife in exchange for her giving an undertaking not to take any other steps to obtain maintenance from him. An application for maintenance in other matrimonial proceedings might also be compromised by the wife's promising to withdraw it in consideration of the husband's paying her maintenance or transferring property to her. In *Hyman v Hyman*,[20] however, the House of Lords held that no arrangement of this sort can preclude her from applying for financial relief in divorce proceedings. The reason for this decision is that the court's power to order the husband to maintain his former wife after divorce is intended to protect not only her but also any person dealing with her and, indirectly, the state in view of the possibility of her having to apply for state benefit. Consequently it would be contrary to public policy to permit the parties to oust the court's jurisdiction by agreement.[1] This reasoning is equally applicable in nullity proceedings and, despite earlier authority to the contrary in the Court of Appeal,[2] it is submitted that the same principle must also be applied in the case of judicial separation. This does not mean that the court will ignore the agreement in subsequent proceedings and the wife may well be held to it.[3] It must also be stressed that, unless the

---

[18] Matrimonial Causes Act 1973, s 34(2). It has been held that this does not include the making of a lump sum payment: *Furneaux v Furneaux* (1973) 118 Sol Jo 204. Sed quaere? A lump sum is a 'payment'. The point was left open in *Pace v Doe* [1977] Fam 18, 23, [1977] 1 All ER 176, 181.

[19] (1973) 117 Sol Jo 204.

[20] [1929] AC 601, HL.

[1] Ibid, at 608 and 629.

[2] *Gandy v Gandy* (1882) 7 PD 168, CA. Cf *Gaisberg v Storr* [1950] 1 KB 107, [1949] 2 All ER 411, CA (promise not to sue for alimony pending suit on divorce binding).

[3] See post, pp 745–746.

wife's undertaking not to claim financial provision is the sole or main consideration, it does not make the whole agreement illegal, so that she may still elect to sue the husband on his covenant rather than to apply for maintenance.[4]

Section 34 of the Matrimonial Causes Act 1973 provides that any term in a 'maintenance agreement' purporting to restrict any right to apply to a court for an order containing financial agreements shall be void. It also provides that any other financial arrangements in the agreement shall not *thereby* be rendered void or unenforceable but shall be binding on the parties unless void or unenforceable for any other reason.[5] The precise effect of this section is uncertain. Clearly the inclusion of the offensive term no longer makes the whole agreement illegal: consequently even if the wife's undertaking not to apply for an order is the sole consideration, the husband can be sued if his covenant to pay her maintenance is made by deed. If it is not made by deed, however, it is submitted that the husband's promise is still not actionable if the sole consideration is the wife's undertaking not to institute other proceedings for the further reason that, as her promise is void, his promise is supported by no valuable consideration at all.[6]

(c) Alteration of agreements

Although any sum agreed on by the parties by way of maintenance might well have been reasonable at the time the agreement was made, it is obvious that in some cases an adherence to this in the light of subsequent events could work serious hardship. The husband's earning capacity may be reduced, which will make reasonable a reduction in the sum he has undertaken to pay the wife; alternatively, the wife's illness or the constant increase in the cost of living may well make the sum absurdly small, particularly if it was agreed on some years ago. To overcome difficulties such as these, sections 35 and 36 of the Matrimonial Causes Act 1973 empower the court in certain circumstances to alter any agreement which is a maintenance agreement for the purpose of section 34.[7]

(d) Alteration during the lifetime of both parties

Either party may apply to a divorce county court to have a subsisting agreement altered if each of them is either domiciled or resident in England.[8]

---

[4] *Goodinson v Goodinson* [1954] 2 QB 118, [1954] 2 All ER 255, CA, followed in *Williams v Williams* [1957] 1 All ER 305, CA. But if this is the sole or main consideration for the husband's promise to pay her maintenance, the whole agreement is illegal and unenforceable even if it is by deed: *Bennett v Bennett* [1952] 1 KB 249, [1952] 1 All ER 413, CA; *Combe v Combe* [1951] 2 KB 215, [1951] 1 All ER 767, CA, following *Gaisberg v Storr* (supra). But an agreement by which the jurisdiction of a foreign divorce court is ousted is not contrary to English public policy and consequently the husband's covenant may be enforced here: *Addison v Brown* [1954] 2 All ER 213.

[5] S 34(1), replacing provisions originally contained in the Maintenance Agreement Act 1957, s 1(2).

[6] See Dew 56 Law Soc Gaz 365. For the contrary view that the statute has made the husband liable on a promise for which there is no consideration, see Treitel *Mutuality in Contract* 77 LQR 83, at pp 92–95.

[7] For the definition of a maintenance agreement, see ante, p 656. The power was originally given by the Maintenance Agreement Act 1957. Cf the automatic reviews of child support provided for by the Child Support Act 1991, s 16, discussed post, p 715.

[8] Matrimonial Causes Act 1973, s 35(1) and Sch 2, para 6(1)(a); Matrimonial Causes Act 1967, s 2, *Pace v Doe* [1977] Fam 18, [1977] 1 All ER 176. A county court may order

Alternatively, the application may be made to a magistrates' court, in which case both parties must reside in England.[9]

No alteration is possible unless one of two conditions is satisfied: either there must have been a change in the circumstances in the light of which the particular financial agreements were made (or financial arrangements were omitted) or the agreement must fail to contain proper financial arrangements with respect to any child of the family.[10] It will be observed that in the latter case the party seeking the alteration does not have to prove any change of circumstances; but where such a change has to be shown, the Act places the court and the parties in a dilemma. On the one hand, if they are not held to the terms that they have freely entered into, there is no incentive to settle differences out of court; on the other hand, if the courts are slow to make alterations, legal advisers are bound to recommend their clients not to enter into an agreement but to obtain a court order which can be varied from time to time to take account of changes in their financial circumstances. With this difficulty in mind, the Court of Appeal has established two principles. First, as they held in *Gorman v Gorman*,[11] the circumstances in the light of which the financial arrangements were agreed must prima facie be viewed objectively. Although in some cases it might be right to have regard only to those circumstances which the evidence shows did influence the parties, normally the court must look at the circumstances which reasonable people in their position would have taken into account. This at least prevents a party from arguing in most cases that the court cannot make an alteration because he did not have particular circumstances in contemplation even though they would clearly have affected the action of a reasonable person. Secondly, the court must be satisfied that the agreement has become unjust as a result of the change. In *D v D*,[12] for example, where having initiated the negotiations and being advised by competent lawyers, a wife agreed to transfer her interest in the matrimonial home for a fixed sum, the court did not think that the agreement had become unjust following an increase in the value of the house. The Act expressly provides that the court is not to be precluded from making an alteration merely because the change was foreseen;[13] if this were not so, a party could rarely rely on an increase in the cost of living or the covenantor's income or on a deterioration in earning capacity due to advancing age. Of course if a change of income is unforeseen then the case for arguing that the agreement has become unjust is stronger. In *Simister v Simister (No 2)*[14] a husband agreed inter alia to pay his wife one-third of his annual gross salary. At the time of the agreement the husband's salary was £16,000 a year but within four years it had risen to £40,000. This meant that the husband was being forced to pay his wife at a rate in excess of her maximum reasonable needs. It was held that the

---

the application to be transferred to the High Court under the Matrimonial and Family Proceedings Act 1984, s 39: see *Practice Direction* [1992] 3 All ER 151.
[9] Matrimonial Causes Act 1973, s 35(3).
[10] Ibid, s 35(2). For the meaning of 'child of the family', see ante, pp 368 et seq.
[11] [1964] 3 All ER 739, CA.
[12] (1974) 118 Sol Jo 715.
[13] S 35(2)(a), reversing the decision in *K v K* [1961] 2 All ER 266, CA.
[14] [1987] 1 FLR 194.

agreement had thereby become unjust.[15] On the other hand, it is unlikely that he will be able to rely on a change brought about by himself, and in *Ratcliffe v Ratcliffe*[16] the court refused to relieve a husband of his obligations under a covenant to pay his wife £450 a year when he voluntarily threw up a post bringing him in £1,400 a year to become a schoolmaster at £550 a year. Similarly in *Gorman v Gorman* they declined to order the husband to pay anything to his wife in view of the fact that he was voluntarily making her an allowance and permitting her to reside in the matrimonial home, whilst she in turn was receiving weekly payments from national insurance and was living with adult children who could be expected to help her financially.

(e) Powers of the court

All courts may alter the agreement by varying or revoking any financial arrangements contained in it or by inserting in it financial arrangements for the benefit of either of the parties or a child of the family. In deciding whether to make an order against a party in favour of a child who is not his biological or adopted child, the court must take into account the same matters as it would on an application for maintenance on divorce.[17]

The High Court and county courts may alter and insert any provisions so long as they are 'financial arrangements' within the meaning of the section. There are, however, some restrictions on their powers. If the court inserts a provision for the making or securing of periodical payments by one party to the other or increases the rate of such payments, the period for which they (or the increase) are to be made must not exceed the parties' joint lives if they are unsecured or the payee's life if they are secured and, in either case, must cease on the payee's remarriage.[18] Secondly, if it inserts a provision for the making or securing of periodical payments for the maintenance of a child of the family or increases the rate of such payments, they (or the increase) may not last for a period longer than the court could order on divorce.[19] Further, in *Pace v Doe*[20] Baker P was of the opinion that it would be contrary to the policy of the Matrimonial Causes Act to enable a spouse to obtain under this section financial relief which she (or he) could not have obtained in divorce proceedings. He therefore held that no alteration at all could be in favour of a divorced wife (as distinct from a child of the family) after she had remarried. Whilst it may be good sense not to permit her to do indirectly that which she cannot do directly, there is no express provision in the Act depriving the court of jurisdiction in these circumstances, and consequently the decision must be treated with

---

[15] In fact because of the terms of the agreement it was held that the agreement should be revoked and an order under the Matrimonial Causes Act 1973, s 23, should replace it (the parties having subsequently divorced). Whether it is wise to make agreements that endure after the divorce has been questioned: see the comment at [1987] Fam Law 52.

[16] [1962] 3 All ER 993, CA.

[17] Matrimonial Causes Act 1973, s 35(2). See post, p 678. For the meaning of 'financial arrangements' see ante, p 656.

[18] Matrimonial Causes Act 1973, s 35(4). Remarriage includes a void or voidable marriage: ibid, s 52(3). Cf the duration of orders after divorce, etc, post, p 728.

[19] Ibid, s 35(5).

[20] [1977] Fam 18, [1977] 1 All ER 176. For the court's powers on divorce, see post, p 723.

reserve. Even if it is not followed, however, there will be few cases where it would be proper to make an alteration in these circumstances.

The powers of magistrates' courts are more circumscribed. If the agreement contains no provision for the making of periodical payments at all, the courts can insert a provision for the payment of *unsecured* periodical payments for the benefit of the other party or for any child of the family. If it contains a provision that one of the parties shall make *unsecured* periodical payments, the court may increase or reduce their rate or terminate them altogether. The maximum period for which any such payments (or increase) may be ordered is the same as in other courts.[1] This limitation is unfortunately narrow. It means, for example, that if the husband has undertaken to maintain the children but not the wife, a magistrates' court cannot insert a term in her favour: there seems no justification for compelling her to go to a county court in these circumstances.

If any agreement is altered, it has effect thereafter as though the alteration had been made by the parties themselves for valuable consideration, so that any person to whom money is due or property is to be transferred under the amended agreement has the normal remedies for breach of contract.[2] It is now established that an order for alteration of a maintenance agreement may be backdated to the point at which in justice the alteration should be made.[3] A further valuable power that the payee has is to apply to have set aside any disposition made by the other party with the intention of defeating a claim for alteration or to restrain him from making such a disposition in the future.[4] The alteration does not affect the powers of any court to make any other order containing financial arrangements or of the parties to apply for such an order.[5]

(f) Alteration after the death of one of the parties

If either party dies domiciled in England and the agreement provides for the continuation of payments, either that party's personal representatives or the survivor may apply for an alteration. In such a case only the High Court or a county court has jurisdiction and the application must not be made more than six months after the date when representation was first taken out except with the permission of the court.[6] The court's powers are the same as they are when an application is made during both parties' lifetime, and any alteration takes effect as though the agreement had been

---

[1] Matrimonial Causes Act 1973, s 35(3)–(5).

[2] Ibid, s 35(2).

[3] *Warden v Warden* [1982] Fam 10, [1981] 3 All ER 193, CA, overruling *Carr v Carr* [1974] Fam 65, [1974] 3 All ER 366.

[4] Matrimonial Causes Act 1973, s 37. See further post, pp 801–804. This presumably does not apply if the alteration is made by a magistrates' court.

[5] Ibid, s 35(6).

[6] Matrimonial Causes Act 1973, s 36, as amended by the Inheritance (Provision for Family and Dependants) Act 1975, s 26(1). The former financial limit on the jurisdiction of a county court has now been abolished by the High Court and County Court Jurisdiction Order 1991. If the court permits an application after six months, the personal representatives will not be personally liable but assets may be traced in the hands of beneficiaries. The court also has power to alter an agreement if the surviving party applies for an order against the other's estate under the Inheritance (Provision for Family and Dependants) Act 1975: see post, p 840.

varied by the parties themselves for valuable consideration immediately before the death.[7]

2. BETWEEN PARENTS

(a) Validity

As we have seen from the foregoing discussion, binding agreements made between spouses can include making provision for their children but there is no doubt that spouses can make binding agreements solely for the benefit of their children. It is equally established that binding agreements can be made between unmarried parents for the benefit of their children. Indeed as early as 1842 it was recognised that an agreement between the mother and father of an illegitimate child that the latter should pay the former maintenance for the child was actionable.[8] The consideration for the father's promise has been variously stated: it is usually recognised as a counter promise on the mother's part either to maintain the child herself (notwithstanding her liability to do so under what is now the Social Security Act 1986)[9] or to refrain from taking proceedings.[10] If there is no agreement as to the time for which the father is to remain bound, it would seem that either side may terminate the contract by giving the other reasonable notice.[11] The father's liability will automatically terminate on the mother's death unless the parties otherwise agree, for her personal representatives cannot claim the benefit of the agreement without at the same time accepting the burden of maintaining the child—an obligation which will not normally have been contemplated.[12] On the other hand, since the father's obligation is not personal but can be met out of his estate, there seems to be no reason why his personal representatives should not be bound.[13]

In one respect agreements of the type seem singular, for it was held in *Follitt v Koetzow*[14] that although the mother may sue the father on his promise to pay her maintenance made in consideration of her counter promise not to take proceedings, this does not prevent her from commencing proceedings to obtain an order. Like the power to award maintenance in a matrimonial cause, the power to order the father to pay maintenance under an order is not given for the benefit of the mother alone and consequently she cannot by agreement deprive herself of the right to apply for it. Unlike agreements made in consideration of the wife's undertaking not to apply for maintenance in a matrimonial cause, however, these agreements are valid in so far as the mother may sue the father upon them: they therefore present what is probably a unique example of a promise

---

[7] But there is no power to avoid transactions intended to defeat the claim unless the court exercises its powers under the Inheritance (Provision for Family and Dependants) Act 1975, s 18, to deem the survivor to have made an application under that Act: see post, pp 840–841.

[8] *Jennings v Brown* (1842) 9 M & W 496. Cf *Tanner v Tanner* [1975] 3 All ER 776, CA.

[9] *Ward v Byham* [1956] 2 All ER 318, CA.

[10] *Jennings v Brown* (supra); *Linnegar v Hodd* (1848) 5 CB 437.

[11] *Knowlman v Bluett* (1873) LR 9 Exch 1, Ex; ibid, 307, Ex Ch.

[12] *James v Morgan* [1909] 1 KB 564.

[13] This was apparently accepted in *Jennings v Brown* (supra). In each case, of course, it will be a question of the construction of the particular contract.

[14] (1860) 2 E & E 730.

which is valid for one purpose but contrary to public policy for another. But if the mother takes proceedings, this will obviously entitle the father to treat himself as discharged from his promise to pay maintenance and he could also presumably sue the mother for damages for breach of the contract. Moreover, the existence of the agreement is one of the factors which the court should take into consideration in determining the amount of maintenance to award.[15]

(b) Alteration of agreements

(i) During the parties' lifetime

The reforms under the Children Act 1989 do not affect the validity of maintenance agreements made between parents. However, powers to alter agreements made between fathers and mothers (regardless of whether they are married to each other) first introduced by the Family Law Reform Act 1987[16] are now contained in Schedule 1, paragraphs 10 and 11 to the 1989 Act. As under section 35 of the Matrimonial Causes Act 1973, only written agreements[17] may be altered and only where the court is satisfied either:[18]

'(a) that, by reason of a change in the circumstances in the light of which any financial arrangements contained in the agreement were made (including a change foreseen by the parties when making the agreement) the agreement should be altered so as to make different financial arrangements; or

(b) that the agreement does not contain proper financial arrangements with respect to the child.'

Provided it is satisfied, the court may vary or revoke any financial arrangements as may appear just.[19] These powers are retrospective applying to agreements made before as well as after the commencement of the provision.[20]

Application can be made by either parent to the High Court, a county court or a magistrates' court, but the last named only has power to increase, reduce or terminate periodical payments, having no power to alter arrangements made in connection with property.[1] If any agreement is altered, it has the effect thereafter as though the alteration had been made by the parties themselves for valuable consideration,[2] thereby preserving the normal contractual remedies for any breach.

(ii) After the death of one of the parties

In the case of an agreement designed to continue after the death of one of the parties if the parent dies domiciled in England and Wales, the surviving parent or personal representatives of the deceased parent may apply to the

---

[15] *Follitt v Koetzow* (supra).

[16] Ss 15 and 16, introduced following the recommendations of the Law Commission, Law Com No 118, paras 6.42–6.46.

[17] Defined by Sch 1, para 10(b) as those containing: 'provision with respect to the making or securing of payments or the disposition or use of any property, for the maintenance or education of the child...'

[18] Sch 1, para 10(3).

[19] Any altered periodical payment provision should not in the first instance extend beyond the child's seventeenth birthday save where the child is or will be receiving instruction at an educational establishment or undergoing training for a trade or profession or where there are special circumstances: Sch 1, para 10(5).

[20] Sch 1, para 10(1).

[1] Sch 1, para 10(6)(a) and (b).

[2] Sch 1, para 10(4).

High Court or a county court to alter the agreement.[3] An application may not be made, save with leave of the High Court or a county court, more than six months after the date when representation in regard to the deceased's estate was first taken out.[4] The court's powers are the same as they are when an application is made during the parties' lifetime, and any variation takes effect as though the agreement had been varied by the parties themselves for valuable consideration immediately before the death.[5]

C. State support

SOCIAL SECURITY BENEFITS[6]

(a) Introduction

The social security system is a crucial aspect of the financial position of families. It provides a means of supporting family members whose income would otherwise be inadequate to meet their needs, for example, owing to unemployment or disability. It also provides additional income for certain families such as those with dependent children. The present system derives in part from the Beveridge reforms enacted in the National Assistance Act 1948 which abolished the old Poor Law. Since then, however, there have been substantial changes, including the creation of the Benefits Agency, a 'next steps' agency under the aegis of the Department of Social Security to run the system. The present structure for the benefits of particular relevance to families was established by the Social Security Act 1986.[7] Social security benefits comprise: contributory benefits dependent upon the National Insurance contributions paid by the beneficiary,[8] such as unemployment benefit and retirement pension; non-contributory income related benefits dependent upon a means test, such as income support; and non-contributory, non-income related benefits—'universal' benefits to which all who fit within the category are entitled, most notably child benefit.

Contributory benefits are not discussed in detail since they do not relate directly to support for families.[9] However, it should be noted that the requirement to have made contributions to be eligible for the benefit (or for the full benefit) means that those unable to build up contributions, in particular women who give up work to have children,[10] may be disadvantaged. They may be ineligible for a full retirement pension based on their own contributions, and be dependent upon their husbands' contribution record, in which case, a reduced pension is payable to them.

[3] Sch 1, para 11(1).
[4] Sch 1, para 11(3). A claim may be overtaken by proceedings under the Inheritance (Provision for Family and Dependants) Act 1975, discussed post, pp 822 et seq.
[5] Sch 1, para 11(2).
[6] See Ogus and Barendt, *The Law of Social Security* (3rd Edn). See also the Report of the Committee on One-Parent Families (the Finer Report) Cmnd 5629.
[7] For the background see the *Fowler Review*: Green Papers: Reform of Social Security, Vols 1,2,3 (Cmnd 9517, 9518, 9519, 1985); see now the Social Security Contributions and Benefits Act 1992 and the Social Security Administration Act 1992.
[8] The benefits may also be payable to a spouse or dependant of the contributor.
[9] For a detailed account, see Ogus and Barendt, op cit.
[10] Interrupted contributions may be supplemented by counting years of 'home responsibility': see Social Security Contributions and Benefits Act 1992, s 60.

Women's career breaks, lower average earnings and concentration in lower status employment all combine to mean that they are also less likely to have access to valuable occupational pensions.[11] If their marriages are terminated by divorce, they will be unable to take advantage of the former husband's pension unless he nominates his ex-wife as a beneficiary. They will accordingly be more likely to have recourse to the non-contributory income related benefits, to which we now turn.

Means-tested benefits are intended to provide a safety-net through which no person should fall into destitution. There are two main types of such benefits; income support and family credit. Income support is frequently the first line of support for a parent who is on her own with a child and unable to work full-time when her partner has left her. If she is later able to obtain a job, but one which is low-paid, she may be eligible for family credit to boost her income. The aim of the government is to reduce dependence upon income support by encouraging the take-up of lower paid work and family credit. Such a strategy is said to reflect what single parents themselves want, and to teach a more positive attitude to work and independence among children.[12]

(b) Income support[13]

(i) Eligibility

Section 124 of the Social Security Contributions and Benefits Act 1992 provides that to be eligible for income support and other income-related benefits, a claimant must be in Great Britain and at least 18-years-old (although the Secretary of State has a discretion to award benefit to those aged 16 or over who would otherwise suffer severe hardship,[14] and those who have a child will qualify).[15] The claimant claims not just for him or herself, but for the family unit, including the spouse or partner living with the claimant, and dependent children under 19 living at home for whom the claimant is responsible. The claimant must: (a) have no income, or an income below the 'applicable amount'; (b) not be engaged in remunerative work; (c) except in prescribed circumstances, be available for and actively seeking employment; and (d) not be receiving relevant education.

The applicable amount is set by regulations, and comprises the 'personal allowance' for which the claimant would be eligible (for example, allowance for a single adult, or married couple, allowance for each child in the family, dependent upon age); any appropriate 'premiums' (for example, an extra sum for a family including a child or young person, and a lone parent premium for one-parent families); and eligible housing costs made up of mortgage interest repayments, so long as these are not regarded as 'excessive'.[16]

[11] See Maclean *Surviving Divorce*.
[12] White Paper, *Children Come First*, Vol 1 (Cm 1264) para 6.1.
[13] See Mesher *Income Support, The Social Fund and Family Credit: The Legislation*.
[14] Social Security Contributions and Benefits Act 1992, s 125.
[15] The Income Support (General) Regulations 1987, Sch 1A, Part I.
[16] Capital repayments are not included, and only half of the interest repayments will be met during the first 16 weeks of entitlement—Income Support (General) Regulations 1987, Sch 3, para 7. Help with rent may be available through housing benefit, administered by local authorities under s 130 of the Social Security Contributions and Benefits Act 1992; see Ogus and Barendt, op cit, ch 13.

If the claimant's income is below the applicable amount, the benefit received is the difference between the two sums. Apart from the claimant's home and certain other assets, capital will be taken into account in assessing eligibility. Capital above £8,000 renders the claimant ineligible for income support, while that between £3,000 and £8,000 will be treated as generating income which will then reduce the amount of benefit payable.[17]

Since the claim is for the family unit, the income and capital of the whole unit (except capital of the children) are 'aggregated'. Spouses no longer living together may claim separately as they live in separate units. In contrast, a man and woman living together as husband and wife will be treated as a couple and their resources aggregated. The investigation of whether a claimant is living with another adult *as husband and wife* is a controversial and complicated exercise. Detailed guidance has been given to adjudication officers in the Benefits Agency.[18] The income to be taken into account includes net earnings (with the first £15 per week disregarded for those in receipt of lone parent premium) and all other gross income. Maintenance payments (even those intended to be made for the benefit of a child, and not the parent)[19] are fully taken into account and reduce income support entitlement pound for pound.[20]

Claimants must not be engaged in remunerative work which for these purposes means 'work in which a person is engaged ... for not less than 16 hours a week being work for which payment is made...'.[1] Limited part-time working, can therefore be undertaken although earnings received will affect eligibility.[2] Claimants should normally be available for work but among the exceptions are lone parents responsible for a child who is a member of their household.[3]

(ii) 'Liable relatives'

Under sections 78(6) and 105(3) of the Social Security Administration Act 1992,

'(a) a man shall be liable to maintain his wife and any children of whom he is the father; and

(b) a woman shall be liable to maintain her husband and any children of whom she is the mother.'

Although liability to support a *spouse* terminates on divorce, liability to support children continues, and may not be excluded by a consent order.[4] Liability exists only in relation to a person's own children; there is no

[17] Income Support (General) Regulations 1987, rr 45, 53.
[18] See Mesher, op cit, pp 9–12 and cases and Commissioners' decisions cited therein.
[19] *Supplementary Benefits Commission v Jull, Y v Supplementary Benefits Commission* [1981] AC 1025, [1980] 3 All ER 65, HL.
[20] Income Support (General) Regulations 1987, r 55.
[1] Ibid, r 5(1) as amended.
[2] Interestingly, and reinforcing stereotyped images of women's work, childminding is not treated as remunerative work, and only one-third of the earnings from childminding are taken into account in assessing the claimant's income: ibid, r 6(b) and r 38(9).
[3] Ibid, Sch 1, para 1.
[4] *Hulley v Thompson* [1981] 1 All ER 1128. Such an order is very unlikely to be made now, as the courts have reiterated the continuing parental obligation to maintain, eg in *Minton v Minton* [1979] AC 593, [1979] 1 All ER 79, HL. Under the Child Support Act 1991, such an order could not be made, by virtue of s 8; see pp 717–719.

concept of 'child of the family' as in matrimonial proceedings.[5] A 'liable relative' may be traced by the Agency, and asked to meet the obligation to maintain. In deciding how much to expect the liable relative to contribute to the claimant's support, the Agency applies a formula, whereby the relative will be allowed to keep an amount equal to the income support payable for him or herself and any partner or children living with him, rent or mortgage costs, and one-quarter of net earnings. If the relative has extra commitments, the Agency may negotiate a lower sum.[6] In future, where the Child Support Act 1991 is applicable, it will replace this approach.[7]

Failure to make a contribution may result in proceedings being taken against the liable person in the magistrates' court under sections 105 or 106 of the Social Security Administration Act 1992. The latter is a civil proceeding which results in an order to pay a sum, weekly or otherwise, to the Secretary of State to meet the income support being claimed. The former is a criminal prosecution whereby a person who persistently refuses or neglects to maintain himself or anyone he is liable to maintain, is guilty of an offence. Criminal proceedings are rarely taken.

To improve the recovery of maintenance from absent parents, section 107 provides that where a parent is claiming income support for herself and her children, the Department of Social Security may seek recovery from the other parent of an amount to meet the claimant's income support personal allowance, even though the parents are not married to each other so that there is no liability to support the claimant herself. If the claimant ceases to claim benefit, the order may be transferred to her under section 107(3), but the element covering her allowance will not be included. This provision therefore enables the Department to recover more of the actual costs of supporting the lone parent. Furthermore, section 108 enables it to enforce a *private* maintenance order obtained by the claimant, even without her consent to such action being taken. There is usually little incentive for a benefits recipient to take or enforce private proceedings (as the maintenance recovered simply reduces the benefit she would receive), but section 108 sidesteps this difficulty, by enabling the Department to pursue the absent parent of its own volition.

(iii) The 'diversion procedure'

Where the amount of maintenance ordered by a court is less than the amount of benefit due, the Agency may agree to the payee authorising the court to pay the maintenance received direct to the Agency, which continues to pay her the full amount of benefit due, whether or not the maintenance is paid, or paid in full. Under this procedure, any shortfall in maintenance is borne by the Agency, rather than the claimant. Without the procedure, a claimant would have to make a fresh claim for extra benefit each time the payment was late or inadequate. The procedure is a valuable one, though apparently some offices administering benefits refuse to apply it except where the liable person has shown persistent default.[8]

[5] See post, p 674.
[6] Supplementary Benefits Handbook (1984).
[7] See pp 707 et seq.
[8] See Cretney and Masson, *Principles of Family Law* (5th Edn) p 342.

(c) The social fund

Income support is intended to meet the weekly needs of those with no, or very low, income. The 'applicable amounts' do not take into account the need for larger purchases, such as for furniture, or even substantial items of clothing such as a winter coat. Before the 1986 Act, help to purchase such items could be obtained by seeking a 'single payment', eligibility for which was subject to highly complex rules. Refusals led to numerous appeals to social security appeal tribunals. The cost of meeting single payments grew rapidly and was 'demand-led'. The Social Fund operates quite differently, in two parts. One part is non-discretionary, based on regulations, and provides maternity, funeral and cold weather payments to those on income support or family credit. Such payments are in the form of grants. The other part is a discretionary fund available generally to income support recipients only, who may be granted repayable *loans* for 'important intermittent expenses' (for example, essential furniture, bedclothes, reconnection charges) or for expenses caused by an emergency or a disaster (in which case, the recipient need not have been in receipt of income support), or to meet short-term needs or living expenses for a period not exceeding 14 days.[9] Its discretionary nature with no right of appeal against decisions taken by Social Fund Officers in local offices together with a cash-limit on the amount of money available to be lent to applicants,[10] have combined to make the Social Fund the most controversial of the reforms in the social security system.[11]

(d) Family credit

Unlike income support which, as we have seen, requires a claimant not to be working, family credit is designed as an alternative benefit for low-income families where the claimant or partner is working. The claimant must in any case be in Great Britain and in the case of a couple seeking the benefit, be the woman. She, or her partner, must be 'normally engaged in remunerative work' defined,[12] from April 1992, as 16 hours-a-week and responsible for a child member of the same household. To attract *maximum* family credit, the net income of the family (excluding child benefit, the first £15 of any maintenance payments and earnings of the children) must be below the 'applicable amount' set by regulations. Where net income exceeds this amount, credit is reduced by 70 per cent of the amount of excess.[13] A family is ineligible if they have capital over £8,000, and capital between £3,000 and £8,000 is treated in the same way as for income support. Once assessed, the amount is payable for 26 weeks, even if the recipient's circumstances change.

There has been concern about the low take-up of this benefit with only

---

[9] See Mesher, op cit, pp 387–395. Community care *grants* are also available, on a discretionary basis, to those leaving institutional or residential care.

[10] £160 million was allocated for loans, and £68 million for grants in 1990–91, compared with £346 million for single payments in 1985–86; see Ogus and Barendt, op cit, p 513, n 10; *Annual Report by the Secretary of State for Social Security on the Social Fund 1990–91*, Cm 1580 (1991).

[11] See the dicta in *R v Secretary of State for Social Services, ex p Healey* (1991) Times, 31 December, CA.

[12] The Family Credit (General) Amendment Regulations 1991, r 2.

[13] The Family Credit (General) Regulations 1987, rr 46–48 (as amended).

half of those families estimated to be eligible having applied. However, the reduction in the number of hours to be worked in order to qualify for family credit and to become ineligible for income support, is likely to lead to higher numbers of families becoming recipients in future.

(e) Child benefit[14]

Direct financial aid to families bringing up children was proposed as long ago as 1796, by William Pitt. However it was not until the Family Allowances Act 1945 that such a scheme was put into practice. Under the 1945 Act family allowance was paid to the mother, but only to families with at least two children. The amount hardly changed in twenty years. Tax allowances for all children were also available to set against income tax. Since married women were less likely to be in paid employment than is now the case, such allowances generally enhanced the take-home pay of the father and it was argued that the children did not always receive the benefit of them. Integration and reform of the two schemes were called for in the late 1960s, and finally achieved under the Child Benefit Act 1975, after which child tax allowances were phased out.

The basic scheme is that child benefit is paid as a flat-rate benefit regardless of need for each child (including the first),[15] usually to the mother.

Section 141 of the Social Security Contributions and Benefits Act 1992 now provides:

'A person who is responsible for one or more children in any week shall be entitled ... to a benefit ... for that week in respect of the child or each of the children for whom he is responsible.'[16]

A child is defined by section 142 as a person under the age of 16; or under the age of 18 and not receiving full-time education, in respect of whom prescribed conditions are satisfied; or under the age of 19 and receiving full-time non-advanced (ie non-degree, or Higher National Diploma) education. Child benefit is not payable in respect of children on youth training schemes.[17]

Under section 143 a person is treated as responsible for a child if he has the child living with him or is contributing to the cost of providing for the child at a weekly rate not less than the child benefit payable for that child. Where care of a child is split between parents, for example where there is a joint residence order, or extensive staying contact, they may agree between themselves who is to receive the benefit, or, in default of agreement, the Secretary of State may decide.[18] The recipient need not be a parent of the child, or even a relative, and there may be many cases where there are competing claims. Schedule 10 to the 1992 Act sets out an order of priority, so that the person having the child living with him or her has priority over a person contributing to the cost of providing for the child; a wife has

[14] See Bonner, I Hooker and White *Non-Means Tested Benefits: The Legislation* and Ogus and Barendt, op cit, ch 10.
[15] Thus reversing the old family allowance rule excluding the first child altogether. In fact a higher amount is paid for the first child: see the Child Benefit and Social Security (Fixing and Adjustment of Rates) Regulations 1976 (as amended), r 2(1).
[16] There are also regulations setting out residence requirements: the Child Benefit (Residence and Persons Abroad) Regulations 1976 (as amended).
[17] The Child Benefit (General) Regulations 1976 (as amended), rr 7A, 7B.
[18] Social Security Contributions and Benefits Act 1992, Sch 10, para 5.

priority over her husband where they are residing together; a parent takes priority over a non-parent; and a mother takes priority over an unmarried father where they are residing together.

In recognition of the extra financial burdens on lone parents, an additional 'one-parent benefit' is payable in respect of the first child of a claimant who is (a) receiving child benefit, (b) has no spouse or is not residing with his or her spouse, and (c) is not living with any other person as his or her spouse.[19]

Child benefit is not taxable, and is not counted when assessing eligibility for family credit. It is, however, included as income for the purposes of calculating income support.

D. Maintenance orders made by magistrates' courts[20]

1. JURISDICTION

A magistrates' court may make an order under the Domestic Proceedings and Magistrates' Courts Act 1978 if, at the date of the making of the application, either the applicant or the respondent ordinarily resides within the commission area for which the court is appointed.[1]

2. ORDERS FOR FINANCIAL PROVISION

Application for financial provision may be made in one of three different sets of circumstances. First, there is what one might term the 'normal' application, when the applicant must establish one of the four grounds set out in section 1 of the Act. Secondly, if the spouses have agreed what financial provision should be made, either may apply to have the terms of the agreement embodied in a court order. Thirdly, the court may make an order if the spouses are living apart (otherwise than as a result of desertion) and the respondent has been making periodical payments to the applicant.

(a) Applications under section 1

Either party to a marriage may apply to a magistrates' court for an order on the ground that the respondent spouse:

  (a) has failed to provide reasonable maintenance for the applicant;
  (b) has failed to provide, or to make a proper contribution towards, reasonable maintenance for any child of the family;
  (c) has behaved in such a way that the applicant cannot reasonably be expected to live with the respondent; or

---

[19] For further details, see D Bonner, I Hooker and R White, op cit.
[20] For the background to the legislation see generally McGregor, Blom-Cooper and Gibson *Separated Spouses*; Report of the Committee on One-Parent Families, Cmnd 5629, passim; Law Com No 77 (Matrimonial Proceedings in Magistrates' Courts), Pt II.
[1] S 30(1). See Law Com No 77, paras 4.77–4.90. As the jurisdiction is statutory, it cannot be enlarged by agreement or submission: *Forsyth v Forsyth* [1948] P 125, 132, [1947] 2 All ER 623, 624, CA.

(d) has deserted the applicant.

In all cases the ground must exist when the application[2] is made and also at the time of adjudication. Hence, for example, an order cannot be made on the ground of desertion if the spouses resume cohabitation before the hearing.[3]

The last two grounds may appear to be unnecessary for, if the respondent is making reasonable provision for the applicant, there will be no occasion to make an order. However, the respondent's behaviour is included to cover the case of the wife who is anxious to leave her husband on account of his conduct but knows that, if she does so, she will receive no maintenance from him. Desertion is included to enable a deserted wife whose husband is providing her with reasonable maintenance to obtain an order immediately without having to wait for him to stop paying her.[4]

(i) Failure to provide reasonable maintenance

Under former Acts the applicant had to show that the respondent had been guilty of wilful neglect to provide reasonable maintenance. This implied that he had failed to comply with his common law duty, and as a husband was under no duty to maintain his wife if she had committed adultery or was in desertion, there could be no wilful neglect in these circumstances.[5] This meant that a wife might fail to obtain maintenance before magistrates although she might claim financial relief on divorce. This argument is no longer valid, and the applicant's own conduct is now only one of the facts to be taken into account in determining whether this ground has been established.

Whether the respondent has provided reasonable maintenance for the applicant or any child of the family is clearly a question of fact. To answer it the bench must ask itself a hypothetical question: assuming that a ground for applying for an order existed, what order should we make? If the provision in fact being made by the respondent is lower—or at least significantly lower—than this, then he must be failing to provide reasonable maintenance. The word 'failure' implies culpability only in so far as it suggests that the respondent has the means to make the provision; and as his resources must be taken into account in deciding what sum to order, the court must ex hypothesi be satisfied that he has the capacity to make the payments.

(ii) The respondent's behaviour

The wording of this ground is the same as that of the second fact upon which a petitioner can rely to establish the ground for divorce and it must be interpreted in the same way.[6] It is not necessary, of course, for the applicant to show that the marriage has irretrievably broken down.

In common with other matters of summary jurisdiction, an application

---

[2] Proceedings are now by way of application and not complaint. For the procedure generally see the Family Proceedings Courts (Matrimonial Proceedings Etc) Rules 1991.
[3] *Irvin v Irvin* [1968] 1 All ER 271.
[4] Law Com No 77, paras 2.6–2.11. It may also enable the applicant to obtain a determination of whether the respondent is in desertion with a view to future divorce proceedings.
[5] *Chilton v Chilton* [1952] P 196, [1952] 1 All ER 1322.
[6] *Bergin v Bergin* [1983] 1 All ER 905. For further discussion see ante, pp 192–199.

must be made under the Domestic Proceedings and Magistrates' Courts Act within six months of the occurrence of the act complained of.[7] This means that the applicant must rely on at least one incident that has occurred during this period, although acts committed more than six months before may be relevant in putting the respondent's conduct in the correct setting.[8]

(iii) The respondent's desertion

Reference should be made to desertion in connection with the law of divorce.[9] Three differences between the law applicable in magistrates' courts and that applicable in divorce proceedings should be noted, however. As a ground for a magistrates' order desertion does not have to run for any minimum period of time: all that is necessary is that it should be running at the time of the application and the hearing. Further, if the respondent becomes incapable of retaining the animus deserendi owning to mental illness, magistrates may not treat desertion as continuing. Finally, the provision relating to the continuation of desertion whilst certain orders are in force does not apply: in such circumstances it will be necessary for the applicant to rely on one of the other grounds.

(iv) Reconciliation

When hearing an application under section 1, the court is required to consider whether there is any possibility of a reconciliation between the parties and if, either then or later, it appears that there is a reasonable possibility, it may adjourn the proceedings and, if it sees fit, request a probation officer or other person to attempt to effect one.[10] In the past courts claimed to have achieved a measure of success in this regard by holding an 'application court' at which the applicant meets the justices' clerk, a magistrate and, perhaps, a probation officer before the summons is issued.[11] The opportunity for doing this will now arise at the directions hearing[12] but, as in the case of divorce, it may be more practicable in most cases to concentrate on conciliation rather than reconciliation.[13]

(v) Cases more suitable for the High Court

A magistrates' court may refuse to deal with an application made under section 1 if it considers that it would be more conveniently dealt with by the High Court.[14] This power may be exercised only if the High Court itself could assume jurisdiction;[15] in other cases justices have an absolute

---

[7] Magistrates' Courts Act 1980, s 127(1).
[8] Cf Buxton v Buxton [1967] P 48, [1965] 3 All ER 150.
[9] See ante, pp 199–211.
[10] Domestic Proceedings and Magistrates' Courts Act 1978, s 26.
[11] See Law Com No 77, paras 4.9–4.17.
[12] Provided for in r 6 of the Family Proceedings Courts (Matrimonial Proceedings Etc) Rules 1991.
[13] See ante, pp 221 et seq.
[14] Domestic Proceedings and Magistrates' Courts Act 1978, s 27. No appeal lies from the justices' decision but the High Court may remit any subsequent proceedings to a magistrates' court: ibid.
[15] Consequently, a magistrates' court should not refuse to deal with an application to vary or discharge an existing order, for the High Court has no jurisdiction to do so: Smyth v Smyth [1956] P 427, [1956] 2 All ER 476. See also Davies v Davies [1957] P 357, [1957] 2 All ER 444.

discretion, but they rarely refuse to hear a case, nor indeed should they do so, for otherwise the whole purpose of providing a summary procedure would be lost. But there is one class of case where a magistrates' court should make an order only in exceptional circumstances, viz if the High Court or a county court is already seised of substantially the same matter and there is an actual or potential conflict of jurisdiction. If a husband is petitioning for divorce or other matrimonial relief and a magistrates' court entertains an application from his wife, there is a danger that the two courts might well find themselves embarrassed by diametrically opposed orders relating to substantially the same issue.[16] For the same reason a magistrates' court normally ought not to make an order if one of the spouses is about to commence proceedings in a divorce county court.[17] There is, of course, a danger that an unscrupulous husband might try to frustrate the wife's attempts to obtain a magistrates' order by the simple expedient of commencing proceedings in a county court. This led the Divisional Court to hold in *Lanitis v Lanitis*[18] that the wife's need to obtain an order quickly and her anxiety about her children (whom the husband had taken away) could—and on the particular facts did—amount to exceptional circumstances entitling the magistrates to make maintenance and (what was then) a custody order in her favour. Even if they make no order in favour of the applicant, they should at least consider whether they should make a section 8 order under the Children Act 1989 (and, where appropriate, a maintenance order) for the children, as failure to do so may lead to intolerable and harmful delay.[19]

(vi) Orders that may be made

On proof of any of the grounds set out above, the court may order the respondent to do one or more of the following:

    (a) to make periodical payments to the applicant;
    (b) to pay a lump sum not exceeding £1,000 for the applicant;
    (c) to make periodical payments to or for a child of the family to whom the application relates;
    (d) to pay a lump sum not exceeding £1,000 for such a child.[20]

---

[16] *Kaye v Kaye* [1965] P 100, [1964] 1 All ER 620. But there is no reason why magistrates should not make an order if the wife has made it clear that she does not propose to apply for maintenance in the divorce court: *Cooper v Cooper* [1953] P 26, [1952] 2 All ER 857.

[17] See *Sanders v Sanders* [1952] 2 All ER 767, at 770, 771.

[18] [1970] 1 All ER 466. An alternative way of dealing with the situation would be to make an interim order and then give the husband the choice of letting the court go into the merits: ibid at 472.

[19] *Jones v Jones* [1974] 3 All ER 702, 703, CA (where, as a consequence of the magistrates' adjourning the case, it was 12 months before a custody order was made). See also *Re S (A Minor) (Care Proceedings: Wardship Summons)* [1987] 1 FLR 479, CA where it was held that justices were not bound to adjourn care proceedings simply because wardship proceedings had been initiated.

[20] Domestic Proceedings and Magistrates' Courts Act 1978, s 2(1), (3). The lump sum figure was raised to £1,000 by the Secretary of State acting under the powers vested in him by s 2: Magistrates' Courts (Increase of Lump Sum) Order 1988. The court may also make an order for costs: Magistrates' Courts Act 1980, s 64. For the court's powers to make orders to or for the benefit of children of the family once the Child Support Act 1991 is fully in force, see post, pp 717–719.

It may allow the respondent to pay a lump sum or may order him to pay it by instalments.[1]

Orders can be made payable both to the applicant and to, or for the benefit of, any 'child of the family'. We have already considered the meaning of 'child of the family',[2] but it should be emphasised that just because a child is found to be a child of the family does not ipso facto mean that the respondent will be ordered to make financial provision for him. In the case of a child who is not that of the respondent, regard has to be had as to whether he had assumed responsibility for the child's maintenance and, if so, upon what basis and for how long that responsibility was discharged.[3]

The court may make an order for financial provision for a child whether or not it makes any other order relating to the child. However, even if the court is not satisfied that any ground for an application has been made out under section 1 but nonetheless makes a residence order under section 8 of the Children Act 1989,[4] it can make financial provision for the child pursuant to the powers under Schedule 1 to the 1989 Act.[5]

All orders for periodical payments may run from the date of the application and may be made for a limited period of time.[6] In the case of an order for a wife, this may be useful if she is likely to need money for a comparatively short period whilst she adjusts to living alone, because the husband will not have to go back to the court at a later date to seek a variation or discharge. Similarly magistrates may deliberately use this device as a means of getting the wife to obtain paid employment if they consider this to be the proper course (though before doing this justices should be confident that the wife can reasonably obtain employment).[7] If she will continue to need maintenance after the end of the period stipulated, she should take care to have the order varied before it runs out, because otherwise it will automatically lapse and she will have to start fresh proceedings.[8] The court may also order that the payments should begin from a future date and it may wish to use this power if, for example, the husband is unemployed but is to start work in a short time.

As far as orders for children are concerned, since some will start earning when they reach the upper limit of the compulsory school age, no order for periodical payments is to extend in the first instance beyond the date

[1] Magistrates' Courts Act 1980, s 75.

[2] Ante, p 368.

[3] Domestic Proceedings and Magistrates' Court Act 1978, s 3(4), discussed post, p 679.

[4] Under s 8 of the 1978 Act (as amended by the Children Act 1989, Sch 13, para 36) the court is enjoined not to dismiss or make a final order inter alia on application under s 2, until it has decided whether or not to exercise any of its powers under the 1989 Act with respect to the child. See the discussion ante, p 370.

[5] Discussed post, p 694.

[6] Domestic Proceedings and Magistrates' Courts Act 1978, ss 2(1)(a) and (c), 4(1) and 5(2).

[7] It is to be noted that as in judicial separation proceedings (see post, p 760) magistrates are not directed to consider whether liability should be terminated as soon as possible, ie the 'self-sufficiency' principle does not apply in these proceedings.

[8] It is doubtful whether a court can revive such an order after it has lapsed. However, under s 20A (as substituted by the Children Act 1989, Sch 13, para 39), where an order (other than an interim order) ceases to have effect upon the child reaching 16 or at any time after that date but before the child reaches 18, the child will be able to apply for the revival of the order if he is receiving instruction at an educational establishment or undergoing training for a trade, profession or vocation or where there are special circumstances justifying the revival.

of the child's birthday next following his attaining that age unless the court thinks it right to specify a later date (as it obviously must if he is already over that age). No order may be made at all, however, if the child is over the age of 18 and an existing order may not continue after his eighteenth birthday. To both limbs of this rule there are two exceptions: there is no age limit on the making or continuation of orders so long as the child is (or, if an order were made, would be) receiving instruction at an educational establishment or undergoing training for a trade, profession or vocation (whether or not he is also gainfully employed) or, in any event, if there are special circumstances justifying this.[9] Periodical payments could therefore continue indefinitely, if, say the child were incapable of earning his own living owing to some physical or mental handicap.

All orders for periodical payments terminate on the death of the spouse or the child or of the person liable to make the payments.[10]

(b) Consent orders

Following the Law Commission's recommendation[11] magistrates are able to make a consent order without the applicant's having to establish any other ground. Under section 6[12] upon either party's application and provided the court is satisfied that either the applicant or the respondent has agreed to make the financial provision[13] specified in the application, it may make an order giving effect to the agreement.[14] The order may contain precisely the same terms as an order made following an application under section 1 except that, as the respondent has agreed to it, a lump sum may be for *any amount* and is not limited to £1,000.

The court may not make the order proposed if it considers that it would be contrary to the interests of justice to do so.[15] This seems most likely to occur if the amount specified in the application looks far too low: there is always the danger of collusion between the parties in an attempt to switch the liability to maintain the wife on to public funds. Obviously other facts may be taken into account as well. Thus the court should refuse to make the order if it appears that undue pressure has been put on either party. In particular, the court must not implement the proposals if they do not provide for, or make a proper contribution towards, the financial needs of any child of the marriage.[16] In such cases, however, it is open to the parties to come forward with a fresh agreement. Alternatively the court itself might

[9] Ss 5(1)–(3), 6(7) and 7(7).
[10] Ss 5(4), 6(7), 7(7).
[11] See Law Com No 77, paras 4.1–4.8.
[12] As substituted by the Matrimonial and Family Proceedings Act 1984, s 10, which was implemented on 1 October 1986: SI 1986/1049.
[13] Defined by s 6(2) as the making of periodical or lump sum payments by one party to the other or by one party to a child of the family or to the other party for the benefit of such a child.
[14] The Act requires that the applicant or respondent should have agreed to make the provision, not that he should have agreed to its being embodied in a court order: see s 6(1). This suggests that the applicant could seek to have the terms of a separation agreement implemented without the respondent's consent. On the other hand, s 6(8) implies consent to the making of the order, and this construction is more in line with the obvious intention of the section. If proceedings are begun under s 1 and the respondent then agrees to the order, the applicant may apply for an order under s 6: s 6(4).
[15] S 6(1)(b).
[16] S 6(3).

take the initiative and suggest what order would be appropriate: if the parties both agree, this may be embodied in an order.[17]

(c) Orders following separation

As we have said, the reason that desertion has been retained as a ground for applying for an order under section 1 of the Act is to enable a wife, who has been deserted but whose husband is in fact providing her with reasonable maintenance, to secure her position. She will not have this advantage, however, if, for example, she has agreed to the separation; if her husband has not agreed to make financial provision she cannot apply under section 6 either. This gap has been partly closed by the provisions of section 7. To bring these into play, the parties must have lived apart for a continuous period exceeding three months, neither must be in desertion, and the respondent must have been making periodical payments for the benefit of the applicant or a child of the family.[18] 'Living apart' is not defined but it presumably bears the same meaning as under the law of divorce.[19] There are, however, no provisions akin to those in the Matrimonial Causes Act 1973 enabling two or more periods to be added together. Although applications under this section will normally be made when the spouses are living apart by agreement, they could be made exceptionally in other circumstances too, for example if one of the spouses was incapable of forming an animus deserendi because of mental illness.[20] The requirement that neither spouse must be in desertion means that if the applicant has deserted the respondent and the latter has continued to make reasonable provision for her or a child of the family, she cannot apply for an order under section 1 or section 7.

If the conditions set out above are satisfied, the court may make an order for periodical payments for the benefit of the applicant or any child of the family for such term as may be specified. The purpose of section 7 is to enable legal effect to be given to the de facto situation. Consequently, no order may be made for a lump sum payment and the court may not require the respondent to make payments which exceed in aggregate during any period of three months the amount actually paid by him for the benefit of the applicant or a child of the family during the three months immediately preceding the making of the application. If this is greater than the sum which the court would have ordered on an application under section 1, the respondent is protected by the further provision that the order must not be for more than this smaller sum.[1] Conversely, if the court considers that the sums paid fail to provide reasonable maintenance for the applicant or a child of the family, the first ground under section 1 must necessarily be made out; the court may therefore treat the application as though made

---

[17] S 6(5).
[18] S 7(1). The payments need not have been made to the applicant. Hence, for example, the payment of rent could amount to periodical payments for this purpose.
[19] See ante, p 211.
[20] Although the side note to this section refers to 'powers of court where parties are living apart by agreement', this cannot limit its unambiguous wording: see *Chandler v DPP* [1964] AC 763, [1962] 3 All ER 142, HL.
[1] S 7(3). Nor may the court require payments to be made for the benefit of a child who is not the child of the respondent if it would not have made an order in its favour on an application under s 1.

under that section and will then have full powers to make such orders for periodical payments and lump sum payments as it thinks fit.[2]

(d) Interim orders

The court may make an interim order at any time before making a final order or dismissing the application. It has a similar power if it refuses to make an order on the ground that the case would be more conveniently dealt with by the High Court. If in the latter case or on appeal the High Court remits the case to a magistrates' court, the High Court may make an interim order, in which case it is deemed to have been made by a magistrates' court for the purpose of enforcement, revocation, suspension, revival and variation.[3]

An interim order may require the respondent[4] to make periodical payments to the applicant or for the benefit of any child of the family under the age of 18. These may be backdated to the making of the application.

The court may put a limit on the time for which the order is to remain in force, and it will cease to have effect when a final order is made (or, alternatively, when the application is dismissed) or, in any case, after three months. If a final adjudication has not been made, the court may extend the order for any period or periods not exceeding in total three months from the first extension.[5]

(e) Income tax

The tax position is discussed in chapter 21.

(f) Payment of maintenance

Upon the making of a periodical payments order, magistrates' courts are required to specify the method of payment.[6] The specified method of payment must be one of the following, namely, payments made directly by the debtor to the creditor; payments made to the clerk of the court or the clerk of any other magistrates' court; payment by standing order or 'by any other method which requires one person to give his authority for payment of a specific amount to be made from an account of his to an account of another, on specific dates during the period for which the authority is in force and without the need for any further authority from him,' and payments by way of an attachment of earnings order.[7]

---

[2] S 7(4).

[3] Domestic Proceedings and Magistrates' Courts Act 1978, s 19(1), (9).

[4] Or applicant in the case of an application made under s 6 by the person who has agreed to make the financial provision: Domestic Proceedings and Magistrates' Courts Act 1978, s 19(3A), added by the Matrimonial and Family Proceedings Act 1984, Sch 1, para 24 and amended by the Children Act 1989, Sch 13, para 31.

[5] S 19(5), (6). No appeal lies from the making of or refusal to make an interim maintenance order or from the variation, revocation, etc of such an order: s 19(8). Only one interim maintenance order may be made, but this is without prejudice to make an interim order upon a subsequent application for an order under ss 2, 6 or 7: s 19(7).

[6] Magistrates' Courts Act 1980, s 59(1), as substituted by the Maintenance Enforcement Act 1991, s 2. This requirement is contingent on the 'debtor' (ie the person against whom the order is made) being ordinarily resident in England and Wales at the time that the order was made: ibid, s 59(2).

[7] Ibid, s 59(6). Attachment of earnings orders are discussed post, p 690.

The power to order payment by standing order (or some similar method) was introduced by the Maintenance Enforcement Act 1991[8] and is intended to ensure prompt payments without the parties having to come face to face. The more traditional method of providing for this is for payment to be made to the clerk of the magistrates' court on behalf of the recipient. Indeed if payment is not ordered to be made by standing order (or its equivalent) or under an attachment of earnings order then it must be ordered to be paid to the clerk unless the recipient can show that for some reason this would be undesirable.[9] Alternatively, the court may order the payments to be made to some other person to the recipient's use.[10] To avoid unnecessary waste of time on the recipient's part (perhaps involving loss of working time and therefore of wages) the clerk is obliged to forward by post all payments received unless the recipient asks for other arrangements to be made.[11]

If the recipient is also in receipt of income support then, as we have seen,[12] payments can be requested to be 'diverted' to the Benefits Agency; the Agency then keeps the payments received and pays the support in full. This has the advantage that the recipient receives the full amount each week regardless of whether the maintenance order is paid in full or on time.

Maintenance payable under a magistrates' order is inalienable like unsecured periodical payments made under the Matrimonial Causes Act.[13] As a lump sum is more in the nature of a debt owed by the respondent, it is possible that it may be assigned.

3. ASSESSMENT

The Domestic Proceedings and Magistrates' Courts Act broke new ground in setting out, for the first time, a comprehensive list of the matters which a magistrates' court is to take into account when making an order. These guidelines have since been amended by the Matrimonial and Family Proceedings Act 1984[14] so that now in deciding what, if any, financial order should be made, the court must 'have regard to all the circumstances of the case, first consideration being given to the welfare while a minor of any child of the family who has not attained the age of 18'.[15] In addition, in determining whether the respondent is to be required to make periodical payments or to pay a lump sum to the applicant and, if so, how much he is to pay, the court is directed 'in particular' to have regard to:[16]

'(a)   the income, earning capacity, property and other financial resources which each of the parties to the marriage has or is likely to have in the foreseeable future, including in the case of earning capacity any increase in that capacity

---

[8] Where payment is so ordered the court can require the debtor to open an account: ibid, s 59(4).
[9] Ibid, s 59(7).
[10] Domestic Proceedings and Magistrates' Courts Act 1978, s 32(2).
[11] Magistrates' Courts Rules 1981, r 39 as substituted by the Magistrates' Courts (Maintenance Enforcement Act 1991) (Miscellaneous Amendments) Rules 1992, r 16.
[12] Ante, p 667.
[13] *Paquine v Snary* [1909] 1 KB 688, CA. See further post, p 731.
[14] S 9.
[15] S 3(1) of the 1978 Act.
[16] S 3(2). In the case of applications made under s 7, para (c) is amended to read: 'the standard of living enjoyed by the parties to the marriage before they lived apart' (s 7(5)).

which it would in the opinion of the court be reasonable to expect a party
to the marriage to take steps to acquire;

(b)   the financial needs, obligations and responsibilities which each of the parties
to the marriage has or is likely to have in the foreseeable future;

(c)   the standard of living enjoyed by the parties to the marriage before the
occurrence of the conduct which is alleged as the ground of the application;

(d)   the age of each party to the marriage and the duration of the marriage;

(e)   any physical or mental disability of either of the parties to the marriage;

(f)   the contributions which each of the parties has made or is likely in the
foreseeable future to make to the welfare of the family, including any
contribution by looking after the home or caring for the family;

(g)   the conduct of each of the parties, if that conduct is such that it would in
the opinion of the court be inequitable to disregard it.'

In deciding what, if any, orders should be made in favour of any child
of the family, in addition to the foregoing considerations, the court must
also have regard to:[17]

'(a)   the financial needs of the child;

(b)   the income, earning capacity (if any), property and other financial resources
of the child;

(c)   any physical or mental disability of the child;

(d)   the standard of living enjoyed by the family before the occurrence of the
conduct which is alleged as the ground of the application (or before the
parties to the marriage lived apart); and

(e)   the manner in which the child was being and in which the parties to the
marriage expected him to be educated or trained.'

The wide definition of the term 'child of the family'[18] means that the
court has power to make an order against a spouse who would be under
no other legal obligation to make financial provision for him and who may
have assumed no responsibility for his maintenance. Consequently a measure
of protection is necessary and, in deciding whether to make an order against
a party to the marriage in favour of a child who is not his natural or
adopted child and, if so, how much to award, the court must further have
regard:[19]

'(a)   to whether [he] has assumed responsibility for the child's maintenance and,
if he did, to the extent to which, and the basis on which, he assumed that
responsibility and to the length of time during which he discharged that
responsibility;

(b)   to whether in assuming and discharging that responsibility [he] did so knowing
that the child was not his own child; and

(c)   to the liability of any other person to maintain the child.'

Whether a spouse assumed responsibility for a child must be judged
objectively, and in the absence of a clear contrary indication the payment
of the expenses of a family unit including the child implies an assumption
of responsibility even though other resources may be available for his
maintenance.[20] In paragraph (a) the word 'extent' refers to the amount of
his contribution in contradistinction to the length of time during which he

---

[17] S 3(3). But for the powers of the court once the Child Support Act 1991 is in force, see post,
pp 717–719.

[18] Discussed ante, p 368.

[19] Ss 3(4), 7(5).

[20] *Snow v Snow* [1972] Fam 74, 111–112, [1971] 3 All ER 833, 863, CA.

made it.[1] The reference in paragraph (c) to the liability of any other person to maintain the child covers any liability enforceable at law and thus embraces the potential liability of a parent or of a party to another marriage who has treated the child as a child of the family.[2] It will be seen that the need to take all these matters into account means that the court might well conclude, for example, that no order should be made against a husband who had married the wife in the mistaken belief that he was the father of her child or who had made it clear at the time of the marriage that he was undertaking no financial responsibility for her children by a previous marriage if their own father was quite capable of providing for them.[3]

Comparison with the matters which the court must take into account in making an order for financial relief after divorce shows that, with one minor exception,[4] the guidelines are identical. This follows the recommendation of the Law Commission who took the view that, as far as possible, the same principles should govern both sets of proceedings.[5] As the law has been much more fully worked out in connection with divorce, detailed examination of these matters will be deferred until chapter 21 but some general principles and certain points of dissimilarity should be mentioned here.

(a) Absence of power to adjust property rights

The main difference between the powers of magistrates' courts and those of divorce courts is that magistrates cannot make property adjustment orders. Furthermore, they should resist any suggestion that they should do so indirectly by using their power to order lump sum payments. It would be wholly improper, for example, to compel a husband to buy his wife's half share in household goods by ordering him to pay her half their value. In the first place, magistrates have no power to make the necessary consequential orders extinguishing and transferring rights in property. More fundamentally, the making of property adjustment orders is inconsistent with the principle that magistrates should regulate the parties' financial position during a period of marital breakdown which is not necessarily permanent or irretrievable.[6] It is to be assumed that whichever spouse is in the matrimonial home will stay there for the time being: if either of them

---

[1] *Roberts v Roberts* [1962] P 212, [1962] 2 All ER 967. See Samuels 26 MLR 92.

[2] *Snow v Snow* (supra) at 112 and 863 respectively. The court may adjourn the hearing to enable proceedings to be taken against the person liable: *Caller v Caller* [1968] P 39, [1966] 2 All ER 754; *Snow v Snow*. This may cause difficulty because, if, for example, the child in question is the wife's illegitimate child or her child by a previous marriage, her present husband has no power to institute or intervene in the proceedings.

[3] See *Bowlas v Bowlas* [1965] P 450, [1965] 3 All ER 40, CA. In the case of an application under s 7 the court shall not require the respondent to make payments for the benefit of a child of the family who is not his child if it would not have made an order in the child's favour in proceedings brought under s 1: s 7(3)(c).

[4] Para (c) of s 25(1) of the Matrimonial Causes Act 1973 refers to 'the standard of living enjoyed by the family before the breakdown of the marriage'. The divorce court is additionally required to consider the loss, inter alia, of pension rights. See post, p 784.

[5] Law Com No 77, paras 2.12–2.29.

[6] See ante, p 654.

wishes to bring about a change, he or she must invoke the jurisdiction of the High Court or a county court in some other way.[7]

(b) No requirement to consider 'self-sufficiency'

Another important difference between magistrates' powers and those of the divorce court is that the former are not directed to consider whether the parties could become self-sufficient. Magistrates have no powers to make a 'clean break' order, that is, an order which settles the financial liability in a once-and-for-all order. On the other hand, they are directed to have regard to whether it is reasonable to expect a party to take steps to increase his earning capacity. This could justify, for example, making a periodical payments order to last for a limited time in a case where the applicant could reasonably be expected to start work or to obtain higher paid work. However, it must be stressed that such an order should not lightly be made. There would need to be evidence, for example, that there is work available in the locality and that it is reasonable to assume that the applicant could become employed.[8] Even if such a limited term order were to be made the applicant could still return to the court to seek an extension of the order, or, if the order had already expired, could bring fresh proceedings to seek a new order.

(c) First consideration to be given to the welfare while a minor of a child of the family who has not attained the age of 18

This requirement, which was introduced under the Matrimonial and Family Proceedings Act 1984, is the same as on divorce[9] and we discuss this more fully in that context.[10] Suffice to say here that (a) priority is only given to children of the spouses' family,[11] (b) the court is only required to give first and not paramount consideration to the child's welfare.[12] This means that other considerations should be taken into account and in some circumstances could be overriding. The enjoinder does not mean, for instance, that the husband's moral obligations towards his second family should be ignored.[13]

(d) The parties' needs

According to Dunn LJ in *Vasey v Vasey*[14] the proper approach for magistrates, when considering an application for financial provision, is to make findings seriatim upon each of the matters set out in what is now section 3(2) and to balance the factors against one another to arrive at an order which is just and reasonable. But as Dunn LJ also pointed out the most important function of magistrates is to balance the needs and responsibilities against the financial resources.

---

[7] Except that magistrates may exclude the respondent from the matrimonial home if he has used or threatened to use violence against the applicant or a child of the family. See ante, p 174.

[8] Cf *Munt v Munt* (1983) 13 Fam Law 81, where an order was made against an unemployed husband on the basis that there were good prospects of obtaining seasonal unskilled work in the area. See further post, p 771.

[9] Thereby implementing the Law Commission's recommendations: Law Com No 112, para 24.

[10] See ch 21.

[11] Ie not those of the parent's second family.

[12] On which see *Suter v Suter and Jones* [1987] Fam 111, [1987] 2 All ER 336, CA.

[13] See *Blower v Blower* [1986] 1 FLR 292; *Roberts v Roberts* [1970] P 1, [1968] 3 All ER 479.

[14] [1985] FLR 596 at 603, CA.

Only the family's reasonable needs should be taken into account. With regard to children, as Bagnall J said in a comment approved by the Court of Appeal in *Lilford v Glynn*:[15]

> 'In the vast majority of cases the financial position of a child of a subsisting marriage is simply to be afforded shelter, food and education, according to the means of his parents.'

The parents similarly require shelter and food, but over and above this there can be no hard and fast rules since what amounts to 'reasonable' needs inevitably has to be judged against the available resources.[16]

Commonly in cases before magistrates the parties' means will be so slight that all the court can do is to concentrate on their needs. Priority must be given to trying to secure the children's position; what is left will frequently have to be divided in the best way possible to ensure that each spouse will at least have enough to cover his or her essential expenses. The need to support two families will often mean that the husband will not be able to keep both above subsistence level; in that case any order made must not reduce his resources to such an extent that, were he unemployed, he would be entitled to income support. Given that he can be ordered to pay something, however, magistrates should make a full assessment of the sum notwithstanding that it will be so small that the wife will still have to look to the Benefits Agency to make up the balance.[17] To this extent the court must know what the benefits payable to both parties would be;[18] similarly it must be told what other social security benefits they can claim, such as child benefit and family income supplement.

(e) Judging the overall fairness of orders

One of the problems of the guidelines is that although they set out the considerations to which the court must have regard, ultimately they do not provide guidance on what may be regarded as a fair and just order overall. A similar problem is faced by the divorce courts, though it is arguably more important to give firmer guidance to magistrates. The courts themselves have used a variety of approaches and it is important to appreciate that, at any rate with regard to the starting point, none of them should be regarded as laying down rigid rules. At various times the courts have used the so-called 'one-third rule' by which, as a starting point, the wife's income should be brought up to one-third of the spouses' joint income.[19] The resulting sum is then tested against the parties' needs. It is now established that this approach is not useful in the case of very low incomes (the situation most

---

[15] [1979] 1 All ER 441 at 447.

[16] One problem is the need for a car. Whether this is a reasonable need depends in part upon whether it is genuinely needed to get to work: cf *Clarke v Clarke* (1979) 9 Fam Law 15, where a car was not thought to be needed, and *Slater v Slater* (1982) 3 FLR 364, where it was. In *Girvan v Girvan* (1983) 13 Fam Law 213, where a husband had just been made redundant, it was thought that a television was a reasonable need but not a video.

[17] *Ashley v Ashley* [1968] P 582, [1965] 3 All ER 554; *Barnes v Barnes* [1972] 3 All ER 872, CA; Bisset-Johnson and Pollard 38 MLR 449. Cf *Freeman v Swatridge* [1984] FLR 762, CA (where a father receiving State benefit was nevertheless ordered to pay 50p a week for each of his two children). But see *Delaney v Delaney* [1990] 2 FLR 457, CA, discussed post, p 769.

[18] Cf *Williams v Williams* [1974] Fam 55, [1974] 3 All ER 377.

[19] The court uses the parties' *gross* earnings in making this computation: *Rodewald v Rodewald* [1977] Fam 192, [1977] 2 All ER 609, CA.

commonly facing magistrates)[20] nor very high incomes.[1] Between these two points, however, this approach can remain useful in giving a 'ranging shot'. The currently favoured method of arriving at a fair order is to adopt the 'net effect' approach. According to Ormrod LJ in *Stockford v Stockford*[2] this involves working out the respondent's liability to tax on the basis of a hypothetical order and deducting from his gross income the aggregate of national insurance contributions,[3] the amount of the proposed order and his tax liability. On the other side of the coin, the applicant's earnings, any allowances and the amount of the hypothetical order (taking into account any tax liability) should also be aggregated. The resulting two figures can then be compared and related to the parties' needs, and the hypothetical order adjusted accordingly. One problem with this approach is that it leaves open what starting point should be used, but in *Slater v Slater*[4] Arnold P commented that the guideline could be the level of maintenance currently being provided voluntarily, any offer which has been made, or if there be no other guideline and it is not a case of great wealth or unusual poverty, the one-third guideline may be taken. In the final analysis it seems that there is no hard and fast starting point, the crucial point being to test the result of whatever order is being proposed.

(f) Some distorting factors

The net effect approach assumes that wherever possible the parties' final financial position should be roughly comparable. However, this standpoint may not apply in cases where it is thought right to take the parties' conduct into account or where the parties' marriage has been short-lived. Both these facts are relevant on divorce and will be discussed in detail in chapter 21. Suffice it here to say that the generally held view is that conduct will only be relevant in exceptional cases. As Dunn LJ said, in *Vasey v Vasey*,[5] conduct should only be taken into account in exceptional cases because 'experience has shown that it is dangerous to make judgments about the cause of breakdown of a marriage without full inquiry, since the conduct of one spouse can only be measured against the conduct of the other, and marriages seldom break down without faults on both sides'. Even if conduct is thought to be relevant, magistrates should still balance that fact against all the others laid down by statute and in particular against each party's needs.[6] It might also be observed that the courts should not prejudice any child (whose welfare is the court's first consideration) because of their parent's misconduct.

In cases where the marriage has been short-lived, reduced orders may be justified.[7]

---

[20] See eg *Cann v Cann* [1977] 3 All ER 957.
[1] See eg *Preston v Preston* [1982] Fam 17, [1982] 1 All ER 41, CA.
[2] (1981) 3 FLR 58 at 63, CA.
[3] Quaere whether union dues may also be deducted?
[4] (1982) 3 FLR 364 at 370.
[5] [1985] FLR 596 at 603, CA.
[6] *Vasey v Vasey*, supra. Even so the wife conceded that a reduced order should be made, since she had deserted her husband after nine months of marriage. See also *Robinson v Robinson* [1983] Fam 42, [1983] 1 All ER 391, CA, discussed post, p 782.
[7] See eg *Khan v Khan* [1980] 1 All ER 497; *Graves v Graves* (1974) 4 Fam Law 124 and *Brady v Brady* (1973) 3 Fam Law 78.

(g) Remarriage and cohabitation

The payer's remarriage will not normally be relevant in magistrates' proceedings, but it may become so if the order continues in force after a later divorce.[8] In this case it may be proper to reduce the order because of his increased financial responsibilities; the same result will follow if he lives with another woman, particularly if they have children whom he has to support.[9] Likewise the wife's living with another man may lead the court to make a much smaller order or no order at all, not because she is committing adultery but because the man will be supporting her himself or, alternatively, because she should look to him for maintenance rather than to her husband.

(h) Lump sum payments

The power conferred on magistrates to order lump sum payments was introduced by the 1978 Act. Such a power, of course, is of no practical value unless the respondent has the necessary capital, or possibly, income;[10] if he has it available, however, there are a number of situations in which relatively small orders may be made. The Act itself provides that a lump sum may be ordered to meet any liability or expenses already incurred in maintaining the applicant or any child of the family:[11] in other words in appropriate cases it will be an alternative to backdating the order. It might also be used to enable a wife to take a course of training, for example to pay the fees of a secretarial course, or even to help provide the capital to set her up in business. If the spouses have low incomes but the respondent has some savings, a just solution might be to order part of the savings to be paid to the applicant.[12] Most applications, however, are likely to be made to pay for children's expenses, for example, to buy a uniform or other clothes for a new school or to pay for fees and other incidental expenses on starting, for example, a course of training.

4. VARIATION, SUSPENSION, REVIVAL, REVOCATION AND CESSATION OF ORDERS

(a) Cohabitation

As under earlier legislation, the 1978 Act permits the court to make an order both as an application under section 1 and section 6 requiring either

[8] The payee's remarriage will automatically discharge an order made in his favour: see post, p 686.
[9] Cf *Delaney v Delaney* [1990] 2 FLR 457, CA, discussed post, p 769.
[10] See *Burridge v Burridge* [1983] Fam 9, [1982] 3 All ER 80, where the court ordered an unemployed husband to pay a lump sum by instalments, expecting him to obtain employment within six weeks.
[11] Domestic Proceedings and Magistrates' Courts Act 1978, s 2(2).
[12] Cf the facts of *Cann v Cann* [1977] 3 All ER 957, where the parties (who were aged 70 and 67) were both living on small pensions and the husband had some savings. The case was decided before magistrates had the power to order the payment of a lump sum, and it was suggested that one solution might be to find out what annuity could be purchased and to take that into account. Alternatively, the husband could be notionally attributed with whatever income the capital would bring in if wisely invested.

party to the marriage to make periodical payments to the other (whether for the spouse's benefit or for the benefit of any child of the family), whilst the spouses are living together.[13] However, if the parties are living with each other in the same household when the order is made, it will cease to have effect if they continue to live with each other for a continuous period exceeding six months. Similarly, if they resume living with each other in the same household at a later date (whether or not they were cohabiting when the order was made), it will cease to have effect only if the same condition is fulfilled. 'Living with each other in the same household' must have the same meaning as it has in the law of divorce: consequently the parties may not be living with each other even though they are physically resident under the same roof.[14] It will also be observed that the period must be continuous: the spouses may live with each other for any length of time in the aggregate provided that no single period lasts for more than six months.[15] The reason for this is that cohabitation should bring an order to an end only if it indicates a permanent reconciliation and this could not be inferred if the period were shorter.[16]

Until an order ceases to have effect under the provisions just considered, it is enforceable notwithstanding that the parties are living together. The justification for this has been said to be that the basic cause of many marital difficulties is the husband's carelessness in financial matters and that it is wrong that a wife who is compelled to obtain an order should be in a worse position if she stays with her husband than if she leaves him.[17] While this may be true, the fact of her obtaining an order at all may well exacerbate the position, particularly in cases where payments have to be made through a magistrates' clerk.[18]

As the parties must be living apart before an order can be made under section 7, the provisions relating to cohabitation when the order is made cannot apply. If the parties resume living with each other in the same household, any interim or final order for periodical payments made under that section will cease to have effect immediately.[19]

Where payments are ordered to be made (except under section 7) *to the child himself* neither the continuation nor the resumption of cohabitation will have any effect on the order unless the court otherwise directs.[20] This gives the court a discretion to distinguish between orders made payable to

---

[13] Ss 25(1) and 88(2).

[14] See ante, p 211. Under earlier Acts orders automatically ceased to have effect if the parties resumed cohabitation.

[15] But if the wife were to leave the husband for a short period solely for the purpose of keeping the order alive, this might be a ground for him to apply to have it revoked.

[16] See Law Com No 77, para 2.55. If there is doubt whether an order has ceased to have effect as a result of the parties' living together, the court may determine the matter: Domestic Proceedings and Magistrates' Courts Act 1978, s 25(4).

[17] See Law Com No 77, paras 2.58–2.65.

[18] See ante, p 677. Another possibility is that a wife who claims that her husband is giving her too little housekeeping money but who has no intention of leaving him might use this procedure to ask the court to 'fix the housekeeping'. It is open to debate whether this is a proper use of magistrates' time.

[19] Domestic Proceedings and Magistrates' Court Act 1978, s 25(3).

[20] Ss 25(2).

the child personally because he is not living with either of the spouses and those made to the child for tax or other financial advantage[1] where the reality is that they are being made to one of the parties to the marriage. Whereas in the former case the order should obviously continue notwithstanding the spouses' cohabitation, in the latter the order should normally be discharged.[2]

(b) Divorce, nullity and remarriage

A decree of divorce does not automatically terminate an order made under the Domestic Proceedings and Magistrates' Courts Act. In some cases the recipient will prefer to have the order discharged and replaced by an order made by the divorce court.[3] In other cases (or if the marriage is dissolved by a foreign court) it will be open to either party to apply for the order to be varied or revoked if the decree has changed their financial position.[4]

If a marriage is void, the whole order must be inoperative as it rests on the false assumption that the parties were in fact married. If the marriage is voidable, the decree will have the same effect as a decree of divorce.[5]

The remarriage of the party required to make periodical payments will not affect the order although it may give him a ground to have it varied in the light of his new financial position. If the other party remarries, she (or he) can make financial claims against her new spouse; consequently the magistrates' order for periodical payments in her favour will automatically cease to have effect even though the second marriage proves to be void or voidable.[6] If the person liable to make payments continues to do so in the mistaken belief that the order is still subsisting, he (or his personal representatives, if he has died) may recover them from the payee (or the payee's personal representatives) in an action in a county court.[7] In some cases an order for the repayment of the whole sum might be unjust, for example if the payee had received the sums paid in good faith and had already spent them; accordingly the court has power to order the repayment of such smaller sum as it thinks fit or to dismiss the application altogether. Magistrates' clerks and collecting officers under attachment of earnings orders are given statutory protection unless they receive written notice of the remarriage from one of the former spouses (or their personal representatives).[8]

---

[1] As there is no longer any tax advantage in making orders payable to the child, see post, p 732, such orders are only likely to have been made before 15 March 1988.

[2] See Law Com No 77, paras 5.97–5.113.

[3] See further ante, p 655.

[4] *Wood v Wood* [1957] P 254, [1957] 2 All ER 14, CA, where the court increased an order made in the wife's favour because of the husband's improved financial position even though he had obtained a divorce in Nevada. Contrast *Sternberg v Sternberg* [1963] 3 All ER 319, where, after the wife had obtained a maintenance order on the ground of the husband's desertion, he obtained a divorce on the ground of her desertion. The Divisional Court held that, as the findings of the High Court in the divorce proceedings bound the magistrates' court, it must be conclusively presumed that the latter had no jurisdiction to make the order which must therefore be discharged.

[5] See ante, pp 100–102.

[6] Domestic Proceedings and Magistrates' Courts Act 1978, ss 4(2), 6(6), 7(6) and 88(3).

[7] Or in the High Court if the order is registered there and proceedings are being brought there for its enforcement.

[8] Domestic Proceedings and Magistrates' Courts Act 1978, s 35.

(c) Party's death

The death of either party automatically bring the order to an end.[9]

(d) Variation, revival and revocation of orders

In addition to the cases already considered, the court has a general power to vary or revoke an order for periodical payments (including an interim order) on the application of either spouse.[10] The child himself may apply for a variation if he has attained the age of 16. He may also, once he has attained the age of 16 but before he reaches 18, apply for an order to be revived.[11] He may well wish to take advantage of the last-mentioned provision if he decides to undergo further education or training at some stage after leaving school and beginning to earn his own living. The court's powers depend on the section under which the original order was made. In all cases it may increase or reduce the amount of the payments or extinguish them entirely. It may also suspend any order temporarily and revive any order which has been suspended, a power which it might wish to use, for example, if the husband is temporarily unemployed.[12] If the order was made following an application under section 1, the court may also make an order for the payment of a lump sum not exceeding £1,000 for the benefit of the applicant or any child of the family, whether or not it has previously made such an order.[13] The applicant may therefore bring proceedings for variation simply to obtain a lump sum. In the case of an order made under section 6 the court can order the respondent to pay a lump sum only if the original order provided for a lump sum payment; if it did contain such a provision, however, the lump sum ordered in proceedings for variation need not be for the benefit of the same person. Thus, if under the original order the husband paid a lump sum to the wife, he may be ordered on variation to pay a lump sum to her or to a child of the family. Whatever the amount of the original payment, in proceedings for variation the court may order him to pay up to £1,000 or, if he consents, any larger sum.[14] As the court has no power to include a lump sum payment in an order made under section 7, it has no power to order such a provision in proceedings for variation.

In considering how to exercise its powers on an application for a variation or revocation, the court must give effect to any agreement reached between the parties if it appears just to do so. If there is no such agreement or, if the court declines to give effect to it, the court should start with the existing order and decide how far it should be varied as a result of any change in the relevant circumstances, first consideration being given to the welfare, while a minor, of any child of the family who has not attained the age of

---

[9] Ibid, ss 4(1), 6(6) and 7(6).

[10] Ibid, s 20(5), (12)(a) as amended by the Children Act 1989, Sch 13, para 38.

[11] S 20(12)(b), as amended by the Children Act 1989 Sch 13, para 38 and s 20A, as added by the Family Law Reform Act 1987 and substituted by the Children Act 1989, Sch 13, para 39.

[12] Ibid, s 20(1), (2), (3), (6). The variation may be backdated to the application: s 20(9). As with an original order any varied or revived periodical payments order can be ordered to be paid by standing order or direct to the clerk, or the court can make an attachment of earnings order: s 20ZA added by the Maintenance Enforcement Act 1991, s 5.

[13] Ibid, s 20(1), (7).

[14] Domestic Proceedings and Magistrates' Courts Act 1978, s 20(2), (7), (8).

18, taking into account the same matters as it does when making a fresh order.[15] It could therefore properly reduce or revoke an order if the party to whom payments were being made had been guilty of 'obvious and gross' conduct. Although 'fresh evidence' is not required before any alteration can be made to the original order, neither party will probably be permitted to adduce any evidence which he could have adduced in earlier proceedings.[16]

(e) Lump sums

A lump sum payment is made once and for all and consequently there is no express power to vary it (except on appeal). The court has, however, a general power to remit arrears in proceedings for enforcement,[17] and this must effectively give it the power to reduce or extinguish a lump sum order although it clearly cannot increase it. In any case, if the sum is payable in instalments, the amount of any instalment and the date on which any instalment is to be paid, may be varied.[18]

5. ENFORCEMENT OF ORDERS[19]

(a) Methods of enforcement

Money due under magistrates' courts maintenance orders may be enforced by distress or committal to prison. They may also be enforced by the attachment of earnings procedure. In addition, following implementation of the Maintenance Enforcement Act 1991, a new option is now available, namely to seek to have the defaulting payer (the debtor) fined for his default to make periodical payments. In this latter case the payee (or creditor) can make a complaint to a justice, who upon being satisfied that the alleged failure to comply with the order justifies the imposition of a penalty, must issue a summons directing the debtor to appear before the court to answer the complaint. After hearing the complaint the court may order the debtor to pay a sum not exceeding £1,000.[20]

(b) Procedure and general consideration for recovering arrears

The 1978 Act provides that orders for periodical payments and for lump sum payments shall be enforceable as magistrates' courts maintenance orders.[21] The procedure is laid down by the Magistrates' Court Act 1980. If payments are being made to a magistrates' clerk, or by standing order (or its equivalent) the clerk himself may take proceedings provided that he

---

[15] Ibid, s 20(11) as amended by the Matrimonial and Family Proceedings Act 1984, s 9(3). See also *Blower v Blower* [1986] 1 FLR 292; *McEwan v McEwan* [1972] 2 All ER 708.
[16] Cf variation, etc in the divorce court, post, p 790.
[17] This is the combined effect of s 32(1) of the Domestic Proceedings and Magistrates' Courts Act 1978 and s 95 of the Magistrates' Courts Act 1980.
[18] Domestic Proceedings and Magistrates' Courts Act 1978, s 22.
[19] See *Children Come First* Vol 2 (HMSO, Cm 1264) ch 5; Gibson 12 Fam Law 138 who found that only a minority of husbands pay regularly under their court orders. See also the Finer Report, Cmnd 5629, Part 4, section 9.
[20] Magistrates' Courts Act 1980, s 59B added by the Maintenance Enforcement Act 1991, s 3.
[21] S 32(1), as amended by the Family Law Reform Act 1987, Sch 2, para 70.

has the written consent of the person to whom the money is to be paid.[1] No order for enforcement may be made except by an order on complaint.[2] On hearing such complaint the court must first decide whether to enforce the arrears in toto or to remit the whole or any part of them;[3] the answer to this question must obviously depend upon the spouses' financial position, their conduct and all the circumstances of the case. The court may then issue a warrant of distress, a warrant committing the payer to prison or make an attachment of earnings order.[4]

(i) Distress

Distress is little used in practice. The warrant directs the police to distrain on the husband's goods and to sell them to raise the sum adjudged to be paid.[5]

(ii) Committal

A warrant of committal (which may also be issued if payment is insufficient to satisfy the debt) commits the husband to prison for a period varying from five days to six weeks, the maximum period being graduated according to the sum owed.[6] But since committal proceedings are in effect designed to punish the husband for failing to carry out the order, he may be imprisoned only if the default was due to his wilful refusal or culpable neglect and the court feels that it is inappropriate to make an attachment of earnings order.[7]

Two further powers that the court possesses are those of ordering the payment of arrears by instalments and of postponing the issue of a warrant of committal upon conditions.[8] Used together these powers constitute a

---

[1] Magistrates' Courts Act 1980, s 59A(3), added by the Maintenance Enforcement Act 1991, s 3.

[2] Magistrates' Courts Act 1980, s 93(1), (2).

[3] Ibid, s 95, as substituted by the Maintenance Enforcement Act 1991, Sch 2, para 8. The court may also remit arrears on hearing an application to vary, discharge or revive the order provided that the wife has been given notice: Magistrates' Courts Rules 1981, r 44. The six months' limitation period does not apply so that arrears up to any amount may be recovered, but normally they should not be enforced if they have been due for more than a year: *Ross v Pearson* [1976] 1 All ER 790 and *Dickens v Pattison* [1985] FLR 610, though this is a rule of practice rather than law: see *Russell v Russell* [1986] 1 FLR 465, CA. Appeals against refusals to remit arrears can only be made pursuant to the Magistrates' Courts Act 1980, s 111, which means that they can only be made on the grounds of errors of law or want of jurisdiction: *Berry v Berry* [1987] Fam 1, [1986] 2 All ER 948, CA. Because arrears can be remitted, they are not provable in the husband's bankruptcy but continue to be enforceable in the same way as before: *James v James* [1964] P 303, [1963] 2 All ER 465. Cf post, p 799, n 8. Provision is made for the Secretary of State to provide for payment of interest on arrears: Magistrates' Courts Act 1980, s 94A, added by the Maintenance Enforcement Act 1991, s 8.

[4] Magistrates' Courts Act 1980, s 76(1); Attachment of Earnings Act 1971, s 1(3)(a).

[5] Magistrates' Courts Rules 1981, r 54. Clothing and bedding are exempt from distress as are tools of the husband's trade up to the value of £150. The court may also order the husband to be searched and any money belonging to him and found on him to be applied towards payment of the arrears: Magistrates' Courts Act 1980, s 80.

[6] Magistrates' Courts Act 1980, ss 76(2), 93(7) and 132, Sch 4.

[7] Magistrates' Courts Act 1980, s 93(6). No order for committal may be made unless the husband has appeared in court; he may be arrested if he fails to answer the summons.

[8] Ibid, ss 75 and 77; Maintenance Orders Act 1958, s 18.

valuable weapon, particularly when it is financially impossible for the husband to pay off all the arrears at once. For example, suppose that £200 is due under the order: the court may order the husband to be imprisoned for 14 days but the issue of the warrant of committal to be postponed on condition, say, that he pays off the arrears at the rate of £10 per week.

If the husband pays the arrears, the order of committal immediately ceases to have effect, and if he pays a part of the sum due, the period of imprisonment is proportionately reduced.[9] But serving the sentence does not wipe off the arrears[10] although no further arrears accrue whilst the husband is in custody unless the court orders otherwise.[11] A husband who is in prison may apply to have the warrant of committal cancelled, in which case the court has power to release him either absolutely or with a postponed warrant of committal for a period not exceeding the balance of the term to be served and may at the same time remit the whole or any part of the sum still unpaid.[12]

(iii) Attachment of earnings

The Maintenance Orders Act 1958 introduced a wholly new means of enforcing an order for maintenance—that of attaching the husband's earnings. The relevant part of that Act has now been replaced by the Attachment of Earnings Act 1971, which extended the power to apply for such an order to judgment debtors generally. The payment of any order for maintenance made under the Domestic Proceedings and Magistrates' Courts Act may be secured in this way.[13] Until the implementation of the Maintenance Enforcement Act 1991, attachment of earnings orders could only be made when an existing maintenance order was in arrears but now such orders can be made by the court itself when making a maintenance order in the first place.[14]

In cases where it is sought to recover arrears, application may be made by the person to whom payments are due under the maintenance order, by a magistrates' clerk if an order is in force directing payments to be made through him, or by the debtor himself.[15]

---

[9] Magistrates' Courts Act 1980, s 79.

[10] Ibid, s 93(8). But a husband cannot be imprisoned more than once for failure to pay the same sum: Maintenance Orders Act 1958, s 17.

[11] Magistrates' Courts Act 1980, s 94, for the committal will probably deprive the husband of the power of earning his living in the meantime.

[12] Maintenance Orders Act 1958, s 18(4), (5), (6). The order cannot be enforced against the husband's personal representatives after his death: *Re Bidie* [1948] Ch 697, [1948] 1 All ER 885; affd [1949] Ch 121, [1948] 2 All ER 995, CA. It is doubtful whether an order can ever be enforced after it has been discharged: per Avory J in *Outerbridge v Outerbridge* [1927] 1 KB 368; consequently the wife should resist an order for discharge until all arrears have been paid or remitted.

[13] Attachment of Earnings Order Act 1971, Sch 1, para 4, as amended by the Domestic Proceedings and Magistrates' Courts Act 1978, Sch 2. Attachment of earnings orders may also be made by the High Court and a county court: ibid, s 1.

[14] Magistrates' Courts Act 1980, s 59(4) as substituted by the Maintenance Enforcement Act 1991, s 2, ante, p 677.

[15] Attachment of Earnings Act 1971, s 3(1), as amended by the Maintenance Enforcement Act 1991, Sch 2, para 1(1).

If an attachment of earnings order is made, it is directed to the debtor's employer, not to the debtor himself. It orders the employer to make periodical deductions from the debtor's earnings[16] and to remit the amount deducted to the collecting officer of the court.[17] The officer must then pay the money received to the person to whom the money is due under the order.[18]

The order must specify two rates: the *normal deduction rate*, which is the amount which the court thinks is reasonable to secure the payment of sums falling due under the order in the future together with the arrears already accrued, and the *protected earnings rate*, that is, the rate below which the husband's earnings shall not in any event be reduced by payments deducted under the order.[19] The purpose of the latter is to keep the husband's remaining income above subsistence level; consequently only in exceptional circumstances would it be reasonable to fix it below the figure which, if it represented the husband's total resources, would entitle him to apply for income support.[20] In assessing the protected earnings rate, the court must take into account the husband's resources and needs and the needs of others for whom he is bound to provide or may reasonably be expected to provide[1] but may consider only his actual earnings from his particular employer at the time and not his potential earnings in some other occupation.[2]

Once an attachment of earnings order has been made, no committal order may be made as a consequence of proceedings begun beforehand; similarly if a committal order is made or a warrant is issued after an attachment of earnings order has been made, the latter will automatically be discharged.[3] A court before which proceedings for committal or distress are brought may always make an attachment of earnings order instead if it thinks that that would be a more efficacious means of securing payment.[4]

The court has a general power to order the variation or discharge of an attachment of earnings order and must vary or discharge it when the debtor has paid off the arrears and the sum attachable is greater than that payable under the related maintenance order.[5] If the debtor ceases to be employed by the person to whom the order has been directed, it lapses until the court

---

[16] 'Earnings' means any salary, wage or pension and includes sums payable by the Crown or out of public revenue in the United Kingdom (except Northern Ireland); it does not include sums payable by any other government, pay or allowances payable to members of HM forces, wages payable to seamen (other than seamen of fishing boats), or pensions, allowances or benefit payable under enactments relating to social security or in respect of the debtor's disablement or disability: Attachment of Earnings Act 1971, ss 22 and 24 and Sch 4, as subsequently amended. It also includes payments made at irregular intervals or under discretionary powers: *Edmonds v Edmonds* [1965] 1 All ER 379 n.

[17] Ie, the clerk of that or another magistrates' court: Attachment of Earnings Act 1971, s 6(7).

[18] Ibid, s 13(1). The sums paid must first go in payment of arrears and then in payment of costs: s 13(2).

[19] Ibid, s 6(5), (6).

[20] *Billington v Billington* [1974] Fam 24, [1974] 1 All ER 546. But this is not a rigid rule of law. There might be exceptional circumstances, eg, if the husband was living with his parents at no personal expense.

[1] Domestic Proceedings and Magistrates' Courts Act 1978, s 25(3).

[2] *Pepper v Pepper* [1960] 1 All ER 529, 534–535.

[3] Ibid, s 8(1), (3).

[4] Ibid, s 3(4).

[5] Ibid, ss 9 and 10. To cope with emergencies a single justice (or a justices' clerk) may increase

directs it to a fresh employer,[6] and it ceases to have effect if the related maintenance order is discharged unless arrears are still unpaid and the court directs that the attachment order shall remain alive.[7]

In many cases it may be questioned whether the value of an order to the wife is worth the administrative trouble that it causes. In the words of the Finer Report, 'the early promise of attachment of earnings orders was not sustained, and ... they have not become established as a major mode of enforcing maintenance orders in magistrates' courts'.[8] The procedure will be most effective when the husband is in steady employment, but when he is in casual employment, he may be able to escape the order by the simple expedient of changing jobs frequently if they are available to him.

E. Orders for financial provision under section 27 of the Matrimonial Causes Act 1973

Section 27 of the Matrimonial Causes Act 1973 (as amended)[9] provides that either party to a marriage may apply to a divorce court for an order on the ground that the other party to the marriage has failed to provide reasonable maintenance for the applicant or has failed to provide, or to make a proper contribution towards, reasonable maintenance for any child of the family. The court has jurisdiction if either party is domiciled in England and Wales, if the applicant has been habitually resident here for one year, or if the respondent is resident here.[10] The proceedings must be commenced in a divorce county court[11] but the court has the power, either upon its own motion or upon application by a party, to order the transfer of the whole or any part of the proceedings to the High Court.[12]

The grounds upon which an application may be made are identical with the first two grounds on which a spouse may apply to a magistrates' court for an order under the Domestic Proceedings and Magistrates' Courts Act 1978, section 1, and the court is enjoined to take the same matters into account in determining whether the respondent has failed to provide reasonable maintenance for the applicant and, if so, what order to make,[13]

---

the protected earnings rate for a period of not more than four weeks: s 9(3) and the Magistrates' Courts (Attachment of Earnings) Rules 1971, rr 14 and 22.

[6] Ibid, s 9(4). For the duties of the debtor, the old employer and a new employer who knows that the order is in force, see ibid, ss 7(2) and 15.

[7] Ibid, s 11(c), (3). For the effect of registration of the maintenance order in another court on an attachment of earnings order, see post, pp 804–805.

[8] Cmnd 562, para 4.146. See also Brown *Attachment of Earnings Orders in Practice* 24 MLR 486.

[9] By the Domestic Proceedings and Magistrates' Courts Act 1978, s 63, and the Matrimonial and Family Proceedings Act 1984, s 4.

[10] Domicile and Matrimonial Proceedings Act 1973, s 6(1).

[11] Matrimonial and Family Proceedings Act 1984, s 33(3).

[12] Ibid, s 39; *Practice Direction* [1992] 3 All ER 151.

[13] In fact the court is directed to have regard to the matters contained in the Matrimonial Causes Act 1973, s 25(2), which are the same in this respect as under the 1978 Act: Matrimonial Causes Act 1973, s 27(3), as substituted by the Domestic Proceedings and Magistrates' Courts Act 1978, ss 63(3) and 89(2), as amended by the Matrimonial and Family Proceedings Act 1984, s 4; (3A) and (3B) as substituted by ss 63(2) and 89(2) of the 1978 Act.

except that the court is enjoined to give first consideration to the welfare while a minor of any child of the family under the age of 18, only if an order is sought for such a child.[14] Readers are referred to discussion of applications in magistrates' courts.[15]

The court may make an interim order for periodical payments to the applicant if it appears that the latter or any child to whom the application relates is in immediate need of financial assistance.[16] If one of the grounds mentioned above is made out, the court may order the respondent to make any one or more of the following payments:[17]

(1) unsecured periodical payments to the applicant;
(2) secured periodical payments to the applicant;
(3) a lump sum payment to the applicant;
(4) unsecured periodical payments for any child to whom the application relates;
(5) secured periodical payments for such a child;
(6) a lump sum payment for such a child.

The question of the assessment of orders is essentially the same as that of orders made in magistrates' courts with the obvious exception that periodical payments may be secured and there is an unlimited power to order lump sum payments. Both these questions will be dealt with more fully when we consider financial provision after divorce;[18] in the case of lump sum payments, however, it should be borne in mind that the court has no power to make property adjustment orders under section 27 and consequently a lump sum order should not be used as a means of circumventing this restriction. The Act specifically provides that a lump sum may be ordered to enable the applicant to meet any liabilities or expenses already incurred in maintaining herself (or himself) or any child of the family to whom the application relates;[19] in addition, it may properly be ordered (as on divorce) whenever a capital sum is more valuable to the applicant than periodical payments.[20] A lump sum may be made payable in instalments and the instalments may be secured.[1]

Interim orders and orders for periodical payments may be varied, discharged, suspended and revived.[2] In the case of a lump sum payable by instalments, the provisions relating to the instalments may be varied but not the total sum payable.[3]

---

[14] S 27(3), as amended. Quaere why it is different and what effect, if any, the difference makes.
[15] Ante, p 670 (grounds) and p 678 (matters to be taken into account).
[16] S 27(5).
[17] S 27(6). But for the court's powers when the Child Support Act 1991 is fully in force, see post, pp 717–719.
[18] See post, p 729 (secured payments) and 733 (lump sum payments).
[19] S 27(7)(a). Cf post, p 733.
[20] See post, p 734.
[1] S 27(7)(b).
[2] For the power of the child aged between 16 and 18 to apply to revive an order, see the Matrimonial Causes Act 1973, s 27(6B), substituted by the Family Law Reform Act 1987, Sch 2, para 52.
[3] Matrimonial Causes Act 1973, s 31. See further post, pp 790–798.

Orders are payable[4] and enforceable in the same way as orders for periodical payments on divorce.[5]

Few applications are made for orders under section 27.[6] Most spouses prefer to take the cheaper and speedier proceedings available in magistrates' courts unless they are also petitioning for divorce or other matrimonial relief in the divorce court. The advantage of proceedings under section 27 is that the court may order periodical payments to be secured and has an unlimited power to order a lump sum payment. Now that the High Court and county courts are empowered to make property transfer orders in favour of children in applications made under Schedule 1 to the Children Act 1989 (discussed below), it is possible that a spouse might couple such an application with one under section 27 of the 1973 Act so as to be able to claim relief for him or herself.

F. Obtaining financial relief solely for the benefit of children

In addition to proceedings under which spouses may obtain financial relief both for themselves and any child of the family, courts are also empowered by the Children Act 1989 to make financial provision *solely* for the benefit of children. The general scheme is that where proceedings concern the child alone individuals seeking financial provision from either or both parents must seek redress under the 1989 Act. This Act therefore provides the only means by which unmarried parents and individuals[7] other than parents can seek financial provision for children from either or both parents. The 1989 Act also permits in certain circumstances children over the age of 18 to seek financial orders against their parents. We shall discuss these proceedings in turn.

1. FREE STANDING ORDERS FOR FINANCIAL RELIEF AGAINST PARENTS

Power to make financial provision solely for the benefit of children is contained in section 15 of and Schedule 1 to the Children Act 1989. Implementing the recommendations of the Law Commission[8] both to simplify and rationalise the law, Schedule 1 provides a single set of provisions to replace those under the Family Law Reform Act 1969, the Guardianship of Minors Act 1971 and 1973, the Children Act 1975 and the Family Law Reform Act 1987.[9]

---

[4] Maintenance Enforcement Act 1991, s 2, discussed post, p 799.

[5] Matrimonial Causes Act 1973, ss 31–33 and 37. See post, pp 801–804.

[6] The average number of applications in the years 1981–1985 was 259 per year. In 1985 there were 121 applications, while in 1989 there were only 51 applications.

[7] Cf under the Social Security Act 1986 by which the Department of Social Security can bring a court action against a 'liable relative' to recover money paid as income support, discussed ante, p 666. Local authorities can also bring court proceedings to recover contributions from a 'contributor' in respect of maintenance of a child looked after by them: Children Act 1989, Sch 2, Part III. For the court's powers once the Child Support Act 1991 is fully in force, see post, pp 717-719.

[8] Law Com No 172, *Guardianship and Custody*, paras 4.59–4.79.

[9] For discussion of which, see pp 632–637 and 641–643 of the seventh edition of this work.

(a) Jurisdiction

(i) When orders may be made

The court may make financial provision for children either upon application[10] or upon its own motion when making, varying or discharging a residence order.[11] Unless the child is a ward of court,[12] the court cannot make a Schedule 1 order upon its own motion if it has not made a residence order.

(ii) Who can apply

Applications may be made by parents, guardians and any person in whose favour a residence order is in force.[13] For these purposes 'parents' includes both married and unmarried parents (including the unmarried father)[14] and 'any party to a marriage (whether or not subsisting) in relation to whom the child concerned is a child of the family'.[15]

Although guardians are entitled to apply they are unlikely to do so very often since they can only take office during the lifetime of the surviving spouse when the deceased appointing parent had a residence order in his favour at the time of death.[16]

(iii) Against whom orders can be made

Orders may be made against either or both parents of the child. As with applicants 'parents', for these purposes, include unmarried fathers and step-parents of 'children of the family'.

With regard to unmarried fathers these provisions are a virtual re-enactment of those under the Guardianship of Minors Act 1971 as amended by the Family Law Reform Act 1987, which in turn replaced affiliation proceedings. As under the 1971 Act,[17] as amended, these proceedings operate retrospectively so that unmarried fathers who were previously immune from liability under the Affiliation Proceedings Act 1957, because no action had been brought within three years of the child's birth,[18] are no longer so. Indeed in *Hager v Osborne*[19] it was held that the equivalent provisions

---

[10] Children Act 1989, Sch 1, para 1(1).

[11] Sch 1, para 1(6). Note also the powers under para 8 when making a residence order to vary or revoke any existing financial relief order made under any enactment other than the Children Act 1989; see further post, p 697.

[12] See Sch 1, para 1(7), added by the Courts and Legal Services Act 1990, Sch 16, para 10(2).

[13] Sch 1, para 1(1). Although a residence order must be in force before a financial order may be made in favour of a person other than a parent, an *application* may be made together with an application for a residence order: cf Family Proceedings Rules 1991, r 4.3(4). For the procedure generally see Family Proceedings Rules 1991, r 4.46 and Family Proceedings Courts (Children Act 1989) Rules 1991, r 4(6).

[14] This is in line with the general interpretation of the term 'parents'; see s 2(3) and the Family Law Reform Act 1987, s 1. See ante, p 287.

[15] Ie a step-parent: Sch 1, para 16(2).

[16] See ante, p 402.

[17] See Law Com No 118, *Illegitimacy*, para 6.55.

[18] Affiliation Proceedings Act 1957, ss 1 and 2, discussed in the sixth edition of this work at p 597.

[19] [1992] 2 All ER 494.

under the 1971 Act were retrospective in the sense that they applied to children born before they came into force and that the dismissal of a previous affiliation application following inconclusive blood tests did not preclude a fresh application being made under the new legislation when advantage could be taken of DNA testing.[20]

The power to order step-parents of children who are children of the family to make financial provision is new and implements the recommendation of the Law Commission.[1] As the Commission pointed out, such persons could already be ordered to make payments inter alia under the Matrimonial Causes Act 1973 and the Domestic Proceedings and Magistrates' Courts Act 1978 and there seemed no logical reason for not making them similarly liable where proceedings have been brought under the 1989 Act. However, although this means that application may be made against step-parents the Commission envisaged that applications are more likely to be made by them. No orders may be made against a guardian. This is in line with the general policy of not making such persons liable to make financial provision or property transfers in the same way as a parent.[2] Similarly, no orders can be made against those other than parents who have residence orders in their favour.[3]

(b) Powers

The High Court, county courts and magistrates' courts all have jurisdiction to make Schedule 1 orders, though magistrates' powers are more restricted than those of the higher courts.

All courts may order the making of unsecured periodical payments either to the applicant for the benefit of the child or to the child himself, for such term as may be specified in the order.[4] Similarly, they can order lump sum payments[5] although in the case of magistrates' orders there is a prescribed maximum limit of £1000 or such larger amount as the Secretary of State shall fix.[6] Lump sum orders may provide for payment to be made by instalments.[7] An order for periodical payments or lump sums may be made, notwithstanding that the child is living outside England and Wales, provided it is sought against a parent living in England and Wales.[8]

The High Court and county courts may additionally order the making of secured periodical payments, settlements of property and property transfers.[9] Where any of these latter orders are made, the court may direct that the matter be referred to one of the court's conveyancing counsel to settle a proper instrument to be executed by all necessary parties.[10] The £2500 exemption from the statutory legal aid charge and the postponement of the charge over orders for money where it is to be used to purchase a new

---

[20] DNA testing is discussed ante, p 274.
[1] Law Com No 172, para 4.63.
[2] See ibid, para 2.25.
[3] Cf *S v X and X (Interveners)* [1990] 2 FLR 187 (third party interveners who had been granted custody were held not liable to maintain the child).
[4] Sch 1, para 1(1)(a), (b) and (2)(a).
[5] Sch 1, para 1(1)(a), (b) and (2)(c).
[6] Sch 1, para 5(2).
[7] Sch 1, para 5(5).
[8] Sch 1, para 14.
[9] Sch 1, paras 1(1)(a) and respectively (2)(b), (d) and (e).
[10] Sch 1, para 13.

home, has been extended to orders made under Schedule 1.[11]

All orders may be made either in favour of the applicant for the benefit of the child or to the child himself. However, in the light of the Finance Act 1988 there are no longer any fiscal advantages in making payments direct to the child[12] although there may be in making payments to the payer's spouse or former spouse[13] in favour of the child.

In *K v K (Minors: Property Transfer)*[14] it was held that the words 'the benefit of the child' were not confined to financial benefit for the child so that powers to order a transfer were not restricted to orders giving the child a beneficial interest in the property. Accordingly, it was held that there was power to order an unmarried father to transfer to the mother for the benefit of the children his interest in the family home, namely, a joint council tenancy.

K v K is the first reported case on the higher courts' powers to make property transfer orders for the benefit of children born outside marriage. The general use of these powers in this context therefore remains a matter of conjecture. In recommending the power the Law Commission thought[15] the transfer provisions could be useful to enable the court to make a once-and-for-all settlement in cases where the father did not intend to have anything to do with the child. However, they did not envisage the power being used at all frequently, relying on the practice of the divorce courts to lean against making such orders.[16] Against this it has been pointed out[17] that, unlike divorce proceedings, where the court can make orders in favour of the spouse, in these proceedings there is no such power so that there is a stark choice between making an order for the child's benefit or no order at all. As *K v K* shows, at any rate, where the parents have cohabited for any length of time, the courts are likely to accept the need to preserve the parties' home as a home for the children. Indeed the Law Commission itself said[18] that few commentators thought it a valid objection that a transfer was tantamount to giving the unmarried mother a right to support for her own benefit. Even if the court is not prepared to make an outright transfer for the child's benefit, it might be disposed to make a limited transfer (not dissimilar to *Mesher* orders in the divorce context)[19] until the child has grown up.

Where the court makes a residence order with respect to a child at a time when there is in force a financial relief order made under any enactment other than the Children Act 1989 (for example an affiliation order or an order made under the Domestic Proceedings and Magistrates' Courts Act

---

[11] Civil Legal Aid (General) (Amendment) (No 2) Regulations 1991, regs 15 and 16. The legal aid charge is discussed post, p 746.

[12] Ie tax relief for payments to children have been abolished, see post, p 732.

[13] But *not* to former cohabitants or third parties with residence orders in their favour.

[14] [1992] 2 All ER 727, CA. This case was brought under the Guardianship of Minors Act 1971, but it was accepted (see at 733 per Nourse LJ) that the provisions of the Children Act 1989 were not materially different in this respect.

[15] Law Com No 118, para 6.6.

[16] See *Chamberlain v Chamberlain* [1974] 1 All ER 33, 38, CA per Scarman LJ and *Draskovic v Draskovic* (1980) 11 Fam Law 87.

[17] Lowe *Family Law Reform Act 1987—Useful Reform but an Unhappy Compromise* (1988) Denning LJ 77, 85.

[18] Law Com No 118, para 6.7.

[19] See post, p 787.

1978) then upon application either by the person required by the financial relief order to contribute to the child's maintenance or the person in whose favour the residence order has been made, the court may revoke or vary the financial relief order.[20] Such orders may be varied either by altering the amount of any sum payable or by substituting the applicant for the person to whom such order is otherwise payable.

Under its power to make interim orders[1] the court may order either or both parents to make such periodical payments as the court thinks fit, and to give any other direction. No order may take effect earlier than the date of application and shall cease to have effect either upon the final disposal of the application or, if earlier, upon the date specified by the court. There is no limit on the number of interim periodical payments orders that may be made but unlike other orders there is no right of appeal against the making or refusal to make an interim order.[2]

Although it is perhaps an arguable point, applications for financial relief under the 1989 Act would appear to rank as 'family proceedings' for the purposes of section 8.[3] Accordingly, the court has power to make any section 8 order upon its own motion as well as being able to exercise its powers under section 37 to direct the local authority to undertake an investigation into the child's circumstances. If this is so, it is an important change from the previous law in which applications could be made for financial relief without putting the child's upbringing into issue at all.[4] Whether this change will deter potential applicants (particularly unmarried mothers) remains to be seen.

(c) Exercising the powers

In assessing what, if any, order to make and what amount will be appropriate, the court is directed[5] to have regard to all the circumstances of the case including the following matters:

'(a) The income, earning capacity, property and other financial resources which [any parent, the applicant and any other person in whose favour the court proposes to make the order][6] has or is likely to have in the foreseeable future.
(b) The financial needs, obligations and responsibilities which [any parent, the applicant and any other person in whose favour the court proposes to make the order][6] has or is likely to have in the foreseeable future.
(c) The financial needs of the child.
(d) The income, earning capacity (if any), property and other financial resources of the child.
(e) Any physical or mental disability of the child.

---

[20] Sch 1, para 8.
[1] Sch 1, para 9.
[2] S 94(3).
[3] The Department of Health's *Guidance and Regulations*, Vol 1, Court Orders, para 2.66 assumes that they are. The argument centres on whether technically applications are made under s 15, which is within Part II of the 1989 Act and clearly 'family proceedings', or under Sch 1 which falls outside the definition of 'family proceedings' in s 8(3), (4).
[4] See Law Com No 118, paras 6.26–6.27, discussed at p 633 of the seventh edition of this work.
[5] Sch, 1 para 4(1).
[6] Sch, 1 para 4(4).

(f) The manner in which the child was being, or was expected to be educated or trained.'

These guidelines are the same as under Domestic Proceedings and Magistrates' Courts Act 1978 save that the court is not specifically enjoined to have regard to the family's standard of living and no weighting of the child's welfare is specified.[7] The direction to have regard to the manner in which the child was being or expected to be educated is new in the context of orders being made solely for the benefit of the child. The absence of a direction concerning standard of living leaves open the question of whose standard of living an order should judge. This is likely to be a particularly difficult issue where an unmarried couple have never lived together. Where, for example, the mother is a woman who is never likely to enjoy a high income and the father earns a high salary, it is tempting to say that the child (for whose benefit the order is being made) ought not to be prejudiced by his mother's position yet it might be thought unwise to drive a wedge between him and siblings that he might have by giving him an undue advantage over them.[8]

Where an order against a step-parent of a child of the family is contemplated, then, as under the 1978 Act, the court is directed[9] to have regard to:

'(a) Whether that person had assumed responsibility for the maintenance of the child and, if so, the extent to which and the basis on which he assumed that responsibility and the length of the period during which he met that responsibility.
(b) Whether he did so knowing that the child was not his child.
(c) The liability of any other person to maintain the child.'

If the court makes an order against a person who is not the father of the child, it must record in the order that the order is made on that basis.[10] Lump sum orders may be made to enable the applicant to meet any liabilities or expenses incurred in connection with the birth of the child or in maintaining the child or those reasonably incurred before the making of the order.[11]

(d) Duration, variation and enforcement

Orders for periodical payments may begin with the date of the making of the application and shall not in the first instance extend beyond the child's seventeenth birthday and shall not in any event extend beyond his eighteenth birthday save where the child is receiving instruction at an educational institution or undergoing training for a trade, profession or vocation 'whether or not he also is, will be or would be in gainful employment' or where there are other exceptional circumstances.[12] Periodical payment orders

---

[7] The child's welfare is not the paramount consideration because s 105(1) expressly excludes maintenance from the definition of upbringing (cf under the Guardianship of Minors Act 1971 where the child's welfare was the first and paramount consideration), and unlike the 1978 Act there is no direction in Sch 1 to treat the child's welfare as the first consideration.
[8] *Haroutunian v Jennings* (1977) 1 FLR 62, at 67 nevertheless supports the view that the father's higher standard of living should be the yardstick.
[9] Sch 1, para 4(2).
[10] Sch 1, para 4(3).
[11] Sch 1, para 5.
[12] Sch 1, para 3(1), (2).

may be made notwithstanding that the parents are living together but, as under the 1978 Act, cease to have effect if they continue to live together or subsequently resume living together for a continuous period of more than six months.[13] Unsecured orders cease upon the death of the payer.[14]

There is a general power to vary, suspend, revive and revoke orders for periodical payments, and the court may order the payment of a lump sum on an application for a variation. The power of a child over the age of 16 to apply for a variation or to revive an order is similar to that under the 1978 Act.[15] If satisfied that payment has not been made in accordance with the order, magistrates' courts may in addition to ordering a variation, order that payments be made directly to the payee or the clerk to the court or that they be paid by standing order. It may also make an attachment of earnings order.[16]

The usual means of enforcement are open if the order is made in the High Court or in a county court. Any person obliged to make payments under a magistrates' court order is obliged to give notice of any change of address to any person specified in the order. Failure to do so is an offence.[17] Magistrates' court orders are enforceable in the same way as any other magistrates' court maintenance order.[18] In all cases the order may be registered and enforced in another court and an attachment of earnings order may be made.

2. THE INDEPENDENT RIGHT OF A CHILD OVER THE AGE OF 18 TO SEEK FINANCIAL RELIEF FROM HIS PARENTS

Schedule 1, paragraph 2 to the Children Act 1989 preserves the independent right, first introduced by the Family Law Reform Act 1987,[19] of a person who has attained 18 years of age to apply for an order requiring either or both of his parents to make periodical and/or lump sum payments to him. Applications may now be made in the magistrates' court as well as the county court or the High Court. Before any order may be made, the court must be satisfied that the applicant is or will be (or would be if an order was made) receiving instruction at an educational institution or undergoing training for a trade, profession or vocation, or that[20] there are other exceptional circumstances justifying an order. An order may not be made if, immediately before the applicant reached the age of 16, a periodical payments order was in force,[21] nor may an order be made if the applicant's parents are living together in the same household.[1] In deciding what order to make, the court is to have regard to the same circumstances as it would

---

[13] Sch 1, para 3(4).
[14] Sch 1, para 3(3).
[15] Sch 1, para 6(4).
[16] Sch 1, para 6A, added by the Maintenance Enforcement Act 1991, s 6.
[17] Sch 1, para 12(1), (2).
[18] Sch 1, para 12(3).
[19] Following the Law Commission's recommendations, Law Com No 118, paras 6.29–6.33.
[20] Children Act 1989, Sch 1, para 2(1).
[21] Sch 1, para 2(3). As we have seen ante, p 687, if such an order is in force the child, once he has attained 16, may himself apply for a variation, or if the order has ceased to have effect, can apply for a revival of the order.
[1] Sch 1, para 2(4).

have in the case of other applications for financial orders under the Children Act 1989.[2]

Both the child and the parent (or parents) ordered to pay, may subsequently seek a variation or discharge of a periodical payments order.[3] There is no power to vary a lump sum payments order save, where the sum has been ordered to be paid in instalments, to vary the number or amount or date of those instalments.[4]

G. Registration of orders in other courts

Orders made by a magistrates' court may be registered in the High Court and orders made by the High Court or a divorce county court under section 27 of the Matrimonial Causes Act may be registered in a magistrates' court. The order must then be paid and can be enforced as though it had been made by the court in which it is registered. The purpose and details of this procedure will be considered in chapter 21.[5]

H. Financial relief when one party is out of the jurisdiction

The powers of an English court to make or enforce an order for financial relief when one of the parties is out of the jurisdiction have become increasingly important with the greater mobility of population, which has become more marked with our entry into the European Community. Two questions have to be answered:

(1) In what circumstances can financial relief be obtained by or against the party in England?
(2) In what circumstances can an order, already in existence, be enforced by or against this party?

Whether an order obtained here can be enforced in the country in which the other party resides and whether an order can be obtained there depends of course on the law of that county. An order obtained abroad may be enforced here in the same way as any other judgment in personam provided it is 'final and conclusive'. If, however, the foreign court retains the same power as an English court to vary the order, it will lack this quality and so will not be enforceable under the general law.[6] Because of this difficulty a number of statutes have been passed to help dependants who might otherwise find themselves without effective relief. One, the Maintenance Orders Act 1950, provides machinery for the reciprocal enforcement of

---

[2] Sch 1, para 4.
[3] Sch 1, para 2(5).
[4] Sch 1, para 6(6).
[5] See post, pp 804–805.
[6] *Harrop v Harrop* [1920] 3 KB 386. But if the court has no power to remit arrears, it may be enforced as a final and conclusive judgment: *Beatty v Beatty* [1924] 1 KB 807, CA. An order may also be enforceable under the Colonial and Other Territories (Divorce Jurisdiction) Acts 1926–1950.

orders within the three jurisdictions of the United Kingdom; the others apply when one party is outside the United Kingdom.

1. MAINTENANCE ORDERS ACT 1950

Under Part II of this Act if a person entitled to payments under a maintenance order[7] obtained in one part of the United Kingdom wishes to enforce it in another part, she (or he) must apply to the court that made the order. If that court is satisfied that the person liable to make the payments resides in another part of the United Kingdom and that it is convenient that the order should be enforceable there, a copy of the order is sent to the relevant court in that jurisdiction, which must then register it.[8] The order is then enforceable as though it had been made by the court in which it is registered.[9]

Variation and discharge of orders remain within the jurisdiction of the court that made the order except that, if any order for periodical payments is registered in a magistrates' court,[10] only the latter has power to vary the rate of payments.[11] To prevent parties to an order registered in a magistrates' court having to travel from one jurisdiction to another to give evidence in proceedings for variation or discharge, the payee's evidence may be given in the court which made the order, and the payer's evidence may be given in the court in which it is registered; in each case a transcript or summary of the evidence is then sent to the other court.[12]

The payee may apply to have the registration cancelled at any time.[13]

2. MAINTENANCE ORDERS (FACILITIES FOR ENFORCEMENT) ACT 1920

The object of this Act is to facilitate the reciprocal enforcement of maintenance orders[14] made in this country and other countries to which the Act applies to obtain a maintenance order against a person resident in one of

---

[7] These are defined in s 16 (as amended). They are all orders for periodical payments and lump sum payments.

[8] S 17. If the order was made by a superior court (ie the Supreme Court in England or Northern Ireland or the Court of Session in Scotland), it is to be registered in the corresponding superior court. Other orders are to be registered in a magistrates' court in England, the sheriff court in Scotland, or a court of summary jurisdiction in Northern Ireland, in the jurisdiction of which the payer appears to be.

[9] Ss 18–20. This includes enforcement of arrears accrued before the registration: s 20. The order may be further registered under the Maintenance Orders Act 1958: Administration of Justice Act 1977, s 3 and Sch 3.

[10] Or in a sheriff court in Scotland or a court of summary jurisdiction in Northern Ireland.

[11] S 22. But the sum as varied must not exceed the maximum which could have been ordered originally: s 22(1).

[12] S 22(5). This also applies to orders registered in sheriff courts in Scotland and courts of summary jurisdiction in Northern Ireland but not to orders registered in superior courts. There is no reason why it should not be extended to them.

[13] S 24. The registration must be cancelled unless proceedings for variation are pending in the court of registration. The payer may apply for cancellation of the registration of an order in a magistrates' court (or sheriff court in Scotland) if he has ceased to reside in the country in which the order is registered: s 24(2).

[14] Ie an order (other than an affiliation order) for periodical payments for a dependant: s 10.

those countries and vice versa. It is intended that the Act should be superseded by the Maintenance Orders (Reciprocal Enforcement) Act 1972 and it no longer applies to any country which is a reciprocating country for the purpose of Part I of that Act. The procedure is similar to that under Part I of the 1972 Act.[15]

3. MAINTENANCE ORDERS (RECIPROCAL ENFORCEMENT) ACT 1972

This Act deals with two entirely different types of proceedings. Part I enables a person to obtain an order in this country against a person resident in another country and to enforce it there or to enforce in another country an order already made here. Conversely it enables a person in another country to obtain and enforce an order against a person resident here. Under Part II a person in this country can obtain an order in another country which will then be enforceable there and a person in another country can obtain and enforce an order in this country.

(a) Part I

Any country or territory outside the United Kingdom may be designated a 'reciprocating country' by Order in Council if reciprocal facilities will be accorded there for British maintenance orders.[16] For the purpose of this Part of the Act a maintenance order is an order (including an affiliation order) providing for the payment of a lump sum or the making of periodical payments towards the maintenance of any person whom the payer is liable to maintain under the law of the place where the order was made.[17] If an order has already been made by an English court, the payee may apply to the court that made it to have it transmitted to a reciprocating country for enforcement if the payer resides or has assets there.[18] If a copy of an order made in a reciprocating country is received here, it will be sent for registration in the magistrates' court within the jurisdiction of which the payer resides or has assets.[19]

Part I also provides machinery whereby an applicant may obtain in the country in which she (or he) resides an order against a person resident in a reciprocating country. To prevent either party having to go to the other country, the proceedings are split between the two countries involved. The applicant starts proceedings in a court in her own country, and if that court is satisfied that she has made out a prima facie case under the law administered there, it may make a provisional order. This is then transmitted to the appropriate court of the reciprocating country in which the other party resides or has assets together with a transcript or summary of the

---

[15] For the countries to which the Act still applies, see *Butterworths Family Law Service*, para D[352].

[16] S 1. The order may limit the operation of the Act to certain types of maintenance order in any given case. For the countries and territories already designated as reciprocating countries, see *Butterworths Family Law Service*, para D[363]. Except for South Africa they are all in the Commonwealth.

[17] S 22(1) (as amended by the Civil Jurisdiction and Judgments Act 1982, Sch 11).

[18] S 2 (as amended).

[19] Ss 6 (as amended) and 21.

evidence given. After hearing the defendant and any evidence he wishes to adduce, that court may confirm the order.[20]

In England the appropriate court is the magistrates' court. Consequently any proceedings started here must be brought under the Domestic Proceedings and Magistrates' Courts Act 1978 or Sch 1 to the Children Act 1989.[1] As the cause for complaint does not have to arise within the jurisdiction,[2] a woman newly arrived in this country may bring proceedings alleging, for example, her husband's behaviour or desertion notwithstanding that he has never set foot in the United Kingdom. Whether it is desirable to give a wife a remedy when she might have none under the law of the country in which the spouses have been living is debatable.[3] A provisional order made in a reciprocating country must be sent to the magistrates' court within whose jurisdiction the respondent resides or has assets. The court must refuse to confirm the order if he establishes that he has a defence to the proceedings under the law of the country that made it; in other cases it must confirm the order but may make any alterations to it that it thinks reasonable. A confirmed order is then registered in the court that confirmed it.[4]

Any order registered in this country, whether already made in a reciprocating country or after confirmation, can be enforced as though it had been made by the registering court.[5] Both the court and the court that made the order (or provisional order) may vary or revoke it; to protect the other party, however, this can be done in most cases only by a provisional order which will not take effect until it is confirmed by the other court, in which case the rules relating to the taking of evidence in one court and its transmission to the other apply.[6]

No appeal lies from the making of a provisional order, but the applicant may appeal if the court refuses to make one. Either party may appeal if a magistrates' court confirms a provisional order made in a reciprocating country (including a provisional order for variation or revocation) or varies or revokes any order (otherwise than by a provisional order) or refuses to confirm, vary or revoke it.[7]

---

[20] Ss 3 and 7. For evidence generally, see ss 13–15. The court may not direct blood tests to determine paternity in any proceedings brought under this Act: s 44(1).

[1] The court may not refuse to make an order on the ground that the case would be more conveniently dealt with by the High Court: s 3(4).

[2] *Collister v Collister* [1972] 1 All ER 334.

[3] It must be remembered that the court has power to deal with de facto polygamous marriages: see ante, p 65.

[4] S 7.

[5] This includes the payer's power to apply for the order to be registered in the High Court under Part I of the Maintenance Orders Act 1958 and the court's power to remit arrears— a matter of importance because there may be a long delay between an application to have the order varied or revoked and its confirmation. See s 8 (as amended by the Domestic Proceedings and Magistrates' Courts Act 1978, s 54, and the Civil Jurisdiction and Judgments Act 1982, Sch 11). For payment of orders registered in this country and the conversion of foreign currency, see s 16.

[6] For details see ss 5 and 9, as amended by the Domestic Proceedings and Magistrates' Courts Act 1978, s 54 and the Civil Jurisdiction and Judgments Act 1982, Sch 11. A provisional order made by a magistrates' court requiring the payer to make periodical payments for his or her spouse will cease to have effect if the payee remarries: s 42, as amended by the Domestic Proceedings and Magistrates' Courts Act 1978, Sch 2. For the cancellation of registration following revocation and the transfer of registered orders if the payer ceases to reside within the court's jurisdiction or has no assets in the United Kingdom, see ss 10 and 11 (as amended).

[7] S 12.

(b) Part II

Part II of the Act gives effect to the United Nations Convention on the Recovery Abroad of Maintenance of 1956. Any country to which this Convention extends may be designated a 'convention country' by Order in Council.[8] Once this has been done, an applicant may start proceedings in this country to obtain maintenance from a person subject to the jurisdiction of a convention country, and an applicant in a convention country may start proceedings there to obtain maintenance from a person resident in any part of the United Kingdom. At first sight this looks similar to the procedure laid down in Part I, but there is an important difference between them. Under Part I the order is made by the court in which the applicant starts the proceedings (even though it will not take effect until it is confirmed in the reciprocating country) and that court must apply its own law; under Part II, however, the order is made by the court of the country in which the respondent resides and the law of that country applies. The relevant authority in the applicant's country is no more than an agent for transmitting the application to the other country.

An application in England is made through the clerk of a magistrates' court and is then transmitted to the convention country.[9] An application received from a convention country is sent to the magistrates' court acting for the area in which the respondent resides and is treated as though it were an application made under the Domestic Proceedings and Magistrates' Courts Act 1978 or Schedule 1 to the Children Act 1989.[10] As proceedings under the former Act are confined to spouses, a person whose marriage has been dissolved or annulled in a convention country may apply for an order against her (or his) former spouse resident here provided that an order for maintenance for the benefit of the applicant or a child of the family has been made in a convention country by reason of the divorce or nullity and the defendant has failed to comply with it. On such an application the court has the same powers as it has on an application under section 1 of that Act except that it may make an order for periodical payments or lump sum payments for the applicant or a child of the family only if the order made in the convention country contained a similar provision.[11]

In all cases the application should be accompanied by a transcript or summary of evidence; if the court requires further evidence, it may ask the

[8] S 24. For the countries already designated as convention countries, see *Butterworths Family Law Service*, para D[371]. They include all the countries of Western and Central Europe.

[9] S 26. If the respondent is domiciled (according to the law of the country concerned) in a contracting state within the meaning of the Civil Jurisdiction and Judgments Act 1982, he may be sued only (i) in that state, (ii) in the country in which the applicant is domiciled or habitually resident, or (iii) in any court which the parties have agreed in writing is to have exclusive jurisdiction. A person is to be regarded as domiciled within the United Kingdom only if he is domiciled there for the purpose of the Civil Jurisdiction and Judgments Act. A court in a contracting state will also have jurisdiction if the defendant enters an appearance unless he does so solely to contest jurisdiction. See the Civil Jurisdiction and Judgments Act 1982, s 41 (meaning of domicile) and Sch 1, arts 2, 5(2), 17, 18 and 52.

[10] S 27, as amended by the Domestic Proceedings and Magistrates' Courts Act 1978, s 56 and Sch 2.

[11] S 28A (added by the Domestic Proceedings and Magistrates' Courts Act 1978, s 58). For the powers of the court, see ante, p 673. The court may also make an interim order. The decree of divorce or nullity must be recognised here but its validity will be presumed and it is for the respondent to prove that an English court will not recognise it.

Secretary of State to request the appropriate body or court in the convention country to take it.[12] The only orders that may be made are for the payment of money; in particular, the court may not make an order for personal protection under section 16 of the Domestic Proceedings and Magistrates' Courts Act or any order under section 8 of the Children Act.[13] Any order made must be registered and may be enforced in the same way as other orders made in magistrates' courts.[14]

An order made in this country may be varied or revoked by the registering court on the application of either party, and the court may hear a complaint notwithstanding that the other party is outside England and Wales provided that he has been given notice of the proceedings.[15] An application for variation by a payee in England may be transmitted to a convention country and vice versa in the same way as an initial application for an order.[16] Either party may appeal against an order or the refusal to make one (including an order for variation or revocation) in the usual way.

(c) Modified schemes for reciprocal enforcement

The schemes laid down in Parts I and II may not be apposite in all cases. Some countries may be unwilling or unable to become parties to the Convention (for example, federal states like the USA, where maintenance orders come within the jurisdiction of individual states and not of the federal government). To overcome this and similar difficulties section 40 of the Act enables modified arrangements to be made under Part I with the Republic of Ireland and 12 other European countries and under Part II with 46 states of the USA.[17]

4. CIVIL JURISDICTION AND JUDGMENTS ACT 1982

This Act gives effect to the Convention on Jurisdiction and the Enforcement of Judgments in Civil and Commercial Matters of 1968 and the Protocol on the Interpretation of the Convention by the European Court of 1971, which are set out in Schedules 1 and 2. The purpose of the Convention is to establish a uniform law of jurisdiction in civil matters within the European Community and to ensure that judgments given in one member state are recognised and enforced in another. The Act applies to proceedings in 'contracting states', that is the member states of the Community except at present Portugal and Spain.[18]

---

[12] Ss 36 and 37. There is a complementary power enabling the Secretary of State to request a court in this country to take evidence to be sent to a court in a convention country dealing with an application originating in this country: s 38.

[13] Nor can the court make an agreed order under s 6 of the Domestic Proceedings and Magistrates' Courts Act 1978 or an order for payments under s 7 of that Act when the parties have been living apart: s 28, as substituted by the Domestic Proceedings and Magistrates' Courts Act 1978, s 57. The court has no power to direct a blood test to determine paternity: s 44.

[14] S 33. Arrears may be remitted and the order may be registered in the High Court under the Maintenance Orders Act 1958.

[15] Ss 34 and 35. For the transfer of an order after the payer has ceased to reside within the jurisdiction of the magistrates' court, see s 32.

[16] Ss 26(2), 34(3) and 35(2).

[17] For details, see *Butterworths Family Law Service*, paras D[368], [369], [372], [896] and [896.1].

[18] S 1(3).

If an application is made in this country for an order against a defendant residing in another contracting state,[19] rules made under the Act provide machinery for giving him notice of the proceedings and for enabling him to adduce written evidence to the English court. The court may also request a court in another contracting state to take further evidence.[20] There are similar provisions if there is an application to vary or revoke the order.[1]

Subject to certain exceptions (for example that recognition would be contrary to public policy in the country in which it is sought or that the order is irreconcilable with a judgment given in a dispute between the same parties in that country)[2] a judgment given in one contracting state is to be recognised and enforced in all the others.[3] The means by which this is to be effected is a matter for the country in which recognition is sought. If the payee under an order made in another state wishes to enforce it in this country, the application must be transmitted through the Secretary of State to the clerk of the magistrates' court having jurisdiction where the person liable to make payments is domiciled for the purpose of the Act. The clerk must register the order unless he is satisfied that it is to be refused recognition or that the payer is not resident within the jurisdiction and has no assets in this country.[4] A registered order may be enforced as though it had been made by the registering court.[5] An order may be varied or revoked only by the court that made it.[6]

I. Maintenance under the Child Support Act 1991[7]

1. BACKGROUND

During the 1980s, increasing attention was paid to the question of whether the existing provision for the assessment and collection of child maintenance through private law mechanisms was satisfactory. The Matrimonial and Family Proceedings Act 1984 amended the Matrimonial Causes Act 1973 to require that, in deciding what orders should be made, the court should give first consideration to the welfare whilst a minor of any child of the family, and attempts were made to increase the awareness of the courts as

---

[19] For jurisdiction if the defendant is domiciled in another contracting state according to that state's law, see ante, p 705, n 9.
[20] Magistrates' Courts (Civil Jurisdiction and Judgments Act 1982) Rules 1986, rr 10 and 13. There is a corresponding power to take evidence for use in proceedings in another state: ibid, r 14.
[1] Ibid, r 11.
[2] For the full list of grounds on which recognition may be refused, see the Civil Jurisdiction and Judgments Act 1982, Sch 1, art 27.
[3] Ibid, Sch 1, arts 26 and 31.
[4] Magistrates' Courts (Civil Jurisdiction and Judgments Act 1982) Rules 1986, r 4. An appeal lies against registration or refusal to register to the magistrates' court and thence on a point of law only to the Family Division of the High Court: ibid, r 5; Civil Jurisdiction and Judgments Act 1982, s 6(3) and Sch 1, arts 37, 40 and 41.
[5] Civil Jurisdiction and Judgments Act 1982, ss 5 and 7(4) and Sch 1, art 39; Magistrates' Courts (Civil Jurisdiction and Judgments Act 1982) Rules 1986, r 6.
[6] Magistrates' Courts (Civil Jurisdiction and Judgments Act 1982) Rules 1986, rr 7 and 11. For the transfer and cancellation of registration if the payer is not residing within the jurisdiction of the court, see ibid, rr 8 and 9.
[7] See R Bird *Child Maintenance: The New Law* (1991).

to the real costs of raising children, by circulating them with information on current income support rates, and the National Foster Care Association's recommended rates for paying foster-parents. Notwithstanding the availability of such information, the government found that the 'going rate' for maintenance for one child, of any age up to 18, was £18 per week in 1990,[8] at a time when the National Foster Care Association was recommending a payment of £34.02 per week for a child under the age of 5. Such disparity is hardly surprising, given the finding by Eekelaar that, in his survey of 38 registrars (now district judges) handling financial provision, 14 rejected the National Foster Care Association rates as irrelevant because they were regarded as unrealistically high.[9] The government found that maintenance awards represented only about 11 per cent of total net incomes of absent parents on above average incomes.[10] It further found wide variations in the amounts of maintenance being awarded, one example being of two fathers, each earning £150 per week net. One was required to pay £5 per week in maintenance, and the other £50 per week.[11]

Not only was there concern that the amounts of maintenance awarded might be too low, but also that awards were not being complied with nor adequately enforced. Edwards, Gould and Halpern found, in a survey of orders in one West London court, that 55 per cent were in arrears, of which 57 per cent involved sums in excess of £1,000. Their study of an Inner London court found that 72 per cent of orders had at some time been in arrears, with 49.5 per cent in arrears at the time of the study, 76 per cent of these involving over £1,000.[12] Where maintenance awards are low, there is little incentive to seek their enforcement, especially where the recipient is in any event dependent upon social security benefits. Yet even where the Department of Social Security has the power to seek enforcement against liable relatives, in only 23 per cent of cases was the full amount of arrears of maintenance recovered.[13]

While low levels of maintenance, and high proportions of orders in arrears were not particularly new, a further element which led to a determination to alter the law was the impact of these factors on the social security budget. The government found that about 770,000 single parents, or around two-thirds of the total number, were dependent upon income support in 1989, up from 330,000 such families in 1980.[14] Fewer than one quarter of these were receiving any maintenance, while the cost to the Treasury of their benefits was £3.2 billion in 1988/89. The cost of supporting lone parent families appeared incompatible with the renewed emphasis upon asserting and strengthening parental responsibility for children represented by the new Children Act 1989.

The desire to do something more fundamental about parental obligations to support children was translated into the Government's White Paper,

[8] White Paper, *Children Come First* Cm 1264 Vol 1, para 1.5.
[9] Eekelaar *Regulating Divorce*, p 95.
[10] Op cit.
[11] White Paper, loc cit.
[12] Edwards, Gould and Halpern *The Continuing Saga of Maintaining the Family after Divorce* [1990] Fam Law 31.
[13] White Paper, Vol 2, para 5.1.2, and see Gibson *The Future for Maintenance* [1991] CJQ 330.
[14] White Paper, Vol 2, p i.

Children Come First, published in 1990,[15] and followed by the Child Support Act 1991.[16] The scheme set up by the Act draws, to some extent, upon similar initiatives in both the United States of America and Australia.[17]

2. THE SCHEME OF THE ACT

The two key characteristics of the new law are first, that it lays down a *formula* to be applied to calculate the amount of maintenance needed by the child and to be met by the absent parent. The aim of the formula is to ensure that adequate amounts of maintenance are awarded, and to achieve consistency so that families in similar circumstances will be assessed for similar amounts of maintenance. Secondly, the assessment, collection and enforcement of maintenance are to be carried out, not by the courts, but by the Child Support Agency, a 'next steps' agency like the Benefits Agency and responsible to the Department of Social Security. The courts will have a residual role to play in relation to child maintenance, with significant implications for the way they will deal with spousal support and property adjustment in future.

(a) The Child Support Agency

The Child Support Agency is to be staffed by child support officers, headed by a Chief Child Support Officer whose duty is to advise them on their functions, to keep under review the operation of the Act, and to make annual reports to the Secretary of State.[18] Where a child support officer is considering the exercise of any discretionary power conferred by the Act, he shall, under section 2, 'have regard to the welfare of any child likely to be affected by his decision'. This requirement is both narrower and wider than similar conditions in other legislation. Since welfare is not made the first consideration, still less the paramount consideration, section 2 is narrower than section 25(1) of the Matrimonial Causes Act 1973, or section 1 of the Children Act 1989. On the other hand, the duty to consider welfare lies in respect of *any* child who may be affected by the decision, and not just the child directly in issue. The Act gives no guidance on how welfare is to be taken into account, nor on how a balance should be struck between different children who may be affected.

(b) The relevant parties

Section 1(1) provides that 'each parent of a qualifying child is responsible for maintaining him'. A child is defined in section 55 as a person under the age of 16, or under the age of 19 and receiving full-time non-advanced education, who has not been married. Such a child is a 'qualifying child' within section 3(1) if:

[15] See Eekelaar *A Child Support Scheme for the United Kingdom* [1991] Fam Law 15; Hayes *Making and Enforcing Child Maintenance Obligations* [1991] Fam Law 105.
[16] Eekelaar notes that the question of *why* parents should be regarded as being under a legal obligation to maintain their children is rarely articulated (op cit, chap 5, n 2), and their obligation to do so was assumed in the White Paper.
[17] See Weitzman and Maclean (eds) *Economic Consequences of Divorce: The International Perspective* Part Four; Parker *Child Support in Australia: Children's Rights or Public Interest?* (1991) 5 International Journal of Law and the Family 24.
[18] Child Support Act 1991, s 13.

'(a) one of his parents is, in relation to him, an absent parent; or
(b) both of his parents are, in relation to him, absent parents.'

A parent is an 'absent parent' under section 3(2) if:

'(a) the parent is not living in the same household with the child; and
(b) the child has his home with a person who is, in relation to him, a person with care.'

A parent is defined in section 54 as 'any person who is in law the mother or father of the child'. This definition covers natural parents, parents by virtue of adoption, and parents by virtue of the Human Fertilisation and Embryology Act 1990. There is no concept of 'child of the family' which underpins private support obligations. The approach of the Act is, like the Social Security Act 1986, to attach liability to those with the legal status of parents only.

A person with care is defined as a person:

'(a) with whom the child has his home;
(b) who usually provides day to day care for the child (whether exclusively or in conjunction with any other person); and
(c) is a parent, guardian or person who has a residence order under section 8 of the Children Act 1989 in his favour.'

More than one person may be a person with care in relation to the child under section 3(5).

The person with care or an absent parent may apply to the Child Support Agency, under section 4(1), for a 'maintenance assessment' to be made by a child support officer with respect to the qualifying child. Unless section 6 applies, application may[19] be made for the Agency to arrange for the collection and enforcement of the 'child support maintenance' so assessed. If, however, the person with care is the child's parent, and she is claiming income support, family credit or any other benefit of a prescribed kind, she *must* authorise the Agency, by completing a 'maintenance application form' under section 6(6), to take action under the Act to recover child support maintenance from the absent parent.

(c) Obtaining information to make the assessment

A person applying under section 4, or under a duty to authorise action under section 6, must, so far as she reasonably can, supply information to the Agency to enable the absent parent to be traced (if necessary), and for the Agency to make the maintenance assessment. To accommodate the concern that a parent dependent upon benefits (and therefore obliged to authorise action under section 6), might not wish to reveal the identity of the absent parent to the Agency, because she fears violence from him, or wishes to put an unhappy relationship behind her, sections 6(2) and 46(3) provide that the requirements to give authorisation, or provide information, can be waived by the Agency where they consider that there are reasonable grounds for believing that compliance would lead to a risk of the claimant, or any child living with her, suffering harm or undue distress as a result. In deciding this, the requirement to consider the child's welfare under section 2 will be relevant. However, as a deterrent to claimants who might

---

[19] But see s 8, discussed below.

prefer to withhold information, section 46(5) provides that, where the child support officer considers that there are no reasonable grounds for non-compliance, he may give a 'reduced benefit direction' whereby the amount of benefit otherwise payable will be reduced by such amount and for such period as may be prescribed by regulations. The White Paper proposed that up to 20 per cent of the claimant's adult allowance could be withheld under this power.

Information will also be needed from the absent parent in order to discover his means and liabilities. Under section 14, regulations may be made requiring any information or evidence needed to determine an application under the Act, to be furnished by persons specified in the regulations. Absent parents and their employers will presumably be so specified and required to provide information. Under Schedule 2, the Agency may also obtain information from the Inland Revenue, and local authorities administering housing benefit, as to the income or housing costs of an absent parent or person with care. Section 15 provides that inspectors may be appointed to exercise powers of entry and enquiry with a view to obtaining information required under the Act. Under section 15(4) inspectors can, at all reasonable times, enter any premises other than those used solely as a dwelling-house and to question any person aged 18 or over on the premises. An occupier of the premises, an employer or employee working there, a person carrying on a trade, profession, vocation or business there, or an employee or agent of any of these, is obliged, under section 15(6) to furnish to the inspector all such information and documents as he may reasonably require. The primary aim is no doubt to obtain information from the absent parent's employer, but it has been pointed out that there appears to be nothing to prevent the inspector going to other premises, such as the parent's bank, or solicitor.[20]

Under section 12 the officer may, after giving written notice of his intention, where it is reasonably practicable to do so, make an *interim* maintenance assessment where it appears to him that he does not have sufficient information to form a final judgment. The intention would seem to be that, by making a higher assessment than might otherwise have been expected, the officer will be able to prompt the provision of additional information so that the final assessment can be reduced.

(d) Disputes about parentage

About one-third of the cases surveyed by the Government for the White Paper involved couples who had never married.[1] For such cases in particular, a question may arise as to whether the absent parent is the father of the qualifying child. Under section 26, if the alleged parent denies parentage, the child support officer shall not make a maintenance assessment unless the case falls within one of a number of categories. These are:

Case A: the parent has adopted the child;
Case B: the parent has a parental order under section 30 of the Human Fertilisation and Embryology Act 1990;

[20] Bird, op cit, para 4.29.
[1] White Paper, Vol 2, para 3.5.1.

Case C: a declaration that the alleged parent is the parent is in force under section 56 of the Family Law Act 1986 and the child has not subsequently been adopted;

Case D: a declaration is in force under section 27 of the Act[2] and the child has not subsequently been adopted;

Case F:[3] the alleged parent has been found, or adjudged to be the father of the child in relevant proceedings in England and Wales[4] or in affiliation proceedings in the United Kingdom the finding still subsists and the child has not subsequently been adopted.

Where the alleged parent denies parentage and falls outside these categories, then under section 27 the officer or the person with care may apply to the court[5] for a declaration that he is, or is not, a parent of the child. Such a declaration will have effect only for the purposes of the Child Support Act, by virtue of section 27(3).

(e) The formula

The formula for calculating the amount of child support maintenance which the absent parent must pay for the qualifying child is set out in Schedule 1 to the Act. It is expressed in mathematical terms, but the amounts or percentages of income which these represent are to be left to delegated legislation.

(i) The maintenance requirement

The starting point is to calculate the child's maintenance requirement, defined[6] as 'the minimum amount necessary for the maintenance of the qualifying child, or, where there is more than one qualifying child, all of them'. The formula used is:

$$MR = AG - CB$$

MR means the maintenance requirement, AG means the aggregate of amounts to be taken into account under paragraph 1(3) of the Schedule, which are expected to be the amount of income support which would be payable for the child and for the child's carer, plus family premium and lone parent premium. CB is the child benefit payable for the child. So the maintenance requirement is the amount of income support the carer would receive for herself and the child or children, less child benefit. Housing costs are not included since, according to the White Paper, the courts will determine what is to happen to the home when the parties' relationship breaks down. For unmarried parties who have not lived together, the only jurisdiction which could be used to determine that a parent should assist in housing costs for the parent with care, is Schedule 1 to the Children Act 1989. That jurisdiction is excluded where the Child Support Act is applicable, except in certain situations detailed below.[7] Yet such a parent might have to live in more expensive accommodation because of having to take care

---

[2] See below.
[3] Case E applies to Scotland.
[4] Within s 12 of the Civil Evidence Act 1968.
[5] By s 27(4), 'court' means, subject to any provision made under Sch 11 to the Children Act 1989, the High Court, county court or magistrates' court.
[6] By Sch 1, para 1.
[7] S 8(3).

of the child. It is unclear why, if this is the case, the absent parent should not be expected to contribute to the extra expense through the formula.

(ii) Assessable income

The next step is to calculate the contribution to this figure to be met by the absent parent. This is done by working out his 'assessable income' and that of the person with care. By paragraph 5(1):

$$A = N - E$$

where A means the absent parent's assessable income, and N 'is the amount of that parent's net income, calculated or estimated in accordance with regulations made by the Secretary of State'. These regulations are expected to provide for income tax and national insurance contributions to be deducted to arrive at net income. E means the absent parent's 'exempt income'. This represents a parent's 'own essential expenses which must be met before maintenance is paid'.[8] It is expected that it will be set as the sum of the income support personal allowance which would be payable to him (but not including an allowance for a new partner), income support allowances for any of the absent parent's own children living with him in his new home (but not step-children) and any premiums payable for such children, *reasonable* housing costs, and possibly a proportion of any superannuation payments made by the absent parent. Other allowances might be made for further costs, such as council tax. The absent parent's assessable income will therefore be his net income less his exempt income which will cover his basic expenses for himself and his own children living with him.

A similar calculation is then carried out for the person with care, using the formula:

$$C = M - F$$

where C is the assessable income of the person with care, M is defined as that person's net income, and F is their exempt income. It is possible that regulations will ascribe amounts different to those used for the absent parent to these values.

(iii) The maintenance assessment

Having calculated the child's maintenance requirement and the parents' assessable incomes, the child support officer must then calculate:

$$(A + C) \times P$$

In other words, the two assessable incomes are added together, and multiplied by P, which will be a number, specified by regulations, less than 1. In the White Paper, it was set as 0.5 or 50 per cent. If the result of this calculation is a sum equal to, or less than the child's maintenance requirement, then, by paragraph 2(2), the absent parent must pay an amount equal to $A \times P$, ie (if 0.5 is the prescribed number for P) half his assessable income.

It was considered in the White Paper that where the child's maintenance

[8] White Paper, Vol 1, para 3.8.

requirement could be met without exhausting the absent parent's assessable income, he should pay something over and above that amount, so that his children could share in his higher standard of living. The question was how much of his excess assessable income should be diverted to his children. In Australia, a ceiling of two and a half times average earnings is imposed.[9] The White Paper suggested that a rate of 15 per cent of such excess income could be used, but, for exceptionally wealthy parents, this could result in unduly high amounts of maintenance being assessed. The Act accordingly imports a different formula for such cases, comprising a basic element and additional element and setting a ceiling on the final figure through use of a further alternative formula, with the exact values involved in these to be left to regulations.[10]

Where income support or other prescribed benefit is paid to an absent parent or parent who is a person with care, he shall be taken to have no assessable income.[11] However, the White Paper envisaged that an absent parent receiving benefit should still make some contribution to his child's maintenance, and suggested that, unless the parent is sick or disabled and unable to work, 5 per cent of his income support should be deducted in order to stress the importance of his responsibility to his children. Provision for such deduction is made by section 43. During debate in the House of Lords, the government undertook that where the absent parent is receiving benefit for children living with him, he will be 'zero-rated' and no deductions will be made.[12]

(iv) 'Protected income'

To prevent payment of child support maintenance leaving the absent parents with a disposable income equivalent to, or below what he would be entitled to if claiming income support,[13] paragraph 6 states that the amount of the assessment shall be adjusted:

'with a view to securing so far as is reasonably practicable that payment by the absent parent of the amount ... so assessed will not reduce his disposable income below his protected income level'.

The 'protected income level' is expected to be the amount of income support which would be payable to the absent parent to cover his own needs, those of his children living with him and any other dependants such as a new partner and step-children, his housing costs and an earnings disregard of £5 per week. In this way, the true financial obligations of the absent parent are taken into account, having been disregarded when assessing his exempt income earlier. Nonetheless, where the absent parent is not receiving benefit, but his assessable income is calculated as a negative

---

[9] See Parker *The Australian Child Support Scheme* [1990] Fam Law 210.
[10] Sch 1, paras 3, 4. For detailed discussion, see Bird, op cit, paras 5.15–5.18.
[11] Sch 1, para 5(4).
[12] HL Official Report Debs 29 April 1991, cols 593, 594.
[13] For as the White Paper comments (at Vol 1, para 3.23): 'There is no point in alleviating one family's possible dependence on Income Support at the expense of creating such dependence for another family.'

amount and is therefore taken to be nil under paragraph 5(3), the Secretary of State may prescribe a minimum amount of child support maintenance to be paid, even by a parent who is assessed as having insufficient income to pay it.[14]

(f) Termination of assessments

Under Schedule 1, paragraph 16, the assessment will cease to have effect on the death of the absent parent or person with care; on there no longer being a qualifying child with respect to whom it would have effect; on the absent parent ceasing to be the child's parent (that is, if the child is adopted); where the absent parent and person with care have been living together for a continuous period of six months; and where a new maintenance assessment is made. Additionally, under paragraph 2, a person who applied for the assessment under section 4 may ask for it to be cancelled and the child support officer must comply. Similarly, paragraph 3 requires the child support officer to cancel an assessment where it was made under section 6 and the person who had been claiming benefits asks for the cancellation and is no longer dependent upon benefits. Under paragraph 6, where the absent parent and person with care both ask for the assessment to be cancelled, the child support officer *may* do so, if satisfied they are living together.[15]

(g) Reviews of assessments

To remedy the problem of maintenance awards failing to keep pace with inflation or to be uprated to meet changed circumstances, section 16 provides that the Secretary of State shall make arrangements for the maintenance assessment to be reviewed by a child support officer as soon as is reasonably practicable after the end of a prescribed period. The period is expected to be one year, in line with the annual adjustment of benefit rates and the fact that employees generally receive annual pay rises. Thus, where the person with care is receiving benefits, the extra money paid through the social security system due to increased rates of benefit can be recouped promptly from the absent parent, and when his income rises due to a pay increase, that too can be brought into account before a long interval has elapsed.

Under section 17, the absent parent or the person with care may himself seek a review of a maintenance assessment, upon the ground that by reason of a change of circumstances since the original assessment was made, the amount of child support maintenance payable would be significantly different if it were to be re-assessed, for example, where the absent parent becomes unemployed, or has another child with a new partner and therefore seeks a downward revision of his maintenance assessment. Equally, the person with care might seek an increased assessment if the absent parent was known to have obtained higher paid employment, or acquired some other gain. Under either section 16 or section 17, where a review is completed, the child support officer must then make a fresh maintenance assessment, unless satisfied that the original assessment has ceased to have effect or should be brought to an end. In the case of a section 17 review, however, this need not be done if the difference in amounts between the

[14] Para 7(1).
[15] Query the application of this provision given the mandatory nature of paras 2 and 3.

original assessment and that of the review is less than an amount to be prescribed.

To enable mistakes in assessment to be corrected, and to obviate the need for a person with care or absent parent to seek a review, section 19 enables the child support officer himself to make a fresh maintenance assessment where he is satisfied that the one currently in force is defective by reason of having been made in ignorance of a material fact, based on a mistake as to a material fact, or being wrong in law; or that it would be appropriate to make a fresh assessment if application to do so were made under sections 17 or 18.

(h) Challenging the child support officer

Under section 18, a person who is aggrieved by a child support officer's decision may seek a review by another officer who was not involved in the original decision. A review may be sought against a refusal to grant an application for a maintenance assessment under section 4 or to carry out a review under section 17 or to challenge a maintenance assessment presently in force, or a cancellation or refusal of cancellation, of such an assessment. The officer need not carry out the review if satisfied that there are no reasonable grounds for supposing that the decision was made in ignorance of a material fact, was based on a mistake as to a material fact, or was wrong in law. If, as a result of the review, the officer is satisfied that a maintenance assessment, or fresh assessment, should be made, then he shall make it.[16]

Appeals against a child support officer's review or his refusal to carry one out, lie to a child support appeal tribunal.[17] If the appeal succeeds, the tribunal must remit the case to be dealt with by a child support officer, and may give such directions as it considers appropriate. Further appeals on questions of law may be made to a Child Support Commissioner,[18] with a further appeal to the Court of Appeal.[19]

(i) Collection and enforcement of assessments

One of the main objectives of the Act is to improve the collection and enforcement of maintenance. The Agency may carry out the collection and enforcement of assessments where this is requested by those applying for assessment under section 4, and in respect of all section 6 assessments.[20] Section 30 gives the Secretary of State power to make regulations to collect and enforce other types of maintenance, such as periodical payments. Section 30(2) provides that, even if child support maintenance under the Act is not being collected, payments payable for the benefit of a child may be collected through the machinery provided by the Act, and it is likely that, ultimately, periodical payments for a spouse may be prescribed as

[16] S 18(a).
[17] S 20. The tribunal is set up under s 21 and is similar in composition and function to social security appeal tribunals. (S 45 enables the Lord Chancellor, by order, to provide for appeals to be made to a court instead.) The appeal must be sought within 28 days of the application of the child unless leave is obtained from the chairman of the tribunal: s 20(2).
[18] Office created by s 22.
[19] Ss 24 and 25.
[20] S 29.

within the section as well, at least where the recipient is claiming benefits or has a child.

Section 31 empowers the Secretary of State to make a 'deduction from earnings' order, akin to an attachment of earnings order, directed to the liable person's employer, instructing him to make deductions from earnings and pay them to the Secretary of State. However, the order is made by the Secretary of State (or, in practice, the Agency), and not by a court, although regulations may provide for an appeal to be made to a magistrates' court by a liable person who is aggrieved by the making of the order, or by its terms.[1] Like attachment of earnings orders, the order can be made before any arrears of payments have accrued.

Where a payment has been missed, the Secretary of State may apply to a magistrates' court for a liability order against the liable person under section 33. This enables the Secretary of State either to levy 'the appropriate amount' (the amount of maintenance unpaid together with charges connected with the distress) through seizure of goods,[2] or to apply to the county court for a garnishee or charging order as if the amount unpaid were payable under a county court order.[3] The ultimate sanction for non-payment will be committal to prison for a maximum of six weeks by a magistrates' court, but only if the court is of the opinion that there has been wilful refusal or culpable neglect on the part of the liable person.[4]

3. THE RESIDUAL ROLE OF THE COURTS

Section 8(1) and (3) provide that:

'... in any case where a child support officer would have jurisdiction to make a maintenance assessment with respect to a qualifying child and an absent parent of his on an application duly made by a person entitled to apply for such an assessment with respect to that child ... no court shall exercise any power which it would otherwise have to make, vary or revive any maintenance order in relation to the child and absent parent concerned.'[5]

In other words it is only where the child support officer does *not* have jurisdiction that the court can continue to make maintenance or periodical payments orders. Under section 44 the officer only has jurisdiction if the person with care, the absent parent, or the qualifying child is habitually resident in the United Kingdom. Where any of these is not so resident, the jurisdiction of the officer is therefore excluded and the court may make an order. Secondly, an assessment may only be made against an absent parent who is the parent of the qualifying child. Where maintenance is sought for a step-child, the jurisdiction of the courts based on the concept of the 'child of the family' will be the only applicable jurisdiction and the Act will not apply.[6] Thirdly, where a child is over the age of 16, or is not a qualifying child within s 3(1), the courts' jurisdiction may still apply (for example, if the child is not in full-time education but still needs financial support).

---

[1] S 32(5).
[2] S 35.
[3] S 36.
[4] S 40(3).
[5] However, s 8(4) permits the court to *revoke* a maintenance order.
[6] Although it might be possible to utilise the Act's provisions on collection and enforcement of other forms of maintenance under s 30(2).

Finally, it may be noted that, since the scheme of the Act imposes liability to pay child support maintenance only on an absent parent, where maintenance is sought from the person with care instead, the courts may continue to be used.[7]

In some situations notwithstanding the fact that a maintenance assessment may be carried out, it will remain possible to utilise the courts' jurisdiction. First, where there is a maintenance assessment in force, which was set at the ceiling fixed by Schedule 1, and 'the court is satisfied that the circumstances of the case make it appropriate for the absent parent to make or secure the making of periodical payments under a maintenance order in addition to the child support maintenance' the court may continue to exercise its powers to award maintenance.[8] In the case of a very wealthy absent parent it will therefore still be possible to increase the amount of maintenance to be paid by recourse to the court. The court, however, can only 'top-up' the assessment; it cannot carry out a whole maintenance assessment exercise itself. Similar powers exist in section 8(7) and (8) to enable the court to make a maintenance order where this is *solely* to meet costs incurred in receiving education or training, or to cover expenses attributable to the child's disability. School fees, support for a student, and special expenses connected with a child's disability may therefore be met through the court system.

The 1991 Act defines a maintenance order as 'an order which requires the making or securing of periodical payments' and so does not affect the court's power to make an order for the payment of a lump sum or property adjustment.[9] Although traditionally the courts have not approved of such orders as being appropriate for children,[10] the jurisdiction to make them is unaffected by the Act, and there may be situations where they will be suitable.

Section 9(2) provides that maintenance *agreements* to or for the benefit of a child are not restricted by the Act. However, section 9(3) and (4) state that the existence of such an agreement cannot prevent a party, or any other person, from seeking a maintenance assessment under the Act, and any clause in the agreement purporting to restrict the right of any person to seek an assessment shall be void. Furthermore, a court will not be able to vary the agreement where the child support officer would have jurisdiction, so that the utility of making such agreements would appear to be limited. In practice, rather than making agreements enforceable only by civil suits, consent orders have been obtained from the court, usually, of course, as part of a package dealing with the financial position of the parties as well as the maintenance of their children. Section 8(5) empowers the Lord Chancellor by order to provide that courts may continue to make consent orders including periodical payments for children, notwithstanding the rest of section 8. It is unclear whether the regulations will permit such an order to take precedence over a maintenance assessment. If they do not, there will seem little point in negotiating for such an order. On the other hand, it is unlikely that an order fixing periodical payments below, or

---

[7] S 8(10).
[8] S 8(6).
[9] S 8(11).
[10] See ante, p 697.

significantly below, the amount which would be fixed by use of the formula would be permitted to endure, especially where the person with care is in receipt of social security benefits.[11]

The broader question of what the impact of the new Act will be upon financial provision settlements inevitably arises. Clean break agreements, whereby the wife forgoes periodical payments in return for a larger share of the capital assets, would seem to be in jeopardy.[12] Even before the 1991 Act, clean break settlements could not prevent the care-giving parent from later seeking maintenance for the children but in future, the husband will be unable to ensure that the wife will not, at some point, seek child support maintenance through the Agency, and such maintenance will, under the formula, include an element for the care-giver's support. Even where he has attempted to satisfy the wife's claim to such support through capital provision, therefore, he will be at risk of having to make payments for his wife, albeit indirectly. A judgment will have to be made (although it is hard to see how), at the time of negotiating the settlement, as to the chances of the wife becoming dissatisfied with any maintenance agreement and later seeking child support, or in particular becoming dependent upon income support or claiming family credit, in which case, section 6 will *require* her to utilise the Act.

One of the objections to clean break arrangements is that it is unrealistic to assume that the care-giving parent's own needs can be separated out from those of the children. Instead, it is argued that the total finances of the lone-parent family must be viewed together. Indeed, the formula itself recognises precisely this point by requiring account to be taken of the care-giver's income support allowance. It therefore seems retrograde to force the parties into using two distinct processes to resolve their financial disputes— the court for financial provision between themselves, and property adjustment for the whole family on the one hand, and the Agency for child support plus indirect spousal support on the other. However, it could be argued that if regulations are made permitting the courts to continue to make consent orders, provided perhaps that they conform with the formula, the result may be to exert a strong upward pressure upon the amounts of periodical payments settled upon for children, thus achieving the objective of the Act of producing more realistic levels of child support.

In straightforward cases, and especially those involving unmarried couples, the 1991 Act is likely to enable a speedy resolution of any disputes over child support. There should at least be little excuse for the Agency if it fails to recoup significantly higher amounts of maintenance from absent parents, to set against the spiralling social security budget. Whatever the outcome, the Act will prove a bold experiment in the replacement of a judicial procedure for enforcing what has hitherto been seen as a primarily private familial obligation by an administrative mechanism instead.

---

[11] For discussion, see Eekelaar *Child Support—An Evaluation* [1991] Fam Law 511.
[12] See post, pp 761 et seq, for a discussion of 'clean breaks'.

Chapter 21

Financial relief for members of the family on divorce, nullity and judicial separation

A. Introductory[1]

Development of the court's powers

The ecclesiastical courts were able to give financial protection to a wife by ordering the husband to pay her alimony pending suit (or pendente lite) and permanent alimony after granting a decree of divorce a mensa et thoro. After 1857 this power was vested in the Divorce Court and subsequently in the High Court and divorce county courts. The Divorce Court set up in 1857 was also empowered on granting a decree of divorce to order the husband to secure maintenance for the wife's life.[2] If the husband had no capital which could be secured, hardship was likely to be caused to the wife; this was cured in 1866, when the court was given the power to order the husband to pay unsecured maintenance to the wife. As this would have to come out of his income, however, the maximum term for which it could be ordered was the spouses' joint lives.[3] In 1907 these powers were extended to nullity.[4] After 1937 a wife petitioning for divorce or judicial separation on the ground of her husband's insanity could be ordered to pay him alimony pending suit and, if the decree was granted, maintenance (secured or unsecured) or permanent alimony.[5] In 1963 the courts were given a power, long overdue, to order the payment of a lump sum in addition to or instead of maintenance or alimony on divorce, nullity and judicial separation.[6] Ancillary orders could also be made by a court granting a decree of restitution of conjugal rights to a wife.[7]

Except when the husband was incurably of unsound mind, orders for alimony and maintenance could be made only against him. This of course reflected the fact that in the middle of the nineteenth century it was very unlikely that a wife would have an income. She might have property settled to her own use, however, and as early as 1857 the court was empowered

---

[1] See generally Jackson's *Matrimonial Finance and Taxation* (5th Edn) by Jackson and Davies. For an account of two empirical studies see Barrington Baker, Eekelaar, Gibson and Raikes *The Matrimonial Jurisdiction of Registrars* and Eekelaar and Maclean *Maintenance After Divorce*. See, too, Eekelaar *Regulating Divorce* and *Economic Consequences of Divorce: The International Perspective* (eds Weitzman and Maclean). The latter is a particularly interesting collection of recent essays, whose contributors are drawn from a variety of different disciplines and countries.
[2] Matrimonial Causes Act 1857, s 32.
[3] Matrimonial Causes Act 1866, s 1.
[4] Matrimonial Causes Act 1907, s 1.
[5] Matrimonial Causes Act 1937, s 10(2).
[6] Matrimonial Causes Act 1963, s 5.
[7] Alimony pending suit, alimony on making the decree on the wife's application, and periodical payments (which could be secured) if the husband failed to comply with the decree: Matrimonial Causes Act 1857, s 17; Matrimonial Causes Act 1884, s 2.

to order this to be settled for the benefit of the husband or children if he obtained a divorce or judicial separation on the ground of her adultery. This power was later extended to the property of wives who were divorced for cruelty or desertion or whose husbands obtained a decree for restitution of conjugal rights.[8] On divorce or nullity, either party could benefit from the exercise of the court's jurisdiction, going back to 1859,[9] to vary ante-nuptial and post-nuptial settlements.

The Matrimonial Causes Act 1973

As often happens, piecemeal modifications of the law spread over more than a century produced confusing anomalies. Whatever reasons there might originally have been for giving the courts different powers according to the nature of the decree, they had largely become obscure by the middle of the present century. Why, for example, could a wife obtain secured maintenance if she petitioned for restitution of conjugal rights but not if she petitioned for judicial separation? Why could the court order maintenance to be secured for the wife's life on divorce or nullity but only for the spouses' joint lives in proceedings for restitution of conjugal rights? It was as difficult for the layman to grasp these subtleties in a branch of the law that was more likely to affect him than most as it was for the lawyer to justify them.

Pressure for immediate reform increased after the passing of the Divorce Reform Act 1969, when the fear was expressed that many innocent wives, divorced against their will, would be left with inadequate provision. The result was the passing of the Matrimonial Proceedings and Property Act 1970, which was based upon the recommendations of the Law Commission.[10] Most of its provisions have been repealed and re-enacted in Part II of the Matrimonial Causes Act 1973, which, in its amended form,[11] now governs the award of financial relief in the High Court and divorce county courts. Some of the more important changes resulting from this legislation are to be noted, namely:

(1) The old confusing terminology (alimony, maintenance and periodical payments) is abolished. All are now described as financial provision and may take the form of periodical payments or a lump sum payment.

(2) The court is no longer virtually restricted to ordering maintenance in favour of the wife. It now has equal powers to order either spouse to make financial provision for the other.

(3) There is no distinction between the court's powers to order financial provision for the petitioner and its powers to order financial provision for the respondent. This is an essential consequence of the passing of the Divorce Reform Act, because the fact that the petitioner has obtained a decree does not necessarily indicate that the respondent has been responsible for the breakdown of the marriage.

---

[8] Matrimonial Causes Act 1857, s 45; Matrimonial Causes Act 1884, s 3; Matrimonial Causes Act 1937, s 10(3).

[9] Matrimonial Causes Act 1859, s 5.

[10] Law Com No 25, Report on Financial Provision in Matrimonial Proceedings, 1969. For critical reviews of the provisions of the Act, see Cretney *The Maintenance Quagmire* 33 MLR 662; Kahn-Freund *Recent Legislation on Matrimonial Property*, ibid pp 601 et seq, particularly at pp 615 et seq.

[11] Ie principally by the Matrimonial Homes and Property Act 1981 and the Matrimonial and Family Proceedings Act 1984.

(4) The court's powers to order financial provision, the transfer and settlement of property, and the variation of ante-nuptial and post-nuptial settlements are the same in divorce, nullity and judicial separation.[12]

It should also be added that the new legislation widened the court's powers in two important respects. First, the court's redistributive powers extend to all the assets that either or both the spouses own, irrespective of when and from whom they acquired them. Secondly, in making orders in respect of the spouses' property, the court is not bound to enforce existing rights and can, for instance, order the transfer of ownership from one spouse to another. This latter power was vested in the court partly in response to the decisions in *Pettitt v Pettitt*[13] and *Gissing v Gissing*[14] which, as we have seen,[15] established that the powers under the Married Women's Property Act 1882, section 17, are declaratory only and that therefore the courts had no power to transfer ownership of property between spouses.

These wider redistributive powers represent one of the key remaining distinctions between the ending of a marriage by divorce or nullity and the ending of cohabitation.

The Matrimonial and Family Proceedings Act 1984

The Matrimonial Causes Act 1973 has not remained unamended. Under the Matrimonial Homes and Property Act 1981, for example, the divorce courts were given the express statutory power to order the sale of any of the spouses' property.[16] The most important change, however, has been brought about by the Matrimonial and Family Proceedings Act 1984.[17] Although this Act does, to a limited extent, extend the courts' powers, for example, to enable them to *impose* a clean break (that is, once-and-for-all settlement between the spouses) upon a spouse,[18] its main concern is to introduce changes in the way that the powers are to be exercised. Two of the most important changes are: (1) in deciding what orders should be made first consideration must be given to the welfare whilst a minor of any child of the family under 18[19] and (2) the court is under a duty to consider whether it is appropriate so to exercise its powers that the financial obligations of each party terminates immediately or as soon as possible.[20] The Act also ended the obligation of the court to place the parties in the position that they would have been had the marriage not broken down.

---

[12] The 1970 Act abolished decrees for restitution of conjugal rights: see ante, p 119.

[13] [1970] AC 777, [1969] 2 All ER 385, HL.

[14] [1971] AC 886, [1970] 2 All ER 780, HL. See also Law Com No 25, paras 64–75.

[15] Ante, p 586.

[16] By s 7 which added s 24A to the 1973 Act. See also Law Com No 99 (Orders for the Sale of Property under the Matrimonial Causes Act 1973).

[17] This Act is based on the Law Commission's recommendations: see Law Com No 112 (The Financial Consequences of Divorce). See also their earlier paper, Law Com No 112 (The Financial Consequences of Divorce: The Basic Policy). For an interesting account of the background and reasons for the Law Commission recommending changes, see Cretney *Money After Divorce—The Mistakes We Have Made?* in *Essays in Family Law 1985* (ed Freeman) pp 34 et seq, particularly at pp 36–42.

[18] Under the Matrimonial Causes Act 1973, s 25A(3) as added by s 3(4) of the Matrimonial and Family Proceedings Act 1984. There is also power to impose a 'deferred clean break' under s 28(1A) as added by s 5(2) of the 1984 Act.

[19] S 25(1) as substituted by s 3 of the 1984 Act.

[20] S 25A(2), (3) as substituted by s 3(4) of the 1984 Act.

Powers of the court

A court hearing a petition for divorce, nullity or judicial separation has statutory power[1] to make an order against *either spouse* with respect to any one or more of the following matters:[2]

(1) Maintenance pending suit;
(2) Unsecured periodical payments to the other spouse;
(3) Secured periodical payments to the other spouse;
(4) Lump sum payments to the other spouse;
(5) Unsecured periodical payments for any child of the family;
(6) Secured periodical payments for any child of the family;
(7) A lump sum payment for any child of the family;
(8) Transfer of property to the other spouse or for the benefit of any child of the family;
(9) Settlement of property for the benefit of the other spouse or any child of the family;
(10) Variation of any ante-nuptial or post-nuptial settlement;
(11) Where a court makes a secured periodical payments order, a lump sum order or a property transfer order, it can further order a sale of property belonging to either or both spouses.

Orders coming within (2)–(7) are collectively known as financial provision orders and those coming within (8), (9) and (10) as property adjustment orders.[3]

The court has similar powers in those rare cases where a marriage has been dissolved on the ground that one spouse is presumed to be dead and he or she is later found to be still alive.[4]

Although, as we shall see, there are statutory guidelines on the matters to be taken into account when exercising these powers, it should be appreciated at the outset that considerable discretion is left to the judge in deciding what order should be made in any individual case. This discretion applies equally to determining what order should be made with regard to the spouses' property and with regard to their income. This vesting of wide discretion in the courts is in contrast to the position taken even in some other common law jurisdictions.[5] In New Zealand, for instance, the

---

[1] But the court can accept a party's undertaking to accept other obligations, see post, p 746.
[2] Under the Matrimonial Causes Act 1973, respectively ss 22, 23, 24 and 24A (added by the Matrimonial Homes and Property Act 1981, s 7).
[3] Ibid, s 21. It will be noted that orders for the sale of property are neither classified as financial provision nor property adjustment.
[4] *Deacock v Deacock* [1958] P 230, [1958] 2 All ER 633, CA. (Overruling *Wall v Wall* [1950] P 112, [1949] 2 All ER 927.)
[5] In most continental legal systems there is some form of community of property which severely restricts or even precludes the court from being able to redistribute the parties' property or even income. For an account of various community of property regimes, see Law Com Working Paper No 42, Part 5 and Appendix C. In most States of the USA there is a principle of equal division of property between the spouses. For research into the effects of this, see eg Weitzman *The Divorce Revolution: The Unexpected Social and Economic Consequences for Women and Children in America*, summarised by her in *The Divorce Revolution and Illusion of Equality: a View from the United States* in *Essays in Family Law 1985* (ed Freeman) p 91. See also now, a more recent essay by the same author, Weitzman, *Marital Property: Its Transformation and Division in the United States* in *Economic Consequences of Divorce—the International Perspective* (eds Weitzman and Maclean) p 85.

matrimonial home and family chattels must be divided equally,[6] while in Scotland, the courts may order one spouse to support the other to the extent that 'is reasonable to enable him [ie the dependent spouse] to adjust over a period of not more than three years'.[7]

Application for relief, discovery and hearing

A petitioner seeking financial relief should apply for it in the petition; a respondent who files an answer should apply in the answer. Once the prayer for relief is included in the petition, it has been held[8] that the petitioner may come back to court at any time thereafter to apply for additional relief (such as a lump sum) or for the amendment or alteration of an award previously made. Inordinate or inexcusable delay by the petitioner may be relevant to the exercise of the court's discretion in deciding whether to grant relief, but it will not oust the court's jurisdiction at least to consider the application. If a spouse does not apply for financial relief in the petition or (as the case may be) in the answer, the party in question must obtain leave of the court unless the parties are agreed on the proposed order.[9] There is no limit on the time in which leave may be sought, but as failure to apply really amounts to no more than a technical omission, the courts tend to look sympathetically at a request for leave if the applicant has a reasonable prospect of success or an arguable case. On the other hand, delay would be fatal if the other party had ordered his affairs in the belief that no application would be made, or was being harassed or would be prejudiced in some other way.[10]

If a respondent does not file an answer claiming relief (as will be the case in all undefended suits), he may apply for financial relief at any time without leave.[11]

It is a general principle of the Matrimonial Causes Act 1973 that, if a former spouse remarries, she (or he) must look to her new partner for financial provision for herself, and not to the old one. Consequently, whether leave is required or not, a party who has remarried cannot apply for an order at all except for periodical payments or a lump sum payment

---

[6] Under the Family Property Act 1976, save in certain defined circumstances, for example, where the marriage has been of short duration. There is also a more restricted power than in England to award income support for a spouse. For further details see eg *Butterworths Family Law Cases (NZ)* (2nd Edn) paras 7.33 et seq. In Australia, the courts have, under the Family Law Act 1975, a wide discretion to redistribute property (though it seems established that equal division should be the starting point) but as in New Zealand a more restricted power to award income support for a spouse. For a comparison of New Zealand law with that of Australia, see the Australian Law Reform Commission: *Matrimonial Property Law* (1985) paras 111–126.

[7] Family Law (Scotland) Act 1985, s 9(d), though under s 9(e) there is power, in cases where a party seems likely to suffer serious financial hardship, to make 'such financial provision as is reasonable to relieve him of the hardship over a reasonable period'.

[8] *Twiname v Twiname* [1992] 1 FLR 29, CA. See the comment by Cretney [1991] Fam Law 520. Presumably the same principle applies to a respondent who makes application for financial relief in the answer.

[9] Family Proceedings Rules 1991, r 2.53(1), (2).

[10] *Chaterjee v Chaterjee* [1976] Fam 199, [1976] 1 All ER 719, CA.

[11] Family Proceedings Rules 1991, r 2.53(3).

for a child of the family,[12] although an application already made can be entertained notwithstanding the remarriage.[13] This rule applies even though the second marriage is void or voidable:[14] the party's remedy lies in seeking financial provision in nullity proceedings.

An application for financial relief is not a cause of action which survives against the other party's estate, so that no order can be made after the death of either of them.[15] The effect of this is now mitigated by the extensive powers given to the court by the Inheritance (Provision for Family and Dependants) Act 1975.[16]

Except for maintenance pending suit and orders with respect to children, no order may be made unless a decree nisi of divorce or nullity or a decree of judicial separation has been granted and, in the case of divorce or nullity, it may not take effect until the decree is made absolute.[17] Unless the parties are agreed on the order to be made, each of them is required to file an affidavit of means setting out full particulars of their property and income.[18] Both spouses are under a duty to make full, frank and up-to-date disclosure of their assets[19] but in practice it is notorious that some spouses, particularly wealthy men, seek to conceal the full extent of their property and means. The courts do possess extensive powers to enable one party to obtain additional information from the other[20] and may (and frequently do) make orders for discovery[1] where financial and other documents and records are required to be produced. While resort to such powers may be necessary in appropriate cases, there has recently been a number of judicial criticisms of excessive and unnecessary enquiries into the means of the parties,

[12] Matrimonial Causes Act 1973, s 28(3), as amended by the Matrimonial and Family Proceedings Act 1984, s 5(3). The Law Commission, who assumed that this proposal would be highly controversial, found that it received almost unanimous support; Law Com No 25, para 14. It may, however, act as a trap and what is no more than a pleading slip may prevent a property adjustment order from being made when this would be proper: see generally *Hargood v Jenkins* [1978] Fam 148, [1978] 3 All ER 1001. See also *Nixon v Fox* [1978] Fam 173, [1978] 3 All ER 995. If the embargo applies and the former spouse wishes to dispute ownership of any matrimonial property, he can, within three years after the divorce, seek a declaration under the Married Women's Property Act 1882, s 17, in which case ownership will be determined upon strict property principles: *Bothe v Amos* [1976] Fam 46, [1975] 2 All ER 321, CA. The amendment makes it clear that the embargo applies whenever the applicant remarried, even if the marriage took place before the implementation of the Matrimonial Causes Act 1973, thereby reversing *Bonning v Dodsley* [1982] 1 All ER 612, CA.
[13] *Jackson v Jackson* [1973] Fam 99, [1973] 2 All ER 395. This does not apply to an application for periodical payments for the spouse which will in any case cease on remarriage: see post, p 728.
[14] Matrimonial Causes Act 1973, s 52(3). This means that, if the second husband is a person of no substance, the taxpayer may have to support the wife even though the first husband is capable of doing so.
[15] *Dipple v Dipple* [1942] P 65, [1942] 1 All ER 234.
[16] See post, pp 821 et seq.
[17] Matrimonial Causes Act 1973, ss 23 and 24.
[18] Family Proceedings Rules 1991, r 2.58(2), (3).
[19] *Livesey (formerly Jenkins) v Jenkins* [1985] AC 424, [1985] 1 All ER 106, HL.
[20] Family Proceedings Rules 1991, r 2.63.
[1] Family Proceedings Rules 1991, r 2.62. Note also the 'millionaire's defence' where the respondent, conceding that his wealth is more than sufficient to support any order the court may make, will not be ordered to make full disclosure: *Thyssen-Bornemisza v Thyssen-Bornemisza (No 2)* [1985] FLR 1069, CA, *S v S* [1986] Fam 189, [1986] 3 All ER 566; *B v B (Discovery: Financial Provision)* [1990] 2 FLR 180; *Primavera v Primavera* [1992] 1 FLR 16, CA.

which can be time-consuming, acrimonious, and above all expensive, with enormous legal and other professional costs swallowing up the value of the family assets available for distribution.[2] In *Evans v Evans*,[3] Booth J, with the concurrence of the President of the Family Division, issued a number of guidelines designed to be followed by practitioners involved in the preparation of substantial ancillary relief cases. These have now been embodied in a Practice Direction.[4] Although these guidelines[5] are undoubtedly of assistance, a practitioner's task is far from easy.[6] On the one hand, he must avoid excessive enquiries and incurring heavy professional costs, while on the other, he can only properly advise his client on the basis of information which is complete and accurate. In this latter context, it has been held that a solicitor's failure properly to investigate a husband's financial and property resources before advising the wife to settle her claims for ancillary relief may constitute negligence, for which substantial damages may be awarded.[7]

The hearing will normally be before a district judge who may, however, refer the application to a judge.[8] Cases are normally heard in the divorce county court but there is power to transfer proceedings to the High Court.[9] In general terms a transfer ought to be ordered in cases of complexity, difficulty or gravity. With regard to proceedings where periodical payments, a lump sum or property are in issue, the court is directed to have regard to the following factors when considering whether the complexity, difficulty or gravity of issues are such that they ought to be tried in the High Court, namely:

'(a) the capital values of assets involved and the extent to which they are available for, or susceptible to, distribution or adjustment;
(b) any substantial allegation of fraud or deception or non disclosure;
(c) any substantial contested allegations of conduct.'[10]

---

[2] See eg *B v B (Financial Provision)* [1989] 1 FLR 119; *P v P* [1989] 2 FLR 241; *Newton v Newton* [1990] 1 FLR 33, CA, *Re T (Divorce: Interim Maintenance: Discovery)* [1990] 1 FLR 1.
[3] [1990] 2 All ER 147.
[4] [1990] 1 WLR 575n. Subsequently, Booth J has advocated court control of ancillary relief proceedings, see her address to the Solicitor's Family Law Association annual conference 1992 entitled *Life After Evans* reprinted at [1992] Fam Law 178.
[5] See also Solicitors Family Law Association *Guidelines for Use by Solicitors in the Conduct of Ancillary Relief Claims.*
[6] For an expression of concern by two family practitioners, see Collis and Kleanthous *Should Evans be Ignored? A No-Win Situation* [1991] Fam Law 466.
[7] *Dickinson v Jones Alexander & Co* [1990] Fam Law 137. CF *Dutfield v Gilbert H Stephens & Sons* [1988] Fam Law 473.
[8] Family Proceedings Rules 1991, r 2.65. An invaluable description of the work of registrars (now district judges) in this field is to be found in Barrington, Baker et al *Matrimonial Jurisdiction of Registrars.*
[9] Under the Matrimonial and Family Proceedings Act 1984, s 39.
[10] *Practice Direction* [1992] 3 All ER 151.

B. Orders that may be made

1. MAINTENANCE PENDING SUIT[11]

On any petition for divorce, nullity or judicial separation, the court may order either spouse to make such periodical payments to the other pending suit as it thinks reasonable.[12] It is clear that the court can also make the following orders in favour of a 'child of the family' pending the suit in divorce or nullity, namely, secured or unsecured periodical payments or a lump sum.[13]

The power to order the husband to pay maintenance pending suit (or alimony pendente lite, as it was formerly called) goes back to the ecclesiastical courts. It was based on the fact that the wife as such was entitled to be maintained by her husband so long as the marriage was still in existence, and the purpose of interim orders of this sort was to ensure that she and any children of the marriage living with her obtained a sufficient allowance until the outcome of the proceedings. Consequently she was entitled to an order even though she was alleged to have been guilty of adultery or desertion or the marriage was alleged to be void, so long as the issue was sub judice.

The modern powers are considerably wider and can no longer be related to the obligation to maintain at common law. No guidelines are laid down to indicate the circumstances in which an order should be made or the facts to be taken into account in assessing the amount to be paid,[14] but even under the old law the courts had a wide and largely unfettered discretion.[15] As in the case of an application under section 27 of the Matrimonial Causes Act,[16] the court should obviously make an order whenever a spouse or child of the family is in immediate need which the other spouse has the means to alleviate.[17] All the circumstances must be taken into account, but it will be appreciated that at this stage there will have been no extensive investigation of the parties' means or conduct[18] and the court must obviously pay most attention to their immediate financial position and the needs of the children of the family.[19] In *Re T (Divorce: Interim Maintenance: Discovery)*[20] the court, having balanced the parties' needs and obligations

[11] See generally Jackson's *Matrimonial Finance and Taxation* (5th Edn by Jackson and Davies) ch 2.

[12] Matrimonial Causes Act 1973, s 22.

[13] Ibid, s 23(1)(d), (e) and (f). For the meaning of 'child of the family' see ante, p 368. But for the court's powers once the Child Support Act 1991 is fully in force, see ante, p 719.

[14] Ie the guidelines under s 25 do not apply to orders made under s 22. Aliter if orders are made in favour of a child of the family.

[15] *Waller v Waller* [1956] P 300, [1956] 2 All ER 234, CA; *Slater v Slater* [1962] P 94, [1960] 3 All ER 217, CA.

[16] See ante, p 692.

[17] See eg *Peacock v Peacock* [1984] 1 All ER 1069. It was held in that case that the principles on which the court has to act with regard to welfare benefits (discussed post, p 768) apply equally to applications for maintenance pending suit.

[18] Orders may be made notwithstanding a claim that the court has no jurisdiction: *Cammell v Cammell* [1965] P 467, [1964] 3 All ER 255 or if the applicant is committing adultery: *Offord v Offord* (1981) 3 FLR 309, 11 Fam Law 208.

[19] The old practice (long since discontinued) was to bring the wife's income (if any) up to one-fifth of the spouses' joint income.

[20] [1990] 1 FLR 1.

against their resources, ordered a wealthy husband to pay his wife £25,000 per annum by way of interim maintenance pending suit. The parties had previously reached an agreement on the amount to be paid which the court considered to be compelling evidence of the sum which it was reasonable to award.[1]

Maintenance pending suit may be ordered to be paid retrospectively from the presentation of the petition. Unless the court orders otherwise, it remains payable until the determination of the suit, that is, until decree absolute in the case of divorce and nullity, or the decree in the case of judicial separation, or alternatively, until the petition is dismissed or the suit abates by reason of the death of either party.[2] If no other order has been made when the decree is made absolute (as will often be the case, because the necessary investigations will still be incomplete), a former spouse may be given temporary relief by means of an interim order.[3] In the event of an appeal, the court may order the payment of maintenance pending suit to be continued if it is fair and reasonable to do so in the circumstances.[4]

2. PERIODICAL PAYMENTS[5]

(a) Orders in favour of spouses

(i) Unsecured payments

On granting a decree of divorce, nullity or judicial separation, the court may order either spouse to make unsecured periodical payments to the other and to secure periodical payments to the other.[6] Any order for periodical payments may be backdated to the making of the application for the order, and a party may properly ask for this to be done if no order was made for maintenance pending suit or if the sum ordered proves to have been disproportionately low.

As periodical payments are intended for the payee's maintenance, they must in any event terminate on her (or his) death. Unsecured periodical payments will normally come out of the payer's income which will presumably come to an end on his death; consequently an order for their payment cannot extend beyond the joint lives of the parties.[7] There is, however, no reason why secured payments should not continue after the payer's death, as the capital will already have been charged; consequently

---

[1] At one time the courts were reluctant to give a wife who had entered into a maintenance agreement more than the husband had covenanted to pay her (see *Birch v Birch* [1908] WN 81, CA). Subject, of course, to the court's assessment of the reasonableness of the covenanted amount, it is highly doubtful whether the court would feel itself so bound today. If a magistrates' order is in force, it will be unusual to make an order for maintenance pending suit.

[2] Matrimonial Causes Act 1973, s 22; *Scott v Scott* [1952] 2 All ER 890 (husband's death).

[3] Family Proceedings Rules 1991, r 2.64(2).

[4] *Corbett v Corbett (No 2)* [1971] P 110, 113, [1970] 2 All ER 654, 656.

[5] See generally Jackson's *Matrimonial Finance and Taxation* (5th Edn) chs 3 and 4.

[6] Matrimonial Causes Act 1973, s 23(1)(a), (b). But orders cannot be made *before* the granting of the decree nisi. The court has no jurisdiction, even if the parties consent, and a purported order cannot be saved either by the slip rule or by the exercise of the inherent jurisdiction of the court: *Board (Board Intervening) v Checkland* [1987] 2 FLR 257, CA.

[7] The survivor can then apply for an order under the Inheritance (Provision for Family and Dependants) Act 1975: see post, pp 821 et seq.

in this case the order can last for the payee's life. Furthermore, on divorce or nullity (whether the payments are secured or not) the order must also provide for their termination on the payee's marriage; if an order made on judicial separation remains in force notwithstanding the subsequent dissolution or annulment of the marriage, it will automatically come to an end on the payee's remarriage.[8] She (or he) must thereafter look to her new partner for support.

Formerly, it seemed doubtful whether a claim for periodical payments could be dismissed without the applicant's consent so as to preclude the latter from making further application.[9] This meant that the courts had no power to impose a 'clean break' order upon the parties, that is, to make a once-and-for-all order. However, in line with the policy introduced by the Matrimonial and Family Proceedings Act 1984, of directing the courts to consider whether the parties could become self-sufficient either immediately after the divorce or nullity[10] or within a reasonable time thereafter,[11] there is now express statutory power to dismiss applications. Under section 25A(3) of the Matrimonial Causes Act 1973,[12] if the court considers that no continuing obligation should be imposed on either party it may 'dismiss the application with a direction that the applicant shall not be entitled to make any further application' for periodical payments.[13] There is also power to make a 'deferred clean break order', that is, to order periodical payments to be made for a specified period with a direction that the applicant cannot apply for an extension of that period.[14]

(ii) Secured payments

The very fact of security obviously makes secured payments more attractive to the payee, for there is no problem of enforcement. By tying up the payer's capital, it also prevents him from trying to frustrate the order by disposing of his assets, and the payee will be protected even though the payer becomes bankrupt.[15] We have also seen that the payee can continue to benefit from a secured order after the other's death; moreover, although the survivor cannot apply for an order after the other party's death, an order made before his death may be implemented by his personal representatives who may therefore be called upon to carry it out.[16] Because

---

[8] Matrimonial Causes Act 1973, s 28(1), (2). It is immaterial that the second marriage is void or voidable: ibid, s 52(3).

[9] Following the decision in *Dipper v Dipper* [1981] Fam 31, [1980] 2 All ER 722, CA.

[10] Ie the provisions do not apply to applications for financial orders following judicial separation.

[11] Discussed post, pp 760 et seq.

[12] Added by the Matrimonial and Family Proceedings Act 1984, s 3(4).

[13] Despite the ambiguity of the language used by s 25A(3) ('if the court considers that *no* continuing obligation should be imposed on *either* (sic) party to make or secure periodical payments in favour of the other') the section *does* confer power to dismiss the claims of one spouse to periodical payments while leaving those of the other alive: *Thompson v Thompson* [1988] 2 All ER 376.

[14] S 28(1A) of the Matrimonial Causes Act 1973, added by s 5(2) of the Matrimonial and Family Proceedings Act 1984.

[15] Passingham and Harmer *Law and Practice in Matrimonial Causes* (4th Edn) p 147.

[16] *Hyde v Hyde* [1948] P 198, [1948] 1 All ER 362; *Mosey v Mosey* [1956] P 26, [1955] 2 All ER 391.

of these advantages, the court may order a smaller sum to be secured than it would have ordered by way of unsecured provision.[17]

Payments are normally secured by ordering the spouse against whom the order is made to transfer specified assets to trustees. They hold them on trust to pay the sum ordered to the payee and the balance to the payer or, alternatively, to pay the income to the payer so long as he complies with the order but to use the income and, if necessary, the capital if he defaults. The court may instead order specific property to be charged with the payment of the sum in question.[18] When the order comes to an end, the capital must be returned to the payer (or his estate, if he has already died) and any charge must be cancelled.

The court is naturally anxious to give the maximum protection, particularly to a wife whom the husband has maltreated and is likely to leave penniless.[19] Whether periodical payments can be secured, however, must depend on the capital or secured income which the other has available, and the number of spouses against whom such an order can be made is obviously small. A party cannot normally be expected to use all his property for this purpose, for example to sell up all his furniture.[20] The court may order both secured and unsecured periodical payments, and under the old law it was unusual for more than a third or a half of the total sum to be secured.

If a party is not in need of immediate provision but may require it in the future, a nominal order may be made secured on assets yielding a substantial income. She (or he) can then apply for a suitable variation if necessary; in the meantime the income can be paid over to the other party.[1]

(b) Orders in favour of children of the family[2]

As well as having power to make orders in favour of a spouse the court can, in proceedings for divorce, nullity and judicial separation, make periodical payment orders (which may be secured or unsecured) in favour of a 'child of the family'. The court's power to make an order for a child over the age of 18 and the term for which periodical payments may be ordered are the same as under the Domestic Proceedings and Magistrates'

---

[17] *Chichester v Chichester* [1936] P 129, [1936] 1 All ER 271.

[18] The court may refer the matter to one of the conveyancing counsel of the court to settle a proper instrument to be executed by all necessary parties and has power to defer the grant of the decree in question until the instrument has been duly executed: Matrimonial Causes Act 1973, s 30.

[19] See *Aggett v Aggett* [1962] 1 All ER 190, CA.

[20] *Barker v Barker* [1952] P 184, 194-195, [1952] 1 All ER 1128, 1134, CA. The security must be on specific assets and not a general charge on all the party's property: *Barker v Barker*. It is doubtful whether reversionary interests should be charged because they cannot be used to secure present payments: *Allison v Allison* [1927] P 308; but see *Harrison v Harrison* (1887) 12 PD 130. The applicant could apply for a variation of the order when the interest fell in. Capital held on protective trusts should not be secured for the order will automatically terminate the interest: cf *Re Richardson's Will Trusts* [1958] Ch 504, [1958] 1 All ER 538. For a case where the court ordered payments to be secured on a party's sole asset (the former matrimonial home), see *Aggett v Aggett* (supra).

[1] *Foard v Foard* [1967] 2 All ER 660.

[2] Readers are advised that when the Child Support Act 1991 is fully in force the court's powers to make orders in favour of children will be very restricted. See ante, pp 717-719.

Courts Act 1978.[3] The order may be made before the decree is granted, when it is granted, or at any time afterwards;[4] alternatively, to avoid a party having to take fresh proceedings for financial provision for the children if the petition is unsuccessful, an order may be made on the dismissal of the petition or within a reasonable time thereafter.[5] Normally, the sums will be payable by one spouse (or former spouse) to the other, but either (or presumably both)[6] of them may be ordered to make payments to a third person, if the child is living with that person, or to the child himself.[7] As will be seen, orders payable to the child no longer have tax advantages. However, unlike orders in favour of spouses there is no power to dismiss an application for periodical payments to or in favour of the child.

3. ASSIGNMENT OF PERIODICAL PAYMENTS

Unsecured periodical payments have always been regarded as inalienable.[8] Two reasons are given for this rule: they are intended as personal provision for the payee and, as they can be varied at any time, no absolute transfer is possible. Consequently any purported assignment of future payments or charge upon them will be completely void and, for the same reason, the payee may not release them by agreement with the other party.[9] Whilst this restriction fetters the fund in the hands of the payee, it also protects her, for a judgment creditor has no power to seize it in satisfaction of his debts.[10]

Secured payments are regarded more in the nature of the payee's property and consequently it has been held that she can assign them and release the other party from further liability in respect of them.[11] One of the reasons formerly advanced for distinguishing secured from unsecured payments in this respect was that the court had no power to vary the former;[12] it is therefore arguable that the power, introduced in 1949, to vary orders for secured maintenance has had the incidental effect of making them inalienable.

---

[3] S 29. For the comparable provisions under the 1978 Act, see ante, p 674. 'Child of the family' is defined by the Matrimonial Causes Act 1973, s 52(1), as amended by the Children Act 1989, Sch 12, para 33, discussed ante, p 368.
[4] Ss 23(1)(d), (e) and 23(2)(a).
[5] S 23(2)(b).
[6] The court had power under previous legislation to make an order against both spouses: *Freckleton v Freckleton* [1966] CLY 3938.
[7] An application for an order may be made by a parent; of any child of the family guardian; any person in whose favour a residence order has been made with respect to the child or any other person who is entitled to apply for a residence order with respect to the child; a local authority, the Official Solicitor as guardian ad litem, or the child himself, if given leave: Family Proceedings Rules 1991, r 2.54.
[8] *Re Robinson* (1884) 27 Ch D 160, CA; *Watkins v Watkins* [1896] P 222, CA.
[9] *Campbell v Campbell* [1922] P 187. But an agreement to release payments will be taken into consideration in deciding what arrears are to be enforced against the other party.
[10] *J Walls Ltd v Legge* [1923] 2 KB 240, CA.
[11] *Harrison v Harrison* (1888) 13 PD 180, CA; *Maclurcan v Maclurcan* (1897) 77 LT 474, CA. The terms of the deed securing the payments may, however, expressly prohibit the payee from assigning them.
[12] *Watkins v Watkins* (supra); *Harrison v Harrison* (supra).

4. INCOME TAX[13]

The tax treatment of maintenance payments was both simplified and fundamentally changed by the Finance Act 1988. Formerly, a binding obligation[14] upon one spouse or former spouse to pay the other maintenance attracted tax relief at both basic and higher rates for the payer. Such payments correspondingly counted as the recipient's taxable income. Furthermore payments made direct to a child, pursuant to a court order to do so,[15] also attracted tax relief for the payer while the receipt of such monies ranked as the child's income for tax purposes. Under the new rules, however, only payments to a spouse or former spouse now attract limited tax relief,[16] while payments to children attract no tax relief at all.

The new provisions apply to maintenance orders and maintenance agreements made on or after 15 March 1988.[17] Payments are made gross (ie without deduction of tax) and are not taxable in the hands of the recipient.[18] Because of this change, it follows that it no longer matters in new orders whether they are expressed to be 'free of tax' though it might be preferable to avoid such references.[19] The payer will only qualify for tax relief (at basic and higher rates) for 'qualifying maintenance payments' to a divorced or separated spouse up to a limit equal to the difference between the married persons' relief and the single person's relief (which is the equivalent to the amount of the married couple's allowance ie £1,720 for 1992–1993) until the recipient re-marries.[20]

As we have said, the payer cannot claim tax relief for payments direct to children.[1] However, payments payable to a divorced or separated spouse expressed to be for the benefit of a child of the family do attract relief. Hence if no order would otherwise be made in the spouse's favour or, if any such order amounted to less than the difference between the single and married person's allowance, then there would be tax advantages in making an order for the benefit of the child. It should be added that although such an order ceases to attract tax relief upon the recipient's remarriage, the order itself apparently remains enforceable against the payer.[2]

---

[13] See generally Jackson's *Matrimonial Finance and Taxation* (5th Edn) ch 6 and Wylie *Taxation of Husband and Wife*.

[14] Whether under a binding maintenance agreement, a court order or (see *Gandolfo v Gandolfo* [1981] QB 359, [1980] 1 All ER 833, CA) pursuant to an undertaking formally given to the court.

[15] Even one made against the parent looking after the child, see *Sherdley v Sherdley* [1988] AC 213, [1987] 2 All ER 54, HL.

[16] Under the Finance Act 1992 binding maintenance payments under European Community court orders or agreements attract tax relief.

[17] Obligations arising before that (but including cases where an order was made before 1 July 1988 for which an application had been made before 15 March) continue to be governed by the old law.

[18] Income and Corporation Taxes Act 1988, s 347A(1)(b).

[19] Aliter if orders are governed by the old rules see p 659 of the seventh edition of this work.

[20] Income and Corporation Taxes Act 1988, s 347B.

[1] Income and Corporation Taxes Act 1988, s 347B.

[2] See Butterworths *Family Law Service* D[668].

5. LUMP SUM PAYMENTS[3]

On divorce, nullity or judicial separation the court may order either party to pay a lump sum or lump sums to the other.[4] It can also order a lump sum to be paid to a specified person for the benefit of any child of the family or to the child himself.[5] In practice, lump sum orders in favour of children, and in particular of children whose parents are of limited means, are rare.[6]

The power to order the payment of a lump sum was first given to the courts in 1963 and was initially little used. The reason is perhaps to be found in a dictum of Willmer LJ in the Court of Appeal in *Davis v Davis*,[7] where he said that it was likely to be used only in relatively rare cases where the party had sufficient assets to justify it.

The Law Commission's hope[8] that following the passing of the Matrimonial Proceedings and Property Act 1970 wider use might be made of lump sums in favour of spouses seems now to have been fulfilled, though initially the number of orders, at any rate, remained comparatively small.[9]

It is provided by the Matrimonial Causes Act 1973 that, without prejudice to the general power, a lump sum may be ordered to enable the payee to meet any liabilities or expenses already incurred in maintaining herself (or himself) or any child of the family or those incurred by or for the benefit of that child.[10] By this means the court can compensate a party (usually the wife) if the other spouse failed to provide proper maintenance before the proceedings were launched or if there was no order for adequate maintenance pending suit.

The more important use of the power, however, is to adjust the parties' capital assets. If, for example, the husband owns shares, the court may wish the benefit of a proportion of these to be given to the wife. As we shall see, it may do this directly by ordering them to be transferred to her in specie; it will be much more common, however, to order him to make a lump sum payment to her. It makes no financial difference to the wife and it will leave the husband free to sell some of his shares or to raise the

---

[3] See generally Jackson's *Matrimonial Finance and Taxation* (5th Edn) ch 5.
[4] Matrimonial Causes Act 1973, s 23(1)(c). The court may *in the same order* direct the payment of more than one lump sum. These may be payable at different dates (eg one payable immediately to enable the wife to put down the deposit on a house and another payable when the husband sells the former matrimonial home); one may be payable by instalments and the other not. But there is no power to make a second or subsequent order for a lump sum in favour of a spouse: *Coleman v Coleman* [1973] Fam 10, [1972] 3 All ER 886. Orders cannot be made in favour of a spouse before the granting of the decree nisi: *Board (Board Intervening) v Checkland* [1987] 2 FLR 257, CA; *Munks v Munks* [1985] FLR 576, CA.
[5] Ibid, s 23(1)(f) under which orders can be made before the granting of the decree: s 23(2).
[6] Per Booth J in *Kiely v Kiely* [1988] 1 FLR 248, 251, CA.
[7] [1967] P 185 at 192, [1967] 1 All ER 123 at 126, CA.
[8] Law Com No 25, para 9.
[9] Barrington, Baker et al *Matrimonial Jurisdiction of Registrars* paras 3.7–3.10. Initially Willmer LJ's dictum was applied under the new law; see *Millward v Millward* [1971] 3 All ER 526, CA. See further Miller *Maintenance and Property* 87 LQR 66; Cretney 121 New LJ 218. Cf Eekelaar and Maclean *Maintenance After Divorce* Tables 5.6 and 5.7 and pp 74–79 who found that in their sample nearly half of owner occupied homes were sold principally to give the wife a lump sum. If the home was not sold, husbands not uncommonly bought out the wife's share.
[10] Matrimonial Causes Act 1973, s 23(3)(a),(b).

money in some other way if he prefers to do so.[11] When the matrimonial home is the only capital asset and it is sold or the wife leaves and the husband remains,[12] the court will commonly make an order for the payment of a lump sum representing the value of that part of the assets of which the other party is to be given the benefit.[13]

The award of a lump sum is not confined to these two situations, however. It is, of course, still true that an order will not be made if the consequence would be to deprive the payer of his livelihood, for example, if a partner would have to realize his share of the partnership.[14] Nor is a lump sum order appropriate where the payer's wealth is locked up in assets which cannot readily be sold to raise capital, for example, in a shareholding in a private family company.[15] But given these restrictions a lump sum will be ordered whenever it is more valuable to the payee than periodical payments, and it is impossible to lay down any hard and fast rules.[16]

Normally a lump sum payment should not be regarded as the capitalisation of periodical payments but rather as a separate provision on its own.[17] In computing the sum regard is to be had to the paying spouse's means and the reasonable needs of the other spouse and child. In the case of lengthy marriages the view may commonly be taken that the recipient spouse has earned a share in the matrimonial property and that therefore the contingency of remarriage should normally be irrelevant.[18] In *Duxbury*

---

[11] But the tax implications should not be ignored. If the husband has to sell property to raise the money to satisfy a lump sum order, he will have to pay capital gains tax on the disposal of the property. The Law Commission are of the view that, if the court orders the transfer of property, it is 'reallocating the property so as to give effect to the existing equitable rights of the marital unit' and consequently no capital gains tax will be payable: Law Com No 25, para 76. Sed quaere? The wife is acquiring something to which she was formerly not entitled and consequently there appears to be a disposal for the purpose of the TCGA 1992. There will normally be no chargeable gain on the transfer of the matrimonial home by one spouse to another: ibid, ss 222–226, and the Inland Revenue Concession No D6 (reprinted in 117 Sol Jo 800). But a tax liability may sometimes arise. In *M v M (Sale of Property)* [1988] 1 FLR 389, CA the judge ordered the wife to transfer her interest in the home to the husband in return for a lump sum of £50,000 which, he assumed, would be free of capital gains tax. On an examination of the facts, the Court of Appeal doubted the availability of the 'principal residence' tax exemption. It ordered the property be sold, with a lump sum of £60,000 being paid to the wife from the net sale proceeds.

[12] See Lord Denning MR in *Wachtel v Wachtel* [1973] Fam 72 at 96, [1973] 1 All ER 829 at 840–841, CA. As has been seen, at n 9 above, it is common for the matrimonial home to be sold or for the husband to buy out the wife's share: Eekelaar and Maclean, op cit, pp 74–79.

[13] In making such orders the court must, however, be aware of the Law Society's charge, discussed post, p 746.

[14] *P v P* [1978] 3 All ER 70, CA; *B v B (Financial Provision)* [1989] 1 FLR 119 (aliter if the partnership is breaking up: cf *Davies v Davies* [1986] 1 FLR 497, CA). An order should not be made if there is no prospect that the party will be able to comply with it: *Martin v Martin* [1976] Fam 335, [1976] 3 All ER 625, CA.

[15] *P v P* [1989] 2 FLR 241. Even if there is a liquidity problem, however, a lump sum may be ordered if the payer does not produce evidence that he cannot raise the necessary capital by borrowing upon the security of his assets rather than by selling them: *Newton v Newton* [1990] 1 FLR 33, CA.

[16] Per Davies LJ in *Jones v Jones* [1971] 3 All ER 1201 at 1206, CA.

[17] *Trippas v Trippas* [1973] Fam 134, 139, [1973] 2 All ER 1, 4 per Lord Denning MR, CA.

[18] Cf periodical payments, which will automatically cease upon the recipient spouse's Remarriage. Occasionally a party's remarriage plans will be a relevant factor (provided there are very real prospects: see *H v H (Family Provision: Remarriage)* [1975] Fam 9, [1975] 1 All

v Duxbury,[19] for instance, the wife had been married to a wealthy man for twenty two years but was now cohabiting with a man of modest means. Conceding that during the marriage his wife had done all that was required of her as a wife, the husband nevertheless argued that a smaller lump sum than that required to meet her reasonable needs should be made (together with a secured periodical payments order) to take account of the cohabitation and the possibility of remarriage. His argument was rejected, it being held that in these circumstances the assessment of the lump sum should be based solely on the wife's reasonable needs. A rather different approach was taken in *Gojkovic v Gojkovic,*[20] another case involving a long relationship and substantial family assets. In 1966 the couple had arrived in England as penniless immigrants and, by their efforts, had built up an hotel and property business valued at over £4 million. The Court of Appeal held that *Duxbury* should not be taken as laying down a binding precedent on the assessment of lump sum payments for the former wife of every millionaire. Here, equally important to the wife's 'needs' was a recognition of her outstanding contribution to the wealth generated during the marriage. The court upheld an award to the wife of £1 million to enable her to acquire and run her own hotel.

Lump sums will be commonly ordered where one party has substantial means but such an order might also be the best solution if the husband has a little capital (for example, the proceeds of sale of the matrimonial home) but little or no income: the capital may be of real value to the wife, because it will give her some financial base, whilst the husband will be relieved of the obligation of finding continuing support for her out meagre earnings.[1] A lump sum payment with consequent reduction in periodical payments may also be ordered if the wife (or husband) has particular need of capital, for example to enable her to purchase a house, furniture[2] or the goodwill of a business[3] or to clear off a mortgage with which she is buying a new house so that she can make a fresh start.[4] A further use is to protect the payee against probable default on the other's part, for example if it appears that the party against whom financial provision is being sought is likely to remove his assets out of the jurisdiction,[5] or to enable the payee to take

---

ER 367). For example, if the party's financial resources are limited and a decision to give the wife capital (eg the matrimonial home) rather than periodical payments is regarded as the most satisfactory way of meeting her needs, it will be material to know if those needs will change as a result of remarriage.

[19] [1992] Fam 62n, [1990] 2 All ER 77 CA. Cf *H v H (Family Provision: Remarriage)*, supra.

[20] [1992] Fam 40, [1990] 2 All ER 84, CA.

[1] Their total income will also be increased if the wife can claim welfare benefits. Cf *Hunter v Hunter* [1973] 3 All ER 362, CA. See also *Chamberlain v Chamberlain* [1974] 1 All ER 33, CA, and *Hector v Hector* [1973] 3 All ER 1070, CA, in each of which the husband's interest in the proceeds of sale of the matrimonial home was reduced to compensate the wife for loss of other financial provision.

[2] *S v S* [1977] Fam 127, [1977] 1 All ER 56, CA.

[3] *Von Mehren v Von Mehren* [1970] 1 All ER 153, CA (husband ordered to pay £4,000 to his former wife to enable her to purchase a house which she intended to run as a boarding house). *Gojkovic v Gojkovic*, supra (lump sum order of £1 million to wife to buy hotel).

[4] *Harnett v Harnett* [1974] 1 All ER 764, CA. Cf *Calderbank v Calderbank* [1976] Fam 93, [1975] 3 All ER 333, CA (husband given lump sum to enable him to buy house in which to live and see children to whom he had been granted access).

[5] *Brett v Brett* [1969] 1 All ER 1007, CA.

bankruptcy proceedings against a contumacious party.[6] Further advantages of a lump sum are that, as the payment is final, there are no continuing problems of enforcement and the wife is left completely free of her former husband—a consideration that may be of particular importance if the parties' relationship is unusually bitter.[7]

Lump sum applications should ordinarily be disposed of once and for all, but there is jurisdiction to adjourn the application where there is a *real* possibility of capital from a specific source becoming available in the near future.[8]

The court can order the sum to be paid in instalments and may also require the payment of instalments to be secured[9] and to carry interest.[10] This differs from periodical payments because the total sum will be fixed and cannot be varied, and the balance will still be payable even if one of the parties dies before the whole sum has been paid.

6. TRANSFER AND SETTLEMENT OF PROPERTY

On granting a decree of divorce, nullity or judicial separation, the court may order either party to the marriage to transfer such property as may be specified to the other party or to or for the benefit of a child of the family. The court may also order either of them to settle any property for the benefit of the other party or any child of the family.[11] The court's power to transfer (but not to settle) property on a child over the age of 18 is limited to where the child is receiving instruction at an educational establishment or is undergoing training for a trade, profession or vocation or where there are other special circumstances (eg the child is suffering from some physical or mental disability).[12] These orders represent a final adjustment of rights in property when the marriage has broken down: the reason that the court is empowered to make them on judicial separation is that this may be the final severance of the matrimonial bond if the parties have a conscientious objection to divorce.[13]

---

[6] *Curtis v Curtis* [1969] 2 All ER 207, CA (husband, who had considerable means and was taking delaying tactics, ordered to pay wife £33,600, capitalising an annual sum of £2,400). Cf *Bryant v Bryant* (1976) 120 Sol Jo 165, CA. It will also be the only effective order that can be made if the husband has disappeared so that there is no hope of obtaining periodical payments from him: *Ally v Ally* (1971) Times, 24 August.

[7] Cf *Griffiths v Griffiths* [1974] 1 All ER 932 at 942, CA; Cretney 117 Sol Jo 347.

[8] *Davies v Davies* [1986] 1 FLR 497, CA, where the break up of the husband's business partnership seemed imminent and upon its dissolution the husband's capital would be unlocked. Cf *Burgess v Burgess* [1986] Fam Law 155 where the husband's prospects of obtaining substantial assets from the disposal of his business was not taken into account since there was no real prospect of a sale. In *Michael v Michael* [1986] 2 FLR 389, CA and *K v K* [1990] 2 FLR 225 the wife's inheritance expectancy was held to be too uncertain to justify an adjournment while in *MT v MT (Financial Provision: Lump Sum)* [1992] 1 FLR 362, the wife's application was adjourned until the death of her 83-year-old German father-in-law. Under German law, the husband would automatically inherit one eighth of his father's estate.

[9] Matrimonial Causes Act 1973, s 23(3)(c).

[10] Matrimonial Causes Act 1973, s 23(6) as added by the Administration of Justice Act 1982, s 16. See Salter *When Can Interest be Ordered in respect of a Lump Sum?* [1989] Fam Law 379.

[11] Matrimonial Causes Act 1973, s 24(1)(a), (b).

[12] S 29(1), (3).

[13] Law Com No 25, para 65.

The transfer power is currently of particular importance to enable the court to make appropriate orders with respect to the matrimonial home and similar assets, for example furniture or the family car,[14] but it may also be ordered as an alternative to the payment of a lump sum when it is more sensible to order one spouse to transfer investments than to compel him to sell them to raise the necessary capital or to supplement or replace periodical payments when the party in question has a limited interest (for example, a life interest under a family settlement) which can conveniently be used for this purpose.

Property that may be the subject of an order

The Act empowers the court to make an order with respect to any property to which the spouse in question is entitled either in possession or in reversion.[15] This form of words follows that of earlier Acts dealing with settlements of the wife's property, under which it was held that 'property' included income as well as capital[16] and 'reversionary interests' embraced those to which the wife was contingently entitled as well as those already vested in interest.[17] Apparently there is no power to order a transfer or settlement that the party could not make voluntarily, for example of a protected life interest (which is determinable on the occurrence of any event which will deprive the beneficiary of the right to receive any part of the income) or of a lease containing a covenant against assignment.[18] The latter limitation may be of particular importance when the court is dealing with rights in the matrimonial home. Similarly it seems that the party must be able to claim the property *as of right*; hence, if he is a beneficiary under a discretionary trust, the court apparently has no power to order the settlement of any income which the trustees *may* in their discretion pay him,[19] nor presumably could it order the settlement of any property which *might* come to him as the result of the exercise of a power of appointment vested in another.

No transfer or settlement will be ordered if the property is outside the jurisdiction and effective control of the court.[20] But the fact that the property is situated abroad will not prevent the order from being made provided that it can be effectively enforced; and so the court might order the settlement of income receivable in this country from capital invested elsewhere. But if such an order might prove to be difficult to enforce, the court will prefer to make an order with respect to property in England.[1]

[14] See post, pp 785–790.
[15] For a recent illustration of the breadth of the courts' powers in this regard see *Harwood v Harwood* [1991] 2 FLR 274, CA (husband ordered to transfer to wife his interest in assets of a dissolved partnership with a third party).
[16] See *Savary v Savary* (1898) 79 LT 607, 610, CA; *Style v Style* [1954] P 209, [1954] 1 All ER 442, CA.
[17] *Stedall v Stedall* (1902) 86 LT 124; *Savary v Savary* (supra).
[18] See *Hale v Hale* [1975] 2 All ER 1090, CA. The question was left open by Lord Penzance in *Milne v Milne* (1871) LR 2 P & D 295, but cf *Loraine v Loraine* [1912] P 222, CA.
[19] *Milne v Milne* (1871) LR 2 P & D 295. Nevertheless the existence of the interest can be taken into account; cf *Browne v Browne* [1989] 1 FLR 291, CA.
[20] *Tallack v Tallack* [1927] P 211 (property situated in Holland and Dutch court would disregard any order made by the English court).
[1] See *Style v Style* (supra).

Orders that can be made

The court can apparently order an absolute transfer of the whole of the party's interest in the property specified or any part of it. It has equally wide powers when ordering a settlement and may either divest the spouse of his whole interest[2] or grant a limited interest to the other spouse or children, leaving the beneficial owner with the reversion.[3] Although the facts which the court should take into account when deciding what order (if any) to make will be considered later,[4] it might be said here that the courts rarely make substantial capital orders in favour of children.[5]

7. VARIATION OF ANTE-NUPTIAL AND POST-NUPTIAL SETTLEMENTS

On granting a decree of divorce, nullity or judicial separation the court may make:

'an order varying for the benefit of the parties to the marriage and of the children of the family or either or any of them any ante-nuptial and post-nuptial settlement (including such a settlement made by will or codicil) made on the parties to the marriage; and

an order extinguishing or reducing the interest of either of the parties to the marriage under any such settlement;

and the court may make an order ... notwithstanding that there are no children of the family.'[6]

The court's powers are wider than they were before 1971 in two respects: they can be exercised on judicial separation, and the court can now extinguish or reduce a party's interest even though neither the other party nor the children are benefited as a result. These powers are complementary to those already discussed and will now be used less in view of the wider powers to order transfer and settlements of property. For example, a conveyance of a house to the husband and wife jointly clearly constitutes a post-nuptial settlement because it will be held on trust for sale.[7] If it was desired to extinguish the husband's interest on divorce before 1971, this could be done by varying the settlement; now he should be ordered to transfer his interest to his wife.[8] But there are still cases where the only power that can be exercised is that of varying a settlement, for example if one party has an interest that cannot be transferred (such as a protected life interest) or if it is desired to vary or destroy limitations in favour of children or other beneficiaries.

[2] As in *Compton v Compton* [1960] P 201, [1960] 2 All ER 70, where property was settled on children for life with remainder to grandchildren. Quaere whether the remainder to the grandchildren was not ultra vires as this does not benefit *children of the family*.
[3] *Style v Style* [1954] P 209, [1954] 1 All ER 422, CA (settlement on husband for life).
[4] See pp 755–790.
[5] See *Kiely v Kiely* [1988] 1 FLR 248, CA; *Chamberlain v Chamberlain* [1974] 1 All ER 33, CA; *Liford v Glynn* [1979] 1 All ER 441, CA and *Draskovic v Draskovic* (1980) 11 Fam Law 87.
[6] Matrimonial Causes Act 1973, s 24(1)(c), (d), (2).
[7] *Ulrich v Ulrich* [1968] 1 All ER 67, CA. Similarly if the legal estate was vested in the husband alone but the wife could claim an interest because she had contributed to the purchase (see ante, pp 585 et seq): *Cook v Cook* [1962] P 235, [1962] 2 All ER 811, CA.
[8] Per Ormrod LJ in *Guerrera v Guerrera* [1974] 1 WLR 1542, 1547, CA.

The parties cannot oust the court's jurisdiction by agreement, nor apparently is this jurisdiction in any way fettered by express provisions in the settlement as to how the property is to be held if the marriage is terminated.[9] In nullity proceedings a settlement may be varied even though the marriage is void,[10] but if it is not to take effect until the celebration of the marriage, it would appear not yet to be in existence and therefore to be incapable of variation.

The court has power to vary any settlement in existence at the time of the decree absolute.[11] Although a party who remarries cannot apply for an order against the other,[12] an application already made can be entertained and an order made notwithstanding the remarriage.[13] The court's jurisdiction is in no way fettered by the remarriage of the *other* party or by the death of either of them[14] although in the latter case no order will be made if its sole effect would be to benefit someone other than the surviving party or a child of the marriage.[15]

Transactions to which the Act applies

The terms 'ante-nuptial and post-nuptial settlements' are used in a sense much wider than that usually given to them by conveyancers, the essential condition being that the benefit must be conferred on either or both of the spouses *in the character of spouse or spouses*.[16] It is immaterial whether it comes from one of the spouses or from a third person, provided that this condition is satisfied.[17] It is possible that a transaction may be a settlement for this purpose if it confers a benefit upon the children of the marriage, even though it confers none upon either spouse, provided that the beneficiaries take *in the character of children of the family*.[18] Conversely, a transaction which would otherwise be a settlement will not cease to be one

---

[9] Cf *Prinsep v Prinsep* [1930] P 35, 49, CA; *Woodcock v Woodcock* (1914) 111 LT 924, CA; Denning LJ in *Egerton v Egerton* [1949] 2 All ER 238, 242, CA. The decision to the contrary in the early case of *Stone v Stone* (1864) 3 Sw & Tr 608, cannot now be regarded as good law.

[10] Cf *Radziej v Radziej* [1967] 1 All ER 944; affirmed [1968] 3 All ER 624, CA.

[11] *Dormer v Ward* [1901] P 20, CA.

[12] Matrimonial Causes Act 1973, s 28(3). See ante, p 725.

[13] *Jackson v Jackson* [1973] Fam 99, [1973] 2 All ER 395. See also *H v H* [1975] Fam 9, [1975] 1 All ER 367.

[14] *Churchward v Churchward* [1910] P 195 (remarriage); *Jacobs v Jacobs* [1943] P 7, [1942] 2 All ER 471, CA (death). The latter case was not cited in *D(J) v D(S)* [1973] Fam 55, [1973] 1 All ER 349, where it was said that both parties must still be alive unless the application is made on behalf of the children. It is submitted that this is wrong.

[15] *Thomson v Thomson* [1896] P 263, CA; followed in *D(J) v D(S)* (supra) (where variation could benefit only the deceased party's estate). In the latter case Ormrod J did not consider whether the express power to extinguish a party's interest first conferred in 1970 now gives the court jurisdiction to make an order in such circumstances. It is submitted that it could do so.

[16] Per Hill J in *Prinsep v Prinsep* [1929] P 225 at 232. See also *Bosworthick v Bosworthick* [1927] P 64, 69, CA; *Worsley v Worsley* (1869) LR 1 P & D 648, 651.

[17] *Prinsep v Prinsep* (supra).

[18] Apparently so held in *Compton v Compton* [1960] P 201, [1960] 2 All ER 70 (where, however, wife was trustee and had a power of appointment in favour of children). Cf Greer LJ in *Melvill v Melvill* [1930] P 159, at 176, 177. But it is difficult to see how this could be a 'settlement *made on the parties to the marriage*'.

merely because it makes provision for any future spouse of either of the parties or the children of such a marriage.[19]

Provided that the condition stated above is fulfilled, it is immaterial that one or both of the spouses are merely the objects of a discretionary trust and can therefore claim nothing as of right.[20] A separation agreement comes within the section even if it is not in writing.[1] Similarly a bond by which a wife undertakes to pay an annuity to her husband[2] and a policy of life assurance taken out by a husband for the benefit of his wife[3] have been held to be post-nuptial settlements. But there cannot be a settlement for this purpose if there has been an absolute and unqualified transfer of property unless payments of some sort still have to be made at the time that the court has to enquire into the existence of the settlement.[4]

The meaning of 'ante-nuptial' and 'post-nuptial'

The court may vary a settlement only if it was made on the footing that the marriage *which is the subject of the decree* should continue.[5] Thus, if a husband marries successively W1 and W2, a settlement made by him on the eve of his marriage to W1 cannot be varied in divorce proceedings brought by W2.[6] But if a particular transaction appears on the face of it to satisfy this condition, then in accordance with the usual rules of construction other evidence may not be adduced to show that this was not the parties' intention.[7] Conversely, if an agreement was ostensibly entered into on the footing that the marriage would be dissolved, it cannot be a post-nuptial settlement.[8]

---

[19] As in *Prinsep v Prinsep* (supra).

[20] *E v E (Financial Provision)* [1990] 2 FLR 233 (post-nuptial settlement constituted where, during the subsistence of a marriage, property purchased by husband's father was settled on discretionary trust whose beneficiaries were the husband, the wife, the husband's children and remoter issue by any subsequent wife). See also *Janion v Janion* [1929] P 237n. A protected life interest can also be varied without producing a forfeiture: *General Accident, Fire and Life Assurance Corpn Ltd v IRC* [1963] 3 All ER 259, CA. In *Howard v Howard* [1945] P 1, [1945] 1 All ER 91, CA, MacKinnon LJ left open the question whether a discretionary trust can be a post-nuptial settlement merely because one of the spouses comes within the class of possible beneficiaries. The court may vary such a settlement even though it is in a foreign form because the parties were domiciled elsewhere at the time of the marriage: *Forsyth v Forsyth* [1891] P 363.

[1] *Tomkins v Tomkins* [1948] P 170, [1948] 1 All ER 237, CA. *Jeffrey v Jeffrey (No 2)* [1952] P 122, [1952] 1 All ER 790, CA. If it were in writing it could also be varied under s 35 of the Matrimonial Causes Act (ante, p 658).

[2] *Bosworthick v Bosworthick* [1927] P 64, CA. Cf *Parrington v Parrington* [1951] 2 All ER 916.

[3] *Gunner v Gunner* [1949] P 77, [1948] 2 All ER 771, followed in *Bown v Bown* [1949] P 91, [1948] 2 All ER 778.

[4] *Prescott v Fellowes* [1958] P 260, [1958] 3 All ER 55, CA.

[5] *Young v Young* [1962] P 27, [1961] 3 All ER 695, CA.

[6] *Burnett v Burnett* [1936] P 1. See also *Hargreaves v Hargreaves* [1926] P 42.

[7] *Melvill v Melvill* [1930] P 159, CA.

[8] *Young v Young* (supra). Surrounding circumstances may be taken into consideration if they do not contradict the written agreement, although the settlor's motive is *per se* immaterial: *Joss v Joss* [1943] P 18, [1943] 1 All ER 102; *Parrington v Parrington* [1951] 2 All ER 916, 919; *Prinsep v Prinsep* [1929] P 225, 236.

Powers of the court

The court may exercise its powers so as to benefit the spouses or the children of the family or to reduce or extinguish the interest of either spouse. This raises the question whether the court may make a variation which may adversely affect a child or any other beneficiary.

A child is most likely to have his interest potentially cut down by the insertion of a power of appointment in favour of a future spouse or the children of a subsequent marriage. Whilst the court is bound to look after the interests of existing children of the family, it must also be borne in mind that to refuse a request to insert such a power of appointment may well cause the applicant and any future spouse and children to feel that they have been unjustly treated and thus cause friction and ill-feeling in the family.[9]

Before 1971 it was clearly established that whatever intangible advantage the children of the first marriage may get out of permitting their parent to exercise a power to appoint among children of a second marriage, nothing must be done which on the whole would be for the disadvantage of the former; consequently the settlement will not be varied to enable a benefit to be conferred upon a stranger to it unless at the same time some approximately equivalent financial benefit is also conferred upon the child or children of the first marriage as a quid pro quo.[10] Whilst the extinction of one spouse's life interest in remainder gives some advantage to the child insofar as it may accelerate the vesting of his own remainder, this is so slight that it cannot now be regarded as sufficient in itself.[11] But the following, either singly or in combination, have been held to be enough to support such a variation: giving the child an additional vested annuity,[12] giving the child a vested interest instead of a contingent interest under the settlement,[13] increasing the child's share by reducing the portion which the parent is permitted to settle on the children of a subsequent marriage,[14] and by making a consent order under which a spouse settles another fund on the children[15] or a third person covenanting to make payments towards the child's maintenance or education.[16]

Third parties' rights are most likely to be affected if there is an ultimate gift to them in the absence of any children of the marriage. The court can apparently strike out this remainder and destroy their interest provided that

[9] *Garforth-Bles v Garforth-Bles* [1951] P 218, 222, [1951] 1 All ER 308, 310; *Best v Best* [1956] P 76, [1955] 2 All ER 839, 843.
[10] See *Purnell v Purnell* [1961] P 141, [1961] 1 All ER 369. In this case, as in *Best v Best* [1956] P 76, [1955] 2 All ER 839, the situation was unusual because the wife wished to have the settlement varied so as to be able to exercise the power in favour of a child whom she and her first husband had adopted.
[11] *Best v Best* (supra); *Tagart v Tagart* (1934) 50 TLR 399.
[12] *Newson v Newson* (1934) 50 TLR 399; *Wadham v Wadham* [1938] 1 All ER 206; *Maxwell v Maxwell* [1951] P 212, [1950] 2 All ER 979.
[13] *Scollick v Scollick* [1927] P 205; *Garforth-Bles v Garforth-Bles* (supra); *Purnell v Purnell* (supra).
[14] *Wadham v Wadham* (supra); *Hodgson Roberts v Hodgson Roberts* [1906] P 142; *Colclough v Colclough* [1933] P 143. In *Newson v Newson* (supra), as a quid pro quo the mother's power to limit the sum which the child should take under his grandmother's settlement was extinguished.
[15] *Purnell v Purnell* (supra).
[16] *Newson v Newson* (supra) (covenant by the wife's mother); *Scollick v Scollick* (supra) (covenant by the wife's second husband).

all the persons now alive who have an interest in the fund consent, even though this may have the effect of extinguishing contingent interests of persons as yet unborn.[17] This has even been done where the remainder was in favour of the children of any subsequent marriage of the applicant on the ground that he could be expected to make provision for them himself in any case.[18] But the court will not accede to the proposal if this would extinguish the interest of a living person who does not consent to the order.[19]

It seems that, as part of an variation order, the court may replace a trustee, at least where the trustee removed is a trust company, or distinct from an individual, and there is no suggestion that the trustee has exercised its powers wrongly.[20]

Retrospective variations

The court apparently has no power to order a retrospective variation. But if a spouse is prejudiced by the delay, the court can compensate for this by giving him or her a temporary or permanent increased benefit.[1]

8. ORDERS FOR THE SALE OF PROPERTY

As originally enacted, the Matrimonial Causes Act 1973 conferred no *express* power to order a sale of spouses' property. One way round this was to issue a summons under the Married Women's Property Act 1882, section 17,[2] but in *Ward v Ward and Greene*[3] even this was thought to be unnecessary since it was suggested that there was an *implicit* power to order a sale under the 1973 Act. However, following the Law Commission's recommendation,[4] it is now expressly provided by section 24A of the 1973 Act[5] that where the court makes a secured periodical payments order, a lump sum order or a property adjustment order then it may make:

> '... a further order for the sale of such property as may be specified in the order, being property in which or in the proceeds of sale of which either or both of the parties to the marriage has or have a beneficial interest, either in possession or reversion.'

It should be noted that the power to order a sale is a consequential or ancillary power and not an independent one. In other words it can only be made where an order relating to the parties' capital has already been made

---

[17] *Morrissey v Morrissey* [1905] P 90; *Bowles v Bowles* [1937] P 127, [1937] 2 All ER 263.
[18] *Meredyth v Meredyth* [1895] P 92.
[19] *Webb v Webb* [1929] P 159, distinguishing *Wynne v Wynne* (1898) 78 LT 796, where the wife could have defeated the remaindermen in any case by exercising a power of appointment by will.
[20] *E v E (Financial Provision)* [1990] 2 FLR 233, where *Compton v Compton and Hussey* [1960] P 201, [1960] 2 All ER 70, was not followed. This recent case amply illustrates the court's extensive powers of variation. If, however, all that is sought is the removal of a trustee or trustees, it is submitted that proceedings should be brought in (or transferred to) the Chancery Division.
[1] See *Constantinidi v Constantinidi* [1905] P 253, 276, CA.
[2] According to Dunn J in *G v G (Practice: Transfer of Application)* [1973] 2 All ER 1187.
[3] [1980] 1 All ER 176n, CA.
[4] Law Com No 99 (Orders for Sale of Property under the Matrimonial Causes Act 1973).
[5] Added by the Matrimonial Homes and Property Act 1981, s 7.

under sections 23 and 24; it does not confer a jurisdiction to order a sale 'in the air'. That section 24A does not extend the court's powers has been emphasised in *Burton v Burton*.[6] In that case it was held that the section conferred no jurisdiction to order one party to pay out of the proceeds of sale of the matrimonial home debts of either party that were unconnected with the interest in the property.

In *Crosthwaite v Crosthwaite*,[7] the Court of Appeal held that there is no power, under section 24A, to make an order for vacant possession against a wife who was joint owner of the matrimonial home pending the completion of its sale. The appropriate course was to make an order, under section 24, requiring the wife to transfer her interest to her husband and *then* make a vacant possession order against her. The effect of this decision, which could enable a co-owning spouse in residence to frustrate an order for sale under section 24A, has been reversed by the Family Proceedings Rules 1991.[8]

Although the power to order a sale is an ancillary power it nevertheless is different in kind from a property transfer order. This is illustrated by *R v Rushmoor Borough Council, ex p Barrett*[9] which concerned a former council house that had been purchased by the parties at a discount from the local authority. It is statutorily provided that that discount has to be repaid if the house is sold within five years of its purchase, except where the court makes a transfer order under section 24 of the 1973 Act.[10] In this case the house was, under a consent order, ordered to be sold and the proceeds divided equally between the spouses. It was held that the exemption did not apply to the sale since it was not a 'disposal in pursuance of an order under section 24' and that therefore the discount was repayable.

In the case of property belonging to one spouse and a third party, the court is directed that before it decides whether to order a sale, the third party must be given the opportunity to make representations and any such representations are then to be included in the circumstances to which the court must have regard under section 25 of the 1973 Act.[11]

9. CONSENT ORDERS

There is nothing to prevent the parties themselves from agreeing to the financial provision and property adjustment to be made: indeed the whole trend during recent years has been to encourage them to do so.[12] From the point of view of costs alone it makes obvious sense for the parties to agree with each other wherever possible. In cases where the parties have come to

[6] [1986] 2 FLR 419. See also *Thompson v Thompson* [1986] Fam 38, [1985] 2 All ER 243, CA in which, approving *Norman v Norman* [1983] 1 All ER 486 on this point, it was held that s 24A was an ancillary and not a varying power.

[7] [1989] 2 FLR 86, CA.

[8] R 2.64(3), incorporating RSC Ord 31, r 1, whereby (inter alia) as ancillary to an order for sale, the court may order an owner of land to give up possession of it, or any part thereof.

[9] [1987] QB 275, [1987] 1 All ER 353. There is also a difference with regard to liability of legally assisted parties to pay the Law Society's charge, see the discussion post at p 746.

[10] Housing Act 1985, ss 118 and 160(1)(c).

[11] Matrimonial Causes Act 1973, s 24A(6), added by the Matrimonial and Family Proceedings Act 1984, Sch 1, para 11.

[12] As Lord Scarman said in *Minton v Minton* [1979] AC 593 at 608, [1979] 1 All ER 79 at 87, HL: 'The law now encourages spouses to avoid bitterness after family break-down and to settle their property and money problems'.

terms, it is commonly sought to have the agreement incorporated into a court order.

To facilitate quicker and therefore cheaper arrangements, the court can make an order in the terms agreed on the basis only of prescribed information furnished with the application.[13] This procedure eliminates the need for the parties to attend the hearing.[14] Despite this procedure, however, it is important not to lose sight of the fact that the court retains the power and indeed the duty to scrutinise the proposed arrangements. In particular it must still have regard to the considerations set out in section 25 of the 1973 Act.[15] In the absence of any change of circumstances or of any allegation of mistake or undue influence, however, the fact that the parties have arrived at a settlement will itself be prima facie evidence that it is reasonable, at least, if they were at arm's length and were both legally advised. Consequently the court will normally approve such an agreement, provided that it is not contrary to public policy, and will incorporate it in an order.[16]

It should also be appreciated that once the agreement has been embodied in a court order it derives its authority from the order and not the agreement. It has been held by the House of Lords in *Livesey (Formerly Jenkins) v Jenkins*[17] that because the court cannot properly discharge its function under section 25 without complete and up-to-date information, the parties owe a duty to the court to make full and frank disclosure of material facts to each other not simply up to the time of the agreement but right up until the time of the court order. Failure to make such disclosure can lead to the order being set aside. In *Livesey v Jenkins* the wife agreed to relinquish all claims for maintenance in return for the husband's agreeing to transfer to her his half share in the matrimonial home. After the agreement had been reached but before it had been embodied in a court order the wife became engaged to be married but this was not disclosed to the husband or the court. It was held that this failure to disclose was so important[18] that the order should be set aside. Lord Brandon, however, emphasised[19] that not every failure of disclosure would justify setting a consent order aside. On the contrary, to justify setting an order aside the absence of disclosure must have led the court to make a substantially different order from that which it would have made had there been full disclosure.[20] This test has been strictly applied, no doubt to prevent a flood of applications

---

[13] Matrimonial Causes Act 1973, s 33A, added by the Matrimonial and Family Proceedings Act 1984, s 7. For the prescribed information see the Family Proceedings Rules 1991, r 2.61.

[14] Though it remains a requirement that the respondent signifies in writing his agreement to the proposed order.

[15] Discussed, post, pp 755 et seq.

[16] *Dean v Dean* [1978] Fam 161, [1978] 3 All ER 758, following *Brockwell v Brockwell* (1975) 6 Fam Law 46, CA. See Miller 10 Fam Law 196, 232.

[17] [1985] AC 424, [1985] 1 All ER 106, HL, approving *de Lasala v de Lasala* [1980] AC 546, [1979] 2 All ER 1146, PC, and disapproving on this point *Wales v Wadham* [1977] 2 All ER 125.

[18] It will be appreciated that once the wife had remarried she would no longer be entitled to receive periodical payments, so that she was not relinquishing very much.

[19] Ibid at 445 and 119 respectively.

[20] A similar rule applies to contested orders and to justify appealing out of time see post, p 795. On the procedure of setting aside a consent order for non-disclosure see *B-T v B-T (Divorce: Procedure)* [1990] 2 FLR 1, and Scott and White *Setting Aside for Non-Disclosure: Practice and Procedure* [1990] Fam Law 326.

to set aside on the basis of material non-disclosure. In *Cook v Cook*,[1] for example, the court refused to set aside a consent order where, it was alleged, the wife had failed to disclose the depth of her relationship with a third party. It was held that any change in the quality of the wife's relationship would not have substantially affected the terms of the original order.

A further problem arises if one of the parties wishes to go back on an agreement before the court approves it and embodies it in an order. We have already seen that the agreement cannot preclude an application to the court,[2] but as the Court of Appeal held in *Edgar v Edgar*,[3] considerable attention will be paid to it if it was entered into with full knowledge of all the relevant facts and on legal advice. Obviously a party will not be bound if the agreement was made under duress or undue influence, but the fact that one of the parties was in a superior bargaining position will not justify the other in going back on it unless the former took an unfair advantage by exploiting the position. In *Edgar v Edgar* a multi-millionaire and his wife entered into a separation deed in which the husband made capital provision for her amounting to some £100,000 and undertook to make periodical payments to her of £16,000 a year together with periodical payments for the children. In return she covenanted not to seek financial relief in any divorce proceedings that might take place in the future. She executed the deed after being warned by her legal advisers that she would probably obtain a much better order from the court. When divorce proceedings were launched, she attempted to resile from the agreement and claimed a lump sum payment. Dismissing her application, the Court of Appeal held that, although the husband's financial position put him in a much stronger bargaining position, there was no evidence that he had exploited it, and consequently the wife must be held to her agreement. The court might be justified in ignoring an agreement if the wife found it impossible to maintain herself owing to unforeseen circumstances[4] or, possibly, if injustice would be done for some other reason, but the facts of *Edgar v Edgar* make it clear that a large disparity between the sum that a wife stipulated for and that which the court might have awarded her will not itself be a ground for releasing her from the contract she made.

The fact that the agreement derives its authority from the court order has two other important consequences. First, the court is no more entitled to make orders outside the terms of the 1973 Act than it is in respect of contested orders.[5] Secondly, the rules against reopening 'clean break' orders[6] and varying property adjustment orders[7] apply equally to consent orders as they do to a contested order.[8] The courts have on more than one occasion

---

[1] [1988] 1 FLR 521, CA.
[2] Ante, p 657.
[3] [1980] 3 All ER 887, CA.
[4] *Wright v Wright* [1970] 3 All ER 209, 214, CA.
[5] See Lord Brandon in *Livesey v Jenkins* [1985] AC 424, 444, [1985] 1 All ER 1060, at 118–119.
[6] Discussed post, p 795. The most common form of consent orders provides for a clean break.
[7] See post, pp 790 et seq.
[8] See *Minton v Minton* [1979] AC 593, [1979] 1 All ER 79, HL. For a good example of the harsh realities of the binding nature of a consent order see *Dinch v Dinch* [1987] 1 All ER 818, HL, in which it was held that there was no power to interfere with an agreement to a delayed sale of the matrimonial home even though the husband by accepting voluntary redundancy had been unable to meet his maintenance commitments under the agreement.

warned of the need for legal representatives to be especially careful in drafting the terms of proposed consent orders and to advise their clients on precisely what impact their agreement will have.[9] The failure by a solicitor to protect his client's interests in respect of a consent order may constitute professional negligence for which substantial damages are awarded.[10]

It will not infrequently be the case that the parties will have reached an agreement which is perfectly proper in itself but which is outside the terms of the Matrimonial Causes Act 1973, for example, as in *Livesey v Jenkins*, where after the transfer of the husband's share in the matrimonial home, the wife agreed to be solely responsible for the mortgage and all other outgoings on the house and to be solely responsible for certain specific bank overdrafts. As we have said, the court has no power to incorporate such agreements in a consent order. However, it is possible to make such agreements binding by, for example, including them in an undertaking to the court (which could be enforced by committal in the event of non-compliance)[11] or the court could dismiss the application conditionally upon the parties' entering into the agreement in question.[12]

10. THE LEGAL AID BOARD'S STATUTORY CHARGE

In cases where either or both parties have been granted legal aid, an important factor to be borne in mind in deciding what orders should be made or agreed to, is the Legal Aid Board's charge. Under the Legal Aid Act 1988, section 16(6), in return for the responsibility for all the legally aided party's appropriately taxed legal costs, the Legal Aid Board has a charge, to the extent of those costs, over property 'recovered or preserved'. Periodical payments are expressly exempted from this charge, as is the first £2,500 of any lump sum or property adjustment order.[13] In effect therefore

[9] See eg *Dinch v Dinch*, supra at 820 per Lord Oliver and *Sandford v Sandford* [1986] 1 FLR 412 at 425 per Oliver LJ (as he then was). See also Cleary *Icebergs and Elephant Traps* [1987] Fam Law 43 and, by the same author, *Icebergs and Elephant Traps Revisited* [1990] Fam Law 102.

[10] *Dickinson v Jones Alexander & Co* [1990] Fam Law 137 (£330,238 damages awarded to a wife for being deprived, through her solicitor's negligence, of proper and reasonable financial provision). On the approach to be adopted in assessing whether a solicitor has shown a proper standard of professional competence, see *Dutfield v Gilbert H Stephens & Sons* [1988] Fam Law 473.

[11] Per Lord Brandon in *Jenkins v Livesey*, ibid at 444 and 119 respectively. But an undertaking given neither by deed nor for valuable consideration (and therefore not a contract) creates an obligation only towards the court. Consequently it can be enforced, eg, by committal but not by an action for arrears by the payee: *Re Hudson* [1966] Ch 209, [1966] 1 All ER 110. This may leave the payee completely unprotected on the other party's death, as in *Re Hudson*.

[12] This is known as a 'Tomlin order': see *Butterworths Family Law Service* D [741]. In cases where the parties reach a settlement early in the proceedings the court cannot normally give effect to it before the decree nisi, see *Board (Board Intervening) v Checkland* [1987] 2 FLR, 257, CA but it can order it to be made into a Rule of Court, see further *Butterworths Family Law Service* D [741]. Whether the court would be prepared to accept an undertaking in respect of a provision which it *is* empowered to order has yet to be determined. If it would, then subject to the consent of the party giving the undertaking, it may be that a court could subsequently vary eg a property transfer order, which under the Matrimonial Causes Act 1973 is not variable: see the comment at [1985] Fam Law 227.

[13] Civil Legal Aid (General) Regulations 1989, reg 94(c), (d)(i).

the Legal Aid Board is entitled to recover its costs out of lump sums, property adjustment orders or proceeds of sale insofar as in the first two instances they exceed £2,500 and in any event can be regarded as property 'recovered or preserved'. Given the high costs of proceedings, this charge can be substantial.

In *Hanlon v Hanlon*,[14] for example, where the matrimonial home with an equity worth £10,000 was transferred to the wife, the wife's legal aid costs amounted to £8,025. The courts have, on more than one occasion, warned advisers to explain to their clients the folly of protracted argument and litigation.[15]

In cases where the matrimonial home is transferred to the legally aided party the charge arises and vests in the Legal Aid Board and may be enforced as a charging order.[16] Before 1 December 1988, and the entry into force of the regulations referred to below, the statutory charge vested in the Law Society which, in the exercise of its discretionary power,[17] would postpone the enforcement of the charge on the dwelling house of the legally assisted person. The Law Society would also permit the transfer of the charge to substituted property in cases where a person wished to sell the dwelling house to which the charge attached, and to use the proceeds of sale to buy another dwelling house. The Law Society, however, had *no* discretion to postpone the charge in cases where the property recovered or preserved was *money*, either in the form of a lump sum or from the proceeds of sale.[18] This was so even if the sum ordered represented the spouse's share of the matrimonial home and was intended for the purchase of a dwelling house for that party.

The Civil Legal Aid (General) Regulations 1989, Part XI,[19] now codify and extend the previous discretion in relation to the postponement of the enforcement of the statutory charge on property and on the transfer of the charge to substituted property. The regulations provide that enforcement may be deferred on condition that, from the date of registration of the charge, simple interest at 10.5 per cent per annum will accrue for the benefit of the Legal Aid Board,[20] where:

(1) in the case of *money* recovered or preserved the order or agreement made provides for its use by the assisted person for the purpose of

---

[14] [1978] 2 All ER 889, CA. See also *Stewart v Law Society* [1987] 1 FLR 223, where costs amounted to £4,600 in a case where a wife was awarded £7,000 in full and final settlement of her rights to receive and claim periodical payments. As was pointed out in a commentary on that case (at [1987] Fam Law 53), the wife lost £1,820 annually (the value of the original periodical payments order) for a single payment of £2,400.
[15] Eg in *Anthony v Anthony* [1986] 2 FLR 353 at 355, CA, per Parker LJ, and *Mason v Mason* [1986] 2 FLR 212 at 223–224, per Purchas LJ. For a statement of the duty of practitioners to advise their clients on the impact of costs and the incidence of the Legal Aid Board's charge, see *Evans v Evans* [1990] 1 FLR 319, sub nom *Practice Note* [1990] 1 WLR 575n.
[16] Civil Legal Aid (General) Regulations 1989, reg 95.
[17] *Hanlon v Law Society* [1981] AC 124, [1980] 2 All ER 199, HL.
[18] *Simpson v Law Society* [1987] AC 861, [1987] 2 All ER 481, HL; *Simmons v Simmons* [1984] Fam 17, [1984] 1 All ER 83, CA; *R v Law Society, ex p Sexton* [1984] QB 360, [1984] 1 All ER 92; *Curling v Law Society* [1985] 1 All ER 705.
[19] First introduced as the Legal Aid (General) (Amendment) (No 2) Regulations 1988.
[20] Civil Legal Aid (General) Regulations 1989, reg 96(3)(b) and 97(4). The rate of interest payable on postponement of the charge was reduced, with effect from 1 January 1992, from 12 per cent per annum to 10.5 per cent by the Civil Legal Aid (General)(Amendment) (No 3) Regulations 1991, reg 4.

purchasing a home for himself or his dependants;[1] or

(2) in the case of *property* recovered or preserved the order or agreement provides that it is to be used as a home for the assisted person or his dependants.[2]

If money recovered or preserved has not been used within one year of the date of the order or agreement, the assisted person's solicitor must pay it to the Legal Aid Board.[3] The substitution of another property, in place of that originally charged, is permissible, provided the assisted person agrees to comply with certain conditions, including the execution of a registered charge, in respect of the substituted property, in favour of the Legal Aid Board, and the payment of interest.[4] In *Scallon v Scallon*[5] it was held that a court may assume that the Legal Aid Board will exercise its statutory discretion, to defer enforcement of the charge, so as not to frustrate the purpose of a court order.

The ambit of the Legal Aid Board's statutory charge is both wide and at times bizarre. It has been held to apply, for example, to a lump sum payment in commutation and in full and final settlement of a spouse's rights to claim and receive periodical payments[6] and to the obtaining of possession of an amount representing the share of the matrimonial home, even though title had not been in issue and the final order was a consent order.[7] While in another case,[8] where both parties were legally aided and an order was made dividing the proceeds of the matrimonial home equally, the charge only attached to the husband's share because he had successfully resisted his wife's claim for a larger share, whereas it did not attach to the wife's share since the husband had made no claim to it.

Although it is clear that the existence of the charge can materially alter the effect or even destroy the intention of the orders, it seems established that the court is not allowed to compensate for this, even where the higher costs are attributable to one side's intransigence, by making a larger award than would be the case had the parties' needs been considered without reference to the charge.[9] On the other hand, it would seem proper to make a different *type* of order if that would be a more efficient use of the parties'

---

[1] Ibid, reg 96—thereby reversing the effect of the decisions referred to in n18 above.

[2] Ibid, reg 97.

[3] Ibid, reg 96(6).

[4] Ibid, reg 98.

[5] [1990] 1 FLR 194, CA. It will be appreciated that the new regulations require that the agreement or court order must *expressly provide* that the money or property be used for a *specific purpose*, namely, the purchase or use of a home for the assisted person or his dependants. A court order in these terms was approved, without judicial comment, by the Court of Appeal in *Scallon v Scallon*, although there appears to be no express authority for making such an order in Part II of the Matrimonial Causes Act 1973.

[6] *Stewart v Law Society* [1987] 1 FLR 223, *Watkinson v Legal Aid Board* [1991] 2 All ER 953, CA.

[7] *Curling v Law Society* [1985] 1 All ER 705, CA.

[8] *Parry v Parry* [1986] 2 FLR 96, CA.

[9] *Parry v Parry* supra and *Collins v Collins* [1987] 1 FLR 226, CA. Sed quaere whether the potential liability could be regarded as a potential liability within the meaning of s 25(2)(b) of the Matrimonial Causes Act 1973 (discussed post, p 774); see the comment at [1987] Fam Law 53. The decision in *Collins v Collins* appears to have been overlooked by Anthony Lincoln J in *B v B (Real Property: Assessment of Interest)* [1988] 2 FLR 490, where he expressly enlarged the award of a lump sum to a wife 'to allow for the legal aid charge'.

resources as, for example, a property transfer order rather than a lump sum order.[10]

11. THE LIMITS OF THE COURT'S POWER

Although the powers to redistribute spouses' property upon divorce etc, are extremely wide, they are not unlimited. One obvious limitation is that the court has no power over property that does not belong to either of the spouses.[11] It cannot, for example, order the sale of the matrimonial home which is owned by someone else as, for example, where the parties live in tied accommodation.[12] Similarly, there is no power to order the transfer of a spouse's interest under a discretionary trust,[13] though the existence of the interest can be taken into account in determining that spouse's needs.[14]

The court also has no power to make an order against a third party which seems to include a limited company in which one or both the spouses hold shares.[15] One important consequence of this is that no order should be made which will effectively have to be paid out of a spouse's new partner's capital or income, though again that partner's assets are relevant to the extent that they relieve the spouse's needs.[16]

A further limitation of the court's powers is that the relief granted must come within the terms of sections 23, 24 and 24A of the Matrimonial Causes Act 1973. In *Milne v Milne*,[17] for instance, it was held that there was no power to order a husband to take out an insurance policy to make capital provision for his wife because section 23(1) only empowered payments to be made to a spouse or child of the family and not to a third party. It has been similarly held that there is no power to order one party to pay out of the proceeds of sale of the matrimonial home the debts of

---

[10] Or a periodical payments order instead of a lump sum order—see eg *Anthony v Anthony* [1986] 2 FLR 353, CA. Lawyers must not try and manipulate the destination of money payable to an assisted person so as to avoid the statutory charge: *Manley v Law Society* [1981] 1 All ER 401, *Clarke v Clarke* [1989] 1 FLR 174. A solicitor owes a duty of care to the legal aid fund, and the court has an inherent jurisdiction to order a solicitor personally to pay costs to the legal aid fund where it has suffered loss as a result of the solicitor's serious dereliction of duty: *Clark v Clark (No 2)* [1991] 1 FLR 179, CA.

[11] *Crittenden v Crittenden* [1990] 2 FLR 361, CA.

[12] Exceptionally, where one or both of the spouses own property together with a third party, the court will have to determine the parties' respective beneficial entitlements before it can exercise its adjustive powers: see *Harwood v Harwood* [1991] 2 FLR 274, CA.

[13] Cf ante, p 737.

[14] *Browne v Browne* [1989] 1 FLR 291, CA. But the court must not place any improper pressure upon the trustees to exercise their discretion in such a way that they would not otherwise have thought it right: *Howard v Howard* [1945] P 1, [1945] 1 All ER 91, CA. In *J v J (C Intervening)* [1989] Fam 29, [1989] 1 All ER 1121, CA, a similar approach to that in *Browne v Browne* was adopted in the assessment of financial provision for children who had interests under a discretionary will trust.

[15] *Crittenden v Crittenden*, supra. (No statutory power to order a company, whose issued shares were held by the spouses, to sell its assets and goodwill, or to require the husband to enter into a covenant not to compete with the proposed purchaser.)

[16] *Macey v Macey* (1981) 3 FLR 7, and *Brown v Brown* (1981) 3 FLR 161. See further post, p 774.

[17] (1981) 2 FLR 286, CA.

either party which were unconnected to the interest in the property.[18]

At first sight these latter limitations may seem an unfortunate gap in the court's powers particularly as in some cases, in order to do justice between the parties, a complete restructuring of their financial affairs may be required.[19] However, as we have seen,[20] in practice this type of restructuring can be achieved by the parties giving binding undertakings to the court or on a Tomlin order.

C. Financial relief after foreign divorce, annulment or legal separation[1]

1. BACKGROUND TO THE NEW LEGISLATION

Formerly, the court could only make financial provision or property adjustment orders under the Matrimonial Causes Act 1973 in the course of divorce, nullity or judicial separation proceedings instituted in England and Wales. This meant that spouses who had been divorced, or whose marriage had been annulled, abroad could not seek such relief from the English divorce courts.[2] Though logical, this rule could nevertheless cause hardship particularly to those who were habitually resident in England and Wales and who, having been divorced abroad, sometimes without their knowledge,[3] had no other means of redress.[4] Responding to pleas for reform[5] the Law Commission[6] recommended widening the jurisdiction of the Divorce Courts to give redress to such applicants. These recommendations have now been enacted in the Matrimonial and Family Proceedings Act 1984, Part III, which came into force in 1985. Jurisdiction

---

[18] *Burton v Burton* [1986] 2 FLR 419, and *Mullard v Mullard* (1981) 3 FLR 330. See also *Livesey (formerly Jenkins) v Jenkins* [1985] AC 424, [1985] 2 All ER 106, HL (wife agreeing to be solely responsible for discharging a bank overdraft and for mortgage repayments, held to be outside the court's powers to order: see ante, p 746]. There appears to be no power to order a spouse to use money or property for a *designated purpose*. However, as was noted earlier (pp 747–748) such an order appears to be *required* under the new regulations relating to the postponement of the statutory charge, and an order in those terms was approved, sub silentio, by the Court of Appeal in *Scallon v Scallon* [1990] 1 FLR 194, CA. Similarly, there is no express statutory power to require a spouse to execute a charge over the former matrimonial home although such orders appear to be frequently made in practice, see Bird *Problems in Ancillary Relief Orders* [1990] Fam Law 421 and the discussion post at p 789.
[19] See the comment at [1986] Fam Law 331.
[20] Ante, p 746.
[1] See generally Canton *The Matrimonial and Family Proceedings Act 1984: Financial Relief After Foreign Divorce* [1985] Fam Law 13 and Gordon *Part III of the MFPA 1984: A Panacea for Foreign Divorcees?* [1986] JSWL 329.
[2] Similarly, since they were no longer married, they could not seek maintenance under the Matrimonial Causes Act 1973, s 27, or under the Domestic Proceedings and Magistrates' Courts Act 1978.
[3] As could happen, for example, where divorce by talaq is permitted.
[4] See, for example, *Torok v Torok* [1973] 3 All ER 101 and *Quazi v Quazi* [1980] AC 744, [1979] 3 All ER 897, HL.
[5] Not least by the Law Lords in *Quazi v Quazi*, supra.
[6] Law Com No 117 (Financial Relief after Foreign Divorce).

is vested in the Family Division of the High Court and any county court designated by the Lord Chancellor.[7]

2. WHEN RELIEF MAY BE SOUGHT

Under section 12(1) of the 1984 Act where a marriage has been dissolved or annulled, or the parties to the marriage are legally separated, by means of judicial or other proceedings in an overseas country, and the divorce, annulment or legal separation is entitled to be recognised as valid in England and Wales,[8] then either party may apply to the court for financial relief. It will be noted that under this provision:

(1) The divorce etc must have been granted in an 'overseas country' which means a country or territory outside the British Islands.[9] Hence, for example, a spouse who has been divorced in Scotland cannot, under these provisions, subsequently seek financial relief in the English court.

(2) The divorce etc must have been by means of 'judicial or other proceedings'. The phrase 'other proceedings' is intended to cover cases where the marriage has been terminated extrajudicially, for example, by talaq.[10] This view would seem to be in line with the House of Lords' interpretation in *Quazi v Quazi*[11] of the similarly worded provision in the Recognition of Divorces and Legal Separations Act 1971, section 2(a).[12]

(3) It is established that Part III is retrospective and that therefore applicants whose marriage had been dissolved etc before Part II came into force, can apply for relief.[13]

(4) Provided the above criteria are satisfied *either* party can apply for relief.

(5) A party who has been legally separated abroad can apply for relief even though he may be able to petition for divorce etc in an English Court.[14]

(6) A party who remarries (but not the other party) loses the right to apply for relief.[15]

---

[7] Ss 27, 33(4) and 34(1)(b) of the 1984 Act. Proceedings cannot be transferred under the provisions of s 38 of the Matrimonial and Family Proceedings Act 1984: *Practice Direction* [1992] 3 All ER 151.

[8] For a discussion of the rules of recognition see eg Cheshire and North *Private International Law* (11th Edn by North and Fawcett).

[9] Matrimonial and Family Proceedings Act 1984, s 27. British Islands means England and Wales, Scotland, Northern Ireland, the Isle of Man and the Channel Islands: Interpretation Act 1978, Sch 1.

[10] See Law Com, op cit, at p 21 in their explanatory notes on clause 1 of their draft Bill.

[11] [1980] AC 744, [1979] 3 All ER 897, HL.

[12] But cf the arguments of Gordon, loc cit, at pp 336–338.

[13] *Chebaro v Chebaro* [1987] Fam 127, [1987] 1 All ER 999, CA.

[14] The need for this provision has been questioned in *Butterworths Family Law Service* at D [861, n 1] but it could be useful in cases where the matrimonial home is situated in England and Wales but the applicant is neither domiciled nor habitually resident here.

[15] Matrimonial and Family Proceedings Act 1984, s 12(2). The right is lost even if the subsequent marriage is void or voidable: s 12(3).

3. APPLICANTS ARE REQUIRED TO OBTAIN LEAVE

(a) Procedure

Before any substantive claim may be made, applicants must first obtain the court's leave to make an application for a financial order. The court cannot grant leave unless it considers that there is a substantial ground for making the application and that there is jurisdiction to make the order.[16] In *Holmes v Holmes*,[17] the Court of Appeal held that this requirement means that a court, in considering whether to grant leave, must take into account the statutory criteria contained in section 16 (discussed below) which apply in relation to the determination of the substantive application. If it is clear that, if leave were given, the application must founder 'at the first hurdle of section 16(1)' then it would be wrong to grant leave. Applications for leave are made ex parte and should be accompanied by an affidavit stating the facts relied upon and the grounds upon which it is alleged the court has jurisdiction.[18] Leave can be granted notwithstanding that an order has been made by a court outside England and Wales requiring the respondent to make financial provision for or to transfer property to the applicant or a child of the family.[19] Leave may be granted upon such conditions as the court sees fit.[20]

The requirement to obtain leave is intended to filter applications whilst at the same time providing maximum protection for all those concerned. The idea of the ex parte procedure is to save the potential respondent the time and expense of being involved in the case before the bona fides of the application have been tested. Given the one-sided nature of the application, there are those that doubt whether the potential respondent is well protected by this procedure.[1] It is, however, essential for a judge hearing the ex parte application to have all the material facts before him to consider whether a substantial ground exists for the making of the order and in order to estimate the applicant's prospects of success. If the applicant fails to make a full and frank disclosure of all relevant facts then the leave granted ex parte will be set aside.[2]

---

[16] Ibid, ss 13(1) and 15.

[17] [1989] Fam 47, [1989] 3 All ER 786, CA.

[18] Family Proceedings Rules 1991, r 3.18. It seems that the court has a discretion to allow the potential respondent to be heard, at any rate, where objection is taken to jurisdiction: *Chebaro v Chebaro* [1986] Fam 71 at 72, [1986] 2 All ER 897 at 898 per Sheldon J at first instance. The affidavit should pay particular reference to the matters set out in s 16(2) of the 1984 Act, see below.

[19] 1984 Act, s 13(2), though this is a factor to be taken into account in deciding whether to make an order: s 16(2), discussed below. The reference to a court outside England and Wales means that there is jurisdiction even if a court in another part of the United Kingdom has made an order. This could happen, for example, where the divorce takes place abroad, the applicant is domiciled in Scotland and the matrimonial home is in England.

[20] Ibid, s 13(3).

[1] See eg Scot Law Com No 72, para 2.13. Quaere whether the procedure would be improved by allowing potential respondents to be heard if they so desired. Cf *Chebaro v Chebaro*, supra.

[2] *W v W (Financial Provision)* [1989] 1 FLR 22.

(b) Jurisdiction

Before leave can be granted the court must be satisfied that there is jurisdiction to make the order.[3] Subject to the provisions of the Civil Jurisdiction and Judgments Act 1982 (discussed below) the court has jurisdiction if: (a) either party to the marriage was domiciled in England and Wales on the date of the application for leave or when the divorce, nullity or judicial separation took effect; or (b) either party was habitually resident there throughout the period of one year ending on the date of the application for leave or when the divorce etc took effect; or (c) either or both parties had at the date of the application for leave a beneficial interest in possession[4] in a dwelling house[5] situated in England and Wales which was at some time during the marriage a matrimonial home of the parties to the marriage.[6] If jurisdiction is taken on this latter basis then the court's powers are more limited.[7]

In cases where Part I of the Civil Jurisdiction and Judgments Act 1982 (by which the United Kingdom has implemented the Brussels Convention on the enforcement of civil and commercial judgments) applies[8] jurisdiction is determined by the rules of that Act rather than the 1984 Act. Effectively this increases jurisdiction since, under the Convention, in matters relating to maintenance,[9] a person who is domiciled in one Contracting State may be sued in the court of the place where the maintenance creditor is domiciled or habitually resident or, in the case of ancillary proceedings, in the court of the State which by its own law has jurisdiction to hear the divorce etc.[10]

(c) Interim orders

Once leave has been granted, then save where jurisdiction has been taken solely upon the matrimonial home basis and provided that it appears to the court that the applicant or any child of the family is in need of immediate financial assistance, the court may make an interim order for maintenance.[11]

4. APPLYING FOR AN ORDER

Once leave has been granted application may be made for financial relief.[12] It should be stressed that the granting of leave does not ipso facto mean that an order will be made. Indeed before an order will be made the court

[3] Pursuant to s 15(1) of the 1984 Act.
[4] This includes the receipt of or the right to receive rent or profits: s 27.
[5] This includes any building or part thereof which is occupied as a dwelling, and any yard, garden, garage or outhouse belonging to the dwelling-house and occupied therewith: s 27.
[6] This latter requirement implies that the married parties must have lived together in the property in question.
[7] Under s 20, see below.
[8] Pt I of the 1982 Act came into force in January 1987.
[9] This expression is not without its difficulties; see Law Com, op cit, para 2.11.
[10] This explanation is taken from that of the Law Commission, op cit, at para 2.11. For a detailed account of the Brussels Convention see eg Cheshire and North, op cit.
[11] S 14 of the 1984 Act. Under this provision the court can order the respondent to make periodical payments to the applicant or any child of the family for such term as the court thinks fit but beginning no earlier than the date of the grant of leave and ending with the date of the determination of the application for the order.
[12] For the procedure, see the Family Proceedings Rules 1991, r 3.18.

must consider whether in all the circumstances it is appropriate for an English court to do so.[13] In deciding that issue the court is directed[14] to have regard to a number of matters, namely: the connection the parties have with England and Wales, the country in which the marriage was dissolved etc and any other country outside England and Wales; any financial benefit which the applicant or any child of the family has received or is likely to receive in consequence of any agreement or operation of law of a country outside England and Wales; if any overseas order has been made, the extent to which it has been or is likely to be complied with; what rights the applicant has to apply for financial relief in a country outside England and Wales and, if an application was not pursued, the reasons why; the availability of property in England and Wales; the extent to which an order made here is likely to be enforceable, and the length of time since the divorce etc has been granted.

It can be seen that these considerations are designed to test whether the parties have any real connection with England and Wales; whether adequate relief has been or could be obtained elsewhere and whether in any event it would be worthwhile making an order here. It was said in *Holmes v Holmes*[15] that the requirements in section 16 reflect the fundamental rule of comity as between competent courts dealing with matters of this kind. The Court of Appeal stressed that an English court must always be slow to interfere with a competent court seized of the matter, which has made orders which are clearly enforceable and which has dealt with the matter on a reasonably careful assessment of all its features.

5. ORDERS THAT CAN BE MADE

Provided it is satisfied that it should make an order, the court has the same powers (save where jurisdiction is taken on the matrimonial home basis) as under the Matrimonial Causes Act 1973, Part II, viz: it can make periodical payments or lump sum orders, property transfer orders and orders for the sale of property.[16] In deciding what orders to make the court must have regard to the same considerations as it would when dealing with a domestic application,[17] though in addition it must consider the extent to which any overseas order has been or is likely to be complied with.[18]

Where jurisdiction is assumed on the matrimonial home basis, the court's powers are confined to making orders concerning that property or to making lump sum orders not exceeding the paying party's interest in it.[19]

There are also similar provisions to domestic proceedings for dealing with consent orders[20] and for variation and discharge.[1]

In addition to the above powers, the court can, provided leave has been given, make such orders as it thinks fit restraining any disposition about

---

[13] S 16(1) of the 1984 Act.
[14] By s 16(2).
[15] Per Purchas LJ [1989] Fam 47 at 53, [1989] 3 All ER 786 at 791, CA.
[16] S 17.
[17] Ss 18(1)–(5).
[18] S 18(6).
[19] S 20.
[20] Ie orders can be made in the terms agreed on the basis only of prescribed information furnished with the application: s 19.
[1] S 21.

to be made with the intention of defeating the claim for financial relief or setting aside any such disposition already made.[2] This power can be exercised even where the jurisdictional requirements are not satisfied provided the court is satisfied that the marriage has been dissolved etc abroad and that the applicant intends to apply for leave for financial relief as soon as he has been habitually resident in England and Wales for one year.[3]

D. Assessment of financial provision

1. GENERAL PRINCIPLES

Following the reform of the law in 1971, the general principles to be applied when the court is making an order for financial provision or the adjustment of property rights on divorce, nullity or judicial separation were contained in section 5 of the Matrimonial Proceedings and Property Act 1970 and re-enacted in section 25 of the Matrimonial Causes Act 1973. As the Act of 1970 was a reforming statute which had introduced a new code, cases decided before 1971 were to be applied only insofar as they laid down commonsense principles.[4]

Section 25 remained unamended for over a decade though by no means everyone was happy with its principles or underlying assumption.[5] In 1980, however, much wider discussion was stimulated when the Law Commission published a discussion paper questioning the basic policy of the then law.[6] In the following year the Law Commission published their final report[7] in which they concluded that on the material available to them[8] radical change in the law could not be justified.[9] Instead they recommended that there should be changes in emphasis in the way in which the court's discretionary powers should be exercised, such changes being 'evolutionary rather than revolutionary'.[10]

Following the Law Commission's recommendations, the Matrimonial and Family Proceedings Act 1984 introduced three changes in the ways

---

[2] S 23. Where jurisdiction is taken upon the matrimonial home basis the court's powers are confined to restraining or setting aside dispositions of the property: s 23(4). See also s 37 discussed post, pp 801–804.

[3] S 24.

[4] *Wachtel v Wachtel* [1973] Fam 72, 91, [1973] 1 All ER 829, 836, CA. Cf *Trippas v Trippas* [1973] Fam 134, 144, [1973] 2 All ER 1, 7, CA.

[5] See in particular the stimulating discussion by Gray *Reallocation of Property on Divorce*. See also Eekelaar *Family Law and Social Policy* (1st Edn) ch 9; Deech 7 Fam Law 229 (in turn criticised by O'Donovan 8 Fam Law 180).

[6] Law Com No 103 (The Financial Consequences of Divorce: the Basic Policy).

[7] Law Com No 112 (The Financial Consequences of Divorce, The Response to the Discussion Paper). For an interesting account of the Law Commission's role in promoting reform, see Cretney *Money After Divorce—The Mistakes We Have Made?* in *Essays in Family Law 1985* (ed Freeman) pp 34–42. For a commentary on the two Law Commission's papers see Deech *Financial Relief: The Retreat from Precedent and Principle* 98 LQR 621, 639–652; Eekelaar 45 MLR 420.

[8] The Law Commission were concerned about the general absence of empirical information about the working of divorce law and recommended (Law Com No 112 at para 46) that provision be made for monitoring any amending legislation. This recommendation has not been implemented.

[9] Law Com No 112, para 11, but see the criticisms of Symes *Indissolubility and the Clean Break* 48 MLR 44.

[10] Law Com No 112, para 23.

that courts are directed to exercise their powers. These can be summarised as being: (1) the removal of the status quo ideal or minimal loss principle; (2) giving priority to the welfare of any child of the family; and (3) placing greater emphasis on the parties becoming self-sufficient.

(a) The removal of the status quo ideal or minimal loss principle

Under section 25 of the Matrimonial Causes Act 1973, as originally enacted, the court was directed, as its overall object, to have regard to all the circumstances of the case and so to exercise its powers 'as to place the parties, so far as it is practicable and, having regard to their conduct, just to do so, in the financial position in which they would have been if the marriage had not broken down and each had properly discharged his or her financial obligations and responsibilities towards the other'. In most cases this objective or target (variously referred to as the status quo ideal or the minimal loss principle)[11] was impossible to achieve since few, if any, can afford to support two households at the same standard as the former one. One judge[12] described it as 'an elusive concept based on a difficult hypothesis', while one commentator[13] criticised it as being 'the mandate of restitution ... misconceived [and] ... almost always incapable of fulfilment'.

It was implicit in the status quo principle that a spouse had a right to life-long support from the other spouse even after divorce, but in their Discussion Paper the Law Commission questioned whether such a principle could now be justified, given, inter alia, the change to irretrievable break-down as the basis of divorce, the impossibility in most cases of attaining the objective and the changed economic role of women. Although perhaps initially more cautious as to what, if any, reform might be appropriate, the replies received by the Law Commission were overwhelmingly of the view that the status quo directive was no longer appropriate. Accordingly, in their final report, the Commission felt able to recommend its removal.

Another issue connected with the removal of the status quo objective and raised by the Law Commission in their Discussion Paper, was whether it was right simply to remove it with the result that the courts would be given no overall target. As the Commission pointed out[14] such a change could be seen as an abdication of responsibility by Parliament to the judiciary. This point drew conflicting responses from the Family Division judges and the Association of County Court and District Registrars.[15] The former thought that any satisfactory solution to the problem necessarily involved the court retaining a wide discretion. The latter thought that without a guiding principle it would be difficult to find a just solution and argued that 'to remove the guiding light is to allow flexibility to go mad'. The Commission did not think it possible to reconcile the objectives of certainty and flexibility and in the event recommended the simple removal of the status quo objective. This recommendation has been enacted by the 1984 Act.

Although at first sight it seems odd not to have statutory guidance on

---

[11] See eg Eekelaar *Family Law and Social Policy* (2nd Edn) p 109.
[12] Bagnall J in *Harnett v Harnett* [1973] Fam 156 at 161, [1973] 2 All ER 593 at 598.
[13] Gray *Reallocation of Property on Divorce* at p 319.
[14] Law Com No 103, para 69.
[15] See Law Com No 112, para 20.

the basic objective for the redistribution of resources after divorce,[16] it may be pointed out that even before the removal of the basic objective, the courts regarded themselves as being vested with very flexible and wide ranging powers and that therefore even Court of Appeal decisions should be regarded as guidelines rather than precedents.[17]

Precisely what impact the removal of the status quo objective has had or will have, is hard to say. However, it seems reasonable to suppose that it will affect previous decisions where express reliance had been made on the objective. One such decision is *Potter v Potter*.[18] In that case the parties were divorced after six years of marriage. They had no children and both had worked throughout the marriage. At the time of the divorce the husband ran a flourishing business and the wife was a personal secretary to a local authority executive earning sufficient money to support herself. During the marriage she had contributed to the home (which was in joint names). She did not apply for periodical payments and the eventual order was that the matrimonial home should be transferred to her and that she should receive a lump sum. However, Ormrod LJ commented that, had it not been for the need to put the parties in the position that they would have been in had the marriage not broken down, this case would not have been one for a lump sum at all. As he put it:[19]

'The marriage which has only lasted six years and in which neither party has suffered any handicaps so far as career and earnings are concerned and where there are no children is not one which in the ordinary way should attract very much in the way of payment as between one spouse and the other after the marriage has broken down.'

Another possible effect of the removal of the status quo objective is that it must in theory be harder for a spouse to claim a share in the other's future income or capital, at any rate where there is an unexpected increase in wealth after the divorce. Whereas under the old law it could simply have been argued that had the marriage not broken down the spouse would have had a share in that newly acquired wealth,[20] under the current law any claim will have to be based upon the claimant's reasonable needs. This is not to say that future income or capital is irrelevant. On the contrary, as will be seen, it is a factor that the courts are expressly enjoined to take into account since it will be obviously relevant to determining the future needs of the parties and of their ability to meet those needs.

---

[16] Cf the approach of the Scottish Law Commission, Scot Law Com No 67 (Report on Aliment and Financial Relief) para 3.37.

[17] See *Chamberlain v Chamberlain* [1974] 1 All ER 33 at 38, CA, per Scarman LJ and *Sharpe v Sharpe* (1981) Times, 17 February, CA per Ormrod LJ.

[18] [1982] 3 All ER 321, CA.

[19] Ibid at 326.

[20] Cf *Trippas v Trippas* [1973] Fam 134, [1973] 2 All ER 1, CA, where after the divorce the husband sold his business and thereby freed his capital and he was ordered to pay his wife a lump sum, inter alia, because, had they remained married, the wife would have had a 'good chance of receiving financial benefit on the sale of the business'. In *Schuller v Schuller* [1990] 2 FLR 193, CA, the court adopted the approach in *Trippas v Trippas* to reduce, rather than increase the financial award to a spouse. A wife inherited substantial property after the decree absolute, which was taken into account in that she was awarded a correspondingly smaller lump sum.

(b) Treating the welfare of any child of the family as the first consideration

As we have said, with the removal of the status quo objective the court no longer has an overall statutory target. Instead under section 25(1) of the Matrimonial Causes Act 1973[1] the court is directed, when considering whether to exercise its powers and, if so, in what manner:

'to have regard to all the circumstances of the case, first consideration being given to the welfare while a minor of any child of the family who has not attained the age of eighteen.'

The statutory enshrinement of the principle that priority is to be given to the welfare of any child of the family is an outstanding feature of English law[2] and has resulted from the Law Commission's recommendation. The Commission saw[3] the following advantages in making the children's position avowedly a priority, namely, it gives adequate recognition to the value of the care-giving parent's role whilst discouraging the belief that such payments may be regarded as an automatic life-time provision for the care-giving parent, and it has the psychological advantage that payments to or for children are more likely to be paid.

It will be observed that the court is required to give first and not paramount consideration to the welfare of any child of the family. This means, as was emphasised in *Suter v Suter and Jones*,[4] that the child's welfare is not the overriding consideration, though of course it is an important one.[5]

It should also be noted that priority is only accorded to children of the family[6] and not, for example, to any children of the spouses' second families, though a spouse's obligation to the second family is a relevant consideration in deciding what order to make.[7] It might be added that not even all children of the family are necessarily accorded priority. Where, for example, the child is not that of the husband, then even if he has 'treated' the child as one of the family he is not ipso facto liable to maintain him. In determining this the court is directed by section 25(4) of the Matrimonial Causes Act to have regard:

'(a) to whether that party assumed any responsibility for the child's maintenance, and, if so, to the extent to which, and the basis upon which, that party assumed such responsibility and to the length of time for which that party discharged such responsibility;
(b) to whether in assuming and discharging such responsibility that party did so knowing that the child was not his or her own;
(c) to the liability of any other person to maintain the child.'

If the court decides that the father is not liable[8] to maintain the child at all

---

[1] As amended by the Matrimonial and Family Proceedings Act 1984, s 3.
[2] Eg there is no comparable provision in Scotland, Australia or New Zealand.
[3] Law Com No 112, para 24.
[4] [1987] Fam 111, [1987] 2 All ER 336, CA. Cf *Anthony v Anthony* [1986] 2 FLR 353, CA, where not all the children's interests were necessarily identical.
[5] The statutory weighting is the same as for instance, in the adoption legislation: see ante, p 417.
[6] For a detailed discussion of the meaning of 'child of the family', see ante, p 368.
[7] See, for example, *Fisher v Fisher* [1989] 1 FLR 423, CA where a wife's responsibility to a child born after the marriage was dissolved was taken into account to increase a periodical payments order.
[8] As in *W v W (Child of the Family)* [1984] FLR 796, CA, see ante, p 369, and *Leadbeater v Leadbeater* [1985] FLR 789.

then of course that child's welfare ceases to be of any relevance in that case.

Finally, it will be noted that priority is only to be given to the child's welfare during his minority. This reflects the previously well established principle that orders for children should be related to their dependency and should not, in the absence of special needs such as mental or physical handicap, provide for continuing support during adulthood.[9]

Of course the principle of according priority to children of the family leaves open how that is to be achieved. However, in deciding what orders should be made for children, in addition to taking into account all the circumstances of the case, including the income, earning capacity, property and other financial resources which each of the spouses has or is likely to have in the foreseeable future together with their present and foreseeable financial needs, obligations and responsibilities, the court is directed[10] to have particular regard to:

'(a) the financial needs of the child;
(b) the income, earning capacity (if any), property and other financial resources of the child;
(c) any physical or mental disability of the child;
(d) the manner in which he was being and in which the parties to the marriage expected him to be educated or trained.'

These guidelines have remained the same since 1971 and even then were thought to do no more than spell out the principles which the courts have always applied. Their effect is summarised in the words of Bagnall J[11] approved by the Court of Appeal in *Lilford v Glynn*:[12]

'In the vast majority of cases the financial position of a child of a subsisting marriage is simply to be afforded shelter, food and education, according to the means of his parents.'

In practice the courts have long regarded their priority task as securing a roof over the children's heads though they have of course been aware of the need to maintain them. In this latter regard, however, before the 1984 reforms there seemed to have been a tendency to consider what order was appropriate for the spouse and then to consider what order could be made for the child out of the remaining resources.[13] Now that priority is to be given to the children it would seem that the appropriate order for the child should be considered first, though the financial position of the care-giving spouse and the child should not be treated as an entirely separate issue. One result of this could be that the amount of periodical sums made in favour of children will increase. In this regard it should be noted that, following the Law Commission's recommendation,[14] the courts have been circulated with figures compiled by the National Foster Care Association as to the costs of looking after children. As at April 1992 these figures were as follows:

---

[9] See eg *Lilford v Glynn* [1979] 1 All ER 441, CA. It is on this basis that capital orders for children are not common: see *Kiely v Kiely* [1988] 1 FLR 248, CA, *Chamberlain v Chamberlain* [1974] 1 All ER 33, CA. Cf *Griffiths v Griffiths* [1984] Fam 70, [1984] 2 All ER 626, CA.
[10] Matrimonial Causes Act 1973, s 25(3).
[11] *Harnett v Harnett* [1973] Fam 156, 161, [1973] 2 All ER 593, 598.
[12] [1979] 1 All ER 441, 447, CA.
[13] See Law Com No 112, para 24.
[14] Ibid at para 25, though they did comment that it would be preferable if the guidance was more specifically directed to the special needs of one parent families.

Child	National Recommended	London
0–4 years	£47.46	£55.79
5–7 years	£55.44	£65.10
8–10 years	£60.69	£71.33
11–12 years	£66.01	£77.56
13–15 years	£71.26	£83.72
16–18 years	£94.99	£111.72

While these figures are probably best regarded as optimum figures since in many cases (particularly where there is more than one child of the family) there will be insufficient resources to make such payments, they do nevertheless serve as an important reminder of the real cost of looking after children.[15]

How significant the introduction of a statutory principle of according priority to children has been, or will prove to be, is hard to say. Some commentators[16] take the view that it merely built upon existing practice and will not therefore have dramatic effect on the orders that are made. In any event some say that the change is merely a cosmetic one in the sense that since of course it does nothing to increase the resources available to the parties, at best it will simply alter the way that those resources are allocated. Others[17] take the view that it represents an important change in principle and may yet prove of practical significance. What can certainly be said is that there are a number of recent reported cases where the interests of children have directly influenced the order which the court has made.[18]

(c) Placing greater emphasis on the parties becoming self-sufficient

Inextricably bound up with the idea that it is no longer appropriate to have a right to life-long support from a former spouse, is that of expecting the former spouses to become financially independent of each other wherever, and as soon as, possible after the divorce. The Law Commission found that there was widespread support for the view that the courts should be more clearly directed to the desirability of 'promoting the severance of financial obligations between the parties at the time of divorce' and to give greater weight to the view that periodical payments in favour of one spouse 'should be primarily directed to secure wherever possible a smooth transition from marriage to the status of independence'.[19]

Following the Commission's recommendations, the courts are now, pursuant to section 25A(1) of the Matrimonial Causes Act 1973,[20] under a *duty* in all cases following the granting of a decree of divorce or nullity[1] to consider:

'... whether it would be appropriate so to exercise those powers that the financial

[15] But the Government's findings show that these rates are frequently ignored, see *Children Come First* (1990, Cm 1264) Vol 1, para 1.5, discussed ante, p 708.
[16] Eg Eekelaar 45 MLR 420, 423.
[17] Notably Cretney *Money After Divorce* in *Essays in Family Law* (1985) pp 43–44.
[18] See, for example, *M v M (Sale of Property)* [1988] 1 FLR 389, CA, *E v E (Financial Provision)* [1990] 2 FLR 233.
[19] Law Com No 112, para 30.
[20] Added by the Matrimonial and Family Proceedings Act 1984, s 3.
[1] But not judicial separation, since the marriage is not terminated.

obligations of each party towards the other will be terminated as soon after the grant of the decree as the court considers just and reasonable'.

If a periodical payments order is thought appropriate, the court is directed by section 25A(2) to consider:

'whether it would be appropriate to require those payments to be made or secured only for such term as would in the opinion of the court be sufficient to enable the party in whose favour the order is made to adjust without undue hardship to the termination of his or her financial dependence on the other party'.

In effect, under section 25A(1) the court is directed to consider whether it can make an immediate 'clean break' order, that is, an order which will settle once and for all the parties' financial liability to each other. If this is not thought possible, then under section 25A(2) the court is directed to consider whether it can nevertheless make a periodical payments order for a limited term rather than for an indefinite period. As we have seen,[2] in order to achieve these objectives the court has been given the power under section 25A(3) to impose a clean break order upon the parties, by which it is empowered to dismiss a spouse's claim for periodical payments without the applicant's consent,[3] and under section 28(1A) to make a 'deferred clean break order' by directing that a party is not entitled to apply for an extension of a fixed term periodical payments order.[4] In its most extended form, either type of clean break order will incorporate a declaration that neither party may make any further application for a lump sum or property adjustment order[5] nor be entitled to apply for financial provision out of the other's estate under the Inheritance (Provision for Family and Dependants) Act 1975.[6]

(i) Imposing an immediate clean break

Although the courts had previously been able to make clean break orders, until 1984, they could not do so against a spouse's will. It was not expected, however, that the new power would lead to a sudden increase in the number of clean break orders. For example, in his evidence to the Special Standing Committee on the 1984 Bill,[7] the President of the Family Division said that an immediate clean break would be:

'... entirely inappropriate in cases in which the wife has a continuing charge of young children, or where the marriage has been long and the wife has not worked during it or during the larger part of it and is middle aged at the time of the divorce'.

---

[2] Ante, p 729.
[3] It should be noted that there is no comparable power to dismiss an application for periodical payments to or for the benefit of any child of the family.
[4] See also s 25(2)(a), discussed post, p 771 et seq, under which the court is directed to consider whether there is any increase in earning capacity which it is reasonable to expect a party to take steps to acquire.
[5] The court may make such a declaration despite the absence of express statutory authority: *H v H (Financial Provision)* [1988] 2 FLR 114.
[6] Inheritance (Provision for Family and Dependants) Act 1975, s 15 as amended by Matrimonial and Family Proceedings Act 1984, s 8. The court will only make this order if it considers it just to do so. It must therefore have evidence as to the likely size of the spouse's estate and an indication of those who are likely to have claims upon it: *Whiting v Whiting* [1988] 2 All ER 275, CA.
[7] HC Official Report, Col 78, 22 March 1984.

He added:

> '... it would be equally inappropriate where the evidence suggests an impossibility in obtaining employment however well equipped for this purpose the spouse may be'.

In the Information Pamphlet issued by the Lord Chancellor's Department,[8] it was suggested that in most cases where there were dependent children a clean break order would not be appropriate and that the most likely cases (though each one had to be judged upon its merits) were short childless marriages where the parties were able to support themselves or those where there were no longer dependent children and there was a sufficient measure of capital to make a just division.

Since the enactment of section 25A, there have been a number of general judicial statements made about its effect. In *Harman v Glencross*,[9] for example, Balcombe LJ commented that the modern practice is to 'favour the clean break wherever possible', while in *Morris v Morris*[10] May LJ said that as a general principle the clean break thinking had parliamentary approval. More recently, in *B v B (Financial Provision)*[11] Ward J said that the primary object of the new law is to strive to make the parties self-sufficient. However, while emphasising the importance of section 25A, the higher courts have declined to offer any definitive guidance on how the statutory power is to be exercised. Indeed in one of the few cases where a clean break was imposed, namely, *Seaton v Seaton*,[12] the Court of Appeal refused to lay down any general guidelines, in part because the facts of the case before them were so unusual. In that case the wife had borne the financial burden of the marriage after the husband lost his job and because of a drink problem could not subsequently obtain another steady job. Eventually she left him and some time after the separation the husband suffered a stroke which left him with permanent disabilities. At the time of the divorce the husband was living with his parents and because of his limited capacity to enjoy life his income, derived from his disability pension, was sufficient to meet his needs. It was held that in the circumstances it would be wrong to impose upon the wife a continuing obligation to support her husband and accordingly the husband's application for periodical payments was dismissed under section 25A(3).

A more significant decision, however, is *Suter v Suter and Jones*.[13] Earlier cases[14] seemed to have established that where there were children for whom the parties shared a continuing obligation there was, in the absence of capital resources, little or no scope for the parents to have a clean break from each other. According to *Suter*, however, these cases must now be read subject to the new enjoinder under section 25A. Hence, it was held to be wrong in that case for the judge not to consider the issue of the possible financial independence of the wife simply because there were dependent children. On the facts, however, it was held that the husband should pay

[8] *The Matrimonial and Family Proceedings Act 1984: Your Questions Answered.*
[9] [1986] 1 All ER 545 at 557, CA.
[10] [1985] FLR 1176 at 1179, CA.
[11] [1990] 1 FLR 20, 26.
[12] [1986] 2 FLR 398, CA.
[13] [1987] Fam 111, [1987] 2 All ER 336, CA.
[14] Viz *Pearce v Pearce* (1979) 1 FLR 261, CA, and *Moore v Moore* (1981) 11 Fam Law 108, CA.

periodical payments to his wife albeit at the nominal rate of one pound a year.[15] The significance of a nominal order (as distinct from no order) is that the recipient may apply subsequently for an upward variation if circumstances change. For the payee it provides a 'last backstop' against unforeseen contingencies or disasters in the future; but the payer is subject to the continuing risk that his financial liabilities may be increased in a later variation application.

In *Whiting v Whiting*,[16] the judge at first instance accepted the 'last backstop' argument, and dismissed the husband's application to discharge a nominal periodical payment order in favour of the wife. The wife, after the divorce, had completed teacher training and, at the time of the hearing was earning over £10,500 per annum. The husband had remarried, but had been made redundant and received less than £4,500 per annum as a self-employed consultant. The Court of Appeal unanimously indicated they would have reached a different decision, on the merits, from the judge. However, only Balcombe LJ (to whom the making of a nominal order 'negated entirely' the clean break principle) was prepared to allow the husband's appeal. The majority would not overturn the judge's decision on the basis that it was not 'clearly wrong'.[17] Slade LJ nonetheless stressed that the court's duty to consider imposing a clean break was real and substantial: the easy course of declining a clean break order would not always be the right one.[18]

In *Barrett v Barrett*,[19] the Court of Appeal held that, although consideration of section 25A was mandatory, this does not mean the section should necessarily be given priority. The requirements of section 25A must be brought into balance with the specific factors in section 25,[20] and an immediate clean break imposed only if appropriate in the circumstances of a given case. This approach, which gives the court an extended scope to exercise its broad statutory discretion, has been expressly approved in at least one later case,[1] and followed in several others.[2] In general and despite one or two apparent inconsistencies in individual cases,[3] it remains true to say that the most obvious cases for imposing an immediate clean break are short childless marriages and those where there are adequate resources to cater for each spouse's reasonable needs.[4] In the latter case, particularly where there is evidence of bitterness between the parties, an immediate

---

[15] Cf *Mortimer v Mortimer-Griffin* [1986] 2 FLR 315, CA, where a clean break order was made even though there were dependent children but the fact that there were dependent children was not even commented upon in the Court of Appeal.

[16] [1988] 2 All ER 275, CA.

[17] Applying *G v G (Minors: Custody Appeal)* [1985] 2 All ER 225, HL (appellate court only to interfere with first instance judge's decision if satisfied that the judge has exceeded the generous ambit within which judicial disagreement was reasonably possible, or was otherwise 'plainly wrong').

[18] [1988] 2 All ER 275, at 287, CA.

[19] [1988] 2 FLR 516, CA.

[20] Post, p 771.

[1] *Fisher v Fisher* [1989] 1 FLR 423, CA.

[2] Eg *Hepburn v Hepburn* [1989] 1 FLR 373; CA, *B v B (Financial Provision)* [1990] 1 FLR 20.

[3] See Wright *Financial Provision, the Clean Break and the Search for Consistency* [1991] Fam Law 76.

[4] *Attar v Attar (No 2)* [1985] FLR 653, *Preston v Preston* [1982] Fam 17 [1982] 1 All ER 41, CA *Gojkovic v Gojkovic* [1992] Fam 40, [1990] 2 All ER 84, CA.

clean break may remove the tension which can be incidental to enduring financial dependence.[5] Even in cases which seem appropriate for the imposition of an immediate clean break, however, the individual merits need to be examined. If, as in *Soni v Soni*,[6] for example, a spouse, however well qualified, cannot obtain employment, then even in short childless marriages an immediate clean break is not the inevitable order.

(ii) Making limited term orders or deferred clean break orders

Even before 1984, the courts had the power to order a limited term periodical payments order but the injunction to consider whether such an order should be made is new. Similarly, the power under section 28(1A) to make a deferred clean break order by adding the direction that no application can be made to extend the term provided for in the original order is also new. It should be understood, however, that unless the court expressly adds a section 28(1A) direction, there is nothing to stop a spouse from returning to the court to ask that periodical payments be extended beyond the term originally fixed by the court.[7]

In considering whether to make a limited term order, the court is directed under section 25A(2) to consider whether the party, in whose favour an order is made, can adjust *without undue hardship* to the termination of financial dependence on the other party. As was stressed in *Morris v Morris*,[8] this is a mandatory requirement needing specific evidence. Although it is unclear precisely what is meant by 'undue hardship' (though it is implicit that a party can expect some hardship), it is evident that a limited order and a fortiori, a section 28(1A) direction, should not be made upon some vague expectation that the dependent spouse will be able to obtain a job, nor should that spouse's potential earning capacity be unrealistically viewed. As was recognised, for example, in *M v M (Financial Provision)*,[9] the prospects of a middle aged woman returning to the job market after several years' absence are far from good. In the same way, if a wife has a young child, it may be appropriate to make a limited term order in her favour to continue whilst the wife devotes herself to child care responsibilities rather than paid employment.[10] Ultimately, the facts of each case must be scrutinised carefully, bearing in mind that there is a presumption that periodical payments should be terminated as soon as possible unless the payee can show some good reason why they should not be.[11]

[5] *CB v CB* [1988] Fam Law 471.
[6] [1984] FLR 294.
[7] See eg *Sandford v Sandford* [1986] 1 FLR 412, CA.
[8] [1985] FLR 1176, CA.
[9] [1987] 2 FLR 1. See also the discussion of s 25(2)(a) post, p 771.
[10] *Waterman v Waterman* [1989] 1 FLR 380, CA; *C v C (Financial Provision)* [1989] 1 FLR 11. Cf *Fisher v Fisher* [1989] 1 FLR 423, CA where the court increased periodical payments in favour of a wife and child and refused to impose a time limit on the order notwithstanding the fact that the child was born after the divorce, and was not the husband's. It was 'quite unsupportable' for the husband to argue that by becoming pregnant, the wife had released the husband from his obligation to support her. Nor could the court ignore the wife's responsibility to the child because it was not a 'child of the family'.
[11] *Barrett v Barrett* [1988] 2 FLR 516, CA.

Of course if there are substantial assets available, then any potential hardship can be offset by appropriate sums.[12]

(iii) Commentary

Despite the widespread support received by the Law Commission for the change, the self-sufficiency principle is perhaps the most controversial of the reforms introduced by the 1984 Act. Some might see the introduction of the principle as being motivated by the spectre of the so-called 'alimony drone', that is, a woman who though perfectly capable of work, is wholly maintained by her former husband.[13] Whether this claim can be substantiated seems doubtful; at any rate while the Law Commission did use the term, they were also aware that 'alimony drones' did not exist to any great extent.[14]

Others question whether, in a society in which women are commonly dependent and encouraged to be dependent upon their husbands,[15] it is at all sensible or even desirable to have a principle of self-sufficiency.[16] Without gainsaying these arguments nor denying the harsh realities of women trying to enter the job market (which is something that the courts have been acutely aware of) there is surely something to be said for encouraging economic independence wherever possible and particularly where the spouses are young and have no children.[17]

(d) The duty of support is reciprocal

Generally speaking the wife is potentially likely to suffer greater financial loss from the breakdown of the marriage than the husband. In many cases he will have been the sole breadwinner and, in any event, her earning capacity is usually less than his and may be diminished even further (if not entirely extinguished) if she has a young family to look after. Even if she later returns to full-time employment, her prospects of promotion and advancement will often have been greatly reduced. For convenience in the following discussion, therefore, it will be assumed that the wife is the financially dependent spouse. It must be remembered, however, that when the position is reversed and the husband has been supported by the wife, the court will apply the same principles in assessing what periodical payments or lump sum payment she should make for him as it will when

[12] In *Attar v Attar (No 2)* [1985] FLR 653, after a marriage lasting six months, a millionaire husband was ordered to pay a £30,000 lump sum to his wife who, during the marriage, had given up her job as an air hostess, to enable her to adjust over a period of two years. In *S v S* [1986] Fam 189, [1985] 3 All ER 566 it was thought that £400,000 was the appropriate figure to compensate the divorced wife of a millionaire pop star for the loss of periodic payments estimated at £70,000 per year.
[13] This expression was originally coined by Hofstadter J in *Doyle v Doyle* 158 NYS 2d 907 at 912 (1957) and was said to have been introduced into English literature by Cretney in *The Maintenance Quagmire* 33 MLR 662, 666: see Cretney *Principles of Family Law* (4th Edn) p 778, n 53.
[14] See Law Com No 103, para 46, and the evidence of Cretney to the Special Standing Committee, HC Official Report, col 62, 20 March 1984.
[15] See eg Smart *The Ties that Bind* and Smart *Marriage, Divorce, and Women's Economic Dependency: A Discussion of the Politics of Private Maintenance* in *State, Law and the Family* (ed Freeman) ch 1. See also Maclean *Surviving Divorce—Women's Resources after Separation*.
[16] For a powerful criticism see Symes *Indissolubility and the Clean Break* 48 MLR 44.
[17] See also Cretney *Money After Divorce: Essays in Family Law* 1985 (ed Freeman) 43–45.

making an order in favour of a wife. 'I rejoice,' said Scarman LJ, 'that it should be made abundantly plain that husbands and wives come to the judgment seat in matters of money and property upon a basis of complete equality.'[18]

(e) Judging the overall fairness of orders

(i) Satisfying the needs of the members of the family

As we have said, the courts no longer have an overall statutory objective and although, as will be seen, there are guidelines setting out the considerations to which the court must have regard, ultimately they do not provide guidance on what may be regarded as a fair and just order overall. It is obvious, however, that the court's primary concern must be for the needs of all the members of the family with priority having to be given to the needs of any child of the family. Clearly, the most important need is for adequate accommodation and support. In cases where there are dependent children these needs will frequently determine what is to be done with the matrimonial home, for it will usually be necessary to permit the spouse with day to day responsibility for the children to remain in the home to provide a roof over their heads.[19] Even if there are no children the matrimonial home, which will commonly be the parties' major capital asset, may be preserved as a home for one of the spouses. The various orders relating to the matrimonial home will be considered separately at the end of this section.

Satisfying the parties' needs, though an important objective, does not, however, provide an overall guideline in all cases. In any event a party's reasonable needs depend in large measure upon the standard of living that he is used to. Furthermore there will be cases where a spouse can adequately cater for his own needs, yet there ought to be a redistribution of the capital assets to reflect each party's past contributions. What yardstick of fairness might be appropriate in these cases?

(ii) The one-third rule[20]

One guideline, apparently commonly used in practice,[1] which has had a chequered history in the courts, is the so-called one-third rule. After its surprising reintroduction in the divorce courts by *Ackerman v Ackerman*[2] and its subsequent endorsement in *Wachtel v Wachtel*,[3] the one-third approach was, for a time, widely used by the courts as a convenient starting point in respect of the parties' income and their capital. Insofar as it is applied to income, the approach is to order the husband to pay such sums

---

[18] *Calderbank v Calderbank* [1976] Fam 93, 103, [1975] 3 All ER 333, 340, CA. See also the views of Butler-Sloss LJ in *Browne v Browne* [1989] 1 FLR 291 at 296, CA.

[19] But cf the findings of Eekelaar and Maclean *Maintenance after Divorce*, Table 5.7.

[20] See generally Deech *Financial Relief: The Retreat from Precedent and Principle* 98 LQR 621, 623–630.

[1] See eg Smart *Interviewing solicitors: a discussion of the results from interviews on matrimonial law with 34 solicitors in Sheffield*, referred to by Cretney in *Principles of Family Law* (4th Edn) at p829, n2.

[2] [1972] Fam 225, 234, [1972] 2 All ER 420, 426, CA. See Hall [1973] CLJ 230; Maidment 4 Fam Law 172.

[3] [1973] Fam 72, [1973] 1 All ER 829, CA. See also *O'D v O'D* [1976] Fam 83, sub nom *O'Donnell v O'Donnell* [1975] 2 All ER 993, CA.

as will bring the wife's income (if any) up to one-third of the spouses' joint income. Thus, if the husband is earning £6,000 a year and the wife is earning £1,500 a year (giving a joint income of £7,500), he will be ordered to pay her £1,000 a year so as to bring her income up to £2,500. The reason for starting with a third rather than, say, a half was defended by Lord Denning, MR in *Wachtel v Wachtel*[4] on the ground that the husband was likely to have greater expenses than the wife (for example, in having to maintain the children and to pay a housekeeper) and that both might remarry (thus increasing the husband's liabilities and the wife's financial resources). This argument is frankly unconvincing: the reference to paying a housekeeper is unrealistic in most cases and, if it is relevant, the wife should be allowed the value of her services in kind; the husband could apply for a variation in the order if he later remarried and the wife's marriage would automatically terminate it. It is clear, however, that this approach is frequently adopted in practice.

Although in *Wachtel v Wachtel*, the Court of Appeal applied the rule to capital assets, Lord Denning MR[5] pointed out that if it were possible to close the account between the spouses completely, it would be fair to divide their capital equally between them, but the husband must be given some compensation for the fact that he will usually have to continue to make periodical payments for the wife and children. It follows that, if a lump sum represents not only a division of capital assets but also the capitalisation of income (so that no periodical payments are ordered), the court may award a sum which will equalise their financial position rather than apply the one-third rule.

However, the one-third approach was never regarded as a rigid rule but merely a starting point against which the needs and resources of the particular parties could then be tested and the resulting sum adjusted upwards or downwards. It became recognised, however, that even as a starting point the one-third approach was not very useful in respect of very low incomes,[6] nor was it thought appropriate in the cases involving large capital assets.[7] As Sir John Arnold P put it in *Slater v Slater*,[8] the guideline was useful provided the cases did not involve great wealth or unusual poverty. However, in a number of decisions during the early 1980s, the Court of Appeal seemed to cast doubt on the utility of the approach altogether[9] and in *Potter v Potter*[10] the one-third rule was expressly said to be inappropriate in cases involving the redistribution of the parties' capital assets. As a result of these later decisions, the one-third approach seemed once again to have become discredited in the eyes of the courts and there was genuine doubt whether the rule had survived the 1984 Act. However, it is apparent that it has. It was applied, for example, in *Bullock v Bullock*,[11]

---

[4] [1973] Fam 72 at 94, [1973] 1 All ER 829 at 839, CA.
[5] Ibid at 95 and 839–840 respectively.
[6] See eg *Cann v Cann* [1977] 3 All ER 957.
[7] See eg *Preston v Preston* [1982] Fam 17, [1982] 1 All ER 41, CA.
[8] (1982) 3 FLR 364 at 370, CA.
[9] Viz *Furniss v Furniss* (1981) 3 FLR 46, CA, *Stockford v Stockford* (1981) 3 FLR 58, CA and *Hall v Hall* [1984] FLR 631.
[10] [1982] 3 All ER 321, CA.
[11] [1986] 1 FLR 372, CA.

ironically in connection with assessing what lump sum the wife, who had no capital assets and, at the date of the hearing, no income, should receive. In that case the Court of Appeal expressly rejected the contention that following cases like *Potter v Potter* it was improper to apply the one-third approach. Similarly, in *Dew v Dew*[12] it was again held that the one-third apportionment principle can be applied to capital redistribution provided it is regarded as a starting point for the considerations set out in section 25.

On the strength of the last two decisions it can be said that the one-third approach still has a place in determining what orders are appropriate though it should not be regarded as a rigid rule nor should it be divorced from the other considerations to which the court is bound to have regard under section 25(2). It would seem to have no application in cases where the parties are either poor or very rich or in cases involving short childless marriages[13] and it is possible that the approach will have less relevance in cases involving children of the family, given the injunction to consider their interests first.[14]

(iii) Other approaches

As Anthony Lincoln J said in *Dew v Dew*[15] the one-third approach is but one approach that a court can properly apply in arriving at a fair order. Another approach and the one more currently favoured is the so-called 'net effect' approach. This involves working out the position of the respective parties on the assumption that a hypothetical order is made and taking into account, inter alia, their respective tax liability. The resulting figures are then compared and related to the parties' respective needs. We examined this approach when discussing magistrates' powers to make maintenance orders and readers are referred to that section for the details.[16]

In the case of very low incomes, where the parties' resources are insufficient to keep both households above subsistence level,[17] even the net effect method may be inappropriate. In these cases two points of principle have been established.[18] The first is the fact that the wife is receiving (or could claim) income support should prima facie be ignored in assessing the amount the husband should pay her: otherwise he would be able to shift his duty to provide for her on to the community as a whole. This will apply even though the maximum sum that could possibly be ordered will be less than the benefit she is receiving, so that there will be no personal advantage to her at all.[19] Secondly, since the husband, if he is in full-time employment,

---

[12] [1986] 2 FLR 341.

[13] See *B v B (Real Property: Assessment of Interests)* [1988] 2 FLR 490.

[14] It might be noted that there were no children involved in either *Bullock v Bullock* or *Dew v Dew*.

[15] [1986] 2 FLR 341 at 344.

[16] Ante, pp 682–683.

[17] That is the level by reference to the income support rates. At the time of writing the weekly rates (effective from 8 April 1992) are: for a married couple £66.60 (premium £9.30), for a single person over 25, £42.45, for a single person aged 18–24, £33.60. Rates for dependants range from £14.55 for those under 11 to £33.60 for those over 18.

[18] *Barnes v Barnes* [1972] 3 All ER 872, CA, approving *Ashley v Ashley* [1968] P 582, [1965] 3 All ER 554; *Shallow v Shallow* [1979] Fam 1, [1978] 2 All ER 483, CA. See further Cretney 127 New LJ 555; Bissett-Johnson and Pollard 38 MLR 449.

[19] As in eg *Peacock v Peacock* [1984] 1 All ER 1069.

will not be able to claim income support, the courts should not normally[20] make an order which depresses him below subsistence level. In assessing what order should be made, it seems that the proper approach[1] is to calculate the husband's net available income, consider the effect of the proposed order on his living expenses and compare the sum that he would receive, if in receipt of income support, to ensure that he is not left with a sum below that amount. It seems that it is appropriate to allow the husband a margin above subsistence level (to meet his particular requirements and provide some incentive to remain in employment) though this is a matter for the court's discretion and is not to be rigidly related to the incentive allowance permitted by the Department of Social Security.[2]

Two recent decisions, however, have marked a significant departure from the approach outlined above. In both cases, the court imposed a clean break, even though its direct effect was to enable the less impoverished spouse to throw upon the taxpayer the financial burden of supporting his dependants. In *Ashley v Blackman*[3] Waite J dismissed a husband's liability for maintenance where a wife, aged 48, was a long-term schizophrenic in receipt of state benefits. The husband, aged 55, had remarried, and had two young children but an income of just £7,000 per annum. The judge drew a distinction between the 'devious and feckless' husband and the 'genuine struggler'. The latter was to be allowed to see 'light at the end of the tunnel' by being spared the obligation to pay to his ex-wife, with no commensurate financial benefit to her, the few pounds which separated him from penury. In the second case, *Delaney v Delaney*,[4] the husband purchased a home with his cohabitant but, after paying the mortgage, was left with insufficient to support his former wife and children. The Court of Appeal held that the needs of the wife and children had to be balanced with the husband's ability to pay, and the availability of social security benefits (including income support) should be considered. It discharged the wife's periodical payments order and made nominal orders for the children. Ward J[5] stated that a former husband was entitled so to order his life as to fulfil his aspirations for the future: there is, after all, 'life after divorce'.

If these cases indicate the court's willingness to recognise the underlying financial realities, the potential for making clean break orders in similar situations in the future has been restricted by recent changes in social security legislation.[6] The new provisions[7] entitle the Department of Social Security effectively to side-step a clean break order by proceeding in the

---

[20] But cf *Billington v Billington* [1974] Fam 24, [1974] 1 All ER 546.
[1] See *Allen v Allen* [1986] 2 FLR 265, CA and *Peacock v Peacock*, supra.
[2] In *Shallow v Shallow* (supra), the Court of Appeal rejected an argument that the courts should apply the same principle as that applied by officers administering (what was then) the supplementary benefits scheme. In negotiating with a husband who is failing to support his wife, the Benefits Agency will leave him with a quarter of his net income (or £5, whichever is the greater) over and above the subsistence sum. This would give the husband an incentive to work which he might lack if any increase in his earnings would go straight to his wife and thus merely reduce the burden on the social security fund: see Hayes [1978–9] JSWL 216.
[3] [1988] Fam 85, [1988] 3 WLR 222.
[4] [1990] 2 FLR 457, CA.
[5] [1990] 2 FLR 457 at 461, CA.
[6] See Wood *The Social Security Act 1990—the Clean Break Rejoined* [1991] Fam Law 31. .
[7] Now the Social Security Aministration Act 1992, ss 107 and 108. Income Support (Liable Relatives) Regulations 1990. See also ante, p 667.

magistrates' court against a husband, as a liable relative, should a former wife become dependent upon income support for her children and her own needs. This divergence in approach between the judiciary and the executive and between public and private law maintenance provisions creates what has been described as a 'crazily uncertain position'[8] for practitioners, and those whom they advise.

(f) The courts should not have an ulterior purpose for making orders

It must be stressed that it is quite wrong for the court to make an order with some ulterior purpose in view, and cases laying down this principle decided before 1971 must still be good law. An award to a wife will not be reduced merely because she chooses to petition for judicial separation rather than divorce and thus prevents the other party from remarrying until he is in a position to petition for divorce himself. She may have a number of reasons for her action apart from spite: the Act has given her the right to pursue either remedy and her motive is no concern of the court.[9] Similarly, periodical payments should not be kept low in order to starve the wife into a reconciliation.[10]

(g) Financial relief after a decree of nullity

There is clearly power to order financial relief after a decree of nullity even though the marriage is void.[11] But it must be appreciated that a claim must be weaker because neither of the parties is losing a right to be maintained either at common law or by statute. Obviously the parties' knowledge and belief at the time of the ceremony will be of particular importance. There is every difference between, say, a woman who unwittingly contracts a marriage which, as the man knows, is bigamous and therefore void, and a woman who takes a risk because she does not know what has happened to her former husband.[12] Consequently the court may be reluctant to make an order in favour of a party who has contracted a marriage knowing it to be void; on the other hand, it must be remembered that if she (or he) has been previously married and divorced, any periodical payments ordered on the divorce will automatically come to an end and her sole source of support for the future will be the other party to the void marriage.

---

[8] *Butterworths Family Law Service* D [1151].
[9] *Lombardi v Lombardi* [1973] 3 All ER 625, 630, CA, following *Sansom v Sansom* [1966] P 52, 55–56, [1986] 2 All ER 396, 399.
[10] *Wharton v Wharton* [1952] 2 All ER 939n. But see *Brett v Brett* [1969] 1 All ER 1007, CA, where the husband was ordered to pay his former wife £5,000 if he did not obtain a Jewish gett within three months, which would enable her to remarry in accordance with her religious beliefs. Could it be argued that, if she remarried, her financial position would be improved so that in effect the court was compensating her for this loss?
[11] A fortiori there is power to order financial relief if the marriage is voidable: see *Johnston v Johnston* (1976) 6 Fam Law 17, CA.
[12] Cf applications under the Inheritance (Provision for Family and Dependants) Act by persons who have in *good faith* entered into a void marriage: post, p 823.

2. FACTS TO BE TAKEN INTO ACCOUNT WHEN ASSESSING WHAT ORDERS SHOULD BE MADE FOR A SPOUSE

Reference has already been made to the fact that, whilst the court must have regard to all the circumstances of the case, it must also take into account certain specific facts. Some of these are relevant to calculating the parties' resources and needs; others will lead the court to make a greater or smaller award than it otherwise would have done. Although the list is not intended to be exhaustive,[13] it covers almost all the matters to which the court had always had regard in the past. It is proposed to consider the facts in the order in which they are set out in section 25(2) of the Matrimonial Causes Act.[14]

(a) '... the income, earning capacity, property and other financial resources which each of the parties to the marriage has or is likely to have in the foreseeable future, including in the case of earning capacity any increase in that capacity which it would in the opinion of the court be reasonable to expect a party to the marriage to take steps to acquire'

The court must have regard to all the income and capital belonging to the spouses. So far as capital is concerned, provided it belongs to one of the spouses, it must be taken into account and it is irrelevant how the spouse came to own it. Hence, inherited property is included and even damages recovered for loss of earnings or damage to property forms part of the recipient's assets. Insofar as damages for personal injuries represent compensation for pain and suffering and loss of amenity, the position was formerly not so clear. Earlier decisions indicated that they should be left out of account,[15] but after a detailed consideration of the authorities the Court of Appeal concluded in *Daubney v Daubney*[16] that the views expressed in those cases had not been necessary to the decisions and that such damages were assets which should be brought into account. However, Scarman LJ was careful to point out that it would not be a correct exercise of the court's discretion to make an order which would in effect deprive the spouse of all benefit of the compensation:[17] the court apparently must decide in each case what would be a fair sum to bring into account. In *Wagstaff v Wagstaff*[18] the Court of Appeal recently held that the fact that substantial damages had been received by a husband as compensation for pain and suffering and loss of amenity did not *necessarily* make that sum unavailable to a wife. The fact that an injured spouse may have special needs, or an

---

[13] Cf *Collins v Collins* [1987] 1 FLR 226, CA, in which it was held wrong to take the Legal Aid Boards statutory charge into account in determining what the order should be, inter alia (see May LJ at 236) because it fell outside the terms of s 25. This could be taken to indicate that the facts are exhaustive, though it is doubtful whether this inference was intended. In any event it could be argued that the charge could have been considered under s 25(2)(b) as an obligation that the recipient would have in the foreseeable future: see the comment at [1987] Fam Law 55. See also *B v B (Real Property)* [1988] 2 FLR 490 where the judge increased a lump sum order to the wife 'to allow for the legal aid charge'. *Collins v Collins* does not appear to have been cited before the court, so (presumably) was overlooked.

[14] As amended by the Matrimonial and Family Proceedings Act 1984.

[15] Eg *Jones v Jones* [1976] Fam 8, [1975] 2 All ER 12, CA.

[16] [1976] Fam 267, [1976] 2 All ER 453, CA.

[17] At 277 and 459, respectively.

[18] [1992] 1 All ER 275, CA.

impaired future earning capacity would, of course, be considered by the court in the exercise of its discretion. But subject to this, damages for personal injury are properly to be regarded as part of the financial resources available to the parties.

In appropriate cases regard must be had to the husband's ability to earn higher wages by working overtime,[19] to raise money by overdrafts,[20] or loans secured on his property[1] or, if he is unemployed, to obtain work if he wishes.[2] Increases in either spouse's income or capital after their separation must also be considered as this is properly to be regarded as part of their resources.[3] In the case of a very rich man, who may well live largely on capital and capital profits, his capital assets will be of particular importance,[4] and such a person's standard of living may be the best guide to the level of his real income.[5]

The court must have regard not only to the resources which each party has at the time of the hearing[6] but also to those which they are likely to have in the foreseeable future. If the benefit is one to which a party may be contingently entitled in the future, the court may take it into account by ordering him to pay an appropriate lump sum if and when he acquires the interest.[7] On the other hand if the contingency is too

---

[19] *Kluchinski v Kluchinski* [1953] 1 All ER 683. It is not unknown for husbands deliberately to refuse overtime before the hearing so as to give a false picture of their normal earnings.

[20] *J v J* [1955] P 215, [1955] 2 All ER 617, CA.

[1] *Newton v Newton* [1990] 1 FLR 33, CA.

[2] *McEwan v McEwan* [1972] 2 All ER 708. Cf *Bromilow v Bromilow* (1976) 7 Fam Law 16. If the husband is in receipt of income support and the payments made to him have not been reduced or stopped, this indicates that the Agency's officers are satisfied after extensive enquiries that he is genuinely unable to find work and, whilst this does not bind any court, is a valuable piece of evidence which should be taken into account: *Williams v Williams* [1974] Fam 55, [1974] 3 All ER 377.

[3] *Schuller v Schuller* [1990] 2 FLR 193 (wife's property inheritance after decree absolute taken into account to reduce her lump sum).

[4] *Brett v Brett* [1969] 1 All ER 1007, CA.

[5] Cf *W v W (No 3)* [1962] P 124.

[6] If a party's income is liable to fluctuate, it is customary to take an average to assess future earnings: *Sherwood v Sherwood* [1929] P 120, CA; and the fact that these fluctuations make it precarious may be a reason for reducing the amount of periodical payments ordered: *Dean v Dean* [1923] P 172. On the question of allowances of men serving in the armed forces, see *Powell v Powell* [1951] P 257, CA; *Collins v Collins* [1943] P 106, [1943] 2 All ER 474; *Buttle v Buttle* [1953] 2 All ER 646.

[7] *Calder v Calder* (1975) 6 Fam Law 242, CA (interest contingent on husband's surviving his mother); cf *MT v MT (Financial Provision)* [1992] 1 FLR 362 (wife's application adjourned pending the death of her 83-year-old German father-in-law. Under German law, husband entitled to fixed portion of his father's substantial estate). In *Priest v Priest* (1978) 1 FLR 189, CA, a husband was ordered to pay one-third of the gratuity payable on completion of his service in the Royal Marines some five years later. It has since been held that because of the terms of the Army Act 1955, s 203, the court has no power to order payments to be made *specifically* out of an army terminal gratuity or resettlement grant, see *Walker v Walker* [1983] Fam 68, [1983] 2 All ER 909, CA, and *Roberts v Roberts* [1986] 2 All ER 483. Nor should the court make an order which indirectly has this effect, for example, by making a lump sum payment order equivalent to a percentage of a terminal grant, see *Ranson v Ranson* [1988] 1 WLR 183, CA (a case involving an RAF serviceman where the legislation, Air Force Act 1955, s 203, is in similar terms to the Army Act). The position in relation to the Royal Navy was different, see *Cotgrave v Cotgrave* [1992] Fam 33, [1991] 4 All ER 537, CA although recent legislation puts seamen on the same footing as other servicemen (Naval Discipline Act 1957, s 128G, as inserted by the Armed Forces Act 1991, s 16, replacing the Naval and Marine Pay and Pensions Act 1865, s 4 and s 5). Despite the special legislation affecting servicemen's gratuities, it is submitted that the court may still take such entitlements

uncertain or remote, it may be left out of account altogether.[8]

Although the courts have had in the past the power to consider whether a spouse could increase his or her earning capacity,[9] the specific injunction to consider this requirement is new and results from an amendment introduced by the Matrimonial and Family Proceedings Act 1984, section 3.

In his evidence to the Special Standing Committee[10] the President of the Family Division instanced what he described as the 'obvious case' of a husband who had reached the point in his career at which he had the right or an opportunity to take some examination which would lead to a higher grade or a better remunerated appointment. While this is an example of how the provision could be relevant, it is much more likely that attention will be directed to the wife's potential earning capacity. The provision is clearly related to the general requirement to consider whether the spouses can become self-sufficient.

It is to be noted that the court should only pay regard to any increase in earning capacity that it is 'reasonable' to expect the spouse to take steps to acquire. Obviously in deciding this, the court must take into account all the circumstances of the case, but particularly relevant will be any commitments to look after any children;[11] the age, health and qualifications of the spouse and the time since the spouse last worked. The courts seem acutely aware of the difficulties that older women may experience in obtaining suitable employment. In *Leadbeater v Leadbeater*,[12] for example, it was held to be unreasonable to expect a 47-year-old woman with no particular skills (she was, at the time of the marriage, the secretary to her former husband) to adapt to new methods used in offices, namely, word processors and so on. On the other hand, it was thought that she could increase the number of hours that she was currently working as a receptionist. Hence, her earnings were assessed at £2,500 per year as against her actual earnings of £1,680.[13] On the other hand in *Mitchell v Mitchell*[14] it was held that a wife who was an experienced secretary but who had taken a part-time job in a canteen could, when the children had left school (the younger child was 13), reasonably be expected to increase her earning

---

into account when considering the parties' resources—perhaps (say) by making a larger lump sum order in favour of a wife (if other capital is available) on the basis that a husband's needs will be met by a terminal grant upon his discharge. Once a terminal grant has been *received* by an ex-serviceman, the Army Act 1955 does not prevent the court from making an order in respect of what has become free and available capital, see *Happé v Happé* [1991] 4 All ER 527, CA.

[8] See eg *Michael v Michael* [1986] 2 FLR 389 where, because of the uncertainty of whether and when the wife would receive an interest under her mother's will, it was left out of account. This was followed in *K v K* [1990] 2 FLR 225. See also *Priest v Priest*, supra, where a gratuity that could arise 15 years after the hearing was thought to be too far in the future to be taken into account.

[9] See eg *Mitchell v Mitchell* [1984] FLR 387, CA.

[10] HC Official Report, col 77, 22nd March 1984.

[11] This may include, it seems, a child which is *not* the husband's, and which was born after the breakdown of the marriage: see *Fisher v Fisher* [1989] 1 FLR 423, CA.

[12] [1985] FLR 789.

[13] See also *M v M (Financial Provision)* [1987] 2 FLR 1 in which the difficulties of another 47-year-old wife were discussed. See also *Boylan v Boylan* [1988] 1 FLR 282 and *Barrett v Barrett* [1988] 2 FLR 516, CA.

[14] [1984] FLR 387, CA.

capacity and the resulting lump sum awarded her reflected this.

Another issue is the presence of a new partner.[15] The fact that the wife has remarried or is about to remarry or is living with another man who is supporting her clearly affects her financial position. Remarriage automatically terminates periodical payments[16] and although, for this purpose, cohabitation is not necessarily to be equated with remarriage,[17] it may nonetheless lead the court to conclude that the wife no longer needs the husband's support; but leaving aside the question of the matrimonial home, all these facts should generally be disregarded in dividing capital assets unless a lump sum award represents the capitalisation of periodical payments.[18] The wife is withdrawing her part of the capital from the former family partnership, and the amount she receives should not depend on what she proposes to do with it.[19] That the mere chance that the wife may remarry at some time in the future should be ignored when dividing capital assets.[20]

So far as the husband's second wife's means are concerned, it is established that they are relevant (though there can be difficulties in discovering those means)[1] but only to the extent that they diminish the needs of the husband, thereby extending his resources to support his first family. An order cannot be made which has the effect of making the new partner pay out of her income or capital.[2]

(b) 'The financial needs, obligations and responsibilities which each of the parties to the marriage has or is likely to have in the foreseeable future'

The most obvious examples of facts to be considered under this head are the parties' need to maintain themselves and their responsibility to provide for their dependants. The maintenance of children must come first; in addition one must take into account the needs of a second spouse,[3] infirm parents, brothers and sisters unable to work, and any other person whom it is reasonable to expect either party to look after in the circumstances. It will be seen that not all these obligations are legally enforceable: in this context a moral obligation and the voluntary assumption of a responsibility (provided that it is reasonable) may be as relevant as a legal obligation. For example, a father's moral duty to make voluntary payments for the upkeep of his child born outside the marriage is indistinguishable for this

---

[15] See Hodson *The New Partner After Divorce* [1990] Fam Law 27.
[16] See ante, p 729.
[17] *Atkinson v Atkinson* [1987] 3 All ER 849, CA.
[18] See for example, *Duxbury v Duxbury* [1992] Fam 62n, [1990] 2 All ER 77, CA.
[19] See eg *Duxbury v Duxbury* supra (irrelevant that wife would spend part of lump sum award to benefit cohabitant); *Gojkovic v Gojkovic* [1992] Fam 40, [1990] 2 All ER 84, CA (wife had earned her share of family wealth and entitled to use lump sum to purchase hotel to run as business).
[20] *Smith v Smith* [1976] Fam 18n at 23, [1975] 2 All ER 19n at 22.
[1] See *Wynn v Wynn and Jeffers* [1980] 3 All ER 659, CA, *W v W* (1981) 2 FLR 291 and the discussion in *Butterworths Family Law Service* at p [771].
[2] *Macey v Macey* (1981) 3 FLR 7, and *Brown v Brown* (1981) 3 FLR 161.
[3] *Barnes v Barnes* [1972] 3 All ER 872, CA. But that does not justify postponing the interests of the first family (and *a fortiori* any child of the family) to those of the second family: *Roberts v Roberts* [1970] P 1, [1968] 3 All ER 479.

purpose from his legal liability to comply with a court order.[4] But if the liability has been assumed in a purely voluntary way, the court can obviously take it into account only if it is reasonable. Thus repayment of a mortgage entered into after the parties separated in order to enable one of them to buy an expensive house may be disregarded if their financial position does not justify the purchase.[5]

As in the case of the parties' resources, the court must have regard to the needs, obligations and liabilities that they are likely to have in the foreseeable future as well as those already incurred at the time of the order.

In all cases the spouses are entitled to have only their *reasonable* needs taken into account but, of course, what is 'reasonable' very much depends upon the circumstances of each case. At the poverty end of the spectrum, for example, it has been held that a video recorder is not a reasonable need[6] and running a car can only be a justified expense if it is needed to get to work.[7] Even if there are ample resources the claims must still be reasonable. In *Leadbeater v Leadbeater*,[8] for example, where the husband's assets amounted to some £250,000, it was held that while the wife could reasonably justify the purchase of a two bedroomed house, given that she would live in it by herself, she could nót justify the need for a three bedroomed property. At the very wealthiest end of the spectrum it has been said that it is impossible to lay down guidelines to help calculate the appropriate levels of lump sum payments,[9] though in *Preston v Preston*[10] the Court of Appeal seemed to hint that there might be some ceiling to awards that might be made. In that case the husband, who had capital assets estimated at £2.3 million, was ordered to pay a lump sum of £600,000 to produce an annual income of £20,000 after tax. In *Duxbury v Duxbury*,[11] the *Preston* decision was followed to the extent that a capital sum was ordered that would produce an annual income of £28,000 (a figure calculated on the basis of *Preston* suitably adjusted to take account of inflation), which was thought to be a reasonable sum to preserve a luxurious standard of living.

In *Duxbury v Duxbury*[12] the firm of accountants acting for the wife devised a sophisticated computer program, designed to take account of a number of financial and other variables, including life expectancy, inflation, tax, investment return and capital growth and produced an estimate of the

---

[4] *Blower v Blower* [1986] 1 FLR 292; *Roberts v Roberts*, supra. See also *Williams v Williams* [1965] P 125, [1964] 3 All ER 526, CA, and *P (JR) v P (GL)* [1966] 1 All ER 439 (liability to educate children of a previous marriage). Cf *Fisher v Fisher* [1989] 1 FLR 423, CA, for a mother's responsibility towards a child born outside the marriage.
[5] Cf *G v P* [1978] 1 All ER 1099, CA.
[6] *Girvan v Girvan* (1983) 13 Fam Law 213.
[7] See eg *Clarke v Clarke* (1979) 9 Fam Law 15; *Delaney v Delaney* [1990] 2 FLR 457, CA. Cf *Slater v Slater* (1981) 3 FLR 58.
[8] [1985] FLR 789.
[9] *Gojkovic v Gojkovic* [1992] Fam 40, 50, [1990] 2 All ER 84, 90, CA per Russell LJ.
[10] [1982] Fam 17, [1982] 1 All ER 41, CA. See also *Thyssen-Bornemisza v Thyssen-Bornemisza (No 2)* [1985] FLR 1069, CA, where it was held that the contention that the husband's assets were £1,000 million rather than the £400 million that he had deposed could not make any difference to the final order for the wife and that therefore further disclosure of means should not be ordered. A similar approach was adopted in *B v B* [1990] 2 FLR 180.
[11] [1992] Fam 62n, [1990] 2 All ER 77, CA. Cf *S v S* [1986] Fam 189, [1986] 3 All ER 566, where an annual income of £70,000 was thought appropriate.
[12] [1992] Fam 62n, [1990] 2 All ER 77, CA.

lump sum required to meet the recipient's needs for life.[13] This so-called 'Duxbury calculation' may provide a helpful guide to the assessment of the needs and reasonable requirements of a wife whose husband is wealthy. However, as Butler-Sloss LJ explained in *Gojkovic v Gojkovic*[14] it ought not to be elevated to a rigid matrimonial calculation: each case must be decided on its own facts, and in accordance with the principles set out in section 25 of the Matrimonial Causes Act 1973 (as amended).[15] In *Gojkovic v Gojkovic*[16] the husband and wife had, by dint of their efforts, built up a hotel and property business worth over £4 million. The Court of Appeal rejected contentions that, (a) there was, in principle, a ceiling for lump sum awards, and, (b) that *Duxbury v Duxbury* laid down any binding authority as to the requirements of every millionaire's former wife. Quite apart from the wife's reasonable needs, her outstanding contribution should be recognised. The Court of Appeal upheld the award of a lump sum of £1 million to the wife, which she intended to use to acquire and run her own hotel.

Two matters require special comment. It may be possible to meet the needs of a wife who is unable to work (either because of her own physical condition or the necessity of looking after a child or other dependant who requires constant care) only by transferring the former matrimonial home to her so that she has at least the security of roof over her head.[17] Secondly, in its anxiety to protect the wife and children, the court should not lose sight of the difficulties likely to be faced by the husband, particularly if he has remarried. He should never be left in a position where the effect of the order will have a crippling effect on him. In *Backhouse v Backhouse*,[18] for example, Balcombe J said that it would be repugnant to the court's sense of justice to make an order which would have necessitated the husband's selling the former matrimonial home in which he was living with his second wife and two children, and he limited the husband's liability to paying a lump sum which he could reasonably be expected to raise by a mortgage.

(c) 'The standard of living enjoyed by the family before the breakdown of the marriage'

This is particularly important when substantial assets are available and one of the spouses has been living at a much higher level than he or she did before the marriage. In *Calderbank v Calderbank*[19] the wife, a relatively rich woman, was ordered to pay a lump sum of £10,000 to the husband (who had no capital and had remarried) so that he might buy a house suitable to the former spouses' ways of life in which he might see his children. But neither party's standard of living should be raised above what it otherwise

---

[13] For a fuller explanation by the program's inventor see Lawrence *Duxbury Disclosure and Other Matters* [1990] Fam Law 12.

[14] [1992] Fam 40, 48, [1990] 2 All ER 84, 87, CA.

[15] A similar approach was taken by Ward J in *B v B (Financial Provision)* [1990] 1 FLR 20 who discusses the limitations and restrictions of the 'Duxbury calculation' and the dangers of its 'unblinkered application'. See also *Newton v Newton* [1990] 1 FLR 33, CA.

[16] Supra.

[17] *Jones v Jones* [1976] Fam 8, [1975] 2 All ER 12, CA; *Smith v Smith* [1976] Fam 18n, [1975] 2 All ER 19n.

[18] [1978] 1 All ER 1158. See also *Wachtel v Wachtel* [1973] Fam 72, 96, [1973] 1 All ER 829, 841, CA; *H v H* [1975] Fam 9, 14 [1975] 1 All ER 367, 371.

[19] [1976] Fam 93, [1975] 3 All ER 333, CA.

would have been, for this would in effect mean that the order was being used as a means of punishing the other.[20]

(d) 'The age of each party and the duration of the marriage'

This must be looked at in conjunction with the contribution made by each of them to the welfare of the family (considered below). Even before 1971 it was clear that a young wife, whose marriage has lasted for only a short time, would generally get much less favourable terms that one who had been deserted after years of married life. Today the courts are not likely to make more than a nominal order if the marriage is childless and has lasted only a matter of months and the wife has made virtually no contribution to the home and is young, fit and capable of earning her own living.[1] They are, however, more sympathetic to such a wife if the breakdown has caused her financial loss, in which case she can expect a substantial order in her favour.[2] In the case of an older woman who may find it difficult to return to work, it was said in *S v S*[3] that the court should concentrate on the parties' needs and try at least to restore them to the position they were in before the marriage. In that case both parties were over 50 when they married and the marriage lasted only two years. The court ordered the husband to settle on the wife a sum which would enable her to buy a house similar to that which she had sold on her marriage and which would revert to the husband or his estate on her death; to pay her a lump sum to enable her to furnish it, and to make periodical payments (which would bring her income up to something less than a fifth of their joint incomes) to compensate her for loss of pension rights and the comfortable old age she could have looked forward to had the marriage continued.

In *Leadbeater v Leadbeater*[4] it was held that 25 per cent should be discounted from the sum that was thought appropriate to meet the wife's reasonable needs since the marriage had been short, lasting only four years. It is tempting to say that what is important is the length of cohabitation rather than the length of the marriage.[5] In *Krystman v Krystman*[6] no order was made at all when the parties had cohabited for only a fortnight at the beginning of a marriage which had taken place 26 years earlier. It should be noted, however, that the wife had made no claim on the husband during the intervening period, and a number of cases have laid down the principle that, if the wife delays making a claim for financial provision without reason so as to lull the husband into assuming that she will not do so, he is entitled to arrange his financial affairs accordingly and the court is

---

[20] Cf *Attwood v Attwood* [1968] P 591, 595, [1968] 3 All ER 385, 388.
[1] See *Khan v Khan* [1980] 1 All ER 497; *Taylor v Taylor* (1974) 119 Sol Jo 30; *Warder v Warder* (1978) 122 Sol Jo 713; *West v West* [1978] Fam 1, [1977] 2 All ER 705, CA. In *Browne v Pritchard* [1975] 3 All ER 721, CA, the wife's half share in the matrimonial home (to the purchase of which she had contributed nothing) was reduced to a third after a marriage which lasted only three years.
[2] *Whyte-Smith v Whyte-Smith* (1974) 5 Fam Law 20 (separation after three months; breakdown caused wife illness and loss of job); *Abdureman v Abdureman* (1978) 122 Sol Jo 663 (separation after 12 weeks; wife had given up job and lost pension on marriage).
[3] [1977] Fam 127, [1977] 1 All ER 56, CA.
[4] [1985] FLR 789.
[5] See generally Deech *Financial Relief: The Retreat from Precedent and Principle* 98 LQR 621, 630–632.
[6] [1973] 3 All ER 247, CA.

unlikely to make any order in her favour.[7] This, of course, is a matter for the court's discretion. There is no limitation period applicable to section 23(1) of the Matrimonial Causes Act 1973, which enables a court to order financial relief on the grant of a decree or *at any time thereafter*. Subject only to the procedural rules which require, prima facie, that the application for financial relief be contained in the divorce petition,[8] a party may come back to court at any time to seek an additional order or an amendment of an award already made. The existence of inexcusable or inordinate delay will not of itself oust the court's jurisdiction, nor will it prevent the court, in the exercise of its discretion, from at least considering an application.[9] A more difficult problem arises if the parties cohabited before the marriage. Obviously this cannot be taken into account under this heading, but it may be relevant under the general requirement that the court should have regard to all the circumstances of the case. Two different situations have to be considered. If the spouses lived together from choice simply because they could not be bothered 'to get round to the paper work' of going through a ceremony of marriage, their cohabitation will generally be disregarded in determining financial provision. Marital rights and duties do not begin before the celebration and it would cheapen marriage to permit such a wife to take advantage of the earlier relationship.[10] This must be distinguished from the case where the parties could not get married because one of them was unable to obtain a divorce, particularly if they lived together for a long time before the marriage and there were children of the union. This occurred in *Kokosinski v Kokosinski*.[11] The husband was a Polish refugee who had lived in this country since the Second World War. He started to live with the petitioner in 1947 and a son was born in 1950. He could not marry her until his first wife (who was still living in Poland) divorced him, which she did not do until 1969. In the meantime the petitioner had been loving, faithful and hardworking, had brought up their child and had played a substantial part in building up the husband's business. The parties married in 1971 but separated in the following year. Wood J was of the opinion that in these circumstances it would offend a reasonable person's sense of justice to ignore this long period of cohabitation and took it into account in deciding what order to make. A similar problem arose in *Chaterjee v Chaterjee*,[12] where the parties lived together for 12 or 13 years *after* being divorced. Following their final separation the wife pursued a claim for financial relief. It was held that this cohabitation was akin to marriage for

---

[7] *Potts v Potts* (1976) 6 Fam Law 217, CA (delay of five years); *Foster v Foster* (1977) 7 Fam Law 112, CA (divorce 23 years after separation); *Chambers v Chambers* (1979) 1 FLR 10 (divorce after 21 years after separation). See also *S v S (Financial Provision)* [1990] 2 FLR 252, CA where a wife, who delayed her application for 9 years after the divorce, was not to be treated as if the divorce had just been obtained.

[8] Ante, p 724. Or answer if the petition is defended.

[9] *Twiname v Twiname* [1992] 1 FLR 29, CA.

[10] *Campbell v Campbell* [1976] Fam 347, [1977] 1 All ER 1. Cf *Gojkovic v Gojkovic* [1992] Fam 40, [1990] 2 All ER 84, where the substantial award to the wife was in large part based upon her outstanding contribution to the family business and much of her effort was made during pre-marital cohabitation.

[11] [1980] Fam 72, [1980] 1 All ER 1106. The facts are not dissimilar from those which would entitle a cohabitant to an order under the Inheritance (Provision for Family and Dependants) Act 1975 after the man's death. (See post, p 825).

[12] [1976] Fam 199, [1976] 1 All ER 719, CA.

this purpose and consequently that the court could deal with property acquired since the divorce. It must be emphasised, however, that it is only in the somewhat unusual circumstances of cases like these that cohabitation outside marriage (whether before or after) is likely to affect the order made.

(e) '... any physical or mental disability of either of the parties to the marriage'

(f) '... the contributions which each of the parties has made or is likely in the foreseeable future to make to the welfare of the family, including any contribution by looking after the home or caring for the family'

It is expressly provided that this is to include any contribution made by looking after the home or caring for the family,[13] but it could no doubt include a financial contribution as well.[14] Although this principle enables the court to recognise the exceptional contribution of a spouse to the family business,[15] it was primarily introduced to give the wife credit for her contribution in kind as housekeeper, wife and mother.[16] Before 1971 the courts were taking this into account to a limited extent, but their hands were partly tied by their restricted powers to make adjustments to rights in property. The result was that a wife who continued to work and hired domestic help was usually in a better position than the wife who stayed at home and did the job herself because her indirect contribution to the acquisition of the matrimonial home might well give her an equitable interest in it. There seem to be few cases where the court has expressly given the wife a larger award because of her contribution to the welfare of the family,[17] but there can be little doubt that this fact is taken into account when, for example, she is given more than a one-third interest in the matrimonial home. Conversely in *H v H*[18] a wife who had left her husband for another man after 15 years of married life and bringing up four children was given a smaller award on the ground that she had 'left the job unfinished'. The enjoinder to consider what contributions each party is likely to make in the foreseeable future was introduced as a result of the amendment by the Matrimonial and Family Proceedings Act 1984, section 3. It is intended to emphasise in particular the continuing role a parent (usually the mother) may have in looking after any children of the family. As such, it may be a useful counter weight to any contention that there should be a 'clean break' order.

---

[13] In *Kokosinski v Kokosinkski* (supra), Wood J was of the opinion (at 1115) that this referred only to contributions made after the marriage had taken place. The point is of little importance as any pre-marital contribution will be taken into account (if at all) under the heading of 'all the circumstances of the case': see supra.

[14] So held by Ormrod LJ in *P v P* [1978] 3 All ER 70, 74, CA. Normally this would form part of the parties' property, but this would not be the case if for some reason the capital had disappeared.

[15] *Gojkovic v Gojkovic* [1992] Fam 40, [1990] 2 All ER 84, CA.

[16] See eg *Duxbury v Duxbury* [1992] Fam 62n, [1990] 2 All ER 77, CA (wife who had done 'everything expected of her as wife and mother' entitled to have reasonable requirements recognised by the court).

[17] But see *Brisdion v Brisdion* (1974) 5 Fam Law 92, CA.

[18] [1975] Fam 9, [1975] 1 All ER 367. Cf *West v West* [1978] Fam 1, [1977] 2 All ER 705, CA.

(g) '... the conduct of each of the parties, if that conduct is such that it would in the opinion of the court be inequitable to disregard it'[19]

The extent to which the court should take a spouse's conduct during the marriage into account when assessing the order should be made, is understandably an emotionally charged issue. Yet even before 1971, when the substantive law was based upon the concept of matrimonial fault, there had been a tendency by the courts, when hearing undefended cases, to place much less stress on the technical finding of innocence or guilt in the decree. When irretrievable breakdown became the sole ground for divorce in 1971, conduct arguably became of much less significance. However, even under the post-1971 law, the courts have always been empowered to take conduct into account in assessing what orders should be made, but the specific enjoinder to do so under section 25(2)(g), cited above, is the result of an amendment made under the Matrimonial and Family Proceedings Act 1984, section 3. At the time of its enactment there was considerable controversy as to whether the new provision had altered the previous law, and to appreciate the arguments it will be necessary to examine the law as it stood before the implementation of the 1984 Act.

(i) The law before the 1984 reform

Under the Matrimonial Causes Act 1973, section 25, as originally enacted, the court was directed, inter alia, to exercise its powers so:

'... to place the parties, so far as it is practicable and, *having regard to their conduct just to do so*, in the financial position in which they would have been if the marriage had not broken down and each had properly discharged his or her financial obligation and responsibilities towards the other.'[20]

It soon became apparent that 'conduct' should not often be taken into account. The basic principle was established in the leading case of *Wachtel v Wachtel*[1] in which Lord Denning MR, delivering the judgment of the court, said:[2]

'It has been suggested that there should be a "discount" or "reduction" in what the wife is to receive because of her supposed misconduct, guilt or blame (whatever word is used). We cannot accept this argument. In the vast majority of cases it is repugnant to the principles underlying the new legislation... There will be many cases in which a wife (though once considered guilty or blameworthy) will have cared for the home and looked after the family for many years. Is she to be deprived of the benefit otherwise to be accorded to her by section [25(1)(f)] because she may share responsibility for the breakdown with her husband? There will no doubt be a residue of cases where the conduct of one of the parties is ... "both obvious and gross", so much so that to order one party to support another whose conduct falls into this category is repugnant to anyone's sense of justice. In such a case the court remains free to decline to afford financial support or to reduce the support which it would otherwise have ordered. But, short of cases falling into this category, the court should not reduce its order for financial

---

[19] See generally Lowe *Conduct Unbecoming—Advising Clients in the Light of the 'Conduct' Provisions in the Matrimonial and Family Proceedings Act 1984* (1985) 1 Professional Negligence 61.
[20] Emphasis added.
[1] [1973] Fam 72, [1973] 1 All ER 829, CA.
[2] At 90 and 835–836, respectively.

provision merely because of what was formerly regarded as guilt or blame. To do so would be to impose a fine for supposed misbehaviour in the course of an unhappy married life... In the financial adjustments consequent upon the dissolution of a marriage which has irretrievably broken down, the imposition of financial penalties ought seldom to find a place.'

In *Harnett v Harnett* Bagnall J commented:[3]

'In my view to satisfy the test the conduct must be obvious and gross in the sense that the party concerned must be plainly seen to have wilfully persisted in conduct, or a course of conduct, calculated to destroy the marriage in circumstances in which the party is substantially blameless.'

In the Court of Appeal in the same case Cairns LJ said:[4]

'Conduct should be taken into account only in a very broad way—that is to say, only where there is something in the conduct of one party which would make it quite inequitable to leave that out of account having regard to the conduct of the other party as well in the course of the marriage.'

In brief, conduct will not affect the order made unless it would be offensive to one's sense of justice to ignore it.[5]

In view of the above comments it is hardly surprising that conduct was rarely taken into account.[6] Matrimonial misconduct such as adultery was usually ignored[7] as were 'brief periods of callous unkindness or brutality'.[8] But of course there were some cases where conduct was held to be relevant. Amongst reported cases the wife's share was reduced where she had accepted a half share of the matrimonial home whilst carrying on an adulterous affair,[9] where she had fired a shotgun at her husband,[10] and where she had twice wounded her husband and damaged his career by her behaviour.[11] In all these cases the conduct was morally blameworthy, but in *West v West*[12] it was held that 'obvious and gross conduct' was not confined to misconduct in the moral sense but covered conduct which was of great importance to the marriage. In that case the wife refused to live in the house which the husband had purchased with her agreement and returned to her parents' home immediately after the marriage. The parties cohabited for only seven weeks in the five years which elapsed before the husband petitioned for divorce. The reason for the wife's misconduct was that she was unable to break away from her own family and 'to cross the threshold into marriage in any effective sense'. The Court of Appeal was unanimously of the opinion that it was 'obvious and gross' and upheld the judge's award of periodical payments to bring her income up to one-eighth rather than one-third of

[3] [1973] Fam 156, 165, [1973] 2 All ER 593, 601.
[4] [1974] 1 All ER 764, 767–768, CA.
[5] Per Orr LJ in *Jones v Jones* [1976] Fam 8, 15, [1975] 2 All ER 12, 17, CA. See also *Armstrong v Armstrong* (1974) 4 Fam Law 156, CA.
[6] See Barrington, Baker et al, op cit, paras 2.19–2.23.
[7] See eg *Trippas v Trippas* [1973] Fam 134, [1973] 2 All ER 1, CA, and *Harnett v Harnett*, supra.
[8] *Griffiths v Griffiths* [1974] 1 All ER 932.
[9] *Cuzner v Underdown* [1974] 2 All ER 351, CA (wife ordered to transfer the half share to husband).
[10] *Armstrong v Armstrong* (1974) 4 Fam Law 156, CA (wife's share reduced to a quarter). A comparison of this case with the last suggests that the courts look more leniently on a wife who intends to inflict serious injury on a husband than on one who is unfaithful!
[11] *Bateman v Bateman* [1979] Fam 25, [1979] 2 WLR 377.
[12] [1978] Fam 1, [1977] 2 All ER 705, CA.

their joint incomes. Similarly, conduct may be taken into account even though it is due to the party's mental illness if it is of sufficient gravity to affect the issue after making allowances for the cause.[13]

Some decisions did give rise to speculation whether conduct was becoming more important. In *Blezard v Blezard*,[14] for instance, Lawton LJ said that it would be gross conduct on the husband's part if he went off with another woman and that in these circumstances the wife's standard of living should not fall as far as the husband's if he has brought about a situation where both will have to be reduced. Had that dictum been followed, much of the old law relating to the 'guilty spouse' could well have been reintroduced. In another case *Robinson v Robinson*[15] the Court of Appeal upheld the decision that a wife who had become disenchanted with army life and who had deserted her husband whilst he was serving in Belize was 'guilty' of conduct that should be taken into account. On the face of it, if simple desertion can constitute relevant conduct then *Robinson* would have opened the floodgates but in fact the Court of Appeal stressed that the case was 'exceptional' because the husband had been 'blameless'.

Despite these cases, in general, conduct seemed rarely to have been taken into account.[16]

(ii) The current position

In his evidence to the Special Standing Committee, the President of the Family Division said of the new provision:[17]

'In case some attempt were made to argue that the new provision enlarged the extent to which conduct should be taken into account I do not anticipate that this would be likely to be the subject of more than one appeal in the judgment of which I would expect it to be firmly rejected.'

Others[18] felt that the new provision represented a change in emphasis and that it was likely to be seen as a signal to the courts to pay a much greater regard to matrimonial conduct. They shared the view of Lord Denning[19] that the courts would have to inquire into the conduct of the parties before it could be said whether or not it was inequitable to disregard it.

It could also have been said that now that conduct stands as a separate circumstance to which the court must 'in particular' have regard, not only does it have a higher profile than before (though that was the necessary

---

[13] *J (HD) v J (AM)* [1980] 1 All ER 156 (repeated molestation of husband by schizophrenic wife taken into account). Cf Matrimonial Causes Act 1973, s 1(2)(b), discussed ante, pp 192–199.

[14] (1978) 9 Fam Law 249, CA. Orr LJ came to the same decision without mentioning conduct. See Berkovits 10 Fam Law 164.

[15] [1983] Fam 42, [1983] 1 All ER 391, CA. This was a maintenance application under the Domestic Proceedings and Magistrates' Courts Act 1978.

[16] Though there were those, see eg Levin [1984] LAG 101–3 who believed that there had been a shift of emphasis. See also *Kokosinski v Kokosinski* [1980] Fam 72, [1980] 1 All ER 1106 where 'good' conduct was taken into account. Cf *E v E (Financial Provision)* [1990] 2 FLR 233 where the wife's adultery and disengagement from family life amounted to a 'negative contribution' which was taken into account.

[17] HC Official Report, cols 77–78, 22nd March 1984. See also Cretney's submission at cols 68, 69.

[18] Notably the Law Society: see their evidence to the Special Standing Committee at cols 206–207.

[19] 445 HL Official Report, col 967, 1983–4.

drafting consequence of the removal of the 'tail piece' of the original section 25) but it has been given greater statutory emphasis. In the event, however, there seems to have been no change in practice. In one reported case, *Anthony v Anthony*,[20] where the trial judge took conduct into account because, in his view, the wife 'broke up the marriage', the Court of Appeal held that there was nothing in her conduct of such a serious nature to justify any reliance upon it. In *Leadbeater v Leadbeater*,[1] conduct was again dismissed as an issue in part because the spouses' conduct cancelled each other out but mainly because the judge did not think it inequitable to ignore it. The leading recent authority in *Kyte v Kyte*[2] where the husband suffered from manic depression, which caused the wife suffering and unhappiness. On several occasions, the husband tried, unsuccessfully, to commit suicide. The registrar found that on one of these occasions the wife (who knew she stood to inherit on the husband's death) did nothing to stop him. On another, she provided drugs and alcohol to facilitate the attempt. The wife had also formed 'a deceitful relationship' with another man. In the Court of Appeal, Purchas LJ (giving the judgment of the court) said[3] that the court must look at the whole picture including conduct during the marriage and after the marriage[4] which might or might not have contributed to the breakdown. Although the parties may not each have been blameless, a spouse should only be penalised where the imbalance of conduct, one way or the other, would make it inequitable it ignore the comparative conduct of the parties. On this basis, the wife's behaviour (even when considered in the context of the husband's) was gross and obvious and so her lump sum award was reduced from £14,000 to just £5,000. In the later case of *Evans v Evans*[5] (where conduct would surely have been relevant whatever approach was adopted) the Court of Appeal upheld the discharge of a periodical payment order in favour of a wife when she was convicted of inciting others to kill her husband. The test propounded in *Kyte v Kyte*, in terms of the 'comparability' of the spouses' behaviour, has recently been applied in *K v K (Financial Provision)*.[6] Here the wife had made great efforts to improve herself in contrast to the husband who had failed to make adequate efforts to find employment and had a serious drink problem which resulted in disagreeable behaviour and his neglect of the matrimonial home. The lump sum payable to the husband was reduced.

---

[20] [1986] 2 FLR 353, CA.

[1] [1985] FLR 789. Cf *Suter v Suter and Jones* [1987] Fam 111, [1987] 2 All ER 336, CA, where there is some suggestion that introducing a lover into the former matrimonial home could be taken into account under s 25(2)(g), but cf *Duxbury v Duxbury* [1992] Fam 62n, [1990] 2 All ER 77, CA, where Ackner LJ said that applying s 25 is essentially a 'financial not a moral exercise'. In *Atkinson v Atkinson* [1988] Fam 93, [1987] 3 All ER 849, CA it was said that, in general, a former spouse's cohabitation with a third party after divorce is to be disregarded since the court ought not to impose an unjustifiable fetter on the freedom of the former spouses to live their lives as they chose. On the other hand, the court did suggest that there may be cases where the conduct of a former spouse in the context of cohabitation, such as financial or sexual or other conduct, may mean that it cannot be ignored.

[2] [1988] Fam 145, [1987] 3 All ER 1041, CA.

[3] At 155 and 1048 respectively.

[4] See *B v B (Real Property: Assessment of Interests)* [1988] 2 FLR 490 where a wife's behaviour after divorce (deceitful behaviour in relation to discovery) was held to be conduct which it would be inequitable to disregard.

[5] [1989] 1 FLR 351, CA.

[6] [1990] 2 FLR 225.

In general terms, it seems that the current position is that conduct is only rarely relevant and even then it is questionable whether it is in a party's interest to pursue it since it is likely to be contested and in consequence, of course, the costs will be higher.

(h) 'in the case of proceedings for divorce or nullity of marriage, the value to each of the parties to the marriage of any benefit (for example, a pension) which, by reason of the dissolution or annulment of the marriage, that party will lose the chance of acquiring'[7]

The obvious example of such a benefit (which the Act specifies) is a pension which can no longer enure for the benefit of the wife as the husband's widow. Another right which the divorced wife loses is that of claiming social security benefits by virtue of her husband's contributions. These problems were made more acute by the passing of the Divorce Reform Act which permits a husband to divorce his wife even though he has been wholly to blame for the breakdown of the marriage; before 1971 an innocent wife could take these potential losses into account before deciding whether to take proceedings for divorce. It is clearly difficult to assess the value of the benefit lost. Not only are there many imponderables (some of which, such as the expectation of life of each spouse, can be actuarially assessed) but in many pension schemes the benefits are held on discretionary trusts which the widow could not claim as of right. In days of inflation the purchase of an annuity for the wife will not give her protection (even if the husband has sufficient assets to make the necessary payment) when his pension will depend upon his final salary, particularly if it is also linked to the cost of living. If the husband has capital, the best solution may be to make an order for secured periodical payments which can be varied from time to time and will also continue if he predeceases his former wife. The truth is that it is virtually impossible to give adequate compensation to a woman who would have depended largely on a widow's pension or retirement pension for her support on her husband's death.[8]

Another example of a lost benefit is to be seen in *Trippas v Trippas*.[9] After the parties had separated, the husband received a considerable sum from the sale of a family business. The court awarded the wife a lump sum of £10,000 on the ground that, had the marriage still been on foot, she would have received such a benefit either directly in cash or indirectly in kind; furthermore the husband could have been expected to leave her a large sum if he had predeceased her, so that she had lost something analogous to a pension.

---

[7] See *Occupational Pension Rights in Divorce* (a Lord Chancellor's Department Consultation Paper); Davies and Joshi *Pensions in Divorce* [1992] Fam Law 1; Ellison *Pensions in Divorce* Parts I–IV [1991] Fam Law 252, 289, 346, and 398.

[8] Cf ante, pp 214–218 (grave financial hardship caused by divorce). A wife aged 50 or over when the decree is absolute will be able to claim a state retirement benefit by virtue of her husband's contributions: see ibid.

[9] [1973] Fam 134, [1973] 2 All ER 1, CA. See also *Kokosinski v Kokosinski* [1980] Fam 72, [1980] 1 All ER 1106. This approach is open to criticism on the ground that the express limitation of the operation of this paragraph to cases of divorce and nullity implies that the chance of acquiring the benefit must be lost as a result of the dissolution or annulment and not as the result of the breakdown of the marriage: see *O'Donnell v O'Donnell* [1976] Fam 83, 89–90, [1975] 2 All ER 993, 996, CA. If this is correct, the husband's increased capital could still have been taken into account as part of his resources.

3. THE MATRIMONIAL HOME[10]

We have already noticed that the matrimonial home presents particular problems. In many cases it will be the only asset of any value owned by either spouse. It may be the only means of giving one of the spouses (whom, for the sake of argument, we shall assume to be the wife) the security of a home with the children in the future. Consequently the parties' interests will often be in direct conflict: the wife will wish to be given the right to occupy the house, whilst the husband will want an immediate sale so as to realise his capital, without which he may be unable to buy another home for his second family. Faced with this, the court's first concern must be to ensure that the children (and therefore the spouse with whom the children are living) have a home.[11] It should certainly do its utmost to avoid ordering a sale of the matrimonial home if this will merely result in having to rehouse the party in occupation.[12]

Once the children's accommodation has been secured, the court must try to make an order which will give the other spouse (or both spouses, if there are no children) a home as well. In many cases this will be impossible because, if the house is sold and the proceeds divided, there will not be sufficient to enable either of them to buy anything else. A temporary solution is to defer the sale of the house until the children have left home so that the parent with whom they have been living can reasonably be expected to move into smaller accommodation. By that time, of course, she (or he) may find it difficult to raise a mortgage, and if it is impossible to find a way of giving them both a home, either immediately or in the future, the court will have no alternative to leaving one of them in occupation indefinitely. This occurred in *Martin v Martin*.[13] The husband had gone to live with another woman in a council house of which the latter was the tenant and which would apparently be transferred to them both jointly. The wife was left alone in the former matrimonial home which belonged to both spouses beneficially in equal shares. The Court of Appeal affirmed the judge's order that the house should be held on trust for the wife during her life, or until her remarriage or such earlier date as she should cease to live there and thereafter on trust for them both in equal shares. The husband was already provided with another home and consequently had no need of the capital; the wife on the other hand would have been unable to purchase alternative accommodation with her half share of the capital and so an immediate sale would have deprived her of the modest comfortable home that she had before the marriage broke down.[14]

We must now consider the various ways in which the court may use the wide range of powers that it has at its disposal.

[10] See generally Jackson *Matrimonial Finance and Taxation* (5th Edn by Jackson and Davies) ch 15 and Hayes and Battersby *Property Adjustment: Order or Disorder in the Former Matrimonial Home?* [1985] Fam Law 213 and Hayes and Battersby *Property Adjustment: Further Thoughts on Charge Orders* [1986] Fam Law 142.
[11] *Browne v Pritchard* [1975] 3 All ER 721, 724, CA; *Scott v Scott* [1978] 3 All ER 65, CA.
[12] See eg *Ross v Ross* [1989] 2 FLR 257, CA.
[13] [1978] Fam 12, [1977] 3 All ER 762, CA. Cf *Eshak v Nowojewski* (1980) 11 Fam Law 115, CA. (Sale deferred until death of husband who had custody of children and was unable to work. Wife had remarried and her second husband was catering for her needs.)
[14] The implications for legally aided parties of the Legal Aid Board's statutory charge (discussed ante, p 746) must not be overlooked.

(1) It may force the wife to buy out the husband's interest by ordering him to transfer his share to her and ordering her to pay him a lump sum equal to its value. This is the ideal solution because she retains a roof over her head and he gets the immediate use of his money. Obviously, however, such an order can be made only if the wife has sufficient capital or, alternatively, a large enough income to pay the sum in instalments,[15] and consequently it is not likely to be met often in practice. If, however, the husband does not need the capital immediately, the payment can be deferred until the house is sold.

(2) The court can order the husband to transfer his share of the home to the wife without any compensating payment on her part. There are a number of quite dissimilar situations in which this may offer the best solution. If the house forms only part of the capital assets which have to be apportioned, it may be transferred to the wife in part or complete extinction of her claim for a lump sum or other capital settlement. Again, if the husband is a rich man, the wife might take the house as representing the capitalisation of part, or all of her claim for periodical payments which will be proportionately reduced or, in a suitable case, discharged altogether, thereby achieving an 'immediate' clean break. It might also be felt desirable to capitalise periodical payments if the husband's past behaviour indicated that any other order might prove to be ineffective.[16] At the other end of the economic scale, if the husband's earnings are so small that it will be impossible for him to make an adequate contribution towards the support of the wife and children of the family, the only possible solution might be to transfer the matrimonial home to her unconditionally and make no order, or only a minimal order, against him for periodical payments. This occurred, for example, in *S v S*,[17] where the husband was ordered to pay a total of £4 a week for his wife and daughter and to transfer his half share in the matrimonial home to the former. This may prove to be much more valuable to the wife than a relatively greater order for periodical payments if she can claim income support because the value of the house will not be taken into account in assessing the benefit payable. Even if the parties are not at either extreme of the economic spectrum, the particular circumstances may make it necessary to order a transfer of the matrimonial home without payment, but with a compensating reduction in periodical payments, as the only way of ensuring that either of them has a home. In *Hanlon v Hanlon*[18] the husband was a police officer who, since separating from his wife, was living rent-free in a police house. On his retirement he could expect a lump sum payment of up to £7,000. The wife was living in the matrimonial home with the two sons of the marriage (then both apprentices over the age of 18) and the two daughters, who were still at school. The most that the parties could expect from the sale of the house was £10,000[19] which, if divided equally, would give neither of them enough to buy any other accommodation. In these circumstances the Court of Appeal ordered that the

---

[15] The house itself could be used as security for the instalments.
[16] As in *Bryant v Bryant* (1976) 6 Fam Law 108, CA.
[17] [1976] Fam 18n, [1975] 2 All ER 19n.
[18] [1978] 2 All ER 889, CA.
[19] In point of fact, because of (what was then) the Law Society's legal aid charge for costs this expectation was considerably reduced: see the later case of *Hanlon v Law Society* [1981] AC 124, [1980] 2 All ER 199, HL; discussed ante, p 747.

husband's half share should be transferred to the wife in return for which she was prepared to forgo any further periodical payments for the two girls.

A transfer of the husband's interests without compensation might also be appropriate if his conduct justified the extinction of his share.[20] In conjunction with other facts this order has also been made when the wife's earning capacity has been so seriously impaired that she is in greater need of security than usual: in *Jones v Jones*[1] this was the result of the husband's conduct in inflicting an injury on her, and in *S v S*[2] of having to nurse a young daughter suffering from kidney trouble.

Two further points should be borne in mind which may be of particular importance when dealing with the property of less affluent spouses. In the first place, it will be recalled that on divorce or nullity (but not judicial separation) the court may make an order transferring a protected statutory, secure or assured tenancy from one spouse to the other.[3] Secondly, like any other lease, a council tenancy is 'property' for the purpose of section 24 of the Matrimonial Causes Act and the court may therefore make an order in relation to it.[4] The court must use its powers under the Matrimonial Homes Act 1983 (except on judicial separation) because, as the order cannot take effect until after the decree absolute, the wife could no longer be a qualified successor and therefore the tenancy could not be assigned to her.[5]

(3) The order may provide that both spouses shall keep or acquire an interest in the house as equitable tenants in common, which will involve settling it on them on trust for sale (if it is not already so held), but that the sale should be deferred until some specified time in the future. In the meantime the wife will be given exclusive possession. Such an order enables both spouses to keep their interest in the capital but also resolves the immediate problem of accommodation for the wife and the children. For some years, perhaps the commonest type of order made was referred to as a *Mesher* order.[6] Here, it was normal to order that the sale of the property should not take place until the youngest child reached a specified age (often 17) or, perhaps, until all the children completed their education, or until the wife died, or until further order.[7] Although frequently made in practice, *Mesher* orders have a number of defects and have been heavily criticised by the courts.[8]

In the first place, the husband and wife will have to act together to effect the sale, perhaps many years after the divorce, and this may cause difficulties,

---

[20] See *Bryant v Bryant* (supra); *S v S* (infra).

[1] [1976] Fam 8, [1975] 2 All ER 12, CA. See Ellis 39 MLR 97.

[2] [1976] Fam 18n, [1975] 2 All ER 19n followed in *Jones v Jones* (supra).

[3] Under s 7 of the Matrimonial Homes Act 1983. See ante, p 640.

[4] *Thompson v Thompson* [1976] Fam 25, [1975] 2 All ER 208, CA. Cf *Hale v Hale* [1975] 2 All ER 1090, CA.

[5] Unless the lease was granted before 5 November 1982, in which case she could not be a secure tenant: see ante, pp 638–639.

[6] From the name of the case in which such an order was made, *Mesher v Mesher and Hall* (1973) reported [1980] 1 All ER 126n, CA.

[7] It is important that the court should retain the power of ordering an earlier sale in case the wife remarries or some unforeseen event occurs. See further post, p 793. The power of sale should not be automatically exercisable on the wife's remarriage because it may still be necessary to give her protection until the children have ceased to be dependants.

[8] See eg *Hanlon v Hanlon* [1978] 2 All ER 889 at 892–893, CA, per Ormrod LJ; *Carson v Carson* [1983] 1 All ER 478 at 482–483, CA, per Ormrod LJ; and *Harman v Glencross* [1986] Fam 81, [1986] 1 All ER 545, 556, CA per Balcombe LJ.

particularly if their relationship is bitter.[9] Secondly, children often do not leave home until long after they have completed their education and may therefore still need the house as their home. Thirdly, being 'property transfer orders' they are not variable even if, for example, the husband reneges on his obligation to make periodical payments.[10] Finally, and perhaps most significantly, a *Mesher* order may lead to a wife being thrown on the housing market in middle age, after her children have left home, without the capital or income to secure adequate alternative accommodation for herself. In short, as Parker LJ said in *Mortimer v Mortimer-Griffin*,[11] such orders are likely to produce harsh and unsatisfactory results. There may be exceptional cases where the *Mesher* order continues to produce the best solution,[12] but where there is doubt as to a wife's ability to rehouse herself, then a *Mesher* order should not be made.[13]

A rather different order, in effect, if not in form, is the *Martin* order named after the case discussed earlier.[14] As with the *Mesher* order, the matrimonial home is settled upon the spouses on trust for sale for themselves as beneficial tenants in common. However, the contingent events specified in the order as triggering a sale are designed to ensure that the wife remains in occupation of the house for as long as she needs a roof over her head. In *Harvey v Harvey*,[15] for example, the court ordered the sale to be postponed until the wife's death or remarriage, or until she voluntarily left home or became dependent upon another man. In *Clutton v Clutton*[16] the Court of Appeal gave its approval to a *Martin* order in a slightly different form. The sale was to take place on the death, remarriage or cohabitation of the wife whereupon the proceeds were to be divided, two-thirds to the wife and one-third to the husband. The court held that a *Martin* order in these terms did not suffer from the same disadvantages as a *Mesher* order as far as the occupying spouse was concerned. Nor did it offend against the clean break principle which ought not to mean that one of the spouses was to be deprived of any share in an asset acquired by the joint efforts of both. The wife had argued that the effect of the order would be to make her subject to 'perpetual supervision' by the husband, who would be anxious to establish cohabitation and trigger a sale. While accepting the force of this argument, Lloyd LJ[17] suggested that the bitterness the wife might feel on being 'spied on' was far outweighed by the bitterness the husband would feel if the wife, despite her present assertions, soon remarried or cohabited and continued to occupy the former matrimonial home.

---

[9] For problems relating to the need for repairs to the house: see *Harvey v Harvey* [1987] 1 FLR 67. But see *Teschner v Teschner* [1985] FLR 627, CA.

[10] As in *Carson v Carson*, supra. See also *Dinch v Dinch* [1987] 1 All ER 818, HL.

[11] [1986] 2 FLR 315 at 319, CA.

[12] See eg *Rushton v Rushton* (1978) 1 FLR 195, CA, where Ormrod LJ said that the right order 'for once' seemed to be a *Mesher* order.

[13] *Clutton v Clutton* [1991] 1 All ER 340 at 346, CA (per Lloyd LJ). A similar approach can be seen, by way of analogy in *Greenham v Greenham* [1989] 1 FLR 105, CA where it was said to be 'wrong' to order a husband to sell his home, and pay a lump sum to wife, on his attaining the age of 70. The Court of Appeal varied the order to provide for a lump sum to be payable on the husband's death or on the earlier sale of the property.

[14] See ante, p 785.

[15] [1982] Fam 83, [1982] 1 All ER 693, CA. See also *Brown v Brown* (1981) 3 FLR 161, CA.

[16] [1991] 1 All ER 340, CA.

[17] Ibid at 344 and 345.

(4) As an alternative to (3), the court may order the husband to transfer his interest to the wife and give him a charge on the house equal to the value of his share.[18] As in (3), the charge should not be realised until the wife no longer needs to live in the house and it can be sold. This solution is to be preferred because the husband will not have to concur in the sale and the spouses can make a clean break.[19] His charge should represent a given fraction of the value of the house at the time of the sale;[20] if it is fixed by reference to its present value, the sum which the husband will eventually receive will not have increased to take account of inflation.[1]

(5) The possibility of settling the house for the benefit of the wife and children[2] appears to be little used in practice. It would usually involve giving the wife a life interest with remainder to children and consequently will rarely provide the best solution because neither spouse will ever have the use of the capital and, save in exceptional circumstances, the court does not make an order providing for children after they have completed their education or training.[3]

(6) The court could leave the whole beneficial interest in the house with the husband and give the wife exclusive occupation until she no longer needs the security of the house to bring up the children (for example, until all the children have completed their full-time education) or until further order. This will of course in the end leave her homeless and consequently should be used only if she will be able to make provision for her own accommodation when her right to occupation comes to an end or if the circumstances are such that she should be given no part of the capital value. It may also be necessary to make such an order if the husband has no power to assign the matrimonial home so that the court cannot order it to be transferred or settled.[4] There is apparently no power to make an order relating to occupation alone under the Matrimonial Causes Act 1973, and a wife seeking such an order would have to apply for it under section 17 of the Married Women's Property Act 1882 or ask the court to continue her right of occupation under the Matrimonial Homes Act 1983 after the dissolution or annulment of the marriage.[5]

---

[18] Although such orders appear to be frequently made in practice there is no express statutory power in the Matrimonial Causes Act 1973, Part II to *order* a spouse to execute a charge over the former matrimonial home, or *impose* a charge on property ordered to be transferred from one spouse to another. However, it appears such orders can be effected by imposing conditions on the exercise of the express powers in ss 21–24A (eg H can be ordered to *transfer* Whiteacre to W *upon condition* W executes a charge in favour of H) or, alternatively, they can be incorporated into consent orders formulated as undertakings given to the court following *Livesey (formerly Jenkins) v Jenkins* [1985] AC 424, [1985] 1 All ER 106, HL. See further, Bird *Problems in Ancillary Relief Orders* [1990] Fam Law 420.
[19] Cf *Schuller v Schuller* [1990] 2 FLR 193, CA where, on the facts, the court refused to order a deferred charge which was to be enforceable on the death of the elderly husband or on earlier sale of the property. Butler-Sloss LJ said (at 199) that such an order would 'fly in the face of the duty upon the court to try, wherever possible, to create a clean break'.
[20] As in *Browne v Pritchard* [1975] 3 All ER 721, CA. See also *H v H* [1975] Fam 9, [1975] 1 All ER 367.
[1] Such an order was made in *Hector v Hector* [1973] 3 All ER 1070, CA but was regarded as out of line by Latey J in *Smith v Smith* [1976] Fam 18n, 21, [1975] 2 All ER 19n, 21.
[2] Cf *Wachtel v Wachtel* [1973] Fam 72, 96, [1973] 1 All ER 829, CA, where Lord Denning MR referred to settling a lump sum.
[3] *Chamberlain v Chamberlain* [1974] 1 All ER 33, CA, allowing an appeal against such an order, and *Kiely v Kiely* [1988] 1 FLR 248, CA.
[4] See ante, p 737.
[5] See ante, pp 567–569 (Married Women's Property Act) and 613 (Matrimonial Homes Act). An application under the former may be made for three years after dissolution or annulment

(7) The court could order the house to be sold[6] and the proceeds to be divided in such proportions as it thinks fit. This might be the best way of dealing with the situation if there were no children living at home and the house was too big for either spouse to live in alone. The money should be sufficient to give at least one of them (and preferably both) enough to put down as a deposit on the purchase of a new house or flat. This solution is not appropriate if its effect would be to deprive both of them of a home.

If there is any danger that the husband will try to dispose of the home before an order is made, the wife's simplest remedy before decree absolute is to register her right of occupation as a Class F land charge under the Land Charges Act 1972 or, in the case of registered land, by notice under the Land Registration Act 1925; alternatively she could apply to have the husband restrained from selling it on the ground that the disposition would defeat her claim for financial relief.[7] A further problem arises if the house is subject to a mortgage (as will often be the case). If the husband is to continue to pay the instalments, in theory any periodical payments should be reduced by the amount of interest repaid (which can be regarded as equivalent to rent)[8] whilst he ought to be given an enlarged share of the proceeds of sale representing the capital repaid. This would involve highly complex calculations and constant variations of periodical payments as a progressively larger fraction of the instalments represented the repayment of capital; in practice, therefore, the husband will be compensated by being ordered to make smaller periodical payments or given a larger share of the capital on sale.

E. Variation, discharge, suspension and revival of orders

Orders that may be varied

The court has power to vary, discharge or suspend any of the following orders and to revive any term suspended:[9]

maintenance pending suit;
periodical payments (secured and unsecured);
an order relating to instalments in the case of lump sum payments;
the settlement (but not the transfer) of property on judicial separation;
the variation of ante-nuptial and post-nuptial settlements on judicial separation;
any order for the sale of property.

Periodical payments are normally variable because they are intended as maintenance for the payee and, if either party's needs or resources change,

---

but an order under the latter must be made before decree absolute. Neither remedy is available if the marriage is void.

[6] Under s 24A of the Matrimonial Causes Act 1973, as added by the Matrimonial Homes and Property Act 1981, s 7.

[7] See ante, p 616 (right to occupation) and post, pp 801–804 (restraining dispositions). But registration of a Class F land charge will be set aside as an abuse of process if the wife has no intention of occupying the house: *Barnett v Hassett* [1982] 1 All ER 80.

[8] Cretney and Masson *Principles of Family Law* (5th Edn) pp 252–254.

[9] Matrimonial Causes Act 1973, s 31(1), (2), as amended by the Matrimonial Homes and Property Act 1981, s 8(2). The court may also order any instrument to be varied, etc: s 31(3).

justice may demand a corresponding change in the amount payable. The principal exception is where the court has expressly added a section 28(1A) direction, namely, that the period fixed for the order cannot be extended.[10] As we have seen,[11] such orders are intended to provide for a 'deferred clean break' between the parties where it is thought that the parties can be financially independent of one another. On the other hand, once a lump sum has been paid, it cannot be discharged or varied; it would therefore, be unfair to the payee if her right to a sum not yet paid could be prejudiced on the ground that the court had softened the blow to the payer by providing that he could pay the sum in question over a period of time. The same objection cannot be raised, however, to a change in the period or manner in which the instalments are paid, and consequently these can be varied by an alteration of their size or frequency. In *Tilley v Tilley*[12] the Court of Appeal held that this power enables the court to remit future instalments entirely; although this seems questionable, it was pointed out in that case that this object could be achieved in any event by ordering the payee to make periodical payments of equal value to the payer. The reason that, generally speaking, orders relating to property cannot be varied is that they are designed to make a final adjustment of the spouses' rights at the time of the decree so that any subsequent change in their needs and resources is irrelevant. Settlements of property and variations of ante-nuptial and post-nuptial settlements made on judicial separation come into a different category, however, because a further adjustment may have to be made if the marriage is later dissolved, and the spouses themselves may wish to have the order varied if they become reconciled. Consequently variations of these orders may be made only in proceedings for the rescission of the decree or for the dissolution of the marriage.[13]

Section 31(5) of the Matrimonial Causes Act 1973 provides that the court cannot make a property adjustment or lump sum order on an application to vary a periodical payments order.[14] However, in *S v S*,[15] Waite J held that as a matter of law, it was open to the court to terminate a wife's periodical payments order on the basis of a capital offer made by the husband even though there is no statutory power (by reason of section 31(5)) to *order* him to pay a lump sum in variation proceedings. Although this point was not discussed by the Court of Appeal in the same case,[16] the

---

[10] The court may however (without making a statutory direction) expressly stipulate events upon the happening of which the periodical payment orders are to end. In this event, an application for variation must be made *before* the specified events occur. In *T v T (Financial Provision)* [1988] 1 FLR 480 a periodical payments order in favour of a wife was expressed to take effect until the wife remarried, or the husband retired or further order. It was held the wife could not apply for a variation *after* the husband had retired. The words 'or further order' could only be relied on for an *earlier* variation, that is, *before* the happening of a specified event but not afterwards. This approach is consistent with that in *Thompson v Thompson* [1986] Fam 38, [1985] 2 All ER 243, CA discussed below, p 792, in the context of a property transfer order.

[11] Ante, p 764. There is no power to vary an order dismissing an application for periodical payments made under s 24A(3).

[12] (1979) 10 Fam Law 89, CA.

[13] Matrimonial Causes Act 1973, s 31(4).

[14] *Sandford v Sandford* [1986] 1 FLR 412, CA. The court can, however, order a lump sum payment to a child because this might be used, for example, for his education.

[15] [1986] Fam 189, [1986] 3 All ER 566.

[16] [1987] 2 All ER 312, CA.

approach has been adopted in later cases.[17] In considering whether the capital offer is adequate, the court should take as its starting point the income to which it is agreed or held that the wife is entitled under the periodical payments order (usually for joint lives) and set this against the advantage to the wife of having a capital sum which will provide her with a secured income.[18] When dealing with substantial figures, it may be wise for the parties to receive expert financial advice on the fair level of capital commutation[19] perhaps by the application of a *Duxbury* type calculation[20] in the appropriate case. Where there is *no* capital offer made by one spouse to another, section 31(5) seems to preclude the court from ordering an unwilling spouse to make capital provision in commutation of periodical payments in variation proceedings. However in *Peacock v Peacock*,[1] Thorpe J suggested that an exception exists where the court has made no previous order for determining capital claims. In such a case, section 24 of the Matrimonial Causes Act 1973 (which permits the court to make (inter alia) lump sum orders on granting a decree ... *or at any time thereafter*), may be used to order the payment of the appropriate capital sum.

A *Mesher* order, being a property adjustment order, cannot be varied.[2] In *Norman v Norman*[3] a husband attempted to invoke the court's powers of sale under section 24A to accelerate a sale following a *Mesher* order but the court rejected this on the ground that such an order would in reality be a variation of the *Mesher* order. It was held that the proper procedure was to apply for a sale under the Law of Property Act 1925, section 30. In *Thompson v Thompson*,[4] however, it was held that provided the sale was deferred inter alia 'until further order',[5] there was power to order an earlier sale under s 24A,[6] at any rate on the application of the party in occupation since, in the court's view, that did not amount to a variation.[7] On the other hand, in *Taylor v Taylor*,[8] in which the matrimonial home was made subject to a charge in favour of the wife who retained exclusive right of occupation, the husband applied under section 24A for an earlier sale and the Court of Appeal seemed to take the view that this was a matter which went to the court's discretion rather than jurisdiction. In other words there was power to order the sale under section 24A but the question remained whether, on the merits, that power should be exercised. The complex position in relation to early sale stands contrasted to that where one spouse seeks early redemption of a charge over the matrimonial home in favour of the other. In *Popat v Popat*,[9] the Court of Appeal held the only purpose

---

[17] *Boylan v Boylan* [1988] 1 FLR 282; *Peacock v Peacock* [1991] 1 FLR 324.
[18] *Boylan v Boylan* [1988] 1 FLR 282 at 292 per Booth J.
[19] Ibid.
[20] See the discussion ante at p 775–776.
[1] [1991] 1 FLR 324 at 331.
[2] *Carson v Carson* [1983] 1 All ER 478.
[3] [1983] 1 All ER 486.
[4] [1986] Fam 38, [1985] 2 All ER 243, CA.
[5] Or words to similar effect. Express authority can be given to allow the parties to come back to the court to ask for an earlier sale: see eg *Anthony v Anthony* [1986] 2 FLR 353 at 359, CA.
[6] The court held that the power to order a sale was retrospective.
[7] *Aliter* if it was sought to *delay* the sale or if the party not in occupation sought the sale.
[8] [1987] 1 FLR 142, CA.
[9] [1991] 2 FLR 163, CA.

of such a charge was to provide security, and once the amount secured had been tendered and paid, the charge could be redeemed. In the absence of any express restriction in the terms of the order, an accelerated redemption did not amount to a variation and so did not require any application to court. The charge-holding spouse had to take his money immediately even though this may be inconvenient to him. The court's only function was to satisfy itself that the amount tendered was correct in the event of disagreement.

An order for the variation, etc, of periodical payments may be retrospective.[10] Although the court's power is unlimited in this regard, it should be exercised reasonably; save in exceptional circumstances, it will be sufficient to backdate the variation to the previous April, and the beginning of the income tax year.[11] If an order for secured periodical payments continues in force after the death of the party against whom it was made, either his personal representatives or the person entitled to the payments may apply for a variation, etc. Except with the leave of the court this may not be done more than six months after representation was first taken out; if leave is given, the personal representatives will not be liable for having failed to anticipate the possibility of such an application but a claim may be made against beneficiaries to whom any part of the estate has been transferred.[12]

Facts to be taken into consideration

The Act expressly provides that, on hearing an application for variation, the court shall have regard to all the circumstances of the case, first consideration being given to the welfare while a minor of any child of the family who has not attained the age of 18, and the circumstances of the case shall include any change in the matters to which it was required to have regard when making the order in the first place. If the application is made after the death of the party against whom the order was originally made, the court must also take into account the changed circumstances resulting from the death.[13] Although in most cases the order itself will be taken as the starting point and most emphasis will be laid on any changes in the parties' financial situation,[14] the court's discretion is completely unfettered.[15] Thus the parties' conduct following the original order may be taken into account if it would have affected the original order had it occurred before it was made.[16]

Two judicial limitations have been placed on the court's power, however.

[10] *MacDonald v MacDonald* [1964] P 1, [1963] 2 All ER 857, CA.
[11] *S v S* [1987] 2 All ER 312, CA.
[12] Matrimonial Causes Act 1973, s 31(6), (8) and (9). The court also has power to vary, discharge or revive an order for secured periodical payments if the payee applies for an order under the Inheritance (Provision for Family and Dependants) Act 1975: see post, pp 840–841. For variation generally, see Law Com No 25, paras 85–93.
[13] Ibid, s 31(7) as amended by the Matrimonial and Family Proceedings Act 1984, s 6(3). See *Jones v Jones* [1971] 3 All ER 1201, 1206–1207. Neither party is under any duty to make a voluntary disclosure of any change in his or her means: *Hayfield v Hayfield* [1957] 1 All ER 598.
[14] Cf *Primavera v Primavera* [1992] 1 FLR 16, CA.
[15] *Lewis v Lewis* [1977] 3 All ER 992, CA.
[16] *J (HD) v J (AM)* [1980] 1 All ER 156, in which it was also held that the fact that the party seeking a variation is in arrears or in breach of an injunction will not preclude an application unless the non-payment or breach is such as to impede the course of justice and there is no other effective means of securing compliance.

First, the parties are still estopped per rem judicatem from raising matters inconsistent with a previous decree or order and neither party may adduce evidence which could have been put before the court when the original order was made.[17] Secondly, a party who has led the other to act to his or her detriment on the assumption that he will continue to honour the order may not later apply to have it reduced or discharged. In *B (MAL) v B (NE)*[18] the husband and the wife had entered into a separation agreement before the wife petitioned for divorce, with the result that she did not immediately seek financial provision. Some years later the husband was adjudicated bankrupt and the wife agreed to consent to his discharge on his undertaking not to oppose an application by her for leave to apply to the court for maintenance. In the maintenance proceedings the husband alleged that the wife had been guilty of adultery but in the event he did not pursue these allegations and submitted to a consent order for periodical payments against himself. He later established that the wife's youngest child was illegitimate and then sought to have the maintenance order discharged on the ground that the wife had obtained it by fraud. It was held that he must fail for two reasons. Having raised the matter of the wife's adultery at a time when he had evidence to prove it and then submitted to judgment by consent, he was estopped from opening the question again: it certainly did not lie in his mouth to say that she had misled the court. Furthermore, having induced the wife to consent to his discharge in bankruptcy by undertaking to maintain her, he could not now argue that he was under no liability to do so.

If the change of circumstances on which the application is based is not likely to be permanent (for example, the husband's temporary unemployment), the order should be suspended rather than discharged, so that it can be revived later if necessary.[19]

As with original orders, the court is under a duty to consider whether it would be appropriate to make a limited term order which 'will in the opinion of the court be sufficient to enable the party in whose favour the order was made to adjust without undue hardship to the termination of those payments.'[20] There is some doubt whether the court has the power, upon a variation application, to make a section 28(1A) direction preventing the party seeking an extension of a limited term order,[1] or even a section 25A(3) order dismissing the application. However, it seems probable that the same effect can be achieved under section 31(10)[2] by ordering a discharge to take effect either at a future date or immediately.

Variation of consent orders

The fact that a party has consented to an order being made against him cannot act as an estoppel or give the other party a contractual right to have the order kept in force indefinitely, and a consent order can generally

---

[17] *Hall v Hall* (1914) 111 LT 403, CA.
[18] [1968] 1 WLR 1109.
[19] Cf *Mills v Mills* [1940] P 124, [1940] 2 All ER 254, CA.
[20] S 31(7)(a), as amended by the Matrimonial and Family Proceedings Act 1984, s 6(3). For the factors to be taken into account see eg *S v S* [1986] Fam 189, [1986] 3 All ER 566. See also the discussion ante, p 764.
[1] See *Sandford v Sandford* [1986] 1 FLR 412, CA.
[2] Added by the Matrimonial and Family Proceedings Act 1984, s 6(4).

be varied in the same circumstances as any other order.[3] This is so even though the order provides that the parties shall not apply for a variation: it is doubtful whether such a provision is valid and, even if it is, it may itself be suspended along with the other provisions of the order.[4] Usually, however, the court should be slower to accede to an application to vary consent orders because otherwise parties and their solicitors might be deterred from negotiating them altogether. Hence a variation sought on the ground that the applicant's consent was given as the result of a mistake (for example, about the other party's income) should be made only if justice demands it and a substantially different order would be made.[5] The court might also exercise its power if the applicant had not been independently and competently advised[6] or if, for whatever reason, the order was grossly unjust.[7] In any case, it is doubtful whether the court can vary or discharge an order which it has no power to make in the first place, for example, an order for unsecured periodical payments for the payee's life.[8]

Appealing out of time

All the orders that we have been discussing are appealable. In exceptional circumstances it is possible to obtain leave to appeal out of time. This may be the only option in cases where, whether upon a consent order or a contested one, a clean break order has been made. Of course the whole point of a clean break order or a property adjustment order is that there should be a final settlement between the parties. Nevertheless circumstances may subsequently occur that so fundamentally change the position that in all justice the order should be reopened. It seems established, however, that in the absence of fraud, misrepresentation or material non-disclosure, or a fundamental mistake common to both parties, events occurring after the making of an order only give grounds for appeal in exceptional circumstances. The leading case is *Barder v Calouri*.[9] Here, in a full and final settlement made in a consent order the husband agreed to transfer to his wife his half interest in the matrimonial home subject to her undertaking responsibility for two outstanding mortgages. The order specified that the transfer should take place within 28 days. Neither party gave notice of appeal but before the order was executed, the wife killed both the children and committed suicide. It was held by the House of Lords that because the fundamental assumption on which the order had been made, namely, that the wife and children would require a suitable home for a substantial period, had been totally invalidated within so short a time of the original order

[3] *B (GC) v B (BA)* [1970] 1 All ER 913.
[4] *Jessel v Jessel* [1979] 3 All ER 645, CA. See Douglas 96 LQR 196.
[5] *B (GC) v B (BA)* (supra).
[6] Per Baker P in *Wilkins v Wilkins* [1969] 2 All ER 463. Cf *Peacock v Peacock* [1991] 1 FLR 324 where Thorpe J said (at 328) that he would not hold the parties to any agreement they may have concluded since the area of negotiation was complicated, neither spouse had had the benefit of legal advice, and both were 'way out of their depth'.
[7] As in *Smethurst v Smethurst* [1978] Fam 52, [1977] 3 All ER 1110 where, for reasons which were not apparent, the sum originally ordered was about twice that which the husband could reasonably afford to pay. See Miller 10 Fam Law 196, 252.
[8] Cf *Mills v Mills* supra, and *Hinde v Hinde* [1953] 1 All ER 171, CA. But they probably can be varied, etc, by consent, and an undertaking given to the court may be discharged: *Russell v Russell* [1956] P 283, [1956] 1 All ER 466, CA.
[9] [1988] AC 20, [1987] 2 All ER 440, HL.

being made, leave to appeal should be granted. It was further held that the original order should be set aside.

The House of Lords laid down four conditions which must be satisfied if leave to appeal out of time is to be granted from an order for financial provision or property adjustment (whether or not made by consent):

(1) new events must have occurred since the making of the order which have invalidated the basis or assumption upon which the order was made so that the appeal would be certain, or very likely, to succeed;
(2) the new events should have occurred within a relatively short time of the order being made;
(3) the application for leave should be made reasonably promptly;
(4) the grant of leave should not prejudice third parties who have acquired interests in good faith and for value in the property which is the subject of the order.

In Lord Brandon's view, these conditions sought to reconcile two conflicting principles: on the one hand, that there should be finality in litigation, and on the other that justice requires cases be decided on their true facts rather than on assumptions or estimates which turn out to be erroneous.[10]

Perhaps not surprisingly, there have now been a number of cases on the application of the *Barder* criteria, which may be categorised into three broad groups.[11] In the first, as in *Barder v Calouri* itself, the supervening event has been the unexpected death of one of the spouses. In *Smith v Smith (Smith Intervening)*[12] for example, the wife committed suicide just six months after the making of a 'clean break' consent order, and the Court of Appeal set the original order aside. In contrast, in *Amey v Amey*,[13] the court refused to set aside a 'clean break' agreement under which the husband paid a £120,000 lump sum to the wife, and, just two months later, before the agreement could be approved by the court, the wife died of a heart attack. Scott Baker J held that, since the wife had died, it was no longer open to the court to affirm or vary the agreement under the Matrimonial Causes Act 1973. Nor was the agreement vitiated at common law by common mistake or frustration; the parties had divided their capital entitlements without making any assumption as to the wife's future health, so her unexpected death did not entitle the court to intervene.

In the second category, there are two cases where a spouse has sought leave to appeal out of time where, subsequent to the making of the original order, the other spouse has remarried, and vacated the former matrimonial home. In *Wells v Wells*,[14] just six months after the husband had been ordered to make a property transfer to provide a home for the wife and children, the wife remarried and began living with her second husband. The Court of Appeal held that these new events had invalidated the basis of the original order, and substituted an order for the sale of the property and the division of the proceeds of sale. In *Chaudhuri v Chaudhuri*[15] the husband's

---

[10] Ibid at 41 and 451 respectively.
[11] For a useful short summary of the cases see Salter [1992] Fam Law 50.
[12] [1992] Fam 69, [1991] 2 All ER 306, CA. See also *Passmore v Gill and Gill* [1987] 1 FLR 441, CA.
[13] [1992] 1 FCR 289.
[14] [1992] 2 FLR 66, CA (decided in 1980).
[15] [1992] 2 FLR 73, CA.

application was dismissed where the wife had remarried and moved out of the former matrimonial home fifteen months after the making of the property transfer order in her favour. The original order had expressly contemplated the possibility of the wife's remarriage,[16] and the change of circumstances was said to be much less drastic than that in *Wells v Wells*.

In the third, and by far the largest group of cases, a change in circumstances or a new event has meant that the property valuation, which was used by the court in making its original order, has turned out to be inaccurate or unreliable. In *Hope-Smith v Hope-Smith*[17] the husband was ordered to pay to the wife £32,000 out of the proceeds of sale of the former matrimonial home, then valued at £116,000. As a result of the husband's 'wilful conduct and dilatory tactics' the house remained unsold some two years later when it was worth over £200,000. The Court of Appeal held that the *Barder* conditions were satisfied through no fault of the wife.[18] It substituted an order that the wife was to receive 40 per cent of the ultimate net sale proceeds, which would be sufficient to enable her to rehouse herself. In contrast, in *Rooker v Rooker*,[19] on broadly similar facts, the court dismissed the wife's appeal because, although the husband had delayed the sale, the wife had not taken proper steps to enforce the original order. In *Edmonds v Edmonds*[20] the Court of Appeal refused to reopen a case where a house, valued by the judge at £70,000 and which the wife had claimed she intended to keep as her home, was sold by her for £110,000 six months later. Although the husband had asserted throughout his belief that the valuation should be higher, he had failed to produce any corroborative expert evidence to support his view. It was held that, since the husband had not taken the opportunity to challenge the false assumption upon which the judge had proceeded, he could not subsequently be heard to say that the new events had invalidated the judge's decision.[1] In a later decision, *Thompson v Thompson*,[2] the Court of Appeal granted leave to appeal out of time against a clean break order where the husband's business had been valued at £20,000, and just one week later was sold for £45,000. The circuit judge dismissed the wife's application for leave because she had agreed the valuation of £20,000 despite having previously received a valuation report of the business at £45,000. On appeal, however, Mustill LJ drew a distinction between the situation where a valuation was unsound when made and that

---

[16] The original order provided for a transfer of the property to the wife subject to a charge in favour of the husband enforceable upon the happening of the following events: the children ceasing full-time education, the death or remarriage of the wife, or her permanent cohabitation with another man.

[17] [1989] 2 FLR 56, CA.

[18] The case demonstrates the flexibility of the court in applying the second of the *Barder* criteria. The wife's successful application was not made until two years after the making of the original order. In *Barder v Caluori*, Lord Brandon had suggested ([1988] AC 20 at 43) that although the length of time could not be laid down precisely, he regarded it as 'extremely unlikely' that it could be as much as a year and that 'in most cases it will be no more than a few months'.

[19] [1988] 1 FLR 219, CA.

[20] [1990] 2 FLR 202, CA.

[1] Cf *Warren v Warren* (1982) 4 FLR 529, CA where there was a 'gross error', through no-one's fault, of almost 100 per cent in the property valuation agreed to by the parties. Since neither party had had the opportunity to correct the false assumption upon which the order was made, it was held to be unfair to hold them to it, so the order was set aside.

[2] [1991] 2 FLR 530, CA.

where a reasonable estimate had been falsified by new events. In the first situation, the court must inquire whether the applicant was in some way responsible for the error. If she was, then as in *Edmonds v Edmonds*, she may not succeed. The mere fact that a valuation report had been agreed, however, cannot be conclusive against an order being reopened, but deliberate fault on the part of the applicant would prevent leave being granted. The second situation is clearly a new event regardless of how the valuation came into existence. Provided that the other criteria in *Barder v Caluori* were satisfied, leave to appeal out of time would be given.

Mustill LJ, concerned lest his decision be seen as opening the floodgates and encouraging applicants to seek leave to appeal out of time, emphasised the severity of the requirements laid down in *Barder v Caluori*, adding:[3]

'... advisers must be alert, and the circuit judge will be alert if they are not, to make sure that the courts are not swamped with meritless applications for leave to appeal out of time.'

Where the court grants leave to appeal out of time, it should reassess the order for financial provision or property adjustment afresh, and consider the criteria in section 25(2) of the Matrimonial Causes Act 1973 having regard to *all* the facts as they are known at the time of the appeal hearing.[4]

F. Enforcement of orders

1. METHODS OF ENFORCEMENT

Periodical payments

If periodical payments are secured, there is of course no question of enforcement. When arrears of unsecured periodical payments accrue, the payee has a number of means of enforcing the order at his or her disposal. But his position is basically different from that of a successful plaintiff in an action for damages for tort or breach of contract for the order is not a final judgment and he does not have the full rights of judgment creditor.

In the first place, if the party in default applies to have the order varied or discharged, the court in effect has a discretion to remit the arrears in part or even entirely by making a retrospective order.[5] In order to prevent large sums from mounting up, arrears which have been due for twelve months or more may not be enforced without the leave of the court: this gives some protection to a party who has stopped paying the full sum ordered and has been mistakenly led to believe by the other's acquiescence that he will not enforce the rest.[6] The court can also give the debtor time to pay and, in particular, may order payment by instalments. Because of this discretion, the arrears do not constitute a legal debt and cannot be sued for as such,[7] nor may the payee institute bankruptcy proceedings as

---

[3] [1991] 2 FLR 530 at 539, CA.
[4] *Smith v Smith (Smith Intervening)* [1992] Fam 69, [1991] 2 All ER 306, CA. *Garner v Garner* [1992] 1 FLR 573, CA.
[5] *MacDonald v MacDonald* [1964] P 1, [1963] 2 All ER 857, CA.
[6] Matrimonial Causes Act 1973, s 32. See further Law Com No 25, para 92.
[7] *Bailey v Bailey* (1884) 13 QBD 855, CA; *Robins v Robins* [1907] 2 KB 13.

a means of execution or prove in the other party's bankruptcy for arrears.[8] But with these important exceptions he has available all the usual means of execution open to a judgment creditor in the High Court or a county court, as the case may be.[9]

One of the most useful ways of enforcing the payment of arrears is by issuing a judgment summons under the Debtors Act 1869, when the court can make an order for the payment by instalments and commit the payer for contempt if he wilfully fails to pay them.[10] Alternatively, the payee may apply for an attachment of earnings order. The detailed provisions are mutatis mutandis the same as those relating to attachment orders made in a magistrates' court.[11] It should be noted that the Maintenance Enforcement Act 1991 extends the enforcement powers of the High Court and county courts as regards maintenance orders (which include orders for periodical payments). The new powers apply when the court makes a maintenance order, or in subsequent proceedings for its revocation or variation. The first is to order payment by standing order, or by other similar method.[12] A debtor who has unreasonably refused to open a bank account can be ordered to do so for this purpose.[13] The second is an unrestricted power to make an attachment of earnings order.[14] Previously, the latter could only be made if the debtor consented, or if he was guilty of wilful neglect or culpable default in failing to meet the order.[15]

In view of the personal nature of the obligation and the fact that arrears do not constitute a legal debt, there is some doubt whether they can be enforced against the payer's personal representatives after his death.[16]

Recovery of overpayments

The court may well feel that, because of some change of circumstances, the payee has been overpaid. To take two examples: the payee may have failed to inform the other party of an unexpected improvement in her financial position, or the payer may not have realised that a decrease in his income entitled him to apply for a variation. In some cases justice may demand that the payee should repay some or all of the money received since the

---

[8] Consequently the arrears are not affected by bankruptcy and may be enforced by other methods: *Linton v Linton* (1885) 15 QBD 239, CA; *Re Henderson* (1888) 20 QBD 509, CA.

[9] An undertaking to make payments given to the court may be enforced in the same way as an order (at least if the court would have had jurisdiction to make a similar order): *Gandolfo v Gandolfo* [1981] QB 359, [1980] 1 All ER 833, CA. An order made by a divorce county court can be transferred to the High Court if it cannot be conveniently enforced in the county court. It is then enforceable as though it had been made by the High Court: Family Proceedings Rules 1991, r 7.3.

[10] For the procedure, see the Family Proceedings Rules 1991, rr 7.2, 7.4, 7.5, 7.6.

[11] See ante, pp 690–692. If the order is a High Court order, the collecting officer is the proper officer of the High Court or the appropriate officer of a county court specified in the order: Attachment of Earnings Act 1971, s 6(7).

[12] Maintenance Enforcement Act 1991, s 1(5).

[13] Ibid, s 1(6).

[14] Ibid, s 1(4)(b).

[15] Attachment of Earnings Act 1971, s 3(5), now repealed by Maintenance Enforcement Act 1991, Sch 3.

[16] In *Re Stillwell* [1916] 1 Ch 365, it was held that arrears could not be recovered against a solvent estate, but the decision of the Court of Appeal in *Sugden v Sugden* [1957] P 120, [1957] 1 All ER 300 suggests the contrary. By analogy with the law of bankruptcy, the payee presumably could not claim in any event if the estate were insolvent.

change in circumstances; in others (for example, where the payee was unaware of the change in the payer's circumstances and has already spent the money) justice may demand that the loss should continue to lie where it has fallen. Consequently by section 33 of the Matrimonial Causes Act, where there has been a change in the circumstances of either the person entitled to the payments or the person liable to make them (including a change produced by the death of the latter) so that the amount received by the payee since then has exceeded the amount which the other should have been required to pay, the court may order the repayment of the whole or any part of the excess as it thinks just. Alternatively it may decide that nothing should be repaid at all. Section 38 of the Act gives the court precisely the same powers if the payee has remarried and the other party (or his personal representatives) has continued to make payments in the mistaken belief that the order was still subsisting. Both sections apply to periodical payments (secured and unsecured); section 33 also applies to maintenance pending suit and interim payments under section 27. In both cases the action may be brought by and against personal representatives and the court may order any sum to be repaid by instalments.

The High Court or a county court may make an order for repayment in proceedings for variation or discharge or for the enforcement of arrears.[17] Alternatively the payer or his personal representatives may bring an action for repayment in a county court.[18]

Other orders

An order for the payment of a lump sum is more in the nature of a judgment for damages and may be enforced in the same way. This means that, if the party against whom it is made becomes insolvent before he implements it, the other party may prove in his bankruptcy.[19] The payee may also issue a judgment summons or apply for an attachment of earnings order.[20] As in the case of periodical payments, a lump sum payment (or any part payable by instalment) cannot be enforced more than twelve months after it falls due without the leave of the court.[1]

Failure to comply with an order to transfer or settle property may be enforced in the same way as any other similar order in the High Court or a county court.

---

[17] But a magistrates' court has no power to make an order for repayment in the case of a High Court or county court order registered there. See further post, p 804.
[18] Cf the recovery of overpayments under a magistrates' order, ante, p 686.
[19] See *Curtis v Curtis* [1969] 2 All ER 207, CA, where the court ordered the husband to pay the wife £33,600 capitalising an annual sum of £2,400 to enable her to take bankruptcy proceedings if he remained contumacious.
[20] See the definition of 'maintenance order' in the Administration of Justice Act 1970, s 28 and Sch 8, and the Attachment of Earnings Act 1971, Sch 1, para 3, as amended in each case by the Matrimonial Causes Act 1973, Sch 2, and the Domestic Proceedings and Magistrates' Courts Act 1978, Sch 2.
[1] Matrimonial Causes Act 1973, s 32.

2. ATTEMPTS TO DEFEAT CLAIMS FOR FINANCIAL RELIEF

A spouse might well try to defeat an application for financial relief by disposing of his property or transferring it out of the jurisdiction. He might do this beforehand in anticipation of an application or order or, alternatively, after an order has been made in order to reduce the property available to meet it. To prevent fraudulent dispositions of this kind, a measure of protection is given by section 37 of the Matrimonial Causes Act 1973.[2] This applies to any order for maintenance pending suit, financial provision or property adjustment made in proceedings for divorce, nullity and judicial separation, any order made under section 27 of the Act on the ground of failure to provide reasonable maintenance, the variation of any of these orders during the payer's lifetime, and the alteration of a maintenance agreement during the parties' joint lives. For the sake of convenience, it will be assumed throughout the following discussion that the wife (or former wife) is applying for or has obtained an order against the husband; it must be appreciated, however, that exactly the same principles apply if the husband is seeking financial provision from the wife or if anyone is seeking it for the children of the family.

If the court is satisfied that the husband is about to make any disposition or to transfer out of the jurisdiction or otherwise deal with any property with the intention of defeating the wife's claim, it may make such an order as it thinks fit to restrain him from doing so and to protect the claim.[3] In *Crittenden v Crittenden*[4] the Court of Appeal held that, for the purpose of section 37, 'property' means property in which either or both spouses has or had a beneficial interest, in possession or reversion, while 'dealing with' refers to some *positive* dealing with property, and not to anything which is purely negative, such as failing to deal with property.[5] It followed that the court had no power, under section 37, to make orders relating to assets owned by a *company* in which the husband held the issued shares. Nor could the court make an order under section 37 requiring the husband to enter into a covenant not to compete with a proposed purchaser of the company's assets.

If the court is satisfied that the husband has already made a disposition with the intention of defeating the wife's claim, the court may make an order setting the disposition aside. In this case, however, a wife who has not yet obtained an order for financial relief must also show that, if the disposition were set aside, the court would make a different order from that which it would otherwise make. Defeating the wife's claim may take the

---

[2] The power was originally given by the Matrimonial Causes (Property and Maintenance) Act 1958, s 2.

[3] It has been held that this power extends to restraining dispositions of property already situated abroad: *Hamlin v Hamlin* [1986] Fam 11, [1985] 2 All ER 1037, CA. However, the court will only make an order if it can be enforced.

[4] [1990] 2 FLR 361, CA.

[5] On the other hand, 'dealing with' in s 37 does *not* require there to be a disposition in favour of a third party: *Shipman v Shipman* [1991] 1 FLR 250, where Anthony Lincoln J held that a husband's use of his funds as a deposit on the purchase of a house, to maintain himself and to pay off existing debts was caught by s 37. The judge also held, following *Roche v Roche* (1981) 11 Fam Law 243, CA, that the court has an inherent jurisdiction to grant injunctions freezing assets which might otherwise be put beyond reach of an applicant, notwithstanding the enactment of s 37. See the comment by Cretney [1991] Fam Law 146.

form of preventing her from obtaining an order at all, reducing the amount that might be ordered, or impeding or frustrating the enforcement of any order that might be made or has been made.

In many cases it may be difficult to establish what the husband's intention was when he made a disposition. Consequently the Act has introduced a compromise designed to protect in part the interests of the wife, the husband and the transferee. If the husband made the disposition three years or more before the application to set it aside, the wife must prove affirmatively that he had the intention to defeat her claim. If he made it less than three years before or is about to make it, this intention will be presumed if the effect of the transaction would be to defeat her claim or, where the disposition has already taken place and an order is in force, if it has had this effect: the burden then shifts on to him to prove that this was not his intention. In *Kemmis v Kemmis (Welland Intervening)*[6] it was held that the husband's intention to defeat the wife's claim has to be a subjective intention, but does not have to be the husband's sole or even dominant intention. It suffices if it plays a *substantial* part in the husband's intention as a whole.

Certain transactions may not be upset at all. No order may be made after the husband's death with respect to any disposition made by him by will or codicil. A disposition inter vivos *already* made may not be set aside if it was made for valuable consideration (other than marriage) to a third party acting in good faith and without notice of the husband's intention to defeat the wife's claim.[7] Where a third party had *actual* knowledge of the husband's intention it is difficult to see how he could claim to act in good faith, and so the transaction will be set aside. However in *Kemmis v Kemmis (Welland Intervening)*[8] the Court of Appeal held the defence is not available to a third party who has *constructive* notice of the husband's intentions. Here, the position is rather more complex, but the test was laid down by Purchas LJ who cited,[9] with approval, a passage from the judgment of Farwell J in *Hunt v Luck*:[10]

'Constructive notice is the knowledge which the courts impute to a person upon presumption so strong of the existence of knowledge that it cannot be allowed to be rebutted either from his knowing something which ought to have put him to further inquiry or from his wilfully abstaining from inquiry to avoid notice.'

Purchas LJ continued:[11]

'The basic concepts are "knowing something" which ought to have stimulated inquiry, or "wilfully abstaining from inquiry to avoid notice". Both import that inquiry, if made, would necessarily have revealed the knowledge, constructive notice of which is to be imported.'

The application of these criteria can be seen in the later case of *Sherry v*

---

[6] [1988] 1 WLR 1307, CA.
[7] A purchaser acts in good faith provided that he acts honestly: *Central Estates (Belgravia) Ltd v Woolgar* [1972] 1 QB 48, [1971] 3 All ER 647, CA. No order may be made if the disposition took place before 1 January 1968, as there was an absolute limitation of three years before the Matrimonial Proceedings and Property Act 1970 came into force: Matrimonial Causes Act 1973, s 37(7). See also *Walker v Walker* [1983] Fam 68, [1983] 2 All ER 909, CA (no power to restrain a serviceman from disposing of his resettlement grant since that would be contrary to the Army Act 1955, s 203).
[8] [1988] 1 WLR 1307, CA. See Fortin [1989] Conv 24.
[9] [1988] 1 WLR 1307 at 1317, CA.
[10] [1901] 1 Ch 45, at 52.
[11] [1988] 1 WLR 1307 at 1317, CA.

Sherry,[12] where the wife obtained injunctions, under section 37, restraining the husband from selling or disposing of certain properties, and had subsequently registered inhibitions against the properties at HM Land Registry. Later, by consent, the injunctions were discharged. The husband then entered into contracts for sale and mortgage of the properties with a purchaser, whose solicitor's searches revealed the existence of the inhibitions whose registration had not been cancelled. On being shown the order discharging the injunctions, the solicitor advised the purchaser to proceed and the transactions were completed. The Court of Appeal adopted the test in *Kemmis v Kemmis*, and set the transactions aside on the basis that the purchaser had constructive notice of the husband's intentions. The purchaser knew of the acrimonious dispute between the spouses, and his discovery that injunctions had been made, and the inhibitions registered, should have caused him to make simple enquiries as regards the properties. His failure to do so meant he was bound by constructive notice, and the transactions were reviewable under section 37.

A wife's application for a property adjustment order relating to a *specific* piece of land (for example, the matrimonial home) is registrable as a pending land action.[13] Once registered, the wife's claims will take priority over subsequent purchasers or mortgagees, regardless of whether they make the appropriate land charges or land registry search, or whether they have notice of the husband's intentions to defeat the wife's claims.[14] If a wife *fails* to register, then the Court of Appeal has held in *Whittingham v Whittingham*[15] that she cannot attack any subsequent transfer to any person taking any interest in the land, or any charge on it for valuable consideration, unless he had actual notice that she had made an application for a property transfer. In *Kemmis v Kemmis*, however, both Purchas LJ and Lloyd LJ expressed doubts about the decision in *Whittingham v Whittingham*. The former said:[16]

'Although this court is bound by the decision of the Court of Appeal in *Whittingham's case* in regard to the wife's failure to register... I feel constrained to comment that if the [third party] had either actual or constructive notice of the husband's intention to prejudice the powers to make orders for financial relief, the court's powers under section 37 should not be frustrated by the failure to register a *lis pendens* by the wife.'

The disposition is voidable, and not void, and consequently, even if it is set aside, this cannot affect any subsequent dealings with the property in good faith. Hence if the husband's immediate transferee is not protected but disposes of the property to a bona fide purchaser for value without notice, the latter's title cannot be upset by the order. In *National Provincial*

---

[12] [1991] 1 FLR 307, CA.
[13] Under the Land Charges Act 1972, s 5(7). If the land is registered, a pending action is protected by lodging a caution: Land Registration Act 1925, s 59.
[14] *Perez-Adamson v Perez-Rivas* [1987] Fam 89, [1987] 3 All ER 20, CA where it was held sufficient for a wife to particularise the property to be charged at the time of *registering* the land charge entry. The wife's application for a property adjustment order had not specified any particular property.
[15] [1979] Fam 9, [1978] 3 All ER 805, CA.
[16] [1988] 1 WLR 1307 at 1320, CA.

Bank Ltd v Hastings Car Mart Ltd[17] the husband, who had deserted the wife, conveyed the matrimonial home to the defendant company who immediately charged it to the plaintiff bank. Although the conveyance to the defendants was set aside on the grounds that it was made with the intention of defeating the wife's claim to maintenance, it was held by the Court of Appeal that this did not extinguish the plaintiff's mortgage which remained a valid charge.

G. Registration of orders in other courts

It will readily be seen that if the spouse ordered to pay money duly fulfils his or her obligations, orders made in magistrates' courts have the advantage that payment may be made through the clerk of the court; conversely, if he fails to fulfil them, a spouse who has an order made in the High Court or a county court has superior means of enforcing it at his or her disposal. Consequently the Maintenance Orders Act of 1958 introduced the means of registering in one court a 'maintenance order'[18] made by another. Under this Act a person entitled to payments under a maintenance order made by the High Court or a county court may apply to the court that made the order to have it registered in a magistrates' court; whether or not the application is granted lies completely in the discretion of the court.[19] In the same way a person entitled to payments under a maintenance order made by the magistrates' court may apply to that court to have it registered in the High Court; again, the court has a discretion[20] whether or not to grant the application.

If the application is granted, no proceedings may be begun or continued to enforce the order in the original court and any attachment of earnings order already in force ceases to have effect.[1] Once the order has been registered, it may be enforced only as though it had been made by the court in which it is registered.[2]

An order may be varied, revoked, suspended and revived only by the original court except that, in the case of orders made by the High Court or a county court and registered in a magistrates' court, variation of rates

---

[17] [1964] Ch 665, [1964] 3 All ER 93, CA. See further the same case in the House of Lords, *National Provincial Bank Ltd v Ainsworth*, ante, p 614. There was no appeal on the point discussed here. Presumably in circumstances such as these the immediate transferee may be ordered to pay over the value of the property.

[18] As defined by the Maintenance Orders Act 1958, s 1(1A) added by the Administration of Justice Act 1970, s 27(3) and Sch 8 as subsequently amended. The statutory definition includes (inter alia) orders for periodical or other payments made, or having effect if made, under the Matrimonial Causes Act 1973, Part III, the Domestic Proceedings and Magistrates' Courts Act 1978 and the Children Act 1989.

[19] Ss 1(1)(a), 2(1).

[20] Ss 1(1)(b), 2(3).

[1] S 2(2), (4); Attachment of Earnings Act 1971, s 11(1)(a), (2). But a warrant of committal remains in force if the defendant is *already* detained under it: s 2(4)(b).

[2] S 3. This includes the power to remit the whole or any part of arrears due. In the case of an order made under the Domestic Proceedings and Magistrates' Courts Act and registered in the High Court, the leave of that court must be obtained to enforce arrears which have been due for more than twelve months: see the Domestic Proceedings and Magistrates' Courts Act 1978, s 32(4)–(6).

of payment (as distinct from a variation of other provisions and complete revocation, suspension and revival of the order) may be made only by the magistrates' court in which it is registered[3] if both parties are in England.[4]

The party entitled to payments under a registered order may give notice to have the registration cancelled. This has a similar effect to an application to have the order registered in the sense that no proceedings may be begun or continued to enforce the order in the court of registration[5] and any attachment of earnings order is automatically discharged. The court in which the order is registered must then cancel the registration provided that no process for the enforcement of the order is in force and, in the case of an order registered in a magistrates' court, no proceedings for variation are pending in that court. If the court that originally made an order registered in a magistrates' court varies or discharges it, it may itself direct that the registration be cancelled; if a magistrates' court discharges an order registered in the High Court, it must direct that the registration be cancelled if there are no arrears remaining to be recovered.[6]

---

[3] Or any other magistrates' court having jurisdiction in the place where the complainant is for the time being: Magistrates' Courts (Maintenance Orders Act 1958) Rules 1959, r 9.

[4] S 4, as amended by the Administration of Justice Act 1970, Sch 11. Hence an order for maintenance pending suit and an interim order made under s 27 of the Matrimonial Causes Act 1973 should normally not be registered in a magistrates' court because this removes control from the divorce court: *Armsby v Armsby* (1973) 118 Sol Jo 183. Cf *Practice Direction* [1980] 1 All ER 1007. The magistrates' court has a discretion to remit the application to the original court and the original court may vary the rate of payment in proceedings to vary other provisions of the order.

[5] Save that a warrant of committal remains in force if the defendant is *already* detained under it.

[6] S 5; Attachment of Earnings Act 1971, s 11(1)(b).

Chapter 22

Property and financial provision on the death of a member of the family

A. Testate succession

The law relating to wills and testate succession generally presents few problems peculiar to family law. Until the beginning of this century the most important question was the testamentary capacity of a married woman. At common law she had virtually no power to make a will at all,[1] although she could always devise and bequeath property held to her separate use in equity even if it were subject to a restraint upon anticipation.[2] When the equitable concept of separate property was extended to legal separate property by the Married Women's Property Act 1882, her power to dispose of it by will was likewise extended, so that her testamentary incapacity remained only with respect to property acquired by her before 1883. Now by the Law Reform (Married Women and Tortfeasors) Act 1935 she has full power to dispose of all her property as if she were a feme sole.

There are, however, still one or two matters of particular importance to spouses and children which we must note.

Revocation of wills by marriage

By section 18 of the Wills Act 1837 (as substituted by section 18 of the Administration of Justice Act 1982) every will made by a man or woman is revoked by his or her marriage.[3] This applies only to persons domiciled in England and Wales at the time of the marriage; consequently if by the testator's lex domicilii his will was not revoked by his marriage, it will not

---

[1] She had no power at all to dispose of realty and leaseholds, although she could exercise a power of appointment by will. With the consent of her husband copyholds could be surrendered to the use of her will. Although all her choses in possession vested in her husband, she could bequeath personalty if there were an ante-nuptial contract to that effect or if her husband assented to the bequest and did not revoke his consent before probate was granted. For further details, reference must be made to the editions of standard works on property, wills and married women published in the late nineteenth and early twentieth centuries.

[2] But until the passing of the Married Women's Property Act 1893, s 3, a will made by a woman during marriage would not pass property acquired after the marriage was terminated unless it was subsequently republished.

[3] But this will not be a breach of an ante-nuptial contract not to revoke a will already made: Re Marsland [1939] Ch 820, [1939] 3 All ER 148, CA. The changes made by the Administration of Justice Act implement the recommendations made in the 22nd Report of the Law Reform Committee (The Making and Revocation of Wills) 1980 (Cmnd 7902) and do not apply to wills *made* before 1st January 1983: ibid, s 73(3).

be automatically revoked if he later acquires an English domicile.[4] Nor will the section apply if the marriage is void.[5]

There are, however, a number of exceptions to the general rule. First, a will is not to be revoked by marriage insofar as it is made in exercise of a power of appointment if the property thereby appointed would not pass in default of appointment to the testator's personal representatives.[6] The reason for this exception is obvious: the marriage cannot possibly affect the devolution of the property involved. The other exceptions are designed to fulfil the intention of a testator who makes his will on the eve of his wedding. If it appears from a will that at the time it was made the testator was expecting to be married to a particular person and that he intended that the will should not be revoked by the marriage, the marriage to that person is not to revoke it. The same rule applies if it appears that the testator intended that a particular disposition should not be revoked by the marriage; in that case the disposition in question is to take effect as are all other dispositions in the will unless it appears that the testator intended that a particular disposition was to be revoked.[7]

The exceptions relating to wills made in contemplation of marriage replace an exception (couched in significantly different terms) contained in section 177 of the Law of Property Act 1925. This section was liberally construed. Thus in *In the Estate of Langston*[8] a will by which the testator left his whole estate to 'my fiancée MEB' was held not to have been revoked by his marriage to that lady two months later. Similarly a will would now be saved if the testator made a bequest 'to my fiancée ABC' but gave the residue of his estate to others.[9] Difficulty arises because it is frequently impossible to tell whether, by making a gift to his fiancée, a testator was intending to provide for his future wife or was merely making a temporary arrangement in case he should die before the proposed marriage took place. It would appear that in many cases this problem will now be resolved by section 21 of the Administration of Justice Act 1982 which permits extrinsic evidence to be admitted to resolve ambiguities in the wording of a will.[10]

---

[4] *In the Goods of Reid* (1886) LR 1 P & D 74; *In the Goods of Groos* [1904] P 269. Contrast *Re Martin* [1900] P 211, CA (woman's will revoked by her acquisition of English domicile on marriage).

[5] *Mette v Mette* (1859) 1 Sw & Tr 416.

[6] S 18(2). Hence the will may be revoked in part but not insofar as the power is exercised: *In the Goods of Russell* (1890) 15 PD 111. See also *In the Goods of Gilligan*, [1950] P 32, [1949] 2 All ER 401; Mitchell, *The Revocation of Testamentary Appointments on Marriage*, 67 LQR 351.

[7] S 18(3), (4). This provision does not apply to wills made before 1st January 1983 (Administration of Justice Act 1982, ss 73(7) and 76(11)) which will still be governed by s 177 of the Law of Property Act 1925.

[8] [1953] P 100, [1953] 1 All ER 928. See also *Pilot v Gainfort* [1931] P 103, where the testator made a will by which he bequeathed his personalty to 'DFP my wife'. Although he was living with her at the time, he did not marry her until 18 months later. It was held that the will was not revoked by the marriage. Sed quaere? On the face of the will it appeared that the testator was *already* married. Contrast *In the Estate of Gray* (1963) 107 Sol Jo 156.

[9] Thus reversing *Re Coleman* [1976] Ch 1, [1975] 1 All ER 675.

[10] It is submitted that the language used is ambiguous *on the face of the will* so that extrinsic evidence, including evidence of the testator's intention, can always be admitted: s 21(1)(b) and (2). In any case the surviving spouse now needs less protection because of the substantial sums that she (or he) takes on intestacy and the court's wide powers to make financial provision for a dependant under the Inheritance (Provision for Family and Dependants) Act 1975 (see post, pp 815–817 and 821 et seq). But other beneficiaries, with no alternative

Revocation of wills by decrees of divorce and nullity

Whereas the contracting of marriage automatically revokes a will (unless one of the exceptions just considered applies), its dissolution used not to do so. Consequently if the testator did not make another will, his estate might pass to a former wife from whom he had long been divorced and who might have remarried. To overcome this difficulty, section 18A of the Wills Act (added by the Administration of Justice Act 1982)[11] now provides that, if a testator's marriage is dissolved or annulled by a decree of a court, any will previously made by him (or her) shall take effect as if any appointment of the former spouse as executor (or executor and trustee) were omitted and any devise or bequest to the former spouse shall lapse unless (in either case) a contrary intention appears in the will. The section will operate if the marriage was dissolved or annulled by a court of civil jurisdiction in England and Wales or by a divorce or annulment obtained elsewhere and entitled to recognition in this country by virtue of Part II of the Family Law Act 1986.[12] It will not operate, however, if no proceedings are taken for the annulment of a void marriage.

In *Re Sinclair*[13] the Court of Appeal held that the word 'lapse' must be given its ordinary meaning of 'fail' and that the former spouse is not to be deemed to have predeceased the testator. This produces an anomalous result. The section expressly provides that any interest subject to a lapsed life interest shall take immediate effect and that, if it is contingent upon the termination of the life interest, it shall be treated as if it were not so contingent.[14] Suppose a testator gives a legacy 'to my wife W for life with remainder to such of my children as are alive at her death'. If the marriage is then dissolved but W is still alive at the testator's death, all the children *then* alive will take immediately for the contingency (that those taking shall survive W) is to be disregarded. But if there is a gift in the form 'To my wife W, but if she predecease me, to X' or in the common survivorship form 'To W provided that she survives me for one month, but if she does not, to X', X can claim nothing because W's interest was not a life interest and the condition precedent to X's taking (that W should die before the testator or within a month of his death) is not satisfied.[15] This is unfortunate and probably an unintended result of the Act. The inference is that the testator wished X to take if W did not; the resulting intestacy therefore defeats his intention.

---

claim, may be deprived of their gifts by revocation. See Tiley [1975] CLJ 205; Bates 129 New LJ 547.

[11] S 18(2). The question was considered by the Law Reform Committee who were unable to agree: 22nd Report (Cmnd 7902), paras 3.26–3.38. The section does not apply to testators dying before 1983 (Administration of Justice Act 1982, s 73(6)(b)) but it will apply even though the decree was obtained before that year.

[12] Family Law Act 1986, s 53. For recognition of divorces and annulments see Cheshire and North *Private International Law* (11th Edn) pp 648–685. In certain circumstances an overseas divorce or annulment will be recognised even though it was not obtained by means of any formal proceedings (eg a Muslim talaq).

[13] [1985] Ch 446, [1985] 1 All ER 1066. See Prime 49 MLR 108.

[14] S 18A(3).

[15] *Re Sinclair* (supra). Similarly, if there is a gift to those members of a group including the spouse alive at the testator's death as tenants in common, the spouse's share will fall into residue and will not pass to the other survivors. Nor will divorce or annulment affect a power of appointment granted by the will. See Oerton 129 Sol Jo 646.

Mutual wills

Although mutual wills are rare, they are still made occasionally, and they are of particular interest in family law as mutual testators are usually (although not invariably) husband and wife. They can take one of two forms. Each testator may leave a life interest to the other with an identical remainder over; alternatively each can give an absolute interest to the other with identical provisions in case the beneficiary predeceases the testator.

It is not sufficient that the testators agreed to make identical wills: it must also be established that they agreed that neither would revoke his or her will without the consent of the other or, at least, without giving notice to the other so that the latter could make fresh testamentary dispositions.[16] Although English law knows of no such thing as an irrevocable will, equity takes the view that it would be inequitable to permit the survivor to take the benefits under the other's will without giving effect to the agreement himself and it protects the other beneficiaries by attaching a trust to the property on the first testator's death.

Let us suppose that a husband, H, and wife, W, agree to make mutual wills in the following form: 'I devise and bequeath the whole of my estate to trustees on trust for my wife W (or my husband H) for life and then on trust for my son S absolutely' or alternatively '... to W (or H) provided that she (or he) survives me, and if she (or he) does not, to S'. The following illustrations will show how the equitable principle operates.

(1) H and W agree that they will no longer be bound by their agreement. Both are free to revoke their wills and no trust is created on the death of either.

(2) H revokes his will and tells W that he has done so. W is free to revoke her will and no trust is created.[17]

(3) H revokes his will without telling W. H dies first and W discovers the revocation. As she is still free to make other testamentary dispositions, she may do so and no trust is created.[18]

(4) W dies first without having revoked her will. As it would be unconscionable to permit H to take the interest given by W's will without adhering to the agreement which effectively gave it to him, equity imposes an obligation on him to observe it and regards him as holding both estates on trust to carry out its terms. Consequently if he later revokes his will[19] (or revoked it before W's death without apprising her of this fact) his personal representatives are bound to give effect to the agreement and take his estate with a trust impressed on it for the benefit of S.[20] It is not clear whether H would still be bound by the agreement if he repudiated it by disclaiming

---

[16] *Re Cleaver* [1981] 2 All ER 1018; *Re Oldham* [1925] Ch 75; *Gray v Perpetual Trustee Co Ltd* [1928] AC 391, PC.

[17] *Birmingham v Renfrew* (1937) 57 CLR 666, 682, cited with approval in *Re Cleaver* (supra) at 1023.

[18] *Stone v Hoskins* [1905] P 194.

[19] Quaere if the will is revoked by operation of law if H remarries. In *Re Marsland* [1939] Ch 820, CA, it was held that this did not amount to a breach of an express covenant not to revoke a will. It is submitted that this principle should not be applied to mutual wills, because the trusts attach on the death of the first testator and, if it were applied, they would frequently fail.

[20] *Dufour v Pereira* (1769) 1 Dick 419, Hargr Jurid Arg 304.

the gift to himself. The dicta are conflicting,[1] but since the trust arises from the prior agreement, the better view is that it is automatically impressed on the property on the first party's death and the survivor's accepting the gift is therefore immaterial.[2]

If these conditions are satisfied, the trust takes effect from the moment the first testator dies.[3] Consequently the remaindermen have a vested interest from this time, and the gifts to them will not lapse if they die after this date but before the surviving testator.[4] But even now it is not settled whether any property acquired by the survivor after the first party's death is also subject to the trust or whether this will attach only to the property which he has at that time.[5] Whatever the answer, there are considerable problems. For example, may the survivor deal with his own property as he wishes or is he, as a trustee, bound to convert it into authorised investments?[6] If the wills appear to give an absolute interest to the survivor, the following practical solution was propounded by Dixon J in *Birmingham v Renfrew*:[7]

'The object of the transaction is to put the survivor in a position to enjoy for his own benefit the full ownership so that, for instance, he may convert [the property passing under the will of the party first dying] and expend the proceeds if he choose... No doubt gifts and settlements, inter vivos, if calculated to defeat the intention of the compact, could not be made by the survivor and his right of disposition, inter vivos, is, therefore, not unqualified. But, substantially, the purpose of the arrangement will often be to allow full enjoyment for the survivor's own benefit and advantage upon condition that at his death the residue shall pass as arranged.'

Since the beneficiaries may not know that the wills were mutual until the death of the surviving testator, not the least of the practical difficulties is to see how he can effectively be prevented from disposing of the trust property inter vivos.[8]

Gifts to the testator's wife or husband

Provided that this was obviously the testator's intention, a gift to the testator's wife (or husband) will take effect in favour of a woman (or man) with whom he (or she) is living as husband and wife even though they are not legally married.[9] Such a gift will even be valid if it is directed to be held on trust during widowhood; in this case it will be construed as

[1] See the different interpretations placed on Lord Camden's judgment in *Dufour v Pereira* (supra) by Lord Hailsham LC in *Gray v Perpetual Trustee Co Ltd* (supra) at 399, and by Clauson J in *Re Hagger* [1930] 2 Ch 190, 195. See Mitchell *Some Aspects of Mutual Wills*, 14 MLR 136.
[2] If this were not so and the survivor were the widow or widower of the other, he or she might disclaim the legacy and take the estate on intestacy, thus obtaining the benefit whilst going back on the agreement: Mitchell, loc cit. See also Burgess *A Fresh Look at Mutual Wills* 34 Conv 230, at p 240.
[3] *Re Hagger* (supra); *Re Green* [1951] Ch 148, [1950] 2 All ER 913.
[4] *Re Hagger* (supra).
[5] See Mitchell, loc cit, for a fuller discussion of this and other difficulties.
[6] See Mellows *Law of Succession* (4th Edn) pp 28–30.
[7] (1937) 57 CLR 666, 689, cited with approval in *Re Cleaver* (supra) at 1023 and 946, respectively.
[8] Mitchell, loc cit.
[9] *Re Brown* (1910) 26 TLR 257. A fortiori if he names her (eg, 'to my wife EAS'): *Re Smalley* [1929] 2 Ch 112, CA.

being determinable upon the other's contracting a valid marriage after the testator's death.[10]

In a home-made will it is not uncommon for a testator to make a bequest in the form: 'I give my whole estate to my wife, W, and after her death to my children'. His probable intention was that she should have full power to dispose of capital and income but that anything that was left at her death should go to the children.[11] The effect, however, would be to give her an only life interest because an absolute interest would be incompatible with the gift over. To remedy this, section 22 of the Administration of Justice Act 1982[12] now provides that, if a testator makes a gift to his or her spouse in terms which in themselves would confer an absolute interest and *by the same instrument*[13] gives an interest in the same property to his or her issue, the gift to the spouse takes effect absolutely unless a contrary intention is shown.[14] The section is not well drafted. The absolute gift to the spouse presumably destroys the gift to the issue; if, therefore, the wife predeceases the testator, the gift will fall into residue and may not pass to the issue, which will again defeat the testator's intention. It will also be observed that the section does not apply to a gift to an unmarried cohabitant or if the gift over is to someone other than the testator's issue (as might be the case if he were childless).

Unlike the position on intestacy,[15] the surviving spouse cannot demand that the matrimonial home or personal chattels should be appropriated as part of a gift (for example, a residuary bequest). If they have not been specifically disposed of by the will, the only thing a widow or widower wishing to retain such property can do is to ask the personal representatives to exercise their power of appropriation in this way.[16]

Gifts to children

The only problem that arises here is over the power of illegitimate, legitimated and adopted children to take under a testamentary disposition. This has already been discussed.[17]

---

[10] Even though the 'wife' is already married to another man: *Re Wagstaff* [1908] 1 Ch 162, CA; *Re Hammond* [1911] 2 Ch 342. Cf *Re Lynch* [1943] 1 All ER 168. The decision to the contrary in *Re Gale* [1941] Ch 209, [1941] 1 All ER 329, cannot be reconciled with these decisions and must be wrong.

[11] See the 19th Report of the Law Reform Committee (Interpretation of Wills) 1973 (Cmnd 5301), para 60.

[12] Implementing the recommendations of the Law Reform Committee: ibid, para 62.

[13] Hence not if one interest is conferred by will and the other by a codicil. The codicil will prevail.

[14] The most effective way of fulfilling the testator's presumed intention would have been to give the spouse a life interest with power to dispose of the capital inter vivos but not by will. The Law Reform Committee rejected this proposal because it would have produced an undesirable complexity: Cmnd 5301, para 62.

[15] See post, pp 815–817.

[16] For the personal representatives' powers of appropriation, see the Administration of Estates Act 1925, s 41.

[17] Ante, pp 646–648.

Testamentary gift to a deceased child

In the normal way if a devisee or legatee predeceases the testator, the gift lapses and either it drops into residue or the testator is deemed to die intestate with respect to it. The application of this rule to a testamentary gift to a child, however, might well defeat the intention of a testator who had failed to foresee the possibility of the child's predeceasing him. If, for example, a father left a substantial legacy to a daughter with a residual gift to a charity, it is probable that he would wish the daughter's legacy to go to her children rather than to the charity in the event of her untimely death. If he himself dies before changing his will, his wishes will be defeated. Consequently section 33 of the Wills Act 1837 (as substituted by section 19 of the Administration of Justice Act 1982)[18] provides that a devise or bequest to a child or remoter descendant who predeceases the testator[19] and leaves issue shall take effect as a gift to the intended beneficiary's issue living at the testator's death. A similar rule operates if there is a gift to a class consisting of the testator's children or remoter descendants: in such a case the deceased member's issue take the share to which he or she would have been entitled.

The issue surviving the testator need not be the same as those surviving the intended beneficiary: indeed they may have been born after the latter's death. Suppose that T by his will made in 1988 bequeathed property to his son, S, and that S died in 1989 leaving an only child, G, who in turn had a child, X, born in 1990. If G died in 1991 and T died in 1992, X could claim S's legacy because he is issue of S living at T's death.[20] For the purpose of this section a person's illegitimacy is to be disregarded[1] and a child en ventre sa mere at the testator's death is to be regarded as living.[2]

If there is more than one descendant of the intended beneficiary, the issue take per stirpes and no one can take if he has a parent (or presumably a remoter ancestor) alive at the testator's death who can take.[3] The following illustrations may make the operation of the section clearer.

(1) T leaves a legacy of £20,000 to his child, C. C predeceases T leaving two children, K and L. K and L each take £10,000. If L had also predeceased T leaving two children, X and Y, K would still take £10,000 and X and Y would each take £5,000. X and Y would have been entitled to nothing, however, if L had survived T.

(2) T leaves a legacy of £60,000 to his children as a class and one of his three children, C, predeceases him. C's share of £20,000 will be divided in the same way.

A testator may prevent the operation of this section by stating a contrary intention in his will. Such an intention could also be implied: the issue of

---

[18] For the section as originally enacted, which applies to the wills of testators dying before 1983 (see the Administration of Justice Act 1982, ss 73(6) and 76(11)), see the 6th edition of this book, pp 608–609.
[19] Including a person who had died before the will was made: *Wisden v Wisden* (1854) 2 Sm & G 396.
[20] See *In the Goods of Parker* (1860) 1 Sw & Tr 523.
[1] For the difficulties that this may cause, see Ryder *Property Law Aspects of the Family Law Reform Act 1969*, Current Legal Problems 1971, 157 at pp 174–177.
[2] S 33(4) of the 1837 Act as substituted by s 19(4) of the 1982 Act.
[3] S 33(3) of the 1837 Act as substituted by s 19(3) of the 1982 Act.

a deceased child could claim nothing, for example, if the gift were to the testator's *surviving* children or conferred a life interest on the intended beneficiary. Further, although the testamentary exercise of a *general* power of appointment in favour of a child or other issue will not lapse if the person in whose favour the donee has exercised it predeceases him, the provision does not apply to the exercise of a *special* power which is not technically a devise or bequest for the purpose of the section and which will therefore lapse.[4]

The rule against double portions

This rule is a direct application of the equitable presumption that a father or other person in loco parentis intends to favour none of his children at the expense of the others and in particular intends to divide his estate or fortune amongst them all equally. They may obviously take a share of this in two ways: by payments made to the child by the parent during the latter's lifetime, and by a gift to the child in the parent's will.[5] Consequently in certain circumstances, unless the presumption that all the children were to share alike can be rebutted, they must bring into account what they have received during the testator's lifetime before they can take the gift under the will. Hence equity is said 'to lean against double portions'.

But it is not every gift that the child received from the testator while he was alive that must be brought into account. Like the presumption of advancement, this rule applies only to gifts and payments made by his father or other person in loco parentis to him.[6] Further, it would clearly be impractical to make the beneficiary account for every penny received, and consequently he must bring in only such gifts as may fairly be called advancements by way of portion, that is, something given to the child to establish him in life. Whether or not this is the purpose of any particular payment must be a question of fact in each case: payments made to a child on his marriage always come into this category, and the gift of a substantial sum raises a presumption that it was intended as an advancement by way of portion.[7] On the other hand, a mere bounty is not a portion,[8] nor is a payment made to extricate a child from financial embarrassment;[9] and a gift will not prima facie amount to an advancement by way of portion unless it is made early in life.[10] For details of the operation of this principle reference should be made to the sixth edition of this book[11] and to works on equity and succession generally.[12]

[4] *Eccles v Cheyne* (1856) 2 K & J 676 (general power); *Holyland v Lewin* (1884) 26 Ch D 266, CA (special power).
[5] Or, of course, by the child's taking a benefit on the latter's intestacy: see post, p 817.
[4] For the meaning of 'person in loco parentis', see ante, pp 643–644.
[7] *Re Hayward* [1957] Ch 528, [1957] 2 All ER 474, CA.
[8] *Re Livesey* [1953] 2 All ER 723; *Re Vaux* [1939] Ch 465, 481, [1938] 4 All ER 703, 709, CA.
[9] *Taylor v Taylor* (1875) LR 20 Eq 155; *Re Scott* [1903] 1 Ch 1, CA.
[10] *Re Hayward* (supra), at 538 and 479, respectively. See also *Re George's Will Trusts* [1949] Ch 154, [1948] 2 All ER 1004 (gift of live and dead stock with which son was to set up as a farmer held to be a portion); *Hardy v Shaw* [1976] Ch 82, [1975] 2 All ER 1052 (substantial gift of shares giving children controlling interest in family printing business held to be portions).
[11] Pp 609–615.
[12] See eg Pettit *Equity and the Law of Trusts* (5th Edn) pp 600–615.

B. Intestate succession

Intestate succession before 1926

Before the Administration of Estates Act 1925 came into force, there was a considerable difference between the descent of realty and the descent of personalty. All inheritable estates of freehold descended to the heir at law subject to the husband's curtesy and the wife's dower.[13] The husband took all his wife's personalty (including her separate estate if she had not disposed of it by will).[14] On the death of a married man his widow took one third of his personalty if he left issue and one half if he did not; the remainder of his estate was divided among his issue or, in default of issue, among his next-of-kin as defined by the Statutes of Distribution of 1670 and 1685.[15] Under the Intestates' Estates Act of 1890, which was passed to give a widow a larger provision if the estate was small and the intestate left no issue, she took the whole of the real and personal estate if the total value did not exceed £500; if it exceeded this sum, the estate was to stand charged with the payment to her of £500.

Administration of Estates Act 1925

This Act radically overhauled the law relating to intestate succession in two respects. First, the law relating to realty and personalty has been put on exactly the same footing; and secondly the distribution of estates has been completely changed. The principal effect of this Act has been to give the surviving widow a much greater interest than she had before 1926 and to give the surviving widower the same rights as the surviving widow. The details of this have been modified by the Intestates' Estates Act 1952 and the Family Provision Act 1966, which have given the surviving spouse an even larger share of the estate and, as will be seen, have made him or her in many cases the universal successor.[16]

It must be remembered that the general law of intestate succession does not apply to entailed interests, which still descend according to the old laws of intestate succession applicable to entailed realty.[17] For the rest, the whole of the intestate's estate vests in his personal representatives on trust for sale and conversion, and after the payment of all expenses and debts they must then distribute it in the way about to be described.[18] It must also be borne in mind that the distribution is liable to be upset by claims under the Inheritance (Provision for Family and Dependants) Act.[19]

---

[13] See ante, pp 555 and 556. See works on real property for a fuller discussion.
[14] See ante, p 558.
[15] For a fuller discussion, see works on the law of personal property.
[16] Ss 46–49 of the Administration of Estates Act, as amended by the Intestates' Estates Act, are now set out in the 1st Sch to the latter Act. References to these sections '(as amended)' are to the sections as set out in that Schedule.
[17] The widower of a deceased female tenant in tail is still entitled to a life interest by the curtesy, see ante, p 561, n 12.
[18] Administration of Estates Act 1925, s 33.
[19] See post, section C.

The rights of the surviving spouse

The surviving widow or widower now takes the following interests.[20]

Personal chattels

The surviving spouse is always entitled to the personal chattels (provided that the estate is solvent), and personal representatives may not sell them unless this is necessary to pay debts and expenses.[1] Personal chattels are defined as:[2]

'Carriages, horses, stable furniture and effects (not used for business purposes), motor cars and accessories (not used for business purposes), garden effects, domestic animals, plate, plated articles, linen, china, glass, books, pictures, prints, furniture, jewellery,[3] articles of household or personal use or ornament, musical and scientific instruments and apparatus, wines, liquors and consumable stores, but [they] do not include any chattels used at the death of the intestate for business purposes[4] nor money or securities for money.'

Residuary interests

The interest which the surviving spouse takes over and above the personal chattels depends upon what other relatives the intestate leaves surviving.

If he leaves any children or remoter issue, the spouse takes what is usually termed a 'statutory legacy' of £75,000 with interest at 6 per cent per annum until it is paid and a *life* interest in half the residue.

If he leaves no issue but a parent or a brother or sister of the whole blood or issue of such a brother or sister, the surviving spouse takes a 'statutory legacy' of £125,000 with interest at 6 per cent per annum until it is paid and an *absolute* interest in half the residue.

If he leaves neither issue nor any of the above relations, the surviving spouse takes the whole of the residue absolutely.

In view of the large interest which the surviving spouse takes in the other's estate, the rule that, where it is uncertain which of two persons died first, the younger shall be deemed to have survived the elder does not apply as between a person dying intestate and his or her spouse, and the estate of each is to be distributed as though he or she had survived the other.[5] Where there are no issue, it is obviously not desirable that the presumption should operate so as to put £125,000 or more at the disposal of a man's parents-in-law rather than at the disposal of his own parents.

[20] Administration of Estates Act 1925, s 46 (as amended); Family Provision Act 1966, s 1; Administration of Justice Act 1977, s 28(1); Family Provision (Intestate Succession) Order, SI 1987/799; Intestate Succession (Interest and Capitalisation) Order, SI 1977/1491, as amended by SI 1983/1374.

[1] Administration of Estates Act 1925, s 33(1).

[2] Ibid, s 55(1)(x). This section has been widely construed and has been held to include a 60-foot motor yacht (*Re Chaplin* [1950] Ch 507, [1950] 2 All ER 155) and a collection of clocks and watches (*Re Crispin's Will Trusts* [1975] Ch 245, [1974] 3 All ER 772, CA). The mere fact that the property might be regarded as an investment does not prevent it from being a personal chattel too: *Re Reynold's Will Trusts* [1965] 3 All ER 686 (valuable stamp collection, which was deceased's principal hobby, held to be an article of personal use). See REM in 82 LQR 18.

[3] Including cut but unmounted jewels: *Re Whitby* [1944] Ch 210, [1944] 1 All ER 299, CA.

[4] See *Re Ogilby* [1942] Ch 288, [1942] 1 All ER 524.

[5] Administration of Estates Act 1925, s 46(3) (as amended).

Redemption of life interest

The spouse may, if he wishes to do so, insist on the personal representatives' redeeming his life interest by paying the capital value to him.[6] He must elect to do so within 12 months after representation is taken out, but the court may extend this period if it considers that the limit will operate unfairly because a previous will was revoked or invalid, or because the interest of some person in the estate had not been determined when representation was taken out, or because of any other circumstances affecting the administration or distribution of the estate.[7]

Rights with respect to the matrimonial home

The Act of 1952 has given the surviving spouse a right within certain limits to retain the matrimonial home in specie.[8] Where the intestate's estate comprises an interest in a dwelling-house in which the surviving spouse was resident at the time of the intestate's death, the survivor may require the personal representatives to appropriate the house in or towards satisfaction of any absolute interest that the survivor has in the estate,[9] and if the value of the house exceeds the value of the survivor's interest, he may exercise this option if he pays the excess value to the representatives.[10] He must exercise this option within 12 months of representation being taken out, but this period may be extended by the court as in the case of an application to have a life interest redeemed.[11] Consequently the personal representatives are forbidden to sell the house within this period without the written consent of the surviving spouse unless this is necessary for the payment of expenses or debts.[12]

There are two limitations upon this power. First, these provisions normally do not apply if the house is held upon a lease which had less than two years to run from the date of the intestate's death or which could be determined by the landlord within this period.[13] This means that many houses (for example, those held on periodic tenancies) come outside these provisions, but to offset this it must be remembered that there will usually be a statutory transmission to the surviving spouse.[14] Secondly, the spouse cannot require the personal representatives to appropriate the house in the following cases except on an order of the court which must be satisfied that the appropriation is not likely to diminish the value of assets in the residuary

---

[6] Administration of Estates Act 1925, s 47A (as amended) and as further amended by the Administration of Justice Act 1977, s 28(2), (3), and SI 1977/1491.

[7] Ibid, s 47A(5) (as amended).

[8] Intestates' Estates Act 1952, Sch 2.

[9] Ibid, para 1(1). 'Dwelling-house' includes part of a building occupied as a separate dwelling and an absolute interest includes a redeemed life interest: ibid, para 1(4), (5).

[10] Ibid, para 5(2); *Re Phelps* [1980] Ch 275, [1979] 3 All ER 373, CA. The value is to be assessed at the date of appropriation: *Robinson v Collins* [1975] 1 All ER 321.

[11] Ibid, para 3. It cannot be exercised after the surviving spouse's death by his or her personal representatives: ibid, para 3(1)(b).

[12] Ibid, para 4. But if they fail to observe this provision, the spouse has no right to claim the house from the purchaser: ibid, para 4(5).

[13] Ibid, para 1(2). But the personal representatives have a discretionary power to appropriate the lease under s 41 of the Administration of Estates Act 1925: ibid, para 5(2). For exceptional cases (where the surviving spouse would be entitled to acquire the freehold or an extended lease), see the Leasehold Reform Act 1967, s 7(8).

[14] See post, section D.

estate (other than the interest in the house) or make these assets more difficult to dispose of.[15] This is where:

'(a) the dwelling-house forms part of a building and an interest in the whole of the building is comprised in the residuary estate;[16] or
(b) the dwelling-house is held with agricultural land and an interest in the agricultural land is comprised in the residuary estate; or
(c) the whole or part of the dwelling-house was at the time of the intestate's death used as a hotel or lodging house; or
(d) a part of the dwelling-house was at the time of the intestate's death used for purposes other than domestic purposes.'

Judicial separation

By section 18(2) of the Matrimonial Causes Act 1973, if either spouse dies wholly or partially intestate whilst a decree of judicial separation is in force and the separation is continuing, his or her property is to devolve as though the other were dead. The reason for this provision is that the rules of intestate succession are intended to reflect the testamentary dispositions the deceased might reasonably be expected to have made, and as judicial separation almost always marks the de facto end of the marriage, it is highly unlikely that either would have left anything to the other.[17]

Interests taken by the intestate's children and remoter issue

If the intestate leaves a surviving spouse, the personal representatives must hold one half of the residue (after taking out the personal chattels and the spouse's £75,000) on the statutory trusts for the intestate's issue and the other half on the same trusts subject to the surviving spouse's life interest. If the intestate leaves no surviving spouse, the personal representatives must hold the whole of the residue on the statutory trusts for the issue.[18]

The statutory trusts

The property is to be held on trust for all the children alive at the intestate's death who reach the age of 18 or marry under that age in equal shares. But if any of his children has predeceased him, that child's share is held upon the same trusts for his own children or remoter issue.[19]

Thus suppose that the intestate had four children, A, B, C and D. The first three are alive at their parent's death but D is already dead. D had two children, K and L, of whom K is still alive but L is also dead, leaving two children, X and Y. By applying the above rules, we see that A, B and C each take one quarter; K takes half of D's share (ie, one-eighth) and the other half of D's share goes to X and Y, who thus get one-sixteenth each.

---

[15] Intestates' Estates Act 1952, Sch 2, para 2.
[16] Eg, if the house is attached to a shop and the owner would normally live in it.
[17] This does not apply to separation orders made by magistrates' courts under earlier statutes (which in other respects had the same effect as decrees of judicial separation) because they might well be followed by a reconciliation: Matrimonial Causes Act 1973, s 18(3). See further Law Com No 25, pp 107–109. S 18(2) replaces earlier legislation going back to 1857 which applied only to certain property with respect to which the wife died intestate.
[18] Administration of Estates Act 1925, s 46(1) (as amended).
[19] Ibid, s 47(1)(i) (as amended); Family Law Reform Act 1969, s 3(2).

If the share of any of the above fails to vest because he dies a minor and unmarried, his share will go over to the others as if he had predeceased the testator.[20] Thus if A were to die in such circumstances, B and C would each take one third of his share, K would take a sixth, and X and Y would each take a twelfth. If K were to die, his share would pass to X and Y equally; and if X were to die, his share would go to Y.

Until a beneficiary obtains a vested interest by attaining his majority or marrying, the trustees may use the whole of the income of the part to which he is contingently entitled for his maintenance, education or benefit, and they may use one half of the capital to which he is contingently entitled for his advancement.[1] Subject to this they must accumulate the income at compound interest.[2] They may also at their discretion permit him to have the use of any personal chattels.[3]

Hotchpot

The Administration of Estates Act expressly brings the rule against double portions into operation by enacting that any portion or portion debt must be brought into account in satisfaction in whole or part of that child's share of the intestacy unless a contrary intention on the part of the intestate can be inferred.[4] This is frequently known as 'bringing into hotchpot'.

Interests taken by other members of the family

If the intestate dies leaving a surviving spouse but no issue, the other half of the residue (after taking out the personal chattels, the £125,000 and the half interest which has gone to the surviving spouse) is to be held on trust for the intestate's parents in equal shares (or for one parent absolutely if only one parent survives the intestate), and if neither of his parents survives him, on the statutory trusts for his brothers and sisters of the whole blood and their issue.

If the intestate leaves neither a spouse nor issue surviving, his whole estate must be held on trust for the persons coming into the first of the following classes that can be satisfied. In other words, if neither of the parents (who come in class (1)) is alive, then the persons coming into class (2) will take and so forth. If none of these classes is filled, the whole estate will go to the Crown as bona vacantia.[5]

(1) For the intestate's parents (if they are both alive) in equal shares, or, if one only is still alive, for that parent absolutely.

(2) On the statutory trusts for the brothers and sisters of the whole blood of the intestate and their issue.

(3) On the statutory trusts for the brothers and sisters of the half blood of the intestate and their issue.

(4) For the surviving grandparents of the intestate in equal shares.

---

[20] *Re Young* [1951] Ch 185, [1950] 2 All ER 1040.
[1] Administration of Estates Act 1925, s 47(1)(ii) (as amended); Trustee Act 1925, ss 31(1), 32(1).
[2] Trustee Act 1925, s 31(2).
[3] Administration of Estates Act 1925, s 47(1)(iv) (as amended).
[4] Ibid, s 47(1)(iii) (as amended); *Hardy v Shaw* [1976] Ch 82, [1975] 2 All ER 1052.
[5] Administration of Estates Act 1925, s 46(1) (as amended).

(5) On the statutory trusts for the uncles and aunts of the intestate (being brothers or sisters of the whole blood of one of his parents) and their issue.

(6) On the statutory trusts for the uncles and aunts of the intestate (being brothers or sisters of the half blood of one of his parents) and their issue.

The statutory trusts are exactly the same in the above cases as the statutory trusts for the intestate's children and issue except that the hotchpot rule does not apply. Hence the members of each class take per capita and the issue of any deceased member of the class take per stirpes. All the interests are contingent upon the beneficiary's attaining his majority or marrying, and if no member of any class takes a vested interest, the members of the next class will take.[6]

Children of unmarried parents and adopted children

Originally, in accordance with the general rule at common law, only legitimate persons and those claiming a relationship through legitimate persons, could participate in intestate succession. Those who had been legitimated could claim after the passing of the Legitimacy Act of 1926,[7] and the Family Law Reform Act of 1969 permitted illegitimate children and their parents to succeed to each other.[8] In pursuance of the policy of removing the disadvantages flowing from birth outside marriage, section 18 of the Family Law Reform Act 1987 now provides that, for the purposes of the distribution of the estate of an intestate, any relationship shall be construed without regard to whether the parents of the deceased, the claimant or any person through whom the claimant is related to the deceased were married to each other.[9] But because of the difficulty in tracing some fathers, whose identity might not be known, a person whose parents were not married to each other is to be presumed not to have been survived by his father or by anyone related to him through his father unless the contrary is shown.[10]

An adopted child is treated as though he were the child of his adopters

---

[6] Administration of Estates Act 1925, s 46(4), (5) (as amended). If all the members of a particular class (except (1) and (4)) are dead, but one or more have left issue, the issue will take in preference to the members of a more remote class: *Re Lockwood* [1958] Ch 231, [1957] 3 All ER 520. Thus, eg, issue of a brother or sister of the whole blood will take before a brother and sister of the half blood.

[7] See the Legitimacy Act 1976, s 5. This also applied to the issue of a person who would have been legitimated had he not died before his parents' marriage. If the intestate died before 1976, the claimant could succeed only if he was legitimated before the death and, if an entailed interest was created before 1976, he can still claim by descent only if it was *created* after his legitimation: Legitimacy Act 1926, s 3(1)(a), (c).

[8] S 14. Except that the legitimate issue of a deceased illegitimate person could succeed on the death intestate of that person's parent, succession was limited to these two cases. Hence an illegitimate person could claim nothing on the intestacy of a grandparent or collateral relative and the latter could claim nothing on his intestacy. This provision implemented the recommendations of the majority of the Committee on the Law of Succession in Relation to Illegitimate Persons 1966, Cmnd 3051, and applied to deaths occurring on or after 1st January 1970.

[9] Applying ibid, s 1. The section applies if the intestate died on or after 4th April 1988. Any reference to statutory next of kin in an instrument taking effect on or after this date is to be construed likewise: s 18(3).

[10] Family Law Reform Act 1987, s 18(2). See Miller *The Family Law Reform Act 1987 and the Law of Succession* [1988] Conv 410.

and of no other person.[11] If he was adopted by two spouses jointly, he will be in the position of a brother (or sister) of the whole blood of any other child or adopted child of both the adopters and a brother of the half blood of any child or adopted child of one of them; if he was adopted by one person only, he will be in the position of a brother of the half blood of any child or adopted child of his adopter. He has no claims on the death of his natural parents or anyone related to them.

Partial intestacy

These rules apply equally to a partial intestacy. But in this case if the deceased devises or bequeaths property to the surviving spouse (other than personal chattels or under the exercise of a special power of appointment), the spouse must take this in partial or total satisfaction of the £75,000 or £125,000 to which he is entitled under the intestacy. Similarly a child *or any remoter issue* of the deceased must bring into hotchpot any beneficial interests acquired by him under the will (except those acquired by virtue of the exercise of a special power of appointment).[12]

Proposals for reform

In their examination of the law relating to intestacy[13] the Law Commission concluded that the main criticism to be levelled against the present rules was that they could operate unjustly in the case of a surviving spouse and, as a consequence, of the children also. In many cases the most valuable asset contained in the estate is the matrimonial home: if this was held by the spouses jointly, it will devolve jure accrescendi on the survivor who will thus take the statutory legacy together with the whole interest in the house; if, on the other hand, they held it as tenants in common, the deceased's undivided share will form part of his estate and so will have to be taken in partial or total satisfaction of the statutory legacy; and if he was the sole beneficial owner, this may be insufficient to enable the survivor to remain in the house.[14] It is generally accepted that the latter should be able to do

---

[11] Adoption Act 1976, ss 39, 42 and 46(4). Hence a child adopted by one of his natural parents cannot claim on the death of the other.

[12] Administration of Estates Act 1925, s 49 (as amended). In *Re Young* [1951] Ch 185, [1950] 2 All ER 1040, and *Re Grover's Will Trusts* [1971] Ch 168, [1970] 1 All ER 1185, it was held that, if the will confers a life interest on the testator's child with remainder over to his children, the capital value of the *whole* fund must be brought into account if the child also claims on a partial intestacy. This is based on the principle that the interest taken by the whole *stirps* must be regarded as a gift to the testator's issue. Quaere whether the child should not have to bring into account only the capitalised value of the life interest which is all that *he* takes under the will: cf *Re Morton* [1956] Ch 644, [1956] 3 All ER 259. For difficulties presented by these decisions, see Ryder *Hotchpot on a Partial Intestacy* Current Legal Problems 1973, 208; Scott 120 New LJ 848. If the surviving spouse is given a life interest in the estate and the testator dies intestate with respect to the remainder, the spouse is entitled to £75,000 or £125,000 less the capitalised value of the life interest immediately: *Re Bowen-Buscarlet's Will Trusts* [1972] Ch 463, [1971] 3 All ER 636. In this case the testator left issue so that his widow's life interest in the rest of the residue merged with her life interest under the bequest. But if there had been no issue, she could presumably also have claimed her absolute half interest in the rest immediately. The trustees will have to sell sufficient of the reversion to raise the sum presently due.

[13] Law Com No 187 (Distribution on Intestacy), 1989.

[14] Ibid, paras 18–21.

so and should also receive a sufficient income without having to suffer the delay and expense of an application under the Inheritance (Provision for Family and Dependants) Act.[15] To ensure this the Commission recommend that the surviving spouse should take the whole estate, whether or not the deceased left children or other issue or close relations. It would no longer be necessary to retain the power to appropriate the matrimonial home and the disappearance of the surviving spouse's life interest would simplify administration and reduce its cost.[16] To prevent the estates of both spouses going to the family of the survivor if, for example, they were both fatally injured in the same accident but did not die simultaneously, a spouse should take nothing unless he or she survived the other by 14 days.[17] Although a strong case can be made out for treating a surviving unmarried cohabitant like a surviving spouse, the proposal was rejected because it would increase the complexity and cost of administration and special rules would have to be introduced to deal with the situation where both a spouse and a cohabitant survived. Instead it is proposed that a cohabitant's power to apply for an order under the Inheritance (Provision for Family and Dependants) Act should be strengthened.[18] The Commission also recommend that the hotchpot rules should be abolished on the ground that they are complicated, difficult to administer and unjust in that they apply only to issue and not to other relations.[19]

C. Provision for members of the family and other dependants

By permitting a husband to extinguish his wife's right to dower, the Dower Act 1833 abolished the last vestige of family provision in English law.[20] After that there was nothing to stop a man (or a woman with respect to her separate property) from devising and bequeathing his whole estate to a charity or a complete stranger and leaving his widow and children penniless. To prevent this evil, in 1938 Parliament passed the Inheritance (Family Provision) Act.[1] This did not cast upon a testator any positive duty to make reasonable provision for his dependants—indeed it would have been impossible to do so—but enacted that, if he failed to do so, the court might order such reasonable provision as it thought fit to be made out of his estate for the benefit of the surviving spouse and certain classes of children. In 1952 the principle underlying this Act was applied to cases of

[15] Para 26.
[16] Paras 33–45. The Commission felt that any other solution would produce anomalies. They appreciated that problems might arise if the survivor were a second (or further) spouse and the deceased also left children of an earlier marriage, but they pointed out that if there were special rules to deal with this case, they would have to cover other situations as well (for example, if the deceased left illegitimate children). This would complicate administration and militate against the principle that the rules should be as simple as possible.
[17] Para 57.
[18] Paras 58–60. See post, p 826, n 8.
[19] Para 47.
[20] See ante, p 556; Unger *The Inheritance Act and the Family* 6 MLR 215.
[1] For a full discussion of the history of family provision and the policy underlying the Inheritance (Provision for Family and Dependants) Act 1975, see Tyler's *Family Provision* (2nd Edn) chs 1 and 2. See also Green *The Englishman's Castle* 51 MLR 187.

intestacy.[2] It is easy to see that the law of intestate succession might leave a child without adequate support: the whole estate might go to a widow who refused to make any provision for the children of a previous marriage or might be divided between a daughter married to a rich man and a minor son whose education was incomplete. In 1958 a similar power to apply for provision was given to a former spouse, that is, one whose marriage to the deceased had been dissolved or annulled and who had not remarried.[3] This, of course, was of particular value to a divorced wife who had obtained an order for unsecured periodical payments which would cease on her former husband's death.

Notwithstanding these extensions there were still many gaps and deficiencies in the law. The term 'dependant' was so narrowly defined that it excluded many who had been supported by another during his lifetime and who had a moral, if not a legal, claim on his estate. Thus no application could be made, for example, by a parent, brother or sister, another's children who had been treated as members of the deceased's family, or a person with whom he had been cohabiting outside marriage. Provision could be ordered only out of property which the deceased had power to dispose of by will, so that he could defeat the operation of the Act altogether by settling his property during his lifetime or by contracting to leave it to a third person after his death.[4] Furthermore, the court was limited to ordering reasonable provision for the dependant's maintenance and had no power to divide capital assets: the result was that a surviving wife could be in a worse position than a divorced wife who obtained a property adjustment order. When the Law Commission examined the whole question of family property law, they rejected the proposal that a surviving spouse should have a right to inherit a fixed proportion of the deceased's estate in favour of the much more flexible approach of family provision. They added, however, that this would need considerable strengthening, and in particular 'the surviving partner of a marriage should have a claim upon the family assets at least equivalent to that of a divorced person'.[5] Their detailed recommendations, overhauling the whole of the law, were published in 1974[6] and effect was given to them by the Inheritance (Provision for Family and Dependants) Act 1975, which came into force on 1st April 1976. This repealed all the existing relevant legislation and replaced it by a new and comprehensive code.

The Act applies only if the person against whose estate the claim is being made died domiciled in England and Wales.[7]

---

[2] Intestates' Estates Act 1952.
[3] Matrimonial Causes (Property and Maintenance) Act 1958, subsequently re-enacted in the Matrimonial Causes Act 1965, ss 26–28.
[4] *Schaefer v Schuhmann* [1972] AC 572, [1972] 1 All ER 621, PC. But the disposition might possibly have been set aside had it been fraudulent: see post, p 834, n 4.
[5] Law Com No 52, First Report on Family Property: a New Approach, paras 31–45.
[6] Law Com No 61, Second Report on Family Property: Family Provision on Death.
[7] S 1(1). See Law Com No 61, paras 258–262.

Who may apply for an order

Application for provision may be made only by the following persons:[8]

(1) The deceased's wife or husband. This category includes a person who had in good faith entered into a void marriage with the deceased. The reason is that such a person is de facto in the position of a surviving spouse and may not discover that the marriage is void until after the other party's death, when it will be too late to apply for financial relief in nullity proceedings. Consequently the survivor may not make an application under this head if during the deceased's lifetime the marriage has been dissolved or annulled by a decree recognised in England or he has entered into a later marriage and thus in effect treated the first marriage as at an end.[9]

(2) A former wife or husband of the deceased, that is, a person whose marriage with the deceased was dissolved or annulled during his lifetime by a decree granted under the law of any part of the British Isles or recognised as valid in England and who, in either case, has not remarried.[10] This enables the court to make or continue financial provision for those to whom it could award financial relief under the Matrimonial Causes Act. It should be appreciated, however, that an application by a former spouse will rarely be successful, as the Court of Appeal pointed out in *Re Fullard*.[11] In that case it refused to make an order in favour of the plaintiff who had accepted a half share of the matrimonial home (the parties' only asset) only a few months before her former husband's death. Normally, the court said, it would be appropriate to make an award in such circumstances only if the sole order made in previous proceedings had been for periodical payments which had been running for a long time and the deceased's estate could support their continuation[12] or if the death had released a substantial capital sum, such as the payment of an insurance policy, of which the deceased was aware and which therefore should be taken into account in deciding whether he had made reasonable provision for the applicant.[13]

(3) A child of the deceased. This includes a child whose parents were not married to each other, an adopted child, and a child en ventre sa mere at the time of the death.[14]

---

[8] S 1(1). See Hand 10 Fam Law 141. The forfeiture rule, which prohibits a person who has unlawfully killed another from acquiring a benefit in consequence of the killing, does not apply to claims under the Inheritance Act unless the applicant has been convicted of murdering the deceased: Forfeiture Act 1982, ss 3 and 5. But if the deceased's will or the law relating to intestacy made reasonable provision for the applicant, the latter cannot apply under the Act if he cannot claim under the will or intestacy because he failed to apply to the court for an order within three months of being convicted of killing the deceased as required by s 2(3) of the Forfeiture Act: *Re Royse* [1985] Ch 22, [1984] 3 All ER 339, CA.

[9] S 25(4). A later marriage includes a void or voidable marriage (because the person in question would have a claim against the other party to it): s 25(5). This category was originally added by the Law Reform (Miscellaneous Provisions) Act 1970 which, by abolishing actions for breach of promise of marriage, took away the remedy formerly possessed by the survivor.

[10] S 25(1), as amended by the Matrimonial and Family Proceedings Act 1984, s 25(2). Remarriage includes a void or voidable marriage: s 25(2). The lapse of a gift to a former spouse under s 18A of the Wills Act 1837 (see ante, p 808) does not preclude an application under the Inheritance Act: ibid, s 18A(2).

[11] [1982] Fam 42, 49, 52, [1981] 2 All ER 796, 801–802, 804, CA. See Prime 12 Fam Law 53, Shindler [1985] Conv 75.

[12] As in *Re Crawford* (1982) 4 FLR 273.

[13] But not other accretions of wealth since the divorce: *Re Fullard* (supra) at 52 and 804 respectively.

[14] S 25(1); Adoption Act 1976, s 39. Conversely, if the deceased's natural child is adopted after

(4) Any other person whom the deceased had treated as a child of the family in relation to any marriage to which he had at any time been a party. This corresponds to the court's power to award financial relief to a child of the family under the Matrimonial Causes Act. Obviously anyone who is a child of the family for the purpose of that Act will qualify as an applicant under the Inheritance Act. It will be immediately apparent, however, that the category of persons able to apply for provision after death is wider, for only the deceased (and not his or her spouse) need have treated the applicant as a child of the family and children placed as foster children are not automatically excluded. The decision of the Court of Appeal in *Re Leach*[15] shows how wide the category can be. The applicant was a spinster aged 53 on her stepmother's death. She frequently visited her father after his remarriage and had a room in his bungalow. After his death she continued to visit her stepmother and the latter regarded her as a daughter rather than as a stepdaughter. The old lady had asked her to make arrangements if she became incapable of looking after herself and the applicant considered the possibility of her stepmother's coming to live with her. The Court of Appeal held that it is not necessary for the applicant to have been treated as a child of the family by the deceased during the latter's marriage; as Slade LJ, delivering the judgment of the court, pointed out, a young child, who had lived with others during his father's second marriage and came to live with his stepmother after his father's death, would properly be regarded as a member of her family in relation to that marriage.[16] A display of affection, kindness or hospitality is not of itself sufficient to constitute treatment for this purpose: the question is whether 'the deceased has, *as wife or husband* (or widow or widower) under the relevant marriage, expressly or impliedly, assumed the position of a parent towards the applicant, with the attendant *responsibilities and privileges* of that relationship'.[17] The deceased's privileges might well increase and his or her responsibilities diminish with age, and it follows from this approach that the applicant can qualify even though he was treated as a child of the family only when he was an adult[18] and the treatment ceased before the death. Applying this test, the court concluded that the applicant in this case had clearly been treated as a child of the family.

(5) Any other person who was being maintained, either wholly or in part, by the deceased immediately before his death. This provision is entirely new. Its most striking aspect is that the applicant now has a legal claim after the deceased's death whereas she (or he) may have had no claim at all during his lifetime. However anomalous this may be, it can be justified on the ground that the deceased would presumably have continued to provide for the applicant had he survived. In many cases there will be a clear moral claim, and the deceased's failure to provide for her after his death may be due to oversight or accident, for example the failure to make a will in time or the revocation of an earlier will by marriage.[19] Although

---

the deceased's death, he cannot subsequently apply for an order under the Act as the deceased's child: *Re Collins* [1990] Fam 56, [1990] 2 All ER 47.
[15] [1986] Ch 226, [1985] 2 All ER 754, CA.
[16] At 234 and 760 respectively.
[17] At 237 and 762 respectively.
[18] See also *Re Callaghan* [1985] Fam 1, [1984] 3 All ER 790.
[19] See Law Com No 61, paras 85–94.

in some cases the applicant and the deceased will have been members of the same family—for example, two sisters who lived together—it is not necessary to establish such a relationship. What is essential is a de facto dependence, and the commonest example is likely to be that of the woman (or man) with whom the deceased had been living but to whom he or she was not married.

For the purpose of this provision, the applicant will be regarded as having been maintained by the deceased only if the latter had been making a substantial contribution in money or money's worth towards his or her reasonable needs otherwise than for full valuable consideration.[20] Two classes of possible claimant are immediately seen to be outside this definition. The first are those who have not been in receipt of a *substantial* contribution. This means that the deceased's mistress may have a claim if he set her up in her own home and paid all her domestic bills[1] but not if he did no more than make her casual payments and gifts. Secondly, the requirement that the contribution must have been made otherwise than for full valuable consideration clearly excludes claims by, for example, a housekeeper or companion who worked for an economic salary. It is not essential, however, that the consideration should have been provided under a contract between the applicant and the deceased.[2] The test to be applied was formulated by Stephenson LJ in *Jelley v Iliffe* in the following words:[3]

'The court has to balance what [the deceased] was contributing against what [the applicant] was contributing, and if there is any doubt about the balance tipping in favour of [the deceased's] being the greater contribution, the matter must … go to trial. If, however, the balance is bound to come down in favour of [the applicant's] being the greater contribution, or if the contributions are clearly equal, there is no dependency.'

So long as one is dealing with tangible matters such as the provision of accommodation[4] or board and lodging, this is a relatively simple matter of assessment and accounting. Difficulty arises because Stephenson LJ added that the court must put a financial value on imponderables like companionship and weigh these against contributions of money and accommodation.[5] Bearing in mind that the Act speaks of contributions *in money or money's worth*, it is submitted that companionship and the like should be brought into account only in so far as they involve services which can and should be evaluated. The court would be put in an impossible position if it had to place a price on the emotional and other support which the two gave each other, and one would be forced to the absurd conclusion that, the more the applicant had offered the deceased, the less chance he would have of succeeding.[6] If a claim is made by a relative or friend who lived with the deceased and performed domestic services for him in exchange for free board and lodging, the obvious approach is to assess what the

---

[20] S 1(3); *Jelley v Iliffe* [1981] Fam 128, [1981] 2 All ER 29, CA; *Bishop v Plumley* [1991] 1 All ER 236, CA. See further Sachs *Recent Working of the Inheritance Act 1975* [1985] Conv 258; Green *The Englishman's Castle* 51 MLR 187, 199 et seq; Naresh *Dependants' Applications under the Inheritance (Provision for Family and Dependants) Act 1975* 96 LQR 534 (written before *Jelley v Iliffe*).

[1] As in *Malone v Harrison* [1979] 1 WLR 1353.

[2] *Jelley v Iliffe* (supra) at 136, 141 and 35, 38 respectively.

[3] At 138 and 36 respectively.

[4] *Jelley v Iliffe* (supra); *Bishop v Plumley* (supra).

[5] Following *Re Wilkinson* [1978] Fam 22, [1978] 1 All ER 221.

[6] *Bishop v Plumley* (supra) at 242.

latter would have had to pay for the benefit he received. But this would produce an unacceptable result in the case of a cohabitant. As Griffiths LJ stressed in *Jelley v Iliffe*,[7] it is essential to use common sense and ask whether the applicant could fairly be called a dependant: it would not be right to deprive a woman, with whom a man had been living as his wife, of a claim by arguing that she had been performing the duties of a housekeeper whom it would have cost more to employ.[8]

The applicant must also prove that the deceased was maintaining him (or her) immediately before his death. This requirement was subject to a detailed examination by the Court of Appeal in *Jelley v Iliffe*.[9] As Stephenson LJ said:[10]

'In considering whether a person is being maintained "immediately before the death of the deceased" it is the settled basis or general arrangement between the parties as regards maintenance during the lifetime of the deceased which has to be looked at, not the actual, perhaps fluctuating, variation of it which exists immediately before his or her death. It is, I think, not disputed that a relationship of dependence which has persisted for years will not be defeated by its termination during a few weeks of mortal sickness.'

On the other hand, if the deceased had clearly abandoned responsibility for the applicant's maintenance before his death, the latter will have no claim.[11] Nor will he have one if he was being maintained on a purely temporary basis or by chance at the time of his death, for example if he was a friend whom the deceased had taken in for a few days whilst he recovered from an illness. It is not sufficient, however, for the applicant to establish the fact of maintenance: he must also prove that the deceased had assumed responsibility for his maintenance and show 'some act or acts which demonstrate an undertaking of responsibility'.[12] Admittedly the best evidence of this is the actual provision of financial support or a home: this raises a presumption in favour of the applicant which may be rebutted, of course, by an express disclaimer of an intention to maintain or by other circumstances. It cannot have been Parliament's intention to give a claim to everyone who receives maintenance out of kindness or charity; if, for example, two friends agreed to share accommodation and the deceased

---

[7] At 141 and 38 respectively. Applied in *Bishop v Plumley* (supra).
[8] To overcome these difficulties the Law Commission recommend the creation of a new category of applicant: a person who was living with the deceased in the same household immediately before the latter's death and who had been so living for not less than two years as his or her wife or husband. (Cf the definition of 'dependant' for the purposes of the Fatal Accidents Act, ante, p 125.) They further recommend that, although reasonable financial provision should be confined to provision for the applicant's maintenance, the court should be specifically required to take into account the duration of the cohabitation, the applicant's age and the contribution that he or she made to the welfare of the deceased's family. See Law Com No 187 (Distribution on Intestacy), 1989, and ante, p 821. If the effect of this were to exclude an applicant who had been cohabiting with the deceased for less than two years, it could put her (or him) in a worse position than, say, a relative who had lived with the deceased for a shorter period.
[9] [1981] Fam 128, [1981] 2 All ER 29, CA.
[10] At 136 and 34–35 respectively, following *Re Beaumont* [1980] Ch 444, 456, [1980] 1 All ER 266, 272. Griffiths LJ expressed the same view at 141 and 38 respectively. Cumming-Bruce LJ agreed with both judgments.
[11] *Kourkgy v Lusher* (1981) 4 FLR 65 (claimant unsuccessful when deceased had stopped cohabiting with her and returned to his wife three weeks before his death).
[12] Per Megarry V-C in *Re Beaumont* (supra) at 458 and 276 respectively, followed in *Jelley v Iliffe* (supra) at 137 and 35 respectively.

made a greater contribution towards the expenses because he was better off than the other, the latter could have no claim against the richer man's estate.[13] At the same time it must be stressed that the question is whether the applicant was being maintained by the deceased *before* his death: consequently there is no need to prove that he had intended to provide for the applicant's continuing support *after* his death. If it were necessary to do this, there would be few cases where a claim would succeed.[14]

Death of applicant

As the claim is essentially for a dependant's provision, an application automatically abates if the applicant dies before an order is made.[15]

Reasonable provision

The applicant must also show that the provisions of the deceased's will or the law relating to intestacy (or the combination of both if there is a partial intestacy) is not such as to make reasonable financial provision for him.[16] This, of course, is a question of fact, but if the applicant cannot discharge the burden of proof, he has no claim at all. It is not the purpose of the Act merely to enable the court to provide legacies or rewards for meritorious conduct.[17]

In defining reasonable provision, the Act draws a significant distinction between surviving spouses and all other applicants. If the application is made by a surviving husband or wife (except where a decree of judicial separation had been pronounced and the decree was in force and the separation continuing at the deceased's death), reasonable financial provision means such financial provision as it would be reasonable in all the circumstances of the case for a husband or wife to receive, *whether or not that provision is required for his or her maintenance*: in all other cases it means such financial provision as it would be reasonable in all the circumstances of the case for the applicant to receive *for his maintenance*.[18] The reason for this difference is that a surviving widow or widower would normally expect to receive a share of the deceased spouse's estate and it would be anomalous if the court could give her (or him) less after the other spouse's death than

---

[13] *Re Beaumont* (supra) at 458 and 276 respectively.
[14] *Jelley v Iliffe* (supra) at 137 and 35–36 respectively.
[15] *Whytte v Ticehurst* [1986] Fam 64, [1986] 2 All ER 158; *Re Bramwell* [1988] 2 FLR 263. Cf applications for financial provision under the Matrimonial Causes Act 1973, ante, p 725. Presumably an order (eg for a lump sum) once made can be enforced after the applicant's death, although the death should be a ground for giving personal representatives leave to appeal out of time: cf *Barder v Caluori* [1988] AC 20, [1987] 2 All ER 440, HL (ante, p 795), and see 102 LQR 483.
[16] Ss 1(1) and 2(1).
[17] *Re Coventry* [1980] Ch 461, at 486 and 495, [1979] 3 All ER 815, at 821 and 828, CA. In *Re Christie* [1979] Ch 168, [1979] 1 All ER 546, the court appears to have done this. The deceased devised her house to her son and left her interest in another house to her daughter. The devise was adeemed because, after making her will, the testatrix sold the house in question and bought another which, under a residuary gift, was held in trust for both children in equal shares. It was held that the son was entitled to this house in a claim under the Inheritance Act because it had been the testatrix's intention that he should take it and it was fair and just to redress the balance in this way. Goff LJ questioned the decision in *Re Coventry* at 490 and 824, respectively: it is submitted that it should not be followed.
[18] S 1(2). See *Re Besterman* [1984] Ch 458, [1984] 2 All ER 656, CA; *Re Bunning* [1984] Ch 480, [1984] 3 All ER 1.

it could on divorce. (This accounts for the exception where a judicial separation is in force, because the survivor will already have had an opportunity of applying to the court for a lump sum or property adjustment order.)[19] In other words, the Act has two distinct objects: to provide appropriate support for a dependant (including a surviving spouse) and to make a fair division of assets between the spouses, although it is apparent that the courts do not always keep these two objects distinct.[20] When considering the provision of maintenance, the court is not limited to assessing the amount needed for bare necessities nor must it take into account everything which the applicant might regard as reasonably desirable for his benefit or welfare. One must ask whether he will be able to maintain himself in a manner suitable to the circumstances.[1] 'Is the provision sufficient to enable the dependant to live neither luxuriously nor miserably but decently and comfortably according to his or her station in life?'[2]

The Act specifically requires the court to have regard to the following matters when determining whether reasonable financial provision has been made for the applicant.[3]

(a) The financial resources and needs[4] of the applicant, any other applicant for an order, and any beneficiary of the estate;[5] any obligations and responsibilities which the deceased had towards any of these people; and any physical or mental disability from which any of them suffers. In this connection the court must take into account the individual's earning capacity, any resources and needs which he is likely to have in the foreseeable future, and his financial obligations and responsibilities. It is of course necessary to consider the position of other applicants and beneficiaries because any order made will limit the property available for them; consequently an applicant is more likely to succeed if an order in his favour can be made at the expense of a beneficiary towards whom the deceased had no obligations.[6] Generally speaking, the court must pay regard to similar matters when considering the question of financial relief on divorce and they have already been considered more fully in the discussion of that problem,[7]

---

[19] Hence if the deceased's marriage had been dissolved or annulled and he died within twelve months of the decree absolute (or if he died within twelve months of a decree of judicial separation) and no application for financial relief has been made or, if it has, the proceedings have not been determined, the court may consider an application for an order under the Inheritance Act as though no decree had been made: s 14. Otherwise the applicant would lose the benefit of both statutes.
[20] See Miller *Provision for a Surviving Spouse* 102 LQR 445.
[1] *Re Coventry* (supra), at pp 485 and 819–820 (per Goff LJ), and 494 and 827, respectively (per Buckley LJ). Hence if a rich man's bounty has enabled his parents to live in luxury whilst their own income would keep them in comfort, it might be reasonable to give them such provision as would permit them to maintain their previous standard of living.
[2] Per Roach JA in *Re Duranceau* [1952] 3 DLR 714 at 720, cited by Goff LJ in *Re Coventry* (supra) at pp 485 and 819, respectively, and Slade LJ in *Re Leach* [1986] Ch 226, 240, [1985] 2 All ER 754, 764, CA.
[3] S 3(1), (6).
[4] Ie reasonable requirements: *Harrington v Gill* (1983) 4 FLR 265, CA.
[5] Beneficiary includes not only a person claiming under the deceased's will or on his intestacy but also anyone nominated by him to receive money or property after his death and any recipient of a donatio mortis causa, because all this property forms part of the net estate: s 25(1).
[6] As in *Re Besterman* (supra) and *Re Bunning* (supra). In both these cases the residuary legatees were charities.
[7] See ante, pp 771–776.

but in one or two respects the court's approach must be different. The standard at which the applicant lived whilst the deceased was alive is clearly relevant but cannot be conclusive in the changed circumstances brought about by the death; for example, money will no longer be needed to maintain the deceased.[8] It will usually be much more reasonable to expect a woman to make provision for her widower, particularly if his earning capacity is reduced, than to support her divorced husband.[9] In the case of a small estate it is particularly important to consider the extent to which an applicant can claim income support or may be expected to make use of free hospital facilities under the National Health Act. If an order for financial provision would be so small that it would merely reduce the amount payable to him out of public funds without giving him any advantage, it may be eminently reasonable to use the whole estate to give a benefit to another applicant or beneficiary.[10] Conversely, if the estate is large and the applicant is in later middle age or elderly, consideration should be given to his or her provision in later life or possible infirmity.[11]

(b) The size and nature of the estate.[12] If, for example, the deceased had a large income but little capital, it might be reasonable for him to leave the whole of his estate to his widow to the total exclusion of others whom he had supported during his lifetime. Likewise the source of the deceased's capital may be relevant; for example, if it came largely from a former spouse, the children of that spouse may have a stronger claim than the deceased's spouse or relations.[13] If the estate is small, the courts discourage applications altogether because of the danger that it will be entirely swallowed up by the costs of the action.[14]

(c) Any other relevant matter, including the conduct of the applicant or any other person.[15] In the case of a former spouse the test should be the same whether the application is made on divorce or after the other party's death.[16] It is submitted that this should be applied if the applicant is a widow or widower because he should be in no worse position than he would have been in if the marriage had been dissolved.[17] It is accepted that

---

[8] Cf (under the old law) *Re Inns* [1947] Ch 576, 581, [1947] 2 All ER 308, 311, and contrast *Re Charman* [1951] 2 TLR 1095 with *Re Borthwick* [1949] Ch 395, [1949] 1 All ER 472.

[9] Cf *Re Clayton* [1966] 2 All ER 370 (widower crippled and earning only £10 a week); *Re Wilson* (1969) 113 Sol Jo 794 (widower aged 92).

[10] Cf *Re E* [1966] 2 All ER 44; *Re Clayton* (supra); *Re Watkins* [1949] 1 All ER 695. Contrast *Re Collins* [1990] Fam 56, [1990] 2 All ER 47 (lump sum ordered for applicant on income support). (It should be noted, however, that Hollings J seems to have misstated Stamp LJ's conclusions in *Re E* (at pp 62 and 52 respectively).)

[11] *Re Besterman* (supra).

[12] Including property forming part of an unsevered joint tenancy or a transaction or contract intended to defeat an application under the Act which may be made available for financial provision (see post, pp 733–736): *Kourkgy v Lusher* (1981) 4 FLR 65, 81.

[13] *Re Callaghan* [1985] Fam 1, [1984] 3 All ER 790.

[14] See *Re Coventry* (supra), at pp 486 and 820–821 (per Goff LJ); *Re Fullard* [1982] Fam 42, 46, [1981] 2 All ER 796, 799, CA (per Ormrod LJ).

[15] But this does not include undertakings given by other beneficiaries not to claim their rights under the will because the question is whether *the will* (or the law of intestacy) makes reasonable financial provision for the applicant: *Rajabally v Rajabally* [1987] 2 FLR 390, CA.

[16] *Re Snoek* (1982) 13 Fam Law 18. This case was decided before s 25 of the Matrimonial Causes Act 1973 was amended by the Matrimonial and Family Proceedings 1984 (see ante, p 780) but this cannot have affected the principle involved.

[17] See infra.

the court should take into account the fact that a child has given up work to look after a parent,[18] but it is not easy to see what weight should be given to a child's hurtful conduct. It is submitted that the test should be this: bearing in mind the deceased's treatment of the applicant, was the latter's conduct towards him such that a reasonable parent would have considered that he had forfeited any further claim to financial provision?[19]

If the applicant is a surviving spouse or a former spouse, the court must also have regard to the duration of the marriage, the applicant's age, and the contribution he or she made to the welfare of the deceased's family including any contribution by looking after the home or caring for the family. If the spouses have been living apart, the length of their separation will also be relevant.[20] Again the similarity with the law of divorce will be seen. In the case of a surviving spouse (except when a judicial separation was in force and the separation was continuing at the deceased's death), the court must also consider what provision the applicant might reasonably have expected to receive had the marriage been terminated by divorce instead of death[21] on the ground that it would be anomalous if the latter could expect less on death than she would have got on divorce. In *Re Moody*[1] the Court of Appeal seems to have applied this principle to the letter. The testatrix, who was aged 85, owned the matrimonial home in which she had lived with her husband, aged 81. About four years before her death she had had to move into a nursing home. She left the whole of her estate, comprising the house and savings of £1,000 to her stepdaughter by a previous marriage. The court held that, had the marriage ended by divorce and not death, an order would have been made enabling the husband to spend the rest of his life in the house but obliging him to pay a lump sum to his wife to give her additional comforts. They therefore made a similar order, pointing out that the lump sum, which was to be paid to the stepdaughter, could be used to keep the property in repair. (This does not apply to former spouses and judicially separated spouses who will already have had an opportunity of applying for financial relief in the matrimonial proceedings in question.[2])

If the applicant is a child of the deceased or a person whom he treated as a child of the family, in addition to the general matters set out above the court must also have regard to the manner in which he was being or might expect to be educated or trained. If he is a child of the family but not the deceased's own child, the court must also consider the same matters as it has to take into account when deciding whether to make an order in favour of such a child on divorce.[3]

If the applicant comes within none of these categories but is relying on

---

[18] Cf *Re Coventry* [1980] Ch 461 at 489–490, [1979] 3 All ER 815 at 823.
[19] Cf *Williams v Johns* [1988] 2 FLR 475.
[20] *Re Rowlands* [1984] FLR 813, CA.
[21] S 3(2). See *Re Besterman* (supra); *Re Bunning* (supra); *Jessop v Jessop* [1992] 1 FLR 591, 597, CA.
[1] [1992] 2 All ER 524, CA. The order to pay the stepdaughter a lump sum was presumably made under the court's power to make consequential provisions under s 2(4) (see post, pp 838–839). See also *Re Besterman* (supra); *Re Bunning* (supra).
[2] For the position where the deceased died within twelve months of the decree absolute (or the decree in the case of a judicial separation) and no application for financial relief has been made or, if it has, the proceedings have not been determined, see ante, p 828, n 19.
[3] S 3(3). For the matters to be taken into account on divorce, see the Matrimonial Causes Act 1973, s 25(4), ante, p 758.

a de facto dependence during the deceased's lifetime, the court must specifically have regard to the extent to which the deceased had assumed responsibility for his maintenance, the basis upon which he had done so, and the length of time for which he had discharged it.[4] These are three of the matters which the court has to take into account when considering applications from persons who have been treated as children of the family and the similarity of their position is obvious. Bearing these points in mind, the court might well decide in a given case that the deceased had acted reasonably in leaving his estate to his wife and children to the exclusion of, say, the woman with whom he had been living.

Under the old law the most important consideration in all cases was the extent to which the deceased was under a moral obligation to make provision for the applicant.[5] So, for example, a father was held to be under no obligation to provide for his unmarried daughter who had lived with a married man as his wife for 42 years.[6] It was at first believed that in *Re Coventry*[7] the Court of Appeal had cast doubt on whether this was the correct approach, but as Ormrod LJ pointed out in *Re Fullard:*[8]

'It is impossible to answer the question, is the provision reasonable or alternatively is it reasonable to make no provision, without considering what ought to have been done for the plaintiff. Once one introduces the word "ought", one inevitably introduces in some way or other some moral question.'

The true distinction, it is submitted, is that it is not necessary for the plaintiff to prove any legal or moral obligation to qualify as an applicant but that, in the absence of such an obligation, he is likely to succeed only in the most exceptional circumstances.[9] Thus in *Re Coventry* the plaintiff, who at the time of the application was aged 48 and divorced, had left the Royal Navy and lived with his father for the last 19 years of the latter's life. Shortly after he returned home, his mother left because of the way in which her husband and son treated her. The plaintiff ran the house and looked after his father, and sought an order under the Act on the latter's death intestate. His disposable income was about £40 a week; his mother (who was the only other person interested in the estate which was worth about £7,000) lived entirely on social security benefits. The Court of Appeal held that it would be rare for a relatively young and able-bodied man in employment to succeed in a claim under the Act,[10] and even though the plaintiff was a qualified claimant as the deceased's son, he would have to

[4] S 3(4). This could include an indication by the deceased that the applicant was not to expect provision to continue after his death. See Law Com No 61, paras 91–93, and cf ante, pp 826–827.
[5] Per Wynn-Parry J in *Re Andrews* [1955] 3 All ER 248, 249. See also *Re Joslin* [1941] Ch 200, [1941] 1 All ER 302; *Re Bellman* [1963] P 239, [1963] 1 All ER 513; *Roberts v Roberts* [1964] 3 All ER 503.
[6] *Re Andrews* (supra). But in an appropriate case the court might make an order in favour of an adult child who had chosen to follow an unremunerative career: *Re Ducksbury* [1966] 2 All ER 374.
[7] [1980] Ch 461, 475, [1979] 2 All ER 408, 418.
[8] [1982] Fam 42, 47, [1981] 2 All ER 796, 800, CA.
[9] See *Jelley v Iliffe* [1981] Fam 128 at 138, [1981] 2 All ER 29 at 36, CA (per Stephenson LJ). See also *Re Debenham* [1986] 1 FLR 404 (order made in favour of 58 year old married daughter for whom deceased had obligation to provide when she developed epilepsy).
[10] Prima facie it is not unreasonable for the deceased not to make financial provision for any adult (other than his or her spouse) capable of maintaining himself: *Re Dennis* [1981] 2 All ER 140, 145; *Williams v Johns* [1988] 2 FLR 475.

establish some special circumstances over and above his relationship to be successful. This he failed to do, and it is not surprising that the court upheld Oliver J's decision to dismiss his claim.

Objective test

There was doubt under the old legislation whether it had to be shown that the testator had acted unreasonably in failing to make provision for the applicant, in which case his conduct must be judged by the circumstances known to him at the time of his death, or whether the court could take an objective view and enquire whether the provision was reasonable in the light of the facts as they existed at the time of the hearing.[11] The latter view is to be preferred because it looks at the reality of the applicant's financial position. The doubts have been resolved by the new Act which comes down in favour of the objective test and provides that the court shall take into account the facts as known at the hearing.[12] The injustice that could otherwise be worked can be seen by examining the facts of *Re Goodwin*,[13] which was decided under the old law. A testator provided for his children by making specific bequests in their favour and for his widow, their stepmother, by a legacy and the bequest of the residue of his estate. He expected the residue to be worth over £8,000 whereas it turned out to be worth about £1,500. Had the court applied the subjective test, it would have been bound to conclude that he acted reasonably; Megarry J, however, applying the objective test, concluded that in the event the provision for the widow was not reasonable and made an order in her favour.

Evidence

Earlier legislation gave the court much greater freedom in family provision cases by enabling evidence of the deceased's reasons for making particular provisions in his will (or for failing to make provision for the applicant) to be put in notwithstanding that it would otherwise have been inadmissible as hearsay. The 1975 Act similarly provides that any oral or written statement made by the deceased may be admitted as evidence of any fact stated therein,[14] and a statement made by a testator giving reasons for not making provision for an applicant may be most relevant.[15]

Time in which the application must be made

In order to enable the personal representatives to distribute the estate, an application for provision may not be made more than six months after the date on which representation is first taken out without the permission of

[11] See the fourth edition of this book at pp 510–511.
[12] S 3(5).
[13] [1969] 1 Ch 283, [1968] 3 All ER 12. For other cases, see *Re Franks* [1948] Ch 62, [1947] 2 All ER 638 (testatrix died two days after son's birth without altering will in his favour); *Re Clarke* [1968] 1 All ER 451 (death of legatee immediately after testator); *Re Shanahan* [1973] Fam 1, [1971] 3 All ER 873, and *Lusternik v Lusternik* [1972] Fam 125, [1972] 1 All ER 592, CA (change in value of estate after death).
[14] S 21.
[15] *Williams v Johns* [1988] 2 FLR 475.

the court.[16] Personal representatives will not be personally liable for distribution after this time if no application is then pending, but property may be recovered from the beneficiaries to whom it has been transferred if it is needed to make provision for a dependant to whom the court gives leave to make a late application.[17]

Property available for financial provision

Except for the court's power to order the variation of an ante-nuptial or post-nuptial settlement (which will be considered later), it can only make orders for the payment of money out of the deceased's net estate or affecting property comprised in that estate.[18] Basically, this means such property as the deceased had power to dispose of by will (otherwise than by virtue of a special power of appointment) less the amount of funeral, testamentary and administration expenses and any liabilities.[19] Five other types of property are also comprised within the definition. First, property in respect of which the deceased had a general power of appointment not exercisable by will is included if the power was never exercised, for he could have exercised the power in his own favour and thus brought it within his estate.[20] Secondly, some statutes enable a person to nominate another to take the benefit of a fund (for example, in a trustee savings bank) after his death. This is equivalent to a testamentary disposition and such property is therefore part of his estate for this purpose notwithstanding any nomination.[1] For a similar reason donationes mortis causa made by the deceased are included.[2] Fourthly, the court may order the severance of a joint tenancy or joint interest (for example, in a bank account) or any part of a joint tenancy or interest to which the deceased was entitled immediately before his death and which would therefore otherwise pass to the other joint tenants jure accrescendi, for the same reason that he could have effected a severance himself and thus brought the property into his estate.[3] The undivided share will then form part of the net estate. Finally, the estate includes any money or property ordered to be restored or provided if a disposition or contract is set aside under the provisions now to be considered.

[16] Ss 4 and 23. If a grant of probate is revoked, the time begins to run from the making of the second and effective grant: *Re Freeman* [1984] 3 All ER 906. The applicant must establish grounds for taking the case out of the general rule. For the facts which the court will take into account, see *Re Stone* (1970) 114 Sol Jo 36, CA; *Re Salmon* [1981] Ch 167, [1980] 3 All ER 532; *Re Dennis* [1981] 2 All ER 140; Prime, 129 Sol Jo 659. In particular permission is more likely to be given if the delay is slight, negotiations were begun before the time limit expired and the estate has not been distributed, and it will not be given if the applicant has no arguable case.
[17] S 20(1). On the question of distribution before the hearing of the application, see *Re Ralphs* [1968] 3 All ER 285.
[18] S 2(1). For net estate generally, see Law Com No 61, paras 127–143.
[19] S 25(1), (2).
[20] S 25(1).
[1] S 8(1). But not if the power arises purely under a contract or trust deed: *Re Cairnes* (1982) 4 FLR 225. It might be possible to have such a nomination set aside as a transaction intended to defeat an application under the Act: see infra.
[2] S 8(2). In this case and the last any person giving effect to the nomination or gift is protected.
[3] S 9. See *Jessop v Jessop* [1992] 1 FLR 591, CA. This power can be exercised only if an application for an order for financial provision was made within six months from the date on which representation was first taken out. Any person dealing with the property before an order for severance is protected.

Transactions intended to defeat applications

We have seen that one of the weaknesses of earlier legislation was that the deceased could defeat an application by settling or disposing of his property during his lifetime so that it never formed part of his estate at all or, alternatively, could contract to leave it to a third person after his death.[4] The 1975 Act contains provisions designed to frustrate such transactions.

Under section 10 the court has a power to set aside a disposition made with the intention of defeating an application for financial provision under the Act which is similar to, but not identical with, the power to set aside transactions made with the intention of defeating an application for financial relief under the Matrimonial Causes Act.[5] There is no presumption of such an intention and the applicant must prove that the deceased intended to prevent an order being made under the Act or to reduce the amount of provision which might otherwise be granted, but this does not have to be his sole intention or, apparently, his principal intention.[6] This will undoubtedly create considerable difficulty in practice: if a man gives a substantial sum to his mistress, his apparent intention is to benefit her; how can it be proved that he also intended to reduce the amount of property available to his wife after his death? In many cases the court will probably have to fall back on the principle that a person may be presumed to have intended the natural and probable consequences of his acts. Because of the difficulty of establishing intention at a remote time in the past, the court has no power to set aside a disposition made more than six years before the deceased's death. Nor, whatever his intention was, can any disposition be set aside if the transferee gave full valuable consideration.[7]

If the court is satisfied that the exercise of the powers given by the section would facilitate the making of financial provision for the applicant, it may order the donee of the property in question to provide such sum of money or other property as it shall direct. It is immaterial that the latter no longer holds any interest in the original property, but he may not be ordered to pay or transfer more than the amount paid to him by the deceased (if the disposition took the form of the payment of money) or the value at the date of the deceased's death of any property transferred in other cases.[8] A

---

[4] If the transaction was effected fraudulently with intent to defeat the dependant's claim, it is arguable that it could be set aside under the court's general power to upset fraudulent transactions or perhaps under s 423 of the Insolvency Act 1986: see *Cadogan v Cadogan* [1977] 3 All ER 831, CA. This might still be relevant eg if the transaction was made more than six years before the deceased's death.

[5] See ante, pp 801–804. See further generally Law Com No 61, Part V.

[6] Ss 10(2)(a) and 12(1). The court must be satisfied on the balance of probabilities that this was the deceased's intention.

[7] S 10(2)(a), (b). Valuable consideration does not include marriage or a promise of marriage: s 25(1). A disposition does not include any testamentary gift, nomination or donatio mortis causa (all of which form part of the net estate) or any appointment made under a special power, but subject to these exceptions it includes any payment of money (including the payment of a premium under a policy of insurance) and any conveyance, assurance, appointment or gift of property: s 10(7). See also *Clifford v Tanner* [1987] CLY 3881, CA.

[8] S 10(2)–(4); *Re Dawkins* [1986] 2 FLR 360 (donee ordered to provide £10,000 for deceased's widow out of proceeds of sale of property of £27,000). The value of any inheritance tax borne by the donee must also be deducted. If the donee has himself disposed of the property, he may not be required to restore more than its value when he disposed of it. If the disposition was made to the donee as trustee, the latter is further protected because the amount he is ordered to pay or transfer must not exceed the money or the value of the

similar order may be made against the donee's personal representatives, in which case it must be limited to the payment of money or transfer of property out of that part of the donee's estate which has not yet been distributed.[9] Some measure of protection is given to the donee by the further provision that, before exercising its powers, the court must have regard to all the circumstances of the case, including particularly the circumstances in which the disposition to him was made, any valuable consideration given for it, the relationship (if any) of the donee to the deceased, and the donee's conduct and financial resources.[10] Thus, even if the deceased intended to defeat an application for financial provision by, say, the deceased's wife, the court is likely to be slower to set aside a gift to his indigent parents than to his unscrupulous mistress.

A person against whom an order is sought may himself seek an order against any other person (or his personal representatives) in whose favour it is alleged that the deceased made a disposition with the intention of defeating an application under the Act.[11] This will enable him to argue that the latter transaction should be set aside rather than the one in his own favour or at least that the burden should be shared.

The court has wide powers to make consequential directions and to secure the adjustment of the rights of persons affected by its orders.[12]

Section 11 deals with contracts by which the deceased agreed that a sum of money or other property would be left by his will or paid or transferred out of his estate. If such a contract were unimpeachable, it would obviously be more valuable than an actual disposition inter vivos which could be set aside. Consequently, if it was made with the intention of defeating an application for financial provision under the Act and full valuable consideration was not given or promised for it, the court may direct the personal representatives not to pay or transfer the whole or any part of the money or property involved. If any payment or transfer has already been made to any person (who, for convenience, is also referred to as the donee), the court may order him to provide such sum of money or other property as may be specified.[13] There is, however, one important qualification to the court's powers under section 11: it may restrain the personal representatives and order restitution only to the extent that the amount of the sum or the value of the property in question exceeds the value of the consideration given or promised under the contract.[14] As in the case of a disposition already made, the deceased's intention to prevent the making of an order or to reduce the amount available need not have been his sole intention, but there is an important difference between contracts and dispositions in that, if no valuable consideration was given or promised for the contract,

---

property in his hands at the time of the order (or the value of any property representing the money or original property): see s 13.
[9] S 12(4). A personal representative will not be liable for having distributed any part of the estate before he has notice that an application is being made for an order.
[10] S 10(6).
[11] Ss 10(5) and 12(4).
[12] S 12(3)
[13] S 11(2). The personal representatives may themselves postpone performance for six months without an order: s 20(3).
[14] S 11(3). Valuable consideration does not include marriage or a promise of marriage: s 25(1). If money or property has already been paid or transferred to the other party as trustee, he has the additional protection conferred by s 13: see n 8, supra.

it will be presumed that he had this intention unless the contrary is shown.[15] A contract may be attacked however long before the deceased's death it was entered into, except that there is no power at all to upset a contract made before the Act came into force (1st April 1976).[16]

In other respects the provisions relating to the two types of transaction are similar. The court may exercise its powers only if there is an application for financial provision under the Act and it must be satisfied that this would facilitate the making of an order.[17] It may make an order against the donee's personal representatives; it must have regard to the same matters before exercising its powers; and it has the same power to give consequential directions, in particular with respect to the rights of any person to sue for breach of contract.[18]

Orders that may be made

If a dependant is in immediate need of financial assistance and property forming part of the net estate can be made available to meet his needs but it is not yet possible to make a final order, the court may make an *interim order*. This may take the form of one payment or of periodical payments, and the court may later direct that any sum paid under an interim order shall be treated as having been paid on account of the final order. As far as possible, the same matters should be taken into account in making an interim order as in making a final order.[19]

If the court is satisfied that reasonable financial provision has not been made for the applicant, it may make a *final order* containing one or more of the provisions set out below.[20] In determining what order (if any) to make, the court must have regard to the same matters as it has when deciding whether reasonable provision has been made.[1]

(1) **An order for periodical payments.**[2] This may be for such a term and subject to such conditions as the court directs. Remarriage of the deceased's widow or widower will not automatically discharge the order (although it may be a ground for an application to have it discharged by the court) because a life interest on intestacy does not come to an end on that event and testators bequeath interests during widowhood much less frequently than they used to do.[3] It would be anomalous, however, to give former spouses and judicially separated spouses greater rights on the deceased's death than they had when the decree was made, and consequently an order for periodical payments made in their favour will terminate automatically

---

[15] S 12(1), (2).
[16] S 11(6).
[17] S 11(1), (2)(d).
[18] Ss 11(4), (5) and 12(3), (4). The donee's personal representatives have the same protection as they have under s 10. A right to sue for breach of contract survives only so far as is consistent with giving effect to the order restraining performance of the contract or directing restitution.
[19] S 5. For the protection of personal representatives, see s 20(2).
[20] S 2(1). See generally Law Com No 61, paras 109–126.
[1] S 3(1). See ante, pp 827–832.
[2] This may be for a specified amount or for an amount equal to the whole or any part of the income of the net estate or of such part of the estate as the court directs to be set aside or appropriated for this purpose, or it may be determined in any other way the court thinks fit: s 2(2), (3).
[3] Law Com No 61, paras 37–43.

on remarriage.[4] In other cases it would normally be reasonable to direct that payment to a child should terminate on his ceasing to receive education or training or that payment to a parent who is temporarily unable to work owing to illness should terminate on his ceasing to be under a disability.[5]

(2) The payment of a lump sum. Such an order would be particularly valuable if the estate is so small that any periodical payments would be valueless. It could also enable, say, a widow to purchase the goodwill of a business: indeed if the estate is large enough, it is submitted that this will normally be the proper order to make in favour of a surviving spouse. This is the usual form of testamentary gift for a widow or widower and it should be immaterial that the capital may ultimately get into the hands of someone who is not a dependant or beneficiary at all.[6] If the order is made at the expense of beneficiaries towards whom the deceased had no obligations, a spouse will probably obtain more under the Inheritance Act than she (or he) would have obtained in divorce proceedings because the estate is no longer needed for the deceased's support and it may be reasonable to give the applicant a cushion to provide against future contingencies.[7] In *Malone v Harrison*,[8] where it was agreed that the most appropriate form of provision for the deceased's mistress was the payment of a lump sum, Hollings J resorted to the practice in claims under the Fatal Accidents Act of assessing her dependency and applying a multiplier to it. Whilst this has the merit of using a recognised principle for the quantification of the award, there are so many imponderables that it is submitted that only in exceptional circumstances should periodical payments be capitalised in this way.

If the applicant is not a surviving spouse (so that the court is concerned solely with his maintenance), it is submitted that the court should approach the making of an order for a lump sum with caution. 'Maintenance' connotes payments which will enable the applicant to discharge the cost of his daily living. Normally, therefore, they will be payments of income, although the payment of a lump sum may be properly given, for example, to enable him to buy a home which will pro tanto reduce his recurrent expenditure.[9] A lump sum may also be valuable if relationships in a family are so bitter that a clean break is desirable.[10] The disadvantage of such an

---

[4] S 19(2). This applies to judicially separated spouses only if the decree was in force and the separation continuing at the time of the deceased's death. Treating such a spouse as though no decree had been made (see ante, p 828, n 19) does not appear to affect the operation of this sub-section and periodical payments would still cease on remarriage. Any other rule would produce a serious anomaly.

[5] For examples of conditions under the old law see *Re Lidington* [1940] Ch 927, [1940] 3 All ER 600 (condition that widow should maintain minor children of the marriage); *Re Hills* [1941] WN 123 (condition that applicant should inform trustees of the will if she became entitled to property worth £100 or more).

[6] Cf *Re Besterman* [1984] Ch 458, [1984] 2 All ER 656, CA. It was said that the sum awarded should take into account the fact that, by taking a lump sum, the recipient is giving up the right to return to the court for a variation of the order in the event of unforeseen contingencies (at 477 and 669 respectively). Sed quaere? There is always a danger that periodical payments could be reduced on the application of another dependant or beneficiary, and if the applicant is the only person in whose favour an order is made, there would be no scope to increase them: see post, p 839.

[7] See *Re Besterman* (supra); *Re Bunning* [1984] Ch 480, [1984] 3 All ER 1; Miller *Provision for a Surviving Spouse* 102 LQR 445; Prime 16 Fam Law 95.

[8] [1979] 1 WLR 1353. See Bryan 96 LQR 165.

[9] *Re Dennis* [1981] 2 All ER 140 at 145.

[10] Cf *Re Collins* [1990] Fam 56, [1990] 2 All ER 47 (need to achieve finality where defendant was violent man and applicant, his daughter, had been fostered).

order is that it cannot be varied to take account of any unforeseen change in the circumstances of the applicant or a beneficiary, and if it represents the capitalisation of periodical payments, events may prove the estimate to have been wildly inaccurate. Consequently the courts are reluctant to order the payment of a lump sum to an applicant who is elderly or in poor health because premature death would often result in the deceased's assets being vested in someone outside his family.[11]

As on divorce, the court may order that a lump sum be paid by instalments.[12]

(3) The transfer or settlement of any property comprised in the net estate to or for the benefit of the applicant. The court might well order that the former matrimonial home be transferred or settled for the benefit of a surviving spouse or unmarried cohabitant who has been living with the deceased,[13] particularly if he or she has to bring up young children. In other cases it may be more convenient, as on divorce, to order the transfer of property in specie than the payment of a lump sum.

(4) The transfer or settlement of property to be acquired out of the estate to or for the benefit of the applicant. This has no counterpart in the Matrimonial Causes Act and is designed particularly to enable a home to be bought for the applicant.[14]

(5) The variation of any ante-nuptial or post-nuptial settlement made on the parties to a marriage of which the deceased was one. This is strictly equivalent to the court's powers on divorce and the variation may be made only for the benefit of the surviving party to the marriage or a child of the family in relation to that marriage.[15]

The similarity with orders that can be made under the Matrimonial Causes Act on divorce will be immediately apparent. It may at first sight appear anomalous that a former spouse can apply for orders for the transfer or settlement of property on the deceased's death when she could not have obtained a property adjustment order if she had sought a variation of an order for periodical payments under the Matrimonial Causes Act. It must be realised, however, that a completely different situation is brought about by the death, which usually produces a major redistribution of capital.

When an order is made, the will or the law relating to intestacy (or both in the case of a partial intestacy) takes effect retrospectively from the deceased's death subject to its provisions.[16] The court has wide powers to give consequential directions and in particular must try to ensure that the

---

[11] Cf *Re Debenham* [1986] 1 FLR 404. In *Stead v Stead* [1985] FLR 16, CA, the lump sum awarded to a widow, aged 82, was limited to the amount needed to cover certain eventualities apparently on the ground that, if she were given more, she would merely save it. But this is not an invariable rule and a lump sum may be ordered in special circumstances; *Kusminow v Barclays Bank Trust Co Ltd* [1989] Fam Law 66.

[12] S 7. The court may subsequently vary the number and amount of instalments and the dates on which they are to be paid but not the total sum payable. A lump sum or the transfer of property could also be of particular benefit to an applicant in receipt of income support because it would have a limited effect on his income and might enable him to make a capital purchase which he might not otherwise be able to afford (for example, a television set): *Millward v Shenton* [1972] 2 All ER 1025, CA.

[13] As in *Harrington v Gill* (1983) 4 FLR 265, CA.

[14] See Law Com No 61, para 116.

[15] For the variation of settlements, see ante, pp 738–742.

[16] Ss 19(1) and 24.

order operates fairly as between the various beneficiaries. To this end it has a general power to vary the dispositions effected by the will and the law of intestacy.[17]

Variation of orders

A change in the financial circumstances of a person in whose favour an order has been made, any other person who comes within the category of those who might apply for an order, or a beneficiary of the deceased's estate, whom the order has deprived of the immediate benefit of his interest, may indicate that it is desirable to vary an order that has already been made. One thing is immediately apparent, however: the whole estate will have been distributed except for that part appropriated for the making of periodical payments. There are three consequences of this: an application for variation can be made only if an order for periodical payments is in existence,[18] it may affect only property presently applicable for the making of such payments,[19] and a variation in favour of another person can be made only at the expense of the recipient.

An application for variation may be made by anyone who has already applied for an order or would be entitled to apply for one if he were not time barred. It may also be made by the deceased's personal representatives, the trustees of any property affected, and any beneficiary of the estate.[20] The court may vary, suspend or discharge any existing order for periodical payments and revive any provision suspended.[1] If the payments are due to cease on the happening of a specified event (other than the remarriage of a former wife or husband) or at the expiration of a specified period of time, the court may direct that they shall continue.[2] It may also make an order for periodical payments, the payment of a lump sum, or the transfer of any part of the property available, to anyone eligible for financial provision (whether or not an order has previously been made in his favour).[3] There is no power to make an order for the settlement of property, the acquisition of other property or the variation of an ante-nuptial or post-nuptial settlement.[4] In exercising its powers, the court must look at all the circumstances of the case, including any change in the matters to which it was

---

[17] S 2(4). Although this appears to give the court a huge discretion, it necessarily had to exercise these powers under the old law: see *Re Preston* [1969] 2 All ER 961. For the meaning of 'beneficiary', see ante, p 828, n 5.

[18] Or within six months of the cessation of an order for periodical payments terminable on the happening of a specified event or the expiration of a specified time (other than the remarriage of a former spouse): s 6(3), (6)(b).

[19] Or applicable for the making of payments under an order of the type mentioned in the last note: s 6(6).

[20] S 6(5). For the meaning of beneficiary, see p 828, n 5, ante. An application may be made notwithstanding that there has been a previous variation: s 6(4).

[1] S 6(1).

[2] S 6(10).

[3] S 6(2). This includes power to make an order in favour of a person who would be entitled to apply for provision if he were not time barred.

[4] Nor may the court order the severance of a joint tenancy or set aside dispositions and contracts made with the intention of defeating a claim for financial provision: s 6(9). Cf the court's powers on an application to vary an order under the Matrimonial Causes Act, ante, p 791.

bound to have regard when making the original order, and it may give such consequential directions as necessary.[5]

Relationship to existing agreements and matrimonial orders

It must not be forgotten that other liabilities to support a dependant may survive the deceased's death. An order for secured periodical payments may have been made in his favour during previous matrimonial proceedings or he may be a party to a maintenance agreement under which payments continue. Not only will the existence of the continuing right affect any order that may be made if he applies for financial relief under the Act but also, in the changed circumstances brought about by the death, it may make unfairly generous provision for him compared with the amount left for other applicants. To prevent the unnecessary duplication of proceedings, the court may vary existing orders and agreements in proceedings under the Inheritance (Provision for Family and Dependants) Act.[6]

If an applicant for financial relief under the Inheritance Act continues to be entitled to secured periodical payments on an order made under the Matrimonial Causes Act, the court may vary or discharge the order or revive the operation of any provision which has been previously suspended.[7] Similarly, if the applicant is still entitled to payments under a maintenance agreement, the court may vary or revoke the agreement.[8] The definition of a maintenance agreement is the same as that contained in section 34 of the Matrimonial Causes Act except that it need not be in writing.[9] These powers are exercisable only on the application of the personal representatives or the payee under the order or agreement and only if the payee brings proceedings under the Inheritance Act. In other cases the court has no power to reduce the sums payable if, in proceedings brought by another applicant under the Act, it comes to the conclusion that they are too large. This can be done only if the personal representatives themselves take proceedings to have the order or agreement varied under the Matrimonial Proceedings Act, which they may be unwilling to do.

Conversely, if the personal representatives, the recipient of secured periodical payments or a party to a maintenance agreement applies for a variation of the order or agreement under the Matrimonial Causes Act,[10] the court may deem the application to have been accompanied by an application for an order under the Inheritance Act and exercise all the powers it has under that Act.[11] This may be of particular importance to a party to an agreement because it will be recalled that under the Matrimonial Causes Act there is no power to set aside a disposition intended to defeat

---

[5] S 6(7), (8).

[6] See further Law Com No 61, Part VII.

[7] S 16. The court must have regard to all the circumstances including any change in the matters to which it was required to have regard when making the order for secured periodical payments.

[8] S 17. The court must have regard to all the circumstances including any change in the circumstances in the light of which the agreement was made.

[9] S 17(4). For the definition of a maintenance agreement under s 34 of the Matrimonial Causes Act, see ante, pp 656–657.

[10] See ante, pp 661 and 793. In this case of course the agreement must be a maintenance agreement within s 34 of the Matrimonial Causes Act.

[11] S 18.

an application for a variation of a maintenance agreement after the payer's death. By invoking this jurisdiction the court can exercise its jurisdiction to set aside dispositions and contracts under sections 10 and 11.

Whether as part of an agreed financial settlement or in pursuance of the principle that a final break should be made if this is desirable, the court dealing with financial provision on divorce, nullity or judicial separation may wish to exclude the possibility of a future application under the Inheritance Act. Accordingly it may make an order having this effect on the application of either party to the marriage if it is satisfied that it is just to do so.[12] The order will take effect only when a decree of divorce or nullity is made absolute or, if it was made on judicial separation, only if the decree is in force and the separation is continuing on the death of one of the parties.[13] The court has the same power if it makes an order for financial relief following a foreign dissolution, annulment or legal separation granted in an overseas country and recognised here.[14]

By analogy with applications for financial relief in matrimonial proceedings, a party presumably cannot contract out of his or her power to apply under the Inheritance Act except by way of a consent order.[15]

D. The statutory transmission of tenancies

We have already seen that the Rent Act, the Rent (Agriculture) Act and the Housing Acts of 1985 and 1988 prevent a landlord from arbitrarily evicting a tenant.[16] In addition to protecting the tenant and his (or her) spouse, this must necessarily give security to members of the tenant's family so long as they are living with him. This secondary purpose of the Acts would be completely defeated if it were possible for the landlord to evict the members of the tenant's family immediately the tenancy was ended by the tenant's death. It is, of course, open to the landlord to grant a fresh contractual tenancy to the person remaining in possession. Whether or not he has done so must be a question of fact in each case, but a contractual tenancy cannot be inferred from the mere receipt of rent as the landlord is bound to accept the new tenant.[17] If he does not grant a new tenancy, the Acts provide that, subject to certain conditions, security shall be given to members of the deceased tenant's family by vesting a tenancy in them.

There must obviously be some limitation on the number of times that a tenancy can be transmitted, for otherwise it could be tied up in the family in perpetuity and the landlord could never obtain possession. The policy

---

[12] Consequently the court must be given some indication of what the estate is likely to consist of and the persons whom the applicant considers to have a prior claim on it: *Whiting v Whiting* [1988] 2 All ER 275, CA.

[13] S 15, as amended by the Matrimonial and Family Proceedings Act 1984, s 8. The order will also prevent the court from deeming that an application for variation under the Matrimonial Causes Act is accompanied by an application for an order under the Inheritance Act: s 18(3).

[14] S 15A, inserted by the Matrimonial and Family Proceedings Act 1984, s 25(3). In this case, however, an order following a legal separation will have effect provided that the separation is in force on the party's death, whether or not the separation is continuing de facto.

[15] Cf *Re M* [1968] P 174, [1967] 3 All ER 412.

[16] Ante, pp 628 et seq.

[17] *Dealex Properties Ltd v Brooks* [1966] 1 QB 542, [1965] 1 All ER 1080, CA.

of successive statutes has been to limit succession in the private sector and the general rule now is that there can be only one transmission although in certain circumstances there can still be two successions to a protected or statutory tenancy under the Rent Act. Only one transmission has ever been possible in the public sector.

1. REGULATED TENANTS UNDER THE RENT ACT

There can be no succession unless the tenancy is still in existence. Hence if it has been terminated by the tenant's vacating the premises or by the landlord's obtaining an order for possession against him before his death, the landlord is entitled to possession against the members of his family remaining on the premises.[18]

Succession by the tenant's spouse or cohabitant

On a protected or statutory tenant's death a statutory tenancy automatically vests in his (or her) surviving spouse or the person who was living with the tenant as his or her wife or husband provided in each case that the survivor was residing in the dwelling house immediately before the death.[19] It will be seen that the residence qualification prevents the spouse or cohabitant from claiming the benefit of the Act if the parties had separated and the survivor left the premises before the tenant's death. The successor remains a statutory tenant so long as she (or he) occupies the dwelling house as her residence even though she subsequently remarries.[20] Like any other statutory tenant, the successor takes the tenancy on the same terms as her predecessor, with all the rights and liabilities unaltered.[1] Thus the burden of paying the same rent, of repairing and of observing restrictive covenants will fall on her as it fell on the deceased tenant.[2]

---

[18] This is so even though the court has suspended the execution of an order for possession and the tenant dies before the order takes effect: *American Economic Laundry Ltd v Little* [1951] 1 KB 400, [1950] 2 All ER 1186, CA. The Court of Appeal left open the question what the position would have been if a conditional order had been made (at 406 and 1190, respectively), but they have subsequently said that, in order to prevent this difficulty from arising, courts should not make orders suspended indefinitely or for a long period of time: *Mills v Allen* [1953] 2 QB 341, at 357, 364, [1953] 2 All ER 534, at 544, 547, CA.

[19] The extension of this provision to a surviving cohabitant, which was introduced by the Housing Act 1988, gives statutory effect to the decision of the Court of Appeal in *Dyson Holdings Ltd v Fox* [1976] QB 503, [1975] 3 All ER 1030, in which the court declined to follow its previous decision in *Gammans v Ekins* [1950] 2 KB 328, [1950] 2 All ER 140, and held that, whatever the position had been 25 years earlier, in 1975 a cohabitant could properly be regarded as a member of the deceased tenant's family. For the meaning of the phrase 'living with the tenant as husband or wife', see ante, p 7. In the unlikely event of a surviving spouse and cohabitant both satisfying the condition, they should decide in which of them the tenancy is to vest; if they cannot agree, the question must be determined by the county court: Housing Act 1988, Sch 4, para 2.

[20] Rent Act 1977, Sch 1, paras 1 and 2, as amended by the Housing Act 1980, s 76, and the Housing Act 1988, Sch 4, paras 1 and 2; *Apsley v Barr* [1928] NI 183.

[1] Ibid, s 3.

[2] *Bolsover Colliery Co Ltd v Abbott* [1946] KB 8, 12, CA, followed in *American Economic Laundry Ltd v Little* (supra). But the new tenant is not liable for arrears of rent owed by her predecessor: *Tickner v Clifton* [1929] 1 KB 207, 211. Consequently she cannot have a possession order made against her for non-payment of it because the rent is not due *from the tenant.*

Succession by a member of the tenant's family

If the tenant leaves neither a surviving spouse nor a surviving cohabitant satisfying the conditions set out above, there can be a transmission to any member of his (or her) family who was residing with him in the dwelling house at the time of, and for a period of two years before, his death. If a surviving spouse or cohabitant became a statutory tenant by succession, there can be a further succession on the death of that person. In this case, however, the claimant must (a) have been a member of the original tenant's family immediately before that tenant's death, (b) have been a member of the successor's family immediately before the successor's death, and (c) have been residing in the dwelling house with the successor at the time of, and for a period of two years before, the latter's death. This will enable, for example, a son or daughter of the original tenant to claim a tenancy if he or she continued to live with the tenant's widow; on the other hand, if the widow remarries, it will not enable her second husband to succeed.[3]

The words 'residing with' must be given their ordinary and popular meaning.[4] This indicates more than 'living at the same premises as' the tenant:[5] what is important is the parties' intention. Although the claimant does not have to establish that he never intended to move away, he must have had his settled home with the tenant. This raises a particular problem if he moved in with the deceased tenant to look after him in sickness or old age. If the parties intended that the arrangement should be permanent, the claimant can be regarded as residing with the other even though the latter is temporarily absent, for example in hospital.[6] If on the other hand the parties contemplated that he would leave when the tenant recovered, the necessary intention will be absent, and although both may be temporarily living in the same premises, the claimant cannot be regarded as residing *with* the tenant.[7] Furthermore, the successor must have 'lived [in] and shared for living purposes the whole of the premises to which he or she claims to have succeeded',[8] so that there can be no succession if the claimant was the sub-tenant of part of the premises.[9]

[3] Rent Act 1977, s 1 and Sch 1; Housing Act 1988, s 39(1)–(3) and Sch 4, Part I. Presumably if the first successor vacates the premises leaving her husband and, say, a daughter in occupation, the attribution of the husband's occupation to the tenant (see ante, p 631) will enable the daughter to claim that she is still residing in the dwelling-house with her mother.

[4] *Edmunds v Jones* [1957] 1 WLR 1118n, CA; *Morgan v Murch* [1970] 2 All ER 100, CA. See Brierley *The Rent Act 1977 and the Absent Tenant—Part II* [1991] Conv 432.

[5] *Foreman v Beagley* [1969] 3 All ER 838, CA; *Swanbrae Ltd v Elliott* (1986) 19 HLR 86, CA.

[6] Even though the tenant is already absent when the other moves in: *Hedgedale Ltd v Hards* (1991) 23 HLR 158, CA. In these circumstances the applicant can apparently be regarded as residing with the tenant even though the latter never returns: per Russell LJ in *Foreman v Beagley* (supra) at p 841.

[7] *Foreman v Beagley* (supra). The claimant's task will be more difficult if he retained an existing home of his own: see *Swanbrae Ltd v Elliott* (supra), at pp 95–96 (per Kerr LJ). In that case the defendant continued to sleep in the house of which she was tenant three or four nights a week, her son still lived there, her post was sent there and she gave it as her usual address. Her claim to succeed to her mother's tenancy failed. Whilst this decision may have the desirable effect of not giving the claimant two protected or statutory tenancies, it overlooks the fact that a person can have more than one residence at the same time. See further Hill *Succession to a Statutory Tenancy* [1987] Conv 349, where it is pointed out that difficulty has arisen because the courts have applied two different tests: (i) did the claimant make his home with the deceased? and (ii) was he part of the deceased's household?

[8] *Edmunds v Jones* (supra) at 1120.

[9] *Edmunds v Jones* (supra).

It is not sufficient that the claimant and the deceased should have been members of the same family: the former must show that he was a member of the latter's family.[10] This expression is not easy to define and has given rise to a spate of litigation. It is not a term of art and must be construed in its ordinary and popular sense.[11] Some judicial limit, however, has been placed upon the term, and either the tenant and the claimant must have been related by blood or marriage or the claimant must have been adopted by the tenant (if not by a legal adoption order at least de facto) as a child. Thus tenancies have been successfully claimed by the tenant's children (together with their husbands or wives),[12] children adopted de facto during minority,[13] and the tenant's brothers and sisters.[14] It has also been suggested that the class includes stepchildren,[15] and there can be no doubt that this is correct.

It does not follow, however, that all persons related to the tenant can be regarded as members of his family. The parties' conduct must be taken into account as well[16] and, the more remote the relationship, the more important this may become. In *Langdon v Horton*,[17] for example, where two sisters had gone to live with their widowed cousin and had stayed with her until she died 29 years later, the Court of Appeal held that they were no more members of her family than would be two strangers to the blood who shared a flat for their convenience. In *Jones v Whitehill*[18] on the other hand, it was held that a niece who had gone to look after her elderly aunt and uncle in their declining years was a member of their family as she had assumed 'out of natural love and affection the duties and offices peculiarly attributable to members of a family'.[19] Where there is no blood relationship or relationship by marriage at all, however, the House of Lords has held that the tenant cannot turn another adult into a member of his family for this purpose simply by treating him as though he were, and it rejected the claim of a young man who, at the age of 25, went to live with and look after a woman more than 50 years older than himself notwithstanding that she treated him as her nephew.[20]

---

[10] *Langdon v Horton* [1951] 1 KB 666, at 669, 671, [1951] 1 All ER 60, at 60, 61, CA.

[11] *Carega Properties SA v Sharratt* [1979] 2 All ER 1084 at 1086, 1088, HL.

[12] *Standingford v Probert* [1950] 1 KB 377, [1949] 2 All ER 861, CA. In *Perry v Dembowski* [1951] 2 KB 420, [1951] 2 All ER 50, CA, the Court of Appeal left open the interesting question where a child of four or five years of age could be a member of his deceased parent's family for the purpose of the Rent Act. A county court has held that a child of 16 can be a statutory tenant: *Portman Registrars and Nominees v Latif* [1987] CLY 2239.

[13] *Brock v Wollams* [1949] 2 KB 388, [1949] 1 All ER 715, CA.

[14] *Price v Gould* (1930) 143 LT 333.

[15] *Brock v Wollams* (supra) at 394 and 717 (per Bucknill LJ), 396 and 718 (per Denning LJ).

[16] *Ross v Collins* [1964] 1 All ER 861, 865, CA.

[17] [1951] 1 KB 666, [1951] 1 All ER 60, CA.

[18] [1950] 2 KB 204, [1950] 1 All ER 71, CA. See further Evershed MR's remarks on this case in *Langdon v Horton* (supra) at 669 and 61, respectively.

[19] At 207 and 72, respectively.

[20] *Carega Properties SA v Sharratt* (supra). Cf *Ross v Collins* (supra). Nor do servants and lodgers come within the definition, for it could not have been the intention of Parliament to protect them: per Cohen LJ in *Brock v Wollams* (supra) at 394 and 718, respectively. Zuckermann *Formality and the Family* 96 LQR 248, proposes a novel test (at 264): was the relationship between the deceased tenant and the claimant such that it may be inferred that the former assumed such a responsibility for the latter's welfare that lack of security for him would have undermined the tenant's own security? This might effectively prevent transmission in some cases where it has been allowed. See Berkovits [1981] JSWL 83.

Nature of transmitted tenancy

The successor (or second successor) will take not a statutory tenancy under the Rent Act but an assured periodic tenancy under the Housing Act 1988. This can vest in only one person;[1] consequently if there are more claimants than one, they should decide amongst themselves who is to succeed. If they cannot come to an agreement, the question must be determined by the county court.[2] The successor's position is not so secure as that of other assured tenants, however, because in addition to the grounds on which the landlord can claim possession from an assured tenant he can also claim possession on any of the other mandatory grounds set out in the Rent Act.[3]

Whether or not there has been a previous succession, there cannot be a further succession after a transmission to a member of the tenant's family.[4]

Concurrent tenancies

We have seen that there can be a succession whether the tenancy is protected or statutory. Originally it was held that there could be no succession if the deceased tenant was a contractual lessee, with the result that the protection given to the widow of a statutory tenant would not be accorded to the widow of a protected tenant if he chose to bequeath his interest to someone else. It was partly because of this anomaly that the House of Lords held in *Moodie v Hosegood*[5] that the widow or other member of the family is entitled to the same protection whether the deceased was a statutory or protected tenant provided, of course, that the dwelling-house is held on a regulated tenancy. This rule has now been given statutory effect.[6] Suppose that a husband, H, dies leaving a widow, W, and a son, S, to whom he has bequeathed the balance of the lease on which H held the matrimonial home. The contractual lease passes to H's personal representatives who must then vest it in S, whilst at the same time a statutory tenancy vests in W. It seems impossible that there should be two adverse tenancies in existence at the same time; the true position is that the contractual tenancy is in abeyance until the statutory tenancy is determined. The result was thus described by Lord Morton of Henryton in *Moodie v Hosegood*:[7]

'If a contractual tenancy is still subsisting at her husband's death and devolves upon someone other than the widow, it is not destroyed, but the rights and

---

[1] *Dealex Properties Ltd v Brooks* [1966] 1 QB 542, [1965] 1 All ER 1080, CA.
[2] The court must take into account the merits of the rival claims, the claimants' needs and perhaps the wishes (or probable wishes) of the original tenant: see *Williams v Williams* [1970] 3 All ER 988.
[3] Rent Act 1977, Sch 1; Housing Act 1988, s 39 and Sch 4, Parts I and III. For the grounds on which a landlord can claim possession under the Rent Act, see ante, p 632. If the original tenancy was a protected shorthold, the successor will take an assured shorthold.
[4] If the court vests a statutory tenancy in the tenant's spouse on divorce, nullity or judicial separation (see ante, p 637), this does not affect the total number of transmissions that can take place: Matrimonial Homes Act 1983, Sch 1, para 3(2). To protect a landlord who might inadvertently have prejudiced his position by granting a fresh tenancy to the first successor, it is expressly provided that this is not to affect the number of successions: Rent Act 1977, Sch 1, para 10, as amended by the Housing Act 1988, Sch 4, para 8.
[5] [1952] AC 61, [1951] 2 All ER 582, HL.
[6] See now the Rent Act 1977, s 2(1)(b), and the Rent (Agriculture) Act 1976, s 4(2).
[7] At 74 and 586, respectively.

obligations which would ordinarily devolve upon the successor in title of the contractual tenant are suspended so long as the widow retains possession of the dwelling-house.

If the contractual tenancy is determinable by notice, the landlord or the contractual tenant can determine it by giving the appropriate notice, but such notice will not affect the widow's rights and obligations ... and, if no notice is given, the contractual tenancy will come into full operation when the widow gives up possession ... If the contractual tenancy is a lease for years, it will remain in being, but so long as the widow remains in possession she, and not the contractual tenant, is bound to observe the terms and conditions of the lease and has the benefit thereof ... At no time are there two tenants, each one entitled to the benefit and subject to the burden of the contractual tenancy. The so-called statutory tenant is not a tenant in the true sense. He or she is merely a person who is given certain protection by the Acts ...'

But whilst this rule removes one anomaly, it creates a number of injustices and difficulties. Thus if H were to devise another house to W with the intention that she should live in that and that S should live in the house bequeathed to him, his intentions can be completely defeated, for W can claim the beneficial interest in the former as devisee and remain in the latter as statutory tenant, and S cannot obtain a possession order against her as he is not the landlord. Moreover, if the lessor determines the contractual tenancy by giving notice to S, S is deprived of the protection of the Rent Act as he is not a contractual tenant in possession. There is little incentive for the landlord to obtain a possession order since this could enure only for the benefit of S whose contractual tenancy will then resume its full force. Nor will the position be eased when the widow dies, for there can be a second transmission to a member of her family residing with her.[8]

2. PROTECTED AND STATUTORY OCCUPANCIES UNDER THE RENT (AGRICULTURE) ACT

The position is similar to that under the Rent Act save in two respects. First, if the tenant's spouse or cohabitant becomes a statutory tenant by succession, there can be no further succession on his or her death. Secondly, the tenancy taken by a member of the tenant's family will be an assured agricultural occupancy.[9]

3. ASSURED TENANCIES AND ASSURED AGRICULTURAL OCCUPANCIES

The circumstances in which there can be a succession to an assured tenancy (including an assured agricultural occupancy) are much more limited.[10]

In the first place, the tenancy must be a periodic one. There is no succession at all to a fixed term tenancy: if the tenant bequeaths the lease to another, a surviving spouse's or cohabitant's sole remedy is to apply for

[8] For a fuller criticism of *Moodie v Hosegood* and the difficulties which it raises, see Megarry *The Rent Acts and the Invention of New Doctrines* 67 LQR 505, 512 et seq.
[9] Rent (Agriculture) Act 1976, s 4; Housing Act 1988, s 39 and Sch 4, Parts II and III. The additional grounds on which the landlord can claim possession are also different.
[10] Housing Act 1988, s 17.

an order under the Inheritance (Provision for Family and Dependants) Act.

Secondly, the tenant must be a sole tenant and must not himself be a successor. This includes not only a person who has himself acquired the lease by succession but also one who acquired it under the will or intestacy of a previous tenant and one who was formerly a joint tenant and has become the sole tenant by survivorship. The reason for this extended definition is that the most likely person to benefit from a bequest or intestacy is a member of the tenant's family and joint tenants will almost certainly be the tenant and his wife or cohabitant, so that there will in effect have been one succession already.

Finally, the only person who can claim to succeed is the tenant's spouse or the person living with him or her as his or her wife or husband. In either case the claimant must have been occupying the dwelling house as his or her only or principal home immediately before the tenant's death.

The successor will become an assured tenant. It is expressly provided that, if the tenancy vests in a spouse or cohabitant by succession, the tenancy is not to devolve under the tenant's will or intestacy and so the principle of *Moodie v Hosegood*[11] will not apply.

4. SECURE TENANCIES

As the legislation relating to secure tenancies in the public sector dates back to 1980, it is to be expected that succession to them is more restricted than it is under the Rent Act but less restricted than succession to assured tenancies. Three points should be noted.

First, there can be a succession only to a periodic tenancy.[12]

Secondly, the tenant must not himself be a successor. This word has an extended meaning for the same reason as it has in the case of an assured periodic tenancy, but its definition is not the same as that in the Housing Act of 1988. A tenant is a successor to a secure tenancy in the following circumstances.[13]

(a) If he succeeded to the tenancy in the way we are now considering.

(b) If he was a joint tenant and had become the sole tenant.[14]

(c) If the periodic tenancy arose on the termination of a term certain and the first tenancy had been granted to another person and the deceased tenant jointly.

(d) If he became tenant by assignment unless the assignment was in pursuance of a property adjustment order under section 24 of the Matrimonial Causes Act or by way of exchange.

(e) If he became tenant on the tenancy being vested in him on the death of the previous tenant.

(f) If the court has made an order under the Matrimonial Homes Act vesting the tenancy in one of the spouses on divorce, nullity or

[11] See ante, p 845.

[12] Housing Act 1985, s 89(1).

[13] Ibid, s 88.

[14] He must have become the sole tenant under the same tenancy by survivorship or release. Hence if a joint tenancy is determined and the landlord then grants a fresh tenancy to one of the joint tenants, the latter is not a successor: *Bassetlaw District Council v Renshaw* [1992] 1 All ER 925, CA.

judicial separation and the transferor was a successor.[15]

Thirdly, there can be a succession only by a *qualified successor*. No person is qualified unless he occupied the dwelling-house as his only or principal home at the time of the tenant's death. In addition he or she must be either the tenant's spouse or another member of his family who, in the latter case, has resided with the tenant throughout the period of twelve months ending with the tenant's death.[16] The term 'residing with' presumably has the same meaning as it has in the Rent Act.[17]

Membership of the tenant's family is precisely defined for the purpose of the Housing Act 1985. A person is a member of the tenant's family if he or she is the tenant's spouse, parent, grandparent, child, grandchild, brother, sister, uncle, aunt, nephew or niece, or if he or she and the tenant lived together as husband and wife. A relationship by marriage is to be treated as a relationship by blood; a relationship of the half-blood as a relationship of the whole blood; a person's stepchild is to be treated as his child; and an illegitimate child is to be treated as the legitimate child of his mother and reputed father.[18] Although this precise wording will obviate the mass of litigation to which the term has given rise under the Rent Act, it is not free from ambiguity. For example, does the fact that a person's stepchild is to be treated as his own child mean that the tenant's stepparent can be treated as his parent?

If there is more than one person qualified to succeed, the surviving spouse is preferred to any other member of his family; if there is no surviving spouse and two or more persons are qualified, they must agree amongst themselves which of them is to succeed and, if they cannot agree, the landlord may select one of them.[19]

The landlord who gives a successor a fresh tenancy is given similar protection under the Housing Act to that given to a landlord under the Rent Act.[20] If a tenant under a periodic secure tenancy to which there could be no (or no further) succession is given a further periodic secure tenancy and either the premises or the landlord (or both) is the same under both tenancies, there can be no succession to the second tenancy provided that it was granted within six months of the termination of the first.[1] Consequently, for example, if the tenant's widow moves to a smaller house on the death of her husband and both houses are leased to her by the same local authority, there can be no succession to the second tenancy on her death.

The successor will become a periodic secure tenant.

[15] Matrimonial Homes Act 1983, Sch 1, para 2(3), as amended by the Housing (Consequential Provisions) Act 1985, Sch 2. Although the position is not clear, the inference is that, if the transferor is not a successor, the transferee will not be one either.
[16] Housing Act 1985, s 87. Provided that these conditions are satisfied, the whole of the residence need not have been in the dwelling-house the tenancy of which the member of the family is claiming: *Waltham Forest London Borough Council v Thomas* [1992] 3 All ER 244, HL. Contrast the position under the Rent Act, ante, p 843.
[17] See ante, p 843.
[18] Housing Act 1985, s 113. For a discussion of the meaning of the phrase 'living together as husband and wife', see ante, p 7. It does not include a homosexual relationship: *Harrogate Borough Council v Simpson* [1986] 2 FLR 91, CA.
[19] Ibid, s 89(1), (2).
[20] See ante, p 845, n 4.
[1] Housing Act 1985, s 88(4). This will not apply if the agreement creating the second tenancy otherwise provides.

5. MOBILE HOMES

The increase in the number of people living in caravans (or other mobile homes) has led Parliament to extend to the members of the family of a deceased occupier the kind of protection afforded by the Rent Act. The Mobile Homes Act 1983 applies to any agreement under which a person is entitled to station a mobile home[2] on land forming part of a protected site[3] and to occupy it as his only or main residence.[4] If he or she dies so occupying it, the agreement enures for the benefit of, and is binding on, the occupier's widow or widower residing with him (or her) at the time of his death or, in default of such a person, any other member of his (or her) family residing with him, at that time.[5] 'Member of the family' has the same meaning as it has in the Housing Act 1985.[6]

Owing to political pressure the Bill in its final form was rushed through Parliament, which accounts for the weaknesses in drafting. Whilst the person claiming to be a successor must have been residing with the deceased occupier at the time of the latter's death, he need not have done so in the mobile home.[7] Consequently if, say, a widowed mother had her main residence in a caravan but resided for part of the year with her daughter, the latter could claim the benefit of the agreement. If more than one person was residing with the occupier at the time of his death (other than the surviving spouse), there is no machinery for deciding which of them may remain there and it seems that they are all entitled to do so. This Act imposes no limitation on the number of times that the benefits and obligations of an agreement may vest in another as the result of an occupier's death, although the owner of the site may always terminate the agreement if the person entitled does not occupy the mobile home as his only or main residence.[8]

---

[2] Ie a structure designed or adapted for human habitation and capable of being moved but excluding rolling stock on a railway system and a tent: Mobile Homes Act 1983, s 5(1); Caravan Sites and Control of Development Act 1960, s 24(1).

[3] Ie land in respect of which a site licence is required (except a licence granted for holiday use only or for limited periods of the year) but excluding land occupied by a local authority as a caravan site for gipsies: ibid.

[4] Mobile Homes Act 1983, s 1(1). A place can be a person's main residence even though he spends relatively short periods there: see *Frost v Feltham* [1981] 1 WLR 452. The occupier's own rights are protected by the very limited circumstances in which the owner of the site can terminate the agreement: see ibid, s 2 and Sch 1.

[5] Ibid, s 3(3).

[6] Ibid, s 5(3). See ante, p 848.

[7] As a person may have more than one residence: see ante, p 630.

[8] Mobile Homes Act 1983, Sch 1, para 5. So long as there is someone who can claim the benefit of the agreement as widow, widower or member of the deceased occupier's family, the person entitled to the property in the mobile home under the occupier's will or on his intestacy apparently can claim no right to it.

Appendices

Summary of contents

Appendix A

Business assigned to the Family Division of the High Court

(The Supreme Court Act 1981, Schedule 1, as amended)

All matrimonial causes and matters (whether at first instance or on appeal).

All causes and matters (whether at first instance or on appeal) relating to:

    (i) legitimacy;
    (ii) the exercise of the inherent jurisdiction of the High Court with respect to minors, the maintenance of minors and any proceedings under the Children Act 1989, except proceedings solely for the appointment of a guardian of a minor's estate;[1]
    (iii) adoption;
    (iv) non-contentious or common form probate business.

Applications for consent to the marriage of a minor or for a declaration under section 27B(5) of the Marriage Act 1949.

Proceedings on appeal under section 13 of the Administration of Justice Act 1960 from an order or decision made under section 63(3) of the Magistrates' Courts Act 1980 to enforce an order of a magistrates' court made in matrimonial proceedings or with respect to the guardianship of a minor.

Applications under Part III of the Family Law Act 1986.

Proceedings under the Children Act 1989.[1]

---

[1] This apparent inconsistency is the result of two separate amendments introduced by the Children Act 1989, Sch 11, para 9, and Sch 13, para 45(3).

Appendix B

Prohibited degrees of kindred and affinity

(The Marriage Act 1949, First Schedule, as amended by the Children Act 1975 and the Marriage Act (Prohibited Degrees of Relationship) Act 1986.)

PART 1

Mother	Father
Adoptive mother or former adoptive mother	Adoptive father or former adoptive father
Daughter	Son
Adoptive daughter or former adoptive daughter	Adoptive son or former adoptive son
Father's mother	Father's father
Mother's mother	Mother's father
Son's daughter	Son's son
Daughter's daughter	Daughter's son
Sister	Brother
Father's sister	Father's brother
Mother's sister	Mother's brother
Brother's daughter	Brother's son
Sister's daughter	Sister's son

PART II

Daughter of former wife	Son of former husband
Former wife of father	Former husband of mother
Former wife of father's father	Former husband of father's mother
Former wife of mother's father	Former husband of mother's mother
Daughter of son of former wife	Son of son of former husband
Daughter of daughter of former wife	Son of daughter of former husband

PART III

Mother of former wife	Father of former husband
Former wife of son	Former husband of daughter

854

Appendix C

Orders relating to financial relief under the Matrimonial Causes Act 1973

Nature of Provision	Proceedings in which it can be ordered	Whether it can be secured	Whether it can be varied	Whether repayment can be ordered	
				(1) after change of circumstances	(2) after remarriage
Maintenance pending suit	Divorce, nullity, judicial separation, s 27	No	Yes	Yes	No
Periodical payments for spouse	Divorce, nullity, judicial separation, s 27	Yes	Yes	Yes	Yes
Lump sum payment for spouse	Divorce, nullity, judicial separation, s 27	Yes, if payable by instalments	Payment by instalments only	No	No
Transfer & settlement of property	Divorce, nullity, judicial separation	–	Only order for settlement made on judicial separation	No	No
Variation of settlements	Divorce, nullity, judicial separation	–	Only if made on judicial separation	No	No
Periodical payments for children of the family	Divorce, nullity, judicial separation, s 27	Yes	Yes	Yes	No
Lump sum payment for children of the family	Divorce, nullity, judicial separation, s 27	Yes, if payable by instalments	Payment by instalments only	No	No

Contracting States to the European and Hague Conventions on International Child Abduction

The European Convention

The Contracting States:		
	Australia	1 August 1986
	Belgium	1 August 1986
	Cyprus	1 October 1986
	Denmark	1 August 1991
	France	1 August 1986
	Germany	1 February 1991
	The Republic of Ireland	1 October 1991
	Luxembourg	1 August 1986
	Netherlands	1 September 1990
	Norway	1 May 1989
	Portugal	1 August 1986
	Spain	1 August 1986
	Sweden	1 July 1989
	Switzerland	1 August 1986

The Hague Convention

The Argentine Republic	–	1 June 1991
Australia	Australian States & mainland Territories	1 January 1987
Austria	–	1 October 1988
Belize	–	1 October 1989
Canada	Ontario	1 August 1986
	New Brunswick	1 August 1986
	British Columbia	1 August 1986
	Manitoba	1 August 1986
	Nova Scotia	1 August 1986
	Newfoundland	1 August 1986
	Prince Edward Island	1 August 1986
	Quebec	1 August 1986
	Yukon Territory	1 August 1986
	Saskatchewan	1 November 1986
	Alberta	1 February 1987
	Northwest Territories	1 April 1988
The Kingdom of Denmark		1 July 1991
Ecuador		1 April 1992
The French Republic		1 August 1986
The Federal Republic of Germany		1 December 1990
The Hungarian People's Republic		1 September 1986
Ireland		1 October 1991
Israel		1 December 1991

The Grand Duchy of Luxembourg	1 January 1987
Mexico	1 September 1991
The Kingdom of the Netherlands	1 September 1990
New Zealand	1 August 1991
Norway	1 April 1989
The Portuguese Republic	1 August 1986
Spain	1 September 1987
Sweden	1 June 1989
The Swiss Confederation	1 August 1986
The United States of America	1 July 1986
The Socialist Federal Republic of Yugoslavia	1 December 1991

Index

868   Index

Guardian—*contd*
appointment of—*contd*
courts, by—*contd*
exercise of power, 404
statutory powers, 398
welfare consideration, 405
effect of, 405
frequency of, 399
private—
disclaimer of, 403
generally, 401
revocation of, 402
taking effect, 402–403
scrutiny of, 400
testamentary, 398
foster parents distinguished, 395–397
functions of, 399
meaning, 253, 395
parents distinguished, 395
person with residence order compared, 397
rights and duties of, 399
unmarried father as, 323
Guardian ad litem
circumstances, investigation of, 520
general duty of, 520
report of, 521
social work qualification, 519
system of, 519
Guardianship
Children Act 1989, before, 398
history of, 398
modern law, 400–401
non-parental, 398
parental, 398
reform, need for, 399–400
role of, 407
termination of—
automatic, 406
court, removal by, 406–407

Habeas corpus
wife, application by, 108
High Court
county court, transfer of case from, 14, 220
Divorce Court, 12
ecclesiastical courts, jurisdiction derived from, 12
Family Division—
business assigned to, 853
establishment of, 12–13
jurisdiction, 13
jurisdiction, 12
Hague Convention, under, 491
Homeless person
accommodation, meaning, 150
homelessness—
domestic violence, as result of, 152
intentional, 151–152
threat of, 150
housing authority, duty to house, 149–151, 153

Homeless person—*contd*
priority need, having, 151–152
meaning, 149
Housing authority
domestic violence victim, duty to, 152
homeless person, duty to house, 149–151, 153
wife, encouraging proceedings by, 153
Human rights
European Convention, 18–19
European Court, application to, 551–552
Husband and wife
agency of necessity, 650
arrest, impeding, 137
assault by, 154
citizenship. *See* BRITISH CITIZENSHIP
community of gains, 564
community of property, 564
consortium, right to. *See* CONSORTIUM
conspiracy between, 106, 135, 138
contracts between, 128
co-ownership of goods, 565
corporal punishment, right to administer, 148
criminal proceedings, instituting, 139
deferred community, 564
equality of rights, 109
evidence by. *See* EVIDENCE
household goods, use and enjoyment of, 565
insurable interests, 581
legal personalities, fusion of, 105–107
life assurance policies, 581–582
maintenance. *See* MAINTENANCE
marital coercion of crime, 136–137
marital confidences, 113–114
mutual wills, 809–810
non-molestation order. *See* NON-MOLESTATION ORDER
property rights—
adjustment. *See* PROPERTY ADJUSTMENT
bankruptcy, effect of, 578–580
chattels, transactions involving, 579
common law, at—
copyholds, 557
freeholds, 555–556
leaseholds, 557
marital rights, fraud on, 557–558
personality, 557
tenancy by entireties, 556
common purse, 570–571
defrauding creditors, transactions used for, 578–579
equity, at—
restraint upon anticipation, 559, 562
settlement, wife's equity to, 558
wife's separate estate, 558
furniture, in, 573
gifts between, 575–577
gifts to, 575
housekeeping allowance, savings from, 572–573

Legal aid
Board's charge, 746–749
matrimonial causes, in, 234
Local authority
care contact order, 354
care proceedings. *See* CARE PROCEEDINGS
children and families, services for, 254
children in need. *See* children in need,
   below
day care, provision on, 502
neglect and abuse, prevention of, 502
racial groups, consideration of, 502
third party, provision of accommodation
   to protect child, 502
upbringing by families, promotion of,
   502
children in care of—
contact with—
   child, position of, 532
   Children Act 1989, changes in, 530
   general presumption, departing from,
     531
   interested persons, position of, 532
   powers of court, 532
   reasonable, presumption of, 531
   variation and discharge of orders, 533
family, maintaining links with, 499–500
legislation, 496–497
section 8 orders, restrictions on, 357–358
wardship jurisdiction, and, 545–547
children in need—
accommodation of—
   agreements, 505
   duty of, 503–504
   limits on, 504
   volunatry care, replacing, 503
   voluntary nature of, 503
   wishes of child, 504
duties to, 500–501
identification of, 501
children looked after by, duties to, 505–
   506
decisions, disputing—
complaints procedure—
   matters complained about, 543
   outcome of, 544
   persons complaining, 542–543
   procedure, 544
   requirement to have, 542
European Court of Human Rights,
   application to, 551–552
generally, 541–542
judicial review—
   circumstances for, 549–550
   claim, substantiating, 549
   function of court, 548
   requirements, 548
local government ombudsman,
   application to, 551
residence order, leave to apply for, 547
Secretary of State, default powers of, 545
wardship jurisdiction, 545–547

Local authority—*contd*
meaning, 496
parental responsibility vested in, 328, 524
parents, working with, 499
powers, development of, 496–498
section 8 order, applying for, 358
supervision proceedings. *See* SUPERVISION
   PROCEEDINGS
wardship jurisdiction, use of, 251

Magistrates' court
binding over, 177
domestic proceedings, hearing, 16
family proceedings courts, as, 16, 256
jurisdiction of—
affiliation orders, 14
children, relating to, 15
criminal law, originating in, 14–15
divorce law, not fitting with, 15
married women, applications by, 15
Law Commission working party, 15
lump sum payment—
enforcement of order, 688–692
power to order, 684
variation of, 688
maintenance order made by. *See*
   MAINTENANCE
matrimonial home, power to exclude
   spouse from, 174–175
non-molestation order by, 160
periodical payments order—
enforcement of, 688–692
power to make, 673–675, 676
personal protection order—
concurrent, 176–177
enforcement, 176
expedited, 175
person applying for, 174
power of arrest attached to, 176
power to make, 174–176
proceedings, evidence of ground for
   divorce in, 187
property adjustment order, no power to
   make, 680
Maintenance
agreement—
alteration of—
   court, powers of, 660–661
   death of one party, after, 661, 663
   lifetime of parties, in, 658–660
   parents, between, 663–664
contract, as, 652, 656
definition, 656–657
financial arrangements, meaning, 656
Inheritance Act, proceedings under, 840–
   841
magistrates' court, alteration by, 660–
   661
parents, between, 662–664
parties to, 656
spouses, between, 656–662
void provisions, 657–658

Marriage—*contd*
  capacity of parties—*contd*
    lack of, 74, 81–82
    monogamy, requirement of, 35
    presumption as to, 68–70
    prohibited degrees. *See* prohibited
      degrees, *below*
    sex of parties, 34–35
  characterisation of rules, 33
  Church of England rites, according to—
    banns, 45–47
    common licence, 47–48
    place of, 49
    solemnization, 49
    special licence, 48
    superintendent registrar's certificate, 49
    time for, 49
    witnesses, 49
  civil, introduction of, 41
  common law, effect of, 105
  common licence, by—
    caveat against, 48
    consent to, 44
    failure to obtain, 82–83
    grant of, 47–48
    oath before, 48
  consent to, 43–45
    age of majority, reduction of, 42–43
    minor, of, 43–45
  consolidation of enactments, 42
  consummation of. *See* CONSUMMATION OF
      MARRIAGE; VOIDABLE MARRIAGE
  contract, as, 20
  defects invalidating, 80, 82–85
  definition, 21
  detained person, of, 42, 53–54
  dissolution on presumption of death, 180–
      181
  divorced person, of, refusal to officiate, 45
  domicile, capacity governed by. *See*
      capacity, *above*
  foreign. *See* FOREIGN MARRIAGE
  formal validity—
    defect, effect of, 80, 82–85
    presumption of, 67
  formalities of—
    Church of England, rites of, 45 *et seq*
    common law, 32
    forces, applying to, 32
    'Gretna Green', 31, 40
    history of, 38–43
    lex loci celebrationis, governed by, 31
    non-observance, 56
    reform, proposals for, 57–59
  gift in contemplation of, 24
  grounds not rendered void on, 82–83
  heterosexual, to be, 22, 34–35
  house-bound person, of, 42, 53–54, 55
  law governing, 26
  life, for, 21
  limping—
    avoidance by statute, 30

Marriage—*contd*
  Lord Hardwicke's Act, 40
  meaning, 21
  minor, of—
    consents to, 43–45
    public dissent to, 84
  monogamous, to be, 23, 35
  mutual declarations, contracted by, 32
  naval, military and air force chapels, in, 56
  persons seriously ill, of, 42, 54–55
  presumption of, 67–70
  private building, in, 42
  prohibited degrees—
    adoption, effect of, 456
    affinity, based on, 37–38
    consanguinity, based on, 36–37
    criminal offence, and, 37
    history of, 36
    illegitimate relationships, 37
    previously void marriage, refusal to
      solemnize, 45
    relaxation of law, 37–38
    step-relationships, 37
    table of, 37, 854
    void, marriage rendered, 81
  publication of banns, after, 45
  register office, in, 52
  registered building, in, 42, 52–53
  Registrar General's licence, on authority
      of—
    consent to, 44
    issue, conditions of, 54
    party expected to die, where, 54
    preliminary formalities, 55
    purpose of, 54
    Quaker and Jewish marriages, 55
    solemnization, 54–56
  registration, 43
  retrospective validation, 56
  seriously ill person, of, 42, 54–55
  solemnization—
    Church of England rites, according to,
      49
    forces, member of, 56
    Jews, between, 51, 54, 55
    person not in Holy Orders, by, 84
    Quakers, between, 51, 54, 55
    registered building, in, 52–53
    Registrar General's licence, on authority
      of, 54–56
    superintendent registrar's certificate, on
      authority of, 49–51
  special licence, grant of, 48, 54
  status, 20–21
    declaration as to, 70–71
  superintendent registrar's certificate, on—
    consent to, 44
    failure to obtain, 83
    introduction of, 41
    licence, issue with, 51
    licence, issue without, 50–51
    register office, in, 52

Matrimonial home—*contd*
  ownership—*contd*
    improvements, effect of, 599–601
    indirect contributions, effect of, 592–594
    profits, accounting for, 601
    proprietary estoppel, 595–596
    shares, quantification of, 596–599
    trust, enforcing, 601–605
  party with dependent children staying in, 602
  pending land action, registration of, 803
  purchaser for value, estate of, 610–612
  rent, entitlement to, 604
  resulting trust in, 590
  sale, court ordering, 602
  statutory co-ownership, 565
  trust for sale, 601
  unmarried cohabitants, provisions not available to, 168
  valuation of, 604
Medical treatment
  consent to—
    child, by, 249
    child not consenting, where, 304–306
    competence of child, 306–309
    prima facie position, 305
Mobile home
  agreement as to stationing, succession to, 849

Nationality
  British citizenship. *See* BRITISH CITIZENSHIP
Non-molestation order
  child, relating to, 167
  divorced person seeking, 166
  High Court, jurisdiction of, 167
  injunction, as, 160–163
    duration of, 172
    enforcement of, 172–173
    ex parte, 169
    exercise of powers to grant, 168–169
    ouster, 163–165
    power of arrest attached to, 173
    provisions in, 166
  jurisdiction to make, 162, 165
  molest, meaning, 166
  other proceedings, sought in, 161–165
  other relief not sought, where, 165
  proposals for reform, 177
  undertaking, as, 160
Nullity of marriage. *See also* VOID MARRIAGE, VOIDABLE MARRIAGE
  ancillary orders, 79, 855
  child, arrangements for—
    child of the family, for, 368–369
    children under 16 years, 368
    duty as to, 366–367
    procedure for, 367–368
  choice of law, 79
  decree—
    absolute, made, 79
    judgement in rem, as, 75

Nullity of marriage—*contd*
  decree—*contd*
    jurisdiction, 75–79
    retrospective effect, 73
  domicile of parties, relevance of, 77–78
  English courts, jurisdiction of, 77–79
  financial provision following. *See* FINANCIAL PROVISION
  law commission, review by, 73–74
  petitions, 76–77
  property adjustment following. *See* PROPERTY ADJUSTMENT
  section 8 orders, jurisdictional rules, 375
  stay of proceedings, 79
  transfer of tenancy on, 637–638, 640
  void and voidable marriages distinguished, 74–76
  will, effect on, 808

Parent
  artificial insemination, by, 260
  child, conveyance of property to, 643
  egg and embryo donation, 261
  father—
    legal—
      genetic not being, 263
      non-genetic treated as, 263–265
    guardian distinguished, 395
  in vitro fertilisation, by, 261
  life assurance policy taken out by, 645
  local authority, working with, 499
  maintenance by. *See* MAINTENANCE
  mother, legal, 261–262
  parentage. *See* CHILD
  parentage rights, sharing, 289
  persons being, 260
  section 30 orders as to, 265–267
  surrogacy—
    agreements, 267–269
    commercial arrangements, prohibition on, 267
    meaning, 261
  undue influence on child, 644–645
Parent-child relationship
  illegitimate children, in relation to, 292
  legal attitude to, 288–289
  legitimate children, in relation to, 289–292
  mother's position, 292–293
Parental responsibility
  absence, effect of, 301
  acts of child, liability for—
    contracts, 318
    crimes, 319
    torts, 318
  adoption order, effect of, 333
  agreements—
    effect of, 326–327
    ending, 327–328
    making, 323–324
  allocation of, 329
  ambit of, 300
  cessation of, 300